AMERICAN INDIAN LAW

CASES AND COMMENTARY

Fourth Edition

■ ■ ■

Robert T. Anderson
Charles I. Stone Professor of Law
Director, Native American Law Center
University of Washington School of Law
Oneida Indian Nation Visiting Professor
Harvard Law School

Sarah A. Krakoff
Moses Lasky Professor of Law
University of Colorado Law School

Bethany Berger
Wallace Stevens Professor of Law
University of Connecticut School of Law

AMERICAN CASEBOOK SERIES®

444 Cedar Street, Suite 700
St. Paul, MN 55101
1-877-888-1330

Printed in the United States of America

ISBN: 978-1-64242-686-1

For Marilyn and Sydney.

RTA

For John and Lucy, who make everything possible.

SK

PREFACE

PREFACE TO THE FOURTH EDITION

■ ■ ■

This edition of the book includes updated cases, statutes, regulations, and analyses since the 2015 publication. The Supreme Court continued to be very active in the Indian law field—handing down seven decisions. The addition of Justice Neal Gorsuch brought a conservative perspective that has so far been favorable to tribal interests. Justice Sotomayor continued to be a serious scholar of Indian law and a voice for a deeper understanding of the field's historic context. We include an updated graphic analysis of Indian law cases during the Roberts Court to help readers see the big picture. In addition to these new cases, in chapter four we add a 1942 Supreme Court case that is a landmark for its recognition of original Indian title, but which has long been overlooked in the field.

Federal and state appellate courts decided many important cases on issues ranging from the Indian Child Welfare Act to tribal taxation immunity, water rights, and tribal jurisdiction over nonmembers. A fair number of these important cases are discussed. We also include amendments to the tribal energy policy act that provide a path to greater self-determination in the natural resources context. The Indian Child Welfare Act section was updated to include Obama-era regulations as well an appellate decision upholding them and the statute itself in the face of a broad constitutional challenge.

We continue to miss Professor Philip P. Frickey, who left us in July of 2010 after the second edition was published. Phil was a great friend and mentor who led us through the production of the first edition, and whose formidable intellect will forever remain at the heart of our book. We were fortunate to know Phil and like so many others are beneficiaries of his life, work and spirit.

This new edition of our casebook would not have been possible without the tremendous effort of Professor Anderson's assistant, Cynthia Fester, of the University of Washington School of Law. She worked way beyond the call of duty to produce this book. We are eternally indebted to her for her dedication and attention to detail. Thank you, Cynthia! Professor Anderson also had stellar assistance from Research Assistants Cory Maguire and Alex Sirio from Harvard Law School. As always, the Reference Librarians at the University of Washington School of Law were of tremendous help in tracking down hard-to-find material, and answering obscure questions. Professor Krakoff is similarly indebted to the University of Colorado law library faculty, and to her excellent research assistants Emilie Kurth and Leah Vasarhelyi.

Robert T. Anderson
Seattle, Washington

Sarah Krakoff
Boulder, Colorado

November 2019

PREFACE TO THE THIRD EDITION

■ ■ ■

Sadly, we produced the Third Edition to our casebook after the passing of Professor Philip P. Frickey, who left us in July of 2010 after the second edition was published. Phil was a great friend and mentor who led us through the production of the first edition, and whose formidable intellect will forever remain at the heart of our book. Phil's short piece, *A Final Toast to My Network*, 98 Cal. L. Rev. 1101 (2010) was published in a California Law Review volume that included tributes from some of Phil's many admirers and friends. He wrote, "I am fascinated with the growing disjunction between my failing physical health and my soaring spirits." We were fortunate to know Phil and like so many others are beneficiaries of his life, work and spirit.

This edition of the book includes updated cases, statutes, regulations, and analyses since the 2010 publication. Of course, we include recent decisions from the Supreme Court, which in general continues to be a dismal place for the vindication of tribal rights—as evidenced by *Adoptive Couple v. Baby Girl*, an Indian Child Welfare Act case, along with *Match-E-Be-Nash-She-Wish Band of Pottawatomi Indians v. Patchak*, which opened to door to more challenges to tribal land acquisitions. The Court also further diminished federal trust obligations to tribes. On the other hand, in *Michigan v. Bay Mills*, many were surprised when the Court adhered to long-standing principles of tribal sovereign immunity. We include a new graphic analysis of Indian law cases in the Roberts Court to help readers follow the big picture. On the congressional front, the Tribal Law and Order Act of 2010 and the Violence Against Women Act Amendments of 2013 are federal statutes that mark the greatest changes in the Indian country criminal jurisdiction regime since 1968. Both are included and analyzed. Obama Administration proposals to support tribal sovereignty in the face of congressional inaction in Alaska, Hawaii and the general tax arena are also highlighted. In international and comparative law, we review the U.S. acceptance of the U.N. Declaration on the Rights of Indigenous Peoples, and victories for indigenous rights in Canada, Japan, Kenya, and other countries.

This new edition of our casebook would not have been possible without the tremendous effort of Professor Anderson's assistant, Cynthia Fester, of the University of Washington School of Law. She worked way beyond the call of duty to produce this book. We are eternally indebted to her for her dedication and attention to detail. Thank you, Cynthia! Professor Anderson also had stellar assistance from Research Assistants, Mark Giuliano, '15, and Nicole Gustine, '14. As always, the Reference Librarians at the University of Washington School of Law were of tremendous help in tracking down hard-to-find material, and answering obscure questions. Finally, UW Law Dean Kellye Testy continues to be a great supporter of the UW Indian Law program and Dean Phil Weiser at the University of Colorado Law School provides invaluable research support for the Indian law program at Colorado Law.

Robert T. Anderson
Seattle, Washington

Bethany Berger
Hartford, Connecticut

Sarah Krakoff
Boulder, Colorado

January 2015

PREFACE TO SECOND EDITION

We produced the second edition of our casebook to incorporate several important new cases from the United States Supreme Court and lower courts. We also created a new section to provide a full introduction to the law governing Indian gaming, and providedmore background information about many of the major Indian law cases. We are thankful for the many constructive comments we received from Indian law teachers throughout the country. We hope that the many additions and edits to the first edition are helpful and look forward to hearing from you as we continue to supplement and improve this book. Finally, we will continue to update and improve our casebook web-site with sample syllabi, lesson plans, and in-class problems. For teacher access to the site, please e-mail any one of us.

Once again, we owe a tremendous debt to Cynthia Fester of the University of Washington School of Law for her skill and willingness to work with us during the evenings and on weekends to meet our deadlines. We could not have done it without her.

Robert T. Anderson
Seattle, Washington

Bethany Berger
Hartford, Connecticut

Sarah Krakoff
Boulder, Colorado

April 2010

PREFACE TO FIRST EDITION

The field of American Indian law has undergone tremendous growth since the first regular course was offered by Professor Ralph Johnson in the 1960s at the University of Washington. Now, nearly all the major law schools offer one or more courses in the subject and the topic is also included on the bar exams of Washington, South Dakota and New Mexico. This casebook is designed to provide an introduction to the history and modern principles of federal law relating to Indian tribes in the United States. Specialized chapters provide opportunities for in-depth study and an introduction to the law affecting indigenous peoples in other countries. We close the book with a survey of the different scholarly approaches taken to the field. We welcome your comments and suggestions about this casebook. We used *** when we omitted material from cases and also as a replacement for ellipses within cases. We did not note when we eliminated footnotes or citations from cases.

We thank the Deans of our law schools, Greg Hicks at Washington, Jeremy Paul at Connecticut, Christopher Edley at Berkeley and David Getches at Colorado. Professor Frickey also thanks his research assistants, Rebecca Hart and Alex Lowther, for their excellent assistance. Professor Anderson thanks Lisa Kremer, who led the charge on research assistance, editing and cite-checking, along with Ben Tramposh, Saza Osawa and Drew Baca. He also thanks Professor William H. Rodgers, Jr., for his optimism and encouragement, and the UW reference librarians for their excellent assistance. Professor Krakoff is grateful to Professor Charles Wilkinson for his generous support and mentoring, to Clinical Professor Jill Tompkins for her inspiring work in shaping contemporary Indian law, and to Jennifer Dill, Amanda Dock, and Vivian Vassall for terrific research assistance. Professor Berger thanks Lee Sims, head reference librarian at Connecticut, as well as the many students who have helped shape her ideas on teaching Indian law.

Our tremendous thanks go out to Cynthia Fester, administrative assistant to Professor Anderson, without whom this casebook would not have been produced. Cynthia labored many nights and weekends to format, edit, and pull together comments from the four of us. Through it all she maintained her wonderful demeanor and kept her sense of humor. Cynthia, in turn, would thank her support staff colleagues at the University of Washington School of Law whose willingness to assume parts of her daily workload allowed her to focus on this project. Additionally, appreciation is extended to her colleagues Claire O'Brien, who assisted in formatting early chapter drafts, and Ann Bates, who provided assistance on the Table of Cases.

Of course, none of us could have made it through this project without the wonderful support of our families and friends. We neglected them at times, but they were still there to encourage us and showed much patience. We are eternally grateful for their support.

Robert T. Anderson
Seattle, Washington

Bethany Berger
Hartford, Connecticut

Philip P. Frickey
Berkeley, California

Sarah Krakoff
Boulder, Colorado

March 2008

ACKNOWLEDGEMENTS

■ ■ ■

The following copyrighted material has been reprinted with permission of the copyright holder.

Anderson, Robert T., *Indian Water Rights and the Federal Trust Responsibility*, 46 Nat. Res. J. 399 (2006). Copyright 2006 by Robert T. Anderson and Natural Resources Journal.

Anderson, Robert T., *Indian Water Rights: Litigation and Settlements*, 42 Tulsa L. R. 23 (2006). Copyright 2006 by Robert T. Anderson. All rights reserved.

Berger, Bethany, *Indian Policy and the Imagined Indian Woman*, 14 Kan. J. L. & Pub. Pol'y 103 (2004). Copyright 2004 by the Kansas Journal of Law & Public Policy. All rights reserved.

Berger, Bethany, United States v. Lara *as a Story of Native Agency*, 40 Tulsa L. Rev. 5 (2004). Copyright 2004 by Bethany Berger. All rights reserved.

Cornell, Stephen, *Sovereignty, Prosperity, and Policy in Indian Country Today,* Community Reinvestment (Fed. Res. Bk. Ks. City Winter 1997). Copyright 1997 by Stephen Cornell. All rights reserved.

Great Documents in American Indian History (Wayne Moquin & Charles Van Doren eds. 1973). Copyright 1973 by Praeger Publishers. Reproduced with permission of Greenwood Publishing Group, Inc. Westport, CT.

Estin, Ann Laquer, Lone Wolf v. Hitchcock: *The Long Shadow, in The Aggressions of Civilization: Federal Indian Policy Since the 1880's* (Sandra L. Cadwalader & Vine Deloria, Jr. eds. 1984). Copyright by Ann Estin. All rights reserved.

Frickey, Philip, P., *(Native) American Exceptionalism in Federal Public Law*, 119 Harv. L. Rev. 431 (2005). Copyright 2005 by the Harvard Law Review. All rights reserved.

Frickey, Philip, P., *Marshalling Past and Present: Colonialism, Constitutionalism, and Interpretation in Federal Indian Law*, 107 Harv. L. Rev. 381 (1993). Copyright 1993 by the Harvard Law Review. All rights reserved.

Goldberg-Ambrose, Carole, *Public Law 280 and the Problem of Lawlessness in Indian Country*, 44 UCLA L. Rev. 1405 (1997). Copyright 1975 by Carole Goldberg. All rights reserved.

Herzberg, Stephen, *The Menominee Indians: Termination to Restoration*, 6 Am. Indian L. Rev. 143 (1978). Copyright 1978 by the American Indian Law Review. Permission also granted by the author. All rights reserved.

Kades, Eric, *The Dark Side of Efficiency*: Johnson v. M'Intosh *and the Expropriation of American Indian Lands*, 148 U. Penn. L. Rev. 1065 (2000). Copyright 2000 by the University of Pennsylvania Press. All rights reserved.

O'Connor, Sandra Day, *Lessons from the Third Sovereign: Indian Tribal Courts*, 33 Tulsa L. J. 1 (1997).

Otis, D.S., The Dawes Act the Allotment of Indian Lands (1934) (Francis P. Prucha ed. 1973).

Porter, Robert Odawi, *Strengthening Tribal Sovereignty Through Peacemaking: How the Anglo-American Legal Tradition Destroys Indigenous Societies*, 28 Colum. Hum. Rts. L. Rev. 235 (1997).

Royster, Judith V., *The Legacy of Allotment*, 27 Ariz. St. L. J. 1 (1995).

Swentzell, Rina, *Testimony of a Santa Clara Woman*, 14 Kan. J. L. & Pub. Pol'y 97 (2004).

Wilkinson, Charles F. & Biggs, Eric R., *The Evolution of the Termination Policy*, 3 Am. Indian L. Rev. 139 (1977).

Yazzie, Robert, *Life Comes from it: Navajo Justice Concepts*, 24 N.M. L. Rev. 175 (1994).

Yazzie, Robert, *"Watch Your Six": An Indian Nation Judge's View of 25 Years of Indian Law, Where We Are and Where We Are Going*, 23 Am. Indian L. Rev. 497 (1998/1999).

SUMMARY OF CONTENTS

■ ■ ■

TABLE OF CONTENTS

■ ■ ■

Page

TABLE OF CASES

The principal cases are in ***bold italic*** type. Cases cited or discussed in the text or excerpted materials are *italic* type. Reference are to pages. Cases cited in principal cases and within other quoted materials are included.

■ ■ ■

American Indian Law

Cases and Commentary

Fourth Edition

CHAPTER 1

INTRODUCTION

■ ■ ■

Introduction: American Indian Law and American Indian Nations and People

I. WHAT IS AMERICAN INDIAN LAW?

> There are few subjects in the history and law of the United States on which public views are more dramatically and flagrantly erroneous than on the subject of Indian affairs. According to the popular view, the Indian is a vanishing race; his lands are steadily dwindling; restricted as to the hunt and denied the warpath, he has nothing to live for and nothing to contribute to our civilization.

Felix Cohen, Handbook of Federal Indian Law v (1941 ed.). These words, written as the foreword to the first treatise on American Indian law, have an uncomfortable resonance even today. The history of American Indians, their unique legal status, and how that legal status has permitted an essential measure of independence for American Indian tribes and their cultures remain obscure to many people. The nature of the misconceptions is somewhat different now than it was in 1941. Then, the stereotype of the American Indian was that "he subsists on 'rations'; and he cannot sign his name without the approval of a reservation superintendent." *Id.* Today, it might be that American Indians are the passive recipients of "special rights" that allow them to take endangered species and own casinos to the detriment of the rest of society. To displace the modern stereotypes, at a minimum, a foundation in American Indian law is required. Again, words from 1941 seem relevant today: "That Indians have legal rights is a matter of little practical consequence unless the Indians themselves and those who deal with them are aware of those rights." *Id.* Awareness of Indian law has certainly increased since 1941. As some indication of this, three states (Washington, New Mexico and South Dakota) include federal Indian law on their bar exams and at least one other state (Wisconsin) has tested on the subject in a performance question. These are small but encouraging signs that the "flagrantly erroneous" views of Indians and their legal status are in retreat.

The legal status of Native nations in the United States is unique domestically, and even globally. At the core is tribal sovereignty. Recognized in thousands of treaties, statutes, executive orders, and court decisions, tribal sovereignty provides tribes with a government-to-government relationship with the federal government of the United States, places limits on state power over tribes and their territories, and affords tribes the ability to generate their own domestic laws. In a very broad sense, all of American Indian law might be described as laws about the sources, meanings and effects of the distinctive sovereign status of American Indian tribes.

Although each Native nation or tribe is in a constant process of defining the distinctive contours of its sovereignty, this book's primary focus is on the federal law that recognizes and limits tribal sovereignty, and governs the relationships between tribal sovereigns and state and federal governments. In many places, however, the book incorporates the diverse ways in which tribes defend and use their sovereignty because these tribal legal actions shape and create a context for Federal Indian Law. Within this broad description, several sub-topics emerge, each of which is explored throughout this casebook. First, the historical origins of tribal legal status provide both necessary context and the essential framework for all the modifications that follow. History is therefore treated separately in the introductory chapters, but is also incorporated throughout the subsequent text. Second, the legal relationship between tribes and the federal government, including questions concerning heightened obligations to tribes and the sources and limitations of federal power over tribes, is a distinctive and ubiquitous theme. Third, the extent of tribal jurisdiction over land and people is a recurring source of legal conflict. Some issues are relatively settled, such as the extent of tribal jurisdiction over tribal members. Others, in particular matters concerning tribal ability to govern non-Indian behavior within tribal territory, are sources of constant litigation and modification in the courts. Fourth, conflicts between state and tribal governments yield evolving and sometimes confusing legal rules. Questions such as which government has the right to tax activity within reservation boundaries recur, yielding clarity in some cases but uncertainty in others. Not all of the material covered in this casebook fits neatly into these four sub-topics. But all of it can be fairly said to relate to the larger encompassing theme of the sources, meanings, and effects of tribal sovereignty. Natural resource issues, for example, can only be understood within the unique context of the rights of tribes as governments that pre-dated non-Indian western settlement. The point of highlighting the central role of tribal sovereignty is not to present the field of American Indian Law as a unified and seamless web, but rather to be clear about the core values and stories that lie at its center.

II. A SNAPSHOT OF AMERICAN INDIAN NATIONS AND PEOPLE IN THE 21ST CENTURY

When American Indian individuals and tribes assert rights stemming from their distinct status, often they must overcome several uninformed presumptions. One is that American Indian nations vanished long ago. This presumption is less prevalent in the western United States, where sizeable Native land holdings and strong tribal and Alaska Native political and business organizations make it harder to relegate Indians to the distant past. But even in communities bordering large reservations, the degree of ignorance about the current political status of tribes remains acute. An obstacle of a different nature is the tendency to romanticize American Indians and their lives, and therefore to obscure the hardships of poverty and its consequences in Indian communities. Yet another misconception is that all American Indian tribes are raking in billions of dollars from gaming operations. A brief review of the "actual state of things" (a phrase which will soon be familiar to you) in Indian country will start the study of American Indian law on more solid footing.

American Indian tribes are numerous and diverse. Today, tribes employ an array of strategies to achieve thriving cultures and economies. There are hardships, often stemming from the historical break-up of tribal land bases and communities, but in general most Indian tribes are building stronger and more independent societies with the understanding and use of federal Indian law playing a critical role. There is an increasing amount of litigation in this area of law, but there is also a great deal of intergovernmental cooperation among tribes, the federal government, along with states and their political subdivisions.

The following overview of some of the key facts about contemporary American Indian nations draws from a variety of sources. Students might find the following on-line sources helpful to their research: the Bureau of Indian Affairs web-site, http://www.bia.gov; Turtle Talk (coordinated by Matthew Fletcher, Kathryn Fort, and Wenona Singel of Michigan State University Law School), http://turtletalk.wordpress.com; Indianz.com, http://www. indianz.com; The Harvard Project on American Indian Economic Development, http://www.hpaied.org; the Native American Constitution and Law Digitization Project (coordinated by the University of Oklahoma Law Library and the National Indian Law Library), http://thorpe.ou.edu; the National Congress of American Indians, http://www.ncai.org; and the United States Government Accountability office, http://www.gao.gov. The National Indian Law Library has an electronic database updated weekly which contains citations and links to every Indian law case decided in the state and federal courts since 2001, http://www.narf.org/nill/bulletins/ilb.htm. To obtain certain categories of information, however, nothing will substitute for a combination of old-fashioned visits to the library and road trips to the many and varied homelands of American Indian nations.

1. *American Indian Tribes and Tribal Governments*. Indian tribes, or nations as many today prefer to be called, have a distinct political status under United States domestic law. From that distinct status flows many of the legal rules, principles, and decisions you will be studying. Treaties were entered into with tribes, and even after treaty-making officially came to an end, federal legislation and executive orders continued to treat American Indians as tribes or nations, not just groups of individual members of a particular ethnicity.

Today, there are 573 federally recognized Indian tribes, including 229 Alaska Native tribes, which are mostly in remote villages. (The Pamunkey Tribe of Virginia was recognized in 2016, and six other Virginia tribes were recognized by Congress in 2018.) *See* Bureau of Indian Affairs, *Indian Entities Recognized and Eligible to Receive Services from the United States Bureau of Indian Affairs*, 83 Fed. Reg. 34863 (2018). For a list of tribes by state, *see* National Conference of State Legislatures, Federal and State Recognized Tribes (2016), http://www.ncsl.org/research/state-tribal-institute/list-of-federal-and-state-recognized-tribes. aspx [https:// perma.cc/9REJ-58SP] (The list of federally recognized tribes is published annually in the Federal Register by the Assistant Secretary of the Interior for Indian Affairs.) There are also a number of tribes that lack federal recognition, and they fall generally into two categories. First, Congress terminated the federal relationship with more than 100 tribes during the 1950's. Most of these tribes lost their land base and ceased to be eligible for federal programs and funding directed towards Indians. Many, though not all, have since been restored to federally recognized status. The second category consists of groups who never received federal recognition.

Today there is an administrative process available to non-federal tribes through which they may petition the federal government for recognition. Non-federal tribes may also pursue recognition through judicial proceedings or from Congress. Through any route, the process is costly, slow, and requires extensive historical and anthropological documentation. In all, although over 200 tribes have submitted letters of intent to pursue administrative recognition, only 18 tribes have received federal recognition through this process since 1978, while 32 have been recognized or restored by Congress. For a helpful study of the federal acknowledgment process, see Mark Edwin Miller, Forgotten Tribes: Unrecognized Tribes and the Federal Acknowledgment Process (2004).

Some tribes that lack federal recognition are nonetheless recognized as having distinct legal attributes under state law. State-recognized tribes include the Little Shell Band of Chippewa of Montana, the Haliwa–Saponi of North Carolina, and the Mattaponi and Pamunkey of Virginia. Some state-recognized tribes also have reservations created and recognized under state law.

Native Hawaiians have status-based rights pursuant to some Hawaiian state laws and programs, and are also eligible for many federal programs and benefits targeting Native people. But the absence of a recognized government-to-government relationship with the United States leaves some of these protections vulnerable to legal challenge. Federal legislation has been introduced to establish a direct federal relationship with Native Hawaiians, but to date no such bill has made it through Congress.

The 573 federally recognized Indian tribes have a range of different governmental structures. Many, including the Navajo, the Jicarilla Apache, and the Cheyenne River Sioux, just to name a few, have a tri-partite form of government, with an executive, legislative, and judicial branch similar to that of the United States federal and state governments. Others, and in particular smaller tribes, have little or no separation of powers, with constitutional provisions that allow executive branch members to participate in the legislative body, and/or provide for legislative review of decisions by the judicial branch. Increasingly, however, tribes are engaging in constitutional or other reform to ensure that their governmental structures both reflect and reinforce their tribal traditions and cultures, and fit with contemporary tribal needs for political and legal accountability. Often this means adopting constitutional requirements for judicial independence. *See* Frank Pommersheim, *A Path Near the Clearing: An Essay on Constitutional Adjudication in Tribal Courts*, 27 Gonz. L. Rev. 393 (1991–1992). A 2000 survey of tribal justice systems found that 93.5% of responding tribes had a judicial appeals process, and only 17.4% of tribes reported that legislative or executive bodies had the power to review court decisions. American Indian Law Center, Survey of Tribal Justice Systems and Courts of Indian Offenses: Final Report Prepared for the U.S. Department of the Interior, Bureau of Indian Affairs 22, 23 (2000).

2. *American Indian Land and Resources*. American Indian land is the most important cultural and economic asset for most tribes. Today approximately 56.2 million acres of land are held in trust by the federal government for American Indian tribes and individuals. *See* Bureau of Indian Affairs, Frequently Asked Questions, *available at* http://www.bia.gov/FAQs/. Alaska Natives hold an additional 45 million acres, set aside pursuant to the Alaska

Native Claims Settlement Act and Alaska Native Allotment Act. Further, many tribes now own some land in fee simple as a result of acquisition programs aimed at restoring the tribal land base. Unfortunately, the Department of Interior has not published a comprehensive review of tribal lands since December 1997, so more recent official figures for amounts and legal status of tribal lands are lacking. For an alternative source, with more recent data collected both from Indian tribes and the Bureau of Indian Affairs, see Tiller's Guide to Indian Country: Economic Profiles of American Indian Reservations (Veronica E. Velarde Tiller, ed., 2005).

Many tribal lands are rich in wildlife and natural resources. In the lower forty-eight states, 44 million acres of tribal lands are range and grazing lands, 5.3 million acres are commercial forest lands, and 2.5 million acres are crop lands. In terms of mineral resources, tribal lands hold 4 percent of U.S. oil and gas reserves, 30 percent of western coal reserves, and 40 percent of U.S. uranium deposits. Cohen's Handbook of Federal Indian Law 995 (2012). Tribal lands also have significant potential as sources for renewable energy. Ninety-three reservations have been identified as having high wind energy potential, and 118 as having high potential for biomass sources of energy. Tribes in the southwest and California have excellent potential for solar electricity, and some tribes have initiated small-scale solar programs. *See* Renewable Resources for America's Future, United States Department of the Interior, *available at* http://www.doi.gov/initiatives/renewable_energy.pdf.

Not all tribal land is located within reservation boundaries, but reservations, as demarcated in treaties, legislation, or executive orders, still play an important jurisdictional role in American Indian law. Tribal authority is not necessarily co-extensive with reservation borders, but some questions of governmental power depend on whether or not a reservation has been diminished or terminated. Today, there are 326 federally recognized Indian reservations, with great variations in size and type of landholdings. The Navajo Nation has the largest land base, with 16 million acres, most of which is in Arizona but with portions in New Mexico and Utah. The following table has the total acreage and type of land for the thirty largest reservations. Note that some tribes have increased their land base since 1985, while others have experienced some diminishment. Note also that such large land bases are unusual: many reservations comprise only a few hundred acres, while other tribes have no land base at all.

TOP THIRTY INDIAN LAND HOLDINGS BY TRIBE

Tribe	**State**	**Total Indian Land 1985, in acres[1]**	**Total Indian Land 2004, in acres[2]**
Navajo	Arizona, New Mexico, Utah	15,432,170	17,028,026
Tohono O'odham	Arizona	2,774,170	2,846,409
Pine Ridge	South Dakota	2,064,507	2,800,000
Cheyenne River	South Dakota	2,023,389	2,796,355
San Carlos	Arizona	1,826,541	1,822,074

TOP THIRTY INDIAN LAND HOLDINGS BY TRIBE

Tribe	State	Total Indian Land	Total Indian Land
Wind River	Wyoming	1,811,365	2,268,008
Ft. Apache / White Mountain	Arizona	1,664,972	1,684,225
Hopi	Arizona	1,561,213	1,862,731
Crow	Montana	1,516,005	1,536,317
Standing Rock	North Dakota, South Dakota	1,248,334	2,300,000
Ft. Berthold	North Dakota	1,200,666	922,750
Rosebud	South Dakota	1,776,239	884,194
Yakama	Washington	1,130,262	1,159,676
Colville	Washington	1,063,036	1,127,649
Uintah & Ouray	Utah	1,021,556	1,021,597
Hualapai	Arizona	992,463	1,015,565
Blackfeet	Montana	937,702	1,534,619
Ft. Peck	Montana	904,683	956,496
Jicarilla	New Mexico	823,580	928,273
Warm Springs	Oregon	643,491	348,000
Flathead	Montana	627,071	817,631
Ft. Belknap	Montana	620,971	655,306
Ute Mountain	Colorado	597,308	606,218
Red Lake	Minnesota	564,452	806,698
Ft. Hall	Idaho	489,878	546,500
Pyramid Lake	Nevada	476,729	464,966
Laguna	New Mexico	461,098	501,018
Mescalero	New Mexico	460,678	462,769
Northern Cheyenne	Montana	436,947	440,882
Gila River	Arizona	371,930	371,822

1. Source: Forest Service National Resource Guide to American Indian and Alaska Native Relations, app. D, 1997, *available at* http://www.fs.fed.us/people/tribal.

2. Sources: Tiller's Guide to Indian Country: Economic Profiles of American Indian Reservations (Veronica E. Velarde Tiller, ed., 2015).

3. *American Indian Demographics (population, income, age, health).* In the 2010 census, 5.2 million individuals, or 1.7 percent of the population, reported that they were American Indian/Alaska Native, either alone or in combination with some other race. Of this group, 2.9 million, or .9%, reported solely American Indian or Alaska Native descent. Forty-one percent of American Indian or Alaska Native respondents to the census lived in the West, 33 percent in the South, 17 percent in the Midwest, and 9.7 percent in the Northeast. The ten

states with the largest native populations (including both respondents who checked "American Indian alone," and "American Indian with at least one other race") were California (723,225), Oklahoma (482,760), Arizona (353,386), Texas (315,264), New York (221,058), New Mexico (219,512), Washington (198,998), North Carolina (184,082), Florida (162,562), and Michigan (139,095). The states in which native people comprised the largest percentage of the population were Alaska (19.5%), Oklahoma (12.9%), New Mexico (10.7%), and South Dakota (10.1%). *See* U.S. Bureau of the Census, *Census 2010, available at* http://www.census.gov.

Native Hawaiians were the largest Pacific Islander group in the United States, with 158,221 respondents reporting Native Hawaiian alone and an additional 491,673 reporting Native Hawaiian with at least one other race, out of a total of 973,336 Native Hawaiian and Pacific Islanders combined.

As of 2010, the Navajo Nation, with 286,731 enrolled members, was the largest tribe; while the Cherokee Nation of Oklahoma, with 284,247 members, was a close second. U.S. Census Bureau, *Census 2010 Summary Files*, United States *available at* http://www.census.gov. Most tribes are far smaller; only 34 tribes, just 5.8% of the total 582, had more than 10,000 members. Bureau of Indian Affairs, U.S. Dep't of the Interior, American Indian Population and Labor Force Report 8, 1-24 (2005). Nearly 2 million individuals were enrolled in a federally recognized American Indian tribe or Alaska Native village. *Id.* at iii.

While still a small percentage of the total United States population, American Indians have a significant enough presence in some regions to be a strong political force:

> Efforts to mobilize Indian voters have been greatest in a few western swing states, where such voters can make the difference between defeat or victory in certain races. *** In 2000, Indian voters had helped Maria Cantwell defeat Senator Slade Gorton, who was widely perceived as anti-Indian, and the Indian vote helped Al Gore carry New Mexico. Two years later, Indian voters again displayed their potential power. In South Dakota they provided the winning margin for Senator Tim Johnson in his very close reelection bid, and they were credited with helping to elect Governor Brad Henry in Oklahoma.

Daniel McCool, Susan M. Olson, and Jennifer L. Robinson, Native Vote: American Indians, the Voting Rights Act, and the Right to Vote 177 (2007).

Despite some indications of socioeconomic gains, American Indians and Alaska Natives remain, as a group, younger and poorer than their white counterparts. In 2014, American Indians and Alaska Natives had a median age of 31 years; the non-Hispanic white population was roughly six years older, with a median age of 37 years. About twenty-eight percent of American Indians and Alaska Natives lived below the poverty level, compared with 9.1% of non-Hispanic whites. About thirty-five percent of American Indian and Alaska Native children lived in poverty, compared to 10.9% percent of non-Hispanic white children. American Indians and Alaska Natives 65 and older had a poverty rate of 18.4%, compared to a seven percent rate for non-Hispanic whites. American Indian/Alaska Native families living in Indian areas (whether on reservations or on off-reservation Indian trust lands) had higher rates of poverty than the rest of the Native population. In 1999, thirty-six percent of American

Indian/Alaska Native families living in Indian areas were below the poverty level, as compared to twenty-two percent of all Native families. *See* Jill Fleury DeVoe, Kristen E. Darling-Churchill, and Thomas D. Snyder, Status and Trends in the Education of American Indians and Alaska Native, U.S. Dep't of Ed., Nat'l Center for Ed. Statistics, U.S. Gov't Printing Office 18, 22, 26 (2008), *available at* http://nces.ed.gov/pubs2008/2008084.pdf.

Health statistics also reveal distinct disparities between American Indians/Alaska Natives and other groups. In 2009–2011, American Indians and Alaska Natives were 15 times more likely to die of tuberculosis, 6.6 times more likely to die of alcohol abuse, 3.2 times more likely to die of cervical cancer, and 3.2 times more likely to die of diabetes than the population as a whole. Diabetes, a leading cause of mortality for American Indians/Alaska Natives, is significantly more prevalent than for all other races, with a 16.1% rate among the Indian Health Service patient population and a national average rate for all races of just 7.1%. While mortality rates for breast cancer declined for all other races between 1992–2002, rates for American Indian/Alaska Native women remained constant. Further, American Indian women diagnosed with breast cancer have lower 5-year survival rates compared to white women. Rates of Fetal Alcohol Syndrome (FAS) are higher among American Indians/Alaska Natives than the general population. In the Southwest, rates for Indians are reported at 9.8 cases of FAS per 1,000 live births, and in Alaska at 5.6 per 1,000, which is well above that for any other racial group. *See* Indian Health Service, 2009 National Summary: Measuring and Improving Quality Healthcare for American Indians/Alaska natives, Government Performance and Results Act (GPRA), *available at* http://www.ihs.gov/.

As the following table reveals, American Indians and Alaska Natives have higher rates of death across many categories, including the strikingly higher rate (more than three times higher than the rest of the population) of death by motor vehicle accidents.

INDIAN HEALTH SERVICE MORTALITY DISPARITIES TABLE			
	Rate	**Rate**	**Ratio:**
	AI/AN1[1]	**U.S. All Races**	**AI/AN:**
	2009-2011	**2010**	**U.S. All Races**
ALL CAUSES	**999.1**	**747.0**	**1.3**
ALCOHOL INDUCED	50.5	7.6	6.6
BREAST CANCER	21.0	25.3	0.8
CEREBROVASCULAR DISEASE	43.6	39.1	1.1
CHRONIC LIVER DISEASE	42.9	9.4	4.6
DIABETES	66.0	25.3	2.9

INDIAN HEALTH SERVICE MORTALITY DISPARITIES TABLE			
	Rate	Rate	Ratio:
	AI/AN1[1]	U.S. All Races	AI/AN:
	2009-2011	2010	U.S. All Races
ALL CAUSES	**999.1**	**747.0**	**1.3**
DISEASES OF THE HEART	231.1	232.3	1.0
HIV INFECTION	3.1	4.7	0.7
HOMICIDE (assault)	12.2	6.0	2.0
MALIGNANT NEOPLASMS (ALL)	180.7	190.1	1.0
MATERNAL DEATHS[2]	11.1	12.1	0.9
MOTOR VEHICLE CRASHES	51.2	15.3	3.3
PNEUMONIA & INFLUENZA	32.2	22.0	1.5
SUICIDE (Intentional self-harm)	17.9	10.8	1.7
TUBERCULOSIS	1.7	0.2	8.5
UNINTENTIONAL INJURIES	94.8	37.3	2.5

1. American Indian and Alaska Natives (AI/AN) in the IHS service area.

2. Rate per 100,000 live births. Rate does not meet the standards of reliability due to small numbers. The break in comparability for maternal mortality has not been quantified by NCHS.

Sources: Indian Health Service, 2018 Indian Health Disparities, Indian Health Service, *available at* https://www.ihs.gov/sites/newsroom/themes/responsive2017/display_objects/documents/factsheets/Disparities.pdf [https:// perma.cc/K7PB-LG4G]; Reilley B. et al., Death rates from human immunodeficiency virus and tuberculosis among American Indians/Alaska Natives in the United States, 1990-2009, Am J Public Health (Jun. 2014).

4. *American Indian Education.* Today, most American Indian families embrace the promise of upward mobility and economic success that education offers, but the history of American Indian education, which you will read about in detail in Chapter 3, is particularly fraught with hardship and government oppression. The United States government's prior policies of forcing American Indian children to separate from their families, shed their languages, and abandon their cultures in the name of assimilative education have left difficult legacies. First, the transition from federal control of American Indian education to local and tribal control is well under way, yet not complete. Second, gaps in attendance, achievement and graduation rates between American Indians and other groups persist, despite signs of progress in some areas.

The official policy of the federal government today is to provide American Indian children with the highest quality education, and to do so by tailoring programs to their unique cultural and linguistic needs. In addition, various federal laws and regulations require American Indian parent and community involvement, and encourage tribal and community control over educational institutions and programs. *See* Cohen's Handbook of Federal Indian Law 1398 (2012). More than ninety percent of American Indian children attend state public schools, reflecting both federal policies of providing funding for public school districts that educate American Indian children, and ongoing skepticism by many American Indian parents of schools funded or run by the BIA under the authority of the Bureau of Indian Education (BIE), which was renamed from the Office of Indian Education Programs in 2006. Less than ten percent of Indian children attend schools that receive some or all of their funding from the BIE. More than two-thirds of the BIE-funded schools are run by Indian communities or tribes, leaving less than one third still operated directly by the BIE. *See id.* at 1400.

In the past twenty years, increasing numbers of Indian students have completed high school and gone on to college. The number of Indian students earning post-secondary degrees more than doubled between 1976 and 2006. *See.* Jill Fleury DeVoe, Kristen E. Darling-Churchill, and Thomas D. Snyder, Status and Trends in the Education of American Indians and Alaska Native, U.S. Dep't of Ed., Nat'l Center for Ed. Statistics, U.S. Gov't Printing Office 126 (2008), *available at* http://nces.ed.gov/pubs2008/2008084.pdf [https://perma.cc/N24R-KLPN]. In spring 2004, some 69 percent of Indian high school seniors expected to attain a bachelor's degree or higher. *Id.* at 60. Also relevant to the increasing prospects of educational success for Indian students, there are now thirty-two tribally controlled colleges, seven of which are four-year institutions and twenty-five of which offer two-year programs. *Id.* at 130. Students who initially enroll in tribal colleges are much more likely to complete a post-secondary degree than those who start off at non-Indian colleges. *See* Cohen's Handbook of Federal Indian Law 1405 (2012). In 2014, the six-year graduation rate for American Indians/Alaska Native students was 41% while the overall graduation rate for full-time undergraduate students was 60%. *See* Lauren Musu-Gillette et al., Status and Trends in the Education of Racial and Ethnic Groups 2017, U.S. Dep't of Ed., Nat'l Center for Ed. Statistics v (2017), *available at* https://nces.ed.gov/pubs2017/2017051.pdf [https://perma.cc/2JC9-WMRM].

Alongside these indications of success are statistics revealing the amount of ground that remains to be covered to achieve equal educational attainment for Native students. In 2014, only fourteen percent of the American Indian/Alaska Native population over twenty-five had a bachelor's degree, compared with thirty percent of the total population. *See* Lauren Musu Gillette et al., *supra* at 129. Absentee, suspension, and drop-out rates remain higher for Indian children than for other groups, and achievement rates, as measured by reading and math tests administered in the fourth and eighth grades, remain lower. *See* DeVoe et al., *supra,* at 148, 52-59, 70-81. In addition, for those Indian children attending BIA-funded schools, the chances that their school facility is dilapidated, crumbling, or otherwise inadequate are unacceptably high. *See* GAO, BIA and DOD Schools: Student Achievement and Other Characteristics Often Different from Public Schools', GAO–01–934, 25 (2001). Something to consider as you study the materials on American Indian law in the following chapters is the extent to which the unique legal relationship between Indian tribes and the federal government has formed the basis of both the deficits Indian students struggle with today, and the promising signs of success that are emerging.

5. *American Indian Economic Conditions and Economic Development.* American Indian tribes are extremely diverse in terms of their economic profiles. Taxation forms the backbone of governmental revenue for many tribes. For tribes with a significant land base, natural resources such as fisheries, range and agricultural lands, recreational and tourism sites, water rights, wind energy and mineral resources provide bases for economic development. Tribes also engage in business activities including banking, telecommunications, manufacturing, retail and service establishments, and gaming. For many tribes, the goal of economic development is not primarily to generate wealth for its own sake. Rather, as found by the Harvard Project on Economic Development, "Native nations are pursuing economic development in order to have the freedom to control their own political, cultural and social destinies and to have the ability to sustain communities where their citizens can and want to live." The Harvard Project on American Indian Economic Development, The State of the Native Nations: Conditions Under U.S. Policies of Self–Determination 112 (2008).

An introductory word or two is required about gaming in particular due to the disproportionate attention that this form of economic development garners from various media sources. The legal framework that recognizes the tribal power to engage in gaming operations, but that also requires tribal/state negotiations and accommodations in the gaming context, is discussed in detail in Chapter 7. As an initial matter, it is important to know a handful of salient facts. First, of the 573 federally recognized Indian tribes, less than half have gaming enterprises. Of the 238 tribes that do have gaming, many use the revenue to reinvest in other forms of economic development as well as cultural and educational programs and institutions. For example, the Oneida Indian Nation of Wisconsin built a school that reflects and teaches about Oneida Culture. The Salt River Pima–Maricopa Indian Community in Arizona constructed a dialysis clinic. The Tohono O'odham Nation, also in Arizona, funds its police and border patrol budget with gaming revenues. The Rosebud Sioux Tribe of South Dakota pays for school clothes for needy students. These are just a few examples. A review by the National Indian Gaming Association found that tribes spent net government revenue from gaming in the following manner: "20% of net revenue is used for education, children and elders, culture, charity and other purposes; 19% goes to economic development; 17% to health care; 17% to police and fire protection; 16% to infrastructure; 11% to housing." National Indian Gaming Association, The Economic Impact of Indian Gaming in 2009, *available at* http://www.indiangaming.org/info/NIGA_2009_Economic_Impact_Report.pdf. While a handful of tribes near population centers have gotten very wealthy from Indian gaming, for most tribes the profits from gaming provide a necessary means to fund some government services but not much more. This is not to say that gaming in the Indian nation context is free of problems. Furthermore, many tribes choose not to engage in gaming for cultural and moral reasons. But for Indian tribes who do choose to adopt this form of economic development, the financial benefits can form the basis of a diverse and healthy program of cultural and social revitalization.

Even with gaming and the other forms of economic development mentioned above, poverty and unemployment remain persistent features of reservation life. In 2005, the average unemployment rate for Indians on or near reservations was 49 percent, and reached as high as 89 percent on the poorest reservations. *See* Cohen's Handbook of Federal Indian Law 1321 (2012). In 2000, average poverty rates were 37 percent in non-gaming areas, and even those reservation areas that had gaming retained a poverty rate of 27 percent. *See* Jonathan B. Taylor & Joseph P. Kalt, American Indians on Reservations: A Databook of Socio-economic Change Between the 1990 and 2000 Censuses 21 (2005), *available at* http://www.ncaiprc.org/pdf/AmericanIndiansonReservationsADatabookofSocioeconomicChange.pdf. As noted in the sections on demographics and education above, health statistics sadly mirror the disproportionate poverty rates, as do the relatively lower levels of educational achievement for Indian children. Even with the impressive amount of economic diversification in recent years, of which gaming is a part, suitable forms of economic development remain a high priority for Indian tribes.

6. *American Indian Language and Culture.* The United States is a place of striking linguistic diversity. This is in large part due to the more than 175 Native languages that are still spoken throughout North America, north of the Mexico border. Yet there is concern among tribal peoples and experts that this diversity is at risk. Of the Native languages still spoken, 74 are considered "almost extinct," with only a handful of elderly speakers remaining; 58 have fewer than 1,000 speakers, 25 have 1,000–10,000 speakers, and only 8 have more than 10,000 speakers. The Native language that is most widely spoken today is Navajo, with 148,530 speakers. While this sounds robust, a challenge for all languages including Navajo is the lack of fluency among young people. Only 20 of the remaining Native languages are spoken widely by children. *See* MIT Indigenous Language Initiative, http://web.mit.edu/linguistics/mitili/language%20loss.html; Indigenous Language Institute, http://www.indigenous-language.org. In addition, approximately 75 Native languages have been lost since European contact, according to a conservative estimate. *See* The Harvard Project on Economic Development, The State of Native Nations: Conditions Under U.S. Policies of Self–Determination 283 (2008).

As with respect to American Indian education generally, the federal government's official policy towards Native languages today is to reverse the harmful effects of prior policies. After centuries of active suppression of Native languages, in 1990 Congress passed the Native American Languages Act, 25 U.S.C. §§ 2901–2906. The Act aligns the policies of self-determination with those of protecting and promoting Native languages, and encourages the support and teaching of Native languages by tribes, as well as by state and other educational institutions. *See* Cohen's Handbook of Federal Indian Law 1302-03 (2012). Many tribes have embarked on language retention programs, requiring their inclusion in school curricula and providing other means of spreading the knowledge of remaining fluent speakers. Tribal programs often rely on the interest and expertise of universities, which can provide human and technical support to back up fluent Native language speakers. The language situation is therefore precarious, but tribes and their supporters are making efforts to make it less so.

The situation with regard to the vitality of American Indian culture is harder to assess. Culture is a moving target in that tribes, like all human communities, evolve as circumstances change. To the extent that land has always played a critical role in American Indian culture and religion, the historic diminishment of the tribal land base, and the accompanying destruction of certain life ways, have had irreversible effects on some cultural groupings and practices. Yet many tribes have found ways to forge living cultures that retain an essence of the past while accommodating drastically changed circumstances. Tribes have successfully recruited federal law, in particular the Native American Graves Protection and Repatriation Act, to aid in these efforts. Battles over sacred sites have also met with some success, though more so in processes of negotiation with federal agencies than in the federal courts. These and other topics related to tribal culture and religion are explored in Chapter 11.

Jonathan Lear, a philosophy professor, has written a moving and thoughtful meditation on how the Crow Tribe managed to come back from the brink of cultural death brought on by their confinement to a reservation. As Lear describes, the leadership of courageous and visionary tribal leaders, in particular Chief Plenty Coups, made it possible to resurrect Crow culture from the ashes of a way of life that had been obliterated. *See* Jonathan Lear, Radical Hope: Ethics in the Face of Cultural Devastation (2006). There have been other such visionary American Indian leaders, many of whom have engaged with and shaped the body of American Indian law as part of their survival strategy. If this were not so, the American Indian tribes that persist as distinct communities today would not be practicing indigenous cultures. Yet it is clear that they are, and that the rhythms of ancient traditions ring truly, not just as memories of times past, but as living ceremonies for today. As you make your way through the materials in this casebook, occasionally stop to ask yourself what, if any, is the connection between all of this law and that reality.

CHAPTER 2

ORIGINS OF FEDERAL INDIAN LAW

■ ■ ■

As the Solicitor for the U.S. Department of the Interior wrote in 1941, "Federal Indian law is a subject that cannot be understood if the historical dimension of existing law is ignored." Nathan Margold, Foreword, in Felix S. Cohen's Handbook of Federal Indian Law xxvii (photo reprint 1986) (1941). Even more than in other fields, centuries of interactions between Indians and non-Indians fundamentally shape modern law. This history is the product of conflicting factors, in particular non-Indian desire to appropriate resources possessed by Indians while ideologically justifying that appropriation, and the desire of American Indian peoples to survive without giving up their tribal and cultural identities. Sociologist Stephen Cornell describes this history as follows:

> For four centuries non-Indians in North America have had an "Indian problem." *** First, it has been an economic problem: how best to secure access to Indian resources, land in particular. Second, it has been a problem in cultural transformation: how best to accomplish the cultural transformation of Indians into non-Indians. Third, and consequently, it has been a political problem: how to maintain an effective system of controls over Indian groups so that problems one and two could be satisfactorily resolved.
>
> ***
>
> Indians, on the other hand, have had what might be called a "Euro–American problem." In its essence this problem seems to have been tribal survival: the maintenance of particular sets of social relations, more or less distinct cultural orders, and some measure of political autonomy in the face of invasion, conquest, and loss of power.
>
> ***
>
> The working out of these two inverse and conflictual agendas has given context and shape to Indian–White relations. The history of those relations can be viewed as a record of the attempts of each group—Indians and Whites—to solve the particular problem they have had to face. Those attempts have not proceeded independently. On the contrary, they have conditioned each other. In the long drama of Indian–White interaction, each actor has been forced to respond to the actions of the other or to the consequences of those actions, manifest in concrete social conditions and relationships.

Stephen Cornell, The Return of the Native: American Indian Political Resurgence 6–7 (1988). Federal Indian Law itself arises from inconsistent principles, "rooted in the fundamental contradiction between the historical fact and continuing realities of colonization, on the one hand, and the constitutional themes of limited government, democracy, inclusion, and fairness that, on the other hand, constitute part of our 'civil religion.'" Philip P. Frickey, *Marshalling Past and Present: Colonialism, Constitutionalism, and Interpretation in Federal Indian* Law, 107 Harv. L. Rev. 381, 384 (1993). In reading the next chapters, think about how these conflicting factors play out in the laws and policies of this formative era.

I. COLONIAL INFLUENCES ON AMERICAN INDIAN POLICY

A. FIRST THEORIES

From the beginning, the "Indian problem" was a legal one: how could European nations assert governmental authority and property rights in land occupied by other peoples?

The first answers developed from medieval justifications for the Crusades. Between the eleventh and thirteenth centuries, Christian kings acting on papal orders led holy wars into Jerusalem and the Middle East. Voluminous legal opinions and commentary sought to legitimize these invasions. Some argued that no ruler had legitimate sovereignty without sanction by the Pope, so invading the lands of these illegitimate rulers violated no legal rights. The more moderate thirteenth-century Pope Innocent IV, himself a lawyer, argued that although the infidel rulers might have legitimate secular authority in their lands, the Pope had the right to punish violations of the universal "law of nature." Deriving this law of nature from biblical sources, Innocent IV declared that the pope could authorize war against countries that worshipped idols or refused to admit preachers of the gospel. *See* Robert A. Williams, Jr., The American Indian in Western Legal Thought: The Discourses of Conquest 13–14 (1990).

In the fifteenth century, these theories were adapted to the colonization of continents discovered by European explorers. European countries competed with each other for profitable trade routes and resources. Presenting the populations they discovered as ripe for conversion to Christ, they obtained papal sanction for their domination of new lands.

Portugal was the first winner in this race. In 1436, Portugal obtained papal permission to colonize the Canary Islands after reporting that its residents "are not unified by a common religion, nor are they bound by the chains of law, they are lacking normal social intercourse, living in the country like animals. They have no houses and no clothing except coverlets of palm leaves or goat skins which are worn as an outer garment by the most honored men." In 1455, Pope Nicolas V extended Portugal's exclusive authority to include all of Africa, noting that the Portuguese king had the right "to invade, search out, capture, vanquish, and subdue all Saracens and pagans whatsoever, and other enemies of Christ wheresoever placed" and to "reduce their persons to perpetual slavery, and to apply and appropriate to himself [their] kingdoms *** and to convert them to his and their use and profit." Reprinted in I European Treaties Bearing on the History of the United States and its Dependencies to 1648 at 23 (Frances Gardiner Davenport, ed. 1917).

The resulting Portuguese monopoly over trade with Africa inspired Spain to seek out new lands and trade routes, including by financing Christopher Columbus' trip to find a new passage to India. Columbus struck landfall in the Caribbean, but believed until his death that he had discovered a new route to South Asia. In 1493, Columbus wrote enthusiastically to his sponsors:

> I found very many islands peopled with inhabitants beyond number. And, of them all, I have taken possession for their highnesses and the royal standard displayed; and I was not gainsaid. *** There could be no believing, without seeing, such harbors as are here, as well as the many and great rivers, and excellent waters, most of which contain gold. *** [T]here are many spiceries, and great mines of gold and other metals. The people of this island and of all other islands which I have found and of which I have found and seen, or not seen, all go naked, men and women, just as their mothers bring them forth. *** Of anything they have, if it be asked for, they never say no, but invite the person to have it. *** And whether it be a thing of value, or of little worth, they are straightaways content with whatever might be given in return for it. *** They took even pieces of broken hoops, and gave whatever they had, like senseless brutes. ***

Columbus' descriptions were only a little more accurate than his geographical sense. But these reports caused King Ferdinand and Queen Isabella to anxiously petition the pope for ownership of these fabled lands. Eager to secure Spanish support in a battle to depose him, the famously corrupt Pope Alexander VI willingly obliged:

> *** [Christopher Columbus has] discovered certain very remote islands and even mainlands that hitherto had not been discovered by others; wherein dwell very many peoples living in peace, and, as reported, going unclothed, and not eating flesh. Moreover *** these very peoples living in the said islands and countries believe in one God, the Creator in heaven, and seem sufficiently disposed to embrace the Catholic faith and be trained in good morals. ***
>
> *** In the islands and countries already discovered are found gold, spices, and very many other precious things of divers kinds and qualities. Wherefore, as becomes Catholic kings and princes *** you have purposed with the favor of divine clemency to bring under your sway the said mainlands and islands with their residents and inhabitants and to bring them to the Catholic faith. ***
>
> [I]n order that you may enter upon so great an undertaking *** we, of our own accord, not at your instance nor the request of anyone else in your regard *** assign to you *** all islands and mainlands found and to be found, discovered and to be discovered towards the west and south, by drawing and establishing a line from the Arctic pole, namely the north, to the Antarctic pole. *** With this proviso however that none of the islands and mainlands *** be in the actual possession of any Christian king or prince. ***

The Bull *Inter Caetera* (May 4, 1493). The following year, Spain began its colonization of the New World.

In 1510, the King's lawyer Palacio Rubios drafted the *Requerimiento* to explain the effect of the papal decree to the native people. The Spanish conquistadors were ordered to read it to any newly discovered people before commencing hostilities:

> Of all the nations God our Lord gave charge to one man, called St. Peter, that he should be Lord and Superior of all the men in the world, that all should obey him, and that he should be the head of the whole human race, wherever men should live, and under whatever law, sect or belief they should be; and he gave him the world for his kingdom and jurisdiction. ***
>
> ***
>
> One of these Pontiffs *** made donation of these isles and mainland to the aforesaid King and Queen and to their successors, our lords, with all that there are in these territories, as is contained in certain writings which passed upon the subject as aforesaid, which you can see if you wish.
>
> *** Wherefore, as best we can, we ask and require you that you consider what we have said to you, and that you take the time that shall be necessary to understand and deliberate upon it, and that you acknowledge the Church as the Ruler and Superior of the whole world, and the high priest called Pope, and in his name the King and Queen Doña Juana our lords, in his place, as superiors and lords and kings of these islands and this Tierra-firme by virtue of the said donation, and that you consent and give place that these religious fathers should declare and preach to you the aforesaid.
>
> ***
>
> But if you do not do this, or if you maliciously delay doing it, I certify to you that with the help of God, we shall forcefully enter into your country, and shall make war against you in all ways and manners that we can, and shall subject you to the yoke and obedience of the Church and of their Highnesses; we shall take you and your wives and your children, and shall make slaves of them, and as such shall sell and dispose of them as their Highnesses may command; and we shall take away your goods, and shall do you all the mischief and damage that we can, as to vassals who do not obey, and refuse to receive their lord, and resist and contradict him; and we protest that the deaths and losses which shall accrue from this are your fault, and not that of their Highnesses, or ours, nor of these cavaliers who come with us. And that we have said this to you and made this *Requerimiento* we request the notary here present to give his testimony in writing, and we ask the rest who are present that they should be witnesses of this *Requerimiento*.

Strange as it may seem, the *requerimiento* was intended to give America's native inhabitants an opportunity to accept the new European authority. Yet both the content and manner of delivery made comprehension, let alone knowing consent, impossible:

> [T]he Requirement was read to trees and empty huts when no Indians were to be found. Captains muttered its theological phrases into their beard on the edge of sleeping Indian settlements, or even a league away before starting the formal attack, and at times some leather-lunged Spanish notary hurled its sonorous phrases after the Indians as they fled into the mountains.

Lewis Hanke, The Spanish Struggle for Justice in America 34 (1949).

NOTES AND QUESTIONS

1. Why did the Europeans place such emphasis on legal formalities in their conquest of the Americas?

2. What was the function of the various descriptions of the peoples of the newly discovered lands? What do you notice about these descriptions?

3. Who was the *Requerimiento* intended to convince? Who was it intended to appease?

B. THE INFLUENCE OF FRANCISCUS DE VICTORIA

The brutality of the Spanish colonization of the New World is famous. Indigenous people that did not succumb to European diseases were often enslaved, indentured, or killed. The protests of Fra. Bartolome de las Casas, a missionary sent to the Indies in 1502, generated Spanish debate on Indian rights. In a series of lectures in 1532, the Dominican scholar Franciscus de Victoria took up the question of Spanish power over the New World and its peoples. His work is widely recognized as laying the foundation for both International Law and Federal Indian Law.

Victoria rejected the arguments with which Spain had justified power over the Indians and their lands:

> The first allegation to consider is that the Emperor is lord of the whole world and therefore of these barbarians also. *** Now, in point of human law, it is manifest that the Emperor is not the lord of the world, because either this would be by the sole authority of some law, and there is none such; or, if there were, it would be void of effect, inasmuch as the law presupposes jurisdiction. *** [T]he Spaniards can not justify on this ground their seizure of the provinces in question.
>
> A second alleged title to the lawful possession of these lands, and one which is vehemently asserted, is traced through the Supreme Pontiff. *** [But] the Pope has no temporal power over the Indian aborigines or over other unbelievers. *** The corollary follows that even if the barbarians refuse to recognize any lordship of the Pope, that furnishes no ground for making war on them and seizing their property.
>
> [T]here is another title which can be set up, namely a right of discovery; *** Not much, however, need be said about this third title of our, because *** the barbarians were true owners, both from the public and from the private standpoint. *** [I]n and by itself [discovery] gives no support to a seizure by the aborigines any more than if it had be they who had discovered us.
>
> There remains another *** title which is put forward, namely, by voluntary choice. For on arrival of the Spaniards, we find them declaring to the aborigines how the King of Spain has sent them for their good and admonishing them to receive and accept him as lord and king; and the

> aborigines replied that they were content to do so. *** This title too is insufficient. This appears, in the first place, because fear and ignorance, which vitiate every choice *** were markedly operative in [these] cases. *** Further, inasmuch as the aborigines, as said above, had real lords and princes, the populace could not procure new lords without other reasonable cause. ***

Franciscus de Victoria, De Indis et de Ivre Belli Relectiones 130–48 (Ernest Nys ed.) (J. Bate trans., Carnegie Institution 1917) (orig. ed. 1557). Although Victoria rejected the common justifications for European title, he proposed certain Spanish rights based on what he asserted were universal rights under the law of nations:

> [T]o keep certain people out of the city or province as being enemies, or to expel them when already there, are acts of war. Inasmuch, then, as the Indians are not making a just war on the Spaniards (it being assumed that the Spaniards are doing no harm), it is not lawful for them to keep the Spaniards away from their territory.
>
> Also *** the Spaniards are the neighbors of the barbarians, as appears from the Gospel parable of the Samaritan (St. Luke, ch. 10). But they are bound to love their neighbors as themselves (St. Matthew, ch. 22). Therefore they may not keep them away from their country without cause: "When it is said 'Love thy neighbor' it is clear that every man is our neighbor" (St. Augustine's De Doctrina Christiana). ***
>
> The Spaniards may lawfully carry on trade among the native Indians, so long as they do no harm to their country. *** [T]he sovereign of the Indians is bound by the law of nature to love the Spaniards. Therefore the Indians may not causelessly prevent the Spaniards from making their profit where this can be done without injury to themselves. ***
>
> If the Indian natives wish to prevent the Spaniards from enjoying any of their above-named rights under the law of nations *** the Spaniards ought in the first place to use reason and persuasion in order to remove scandal and ought to show in all possible methods that they do not come to the hurt of the natives. *** [B]ut, if safety can not otherwise be had *** they may follow it up with war. *** Also, it is a universal rule of the law of nations that whatever is captured in war becomes the property of the conqueror. ***
>
> Another possible title is by way of propagation of Christianity. *** Christians have a right to preach and declare the Gospel in barbarian lands. *** If the Indians—whether it be their lords or the populace—prevent the Spaniards from freely preaching the Gospel *** [the Spanish] may then accept or even make war, until they succeed in obtaining facilities and safety for preaching the Gospel. *** [I]f there is no other way to carry on the work of religion, this furnishes the Spaniards with another justification for seizing the lands and territory of the natives and for setting up new lords there. ***
>
> There is another title *** I dare not affirm it at all, nor do I entirely condemn it. It is this: Although the aborigines in question are *** not wholly unintelligent, yet they are little short of that condition, and so are unfit to found or administer a lawful State up to the standard required by human and civil claims. Accordingly they have no proper laws nor

> magistrates, and are not even capable of controlling their family affairs; they are without literature or arts, not only the liberal arts, but the mechanical arts also; they have no careful agriculture and no artisans. *** It might, therefore, be maintained that in their own interests the sovereigns of Spain might undertake the administration of their country, *** and might even given them new lords, so long as this was clearly for their benefit.

Id. at 151–157.

NOTES AND QUESTIONS

1. Felix S. Cohen, whose 1941 Handbook of Federal Indian Law was the first systematic exploration of the field, saw in the work of Spanish theologians and Victoria in particular the origins of "the humane principles" in Indian law, which he listed as "(1) The principle of equality of all races; (2) The principle of tribal self-government; (3) the principle of Federal sovereignty in Indian affairs; and (4) the principle of governmental protection of Indians." Felix Cohen, *The Spanish Origin of Indian Rights in the Law of the United States*, 31 Geo. L.J. 1, 3 (1942). Robert A. Williams, Jr., a modern authority on the intellectual origins of Federal Indian Law, writes that through Victoria's theories the "[h]ierarchical subjugation of the alien and divergent cultures of the New World could proceed on a 'modern,' desacralized basis, but a basis nonetheless possessed of all the missionary, chauvinistic zeal that had attended Christianity's will to empire in earlier medieval Crusades to distant lands held by unregenerate 'barbarians and infidels.' " Robert A. Williams, Jr., The American Indian in Western Legal Thought: The Discourses of Conquest 107 (1990). How did these two accomplished scholars get such divergent meanings from the same text?

2. Whatever its ultimate impact, Victoria's lectures had an immediate effect on papal and Spanish law. In 1537, Pope Paul III issued the Bull *Sublimeus Deus*:

> [N]otwithstanding whatever may have been or may be said to the contrary, the said Indians and all other people who may later be discovered by Christians, are by no means to be deprived of their liberty or the possession of their property, even though they be outside the faith of Jesus Christ; and that they may and should, freely and legitimately, enjoy their liberty and the possession of their property; nor should they be in any way enslaved; should the contrary happen, it shall be null and of no effect.

Quoted in Felix Cohen, *The Spanish Origin of Indian Rights in the Law of the United States*, 31 Geo. L.J. 1, 12 (1942). In 1542, after consulting Victoria on the rights of Indians, the Spanish King Charles V promulgated laws providing that, "Indians are free persons and vassals of the crown"; "Lawsuits among the Indians are to be decided *** according to their usage and custom"; "for no reason of war or for any other *** is any Indian to be made a slave"; and "Nothing is to be taken from the Indians except in fair trade." D'Arcy McNickle, They Came Here First 125–126 (1975). Although brutalities continued on the ground, these were violations of official Spanish law. This divergence between stated law and actual practice would continue throughout the colonization of the Americas.

C. NORTH AMERICAN DEBATES AND PRACTICES

With Latin America and Africa claimed by Spain and Portugal, other European nations turned their colonial aspirations to North America. In 1606, the English King James I gave the Virginia Company, a joint stock corporation, a license to found a colony in Virginia and other parts of America “which are not now actually possessed by any Christian Prince or People.” The document commended the Company for “their Desires for the Furtherance of so noble a Work, which may, by the Providence of Almighty God, hereafter tend to the Glory of his Divine Majesty, in propagating of Christian Religion to such People, as yet live in Darkness and miserable Ignorance of the true Knowledge and Worship of God, and may in time bring the Infidels and Savages, living in those parts, to human Civility, and to a settled and quiet Government.” But the King and company had more than Indian souls in their sights. The charter provided the right to “dig, mine, and search for all Manner of Mines of Gold, Silver, and Copper *** And to HAVE and enjoy the Gold, Silver, and Copper, to be gotten thereof, to the Use and Behoof of the same Colonies, and the Plantations thereof; YIELDING therefore to Us, our Heirs and Successors, the fifth Part only of all the same Gold and Silver, and the fifteenth Part of all the same Copper, so to be gotten or had.”

Original Massachusetts Seal. Courtesy of Massachusetts Archive

The New England colonies were founded less to produce profit than to establish permanent communities for the emigrants. They too, however, used conversion of the Indians as a justification for their endeavor. The original seal of the Massachusetts colony featured an Indian man with the words “Come Over and Help Us,” written on a ribbon coming from his mouth. Richard Hakluyt was a London lawyer and advocate for English settlement in North America. In a prominent piece of advocacy published in 1585, he stated the goals of colonization: “1. To plant Christian Religion; 2. To trafficke; 3. To Conquer; Or, to doe all three.” Envisioning America: English Plans for the Colonization of North America, 158-1640 at 1, 40 (Peter C. Mancall, ed. 2d ed. 2017).

The initial royal charters suggest little concern for the rights of the peoples occupying the land. But the question was immediately a subject of vehement debate. William Crashaw, one of the ministers to the Virginia Company, preached in 1609 that the "first and fundamental" objection to the colony "is the doubt of lawfulness of the action. *** A Christian may take nothing from a Heathen against his will, but in faire and lawfull bargaine." Hugo Grotius, whose work on International Law would greatly influence the American founders, wrote that is was "shameless to claim for oneself by right of discovery what is held by another, even though the occupant may be wicked, may hold wrong views about God, or may be dull of wit." Hugo Grotius, II On the Law of War and Peace 550 (1625) (Francis W. Kelsey trans. 1964). (Grotius did not write from purely disinterested motives. He first developed his theories as a lawyer for the Dutch East India Company, which desired to trade in areas over which Portugal claimed exclusive dominion by papal grant.)

Others used a combination of religious and economic philosophy to argue that the native residents had no property claims that the colonizers needed to recognize. In his 1609 pamphlet, "A Good Speed to Virginia," minister Robert Gray asked, "By what right or warrant can we enter into the land of these Savages, take away their rightful inheritance from them, and plant ourselves in their place, being unwronged or unprovoked by them?" He provided his own answer:

> In Virginia the people are savage and incredibly rude, they worship the divell, offer their young children in sacrifice unto him, wander up and downe like beastes, and in manners and conditions, differ very little from beastes, having no Arte, nor science, nor trade, to imploy themselves. *** [T]hese Savages have no particular propriety in any part or parcel of that Countrey, but only a general residence there, as wild beasts have in the forest *** so that if the whole land be taken from them, there is not a man that can complaine of any particular wrong done unto him. ***

Robert Gray, A Good Speed to Virginia, quoted in Peter Harrison, *"Fill the Earth and Subdue It": Biblical Warrants for Colonization in Seventeenth Century England*, 29 J. Religious Hist. 1, 15 (2005).

John Winthrop, first governor of the Massachusetts Bay Colony, similarly dismissed the property rights of the Indians:

> That which lies comon, & hath never beene replenished or subdued, is free to any that possesse & improve it: ffor God hath given to the sonnes of men a double right to the earth: theire is a naturall right, & a civill right. The first right was naturall when men held the earth in common every man soweing & feeding where he pleased; then as men and theire cattle increased they appropriated certaine parcells of Ground by inclosinge & peculiar mannerance, & this in tyme gave them a civill right. *** As for the Natives of New England, they inclose noe Land, neither have any setled habytation, nor any tame Cattle to improve the Land by, & soe have noe other but a Naturall Right to those Countries. Soe as if we leave them sufficient for their use, we may lawfully take the rest, there being more then enough for them and us.

I Life and Letters of John Winthrop: Governor of the Massachusetts–Bay Company at their Emigration to New England 311–312 (Robert C. Winthrop ed. 1869). Winthrop wrote these words in 1629, a year before he left England or had ever observed native property use. In 1632, Roger Williams, who had studied indigenous customs and languages, attacked the fiction that the New England tribes had no concept of property rights: "The Natives are very exact and punctuall in the bounds of their lands, belonging to this or that Prince or people. *** And I have known them make sale or bargain amongst themselves for a small piece, or quantity of Ground: notwithstanding a sinfull opinion amongst mauy [sic] that Christians have right to Heathens Lands." I The Complete Writings of Roger Williams 120 (1963). Williams also "related that the Narragansets believed the English had traveled across the sea because they had burned up all their wood. 'Have you no trees?' the Narragansetts asked their new neighbors." Lisa Brooks, The Common Pot: The Recovery of Native Space in the Northeast 7 (2008).

Many other observers reported farming and property rights among the Indian tribes by the early 1600s. In 1603 Martin Pring recorded the "sowne Tobacco, Pompions, Cowcumbers and such like" grown by the native people of Cape Cod, James Smith wrote of the tribes near Jamestown that "Each household knoweth their owne lands & gardens. *** They all know their severall landes, and habitations, and limits, to fish, fowle, or hunt in," while John Lawson wrote that the tribes of North Carolina "have no Fence to part one anothers Lots in their Corn–Fields; but every Man knows his own, and it scarce ever happens, that they rob one another of so much as an Ear of Corn." Quoted in Stuart Banner, How the Indians Lost their Land: Law and Power on the Frontier 19–20 (2005). One historian notes that "Indian peoples reaped the riches of the northeastern woodlands in seasonally mobile and gendered economies that embraced female agriculture and gathering of wild foodstuffs with male hunting and fishing in the interior and coastal waterways. Dense networks of trade connected them to each other and to Native peoples elsewhere." Jean M. O'Brien, Firsting and Lasting: Writing Indians out of Existence in New England 3 (2010). Professor O'Brien explains how the colonists created a false historical view denigrating Indian societies as they existed in order to construct a narrative of Indian disappearance.

Despite the evidence on the ground, the English continued to assert that Indian tribes recognized no property rights and enclosed no land. Perhaps the most famous statement of this idea is that by John Locke in his 1690 *Second Treatise on Civil Government*. Locke, himself an investor in the colonization of North America, fully adopted Winthrop's theory of property, and his assumption that the Indians had no idea of individual property in land:

> As much land as a man tills, plants, improves, cultivates, and can use the product of, so much is his property. He by his labour does, as it were, inclose it from the common. ***
>
> God gave the world to men in common; but since he gave it them for their benefit *** it cannot be supposed he meant it should always remain common and uncultivated. He gave it to the use of the industrious and rational, (and labour was to be his title to it;) ***.
>
> There cannot be a clearer demonstration of any thing, than several nations of the Americans are of this, who are rich in land, and poor in all the comforts of life; whom nature having furnished as liberally as any other people, with the materials of plenty, *i.e.* a fruitful soil, apt to produce in abundance, what might serve for food, raiment, and delight; yet for want of improving it by labour, have not one hundredth part of the conveniences we enjoy. ***

John Locke, Second Treatise on Government, Ch. 5, Sec. 32, 34 & 41 (1690).

Theoretical assertions about native rights were of little use in the actual encounters between Indians and English colonists. Instead of ignorant subjects grateful for religious enlightenment, the English found established native societies that initially outnumbered the settlers. The settlers were also dependent on good relations with the tribes occupying the lands they had "discovered" to facilitate trade for valuable goods and to teach them to farm the crops necessary to survive in this new place. In the face of competition from Dutch, French, and other English settlements, the colonists relied on agreements from the tribes to bolster their claims to the land. Thus whatever they wrote about the rights of Indian tribes, the colonists from the start dealt with them as governments possessed of sovereignty and property, beginning a tradition of negotiation and treaty-making that would continue throughout the nineteenth century. By the early seventeenth century, each of the colonial nations and settlements enacted laws requiring that no land be taken from Indians without their consent. Not long after, Indian land purchases were centralized and governmental representatives were required to authorize private purchases. Although there were many fraudulent and illegal land acquisitions, these laws had a continuing impact on Indian policy.

Most of the early "treaties" consisted less of resulting written documents than the ceremonial negotiation and affirmation of the relationship between Indian and European governments. In entering into these treaties, the colonists were forced to accommodate native interests and ideas of proper procedure, forging a cross cultural diplomacy that was neither Indian nor white but a unique product of this encounter between peoples. *See* Colin G. Calloway, Pen & Ink Witchcraft: Treaties and Treaty-Making in American Indian History (2013); Daniel E. Richter, Facing East From Indian Country: A Native History of Early America 129–149 (2001); Robert A. Williams Jr., Linking Arms Together: American Indian Treaty Visions of Law and Peace, 1600-1800 (1997).

The League of Peace between the Wampanoag Tribe and the Plymouth Colony is an early iteration of this tradition. The treaty concluded after multiple meetings over several days. The treaty process began with the English delivery of gifts to a Wampanoag messenger, who later returned twice with other envoys for shared meals, more gift exchanges, and song and dance. Finally Massassoit, the sachem or king of the Wampanoags, came with a train of sixty men, stopping some distance away from the settlement to request an envoy to parlay with him. A colonial envoy then went to meet with the king, bringing gifts of knives and jewels, and informing him that, "King James saluted him with words of love and Peace, and did accept of his as his Friend and Alie, and that our Governour desired to see him and to confirm a Peace with him as his next neighbor." Finally, after an exchange of hostages to secure the peace of each party, King Massasoit went to meet with the Governor, who greeted him with a fanfare of drum and trumpet and salute by a half dozen musketeers. After salutations and an elaborate meal, the parties concluded the following league of peace.

LEAGUE OF PEACE ENTERED INTO BY MASSASOIT AND THE FIRST SETTLERS OF NEW PLIMOUTH

(March 22, 1621)

---

1. That neyther he nor any of his should injure or doe hurt to any of our people.

2. And if any of his did hurt to any of ours, he should send the offender, that we might punish him.

3. That if any of our Tooles were taken away when our people were at worke, he should cause them to be restored, and if ours did any harme to any of his, wee would doe the like to them.

4. If any did unjustly warre against him, we would ayde him; If any did warre against us, he should ayde us.

5. He should send to his neighbour Confederates, to certifie them of this, that they might not wronge us, but might be likewise comprised in the conditions of Peace.

6. That when their men came to us, they should leave their Bowes and Arrowes behind them, as wee should doe our Peeces when we came to them.

Lastly, that doing thus, King James would esteem of him as his friend and Alie: all which the King [Massasoit] seemed to like well, and it was applauded of his followers.

XIX Early American Indian Documents, Treaties and Laws, 1607–1789 at 26 (Alden T. Vaughan & Deborah A. Rosen, ed., 1998).

NOTES AND QUESTIONS

1. How would you describe the relationship between the Wampanoag and English as reflected in this agreement and the procedure leading to it?

2. The original observer who recorded the 1621 agreement followed his transcription with the above words, "all which the King seemed to like well, and it was applauded of his followers." *Id.* In his 1669 New England's Memorial, Nathanial Morton added this to the account: "All which he liked well, and withal at the same time acknowledged himself content to become the subject of our Sovereign Lord the King aforesaid, his heirs and successors; and gave unto them all the lands adjacent, to them and their heirs forever." Ebenezer Hazard, I Historical Collections: Consisting of State Papers, and other authentic documents; Intended as Materials for an History of the United States of America 146 (1792). What do you make of the difference?

3. The peace did not last. By the 1660s, the Wampanoags were increasingly frustrated at the English livestock that trampled their crops. The Plymouth colony, in turn, resented Wampanoag land sales to Rhode Island, which expanded that colony at the expense of Plymouth. Their own settlements and those of the Massachusetts Bay Colony continued to press harder on

Wampanoag territory on all sides. The English, fearful of growing Wampanoag resentment, sought further concessions and fines from Massassoit's son, the sachem Metacom, whom the English called King Philip. In 1675, the tensions exploded in King Philip's War, a bloody war that left many dead on both sides, and ultimately ended Indian military might in New England. *See* Lisa Brooks, Our Beloved Kin: A New History of King Philip's War (2018); James D. Drake, King Philip's War: Civil War in New England, 1675-1676. (1999). Over 25 English towns were destroyed and the colonizers were nearly forced to the coast, but after the English victory many of the Indian participants were enslaved and shipped to the West Indies. O'Brien, *supra*, 32.

D. THE IMPACT OF DISEASE

Across the Americas, respect for native rights lessened as the European population grew and the Indian population diminished. The most significant factor in this demographic shift was the devastation caused by European diseases like small pox. Across the Americas it is estimated that between 80 and 96 percent of the indigenous population was killed by these diseases. Before these deaths, some scholars believe, the indigenous population of the Americas was about 100 million—more than that in all of Europe. Charles C. Mann, 1491: New Revelations of the Americas before Columbus 104 (2006).

Current research suggests that these epidemics decimated native populations even before Europeans encountered them, as disease was carried from the initial encounter sites to more remote communities through elaborate intertribal trade routes. The first accounts of native peoples in New England show that these early disease waves preceded the first permanent settlements. The Plymouth colony was established in 1621, some years after initial European explorations of the New England coast. On meeting an Indian man that spoke some English, they were informed that "the place where we now live, is called, *Patuxet*, and that about foure yeares agoe, all the Inhabitants dyed of an extraordinary plague, and there is neither man, woman, nor child remaining, as indeed we have found none, so as there is none to hinder our possession, or to lay claime unto it ***." XIX Early American Indian Documents, Treaties and Laws, 1607–1789 at 24 (Alden T. Vaughan & Deborah A. Rosen, ed., 1998). The Massachusett Indians who occupied the territory around present day Boston and Cambridge lost approximately 90% of their population in the epidemic of 1617-1619. 15 Handbook of North American Indians – Northeast, Table 1, 169 (William C. Sturtevant, Bruce G. Trigger eds. 1978). These disease waves did more than decimate populations; they often destabilized tribal governmental and religious systems as traditional leaders found themselves helpless to stem the devastation. Dane Morrison, A Praying People: Massachusett Acculturation and the Failure of the Puritan Mission, 1600-1690 3-8 (1995). Conversely, for some Europeans the waves of death only confirmed the rightness of their cause. King James I of England celebrated the epidemic in his letter patent for the Plymouth Colony:

> [W]ithin these late Yeares there hath by God's Visitation reigned a wonderfull Plague, together with many horrible Slaugthers, and Murthers, committed amoungst the Savages and brutish People there, heertofore inhabiting, in a Manner to the utter Destruction, Devastacion, and

> Depopulacion of that whole Territorye *** whereby We in our Judgment are persuaded and satisfied that the appointed Time is come in which Almighty God in his great Goodness and Bountie towards Us and our People, hath thought fitt and determined, that those large and goodly Territoryes, deserted as it were by their naturall Inhabitants, should be possessed and enjoyed by *** our Subjects and People. ***

James I, Charter of New England to the Plymouth Council (Nov. 3, 1620). Similarly, John Winthrop saw the ongoing plague as a sign of divine aid for the colonial project, as can be seen from his letters during the horrific smallpox outbreak of 1634:

> But for the natives in these parts, Gods hand hath so pursued them, as for 300 miles space, the greatest parte of them are swept awaye by the small poxe which still continues among them: So as God hathe thereby cleared our title to this place, those who remain in these parts, being in all not 50, have putt themselves under our protection. ***

John Winthrop to Sir Simonds Dewes (June 21, 1634), in III Winthrop Papers 171–172 (Massachusetts Historical Society 1943).

> [I]f God were not pleased with our inheriting these parts, why did he drive out the natives before us? and why dothe he still make roome for us, by deminishinge them as we increase? *** If we had no right to this lande, yet our God hath a right to it, and if he be pleased to give it us (takinge it from a people who had so long usurped upon him, and abused his Creatures) who shall control him or his termes?

John Winthrop to John Endecott (January 3, 1634), in III Winthrop Papers 149 (Massachusetts Historical Society 1943).

II. THE REVOLUTIONARY ERA AND ITS AFTERMATH

A. CONFLICTS BETWEEN COLONISTS AND CROWN

While the colonies jealously guarded the right to control Indian land acquisitions within their chartered limits, the British Crown sought to maintain control over such purchases in order to maintain royal authority, facilitate trade, and prevent costly wars and tribal alliances with other European nations. Northern Indian tribes often entered into profitable alliances with the French, who were less interested in acquiring land for settlement than in trading with the Indians. While many of these tribes sided with the French in the French and Indian (or Seven Years) War, the Iroquois Six Nations Confederacy sided with their trading partners, the British. In 1758, the British negotiated a peace with many of the hostile tribes. This was one of the turning points in the war, and by 1760, the French were defeated.

With the defeat of the French, English settlers began to flood into the area north of the Ohio River. By the spring of 1763, tribal anger was so widespread that the Ottawa Chief Pontiac was able to organize numerous tribes into coordinated attacks on every British fort west of the Alleghenies. This military success led the British Crown to issue the Royal Proclamation of 1763, which declared that "great Frauds and Abuses have been committed in purchasing Lands of the Indians, to the great Prejudice of our Interests and to the great Dissatisfaction of the said Indians," and reserved all lands west of the

Appalachians for the Indians, and forbade British citizens or colonies from purchasing lands from the Indians except with the authority and in the name of the Crown.

The Proclamation placated the tribes of the area, but it infuriated the Americans who had begun to perceive speculation in Indian lands as their right. Such speculation was the occupation of the most prominent business men and political leaders of the colonies. George Washington himself entered the enterprise, as can be seen from his 1767 letter to William Crawford:

> The other matter, just now hinted at and which I proposed in my last to join you in attempting to secure some of the most valuable Lands in the King's part which I think may be accomplished after a while notwithstanding the Proclamation that restrains it at present and prohibits the Settling of them at all for I can never look upon that Proclamation in any other light (but this I say between ourselves) than as a temporary expedient to quiet the Minds of the Indians and must fall of course in a few years especially when those Indians are consenting to our Occupying the Lands. Any person therefore who neglects the present opportunity of hunting out good Lands and in some measure marking and distinguishing them for their own (in order to keep others from settling them) will never regain it.

II The Writings of George Washington from the Original Manuscript Sources 468–469 (John Clement Fitzpatrick ed. 1944). Washington became one of fifty shareholders in the Mississippi Land Company, which unsuccessfully sought rights to 2.5 million acres of land flanking the Mississippi River. Benjamin Franklin, Thomas Paine, and constitutional drafter and future Supreme Court Justice James Wilson were also among those invested in Indian land speculation. The Proclamation's assertion of exclusive authority over these land purchases fueled anger against the British crown, and was "the first of many British moves that would lead to the American Revolution." Lindsay Robertson, Conquest by Law: How the Discovery of America Dispossessed Indigenous People of Their Lands 6 (2005). These American protesters against British authority, however, became even more committed to Indian property rights, as they argued that tribes could sell their land to whomever they chose.

In the revolutionary struggle, Indians came to symbolize a rebellious and uniquely American spirit. The 1773 Boston Tea Party, in which colonists costumed as Mohawks boarded British ships and dumped tea into Boston harbor to protest the Tea Tax, was only one of many protests against royal authority by colonists in "Indian" garb. Between 1765 and 1783, the colonies appear represented as an Indian in sixty-five political prints, four times more often than any other symbol of America. Although this identification with an imagined Indian would rarely trump colonial desires when real Indians stood in the way, the use of Indian-ness as an "ideological tool that was essential in propping up American identity" would continue to complicate American Indian policy. *See* Philip J. Deloria, Jr., Playing Indian 28–37 (1998).

Indians were also viewed by the now independent states as important military players in the Revolutionary War. The Massachusetts Bay Colony entered into the Treaty of Watertown with the St. John's (aka Maliseet) and Mi'kmaq Tribes of Nova Scotia just over two weeks after the Declaration of Independence was announced on July 4, 1776. The Treaty provided in part,

1st. [T]that the people of the said State of Massachusetts Bay and of the other United States of America, and of the said Tribes of Indians, shall henceforth be at peace with each other, and be considered as friends and brothers, united and allied together for their mutual defence, safety, and happiness.

2d. That each party to this Treaty shall and will consider the enemies of the other as enemies to themselves; and do hereby solemnly promise and engage to and with each other, that when called upon for that purpose, they shall and will, to the utmost of their abilities, aid and assist each other against their publick enemies; and particularly that the people of the said Tribes of Indians shall and will afford and give to the people of said State of Massachusetts-Bay and the people of the other United States of America, during their present war with the King of Great Britain, all the aid and assistance in their power; and that they, the people of the said Tribes of Indians, shall not and will not, directly or indirectly, give any aid or assistance to the troops or subjects of the said King of Great Britain, or others adhering; to him, or hold any correspondence, or carry on any commerce with them during the present war. ***

6th. That the said Tribes of Indians shall and will furnish and supply six hundred strong men out of the said Tribes, or as many as may be, who shall, without delay, proceed from their several homes up to the town of Boston, within this State, and from thence shall march to join the Army of the United States of America, now at New-York, under the immediate command of his Excellency General Washington, there to take his orders.

Treaty of Watertown (July 19, 1776), *in* 1 Peter Force, American Archives 848-50 (5th Ser., n.d.),

B. THE ARTICLES OF CONFEDERATION AND THE CONSTITUTION

After the Revolutionary War, conflicts arose as to whether the new nation or the states had the power to regulate the Indian trade and acquisition of Indian lands. Early drafts of the Articles of Confederation gave this power exclusively to the federal government. Virginia, however, argued that states should have the power to regulate land sales and trade within their own borders. This was a highly charged issue: the royal charters of Virginia, Connecticut, Georgia, Massachusetts, North Carolina, South Carolina, and Massachusetts had no western boundary other than the Pacific Ocean. Power to regulate land purchases across these thousands of miles would give these states a huge advantage over the states with defined western borders. Maryland, one of the "landless" states, even instructed its delegates not to agree to the Articles unless the western lands were ceded to the national government. (Influential Marylanders also made up most of the shareholders in the Wabash Company of land speculators, and recognition of these private purchases from Indians was one of the Maryland delegates' demands.)

Unable to resolve the disagreement, the Articles of Confederation accommodated both federal and state power in Indian affairs without specifying the limits of either. Article IX provided that

The United States in Congress assembled shall also have the sole and exclusive right and power of *** regulating the trade and managing all

> affairs with Indians not members of any of the states; provided, that the legislative right of any state within its own limits be not infringed or violated.

James Madison derided this provision as "obscure and contradictory" in the Federalist Papers:

> What descriptions of Indians are to be deemed members of a State, is not yet settled; and has been a question of frequent perplexity and contention in the Federal Councils. And how the trade with Indians, though not members of a State, yet residing within its legislative jurisdiction, can be regulated by an external authority, without so far intruding on the internal rights of legislation, is absolutely incomprehensible. *** [T]he articles of confederation have inconsiderately endeavored to accomplish impossibilities; to reconcile a partial sovereignty in the Union, with complete sovereignty in the States; to subvert a mathematical axiom, by taking away a part, and letting the whole remain.

The Federalist No. 42, at 284–285 (James Madison) (J.E. Cooke ed., 1961). The compromise language only created more conflict in Indian affairs. North Carolina, Georgia and New York decried federal treaties signed with the Cherokee, Creek and Iroquois nations, declaring that the treaties violated their legislative rights. States signed treaties with Indians who did not have tribal authorization to cede land, then called on the U.S. military to defend them from the resulting tribal resistance.

By the time the Constitutional Convention convened in May of 1787, the young country was on the brink of Indian warfare on several fronts. The Northwest Ordinance enacted that July shows congressional desire to remove the causes for tribal anger:

> The utmost good faith shall always be observed towards the Indians; their land and property shall never be taken from them without their consent; and in their property, rights and liberty, they never shall be invaded or disturbed, unless in just and lawful wars authorized by Congress; but laws founded in justice and humanity shall from time to time be made, for preventing wrongs being done to them, and for preserving peace and friendship with them.

32 J. Continental Cong. 340–341 (1787). Madison proposed that in order to "prevent encroachments on federal authority," the Constitution provide that Congress had the power to "regulate affairs with the Indians as well within as without the United States." With little debate, a broad grant of federal authority was included in the Commerce Clause:

> The Congress shall have power *** [t]o regulate Commerce with foreign Nations, and among the several States, and with the Indian Tribes.

U.S. Const. art. I, § 8, cl. 3.

NOTES AND QUESTIONS

1. How does the language of the Commerce Clause differ from that of the Articles of Confederation? What do the language and history of the Indian Commerce Clause suggest with respect to state and federal power over Indian

affairs? Does the fact that "Indians not taxed" were excluded from the apportionment clause, U.S. Const. art. I, § 2, cl. [3], tell you anything about the relation of Indians to the federal government?

2. The Second Circuit held that the Articles of Confederation gave states the power to purchase land from tribes within their borders, but that this power ended with the adoption of the Constitution. *Oneida Indian Nation v. New York*, 860 F.2d 1145 (2d Cir. 1988). The challenged sales involved over five million acres made prior to the adoption of the Constitution.

3. How extensive is Congress's Commerce Clause power to regulate tribal matters? Congress and the federal courts have often assumed, as you will see in the coming chapters, that it is quite broad, allowing extensive intermeddling in tribal affairs. So far, can you identify a textual or historical basis for such a reading?

Some scholars, most prominently Robert Clinton, read the constitutional history to suggest that the clause is intended to exclude state power over Indian affairs and grant the federal government authority to engage in diplomatic relations, but not regulate Native nations themselves without their consent. Robert N. Clinton, *The Dormant Indian Commerce Clause*, 27 Conn. L. Rev. 1055 (1995); Robert N. Clinton, *There is no Federal Supremacy Clause for Indian Tribes*, 34 Ariz. St. L.J. 113 (2002). One scholar argues instead that "commerce" is limited to commercial transactions, and that the power does not exclude significant state authority. Robert G. Natelson, *The Original Understanding of the Indian Commerce Clause*, 85 Denv. U. L. Rev. 201 (2007). Historian Gregory Ablavsky concludes that while the first argument is somewhat more compelling, neither the language of the Indian Commerce Clause nor the limited debate on it definitively answer these questions. Other statements and actions by the founders, however, suggest a broad constitutional vision of federal authority and robust preemption of state authority. Gregory E. Ablavsky, *Beyond the Indian Commerce Clause: The Constitutional Origins of Federal Power Over Indians*, 124 Yale L.J. 1012 (2015); *see also* Gregory E. Ablavsky, *The Savage Constitution*, 63 Duke L. Rev. 999 (2014) (arguing that Indian affairs at time of founding influence provisions about federal supremacy and the treaty power generally); Maggie Blackhawk, Federal Indian Law as Paradigm within Public Law, 132 Harv. L. Rev. 1787, 1802 (2019) ("constitutional law shifted power over Natives up the vertical separation of powers to the national government").

C. CONSOLIDATING FEDERAL CONTROL OVER INDIAN LANDS: *JOHNSON V. MCINTOSH*

The new Constitution did not settle the status of prior individual land purchases from Indian tribes. The issue was touched on by the Supreme Court in *Fletcher v. Peck*, 10 U.S. 87, 142-143 (1810) (observing that Georgia could sell land subject to Indian title). It was not resolved until 1823, when the Court decided *Johnson v. McIntosh*, 21 U.S. (8 Wheat) 543 (1823). The case did not involve Indians as parties, but instead pitted white land claimants against each other, the plaintiffs tracing their right to private purchases from the alleged tribal owners in private land sales in 1773 and 1775, and the defendants tracing their right to purchases from the federal government after the tribes had ceded their rights in treaties with the United States. The history of the case provides a colorful illustration of speculation in Indian lands.

ERIC KADES, *THE DARK SIDE OF EFFICIENCY:* JOHNSON V. M'INTOSH *AND THE EXPROPRIATION OF AMERICAN INDIAN LANDS*

148 U. PENN. L. REV. 1065, 1081–1093 (2000)

*** The plaintiffs in *M'Intosh* claimed lands under Indian deeds obtained before the Revolutionary War by two closely related land ventures, the Illinois Land Company and the Wabash Land Company. *** William Murray, [a partner in the Illinois company] arrived at the British fort in Kaskaskia (on the Mississippi River, in southern Illinois) in June 1773. Despite warnings from local British officials of the strictures against private purchases from the Indians, Murray promptly began negotiations with the Illinois tribes.

Murray dealt with the shells that remained of the once great Illinois tribes. Their population had fallen from around 10,500 in 1680 to 2500 in 1736 and to 500 in 1800, as they fell victim to European diseases and Indian enemies on all sides. Unable to prevent neighboring tribes from encroaching on their extensive land, on July 5, 1773, the Kaskaskia, Peoria, and Cahokia tribes deeded two large tracts of land to Murray and the other twenty-one members of the Illinois Company.

Murray and his Philadelphia partners worried about obtaining official recognition for the Illinois Company's deed. Unable to find political support in their own state for their purchase, the Pennsylvanians of the Illinois Company turned to Lord Dunmore, Governor of Virginia. *** An aspiring land speculator himself, the governor apparently agreed to throw his weight behind the Illinois Land Company's claim in return for the opportunity to participate in subsequent transactions. ***

To satisfy the desires of the governor, Murray created the Wabash Land Company, of which Lord Dunmore and several men from Maryland, Philadelphia, and London became members. *** Louis Viviat, [Murray's] partner and an agent *** treated with Piankashaw tribal leaders. *** The Piankashaws were one of six tribes classified as Miami Indians. Like the Illinois tribes, the Miami suffered precipitous population declines after contact with Europeans; their numbers fell from 7500 in 1682 to just over 2000 in 1736.

Viviat reached terms and executed a deed on behalf of the twenty members of the Wabash Company, with the Piankashaw representatives on October 18, 1775. *** Viviat apparently did not make efforts to include all the tribes with colorable claims to the lands purchased. *** In addition, there is evidence that the Piankashaw negotiators did not have the support of their own tribe in making the grant. ***

In order to cure any defects in their title, the Illinois and Wabash Companies did what so many other land speculators did in the early republic: they lobbied the legislature. Lobbying in the early republic was no prettier than lobbying today. In the Continental Congress, land claims formed "the most complicated and embarrassing Subject ***. Infinite pains are taken by a certain sett of men vulgarly called Land robbers [jobbers], or Land–Sharks to have it in their power to engross the best lands."

In the early years of the American Revolution, the Companies took two important steps to obtain legislative confirmation of their titles. First, they attracted influential, well-connected investors to bolster their lobbying efforts. James Wilson, who later became one of the primary architects of the Constitution and a Supreme Court Justice, was the central figure in the United Company's efforts by 1779. *** Second, the members of the Illinois Company and the Wabash Company merged on March 13, 1779, in order to pool their resources. Wilson became chairman of the newly founded company on August 20, 1779. ***

Virginia *** refused to recognize the Companies' Indian deeds. *** The fluid political situation, however, soon gave the United Companies a new body to lobby: the American Continental Congress and its successors. Between 1781 and 1796, Wilson drafted no fewer than five memorials to the national legislature pleading the United Companies' case. *** In 1805, the Secretary of the Treasury summed up the consensus view of the Companies' claims: "[the Companies] have not the shadow of a title to support their claim. *** "

Meanwhile, the United States was busily buying up Indian lands closer and closer to the United Companies' claims. In 1803, [in the Treaty with the Kakaskia, 7 Stat. 78] William Henry Harrison obtained all the lands described in the Illinois Company's deed, and more, in a huge 8.9-million-acre cession from the Illinois tribes. *** Neighboring Indians disputed the title of such a "decimated and impotent tribe" to so vast a territory, and "there was considerable doubt as to their rightful claim to all the land they had ceded." A recent account labeled the 1803 treaty with the Illinois tribes as "[t]he most notorious" of Harrison's dealings with tribes that had only tenuous claims to lands ceded. Harrison dealt with "the remnants of the Kaskaskias under Ducoigne, a band that numbered, according to the United States, only 30 men, women, and children in 1796 but that ceded [all of] southern Illinois [and much of central Illinois] to the United States."

*** In the fall of 1809, the United States acquired 2.8 million acres that included the first (northern) parcel in the Companies' deed from five other tribes, without paying the Piankashaws a cent [in the Treaty with the Delawares, Putawatimies, Miamies and Eel River Miamies, 7 Stat. 113]. *** The United States began surveying these lands, a necessary prerequisite to sale, almost immediately after finalizing the treaties. ***

[The defendant in *Johnson v. M'Intosh*, William M'Intosh] obtained the lands at issue in the case (fifty-three tracts amounting to nearly 12,000 acres) on April 24, 1815, before the first public sale. *** William Henry Harrison, Governor of the territories, identified M'Intosh as one of "the principal councellors of the Kaskaskias Speculators."

[The plaintiffs traced their land title to Thomas Johnson.] Thomas Johnson, an original investor in the Wabash Company, and later a Supreme Court Justice, died on or about November 1, 1819, and the plaintiffs, his son Joshua and grandson Thomas Graham, were the primary beneficiaries in his will. Perhaps more importantly for the commencement of the *M'Intosh* litigation, the will made Robert Goodloe Harper [who, along with Daniel Webster, served as attorney for the plaintiffs] executor of the estate. Harper apparently determined that Johnson owned shares and decided to go to court in a final stab at giving a happy ending to the long and sad story of the United Illinois and Wabash Land Companies.

Looking for a federal patent holder to sue, as a test of the validity of their claim under the Wabash Company's Indian deed, Johnson and Graham, probably led by Harper, appeared to target M'Intosh. As one of the largest landholders in the Illinois and Indiana territories, M'Intosh was a natural adversary, but he does not appear to have been a real one. Mapping the United Companies' claims alongside M'Intosh's purchases, as enumerated in the district court records, shows that the litigants' land claims did not overlap. Hence there was no real "case or controversy," and *M'Intosh*, like another leading early Supreme Court land case, *Fletcher v. Peck*, appears to have been a sham.

M'Intosh did not contest a single fact alleged in the complaint, jurisdictional or otherwise. Perhaps he participated in framing the complaint, which became the stipulated facts of the case. Neither the district court nor the Supreme Court questioned any of these facts. Everyone involved, it seems, wanted a decision on the legal question of the validity of private purchases from the Indians. ***

JOHNSON V. M'INTOSH

21 U.S. (8 Wheat) 543, 5 L. Ed. 681 (1823)

CHIEF JUSTICE MARSHALL delivered the opinion of the Court.

The plaintiffs in this cause claim the land, in their declaration mentioned, under two grants, purporting to be made, the first in 1773, and the last in 1775, by the chiefs of certain Indian tribes, constituting the Illinois and the Piankeshaw nations; and the question is, whether this title can be recognised in the Courts of the United States?

The facts, as stated in the case agreed, show the authority of the chiefs who executed this conveyance, so far as it could be given by their own people; and likewise show, that the particular tribes for whom these chiefs acted were in rightful possession of the land they sold. The inquiry, therefore, is, in a great measure, confined to the power of Indians to give, and of private individuals to receive, a title which can be sustained in the Courts of this country.

As the right of society, to prescribe those rules by which property may be acquired and preserved is not, and cannot be drawn into question; as the title to lands, especially, is and must be admitted to depend entirely on the law of the nation in which they lie; it will be necessary, in pursuing this inquiry, to examine, not singly those principles of abstract justice, which the Creator of all things has impressed on the mind of his creature man, and which are admitted to regulate, in a great degree, the rights of civilized nations, whose perfect independence is acknowledged; but those principles also which our own government has adopted in the particular case, and given us as the rule for our decision.

On the discovery of this immense continent, the great nations of Europe were eager to appropriate to themselves so much of it as they could respectively acquire. Its vast extent offered an ample field to the ambition and enterprise of all; and the character and religion of its inhabitants afforded an apology for considering them as a people over whom the superior genius of Europe might claim an ascendency. The potentates of the old world found no difficulty in convincing themselves that they made ample compensation to the inhabitants of the new, by bestowing on them civilization and Christianity, in exchange for unlimited independence. But, as they were all in pursuit of nearly the same object, it was necessary, in order to avoid conflicting settlements, and consequent war with each other, to establish a principle, which all should acknowledge as the law by which the right of acquisition, which they all asserted, should be regulated as between themselves. This principle was, that discovery gave title to the government by whose subjects, or by whose authority, it was made, against all other European governments, which title might be consummated by possession.

The exclusion of all other Europeans, necessarily gave to the nation making the discovery the sole right of acquiring the soil from the natives, and establishing settlements upon it. It was a right with which no Europeans could interfere. It was a right which all asserted for themselves, and to the assertion of which, by others, all assented.

Those relations which were to exist between the discoverer and the natives, were to be regulated by themselves. The rights thus acquired being exclusive, no other power could interpose between them.

In the establishment of these relations, the rights of the original inhabitants were, in no instance, entirely disregarded; but were necessarily, to a considerable extent, impaired. They were admitted to be the rightful occupants of the soil, with a legal as well as just claim to retain possession of it, and to use it according to their own discretion; but their rights to complete sovereignty, as independent nations, were necessarily diminished, and their power to dispose of the soil at their own will, to whomsoever they pleased, was denied by the original fundamental principle, that discovery gave exclusive title to those who made it.

While the different nations of Europe respected the right of the natives, as occupants, they asserted the ultimate dominion to be in themselves; and claimed and exercised, as a consequence of this ultimate dominion, a power to grant the soil, while yet in possession of the natives. These grants have been understood by all, to convey a title to the grantees, subject only to the Indian right of occupancy.

***

No one of the powers of Europe gave its full assent to this principle, more unequivocally than England. The documents upon this subject are ample and complete. So early as the year 1496, her monarch granted a commission to the Cabots, to discover countries then unknown to *Christian people*, and to take possession of them in the name of the king of England. Two years afterwards, Cabot proceeded on this voyage, and discovered the continent of North America, along which he sailed as far south as Virginia. To this discovery the English trace their title.

In this first effort made by the English government to acquire territory on this continent, we perceive a complete recognition of the principle which has been mentioned. The right of discovery given by this commission, is confined to countries "then unknown to all Christian people;" and of these countries Cabot was empowered to take possession in the name of the king of England. Thus asserting a right to take possession, notwithstanding the occupancy of the natives, who were heathens, and, at the same time, admitting the prior title of any Christian people who may have made a previous discovery. ***

Thus has our whole country been granted by the crown while in the occupation of the Indians. These grants purport to convey the soil as well as the right of dominion to the grantees. ***

Further proofs of the extent to which this principle has been recognised, will be found in the history of the wars, negotiations, and treaties, which the different nations, claiming territory in America, have carried on, and held with each other. ***

Between France and Great Britain, whose discoveries as well as settlements were nearly contemporaneous, contests for the country, actually covered by the Indians, began as soon as their settlements approached each other, and were continued until finally settled in the year 1763, by the treaty of Paris. ***

This treaty expressly cedes, and has always been understood to cede, the whole country, on the English side of the dividing line, between the two nations, although a great and valuable part of it was occupied by the Indians. Great Britain, on her part, surrendered to France all her pretensions to the country west of the Mississippi. It has never been supposed that she surrendered nothing, although she was not in actual possession of a foot of land. She surrendered all right to acquire the country; and any after attempt to purchase it from the Indians, would have been considered and treated as an invasion of the territories of France.

***

Thus, all the nations of Europe, who have acquired territory on this continent, have asserted in themselves, and have recognised in others, the exclusive right of the discoverer to appropriate the lands occupied by the Indians. Have the American States rejected or adopted this principle?

By the treaty which concluded the war of our revolution, Great Britain relinquished all claim, not only to the government, but to the "propriety and territorial rights of the United States," whose boundaries were fixed in the second article. By this treaty, the powers of government, and the right to soil, which had previously been in Great Britain, passed definitively to these States. We had before taken possession of them, by declaring independence; but neither the declaration of independence, nor the treaty confirming it, could give us more than that which we before possessed, or to which Great Britain was before entitled. It has never been doubted, that either the United States, or the several States, had a clear title to all the lands within the boundary lines described in the treaty, subject only to the Indian right of occupancy, and that the exclusive power to extinguish that right, was vested in that government which might constitutionally exercise it. ***

The United States, then, have unequivocally acceded to that great and broad rule by which its civilized inhabitants now hold this country. They hold, and assert in themselves, the title by which it was acquired. They maintain, as all others have maintained, that discovery gave an exclusive right to extinguish the Indian title of occupancy, either by purchase or by conquest; and gave also a right to such a degree of sovereignty, as the circumstances of the people would allow them to exercise.

The power now possessed by the government of the United States to grant lands, resided, while we were colonies, in the crown, or its grantees. The validity of the titles given by either has never been questioned in our Courts. It has been exercised uniformly over territory in possession of the Indians. The existence of this power must negative the existence of any right which may conflict with, and control it. An absolute title to lands cannot exist, at the same time, in different persons, or in different governments. An absolute, must be an exclusive title, or at least a title which excludes all others not compatible with it. All our institutions recognise the absolute title of the crown, subject only to the Indian right of occupancy, and recognise the absolute title of the crown to extinguish that right. This is incompatible with an absolute and complete title in the Indians.

We will not enter into the controversy, whether agriculturists, merchants, and manufacturers, have a right, on abstract principles, to expel hunters from the territory they possess, or to contract their limits. Conquest gives a title which the Courts of the conqueror cannot deny, whatever the private and speculative opinions of individuals may be, respecting the original justice of the claim which has been successfully asserted. The British government, which was then our government, and whose rights have passed to the United States, asserted title to all the lands occupied by Indians, within the chartered limits of the British colonies. It asserted also a limited sovereignty over them, and the exclusive right of extinguishing the title which occupancy gave to them. These claims have been maintained and established as far west as the river Mississippi, by the sword. The title to a vast portion of the lands we now hold, originates in them. It is not for the Courts of this country to question the validity of this title, or to sustain one which is incompatible with it.

Although we do not mean to engage in the defence of those principles which Europeans have applied to Indian title, they may, we think, find some excuse, if not justification, in the character and habits of the people whose rights have been wrested from them.

The title by conquest is acquired and maintained by force. The conqueror prescribes its limits. Humanity, however, acting on public opinion, has established, as a general rule, that the conquered shall not be wantonly oppressed, and that their condition shall remain as eligible as is compatible with the objects of the conquest. Most usually, they are incorporated with the victorious nation, and become subjects or citizens of the government with which they are connected. The new and old members of the society mingle with each other; the distinction between them is gradually lost, and they make one people. Where this incorporation is practicable, humanity demands, and a wise policy requires, that the rights of the conquered to property should remain unimpaired; that the new subjects should be governed as equitably as the old, and that confidence in their security should gradually banish the painful sense of being separated from their ancient connexions, and united by force to strangers.

When the conquest is complete, and the conquered inhabitants can be blended with the conquerors, or safely governed as a distinct people, public opinion, which not even the conqueror can disregard, imposes these restraints upon him; and he cannot neglect them without injury to his fame, and hazard to his power.

But the tribes of Indians inhabiting this country were fierce savages, whose occupation was war, and whose subsistence was drawn chiefly from the forest. To leave them in possession of their country, was to leave the country a wilderness; to govern them as a distinct people, was impossible, because they were as brave and as high spirited as they were fierce, and were ready to repel by arms every attempt on their independence.

What was the inevitable consequence of this state of things? The Europeans were under the necessity either of abandoning the country, and relinquishing their pompous claims to it, or of enforcing those claims by the sword, and by the adoption of principles adapted to the condition of a people with whom it was impossible to mix, and who could not be governed as a distinct society, or of remaining in their neighbourhood, and exposing themselves and their families to the perpetual hazard of being massacred.

Frequent and bloody wars, in which the whites were not always the aggressors, unavoidably ensued. European policy, numbers, and skill, prevailed. As the white population advanced, that of the Indians necessarily receded. The country in the immediate neighbourhood of agriculturists became unfit for them. The game fled into thicker and more unbroken forests, and the Indians followed. The soil, to which the crown originally claimed title, being no longer occupied by its ancient inhabitants, was parcelled out according to the will of the sovereign power, and taken possession of by persons who claimed immediately from the crown, or mediately, through its grantees or deputies.

That law which regulates, and ought to regulate in general, the relations between the conqueror and conquered, was incapable of application to a people under such circumstances. The resort to some new and different rule, better adapted to the actual state of things, was unavoidable. Every rule which can be suggested will be found to be attended with great difficulty.

However extravagant the pretension of converting the discovery of an inhabited country into conquest may appear; if the principle has been asserted in the first instance, and afterwards sustained; if a country has been acquired and held under it; if the property of the great mass of the community originates in it, it becomes the law of the land, and cannot be questioned. So, too, with respect to the concomitant principle, that the Indian inhabitants are to be considered merely as occupants, to be protected, indeed, while in peace, in the possession of their lands, but to be deemed incapable of transferring the absolute title to others. However this restriction may be opposed to natural right, and to the usages of civilized nations, yet, if it be indispensable to that system under which the country has been settled, and be adapted to the actual condition of the two people, it may, perhaps, be supported by reason, and certainly cannot be rejected by Courts of justice. ***

Another view has been taken of this question, which deserves to be considered. The title of the crown, whatever it might be, could be acquired only by a conveyance from the crown. If an individual might extinguish the Indian title for his own benefit, or, in other words, might purchase it, still he could acquire only that title. Admitting their power to change their laws or usages, so far as to allow an individual to separate a portion of their lands from the common stock, and hold it in severalty, still it is a part of their territory, and is held under them, by a title dependent on their laws. The grant derives its efficacy from their will; and, if they choose to resume it, and make a different disposition of the land, the Courts of the United States cannot interpose for the protection of the title. The person who purchases lands from the Indians, within their territory, incorporates himself with them, so far as respects the property purchased; holds their title under their protection, and subject to their laws. If they annul the grant, we know of no tribunal which can revise and set aside the proceeding. We know of no principle which can distinguish this case from a grant made to a native Indian, authorizing him to hold a particular tract of land in severalty.

As such a grant could not separate the Indian from his nation, nor give a title which our Courts could distinguish from the title of his tribe, as it might still be conquered from, or ceded by his tribe, we can perceive no legal principle which will authorize a Court to say, that different consequences are attached to this purchase, because it was made by a stranger. By the treaties concluded between the United States and the Indian nations, whose title the plaintiffs claim, the country comprehending the lands in controversy has been ceded to the United States, without any reservation of their title. These nations had been at war with the United States, and had an unquestionable right to annul any grant they had made to American citizens. Their cession of the country, without a reservation of this land, affords a fair presumption, that they considered it as of no validity. ***

The proclamation issued by the King of Great Britain, in 1763, has been considered, and, we think, with reason, as constituting an additional objection to the title of the plaintiffs. By that proclamation, the crown reserved under its own dominion and protection, for the use of the Indians, "all the land and territories lying to the westward of the sources of the rivers which fall into the sea from the west and northwest," and strictly forbade all British subjects from making any purchases or settlements whatever, or taking possession of the reserved lands. [Chief Justice Marshall rejected the argument that the Proclamation exceeded the powers of the British Crown.]

The acts of the several colonial assemblies, prohibiting purchases from the Indians, have also been relied on, as proving, that, independent of such prohibitions, Indian deeds would be valid. But, we think this fact, at most, equivocal. While the existence of such purchases would justify their prohibition, even by colonies which considered Indian deeds as previously invalid, the fact that such acts have been generally passed, is strong evidence of the general opinion, that such purchases are opposed by the soundest principles of wisdom and national policy.

After bestowing on this subject a degree of attention which was more required by the magnitude of the interest in litigation, and the able and elaborate arguments of the bar, than by its intrinsic difficulty, the Court is decidedly of opinion, that the plaintiffs do not exhibit a title which can be sustained in the Courts of the United States; and that there is no error in the judgment which was rendered against them in the District Court of Illinois.

NOTES AND QUESTIONS

1. What was the purpose of the doctrine of discovery according to Marshall? To whom did it apply?

2. What did the federal government get through the doctrine of discovery? Did it get full rights to native land?

3. What property rights did Indian nations lose through the doctrine? What did they retain? How are those property rights to be extinguished?

4. What does the language and tone of the opinion suggest about Chief Justice Marshall's attitude toward the doctrine of discovery? Why does he uphold it? Why did Marshall resort to the doctrine when the private purchases plainly violated the Royal Proclamation of 1763?

5. How might the opinion have played into the contemporary struggle between states and the federal government and between states and the U.S. Supreme Court?

6. What does the case suggest about tribal law—does it have any effect on non-Indians?

7. The old Supreme Court Reporters often included a summary of the arguments made by the parties to the Court. The argument of the defendants is excerpted below. How does it compare to the reasoning in the *M'Intosh* decision?

> *** [T]he uniform understanding and practice of European nations, and the settled law, as laid down by the tribunals of civilized states, denied the right of the Indians to be considered as independent communities, having a permanent property in the soil, capable of alienation to private individuals. They remain in a state of nature, and have never been admitted into the general society of nations. All the treaties and negotiations between the civilized powers of Europe and of this continent *** have uniformly disregarded their supposed right to the territory included within the jurisdictional limits of those powers. *** Discovery is the foundation of title, in European nations, and this overlooks all proprietary rights in the natives. The sovereignty and eminent domain thus acquired, necessarily precludes the idea of any other sovereignty existing within the same limits. ***
>
> Such, then, being the nature of the Indian title to lands, the extent of their right of alienation must depend upon the laws of the dominion under which they live. *** These statutes seem to define sufficiently the nature of the Indian title to lands; a mere right of usufruct and habitation, without power of alienation. By the law of nature, they had not acquired a fixed property capable of being transferred. The measure of property acquired by occupancy is determined, according to the law of nature, by the extent of men's wants, and their capacity of using it to supply them. It is a violation of the rights of others to exclude them from the use of what we do not want, and they have an occasion for. Upon this principle the North American Indians could have acquired no proprietary interest in the vast tracts of territory which they wandered over; and their right to the lands on which they hunted, could not be considered as superior to that which is acquired to the sea by fishing in it. ***

21 U.S. (8 Wheat) at 567–570.

8. *Johnson v. M'Intosh* has inspired many contrasting opinions of the case and its significance. Here are just two of the perspectives on the case. Which do you find more persuasive?

> [Marshall] proposed a theory that seems to limit tribal power but that actually poses little or no restriction on the tribes. It *** has the function of settling a certain class of non-Indian title conflicts. *** The theory sets out two different relationships: one among European claimants to the New World, the other between each of the European claimants and the Indian inhabitants. As among the Europeans, the doctrine of discovery obtained. As between European and Indian nations, each relationship was to be separately regulated.
>
> ***
>
> Marshall's version of the doctrine of discovery has small consequence for the tribes. The Indian property interest is described as a "title of occupancy." It is recognized and protected. And it can be conveyed to non-Indians. It has all the indicia of fee simple except this: unless a non-Indian purchaser is licensed by the discovering sovereign or that sovereign's successor, the non-Indian purchasers takes only the Indian's interest. ***

Milner S. Ball, *Constitution, Court, Indian Tribes,* 1987 Am. B. Found. Res. J. 1, 23, 25.

> The acceptance of the Doctrine of Discovery into United States law confirmed the superior rights of a European-derived nation to the lands occupied by "infidels, heathens and savages," encouraged further efforts by white society to acquire the Indians' waste lands, and vested authority in a centralized sovereign to regulate the Indians' dispossession according to national interest, security, and sometimes even honor.
>
> Perhaps most important, Johnson's acceptance of the Doctrine of Discovery into United States law represented the legacy of 1,000 years of European racism and colonialism directed against non-Western peoples. *** The Doctrine of Discovery's underlying medievally derived ideology—that normatively divergent "savage" peoples could be denied rights and status equal to those accorded to the civilized nations of Europe—had become an integral part of the fabric of United States federal Indian law.

Robert A. Williams, Jr., The American Indian in Western Legal Thought: The Discourses of Conquest, 316–17 (1990).

9. Lindsay Robertson offers yet another perspective. *See* Lindsay G. Robertson, Conquest by Law: How the Discovery of America Dispossessed Indigenous Peoples of their Lands (2005). Robertson argues that Marshall's goal was to validate the titles of Virginia revolutionary war veterans, to whom the national government had granted rights in land while that land was still occupied by the Chickasaw Nation. These so-called "preemptive rights" faced legal uncertainty. Marshall's father, Thomas Marshall, had served as superintendent of the militia claims and argued for the veterans' preemptive rights before the Virginia Court of Appeals. Although Chief Justice Marshall might have disposed of *Johnson* simply by declaring that the private purchases violated the Royal Proclamation of 1763, by establishing that the government might

"grant the soil, while yet in possession of the natives," and that these grants "convey a title to the grantees, subject only to the Indian right of occupancy," Marshall removed an "obstacle standing between his former colleagues in Virginia's Revolutionary War military and bounty lands promised them in Western Kentucky." One final punch line to this story is that Marshall himself was one of the veterans entitled to a preemptive land right. *Id.* at xi-xii.

10. Notice the assumptions about Indian land used in both the opinion and the defendants' argument: Indians did not farm. Recent scholarship suggests that this inaccurate assumption came in part from the jurists' refusal to acknowledge the work of Indian women:

> [B]y emphasizing hunting and ignoring agriculture, Chief Justice Marshall focused on work that, in many tribes, was traditionally done by men and ignored Indian women and their work. As one scholar has noted, "At the time the Europeans first arrived in North America, and for centuries after, Native American women dominated agricultural production in the tribes of the eastern half of the United States." For example, in the Six Nations of the Iroquois Confederacy, the Algonquians of the Virginia tidewater, and the tribes of Illinois, women were primarily responsible for tribal farming, and their use of the land led to their holding important property rights in the land. Although Indian men provided some assistance to women in farming, their principal contribution to many tribal economies resulted from hunting. By emphasizing Indian men's work and ignoring Indian women's work, Chief Justice Marshall depicted Indians as people whose property rights could be restricted justifiably by the Europeans and their American successors on the grounds that the Indians did not establish title to the land through settled agriculture but instead left it a "wilderness."

Allison Dussias, *Squaw Drudges, Farm Wives, and the Dann Sisters' Last Stand: American Indian Women's Resistance to Domestication and the Denial of their Property Rights*, 77 N.C. L. Rev. 637, 649–51 (1999); *see also* Bethany R. Berger, *Indian Policy and the Imagined Indian Woman*, 14 Kan. J. Law & Public Policy 103, 104–107 (2004) (discussing reasons for disregard of Indian women's work); Bethany R. Berger, *After Pocahontas: Indian Women and the Law, 1830–1934*, 21 Am. Indian L. Rev. 1 (1997). On Indian land enclosure and property rights generally, see Stuart Banner, How the Indians Lost Their Land: Law and Power on the Frontier (2005); Kenneth Bobroff, *Retelling Allotment: Indian Property Rights and the Myth of Common Ownership*, 54 Vand. L. Rev. 1559 (2001). For more on the origins and influence of the Doctrine of Discovery in the nineteenth century, see Robert J. Miller, Native America, Discovered and Conquered: Thomas Jefferson, Lewis & Clark, and Manifest Destiny (2006). Professor O'Brien painstakingly describes the efforts of towns in New England to write Indians out of their histories and to mischaracterize Indian property concepts. O'Brien, *supra*. Professor Brooks also documents Native property concepts, including the role of women, in The Common Pot, *supra*.

III. THE TRADE AND INTERCOURSE ERA: 1785–1817

A. TREATY MAKING AND TRADE AND INTERCOURSE ACTS

The United States initially implemented federal Indian policy through two main vehicles: (1) treaties with Indian nations and (2) trade and intercourse acts to facilitate and implement the treaties. Both were designed to draw and enforce boundary lines between American citizens and the Indian nations. Their purpose was to prevent expensive wars with Indian tribes, avoid tribal alliances with European nations, and conform to the American idea of itself as a just and lawful nation.

Henry Knox, the first Secretary of War, emphasized these goals in his reports to Congress. In 1789 he reported that

> The white inhabitants on the frontiers of North Carolina *** have frequently committed the most direct and unprovoked outrages against the Cherokee Indians. *** [B]y an upright and honorable construction of the treaty of Hopewell the United States have pledged themselves for the protection of the said indians within the boundaries described by the said treaty and that the principles of good Faith and sound policy and every respect which a nation, owes to its own reputation and dignity require if the union possess sufficient power that it be exerted to enforce a due observance of the said treaty.

34 J. Cont. Cong. 342–343 (1788). It was "of the highest importance to the peace of the frontiers that the Indian tribes should be able to rely with security on the treaties. *** " *Id.* at 344. President Washington agreed:

> To conciliate the powerful tribes of Indians in the southern district *** may be regarded as highly worthy of the serious attention of the federal government. The measure includes not only peace and security to the whole southern frontier, but is calculated to form a barrier against the colonies of a European Power, which, in the mutations of policy, may one day become the enemy of the United States. The fate of the Southern States, therefore, or the neighboring colonies, may principally depend on the measures of the Union towards the Southern Indians.

1 Annals of Cong. 13 (Joseph Gales ed., 1834).

The United States also decided to accord Indian treaties the same legal status as treaties with foreign nations, approving them only with the advice and consent of two thirds of the Senate. This was on the urging of President Washington, who declared it "important that all treaties and compacts formed by the United States with another nation, whether civilized or not, should be made with caution and executed with fidelity." 1 Annals of Cong. 83 (1789).

Beginning in 1790 the United States passed a series of Trade and Intercourse Acts. President Washington described the basic goals of this legislation in his 1791 Annual Message to Congress:

> That the mode of alienating their lands, the main source of discontent and war, should be so defined and regulated as to obviate imposition, and *** controversy concerning the reality and extent of the alienations which are made.

> That commerce with them should be promoted under regulations tending to secure an equitable deportment towards them, and that such rational experiments should be made, for imparting to them the blessings of civilization, as may, from time to time, suit their condition.
>
> That the executive of the United States should be enabled to employ the means to which the Indians have been long accustomed for uniting their immediate interests with the preservation of peace.
>
> And that efficacious provision should be made for inflicting adequate penalties upon all those who, by violating their rights, shall infringe the treaties, and endanger the peace of the Union.

1 Jour. Senate 325 (Oct. 25, 1791). This is the first such Act:

> Sec. 1. *** [N]o person shall be permitted to carry on any trade or intercourse with the Indian tribes, without a license for that purpose under the hand and seal of the superintendent of the department, or of such other person as the President of the United States shall appoint for that purpose; ***
>
> Sec. 3. And be it further enacted, That every person who shall attempt to trade with the Indian tribes, or to be found in the Indian country with such merchandise in his possession as are usually vended to the Indians, without a license first had and obtained, as in this act prescribed, and being thereof convicted in any court proper to try the same, shall forfeit all the merchandise so offered for sale to the Indian tribes, or so found in the Indian country, which forfeiture shall be one half to the benefit of the person prosecuting, and the other half to the benefit of the United States.
>
> Sec. 4. And be it enacted and declared, That no sale of lands made by any Indians, or any nation or tribe of Indians the United States, shall be valid to any person or persons, or to any state, whether having the right of pre-emption to such lands or not, unless the same shall be made and duly executed at some public treaty, held under the authority of the United States.
>
> Sec. 5. And be it further enacted, That if any citizen or inhabitant of the United States, or of either of the territorial districts of the United States, shall go into any town, settlement or territory belonging to any nation or tribe of Indians, and shall there commit any crime upon, or trespass against, the person or property of any peaceable and friendly Indian or Indians, which, if committed within the jurisdiction of any state, or within the jurisdiction of either of the said districts, against a citizen or white inhabitant thereof, would be punishable by the laws of such state or district, such offender or offenders shall be subject to the same punishment, and shall be proceeded against in the same manner as if the offence had been committed within the jurisdiction of the state or district to which he or they may belong, against a citizen or white inhabitant thereof. ***

1 Stat. 137–138 (1790).

The 1790 Act was the origin of important elements of modern Federal Indian Law. Section 4 of the Act, prohibiting purchases of lands from Indians or tribes except at public treaties held under the authority of the United States, has remained in effect, with minor modifications, to this day, 25 U.S.C. § 177, and is the basis for modern litigation by tribes seeking return of lands taken without federal consent. *See, e.g., County of Oneida v. Oneida Indian Nation*, 470 U.S. 226 (1985). Section 5, providing punishment for those committing crimes against tribal members, forms the roots of modern federal statutes creating federal jurisdiction over crimes between Indians and non-Indians on Indian land.

NOTES AND QUESTIONS

1. Section 3 of the Trade and Intercourse Act makes it a crime to trade with Indians within "Indian country" without a license. "Indian country" is not defined. How would you determine where the prohibition would apply?

2. Notice that section 5 provides that non-Indians committing crimes within the Indian country are subject to punishment by federal authorities. Does that have any implications for Indian jurisdiction over the perpetrators?

3. The 1785 Treaty negotiated at Hopewell between the United States and the Cherokee Nation is similar to others negotiated soon after the United States had won the Revolutionary War with tribes that had fought against the United States. How does it reflect the policies and concerns described above? What does it suggest about federal perceptions of the Cherokees? What jurisdictional scheme does the treaty establish? When you read *Worcester v. Georgia*, 31 U.S. (6 Pet.) 515 (1832), notice how the Court construes this treaty.

TREATY OF HOPEWELL

(1785)

The Commissioners Plenipotentiary of the United States in Congress assembled, give peace to all the Cherokees, and receive them into the favor and protection of the United States of America, on the following conditions:

Art. I. The Head–Men and Warriors of all the Cherokees shall restore all the prisoners, citizens of the United States, or subjects of their allies, to their entire liberty: They shall also restore all the Negroes, and all other property taken during the late war from the citizens, to such person, and at such time and place, as the Commissioners shall appoint.

Art. II. The Commissioners of the United States in Congress assembled, shall restore all the prisoners taken from the Indians, during the late war, to the Head–Men and Warriors of the Cherokees, as early as is practicable.

Art. III. The said Indians for themselves and their respective tribes and towns do acknowledge all the Cherokees to be under the protection of the United States of America, and of no other sovereign whosoever.

Art. IV. The boundary allotted to the Cherokees for their hunting grounds, between the said Indians and the citizens of the United States, within the limits of the United States of America, is, and shall be the following [specifying boundaries].

Art. V. If any citizen of the United States, or other person not being an Indian, shall attempt to settle on any of the lands westward or southward of the said boundary which are hereby allotted to the Indians for their hunting grounds, or having already settled and will not remove from the same within six months after the ratification of this treaty, such person shall forfeit the protection of the United States, and the Indians may punish him or not as they please ***.

Art. VI. If any Indian or Indians, or person residing among them, or who shall take refuge in their nation, shall commit a robbery, or murder, or other capital crime, on any citizen of the United States, or person under their protection, the nation, or the tribe to which such offender or offenders may belong, shall be bound to deliver him or them up to be punished according to the ordinances of the United States; provided, that the punishment shall not be greater than if the robbery or murder, or other capital crime had been committed by a citizen on a citizen.

Art. VII. If any citizen of the United States, or person under their protection, shall commit a robbery or murder, or other capital crime, on any Indian, such offender or offenders shall be punished in the same manner as if the murder or robbery, or other capital crime, had been committed on a citizen of the United States; and the punishment shall be in presence of some of the Cherokees, if any shall attend at the time and place, and that they may have an opportunity so to do, due notice of the time of such intended punishment shall be sent to some one of the tribes.

Art. VIII. It is understood that the punishment of the innocent under the idea of retaliation, is unjust, and shall not be practiced on either side, except where there is a manifest violation of this treaty; and then it shall be preceded first by a demand of justice, and if refused, then by a declaration of hostilities.

Art. IX. For the benefit and comfort of the Indians, and for the prevention of injuries or oppressions on the part of the citizens or Indians, the United States in Congress assembled shall have the sole and exclusive right of regulating the trade with the Indians, and managing all their affairs in such manner as they think proper.

Art. X. Until the pleasure of Congress be known, respecting the ninth article, all traders, citizens of the United States, shall have liberty to go to any of the tribes or towns of the Cherokees to trade with them, and they shall be protected in their persons and property, and kindly treated.

Art. XI. The said Indians shall give notice to the citizens of the United States, of any designs which they may know or suspect to be formed in any neighboring tribe, or by any person whosoever, against the peace, trade or interest of the United States.

Art. XII. That the Indians may have full confidence in the justice of the United States, respecting their interests, they shall have the right to send a deputy of their choice, whenever they think fit, to Congress.

Art. XIII. The hatchet shall be forever buried, and the peace given by the United States, and friendship re-established between the said states on the one part, and all the Cherokees on the other, shall be universal; and the contracting parties shall use their utmost endeavors to maintain the peace given as aforesaid, and friendship re-established.

In witness of and every thing herein determined, between the United States of America and all the Cherokees, we, their underwritten Commissioners, by virtue of Her full powers, have signed this definitive treaty, and have caused our seals to be hereunto affixed.

Benjamin Hawkins

***

Koatohee, or Corn Tassel of Toquo, his x mark

Seholauetta, or Hanging Man of Chota, his x mark

Tuskegatahu, or Long Fellow of Chistohoe, his x mark

Ooskvrha, or Abraham of Chilkowa, his x mark

Kolakusta, or Prince of Noth, his x mark

[X marks of many other Cherokees and signatures of interpreters follow].

B. RELYING ON THE DISAPPEARING INDIAN

The Indian signers believed that their treaties with the United States created a sacred covenant that would permit Indian and American nations to exist side by side. Federal policymakers, however, expected the Indian tribes to soon disappear, taking the need to respect their territory and sovereignty with them. Secretary of War Knox, while arguing that taking Indian land except by consent or after a just war would be "a gross violation of the federal laws of nature, and of that distributive justice which is the glory of a nation," believed that the tribes would soon voluntarily give up their land:

> As population shall increase and approach the Indian boundaries, game will be diminished and new purchased may be made for small considerations. This has been and probably will be the inevitable consequence of cultivation. It is, however, painful to consider that all the Indian tribes, once existing in those states now best cultivated and most populous, have become extinct. If the same causes continue, the effects will happen and, in a short period the idea of an Indian this side of the Mississippi will be found only in the pages of the historian.

1 Ann. Cong. 13 (1789).

George Washington wrote the same in an early letter on Indian affairs:

> I am clear in my opinion, that policy and economy point very strongly to the expediency of being on good terms with the Indians, and the propriety of purchasing their Lands in preference to attempting to drive them by force of arms out of their Country; which as we have already experienced is like driving the Wild Beasts of the Forest which will return as soon as the pursuit is at an end and fall perhaps on those that are left there; when the gradual extension of our Settlements will as certainly cause the Savage as the Wolf to retire; both being beasts of prey tho' they differ in shape.

George Washington to James Duane, September 7, 1783, reprinted in Documents of United States Indian Policy 2 (Francis P. Prucha ed., 3d ed. 2000).

As early as 1803, moreover, President Thomas Jefferson privately reassured Indiana Governor William Henry Harrison that if the tribes did not leave voluntarily, they would be removed by force:

> [T]his letter being unofficial and private, I may with safety give you a more extensive view of our policy respecting the Indians. *** Our system is to live in perpetual peace with the Indians, to cultivate an affectionate attachment from them, by everything just and liberal which we can do for them within the bounds of reason, and by giving them effectual protection against wrongs from our own people. The decrease of game rendering their subsistence by hunting insufficient, we wish to draw them into agriculture, to spinning and weaving. The latter branches they take up with great readiness, because they fall to the women, who gain by quitting the labors of the field for those which are exercised indoors. When they withdraw themselves to the culture of a small piece of land, they will perceive how useless to them are their extensive forests, and will be willing to pare them off from time to time in exchange for necessaries for their farms and families. *** In this way our settlements will gradually circumscribe and approach the Indians, and they will in time either incorporate with us as citizens of the United States, or remove beyond the Mississippi. *** In the whole course of this, it is essential to cultivate their love. As to their fear, we presume that our strength and their weakness is now so visible that they must see we have only to shut our hand to crush them, and that all our liberalities to them proceed from motives of pure humanity only. Should any tribe be foolhardy enough to take up the hatchet at any time, the seizing the whole country of that tribe, and driving them across the Mississippi, as the only condition of peace, would be an example to others, and a furtherance of our final consolidation.

President Jefferson to William Henry Harrison, February 27, 1803; *see generally* Robert J. Miller, Native America, Discovered and Conquered: Thomas Jefferson, Lewis & Clark, and Manifest Destiny (2006). Harrison was the author of the 1803 treaties that you read about in the description of the land claims at issue in *Johnson v. M'Intosh*. How might this private description of federal policy have influenced his negotiation of these treaties?

The iron fist in the velvet glove may also be seen in the 1819 House Report on the establishment of a permanent fund for the civilization of the Indians: "In the present state of our country one of two things seems to be necessary. Either that those sons of the forest should be moralized or exterminated." Quoted in Alice C. Fletcher, *Indian Education and Civilization*, Bureau of Education Special Report 162 (1888). Federal policy makers expected Indian people to disappear voluntarily, but they were willing to contemplate force to speed along the process.

IV. THE REMOVAL ERA: 1817–1848

A. REMOVAL POLICY

The Louisiana Purchase of 1803 and American success in the War of 1812 removed many federal concerns about foreign claimants to the continent. The white population exploded in the first decades of the nineteenth century, creating more and more pressure for Indian land. The southern states, moreover, saw the presence of the "Five Civilized Tribes" (the Chickasaw, Creek, Choctaw, Cherokee and Seminole), who had established governments with written laws and elaborate western-style courts, as an affront to state sovereignty. Georgia was foremost among these. Under an 1802 compact with the United States, Georgia had agreed to cede its western land claims in exchange for a promise that the federal government would extinguish Indian title within the state as soon as it could be done "peaceably, and on reasonable terms." The state now claimed that the continued presence of Indian tribes was a violation of that compact.

In the 1810s and 1820s, federal treaty commissioners went repeatedly to the southeastern tribes to persuade them to exchange their lands for lands west of the Mississippi. The following 1824 correspondence from the Chiefs of the Creek Nation provides a good idea of tribal reactions to the removal proposals:

> Brothers, we have among us aged and infirm men and women, and helpless children, who cannot bear the fatigues of even a single day's journey. Shall we, can we, leave them behind us? Shall we desert, in their old age, the parents that fostered us? The answer is in your own hearts. No! Again: we feel an affection of the land in which we were born; we wish our bones to rest by the side of our fathers. Considering, then, our now circumscribed limits, the attachments we have to our native soil, and the assurance which we have that our homes will never be forced from us, so long as the government of the United States shall exist, we must positively decline the proposal of a removal beyond the Mississippi or the sale of any more of our territory.

8 American State Papers 571 (Dec. 11, 1824).

These tribes, moreover, had long been seen as civilization success stories by federal policymakers, experiencing success in farming and establishing courts and common school systems. The prosperity of Cherokee country was described by tribal member David Brown in 1825:

> These plains furnish immense pasturage, and numberless herds of cattle are dispersed over them. Horses are plenty, *** [n]umerous flocks of sheep, goats, and swine, cover the valleys and hills. *** The natives carry on considerable trade with the adjoining States. ***
>
> Butter and cheese are seen on Cherokee tables. There are many public roads in the nation, and houses of entertainment kept by natives. *** Cotton and woolen clothes are manufactured here. Blankets, of various dimensions, manufactured by Cherokee hands, are very common. *** Industry and commercial enterprise are extending themselves in every part. *** Nearly all the merchants in the nation are native Cherokees. Agricultural pursuits *** engage the chief attention of the people. Different branches in mechanics are pursued.

Reprinted in Thomas L. M'Kenney, Memoirs, Official and Personal with Sketches of Travels among the Northern and Southern Indians 37–38 (1846). (A disturbing sign of this degree of "civilization" was that the more acculturated members of some of these tribes owned many African slaves.) In the Cherokee Nation, the development of a written syllabary for the Cherokee language in 1821 had encouraged a new and distinctly Cherokee nationalism, and soon gave rise to a national paper, the *Cherokee Phoenix*, written in both Cherokee and English.

One can see this nationalism and the resistance to removal in the 1827 Cherokee Constitution, the first written constitution of any Indian nation:

> Article 1: The boundaries of this nation embracing the lands solemnly guaranteed and reserved forever to the Cherokee Nation by the treaties concluded with the United States is as follows, and which shall forever hereafter remain unalterably the same; ***
>
> The sovereignty & jurisdiction of this Government shall extend over the country within the boundaries above described, and the lands therein is & shall remain the common property of the nation. ***

The Constitution, although modeled in many ways on U.S. and state constitutions, caused alarm and anger among state and federal leaders. In 1828, President John Quincy Adams addressed the situation in his final message to Congress:

> [W]hen we have had the rare good fortune of teaching them the arts of civilization and the doctrines of Christianity we have unexpectedly found them forming in the midst of ourselves communities claiming to be independent of ours and rivals of sovereignty within the territories of the members of our Union. This state of things requires that a remedy should be provided—a remedy which, while it shall do justice to those unfortunate children of nature, may secure to the members of our confederation their rights of sovereignty and soil.

Georgia did not wait for a federal remedy. In 1828, the state enacted laws declaring Georgia's territory to include the Cherokee lands. The discovery of gold in Cherokee country in 1829 fueled this effort. That year, Georgia's laws were amended "to extend the laws of this state over [Cherokee territory], and to annul all laws and ordinances made by the Cherokee nation of Indians." In 1830, the laws were amended again to provide guards for the gold mines and to declare any governmental actions by the Cherokee Nation illegal: "[I]t shall not be lawful for any person or persons, under color or pretence of authority from said Cherokee tribe, or as headmen, chiefs or warriors of said tribe, to cause or procure by any means the assembling of any council or other pretended legislative body of the said Indians or others living among them, for the purpose of legislating (or for any other purpose whatever)." In 1829, Alabama followed suit by extending its laws over the Creek Nation, and by the end of the nineteenth century almost every state east of the Mississippi had passed laws extending jurisdiction over the Indians within their borders. Tim Alan Garrison, The Legal Ideology of Removal: The Southern Judiciary and the Sovereignty of Native American Nations 9 (2002).

These states welcomed Andrew Jackson's victory in the presidential election of 1828. Jackson ran on a states rights' ticket, and as early as 1820 had written to the Secretary of War that it was "high time to do away with the farce of treating with the Indian tribes." Francis Paul Prucha, The Great Father: The United States Government and the American Indians 192 (1984). In his first address to Congress, Jackson declared that it was folly for Indians to claim lands "merely because they had seen them from the mountain or passed them in the chase," and that he had rejected the tribes' plea for federal protection and informed them "that their attempt to establish an independent government would not be countenanced by the Executive of the United States, and advised them to emigrate beyond the Mississippi or submit to the laws of those States." Andrew Jackson, First Annual Message to Congress (Dec. 1829).

In 1830, at Jackson's urging, Congress passed the Indian Removal Act by a narrow margin. The Senate Committee on Indian Affairs wrote that the bill was a liberal measure to remove the Indians to the west "where they can be secured against the intrusion of any other people, where *** they can pursue their plan of civilization, and, ere long, be in the peaceable enjoyment of a civil government of their own choice. *** " Sen. Doc. No. 61, 21st Cong., 1st Sess. (1830). This benevolent plan was accompanied by the belief that the tribes had no real legal or moral claims to the land. The House Report claimed that the bill was a means to secure "the actual enjoyment of property claimed by the right of discovery, and sanctioned by the natural superiority allowed to the claims of civilized communities over those of savage tribes." H. Rep. No. 227, 21st Cong., 1st Sess. (1830). The Act did not authorize forcible removal; rather it allowed the President to provide lands west of the Mississippi in exchange for eastern lands "of such tribes or nations of Indians as may choose to exchange the lands where they now reside," and declared that "nothing in this act contained shall be construed as authorizing or directing the violation of any existing treaty between the United States and any of the Indian tribes." 4 Stat. 411–412, §§ 2 & 7 (May 28, 1830). But it was the final confirmation that tribes could not hope for aid from either the President or from Congress. The tribes had no alternative but to bring their claims to the courts.

B. THE CHEROKEE CASES

The Cherokee cases pitted the Court against the President and the State of Georgia in what a leading Supreme Court historian has called "the most serious crisis in the history of the Court." 2 Charles Warren, The Supreme Court in United States History 189 (Little, Brown & Co. 1923). At the height of the conflict, former President John Quincy Adams declared that "the Union is in the most imminent danger of dissolution. *** The ship is about to founder." 4 Albert J. Beveridge, The Life of John Marshall 544 (Houghton Mifflin Co. 1919). Although the constitutional crisis ultimately diffused with little lasting impact on the nation, the imprint of these decisions on federal Indian law would be permanent.

Johnson v. M'Intosh and *Fletcher v. Peck* had discussed Indian tribes, but the Cherokee cases were the first Supreme Court cases in which a tribe was actively involved. John Ross, the Principal Chief of the Cherokee Nation, worked with William Wirt, a leading member of the Supreme Court bar, in developing the legal strategy. The Cherokee people closely followed the cases, and the plaintiffs' briefs were reprinted in the *Cherokee Phoenix*.

The first difficulty was how to bring the issue before the Court. Federal district courts did not gain general federal question jurisdiction until 1875. The Supreme Court, however, had original jurisdiction over disputes between states and foreign nations, and Wirt hoped that the Cherokee Nation might be able to sue Georgia on this basis. Wirt's concerns about this jurisdictional hook were great enough that he wrote Judge Dabney Carr, a friend of both Marshall and Wirt, to ask about the propriety of asking the Chief Justice about the subject. Marshall (correctly) declined such a consultation, but wrote to Carr that,

"I have followed the debate in both houses of Congress, with profound attention and with deep interest, and have wished, most sincerely, that both the executive and legislative department had thought differently on the subject. Humanity must bewail the course which is pursued, whatever may be the decision of policy." Leonard Baker, John Marshall: A Life in Law 734–735 (Macmillan Publishing Co. 1974).

Although the Supreme Court could review decisions regarding federal law made by the highest court of a state, *State v. Tassels* forcefully illustrated the difficulties with this approach. George (or Corn) Tassel was a Cherokee man living in one of the areas recently annexed by the state. After he was arrested for the murder of another Cherokee, the Cherokee Nation hired attorneys to challenge state jurisdiction. A conference of Georgia judges (unlike the Cherokee Nation, the state did not yet have an appellate court) disdainfully rejected this argument, stating that the "habits, manners, and imbecile intellect" of the Indians opposed their governance as an independent state. *State v. Tassels*, 1 Ga. Rep. Ann. 478, 481, 1 Dud. 229 (Hall Sup. Ct. 1830). Tassel's attorney sought a writ of error to the U.S. Supreme Court. On December 12, 1830, Chief Justice Marshall granted the writ. In response a hastily assembled meeting of the Georgia Legislature authorized Governor Gilmer to use "all the force and means placed at his command *** to resist and repel any and every invasion, from whatever corner, upon the criminal laws of the state." At midnight, the governor sent a messenger to the sheriff. On Christmas Eve, December 24, 1830, Tassel was led from his jail cell and hanged until dead. *See* Tim Alan Garrison, The Legal Ideology of Removal: The Southern Judiciary and the Sovereignty of Native American Nations 111–122 (2002).

The death of Tassel mooted the appeal and dashed hopes of getting to the Supreme Court through a writ of error. On December 27, the attorneys for the Cherokee Nation served Georgia with notice that they would be invoking the Court's original jurisdiction over suits between states and foreign nations and filing a case directly with the Supreme Court. Georgia signaled its disregard for federal authority by refusing to appear or argue before the Court, but could not this time moot the case.

CHEROKEE NATION V. GEORGIA

30 U.S. (5 Pet.) 1, 8 L. Ed. 25 (1831)

CHIEF JUSTICE MARSHALL delivered the opinion of the Court.

This bill is brought by the Cherokee nation, praying an injunction to restrain the state of Georgia from the execution of certain laws of that state, which, as is alleged, go directly to annihilate the Cherokees as a political society, and to seize, for the use of Georgia, the lands of the nation which have been assured to them by the United States in solemn treaties repeatedly made and still in force.

If courts were permitted to indulge their sympathies, a case better calculated to excite them can scarcely be imagined. A people once numerous, powerful, and truly independent, found by our ancestors in the quiet and uncontrolled possession of an ample domain, gradually sinking beneath our superior policy, our arts and our arms, have yielded their lands by successive treaties, each of which contains a solemn guarantee of the residue, until they retain no more of their formerly extensive territory than is deemed necessary to their comfortable subsistence. To preserve this remnant, the present application is made.

Before we can look into the merits of the case, a preliminary inquiry presents itself. Has this court jurisdiction of the cause?

[Article III of the Constitution provides that the "judicial power" of the United States extends to various categories of cases, including those "between a State *** and [a] foreign State." Most cases within the judicial power fall within the Supreme Court's appellate jurisdiction, but cases in which a state is a party come within the Court's original jurisdiction.] The party defendant may then unquestionably be sued in this court. May the plaintiff sue in it? Is the Cherokee nation a foreign state in the sense in which that term is used in the constitution?

The counsel for the plaintiffs have maintained the affirmative of this proposition with great earnestness and ability. So much of the argument as was intended to prove the character of the Cherokees as a state, as a distinct political society, separated from others, capable of managing its own affairs and governing itself, has, in the opinion of a majority of the judges, been completely successful. They have been uniformly treated as a state from the settlement of our country. The numerous treaties made with them by the United States recognize them as a people capable of maintaining the relations of peace and war, of being responsible in their political character for any violation of their engagements, or for any aggression committed on the citizens of the United States by any individual of their community. Laws have been enacted in the spirit of these treaties. The acts of our government plainly recognize the Cherokee nation as a state, and the courts are bound by those acts.

A question of much more difficulty remains. Do the Cherokees constitute a foreign state in the sense of the constitution?

The counsel have shown conclusively that they are not a state of the union, and have insisted that individually they are aliens, not owing allegiance to the United States. An aggregate of aliens composing a state must, they say, be a foreign state. Each individual being foreign, the whole must be foreign.

This argument is imposing, but we must examine it more closely before we yield to it. The condition of the Indians in relation to the United States is perhaps unlike that of any other two people in existence. In the general, nations not owing a common allegiance are foreign to each other. The term *foreign nation* is, with strict propriety, applicable by either to the other. But the relation of the Indians to the United States is marked by peculiar and cardinal distinctions which exist no where else.

The Indian territory is admitted to compose a part of the United States. In all our maps, geographical treatises, histories, and laws, it is so considered. In all our intercourse with foreign nations, in our commercial regulations, in any attempt at intercourse between Indians and foreign nations, they are considered as within the jurisdictional limits of the United States, subject to many of those restraints which are imposed upon our own citizens. They acknowledge themselves in their treaties to be under the protection of the United States; they admit that the United States shall have the sole and exclusive right of regulating the trade with them, and managing all their affairs as they think proper; and the Cherokees in particular were allowed by the treaty of Hopewell, which preceded the constitution, "to send a deputy of their choice, whenever they think fit, to congress." Treaties were made with some tribes by the state of New York, under a then unsettled construction of the confederation, by which they ceded all their lands to that state, taking back a limited grant to themselves, in which they admit their dependence.

Though the Indians are acknowledged to have an unquestionable, and, heretofore, unquestioned right to the lands they occupy, until that right shall be extinguished by a voluntary cession to our government; yet it may well be doubted whether those tribes which reside within the acknowledged boundaries of the United States can, with strict accuracy, be denominated foreign nations. They may, more correctly, perhaps, be denominated domestic dependent nations. They occupy a territory to which we assert a title independent of their will, which must take effect in point of possession when their right of possession ceases. Meanwhile they are in a state of pupilage. Their relation to the United States resembles that of a ward to his guardian.

They look to our government for protection; rely upon its kindness and its power; appeal to it for relief to their wants; and address the president as their great father. They and their country are considered by foreign nations, as well as by ourselves, as being so completely under the sovereignty and dominion of the United States, that any attempt to acquire their lands, or to form a political connexion with them, would be considered by all as an invasion of our territory, and an act of hostility.

These considerations go far to support the opinion, that the framers of our constitution had not the Indian tribes in view, when they opened the courts of the union to controversies between a state or the citizens thereof, and foreign states.

In considering this subject, the habits and usages of the Indians, in their intercourse with their white neighbours, ought not to be entirely disregarded. At the time the constitution was framed, the idea of appealing to an American court of justice for an assertion of right or a redress of wrong, had perhaps never entered the mind of an Indian or of his tribe. Their appeal was to the tomahawk, or to the government. This was well understood by the statesmen who framed the constitution of the United States, and might furnish some reason for omitting to enumerate them among the parties who might sue in the courts of the union. Be this as it may, the peculiar relations between the United States and the Indians occupying our territory are such, that we should feel much difficulty in considering them as designated by the term *foreign state*, were there no other part of the constitution which might shed light on the meaning of these words. But we think that in construing them, considerable aid is furnished by that clause in the eighth section of the third article; which empowers congress to "regulate commerce with foreign nations, and among the several states, and with the Indian tribes."

In this clause they are as clearly contradistinguished by a name appropriate to themselves, from foreign nations, as from the several states composing the union. They are designated by a distinct appellation; and as this appellation can be applied to neither of the others, neither can the appellation distinguishing either of the others be in fair construction applied to them. The objects, to which the power of regulating commerce might be directed, are divided into three distinct classes—foreign nations, the several states, and Indian tribes. When forming this article, the convention considered them as entirely distinct. We cannot assume that the distinction was lost in framing a subsequent article, unless there be something in its language to authorize the assumption.

The counsel for the plaintiffs contend that the words "Indian tribes" were introduced into the article, empowering congress to regulate commerce, for the purpose of removing those doubts in which the management of Indian affairs was involved by the language of the ninth article of the confederation. Intending to give the whole power of managing those affairs to the government about to be instituted, the convention conferred it explicitly; and omitted those qualifications which embarrassed the exercise of it as granted in the confederation. This may be admitted without weakening the construction which has been intimated. Had the Indian tribes been foreign nations, in the view of the convention; this exclusive power of regulating intercourse with them might have been, and most probably would have been, specifically given, in language indicating that idea, not in language contradistinguishing them from foreign nations. Congress might have been empowered "to regulate commerce with foreign nations, including the Indian tribes, and among the several states." This language would have suggested itself to statesmen who considered the Indian tribes as foreign nations, and were yet desirous of mentioning them particularly.

It has been also said, that the same words have not necessarily the same meaning attached to them when found in different parts of the same instrument: their meaning is controlled by the context. This is undoubtedly true. In common language the same word has various meanings, and the peculiar sense in which it is used in any sentence is to be determined by the context. This may not be equally true with respect to proper names. *Foreign nations* is a general term, the application of which to Indian tribes, when used in the American constitution, is at best extremely questionable. In one article in which a power is given to be exercised in regard to foreign nations generally, and to the Indian tribes particularly, they are mentioned as separate in terms clearly contradistinguishing them from each other. We perceive plainly that the constitution in this article does not comprehend Indian tribes in the general term "foreign nations;" not we presume because a tribe may not be a nation, but because it is not foreign to the United States. When, afterwards, the term "foreign state" is introduced, we cannot impute to the convention the intention to desert its former meaning, and to comprehend Indian tribes within it, unless the context force that construction on us. We find nothing in the context, and nothing in the subject of the article, which leads to it.

The court has bestowed its best attention on this question, and, after mature deliberation, the majority is of opinion that an Indian tribe or nation within the United States is not a foreign state in the sense of the constitution, and cannot maintain an action in the courts of the United States.

A serious additional objection exists to the jurisdiction of the court. Is the matter of the bill the proper subject for judicial inquiry and decision? It seeks to restrain a state from the forcible exercise of legislative power over a neighbouring people, asserting their independence; their right to which the state denies. On several of the matters alleged in the bill, for example on the laws making it criminal to exercise the usual powers of self government in their own country by the Cherokee nation, this court cannot interpose; at least in the form in which those matters are presented.

That part of the bill which respects the land occupied by the Indians, and prays the aid of the court to protect their possession, may be more doubtful. The mere question of right might perhaps be decided by this court in a proper case with proper parties. But the court is asked to do more than decide on the title. The bill requires us to control the legislature of Georgia, and to restrain the exertion of its physical force. The propriety of such an interposition by the court may be well questioned. It savours too much of the exercise of political power to be within the proper province of the judicial department. But the opinion on the point respecting parties makes it unnecessary to decide this question.

If it be true that the Cherokee nation have rights, this is not the tribunal in which those rights are to be asserted. If it be true that wrongs have been inflicted, and that still greater are to be apprehended, this is not the tribunal which can redress the past or prevent the future.

The motion for an injunction is denied.

JUSTICE JOHNSON, [concurring in the judgment.]

*** I cannot but think that there are strong reasons for doubting the applicability of the epithet *state*, to a people so low in the grade of organized society as our Indian tribes most generally are. I would not here be understood as speaking of the Cherokees under their present form of government; which certainly must be classed among the most approved forms of civil government. Whether it can be yet said to have received the consistency which entitles that people to admission into the family of nations is, I conceive, yet to be determined by the executive of these states. Until then I must think that we cannot recognize it as an existing state, under any other character than that which it has maintained hitherto as one of the Indian tribes or nations. ***

*** When the eastern coast of this continent, and especially the part we inhabit, was discovered, finding it occupied by a race of hunters, connected in society by scarcely a semblance of organic government; the right was extended to the absolute appropriation of the territory, the annexation of it to the domain of the discoverer. ***

In the very treaty of Hopewell, the language or evidence of which is appealed to as the leading proof of the existence of this supposed state, we find the commissioners of the United States expressing themselves in these terms. "The commissioners plenipotentiary of the United States give peace to all the Cherokees, and receive them into the favour and protection of the United States *on the following conditions*." This is certainly the language of sovereigns and conquerors, and not the address of equals to equals. And again, when designating the country they are to be confined to, comprising the very territory which is the subject of this bill, they say, "Art. 4. *The boundary allotted to the Cherokees for their hunting grounds* shall be as therein described. Certainly this is the language of concession on our part, not theirs; and when the full bearing and effect of those words, "for their hunting grounds," is considered, it is difficult to think that they were then regarded as a state, or even intended to be so regarded. It is clear that it was intended to give them no other rights over the territory than what were needed by a race of hunters; and it is not easy to see how their advancement beyond that state of society could ever have been promoted, or, perhaps, permitted, consistently with the unquestioned rights of the states, or United States, over the territory within their limits. *** The hunter state bore within itself the promise of vacating the territory, because when game ceased, the hunter would go elsewhere to seek it. But a more fixed state of society would amount to a permanent destruction of the hope, and, of consequence, of the beneficial character of the pre-emptive right. ***

*** And almost every attribute of sovereignty is renounced by them in that very treaty. They acknowledge themselves to be under the sole and exclusive protection of the United States. They receive the territory allotted to them as a boon, from a master or conqueror; the right of punishing intruders into that territory is conceded, not asserted as a right; and the sole and exclusive right of regulating their trade and managing all their affairs in such manner as the government of the United States shall think proper; amounting in terms to a relinquishment of all power, legislative, executive and judicial to the United States, is yielded in the ninth article. ***

[If the Cherokees are a state, where] is the rule to stop? Must every petty kraal of Indians, designating themselves a tribe or nation, and having a few hundred acres of land to hunt on exclusively, be recognized as a state? ***

*** They have in Europe sovereign and demi-sovereign states and states of doubtful sovereignty. But this state, if it be a state, is still a grade below them all: for not to be able to alienate without permission of the remainder-man or lord, places them in a state of feudal dependence.

*** I believe, in one view and in one only, if at all, they are or may be deemed a state, though not a sovereign state, at least while they occupy a country within our limits. Their condition is something like that of the Israelites, when inhabiting the deserts. Though without land that they can call theirs in the sense of property, their right of personal self government has never been taken from them; and such a form of government may exist though the land occupied be in fact that of another. The right to expel them may exist in that other, but the alternative of departing and retaining the right of self government may exist in them. And such they certainly do possess; it has never been questioned, nor any attempt made at subjugating them as a people, or restraining their personal liberty except as to their land and trade. ***

*** I think it very clear that the constitution neither speaks of them as states or foreign states, but as just what they were, Indian tribes; an anomaly unknown to the books that treat of states, and which the law of nations would regard as nothing more than wandering hordes, held together only by ties of blood and habit, and having neither laws or government, beyond what is required in a savage state. ***

JUSTICE BALDWIN, [concurring in the judgment].

*** There can be no dependence so antinational, or so utterly subversive of national existence as transferring to a foreign government the regulation of its trade, and the management of all their affairs at their pleasure [as the Cherokee did in Article 9 of the Treaty of Hopewell]. The nation or state, tribe or village, head men or warriors of the Cherokees, call them by what name we please, call the articles they have signed a definitive treaty or an indenture of servitude; they are not by its force or virtue a foreign state capable of calling into legitimate action the judicial power of this union, by the exercise of the original jurisdiction of this court against a sovereign state, a component part of this nation. Unless the constitution has imparted to the Cherokees a national character never recognized under the confederation; and which if they ever enjoyed was surrendered by the treaty of Hopewell; they cannot be deemed in this court plaintiffs in such a case as this. ***

[Georgia's] jurisdiction over the territory in question is as supreme as that of congress over what the nation has acquired by cession from the states or treaties with foreign powers, combining the rights of the state and general government. Within her boundaries there can be no other nation, community, or sovereign power, which this department can judicially recognize as a foreign state, capable of demanding or claiming our interposition, so as to enable them to exercise a jurisdiction incompatible with a sovereignty in Georgia, which has been recognized by the constitution, and every department of this government acting under its authority. Foreign states cannot be created by judicial construction; Indian sovereignty cannot be roused from its long slumber, and awakened to action by our fiat. I find no acknowledgement of it by the legislative or executive power. Till they have done so, I can stretch forth no arm for their relief without violating the constitution.

JUSTICE THOMPSON, dissenting.

[T]he first inquiry is, whether the Cherokee nation is a foreign state within the sense and meaning of the constitution.

The terms *state* and *nation* are used in the law of nations, as well as in common parlance, as importing the same thing; and imply a body of men, united together, to procure their mutual safety and advantage by means of their union. *** Vattel, 1. *** It is sufficient if it be really sovereign and independent: that is, it must govern itself by its own authority and laws. We ought, therefore, to reckon in the number of sovereigns those states that have bound themselves to another more powerful, although by an unequal alliance. The conditions of these unequal alliances may be infinitely varied; but whatever they are, provided the inferior ally reserves to itself the sovereignty or the right to govern its own body, it ought to be considered an independent state. Consequently, a weak state, that, in order to provide for its safety, places itself under the protection of a more powerful one, without stripping itself of the right of government and sovereignty, does not cease on this account to be placed among the sovereigns who acknowledge no other power. Tributary and feudatory states do not thereby cease to be sovereign and independent states, so long as self government, and sovereign and independent authority is left in the administration of the state. Vattel, c. 1, pp. 16, 17. ***

Suppose the Cherokee territory had been occupied by Spaniards or any other civilized people, instead of Indians, and they had from time to time ceded to the United States portions of their lands precisely in the same manner as the Indians have done, and in like manner retained and occupied the part now held by the Cherokees, and having a regular government established there: would it not only be considered a separate and distinct nation or state, but a foreign nation, with reference to the state of Georgia or the United States. ***

And what possible objection can lie to the right of the complainants to sustain an action? The treaties made with this nation purport to secure to it certain rights. These are not gratuitous obligations assumed on the part of the United States. They are obligations founded upon a consideration paid by the Indians by cession of part of their territory. And if they, as a nation, are competent to make a treaty or contract, it would seem to me to be a strange inconsistency to deny to them the right and the power to enforce such a contract. ***

NOTES AND QUESTIONS

1. First, count the votes. Six justices heard the case. Only Justice McLean joined in Justice Marshall's opinion, making it a plurality opinion. Justices Johnson and Baldwin concurred in the judgment in separate opinions, and Justice Thompson wrote a dissent which Justice Story joined. How many justices agreed that the Cherokees were a state or nation? How many that they were a foreign nation entitled to invoke the original jurisdiction of the Supreme Court?

2. How does the portrayal of Indian tribes and their property rights in *Cherokee Nation* compare to that in *Johnson v. McIntosh*?

3. What does Chief Justice Marshall mean when he says, "If it be true that the Cherokee nation have rights, this is not the tribunal in which those rights are to be asserted"? What tribunal is he referring to?

4. *Cherokee Nation v. Georgia* is generally considered to be the origin of the trust relationship in Federal Indian Law, under which the federal government is considered the trustee of Indian tribes. What does it mean to say Indian tribes are "dependent" or that they are "in a state of pupilage" or that "Their relationship to the United States is that of a ward to his guardian"? What creates this dependent relationship? What are the purposes of this guardianship? Does it place any limits on federal power toward Indian tribes? Think about the kinds of guardian relationships you know of, both legal and non-legal; what are the implications of such a relationship for Indian tribes?

5. The fate of the Cherokee Nation was not the only interest of the lawyers and judges. The opponents of President Jackson and the Democratic Party hoped to use the issue to stir up sympathy for the Cherokees and drive the Democrats out of the White House in the 1832 election. Federalist leaders like Daniel Webster had recommended William Wirt to John Ross, and helped persuade him to take the job. When Wirt was U.S. Attorney General for the Monroe administration he had supported tribal removal. But as a candidate running against Jackson on the Antimasonic ticket, Wirt had every incentive to further the Cherokee cause. Chief Justice Marshall, too, hoped the issue would contribute to Jackson's defeat. Marshall was already losing control of the Court as Jackson's appointees split with him on fundamental issues of constitutionalism and the relationship between the federal government and the states. He hoped a Republican president would appoint his protégé, Justice Story, as Chief Justice to replace him, so that he could retire knowing his federalist legacy was safe. The leading contemporary biographer of John Marshall suggests that the Chief Justice actually encouraged Thompson to write his dissent in *Cherokee Nation* (with Story in silent and politically safe concurrence) to highlight the arguments for the Cherokees. R. Kent Newmyer, John Marshall and the Heroic Age of the Supreme Court 450 (2001). In reading *Worcester v. Georgia*, notice how Marshall adopts and uses Thompson's arguments.

The battle between the Cherokee Nation and Georgia was not long out of the Court. Believing that the Cherokee refusal to remove must be the result of non-Indian influence, Georgia had prohibited any non-Indian from going into Indian country without obtaining a license and swearing an oath of loyalty to the state. Several individuals were convicted of violating the law and sentenced to four years hard labor. Two missionaries, Samuel Worcester and Elizur Butler, refused to accept pardons conditioned on their leaving the Cherokee Nation, and their convictions went to the Supreme Court on a writ of error. This time, the Supreme Court accepted jurisdiction and held that Georgia laws had no effect on Cherokee land.

Chief Justice Marshall issued the *Worcester* opinion at the most difficult time in his life. Early in 1831 he had suffered the first of the series of gallstone attacks that would ultimately kill him. Even more painful was the death of his wife at the end of that year. William Wirt noted on another occasion that the chief justice was "badly shaved this morning" and "came into the court with a quantity of egg on his underlip and chin." Quoted in R. Kent Newmyer, John Marshall and the Heroic Age of the Supreme Court 439 (2001). In announcing the decision in *Worcester*, Marshall "read his opinion to a hushed audience in a voice that was barely audible, but the words he spoke were forceful and uncompromising." *Id.* at 451.

WORCESTER V. GEORGIA

31 U.S. 515, 8 L. Ed. 483 (1832)

CHIEF JUSTICE MARSHALL delivered the opinion of the Court.

This cause, in every point of view in which it can be placed, is of the deepest interest.

The defendant is a state, a member of the union, which has exercised the powers of government over a people who deny its jurisdiction, and are under the protection of the United States.

The plaintiff is a citizen of the state of Vermont, condemned to hard labour for four years in the penitentiary of Georgia; under colour of an act which he alleges to be repugnant to the constitution, laws, and treaties of the United States.

The legislative power of a state, the controlling power of the constitution and laws of the United States, the rights, if they have any, the political existence of a once numerous and powerful people, the personal liberty of a citizen, are all involved in the subject now to be considered.

***

The indictment charges the plaintiff in error, and others, being white persons, with the offence of "residing within the limits of the Cherokee nation without a license," and "without having taken the oath to support and defend the constitution and laws of the state of Georgia."

***

It has been said at the bar, that the acts of the legislature of Georgia seize on the whole Cherokee country, parcel it out among the neighbouring counties of the state, extend her code over the whole country, abolish its institutions and its laws, and annihilate its political existence.

If this be the general effect of the system, let us inquire into the effect of the particular statute and section on which the indictment is founded.

It enacts that "all white persons, residing within the limits of the Cherokee nation on the 1st day of March next, or at any time thereafter, without a license or permit from his excellency the governor, or from such agent as his excellency the governor shall authorise to grant such permit or license, and who shall not have taken the oath hereinafter required, shall be guilty of a high misdemeanour, and, upon conviction thereof, shall be punished by confinement to the penitentiary, at hard labour, for a term not less than four years."

The eleventh section authorises the governor, should he deem it necessary for the protection of the mines, or the enforcement of the laws in force within the Cherokee nation, to raise and organize a guard, & c.

The thirteenth section enacts, "that the said guard or any member of them, shall be, and they are hereby authorised and empowered to arrest any person legally charged with or detected in a violation of the laws of this state, and to convey, as soon as practicable, the person so arrested, before a justice of the peace, judge of the superior, or justice of inferior court of this state, to be dealt with according to law."

The extra-territorial power of every legislature being limited in its action, to its own citizens or subjects, the very passage of this act is an assertion of jurisdiction over the Cherokee nation, and of the rights and powers consequent on jurisdiction.

The first step, then, in the inquiry, which the constitution and laws impose on this court, is an examination of the rightfulness of this claim.

America, separated from Europe by a wide ocean, was inhabited by a distinct people, divided into separate nations, independent of each other and of the rest of the world, having institutions of their own, and governing themselves by their own laws. It is difficult to comprehend the proposition, that the inhabitants of either quarter of the globe could have rightful original claims of dominion over the inhabitants of the other, or over the lands they occupied; or that the discovery of either by the other should give the discoverer rights in the country discovered, which annulled the pre-existing rights of its ancient possessors.

After lying concealed for a series of ages, the enterprise of Europe, guided by nautical science, conducted some of her adventurous sons into this western world. They found it in possession of a people who had made small progress in agriculture or manufactures, and whose general employment was war, hunting, and fishing.

Did these adventurers, by sailing along the coast, and occasionally landing on it, acquire for the several governments to whom they belonged, or by whom they were commissioned, a rightful property in the soil, from the Atlantic to the Pacific; or rightful dominion over the numerous people who occupied it? Or has nature, or the great Creator of all things, conferred these rights over hunters and fishermen, on agriculturists and manufacturers?

But power, war, conquest, give rights, which, after possession, are conceded by the world; and which can never be controverted by those on whom they descend. We proceed, then, to the actual state of things, having glanced at their origin; because holding it in our recollection might shed some light on existing pretensions.

The great maritime powers of Europe discovered and visited different parts of this continent at nearly the same time. The object was too immense for any one of them to grasp the whole; and the claimants were too powerful to submit to the exclusive or unreasonable pretensions of any single potentate. To avoid bloody conflicts, which might terminate disastrously to all, it was necessary for the nations of Europe to establish some principle which all would acknowledge, and which should decide their respective rights as between themselves. ***

This principle, acknowledged by all Europeans, because it was the interest of all to acknowledge it, gave to the nation making the discovery, as its inevitable consequence, the sole right of acquiring the soil and of making settlements on it. It was an exclusive principle which shut out the right of competition among those who had agreed to it; not one which could annul the previous rights of those who had not agreed to it. It regulated the right given by discovery among the European discoverers; but could not affect the rights of those already in possession, either as aboriginal occupants, or as occupants by virtue of a discovery made before the memory of man. It gave the exclusive right to purchase, but did not found that right on a denial of the right of the possessor to sell.

The relation between the Europeans and the natives was determined in each case by the particular government which asserted and could maintain this pre-emptive privilege in the particular place. The United States succeeded to all the claims of Great Britain, both territorial and political; but no attempt, so far as is known, has been made to enlarge them. So far as they existed merely in theory, or were in their nature only exclusive of the claims of other European nations, they still retain their original character, and remain dormant. So far as they have been practically exerted, they exist in fact, are understood by both parties, are asserted by the one, and admitted by the other.

Soon after Great Britain determined on planting colonies in America, the king granted charters to companies of his subjects who associated for the purpose of carrying the views of the crown into effect, and of enriching themselves. The first of these charters was made before possession was taken of any part of the country. They purport, generally, to convey the soil, from the Atlantic to the South Sea. This soil was occupied by numerous and warlike nations, equally willing and able to defend their possessions. The extravagant and absurd idea, that the feeble settlements made on the sea coast, or the companies under whom they were made, acquired legitimate power by them to govern the people, or occupy the lands from sea to sea, did not enter the mind of any man. They were well understood to convey the title which, according to the common law of European sovereigns respecting America, they might rightfully convey, and no more. This was the exclusive right of purchasing such lands as the natives were willing to sell. The crown could not be understood to grant what the crown did not affect to claim; nor was it so understood.

***

Certain it is, that our history furnishes no example, from the first settlement of our country, of any attempt on the part of the crown to interfere with the internal affairs of the Indians, farther than to keep out the agents of foreign powers, who, as traders or otherwise, might seduce them into foreign alliances. The king purchased their lands when they were willing to sell, at a price they were willing to take; but never coerced a surrender of them. He also purchased their alliance and dependence by subsidies; but never intruded into the interior of their affairs, or interfered with their self government, so far as respected themselves only.

***

Such was the policy of Great Britain towards the Indian nations inhabiting the territory from which she excluded all other Europeans; such her claims, and such her practical exposition of the charters she had granted: she considered them as nations capable of maintaining the relations of peace and war; of governing themselves, under her protection; and she made treaties with them, the obligation of which she acknowledged.

This was the settled state of things when the war of our revolution commenced. The influence of our enemy was established; her resources enabled her to keep up that influence; and the colonists had much cause for the apprehension that the Indian nations would, as the allies of Great Britain, add their arms to hers. This, as was to be expected, became an object of great solicitude to congress. Far from advancing a claim to their lands, or asserting any right of dominion over them, congress resolved "that the securing and preserving the friendship of the Indian nations appears to be a subject of the utmost moment to these colonies."

The early journals of congress exhibit the most anxious desire to conciliate the Indian nations. Three Indian departments were established; and commissioners appointed in each, "to treat with the Indians in their respective departments, in the name and on the behalf of the United Colonies, in order to preserve peace and friendship with the said Indians, and to prevent their taking any part in the present commotions."

The most strenuous exertions were made to procure those supplies on which Indian friendships were supposed to depend; and every thing which might excite hostility was avoided.

***

During the war of the revolution, the Cherokees took part with the British. After its termination, the United States, though desirous of peace, did not feel its necessity so strongly as while the war continued. Their political situation being changed, they might very well think it advisable to assume a higher tone, and to impress on the Cherokees the same respect for congress which was before felt for the king of Great Britain. This may account for the language of the treaty of Hopewell. There is the more reason for supposing that the Cherokee chiefs were not very critical judges of the language, from the fact that every one makes his mark; no chief was capable of signing his name. It is probable the treaty was interpreted to them.

The treaty is introduced with the declaration, that "the commissioners plenipotentiary of the United States give peace to all the Cherokees, and receive them into the favour and protection of the United States of America, on the following conditions."

When the United States gave peace, did they not also receive it? Were not both parties desirous of it? If we consult the history of the day, does it not inform us that the United States were at least as anxious to obtain it as the Cherokees? We may ask, further: did the Cherokees come to the seat of the American government to solicit peace; or, did the American commissioners go to them to obtain it? The treaty was made at Hopewell, not at New York. The word "give," then, has no real importance attached to it.

The first and second articles stipulate for the mutual restoration of prisoners, and are of course equal.

The third article acknowledges the Cherokees to be under the protection of the United States of America, and of no other power.

This stipulation is found in Indian treaties, generally. It was introduced into their treaties with Great Britain; and may probably be found in those with other European powers. Its origin may be traced to the nature of their connexion with those powers; and its true meaning is discerned in their relative situation.

The general law of European sovereigns, respecting their claims in America, limited the intercourse of Indians, in a great degree, to the particular potentate whose ultimate right of domain was acknowledged by the others. *** The consequence was, that their supplies were derived chiefly from that nation, and their trade confined to it. Goods, indispensable to their comfort, in the shape of presents, were received from the same hand. What was of still more importance, the strong hand of government was interposed to restrain the disorderly and licentious from intrusions into their country, from encroachments on their lands, and from those acts of violence which were often attended by reciprocal murder. The Indians perceived in this protection only what was beneficial to themselves—an engagement to punish aggressions on them. It involved, practically, no claim to their lands, no dominion over their persons. It merely bound the nation to the British crown, as a dependent ally, claiming the protection of a powerful friend and neighbour, and receiving the advantages of that protection, without involving a surrender of their national character.

This is the true meaning of the stipulation, and is undoubtedly the sense in which it was made. Neither the British government, nor the Cherokees, ever understood it otherwise.

The same stipulation entered into with the United States, is undoubtedly to be construed in the same manner. They receive the Cherokee nation into their favor and protection. The Cherokees acknowledge themselves to be under the protection of the United States, and of no other power. Protection does not imply the destruction of the protected. The manner in which this stipulation was understood by the American government, is explained by the language and acts of our first president.

The fourth article draws the boundary between the Indians and the citizens of the United States.† But, in describing this boundary, the term "allotted" and the term "hunting ground" are used.

Is it reasonable to suppose, that the Indians, who could not write, and most probably could not read, who certainly were not critical judges of our language, should distinguish the word "allotted" from the words "marked out." The actual subject of contract was the dividing line between the two nations, and their attention may very well be supposed to have been confined to that subject. When, in fact, they were ceding lands to the United States, and describing the extent of their cession, it may very well be supposed that they might not understand the term employed, as indicating that, instead of granting, they were receiving lands.

***

So with respect to the words "hunting grounds." Hunting was at that time the principal occupation of the Indians, and their land was more used for that purpose than for any other. It could not, however, be supposed, that any intention existed of restricting the full use of the lands they reserved.

To the United States, it could be a matter of no concern, whether their whole territory was devoted to hunting grounds, or whether an occasional village, and an occasional corn field, interrupted, and gave some variety to the scene.

These terms had been used in their treaties with Great Britain, and had never been misunderstood. They had never been supposed to imply a right in the British government to take their lands, or to interfere with their internal government.

The fifth article withdraws the protection of the United States from any citizen who has settled, or shall settle, on the lands allotted to the Indians, for their hunting grounds; and stipulates that, if he shall not remove within six months the Indians may punish him.

The sixth and seventh articles stipulate for the punishment of the citizens of either country, who may commit offences on or against the citizens of the other. The only inference to be drawn from them is, that the United States considered the Cherokees as a nation.

The ninth article is in these words: "for the benefit and comfort of the Indians, and for the prevention of injuries or oppressions on the part of the citizens or Indians, the United States, in congress assembled, shall have the sole and exclusive right of regulating the trade with the Indians, and *managing all their affairs*, as they think proper."

To construe the expression "managing all their affairs," into a surrender of self-government, would be, we think, a perversion of their necessary meaning, and a departure from the construction which has been uniformly put on them. The great subject of the article is the Indian trade. The influence it gave, made it desirable that congress should possess it. The commissioners brought forward the claim, with the profession that their motive was "the benefit and

---

†. [Eds. Article 4, in its sole description of the bounds of Cherokee territory, states "The boundary allotted to the Cherokees for their hunting grounds" would be within the limits described.]

comfort of the Indians, and the prevention of injuries or oppressions." This may be true, as respects the regulation of their trade, and as respects the regulation of all affairs connected with their trade, but cannot be true, as respects the management of all their affairs. The most important of these, are the cession of their lands, and security against intruders on them. Is it credible, that they should have considered themselves as surrendering to the United States the right to dictate their future cessions, and the terms on which they should be made, or to compel their submission to the violence of disorderly and licentious intruders? It is equally inconceivable that they could have supposed themselves, by a phrase thus slipped into an article, on another and most interesting subject, to have divested themselves of the right of self-government on subjects not connected with trade. Such a measure could not be "for their benefit and comfort," or for "the prevention of injuries and oppression." Such a construction would be inconsistent with the spirit of this and of all subsequent treaties; especially of those articles which recognise the right of the Cherokees to declare hostilities, and to make war. It would convert a treaty of peace covertly into an act, annihilating the political existence of one of the parties. Had such a result been intended, it would have been openly avowed.

The treaty of Hopewell seems not to have established a solid peace. To accommodate the differences still existing between the state of Georgia and the Cherokee nation, the treaty of Holston was negotiated in July 1791. The existing constitution of the United States had been then adopted, and the government, having more intrinsic capacity to enforce its just claims, was perhaps less mindful of high sounding expressions, denoting superiority. We hear no more of giving peace to the Cherokees. The mutual desire of establishing permanent peace and friendship, and of removing all causes of war, is honestly avowed. ***

***

This relation was that of a nation claiming and receiving the protection of one more powerful: not that of individuals abandoning their national character, and submitting as subjects to the laws of a master.

***

This treaty, thus explicitly recognizing the national character of the Cherokees, and their right of self government; thus guarantying their lands; assuming the duty of protection, and of course pledging the faith of the United States for that protection; has been frequently renewed, and is now in full force.

***

From the commencement of our government, congress has passed acts to regulate trade and intercourse with the Indians; which treat them as nations, respect their rights, and manifest a firm purpose to afford that protection which treaties stipulate. All these acts, and especially that of 1802, which is still in force, manifestly consider the several Indian nations as distinct political communities, having territorial boundaries, within which their authority is exclusive, and having a right to all the lands within those boundaries, which is not only acknowledged, but guarantied by the United States.

***

The treaties and laws of the United States contemplate the Indian territory as completely separated from that of the states; and provide that all intercourse with them shall be carried on exclusively by the government of the union.

***

[Our Constitution] confers on congress the powers of war and peace; of making treaties, and of regulating commerce with foreign nations, and among the several states, and *with the Indian tribes.* These powers comprehend all that is required for the regulation of our intercourse with the Indians. They are not limited by any restrictions on their free actions. The shackles imposed on this power, in the confederation, are discarded.

The Indian nations had always been considered as distinct, independent political communities, retaining their original natural rights, as the undisputed possessors of the soil, from time immemorial, with the single exception of that imposed by irresistible power, which excluded them from intercourse with any other European potentate than the first discoverer of the coast of the particular region claimed: and this was a restriction which those European potentates imposed on themselves, as well as on the Indians. The very term "nation," so generally applied to them, means "a people distinct from others." The constitution, by declaring treaties already made, as well as those to be made, to be the supreme law of the land, has adopted and sanctioned the previous treaties with the Indian nations, and consequently admits their rank among those powers who are capable of making treaties. The words "treaty" and "nation" are words of our own language, selected in our diplomatic and legislative proceedings, by ourselves, having each a definite and well understood meaning. We have applied them to Indians, as we have applied them to the other nations of the earth. They are applied to all in the same sense.

***

The actual state of things at the time, and all history since, explain these charters; and the king of Great Britain, at the treaty of peace, could cede only what belonged to his crown. These newly asserted titles can derive no aid from the articles so often repeated in Indian treaties; extending to them, first, the protection of Great Britain, and afterwards that of the United States. These articles are associated with others, recognizing their title to self government. The very fact of repeated treaties with them recognizes it; and the settled doctrine of the law of nations is, that a weaker power does not surrender its independence—its right to self government, by associating with a stronger, and taking its protection. A weak state, in order to provide for its safety, may place itself under the protection of one more powerful, without stripping itself of the right of government, and ceasing to be a state. Examples of this kind are not wanting in Europe. "Tributary and feudatory states," says Vattel, "do not thereby cease to be sovereign and independent states, so long as self government and sovereign and independent authority are left in the administration of the state." At the present day, more than one state may be considered as holding its right of self government under the guarantee and protection of one or more allies.

The Cherokee nation, then, is a distinct community occupying its own territory, with boundaries accurately described, in which the laws of Georgia can have no force, and which the citizens of Georgia have no right to enter, but with the assent of the Cherokees themselves, or in conformity with treaties, and with the acts of congress. The whole intercourse between the United States and this nation, is, by our constitution and laws, vested in the government of the United States.

The act of the state of Georgia, under which the plaintiff in error was prosecuted, is consequently void, and the judgment a nullity. Can this court revise, and reverse it?

If the objection to the system of legislation, lately adopted by the legislature of Georgia, in relation to the Cherokee nation, was confined to its extra-territorial operation, the objection, though complete, so far as respected mere right, would give this court no power over the subject. But it goes much further. If the review which has been taken be correct, and we think it is, the acts of Georgia are repugnant to the constitution, laws, and treaties of the United States.

They interfere forcibly with the relations established between the United States and the Cherokee nation, the regulation of which, according to the settled principles of our constitution, are committed exclusively to the government of the union.

They are in direct hostility with treaties, repeated in a succession of years, which mark out the boundary that separates the Cherokee country from Georgia; guaranty to them all the land within their boundary; solemnly pledge the faith of the United States to restrain their citizens from trespassing on it; and recognize the pre-existing power of the nation to govern itself.

They are in equal hostility with the acts of congress for regulating this intercourse, and giving effect to the treaties.

The forcible seizure and abduction of the plaintiff in error, who was residing in the nation with its permission, any by authority of the president of the United States, is also a violation of the acts which authorise the chief magistrate to exercise this authority.

***

It is the opinion of this court that the judgment of the superior court for the county of Gwinnett, in the state of Georgia, condemning Samuel A. Worcester to hard labour, in the penitentiary of the state of Georgia, for four years, was pronounced by that court under colour of a law which is void, as being repugnant to the constitution, treaties, and laws of the United States, and ought, therefore, to be reversed and annulled.

JUSTICE MCLEAN [concurring in the judgment]

Much has been said against the existence of an independent power within a sovereign state; and the conclusion has been drawn, that the Indians, as a matter of right, cannot enforce their own laws within the territorial limits of a state. The refutation of this argument is found in our past history.

***

But the inquiry may be made, is there no end to the exercise of this power over Indians within the limits of a state, by the general government? The answer is, that, in its nature, it must be limited by circumstances.

If a tribe of Indians shall become so degraded or reduced in numbers, as to lose the power of self-government, the protection of the local law, of necessity, must be extended over them. The point at which this exercise of power by a state would be proper, need not now be considered: if indeed it be a judicial question. Such a question does not seem to arise in this case. So long as treaties and laws remain in full force, and apply to Indian nations, exercising the right of self-government, within the limits of a state, the judicial power can exercise no discretion in refusing to give effect to those laws, when questions arise under them, unless they shall be deemed unconstitutional.

The exercise of the power of self-government by the Indians, within a state, is undoubtedly contemplated to be temporary. This is shown by the settled policy of the government, in the extinguishment of their title, and especially by the compact with the state of Georgia. *** [A] sound national policy does require that the Indian tribes within our states should exchange their territories, upon equitable principles, or, eventually, consent to become amalgamated in our political communities.

***

This state of things can only be produced by a co-operation of the state and federal governments. The latter has the exclusive regulation of intercourse with the Indians; and, so long as this power shall be exercised, it cannot be obstructed by the state. It is a power given by the constitution, and sanctioned by the most solemn acts of both the federal and state governments: consequently, it cannot be abrogated at the will of a state. It is one of the powers parted with by the states, and vested in the federal government. But, if a contingency shall occur, which shall render the Indians who reside in a state, incapable of self-government, either by moral degradation or a reduction of their numbers, it would undoubtedly be in the power of a state government to extend to them the aegis of its laws. Under such circumstances, the agency of the general government, of necessity, must cease.

***

[JUSTICE BALDWIN dissented without written opinion, declaring from the bench that "his opinion remained the same as was expressed by him in the case of the *Cherokee Nation v. The State of Georgia*, at the last term."]

NOTES AND QUESTIONS

1. What does the case suggest with respect to state power in Indian country? What are the limits on such power? Do states have jurisdiction over Indian people in Indian country? Over non-Indian people?

2. What does the case suggest with respect to federal power in Indian country? What is the source of such power? What are the limits on such power?

3. What does the case suggest with respect to tribal power in Indian country? What is the source of such power?

4. What role does history play in Chief Justice Marshall's decision? What does he mean by the "actual state of things"?

5. How does Chief Justice Marshall interpret the Treaty of Hopewell? Is it the same way one would interpret a contract? Remember how Justice Johnson interpreted the treaty in his concurrence in *Cherokee Nation*. What

are the interpretive principles Marshall employs to reach a different interpretation? Philip Frickey explains these interpretive moves as follows:

> *** Chief Justice Marshall stressed that the treaty was negotiated and written in English, a language foreign to the tribal negotiators. *** [T]he term "hunting ground" should be construed as the Indians would have understood it—complete land possession and control—rather than as non-Indians would have—at most an exclusive license to hunt.
>
> *** In essence, Chief Justice Marshall placed the responsibility upon the federal treaty negotiators to ensure that tribes understood what they were abandoning through the treaty. ***
>
> Second, Chief Justice Marshall concluded that to give the fourth article the plain meaning of its text—particularly the word "allotted"—would be inconsistent with the fundamental nature of the transactions at the heart of Indian treaties. *** He conceptualized an Indian treaty as a grant of rights from a tribe to the United States, rather than a cession of all tribal rights to the United States, which then granted back certain concessions to the tribe. Chief Justice Marshall reasoned that Indian treaties were not acts of complete tribal surrender to the conquering government. Instead, they were reservations by the tribe of all rights not clearly granted to the United States—hence the term "reservation" for the lands retained by the tribe. ***
>
> [The ninth article of the treaty provides that "Congress assembled shall have the sole and exclusive right of regulating the trade with the Indians, and managing all their affairs in such manner as they think proper."] *** [W]hen the ninth article is read in context with all other parts of the treaty, there is considerable force to Justice Johnson's conclusion in Cherokee Nation that the article amounts to "a relinquishment of all power, legislative, executive and judicial to the United States." ***
>
> *** Chief Justice Marshall concluded that the "spirit," or purpose, of Indian treaties in general, and the Treaty of Hopewell in particular, trumped the apparent plain meaning of the ninth article. Indian treaties, according to this construct, are premised on the continuing nature of tribal sovereignty—they are ongoing arrangements between sovereigns. More specifically, the purpose of the ninth article, according to its own terms, was to protect and benefit the Indians. An interpretation that robbed the tribe of the power of self-government, of the capacity to control future cessions of its lands, and of the ability to safeguard its security interests would stand in stark opposition to these fundamental purposes and would conflict with any plausible assumptions about the tribe's understanding of the treaty.

Philip P. Frickey, *Marshalling Past and Present, Colonialism, Constitutionalism, and Interpretation in Federal Indian* Law, 107 Harv. L. Rev. 381, 400–404 (1993). Identify these interpretive moves in the text of the *Worcester* opinion.

Felix Cohen's Handbook of Federal Indian Law lists four "canons of construction," interpretive rules that must be applied in construing laws regarding Indians:

> [1.] [T]reaties, agreements, statutes, and executive orders [must] be liberally construed in favor of the Indians; and [2.] all ambiguities are to be

> resolved in [their] favor. *** In addition, [3.] treaties and agreements are to be construed as the Indians would have understood them, and [4.] tribal property rights and sovereignty are preserved unless Congress' intent to the contrary is clear and unambiguous.

Cohen's Handbook of Federal Indian Law 113-114 (2012). Can you see the roots of each of these principles in *Worcester*?

6. Justice McLean's opinion that a state could exercise jurisdiction over a tribe that has "become so degraded or reduced in numbers, as to lose the power of self-government" raises interesting questions. Should tribes of a few dozen members have the same rights as tribes like the Cherokee? Who is to decide when a tribe no longer deserves the power of self-government, and how? Although, as you will learn, the federal government has the exclusive power to determine what groups are entitled to the legal rights of tribes, for many years after *Worcester* lower courts relied on McLean's opinion to decide what rights tribes had the capacity to exercise. *See* Sidney Harring, Crow Dog's Case: American Indian Sovereignty, Tribal Law, and United States Law in the Nineteenth Century (1994).

C. AFTERMATH OF THE CHEROKEE CASES: MANY TRAILS OF TEARS

The participants in the *Worcester* decision knew that winning in the Supreme Court was not the most significant challenge; rather, the plaintiffs had to get President Jackson to enforce it. William Wirt had addressed this issue directly in his argument to the Court, saying this concern should not influence its opinion: "What is the value of that government in which the decrees of its courts can be mocked at and defied with impunity? *** It is no government at all." Quoted in Leonard Baker, John Marshall: A Life in Law 736 (Macmillan Publishing Co. 1974). Justice Story suggested the same in a letter to George Ticknor: "The Court has done its duty. Let the nation now do theirs. If we have a Government, let its command be obeyed; if we have not, it is as well to know it at once, and to look to the consequences." *Id.* at 745.

Georgia had no intention of abiding by the decision. Governor Lumpkin told the state legislature he would meet the "usurpation of federal power with the most prompt and determined resistance." The subcommander of the Georgia Guard in Cherokee Country wrote the following letter to the governor about the Cherokee reaction to the decision:

> Rejoicings Dances & Meetings have been held in all [the Cherokee] Towns. They not only believed that the right of Jurisdiction was restored but that they were Sovereign independent nation & the U.S. bound by Treaty to afford them protection. *** In order to arrest the delusion and set these poor deluded people to rights *** [t]hree I have had committed to Jail ***.
>
> I admitted that it was possible for *** the President to send on an Army & whip Georgia into her duty [but if this occurred, the Cherokees] would be swept of the Earth before any assistance could arrive. *** [W]hen their Allies arrived they would find no Cherokees to protect.

William Williamson, Subcommander of the Georgia Guard to Gov. Wilson Lumpkin (Apr. 28, 1832).

As for the United States, President Jackson is famously reported to have said, "John Marshall has made his opinion, now let him enforce it." Although modern historians generally believe that the quote is apocryphal, it aptly embodied the spirit of the times. Although the Supreme Court issued a mandate to the Georgia Superior Court to release the prisoners, the state refused to obey, and the term ended before a writ of execution could be issued to the Georgia sheriff, leaving the federal government without a means of enforcing the decision until the Court met again in the fall; even then, Wirt believed, no statute authorized federal enforcement unless Georgia put its intention to defy the writ in writing. Jill Norgren, The Cherokee Cases: Two Landmark Cases in the Fight for Sovereignty 122–123 (2004); *see* Joseph C. Burke, *The Cherokee Cases: A Study in Law, Politics and Morality*, 21 Stan. L. Rev. 500, 529–30 (1969). The country was not sufficiently moved by the plight of the Cherokees and returned Jackson to office. Another political crisis, however, intervened to change Jackson's perspective on state resistance to federal authority. Supreme Court Justice Stephen Breyer described the volatile political situation surrounding the case:

> The words "civil war" began to appear in the congressional debates. [The president] had made clear that *** the state legislatures "had the power to extend their laws over all persons living within their boundaries," and that he possessed "no authority to interfere." ***
>
> Then, just when all seemed lost, *** Georgia's resistance was overcome. And the missionaries were freed. This change took place because another state—South Carolina—decided that the time was ripe to put Georgia's nullification theory into practice. On November 24, 1832 *** South Carolina promulgated its own "Nullification Ordinance" [forbidding enforcement of federal tariff laws].
>
> [In response,] Jackson immediately supported congressional enactment of a Force Bill that would give federal officials adequate powers to enforce the federal laws. ***
>
> What, then, about Georgia? *** Worcester had said from prison that he might bring his case right back to the Supreme Court; and in light of his new position on the limits of states' rights, Jackson began to say that he would carry into effect any decision that the Supreme Court might make. ***
>
> Before the Supreme Court could meet for its 1833 term, friends of Governor Lumpkin visited Worcester in prison. They said the governor had told them that if the missionaries would withdraw their suit, they would be discharged from prison, immediately and unconditionally. ***

Stephen Breyer, *For Their Own Good*, The New Republic, Aug. 7, 2000, at 30.

As for the Cherokees, they won the battle but lost the war. Although the leaders of the Cherokee government steadfastly refused to sign a removal treaty, in 1835 the United States signed the Treaty of New Echota with individual Cherokees who believed that removal was the only way to save their nation. In 1838, under color of the unauthorized treaty, the federal soldiers joined by state "volunteers" rounded up the Cherokee people and forced them to walk the Trail of Tears to the Oklahoma Territory.

Between 1820 and 1850, the vast majority of Indian tribes were also forced across the Mississippi. In 1830, the Choctaw Nation reluctantly signed a removal treaty. Upon hearing of the ratification of the treaty, Chief David Folsom wrote, "We are exceedingly tired. *** There is no other course for us but to turn our faces to our new homes toward the setting sun." Quoted in Francis Paul Prucha, The Great Father: The United States Government and the American Indians 218 (1984). Alexis de Tocqueville, French chronicler of American democracy, observed the 1831 removal:

> It was then in the depths of winter, and that year the cold was exceptionally severe; the snow was on the ground and huge masses of ice drifted on the river. The Indians brought their families with them; there were among them the wounded, the sick, newborn babies, and old men on the point of death. They had neither tents nor wagons, but only some provisions and weapons. I saw them embark to cross the great river, and the sight will never fade from my memory. Neither sob nor complaint rose from that silent assembly. Their afflictions were of long standing, and they felt them to be irremediable. ***
>
> The conduct of the Americans of the United States towards the aborigines is characterized *** by a singular attachment to the formalities of law. *** The Spaniards were unable to exterminate the Indian race by those unparalleled atrocities which brand them with indelible shame, nor did they succeed even in wholly depriving it of its rights; but the Americans of the United States have accomplished this twofold purpose with singular felicity, tranquilly, legally, philanthropically, without shedding blood, and without violating a single great principle of morality in the eyes of the world. It is impossible to destroy men with more respect for the laws of humanity.

Alexis de Tocqueville, I Democracy in America 352–353, 355 (Alfred A. Knopf 1945).

The Creek Nation had been forced from their lands in Georgia in 1824 under a treaty signed with an unauthorized faction of the tribe. In 1832, the nation signed a treaty that permitted Creek heads of households to take individual allotments of its lands in Alabama, but provided that it was "not to be construed so as to compel any Creek Indian to emigrate, but they shall be free to go or stay, as they please." Treaty with the Creeks, 7 Stat. 366, art. 12 (Mar. 24, 1832). As recorded in an 1851 House Report,

> No sooner had the treaty *** been ratified and proclaimed, than these white persons, in large numbers, commenced flocking into the country of the Indians, in order to select and take possession of the best lands; and there were cases in which the Indians were driven from their habitations and homes by these lawless people, and subjected to great suffering.

H.R. Rep. No. 31–37, at 25 (1851). After individual Creeks resorted to robbery and violence in response, the military forced the entire nation west.

With similar combinations of resignation, military coercion, and fraud, many other tribes were removed during this period. Some tribes, including parts of the Iroquois Confederacy in New York and the Chippewa and Ottawa tribes of Minnesota, Wisconsin, and Michigan, never ceded all their lands east of the Mississippi. Some members of other tribes who did cede their lands fled into remote parts of their territories and ultimately received recognition as independent Indian nations. The Mississippi Band of Choctaw Indians and the Eastern Band of Cherokee Indians of North Carolina are examples of this history. Despite these exceptions, by 1850 the vast majority of Indian people had been removed from the eastern states. Nonetheless, today there are many federally recognized tribes in the original thirteen states that persisted despite the onslaught of removal, disease, and hostile federal policies. In 2018, Congress officially recognized the continued existence of six Indian tribes in the state of Virginia. Thomasina E. Jordan Indian Tribes of Virginia Federal Recognition Act, Pub. L. No. 115-121 (Jan. 29, 2019).

Notwithstanding the hardships imposed by removal, some tribes managed to reconstitute themselves and flourish in their new lands. The Cherokee Nation, for example, experienced a "Golden Age" from 1839 up until just before the Civil War. *See* Robert J. Conley, The Cherokee Nation: A History 167–70 (2005). The Cherokee Nation's ability to revive its political and cultural institutions depended on a number of factors, including strong leadership and fertile lands. Foremost among those factors was a fair amount of independence for the tribe to continue as a separate government. Consider the importance of this as you study the material in the following chapters.

CHAPTER 3

EXPERIMENTS IN FEDERAL INDIAN POLICY

■ ■ ■

In the 150 years since removal, the federal government has tried many different federal Indian policies, flipping from one to the other as each failed to solve what non-Indians saw as the Indian problem. Only well into the twentieth century did the United States finally turn to Indian tribes to define *their* "Indian problem" and to participate in its solutions. The following sections provide definite chronological divisions between one federal Indian policy and another, but in reality the dividing lines were not so crisp. The colonists had begun establishing reservations in the seventeenth century and the United States began urging removal in what we have called the Trade and Intercourse Era and experimented with allotment and assimilation in what we will call the Reservation Era. With that in mind, here is a brief summary of the periods of federal Indian policy.

1. Trade and Intercourse Period—1790 to 1820s or 30s. Treaties and intergovernmental agreements were used to draw boundaries between sovereigns and memorialize rules for interaction; Trade and Intercourse Acts modeled on treaties police boundaries between tribes and others.

2. Removal Period—1820s to 1840s. Tribes were removed from heavily populated areas, with the vast majority of Indian peoples moved west of the Mississippi. Treaties nonetheless remained important aspects of Indian policy throughout this period.

3. Reservation Period—1840s to 1880s. Tribes were concentrated on reservations where they could be groomed for civilization under control of federal Indian agents. In 1871, Congress passed legislation purporting to end treaty making with Indian tribes. The federal government instead began to designate Indian reservations by executive order. Westward expansion ended the notion that there might be a large and permanent geographically distinct "Indian territory."

4. Allotment and Assimilation Period—1880s to 1920s. Congress authorized forcible assimilation measures and the Supreme Court created the plenary power doctrine to sanction these measures. In 1885, Congress passed the Major Crimes Act authorizing federal jurisdiction over crimes committed by Indians; beginning in 1887, Congress generally authorized individual allotment of Indian lands and the opening of unallotted reservation lands to non-Indians; boarding schools were created to facilitate assimilation of Indian children. Allotment reduced Indian landholdings from 138 million acres to 48 million acres.

5. Indian New Deal Period—late 1920s through 1940s. United States sought to prevent bureaucratic domination and abuse and resulting poverty of Native peoples by strengthening tribal governments and economies. The Indian Reorganization Act of 1934 ended allotment and provided tribes with technical assistance to organize as governments; the Department of the Interior published Felix S. Cohen's Handbook of Federal Indian Law in 1941; in 1948, Congress enacted a broad definition of Indian Country.

6. Termination Period—1940s to 1960s. The United States resolved to end special status of Indian tribes and terminated its governmental relationship with some tribes. In 1953, Congress enacted Public Law 280, which unilaterally extended state jurisdiction over Indians on reservations in some states and gave other states the option unilaterally to assume jurisdiction.

7. Self–Determination Period—1960s to Present? Congress and the Executive began the policy of "self-determination without termination," encouraging tribal control of governmental services and tribal resources, economies and culture, and negotiation with tribes regarding tribal problems. Representative legislation included the 1975 Indian Self–Determination and Educational Assistance Act, the 1978 Indian Child Welfare Act, and the 1988 Indian Gaming Regulatory Act. The Violence Against Women Act was amended in 2013 to restore inherent tribal criminal jurisdiction over non-Indian domestic abusers. The period has been accompanied by what some see as an era of judicial backlash, in which the Supreme Court undermines tribal sovereignty over nonmembers in the face of congressional recognition of sovereignty.

I. RESERVATION PERIOD: 1848–1886

A. RESERVATION POLICIES

In 1824, the Creek chiefs responded to the treaty commissioners urging removal that, "It is true, very true, that we are 'surrounded by white people' and that there are encroachments made. What assurances have we that similar ones will not be made on us, should we deem it proper to accept your offer and remove beyond the Mississippi?" 8 Am. State Papers 569 (Dec. 8, 1824). This objection was prescient. Although policymakers in the 1820s presented the west as a vast expanse where Indian tribes could remain undisturbed, by the 1840s it was clear that this promise was illusory. It was the age of Manifest Destiny, in which United States policy was informed not by the struggles of building a new nation, but by the sense that "We are the nation of human progress, and who will, what can, set limits to our onward march?" John O'Sullivan, *The Great Nation of Futurity*, 6 U.S. Mag. & Democratic Rev. 426, 427 (1839). Fueled by belief in a divine American mission, the United States finally attained control over all of the western continent, with the annexation of Texas in 1845, the acquisition of the Oregon Territory from the British in 1846, and the acquisition of New Mexico, Arizona, and California from Mexico in the 1848 Treaty of Guadalupe Hidalgo. In the same decade, the technology developed to build cross-country railroads, beginning a process that would end with the completion of a transcontinental railroad in 1869. In 1849, the discovery of gold in California spurred hordes of would-be prospectors to cross the Indian Territory in search of riches in the west.

By 1848, Commissioner of Indian Affairs William Medill had proposed the "reservation system," a new federal Indian policy under which Indian tribes would be confined on smaller reservations of land under the authority of a federal agent who would, forcibly if need be, lead them toward civilization. The following reports of successive Commissioners of Indian Affairs illustrate the philosophy and methods behind the policy.

ANNUAL REPORT OF COMMISSIONER OF INDIAN AFFAIRS WILLIAM MEDILL (NOV. 30, 1848)

House Exec. Doc. No. 30–1 (1848)

*** Stolid and unyielding in his nature, and inveterately wedded to the savage habits, customs, and prejudices in which he has been reared and trained, it is seldom the case that the full blood Indian of our hemisphere can, in immediate juxtaposition with a white population, be brought farther within the pale of civilization than to adopt its vices; under the corrupting forces of which, too indolent to labor, and too weak to resist, he soon sinks into misery and despair. The inequality of his position in all that secures dignity and respect is too glaring, and the contest he has to make with the superior race with which he is brought into contact, in all the avenues to success and prosperity in life, is too unequal to hope for a better result. *** It must be recollected, too, that our white population has rapidly increased and extended, and, with a widening contact, constantly pressed upon the Indian occupants of territory necessary for the accommodation of our own people; thus engendering prejudices and creating difficulties which have occasionally led to strife and bloodshed—inevitable between different races under such circumstances—in which the weaker party must suffer. *** Cannot this sad and depressing tendency of things be checked, and the past be at least measurably repaired by better results in the future? It is believed they can; and, indeed, it has to some extent been done already, by the wise and beneficent system of policy put in operation some years since and which, if steadily carried out, will soon give to our whole Indian system a very different and much more favorable aspect.

The policy already begun and relied on to accomplish objects so momentous and so desirable to every Christian and philanthropist is, as rapidly as it can safely and judiciously be done, to colonize our Indian tribes beyond the reach, for some years, of our white population; confining each within a small district of country, so that, as the game decreases and becomes scarce, the adults will gradually be compelled to resort to agriculture and other kinds of labor to obtain a subsistence. *** To establish, at the same time, a judicious and well devised system of manual labor schools for the education of the youth of both sexes in letters—the males in practical agriculture and the various necessary and useful mechanic arts, and the females in the different branches of housewifery, including spinning and weaving; and these schools like those already in successful operation, to be in charge of the excellent and active missionary societies of the different Christian denominations of the country. ***

The strongest propensities of an Indian's nature are his desire for war and his love of the chase. *** But anything like labor is distasteful and utterly repugnant to his feelings and natural prejudices. *** [If] it be necessary to cultivate the earth or to manufacture materials for dress, it has to be done by the women, who are their "hewers of wood and drawers of water." Nothing can induce him to resort to labor, unless compelled to do so by a stern necessity; and it is only then that there is ground to work upon for civilizing and Christianizing him. *** When compelled to face the stern necessities of life and to resort to a labor for a maintenance, he in very short time becomes a changed being; and is then willing, and frequently eager to receive information and instruction in all that may aid him in his condition. *** The most marked change, however, when this condition takes place is in the condition of the females. She who had been the drudge and the slave then begins to assume her true position as an equal; and her labor is transferred from the field to her household—to the care of her family and children. This great change in disposition and condition has taken place, to a greater or less extent, in all the tribes that have been removed and permanently settled west of the Mississippi. It is true, that portions of some of them enjoyed a considerable degree of civilization before they were transplanted; but prior to that even they were retrograding in all respects; while now, they and others who have been colonized and confined within reasonable and fixed limits, are rapidly advancing in intelligence and morality, and in all the means and elements of national and individual prosperity; so that before many years, if we sacredly observe all our obligations towards them, they will have reached a point at which they will be able to compete with a white population, and to sustain themselves under any probable circumstances of contact or connection with it. ***

ANNUAL REPORT OF THE COMMISSIONER OF INDIAN AFFAIRS LUKE LEA (NOV. 27, 1850)

Senate Exec. Doc. No. 31–1

Experience *** has conclusively shown that there is but one course of policy by which the great work of regenerating the Indian race may be effected. *** [I]t is indispensably necessary that they be placed in positions where they can be controlled, and finally compelled by stern necessity to resort to agricultural labor or starve. Considering, as the untutored Indian does, that labor is a degradation, and that there is nothing worthy of his ambition but prowess in war, success in the chase, and eloquence in council, it is only under such circumstances that his haughty pride can be subdued, and his wild energies trained to the more ennobling pursuits of civilized life. There should be assigned to each tribe, for a permanent home, a country adapted to agriculture, of limited extent and well-defined boundaries; within which all, with occasional exceptions, should be compelled constantly to remain until such time as their general improvement and good conduct may supersede the necessity of such restrictions. In the meantime the government should cause them to be supplied with stock, agricultural implements, and useful materials for clothing; encourage and assist them in the erection of comfortable dwellings, and secure to them the means and facilities of education, intellectual, moral, and religious. The application of their own funds to such purposes would be far better for them than the present system of paying their annuities in money, which does substantial good to but few, while to the great majority it only furnishes the means and incentive to vicious and depraving indulgence, terminating in destitution and misery, and too frequently in premature death. ***

ANNUAL REPORT OF COMMISSIONER OF INDIAN AFFAIRS GEORGE MANYPENNY (NOV. 22, 1856)

Senate Exec. Doc. 34–5

*** Since the 4th of March, 1853, fifty-two treaties with various Indian tribes have been entered into. These treaties may, with but few exceptions of specified character, be separated into three classes: first, treaties of peace and friendship; second, treaties of acquisition, with a view of colonizing the Indians on reservations; and third, treaties of acquisition, and providing for the permanent settlement of the individuals of the tribes, at once or in the future, on separate tracts of lands or homesteads, and for the gradual abolition of the tribal character. The quantity of land acquired by these treaties *** is about one hundred and seventy-four million of acres. *** In no former equal period of our history have so many treaties been made, or such vast accessions of land been obtained. ***

*** The relation which the federal government sustains towards the Indians, and the duties and obligations flowing from it, cannot be faithfully met and discharged without ample legal provisions, and the necessary power and means to enforce them. The rage for speculation and the wonderful desire to obtain choice lands, which seems to possess so many of those who go into our new territories, causes them to lose sight of and entirely overlook the rights of the aboriginal inhabitants. The most dishonorable expedients have, in many cases, been made use of to dispossess the Indian; demoralizing means employed to obtain his property; and, for the want of adequate laws, the department is often perplexed and embarrassed, because of inability to afford prompt relief and apply the remedy in cases obviously requiring them.

*** That the red man can be transformed in his habits, domesticated, and civilized, and made a useful element of society, there is abundant evidence. With reference to his true character, erroneous opinions very generally prevail. He is, indeed, the victim of prejudice. He is only regarded as the irreclaimable, terrible savage *** committing with exultant delight the most horrible massacres. These are chronicled from year to year, and are, indeed, sad chapters in our annals. But the history of the sufferings of the Indian has never been written; the story of his wrongs never been told. Of these there is not, and can never be, an earthly record. ***

ANNUAL REPORT OF COMMISSIONER ON INDIAN AFFAIRS NATHANIEL G. TAYLOR (NOV. 23, 1868)

House Exec. Doc. No. 40–1

Shall our Indian tribes be civilized? And How?

*** It so happens that under the silent and seemingly slow operation of efficient causes, certain tribes of our Indians have already emerged from a state of pagan barbarism, and are to-day clothed in the garments of civilization, and sitting under the vine and fig tree of an intelligent and scriptural Christianity. *** The Cherokees, Choctaws, Chickasaws, Creeks, and Seminoles are the tribes to which I refer. ***

[T]he mainsprings of Cherokee civilization were, first, the circumscribing of their territorial domain; this resulted in, second, the localization of the members of the tribe, and consequently in, third, the necessity of agriculture and pastoral pursuits instead of the chase as a means of existence; and as a logical sequence, fourth, the introduction of the ideas of property in things, of sale and barter, & c; and hence, fifth, of course, a corresponding change from the ideas, habits and customs of savages to those of civilized life; and sixth, the great coadjutor in the whole work in all its progress, the Christian teacher and missionary, moving *pari passu* with every other cause. ***

What, then, is our duty as the guardian of all the Indians under our jurisdiction? ***

It is beyond question our most solemn duty to protect them and care for, to elevate and civilize them. We have taken their heritage, and it is a grand and magnificent heritage. Now is it too much that we carve for them liberal reservations out of their own lands and guarantee them homes forever? Is it too much that we supply them with agricultural implements, mechanical tools, domestic animals, instructors in the useful arts, teachers, physicians, and Christian missionaries? If we find them fierce, hostile, and revengeful; if they are cruel, and if they sometimes turn upon us and burn, pillage, and desolate our frontiers, and perpetuate atrocities that sicken the soul and paralyze us with horror, let us remember that two hundred and fifty years of injustice, oppression and wrong, heaped upon them by our race with cold, calculating and relentless perseverance, have filled them with the passion of revenge, and made them desperate. ***†

NOTES AND QUESTIONS

1. What were the goals of the reservation policy? How were these goals to be accomplished?

---

†. The foregoing reports are excerpted in Documents of United States Indian Policy (Francis P. Prucha, 3d ed. 2000), Eds.

2. What did the Commissioners think about past treatment of the Indians? What did they state as their intentions toward the Indians? Can you assess their sincerity?

3. Regardless of federal intentions, Indian people often did not welcome the policy or believe that it would be implemented in their interest. At the 1867 Medicine Lodge treaty negotiations, Comanche leader Ten Bears responded to Commissioner Taylor's description of the reservation policy with these words:

> *** [T]here are things which you have said to me which I do not like. They were not sweet like sugar, but bitter like gourds. You said that you wanted to put us upon a reservation, to build our houses and make us medicine lodges. I do not want them. I was born upon the prairie where the wind blew free and there was nothing to break the light of the sun.
>
> I was born where there were no inclosures and where everything drew a free breath. I want to die there and not within walls. I know every stream and every wood between the Rio Grande and the Arkansas, I have hunted and lived over that country. I lived like my fathers before me, and like them, I lived happily.
>
> When I was at Washington the Great Father told me that all the Comanches' land was ours, and that no one should hinder us living upon it. So why do you ask us to leave the rivers and the sun and the wind and live in houses? Do not ask us to give up the buffalo for the sheep. ***
>
> If Texans had kept out of my country there might have been peace. But that which you now say we must live on is too small. The Texans have taken away the places where the grass grew the thickest and the timber the best. Had we kept that, we might have done the things you ask. But it is too late. The white man has the country we loved, and we only wish to wander on the prairies until we die. ***

Reprinted in Great Documents in American Indian History 209 (Wayne Moquin & Charles Van Doren ed. 1973).

Even those that supported the policy complained that corruption prevented its effective implementation. This is the 1865 testimony of Yankton Sioux leader Palaneapope:

> When I went to make my treaty, my grandfather [the U.S. president] agreed *** to furnish one white man for each trade to learn the young men. My grandfather also said that a school should be established for the nation to learn them to read and write; that the young boys and girls should go to school, and that the young men who worked should have the same pay as the whites *** None of this has happened. ***
>
> My friend I think if my young men knew how to sow, farm, carpenter, and do everything else, I could send the white men away; we ourselves should have the money paid the white men ***If we had been learned all these things, we could support ourselves, have plenty of money, have schools, and I could have written my great grandfather, and have got a letter from him; I could have written him myself what I wanted. ***
>
> Every time our goods come I have asked the agent for the invoices, but they never show me the invoices; they can write what they please, and they go and show it to my grandfather, and he thinks it all right. I think,

> my friend, my grandfather tells me lies. My friend, what I give a man I don't try to take back. I think, my friend, there is a great pile of money belonging to us. ***
>
> The agent puts his foot on me as though I were a skunk. And the agents are all getting rich and we are getting poor. ***

Id. at 195–196, 198.

4. Notice the role of agriculture and private property in the reservation policy. The need to inculcate an idea of individual property had long been a theme of the federal policymakers. In 1832, the first Commissioner of Indian Affairs, Elbert Herring, declared that "the absence of *meum* and *tuum* in the general community of possessions, which is the grand conservative principle of the social state, is a perpetual operating cause of the *vis inertiae* of savage life," while in 1838, Commissioner Crawford proclaimed that "[c]ommon property and civilization cannot coexist." Why was private property so significant to these officials? How did private property and farming fit into the American ideology?

5. Also notice the role of gender. Although white officials often portrayed themselves as riding to the rescue of oppressed Indian women,

> such well-meaning policy makers were motivated by a misunderstanding of the role of the Indian woman within many tribes. *** Ironically, despite the frustrated attempts of federal officials to turn Indian men into farmers, it was women who had responsibility for cultivating the land in most American tribes. White observers and federal officials rejected such female participation in what they conceived of as the male sphere of work as a sign of ignoble savagery and of the debasement of the Indian male.
>
> These traditional responsibilities, however, gave Indian women a degree of autonomy unknown to their white counterparts. Women controlled what food would be grown, how it would be prepared, what clothes, shoes, and blankets would be made. Sitting Bull, the powerful Chief of the Sioux, well recognized the power that productive labor gave women when he pleaded with a white woman administrating the Dawes Act. "Take pity on my women. *** The young men can be like the white men, can till the soil, supply the food and clothing. They will take the work out of the hands of women. And the women *** will be stripped of all which gave them power."

Bethany Ruth Berger, *After Pocahontas: Indian Women and the Law, 1830–1934*, 21 Am. Ind. L. Rev. 1, 17 (1997). *See also* Allison Dussias, *Squaw Drudges, Farm Wives, and the Dann Sisters Last Stand, American Indian Women's Resistance to Domestication and the Denial of their Property Rights*, 77 N.C. L. Rev. 637, 649 (1999) ("In actuality, agriculture—in simple terms, "raising things on purpose"—has an extensive history in the Americas, where women may well have been the first agriculturalists.").

6. Reservations were intended to be schools for civilization with the local federal agent as superintendent. Many agents saw their role as protecting the Indians and wrote long reports protesting the abuses perpetrated by the whites surrounding the reservations. Some agents were corrupt, agreeing to contracts for shoddy goods to profit themselves. But all agents, with control over distribution of food and other annuities and the authority of the federal government behind them, had significant power. They could terminate the

rations of those that refused to send their children to school or to work in agricultural pursuits, or give positions of power and authority to "progressives" that went along with the civilization project. Notice the role of the agent in the following treaty with the Navajo in 1868. The treaty is similar to treaties made with the Ute, Sioux, Crow, Northern Cheyenne and Arapahoe, and Eastern Shoshone and Bannock Nations. How does the treaty compare to the Treaty of Hopewell made with the Cherokee Nation in 1785 (*supra* Ch. 2, § III)? Despite the federal government's assimilationist intentions in these treaties, many tribes (including the Navajo) also see them as foundational documents that preserved their hard-fought independence.

TREATY WITH THE NAVAJO

(1868)

Art. 1. From this day forward all war between the parties to this agreement shall forever cease. The Government of the United States desires peace, and its honor is hereby pledged to keep it. The Indians desire peace, and they now pledge their honor to keep it.

If bad men among the whites, or among other people subject to the authority of the United States, shall commit any wrong upon the person or property of the Indians, the United States will, upon proof made to the agent and forwarded to the Commissioner of Indian Affairs at Washington City, proceed at once to cause the offender to be arrested and punished according to the laws of the United States, and also to reimburse the injured persons for the loss sustained.

If the bad men among the Indians shall commit a wrong or depredation upon the person or property of any one, white, black, or Indian, subject to the authority of the United States and at peace therewith, the Navajo tribe agree that they will, on proof made to their agent, and on notice by him, deliver up the wrongdoer to the United States, to be tried and punished according to its laws. ***

Art. 2. The United States agrees that the following district of country *** shall be, and the same is hereby, set apart for the use and occupation of the Navajo tribe of Indians, and for such other friendly tribes or individual Indians as from time to time they may be willing, with the consent of the United States, to admit among them; and the United States agrees that no persons except those herein so authorized to do, and except such officers, soldiers, agents, and employees of the Government, or of the Indians, as may be authorized to enter upon Indian reservations in discharge of duties imposed by law, or the orders of the President, shall ever be permitted to pass over, settle upon, or reside in, the territory described in this article.

Art. 3. The United States agrees to cause to be built, at some point within said reservation *** a warehouse *** and agency building for the residence of the agent *** a carpenter-shop and blacksmith-shop *** and a schoolhouse and chapel, so soon as a sufficient number of children can be induced to attend school. ***

Art. 4. The United States agrees that the agent for the Navajos shall make his home at the agency building; that he shall reside among them, and shall keep an office open at all times for the purpose of prompt and diligent inquiry into such matters of complaint by or against the Indians as may be presented for investigation, as also for the faithful discharge of other duties enjoined by law. In cases of depredation on person or property he shall cause the evidence to be taken in writing and forwarded, together with his finding, to the Commissioner of Indian Affairs, whose decision shall be binding on the parties to this treaty.

Art. 5. If any individual belonging to said tribe, or legally incorporated with it, being the head of a family, shall desire to commence farming, he shall have the privilege to select, in the presence and with the assistance of the agent then in charge, a tract of land within said reservation, not exceeding one hundred and sixty acres in extent, which tract, when so selected, certified, and recorded in the "land-book" as herein described, shall cease to be held in common, but the same may be occupied and held in the exclusive possession of the person selecting it, and of his family, so long as he or they may continue to cultivate it.

Any person over eighteen years of age, not being the head of a family, may in like manner select, and cause to be certified to him or her for purposes of cultivation, a quantity of land, not exceeding eighty acres in extent, and thereupon be entitled to the exclusive possession of the same as above directed. ***

The United States may pass such laws on the subject of alienation and descent of property between the Indians and their descendants as may be thought proper.

Art. 6. In order to insure the civilization of the Indians entering into this treaty, the necessity of education is admitted, especially of such of them as may be settled on said agricultural parts of this reservation, and they therefore pledge themselves to compel their children, male and female, between the ages of six and sixteen years, to attend school; and it is hereby made the duty of the agent for said Indians to see that this stipulation is strictly complied with. ***

Art. 8. In lieu of all sums of money or other annuities provided to be paid to the Indians herein named under any treaty or treaties heretofore made, the United States agrees to deliver at the agency-house on the reservation herein named, on the first day of September of each year for ten years, the following articles, to wit:

Such articles of clothing, goods, or raw materials in lieu thereof, as the agent may make his estimate for, not exceeding in value five dollars per Indian—each Indian being encouraged to manufacture their own clothing, blankets, & c.; to be furnished with no article which they can manufacture themselves. *** And in addition to the articles herein named, the sum of ten dollars for each person entitled to the beneficial effects of this treaty shall be annually appropriated for a period of ten years, for each person who engages in farming or mechanical pursuits, to be used by the Commissioner of Indian Affairs in the purchase of such articles as from time to time the condition and necessities of the Indians may indicate to be proper. ***

Art. 9. In consideration of the advantages and benefits conferred by this treaty, and the many pledges of friendship by the United States, the tribes who are parties to this agreement hereby stipulate that they will relinquish all right to occupy any territory outside their reservation, as herein defined, but retain the right to hunt on any unoccupied lands contiguous to their reservation, so long as the large game may range thereon in such numbers as to justify the chase; and they, the said Indians, further expressly agree:

1st. That they will make no opposition to the construction of railroads now being built or hereafter to be built across the continent. ***

3d. That they will not attack any persons at home or travelling, nor molest or disturb any wagon-trains, coaches, mules, or cattle belonging to the people of the United States, or to persons friendly therewith.

4th. That they will never capture or carry off from the settlements women or children.

5th. They will never kill or scalp white men, nor attempt to do them harm.

6th. They will not in future oppose the construction of railroads, wagon-roads, mail stations, or other works of utility or necessity which may be ordered or permitted by the laws of the United States; but should such roads or other works be constructed on the lands of their reservation, the Government will pay the tribe whatever amount of damage may be assessed by three disinterested commissioners to be appointed by the President for that purpose, one of said commissioners to be a chief or headman of the tribe. ***

Art. 10. No future treaty for the cession of any portion or part of the reservation herein described, which may be held in common, shall be of any validity or force against said Indians unless agreed to and executed by at least three-fourths of all the adult male Indians occupying or interested in the same. ***

Art. 13. The tribe herein named, by their representatives, parties to this treaty, agree to make the reservation herein described their permanent home, and they will not as a tribe make any permanent settlement elsewhere, reserving the right to hunt on the lands adjoining the said reservation formerly called theirs, *** and it is further agreed by the parties to this treaty, that they will do all they can to induce Indians now away from reservations set apart for the exclusive use and occupation of the Indians, leading a nomadic life, or engaged in war against the people of the United States, to abandon such a life and settle permanently in one of the territorial reservations set apart for the exclusive use and occupation of the Indians.

In testimony of all which the said parties have hereunto, on this the first day of June, one thousand eight hundred and sixty-eight, at Fort Sumner, in the Territory of New Mexico, set their hands and seals.

B. THE END OF TREATY MAKING?: 1871

After the 1868 treaties, Congress purported to put an end to treaty making with Indian nations. Legislative history makes clear that a congressional power play was part of the motivation. Under the Constitution, only the Senate has the power to "advise and consent" to treaty terms. U.S. Const., art. II, § 2, cl. 2. Lawmakers in the House of Representatives resented the underfunded mandates the Senate foisted on them in the form of treaty promises. In addition, some representatives were irked that lands ceded by tribes in the 1867 and 1868 treaties had been sold to the railroad companies without being opened to homesteading. *See* Cong. Globe, 40th Cong., 2d sess. 3261–64 (1868), reprinted in Documents of United States Indian Policy, 113–115 (Francis P. Prucha ed., 3d ed. 2000). The House sought to wrest this unilateral power from the Senate by ending the power to make treaties with Indian tribes.

The Indian Department supported this move. Backers of the civilization policy wanted more power to regulate their Indian wards. Federal unwillingness to enforce treaty stipulations against encroaching settlers was also an increasing embarrassment. Commissioner Ely S. Parker, the first tribal member ever to head the Indian Department, was one of these supporters. Parker, whose Iroquois name was Donehogawa, was a member of the Seneca Nation and had been denied the right to sit for the New York Bar exam because of his tribal status. When the Civil War broke out, he was initially refused permission to enlist, but finally joined as a Captain of Engineers after a friend intervened on his behalf. During the War Parker rose to become a Brigadier General, and it was he that wrote out the terms of Confederate surrender at Appomattox. He was embroiled in a controversy because he married a white woman from high society in Washington, D.C. The *Washington Post* ran a story about their relationship on the eve of Valentine's Day, 2019. *The Interracial Love Story that Stunned Washington—Twice*, Wash. Post (Feb. 13, 2019) https://www.washingtonpost.com/history/2019/02/13/interracial-love-story-that-stunned-washington-twice/ ("When Ely Parker married Minnie Sacket, the crème de la crème of Washington came to gawk"). In 1869, he became Commissioner of Indian Affairs under President Ulysses Grant. In 1864, Parker had decried white violations of Indian treaties, and worked as Commissioner to end corruption and abuses in the Indian Service. By 1869, however, he had stopped believing in the viability of Indian treaties:

> A treaty involves the idea of a compact between two or more sovereign powers, each possessing sufficient authority and force to compel a compliance with the obligations incurred. *** It is time that this idea should be dispelled, and the government cease the cruel farce of thus dealing with its helpless and ignorant wards.

Annual Report of the Commissioner of Indian Affairs, H. Exec. Doc. No. 1, 41st Cong., 2d Sess. 448 (Dec. 23, 1869), reprinted in Documents of United States Indian Policy, 133–134 (Francis P. Prucha ed., 3d ed. 2000).

On March 3, 1871, a provision ending treaty-making was slipped in as a rider at the end of a long Indian Appropriations Act:

> *** For insurance and transportation of the Yanktons, one thousand five hundred dollars: *Provided*, That hereafter no Indian nation or tribe within the territory of the United States shall be acknowledged or recognized as an independent nation, tribe, or power with whom the United States may contract by treaty: *Provided, further*, That nothing herein contained shall be construed to invalidate or impair the obligation of any treaty heretofore lawfully made and ratified with any such Indian nation or tribe. ***

16 Stat. 566 (March 3, 1871), codified at 25 U.S.C. § 71.

The prohibition of further treaty-making had little practical significance. The law explicitly recognized the validity of existing treaties, and the United States continued to create reservations by agreements and statutes that have been treated, by reviewing courts and legislators, as the legal equivalent of treaty reservations. Charles Wilkinson coined the term "treaty substitutes" for these many laws that are the functional equivalent of the pre–1871 treaties. See Charles F. Wilkinson, American Indians, Time, and the Law: Native Societies in a Modern Constitutional Democracy 8, 101–02 (1987). Justice Clarence Thomas, however, has suggested that the law may have an impact on the extent of tribal sovereignty:

> *** To be sure, it makes sense to conceptualize the tribes as sovereigns that, due to their unique situation, cannot exercise the full measure of their sovereign powers. ***
>
> [But] federal policy itself could be thought to be inconsistent with this residual-sovereignty theory. In 1871, Congress enacted a statute that purported to prohibit entering into treaties with the "Indian nation[s] or tribe[s]." Although this Act is constitutionally suspect (the Constitution vests in the President both the power to make treaties, Art. II, § 2, and to recognize foreign governments, Art. II, § 3); it nevertheless reflects the view of the political branches that the tribes had become a purely domestic matter.
>
> To be sure, this does not quite suffice to demonstrate that the tribes had lost their sovereignty. After all, States retain sovereignty despite the fact that Congress can regulate States *qua* States in certain limited circumstances. But the States (unlike the tribes) are part of a constitutional framework that allocates sovereignty between the State and Federal Governments and specifically grants Congress authority to legislate with respect to them. ***

U.S. v. Lara, 541 U.S. 193, 217–218 (2004) (Thomas, J., concurring in the judgment) (citations omitted).

What role should the 1871 Act play in how courts interpret tribal sovereignty today? As the legislative history reveals, it was not at all clear that the 1871 rider to an appropriations bill reflected a consensus view about much of anything, let alone the political-legal status of tribes. Even if lawmakers at the time agreed that tribal status was a wholly domestic matter, that would not automatically equate with a view that tribes lacked residual sovereignty. Recall that Justice Marshall folded Indian nations into the domestic legal framework in *Cherokee Nation v. Georgia* while nonetheless recognizing retained inherent tribal sovereignty, which he elaborated on more fully in *Worcester v. Georgia*. Moreover, one might consider how much weight to give to that moment in 1871 as compared to the many moments since the late 1960's, when Congress and Executive agencies have repeatedly referenced and acted on the sovereign status of Indian nations. Finally, as Justice Thomas mentions, the 1871 act is "constitutionally suspect." The Constitution allocates the treaty power to the Senate and President, and the Constitution cannot be changed by ordinary legislation. *See* David P. Currie, *Indian Treaties*, 10 Green Bag 2d 445, 451 (2007) ("In short, the entire enterprise was flatly unconstitutional, and it seems extraordinary that President Grant unblinkingly signed it into law.").

C. THE EMERGENCE OF FEDERAL PLENARY POWER

In the Reservation Era, federal officials began to see themselves as molding Indian lives rather than administering the boundary line between Indians and whites. They wanted more legal power in order to fulfill this role. But tribal members in Indian country were not subject to state jurisdiction, and federal statutes specifically excluded crimes between Indians from federal jurisdiction. As early as 1846, the Indian Department began petitioning Congress for a statute to extend federal jurisdiction over crimes between Indians. S. Doc. 461, 29th Cong., 1st Sess. at 2 (1846). Congress repeatedly rejected these attempts, believing that it did not have the authority to legislate regarding exclusively intratribal affairs. To circumvent this legislative obstacle, the Indian Department participated in a number of cases seeking to establish that crimes between Indians were subject to either federal or state jurisdiction. *Ex Parte Crow Dog*, 109 U.S. 556 (1883), was one of these.

Kangishunca—Crow Dog (left), 1898, by John Alvin Anderson, Library of Congress, and Sintegaleska—Spotted Tail (right), ca. 1880, by CM Bell, Denver Public Library.

Crow Dog, whose Dakota name was Kangi Shunca, and Spotted Tail, whose Dakota name was Sinte Gleska, were both members of the Brûlé Sioux Tribe caught up in the complex tribal political struggles of the reservation period.† Professor Sidney L. Harring has provided the most complete historical excavation of the case and its parties in Crow Dog's Case: American Indian Sovereignty, Tribal Law, and United States Law in the Nineteenth Century (1994). Spotted Tail had fought in and been imprisoned after the Sioux War of 1855, but sought afterwards to keep his band at peace with the United States. Although his efforts to prevent hostilities with the Americans led the Indian

†. The word "Sioux" is believed to be a French corruption of a derogatory name used by the Anishinaabe, historic enemies of this group of Indian tribes. It is, however, the term used in most treaties and decisions regarding this group, and is also the name given to most of their reservations, so we will use it where necessary to avoid confusion. The terms the people called Sioux use to describe themselves are Lakota, Dakota, and Nakota, with the difference in the first letter referring to the dialect of the common language that the group spoke. The Brûlé Sioux were primarily Lakota.

agent to support him as chief, Spotted Tail also resisted federal efforts to undermine the culture of his people. He had caused an uproar among Indian reformers by withdrawing his children from the Carlisle Indian School after finding that instead of learning to read and write they were doing farming and industrial work and marching about dressed in military uniforms. He had also refused to live in the three-story house the government built for him, preferring to remain in his traditional camp, and had blocked the survey of a railroad through his reservation. His conciliatory efforts, however, drew opposition from less accommodating members of the band such as Crow Dog. Crow Dog had fought alongside Crazy Horse at the battle of Little Big Horn and briefly sought exile in Canada rather than accept confinement on the reservation. Crow Dog was also a leader among the Brûlé Sioux, and Spotted Tail had twice appointed him as chief of police, but each time rescinded the appointment within a year. It is not clear who started the fatal fight or why. It is agreed, however, that on August 5, 1881, Crow Dog shot Spotted Tail to death.

The tribe handled the death according to traditional law. At a tribal council meeting the day after the killing, the tribal council "ordered an end to the tribal conflict, sending peacemakers to both parties. The families, in turn, also following Brûlé law, agreed to a payment of $600, eight horses, and one blanket, which Crow Dog's people promptly paid to Spotted Tail's people." Harring at 110. These justice procedures were designed to preserve the community cooperation necessary for the Sioux way of life:

> The process that occurred in the homicide case of Crow Dog, that of a tribal council meeting to arrange for a peaceful reconciliation of the parties with an ordered gift of horses, blankets, money or other property was one of a number of conflict resolution mechanisms available to the Sioux. Apparently it was used only after the most serious of tribal disturbances. The council met not to adjudicate the dispute but to reconcile the parties involved. Hence, the result of the case—the offering of property to one side by the other—does not indicate any substantive resolution of the merits of the case: Crow Dog had been in no way "convicted" by a tribal council. Nor was the offered property "blood money," a payment to relatives to atone for the killing in a substantive way or to take the place of blood revenge. It was an offer of reconciliation and a symbolic commitment to continuation of tribal social relations. Although the family of Spotted Tail accepted the offer, this was not necessary to resolve the conflict. Often the recipients refused to take the offered property, a position that showed the tribe both their pride and their wealth.

Id. at 104–105.

Although the federal Indian agent knew that the tribe had already resolved the dispute, on August 7, 1881 he had Crow Dog arrested and imprisoned at Fort Niobara, Nebraska. *Ex Parte Crow Dog* became one of six parallel murder cases through which the federal Indian Office was trying to extend U.S. criminal law over the Indian tribes. In 1883, the U.S. Supreme Court agreed to hear Crow Dog's appeal.

EX PARTE KAN-GI-SHUN-CA (OTHERWISE KNOWN AS CROW DOG)

109 U.S. 556, 3 S. Ct. 396, 27 L. Ed. 1030 (1883)

MATTHEWS, J.

The petitioner is in the custody of the marshal of the United States for the territory of Dakota, imprisoned in the jail of Lawrence county, in the first judicial district of that territory, under sentence of death, adjudged against him by the district court for that district, to be carried into execution January 14, 1884. That judgment was rendered upon a conviction for the murder of an Indian of the Brûlé Sioux band of the Sioux nation of Indians, by the name of Sin-ta-ge-le-Scka, or in English, Spotted Tail, the prisoner also being an Indian of the same band and nation, and the homicide having occurred, as alleged in the indictment, in the Indian country. *** It is claimed on behalf of the prisoner that the crime charged against him, and of which he stands convicted, is not an offense under the laws of the United States; that the district court had no jurisdiction to try him, and that its judgment and sentence are void. ***

The indictment is framed upon section 5339 of the Revised Statutes [which] provides that "every person who commits murder, *** within any fort, arsenal, dock-yard, magazine, or in any other place or district of country under the exclusive jurisdiction of the United States, *** shall suffer death." Title 28 of the Revised Statutes relates to Indians, and *** embraces many provisions regulating the subject of intercourse and trade with the Indians in the Indian country, and imposes penalties and punishments for various violations of them. *** [Sections 2145 and 2146 of Title 28 provide as follows:]

> Sec. 2145. *** [T]he general laws of the United States as to the punishment of crimes committed in any place within the sole and exclusive jurisdiction of the United States, except the District of Columbia, shall extend to the Indian country.
>
> Sec. 2146. The preceding section shall not be construed to extend to [crimes committed by one Indian against the person or property of another Indian, nor to] any Indian committing any offense in the Indian country who has been punished by the local law of the tribe, or to any case where by treaty stipulations the exclusive jurisdiction over such offenses is or may be secured to the Indian tribes respectively.
>
> ***

The argument in support of the jurisdiction and conviction is, that the exception contained in section 2146 is repealed by [the 1868 treaty with Sioux and an 1877 Act of Congress ratifying an agreement with the tribe.] ***

The following provisions of the treaty of 1868 are relied on:

> Article 1. From this time forward all war between the parties to this agreement shall forever cease. The government of the United States desires peace, and its honor is hereby pledged to keep it. The Indians desire peace, and they now pledge their honor to maintain it.

If bad men among the whites, or among other people subject to the authority of the United States, shall commit any wrong upon the person or property of the Indians, the United States will, upon proof made to the agent and forwarded to the commissioner of Indian affairs at Washington city, proceed at once to cause the offender to be arrested and punished according to the laws of the United States, and also reimburse the injured person for the loss sustained.

If bad men among the Indians shall commit a wrong or depredation upon the person or property of any one, white, black, or Indian, subject to the authority of the United States and at peace therewith, the Indians herein named solemnly agree that they will, upon proof made to their agent and notice by him, deliver up the wrong-doer to the United States, to be tried and punished according to its laws. And in case they wilfully refuse so to do, the person injured shall be reimbursed for his loss from the annuities or other moneys due or to become due to them under this or other treaties made with the United States.

***

[The United States contends that the "bad men among the Indians" provision subjects crimes between Indians to federal jurisdiction.] But it is quite clear from the context that this does not cover the present case of an alleged wrong committed by one Indian upon the person of another of the same tribe. The provision must be construed with its counterpart, just preceding it, which provides for the punishment by the United States of any bad men among the whites, or among other people subject to their authority, who shall commit any wrong upon the person or property of the Indians. Here are two parties, among whom, respectively, there may be individuals guilty of a wrong against one of the other—one is the party of whites and their allies, the other is the tribe of Indians with whom the treaty is made. In each case the guilty party is to be tried and punished by the United States, and in case the offender is one of the Indians who are parties to the treaty, the agreement is that he shall be delivered up. In case of refusal, deduction is to be made from the annuities payable to the tribe, for compensation to the injured person, a provision which points quite distinctly to the conclusion that the injured person cannot himself be one of the same tribe. Similar provisions for the extradition of criminals are to be found in most of the treaties with Indian tribes, as far back, at least, as that concluded at Hopewell with the Cherokees, Nov. 28, 1785. 7 St. 18.

The second of these provisions, that are supposed to justify the jurisdiction asserted in the present case, is the eighth article of the agreement [with the Sioux Nation], embodied in the act of 1877, in which it is declared: "And congress shall, by appropriate legislation, secure to them an orderly government; they shall be subject to the laws of the United States, and each individual shall be protected in his rights of property, person, and life." It is equally clear, in our opinion, that these words can have no such effect as that claimed for them. The pledge to secure to these people, with whom the United States was contracting as a distinct political body, an orderly government, by appropriate legislation thereafter to be framed and enacted, necessarily implies, having regard to all the circumstances attending the transaction, that among the arts of civilized life, which it was the very purpose of all these arrangements to introduce and naturalize among them, was the highest and best of all,—that of self-government, the regulation by themselves of their own domestic affairs, the maintenance of order and peace among their own members by the administration of their own laws and customs. They were nevertheless to be subject to the laws of the United States, not in the sense of citizens, but, as they had always been, as wards, subject to a guardian; not as individuals, constituted members of the political community of the United States, with a voice in the selection of representatives and the framing of the laws, but as a dependent community who were in a state of pupilage, advancing from the condition of a savage tribe to that of a people who, through the discipline of labor, and by education, it was hoped might become a self-supporting and self-governed society. *** The phrase cannot, we think, have any more extensive meaning than an acknowledgement of their allegiance, as Indians, to the laws of the United States, made or to be made in the exercise of legislative authority over them as such. The corresponding obligation of protection on the part of the government is immediately connected with it, in the declaration that each individual shall be protected in his rights of property, person, and life, and that obligation was to be fulfilled by the enforcement of the laws then existing appropriate to those objects, and by that future appropriate legislation which was promised to secure to them an orderly government. The expressions contained in these clauses must be taken in connection with the entire scheme of the agreement as framed, including those parts not finally adopted, as throwing light on the meaning of the remainder; and looking at the purpose, so clearly disclosed in that, of the removal of the whole body of the Sioux nation to the Indian territory proper, which was not consented to, it is manifest that the provisions had reference to their establishment as a people upon a defined reservation as a permanent home, who were to be urged, as far as it could successfully be done, into the practice of agriculture, and whose children were to be taught the arts and industry of civilized life, and that it was no part of the design to treat the individuals as separately responsible and amenable, in all their personal and domestic relations with each other, to the general laws of the United States, outside of those which were enacted expressly with reference to them as members of an Indian tribe.

***

The language of the exception is special and express; the words relied on as a repeal are general and inconclusive. *** "The general principle to be applied *** is that a general act is not to be construed to repeal a previous particular act, unless there is some express reference to the previous legislation on the subject, or unless there is a necessary inconsistency in the two acts standing together." ***

The nature and circumstances of this case strongly reinforce this rule of interpretation in its present application. It is a case involving the judgment of a court of special and limited jurisdiction, not to be assumed without clear warrant of law. It is a case of life and death. It is a case where, against an express exception in the law itself, that law, by argument and inference only, is sought to be extended over aliens and strangers; over the members of a community, separated by race, by tradition, by the instincts of a free though savage life, from the authority and power which seeks to impose upon them the restraints of an external and unknown code, and to subject them to the responsibilities of civil conduct, according to rules and penalties of which they could have no previous warning; which judges them by a standard made by others, and not for them, which takes no account of the conditions which should except them from its exactions, and makes no allowance for their inability to understand it. It tries them not by their peers, nor by the customs of their people, nor the law of their land, but by superiors of a different race, according to the law of a social state of which they have an imperfect conception, and which is opposed to the traditions of their history, to the habits of their lives, to the strongest prejudices of their savage nature; one which measures the red man's revenge by the maxims of the white man's morality. ***

The provisions now contained in sections 2145 and 2146 of the Revised Statutes were first enacted in section 25 of the Indian intercourse act of 1834. 4 St. 733. Prior to that, by the act of 1796, (1 St. 469,) and the act of 1802, (2 St. 139,) offenses committed by Indians against white persons, and by white persons against Indians, were specifically enumerated and defined, and those by Indians against each other were left to be dealt with by each tribe for itself, according to its local customs. The policy of the government in that respect has been uniform. As was said by **JUSTICE MILLER**, delivering the opinion of the court in *United States v. Joseph*, 94 U.S. 614, 617 (1876):

> The tribes for whom the act of 1834 was made were those semi-independent tribes whom our government has always recognized as exempt from our laws, whether within or without the limits of an organized state or territory, and, in regard to their domestic government, left to their own rules and traditions, in whom we have recognized the capacity to make treaties, and with whom the governments, state and national, deal, with a few exceptions only, in their national or tribal character, and not as individuals.

To give to the clauses in the treaty of 1868 and the agreement of 1877 effect, so as to uphold the jurisdiction exercised in this case, would be to reverse in this instance the general policy of the government towards the Indians, as declared in many statutes and treaties, and recognized in many decisions of this court, from the beginning to the present time. To justify such a departure, in such a case, requires a clear expression of the intention of congress, and that we have not been able to find. It results that the first district court of Dakota was without jurisdiction to find or try the indictment against the prisoner; that the conviction and sentence are void, and that his imprisonment is illegal.

The writs of *habeas corpus* and *certiorari* prayed for will accordingly be issued.

NOTES AND QUESTIONS

1. Is *Ex Parte Crow Dog* consistent with *Worcester v. Georgia*? What, if anything, is different? What is the same?

2. What does the case suggest with respect to the limits of federal power in Indian country?

3. Does the Court give effect to the plain meaning of the 1868 Treaty and the 1877 statute? What principles of interpretation does it apply to those laws?

4. Justice Miller contrasts "white man's morality" and "red man's revenge." You have read about the Brûlé Sioux (Lakota) law for dealing with murders. How did American law deal with murder on the frontier?

5. The "bad men" clause is found in nine treaties negotiated in 1867 and 1868 in an effort to secure peace on the Great Plains. Note, *A Bad Man Is Hard to Find*, 127 Harv. L. Rev. 2521, 2525 (2014). The provision has been relied upon by tribal members who suffered harm at the hands of outsiders in several cases. *See Elk v. United States*, 87 Fed. Cl. 70 (2009) and *Richard v. United States*, 677 F.3d 1141 (Fed. Cit. 2012).

The Major Crimes Act (1885)

Crow Dog's acquittal proved to be just as effective in the campaign to extend federal jurisdiction over Indian country as his conviction would have been. Commissioner of Indian Affairs Lamar called attention to the case in his Annual Report, declaring that "If offenses of this character cannot be tried in the courts of the United States, there is no tribunal in which the crime of murder can be punished. *** If the murder is left to be punished according to the old Indian custom, it becomes the duty of the next of kin to avenge the death of his relative or some one of his kinsmen." Quoted in Harring at 137. The Indian Reform Association, a non-Indian organization concerned with the plight of Indian people, argued that federal jurisdiction was necessary to extend to the Indians the benefits of civilized law. Spotted Tail was portrayed as an advocate of the civilization policy killed by Crow Dog to prevent its progress. In 1885, Congress responded by enacting the Major Crimes Act, which, with few modifications, remains in effect today. *See* 18 U.S.C. § 1153. The law extends federal jurisdiction over certain "major" felonies, such as murder, rape, and serious assault, that are committed by Indians against Indians and others in Indian country. In 1886, the Supreme Court heard a case challenging the law.

UNITED STATES V. KAGAMA

118 U.S. 375, 65 S. Ct. 1109, 30 L. Ed. 228 (1886)

MILLER, JUSTICE.

[Two Klamath Indians, Kagama, alias Pactah Billy, and Mahawama, alias Ben, were indicted for the murder of another Klamath man, Iyouse. The alleged crime took place on the California reservation on which the Klamath Tribe was confined. The defendants challenged the Major Crimes Act as outside Congress' lawmaking powers. The district court and circuit court judges disagreed on two questions: first, whether the Major Crimes Act was constitutional, and second, whether the federal government could have jurisdiction over a crime between Indians committed "upon an Indian reservation made and set apart for the use of the Indian tribe to which said Indians both belong."]

[The Major Crimes Act] is new in legislation of Congress. *** It is new, because it now proposes to punish these offenses when they are committed by one Indian on the person or property of another. *** The [statute], which applies *** to offenses by Indians which are committed within the limits of a state and the limits of a reservation, subjects the offenders to the laws of the United States passed for the government of places under the exclusive jurisdiction of those laws, and to trial by the courts of the United States. This is a still further advance, as asserting this jurisdiction over the Indians within the limits of the states of the Union. ***

The constitution of the United States is almost silent in regard to the relations of the government which was established by it to the numerous tribes of Indians within its borders. ***

The mention of Indians in the Constitution which has received most attention is that found in the clause which gives congress "power to regulate commerce with foreign nations, and among the several states, and with the Indian tribes." This clause is relied on in the argument in the present case, the proposition being that the statute under consideration is a regulation of commerce with the Indian tribes. But we think it would be a very strained construction of this clause that a system of criminal laws for Indians living peaceably in their reservations, which left out the entire code of trade and intercourse laws justly enacted under that provision, and established punishments for the common-law crimes of murder, manslaughter, arson, burglary, larceny, and the like, without any reference to their relation to any kind of commerce, was authorized by the grant of power to regulate commerce with the Indian tribes. ***

But these Indians are within the geographical limits of the United States. The soil and the people within these limits are under the political control of the government of the United States, or of the states of the Union. There exists within the broad domain of sovereignty but these two. There may be cities, counties, and other organized bodies, with limited legislative functions, but they are all derived from, or exist in, subordination to one or the other of these. The territorial governments owe all their powers to the statutes of the United States conferring on them the powers which they exercise, and which are liable to be withdrawn, modified, or repealed at any time by congress. What authority the state governments may have to enact criminal laws for the Indians will be presently considered. But this power of congress to organize territorial governments, and make laws for their inhabitants, arises, not so much from the clause in the constitution in regard to disposing of and making rules and regulations concerning the territory and other property of the United States, as from the ownership of the country in which the territories are, and the right of exclusive sovereignty which must exist in the national government, and can be found nowhere else. ***

The relation of the Indian tribes living within the borders of the United States, both before and since the Revolution, to the people of the United States, has always been an anomalous one, and of a complex character. Following the policy of the European governments in the discovery of America, towards the Indians who were found here, the colonies before the Revolution, and the states and the United States since, have recognized in the Indians a possessory right to the soil over which they roamed and hunted and established occasional villages. But they asserted an ultimate title in the land itself, by which the Indian tribes were forbidden to sell or transfer it to other nations or peoples without the consent of this paramount authority. When a tribe wished to dispose of its land, or any part of it, or the state or the United States wished to purchase it, a treaty with the tribe was the only mode in which this could be done. The United States recognized no right in private persons, or in other nations, to make such a purchase by treaty or otherwise. With the Indians themselves these relations are equally difficult to define. They were, and always have been, regarded as having a semi-independent position when they preserved their tribal relations; not as states, not as nations, not as possessed of the full attributes of sovereignty, but as a separate people, with the power of regulating their internal and social relations, and thus far not brought under the laws of the Union or of the state within whose limits they resided.

Perhaps the best statement of their position is found in the two opinions of this court by **CHIEF JUSTICE MARSHALL** in the case of *Cherokee Nation v. Georgia* and *Worcester v. Georgia.* *** In the opinions in these cases they are spoken of as "wards of the nation;" "pupils;" as local dependent communities. In this spirit the United States has conducted its relations to them from its organization to this time. But, after an experience of a hundred years of the treaty-making system of government, congress has determined upon a new departure,—to govern them by acts of congress. This is seen in the act of March 3, 1871, embodied in section 2079 of the Revised Statutes: "No Indian nation or tribe, within the territory of the United States, shall be acknowledged or recognized as an independent nation, tribe, or power, with whom the United States may contract by treaty; but no obligation of any treaty lawfully made and ratified with any such Indian nation or tribe prior to March 3, 1871, shall be hereby invalidated or impaired."

[*Ex Parte Crow Dog*] admits that if the intention of congress had been to punish, by the United States courts, the murder of one Indian by another, the law would have been valid. But the court could not see, in the agreement with the Indians sanctioned by congress, a purpose to repeal section 2146 of the Revised Statutes, which expressly excludes from that jurisdiction the case of a crime committed by one Indian against another in the Indian country. The passage of the act now under consideration was designed to remove that objection, and to go further by including such crimes on reservations lying within a state. Is this latter fact a fatal objection to the law? The statute itself contains no express limitation upon the powers of a state, or the jurisdiction of its courts. If there be any limitation in either of these, it grows out of the implication arising from the fact that congress has defined a crime committed within the state, and made it punishable in the courts of the United States. But congress *has* done this, and *can* do it, with regard to all offenses relating to matters to which the federal authority extends. Does that authority extend to this case?

It will be seen at once that the nature of the offense (murder) is one which in most all cases of its commission is punishable by the laws of the states, and within the jurisdiction of their courts. The distinction is claimed to be that the offense under the statute is committed by an Indian, that it is committed on a reservation set apart within the state for residence of the tribe of Indians by the United States, and the fair inference is that the offending Indian shall belong to that or some other tribe. It does not interfere with the process of the state courts within the reservation, nor with the operation of state laws upon white people found there. Its effect is confined to the acts of an Indian of some tribe, of a criminal character, committed within the limits of the reservation. It seems to us that this is within the competency of congress. These Indian tribes *are* the wards of the nation. They are communities *dependent* on the United States,—dependent largely for their daily food; dependent for their political rights. They owe no allegiance to the states, and receive from them no protection. Because of the local ill feeling, the people of the states where they are found are often their deadliest enemies. From their very weakness and helplessness, so largely due to the course of dealing of the federal government with them, and the treaties in which it has been promised, there arises the duty of protection, and with it the power. This has always been recognized by the executive, and by congress, and by this court, whenever the question has arisen.

***

The power of the general government over these remnants of a race once powerful, now weak and diminished in numbers, is necessary to their protection, as well as to the safety of those among whom they dwell. It must exist in that government, because it never has existed anywhere else; because the theater of its exercise is within the geographical limits of the United States; because it has never been denied; and because it alone can enforce its laws on all the tribes.

[Accordingly, the Major Crimes Act is constitutional, and the federal court had jurisdiction over the offense.]

NOTES AND QUESTIONS

1. Is the decision in *Kagama* consistent with *Ex Parte Crow Dog*?

2. Notice that *Kagama*, like *Cherokee Nation*, refers to Indian tribes as "dependent." The phrase in *Kagama* is "local dependent communities," whereas Chief Justice Marshall referred to tribes as "domestic dependent nations." What is the significance of this different phrasing? What are the different implications of dependence in the opinions?

3. *Beyond Congressional Power?* Outside of Indian affairs, the powers of the federal government are generally limited to those derived from the Constitution. *Kagama* is a remarkable opinion in this sense. It notes that the Indian Commerce Clause is the only likely source of Article I congressional power to legislate—and then rejects the clause as a legitimate basis for the Major Crimes Act on the ground that an intra-tribal murder has nothing to do with commerce. Does the Court locate any particular constitutional provision authorizing Congress to enact the Major Crimes Act? Assuming that no such provision exists, presumably the Court should have held the Major Crimes Act unconstitutional—but then what would follow from that, that tribes are free from Anglo–American legislative power except on commercial matters, or that the states rather than the federal government had a police power in Indian country? The former conclusion seems to have more support from earlier case law and constitutional understandings. *See* Robert N. Clinton, *There is No Supremacy Clause for Indian Tribes*, 34 Ariz. St. L.J. 113 (2002). The latter conclusion would be very difficult for the Court to resist, however, as the states that had Indian country within them would powerfully assert this authority, and it would seem dubious to many non-Indians in the late nineteenth century that no Anglo–American legislature could constitutionally enact a criminal code for Indian country.

In the twentieth century, Congress asserted broad powers to legislate under the authority of the Interstate Commerce Clause. In a 1995 decision, the Court made clear that this power while broad is not unlimited. *U.S. v. Lopez*, 514 U.S. 549 (1995), invalidated a federal criminal law prohibiting gun possession within a school zone, finding that the statute "has nothing to do with 'commerce' or any sort of economic enterprise," and infringed on the "primary authority" of States to define and enforce criminal law. *Id.* at 561 & n.2. More recently, in a fractured opinion, Justice Roberts found that the Affordable Care Act's individual insurance mandate violated the Commerce Clause because it compelled commercial activity rather than regulating existing activity. *National Federation of Independent Business v. Sebelius*, 567 U.S. 519, 558 (2012). Could this reasoning be employed to invalidate the Major Crimes Act? How likely is that to happen? If the Court did take that step, what are the likely legal and political consequences? Would the Court be a step closer to recognize full sovereignty for Indian nations? Or would the Court proceed to second-guess Congress with respect to legislation that supports tribal self-governance?

4. If the *Kagama* Court does not find Congressional power over Indians on reservations in the Constitution, where does it find that power? Does it suggest any limits on that power? The Court faced the same issue in *United States v. Lara*, 541 U.S. 193 (2004) which confirmed congressional power to restore tribal inherent authority to exercise criminal jurisdiction over Indians who are not members of the governing tribe. The Court stated that Congress's authority rests in part "upon the Constitution's adoption of preconstitutional powers necessarily inherent in any Federal Government, namely powers that this Court has described as 'necessary concomitants of nationality.'" The case is in Ch. 8, § II. E., *infra*. *See* Maggie Blackhawk, *Federal Indian Law as Paradigm within Public Law*, 132 Harv. L. Rev. 1787, 1833–34 (2019)("Despite mounting criticism, the inherent powers doctrine has survived into the twenty-first century and was recently reaffirmed by the Court in reviewing the constitutionality of the Trump Administration's Executive Order 13780—the so-called 'travel ban' in *Trump v. Hawaii*, 138 S. Ct. 2392 (2018).").

5. How does the decision portray Indian tribes? How does it portray tribal sovereignty?

6. What does the case suggest with respect to *state* power in Indian country? Over Indian people? Over non-Indian people? Remember that *Worcester v. Georgia* had held that Georgia's laws were invalid with respect to two non-Indians in Cherokee territory. In 1881, however, the Supreme Court held that the state of Colorado had exclusive jurisdiction over a crime between two non-Indians committed on the Ute Reservation, because the federal government had not reserved jurisdiction over Indian country in admitting the state to the union. *U.S. v. McBratney*, 104 U.S. 621 (1881). In 1885, the Court held that the Idaho Territory could impose taxes on a Railroad Company for its right of way running through the Shoshone and Bannock Reservation. *Utah & N. Ry. Co. v. Fisher*, 116 U.S. 28 (1885). In other words, *Worcester*'s blanket exclusion of state law from Indian country was already being eroded in the name of states' rights where tribal interests were perceived not to be at stake. In *Kagama*, therefore, the Court had to respond to the argument that *any* assertion of federal jurisdiction in Indian country violated state sovereignty. That the erosion came at the hand of the Supreme Court, and not Congress, set a precedent that has had disastrous consequences for tribal jurisdiction over nonmembers as you will see in chapter 8.

Courts of Indian Offenses

The Major Crimes Act was not the only method of controlling law on reservations. Local Indian agents began to experiment with reservation courts staffed by accommodating tribal leaders in the 1860s. In 1883 these courts received formal sanction from the Department of the Interior, after Secretary Henry Teller directed the Commissioner of Indian Affairs to establish

> a tribunal at all agencies, except among the civilized Indians, consisting of three Indians, to be known as the court of Indian offenses. The members of this tribunal consist of the first three officers in rank of the police force, if such selection is approved by the agent; otherwise, the agent may select from among the members of the tribe three suitable persons to constitute such tribunal. *** It is believed that such a tribunal, composed as it is of Indians, will not be objectionable to the Indians and will be a step in the direction of bringing the Indians under the civilizing influence of law.

Annual Report of the Secretary of the Interior, H. Exec. Doc. 48–1 at xiii (Nov. 1, 1883). The Rules for Courts of Indian Offenses were published in the Annual Report on Indian Affairs in 1892.

RULES FOR COURTS OF INDIAN OFFENSES

Report on Indian Affairs (1892)

***

2. *Appointment of judges.*—*** The judges must be men of intelligence, integrity, and good moral character, and preference shall be given to Indians who read and write English readily, wear citizens' dress, and engage in civilized pursuits, and no person shall be eligible to such appointment who is a polygamist.

***

4. Offenses. ***

(a) Dances, etc.—Any Indian who shall engage in the sun dance, scalp dance, or war dance, or any other similar feast, so called, shall be guilty of an offense, and upon conviction thereof shall be punished for the first offense by the withholding of his rations for not exceeding ten days or by imprisonment for not exceeding ten days; and for any subsequent offense under this clause he shall be punished by withholding his rations for not less than ten not more than thirty days, or by imprisonment for not less than ten no more than thirty days.

(b) Plural or polygamous marriages.—Any Indian under the supervision of the United States Indian agent who shall hereafter contract or enter into any plural or polygamous marriage shall be deemed guilty of an offense, and upon conviction thereof shall pay a fine of not less than twenty nor more than fifty dollars, or work at hard labor for not less than twenty not more than sixty days, or both, at the discretion of the court, and so long as the person shall continue in such unlawful relation he shall forfeit all right to receive rations from the Government.

(c) Practices of medicine men.—Any Indian who shall engage in the practices of so-called medicine men, or who shall resort to any artifice of device to keep the Indians of the reservation from adopting and following civilized habits and pursuits, or shall adopt any means to prevent the attendance of children at school, or shall use any arts of a conjurer to prevent Indians from abandoning their barbarous rites and customs, shall be deemed to be guilty of an offense, and upon conviction thereof, for the first offense shall be imprisoned for not less than ten nor more than thirty days. ***

(d) Destroying property of other Indians.—Any Indian who shall willfully or wantonly destroy or injure, or, with intent to destroy or injure or appropriate, shall take and carry away any property of any other Indian or Indians, shall without reference to its value, be deemed guilty of an offense *** and the plea that the person convicted or the owner of the property in question was at the time a "mourner," and that thereby the taking, destroying or injuring of the property was justified by the customs or rites of the tribes, shall not be accepted as a sufficient defense.

(e) Immorality.—Any Indian who shall pay, or offer to pay, money or other thing of value to any female Indians, or to her friends or relatives, or to any other persons for the purpose of living or cohabiting with any such female Indian not his wife, shall be guilty of an offense, and upon conviction thereof shall forfeit all right to Government rations for not exceeding ninety days, or be imprisoned for not exceeding ninety days, or both, in the discretion of the court. ***

(f) Intoxication and the introduction of intoxicants [shall be an offense].

5. *Misdemeanors.*—***[I]f any Indian who is subject to road duty shall refuse or neglect to work the roads the required number of days each year, or to furnish a proper substitute therefore, he shall be deemed guilty of a misdemeanor, and shall be liable to a fine of one dollar and fifty cents for every day that he fails to perform road duty, or to imprisonment for not more than five days: *And provided further*, That if an Indian refuses or neglects to adopt habits of industry, or to engage in civilized pursuits of employments but habitually spends his time in idleness and loafing, he shall be deemed a vagrant and guilty of a misdemeanor, and shall, upon the first conviction thereof, be liable to a fine of not more than five dollars, or to imprisonment for not more than ten days, and for any subsequent conviction thereof to a fine of not more than ten dollars, or to imprisonment for not more than thirty days, in the discretion of the court.

6. *Judges to solemnize marriages.*—The said judges shall have power also to solemnize marriages between Indians. ***

H. Exec. Doc. No. 52–1.

NOTES AND QUESTIONS

1. What do the rules reveal about the purposes of the Courts of Indian Offenses?

2. What were the benefits to using tribal members as judges rather than using federal agents or other federal employees?

3. Many modern tribal courts owe their origins to Courts of Indian Offenses. How might this history affect community perceptions of those courts?

4. The courts did not always implement these rules as federal policy makers might have wished. For the courts to succeed, federal agents had to select judges who had some respect within the tribal community. A long-time judge of the Kiowa and Comanche court, for example, was Quanah Parker, who had six wives when he was appointed and took a seventh while in office. One of the cases he heard involved a charge of adultery brought by a man because one of his two wives had gone to live with another man. Parker ordered the woman to return to her husband, but only until the second wife, who was ill, had recovered. *See* William T. Hagan, Indian Police and Judges: Experiments in Acculturation and Control 135–137 (1966). How would this disposition have accorded with federal goals?

5. There was no explicit congressional authorization for these courts, and they were challenged in *United States v. Clapox*, 35 F. 575 (D. Or. 1888). The court upheld their establishment in the following terms.

> These 'courts of Indian offenses' are not the constitutional courts provided for in section 1, art. 3, Const., which congress only has the power to 'ordain and establish,' but mere educational and disciplinary instrumentalities, by which the government of the United States is endeavoring to improve and elevate the condition of these dependent tribes to whom it sustains the relation of guardian. In fact, the reservation itself is in the nature of a school, and the Indians are gathered there, under the charge of an agent, for the purpose of acquiring the habits, ideas, and aspirations which distinguish the civilized from the uncivilized man.

Id. at 577.

6. Congressional authorization of the modern courts was confirmed in the Indian Civil Rights Act of 1968, when Congress directed the Secretary of the Interior to develop a model code for the Courts of Indian Offenses, 25 U.S.C. §1311 and again in the Indian Tribal Justice Act of 1993, which created an Office of Tribal Justice support to "further the development, operation, and enhancement of tribal justice systems and Courts of Indian Offenses." 25 U.S.C. § 3611. There are now 20 tribes with Courts of Indian offenses operating. 25 C.F.R. § 11.100. The regulations are a far cry from those in place in 1892. Their current purpose is "to provide adequate machinery for the administration of justice for Indian tribes in those areas of Indian country where tribes retain jurisdiction over Indians that is exclusive of State jurisdiction but where tribal courts have not been established to exercise that jurisdiction." 25 C.F.R §11.102. In civil actions the courts are directed to follow applicable tribal or federal law. *Id.* § 11.500. The criminal code has a list of offenses ranging from common misdemeanors to sexual assault and domestic violence. *Id.* § 11.400-454. Long gone are the culture and religion-based offenses.

II. ALLOTMENT AND ASSIMILATION: 1887–1928

U.S. v. Kagama, with its portrayal of almost boundless federal power over Indian people, laid the groundwork for the next era in federal Indian policy. While the Reservation Era had aggressively pursued assimilation and conversion to farming by Indian people, this had been done with at least the nominal consent of tribes through treaties, and by a method that preserved the territorial integrity of tribal lands, albeit in a much-diminished form. In the next period in federal Indian policy, reservations would be opened to non-Indian settlement, and Congress and the Court would sanction assimilationist measures without the need for treaty consent.

A. THE DAWES (ALLOTMENT) ACT OF 1887

1. Origins and Provisions of the General Allotment Act

The allotment policy was a cornerstone of federal Indian policy between the 1880s and the 1920s. Tribal reservations would be broken up and divided among individual heads of households. Lands not included in these individual allotments would be opened to non-Indian settlement. As the Supreme Court has acknowledged, "[t]he policy of allotment of Indian lands quickly proved disastrous for the Indians." *Hodel v. Irving*, 481 U.S. 704, 707 (1987). Although greed for reservation land greatly influenced the pace and implementation of allotment, the policy itself was conceived and secured by eastern reformers who believed they were helping the Indians. These self-titled "Friends of the Indian" met in annual conferences at Lake Mohonk, advocated in the press, and lobbied in Congress for the measure. In 1887, these efforts succeeded with the passage of the General Allotment Act, which was also called the Dawes Act after its primary sponsor, Senator Henry Dawes. In 1934, D.S. Otis wrote the following history of allotment for the Bureau of Indian Affairs.

D.S. OTIS, THE DAWES ACT AND THE ALLOTMENT OF INDIAN LANDS

8–11, 13, 16, 17, 18–19, 31–32 (1934) (Francis P. Prucha ed. 1973)

That the leading proponents of allotment were inspired by the highest motives seems conclusively true. *** The new policy was regarded as a panacea which would make restitution to the Indian for all that the white man had done to him in the past. ***

Supporters of allotment showed themselves children of their age in their deference to the principle of individualism. In 1873 the Commissioner of Indian Affairs wrote, "A fundamental difference between barbarians and a civilized people is the difference between a herd and an individual."

The Indian, then was to learn to go his own independent, industrious way and he would become civilized. Probably most citizens would have applauded Senator George H. Pendleton when in debating the Coke bill [the failed precursor to the Allotment Act] he *** said, "It must be our part to seek to foster and to encourage within them *** this trinity upon which all civilization depends—family, and home, and property." One cannot but wonder how many would have subscribed to the astounding utterances of Senator Dawes, himself, in an address to the 1885 Lake Mohonk Conference:

> The head chief told us that there was not a family in that whole Nation [one of the Five Civilized Tribes] that had not a home of its own. There was not a pauper in that Nation, and the Nation did not owe a dollar. It built its own capitol *** and it built its schools and its hospitals. Yet the defect of the system was apparent. They have got as far as they can go, because they own their land in common. It is Henry George's system, and under that there is no enterprise to make your home any better than that of your neighbors. There is no selfishness, which is at the bottom of civilization. Till this people will consent to give up their lands, and divide them among their citizens so that each can own the land he cultivates, they will not make much more progress.

***

The believers in allotment had another philanthropic aim, which was to protect the Indian in his present land holding. They were confident that if every Indian had his own strip of land, guaranteed by a patent from the Government, he would enjoy a security which no tribal possession could afford him. *** The age-old process of dispossessing the Indian was in this period rapidly accelerating. The railroads were giving powerful impetus to the westward march of land-hungry native Americans and even more voracious European immigrants. ***

It must also be noted that while the advocates of allotment were primarily and sincerely concerned with the advancement of the Indian they at the same time regarded the scheme as promoting the best interests of the whites as well. For one thing, it was fondly but erroneously hoped that setting the Indian on his own feet would relieve the Government of a great expense. ***

The chief advantages that the new system was to bring to the country as a whole were to be found in the opening up of surplus lands on the reservations and in the attendant march of progress and civilization westward. In his report of 1880, Secretary Schurz wrote:

> [Allotment] will eventually open to settlement by white men the large tracts of land now belonging to the reservations, but not used by Indians. It will thus put the relations between the Indians and their white neighbors upon a new basis, by gradually doing away with the system of large reservations, which has so frequently provoked those encroachments which in the past have led to so much cruel injustice and so many disastrous collisions. ***

But doubters of the allotment system could see nothing but dire consequences for the Indian. Senator Teller in 1881 called the Coke bill "a bill to despoil the Indians of their lands and to make them vagabonds on the face of the earth." At another time he said:

> If I stand alone in the Senate, I want to put upon the record my prophecy in this matter, that when thirty or forty years have passed and these Indians shall have parted with their title, they will curse the hand that

> was raised professedly in their defense to secure this kind of legislation and if the people who are clamoring for it understood Indian character, and Indian laws, and Indian morals, and Indian religion, they would not be here clamoring for this at all. ***

[T]he minority report of the House Indian Affairs Committee in 1880 had gone even further in its accusations. It said:

> The real aim of this bill is to get at the Indian lands and open them up to settlement. The provisions for the apparent benefit of the Indian are but the pretext to get at his lands and occupy them. *** If this were done in the name of Greed, it would be bad enough; but to do it in the name of Humanity, and under the cloak of an ardent desire to promote the Indian's welfare by making him like ourselves, whether he will or not, is infinitely worse.

This statement is hardly fair to all the supporters of the allotment policy. [I]t is true that even the genuine friends of the Indian favored opening up his "surplus" lands in the interests of spreading civilization. But there is no doubt that they believed that the allotment policy would promote the Indian's economic and spiritual welfare. ***

[T]here is plenty of evidence to indicate that there were definite and powerful interests behind allotment which were not philanthropic at all; that homesteaders, land companies, and perhaps railroads, saw allotment as a legal way of getting at wide areas of Indian lands. *** There is no evidence that any of these private interests originated the allotment idea. Had it been for them to choose, they would have probably preferred outright dispossession. But they were certainly not hostile to allotment or there would have been western opposition to it in Congress; and the Dawes bill would not have progressed through its final stages almost without debate and passed without a roll call. ***

The General Allotment Act authorized the President "whenever in his opinion any reservation or any part thereof of such Indians is advantageous, for agricultural and grazing purposes, to cause said reservation *** to be surveyed *** and to allot the lands in severalty." ***, 24 Stat. 388 (Feb. 8, 1887). The Act was implemented through individual acts regarding specific reservations and regions. Although there were some changes to the Act in its initial years, the basic provisions of the Allotment Act and its implementing acts were as follows:

1. Each individual Indian on a given reservation would be issued an allotment of up to 160 acres of land. The Indians were to choose the portion of land allotted to them, but if they did not choose within a period of four years, the local agent would select an allotment for them.

2. The federal government would hold allotments in trust for their Indian owners for twenty-five years, during which time the land could not be sold or encumbered. Upon the expiration of the twenty-five year period, the allottee would be issued a "fee patent," indicating that they owned the land in fee simple. In the 1906 Burke Act, Congress authorized the Secretary of the Interior to issue a patent before twenty-five years had expired "whenever he shall be satisfied that any Indian allottee is competent and

capable of managing his or her affairs" and provided that a patent removed all restrictions on "sale, incumbrance, or taxation" of the land. 34 Stat. 182, § 6.

3. The descent and inheritance of allotted lands would be governed by the laws of the state or territory within which the allotment was located, but administered by the Bureau of Indian Affairs.

4. Lands not allotted would be opened to non-Indian purchase and settlement as "surplus" lands.

2. Allotment and Tribal Land Loss

Legislators, courts, and historians agree: allotment was an unmitigated disaster. Between 1887 and 1934, a period of just forty-seven years, it cut the Indian land base by two-thirds, from 138 million acres to 48 million, with 84% of the remaining tribal land located on unallotted reservations in Arizona, New Mexico, Utah, Wyoming, and Montana. Professor Judith Royster documents this land loss.

JUDITH V. ROYSTER, *THE LEGACY OF ALLOTMENT*

27 Ariz. St. L. J. 1 (1995)

*** The twenty-five year trust period came under attack *** by those who viewed the continued federal guardianship as an obstacle to the goal of assimilation. As a result, Congress amended the General Allotment Act in 1906 to authorize the early issuance of fee patents. The Burke Act authorized the Secretary of the Interior to issue a fee patent to an allottee at any time, upon a determination that the individual was "competent and capable of managing his or her affairs." Upon the issuance of one of these premature patents, the land was expressly subject to alienation, encumbrance, and taxation.

The effect of the Burke Act was immediate and substantial. In the three years following the passage of the 1906 act, patents were issued upon the recommendation of the Indian superintendent. Of the 2744 applications made during those years, all but 68 were granted. Surveys in 1908 showed that more than 60 percent of the premature patentees lost their lands. In 1909, an alarmed Commissioner of Indian Affairs began requiring a more detailed showing that the allottee was competent, and the approval rate dropped to approximately seventy percent of all applicants.

That relief was short-lived. In 1913, a new Commissioner of Indian Affairs not only reinstated the liberalized policy, but expanded upon it. Initially, the Indian superintendents were ordered to submit the names of competent Indians, but that procedure was soon replaced by "competency commissions," charged with roaming the reservations in search of allottees who could be issued premature patents. Under pressure to liberate the Indians from federal guardianship, the Indian Office issued patents to unqualified allottees and, in many cases, to allottees who neither applied for nor wanted to accept them. Despite reports showing that in many cases 90 percent or more of premature and forced-fee allottees lost their lands, the liberalized policy was formalized and further expanded in 1917.

In that year, Indian Commissioner Sells announced that fee patents would simply be issued to all allottees of less than one-half Indian ancestry, while competency determinations would still be required for those of one-half or more Indian blood. *** The havoc caused by Sells' policy resulted in a loss of support for liberalized patenting, and in 1920 a new Commissioner abolished the competency commissions and declared that no fee patents would issue without a determination of competency regardless of blood quantum.

Between the two methods—expiration of the trust period and premature patents—thousands of patents in fee were issued, often amounting to several thousand in a single year. Once a patent in fee was issued, the land could be alienated, encumbered, and at least as to Burke Act patents, taxed. Thousands of Indian owners disposed of their lands by voluntary or fraudulent sales; many others lost their lands at sheriffs' sales for nonpayment of taxes or other liens. By the end of the allotment era, two-thirds of all the land—allotted approximately 27 million acres—had passed into non-Indian ownership.

***

Despite the devastating effect of fee patents, the 27 million patented acres lost to non-Indians represented only about one-third of the tribal losses during the allotment era. More than twice as much land—some 60 million acres—was lost under the surplus lands program. The General Allotment Act provided that, once reservation lands were allotted in severalty, the remaining "surplus" lands could, at the discretion of the President, be opened to non-Indian settlement. Non–Indian settlement interspersed with Indian allotments, assimilation advocates believed, would promote interaction between citizens and Indians and encourage the allottees to adopt white ways. Allotment would remove the "dead weight" of communal tribal lands that kept the Indians from full participatory citizenship.

As enacted, the General Allotment Act called for tribal consent to cession of the surplus lands. Although multiple cession agreements were negotiated with tribes, many of the early efforts were thwarted by the tribes' refusal to sell or their demand of a high price. In 1903, however, the Supreme Court held in *Lone Wolf v. Hitchcock* that tribal consent to the loss of surplus lands was not required, notwithstanding either the General Allotment Act or a specific treaty provision requiring written consent to any cession agreement. Thereafter, Congress unilaterally enacted surplus lands acts. ***

The post-Lone Wolf surplus lands acts followed a pattern. "They were proposed by western politicians, approved by a voice vote in Congress, and greeted with cheers from local settlers and businessmen." Tribal advocates were reduced to campaigning for adequate compensation for the homesteaded lands. Once tribal consent was no longer at issue, the focus of the surplus lands program had shifted from assimilation of the Indians to the development and white settlement of the western states.

***

---

3. Allotment and Farming

Allotment also failed to encourage Indian farming. Much reservation land was unsuitable for farming to begin with. Corrupt local allotting agents, under the influence of non-Indian interests, might designate fertile land as surplus, allotting only land that was not profitable to farm. Where valuable lands were allotted to Indians, pressure to issue fee patents for the lands and sell them to non-Indians quickly took the land out of Indian hands. In addition, although successful farming required capital for plows, livestock, and seed, in practice almost no aid was provided. In 1888, for example, the appropriations for this purpose amounted to less than ten dollars per allottee. Professor Charles C. Painter told the 1889 Lake Mohonk Conference of an allottee who found himself with "a vast but unusable possession: a large land estate, but without teams, implements, money, houses or experience, and consequently without power to utilize a foot of it." Quoted in Otis, at 101. As a result, the policy actually resulted in a decline in Indian farming:

> Allotment did not perform its primary function: to turn the Indians generally into agriculturalists. Many Indians had farmed successfully under their communal land patterns, with individuals and families using designated sections of tribal land for their cultivation, and as allotment began it was hoped that more and more Indians would become self-sufficient through the land. Yet in fact, under allotment, the amount of Indian farming declined rather than grew. *** In the ten states in which the great majority of Indians allotments were made, excluding Oklahoma, the total area farmed by Indians in 1910 was estimated at 2,131,477 acres. In the next decade Indian farming declined in all the states except Montana, with a total of 1,836,191 acres in 1920, and in the 1920s the decline was universal, with a total of 1,519,368 acres farmed by Indians in 1930. Moreover, the position of Indians in relation to white farmers deteriorated. In 1910 the value of land and buildings on an Indian farm was 44 percent of that on the average white farm; in 1930, it was only 31 percent. A similar decline occurred in the relative value of machinery and implements on Indian and white farms. "Allotment in severalty, judged either as a program to advance the welfare of American Indians or to promote economic development among the reservation Indians," a careful economic study has concluded, "was a disaster. Rather than encourage Indian farming, it led to a significant decline in Indian farming."

Francis P. Prucha, The Great Father: The United States Government and the American Indians 895 (1984).

4. Allotment and the Checkerboarded Reservation

One of the most important legacies of allotment for modern federal Indian law is its impact on land ownership on Indian reservations. Both sales of surplus lands and the practice of fee patenting and selling allotted lands have transformed many Indian reservations from contiguous territories into "checkerboards" of trust land, Indian fee patent land, and non-Indian land. Congress sought to address the jurisdictional questions this created in 1948 by declaring that all land within reservation boundaries, regardless of ownership, was considered "Indian country." 18 U.S.C. § 1151(a). More recent Supreme Court decisions have complicated this rule, however, by holding that some allotment acts removed or diminished reservation boundaries, *see Hagen v. Utah*, 510 U.S. 399, 410 (1994); that allotted Indian-owned fee land within reservations is subject to state property taxes, *County of Yakima v. Yakima Indian Nation*, 502 U.S. 251, 263–264 (1992); *Cass County v. Leech Lake Band of Chippewa*

Indians, 524 U.S. 103 (1998); and that tribes have only limited jurisdiction over non-Indians on non-Indian owned land on reservations. *See Atkinson Trading Company v. Shirley*, 532 U.S. 645, 654 (2001).

5. Allotment and Fractionation

The provision that allotted land would be subject to state inheritance laws further diminished the value of allotted lands. Because most Indian allottees did not make written wills, their estates passed in shares to each of their descendants specified in state intestacy acts. This division of ownership among numerous heirs made the resulting fractionated land virtually unusable. Although the federal government might respond by leasing the land, the administrative costs of such leasing could outweigh the value to the share-owner. By 1934, Representative Edgar Howard declared in Congress,

> On allotted reservations, numerous cases exist where the shares of each individual heir from lease money may be 1 cent a month. Or one heir may own minute fractional shares in 30 or 40 different allotments. The cost of leasing, bookkeeping, and distributing the proceeds in many cases far exceeds the total income. The Indians and the Indian Service personnel are thus trapped in a meaningless system of minute partition in which all thought of the possible use of land to satisfy human needs is lost in a mathematical haze of bookkeeping.

78 Cong. Rec. 11728 (1934). The problem has only gotten worse with time; by 2004, some interests amounted to only 0.0000001 percent, or 1/9 millionth, of the undivided allotment. *Testimony of Ross O. Swimmer*, Special Trustee for American Indians, House Resources Comm. Hrg. on S. 1721 (AIPRA) (June 23, 2004). Congress twice sought to ameliorate the problem of fractionation by providing that certain very fractionated shares whose owners would die intestate would escheat to the tribe rather than be passed to the owner's heirs, but each time the Supreme Court invalidated the measure as a violation of the Fifth Amendment Takings Clause. *See Babbitt v. Youpee*, 519 U.S. 234 (1997) (invalidating escheat provisions of 98 Stat. 3173); *Hodel v. Irving*, 481 U.S. 704 (1987) (invalidating escheat provisions of 96 Stat. 2519 (1984)). In 2004, after much debate, consultation, and criticism from Indian country, Congress made another try, enacting the American Indian Probate Reform Act. The Act provides for a uniform probate code for tribes that do not enact their own codes and provides that where a decedent owns a less than 5% interest in an allotment, the interest descends to a single heir, the closest relative of the decedent. 25 U.S.C. § 2206.

B. ALLOTMENT AND THE ABROGATION OF TREATY RIGHTS

As Professor Royster notes, treaties were initially an obstacle to allotment of land belonging to tribes that refused to consent. In *Lone Wolf v. Hitchcock*, 187 U.S. 553 (1903), the Court considered a challenge to the Kiowa, Comanche and Kiowa–Apache allotment act on the grounds that the act violated a treaty with the tribes. The Court held that Congress had the power to unilaterally abrogate its treaties with Indian tribes. The following article provides both a history of the case and a window into the implementation of allotment and tribal reactions to it.

ANN LAQUER ESTIN, LONE WOLF V. HITCHCOCK: *THE LONG SHADOW*, *IN* THE AGGRESSIONS OF CIVILIZATION: FEDERAL INDIAN POLICY SINCE THE 1880'S

215, 216 (Sandra L. Cadwalader & Vine Deloria, Jr. eds., 1984)

When Commissioner of Indian Affairs J.D.C. Atkins arrived at the Kiowa, Comanche, and Kiowa–Apache reservation during the winter of 1886–1887, his purpose was to enlist Indian support for the allotment acts pending in Congress. ***

Instead of gaining enthusiastic Indian support, Commissioner Atkins encountered the "determined opposition" of the southern plains tribes; his visit in fact spurred the Indian leaders into action. Defying efforts by the local agent to keep them on their reservation, Lone Wolf of the Kiowas and Chief Jake of the Caddoes traveled by train to Washington to fight the proposed legislation. Lone Wolf and Chief Jake arrived too late; the General Allotment Act had been passed on February 8, 1887. ***

For Lone Wolf, called Guipagho by the Kiowa, the fruitless trip to Washington marked the start of a long fight to protect his tribe's land and community. ***

[In 1892] Commissioner David H. Jerome addressed the Kiowa, Comanche, and Apache in council at Fort Sill. He began with a description of the changes in Indian Territory during the twenty-four years since the Medicine Lodge Treaty: the disappearance of the buffalo and other game from the southern plains, growing dependence on government rations, and significantly, a doubling in the region's white population, while the three tribes had not increased in number. Jerome then presented allotment as a means of alleviating the hardships of the past decades.

> If the Indians will do what the Great Father wants them to do, and do their part well, it will result in your having plenty of food and clothing; and instead of having, as you sometimes do, only one meal a day, you will have three meals a day and have plenty of clothing and things that will make you comfortable through the winter. Instead of having to wait for an issue of beef every two weeks, you can go out and kill a beef of your own and have a feast every day if you please. I told you a little while ago that for twenty-four years the Indians had increased very little if any in numbers. Now, if you follow the plan that we have told you about you will not have your babies die from the cold, but you will have them grow up good, strong, healthy men and women, instead of putting them in the ground.

Jerome's cynical reliance on this sort of appeal reflected the increasingly desperate situation of the Plains tribes. During the early reservation years, the Indians had been able to supplement their treaty annuity income and the unreliable government rations with hunting (and periodic raids on Texas ranches). Within a decade of the Medicine Lodge Treaty, however, their subsistence economy had been destroyed, and the tribes were kept under total control by the Indian agents and military at Fort Sill. ***

Disarmed and dismounted, the three tribes faced this fresh assault from the United States government with a new sort of courage. With their tribal autonomy and independence at a nadir, the tribes turned to their treaty, negotiated at Medicine Lodge Creek in 1867, to define their relationship with the federal government. ***

When the Indians were given an opportunity to speak during the second day of the council, the chiefs and headmen of the three tribes rose in turn to speak about the Medicine Lodge Treaty. Although the Indians who spoke called the "white man's road" a good one to travel, the almost unanimous view was that the tribes wished to wait another four years, until the annuity provisions of the treaty expired, before considering a new deal. ***

What terms the commissioners were prepared to offer was not made clear until the middle of the second session. With prodding from [Comanche leader] Quanah Parker, Commissioner Jerome presented a proposal to give every member of the three tribes a 160–acre allotment and to pay $2 million for the surplus land remaining after allotment. Jerome refused to estimate a cost per acre, but his report to the President later put the reservation land base at 2,968,983 acres, with only 453,000 required for the Indian allotments. ***

After Jerome presented the offer, Commissioner Warren Sayre made sure that the Indians assembled in council understood the iron fist in the velvet glove: he claimed that under the Dawes Act the President could order tribes to take allotments whether they wanted to or not. ***

Despite their desperate condition and the strong inducements offered by the commissioners, the three tribes decided in a council held before the third day's session to keep their treaty land. *** At the start of the third day of meetings, Lone Wolf addressed the three commissioners and made the tribes' position clear.

> Look on Quanna's people, they are Indians; look on Lone Wolf's people and Whiteman's people, they are Indians; they are not educated, they do not know how to till the ground. They do not know how to work. Should they be forced to take allotments it means sudden downfall for the three tribes ***

Lone Wolf's pleading were not intended to turn back the clock or attempt to avoid change. The Kiowa chief agreed that the road set out by the Medicine Lodge Treaty "is about the best that we can travel." He described the "good advice" he had received in Washington and the progress the tribes were making in building schools and houses, concluding: "For that reason, because we are making such rapid progress, we ask the commission not to push us ahead too fast on the road we are to take."

But the Indians had serious reasons for questioning the benefits to be obtained by accepting the commissioner's offer. Two Kiowas, Big Tree and Iseeo, spoke about the experience of the nearby Cheyenne–Arapahoe after allotment. Big Tree stated that

> A year ago this commission came to the Cheyenne and Arapahoe Indians; they talked to those Indians very good. These Indians came to the Kiowa and Comanche Reservation; we saw tears in their eyes; we saw they had nothing to their name.
>
> They are poor; they will be poor in the future; they had made a mistake in selling their country; that money was given to them but it was all gone.

Iseeo, a young Kiowa sergeant in the U.S. Cavalry, rose to speak to the commissioners at the request of the chiefs. He apologized for his short hair and uniform, for not being a chief or a wise man, and for belonging both to the United States and the Kiowa tribe, but he spoke eloquently about the Cheyenne's experience.

> [I]t is only a few months ago that the Cheyennes came to this military reservation and brought their wagons and fancy shawls, velvet blankets, and carriages, and told us that the money that the Great Father had given them was all gone—that the money they got was invested in these things. Now the wagons are old, being used very hard, and the velvet shawls will be worn out. ***
>
> In a few years these Cheyenne Indians will be the poorest Indians, and they will be coming all the time for ponies. Look at them today, surrounded by white men; they will get the Indians drunk and get his money; they will make him sign a contract to get anything that the Cheyenne has got, and the Cheyenne's life in the next three years will be worse than when he was an Indian; so that is why we say wait three years till we get some place picked out and some better way to get along in life. ***
>
> Mother earth is something that we Indians love. The Great Father in Washington told us that this reservation was ours; that we would not be disturbed; that this place was for our use, and when you told us the purpose of the Government it made us uneasy. We do not know what to do about selling our mother to the Government. That makes us scared.

Quanah Parker, who had grown rich from his own farms and from his dealings with Texas cattlemen, asked pointed questions about the business aspects of the deal: "How much will be paid for one acre, what the terms will be and when it will be paid." ***

Given the tribes' overwhelming opposition to the selling of the reservation, it is surprising how quickly the [Jerome] Commission completed its task. ***

On the fourth day of the meetings, Quanah broke the impasse with an announcement that he had sent for a lawyer and proposed that a representative of each tribe meet with the lawyer and the commissioners to examine the proposed agreement. Quanah also requested that once the tribes understood the agreement the commissioners adjourn for two months to let the tribes consider.

Without agreeing to Quanah's plan, Jerome set a time the following morning to meet with the representatives and the lawyer. Several days later, the council reconvened; it was announced that the lawyer was unable to help the tribes at this point, and Quanah offered a compromise proposal: that the differences between the tribes and the Commission be resolved directly with Congress by a delegation from the tribes. Quanah thought the tribes should be paid half a million more than the commissioners had offered, and asked the Commission to present both figures to Congress.

Quanah got Lone Wolf and White Man to support his proposal, and the three commissioners announced the following day that they would accept Quanah's proposal. Despite the assurance, the document Jerome prepared for signatures was little different than the terms he had originally offered. The agreement as drafted and signed included the original $2 million figure and gave the tribes only "an opportunity to be heard" in Congress for the balance. There was no provision included to delay implementation. ***

After reviewing the terms of his new draft, Jerome made it clear that he would no longer tolerate opposition. The commissioners raised a final question: which non-Indian people should be "adopted" into tribes as beneficiaries of the agreement? The commissioner's request for a list of non-Indian allottees was a useful device to generate more support for the agreement. The final list totaled twenty-five and included white "squaw-men" as well as two of the interpreters for the Commission, and the wife of a third; Quanah's sharecropper; his son-in-law; Agent George Day; Lieutenant Hugh Scott, commander of the Indian cavalry at Fort Sill; and a Methodist minister who had lived five years on the reservation. ***

Lone Wolf, Big Tree, Komalty, and Iseeo, all Kiowas, had each signed the agreement, based apparently on their understanding that the commissioners had incorporated Quanah's proposals. ***

Before the commissioners left Fort Sill, they were already fighting rumors of foul play. ***

Although Jerome had collected 456 signatures on his "agreement," he left the reservation deeply divided and mistrustful. *** [T]he Indians were already meeting in council to find a way to stop the agreement. Gathered at the Methodist Church, the tribes drafted a memorial protesting the procedures and interpreters used by the commissioner and charging fraud and misrepresentation.

Although Lone Wolf was among the Kiowas who had initially agreed to sign, he reverted to opposition almost immediately. Before the commissioners left the reservation, Lone Wolf paid them a visit with a group of other signers. The Indians suspected that they had been deceived by incorrect translation of the terms of the agreement. Their request to see the document was denied, as was their request to have their names erased. ***

*** At every council after the commissioners left the reservation the subject was raised and debated and the three tribes sent frequent petitions and memorials to Congress expressing their opposition to the proposal. By the time the agreement reached Congress, however, the primary concern was not the consent or even the welfare of the Indians. A clamor to "open" the Kiowa, Comanche, and Apache reservation had brought increasing pressure on Congress to "ratify" any "agreement," regardless of the tribes' view.

*** The first bill [to ratify the agreement] was introduced in September 1893, by Delegate Dennis Flynn from the Oklahoma Territory. ***

The three tribes held a general council the same month and sent another memorial to Congress, this one drafted by a Washington, D.C. attorney, W.C. Shelley. Signed by 323 members of the tribe, the memorial set forth the history of "mendacity, fraud and coercion" in the dealings of the [Jerome] Commission, and repudiated the agreement. ***

[When the bill finally went to the Senate in 1898, Secretary of the Interior C.N. Bliss] reported the census figures that indicated that less than three-fourths of the adult Indian men had signed the agreement. A tribal roll, prepared less than three months after Agent Day's count of 562 adult men, listed 725 Indian men over age 18 and 639 men over 21. ***

The tribes' final memorial was transmitted to the House and Senate when the Fifty–Sixth congress convened in January 1900. Accompanied by letter from Commissioner Jones and Ethan A. Hitchcock, the new Interior Secretary, the petition was a clear and simple statement of the Indians' repudiation.

> [E]ach and every one of us who signed that treaty do solemnly declare that if we had not been deceived we would never have signed it. ***
>
> We now realize that if this treaty is ratified we are doomed to destruction as a people and brought to the same impoverished condition to which the Cheyenne and Arapahoe and other Indian tribes have been brought from the effects of prematurely opening their reservation for the settlement of white men among them.

At the time the Kiowas, Comanches, and Apaches were drafting their petition to Congress, the whites located around the reservation borders began collecting affidavits to submit to the Senate. ***

In February 1900, the House proponents of ratification tried a new approach and added their two year old bill as a rider to another Senate Indian bill that concerned the Fort Hall Reservation in Idaho. *** [T]he bill passed the Senate without debate at the end of the session. No words in the title of the Act of June 6, 1900 indicated that Section VI was a ratification of the long-disputed Jerome agreement. The ratification legislation amended the original Jerome agreement in several critical ways, but the amendments were never submitted to the three tribes for their approval.

[After traveling again to Washington to try to stop implementation of the agreement and being rebuffed, Lone Wolf filed suit against the Secretary of the Interior with the assistance of the Indian Rights Association. By this point the United States would no longer recognize him as a principal chief of this tribe because of his continued opposition to allotment. The trial court refused to enjoin the allotment.] [B]y the time the Court of Appeals heard the case the opening of the Kiowa, Comanche, and Apache reservation was an accomplished fact. By proclamation of President McKinley on July 4, 1901, the date of opening was set for August 6, 1901.

*** Registration of land-hungry whites began on July 10, and after two weeks more than 150,000 people had registered for the 13,000 allotments available. Before the date of opening, a lottery was held to select those who would be allowed to claim 160–acre homesteads at a price of $1.75 per acre.

The *fait accompli* of 13,000 non-Indian homesteads cannot have helped Lone Wolf and [his attorney, William] Springer in their uphill legal battle. On December 4, 1901, the Court of Appeals of the District of Columbia rejected their appeal. ***

Oral argument [in the Supreme Court] was held on October 23, 1902. *** [T]he Supreme Court issued its opinion on January 5, 1903. ***

LONE WOLF V. HITCHCOCK

187 U.S. 553, 23 S. Ct. 216, 47 L. Ed. 299 (1903)

JUSTICE WHITE delivered the opinion of the court.

[In 1867, the Kiowa, Comanche, and Apache Tribes signed a treaty setting apart a reservation for their use. The twelfth article of the treaty reads as follows:]

> Article 12. No treaty for the cession of any portion or part of the reservation herein described, which may be held in common, shall be of any validity or force, as against the said Indians, unless executed and signed by at least three fourths of all the adult male Indians occupying the same. ***

The appellants base their right to relief on the proposition that by the effect of the article just quoted the confederated tribes of Kiowas, Comanches, and Apaches were vested with an interest in the lands held in common within the reservation, which interest could not be divested by Congress in any other mode than that specified in the said twelfth article, and that as a result of the said stipulation the interest of the Indians in the common lands fell within the protection of the 5th Amendment to the Constitution of the United States, and such interest—indirectly at least—came under the control of the judicial branch of the government. We are unable to yield our assent to this view.

The contention in effect ignores the status of the contracting Indians and the relation of dependency they bore and continue to bear towards the government of the United States. To uphold the claim would be to adjudge that the indirect operation of the treaty was to materially limit and qualify the controlling authority of Congress in respect to the care and protection of the Indians, and to deprive Congress, in a possible emergency, when the necessity might be urgent for a partition and disposal of the tribal lands, of all power to act, if the assent of the Indians could not be obtained.

Now, it is true that in decisions of this court, the Indian right of occupancy of tribal lands, whether declared in a treaty or otherwise created, has been stated to be sacred, or, as sometimes expressed, as sacred as the fee of the United States in the same lands. *** But in none of these cases was there involved a controversy between Indians and the government respecting the power of Congress to administer the property of the Indians. ***

Plenary authority over the tribal relations of the Indians has been exercised by Congress from the beginning, and the power has always been deemed a political one, not subject to be controlled by the judicial department of the government. Until the year 1871 the policy was pursued of dealing with the Indian tribes by means of treaties, and, of course, a moral obligation rested upon Congress to act in good faith in performing the stipulations entered into on its behalf. But, as with treaties made with foreign nations (*Chinese Exclusion Case* [*Chae Chan Ping v. United States*], 130 U.S. 581 (1889)), the legislative power might pass laws in conflict with treaties made with the Indians. ***

The power exists to abrogate the provisions of an Indian treaty, though presumably such power will be exercised only when circumstances arise which

Non-PL280 Jurisdictions		**DEFENDANT**		
		Indian		**Non-Indian**
VICTIM	**Non-Indian**	<u>Major Crime:</u> ✓ X ? Federal (MCA) ✓ X ? Tribal ✓ X ? State	<u>Non-Major Crime:</u> ✓ X ? Federal (ICCA & ACA if not already punished by tribe) ✓ X ? Tribal ✓ X ? State	✓ X ? Federal ✓ X ? Tribal ✓ X ? State (*McBratney*)
	Indian	<u>Major Crime</u> ✓ X ? Federal (MCA) ✓ X ? Tribal ✓ X ? State	<u>Non-Major Crime:</u> ✓ X ? Federal ✓ X ? Tribal ✓ X ? State	✓ X ? Federal (ICCA & ACA) ✓ X ? Tribal (VAWA & *Oliphant*) ✓ X ? State (*Castro-Huerta*)
	No Victim	✓ X ? Federal (ACA Fed. type crimes) ✓ X ? Tribal ✓ X ? State		✓ X ? Federal (ICCA) ✓ X ? Tribal (*Oliphant*) ✓ X ? State (*McBratney*)

Category number	**1**	**-2**	**-3**	**-4**	**+5**	**=Tribal sovereignty today**
Nature and limits of sovereignty	Full sovereignty under international law	Loss of sovereignty because of the effects of contact with Europeans	Loss of tribal interests through treaty cessions	Loss of tribal authority because preempted by federal statute	Delegations of federal authority	
Doctrinal aspects	Pre-contact nature of tribes	Doctrine of discovery, requiring approval of Discovering European Sovereign (DES) for land transactions with tribes	Canons of interpretation (supposedly) limit this to clear cessions as the Indians would have understood them	Congressional plenary power; supposedly the canons require explicit preemption before it counts	No violation of nondelegation doctrine	

		requiring tribe to enter into treaties only with the DES				
Illustrative case taking this approach	*Marshall trilogy*	*Johnson v. McIntosh*	*Worcester; Crow Dog*	*Lone Wolf; Mille Lacs*	*Mazurie*	

Jurisdictions		Indian	Non-Indian
VICTIM	Non-Indian	✓ ✗ ? Federal ✓ ✗ ? Tribal ✓ ✗ ? State	✓ ✗ ? Federal ✓ ✗ ? Tribal ✓ ✗ ? State
	Indian	✓ ✗ ? Federal ✓ ✗ ? Tribal ✓ ✗ ? State	✓ ✗ ? Federal ✓ ✗ ? Tribal ✓ ✗ ? State

Major Crimes Act (MCA); Indian Country Crimes Act (ICCA); Assimilative Crimes Act (ACA)

✓ - yes
✗ - no
? - maybe

will not only justify the government in disregarding the stipulations of the treaty, but may demand, in the interest of the country and the Indians themselves, that it should do so. When, therefore, treaties were entered into between the United States and a tribe of Indians it was never doubted that the *power* to abrogate existed in Congress, and that in a contingency such power might be availed of from considerations of governmental policy, particularly if consistent with perfect good faith towards the Indians. ***

In view of the legislative power possessed by Congress over treaties with the Indians and Indian tribal property, we may not specially consider the contentions pressed upon our notice that the signing by the Indians of the agreement of October 6, 1892, was obtained by fraudulent misrepresentations, and concealment, that the requisite three fourths of adult male Indians had not signed, as required by the twelfth article of the treaty of 1867, and that the treaty as signed had been amended by Congress without submitting such amendments to the action of the Indians since all these matters, in any event, were solely within the domain of the legislative authority, and its action is conclusive upon the courts.

The act of June 6, 1900, which is complained of in the bill, was enacted at a time when the tribal relations between the confederated tribes of Kiowas, Comanches, and Apaches still existed, and that statute and the statutes supplementary thereto dealt with the disposition of tribal property, and purported to give an adequate consideration for the surplus lands not allotted among the Indians or reserved for their benefit. Indeed, the controversy which this case presents is concluded by the decision in *Cherokee Nation v. Hitchcock*, 187 U.S. 294 (1903), decided at this term, where it was held that full administrative power was possessed by Congress over Indian tribal property. In effect, the action of Congress now complained of was but an exercise of such power, a mere change in the form of investment of Indian tribal property, the property of those who, as we have held, were in substantial effect the wards of the government. We must presume that Congress acted in perfect good faith in the dealings with the Indians of which complaint is made, and that the legislative branch of the government exercised its best judgment in the premises. In any event, as Congress possessed full power in the matter, the judiciary cannot question or inquire into the motives which prompted the enactment of this legislation. If injury was occasioned, which we do not wish to be understood as implying, by the use made by Congress of its power, relief must be sought by an appeal to that body for redress, and not to the courts. The legislation in question was constitutional, and the demurrer to the bill was therefore rightly sustained.

***

JUSTICE HARLAN concurs in the result.

NOTES AND QUESTIONS

1. Notice that the Court does not decide whether or not the allotment agreement complied with the treaty of 1867. Why not? If the Court had reached that question, what would the answer be?

2. How does the Court describe congressional power with respect to Indian tribes? Are there any limits to that power?

3. How does the Court describe judicial power with respect to congressional actions regarding Indian tribes?

4. The Court cites the Chinese Exclusion Cases in support of its assertion that the United States may unilaterally break treaties with foreign nations, and therefore may also unilaterally abrogate treaties with Indian tribes. In fact *U.S. v. Kagama*, *Lone Wolf v. Hitchcock*, the *Chinese Exclusion Cases*, and the *Insular Cases* regarding the territories of Puerto Rico and the Philippines, were all part of a series of cases decided between 1886 and 1910 in which the Supreme Court upheld almost limitless powers over non-white, quasi-foreign peoples. In each, the Court referred to the cultural difference and supposed inferiority of these groups and the congressional need for freedom in dealing with them in order to hold that these exercises of power were not bound by the strictures of the constitution. *See* Sarah H. Cleveland, *Powers Inherent in Sovereignty: Indians, Aliens, Territories and the Nineteenth Century Origins of Plenary Power in Foreign Affairs*, 81 Tex. L. Rev. 1 (2002); Philip P. Frickey, *Domesticating Federal Indian Law*, 81 Minn. L. Rev. 31 (1996).

5. Much of *Lone Wolf v. Hitchcock* is still good law, although subsequent cases have placed some limitations on it. As you will see in *United States v. Winans*, the next case, treaties remain good law until abrogated by Congress and trump conflicting state law. In addition, although some language in *Lone Wolf* suggests that congressional actions regarding Indians are not subject to judicial review, more recent cases have held that although congressional authority is "plenary" it is not "absolute," and that the courts can subject congressional actions to judicial scrutiny to determine whether they are "tied rationally to the fulfillment of Congress' unique obligation toward the Indians." *See, e.g.*, *Delaware Tribal Bus. Comm. v. Weeks*, 430 U.S. 73, 85 (1977); *United States v. Sioux Nation*, 448 U.S. 371, 413 (1980) ("[T]he idea that relations between this Nation and the Indian tribes are a political matter, not amenable to judicial review *** has long since been discredited in taking cases, and was expressly laid to rest in [*Delaware Tribal Bus. Comm'n v. Weeks*]."). In particular, the Court has held that in taking federally recognized tribal property, the United States must provide fair compensation for the property, and that the Court should scrutinize the factual record to determine whether it has done so. *Sioux Nation*, 448 U.S. at 416–417.

6. Aftermath of *Lone Wolf*. The opinion was alternately celebrated and criticized in Congress, which had a thousand copies printed for distribution among its members. Senator Mathew Quey of Pennsylvania declared: "It is a very remarkable decision. It is the Dred Scott decision no. 2, except that in this case the victim is red instead of black. It practically inculcates the doctrine that the red man has no rights which the white man is bound to respect, and, that no treaty or contract made with him is binding. Is that not about it?" Quoted in David E. Wilkins, American Indian Sovereignty and the U.S. Supreme Court: The Masking of Justice 116 (1997).

The federal government made ample use of the decision in *Lone Wolf v. Hitchcock* as it pressed forward with allotment of reservations. The United States generally attempted to obtain tribal consent to the sale of Indian lands, but did not hesitate to act unilaterally when such consent could not be obtained. Many of these cases are discussed in chapter 5, § II, Allotment and Reservation Boundaries.

C. THE PERSISTENCE OF TREATY RIGHTS

One might think after *Lone Wolf* that Indian treaties were an anachronism of little force in preserving Indian rights. But just two years after issuing its opinion in *Lone Wolf* the Court decided a case affirming the continuing vitality of treaties, at least until abrogated by Congress. The case concerned the treaty right of the Yakima Nation to take fish in all "usual and accustomed places, in common with the citizens of the territory," on the off-reservation land ceded under the treaty. The United States, on behalf of the tribe, claimed that this right had been violated by "fish wheels" placed at the customary fishing sites. Fishing wheels are rotating mechanical scoops that take virtually all fish out of the water and also physically block access to the fishing area. Since the time the treaty had been signed, however, the territory had become a state, and state law specifically authorized the defendants to use the fishing wheels.

UNITED STATES V. WINANS

198 U.S. 371, 25 S. Ct. 662, 49 L. Ed. 1089 (1905)

JUSTICE MCKENNA delivered the opinion of the court:

This suit was brought to enjoin the respondents from obstructing certain Indians of the Yakima Nation, in the state of Washington, from exercising fishing rights and privileges on the Columbia river, in that state, claimed under the provisions of the treaty between the United States and the Indians, made in 1859.

The treaty is as follows:

> Article 1. The aforesaid confederated tribes and bands of Indians hereby cede, relinquish, and convey to the United States all their right, title, and interest in and to the lands and country occupied and claimed by them. ***
>
> Article 2. There is, however, reserved from the lands above ceded, for the use and occupation of the aforesaid confederated tribes and bands of Indians, the tract of land included within the following boundaries: ***
>
> All of which tract shall be set apart *** for the exclusive use and benefit of said confederated tribes and bands of Indians as an Indian reservation; nor shall any white man, excepting those in the employment of the Indian Department, be permitted to reside upon the said reservation without permission of the tribe and the superintendent and agent. And the said confederated tribes and bands agree to remove to and settle upon the same within one year after the ratification of this treaty. ***
>
> Article 3. ***

> The exclusive right of taking fish in all the streams where running through or bordering said reservation is further secured to said confederated tribes and bands of Indians, as also the right of taking fish at all usual and accustomed places, in common with citizens of the territory, and of erecting temporary buildings for curing them, together with the privilege of hunting, gathering roots and berries, and pasturing their horses and cattle upon open and unclaimed land. ***

The respondents or their predecessors in title claim under patents of the United States the lands bordering on the Columbia river, and under grants from the state of Washington to the shore land which, it is alleged, fronts on the patented land. They also introduced in evidence licenses from the state to maintain devices for taking fish, called fish wheels.

At the time the treaty was made the fishing places were part of the Indian country, subject to the occupancy of the Indians, with all the rights such occupancy gave. The object of the treaty was to limit the occupancy to certain lands, and to define rights outside of them.

The pivot of the controversy is the construction of the second paragraph. Respondents contend that the words "the right of taking fish at all usual and accustomed places *in common* with the citizens of the territory" confer only such rights as a white man would have under the conditions of ownership of the lands bordering on the river, and under the laws of the state, and, such being the rights conferred, the respondents further contend that they have the power to exclude the Indians from the river by reason of such ownership. ***

[In the lower court, the] contention of the respondents was sustained. In other words, it was decided that the Indians acquired no rights but what any inhabitant of the territory or state would have. Indeed, acquired no rights but such as they would have without the treaty. This is certainly an impotent outcome to negotiations and a convention which seemed to promise more, and give the word of the nation for more. And we have said we will construe a treaty with the Indians as "that unlettered people" understood it, and "as justice and reason demand, in all cases where power is exerted by the strong over those to whom they owe care and protection," and counterpoise the inequality "by the superior justice which looks only to the substance of the right, without regard to technical rules." [*Choctaw Nation v. United States*, 119 U.S. 1 (1886); *Jones v. Meehan*, 175 U.S. 1 (1899).] How the treaty in question was understood may be gathered from the circumstances.

The right to resort to the fishing places in controversy was a part of larger rights possessed by the Indians, upon the exercise of which there was not a shadow of impediment, and which were not much less necessary to the existence of the Indians than the atmosphere they breathed. New conditions came into existence, to which those rights had to be accommodated. Only a limitation of them, however, was necessary and intended, not a taking away. In other words, the treaty was not a grant of rights to the Indians, but a grant of rights from them—a reservation of those not granted. And the form of the instrument and its language was adapted to that purpose. Reservations were not of particular parcels of land, and could not be expressed in deeds, as dealings between private individuals. The reservations were in large areas of territory, and the negotiations were with the tribe. They reserved rights, however, to every individual Indian, as though named therein. They imposed a servitude upon every piece of land as though described therein. There was an exclusive right of fishing reserved within certain boundaries. There was a right outside of those boundaries reserved "in common with citizens of the territory." As a mere right, it was not exclusive in the Indians. Citizens might share it, but the Indians were secured in its enjoyment by a special provision of means for its exercise. They were given "the right of taking fish at all usual and accustomed places," and the right "of erecting temporary buildings for curing them." The contingency of the future ownership of the lands, therefore, was foreseen and provided for; in other words, the Indians were given a right in the land, the right of crossing it to the river, the right to occupy it to the extent and for the purpose mentioned. No other conclusion would give effect to the treaty. And the right was intended to be continuing against the United States and its grantees as well as against the state and its grantees.

The respondents urge an argument based upon the different capacities of white men and Indians to devise and make use of instrumentalities to enjoy the common right. Counsel say: "The fishing right was in common, and aside from the right of the state to license fish wheels, the wheel fishing is one of the civilized man's methods, as legitimate as the substitution of the modern combined harvester for the ancient sickle and flail." But the result does not follow that the Indians may be absolutely excluded. It needs no argument to show that the superiority of a combined harvester over the ancient sickle neither increased nor decreased rights to the use of land held in common. In the actual taking of fish white men may not be confined to a spear or crude net, but it does not follow that they may construct and use a device which gives them exclusive possession of the fishing places, as it is admitted a fish wheel does. Besides, the fish wheel is not relied on alone. Its monopoly is made complete by a license from the state. The argument based on the inferiority of the Indians is peculiar. If the Indians had not been inferior in capacity and power, what the treaty would have been, or that there would have been any treaty, would be hard to guess.

The construction of the treaty disposes of certain subsidiary contentions of respondents. The Land Department could grant no exemptions from its provisions. It makes no difference, therefore, that the patents issued by the Department are absolute in form. They are subject to the treaty as to the other laws of the land.

It is further contended that the rights conferred upon the Indians are subordinate to the powers acquired by the state upon its admission into the Union. In other words, it is contended that the state acquired by its admission into the Union "upon an equal footing with the original states," the power to grant rights in or to dispose of the shore lands upon navigable streams, and such power is subject only to the paramount authority of Congress with regard to public navigation and commerce. The United States, therefore, it is contended, could neither grant nor retain rights in the shore or to the lands under water.

The elements of this contention and the answer to it are expressed in *Shively v. Bowlby*, 152 U.S. 1 (1894). *** The power and rights of the states in and over shore lands were carefully defined, but the power of the United States, while it held the country as a territory, to create rights which would be binding on the states, was also announced, opposing the *dicta* scattered through the cases, which seemed to assert a contrary view. ***

The extinguishment of the Indian title, opening the land for settlement, and preparing the way for future states, were appropriate to the objects for which the United States held the territory. And surely it was within the competency of the nation to secure to the Indians such a remnant of the great rights they possessed as "taking fish at all usual and accustomed places." Nor does it restrain the state unreasonably, if at all, in the regulation of the right. It only fixes in the land such easements as enable the right to be exercised.

The license from the state, which respondents plead, to maintain a fishing wheel, gives no power to them to exclude the Indians, nor was it intended to give such power. It was the permission of the state to use a particular device. What rights the Indians had were not determined or limited. This was a matter for judicial determination regarding the rights of the Indians and rights of the respondents. *** *Decree reversed*, and the case remanded for further proceedings in accordance with this opinion.

JUSTICE WHITE dissents.

NOTES AND QUESTIONS

1. What does *Winans* hold about the effect of state law on Indian treaty rights?

2. How could the Court within two years reach the result in *Lone Wolf* and the result in *Winans*? Are the decisions inconsistent?

3. What does the case hold about fishing rights off-reservation? How are these rights affected by state law? How are they affected by private property rights?

4. *Winans* is one of many cases in continuing disputes about the treaty fishing rights of tribes in Washington State. These cases are discussed further in Chapter 9, Natural Resources, Hunting, Fishing and Gathering. In these cases, the courts have held that that the treaties guarantee not only the right to fish, but a fair share of the fish harvest, or the right "not only to cast their nets, but to not bring them up empty." In 2018, the Supreme Court affirmed by an equally divided Court a decision holding that Washington State violated tribal treaty rights by constructing and operating culverts that block access by salmon to habitat needed for spawning and rearing, and from getting out to sea when they are young (smolts). *United States v. Washington*, 853 F.3d 946 (9th Cir. 2017), *affirmed by an equally divided court*, 138 S. Ct. 1832 (2018).

5. Consider the sentence "Nor does [the treaty] restrain the state unreasonably, if at all, in the regulation of the right." Is that part of the Court's holding? State power to regulate treaty hunting and fishing rights is covered in chapter 9.

6. Water Rights. In 1908, in a further victory for reserved treaty rights, the Court also held that treaty territory included not only a reservation of land, but also sufficient water to fulfill the purposes of the reservation, prohibiting off-reservation land owners from diverting water from a river that formed the border of the reservation. *Winters v. United States*, 207 U.S. 564 (1908). For discussion of the rules emerging from disputes over reserved water rights, see Chapter 10.

7. In *Herrerra v. Wyoming*, 139 S. Ct. 1686, 1698 (2019), the Supreme Court held that the "Wyoming Statehood Act does not show that Congress

intended to end the 1868 Treaty hunting right [to hunt on the unoccupied lands of the United States so long as game may be found thereon]." The Opinion by Justce Sotomayor made it clear that statehood by itself has no effect on Indian treaty rights: "To avoid any future confusion, we make clear today that [*Ward v.*] *Race Horse* [163 U.S. 504 (1896)] is repudiated to the extent it held that treaty rights can be impliedly extinguished at statehood." *Id.* at 1697. The case is considered more fully in Ch 10. Hunting and Fishing Rights.

D. INDIAN BOARDING SCHOOLS

Federal Indian boarding schools were an important element of the assimilation policy. Although the United States had long been involved in Indian education, its role had been largely limited to providing funding and personnel for educational efforts by missionary societies and tribes themselves. In the 1870s, however, the United States began directly administering schools for Indian children.

Army officer Richard H. Pratt spearheaded the boarding school movement. Pratt had participated in the wars with the Southern plains tribes, and began his educational program with the Kiowa soldiers imprisoned at Fort Marion after the Red River War of 1874. After trying to establish an Indian program at the Hampton Institute for African American students, Pratt won support from the Department of the Interior to establish the Carlisle Indian School at an abandoned military barracks in Pennsylvania. The school became a model for Indian education. Its purpose was to separate children from their families and tribes in order to fully inculcate them with American culture, language and religion. Pratt famously described the purpose of the schools as to "[k]ill the Indian in him to save the man." In 1892, he wrote that the Cherokee, Choctaw, Creek, Chickasaw and Seminole tribes

> have had tribal schools until it is asserted that they are civilized; yet they have no notion of joining us and becoming a part of the United States. Their whole disposition is to prey upon and hatch up claims against the government *** We make our greatest mistake in feeding our civilization to the Indians instead of feeding the Indians to our civilization. *** It is a great mistake to think that the Indian is born an inevitable savage. He is born a blank, like the rest of us. Left in the surroundings of savagery, he grows to possess a savage language, superstition and life. We, left in the surroundings of civilization, grow to possess a civilized language, life, and purpose. *** Carlisle has always planted treason to the tribe and loyalty to the nation at large. It has preached against colonizing Indians, and in favor of individualizing them.

Reprinted in Americanizing the American Indians: Writings by the "Friends of the Indian" 1880–1900 at 263, 268–69 (Francis Paul Prucha ed. 1973).

Physical transformation was an important part of the boarding school process. The first thing the schools did was cut their pupils' hair and exchange their tribal clothes for Anglo clothes. They took "before and after" pictures of their students to illustrate the success of the schools to their Eastern supporters. The below pictures below show a student upon his arrival at Carlisle and after three years there.

Navajo student Tom Torlino upon arriving at Carlisle and after three years there. Photographs courtesy of Yale Collection of Western Americana, Beinecke Rare Book and Manuscript Library.

Zitkala–Sa, a Dakota woman from the Yankton Sioux Reservation, later described her first morning at Carlisle:

> *** The constant clash of harsh noises, with an undercurrent of many voices murmuring an unknown tongue, made a bedlam within which I was securely tied. And though my spirit tore itself in struggling for its lost freedom, all was useless.
>
> *** We were placed in a line of girls who were marching into the dining room. These were Indian girls, in stiff shoes and closely clinging dresses. The small girls wore sleeved aprons and shingled hair. As I walked noiselessly in my soft moccasins, I felt like sinking to the floor, for my blanket had been stripped from my shoulders. I looked hard at the Indian girls, who seemed not to care that they were even more immodestly dressed than I, in their tightly fitting clothes. ***
>
> Late in the morning, my friend Judewin gave me a terrible warning. Judewin knew a few words of English, and she had overheard the paleface woman talk about cutting our long, heavy hair. Our mothers had taught us that only unskilled warriors who were captured had their hair shingled by the enemy. Among our people, short hair was worn by mourners, and shingled hair by cowards! ***
>
> I watched my chance, and when no one noticed I disappeared. *** On my hands and knees I crawled under the bed, and cuddled myself in the dark corner. *** I remember being dragged out, though I resisted by kicking and scratching wildly. In spite of myself, I was carried downstairs and tied fast in a chair.
>
> I cried aloud, shaking my head all the while until I felt the cold blades of the scissors against my neck, and heard them gnaw off one of my thick braids. Then I lost my spirit. Since the day I was taken from my mother I had suffered extreme indignities. People had stared at me. I had been tossed about in the air like a wooden puppet. And now my long hair was shingled like a coward's! In my anguish I moaned for my mother, but no

> one came to comfort me. Not a soul reasoned quietly with me, as my own mother used to do; for now I was only one of many little animals driven by a herder.

Zitkala–Sa, The School Days of an Indian Girl (1900). Zitkala–Sa, also known as Gertrude Bonnin, went on to graduate from Earlham College, became a well-known writer and activist, and was one of the founders of the Society for American Indians in 1911. Although she used her western education to advocate for her people, she felt that it divided her from her family and left her a figure in between, fully at home neither in Indian nor white worlds. *Id.*

The boarding schools were often places of suffering. Children were thrust into a foreign environment in which their cultures and languages were actively repressed. The schools emphasized manual labor, and with insufficient federal funding they relied on students' work to grow sufficient food and maintain school facilities. The crowding together of so many children, sometimes in unsanitary conditions, led to the spread of disease. Some children who were sent to the schools never returned, dying from tuberculosis or other contagious illnesses. Children that did return, like Zitkala–Sa, found themselves everywhere out of place, no longer fully at home in their old lives, but blocked by racism and prejudice from fully joining the non-Indian world. The cycles of mistreatment and abuse of Indian children continued, leaving a damaging legacy for generations. Today, the Boarding School Healing movement, composed of boarding school survivors and organizations that support them, is addressing the deep harm to tribal people through a variety of strategies, including seeking an apology from the United States government. See The National Native American Boarding School Healing Coalition, www.boardingschoolhealing.org.

But the boarding schools also gave their students the tools and support to participate in the non-Indian world as never before. Encouraged by white reformers who mourned the anticipated disappearance of Indian culture but were eager to celebrate successful Indian assimilation, Indian people took center stage in many arenas of American culture. As Philip Deloria has recounted, in 1910, tribal members played on both teams in the World Series, wrote and soloed in opera premiers in Carnegie Hall, and ran film studios in Hollywood. Philip J. Deloria, Indians in Unexpected Places (2006). That same generation of boarding school students began to advocate and write about Indian people from an Indian perspective. And when they turned their attention back to their tribes, this generation laid the path toward a policy where forced boarding schools would be no more. Today, the Bureau of Indian Education still funds 183 schools, including several off-reservation boarding schools and dormitories, but Indian tribes and tribal organizations administer more than two-thirds of these schools.

E. AMERICAN INDIAN CITIZENSHIP

In the pre-Civil War period, the question of American citizenship usually turned on state law, and Indians were generally considered to be members of separate political communities rather than members of the states or of the United States. The Fourteenth Amendment, adopted in the aftermath of the Civil War, provides that "all persons born or naturalized in the United States, and subject to the jurisdiction thereof, are citizens of the United States and of the State wherein they reside." U.S. Const., amend. XIV, § 1. Nonetheless, in

Elk v. Wilkins, 112 U.S. 94 (1884), the Court held that Indians born in a tribal setting did not receive citizenship through the Fourteenth Amendment because they were born under tribal, rather than U.S., authority.

Congress used its naturalization authority to confer citizenship upon particular Indians through treaties and special statutes. In particular, the General Allotment Act conferred citizenship upon Indian allottees. Eventually, in 1924, Congress unilaterally conferred citizenship upon all Indians who still lacked that status. *See* 8 U.S.C. § 1401(b). Under the citizenship clause of the Fourteenth Amendment, this statute also had the effect of making all such Indians citizens of the state in which they resided.

U.S. citizenship was not uniformly welcomed by Indian people. The United States had long looked at citizenship as a reward for assimilation and symbol of the erasure of political separateness of Indian people. This is starkly illustrated by the citizenship ceremony for Indians who had accepted their allotments:

> After the American Indian male renounced allegiance to his tribe, shot his last arrow, and accepted the plow, the federal official said: "This act means that you have chosen to live the life of the white man—and the white man lives by work. From the earth we must all get our living. *** Only by work do we gain a right to the land *** "
>
> After the American Indian female renounced allegiance to her tribe, accepted the work bag and purse, the federal official said: "This means you have chosen the life of the white woman—and the white woman loves her home. The family and home are the foundation of our civilization."

Office of the Secretary, Dep't of the Interior, Doc. 89.94.04b, Attorneys and Agents, Competent Indians 5–6 (Central Classified File 1936–1937), quoted in Gloria Valencia–Weber, *Racial Equality: Old and New Strains and American Indians*, 80 Notre Dame L. Rev. 333, 333 (2004). Some tribes and their members resented this involuntary inclusion in the American polity. The Grand Council of the Iroquois Confederacy, for example, "sent letters to the president and Congress of the United States respectfully declining United States citizenship, rejecting dual citizenship, and stating that the act was written and passed without their knowledge or consent." Robert B. Porter, *The Demise of Ohnegeweh and the Rise of the Native Americans: Redressing the Genocidal Act of Forcing Citizenship on Native American Peoples*, 15 Harv. Blackletter J. 107, 127 (1999). But as Indian people were increasingly physically and economically incorporated into non-Indian society, discrimination in the right to vote, go to school, and otherwise participate in that society became more and more detrimental, and citizenship was an important step in removing legal justifications for that treatment. *See generally* Jeanette Wolfley, *Jim Crow, Indian Style: The Disenfranchisement of Native Americans*, 16 Am. Ind. L. Rev. 167 (1990).

III. THE INDIAN NEW DEAL: 1928–1947

After over a century of federal policies designed to destroy Indian tribes and assimilate Indian people, the Indian New Deal Era represented something truly new in Indian policy. For the first time, the federal government would encourage development of tribal governments, economies, and cultures. The Indian Reorganization Act of 1934, also called the Wheeler–Howard Act, was the centerpiece of this policy. As Senator Wheeler declared, the Act sought "to get away from the bureaucratic control of the Indian Department, and *** give the Indians the control over their own affairs." 78 Cong. Rec. 11125 (1934). While both the Act and its implementation can be criticized for failing to fulfill these goals, the era remains a watershed in federal Indian policy.

Many factors led to this transformation. First, efforts to end Indian adherence to their tribal identities simply had not worked. Although traditional governments were weakened and tribal territories broken up, many Indian people continued to resist full incorporation into the American mainstream. The graduates of Carlisle and Hampton, moreover, used their education to give the hardship experienced by Indian people and the desire to maintain Indian identity a public voice. The Society of American Indians, for example, the first modern supratribal Indian organization, was founded in 1911. In addition, the successful fight against the 1922 Bursum Bill, which would have authorized the taking of Pueblo lands and was characterized by D.H. Lawrence as playing "the Wild West scalping trick a little too brazenly," both galvanized non-Indian reform organizations and resulted in the revitalization of the All Pueblo Council, a coalition of Pueblo villages created in the 1600s to resist Spanish domination.

At the same time, Congress began to resent the explosion in federal expenditures as the Bureau of Indian Affairs took ever greater control over reservation life. Non–Indian pressure for allotment also declined because prices for farmland fell in the 1920s and the valuable Indian lands had already largely been allotted. Public reformers and academics, moreover, began to turn from the aggressive individualism of the Gilded Age toward a socially progressive and culturally pluralist philosophy. The rise of the great corporations and the resulting plight of American workers undermined blind faith in laissez faire capitalism as a great engine of social progress. All of these factors contributed to the pressure for reform leading to the Indian Reorganization Act of 1934.

To respond to the pressure, the government commissioned the Institute for Government Research (which would soon be renamed the Brookings Institution) to write a report on the status of American Indians. In 1928, after two years of research into every aspect of Indian life, the Institute published *The Problem of Indian Administration*, which has been dubbed "The Meriam Report," after its lead author, Lewis Meriam. The report was a devastating critique of federal Indian policy and allotment: "An overwhelming majority of Indians," the report began, "are poor, even extremely poor. *** The number of Indians who are supporting themselves through their own efforts, according to what a white man would regard as the minimum standard of health and decency, is extremely small. *** In justice to the Indians it should be said that many of them are living on lands from which a trained and experienced white man could scarcely wrest a reasonable living. *** "

The blame for this condition was laid squarely at the door of the United States. "Several past policies adopted by the government in dealing with the Indians have been of a type which, if long continued, would tend to pauperize any race. *** When the government adopted the policy of individual ownership of the land on the reservations, the expectation was that the Indians would become farmers. Part of the plan was to instruct and aid them in agriculture, but this vital part was not pressed with vigor and intelligence. It almost seems as if the government assumed that some magic in individual ownership of property would in itself prove an educational civilizing factor, but unfortunately this policy has for the most part operated in the opposite direction."

Nor were other programs free from criticism. "The work of the government directed toward the education and advancement of the Indian himself, as distinguished from the control and conservation of his property, is largely ineffective." Health, housing, economic and community development programs were all deficient. As to education, "[t]he survey staff finds itself obliged to say frankly and unequivocally that the provisions for the care of the Indian children in boarding schools are grossly inadequate."

The authors, for the first time in a major government report, suggested that assimilation should not be the only goal of federal policy, and that Indian policy should be tailored to Indian desires:

> The object of work with or for the Indians is to fit them either to merge into the social and economic life of the prevailing civilization as developed by the whites or to live in the presence of that civilization at least in accordance with a minimum standard of health and decency. ***
>
> Some Indians, proud of their race and devoted to their culture and mode of life, have no desire to be as the white man is. *** In this desire they are supported by intelligent, liberal whites who find real merit in their *** culture. Some of these whites would even go so far, metaphorically speaking, as to enclose these Indians in a glass case to preserve them as museum specimens for future generations to study and enjoy. With this view as a whole, if not in its extremities, the survey staff has great sympathy. It would not recommend the disastrous attempt to force individual Indians or groups of Indians to be what they do not want to be, to break their pride in themselves and their Indian race, or to deprive them of their Indian culture. ***
>
> The fact remains, however, that the hand of the clock cannot be turned backward. The Indians are face to face with the predominating civilization of the whites. This advancing tide of white civilization has as a rule largely destroyed the economic foundation upon which the Indian culture rested. This economic foundation cannot be restored as it was. The Indians cannot be set apart away from contacts with the whites. The glass case policy is impracticable. ***
>
> The position taken, therefore, is that the work with and for the Indians must give consideration to the desires of the individual Indians. He who wishes to merge into the social and economic life of the prevailing civilization of this county should be given all practicable aid and advice in making the necessary adjustments. He who wants to remain an Indian and live according to his old culture should be aided in doing so.

The Problem of Indian Administration at 86–88 (1928).

A. INDIAN NEW DEAL POLICIES AND LEGISLATION

When the Roosevelt Administration assumed the White House, politics and policy united to create a sea change in federal Indian policy. John Collier, a leader in the fight to preserve Pueblo Lands, was appointed Commissioner of Indian Affairs in 1933. The national New Deal was joined by the Indian New Deal. "For the first time, assimilation was not the goal of federal Indian services. Rather, tribal culture and organization were to be preserved while providing Indians with the tools to achieve economically and socially." Cohen's Handbook of Federal Indian Law 1379 (2012).

The centerpiece of the Indian New Deal was the Indian Reorganization Act of 1934 (IRA). 48 Stat. 984 (1934). The IRA was developed in consultation with Indian tribes, and some of its elements, including the power to incorporate, were suggested by tribes themselves. The legislation terminated allotment and sought to facilitate restoration of some Indian lands. It sought to provide assistance to tribal governments and increase Indian presence within the Department of Indian Services. Perhaps most notably, tribal approval was required before any of its provisions could be imposed on the tribe. "For the first time in more than half a century, Native Americans were back in the decision-making process." Stephen Cornell, The Return of the Native: American Indian Political Resurgence 92 (1988).

The key provisions of the **Indian Reorganization Act** were as follows:

Sec 1. After the date of the Act, no land of any Indian reservation could be allotted in severalty.

Sec. 2. The existing periods of trust or restrictions placed upon any Indian lands would continue indefinitely.

Sec. 3. The Secretary of the Interior could restore any surplus lands not yet disposed of to tribal ownership.

Sec. 4. No further sale, devise, gift, exchange, or other transfer of tribal lands would be approved, with the exception of exchanges of tribal for non-tribal lands to encourage consolidation of Indian territories.

Sec. 5. The Secretary of the Interior was authorized to acquire interests in lands for the benefit of tribes and Indians, and these lands would be held in trust for the beneficiaries and exempt from state and local taxation.

Sec. 10. A revolving fund was created to make loans to tribal corporations in order to promote the economic development of tribes and their members.

Sec. 12. The Indian Office was directed to give preference to qualified Indians in appointments to any vacancies in the office.

Sec. 16. Any Indian tribe would have the right to organize for its common welfare and adopt a tribal constitution and by-laws that would become effective when ratified by a majority vote of the adult members of the tribe or the adult Indians residing on the reservation.

Sec. 17. Upon petition of a third of the adult members of the tribe and ratification by a majority vote of the adult Indians living on the reservation, the Secretary of the Interior would issue a certificate of incorporation to the tribe. The resulting Section 17 corporation would have the power to manage and dispose of tribal property, and all other powers necessary to conduct corporate business, except the power to sell, mortgage, or, lease tribal lands for a period exceeding ten years.

> Sec. 18. The Act would not apply to any reservation wherein a majority of the adult Indians, voting at a special election called by the Secretary of the Interior, voted against its application.

Ultimately 258 elections were held, with 181 tribes, about 70% of the total, voting to accept the act, and 77 tribes, about 30%, rejecting it.† Together the number of Indians that chose to come under the Act included 60% of the total 216,115 voting. *See* Theodore H. Haas, Ten Years of Tribal Government Under the Indian Reorganization Act (1947). One of the largest tribes, the Navajo Nation, voted to reject the Act, largely in reaction to the despised stock reduction policy Collier had imposed on the tribe. The Six Nations of the Iroquois Confederacy also rejected the Act as part of their historic battle to avoid federal or state interference with their affairs.

Scholars have argued that despite radical changes under the Indian New Deal,

> the basic assumption of Indian policy was little changed. Neither the IRA nor the Indian New Deal challenged the fundamental belief that Indians would, and probably should, be assimilated ultimately by the society around them. They looked rather for means of easing the process of change and giving Native Americans some measure of control over it. ***
>
> Native culture was no longer to be discouraged—indeed, it was to be given support, and interference in internal tribal affairs was at least somewhat reduced—but the thrust of the policy was acculturational. In the implementation of the IRA, tribes were asked to choose between an alien constitutional form of government and the uncertainties of the pre-IRA period. The institutions provided for through the IRA were Euro-American in origin, applied more or less uniformly to a hugely varied mosaic of cultures and in widely divergent local situations. The form of political organization the tribes were encouraged to adopt, with its representative government, electoral districts, tribal officers, and so forth, was derived from political and legal traditions very different from theirs. As Edward Spicer observes, it was a pattern "in the image of the conquerors' nation[.]"

Stephen Cornell, The Return of the Native: American Indian Political Resurgence 93–94 (1988).

The New Deal Era saw other legislative and policy shifts. In order to prevent discrimination in the provision of services to Indians, the Johnson O'Malley Act, 48 Stat. 596 (1934), authorized the federal government to contract with states and local governments to provide education and other governmental services. The Indian Arts and Crafts Act of 1935, 49 Stat. 891, created measures to encourage Indian arts and crafts as a means of economic development. The Indian Mineral Leasing Act of 1938, 25 U.S.C. §§ 396a–398, 52 Stat. 347, sought to facilitate tribal control over leases of mineral-producing lands and removed the authorization for state taxation of such leases.

---

†. Although the Act did not apply to Alaska Native villages or the Oklahoma tribes, the 1936 Oklahoma Indian Welfare Act, 25 U.S.C. § 5201, et seq., 49 Stat. 1967, and Alaska Reorganization Act, 49 Stat. 1250, applied most of its terms to these peoples. The Act also applied to 14 tribes that did not hold elections on whether or not to accept it.

The New Deal administration began to close the boarding schools and create community day schools in their place. Many Indian children were also enrolled in local public schools. At the same time, the rules for Courts of Indian Offenses were repealed and reissued; tribes were encouraged to develop their own tribal codes and Indian Service officers were "prohibited from controlling, obstructing, or interfering with the functions of the Indian courts." Law and Order Regulations, Nov. 27, 1935.

The Indian Claims Commission Act of 1946 (ICCA) created a special tribunal and process for bringing monetary claims against the United States for takings of land, failures to provide promised treaty funds, other violations of law and "claims based upon fair and honorable dealings that are not recognized by any existing rule of law or equity." 60 Stat. 1049 (Aug. 13, 1946). The ICCA is often regarded as a product of the Termination Era in Indian policy, designed to settle all accounts with Indian tribes in preparation for absolution of responsibility for Indian affairs. But the Act was forwarded by the architects of the New Deal, and as originally conceived (if not implemented) the ICCA was a means to compensate tribes for past injustices and correct a glaring inequality in American law: tribal treaty claims were specifically excluded from the law waiving federal sovereign immunity for claims against the United States. (See Ch.4, Sec. II for more about suits against the United States.) Tribes, therefore, could not sue for damages from failures to abide by its agreements unless Congress passed a law permitting the individual tribe to sue. As the Meriam Report had noted, "the simple canons of justice and morality demand that no Indian tribe should be denied an opportunity to present for adjustment before an appropriate tribunal the rights which the tribe claims under recognized principles of law and government." The Institute for Government Research, The Problem of Indian Administration 805 (1928). For a comprehensive study of the implementation of the Act, *see* Nell Jessup Newton, *Indian Claims in the Courts of the Conqueror*, 41 Am. U. L. Rev. 753 (1992).

One of the most lasting products of the Indian New Deal was Felix S. Cohen's Handbook of Federal Indian Law, published by the Department of the Interior in 1941. The book began as a joint project of the Department of Justice and the Department of the Interior under the supervision of Felix S. Cohen. Cohen, a lawyer and philosopher by training, was one of the prominent young members of the new legal realist school, and had coined the phrase "transcendental nonsense" to describe a formalist jurisprudence that approached abstract principles as though they were divorced from their impact on society. *See* Felix S. Cohen, *Transcendental Nonsense and the Functional Approach*, 35 Colum. L. Rev. 809 (1935). As Assistant Solicitor for the Department of the Interior, Cohen was one of the principal legal architects of the Indian New Deal. His task in writing the Handbook was to supervise the consolidation of forty-seven surveys of federal Indian law into a single compendium to guide federal work in Indian affairs.

The Justice Department had hoped for a book that would aid its lawyers in defending land cases brought by Indian tribes. When Justice realized that the resulting volume would be of equal assistance to tribes themselves, it sought to stop the project, firing Cohen as supervisor of Justice Department staff, refusing to provide copies of materials for the Handbook team, and blocking their after-hours access to department archives. The Department of the Interior, however, continued to support the project, and the Handbook was published in 1941 by Interior alone. *See* Dalia Tsuk, Architect of Justice: Felix S. Cohen and the Founding of American Legal Pluralism (2007).

The Handbook was the first attempt to, as Justice Felix Frankfurter later wrote, draw "meaning and reason out of the vast hodge-podge of treaties, statutes, judicial and administrative rulings, and unrecorded practice in which the intricacies and perplexities, the confusions and injustices of the law governing Indians lay concealed." Felix Frankfurter, *Foreword to Symposium: Felix S. Cohen*, 9 Rutgers L. Rev. 355, 356 (1954). The introduction to the 2012 edition records its impact: "Felix Cohen's *Handbook* brought focus and coherence to this confusing welter of sources and, in effect, created the field of federal Indian law." Board of Editors, *Foreword*, in Cohen's Handbook of Federal Indian Law vii (2012).

At the core of the Handbook is its description of tribal power and its relationship to federal power:

> Perhaps the most basic principle of all Indian law, supported by a host of decisions hereinafter analyzed, is the principle that *those powers which are lawfully vested in an Indian tribe are not, in general, delegated powers granted by express acts of Congress, but rather inherent powers of a limited sovereignty which has never been extinguished.* Each Indian tribe begins its relationship with the Federal Government as a sovereign power, recognized as such in treaty and legislation. The powers of sovereignty have been limited from time to time by special treaties and laws designed to take from the Indian tribes control of matters which, in the judgment of Congress, these tribes could no longer be safely permitted to handle. The statutes of Congress, then, must be examined to determine the limitations of tribal sovereignty rather than to determine its sources or its positive content. What is not expressly limited remains within the domain of tribal sovereignty.
>
> ***
>
> The whole course of judicial decision on the nature of Indian tribal powers is marked by adherence to three fundamental principles: (1) An Indian tribe possesses, in the first instance, all the powers of any sovereign state. (2) Conquest renders the tribe subject to the legislative power of the United States and, in substance, terminates the external powers of sovereignty of the tribe, e.g., its power to enter into treaties with foreign nations, but does not by itself affect the internal sovereignty of the tribe, i.e., its powers of local self-government. (3) These powers are subject to qualification by treaties and by express legislation by Congress, but save as thus expressly qualified, full powers of internal sovereignty are vested in the Indian tribes and in their duly constituted organs of government.

Felix S. Cohen, Handbook of Federal Indian Law 122–123 (1941) (emphasis in original).

NOTES AND QUESTIONS

1. What did tribes get by adopting the Indian Reorganization Act? The federal government stopped allotment and applied the other provisions of the Act regarding tribal land to all tribes. The Handbook's formulation of the

nature and limitation on tribal powers was largely drawn from the *Solicitor's Opinion on the Powers of Indian Tribes*, 55 Interior Dec. 14 (Oct. 25, 1934). The Solicitor of the Department of the Interior had been asked to opine on what were the "powers vested in any Indian tribe or tribal council by existing law," to which the IRA added. *See* 48 Stat. 984 § 16. After an encyclopedic review of the case law, the opinion concluded that those powers included all powers of self-government that had never been terminated by law or waived by treaty. 55 Interior Dec. 14, 42. Thus adoption of the Indian Reorganization Act was not necessary to exercise tribal powers of self-government, but simply to add any of the enumerated powers which had been expressly removed, and to take advantage of the monetary and technical assistance provided by the Act. Subsequent decisions have confirmed this. *See Kerr–McGee Corp. v. Navajo Tribe of Indians*, 471 U.S. 195, 198–199 (1985) (holding that the fact that Navajo Nation had not organized or enacted constitution under IRA did not limit tribal power to levy taxes on nonmembers); *Harjo v. Kleppe*, 420 F. Supp. 1110, 1136 n.87 (D.D.C. 1976) (stating that failure of Creek Nation to organize under the Oklahoma Indian Welfare Act did not lessen tribal powers of government).

2. Felix Cohen's formulation has been criticized by contemporary scholars, who write that by "resurrecting the fiction of conquest, it dispels any lingering hopes that congressional intervention in tribes' domestic affairs could be limited by treaties." Russel Barsh & James Youngblood Henderson, The Road: Indian Tribes and Political Liberty 112 (1980). Do you see the basis for their criticism in the above excerpt? Why might Cohen not have written that Congress was prevented from acting in the face of an inconsistent treaty?

3. Think about the Supreme Court decisions you have read so far in this course. How do they support Cohen's description of tribal and federal power?

B. TRIBAL CONSTITUTIONS ADOPTED UNDER THE IRA

One hundred and five tribes chose to adopt constitutions under Section 16 of the IRA. These constitutions have been criticized as "boilerplate" constitutions with little individual tailoring to particular tribal circumstances. *See* Stephen Cornell & Joseph P. Kalt, *Where Does Economic Development Really Come From? Constitutional Rule Among the Contemporary Sioux and Apache*, 33 Econ. Inquiry 402, 423–24 (1995). Below is one of these constitutions, the 1936 constitution adopted by the Hopi Tribe. Although otherwise similar to many IRA constitutions, the constitution acknowledges the unique village government of the Hopi people.

CONSTITUTION AND BY–LAWS OF THE HOPI TRIBE

(Approved Dec. 1936)

Preamble. This Constitution, to be known as the Constitution and By-laws of the Hopi Tribe, is adopted by the self-governing Hopi and Tewa villages of Arizona to provide a way of working together for peace and agreement between the villages, and of preserving the good things of Hopi life, and to provide a way of organizing to deal with modern problems, with the United States government and with the outside world generally.

Art. I—Jurisdiction. The authority of the Tribe under this Constitution shall cover the Hopi villages and such land as shall be determined by the Hopi Tribal Council in agreement with the United States Government and the Navajo Tribe, and such lands as may be added thereto in the future. ***

Art. II—Membership.

Sec. 1. Membership in the Hopi Tribe shall be as follows:

(a) All persons whose names appear on the census roll of the Hopi Tribe as of January 1st, 1936. ***

(b) All children born after January 1, 1936, whose father and mother are both members of the Hopi Tribe.

(c) All children born after January 1, 1936, whose mother is a member of the Tribe and whose father is a member of some other tribe.

(d) All persons adopted into the Tribe as provided in Section 2.

Sec. 2. Non-members of one-fourth degree of Indian blood, or more, who are married to members of the Hopi Tribe, and adult persons of one-fourth degree of Indian blood or more whose fathers are members of the Hopi Tribe, may be adopted in the following manner: Such person may apply to the Kikmongwi of the village to which he is to belong, for acceptance. According to the way of doing established in that Village, the Kikmongwi may accept him, and shall tell the Tribal Council. The Council may then by a majority vote have that person's name put on the roll of the Tribe, but before he is enrolled he must officially give up membership in any other tribe.

Sec. 3. Resident members shall be those who actually live in the Hopi jurisdiction and who have been living therein for not less than six months. Only resident members of twenty-one years of age or over shall be qualified to vote in any election or referendum. Any adult member who is away from the jurisdiction for six months continuously, shall cease to be a resident member until he has again lived in the jurisdiction for the necessary time.

Art III—Organization

Sec. 1. The Hopi Tribe is a union of self-governing villages sharing common interests and working for the common welfare of all. It consists of the following recognized villages: First Mesa (consolidated villages of Walpi, Shitchumovi, and Tewa), Mishongnovi, Sipaulavi, Shungopavi, Oraibi, Kyakotsmovi, Bakabi, Hotevilla, Moenkopi.

Sec. 2. The following powers which the Tribe now has under existing law or which have been given by the Act of June 18, 1934, (48 Stat. 984) and acts amendatory thereof or supplemental thereto, are reserved to the individual villages:

(a) To appoint guardians for orphan children and incompetent members.

(b) To adjust family disputes and regulate family relations of members of the villages.

(c) To regulate the inheritance of property of the members of the villages.

(d) To assign farming land, subject to the provisions of Article VII.

Sec. 3. Each village shall decide for itself how it shall be organized. ***

Art. IV—The Tribal Council

Sec. 1. The Hopi Tribal Council shall consist of representatives from the various villages. The number of representatives from each village shall be determined according to its populations as follows ***.

Sec. 3. Each representative must be a member of the village which he represents. He must be twenty-five years or more of age, and must have lived in the Hopi jurisdiction for not less than two years before taking office, and must be able to speak the Hopi language fluently. ***

Sec. 7. The Tribal Council shall choose from its own members a Chairman and Vice–Chairman, and from the Council or from other members of the Tribe, a Secretary, Treasurer, Sergeant-at-Arms, and interpreters, and such other officers and committees as it may think necessary ***.

Art. VI—Powers of the Tribal Council

Sec. 1. The Hopi Tribal Council shall have the following powers which the Tribe now has under existing law or which have been given to the Tribe by the Act of June 18, 1934. The Tribal Council shall exercise these powers subject to the terms of this Constitution and to the Constitution and Statutes of the United States.

(a) To represent and speak for the Hopi Tribe in all matters for the welfare of the Tribe, and to negotiate with the Federal, State, and local governments, and with the councils or governments of other tribes.

(b) To employ lawyers, the choice of lawyers and fixing of fees to be subject to the approval of the Secretary of the Interior.

(c) To prevent the sale, disposition, lease or encumbrance of tribal lands, or other tribal property.

(d) To advise with the Secretary of the Interior and other governmental agencies upon all appropriation estimates or Federal projects for the benefit of the Tribe, before the submission of such estimates to the Bureau of the Budget or to Congress.

(e) To raise and take care of a tribal council fund by accepting grants or gifts from any person, State, or the United States Government, or by charging persons doing business within the Reservation reasonable license fees, subject to the approval of the Secretary of the Interior. ***

(g) To make ordinances, subject to the approval of the Secretary of the Interior, to protect the peace and welfare of the Tribe, and to set up courts for the settlement of claims and disputes, and for the trial and punishment of Indians within the jurisdiction charged with offenses against such ordinances. ***

(i) To provide by ordinance, subject to the approval of the Secretary of the Interior, for removal or exclusion from the jurisdiction of any non-members whose presence may be harmful to the members of the Tribe. ***

(k) To protect the arts, crafts, traditions, and ceremonies of the Hopi Indians. ***

Sec. 2. Any resolution or ordinance which, by the terms of this Constitution, is subject to review by the Secretary of the Interior, shall be given to the Superintendent of the jurisdiction, who shall, within ten days thereafter, approve or disapprove the same. ***

Art. IX—Bill of Rights

Sec. 1. All resident members of the Tribe shall be given equal opportunities to share in the economic resources and activities of the jurisdiction.

Sec. 2. All members of the Tribe worship in their own way, to speak and write their opinion, and to meet together.

Art. X—Amendment

Any representative may propose an amendment to this Constitution and By-laws at any meeting of the Council. Such proposed amendment may be discussed at that meeting, but no vote shall be taken on it until the next following meeting of the Council. If the Council shall then approve such proposed amendment by a majority vote, it shall request the Secretary of the Interior to call such referendum, for accepting or rejecting such amendment. It shall then be the duty of the Secretary of the Interior to call such referendum, at which the proposed amendment may be adopted subject to the Secretary's approval, in the same manner as provided for the adoption and approval of this Constitution and By-laws. ***

Art. XI—Adoption of Constitution and By-Laws

This Constitution and By-laws, when ratified by a majority vote of the adult members of the Hopi Tribe voting at a referendum called for the purpose by the Secretary of the Interior, provided that at least thirty percent of those entitled to vote shall vote at such referendum, shall be submitted to the Secretary of the Interior, and if approved, shall take effect from the date of approval. ***

NOTES AND QUESTIONS

1. What do you notice about this constitution? What governmental institutions or procedures are missing that one would expect to find? What is present that is surprising or unusual?

2. The IRA constitutions created centralized secular governments that clashed with traditional reservation power structures. The new tribal councils were in many instances dominated by more acculturated tribal members that favored assimilation and support of the BIA. At Pine Ridge, this government became a focal point for factional struggles between "traditionalists" and "progressives" that dominated tribal government for many years, causing disruption and even bloodshed on the reservation. On the Blackfeet Reservation, BIA employees reported that "the Indian Reorganization Act has placed a legal tool in the hands of the ruling clique *** that more or less formalizes the struggle for control that makes full-blood resistance almost an act of treason." Quoted in Cornell, The Return of the Native at 99. By making voting the means of choosing to adopt an IRA government, the Act disadvantaged traditional members of tribes whose cultures prohibited this form of decision making. Over 1700 eligible Hopi voters, including all the Kikmongwis, or traditional village

leaders, refused to vote on the constitution because deciding matters by voting violated their clan and village based system. *See* Charles F. Wilkinson, *Home Dance, The Hopi, and Black Mesa Coal: Conquest and Endurance in the American Southwest*, 1996 B.Y.U.L. Rev. 449, 458. The 818 Hopis that did vote (519 for, 299 against) just barely composed the 30 percent of the electorate needed for a valid election. *See* Theodore H. Haas, Ten Years of Tribal Government Under the Indian Reorganization Act, *Table A* (1947).

On other reservations, the new tribal governments helped to unify and focus the tribal political voice. This consolidation often served federal and commercial interests, by creating a single entity that could sign leases for coal and mineral producing lands. Some IRA governments also provided a federally acceptable façade for the traditional power structures continuing beneath federal notice. For at least one group, the Santa Clara Pueblo, adoption of an IRA government helped to resolve a factional struggle. As reported in *Martinez v. Santa Clara Pueblo*, 402 F. Supp. 5 (D.N.M. 1975),

> During the early part of the twentieth century sharp conflicts developed in the Pueblo over the importance of traditional customs and values in the life of the Pueblo. For example, a major source of controversy was whether the Governor should be an older, highly respected man who was well versed in the traditional ways, or a younger man, educated in Anglo–American schools, who could speak English and would be able to deal more effectively with non-Pueblo society. The disagreement literally split the Pueblo, and during the late 1920s and early 1930s the Pueblo had two governors, neither of whom recognized the authority of the other, and two separate Winter and Summer moieties.† ***
>
> The members of the Pueblo did agree to have the resident BIA agent, Elizabeth Sargent, help settle the difference. At her suggestion, and after much discussion, the Pueblo organized pursuant to the authority of the Wheeler–Howard Act, 25 U.S.C. § 476, and adopted a Constitution and By–Laws in 1935. ***

402 F. Supp. at 12–13. Rarely, however, did the new governments mesh with traditional tribal governmental institutions. What might be the implications of this distance between community and written law? How would one develop a tribal constitution that better reflected community notions of justice and government?

3. Felix Cohen himself had argued that a "model constitution" should not be provided to tribes:

> [T]he situation of the various Indian tribes, with respect to experience in self-government, the nature of land ownership, the solidarity of the community, and the extent of the contests with non-Indians, is so variable that no single constitution prepared by the Indian Office could possibly fit the varied needs of the different Indian tribes.

Felix S. Cohen, On the Drafting of Tribal Constitutions 3 (David E. Wilkins ed. 2007). In addition, while a "model furnished by the Indian Office might be 'adopted' by an Indian tribe," it would not be "the natural offspring of Indian hearts and minds." Although "many Indian tribal councils ha[d] tried to

---

†. [Eds. Moiety is derived from the word "half" and represents a kinship-based division of a people into two groups.]

operate under written constitutions prepared by the Indian Office," these constitutions had been "mere scraps of paper. *** This has not been the case where the Indians themselves have determined the forms of their own self government." *Id.*

4. According to one historian, "Whether Indians wanted to salvage traditional governments, modernize governing practices, or maintain political structures approved by federal overseers, Collier promised Interior Department respect for their decisions. *** If BIA practices had been consistent with such rhetoric, Indian disappointment with Collier's administration would have been rarer than it ultimately was, but Indian New Deal realities seldom matched the high expectations he encouraged. In practice, significant restraints on tribal government power persisted." Alexandra Harmon, Reclaiming the Reservation: Histories of Indian Sovereignty Suppressed and Renewed 46 (2019). In the self-determination era many tribes, including the Hopi Tribe, have amended their constitutions to make them better fit their own laws, cultures, and customs.

IV. TERMINATION ERA: 1947–1961

The New Deal revolution in federal Indian policy came to a premature end. Collier's Indian policy had always drawn bitter criticism, and by the 1940s both Senate and House reports expressed fundamental disagreement with its goals. The tone of one such report recalls speeches by Friends of the Indians in the Assimilationist Era: "The goal of Indian education should be to make the Indian child a better American rather than to equip him simply to be a better Indian. *** The present Indian education program tends to operate too much in the direction of perpetuating the Indian as a special status individual rather than preparing him for independent citizenship." H.R. Rep. 78–2091 at 9 (Dec. 3, 1944). The celebrated service of Native soldiers in World War II, in which they enlisted at perhaps greater rates than any other ethnic group, added to the insistence that it was inappropriate to treat Indians differently than other Americans. Continuing inadequacies in health and social services to Indian people and the perennial corruption and inefficiency of the BIA became other justifications for ending special federal responsibility for Indians.

Although Collier beat back proposals to dismantle the Bureau of Indian Affairs and remove the trust protections for tribal lands, he was unable to secure sufficient appropriations to continue his programs. Funding for the Indian service was slashed between 1943 and 1945 even as non-war funding increased. Collier finally resigned in 1945 after threats of even more radical cuts if he remained. His resignation was followed by those of Secretary of the Interior Harold Ickes in 1946 and Felix Cohen in 1947. Other key players in the Indian New Deal, including Theodore Haas, one of the principal contributors to the Handbook of Federal Indian Law, and D'Arcy McNickle, a Cree anthropologist and director of the Office of Tribal Relations, were replaced a few years later.

With the architects of the New Deal gone, Congress and the BIA began moving toward a policy of terminating the special "wardship" status of Indian tribes. Between 1946 and 1950, Congress enacted laws extending state jurisdiction over tribal lands in New York, North Dakota, and Iowa. A similar provision extending state jurisdiction over the Navajo and Hopi reservations was defeated by a presidential veto in 1949. A 1949 Hoover Commission report called for the "complete integration" of Indians "into the mass of the population as full tax-paying citizens."

The effort to terminate the special status of Indian peoples picked up speed with the appointment of Dillon Myer as Indian Commissioner in 1950. Myer's last political appointment was as director of the World War II Japanese relocation and internment program. He enthusiastically embraced a program of "withdrawal" of the federal government from Indian affairs and "liquidation" of Indian property. Although Myer used the rhetoric of freedom from arbitrary control, his actions increased bureaucratic control of tribal self-government: "This time 'winding up the Indian bureau' has meant in practice increased control of Indians' appointment of attorneys, new restrictions upon trips to Washington of tribes with grievances, curtailment of the rights of individual Indians to use or lease their own lands, and denial of the rights of Indian communities to spend their own funds or even to hold their own elections." *Experiment in Immorality*, The Nation, July 26, 1952. A member of the Blackfeet Tribe, testifying at a 1952 Senate hearing on the plans for withdrawal, was even more cynical:

> We have had 97 years of experience with program makers who came out on behalf of the Indian Bureau and sold us programs to do away with the Indian Bureau. *** Now if you look over all of these programs for liquidating the Indian Bureau on the Blackfeet Reservation, you'll find that they all resulted in actually making the Indian Bureau a little fatter and our own land holdings a little leaner. *** So you gentlemen can understand why we on the Blackfeet Reservation are very much worried at the prospect of another expert program-maker from Washington to come out and improve us any further.

Quoted in Felix S. Cohen, *The Erosion of Indian Rights 1950–1953: A Case Study in Bureaucracy*, 62 Yale L. J. 348, 387–388 n.154 (1952–53).

Such protests were swept away by the ethos of the times. Nevada Senator George Malone argued that at the same time that the country was "spending billions of dollars fighting Communism," it was "perpetuating the systems of Indian reservations and tribal governments, which are natural Socialist environments." Quoted in Cornell, The Return of the Native at 121. The rhetoric of racial and political equality in the wake of World War II and the beginning of the Civil Rights movement was even more powerful. Senator Arthur V. Watkins of Utah, the Chair of the Senate Committee on Indian Affairs and the most important legislative advocate of the termination policy, wrote in 1957,

> In view of the historic policy of Congress favoring freedom for the Indians, we may well expect future Congresses to continue to endorse the principle that "as rapidly as possible" we should end the status of Indians as wards of the government and grant them all of the rights and prerogatives pertaining to American citizenship.
>
> With the aim of "equality before the law" in mind our course should rightly be no other. Firm and constant consideration for those of Indian ancestry should lead us all to work diligently and carefully for the full realization of their national citizenship with all other Americans. Following in the footsteps of the Emancipation Proclamation of ninety-four years ago, I see the following words emblazoned in letters of fire above the heads of the Indians—*THESE PEOPLE SHALL BE FREE!*

Arthur V. Watkins, *Termination of Federal Supervision: The Removal of Restrictions over Indian Property and Person*, 311 Annals of the American Academy of Political and Social Science 50, 55 (May 1957).

In 1953, House Resolution 108, the legislative centerpiece of the Termination policy, was approved by both houses without debate. Although it had no independent legal effect, the ominous resolution enshrined termination as congressional policy:

> Whereas it is the policy of Congress, as rapidly as possible, to make the Indians within the territorial limits of the United States subject to the same laws and entitled to the same privileges and responsibilities as are applicable to other citizens of the United States, to end their status as wards of the United States, and to grant them all of the rights and prerogatives pertaining to American citizenship; and
>
> Whereas the Indians within the territorial limits of the United States should assume their full responsibilities as American citizens: Now, therefore, be it
>
> *Resolved by the House of Representatives (the Senate concurring)*
>
> That it is declared to be the sense of congress that, at the earliest possible time, all of the Indian tribes and the individual members thereof located within the States of California, Florida, New York, and Texas, and all of the following named Indian tribes and individual members thereof, should be freed from Federal supervision and control and from all disabilities and limitations specially applicable to Indians. ***

67 Stat. B132 (Aug. 1, 1953). The resolution directed the Secretary of the Interior to examine the legislation regarding these tribes, and report back to Congress with recommendations for legislation to accomplish the purposes of the resolution no later than January 1, 1954.

The table below, from Charles F. Wilkinson & Eric R. Biggs, *The Evolution of the Termination Policy*, 3 Am. Indian L. Rev. 139, 151 (1977), includes the groups whose status was terminated. In all, termination affected 109 tribes and bands together possessing at least 1,362,155 acres and 11,466 members, or approximately 3% of the federally recognized Indian population and 3.2% of Indian trust land.

GROUPS WITH STATUS TERMINATED

Group	*Number*	*Acres*	*State*	*Authorizing statute (date)*	*Effective date*
Menominee	3,270	233,881	Wisconsin	68 Stat. 250 (1954)	1961
Klamath	2,133	862,662	Oregon	68 Stat. 718 (1954)	1961
Western Oregon*	2,091	2,158	Oregon	69 Stat. 724 (1954)	1956
Alabama–Coushatta	450	3,200	Texas	68 Stat. 768 (1954)	1955

GROUPS WITH STATUS TERMINATED

Group	*Number*	*Acres*	*State*	*Authorizing statute (date)*	*Effective date*
Mixed-blood Utes	490	211,430	Utah	68 Stat. 868 (1954)	1955
Southern Paiute	232	42,839	Utah	68 Stat. 1099 (1954)	1961
Lower Lake Rancheria	Unk.	Unk.	California	70 Stat. 58 (1956)	1956
Peoria	Unk.	Unk.	Oklahoma	70 Stat. 963 (1957)	1959
Ottawa	630	0	Oklahoma	70 Stat. 963 (1957)	1959
Coyote Valley Rancheria	Unk.	Unk.	California	71 Stat. 293 (1957)	1957
California Rancheria Act+	1,107	4,317	California	72 Stat. 619 (1958)	1961–70
Catawba	631	3,888	South Carolina	73 Stat. 592 (1959)	1962
Ponca	442	834	Nebraska	76 Stat. 429 (1962)	1966

* 61 tribes and bands. Figures listed are aggregates.

+ 37 to 38 Rancherias. Figures listed are aggregates.

Termination acts provided for the "termination of federal supervision" over the property and members of a tribe and disposition of any tribal or trust property. Tribes had the option of electing for tribal property to be sold, with cash proceeds distributed among their members, divided among the tribal membership, or placed under the control of a state-chartered corporation to manage the property for the members of the tribe. *See, e.g.*, Menominee Termination Act, 68 Stat. 250 (1954); Klamath Termination Act, 68 Stat. 718; 25 U.S.C. § 564. After distribution of all restricted property, tribal members "shall not be entitled to any of the services performed by the United States for Indians because of their status as Indians, all statutes of the United States which affect Indians because of their status as Indians shall no longer be applicable to the members of the tribe, and the laws of the several States shall apply to the tribe and its members in the same manner as they apply to other citizens or persons within their jurisdiction." 68 Stat. 250, Sec. 10.

The story of the Menominee Tribe, the largest tribe subject to termination, demonstrates the abject failure of this policy.

STEPHEN HERZBERG, *THE MENOMINEE INDIANS: TERMINATION TO RESTORATION*

6 Am. Indian L. Rev. 158 (1978)

*** The Menominee *** entered the 1950's a relatively prosperous, self-sufficient tribe. One of a very few tribes to hold assets communally, the Menominee owned a heavily wooded 233,092–acre reservation, a lumber mill, power plants, schools, and medical facilities. Members of the tribe received a broad spectrum of health, education and welfare services. Unlike most other tribes, the Menominee paid, either directly or indirectly, for these benefits. Most Menominee were able to find jobs on the reservation; the tribe's mill was run so as to maximize employment rather than profits. The recent recipients of an $8.5 million legal settlement, the Menominee looked forward to a period of growth and prosperity. ***

*** Identified in Commissioner Zimmerman's 1947 testimony as an "excellent possibility for termination," the Menominee inadvertently placed themselves before a withdrawal oriented Congress when they asked for special legislation to allow a per capita distribution of a portion of their $8.5 million settlement. *** In 1953, [the] bill was brought before Senator Arthur V. Watkins' subcommittee on Indian Affairs. The senator used his control over the subcommittee to turn the appropriation proposal into a termination bill. *** Senator Watkins took a hard line. The Menominee were to be terminated—it was inevitable. If they were wise, and if they wanted their per capita distribution, they would cooperate with the senator and the withdrawal forces. In the heat of the moment, without a full understanding of the concept of termination, and acting under the influence of the senator's threats, a small number of Menominee passed a resolution accepting, in principle, the amorphous idea of termination. Within a month, the tribe recognized that in its haste it had made a mistake. It voted to rescind its support for the withdrawal program, knowing fully that this antitermination position would eliminate its chance of receiving the per capita payments. Congress chose to ignore this latter resolution; instead, Senator Watkins repeatedly told the legislators that the Menominee had consented to their termination. ***

The passage of the Menominee Termination Act brought about an immediate, rapid decline in both the success of the tribe's enterprises and the well-being of the individual Menominee. ***

Of all the termination losses suffered by the Menominee, the depletion of the tribe's cash reserve is most easily observed. When the termination act was passed, the government held $10,437,000 in the Menominee treasury accounts. This apparently secure cash position was an important factor in congress' decision to withdraw federal support from the tribe. A rapid cash drain began immediately. With little federal support, the Menominee had to pay for expensive pretermination studies. In addition, with little help, the tribe had to improve its facilities so they would qualify for state licensing. For the first time, the Menominee were forced to use a system of deficit spending. *** In 1961, on the termination day, the tribal accounts contained $1,750,000; by 1964, they held $300,000; and in 1972, its reserves were down to $58,000. The weakened financial position had its greatest impact on the tribal enterprises. The depletion of capital eliminated an important source of tribal income—the interest payments received on the treasury accounts. The Menominee had previously used these payments to voluntarily reimburse the state and federal governments for services performed on the reservation. With termination, the tribe would have to both provide and pay for these services. No longer able to rely on this traditional source of funding, the Menominee had to place this burden on the struggling tribal enterprises. ***

The Menominee health care system was completely destroyed by the termination program. *** The system had been run by the Menominee; it was reservation-based, comprehensive, and inexpensive. On the reservation, the tribe owned and maintained both a hospital and a clinic. Each member was entitled to complete medical, surgical, and dental care. And, in sharp contrast to the cost of non-reservation health care, each Menominee family paid only $38 per year for complete coverage. ***

On January 1, 1961, the 45–bed Menominee hospital, the symbolic center of the health care program, was closed, a victim of the tribe's inability to comply with state licensing standards. *** The Menominee made a real effort to save the hospital; they spent more than $300,000 on renovation projects. After the work was completed, the building was inspected and found to have at least ten major code violations. In June 1960, nine months before they were to be terminated, the General Council asked the Department of the Interior for help. Two months later, a Department official reported that the hospital could be brought into compliance at a cost of $50,000. When the federal government refused to give the assistance necessary to finish the repairs, the Menominee were forced to close the hospital. ***

In like manner, termination brought the close of the other reservation medical and dental facilities. With no resident doctors in Menominee County, the people had to go to the private doctors in Shawano County for treatment. *** Although some who worked for the mill or the county had health insurance, and others received medical care cards from the welfare department, many Menominee fell in between and could not afford health care. ***

*** Before termination the tribes owned and operated three power plants. Each Menominee household received free electricity and water. Not regulated by the federal government and exempt from state control, the plants were never licensed. Termination would end the exemption. To conform with the state's standards, the Menominee would have had to spend at least $40,000 on physical plant improvements. Had they the money to make these changes, they still could not have complied with two other state regulations: utility companies had to post a sizable cash bond, and Wisconsin prohibited the operation of a utility company at a financial loss. To make the improvements, to post the bond, and to operate at a profit, the small-scale Menominee power companies would have had to charge very high rates. In the face of this reality, the Menominee sold their power plants to the Wisconsin Power and Light Company. *** Many Menominee were not able to pay their power bills. The private power company discontinued their service. Once a relic, the kerosene lamp became a fixture in many Menominee homes.

One of the central assumptions that dominated the rhetoric of the bureaucrats and congressmen who supported the termination of the Menominee was that the tribe's lumber industry would provide an economic base capable of supporting both individual Menominee and a new, reservation-based county.

There was no factual support for this assumption. That it was without merit became clear soon after the withdrawal program took effect. Forced to comply with state regulations, taxed on its income and property, and placed in a highly competitive market in which it was asked to turn a profit, the mill foundered and threw the tribe and the county into a period of economic chaos. ***

Perhaps more than any other factor, the lack of reservation employment opportunities lead to the sharp decline in the quality of Menominee life. After termination, *** the mill, the reservation's major employer, was laying off people. From 1954 to 1964, the number of reservation jobs decreased. *** Spokeswoman Ada Deer gave meaning to those numbers when she testified about the impact the high unemployment rate was having on the Menominee:

> Let us tell you about our people's far reaching poverty, which extends beyond mere income levels to practically all other areas of our life.
>
> Today, Menominee County is the poorest county in Wisconsin. It has the highest birthrate in the state and ranks at or near the bottom of Wisconsin counties in income, housing, property value, education, employment, sanitation and health. [1967 figures] show that the annual income of nearly 80 percent of our families falls below the federal poverty level of $3,000. ***
>
> This lack of employment opportunities, combined with our high birthrate, forced nearly 50 percent of our county residents to go on welfare in 1968. Welfare costs in the county for 1968 were over $766,000 and our per capita welfare payment was the highest in the state. ***

As the post-termination years passed, both the individual Menominee and the county became dependent on the assistance provided by the federal and state governments. *** The Menominee had not needed this help before. In 1953, they had paid the federal government for all but $59,000 of their reservation expenses. But with termination, this changed. From June 17, 1954, to June 27, 1973, the Menominee and the county received more than $20,000,000 in federal and state aid. ***

NOTES AND QUESTIONS

1. *Experience of other tribes.* Although the experience of the Menominee is the best documented, other tribes also suffered under termination. The Siletz Confederated Tribes of Indians, for example, who were among the Western Oregon tribes terminated in 1954, had a similar post-termination experience:

> After the enactment of that legislation, the tribal land was sold by the Federal Government and lands which had been used by the Bureau of Indian Affairs and as a tribal cemetery were transferred to the town of Siletz, because the Tribe was unable to pay the required property taxes.
>
> In the years that followed termination, tribal activities generally ceased and many tribal members left the area. Conditions did not improve and recent studies show that the unemployment rate for the Siletz Indians living in the former reservation area is over 40 percent and that the median family income for Siletz families remaining in the area is only $3,333. Members of this tribal group are handicapped by many other problems, as

well. Nearly half of the youths between the ages of 17 and 25 had not finished high school in 1974 and alcoholism and other health problems plague tribal members who cannot afford proper medical attention.

Report on the Siletz Tribe Restoration Act, H.R. Rep. 95–923 at 3 (1977).

2. *Termination and Equality?* Senator Watkins used the rhetoric of Indian equality and rights to argue for the termination policy, declaring "LET THESE PEOPLE BE FREE." Felix Cohen, in his blistering critique of the emerging termination policy, used a similar rhetoric, writing, "the Indian plays much the same role in our American society that the Jews played in Germany. Like the miner's canary, the Indian marks the shift from fresh air to poison gas in our political atmosphere; and our treatment of Indians, even more than our treatment of other minorities, reflects the rise and fall in our democratic faith." Felix S. Cohen, *The Erosion of Indian Rights 1950–1953: A Case Study in Bureaucracy*, 62 Yale L. J. 348, 390 (1952–1953). What aspects of federal Indian policy lent themselves to such a critique both for and against termination policy? *See* Bethany R. Berger, *Williams v. Lee and the Debate over Indian Equality*, 109 Mich. L. Rev. 1463 (2011). For more on the complicated factors behind the termination policy, see Kenneth R. Philp, Termination Revisited: American Indians on the Trail to Self–Determination, 1933–1953 (1999).

3. *Termination to Restoration.* After a long tribal campaign, the Menominee Tribe was finally restored to federal recognition in 1973, 87 Stat. 770 (1973), although it had been forced to sell ten thousand acres of its property to meet expenses and other tribal assets were permanently lost. In 1979, the Court of Claims held that there was no cause of action to sue for damages caused by the termination act. *Menominee Tribe v. United States*, 221 Ct. Cl. 506, 607 F.2d 1335 (Ct. Cl. 1979). Numerous other tribes were also restored to recognition, albeit poorer than before. The Siletz Tribe, for example, was restored to federal recognition in 1977, although its reservation had been lost. Siletz Indian Tribe Restoration Act, 91 Stat. 1415 (1977); *see also* Klamath Tribe Restoration Act, 100 Stat. 849 (1986); 92 Stat. 246 (1978) (restoring federal recognition of the Wyandotte, Ottawa and Peoria Tribes of Oklahoma). A number of California tribes were also "restored" to recognition after judicial findings that the Secretary of the Interior had never provided the sanitation and irrigation facilities required before termination would become effective under the California Rancheria Act. *See Table Bluff Band of Indians v. Andrus*, 532 F. Supp. 255, 260 (N.D. Cal. 1981); *Smith v. United States*, 515 F. Supp. 56 (N.D. Cal. 1978); *Duncan v. Andrus*, 517 F. Supp. 1 (N.D. Cal. 1977).

4. *What was left after termination?* Although the termination acts ended the federal relationship with the tribes as well as the benefits and protections provided by federal law, they did not terminate the tribes themselves. *See Kimball v. Callahan*, 590 F.2d 768, 776 (9th Cir. 1979) ("Although the [Klamath Termination] Act terminated federal supervision over trust and restricted property of the Klamath Indians *** it did not affect the power of the tribe to take any action under its constitution and bylaws consistent with the Act. The Klamaths still maintain a tribal constitution and tribal government, which among other things establishes criteria for membership in the Tribe."); *Menominee Tribe of Indians v. U.S.*, 179 Ct. Cl. 496, 388 F.2d 998 (Ct. Cl. 1967) ("The Termination Act did not abolish the *tribe* or its membership. It merely terminated Federal supervision over and responsibility for the property and members of the tribe. The Menominee Indians continue to constitute a tribe

whose membership is composed of those persons whose names appear on the official roll of the tribe ***."). Thus several courts have held that members of terminated tribes retain treaty rights to hunt and fish that were not specifically abrogated by the relevant termination acts. *See Menominee Tribe of Indians v. United States*, 391 U.S. 404 (1968), *infra* Ch. 4; *Kimball v. Callahan*, 590 F.2d 768 (9th Cir. 1979).

5. *Other Products of the Termination Era.* Termination was not the only, or even necessarily the most important, product of the Termination Era. Two weeks after passing House Resolution 108, Congress enacted Public Law 280, which extended state criminal and civil jurisdiction over most reservations in California, Minnesota, Nebraska, Oregon, and Wisconsin, and permitted other states to assume such jurisdiction if they chose. 18 U.S.C. §§ 1162 & 1163. (When Alaska became a state, it was included as well.) As you will read later, Pub. L. 280 has greatly complicated the jurisdictional situation in Indian country, and has often resulted in lawlessness as the federal government has withdrawn from providing law enforcement or providing funds for tribes to do so, while states have been unable or unwilling to take up the slack. *See* Carole Goldberg–Ambrose, *Public Law 280 and the Problem of Lawlessness in California Indian Country*, 44 UCLA L. Rev. 1405 (1997).

Felix Cohen died in October 1953, at the age of forty-six. The Department of the Interior found the Handbook he had authored, with its legal support for tribal sovereignty, inconvenient in implementing the new Indian policy. In 1958, the Department of the Interior issued a new Handbook of Federal Indian Law. The book was not a true updating and revision, but instead simply cut and pasted in useful sentences to undermine the whole. *See* U.S. Dept. of Interior, Federal Indian Law 501 (1958).

Other programs were aimed at moving Indian people from their reservations and encouraging integration in off-reservation communities. The BIA partnered with the Child Welfare League of America in an effort to move children from "broken" Indian homes to off-reservation placements. A BIA news release of 1966 declared, "One little, two little, three little Indians—and 206 more—are brightening the homes and lives of 172 American families, mostly non-Indians, who have taken the Indian waifs as their own. *** Almost all the placements have been in the east and midwest," far from most reservations, "with 49 in New York alone." Bureau of Indian Affairs, news release, March 14, 1966, quoted in Francis Paul Prucha, The Great Father: The United States Government and the American Indians 1154 (1984).

The Urban Relocation Program moved Indian people on a much larger scale by providing financial incentives and encouragement for adults to leave their reservations and settle in cities where employment opportunities might be greater. Relocation was clearly part of the termination policy. Senator Watkins declared, "The sooner we can get the Indians into cities the sooner the government can get out of the Indian business." A total of 33,000 individuals were relocated under the program between 1953 and 1960, mostly to very large cities like Los Angeles and Chicago. The program was not necessarily coercive; given the poverty and lack of opportunity on many reservations, Indian people had been seeking employment in cities for decades, a process that picked up after World War II. But the BIA moved thousands of reservation people to unfamiliar cities and left them there with little assistance to grapple with the vast change from their reservations; these urban Indians, separated from the support networks of their tribes and from federal services, often fell into unemployment, poverty, and alcoholism.

The growth of urban Indian populations had another effect not anticipated by Senator Watkins. Members of different tribes, thrown together in the cities and together experiencing discrimination and disadvantage, began to organize as a unified arm to change federal Indian policy. This increase in political organization continued a process catalyzed by the termination era itself. The National Congress of American Indians, the first national organization of tribal leaders, had formed in 1944, and with the Termination Era found a common cause to galvanize Indian country.

> *** Termination had touched a nerve, drawing Indian groups and leadership together in a concerted effort—much of it waged through the NCAI—to defeat or modify the termination program. In the summer of 1961, when nearly five hundred Indians from seventy tribes gathered in Chicago for the American Indian Chicago Conference, they had in common, wrote D'Arcy McNickle, an anthropologist who was one of them, "a sense of being under attack, and it was this shared experience which drew them together." In its concluding statement the conference rejected termination and asserted the right of Indian communities to choose their own ways of life. It was the largest multitribal gathering in decades, the most striking evidence to date of a supratribal consciousness making its way into politics.
>
> And it had an effect. It was a long struggle, but the opposition to termination gradually grew. State governments, at first in favor, had second thoughts once they realized what was involved in assuming the responsibilities once borne by the feds, while other critics attacked the lack of Indian input and the haste with which the policy was adopted. In 1958, signaling the beginning of retreat, the secretary of the interior called termination without tribal consent—once official practice—"unthinkable," although termination remained government policy for another decade. But by the early 1960s Indian and non-Indian protest, coupled with the policy's failure to deal effectively with Indian problems, had killed its momentum.

Cornell, The Return of the Native at 124. Thus the termination policy sowed the seeds for its own demise by spurring Indian people to newly strategic and effective demands for meaningful self-determination.

V. THE SELF-DETERMINATION ERA: 1961 TO PRESENT?

A. THE PATH TO SELF-DETERMINATION

The 1960s began in a spirit of resistance to the termination policy. John Kennedy's presidential platform included a promise to protect the tribal land base and encourage tribal participation in economic development. In June of 1961, 450 Indian delegates from 90 tribes met at the American Indian Chicago Conference, and in 1962, presented a bound copy of their Declaration of Purpose to President Kennedy at the White House. And in July of 1961, the federal Task Force on Indian Affairs presented its report based on information gathered from hearings on reservations, interviews with the Bureau of Indian Affairs, and attendance at the Chicago conference. The report did not repudiate the goals of "equal citizenship" and "full participation in American life," but concluded that emphasis on termination rather than tribal collaboration and development only impeded these goals. No tribes were terminated after 1962, although Washington Senator Henry "Scoop" Jackson led an effort to terminate the 1.1 million acre Colville reservation in the late 1960s. *See* Charles Wilkinson, Blood Struggle 178–182 (2005).

President Johnson's War on Poverty also furthered the move toward a self-determination policy. War on Poverty programs emphasized local control and experimentation to attack social problems, and Indian tribes were among their beneficiaries. With funding from the Economic Opportunity Act of 1964, tribes began demonstration projects to run their own schools, colleges, and social service programs. The Office of Economic Opportunity also funded the first reservation-based legal services programs, and these would prove to become important players in the development of a contemporary legal vision of tribal sovereignty. At the same time, federal studies of social and economic conditions among Indian people revealed the shocking disparities in Indian health, welfare, and education.

The national policy had been turning away from termination and toward tribal self-determination for a decade. In the 1968 Indian Civil Rights Act, Congress amended Public Law 280 to provide that no state could in the future assume jurisdiction over an Indian reservation without the consent of the tribe at a special election. But it was President Richard M. Nixon who, in a special message to Congress, defined the hallmark of the new era: self-determination without termination.

RICHARD M. NIXON, *SPECIAL MESSAGE ON INDIAN AFFAIRS*

(July 8, 1970)

To the Congress of the United States:

*** It is long past time that the Indian policies of the Federal government began to recognize and build upon the capacities and insights of the Indian people. Both as a matter of justice and as a matter of enlightened social policy, we must begin to act on the basis of what the Indians themselves have long been telling us. The time has come to break decisively with the past and to create the conditions for a new era in which the Indian future is determined by Indian acts and Indian decisions.

Self-Determination Without Termination

The first and most basic question that must be answered with respect to Indian policy concerns the historic and legal relationship between the Federal government and Indian communities. In the past, this relationship has oscillated between two equally harsh and unacceptable extremes.

On the one hand, it has—at various times during previous Administrations—been the stated policy objective of both the Executive and Legislative branches of the Federal government eventually to terminate the trusteeship relationship between the Federal government and the Indian people. As recently as August of 1953, in House Concurrent Resolution 108, the Congress declared that termination was the long-range goal of its Indian policies. ***

This policy of forced termination is wrong, in my judgment, for a number of reasons. First, the premises on which it rests are wrong. Termination implies that the Federal government has taken on a trusteeship responsibility for Indian communities as an act of generosity toward a disadvantaged people and that it can therefore discontinue this responsibility on a unilateral basis whenever it sees fit. But the unique status of Indian tribes does not rest on any premise such as this. The special relationship between Indians and the Federal government is the result instead of solemn obligations which have been entered into by the United States Government. Down through the years, through written treaties and through formal and informal agreements, our government has made specific commitments to the Indian people. For their part, the Indians have often surrendered claims to vast tracts of land and have accepted life on government reservations. In exchange, the government has agreed to provide community services such as health, education and public safety, services which would presumably allow Indian communities to enjoy a standard of living comparable to that of other Americans.

This goal, of course, has never been achieved. But the special relationship between the Indian tribes and the Federal government which arises from these agreements continues to carry immense moral and legal force. To terminate this relationship would be no more appropriate than to terminate the citizenship rights of any other American.

The second reason for rejecting forced termination is that the practical results have been clearly harmful in the few instances in which termination actually has been tried. ***

In short, the fear of one extreme policy, forced termination, has often worked to produce the opposite extreme: excessive dependence on the Federal government. In many cases this dependence is so great that the Indian community is almost entirely run by outsiders who are responsible and responsive to Federal officials in Washington, D.C., rather than to the communities they are supposed to be serving. This is the second of the two harsh approaches which have long plagued our Indian policies. Of the Department of the Interior's programs directly serving Indians, for example, only 1.5 percent are presently under Indian control. ***

I believe that both of these policy extremes are wrong. Federal termination errs in one direction, Federal paternalism errs in the other. Only by clearly rejecting both of these extremes can we achieve a policy which truly serves the best interests of the Indian people. Self-determination among the Indian people can and must be encouraged without the threat of eventual termination. In my view, in fact, that is the only way that self-determination can effectively be fostered.

This, then, must be the goal of any new national policy toward the Indian people: to strengthen the Indian's sense of autonomy without threatening his sense of community. We must assure the Indian that he can assume control of his own life without being separated involuntarily from the tribal group. And we must make it clear that Indians can become independent of Federal control without being cut off from Federal concern and Federal support. My specific recommendations to the Congress are designed to carry out this policy.

1. Rejecting Termination

Because termination is morally and legally unacceptable, because it produces bad practical results, and because the mere threat of termination tends to discourage greater self-sufficiency among Indian groups, I am asking the Congress to pass a new Concurrent Resolution which would expressly renounce, repudiate and repeal the termination policy as expressed in House Concurrent Resolution 108 of the 83rd Congress. ***

2. The Right to Control and Operate Federal Programs

*** In the past, we have often assumed that because the government is obliged to provide certain services for Indians, it therefore must administer those same services. And to get rid of Federal administration, by the same token, often meant getting rid of the whole Federal program. But there is no necessary reason for this assumption. Federal support programs for non-Indian communities—hospitals and schools are two ready examples—are ordinarily administered by local authorities. There is no reason why Indian communities should be deprived of the privilege of self-determination merely because they receive monetary support from the Federal government. Nor should they lose Federal money because they reject Federal control.

*** To this end, I am proposing legislation which would empower a tribe or a group of tribes or any other Indian community to take over the control or operation of Federally funded and administered programs in the Department of the Interior and the Department of Health, Education and Welfare whenever the tribal council or comparable community governing group voted to do so.

***

As we move ahead in this important work, it is essential that the Indian people continue to lead the way by participating in policy development to the greatest possible degree. ***

The recommendations of this Administration represent an historic step forward in Indian policy. We are proposing to break sharply with past approaches to Indian problems. In place of a long series of piecemeal reforms, we suggest a new and coherent strategy. ***

But most importantly, we have turned from the question of whether the Federal government has a responsibility to Indians to the question of how that responsibility can best be fulfilled. We have concluded that the Indians will get better programs and that public monies will be more effectively expended if the people who are most affected by these programs are responsible for operating them. ***

President Nixon is routinely praised for this major policy switch, and you can see a presentation by Bobbie Kilberg who, as a White House Fellow, was closely involved in the process. http://youtu.be/Jk02XLzljOY.

Professor Carole Goldberg, however, offers a critical view of President Nixon's legacy on Indian law and policy.

> Scholars of Federal Indian law have often celebrated President Richard Nixon for advancing tribal interests through legislation and policy

> initiatives. Far less attention has been paid to his impact on Federal Indian law through the appointments he made to the U.S. Supreme Court. During the time his four appointees served together, the Supreme Court rendered three decisions that are among the most harmful to tribal interests of the modern era. Whether any President should be held responsible for the decisions of his appointees is no simple question. It is worth noting, however, that President Nixon had every reason to know the issues in those three cases would likely reach the Supreme Court. Yet he did not investigate or take into account his appointees' views on Native issues before making the appointments. Further, for at least one of the appointees—the one most consistently hostile to tribal interests—there was ample evidence of those views had President Nixon cared to check.

Carole Goldberg, *President Nixon's Indian Law Legacy: A Counterstory*, 63 UCLA L. Rev. 1506 (2016).

B. SELF-DETERMINATION LEGISLATION

Since 1970, federal legislation regarding Indian affairs, and largely executive policy, has followed the self-determination policy. This policy has been maintained through an important development:

> Indians have learned how to lobby. Highly effective legislative campaigns have been pursued by individual tribes and by national organizations. *** A skilled network exists to identify opposition proposals and to react to them promptly and professionally. *** [Although] tribal rights remain vulnerable to initiatives backed by well-organized interest groups *** [n]o Indian legislation has been passed over Indian opposition since the Indian Civil Rights Act of 1968.

Charles F. Wilkinson, American Indians, Time and the Law 82–83 (1987).

Self-determination legislation has focused on three areas: furthering tribal control over governmental services to tribal people; increasing tribal control over natural resources and economic development; and protecting tribal culture and community. Major legislation in each area is summarized below. As discussed more fully in Chapter 13, international human rights law is also an increasingly important body self-determination principles, particularly with the 2010 decision of the United States to support the United Nations Declaration on the Rights of Indigenous Peoples.

1. Laws Furthering Tribal Control of Governmental Services to Tribal People

In 1975, Congress passed the legislation that Nixon had envisioned, the Indian Self–Determination and Educational Assistance Act (ISDEA). 25 USC § 5301 *et seq.* The Act permits tribes to enter into contracts with the federal government to take over administration of federally funded governmental services for their tribes.[3] The goals of the Act have been enhanced by the Tribal

3. Contractible programs must be "for the benefit of Indians because of their status as Indians." 25 U.S.C. § 5321(a)(1)(E); *Navajo Nation v. Dept. Health & Human Servs.*, 325 F.3d 1133, 1138 (9th Cir. 2003) (holding that Navajo Nation could not enter into a self-governance compact

Self–Governance Acts of 1988, 1994, and 2000, which make it possible for tribes and tribal consortia to enter into flexible tribal block grants to administer these services. 25 U.S.C. § 5361 *et seq*. The Tribally Controlled Schools Act of 1988 builds on the ISDEA to provide more flexible grants for the administration of federally funded tribal schools. 25 U.S.C. § 2501 *et seq*.

The Tribally Controlled Colleges and Universities Act of 1978 provided funding for tribally controlled colleges on reservations. 25 U.S.C. § 1801 *et seq*. Although the act is underfunded, with its support tribes now run 36 colleges on their reservations.

The Native American Housing Assistance Self–Determination Act, passed in 1996, enhances tribal control of reservation housing projects. 25 U.S.C. § 4101 *et seq*.

More general federal spending legislation frequently authorizes tribes to take over administration of governmental services programs from states. Programs which tribes now administer under these programs include Temporary Assistance for Needy Families, Food Stamps, and Women Infants and Children programs, and child support enforcement. *See* Cohen's Handbook of Federal Indian Law § 22.06[2][b] (2012).

Although more remains to be done, these laws have created substantial progress toward tribal control of governmental services. Nixon reported that in 1970, only 1.5% of federal services for Indians on reservations were under tribal control; today, more than half of such services are administered by tribes and tribal organizations. Cohen at § 22.02[1].

2. Laws Furthering Tribal Control of Natural Resources and Economic Development

The Indian Financing Act of 1974, 25 U.S.C. § 1415 *et seq*., proposed by Nixon in his 1970 speech, enhances the revolving loan fund created in the IRA era. A host of laws, including the Indian Forest Resources Management Act, 25 U.S.C. §§ 3101–3120, the Indian Mineral Development Act of 1982, 25 U.S.C. §§ 2101–2108, and the Indian Tribal Energy Development and Self-Determination Act of 2005, 25 U.S.C. §§ 3501-3506, seek to increase tribal control over valuable natural resources on their reservations. With assistance from these laws, tribal have begun to correct generations of federal bureaucratic domination of these industries, and the inefficiencies and corruption created by this domination. Of course the best known piece of economic development legislation is the Indian Gaming Regulatory Act, 25 U.S.C. §§ 2701–2721, passed in 1988 to regulate and facilitate tribal gaming in their territories.

Federal laws have enhanced tribal control not only over economic development but also tribal territory and environment. Amendments to the Clean Air and Clean Water Acts, for example, provide that tribes shall be treated as states under these laws, and therefore have the option of taking over federal responsibilities for setting and enforcing environmental standards on their reservations. *See* 42 U.S.C. § 7474(c) (Clean Air Act); 33 U.S.C. § 1377(e) (Clean Water Act); Cohen at § 10.02[1].

---

to administer TANF services because it was not solely directed at Indians "because of their status as Indians." Rather, it was a federal program made available to both Indian tribes and states.).

3. Laws Protecting Culture and Community

One of the most important examples of self-determination legislation is the Indian Child Welfare Act of 1978 (ICWA). 25 U.S.C. §§ 1901–1931. The Act seeks to prevent high rates of removal of children from reservation communities by increasing and protecting tribal jurisdiction over child custody decisions and creating procedural safeguards when states decide child custody matters.

The same year it enacted ICWA, Congress also passed the American Indian Religious Freedom Act, 42 U.S.C. § 1996, which is "toothless" in terms of judicial review of agency action, but which has nonetheless proved to be valuable for the protection of Native sacred sites and religious practices. The Act prioritizes federal support for American Indian religious rights, and has been deployed by tribes to educate and influence federal land managers. Similarly, the Native American Languages Act of 1990, 25 U.S.C. §§ 2901–2906, although mostly without judicial enforcement mechanisms, affirms the importance of native languages and facilitates certification of native language instructors.

More significant is the Native American Grave Protection and Repatriation Act of 1990 (NAGPRA). 18 U.S.C. § 1170; 25 U.S.C. §§ 3001–3013. The Act seeks to put a halt to generations of casual acquisition of Native American skeletons and funerary objects. It prevents appropriation and disturbance of Native American graves and their contents, and requires those that possess such objects to consult with tribes for their return or appropriate disposition.

Laws like the Tribal Justice Support Act of 1993, 25 U.S.C. § 3601, *et seq.*, and Tribal Law and Order Act of 2010, 124 Stat. 2258, seek to enhance self-determination with respect to law enforcement and administration. The Violence Against Women Act provided funding to tribes for domestic violence prevention and required that courts give full faith and credit to tribal court orders of protection, 18 U.S.C. § 2265, and the 2013 reauthorization enhances tribal jurisdiction over non-Indian abusers. 25 U.S.C. § 1304(b)(1).

Tribes cannot effectively exercise self-government without federal and state recognition of their sovereignty. Although the recognition process has been justly criticized, federal regulations passed in 1978 provide a formal process through which groups can apply for recognition as tribes entitled to a government-to-government relationship with the United States. 25 CFR Part 83. The 1970s and 1980s have also seen a series of acts restoring terminated tribes to federal recognition and providing for acknowledgement of other tribes never formally recognized by the federal government.

C. BACKLASH AGAINST SELF-DETERMINATION

Non–Indians have not uniformly supported tribal self-determination. Many scholars have commented that even as Congress has been relatively consistent in supporting tribal sovereignty, the Supreme Court has acted to limit that sovereignty. A study of Supreme Court decisions between 1986 and 2001 found that tribal interests won in only 23% of cases decided by the Court during this period, a success rate even lower than the 36% win rate enjoyed by convicted criminals seeking to have their convictions reversed. David H. Getches, *Beyond Indian Law: The Rehnquist Court's Pursuit of States' Rights, Color–Blind Justice and Mainstream Values,* 86 Minn. L. Rev. 267, 280–281 (2001). In a series of decisions since 1976, the Court has increased state jurisdiction to tax and extend other laws on Indian territories and significantly impaired tribal power to exercise jurisdiction over non-Indians and Indians that are not members of the governing tribe. *See* Chs.7 & 8, *infra*. Recent years have seen some important wins and losses for Indian Nations in the Supreme Court. Secretarial decisions to take land in trust are now subject to review under the Administrative Procedures Act, and tribes relying on section 5 of the IRA as authority for the trust acquisition must be able to show that they were "under federal jurisdiction" when the law passed in 1934. On the other hand Northwest Indian tribes in 2018 won their fisheries habitat protection case against the State of Washington when the Court affirmed a favorable 9th circuit decision by an equally divided 4-4 vote. The Crow Tribe in 2019 was on the favorable side of a 5-4 holding that Wyoming's admission to the Union did not abrogate off-reservation hunting rights on unoccupied federal lands.

These judicial developments have been accompanied, in some areas, by non-Indian resentment of tribes and Indian people who exercise what are perceived as "special" rights not available to other individuals and governments. The following case provides a stark example of backlash against tribal rights.

LAC DU FLAMBEAU BAND OF LAKE SUPERIOR CHIPPEWA INDIANS V. STOP TREATY ABUSE–WISCONSIN

843 F. Supp. 1284 (D. Wisc. 1994)

CRABB, CHIEF JUDGE.

In this civil action, plaintiffs are seeking a permanent injunction restraining defendants from interfering with plaintiffs' exercise of their treaty-preserved rights to hunt, fish and gather in the area of northern Wisconsin ceded to the United States by the Lake Superior Chippewa Indians in 1837 and 1842. Plaintiffs allege violations of these rights under 42 U.S.C. §§ 1982 [which prohibits interference with "the same right *** as is enjoyed by white citizens thereof to inherit, purchase, lease, sell, hold and convey real and personal property." The district court initially granted summary judgment for the plaintiffs. On appeal, the Seventh Circuit remanded for a trial on the issue of racial discrimination.] From the evidence adduced at the bench trial *** I find that defendants' interference with plaintiffs' spearfishing was racially motivated, that is, it would not have occurred but for the racial animus of defendants and their followers. ***

Plaintiff Lac du Flambeau band is a band of the Lake Superior Chippewa. *** In 1837 and 1842 the tribe entered into treaties with the United States ceding huge tracts of land in northern Wisconsin, Michigan and Minnesota to the government while reserving the right to hunt, fish and gather throughout the ceded territory. *** Defendant Stop Treaty Abuse–Wisconsin, Inc. is a for-profit corporation organized under the laws of the state of Wisconsin, with its principal place of business in Woodruff, Wisconsin. Its avowed purpose is to stop tribal members from exercising their off-reservation treaty rights including their rights to spear and net fish. Defendant Dean Crist is a member and co-founder of STA and its chief spokesperson. ***

Defendant Crist moved to northern Wisconsin in large part because of the fishing opportunities there. In his opinion, spearing and netting have had a detrimental effect on the inland lakes' populations of game fish although he admits that it may be "a buried detriment because nobody knows all of the effects of the spearing as it is currently practiced." ***

Spearing

Under the applicable treaties, the Lake Superior Chippewa have the right to catch fish by spearing and netting. State law prohibits all other persons from engaging in such activity on any inland lakes, except that non-Chippewas may net buffalo fish and carp on a few very large inland lakes and may engage in winter ice spearing of sturgeon on Lake Winnebago. Chippewa spearing and netting are carefully regulated and monitored by wardens from both the Wisconsin Department of Natural Resources and the Great Lakes Indian Fish and Wildlife Commission, an inter-tribal, interstate organization. For example, spearers are required to obtain a permit for spearing, which is good for only one night and can be obtained only on the day the spearing is to take place.

The majority of Chippewa spearing occurs in the early spring. It begins as soon as the ice thaws from the lakes and lasts as long as spawning is taking place: usually between one to two weeks on any particular lake for walleye and an additional one to two weeks thereafter for muskellunge. To spear the fish, tribal spearers stand in small boats or canoes and use a long metal five-tine spear. Because spearing begins at twilight and continues on into the night, the spearer usually wears a large miner's type hat with a light attached to illuminate the shallow water below him. A spearer standing in a small boat in the dark in the early spring is vulnerable to falling into the icy water if the lake becomes rough or the boat is subjected to high wakes created by motorboats passing near the boat. ***

Before spearing, it is common for the Chippewa to hold a traditional ceremony involving prayers and the placing of a tobacco or "asema" offering into the water.

Defendant Crist's and STA's Operation

STA was formed at the end of the spring spearing season in 1988. During the following winter, articles of incorporation were drawn up and board meetings were held. The first general meetings took place in the spring of 1989. At that time, a "couple hundred" persons had joined, each paying a ten dollar membership fee. At first the board intended to use the money to intervene in the ongoing litigation between the state of Wisconsin and the Chippewa. When that proved impossible, the board decided to organize protests at the landings. ***

Persons who wanted to know where STA would be protesting on a given night could call defendant Crist's restaurant to be directed to a particular boat landing. Generally, defendant Crist would organize protests at the landings where he believed members of the plaintiff band planned to spear. His goal was to reduce the walleye harvest of the tribal members; to that end, he urged persons to come to the landings, to crowd the landing area and to protest the spearing. Also, he organized on-water flotillas of motorboats to crowd the launch area, making it difficult for spearers to launch their boats, and to create wakes near the spearing boats, interfering with the spearing and endangering the spearers while they were spearing. On some landings in 1989 and 1990, defendants Crist and STA attracted as many as 1,000 to 3,000 protesters. ***

*** On many landings in 1990, protesters used whistles to blow directly into the ears of spearing supporters. STA sold whistles at the landings in 1990 and included them in the STA protest kits they sold at their rallies. ***

Immediately following the filing of this lawsuit, the STA board authorized the destruction of all STA membership lists. ***

Incidents at Landings and on Lakes

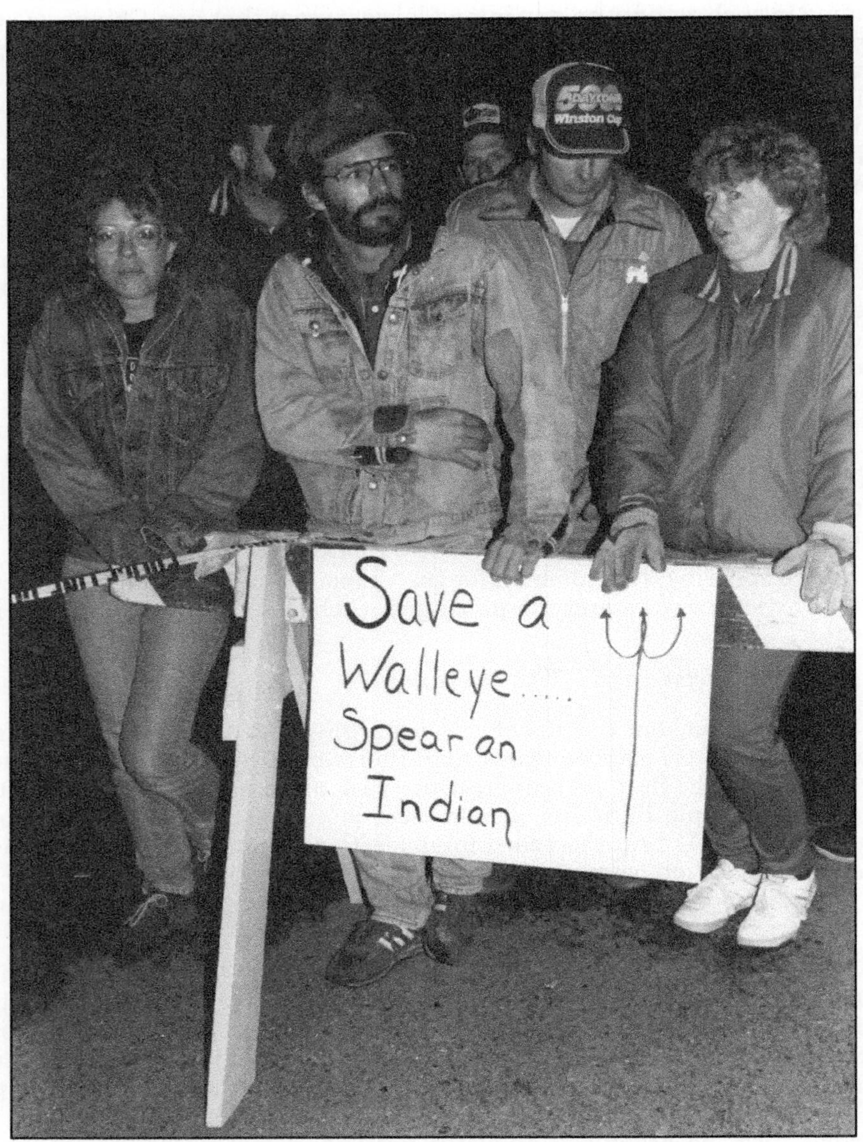

Wisconsin treaty-fishing protests (1989), courtesy of the Great Lakes Indian Fish & Wildlife Commission.

On the lakes where plaintiffs and other tribal members speared in 1989, 1990 and 1991, protesters used high-powered motorboats to create wakes and rock the boats in which spearers were standing, threw stones at the spearers who were trying to launch their boats from the landings, crowded the landings to try to prevent spearers from getting their boats to the water, encircled the launch areas with their motor boats to interfere with the spearers' efforts to launch their boats and move them away from the landings, taunted and threatened spearers and their supporters, yelled racial and sexual insults, shined lights in the eyes of spearers as they were spearing, and mocked the religious and cultural significance of spearing. Often, protesters threw rocks that struck spearers and caused injury. At one lake, protesters used slingshots to hurl rocks at spearers. At another lake, a protester struck a spearer with a fishing lure he cast at the spearer. This interference and harassment took place despite the presence at the lakes of numerous law enforcement officers recruited from the entire state and mobilized into an emergency force for the spearing season and despite the establishment of fenced-off areas intended to separate protesters and supporters from the boat launching areas.

At landings where plaintiffs speared in 1989 and 1990, protesters yelled such comments as, "All you Indians that are on welfare" or "All you Indians that are filling up our jails" and asked Indian women at the landings, "What do you use that spawn for, to douche?" Indians with long hair were called "Tonto" or "redskin." Protesters asked spearers where they got their boats and trailers and made statements to the effect that taxpayers had paid for the boats. At Arbor Vitae Lake, protesters sang a variation of the song, "Tom Dooley," to plaintiff Tom Maulson as he tried to spear: "Hang down your head, Tom Maulson, hang down your head and die." At many landings, STA board member Al Soik and his wife Elaine Soik beat on drums to the chant of "Hey, how are ya? Hey, how are ya?" in mockery of an Indian chant. On several occasions, Elaine Soik wrapped a bandanna around her head, stuck a twig in her hair as a feather, and caricatured an Indian ceremonial dance. On Minocqua Lake, STA leader Jack Lanta stated, "Niggers are better than Indians." At Big Arbor Vita, Jack Lanta said, "Those Indians are all on welfare that are out there spearing." At one landing, protesters commented in reference to some young Indian men who had brought drums to the landing, "The hardest work they've ever done in their life is pounding on that drum."

On one occasion on Trout Lake, STA leader Howie Caputo yelled, "Go home, timber niggers" to plaintiff Maulson while circling Maulson's spearing boat in his own motorboat. Other STA members made comments to the effect that Indians couldn't find their food stamps because they kept them under their work boots. Members of STA, including board member Tommy Handrick, frequently called spearers "welfare warriors," "wagon burners" and "timber niggers." At Squirrel, Willow Springs and Namekagon lakes, protesters yelled, "Timber nigger" and "You're a defeated people; you are a conquered people." At Sand and Dam Lake, protesters chanted, "Spear an Indian, save a walleye. Drown 'em, drown 'em." Especially during the 1990 spearing season, it was customary to reserve the derogatory chants until after 10:30 p.m., by which time most of the press and camera crews had left the landings.

Protesters yelled, "Dead Indian, dead Indian" and sang, "A half breed here; a half breed there," to the tune of "Old McDonald had a farm." At Eau Pleine Reservoir, they referred to Indian women as squaws and bitches and said, "The only good Indian is a dead Indian." In 1989, they said that "Custer had the right idea" and "Tom Maulson is nothing but a fucking Jew. We need another Hitler to take care of him." ***

Spearers were the subject of threats of death and violence to themselves and their families even when they were not at the landings or out on the water. They heard the threats on the street in town, in the media and on the road on the way to the landings. For example, protesters carried signs at the landings that read, "Spear an Indian, save a walleye" and "Spear a pregnant squaw, save two walleyes." Some wore hats or shirts that showed a frontal view of a gun barrel and said, "Spear this." At Eau Pleine Reservoir, a protester carried a mannequin's head made to mimic the head of an Indian mounted on a spear. STA board member Dave Worthen displayed a poster in his tavern that read, "Wanted: Small Indians for mudflaps. Must be flexible and willing to travel." ***

Incidents Involving Defendant Crist

***

On numerous landings during the spearing season in 1989 and 1990, defendant Crist told the crowds of protesters, "You're doing a good job. Keep up the good work. Don't quit; we're winning." He often used the term "squaws" in a derogatory reference to Indian women and made comments about fat, ugly, lazy Indians, Indians on welfare and Indians being unable to hold down jobs. In 1990 at Big Arbor Vitae Lake, Crist pointed to two Indian girls nearby and said, "Look at those fat Indians. Eating all the commodities up at Flambeau there."

***

Protesters saw defendant Crist as their leader. They sang a song to the effect that they would follow defendant Crist wherever he went. It was common for defendant Crist to pull up near a landing in his boat and address the crowd, using his megaphone, with comments such as "Are we having fun yet?" to which the crowd would respond with cheers. Defendant Crist would use his megaphone and yell, "STA" and the crowd would yell back, "STA." Another cheer he used was "What do you get for raping the resource? Indian AIDS."

***

Defendant Crist helped write and distribute a STA-sponsored pamphlet to STA members and the public that contained the following statements:

a. Chippewa spearers use spears "mass produced in China and Korea," and outboard motors "manufactured in Japan";

b. Many speared fish are sold;

c. "Thousands of fish spoil because of warm weather and the lack of ambition to clean them. Each year thousands of spoiled game fish are dumped in dumps and along road sides because tribal member [sic] didn't want to clean them";

d. Tribal members receive "huge amounts of free government surplus food including cheese, butter, milk and other vast amounts of 'commodity' foods. Along with these free foods they receive free food stamps and a cost of living allowance of over $20,000/household/year. They are also eligible for free government housing, subsidized heat and light, a whole list of government entitlements and subsidies, and a host of other government benefits. Tribal members receive 100% free medical and dental care, free pharmaceutical coverage, free day care and free and complete educational subsidies."

***

The statements in the pamphlet are inaccurate. *** Indians are not entitled to surplus food or to food stamps simply by virtue of being Indian. They receive surplus food or food stamps only if they qualify for them under the same program requirements that are imposed upon all applicants for state or federal benefits. Indians are eligible for subsidized housing on the same basis as any other citizen; they do not receive a cost of living allowance of over $20,000 a household; and they do not receive free and complete educational subsidies. Like all other citizens, Indians are eligible for educational grants if their income is below a certain level. ***

Opinion

All citizens of the United States are guaranteed "the same right *** as is enjoyed by white citizens thereof to inherit, purchase, lease, sell, hold and convey real and personal property" under 42 U.S.C. § 1982. To prove a violation of this statute, it is necessary to prove both that property rights were interfered with and that the interference was motivated by racial prejudice. *** The court of appeals has upheld the findings in the January 6, 1992 order that the right of the plaintiff tribe to exercise its usufructuary rights in the ceded territory is a property right, *Lac du Flambeau,* 991 F.2d at 1258–59, and that defendants interfered with plaintiffs' property right when they and others acting in concert with them or at their direction created wakes on waterways to interfere with spearing, planted concrete decoys, shined lights in the eyes of spearers, impeded the progress of boats, blocked spearing boats from moving from the boat landings out to the spawning beds and assaulted and battered members of the plaintiff band, their families and supporters. The only questions remaining to be decided on remand are whether racial prejudice was a motivating factor in the interference and, if it was, whether the interference would not have occurred but for the prejudice. ***

This inquiry is complicated somewhat by the fact that only Indians can spear fish, so that as a consequence, any protest against spearfishing is also directed against Indians. ***

Even when examined critically, the use of racial slurs in this case is so prevalent as to provide overwhelming evidence of "the prohibited intent." This is not a case in which plaintiffs grasp at a few stray statements made over a three or four year period in an attempt to suggest a biased state of mind on the part of the speakers. Plaintiffs have adduced evidence of countless episodes in which defendant Crist or persons acting at his direction or with his knowledge and approval hurled racial epithets at the individual plaintiffs, other tribal members, their families and supporters and taunted them with signs bearing racially offensive messages. *** This is strong evidence of a racial bias on the part of defendants that cannot be dismissed as a coincidence resulting from the fact that only Indians spear fish.

Defendants argue that the court of appeals indicated that statements made at the landings cannot be used to show that defendants' harassment of plaintiffs was racially motivated. *** The court [of appeals] noted the possibility that racially derogatory remarks may be a consequence and not the cause of a protest, but it did not hold that such remarks can never be evidence of racial motivation or that they may not be considered as evidence in this case. The court did not deny that the indications of racist motivation in this case were strong; to the contrary, it noted that "the use of racial slurs *** [is] certainly evidence of the prohibited intent," *id.* at 1263, and that "the stench of racism is unmistakable," *id.* at 1263–64. The court remanded the case for trial to determine whether defendants' "racist acts *conclusively* demonstrate racist motivation." *Id.* at 1260 (emphasis added).

Throughout the trial, defendants tried to show that plaintiffs and their witnesses were unable to identify specific STA members who made racial taunts. Plaintiffs did not need to identify all of the speakers. The statements of the protesters are attributable to defendants. Defendant Crist and the STA board members orchestrated the protests. They held organizational meetings, publicized the lakes that were likely to be speared, encouraged the protesters to go out to the landings, and when the crowds showed up, used spokesperson Crist to direct the protests. ***

Although at trial defendant Crist attempted to distance himself from the acts and statements of persons on the landings, he did not succeed in doing so. *** Not only did he fail to take any effective action to stop the taunts, he repeatedly exhorted the crowds to "keep up the good work." *** In the eyes of the protesters, law enforcement officers and spearers, defendant Crist was the leader of the protests. He was the one with the megaphone. He was the one who played peacekeeper while the TV cameras were present and reviled the Chippewa when the cameras were absent. When he told his supporters not to make racial remarks and not to throw stones at the Indians, they understood him to intend the advice only as a public relations ploy. They knew he was not criticizing them for their racist attitudes. This is why they laughed at the meeting in Arbor Vitae when he made a point of warning STA members not to use slingshots against law enforcement officers but omitted any similar warning about not using the slingshots against Indians. ***

In its opinion remanding this case, the court of appeals noted that there may be circumstances in which racist remarks are an unfortunate outgrowth of a protest rather than an indication of the purpose behind the protest. *Lac du Flambeau,* 991 F.2d at 1262. If, for example, a striking union member were to call the president of the company a racially offensive name in the heat of the strike, the name-calling would not necessarily mean that the strike was racially motivated. That is not the circumstance in this case. Defendant Crist employed racial stereotypes from the beginning, in an obvious attempt to exploit the deep-seated racism that existed in northern Wisconsin for his own purposes. *** By portraying the Indians as undeserving of the rights that they had preserved by treaty, he could justify the efforts to prevent tribal members from exercising those rights. Both in the STA brochure and in his radio appearance in Milwaukee, Crist emphasized the unworthiness of the Indians, perpetuating the idea that they were lazy and wasteful and lacking in respect for conserving nature. He had no compunction about ridiculing the cultural aspects of Indian spearing or the spearers' attempts to engage in religious ceremonies before spearing. ***

*** I conclude that plaintiffs met their burden of showing that defendants' protest activities were motivated by racial animus, and I turn to the question whether defendants established that they would have protested even if they had held no racial bias against plaintiffs.

*** From defendant Crist's testimony and from other evidence in the record, it is clear that defendant Crist is concerned about the effect of Chippewa spearing and netting upon the fish resource in northern Wisconsin. *** The question, however, is whether [this concern] is so compelling that defendants would have engaged in the extended protests on the lakes and landings in the long cold nights of a northern Wisconsin spring had it not been for the racial animus they and their supporters felt toward the Indians who were threatening their sport. I conclude that they did not. Although defendants would have been angry at anyone who restricted their fishing (including the Wisconsin Department of Natural Resources), it was a particular source of irritation that the threat came from persons they despised, whom they saw as fat, lazy, living on welfare at taxpayer expense and lacking appreciation for the wildlife resources of northern Wisconsin. The animosity for Indians as a group is what provided the fuel that kept protesters warm at the landings at ice-out time. Defendant Crist knew this and he employed it to his own ends deliberately. ***

Plaintiffs proved that defendants' protest activities were motivated by racial animus; defendants failed to prove that the protest activities would have occurred in the absence of such animus. Accordingly, I will grant plaintiffs' request for a permanent injunction. ***

NOTES AND QUESTIONS

1. What makes it difficult to prove that racial intent was a "but for" cause of the protests? Do you agree with the court on this issue? What would be the arguments for and against finding that the protests were in part racially motivated if the protests had actively interfered with Chippewa exercises of their treaty fishing rights but had not used such offensive language in doing so?

2. What about the repeated criticisms that modern tribal fishing methods are not "traditional"? Why did Crist and others think this was an effective critique? Are these criticisms motivated by racial intent? Historians have noted that "Indian cultures are the only cultures where it is assumed that if they change they are no longer a culture. In most other cultures, change is viewed as a sign that the culture in vibrant and alive, capable of surviving." Lisa Brooks, The Common Pot: The Recovery of Native Space in the Northeast xxxiii, *quoting* Craig S. Womak.

3. The litigation involving Indian fishing rights in Washington and Oregon was also very controversial, but in addition to rabid anti-Indian activists, a good number of non-Indians rallied in support of the tribal rights. *See* Fay G. Cohen, Treaties on Trial 73–76 (1986) (recounting the support for Indian fishing rights from celebrities like Marlon Brando, Dick Gregory, along with religious organizations). *See also* Uncommon Controversy: A Report Prepared for the American Friends Service Committee 108–111 (1970).

Although few members of the public would condone the methods used by Stop Treaty Abuse and its members, many people actively oppose modern tribal activities such as gaming as unfair and untraditional. Others express concern about the concept of tribes, governments within governments, whose members, like the treaty fishermen at *Lac du Flambeau*, are not subject to the laws that affect most state citizens. Are these critiques simply a more subtle form of the racist attitudes seen in *Lac du Flambeau v. Stop Treaty Abuse*? Or are they the product of the opposite impulse, the desire to ensure equal treatment?

Critics of modern tribal sovereignty are a diverse group with varied arguments and objections. One pragmatic source of critique is great skepticism that a nation—already a federation of fifty states—can operate effectively with over 560 sub-nations within it. Another continuing question is whether special treatment of Indian tribes and their members is consistent with American notions of democracy and equality. As this book turns to the complicated problems of jurisdiction and legal authority that arise in Indian country today, consider how much force there is to these concerns, and how defenders of tribal authority might respond to them. Recall also the inconsistent and unsuccessful attempts to resolve the "Indian problem" over hundreds of years of history; this history should give you pause in evaluating any proposed "quick fixes" to the legal and policy concerns raised in the next chapters

CHAPTER 4

FEDERAL POWER IN INDIAN AFFAIRS: SCOPE, SOURCES AND LIMITATIONS

■ ■ ■

By the end of the nineteenth century, the federal government was exercising vast power over Indian people and their lands. Even today, Indian "lives and activities are governed by the [United States] in a unique fashion." *Morton v. Mancari*, 417 U.S. 535, 554 (1974). Congressional power in particular has frequently been described as both "plenary and exclusive," *United States v. Lara*, 541 U.S. 193, 200 (2004), but there is less agreement about what this means. "Plenary" has several legal meanings, and all have been used in federal Indian law. *See* Nell Jessup Newton, *Plenary Power Over Indians: Its Scope, Sources and Limitations*, 132 U. Pa. L. Rev 195, 196 n.3 (1984). It may indicate a preemptive power, such as the power to preempt inconsistent state laws. *Gibbons v. Ogden*, 22 U.S. (9 Wheat.) 1, 196–97 (1824). It may also indicate a power of unlimited scope, like the general police powers of states to legislate for the health, welfare, and safety of their residents. *United States v. Lara*, 541 U.S. 193, 200 (2004). Finally, it may also indicate a power not subject to other restrictions, including constitutional or judicial review. *Lone Wolf v. Hitchcock*, 187 U.S. 553, 565 (1903).

Scholars have argued that unconstrained federal power is inconsistent with the constitutional text and foundational precedents. Robert N. Clinton, *There is No Federal Supremacy Clause for Indian Tribes*, 34 Ariz. St. L.J. 113 (2002); Philip P. Fricker, *Domesticating Federal Indian Law*, 81 Minn. L. Rev. 31, 55–56 (1996). Others argue that the plenary power doctrine from the beginning has meant wholly unlimited power, and that the doctrine must be rejected as racist at its core: "Animated by a central orienting myth of its own universalized, hierarchical position among all other discourses, the white man's archaic, European-derived law respecting the Indian is ultimately genocidal in both its practice and intent." Robert A. Williams, Jr., *The Algebra of Federal Indian Law: The Hard Trail of Decolonizing and Americanizing the White Man's Indian Jurisprudence*, 1986 Wis. L. Rev. 219, 265. Still others argue that plenary power does not mean absolute power, but simply a power without subject matter limitation, and is acceptable so long as tempered by a "conflicting, and inconsistent, recognition of inherent tribal sovereignty." Robert Laurence, *Learning to Live with the Plenary Power of Congress over the Indian Nations: An Essay in Reaction to Professor Williams' "Algebra,"* 30 Ariz. L. Rev. 413, 422 (1988).

This chapter deals with the sources and limitations for federal power in Indian affairs. Does this power come from the Constitution, from treaties, from historical practice, or from something else? How do the unique interpretive rules applicable to statutes affecting Indians, the Indian law canons of construction, restrain courts in the face of arguments that Congress has limited Indian rights? How have courts dealt with the effects of other constitutional provisions, such as the requirement of equal protection of the laws, or the prohibition on taking property without compensation? Finally, what rights do tribes have with respect to federal takings and mismanagement of tribal property? Although these questions invoke separate legal doctrines, they all concern the broader themes of the tension between constitutionalism, colonialism, and tribal survival raised earlier in the course.

I. CONSTITUTIONAL LIMITS ON FEDERAL POWER

A. SURVEYING CONSTITUTIONAL LIMITS ON FEDERAL POWER

[Review *Lone Wolf* and *Kagama*, ch. 3 *supra*; read Article I of the U.S. Constitution (Appendix *infra*) as well.]

The following overview of the ostensible constitutional sources for and limitations on federal power over Indian affairs highlights the Court's fluctuating views on these issues. Are the twin doctrines of (1), a trust obligation to tribes that the federal government, courts included, is charged with enforcing, and (2), an ill-defined "plenary" power over tribes that appears to act as a limit on judicial review of congressional action, hopelessly incompatible? How has the Court addressed the tension? Is there a coherent story to tell, or is forcing coherence a pointless exercise in a field as inevitably political as American Indian law? We preview these issues for you in the following survey, but you would do well to revisit these questions at the end of the chapter also.

Standard constitutional challenges to federal legislation. Generally, federal legislation may be challenged constitutionally in two ways. First, the statute might be beyond the legislative authority delegated to Congress in Article I or other constitutional provisions. *See, e.g., United States v. Lopez,* 514 U.S. 549 (1995) (Congress lacked authority under the Commerce Clause to enact statute prohibiting possession of guns within 1,000 feet of a school). Second, it might run afoul of limitations upon congressional authority, such as those contained in the Bill of Rights. *See, e.g., United States v. Eichman,* 496 U.S. 310 (1990) (federal statute criminalizing the defacing of U.S. flag violates first amendment protection of freedom of speech). The decisions you have read in earlier chapters suggest some limitations on both avenues of attack in the Indian context.

Nonjusticiability? In 1903 in *Lone Wolf v. Hitchcock,* the Court suggested that courts could not review most federal legislation involving Indian affairs because these statutes raised nonjusticiable political questions. *Lone Wolf* suggests that, similar to international relations, domestic Indian relations are essentially determined by politics and power (by the federal government's national authority to exercise sovereignty and subordination), not by law.

Although *Lone Wolf*'s conclusion that Congress has the authority unilaterally to abrogate an Indian treaty remains good law, its conclusion about nonjusticiability has been repudiated. In *Morton v. Mancari,* 417 U.S. 535 (1974) and *United States v. Antelope,* 430 U.S. 641 (1977), the Court reviewed statutes treating tribal members distinctly from non-tribal members to determine whether those statutes violated equal protection principles. Both statutes were upheld, but in neither case did the Court find that the issue was not justiciable. More fundamentally, in *United States v. Sioux Nation*, 448 U.S. 371 (1980), the Court conclusively rejected the argument that it could not review the claim that congressional abrogation of an Indian treaty and resulting loss of Indian land gave rise to a federal "taking" of property compensable under the Fifth Amendment. Thus, for several decades at least, it has been clear that tribes may litigate claims of the unconstitutionality of federal legislation.

Beyond Congressional Power? In 1886 in *U.S. v. Kagama, supra* the Court suggested that, although the Indian Commerce Clause did not give Congress the power to enact laws regarding crimes between tribal members occurring in Indian country, the Major Crimes Act was nonetheless valid because the dependent relationship between Indian tribes and the federal government created an extra-constitutional power to legislate in Indian affairs.

Despite this aspect of *Kagama*, over thirty years ago the Court stated in dictum that "[t]he source of federal authority over Indian matters has been the subject of some confusion, but it is now generally recognized that the power derives from federal responsibility for regulating commerce with Indian tribes and for treaty making." *McClanahan v. Arizona State Tax Comm'n*, 411 U.S. 164, 172 n.7 (1973). Can this make sense of the results in *Kagama* and *Lone Wolf*? In a somewhat more recent case, again in dictum, the Court stated that "the central function of the Indian Commerce Clause is to provide Congress with plenary power to legislate in the field of Indian affairs." *Cotton Petroleum Corp. v. New Mexico*, 490 U.S. 163, 192 (1989). Read this quotation carefully. Does it make better sense of the earlier cases? Is it a plausible understanding of the U.S. Constitution? *See* Gregory E. Ablavsky, *Beyond the Indian Commerce Clause: The Constitutional Origins of Federal Power Over Indians*, 124 Yale L. J. 1012 (2015).

In a 2004 case, *United States v. Lara*, 541 U.S. 193 (2004), *infra* ch. 8, the Court returned to the puzzle of congressional authority over Indian affairs. That case is best studied later in our course, as it involves a complicated question of tribal criminal jurisdiction.

Transgressing Limits on Congressional Power? Morton v. Mancari, infra, suggested that federal legislation or classifications that treat tribes or tribal members differently from non-Indians would be upheld as consistent with the Fifth Amendment's Due Process Clause if they could be tied rationally to Congress's unique obligations to Indians. In theory, at least, this standard of judicial review should be more stringent than the garden-variety rational basis test under the due process and equal protection clauses, under which a law will be upheld if any facts can be conceived under which the goal of the statute and the means chosen to effectuate that goal are rationally related. Under the *Mancari* "rationally tied" test, the goal of *harming* Indians—as opposed to the goals of furthering tribal-self-determination or supporting treaty rights—should be suspect. Nonetheless, the Supreme Court has not struck down a statute as violating the *Mancari* test. *See Antelope, infra; Delaware Tribal Business Committee v. Weeks*, 430 U.S. 73 (1977) (upholding congressional distribution of judgment to the historic Delaware Nation under which one present-day group, the Kansas Delawares, received nothing; Justice Stevens, in dissent, argued that the distribution scheme was simply the result of legislative oversight). To this day, the only cases in which the Supreme Court has found that a congressional act has violated limitations on congressional power have involved property rights. *See United States v. Sioux Nation, infra* (treaty abrogation and taking of tribal land amounted to a "taking" of property under the Fifth Amendment); *Hodel v. Irving*, 481 U.S. 704 (1987) (statute providing that tiny fractional share of Indian allotment would escheat to the tribe held a taking under Fifth Amendment).

Constitutional Protection for States' Rights? The only case we are aware of in which the Supreme Court has held that Congress exceeded its legislative power in Indian affairs concerned constitutional protection of states' rights. In *Seminole Tribe of Florida v. Florida*, 517 U.S. 44 (1996), the Court invalidated a provision of the Indian Gaming Regulatory Act that authorized a tribe to sue a state in federal court for refusing to negotiate a gaming compact in good faith. The case is understood to be about the state's Eleventh Amendment immunity to suit in federal court, not about Indian law, yet it cannot be wholly marginalized given that the reasoning is grounded in an interpretation of the Indian Commerce Clause. A few late nineteenth-century cases suggested that federal limitations on states' rights to regulate tribal hunting and fishing outside reservations or prosecute crimes between non-Indians on reservations might violate the Equal Footing Doctrine, under which territories are admitted as states of the union with the same rights as the original states. *See Ward v. Race Horse*, 163 U.S. 504, 516 (1896) (treaty right to hunt and fish off-reservation repealed by Enabling Act admitting Wyoming as a state); *Draper v. United States*, 164 U.S. 240, 242–245 (1896) (federal jurisdiction over crimes between non-Indians repealed by admission of Montana as a state). These decisions, however, turned on questions of statutory construction, and have not been followed in subsequent cases. *See Minnesota v. Mille Lacs Band of Chippewa Indians*, 526 U.S. 172, 205 (1999) (treaty rights not irreconcilable with state sovereignty, and so did not violate Equal Footing doctrine); *U.S. v. Winans*, 198 U.S. 371 (1905) (Equal Footing doctrine not inconsistent with right of United States to reserve certain rights and territories in Indians).[†]

Theoretical efforts to make sense of the congressional power over Indian affairs—and to suggest greater limits upon it. See if this argument makes sense: congressional power over Indian affairs can be best understood as an inherent, extra-textual power of sovereignty akin to congressional authority over foreign affairs. The Marshall trilogy recognized that, under the Law of Nations, which eventually became understood as customary international law, European countries had a lawful authority to export their sovereignty and "conquer" Indian tribes in some circumstances and unilaterally alter tribal sovereignty and property rights. *See Johnson v. McIntosh.* That authority to subordinate tribes devolved to the United States as a nation upon its independence, not to the individual states. *Worcester.* But the tribes did not lose all their sovereignty in the process; before contact with Europeans, under the Law of Nations, tribes were full, separate sovereigns (and hence could enter into treaties with European countries); even after colonization, they remained distinct

†. A case involving Indians that is somewhat hard to categorize is *Muskrat v. United States*, 219 U.S. 346 (1911), in which the Supreme Court rejected a federal statute that asked the federal courts to issue an advisory opinion, which the courts cannot do because it would exceed the courts' authority under Article III only to decide "cases" and "controversies." *Muskrat* is best understood as not a violation of Article I, but of Article III.

political communities with the authority of governing their members and their lands as well as to enter treaties with the United States. *Worcester*, again. This backdrop of sovereignty, from international law and foreign affairs, is the only plausible legal way to understand how Congress ended up with a plenary power over Indian affairs that is not provided in the words of the U.S. Constitution. It also makes the plenary power in Indian affairs consistent with the case law providing that Congress has a similar inherent plenary power over immigration, even though that latter power cannot be easily squared with constitutional text, either. The fusion of the power over Indian affairs and over immigration clearly occurred in *Lone Wolf*, which relied upon the *Chinese Exclusion Cases*—the fundamental decision according Congress a plenary power over immigration—to hold that, as with international treaties, Congress may unilaterally abrogate Indian treaties.

There are actually some advantages, normatively, to understanding congressional power this way. If it is legitimate (not as an absolute power, but as a basis for exclusive federal authority), it explains why state authority over tribes and over Indian country is generally preempted and prohibited. It means that tribes generally have one legislature to deal with, not fifty. It provides for a more uniform, national approach to Indian affairs, and this is consistent with what little constitutional text there is about Indian tribes, which consolidates the power to deal with tribes in the federal government.

Conceivably, the international background also provides ways to imagine more limitations upon congressional power. If the international law backdrop can be understood as legitimating congressional power over Indian affairs, it could also suggest limits on that power. This is not to say, necessarily, that international human rights norms about the treatment of indigenous persons should be directly enforceable in federal court. It is to suggest, however, that limitations upon congressional power should be informed by international norms. On such norms, *see, e.g.* S. James Anaya, Indigenous Peoples in International Law (2004 2d ed.).

As an example, note that the Fifth Amendment provides that the federal government may take private property "for public use" upon the payment of "just compensation." The Court has taken a very deferential approach to defining what a "public use" is, applying what amounts to rational basis review. Thus, if Congress authorizes the Corps of Engineers to take Indian reservation land to use in a dam project along a river, the amelioration of flooding easily satisfies the public use requirement; the tribe will receive just compensation, but has no way to stop the taking, and the Corps is probably under no obligation to consider alternative approaches that would limit or avoid the taking of the Indian land. Considering international human rights notions regarding indigenous persons, however, would require taking more seriously the unique importance of a homeland for such persons and the unique ways in which land is intertwined with indigenous culture, religion, and so on. That might lead courts to impose a stricter "public use" requirement for the taking of tribal land. For further elaboration of these arguments, *see* Philip P. Frickey, *Domesticating Federal Indian Law*, 81 Minn. L. Rev. 31 (1996). For another view of the plenary power/trust doctrine conundrum, see Robert Odawi Porter, *The Inapplicability of American Law to the Indian Nations*, 89 Iowa L. Rev. 1595 (2004). Professor Porter concludes that the tension is an inevitable byproduct of the colonial nature of federal Indian law, and that rather than attempt to temper colonialism, tribes should reconsider the validity of federal Indian law.

B. CANONICAL, INTERPRETIVE LIMITS ON CONGRESSIONAL POWER

Because the federal courts have not generally invoked the Constitution to limit congressional authority over Indian affairs, the usual argument for tribes in most cases is at the interpretive, not constitutional level: even if Congress has the authority to damage tribal interests, in this instance the statute is not clear enough to overcome the canonical presumption against such a congressional intent. As explained by Cohen's Handbook of Federal Indian Law 113-14 (2012),

> The theory and practice of interpretation in federal Indian law differs from that of other fields. The Supreme Court has forthrightly acknowledged this, stating for example that "the standard principles of statutory interpretation do not have their usual force in cases involving Indian law." *Montana v. Blackfeet Tribe*, 471 U.S. 759, 766 (1985). The basic Indian law canons of construction require that treaties, agreements, statutes, and executive orders be liberally construed in favor of the Indians; all ambiguities are to be resolved in favor of the Indians; in addition, treaties and agreements are to be construed as the Indians would have understood them; and tribal property rights and sovereignty are preserved unless Congress's intent to the contrary is clear and unambiguous. [citations omitted.]

The canons first arose in treaty interpretation, but have long also been applied to the interpretation of statutes and other laws. *See Ex Parte Crow Dog*, *supra*; *Montana v. Blackfeet Tribe of Indians*, 471 U.S. 759, 766 (1985); *Squire v. Capoeman*, 351 U.S. 1, 6 (1956). Chief Justice Marshall in *Worcester* justified the canons in part by analogy to contract interpretation, especially the special approaches taken to contracts of adhesion (where one party with superior bargaining power has drafted the contract). Can this, or some other, reason justify applying the canons to the interpretation of federal statutes as well? Some observers might view the Indian law canons as mere legalistic veneer for the imposition of liberal judicial values. Others might worry that the canons seem to be just "made up" by judges without any analogy or support in the broader law. Consider the following attempt to make sense of the canons as "law," not simply morality or judicial willfulness. Does this account make sense? Does it adequately explain the different results in cases like *Ex Parte Crow Dog* and *U.S. v. Kagama*? When you read *Menominee* and *Dion*, the next cases in this section, see whether it helps to explain those decisions.

PHILIP P. FRICKEY, *MARSHALLING PAST AND PRESENT: COLONIALISM, CONSTITUTIONALISM AND INTERPRETATION IN FEDERAL INDIAN LAW*

107 Harv. L. Rev. 381, 413–417 (1993)

Interpretive techniques come in many varieties. They can usually be summed up in "canons," which are simply rules of thumb that, by dint of judicial repetition, take on the appearance (though hardly the reality) of rules of law. Some canons are linguistic in nature and purport to guide the construction of a legal document, such as a statute, in accordance with ordinary rules of language. Other canons simply adopt a basic interpretive approach, such as textualism, which follows plain textual meaning; intentionalism, which follows legislative intent; or purposivism, which follows statutory purposes. Both the linguistic canons and the canons that establish a fundamental method of interpretation guide the internal interpretation of the document. By contrast, some other canons go outside the document and create an exception to the basic interpretive approach for cases that implicate certain important values. In most instances, these policy-based canons operate either as tiebreakers at the end of the basic interpretive analysis or as rebuttable presumptions at the outset of the interpretive process. The force this kind of canon has in a given case is likely to be linked to how well a vigorous application of it would promote the canon's underlying purposes on the facts.

Clear-statement rules are policy-based canons of a different order of magnitude. They go beyond end-game tiebreakers, and even beyond initial rebuttable presumptions, to require that a document be interpreted a certain way unless unambiguous statutory text or, perhaps, absolutely compelling legislative history requires a contrary conclusion. In [*McCulloch v. Maryland*, the famous constitutional case upholding congressional authority to establish a Bank of the United States] and *Worcester*, Chief Justice Marshall approached interpretation with this degree of vigor. Because no clear constitutional text denied Congress the discretion to use all feasible means to implement its enumerated powers, *McCulloch* held that Congress had that discretion. Because the Treaty of Hopewell nowhere contained language that terminated the sovereignty of the Cherokee Nation in so many words, that sovereignty survived.

Clear-statement rules, because they can radically bend documents away from their apparent meaning, are used sparingly. Their primary justification today is to guard against the erosion of constitutional structures that are difficult to protect by more direct forms of judicial review. As a recent study demonstrates, the present Supreme Court has adopted particularly stringent clear-statement rules as an aspect of "quasi-constitutional law" in order to protect values rooted in federalism and the separation of powers from evisceration at the hands of Congress. The Court has been especially vigilant in the former context and has held that Congress may invade the states' Eleventh Amendment immunity from suit in federal court or regulate core state functions "only by making its intention unmistakably clear in the language of the statute."

The rationale for these canons is straightforward. Federalism and the separation of powers are fundamental to our system, but the Court cannot easily protect them through constitutional invalidation. Most separation of powers and federalism questions essentially ask whether Congress adopted legislation that "goes too far" in invading the domain of the executive or of the states. It is difficult to find some principled way to draw this line, and in the modern regulatory state there is an evident need for wide-ranging congressional authority. Yet because the values rooted in the separation of powers and in federalism are central to our constitutional system, their very underenforcement at the constitutional level has led the Court, at the statutory interpretive level, to apply stringent clear-statement rules to federal statutes that endanger those values.

This approach has significant institutional implications both for the Court and for Congress. It provides the Court with a structural lodestar to cut through the complexities of a difficult statutory case. The state gets the benefit of a strong presumption in favor of its sovereignty, and the opposing party bears the burden of marshalling the legal complexities and finding clear evidence of congressional support for its position. If, as is often the case, state sovereignty survives the challenge, the burden of combating inertia and seeking legal change lies with the party who sought to intrude upon state authority. If this party undertakes the lobbying effort necessary to obtain federal legislation to overturn the Court's decision, it must do so openly, by clear language in a bill. In theory, at least, this approach encourages a fair fight in Congress, which is structurally better suited than the Court to weigh state sovereignty against other interests. Because it is much easier to kill legislation than to pass it, states ultimately retain all the institutional and procedural advantages in conflicts over their sovereignty, but Congress retains the capacity to erode state sovereignty whenever the national interest is sufficiently strong.

These rationales for employing clear-statement rules in the federalism and separation of powers contexts fit Chief Justice Marshall's methodology in *Worcester* well. The "Courts of the conqueror" cannot realistically be expected to invalidate even harsh colonial measures in the name of the very constitution established by the colonizers. How can such courts determine when Congress or the executive "goes too far" to promote colonization? How could a decree that made such a judgment be enforced, in any event? These concerns do not mean, however, that the courts must slavishly enforce colonial measures to the limits of their plausible meanings. By centralizing the power over Indian affairs in the federal government, by conceptualizing the relationship of tribes with the federal government as a sovereign-to-sovereign one, by envisioning an Indian treaty as the constitutive document of that sovereignty and structure, and by protecting treaty-recognized sovereignty and structure from erosion by all but crystal-clear treaty text, Chief Justice Marshall built a complex, institutionally sensitive interpretive scheme. His approach to the problems of colonization, then, parallels the current Court's efforts to domesticate important but essentially nonjusticiable questions of governmental structure by creating clear-statement rules. Both techniques have been justified by the centrality to these disputes of a constitutive document of sovereignty—an Indian treaty in the first instance, and the American Constitution in the second. ***

MENOMINEE TRIBE OF INDIANS V. UNITED STATES

391 U.S. 404, 88 S. Ct. 1705, 20 L. Ed. 2d 697 (1968)

JUSTICE DOUGLAS delivered the opinion of the Court.

The Menominee Tribe of Indians was granted a reservation in Wisconsin by the Treaty of Wolf River in 1854. 10 Stat. 1064. By this treaty the Menominees retroceded certain lands they had acquired under an earlier treaty and the United States confirmed to them the Wolf River Reservation "for a home, to be held as Indian lands are held." Nothing was said in the 1854 treaty about hunting and fishing rights. Yet we agree with the Court of Claims that the language "to be held as Indian lands are held" includes the right to fish and to hunt. The record shows that the lands covered by the Wolf River Treaty of 1854 were selected precisely because they had an abundance of game. The essence of the Treaty of Wolf River was that the Indians were authorized to maintain on the new lands ceded to them as a reservation their way of life which included hunting and fishing. ***

What the precise nature and extent of those hunting and fishing rights were we need not at this time determine. For the issue tendered by the present decision of the Court of Claims is whether those rights, whatever their precise extent, have been extinguished.

That issue arose because, beginning in 1962, Wisconsin took the position that the Menominees were subject to her hunting and fishing regulations. Wisconsin prosecuted three Menominees for violating those regulations and the Wisconsin Supreme Court held that the state regulations were valid, as the hunting and fishing rights of the Menominees had been abrogated by Congress in the Menominee Indian Termination Act of 1954. 68 Stat. 250, as amended, 25 U.S.C. §§ 891–902.

Thereupon the tribe brought suit in the Court of Claims against the United States to recover just compensation for the loss of those hunting and fishing rights. The Court of Claims by a divided vote held that the tribe possessed hunting and fishing rights under the Wolf River Treaty; but it held, contrary to the Wisconsin Supreme Court, that those rights were not abrogated by the Termination Act of 1954. We granted the petition for a writ of certiorari in order to resolve that conflict between the two courts. On oral argument both petitioner and respondent urged that the judgment of the Court of Claims be affirmed. The State of Wisconsin appeared as amicus curiae and argued that that judgment be reversed.

In 1953 Congress by concurrent resolution instructed the Secretary of the Interior to recommend legislation for the withdrawal of federal supervision over certain American Indian tribes, including the Menominees. Several bills were offered, one for the Menominee Tribe that expressly preserved hunting and fishing rights. But the one that became the Termination Act of 1954 *** did not mention hunting and fishing rights. Moreover, counsel for the Menominees spoke against the bill, arguing that its silence would by implication abolish those hunting and fishing rights. It is therefore argued that they were abolished by the Termination Act.

The purpose of the 1954 Act was by its terms "to provide for orderly termination of Federal supervision over the property and members" of the tribe. Under its provisions, the tribe was to formulate a plan for future control of tribal property and service functions theretofore conducted by the United States. On or before April 30, 1961, the Secretary was to transfer to a tribal corporation or to a trustee chosen by him all property real and personal held in trust for the tribe by the United States.

The Menominees submitted a plan, looking toward the creation of a county in Wisconsin out of the former reservation and the creation by the Indians of a Wisconsin corporation to hold other property of the tribe and its members. The Secretary of the Interior approved the plan with modifications; the Menominee Enterprises, Inc., was incorporated; and numerous ancillary laws were passed by Wisconsin integrating the former reservation into its county system of government. The Termination Act provided that after the transfer by the Secretary of title to the property of the tribe, all federal supervision was to end and "the laws of the several States shall apply to the tribe and its members in the same manner as they apply to other citizens or persons within their jurisdiction."

It is therefore argued with force that the Termination Act of 1954, which became fully effective in 1961, submitted the hunting and fishing rights of the Indians to state regulation and control. We reach, however, the opposite conclusion. The same Congress that passed the Termination Act also passed Public Law 280, 67 Stat. 588, as amended, 18 U.S.C. § 1162. The latter came out of the same committees of the Senate and the House as did the Termination Act; and it was amended in a way that is critical here only two months after the Termination Act became law. As amended, Public Law 280 granted designated States, including Wisconsin, jurisdiction "over offenses committed by or against Indians in the areas of Indian country" named in the Act, which in the case of Wisconsin was described as "All Indian country within the State." But Public Law 280 went on to say that "Nothing in this section *** shall deprive any Indian or any Indian tribe, band, or community of any right, privilege, or immunity afforded under Federal treaty, agreement, or statute *with respect to hunting, trapping, or fishing* or the control, licensing, or regulation thereof." (Emphasis added.) That provision on its face contains no limitation; it protects any hunting, trapping, or fishing right granted by a federal treaty. Public Law 280, as amended, became the law in 1954, nearly seven years before the Termination Act became fully effective in 1961. In 1954, when Public Law 280 became effective, the Menominee Reservation was still "Indian country" within the meaning of Public Law 280.

Public Law 280 must therefore be considered *in pari materia* with the Termination Act. The two Acts read together mean to us that, although federal supervision of the tribe was to cease and all tribal property was to be transferred to new hands, the hunting and fishing rights granted or preserved by the Wolf River Treaty of 1854 survived the Termination Act of 1954. ***

We decline to construe the Termination Act as a backhanded way of abrogating the hunting and fishing rights of these Indians. While the power to abrogate those rights exists, "the intention to abrogate or modify a treaty is not to be lightly imputed to the Congress." [Citing *Pigeon River, etc., Co. v. Charles W. Cox, Limited*, 291 U.S. 138 (1934); *Squire v. Capoeman*, 351 U.S. 1 (1956).]

Our conclusion is buttressed by the remarks of the legislator chiefly responsible for guiding the Termination Act to enactment, Senator Watkins, who stated upon the occasion of the signing of the bill that it "in no way violates any treaty obligation with this tribe." [100 Cong. Rec. 8538.]

We find it difficult to believe that Congress, without explicit statement, would subject the United States to a claim for compensation by destroying property rights conferred by treaty, particularly when Congress was purporting by the Termination Act to settle the Government's financial obligations toward the Indians.

Accordingly the judgment of the Court of Claims is *affirmed.*

JUSTICE MARSHALL took no part in the consideration or decision of this case.

JUSTICE STEWART, with whom JUSTICE BLACK joins, dissenting.

***

The statute is plain on its face: after termination the Menominees are fully subject to state laws just as other citizens are, and no exception is made for hunting and fishing laws. Nor does the legislative history contain any indication that Congress intended to say anything other than what the unqualified words of the statute express. In fact two bills which would have explicitly preserved hunting and fishing rights were rejected in favor of the bill ultimately adopted—a bill which was opposed by counsel for the Menominees because it failed to preserve their treaty rights.[5]

The Court today holds that the Termination Act does not mean what it says. The Court's reason for reaching this remarkable result is that it finds "*in pari materia*" another statute which, I submit, has nothing whatever to do with this case.

That statute, Public Law 280, [18 U.S.C. § 1162 and 28 U.S.C. § 1360] granted to certain States, including Wisconsin, general jurisdiction over "Indian country" within their boundaries. Several exceptions to the general grant were enumerated, including an exception from the grant of criminal jurisdiction for treaty-based hunting and fishing rights. 18 U.S.C. § 1162(b). But this case does not deal with state jurisdiction over Indian country; it deals with state jurisdiction over Indians after Indian country has been terminated. Whereas Public Law 280 provides for the continuation of the special hunting and fishing rights while a reservation exists, the Termination Act provides for the applicability of all state laws without exception after the reservation has disappeared.[7]

The Termination Act by its very terms provides:

---

5. "I think it is clear that (the bill) does affect those treaty rights and that those treaties are abrogated. Certainly it abolishes the tribal right to exclusive hunting and fishing privileges, because automatically upon the final termination date, the Menominee Reservation so far as hunting and fishing is concerned, would become subject to the laws of Wisconsin." Joint Hearings on S. 2813, H.R. 2828, and H.R. 7135, Subcommittees of Committees on Interior and Insular Affairs, 83d Cong., 2d Sess., Pt. 6, pp. 692, 708.

7. The only real relevance of Public Law 280 lies in its demonstration that when Congress wants to except treaty rights from jurisdictional grants, it knows how to do so. *Cf.* Klamath Termination Act, 68 Stat. 718, 25 U.S.C. § 564 *et seq.*, enacted by the same Congress that enacted the Menominee Termination Act, which explicitly preserves fishing rights. 25 U.S.C. § 564m(b).

> [A]ll statutes of the United States which affect Indians because of their status as Indians shall no longer be applicable to the members of the tribe *** 25 U.S.C. § 899.

Public Law 280 is such a statute. It has no application to the Menominees now that their reservation is gone.

UNITED STATES V. DION

476 U.S. 734, 106 S. Ct. 2216, 90 L. Ed. 2d 767 (1986)

JUSTICE MARSHALL delivered the opinion for a unanimous Court.

[Dwight Dion, Sr., a member of the Yankton Sioux Tribe, was convicted of shooting four bald eagles on the Yankton Sioux Reservation. The questions before the Court concerned whether he could be convicted of violating the Endangered Species Act, 16 U.S.C. § 1531 *et seq.*, and the Bald Eagle Protection Act., 16 U.S.C. § 668 *et seq.*, which the Court referred to as the "Eagle Protection Act."]

I.

The Eagle Protection Act by its terms prohibits the hunting of the bald or golden eagle anywhere within the United States, except pursuant to a permit issued by the Secretary of the Interior. The Endangered Species Act imposes an equally stringent ban on the hunting of the bald eagle. The Court of Appeals for the Eighth Circuit, however, sitting *en banc*, held that members of the Yankton Sioux Tribe have a treaty right to hunt bald and golden eagles within the Yankton Reservation for noncommercial purposes. It further held that the Eagle Protection Act and Endangered Species Act did not abrogate this treaty right. It therefore directed that Dion's convictions for shooting bald eagles be vacated, since neither the District Court nor the jury made any explicit finding whether the killings were for commercial or noncommercial purposes.[3]

The Court of Appeals relied on an 1858 treaty signed by the United States and by representatives of the Yankton Tribe. Treaty with the Yancton [1858 spelling] Sioux, Apr. 19, 1858, 11 Stat. 743. Under that treaty, the Yankton ceded to the United States all but 400,000 acres of the land then held by the Tribe. *** The United States in turn agreed to guarantee the Yanktons quiet and undisturbed possession of their reserved land, and to pay to the Yanktons, or expend for their benefit, various moneys in the years to come. The area thus reserved for the Tribe was a legally constituted Indian reservation. The treaty

---

3. *** [A]n Eighth Circuit panel rejected a religious freedom claim raised by Dion. Dion does not pursue that claim here, and accordingly we do not consider it. A statement made by the panel in rejecting that claim, though, casts some doubt on whether the issue of whether Dion had a treaty right to kill eagles for noncommercial purposes is squarely before us. The panel stated: "The record reveals that Dion, Sr. was killing eagles and other protected birds for commercial gain. The Solicitor General argues that Dion's convictions should have been affirmed whether the killings were for commercial or noncommercial purposes. The correctness of the holding below that killing for noncommercial purposes is not punishable, therefore, is squarely before us."

did not place any restriction on the Yanktons' hunting rights on their reserved land.

All parties to this litigation agree that the treaty rights reserved by the Yankton included the exclusive right to hunt and fish on their land. *** As a general rule, Indians enjoy exclusive treaty rights to hunt and fish on lands reserved to them, unless such rights were clearly relinquished by treaty or have been modified by Congress. These rights need not be expressly mentioned in the treaty. *Menominee Tribe.* Those treaty rights, however, little avail Dion if, as the Solicitor General argues, they were subsequently abrogated by Congress. We find that they were.[5]

II.

It is long settled that "the provisions of an act of Congress, passed in the exercise of its constitutional authority, *** if clear and explicit, must be upheld by the courts, even in contravention of express stipulations in an earlier treaty" with a foreign power. [*Chinese Exclusion Cases.*] This Court applied that rule to congressional abrogation of Indian treaties in *Lone Wolf.* Congress, the Court concluded, has the power "to abrogate the provisions of an Indian treaty, though presumably such power will be exercised only when circumstances arise which will not only justify the government in disregarding the stipulations of the treaty, but may demand, in the interest of the country and the Indians themselves, that it should do so."

We have required that Congress' intention to abrogate Indian treaty rights be clear and plain. [Citing *United States v. Santa Fe Pacific R. Co.*, 314 U.S. 339, 353 (1941).] "Absent explicit statutory language, we have been extremely reluctant to find congressional abrogation of treaty rights. *** " *Washington v. Washington Commercial Passenger Fishing Vessel Assn.*, 443 U.S. 658, 690 (1979). We do not construe statutes as abrogating treaty rights in "a backhanded way," *Menominee Tribe*; in the absence of explicit statement, " 'the intention to abrogate or modify a treaty is not to be lightly imputed to the Congress.' " *Id.* Indian treaty rights are too fundamental to be easily cast aside.

We have enunciated, however, different standards over the years for determining how such a clear and plain intent must be demonstrated. In some cases, we have required that Congress make "express declaration" of its intent to abrogate treaty rights. In other cases, we have looked to the statute's " 'legislative history' " and " 'surrounding circumstances' " as well as to " 'the face of the Act.' " *Rosebud Sioux Tribe v. Kneip*, 430 U.S. 584, 587 (1977), quoting *Mattz v. Arnett*, 412 U.S. 481, 505 (1973). Explicit statement by Congress is preferable for the purpose of ensuring legislative accountability for the abrogation of treaty rights[.] We have not rigidly interpreted that preference, however, as a *per se* rule; where the evidence of congressional intent to abrogate is sufficiently compelling, "the weight of authority indicates that such an intent can also be found by a reviewing court from clear and reliable evidence in the legislative history of a statute." [Quoting Felix S. Cohen's Handbook of Federal Indian Law 223 (1982 ed.).] What is essential is clear evidence that Congress actually considered the conflict between its intended action on the

5. We therefore do not address the Solicitor General's argument that Dion's hunting is outside the scope of the treaty right because the right does not protect hunting "to extinction."

one hand and Indian treaty rights on the other, and chose to resolve that conflict by abrogating the treaty.

A

The Eagle Protection Act renders it a federal crime to "take, possess, sell, purchase, barter, offer to sell, purchase or barter, transport, export or import, at any time or in any manner any bald eagle commonly known as the American eagle or any golden eagle, alive or dead, or any part, nest, or egg thereof." 16 U.S.C. § 668(a). *** The Act, however, authorizes the Secretary of the Interior to permit the taking, possession, and transportation of eagles "for the religious purposes of Indian tribes," and for certain other narrow purposes, upon a determination that such taking, possession, or transportation is compatible with the preservation of the bald eagle or the golden eagle.

Congressional intent to abrogate Indian treaty rights to hunt bald and golden eagles is certainly strongly suggested on the face of the Eagle Protection Act. The provision allowing taking of eagles under permit for the religious purposes of Indian tribes is difficult to explain except as a reflection of an understanding that the statute otherwise bans the taking of eagles by Indians, a recognition that such a prohibition would cause hardship for the Indians, and a decision that that problem should be solved not by exempting Indians from the coverage of the statute, but by authorizing the Secretary to issue permits to Indians where appropriate.

The legislative history of the statute supports that view. The Eagle Protection Act was originally passed in 1940, and did not contain any explicit reference to Indians. Its prohibitions related only to bald eagles; it cast no shadow on hunting of the more plentiful golden eagle. In 1962, however, Congress considered amendments to the Eagle Protection Act extending its ban to the golden eagle as well. As originally drafted by the staff of the Subcommittee on Fisheries and Wildlife Conservation of the House Committee on Merchant Marine and Fisheries, the amendments simply would have added the words "or any golden eagle" at two places in the Act where prohibitions relating to the bald eagle were described.

Before the start of hearings on the bill, however, the Subcommittee received a letter from Assistant Secretary of the Interior Frank Briggs on behalf of the Interior Department. The Interior Department supported the proposed bill. It noted, however, the following concern:

> The golden eagle is important in enabling many Indian tribes, particularly those in the Southwest, to continue ancient customs and ceremonies that are of deep religious or emotional significance to them. ***
>
> There are frequent reports of the continued veneration of eagles and of the use of eagle feathers in religious ceremonies of tribal rites. The Hopi, Zuni, and several of the Pueblo groups of Indians in the Southwest have great interest in and strong feelings concerning eagles. In the circumstances, it is evident that the Indians are deeply interested in the preservation of both the golden and the bald eagle. If enacted, the bill should therefore permit the Secretary of the Interior, by regulation, to allow the use of eagles for religious purposes by Indian tribes. House Hearings 2–3.

The House Committee reported out the bill. In setting out the need for the legislation, it explained in part:

Certain feathers of the golden eagle are important in religious ceremonies of some Indian tribes and a large number of the birds are killed to obtain these feathers, as well as to provide souvenirs for tourists in the Indian country. In addition, they are actively hunted by bounty hunters in Texas and some other States. As a result of these activities if steps are not taken as contemplated in this legislation, there is grave danger that the golden eagle will completely disappear. H.R. Rep. No. 1450, 87th Cong., 2d Sess., 2 (1962).

*** The bill as reported out of the House Committee thus made three major changes in the law, along with other more technical ones. It extended the law's ban to golden eagles. It provided that the Secretary may exempt, by permit, takings of bald or golden eagles "for the religious purposes of Indian tribes." And it added a final proviso: "Provided, That bald eagles may not be taken for any purpose unless, prior to such taking, a permit to do so is procured from the Secretary of the Interior." *Id.,* at 7. The bill, as amended, passed the House and was reported to the Senate Committee on Commerce.

At the Senate hearings, representatives of the Interior Department reiterated their position that, because "the golden eagle is an important part of the ceremonies and religion of many Indian tribes," the Secretary should be authorized to allow the use of eagles for religious purposes by Indian tribes. The Senate Committee agreed, and passed the House bill with an additional amendment allowing the Secretary to authorize permits for the taking of golden eagles that were preying on livestock. That Committee *** summarized the bill as follows: "The resolution as hereby reported would bring the golden eagle under the 1940 act, allow their taking under permit for the religious use of the various Indian tribes (their feathers are an important part of Indian religious rituals) and upon request of a Governor of any State, be taken for the protection of livestock and game." The bill passed the Senate, and was concurred in by the House, with little further discussion.

It seems plain to us, upon reading the legislative history as a whole, that Congress in 1962 believed that it was abrogating the rights of Indians to take eagles. Indeed, the House Report cited the demand for eagle feathers for Indian religious ceremonies as one of the threats to the continued survival of the golden eagle that necessitated passage of the bill. Congress expressly chose to set in place a regime in which the Secretary of the Interior had control over Indian hunting, rather than one in which Indian on-reservation hunting was unrestricted. Congress thus considered the special cultural and religious interests of Indians, balanced those needs against the conservation purposes of the statute, and provided a specific, narrow exception that delineated the extent to which Indians would be permitted to hunt the bald and golden eagle.

Respondent argues that the 1962 Congress did not in fact view the Eagle Protection Act as restricting Indian on-reservation hunting. He points to an internal Interior Department memorandum circulated in 1962 stating, with little analysis, that the Eagle Protection Act did not apply within Indian reservations. Memorandum from Assistant Solicitor Vaughn, Branch of Fish and Wildlife, Office of the Solicitor to the Director, Bureau of Sport Fisheries and Wildlife, Apr. 26, 1962. We have no reason to believe that Congress was aware of the contents of the Vaughn memorandum. More importantly, however, we find respondent's contention that the 1962 Congress did not understand the

Act to ban all Indian hunting of eagles simply irreconcilable with the statute on its face.

Respondent argues, and the Eighth Circuit agreed, that the provision of the statute granting permit authority is not necessarily inconsistent with an intention that Indians would have unrestricted ability to hunt eagles while on reservations. Respondent construes that provision to allow the Secretary to issue permits to *non*-Indians to hunt eagles "for Indian religious purposes," and supports this interpretation by pointing out testimony during the hearings to the effect that large-scale eagle bounty hunters sometimes sold eagle feathers to Indian tribes. *** Congress could have felt such a provision necessary only if it believed that Indians, if left free to hunt eagles on reservations, would nonetheless be unable to satisfy their own needs and would be forced to call on non-Indians to hunt on their behalf. Yet there is nothing in the legislative history that even remotely supports that patronizing and strained view. Indeed, the Interior Department immediately after the passage of the 1962 amendments adopted regulations authorizing permits *only* to "individual Indians who are authentic, bona fide practitioners of such religion."

Congress' 1962 action, we conclude, reflected an unmistakable and explicit legislative policy choice that Indian hunting of the bald or golden eagle, except pursuant to permit, is inconsistent with the need to preserve those species. We therefore read the statute as having abrogated that treaty right.

B

Dion also asserts a treaty right to take bald eagles as a defense to his Endangered Species Act prosecution. He argues that the evidence that Congress intended to abrogate treaty rights when it passed the Endangered Species Act is considerably more slim than that relating to the Eagle Protection Act. The Endangered Species Act and its legislative history, he points out, are to a great extent silent regarding Indian hunting rights. In this case, however, we need not resolve the question of whether the Congress in the Endangered Species Act abrogated Indian treaty rights. We conclude that Dion's asserted treaty defense is barred in any event.

Dion asserts that he is immune from Endangered Species Act prosecution because he possesses a treaty right to hunt and kill bald eagles. We have held, however, that Congress in passing and amending the Eagle Protection Act divested Dion of his treaty right to hunt bald eagles. He therefore has no treaty right to hunt bald eagles that he can assert as a defense to an Endangered Species Act charge.

We do not hold that when Congress passed and amended the Eagle Protection Act, it stripped away Indian treaty protection for conduct not expressly prohibited by that statute. But the Eagle Protection Act and the Endangered Species Act, in relevant part, prohibit exactly the same conduct, and for the same reasons. Dion here asserts a treaty right to engage in precisely the conduct that Congress, overriding Indian treaty rights, made criminal in the Eagle Protection Act. Dion's treaty shield for that conduct, we hold, was removed by that statute, and Congress' failure to discuss that shield in the context of the Endangered Species Act did not revive that treaty right.

It would not promote sensible law to hold that while Dion possesses no rights derived from the 1858 treaty that bar his prosecution under the Eagle

Protection Act for killing bald eagles, he nonetheless possesses a right to hunt bald eagles, derived from that same treaty, that bars his Endangered Species Act prosecution for the same conduct. Even if Congress did not address Indian treaty rights in the Endangered Species Act sufficiently expressly to effect a valid abrogation, therefore, respondent can assert no treaty defense to a prosecution under that Act for a taking already explicitly prohibited under the Eagle Protection Act. ***

NOTES AND QUESTIONS

1. *How clear is "clear"?* One might suggest that the courts that decided *Menominee Tribe* and *Dion* were from different planets, let alone different jurisdictions. Which statutory regime is clearer regarding congressional intent to abrogate treaty rights? One might want to approach that question sequentially, moving from more concrete to more abstract sources of potential statutory meaning. In which case was the statutory text clearer on that score? The legislative intent? The purpose of the statute? Public policy considerations, such as whether the statute was consistent with current public values?

2. *Other factors.* Was there some legitimate reason to give less weight to the probable expectations of the Termination Congress in *Menominee* than the environmentally minded Congresses in *Dion*? Recall ch. 3, § IV, *supra* (concerning the effects of termination upon the Menominee). Was there any legitimate reason to consider the tribal interests in *Menominee* stronger than the tribal interests in *Dion*? Were the regulatory interests stronger in one case than the other? Is it legitimate for courts to consider such factors when they "interpret" a statute? Is *Dion* a "bad facts" case? Consider footnote 3 of the Court's opinion. If Dion had killed the eagles for religious or other non-commercial purposes, would this have affected the Court's analysis? Or are all cases presenting clashes between Indian natural resource use and mainstream environmental laws "bad fact" cases for the Indian litigants?

3. *Interpretation of Statutes Implementing Old Policies.* Notice that the *Menominee* Court was considering the impact of the Menominee Termination Act at a time when Congress and the President were beginning to acknowledge that Termination had been a bad idea, and only five years before Congress passed the Menominee Restoration Act. The Eagle Protection and Endangered Species Acts, in contrast, represented an environmental concern still generally embraced by Congress in 1986. Should the policies of current congresses influence statutory interpretation? Wouldn't this allow courts to improperly assume the role of legislators, who can, after all, always amend statutes they don't like? Or might this approach be more legitimate in Indian law than in other fields, given the radically shifting federal policies and their tragic and continuing impact on native people? Questions of what courts should do with statutes representing repudiated policies recur repeatedly in Indian law. You will see them, for example, in questions of the impact of allotment on contemporary land and jurisdictional rights, as well as in the impact of Public Law 280 on present state jurisdiction.

4. *Utility of the canons.* Do the canons ever lead a judge to do what she didn't already want to do? Just six years after writing the article excerpted

above, Professor Frickey wrote that "[t]he canons of interpretation that once seemed to influence strongly, if not control, outcomes in federal Indian law cases have lost their force in the context of significant nonmember interests. *** In place of the canonical method, where only clear treaty or statutory text or congressional intent may displace tribal interests, the Court in *Yankton Sioux*, *Bourland*, and *Strate* [all cases involving tribal jurisdiction over nonmember activity] took a more abstract interpretive approach, under which general congressional [assimilative] purposes control if they have worked their way sufficiently into the adjudicatory context." Philip P. Frickey, *A Common Law for our Age of Colonialism: The Judicial Divestiture of Indian Tribal Authority Over Nonmembers*, 109 Yale L. J. 1, 58 (1999). The canons, in other words, are important but not controlling tools in interpretation.

5. The Supreme Court has affirmed the modern vitality of the canons, at least in some contexts. *Minnesota v. Mille Lacs Band of Chippewa Indians*, 526 U.S. 172 (1999), reprinted in Chapter 9, *infra*, held that a 1837 treaty right to hunt and fish free from state regulation survived to the present day, despite an 1850 Executive Order explicitly revoking the right, an 1855 treaty in which the tribe surrendered "all right, title, and interest, of whatsoever nature the same may be, which they may now have in, and to any other lands in the Territory of Minnesota or elsewhere," and the admission of Minnesota as a state in 1858. In its decision, the Court applied the following canons of interpretation: "treaty ambiguities are to be resolved in favor of the Indians;" treaties should be interpreted "to give effect to the terms as the Indians themselves would have understood them;" and Congress "must clearly express its intent to abrogate treaty rights." 526 U.S. at 195 n.5, 196 & 202.

In 2014, the Court held that the Indian Gaming Regulatory Act, which authorizes states to sue tribes to "enjoin a class III gaming activity located on Indian lands and conducted in violation of any Tribal–State compact," did not encompass suits to enjoin gaming outside Indian lands in violation of a compact. *Michigan v. Bay Mills Indian Community*, 134 S. Ct. 2024, 2033 (2014). The Court relied on the specific principle that to abrogate tribal sovereign immunity, "Congress must 'unequivocally' express that purpose," and the general canon that "[a]lthough Congress has plenary authority over tribes, courts will not lightly assume that Congress in fact intends to undermine Indian self-government." *Id.* at 2031-32.

The Problem of "Generally Applicable" Federal Statutes

The world of American law is filled with federal regulatory and criminal statutes that reach far into the everyday activities of Americans. Most such statutes apply to any person doing certain activity, and then provide specified exceptions. Occasionally, but only rarely, does the federal statute say something clearly about whether tribes are covered, or whether tribal members in Indian country are covered. *Dion* is an example of this problem. The Endangered Species Act prohibits any person from taking an endangered species (with complicated exceptions). It does not say, "any person, including an Indian tribal member exercising treaty rights, shall not take an endangered species." The Eagle Protection Act provided a variant in *Dion*: it did not squarely indicate that tribal members exercising treaty rights are covered, but by providing an exception for such persons operating under a federal permit, a strong inference was created that tribal members taking such a species without a federal permit were violating the statute. This follows from the longstanding canon of statutory interpretation "*exclusio unius est inclusio alterius*"—the expression of specified exceptions raises the inference that they are the only exceptions.

In *Dion*, it seemed natural to the Court to consider the alleged statutory violations as a matter of treaty abrogation. The taking of animals was involved, and the right to take the animals was understood as a pre-existing treaty right. Thus, the Court applied (or at least purported to apply) the Indian law canons.

What about when a treaty right might not be so apparent? Suppose a tribal member in Indian country allegedly commits mail fraud. Should she be subject to prosecution under the federal mail fraud statute, which just generally prohibits any person from engaging in that activity, without saying anything about tribal members or Indian country? Or should the canons apply, on the ground that unless Congress has expressly applied federal criminal laws to Indian country, the presumption is that the tribe will exclusively regulate crime by members? Should it matter if the mail fraud victimized off-reservation non-Indians?

Similarly, should federal regulatory laws that are silent about tribes apply to tribes? This problem is one of the most frequently recurring issues in the practice of federal Indian law, and it has never been satisfactorily resolved. It is complicated by *Federal Power Comm'n v. Tuscarora Indian Nation*, 362 U.S. 99, 120 (1960), in which the Court stated baldly "that general Acts of Congress apply to Indians as well as to all others in the absence of a clear expression to the contrary." The statement was dictum: the case involved the flooding of Tuscarora lands under the Federal Power Act, which specifically mentioned Indian reservations and evidenced congressional intent to include Indian along with other lands. In other words, the statute in *Tuscorara* was not a general Act of Congress, and was not silent with respect to tribes. Furthermore, analytically, the dictum makes no sense in light of fundamental Indian law principles. But the Court has never repudiated it, and it has been left to the lower courts to undertake the task of reconciling the dictum with broader currents in Indian law. Consider the following case, where the majority of a Seventh Circuit panel innovatively—one might say, heroically—tries to do so.

REICH V. GREAT LAKES INDIAN FISH AND WILDLIFE COMM'N

4 F.3d 490 (7th Cir. 1993)

POSNER, CIRCUIT JUDGE.

[The case concerned whether the Department of Labor could enforce the Fair Labor Standards Act against the defendant.] The Great Lakes Indian Fish and Wildlife Commission is a consortium of thirteen Chippewa Indian tribes that inhabit the Great Lakes region. The Commission was created in 1984 in order to enforce the usufructuary rights that the Chippewas retained under a series of nineteenth-century treaties with the United States. The Chippewa surrendered in these treaties most of their rights to the occupation of land outside of Indian reservations, but retained the right to use a great deal of that land for traditional Indian activities (which incidentally have a religious as well as economic significance for the Indians), such as fishing for walleye pike and muskellunge, hunting deer and moose, and gathering wild rice and the sap of maple trees, provided that they could do these things without prejudice to lawful occupiers of the land. Today these retained rights, though greatly curtailed by the spread of white occupation, still extend over tens of thousands of square miles in states abutting the Great Lakes. The Great Lakes Indian Fish and Wildlife Commission supervises these activities. It fixes hunting, fishing, and gathering seasons for the various species of animal and plant covered by the usufructuary rights, sets limits on the amounts and type of catch permitted, and polices compliance with its regulations. The last function is the most labor intensive. It consists not only of assuring that Indian hunters, fishers, and gatherers do not exceed the authorized catch, use unauthorized methods, or fish, hunt, or gather out of season, but also of protecting the Indians from interference by white hunters, fishers, and gatherers. Many white people in the Great Lakes region as elsewhere in the United States either do not understand or do not accept the privileges that the Indian treaties grant Indians. Forbidden themselves to spear fish, for example, white fishermen resent the fact that Indians are permitted to do so. This resentment sometimes boils over into violence. Hence the field employees of the Commission are not only uniformed but also armed. They are in fact a combination of game wardens and policemen. The State of Wisconsin has deputized them to exercise state as well as tribal law enforcement functions in the areas that they patrol.

The work of the Commission is seasonal because the usufructuary rights that it administers are seasonal. And during the seasons for fishing and hunting the principal species, the work of the Commission's field employees—its game warden police—takes place virtually round the clock, not only because the hours of daylight are long and hunting and fishing take place throughout them, but also because the Indians like to spear fish at night, by torchlight. The seven-day-a-week, twenty-four-hour-a-day character of the work of these Indian police is similar to that of law enforcement officers generally, only accentuated by the seasonality of the Commission's responsibilities. If employed by state or local governments these police would have no federal legal entitlement to time and a half for overtime; their employer would be free within broad limits not only to substitute compensatory time off for overtime premium pay but also to measure hours worked by a work month rather than a work week, so that an employee who worked more than 40 hours in a particular week would not be entitled even to compensatory time off unless he had exceeded 160 hours in the entire month. 29 U.S.C. §§ 207(k), 207(o). Because the Fair Labor Standards Act does not mention Indians, the Department of Labor takes the position that these exemptions are inapplicable to the warden-policemen of the Great Lakes Indian Fish and Wildlife Commission. The Department's able counsel acknowledged at argument that the difference in treatment between these tribal law enforcement officers and state or local policemen makes no sense, but contended that the difference can be erased only by Congress. She added reassuringly that it was only a question of money. The Commission's activities are financed primarily by a grant from the Department of the Interior, and if the Commission is required to pay its warden-policemen overtime it can always ask the Department for additional funding and the Department can in turn ask Congress for a supplemental appropriation.

Indian treaties are deemed the legal equivalent of federal statutes and they can therefore be modified or even abrogated by Congress. *Dion*. Nevertheless, partly no doubt out of a sense of guilt for the mistreatment of Indians by the U.S. government, partly in recognition that Indian tribes like states retain at least vestiges of sovereignty, and partly perhaps as a straightforward application of the "canon of construction" that repeals by implication are disfavored, the presumption is that a statute does not modify or abrogate Indian treaty rights. *Id.* The Fair Labor Standards Act does not mention Indians. It was enacted in 1938, at a time when Indian problems were not at the forefront of the national policy agenda. Nothing in the legislative history suggests that Congress thought about the possible impact of the Act on Indian rights, customs, or practices. If therefore the Chippewa had a treaty right to employ law enforcement officers on any terms, the Fair Labor Standards Act would be presumed not to abrogate the right by forcing the Great Lakes Indian Fish and Wildlife Commission to pay time and a half for overtime. But one searches the treaties in vain for such a right. So far as pertains to this case the only rights granted are rights to hunt, fish, and gather. There is no mention of the system for enforcing these rights, let alone any reference to the terms of employment of those hired to enforce it.

But we cannot end our consideration of the appeal with that observation. The ultimate question is the meaning fairly to be attributed to the Fair Labor Standards Act. Obviously the Act is broadly enough worded to apply to the Commission's warden-policemen without semantic strain. Indeed, read literally against the background of the exemption for state and local law enforcement officers, it covers the Commission's law enforcement officers because the Commission is not a state or local agency. And literal readings of statutes—readings that refuse to take into account any ambiguities that are not visible on the face of the statute—are rather in vogue in the Supreme Court these days, [citing recent cases], despite what might seem compelling objections. *Hermann v. Cencom Cable Associates, Inc.*, 978 F.2d 978, 982 (7th Cir. 1992). The Department of Labor's invocation of the "plain meaning" canon, however, is parried by the Commission's invocation of the canon that not only treaties but (other) federal statutes as well are to be construed so far as is reasonable to do in favor of Indians. And even literalists do not interpret statutes literally when doing so would produce a result senseless in the real world. *E.g., Green v. Bock Laundry Machine Co.*, 490 U.S. 504, 527–30 [Scalia, J., concurring in the result]. Even literalists, that is to say, acknowledge the applicability to statutes of the principle of contract interpretation that allows the court to seek meaning beneath the semantic level not only when there is an "intrinsic" ambiguity in the contract but also when there is an "extrinsic" one, that is, when doubt that the literal meaning is the correct one arises only when one knows something about the concrete activities that the contract was intended to regulate. ***

The Department of Labor's lawyer acknowledges what we have described as the statutory analogue of extrinsic ambiguity. A literal reading of the Fair Labor Standards Act would create a senseless distinction between Indian police and all other public police. Nothing in the Act alerts the reader to the problem; you have to know that there are Indian police to recognize it. But once it is recognized, the Act, viewed as a purposive, rational document, becomes ambiguous, creating room for interpretation. We cannot think of any reason other than oversight why Congress failed to extend the law enforcement exemption to Indian police, especially when engaged in the sort of seasonal activities in which the defendant's warden-police engage; more important, no reason has been suggested to us. The Department's lawyer speculated that the Indians must simply have failed to lobby for an exemption; and we know that in legislation as in other areas of life it is the squeaky wheel that gets oiled. As she also said, it is only a question of money, and maybe the Commission can get more money from Congress, although Congress is not at the moment in a very giving mood. It is only a question of money for state and local policemen as well, yet we can imagine the howls that would go up from the state and local law enforcement community if Congress tried to repeal its exemption from the overtime provisions of the Act.

The case for exempting the tribal policemen is stronger than that for exempting ordinary police. We mentioned the intensely seasonal character of their work. An additional consideration is that even though there is no treaty right to employ law enforcement officers on whatever terms the tribal organization sets and the officers are willing to accept, it has been traditional to leave the administration of Indian affairs for the most part to the Indians themselves. They have their own courts, their own tribal governments, their own police. It is true that these institutions are mainly for the regulation of the reservations, but the exercise of usufructuary rights off the reservation is as important to the Indians as the exercise of their occupancy rights within the reservations and maybe more so, since only about a third of all Indians live on reservations. An effective system of property rights, we have long been reminded by skeptics about laissez-faire, depends upon regulations establishing and enforcing those rights. Robert L. Hale, *Coercion and Distribution in a Supposedly Non–Coercive State*, 38 Pol. Sci. Q. 470 (1923); Cass R. Sunstein, After the Rights Revolution: Reconceiving the Regulatory State 20 (1990). The warden-policemen of the Great Lakes Indian Fish and Wildlife Commission are an important element of the scheme for regulating Indian property rights. The courts have spoken of the "inherent sovereignty" of Indian tribes and have held that it extends to the kind of regulatory functions exercised by the Commission with respect to both Indians and non-Indians. The idea of comity—of treating sovereigns, including such quasi-sovereigns as states and Indian tribes, with greater respect than other litigants—counsels us to exercise forbearance in construing legislation as having invaded the central regulatory functions of a sovereign entity.

Of course the Indians have no *constitutional* immunity from such intrusion; after *Garcia v. San Antonio Metropolitan Transit Authority*, 469 U.S. 528 (1985), even the states do not. But even when it has no constitutional backing, comity is a proper consideration in statutory interpretation. So the Supreme Court has held in insisting that if Congress wants to alter the traditional balance between the states and the federal government it make its intention unmistakable. *** *Gregory v. Ashcroft*, 501 U.S. 402 (1991). *** Our dictum in *Smart v. State Farm Ins. Co.*, 868 F.2d 929, 936 (7th Cir. 1989), that "federalism uniquely concerns States; there simply is no Tribe counterpart," goes too far. Indian tribes, like states, are quasi-sovereigns entitled to comity. Comity argues for allowing the Indians to manage their own police as they like, even though no treaty confers such prerogatives, until and unless Congress gives a stronger indication than it has here that it wants to intrude on the sovereign functions of tribal government.

The Department's lawyer argued that application of the overtime provisions of the Fair Labor Standards Act would benefit the Commission's law enforcement officers, who are of course themselves Indians, even if it hurt their employer. Well, it might, but then again it might not—for there is a lively debate over whether regulations of the employment relation such as minimum wage and overtime regulations actually benefit the ostensible beneficiaries, since by making labor more expensive such regulations may cause disemployment. *See, e.g., Mechmet v. Four Seasons Hotel, Ltd.*, 825 F.2d 1173, 1176 (7th Cir.1987); Finis Welch, Minimum Wages: Issues and Evidence (1978). *** It is not our business to try to resolve such a debate, and anyway the resolution would not decide this case. The relevant comity is a duty of forbearance not to individual Indians but to Indian governments, and it would be a conspicuous breach of comity to accuse the latter, as the Labor Department's lawyer came close to doing at the oral argument, of not being guided by a sincere concern for the best interests of the former. We must bear in mind also that the principal beneficiaries of the activities of the Great Lakes Indian Fish and Wildlife Commission are not the Commission's employees; they are the Indian fishermen, hunters, and gatherers whom the Commission serves and protects.

We realize that other general federal statutes regulating employment, notably ERISA and OSHA, have been applied to Indian agencies when, as in the present case, no treaty right was at stake. *Smart, supra*; *Donovan v. Coeur d'Alene Tribal Farm*, 751 F.2d 1113 (9th Cir. 1985); *U.S. Dept. of Labor v. OSHRC*, 935 F.2d 182 (9th Cir. 1991); *Lumber Industry Pension Fund v. Warm Springs Forest Products Industries*, 939 F.2d 683 (9th Cir. 1991). But the employees in those cases were engaged in routine activities of a commercial or service character, namely lumbering and health care, rather than of a governmental character. They were not law enforcement officers, who if they had been employed by a state or local government would have been exempt from the law. Similarly distinguishable is *Confederated Tribes v. Kurtz*, 691 F.2d 878 (9th Cir. 1982), refusing to recognize an implied exemption from federal excise taxation for a tribal sawmill. We do not hold that employees of Indian agencies are exempt from the Fair Labor Standards Act. We hold only that those agencies' law-enforcement employees, and any other employees exercising governmental functions that when exercised by employees of other governments are given special consideration by the Act, are exempt. We have the support of [*EEOC v. Cherokee Nation*, 871 F.2d 937 (10th Cir. 1989).] Noting that Title VII of the Civil Rights Act of 1964 explicitly exempts Indian tribes but that the Age Discrimination in Employment Act does not, the Tenth Circuit held that it would read the Indian tribal exemption into the latter statute. The court was rectifying an oversight. We do the same today, actuated by the same purpose of making federal law bear as lightly on Indian tribal prerogatives as the leeways of statutory interpretation allow.

Affirmed.

[**JUDGE COFFEY** dissented; his views are discussed in the following notes.]

NOTES AND QUESTIONS

1. *What is the holding in* Great Lakes? The attorney for the Fish and Wildlife Commission argued that, because of the Indian law canons, the commission was not covered by the FLSA at all. The attorney for the Department of Labor argued that, under *Tuscarora* and lower-court decisions attempting to interpret it, the commission and its employees were covered by the statute. Judge Posner followed neither argument. What, exactly, did he hold? What did he mean at the end of the opinion when he referred to "the leeways of statutory interpretation"? How can an exception for state and local police be "interpreted" as applying to tribal police?

2. *Menominee* held that treaty rights to hunt and fish are implied in when a reservation is established, and tribes have always regulated hunting and fishing activities through customary and traditional law. The fact that tribes now have written fish and game codes and employ officers should not result in a finding that tribal law enforcement is not part of the treaty right to hunt. Why do you think Judge Posner felt he had to look to the text of the treaty for such a right, but the Supreme Court did not in *Menominee*?

3. *Judge Coffey's Dissent and the Coeur D'Alene Test.* In dissent, Judge Coffey invoked *Tuscarora* and relied upon a test for applicability of general federal laws first developed in *Donovan v. Coeur D'Alene Tribal Farm,* 751 F.2d 1113 (9th Cir. 1985):

> This court has stated "[g]eneral statutes, *** whose concerns are widely inclusive and do not affect traditional Indian or Tribal rights, are typically applied to Indians." *** A statute of general applicability does not apply to the Indians if: "(1) the law touches exclusive rights of self-governance in purely intramural matters; (2) the application of the law to the tribe would abrogate rights guaranteed by Indian treaties; or (3) there is proof by legislative history or some other means that Congress intended [the law] not to apply to Indians on their reservation. *** "

Great Lakes, 4 F.3d at 499 (Coffey, J. dissenting). How does this test attempt to accommodate the Indian law canons and the *Tuscarora* dictum? If forced to apply this test, how would the attorneys on both sides address it?

Bill Soulier, a GLIFWC technician and Bad River Band Member, measures walleye during a 2010 fisheries assessment. Courtesy of C.O. Rasmussen/GLIFWC.

4. *Current case law concerning federal statutes of general applicability.* Applying the *Coeur D'Alene* test, a few circuit courts have found that general federal laws apply to tribal commercial enterprises that serve primarily non-tribal markets and employ significant numbers of non-tribal members. *See Donovan v. Coeur D'Alene Tribal Farm,* 751 F.2d 1113 (9th Cir. 1985) (OSHA applies to a tribal farm because it was a "normal commercial enterprise" operating in interstate commerce and employing both Indians and non-Indians); *Fla. Paraplegic Ass'n, Inc. v. Miccosukee Tribe of Indians of Fla.,* 166 F.3d 1126 (11th Cir. 1999) (ADA applies to accessibility of restaurant at tribal casino); *Reich v. Mashantucket Sand & Gravel,* 95 F.3d 174, 180–81 (2d Cir. 1996) (OSHA applies to tribal business because of the "nature of MSG's work, its employment of non-Indians, and the construction work on a hotel and casino that operates in interstate commerce."). None of these cases involved tribes with treaty rights. In contrast, in *Donovan v. Navajo Forest Products Industries,* the Tenth Circuit held that OSHA did not apply to a Navajo business because the inspections required under OSHA would violate the right to

exclude protected by the 1868 Treaty between the Navajo and the United States and "dilute the principles of tribal sovereignty and self-government recognized in the treaty." *Donovan*, 692 F.2d 709, 712 (10th Cir. 1982). In general the Tenth Circuit has followed an approach more consistent with the Indian law canons of construction, and has been "reluctant to apply statutes which regulate the terms and conditions of employment such as health and safety in the workplace (OSHA), unless the statute expressly includes Indian tribes." *NLRB v. Pueblo of San Juan,* 280 F.3d 1278 (10th Cir. 2000).

Where federal laws would affect tribes engaging in classically governmental functions, or affect relations largely between tribal members, courts have tended to hold that federal statutes of general applicability do not apply. Thus courts have held that the age-discrimination statutes do not apply to tribal employment of tribal members, *EEOC v. Fond du Lac Heavy Equipment and Construction Co.,* 986 F.2d 246, 251 (8th Cir. 1993), to tribal membership decisions, *Nero v. Cherokee Nation of Oklahoma,* 892 F.2d 1457 (10th Cir. 1989), or to classically governmental agencies such as Housing Authorities. *EEOC v. Karuk Tribe Housing Authority,* 260 F.3d 1071, 1082 (9th Cir. 2001) (age discrimination).

Some statutes explicitly or implicitly exclude tribes from their coverage. Title VII and the ADA, for example, exclude tribes from the definition of employers, 42 U.S.C. § 2000e(b); 42 U.S.C. § 12111(B)(i). Courts have held that this exclusion reveals a congressional intent to prohibit employment discrimination actions against tribes under 42 U.S.C. § 1981 as well. *Taylor v. Alabama Intertribal Council Title IV JTPA,* 261 F.3d 1032, 1035 (11th Cir. 2001); *Wardle v. Ute Indian Tribe,* 623 F.2d 670 (10th Cir. 1980).

In *San Manuel Indian Bingo and Casino v. NLRB,* 475 F.3d 1306 (D.C. Cir. 2007), the D.C. Circuit considered whether the National Labor Relations Act applied to a tribal casino. The court noted the conflict between the *Tuscarora* statement and the interpretive canons protecting tribal sovereignty, but held that the two principles did not conflict in the dispute at hand. Although the casino was the tribe's sole source of revenue, the court found that application of the NLRA would have little impact on that revenue. Moreover, the court stated,

> [O]peration of a casino is not a traditional attribute of self-government. Rather, the casino at issue here is virtually identical to scores of purely commercial casinos across the country. Second, the vast majority of the Casino's employees and customers are not members of the Tribe, and they live off the reservation. For these reasons, the Tribe is not simply engaged in internal governance of its territory and members, and its sovereignty over such matters is not called into question. Because applying the NLRA to San Manuel's Casino would not impair tribal sovereignty, federal Indian law does not prevent the Board from exercising jurisdiction.

475 F.3d at 1315. In deciding that the NLRA should apply, the court rejected arguments that because the NLRA does not apply to state or federal governments, it should not be interpreted to apply to tribal governments without further evidence of congressional intent. Was the court correct that application of federal law to the nonmember employees of a tribal business does not affect tribal sovereignty? Why shouldn't Congress' exclusion of other governments

from application of the NLRA influence the question of whether Congress would have intended the act to apply to tribes?

The NLRB, following *San Manuel*, found that the NLRA applies to tribal labor laws and practices in several subsequent decisions. *See Chickasaw Nation Operating Winstar World Casino and International Brotherhood of Teamsters Local 886*, 360 NLRB No. 1 (July 12, 2013); *Soaring Eagle Casino and Resort, an Enterprise of the Saginaw Chippewa Indian Tribe of Michigan and International Union, United Automobile, Aerospace and Agricultural Implement Workers of America*, 359 NLRB No. 92 (April 16, 2013); *Little River Band of Ottawa Indians Tribal Government and Local 406, International Brotherhood of Teamsters*, 359 NLRB No. 84, (March 18, 2013). These decisions were being challenged in the federal circuit courts and were close to resolution when the Supreme Court decided *NLRB v. Noel Canning*, 134 S. Ct. 2550 (2014), which invalidated recess appointments to the NLRB and therefore vacated all NLRB decisions issued during the period that recess appointees served on the board.

The tribal decisions were remanded back to the NLRB for reconsideration, which adhered to its prior position on the application of the NLRA. Two of these cases have since been appealed to the Sixth Circuit, and the first panel to decide the issue upheld the NLRB's position based on application of the *Coeur d'Alene* test. *NLRB v. Little River Band of Ottawa Indians Tribal Government*, 788 F.3d 537 (6th Cir. 2015). The second panel would have reversed the NLRB, but was bound by the first panel's result under Sixth Circuit rules. *Soaring Eagle Casino & Resort v. N.L.R.B.*, 791 F.3d 648 (6th Cir. 2015), *cert. denied*, 136 S. Ct. 2509 (2016). If the timing had been reversed, the panel that issued the opinion in *Soaring Eagle* would have been able to set the Circuit's precedent. *See* Alex T. Skibine, *Practical Reasoning and the Application of General Federal Regulatory Laws to Indian Nations*, 22 Wash. & Lee J. Civil Rts. & Soc. Just. 123, 138-54 (2016) (discussing the approach proposed by the *Soaring Eagle* panel and offering alternatives).

For more on statutes of general applicability, see Vicki J. Limas, *Application of Federal Labor and Employment Statutes to Native American Tribes: Respecting Sovereignty and Achieving Consistency*, 26 Ariz. St. L.J. 681 (1994); Wenona T. Singel, *Labor Relations and Tribal Self–Governance*, 80 N.D.L. Rev. 691 (2004); Cohen's Handbook of Federal Indian Law §§ 2.03 & 21.02[5][c] (2012).

5. *Laws of General Applicability and Individual Indians.* The above cases concern whether federal laws apply to tribes themselves. Courts are more likely to find that federal laws apply to Indian individuals. Thus, individual Indians are subject to federal income taxes unless treaties or other statutes indicate intent to exempt the income from such taxes. *See Squire v. Capoeman*, 351 U.S. 1 (1956) (although Indians were generally subject to federal income tax, General Allotment Act indicated intent to exempt income from allotted land). Similarly, most courts have concluded that general federal criminal statutes, such as those prohibiting interstate commerce in drugs, reach Indians to the same extent they reach others. *See U.S. v. Begay*, 42 F.3d 486, 499 (9th Cir. 1994); *cf. U.S. v. Smiskin*, 487 F.3d 1260 (9th Cir. 2007) ("right to travel" in Yakama treaty barred prosecution of tribal members under Contraband Cigarette Trafficking Act). Within Indian territory, however, this general rule is

complicated by special federal statutes that indicate an intent to leave prosecution of certain crimes to Indians themselves. *See U.S. v. Quiver,* 241 U.S. 602 (1916) (tribal members could not be prosecuted for adultery); *U.S. v. Markiewicz,* 978 F.2d 786, 799 (2d Cir. 1992) (stating that automatic application of federal criminal laws to Indians would violate the spirit of *Quiver*); Ch. 5, § IV.A, *infra.*

6. *Different Analysis for State Laws.* It is important to understand that the general applicability analysis only concerns whether *federal* laws apply. As you will see in Chapter 7, the analysis for state laws is very different, and state law will only rarely apply to Indian tribes or tribal members directly.

C. EQUAL PROTECTION AS A RESTRAINT ON FEDERAL POWER

Federal Indian law, which deals entirely with the special rights of Indians and tribes, might be seen as fundamentally at odds with the equal protection principles which generally prohibit classifications based on race. But is it appropriate to think of tribal and Indian classifications as solely "racial," rather than as classifications of groups with a special political and sovereign status? Still, is it possible to think of such classifications as not racial at all, given that many federal laws and tribal definitions of membership include descent as one criteria for inclusion? Or are these simply the wrong questions—does it really make sense to apply doctrines developed in reaction to the United States' dismal history of enslavement and discrimination against non-white individuals to the government-to-government relationship between the United States and Indian tribes? *Morton v. Mancari* dealt with all of these questions. The *Mancari* plaintiffs' constitutional claims are necessarily described as Fifth Amendment Due Process claims because the Fourteenth Amendment applies to states, not the federal government. But the courts have long held that the Fifth Amendment includes prohibitions against unequal treatment by the federal government, and plaintiffs therefore bring equal protection claims under the Fifth Amendment.

MORTON V. MANCARI

417 U.S. 535, 94 S. Ct. 2474, 41 L. Ed. 2d 290 (1974)

JUSTICE BLACKMUN delivered the opinion of the Court. ***

Section 12 of the Indian Reorganization Act, 48 Stat. 986, 25 U.S.C. § 472, provides:

> The Secretary of the Interior is directed to establish standards of health, age, character, experience, knowledge, and ability for Indians who may be appointed, without regard to civil-service laws, to the various positions maintained, now or hereafter, by the Indian Office, in the administration of functions or services affecting any Indian tribe. Such qualified

Indians shall hereafter have the preference to appointment to vacancies in any such positions.

In June 1972, pursuant to this provision, the Commissioner of Indian Affairs, with the approval of the Secretary of the Interior, issued a directive stating that the BIA's policy would be to grant a preference to qualified Indians not only, as before, in the initial hiring stage, but also in the situation where an Indian and a non-Indian, both already employed by the BIA, were competing for a promotion within the Bureau. The record indicates that this policy was implemented immediately.

Shortly thereafter, appellees, who are non-Indian employees of the BIA at Albuquerque, instituted this class action, on behalf of themselves and other non-Indian employees similarly situated, claiming that the "so-called 'Indian Preference Statutes,'" were repealed by the 1972 Equal Employment Opportunity Act and deprived them of rights to property without due process of law, in violation of the Fifth Amendment. *** [The District Court avoided the constitutional question by deciding the case on statutory grounds. It enjoined the BIA from implementing the preference on the ground that it had been impliedly repealed by the Equal Employment Opportunity Act, which provided that "all personnel actions" in federal agencies "shall be free from any discrimination based on race, color, religion, sex, or national origin."]

The federal policy of according some hiring preference to Indians in the Indian service dates at least as far back as 1834. Since that time, Congress repeatedly has enacted various preferences of the general type here at issue. The purpose of these preferences, as variously expressed in the legislative history, has been to give Indians a greater participation in their own self-government; to further the Government's trust obligation toward the Indian tribes; and to reduce the negative effect of having non-Indians administer matters that affect Indian tribal life.

The preference directly at issue here was enacted as an important part of the sweeping Indian Reorganization Act of 1934. The overriding purpose of that particular Act was to establish machinery whereby Indian tribes would be able to assume a greater degree of self-government, both politically and economically. Congress was seeking to modify the then-existing situation whereby the primarily non-Indian-staffed BIA had plenary control, for all practical purposes, over the lives and destinies of the federally recognized Indian tribes. Initial congressional proposals would have diminished substantially the role of the BIA by turning over to federally chartered self-governing Indian communities many of the functions normally performed by the Bureau. Committee sentiment, however, ran against such a radical change in the role of the BIA. The solution ultimately adopted was to strengthen tribal government while continuing the active role of the BIA, with the understanding that the Bureau would be more responsive to the interests of the people it was created to serve.

One of the primary means by which self-government would be fostered and the Bureau made more responsive was to increase the participation of tribal Indians in the BIA operations. In order to achieve this end, it was recognized that some kind of preference and exemption from otherwise prevailing civil service requirements was necessary. Congressman Howard, the House sponsor, expressed the need for the preference:

> The Indians have not only been thus deprived of civic rights and powers, but they have been largely deprived of the opportunity to enter the more important positions in the service of the very bureau which manages their affairs. Theoretically, the Indians have the right to qualify for the Federal civil service. In actual practice there has been no adequate program of training to qualify Indians to compete in these examinations, especially for technical and higher positions; and even if there were such training, the Indians would have to compete under existing law, on equal terms with multitudes of white applicants. *** The various services on the Indian reservations are actually local rather than Federal services and are comparable to local municipal and county services, since they are dealing with purely local Indian problems. It should be possible for Indians with the requisite vocational and professional training to enter the service of their own people without the necessity of competing with white applicants for these positions. This bill permits them to do so.

78 Cong. Rec. 11729 (1934).

Congress was well aware that the proposed preference would result in employment disadvantages within the BIA for non-Indians. Not only was this displacement unavoidable if room were to be made for Indians, but it was explicitly determined that gradual replacement of non-Indians with Indians within the Bureau was a desirable feature of the entire program for self-government. Since 1934, the BIA has implemented the preference with a fair degree of success. The percentage of Indians employed in the Bureau rose from 34% in 1934 to 57% in 1972.[†] *** The Commissioner's extension of the preference in 1972 to promotions within the BIA was designed to bring more Indians into positions of responsibility and, in that regard, appears to be a logical extension of the congressional intent.

It is against this background that we encounter the first issue in the present case: whether the Indian preference was repealed by the Equal Employment Opportunity Act of 1972. Title VII of the Civil Rights Act of 1964, 78 Stat. 253, was the first major piece of federal legislation prohibiting discrimination in private employment on the basis of "race, color, religion, sex, or national origin." 42 U.S.C. § 2000e–2(a). Significantly, §§ 701(b) and 703(i) of that Act explicitly exempted from its coverage the preferential employment of Indians by Indian tribes or by industries located on or near Indian reservations.[19] This exemption reveals a clear congressional recognition, within the framework of Title VII, of the unique legal status of tribal and reservation-based activities. ***

[The 1964 Act did not outlaw employment discrimination by the federal government; the 1972 Act was the first statute to do so.] Nowhere in the [statutory text or] legislative history of the 1972 Act, however, is there any mention of Indian preference. Appellees assert, and the District Court held, that since the 1972 Act proscribed racial discrimination in Government employment, the

---

†. [Eds.: Today about 95% of the Bureau's employees are Indian.]

19. Section 701(b) excludes "an Indian Tribe" from the Act's definition of "employer." Section 703(i) states: "Nothing contained in this subchapter shall apply to any business or enterprise on or near an Indian reservation with respect to any publicly announced employment practice of such business or enterprise under which a preferential treatment is given to any individual because he is an Indian living on or near a reservation."

Act necessarily, albeit *sub silentio*, repealed the provision of the 1934 Act that called for the preference in the BIA of one racial group, Indians, over non-Indians: ***

We disagree. For several reasons we conclude that Congress did not intend to repeal the Indian preference and that the District Court erred in holding that it was repealed.

First: There are the above-mentioned affirmative provisions in the 1964 Act excluding coverage of tribal employment and of preferential treatment by a business or enterprise on or near a reservation. These 1964 exemptions as to private employment indicate Congress' recognition of the longstanding federal policy of providing a unique legal status to Indians in matters concerning tribal or "on or near" reservation employment. The exemptions reveal a clear congressional sentiment that an Indian preference in the narrow context of tribal or reservation-related employment did not constitute racial discrimination of the type otherwise proscribed. In extending the general anti-discrimination machinery to federal employment in 1972, Congress in no way modified these private employment preferences built into the 1964 Act, and they are still in effect. It would be anomalous to conclude that Congress intended to eliminate the longstanding statutory preferences in BIA employment, as being racially discriminatory, at the very same time it was reaffirming the right of tribal and reservation-related private employers to provide Indian preference. ***

Second: Three months after Congress passed the 1972 amendments, it enacted two new Indian preference laws. These were part of the Education Amendments of 1972, 86 Stat. 235. The new laws explicitly require that Indians be given preference in Government programs for training teachers of Indian children. It is improbable, to say the least, that the same Congress which affirmatively approved and enacted these additional and similar Indian preferences was, at the same time, condemning the BIA preference as racially discriminatory. In the total absence of any manifestation of supportive intent, we are loathe to imply this improbable result.

Third: Indian preferences, for many years, have been treated as exceptions to Executive Orders forbidding Government employment discrimination. The 1972 extension of the Civil Rights Act to Government employment is in large part merely a codification of prior anti-discrimination Executive Orders that had proved ineffective because of inadequate enforcement machinery. There certainly was no indication that the substantive proscription against discrimination was intended to be any broader than that which previously existed. By codifying the existing anti-discrimination provisions, and by providing enforcement machinery for them, there is no reason to presume that Congress affirmatively intended to erase the preferences that previously had coexisted with broad anti-discrimination provisions in Executive Orders.

Fourth: Appellees encounter head-on the "cardinal rule *** that repeals by implication are not favored." *** They and the District Court read the congressional silence as effectuating a repeal by implication. There is nothing in the legislative history, however, that indicates affirmatively any congressional intent to repeal the 1934 preference. Indeed, as explained above, there is ample independent evidence that the legislative intent was to the contrary.

This is a prototypical case where an adjudication of repeal by implication is not appropriate. The preference is a longstanding, important component of the Government's Indian program. The anti-discrimination provision, aimed at alleviating minority discrimination in employment, obviously is designed to deal with an entirely different and, indeed, opposite problem. Any perceived conflict is thus more apparent than real.

In the absence of some affirmative showing of an intention to repeal, the only permissible justification for a repeal by implication is when the earlier and later statutes are irreconcilable. Clearly, this is not the case here. A provision aimed at furthering Indian self-government by according an employment preference within the BIA for qualified members of the governed group can readily co-exist with a general rule prohibiting employment discrimination on the basis of race. Any other conclusion can be reached only by formalistic reasoning that ignores both the history and purposes of the preference and the unique legal relationship between the Federal Government and tribal Indians.

Furthermore, the Indian preference statute is a specific provision applying to a very specific situation. The 1972 Act, on the other hand, is of general application. Where there is no clear intention otherwise, a specific statute will not be controlled or nullified by a general one, regardless of the priority of enactment. ***

The courts are not at liberty to pick and choose among congressional enactments, and when two statutes are capable of co-existence, it is the duty of the courts, absent a clearly expressed congressional intention to the contrary, to regard each as effective. *** In light of the factors indicating no repeal, we simply cannot conclude that Congress consciously abandoned its policy of furthering Indian self-government when it passed the 1972 amendments. ***

IV.

We still must decide whether, as the appellees contend, the preference constitutes invidious racial discrimination in violation of the Due Process Clause of the Fifth Amendment. ***

Resolution of the instant issue turns on the unique legal status of Indian tribes under federal law and upon the plenary power of Congress, based on a history of treaties and the assumption of a "guardian-ward" status, to legislate on behalf of federally recognized Indian tribes. The plenary power of Congress to deal with the special problems of Indians is drawn both explicitly and implicitly from the Constitution itself. Article I, § 8, cl. 3, provides Congress with the power to "regulate Commerce *** with the Indian Tribes," and thus, to this extent, singles Indians out as a proper subject for separate legislation. Article II, § 2, cl. 2, gives the President the power, by and with the advice and consent of the Senate, to make treaties. This has often been the source of the Government's power to deal with the Indian tribes. The Court has described the origin and nature of the special relationship:

> In the exercise of the war and treaty powers, the United States overcame the Indians and took possession of their lands, sometimes by force, leaving them an uneducated, helpless and dependent people, needing protection against the selfishness of others and their own improvidence. Of necessity the United States assumed the duty of furnishing that protection, and with it the authority to do all that was required to perform that obligation and to prepare the Indians to take their place as independent, qualified members of the modern body politic. ***

Board of County Comm'rs v. Seber, 318 U.S. 705, 715 (1943).

Literally every piece of legislation dealing with Indian tribes and reservations, and certainly all legislation dealing with the BIA, single out for special treatment a constituency of tribal Indians living on or near reservations. If these laws, derived from historical relationships and explicitly designed to help only Indians, were deemed invidious racial discrimination, an entire Title of the United States Code (25 U.S.C.) would be effectively erased and the solemn commitment of the Government toward the Indians would be jeopardized. ***

Contrary to the characterization made by appellees, this preference does not constitute "racial discrimination." Indeed, it is not even a "racial" preference.[24] Rather, it is an employment criterion reasonably designed to further the cause of Indian self-government and to make the BIA more responsive to the needs of its constituent groups. It is directed to participation by the governed in the governing agency. The preference is similar in kind to the constitutional requirement that a United States Senator, when elected, be "an Inhabitant of that State for which he shall be chosen," Art. I, § 3, cl. 3, or that a member of a city council reside within the city governed by the council. Congress has sought only to enable the BIA to draw more heavily from among the constituent group in staffing its projects, all of which, either directly or indirectly, affect the lives of tribal Indians. The preference, as applied, is granted to Indians not as a discrete racial group, but, rather, as members of quasi-sovereign tribal entities whose lives and activities are governed by the BIA in a unique fashion. *See* n. 24, *supra*. In the sense that there is no other group of people favored in this manner, the legal status of the BIA is truly *sui generis*. Furthermore, the preference applies only to employment in the Indian service. The preference does not cover any other Government agency or activity, and we need not consider the obviously more difficult question that would be presented by a blanket exemption for Indians from all civil service examinations. Here, the preference is reasonably and directly related to a legitimate, nonracially based goal. This is the principal characteristic that generally is absent from proscribed forms of racial discrimination.

On numerous occasions this Court specifically has upheld legislation that singles out Indians for particular and special treatment. *See, e.g., Board of County Comm'rs v. Seber* (federally granted tax immunity); *** *Simmons v. Chief Eagle Seelatsee*, 384 U.S. 209 (1966), *aff'g* 244 F.Supp. 808 (E.D. Wash. 1965) (statutory definition of tribal membership, with resulting interest in trust estate)[.] This unique legal status is of long standing, see *Cherokee Nation*, and its sources are diverse. As long as the special treatment can be tied rationally to the fulfillment of Congress' unique obligation toward the Indians, such legislative judgments will not be disturbed. Here, where the preference is

---

24. The preference is not directed towards a "racial" group consisting of "Indians"; instead, it applies only to members of "federally recognized" tribes. This operates to exclude many individuals who are racially to be classified as "Indians." In this sense, the preference is political rather than racial in nature. The eligibility criteria appear in 44 BIAM 335, 3.1: "1. Policy—An Indian has preference in appointment in the Bureau. To be eligible for preference in appointment, promotion, and training, an individual must be one-fourth or more degree Indian blood and be a member of a Federally recognized tribe. It is the policy for promotional consideration that where two or more candidates who met the established qualification requirements are available for filling a vacancy, if one of them is an Indian, he shall be given preference in filling the vacancy. *** "

reasonable and rationally designed to further Indian self-government, we cannot say that Congress' classification violates due process. ***

NOTES AND QUESTIONS

1. *Mancari's historical and social context. Mancari* emerged from both the Indian activism of the self-determination era and the growing challenges to affirmative action. In 1970, members of the National Indian Youth Council occupied BIA offices in Denver, challenging BIA hiring practices. Although 57% of BIA employees were Indian, they were mostly in lower-ranked, lower-responsibility positions. Seventy-six percent of employees in General Schedule grades 7 and below were Indian, while only 20% of those in grades 9 and above were. The protesters brought a lawsuit challenging the BIA's failure to apply the 1934 Indian preference, and secured a broad district court judgment ordering the bureau to reform its promotion practices. *Freeman v. Morton*, No. 327–71, 1972 WL 258 (D.D.C. Dec. 21, 1972), *aff'd* 499 F.2d 494 (D.C. Cir. 1974). The new BIA policy, however, was almost immediately greeted by a class action brought by four teachers—two white, one black, and one Hispanic—at the Southwest Indian Polytechnic Institute in Albuquerque. When the case reached the Supreme Court, many thought the Court would take the opportunity to resolve the question of the constitutionality of affirmative action. Instead the Court simply hinted at more general issues—stating that as a policy "reasonably and directly related to a legitimate, nonracially based goal" it had the "the principal characteristic that generally is absent from proscribed forms of racial discrimination"—leaving their resolution for future cases. *See* Carole Goldberg, *What's Race Got to Do with It?: The Story of* Morton v. Mancari, *in* Race Law Stories 237 (Rachel F. Moran & Devon W. Carbado eds., 2008).

2. There are two parts of the *Mancari* opinion, one holding that the Indian preference is not repealed by the Equal Employment Opportunity Act of 1972, and one holding that the Indian preference does not violate the equal protection prohibitions implicit in the Due Process Clause of the Fifth Amendment. What is the Court's rationale for each holding?

3. *Source of Federal Power.* The Court describes the federal government's power in Indian affairs as deriving from two sources: The Commerce Clause and the Treaty Clause. How does locating federal power in both of these clauses affect its scope? Take a close look at the Court's language in those paragraphs of the opinion.

4. *The "political rather than racial" rationale.* The Court in *Mancari* states that the Indian preference, because it applies only to members of federally recognized tribes, is "political rather than racial in nature." This language has sown confusion in later cases because aspects of conventional understandings of "racial" identification exist within classifications that further the special relationship with federally recognized Indian tribes. Read the description of who was eligible for the BIA preference in footnote 24. Shortly after the *Mancari* decision, the BIA reverted to the original IRA definition for Indian preference and also added a category for Alaska Natives. The preference now applies to someone who (1) is a member of a federally-recognized tribe, band or community; (2) is a descendant of enrolled members of federally-recognized

tribes who were residing on a reservation on June 1, 1934; (3) possesses at least one-half degree Indian blood; or (4) is "a member of an Alaska Native Tribe; or, an individual whose name appears on the roll of Alaska Natives prior to July 31, 1981, and not subsequently disenrolled; or, an individual who was issued stock in a Native corporation pursuant to 43 U.S.C. § 1606(g)(1)(B)(i)." The change from *Mancari* allows the BIA to apply the preference to all tribal members, rather than just tribal members who also possess one-quarter or more Indian blood, and also to non-tribal members who possess one-half or more Indian blood. Is the latter addition constitutional under *Mancari*? Does it affect your analysis to know that many Native people were omitted from tribal rolls during the allotment era, sometimes inadvertently and sometimes not?

Today, most federal programs that benefit Indian tribes defer to the tribes' own membership criteria without requiring additional blood-quantum, but some also extend benefits to descendants of tribal members. *See* Sarah Krakoff, *Inextricably Political: Race, Membership, and Tribal Sovereignty*, 87 Wash. L. Rev. 1041, 1083-85 (2012) (reviewing definitions in federal programs benefitting Indians). Similar descent-based criteria are the basis of other laws as well. The Indian Child Welfare Act, for example, applies to children who are the biological children of a tribal member and who are eligible for membership themselves. 25 U.S.C. § 1903(4). Is this descent-based classification constitutional under *Mancari*? So far the courts have held that it is. *See Brackeen v. Bernhardt*, 937 F.3d 406 (5th Cir. 2019) (upholding the ICWA against equal protection and other constitutional challenges brought by non-Indian adoptive parents).

Rather than making too much of *Mancari*'s "political rather than racial" language, the leading Indian law treatise counsels that "[a] sound reading of *Morton v. Mancari* would acknowledge that even though ancestry may figure into some Indian classifications, ultimately the most important inquiry is whether the law can be justified as fulfilling 'Congress' unique obligation toward the Indians.'" Cohen's Handbook of Federal Indian Law § 14.03[2][b] (2012); *see* Bethany R. Berger, *Reconciling Equal Protection and Federal Indian Law*, 98 Cal. L. Rev. 1165 (2010) (justifying this approach as a matter of doctrinal analysis and legal history).

This approach—that *Mancari* stands for the principle that courts should defer to Congress and the Executive branch when they act to further tribes' self-governance regardless of whether the classifications have aspects of descent and ancestry—also fits better with the reality of how the federal government has affected the evolution of tribal membership. Many tribes today have membership criteria that include aspects of blood quantum or lineal descent. For some, these membership rules reflect the legacies of the allotment era, when the federal government insisted on a list of tribal members for the purpose of carving up reservations.

On the other hand, many tribes are composed of distinct ethnic and linguistic groups as a result of the federal government's other coercive policies during the reservation and allotment eras, which at times forced many tribal peoples onto shared reservations and into a shared government. Peoples as distinct as the Mojave, Chemehuevi, Navajo, and Hopi, for example, were consolidated onto a single reservation and became the Colorado River Indian Tribes, a single federally-recognized tribe. *See* Sarah Krakoff, *Inextricably*

Political: Race, Membership, and Tribal Sovereignty, 87 Wash. L. Rev. 1041 (2012). Membership in a federally-recognized tribes is therefore always "political," whether or not the tribe's own rules have aspects of lineal descent or ancestry. *See* Sarah Krakoff, *They Were Here First: Tribes, Race, and the Constitutional Minimum*, 69 Stanford L. Rev. 491, 546 (2017).

5. *Fitting* Mancari *into equal protection doctrine generally.* In other areas of equal protection analysis, the Court refers to rational basis scrutiny, which requires that the classification be rationally related to a legitimate interest; heightened scrutiny, which requires that the classification be substantially related to an important interest; and strict scrutiny, which requires that the classification be narrowly tailored to further a compelling interest. The rational basis test, applied to social and economic classifications that do not affect a fundamental right, is often thought of as an almost anything-goes standard, while the strict scrutiny test has been called " 'strict' in theory but fatal in fact." Gerald Gunther, *Foreword: In Search of an Evolving Doctrine on a Changing Court: A Model for a Newer Equal Protection*, 86 Harv. L. Rev. 1, 8 (1972). *But see Grutter v. Bollinger*, 539 U.S. 306, 326 (2003) ("Strict scrutiny is not 'strict in theory but fatal in fact.' "). *Mancari* states that as long as special treatment of Indians "can be tied rationally to the fulfillment of Congress' unique obligation toward the Indians, such legislative judgments will not be disturbed." What is the basis for this holding? Is this rational basis scrutiny or something else?

Is a general Indian preference in the Bureau of Indian Affairs rationally related to tribal self-government? How, for example, does it further tribal self-government to appoint a Navajo from Arizona to a position working with the Ottawa in Michigan?

6. *Does the* Mancari *standard mean that any federal classification affecting tribal members will be upheld, whether or not it furthers tribal self-governance?* The employment preference in *Mancari* was challenged by non-Indians. It clearly benefited Indian people and furthered Indian self-government by reforming the federal agency that works directly with tribes and tribal programs. What about cases brought by tribal members alleging that they are denied privileges or protections afforded to non-Indians? *Fisher v. District Court*, 424 U.S. 382 (1976), held that a member of the Northern Cheyenne Tribe could not bring a case in Montana state court to regain the custody of her son, also a tribal member, where the case arose on the reservation. The Court rejected the argument that denying her access to the state courts constituted impermissible racial discrimination:

> The exclusive jurisdiction of the Tribal Court does not derive from the race of the plaintiff but rather from the quasi-sovereign status of the Northern Cheyenne Tribe under federal law. Moreover, even if a jurisdictional holding occasionally results in denying an Indian plaintiff a forum to which a non-Indian has access, such disparate treatment of the Indian is justified because it is intended to benefit the class of which he is a member by furthering the congressional policy of Indian self-government.

424 U.S. 382, 390–391. *Fisher* can be seen as a case about jurisdictional rules, rather than individual rights. The Northern Cheyenne tribal member was, for the purposes of accessing the Montana state courts, more similar to a citizen of Wyoming than a citizen of Montana. Allowing her to evade her own court's

jurisdiction would undermine the tribal courts' power to decide matters properly within its jurisdiction.

What about cases in which the distinctive treatment of Indians is not rooted in deference to tribal sovereignty or other obligations to tribes? In *United States v. Antelope*, 430 U.S. 641 (1977), the Court considered the impact of the criminal jurisdiction rules at play in Indian country. Under this scheme, crimes committed by non-Indians against non-Indians on reservations are subject to state jurisdiction, but crimes by Indians against non-Indians are subject to federal jurisdiction. (See Ch. 5, *infra*, for more on this complicated jurisdictional scheme). The defendants, both Coeur D'Alene Indians, had been prosecuted for robbing and killing a non-Indian woman on the Coeur D'Alene reservation in Idaho. Because they were tried under federal law, they were subject to the federal felony-murder rule, under which any death that occurs during the commission of a felony like robbery is automatically considered a murder. Had they been non-Indian, however, they would have been tried under Idaho law, which did not have a felony-murder provision, so the prosecution would have had to prove premeditation to get a murder conviction. The Court held that this distinction did not violate the Constitution:

> [I]n the present case we are dealing, not with matters of tribal self-regulation, but with federal regulation of criminal conduct within Indian country implicating Indian interests. But the principles reaffirmed in *Mancari* and *Fisher* point more broadly to the conclusion that federal regulation of Indian affairs is not based upon impermissible classifications. Rather, such regulation is rooted in the unique status of Indians as "a separate people" with their own political institutions. Federal regulation of Indian tribes, therefore, is governance of once-sovereign political communities; it is not to be viewed as legislation of a " 'racial' group consisting of 'Indians' ***." Indeed, respondents were not subjected to federal criminal jurisdiction because they are of the Indian race but because they are enrolled members of the Coeur d'Alene Tribe. We therefore conclude that the federal criminal statutes enforced here are based neither in whole nor in part upon impermissible racial classifications.

430 U.S. 641, 646–647. Does the Court in *Antelope* follow the *Mancari* standard of determining whether the classification is rationally tied to Congress's unique obligation to the Indians? Could the federal criminal scheme survive that standard?

7. *Affirmative action and the color-blindness paradigm. Mancari, Fisher*, and *Antelope* all preceded several cases in which the Supreme Court called affirmative action programs into question. In *Regents of the University of California v. Bakke*, 438 U.S. 265 (1978), the Court held that an admissions program granting a numeric preference to underrepresented minority students was unconstitutional. *Bakke* led to later decisions holding that even remedies for past discrimination or under-representation must be narrowly tailored to meet a compelling purpose. *See Grutter v. Bollinger*, 539 U.S. 306, 326 (2003). In *Adarand Contractors v. Pena*, 515 U.S. 200 (1995), the Court held that federal affirmative action measures were subject to the same strict constitutional scrutiny as state measures. In dissent, Justice Stevens expressed the concern that the majority's approach "would view the special preferences that the National Government has provided to Native Americans since 1834 as

comparable to the official discrimination against African Americans that was prevalent for much of our history." 515 U.S. at 244 (Stevens, J., dissenting).

A few subsequent lower court cases implied that there should be greater scrutiny of measures benefiting Indians. In *Williams v. Babbitt*, 115 F.3d 657 (9th Cir. 1997), a non-Native challenged an agency determination that he could not import and raise reindeer under the Reindeer Industry Act, which was designed to protect and encourage Alaska Native reindeer farming. Finding that this interpretation "would almost certainly render the Reindeer Act unconstitutional," the Ninth Circuit interpreted the Act "as not precluding non-natives in Alaska from owning and importing reindeer." 115 F.3d at 665–66. Writing for the majority, Judge Kozinski quoted Justice Stevens' dissent in *Adarand* saying, "If Justice Stevens is right about the logical implications of *Adarand*, *Mancari*'s days are numbered." *Id.* at 666.

Kozinski's prediction was premature. More than two decades later, *Mancari* remains good law. The Supreme Court has gestured at concerns about descent-based classifications in the Indian Child Welfare Act context, but so far has stayed its hand. *See Adoptive Couple v. Baby Girl*, 133 S. Ct. 2552, 2565 (2013) (noting equal protection "concerns" with ICWA's application in that case but ruling on other grounds). For criticism of *Williams v. Babbitt* and similar cases, see Carole Goldberg, *Descent into Race*, 49 UCLA L. Rev. 1373 (2002). *See also* Cohen's Handbook of Federal Indian Law at 948-64 (2012) (extensive discussion and collection of authorities); Sarah Krakoff, *Inextricably Political, Race, Membership, and Tribal Sovereignty*, 87 Wash. L. Rev. 1041 (2012) (arguing that judicial second-guessing of federal classifications that benefit tribes is beyond judicial competence); *see also* Sarah Krakoff, *They Were Here First: American Indian Tribes, Race, and the Constitutional Minimum*, 69 Stanford L. Rev. 491 (2017) (critiquing the color-blindness paradigm in general and with regard to its specific application to American Indian law).

8. *State classifications of Indians.* The Court in *Mancari* considered the preference under the Fifth Amendment, which applies to the federal government, rather than the Fourteenth Amendment, which applies to states. What are the other reasons that the rationale of *Mancari* would not apply to state classifications? Courts have held that although states do not have federal authority to classify Indians differently from other citizens, they may do so to further a federal scheme. *See Washington v. Confederated Bands of Yakima Indian Nation*, 439 U.S. 463, 501 (1979) (holding that where federal law permitted states to assume jurisdiction over Indian reservations, state law assuming criminal jurisdiction over Indians only when on non-Indian land did not violate equal protection); *Peyote Way Church of God, Inc. v. Thornburgh*, 922 F.2d 1210, 1281 (5th Cir. 1991) (state exemption of members of Native American Church, whose membership was limited to those of Native American descent, from laws criminalizing Peyote possession did not violate equal protection where state exemption was similar to congruent federal exemption).

At least one court has held that state classifications that recognize tribes as governments, and treat tribes differently from businesses or other non-governmental entities on that basis, are also distinct from racial classifications and should not be subject to strict scrutiny. *See Artichoke Joe's California Grand Casino v. Norton*, 353 F.3d 712 (9th Cir. 2003) (upholding California statute that granted tribes a monopoly on class III gaming against an equal protection challenge.) In *Artichoke Joe's*, the court held that the California statute furthered the federal government's purposes in the Indian Gaming Regulatory Act, but also noted that state (or federal) classifications that treat individual Indians differently from other citizens are distinguishable from state actions that recognize and treat tribes as governments: "The very nature of a Tribal–State compact is political; it is an agreement between an Indian tribe, as one sovereign, and a state, as another." *Id.* at 734. *But see KG Urban Enterprises, LLC v. Patrick*, 693 F.3d 1 (1st Cir. 2012) (suggesting casino preference for Indian tribe with tribal-state compact without IGRA-qualified lands might be subject to strict scrutiny).

State classifications that do not promote a federal statutory scheme or otherwise further the unique relationship between tribes and the federal government are subject to strict scrutiny, and state actions that deprive Indians of rights or services afforded to all other state citizens have repeatedly been found to violate the Fourteenth Amendment. *See Navajo Nation v. New Mexico*, 975 F.2d 741, 744 (10th Cir. 1992); *Natonabah v. Board of Education of Gallup–McKinley County School Dist.*, 355 F. Supp. 716, 724 (D.N.M. 1973); Cohen's Handbook of Federal Indian Law, § 14.02 (2012).

9. *State classifications, voting rights, and Native Hawaiians:* Rice v. Cayetano, 528 U.S. 495 (2000). Hawaii was once an independent kingdom, and entered into treaties with the United States until American forces annexed the islands without Hawaiian consent in 1893. Although recent federal statutes regarding Indian peoples often have parallel provisions regarding Native Hawaiians, the indigenous people of Hawaii have not been recognized as having the same sovereign status as American Indian tribes. Nevertheless, when a state voting regime that permitted only descendants of Hawaii's indigenous peoples to vote for trustees of the Office for Hawaiian Affairs (OHA), which administers a trust for the benefit of Native Hawaiians, was challenged under the Fifteenth Amendment, many were concerned that the Supreme Court might take the opportunity to limit *Morton v. Mancari*. Key to Hawaii's defense of the voting restriction was the historical context of the trust. *Rice*. The United States transferred the trust property that it managed on behalf of Hawaii's indigenous peoples to Hawaii upon statehood and required the new state to take on the administration of those lands for the benefit of Native Hawaiians. Hawaii argued that it had stepped into the United States' trustee role and the voting restriction was therefore directly comparable to classifications benefitting federally-recognized tribes. The Court, in an opinion by Justice Kennedy, dodged the *Mancari* question, holding that the Fifteenth Amendment bars states from enacting any voting restrictions based on ancestry.

> *** Ancestry can be a proxy for race. It is that proxy here. *** For centuries Hawaii was isolated from migration. *** The inhabitants shared common physical characteristics, and by 1778 they had a common culture. *** The very object of the statutory definition in question and of its earlier congressional counterpart in the Hawaiian Homes Commission Act is to treat the early Hawaiians as a distinct people, commanding their own recognition and respect. The State, in enacting the legislation before us, has used ancestry as a racial definition and for a racial purpose.
>
> *** The ancestral inquiry mandated by the State is forbidden by the Fifteenth Amendment for the further reason that the use of racial

classifications is corruptive of the whole legal order democratic elections seek to preserve. The law itself may not become the instrument for generating the prejudice and hostility all too often directed against persons whose particular ancestry is disclosed by their ethnic characteristics and cultural traditions. "Distinctions between citizens solely because of their ancestry are by their very nature odious to a free people whose institutions are founded upon the doctrine of equality." *Hirabayashi v. United States*, 320 U.S. 81, 100 (1943). ***

*** The most far reaching of the State's arguments is that exclusion of non-Hawaiians from voting is permitted under our cases allowing the differential treatment of certain members of Indian tribes. [*Morton v. Mancari*], and the theory upon which it rests, are invoked by the State to defend its decision to restrict voting for the OHA trustees, who are charged so directly with protecting the interests of native Hawaiians.

If Hawaii's restriction were to be sustained under *Mancari* we would be required to accept some beginning premises not yet established in our case law. Among other postulates, it would be necessary to conclude that Congress *** has determined that native Hawaiians have a status like that of Indians in organized tribes, and that it may, and has, delegated to the State a broad authority to preserve that status. These propositions would raise questions of considerable moment and difficulty. *** We can stay far off that difficult terrain, however.

*** Even were we to take the substantial step of finding authority in Congress, delegated to the State, to treat Hawaiians or native Hawaiians as tribes, Congress may not authorize a State to create a voting scheme of this sort.

Of course, as we have established in a series of cases, Congress may fulfill its treaty obligations and its responsibilities to the Indian tribes by enacting legislation dedicated to their circumstances and needs. ***

Mancari, upon which many of the above cases rely, presented the somewhat different issue of a preference in hiring and promoting at the federal Bureau of Indian Affairs (BIA), a preference which favored individuals who were " 'one-fourth or more degree Indian blood and *** member[s] of a Federally-recognized tribe.' " Although the classification had a racial component, the Court found it important that the preference was "not directed towards a 'racial' group consisting of 'Indians,' " but rather "only to members of 'federally recognized' tribes." *** Because the BIA preference could be "tied rationally to the fulfillment of Congress' unique obligation toward the Indians," and was "reasonable and rationally designed to further Indian self-government," the Court held that it did not offend the Constitution. The opinion was careful to note, however, that the case was confined to the authority of the BIA, an agency described as "*sui generis*."

*** It does not follow from *Mancari,* however, that Congress may authorize a State to establish a voting scheme that limits the electorate for its public officials to a class of tribal Indians, to the exclusion of all non-Indian citizens. *** If a non-Indian lacks a right to vote in tribal elections, it is for the reason that such elections are the internal affair of a quasi sovereign. The OHA elections, by contrast, are the affair of the State of Hawaii. ***

*** To extend *Mancari* to this context would be to permit a State, by racial classification, to fence out whole classes of its citizens from decisionmaking in critical state affairs. The Fifteenth Amendment forbids this result. ***

Hawaii's final argument is that the voting restriction does no more than ensure an alignment of interests between the fiduciaries and the beneficiaries of a trust [because the lands that the OHA administers are held in trust for the benefit of Native Hawaiians.] ***

*** The State's position rests, in the end, on the demeaning premise that citizens of a particular race are somehow more qualified than others to vote on certain matters. That reasoning attacks the central meaning of the Fifteenth Amendment. *** Race cannot qualify some and disqualify others from full participation in our democracy. All citizens, regardless of race, have an interest in selecting officials who make policies on their behalf, even if those policies will affect some groups more than others. Under the Fifteenth Amendment voters are treated not as members of a distinct race but as members of the whole citizenry. Hawaii may not assume, based on race, that petitioner or any other of its citizens will not cast a principled vote. To accept the position advanced by the State would give rise to the same indignities, and the same resulting tensions and animosities, the Amendment was designed to eliminate. The voting restriction under review is prohibited by the Fifteenth Amendment. ***

Rice v. Cayetano, 528 U.S. 495 (2000).

Indigenous Hawaiians and their descendants are often multi-racial and multi-ethnic, as is much of the non-Native population of Hawaii. Is the Court right that Hawaii was using ancestry as a "proxy for race?" Was the State instead using ancestry as a proxy for belonging to a displaced polity? Further, can you think of examples where the law uses ancestry as a legitimate classification that is not equated with race? Almost every state has laws of intestate succession that rely on familial relations for devising property in the event that someone dies without a will. *See, e.g.*, Ariz. Rev. Stat. Ann. § 14-2103 (2016); Cal. Prob. Code § 6402 (West 2016); Mich. Comp. Laws § 700.2103 (2016); 20 PA. Cons. Stat. § 2103 (2016) (all requiring decedents' property to pass based on lineage in the absence of a surviving spouse). U.S. citizenship laws also recognize ancestry. *See, e.g.*, 8 C.F.R. § 322.2 (2016) (allowing a child to be eligible for citizenship if he or she has at least one U.S.- citizen parent). Is *Rice* therefore best understood as being confined to the specific context of the Fifteenth Amendment and state voting rights?

EQUAL PROTECTION REVIEW

Hypotheticals

1. Use *Mancari* and/or *Rice* to argue that the following measures are constitutional or unconstitutional:

a. The federal government provides special funds and programs for the education of Native Hawaiians.

b. Congress declares that Hawaii's indigenous peoples have the same legal status as American Indian tribes.

c. The federal government takes over administration of the Office of Hawaiian Affairs and reinstitutes the voting scheme struck down in *Rice*.

d. Congress enacts a measure requiring members of Indian tribes to ride in a separate car on cross-country trains.

e. A state waives the requirement of fishing licenses for members of Indian tribes with off-reservation fishing rights.

f. A state creates a tuition waiver program for all members of federally recognized tribes who attend state institutions of higher education. Does it matter if the state narrows the program to members of tribes whose aboriginal lands were in the state?

g. Congress passes a statute banning possession or consumption of alcohol on Indian reservations without compliance with state and tribal laws—the latter effective only with federal approval.

II. FEDERAL POWER AND INDIAN PROPERTY

A. ORIGINAL INDIAN TITLE

In *Johnson v. McIntosh*, the Supreme Court held that upon "discovery" of the continent by European nations, American Indian tribes lost the right to convey legal title of their property to anyone other than the discovering European sovereign. According to *Johnson*, the United States stepped into England's shoes in that regard after the Revolutionary War, and thereafter tribes within U.S. territorial boundaries could only convey legal title to the federal government. *See Johnson, supra*, Ch. 2. *Johnson* also stands for the corollary proposition that tribes remain in full possession of their traditional property, including the rights to use and occupy their lands, until the United States acquires legal title either by acquisition or conquest. And further, that even after discovery, tribes can convey their rights to use and possess property according to their own laws and enforcement mechanisms. *See Johnson, supra*. What tribes lost, according to *Johnson*, was essentially the right to convey their property to more than just one purchaser, the United States.

The facts of *Johnson* were never contested due to the parties' stipulations. If there had been a dispute about how the two non-Indian litigants acquired their claimed title from the tribes, difficult questions would have arisen regarding who purported to represent the federal government in the initial acquisitions from the Illinois and Piankeshaw tribes. *See* Eric Kades, *The Dark Side of Efficiency*, *supra* Ch.2. Shady dealings and outright fraud were a regular feature of the settlement of the lands outside the original thirteen states. As the United States pushed its territorial boundaries further west, eventually succeeding in establishing a nation from coast to coast, these actions hardly subsided. *See* Patricia Nelson Limerick, The Legacy of Conquest: The Unbroken Past of the American West (1987). Despite *Johnson*'s proscription on non-federal acquisition of Indian title and the parallel prohibitions in the trade and intercourse acts, *see* Ch. 2 *supra*, non-Indian individuals and corporations forced Indians off of their lands through skirmishes, usurpation, and a variety of sub-legal means. The federal government often either looked the other way or blessed these illegal dispossessions by designating small reservations for tribes that represented a fraction of their traditional territory.

As a result, questions eventually arose about how tribes could prove and protect their claims to their traditional territory. In the following case, which the Hualapai Tribe pursued for decades by urging the United States to protect their lands, the Supreme Court held that tribes could prove they retained original Indian title (sometimes referred to as aboriginal title) by showing historic use and occupancy, even without any prior recognition or formalities by the federal government. Further, the Court applied a strong version of the Indian law canons of interpretation to various enactments that the defendant, the Santa Fe-Pacific Railroad, argued had terminated the tribe's aboriginal title. This case, decided during the Indian New Deal era, was litigated before the Supreme Court by Felix Cohen and Nathan Margold. Both were deeply involved in promoting tribal self-governance, and Cohen was simultaneously working on academic articles making the case for original Indian title as a core legal doctrine. *See* Felix S. Cohen, *The Spanish Origin of Indian Rights in the Law of the United States*, 31 Geo. L. J. 1 (1942); *Original Indian Title*, 32 Minn. L. Rev. 28 (1947).

UNITED STATES V. SANTA FE PAC. R. CO.

314 U.S. 339, 62 S. Ct. 248, 86 L.Ed. 260 (1941)

Mr. JUSTICE DOUGLAS delivered the opinion of the Court.

This is a suit brought by the United States, in its own right and as guardian of the Indians of the Walapai (Hualpai) Tribe in Arizona to enjoin respondent from interfering with the possession and occupancy by the Indians of certain land in northwestern Arizona. Respondent claims full title to the lands in question under the grant to its predecessor, the Atlantic and Pacific Railroad Co., provided for in the Act of July 27, 1866, 14 Stat. 292. The [United States] sought to establish that respondent's rights under the grant of 1866 are subject to the Indians' right of occupancy both inside and outside their present reservation which was established by the Executive Order of President Arthur, January 4, 1883. The [lawsuit] consists of two causes of action—the first relating to lands inside, and the second, to lands outside, that reservation. * * * [The District Court and Court of Appeals ruled for the Respondent Santa Fe Pacific.] We granted the petition for certiorari because of the importance of the problems raised in the administration of the Indian laws and the land grants.

Sec. 2 of the Act of July 27, 1866, the Act under which respondent's title to the lands in question derived, provided: 'The United States shall extinguish, as rapidly as may be consistent with public policy and the welfare of the Indians, and only by their voluntary cession, the Indian title to all lands falling under the operation of this act and acquired in the donation to the road named in the act.'

Basic to the present causes of action is the theory that the lands in question were the ancestral home of the Walapais, that such occupancy constituted 'Indian title' within the meaning of § 2 of the 1866 Act, which the United States agreed to extinguish, and that in absence of such extinguishment the grant to the railroad 'conveyed the fee subject to this right of occupancy.' The Circuit Court of Appeals concluded that the United States had never recognized such possessory rights of Indians within the Mexican Cession and that in absence of such recognition the Walapais had no such right good against grantees of the United States.

Occupancy necessary to establish aboriginal possession is a question of fact to be determined as any other question of fact. If it were established as a fact that the lands in question were, or were included in, the ancestral home of the Walapais in the sense that they constituted definable territory occupied exclusively by the Walapais (as distinguished from lands wandered over by many tribes), then the Walapais had 'Indian title' which unless extinguished survived the railroad grant of 1866.

'Unquestionably it has been the policy of the federal government from the beginning to respect the Indian right of occupancy, which could only be interfered with or determined by the United States.' This policy was first recognized in *Johnson v. M'Intosh* and has been repeatedly reaffirmed. As stated in *Mitchel v. United States*, Indian 'right of occupancy is considered as sacred as the fee-simple of the whites.' Whatever may have been the rights of the Walapais under Spanish law, the *Cramer* case assumed that lands within the Mexican Cession were not excepted from the policy to respect Indian right of occupancy. * * * Perhaps the assumption that aboriginal possession would be respected in the Mexican Cession was, like the generalizations in *Johnson v. M'Intosh*, not necessary for the narrow holding of the case. But such generalizations have been so often and so long repeated as respects land under the prior sovereignty of the various European nations including Spain, that like other rules governing titles to property they should now be considered no longer open. Furthermore treaties negotiated with Indian tribes, wholly or partially within the Mexican Cession, for delimitation of their occupancy rights or for the settlement and adjustment of their boundaries, constitute clear recognition that no different policy as respects aboriginal possession obtained in this area than in other areas. Certainly it would take plain and unambiguous action to deprive the Walapais of the benefits of that policy. For it was founded on the desire to maintain just and peaceable relations with Indians. The reasons for its application to other tribes are no less apparent in case of the Walapais, a savage tribe which in early days caused the military no end of trouble.

Nor is it true, as respondent urges, that a tribal claim to any particular lands must be based upon a treaty, statute, or other formal government action. As stated in the *Cramer* case, 'The fact that such right of occupancy finds no recognition in any statute or other formal governmental action is not conclusive.'

Extinguishment of Indian title based on aboriginal possession is of course a different matter. The power of Congress in that regard is supreme. The manner, method and time of such extinguishment raise political not justiciable issues. As stated by Chief Justice Marshall in *Johnson v. M'Intosh*, 'the exclusive right of the United States to extinguish' Indian title has never been doubted. And whether it be done by treaty, by the sword, by purchase, by the exercise of complete dominion adverse to the right of occupancy, or otherwise, its justness is not open to inquiry in the courts.

If the right of occupancy of the Walapais was not extinguished prior to the date of definite location of the railroad in 1872, then the respondent's predecessor took the fee subject to the encumbrance of Indian title.

Certainly prior to 1865 any right of occupancy of the Walapais to the lands in question was not extinguished; nor was the policy of respecting such Indian title changed. The Indian Trade and Intercourse Act of June 30 was extended over 'the Indian tribes in the Territories of New Mexico and Utah' by § 7 of the Act of February 27, 1851. The 1834 Act, which derived from the Act of July 22, 1790, made it an offense to drive stock to range or feed 'on any land belonging to any Indian or Indian tribe without the consent of such tribe'; gave the superintendent of Indian affairs authority 'to remove from the Indian country all persons found therein contrary to law'; made it unlawful to settle on 'any lands belonging, secured, or granted by treaty with the United States to any Indian tribe'; and made invalid any conveyance of lands 'from any Indian nation or tribe of Indians.' The Act of 1851 obviously did not create any Indian right of occupancy which did not previously exist. But it plainly indicates that in 1851 Congress desired to continue in these territories the unquestioned general policy of the Federal government to recognize such right of occupancy. As stated by Chief Justice Marshall in *Worcester v. Georgia*, the Indian trade and intercourse acts 'manifestly consider the several Indian nations as distinct political communities, having territorial boundaries, which their authority is exclusive, and having a right to all the lands within those boundaries, which is not only acknowledged, but guaranteed by the United States.'

[The Court then discussed other acts establishing rules for settlement in the territories acquired by the United States after the Mexican-American War of 1848 and concluded that none of them extinguished "any Indian title based on aboriginal occupancy which the Walapais may have had."] * * *

This brings us to the Act of March 3, 1865, which provided: 'All that part of the public domain in the Territory of Arizona, lying west of a direct line from Half-Way Bend to Corner Rock on the Colorado River, containing about seventy-five thousand acres of land, shall be set apart for an Indian reservation for the Indians of said river and its tributaries.' It is plain that the Indians referred to included the Walapais. The suggestion for removing various Indian tribes in this area to a reservation apparently originated with a former Indian agent, Superintendent Poston, who was a Territorial Representative in Congress in 1865. His explanation on the floor of the House of the bill, which resulted in the creation of the 1865 reservation, indicates that he had called a council of the confederated tribes of the Colorado, including the Walapais, and had told them that 'they should abandon' their lands and confine themselves to the place on the Colorado river which was later proposed for a reservation. He entered into no agreement with them nor did he propose a treaty. He merely stated that if elected to Congress he would try to get Congress to provide for them. As stated by the Commissioner of Indian Affairs in 1864: 'Assuming that the Indians have a right of some kind to the soil, Mr. Poston's arrangement proposes a compromise with these Indians, by which on their confining themselves to their reservation and yielding all claims to lands beyond it, they shall, in lieu of an annuity in money or supplies, be furnished by government with an irrigating canal, at a cost estimated at something near $100,000 which, by insuring them their annual crops, will enable them to support themselves, independently of other aid by the government.'

We search the public records in vain for any clear and plain indication that Congress in creating the Colorado River reservation was doing more than making an offer to the Indians, including the Walapais, which it was hoped would be accepted as a compromise of a troublesome question. We find no indication that Congress by creating that reservation intended to extinguish all of the rights which the Walapais had in their ancestral home. That Congress could have effected such an extinguishment is not doubted. But an extinguishment cannot be lightly implied in view of the avowed solicitude of the Federal Government for the welfare of its Indian wards. [T]he rule of construction recognized without exception for over a century has been that 'doubtful expressions, instead of being resolved in favor of the United States, are to be resolved in favor of a weak and defenseless people, who are wards of the nation, and dependent wholly upon its protection and good faith.' Nor was there any plain intent or agreement on the part of the Walapais to abandon their ancestral lands if Congress would create a reservation. Furthermore, the Walapais did not accept the offer which Congress had tendered. In 1874 they were, however, forcibly removed to the Colorado River reservation on order from the Indian Department. But they left it in a body the next year. And it was decided 'to allow them to remain in their old range during good behavior.' They did thereafter remain in their old country and engaged in no hostilities against the whites. No further attempt was made to force them onto the Colorado River reservation … . On these facts we conclude that the creation of the Colorado River reservation was, so far as the Walapais were concerned, nothing more than an abortive attempt to solve a perplexing problem. Their forcible removal in 1874 was not pursuant to any mandate of Congress. It was a high-handed endeavor to wrest from these Indians lands which Congress had never declared forfeited. No forfeiture can be predicated on an unauthorized attempt to effect a forcible settlement on the reservation unless we are to be insensitive to the high standards for fair dealing in light of which laws dealing with Indian rights have long been read. Certainly a forced abandonment of their ancestral home was not a 'voluntary cession' within the meaning of § 2 of the Act of July 27, 1866.

The situation was, however, quite different in 1881. Between 1875 and that date there were rather continuous suggestions for settling the Walapais on some reservation. In 1881 the matter came to a head. A majority of the tribe, 'in council assembled,' asked an officer of the United States Army in that region 'to aid them and represent to the proper authorities' the following proposal: 'They say that in the country, over which they used to roam so free, the white men have appropriated all the water; that large numbers of cattle have been introduced and have rapidly increased during the past year or two; that in many places the water is fenced in and locked up; and they are driven from all waters. They say that the Railroad is now coming which will require more water, and will bring more men who will take up all the small springs remaining. They urge that the following reservation be set aside for them while there is still time; that the land can never be of any great use to the Whites; that there are no mineral deposits upon it, as it has been thoroughly prospected; that there is little or no arable land; that the water is in such small quantities, and the country is so rocky and void of grass, that it would not be available for stock raising. I am credibly informed, and from my observations believe, the above facts to be true. I, therefore, earnestly recommend that the hereafter described Reservation be, at as early a date as practicable, set aside for them.'

Pursuant to that recommendation the military reservation was constituted on July 8, 1881, subject to the approval of the President. The Executive Order creating the Walapai Indian Reservation was signed by President Arthur on January 4, 1883. There was an indication that the Indians were satisfied with the proposed reservation. * * * [W]e conclude that its creation at the request of the Walapais and its acceptance by them amounted to a relinquishment of any tribal claims to lands which they might have had outside that reservation and that that relinquishment was tantamount to an extinguishment by 'voluntary cession' within the meaning of § 2 of the Act of July 27, 1866. The lands were fast being populated. The Walapais saw their old domain being preempted. They wanted a reservation while there was still time to get one. That solution had long seemed desirable in view of recurring tension between the settlers and the Walapais. In view of the long-standing attempt to settle the Walapais' problem by placing them on a reservation their acceptance of this reservation must be regarded in law as the equivalent of a release of any tribal rights which they may have had in lands outside the reservation. They were in substance acquiescing in the penetration of white settlers on condition that permanent provision was made for them too. In view of this historical setting, it cannot now be fairly implied that tribal rights of the Walapais in lands outside the reservation were preserved. That would make the creation of the 1883 reservation, as an attempted solution of the violent problems created when two civilizations met in this area, illusory indeed. We must give it the definitiveness which the exigencies of that situation seem to demand. Hence, acquiescence in that arrangement must be deemed to have been a relinquishment of tribal rights in lands outside the reservation and notoriously claimed by others. ****

NOTES AND QUESTIONS

1. *A victory for the Hualapai Tribe.* After the Supreme Court's decision, the United States and the railroad arrived at a settlement recognizing as Hualapai lands all of the terrain within the one-million-acre 1883 Executive Order reservation, as well as an additional 6,000 acres adjacent to the reservation. For more on the history of the case and its impact, see Christian McMillen, Making Indian Law: The Hualapai Land Case and the Birth of Ethnohistory (2007).

2. *Proving traditional use and occupancy.* The Court states, almost in an off-hand way, that "[o]ccupancy necessary to establish aboriginal possession is a question of fact to be determined as any other question of fact." The Santa Fe Pacific had argued vehemently, and winningly in the courts below, that the Hualapai Tribe could not prove traditional use and occupancy because tribes had no conception of property that was recognizable in U.S. law. Justice

Douglas revived the pro-tribal aspects of *Johnson v. McIntosh* and, no doubt relying on the arguments marshalled by Margold and Cohen, affirmed that tribes retained original Indian title and could prove it through oral and anthropological means. This aspect of the Court's decision proved crucial to tribes later attempting to prove the illegal taking of their lands before the Indian Claims Commission and the Federal Court of Claims. Those forums are discussed in the next section.

B. FEDERAL TAKING OF TRIBAL PROPERTY

The Hualapai Tribe's success at fending off the railroad was relatively rare. For many tribes, the illegal loss of their aboriginal property was not resolved in a way that allowed them to retain their lands. Tribes therefore sought ways to get compensation for their losses from the federal government. In 1946, Congress passed the Indian Claims Commission Act (ICCA), which created a forum for tribes to pursue takings and other claims against the federal government and eliminated the jurisdictional barriers to bringing suit. The ICCA's waiver of the federal government's immunity from suit was very broad, applying to a wide range of possible claims. If tribes did not have a claim under the ICCA, they had to rely on other jurisdictional statutes and waivers to pursue compensation. For tribes that lacked treaties, the ICCA was crucial for providing a path to compensation for the taking of aboriginal title. For tribes with "recognized title," meaning lands that the United States acknowledged through treaties or legislation, the ICCA is not the only jurisdictional option. The following sections address compensation for aboriginal title, and then compensation for recognized title.

1. Introductory Note on Sovereign Immunity

It is difficult to make sense out of the judicial decisions concerning federal power to take Indian assets without understanding principles of sovereign immunity. Unfortunately, sovereign immunity is a messy and arcane area of the law, and mixing it with federal Indian law leads to a uniquely complicated subject matter.

The place to begin is to recognize that American law inherited the British notion that, in the Crown's own courts, the Crown could do no wrong. In other words, the Crown's courts would not award damages against the Crown unless the government had agreed that the courts had this authority. It is still American law today that someone injured by the federal or state government cannot recover damages in court unless she can demonstrate that the government has waived its sovereign immunity with respect to her claim.

The federal government and every state government have waived sovereign immunity, but not absolutely. For example, a tort claim against the federal government must be analyzed under the Federal Tort Claims Act of 1946 to determine whether monetary relief is available to the claimant. Because of the background rule favoring sovereign immunity, the federal courts, and most state courts, apply a "clear statement" canon of construction to waiver statutes such as the FTCA, under which the court will conclude that the claimant bears the burden of demonstrating a clear waiver of sovereign immunity before her claim can be considered.

Prior to the enactment of the Indian Claims Commission Act of 1946, federal law contained no general waiver of sovereign immunity to benefit tribes or individual Indians who sought to recover damages from the federal government arising out of the federal management of Indian affairs. Before 1946, an attorney representing a tribe that wished to sue the federal government for damages first had to go to Congress and either obtain a private bill awarding the tribe some relief or a private bill waiving the sovereign immunity of the United States and subjecting the government to suit in some federal court for the claim at issue. Needless to say, this was an extraordinarily cumbersome process, and the great majority of viable Indian claims were never paid off or litigated. Under the approach adopted in 1946, tribal claims arising before August 13 of that year were to be filed with the Indian Claims Commission. Newer claims were to be filed with the United States Court of Claims (now called the Court of Federal Claims).

For our purposes, suffice it to say that the claims statute provided a rather broad waiver of federal sovereign immunity for "historical" (*i.e.*, 1946 and earlier) claims, including a waiver for claims of fraud, duress, unconscionable consideration, and lack of fair and honorable dealings. Consider this provision:

> The commission shall hear and determine the following claims against the United States on behalf of any Indian tribe, band, or other identifiable group of American Indians residing within the territorial limits of the United States or Alaska: (1) claims in law or equity arising under the Constitution, laws, treaties of the United States, and Executive orders of the President; (2) all other claims in law or equity, including those sounding in tort, with respect to which the claimant would have been entitled to sue in a court of the United States if the United States was subject to suit; (3) claims which would result if the treaties, contracts, and agreements between the claimant and the United States were revised on the ground of fraud, duress, unconscionable consideration, mutual or unilateral mistake, whether of law or fact, or any other ground cognizable by a court of equity; (4) claims arising from the taking by the United States, whether as the result of a treaty of cession or otherwise, of lands owned or occupied by the claimant without the payment for such lands of compensation agreed to by the claimant; and (5) claims based upon fair and honorable dealings that are not recognized by any existing rule of law or equity.

Indian Claims Commission Act, ch. 959, sec. 2, 60 Stat. 1049, 1050 (1946).

As we shall see, however, the claims commission tempered this apparent generosity by refusing to award interest on any judgment except those rooted in a constitutional violation. Thus, a non-constitutional claim for the loss of a tribal asset would be measured by the fair market value of the asset at the time of the taking, with no interest awarded. The loss of land many years before would, accordingly, be compensated by awarding a few cents on the dollar, when compared to contemporary land value. The reason the commission awarded interest on constitutional claims is that the fifth amendment's just compensation clause has long been held to require that federal takings be compensated according to the formula of fair market value at the time of the taking plus interest (otherwise, the compensation would not be "just"). But when the Fifth Amendment did not apply, the clear-statement canon led to interpreting the ICCA narrowly, as authorizing the award of only fair market value at the time of the taking, with no interest. In her comprehensive examination of the implementation of the Indian Claims Commission Act, Professor Newton notes that the provision promising relief for "claims based upon fair and honorable dealings that are not recognized by any existing rule of law or equity" proved to be illusory as the ICC interpreted the clause as allowing relief only if claims were based on a "treaty, agreement, order or statute which expressly obligated the United States to perform [any] services." Nell Jessup Newton, *Indian Claims in the Courts of the Conqueror*, 41 Am. U.L. Rev. 753, 778 (1992), quoting *Gila River Pima-Maricopa Indian Community v. United States*, 427 F.2d 1194, 1198 (1970).

By 1946, new Indian claims were subject to the following two statutes, 28 U.S.C. § 1491 (the Tucker Act, which had long been the basic jurisdictional provision for the federal Court of Claims) and 28 U.S.C. § 1505 (the so-called Indian Tucker Act). They are reproduced below. Note that § 1505 deals with tribal claims and § 1491 deals with individual Indian claims. Note also that § 1505 incorporates by reference certain provisions of § 1491.

28 U.S.C. § 1491

Claims against United States generally; actions involving Tennessee Valley Authority

---

(a)(1) The United States Court of Federal Claims shall have jurisdiction to render judgment upon any claim against the United States founded either upon the Constitution, or any Act of Congress or any regulation of an executive department, or upon any express or implied contract with the United States, or for liquidated or unliquidated damages in cases not sounding in tort. ***

---

28 U.S.C. § 1505

Indian claims

The United States Court of Federal Claims shall have jurisdiction of any claim against the United States accruing after August 13, 1946, in favor of any tribe, band, or other identifiable group of American Indians residing within the territorial limits of the United States or Alaska whenever such claim is one arising under the Constitution, laws or treaties of the United States, or Executive orders of the President, or is one which otherwise would be cognizable in the Court of Federal Claims if the claimant were not an Indian tribe, band or group.

Consider the interplay of the Indian Claims Commission Act, § 1505, and the Fifth Amendment in the following case.

Tongass National Forest (2004), by Henry Hartley, Creative Commons License.

TEE–HIT–TON INDIANS V. UNITED STATES

348 U.S. 272, 75 S. Ct. 313, 99 L. Ed. 314 (1955)

JUSTICE REED delivered the opinion of the Court.

This case rests upon a claim under the Fifth Amendment by petitioner, an identifiable group of American Indians of between 60 and 70 individuals residing in Alaska, for compensation for a taking by the United States of certain timber from Alaskan lands allegedly belonging to the group. The area claimed is said to contain over 350,000 acres of land and 150 square miles of water. The Tee–Hit–Tons, a clan of the Tlingit Tribe, brought this suit in the Court of Claims under 28 U.S.C. § 1505. The compensation claimed does not arise from any statutory direction to pay. Payment, if it can be compelled, must be based upon a constitutional right of the Indians to recover. This is not a case that is connected with any phase of the policy of the Congress, continued throughout our history, to extinguish Indian title through negotiation rather than by force, and to grant payments from the public purse to needy descendants of exploited Indians. The legislation in support of that policy has received consistent interpretation from this Court in sympathy with its compassionate purpose.

The Court of Claims held that petitioner was an identifiable group of American Indians residing in Alaska; that its interest in the lands prior to purchase of Alaska by the United States in 1867 was "original Indian title" or "Indian right of occupancy". It was further held that if such original Indian title survived the Treaty of 1867, 15 Stat. 539, Arts. III and VI, by which Russia conveyed Alaska to the United States, such title was not sufficient basis to maintain this suit as there had been no recognition by Congress of any legal rights in petitioner to the land in question. The court said that no rights inured to plaintiff by virtue of legislation by Congress. ***

The Alaskan area in which petitioner claims a compensable interest is located near and within the exterior lines of the Tongass National Forest. By Joint Resolution of August 8, 1947, 61 Stat. 920, the Secretary of Agriculture was authorized to contract for the sale of national forest timber located within this National Forest "notwithstanding any claim of possessory rights." The Resolution *** provides for all receipts from the sale of timber to be maintained in a special account in the Treasury until the timber and land rights are finally determined.

Section 3(b) of the Resolution provides:

> Nothing in this resolution shall be construed as recognizing or denying the validity of any claims of possessory rights to lands or timber within the exterior boundaries of the Tongass National Forest.

The Secretary of Agriculture, on August 20, 1951, pursuant to this authority contracted for sale to a private company of all merchantable timber in the area claimed by petitioner. This is the sale of timber which petitioner alleges constitutes a compensable taking by the United States of a portion of its proprietary interest in the land.

The problem presented is the nature of the petitioner's interest in the land, if any. *** It is petitioner's contention that its tribal predecessors have continually claimed, occupied and used the land from time immemorial; that when Russia took Alaska, the Tlingits had a well-developed social order which included a concept of property ownership; that Russia while it possessed Alaska in no manner interfered with their claim to the land; that Congress has by subsequent acts confirmed and recognized petitioner's right to occupy the land permanently and therefore the sale of the timber off such lands constitutes a taking *pro tanto* of its asserted rights in the area.

The Government denies that petitioner has any compensable interest. It asserts that the Tee–Hit–Tons' property interest, if any, is merely that of the right to the use of the land at the Government's will; that Congress has never recognized any legal interest of petitioner in the land and therefore without such recognition no compensation is due the petitioner for any taking by the United States.

I. Recognition.

The question of recognition may be disposed of shortly. Where the Congress by treaty or other agreement has declared that thereafter Indians were to hold the lands permanently, compensation must be paid for subsequent taking. The petitioner contends that Congress has sufficiently "recognized" its possessory rights in the land in question so as to make its interest compensable. Petitioner points specifically to two statutes to sustain this contention. The first is § 8 of the Organic Act for Alaska of May 17, 1884, 23 Stat. 24.[10] The

10. " *** That the Indians or other persons in said district shall not be disturbed in the possession of any lands actually in their use or occupation or now claimed by them but the terms under which such persons may acquire title to such lands is reserved for future legislation by Congress: ***."

second is § 27 of the Act of June 6, 1900, which was to provide for a civil government for Alaska, 31 Stat. 321, 330.[11] ***

We have carefully examined these statutes and the pertinent legislative history and find nothing to indicate any intention by Congress to grant to the Indians any permanent rights in the lands of Alaska occupied by them by permission of Congress. Rather, it clearly appears that what was intended was merely to retain the status quo until further congressional or judicial action was taken. There is no particular form for congressional recognition of Indian right of permanent occupancy. It may be established in a variety of ways but there must be the definite intention by congressional action or authority to accord legal rights, not merely permissive occupation. *Hynes v. Grimes Packing Co.*, 377 U.S. 86, 101.

This policy of Congress toward the Alaskan Indian lands was maintained and reflected by its expression in the Joint Resolution of 1947 under which the timber contracts were made.

II. Indian Title.

(a) The nature of aboriginal Indian interest in land and the various rights as between the Indians and the United States dependent on such interest are far from novel as concerns our Indian inhabitants. It is well settled that in all the States of the Union the tribes who inhabited the lands of the States held claim to such lands after the coming of the white man, under what is sometimes termed original Indian title or permission from the whites to occupy. That description means mere possession not specifically recognized as ownership by Congress. After conquest they were permitted to occupy portions of territory over which they had previously exercised "sovereignty," as we use that term. This is not a property right but amounts to a right of occupancy which the sovereign grants and protects against intrusion by third parties but which right of occupancy may be terminated and such lands fully disposed of by the sovereign itself without any legally enforceable obligation to compensate the Indians.

This position of the Indian has long been rationalized by the legal theory that discovery and conquest gave the conquerors sovereignty over and ownership of the lands thus obtained. The great case of *Johnson v. McIntosh* denied the power of an Indian tribe to pass their right of occupancy to another. It confirmed the practice of two hundred years of American history "that discovery gave an exclusive right to extinguish the Indian title of occupancy, either by purchase or by conquest." ***

No case in this Court has ever held that taking of Indian title or use by Congress required compensation. The American people have compassion for the descendants of those Indians who were deprived of their homes and hunting grounds by the drive of civilization. They seek to have the Indians share the benefits of our society as citizens of this Nation. Generous provision has been willingly made to allow tribes to recover for wrongs, as a matter of grace, not because of legal liability. 60 Stat. 1050 [Indian Claims Commission Act].

---

11. "The Indians or persons conducting schools or missions in the district shall not be disturbed in the possession of any lands now actually in their use or occupation. *** "

(b) There is one opinion in a case decided by this Court that contains language indicating that unrecognized Indian title might be compensable under the Constitution when taken by the United States. *United States v. Alcea Band of Tillamooks*, 329 U.S. 40.

Recovery was allowed under a jurisdictional Act of 1935, 49 Stat. 801, that permitted payments to a few specific Indian tribes for "legal and equitable claims arising under or growing out of the original Indian title" to land, because of some unratified treaties negotiated with them and other tribes. The other tribes had already been compensated. Five years later this Court unanimously held that none of the former opinions in Vol. 329 of the United States Reports expressed the view that recovery was grounded on a taking under the Fifth Amendment. *United States v. Tillamooks*, 341 U.S. 48. Interest, payable on recovery for a taking under the Fifth Amendment, was denied.

We think it must be concluded that the recovery in the *Tillamook* case was based upon statutory direction to pay for the aboriginal title in the special jurisdictional act to equalize the Tillamooks with the neighboring tribes, rather than upon a holding that there had been a compensable taking under the Fifth Amendment. This leaves unimpaired the rule derived from *Johnson v. McIntosh*, that the taking by the United States of unrecognized Indian title is not compensable under the Fifth Amendment.

This is true, not because an Indian or an Indian tribe has no standing to sue or because the United States has not consented to be sued for the taking of original Indian title, but because Indian occupation of land without government recognition of ownership creates no rights against taking or extinction by the United States protected by the Fifth Amendment or any other principle of law.

(c) What has been heretofore set out deals largely with the Indians of the Plains and east of the Mississippi. The Tee–Hit–Tons urge, however, that their stage of civilization and their concept of ownership of property takes them out of the rule applicable to the Indians of the States. They assert that Russia never took their lands in the sense that European nations seized the rest of America. The Court of Claims, however, saw no distinction between their use of the land and that of the Indians of the Eastern United States.

The line of cases adjudicating Indian rights on American soil leads to the conclusion that Indian occupancy, not specifically recognized as ownership by action authorized by Congress, may be extinguished by the Government without compensation. Every American schoolboy knows that the savage tribes of this continent were deprived of their ancestral ranges by force and that, even when the Indians ceded millions of acres by treaty in return for blankets, food and trinkets, it was not a sale but the conquerors' will that deprived them of their land. ***

In the light of the history of Indian relations in this Nation, no other course would meet the problem of the growth of the United States except to make congressional contributions for Indian lands[†] rather than to subject the Government to an obligation to pay the value when taken with interest to the date of payment. Our conclusion does not uphold harshness as against tenderness toward the Indians, but it leaves with Congress, where it belongs, the

†. Eds. Probably should insert "discretionary" here.

policy of Indian gratuities for the termination of Indian occupancy of Government-owned land rather than making compensation for its value a rigid constitutional principle.

The judgment of the Court of Claims is *Affirmed.*

JUSTICE DOUGLAS, with whom **THE CHIEF JUSTICE** and **JUSTICE FRANKFURTER**, concur, dissenting.

The first Organic Act for Alaska became a law on May 17, 1884, 23 Stat. 24. It contained a provision in § 8 which reads as follows:

> the Indians or other persons in said district shall not be disturbed in the possession of any lands actually in their use or occupation or now claimed by them but the terms under which such persons may acquire title to such lands is reserved for future legislation by Congress: And provided further, That parties who have located mines or mineral privileges therein under the laws of the United States applicable to the public domain, or who have occupied and improved or exercised acts of ownership over such claims, shall not be disturbed therein, but shall be allowed to perfect their title to such claims by payment as aforesaid.

Section 12 provided for a report upon "The condition of the Indians residing in said Territory, what lands, if any, should be reserved for their use, what provision shall be made for their education(,) what rights by occupation of settlers should be recognized," *etc.*

Respondent contends, and the Court apparently agrees, that this provision should be read, not as recognizing Indian title, but as reserving the question whether they have any rights in the land.

It is said that since § 8 contemplates the possible future acquisition of "title," it expressly negates any idea that the Indians have any "title." That is the argument; and that apparently is the conclusion of the Court.

There are, it seems to me, two answers to that proposition.

First. The first turns on the words of the Act. The general land laws of the United States were not made applicable to Alaska. § 8. No provision was made for opening up the lands to settlement, for clearing titles, for issuing patents, all as explained in Gruening, The State of Alaska (1954), p. 47 *et seq.* There were, however, at least two classes of claimants to Alaskan lands—one, the Indians; the other, those who had mining claims. Section 8 of the Act did not recognize the "title" of either. Rather, it provided that one group, the miners, should be allowed to "perfect their title"; while the others, the Indians, were to acquire "title" only as provided by future legislation. Obviously the word "title" was used in the conveyancer's sense; and § 8 did service in opening the door to perfection of "title" in the case of miners, and in deferring the perfection of "title" in the case of the Indians.

Second. The second proposition turns on the legislative history of § 8. Section 8 of the Act commands that the Indians "shall not be disturbed in the possession of any lands actually in their use or occupation or now claimed by them". The words "or now claimed by them" were added by an amendment offered during the debates by Senator Plumb of Kansas. 15 Cong. Rec. 627–628. Senator Benjamin Harrison, in accepting the amendment, said, " *** it was the intention of the committee to protect to the fullest extent all the rights of the Indians in Alaska and of any residents who had settled there, but at the same time to allow the development of the mineral resources. *** " *Id.*

The conclusion seems clear that Congress in the 1884 Act recognized the claims of these Indians to their Alaskan lands. What those lands were was not known. Where they were located, what were their metes and bounds were also unknown. Senator Plumb thought they probably were small and restricted. But all agreed that the Indians were to keep them, wherever they lay. It must be remembered that the Congress was legislating about a Territory concerning which little was known. No report was available showing the nature and extent of any claims to the land. No Indian was present to point out his tribe's domain. Therefore, Congress did the humane thing of saving to the Indians all rights claimed; it let them keep what they had prior to the new Act. The future course of action was made clear—conflicting claims would be reconciled and the Indian lands would be put into reservations.

That purpose is wholly at war with the one now attributed to the Congress of reserving for some future day the question whether the Indians were to have any rights to the land.

There remains the question what kind of "title" the right of use and occupancy embraces. Some Indian rights concern fishing alone. *See Tulee v. Washington*, 315 U.S. 681. Others may include only hunting or grazing or other limited uses. Whether the rights recognized in 1884 embraced rights to timber, litigated here, has not been determined by the finders of fact. The case should be remanded for those findings. It is sufficient now only to determine that under the jurisdictional Act the Court of Claims is empowered to entertain the complaint by reason of the recognition afforded the Indian rights by the Act of 1884.

NOTES AND QUESTIONS

1. *Recognized versus Original Indian Title.* All the Justices in *Tee Hit Ton* agreed that, if Congress had "recognized" Indian title in a treaty, statute, or agreement, property in the Fifth Amendment sense existed, such that a taking of it required payment of just compensation. The issue dividing the Court was whether Congress had recognized the title of Alaska Natives. Which opinion, the majority or the dissent, is truer to the Indian law canons in interpreting the statute in question as to whether it recognized Indian title? Is there some good reason why the canons might have less force in this context? What might "every American schoolboy know[]" that is arguably relevant to this question of whether Congress intended to recognize title? What if such boys don't know much about history? *See* Felix S. Cohen, *Original Indian Title*, 32 Minn. L. Rev. 28, 34 (1947) (contrary to what "every American schoolboy knows," the great bulk of Indian lands were lost through transactions in which the tribes received at least some compensation, not through outright confiscation).

2. *Fitting the taking of recognized title into the statutory framework.* Go back to the provisions of the Indian Claims Commission and the Indian Tucker Act. Note that a pre–1946 taking of recognized title would be brought before the Commission; the Indian Claims Commission Act clearly provides a waiver

of sovereign immunity for that claim; just compensation would be required because the Fifth Amendment mandates that when Fifth Amendment property is taken, just compensation is required. The only difference for post–1946 takings is that, under the Indian Tucker Act, the claim is brought in the U.S. Court of Claims. Again, just compensation would be required by the Fifth Amendment.

3. *Fitting the taking of original Indian title into the statutory framework.* A pre–1946 taking of original Indian title would be adjudicated where? Find in the relevant statute the appropriate waiver(s) of sovereign immunity. Would just compensation be available? Is there a waiver of sovereign immunity for a post–1946 taking of original Indian title? Read § 1505 carefully.

4. *Why the sharp distinction between original Indian title and recognized title?* Is the distinction required by *Johnson v. McIntosh*? Review the very different characterization of original Indian title in *Santa Fe Pac. R. Co., supra.* If not required by *Johnson*, was the distinction the result of what some have called "judicial fiscal restraint"? In a portion of the majority opinion we have omitted, the Court noted that in the two *Tillamook* cases the government had asserted the following: "Three million dollars was involved in the *Tillamook* case as the value of the land, and the interest granted by the Court of Claims was $14,000,000. The Government pointed out that if aboriginal Indian title was compensable without specific legislation to that effect, there were claims with estimated interest already pending under the Indian jurisdictional act aggregating $9,000,000,000." Dean Newton has pointed out that, of this $9 billion, $8 billion was interest. Nell Jessup Newton, *At the Whim of the Sovereign: Aboriginal Title Reconsidered*, 31 Hastings L.J. 1215, 1248 (1980). In addition to fiscal considerations, consider (a) the case was decided in the heart of the Termination Era, and (b) the facts emphasized by Justice Reed at the beginning of the opinion seemed motivated by a desire to paint a picture of a relationship between people and property that would not amount to "property rights" in a western sense of the term.

5. *Separation of powers.* Consider also a separation of powers concern: an argument can be made that, for the creation of Fifth Amendment property outside the customary conception of property in western legal thought, Congress must have expressly agreed to bring the property into the domain of U.S. property law. Thus, when Congress and the President by treaty, or Congress by agreement, recognizes Indian tribal property rights, those rights "count" as Fifth Amendment property. When this has not happened, as with original Indian title, the tribe may have certain legally enforceable rights as against third parties—*e.g.*, the tribe could get an injunction forbidding future trespasses by nonmembers—but the right is subject to congressional control. Thus, Congress may require federal consent before the tribe may convey the land in a way that confers U.S. property rights upon the putative purchaser. *See Johnson v. McIntosh*; Trade & Intercourse Act of 1790 and its successors. In addition, under *Johnson*, of course, the tribe has no way to prevent Congress from confiscating the land. Is this analysis a more plausible (and less offensive) way of understanding what the Court was trying to say in *Tee Hit Ton*? Does this analysis necessarily mean that, when Congress takes tribal property held by original Indian title, Congress need pay nothing?

6. *Aftermath of Tee–Hit–Ton*: *The Alaska Native Claims Settlement Act.* Justice Reed declared in *Tee–Hit–Ton* that the decision "leaves with Congress, where it belongs, the policy of Indian gratuities for the termination of Indian occupancy of Government-owned land." 348 U.S. at 291. Congress was not sufficiently moved to decide what "gratuities" the Alaska Natives were owed until oil was discovered in Prudhoe Bay in 1968. After that, oil developers pushed for a firm settlement for all Alaska Native land claims to protect the security of their oil fields. The result was the 1971 Alaska Native Claims Settlement Act, Pub. L. No. 92–203 (1971) (codified as amended at 43 U.S.C. § 1601–1629). ANCSA has been hailed by some as a victory for the tribes; in exchange for relinquishing all claims to nearly 340 million acres in unceded lands, the Native villages were able to reserve 45 million acres of land and to receive 925 million dollars from the federal government and from state petroleum revenues over the next eleven years. Several distinctive features of the Act, however, were tailored to non-Indian interests, and were surely affected by *Tee–Hit–Ton*'s impact on Native negotiating power. They would hold surface and subsurface rights to their lands as stockholders of state-chartered village and regional corporations, facilitating transactions regarding their natural resources. The stock in these corporations would be inalienable for only twenty years. The act included a further poison pill, although it would not take effect for many years. ANCSA declared that it was intended to extinguish native land claims and provide fee simple title to remaining lands "without creating a reservation system." 43 U.S.C. § 1601(b). In 1998, the Supreme Court held that this language meant that Native corporation lands set aside under the act are not "Indian country," and are therefore not lands over which a Native village can exercise territorial jurisdiction. *Alaska v. Native Village of Venetie Tribal Government,* 522 U.S. 520 (1998), *infra* Ch. 5. For more on ANCSA and the distinctive legal questions affecting Alaska Natives, see Ch. 12, *infra*.

---

2. Taking of Recognized Title

UNITED STATES V. SIOUX NATION

448 U.S. 371, 100 S. Ct. 2716, 65 L. Ed. 2d 844 (1980)

JUSTICE BLACKMUN delivered the opinion of the Court.

This case concerns the Black Hills of South Dakota, the Great Sioux Reservation, and a colorful, and in many respects tragic, chapter in the history of the Nation's West. Although the litigation comes down to a claim of interest since 1877 on an award of over $17 million, it is necessary, in order to understand the controversy, to review at some length the chronology of the case and its factual setting.

For over a century now the Sioux Nation has claimed that the United States unlawfully abrogated the Fort Laramie Treaty of April 29, 1868, 15 Stat. 635, in Art. II of which the United States pledged that the Great Sioux Reservation, including the Black Hills, would be "set apart for the absolute and undisturbed use and occupation of the Indians herein named." *Id.*, at 636. The Fort Laramie Treaty was concluded at the culmination of the Powder River War of 1866–1867, a series of military engagements in which the Sioux tribes, led by their great chief, Red Cloud, fought to protect the integrity of earlier-recognized treaty lands from the incursion of white settlers.[1]

The Fort Laramie Treaty included several agreements central to the issues presented in this case. First, it established the Great Sioux Reservation, a tract of land bounded on the east by the Missouri River, on the south by the northern border of the State of Nebraska, on the north by the forty-sixth parallel of north latitude, and on the west by the one hundred and fourth meridian of west longitude, in addition to certain reservations already existing east of the Missouri. The United States "solemnly agree[d]" that no unauthorized persons "shall ever be permitted to pass over, settle upon, or reside in [this] territory." *Ibid.*

Second, the United States permitted members of the Sioux tribes to select lands within the reservation for cultivation. *Id.*, at 637. In order to assist the Sioux in becoming civilized farmers, the Government promised to provide them [with the necessary services and materials, such as seeds and agricultural instruments, assistance from blacksmiths and other relevant artisans, and subsistence rations for four years].

Third, in exchange for the benefits conferred by the treaty, the Sioux agreed to relinquish their rights under the Treaty of September 17, 1851, to occupy territories outside the reservation, while reserving their "right to hunt on any lands north of North Platte, and on the Republican Fork of the Smoky Hill river, so long as the buffalo may range thereon in such numbers as to justify the chase." *Ibid.* The Indians also expressly agreed to withdraw all opposition to the building of railroads that did not pass over their reservation lands, not to engage in attacks on settlers, and to withdraw their opposition to the military posts and roads that had been established south of the North Platte River. *Ibid.*

Fourth, Art. XII of the treaty provided:

> No treaty for the cession of any portion or part of the reservation herein described which may be held in common shall be of any validity or force as against the said Indians, unless executed and signed by at least three fourths of all the adult male Indians, occupying or interested in the same. *Ibid.*

The years following the treaty brought relative peace to the Dakotas, an era of tranquility that was disturbed, however, by renewed speculation that the Black Hills, which were included in the Great Sioux Reservation, contained vast quantities of gold and silver. In 1874 the Army planned and undertook an exploratory expedition into the Hills, both for the purpose of establishing a military outpost from which to control those Sioux who had not accepted the terms of the Fort Laramie Treaty, and for the purpose of investigating "the country about which dreamy stories have been told." Lieutenant Colonel George Armstrong Custer led the expedition of close to 1,000 soldiers and

1. The Sioux territory recognized under the Treaty of September 17, 1851, *see* 11 Stat. 749, included all of the present State of South Dakota, and parts of what is now Nebraska, Wyoming, North Dakota, and Montana. ***

teamsters, and a substantial number of military and civilian aides. Custer's journey began at Fort Abraham Lincoln on the Missouri River on July 2, 1874. By the end of that month they had reached the Black Hills, and by mid-August had confirmed the presence of gold fields in that region. The discovery of gold was widely reported in newspapers across the country. Custer's florid descriptions of the mineral and timber resources of the Black Hills, and the land's suitability for grazing and cultivation, also received wide circulation, and had the effect of creating an intense popular demand for the "opening" of the Hills for settlement. The only obstacle to "progress" was the Fort Laramie Treaty that reserved occupancy of the Hills to the Sioux.

Having promised the Sioux that the Black Hills were reserved to them, the United States Army was placed in the position of having to threaten military force, and occasionally to use it, to prevent prospectors and settlers from trespassing on lands reserved to the Indians. For example, in September 1874, General [Philip H.] Sheridan[, Commander of the Military Division of the Missouri,] sent instructions to Brigadier General Alfred H. Terry, Commander of the Department of Dakota, at Saint Paul, directing him to use force to prevent companies of prospectors from trespassing on the Sioux Reservation. At the same time, Sheridan let it be known that he would "give a cordial support to the settlement of the Black Hills," should Congress decide to "open up the country for settlement, by extinguishing the treaty rights of the Indians." App. 62–63. Sheridan's instructions were published in local newspapers. *See id.* at 63.

Eventually, however, the Executive Branch of the Government decided to abandon the Nation's treaty obligation to preserve the integrity of the Sioux territory. In a letter dated November 9, 1875, to Terry, Sheridan reported that he had met with President Grant, the Secretary of the Interior, and the Secretary of War, and that the President had decided that the military should make no further resistance to the occupation of the Black Hills by miners, "it being his belief that such resistance only increased their desire and complicated the troubles." *Id.* at 59. These orders were to be enforced "quietly," *ibid.*, and the President's decision was to remain "confidential." *Id.* at 59–60 (letter from Sheridan to [William T.] Sherman, [Commanding General of the Army]).

With the Army's withdrawal from its role as enforcer of the Fort Laramie Treaty, the influx of settlers into the Black Hills increased. The Government concluded that the only practical course was to secure to the citizens of the United States the right to mine the Black Hills for gold. Toward that end, the Secretary of the Interior, in the spring of 1875, appointed a commission to negotiate with the Sioux. *** The tribal leaders of the Sioux were aware of the mineral value of the Black Hills and refused to sell the land for a price less than $70 million. The commission offered the Indians an annual rental of $400,000, or payment of $6 million for absolute relinquishment of the Black Hills. The negotiations broke down.

In the winter of 1875–1876, many of the Sioux were hunting in the unceded territory north of the North Platte River, reserved to them for that purpose in the Fort Laramie Treaty. On December 6, 1875, for reasons that are not entirely clear, the Commissioner of Indian Affairs sent instructions to the Indian agents on the reservation to notify those hunters that if they did not return to the reservation agencies by January 31, 1876, they would be treated as "hostiles." Given the severity of the winter, compliance with these instructions was impossible. On February 1, the Secretary of the Interior nonetheless relinquished jurisdiction over all hostile Sioux, including those Indians exercising their treaty-protected hunting rights, to the War Department. The Army's campaign against the "hostiles" led to Sitting Bull's notable victory over Custer's forces at the battle of the Little Big Horn on June 25. That victory, of course, was short-lived, and those Indians who surrendered to the Army were returned to the reservation, and deprived of their weapons and horses, leaving them completely dependent for survival on rations provided them by the Government. ***

In the meantime, Congress was becoming increasingly dissatisfied with the failure of the Sioux living on the reservation to become self-sufficient. Toward this end, Congress requested the President to appoint another commission to negotiate with the Sioux for the cession of the Black Hills.

This commission, headed by George Manypenny, arrived in the Sioux country in early September and commenced meetings with the head men of the various tribes. The members of the commission impressed upon the Indians that the United States no longer had any obligation to provide them with subsistence rations. The commissioners brought with them the text of a treaty that had been prepared in advance. The principal provisions of this treaty were that the Sioux would relinquish their rights to the Black Hills and other lands west of the one hundred and third meridian, and their rights to hunt in the unceded territories to the north, in exchange for subsistence rations for as long as they would be needed to ensure the Sioux' survival. In setting out to obtain the tribes' agreement to this treaty, the commission ignored the stipulation of the Fort Laramie Treaty that any cession of the lands contained within the Great Sioux Reservation would have to be joined in by three-fourths of the adult males. Instead, the treaty was presented just to Sioux chiefs and their leading men. It was signed by only 10% of the adult male Sioux population. ***

Congress resolved the impasse by enacting the 1876 "agreement" into law as the Act of Feb. 28, 1877 (1877 Act), 19 Stat. 254. The Act had the effect of abrogating the earlier Fort Laramie Treaty, and of implementing the terms of the Manypenny Commission's "agreement" with the Sioux leaders.

The passage of the 1877 Act legitimized the settlers' invasion of the Black Hills, but throughout the years it has been regarded by the Sioux as a breach of this Nation's solemn obligation to reserve the Hills in perpetuity for occupation by the Indians. One historian of the Sioux Nation commented on Indian reaction to the Act in the following words:

> The Sioux thus affected have not gotten over talking about that treaty yet, and during the last few years they have maintained an organization called the Black Hills Treaty Association, which holds meetings each year at the various agencies for the purpose of studying the treaty with the intention of presenting a claim against the government for additional reimbursements for the territory ceded under it. Some think that Uncle Sam owes them about $9,000,000 on the deal, but it will probably be a hard matter to prove it.

F. Fiske, The Taming of the Sioux 132 (1917).

Fiske's words were to prove prophetic.

II

[Here Justice Blackmun summarized the tortured procedural history of attempts by the tribe to obtain redress from the federal government. Ultimately, the Court of Claims concluded that the 1877 Act abrogated the 1868 treaty and resulted in a "taking" of the Black Hills. *** The court held that the Sioux were entitled to an award of interest, at the annual rate of 5%, on the principal sum of $17.1 million, dating from 1877.] ***

IV A

In reaching its conclusion that the 1877 Act effected a taking of the Black Hills for which just compensation was due the Sioux under the Fifth Amendment, the Court of Claims relied upon the "good faith effort" test developed in its earlier decision in *Three Tribes of Fort Berthold Reservation v. United States*, 390 F.2d 686 (1968). The *Fort Berthold* test had been designed to reconcile two lines of cases decided by this Court that seemingly were in conflict. The first line, exemplified by *Lone Wolf*, recognizes "that Congress possesse[s] a paramount power over the property of the Indians, by reason of its exercise of guardianship over their interests, and that such authority might be implied, even though opposed to the strict letter of a treaty with the Indians." The second line, exemplified by the more recent decision in *Shoshone Tribe v. United States*, 299 U.S. 476 (1937), concedes Congress' paramount power over Indian property, but holds, nonetheless, that "[t]he power does not extend so far as to enable the Government 'to give the tribal lands to others, or to appropriate them to its own purposes, without rendering, or assuming an obligation to render, just compensation.' " In *Shoshone Tribe*, Mr. Justice Cardozo, in speaking for the Court, expressed the distinction between the conflicting principles in a characteristically pithy phrase: "Spoliation is not management."

The *Fort Berthold* test distinguishes between cases in which one or the other principle is applicable:

> It is obvious that Congress cannot simultaneously (1) act as trustee for the benefit of the Indians, exercising its plenary powers over the Indians and their property, as it thinks is in their best interests, and (2) exercise its sovereign power of eminent domain, taking the Indians' property within the meaning of the Fifth Amendment to the Constitution. In any given situation in which Congress has acted with regard to Indian people, it must have acted either in one capacity or the other. Congress can own two hats, but it cannot wear them both at the same time.
>
> Some guideline must be established so that a court can identify in which capacity Congress is acting. The following guideline would best give recognition to the basic distinction between the two types of congressional action: Where Congress makes a good faith effort to give the Indians the full value of the land and thus merely transmutes the property from land to money, there is no taking. This is a mere substitution of assets or change of form and is a traditional function of a trustee.

Applying the *Fort Berthold* test to the facts of this case, the Court of Claims concluded that, in passing the 1877 Act, Congress had not made a good-faith effort to give the Sioux the full value of the Black Hills. The principal issue presented by this case is whether the legal standard applied by the Court of Claims was erroneous.

B

The Government contends that the Court of Claims erred insofar as its holding that the 1877 Act effected a taking of the Black Hills was based on Congress' failure to indicate affirmatively that the consideration given the Sioux was of equivalent value to the property rights ceded to the Government. It argues that "the true rule is that Congress must be assumed to be acting within its plenary power to manage tribal assets if it reasonably can be concluded that the legislation was intended to promote the welfare of the tribe." Brief for United States 52. The Government derives support for this rule principally from this Court's decision in *Lone Wolf v. Hitchcock*.

*** This Court's principal holding in *Lone Wolf* was that "the legislative power might pass laws in conflict with treaties made with the Indians." The Court stated:

> The power exists to abrogate the provisions of an Indian treaty, though presumably such power will be exercised only when circumstances arise which will not only justify the government in disregarding the stipulations of the treaty, but may demand, in the interest of the country and the Indians themselves, that it should do so. When, therefore, treaties were entered into between the United States and a tribe of Indians it was never doubted that the *power* to abrogate existed in Congress, and that in a contingency such power might be availed of from considerations of governmental policy, particularly if consistent with perfect good faith towards the Indians. *Ibid.* (Emphasis in original.)

The Court, therefore, was not required to consider the contentions of the Indians that the agreement ceding their lands had been obtained by fraud, and had not been signed by the requisite number of adult males. "[A]ll these matters, in any event, were solely within the domain of the legislative authority, and its action is conclusive upon the courts."

In the penultimate paragraph of the opinion, however, the Court in *Lone Wolf* went on to make some observations seemingly directed to the question whether the Act at issue might constitute a taking of Indian property without just compensation. The Court there stated:

> The act of June 6, 1900, which is complained of in the bill, was enacted at a time when the tribal relations between the confederated tribes of Kiowas, Comanches, and Apaches still existed, and that statute and the statutes supplementary thereto dealt with the disposition of tribal property and purported to give an adequate consideration for the surplus lands not allotted among the Indians or reserved for their benefit. Indeed, the controversy which this case presents is concluded by the decision in *Cherokee Nation v. Hitchcock*, 187 U.S. 294, decided at this term, where it was held that full administrative power was possessed by Congress over Indian tribal property. In effect, the action of Congress now complained of was but an exercise of such power, a mere change in the form of investment of Indian tribal property, the property of those who, as we have held, were in substantial effect the wards of the government. *We must presume that Congress acted in perfect good faith in the dealings with the Indians of which complaint is made, and that the legislative branch of the government exercised its best judgment in the premises.* In any event, as Congress possessed full power in the matter, the judiciary cannot question or

inquire into the motives which prompted the enactment of this legislation. If injury was occasioned, which we do not wish to be understood as implying, by the use made by Congress of its power, relief must be sought by an appeal to that body for redress and not to the courts. The legislation in question was constitutional. *Ibid.* (Emphasis supplied.)

The Government relies on the italicized sentence in the quotation above to support its view "that Congress must be assumed to be acting within its plenary power to manage tribal assets if it reasonably can be concluded that the legislation was intended to promote the welfare of the tribe." Several adjoining passages in the paragraph, however, lead us to doubt whether the *Lone Wolf* Court meant to state a general rule applicable to cases such as the one before us.

First, *Lone Wolf* presented a situation in which Congress "purported to give an adequate consideration" for the treaty lands taken from the Indians. In fact, the Act at issue set aside for the Indians a sum certain of $2 million for surplus reservation lands surrendered to the United States. In contrast, the background of the 1877 Act "reveals a situation where Congress did not 'purport' to provide 'adequate consideration,' nor was there any meaningful negotiation or arm's-length bargaining, nor did Congress consider it was paying a fair price."

Second, given the provisions of the Act at issue in *Lone Wolf*, the Court reasonably was able to conclude that "the action of Congress now complained of was but *** a mere change in the form of investment of Indian tribal property." Under the Act of June 6, 1900, each head of a family was to be allotted a tract of land within the reservation of not less than 320 acres, an additional 480,000 acres of grazing land were set aside for the use of the tribes in common, and $2 million was paid to the Indians for the remaining surplus. 31 Stat. 677–678. In contrast, the historical background to the opening of the Black Hills for settlement, and the terms of the 1877 Act itself, see Part I, *supra*, would not lead one to conclude that the Act effected "a mere change in the form of investment of Indian tribal property."

Third, it seems significant that the views of the Court in *Lone Wolf* were based, in part, on a holding that "Congress possessed full power in the matter." Earlier in the opinion the Court stated: "Plenary authority over the tribal relations of the Indians has been exercised by Congress from the beginning, and the power has always been deemed a political one, not subject to be controlled by the judicial department of the government." Thus, it seems that the Court's conclusive presumption of congressional good faith was based in large measure on the idea that relations between this Nation and the Indian tribes are a political matter, not amenable to judicial review. That view, of course, has long since been discredited in taking cases, and was expressly laid to rest in *Delaware Tribal Business Comm. v. Weeks*, 430 U.S. 73, 84 (1977).

Fourth, and following up on the political question holding, the *Lone Wolf* opinion suggests that where the exercise of congressional power results in injury to Indian rights, "relief must be sought by an appeal to that body for redress and not to the courts." Unlike *Lone Wolf*, this case is one in which the Sioux have sought redress from Congress, and the Legislative Branch has responded by referring the matter to the courts for resolution [by providing the courts with authority under a special jurisdictional statute to adjudicate the case]. Where Congress waives the Government's sovereign immunity, and expressly directs the courts to resolve a taking claim on the merits, there would appear to be far less reason to apply *Lone Wolf's* principles of deference.

The foregoing considerations support our conclusion that the passage from *Lone Wolf* here relied upon by the Government has limited relevance to this case. More significantly, *Lone Wolf*'s presumption of congressional good faith has little to commend it as an enduring principle for deciding questions of the kind presented here. In every case where a taking of treaty-protected property is alleged, a reviewing court must recognize that tribal lands are subject to Congress' power to control and manage the tribe's affairs. But the court must also be cognizant that "this power to control and manage [is] not absolute. While extending to all appropriate measures for protecting and advancing the tribe, it [is] subject to limitations inhering in *** a guardianship and to pertinent constitutional restrictions." *United States v. Creek Nation*, 295 U.S. 103, 109–110 (1935).

As the Court of Claims recognized in its decision below, the question whether a particular measure was appropriate for protecting and advancing the tribe's interests, and therefore not subject to the constitutional command of the Just Compensation Clause, is factual in nature. The answer must be based on a consideration of all the evidence presented. We do not mean to imply that a reviewing court is to second-guess, from the perspective of hindsight, a legislative judgment that a particular measure would serve the best interests of the tribe. We do mean to require courts, in considering whether a particular congressional action was taken in pursuance of Congress' power to manage and control tribal lands for the Indians' welfare, to engage in a thoroughgoing and impartial examination of the historical record. A presumption of congressional good faith cannot serve to advance such an inquiry.

C

We turn to the question whether the Court of Claims' inquiry in this case was guided by an appropriate legal standard. We conclude that it was. In fact, we approve that court's formulation of the inquiry as setting a standard that ought to be emulated by courts faced with resolving future cases presenting the question at issue here:

> In determining whether Congress has made a good faith effort to give the Indians the full value of their lands when the government acquired [them], we therefore look to the objective facts as revealed by Acts of Congress, congressional committee reports, statements submitted to Congress by government officials, reports of special commissions appointed by Congress to treat with the Indians, and similar evidence relating to the acquisition. ***
>
> The "good faith effort" and "transmutation of property" concepts referred to in *Fort Berthold* are opposite sides of the same coin. They reflect the traditional rule that a trustee may change the form of trust assets as long as he fairly (or in good faith) attempts to provide his ward with property of equivalent value. If he does that, he cannot be faulted if hindsight should demonstrate a lack of precise equivalence. On the other hand, if a trustee (or the government in its dealings with the Indians) does not attempt to give the ward the fair equivalent of what he acquires from him, the trustee to that extent has taken rather than transmuted the property

of the ward. In other words, an essential element of the inquiry under the *Fort Berthold* guideline is determining the adequacy of the consideration the government gave for the Indian lands it acquired. That inquiry cannot be avoided by the government's simple assertion that it acted in good faith in its dealings with the Indians.

D

We next examine the factual findings made by the Court of Claims, which led it to the conclusion that the 1877 Act effected a taking. First, the Court found that "[t]he only item of 'consideration' that possibly could be viewed as showing an attempt by Congress to give the Sioux the 'full value' of the land the government took from them was the requirement to furnish them with rations until they became self-sufficient." This finding is fully supported by the record, and the Government does not seriously contend otherwise.

Second, the court found, after engaging in an exhaustive review of the historical record, that neither the Manypenny Commission, nor the congressional Committees that approved the 1877 Act, nor the individual legislators who spoke on its behalf on the floor of Congress, ever indicated a belief that the Government's obligation to provide the Sioux with rations constituted a fair equivalent for the value of the Black Hills and the additional property rights the Indians were forced to surrender. This finding is unchallenged by the Government.

A third finding lending some weight to the Court's legal conclusion was that the conditions placed by the Government on the Sioux' entitlement to rations "further show that the government's undertaking to furnish rations to the Indians until they could support themselves did not reflect a congressional decision that the value of the rations was the equivalent of the land the Indians were giving up, but instead was an attempt to coerce the Sioux into capitulating to congressional demands." ***

Finally, the Court of Claims rejected the Government's contention that the fact that it subsequently had spent at least $43 million on rations for the Sioux (over the course of three-quarters of a century) established that the 1877 Act was an act of guardianship taken in the Sioux' best interest. The court concluded: "The critical inquiry is what Congress did—and how it viewed the obligation it was assuming—at the time it acquired the land, and not how much it ultimately cost the United States to fulfill the obligation." It found no basis for believing that Congress, in 1877, anticipated that it would take the Sioux such a lengthy period of time to become self-sufficient, or that the fulfillment of the Government's obligation to feed the Sioux would entail the large expenditures ultimately made on their behalf. We find no basis on which to question the legal standard applied by the Court of Claims, or the findings it reached, concerning Congress' decision to provide the Sioux with rations.

E

The aforementioned findings fully support the Court of Claims' conclusion that the 1877 Act appropriated the Black Hills "in circumstances which involved an implied undertaking by [the United States] to make just compensation to the tribe." [Quoting *United States v. Creek Nation.*] We make only two additional observations about this case. First, dating at least from the decision in *Cherokee Nation v. Southern Kansas R. Co.*, 135 U.S. 641 (1890), this Court has recognized that Indian lands, to which a tribe holds recognized title, "are held subject to the authority of the general government to take them for such objects as are germane to the execution of the powers granted to it; provided only, that they are not taken without just compensation being made to the owner." In the same decision the Court emphasized that the owner of such lands "is entitled to reasonable, certain and adequate provision for obtaining compensation before his occupancy is disturbed." The Court of Claims gave effect to this principle when it held that the Government's uncertain and indefinite obligation to provide the Sioux with rations until they became self-sufficient did not constitute adequate consideration for the Black Hills.

Second, it seems readily apparent to us that the obligation to provide rations to the Sioux was undertaken in order to ensure them a means of surviving their transition from the nomadic life of the hunt to the agrarian lifestyle Congress had chosen for them. Those who have studied the Government's reservation policy during this period of our Nation's history agree. It is important to recognize that the 1877 Act, in addition to removing the Black Hills from the Great Sioux Reservation, also ceded the Sioux' hunting rights in a vast tract of land extending beyond the boundaries of that reservation. Under such circumstances, it is reasonable to conclude that Congress' undertaking of an obligation to provide rations for the Sioux was a *quid pro quo* for depriving them of their chosen way of life, and was not intended to compensate them for the taking of the Black Hills. *** [*Affirmed.*]

JUSTICE REHNQUIST, dissenting.

In 1942, the Sioux Tribe filed a petition for certiorari requesting this Court to review the Court of Claims' ruling that Congress had not unconstitutionally taken the Black Hills in 1877, but had merely exchanged the Black Hills for rations and grazing lands—an exchange Congress believed to be in the best interests of the Sioux and the Nation. This Court declined to review that judgment. *Sioux Tribe v. United States*, 97 Ct. Cl. 613 (1942), *cert. denied*, 318 U.S. 789 (1943). Yet today the Court permits Congress to reopen that judgment which this Court rendered final upon denying certiorari in 1943, and proceeds to reject the 1942 Court of Claims' factual interpretation of the events in 1877. I am convinced that Congress may not constitutionally require the Court of Claims to reopen this proceeding, that there is no judicial principle justifying the decision to afford the respondents an additional opportunity to litigate the same claim, and that the Court of Claims' first interpretation of the events in 1877 was by all accounts the more realistic one. I therefore dissent. ***

[T]his is nothing other than an exercise of judicial power reserved to Art. III courts that may not be performed by the Legislative Branch under its Art. I authority. ***

Even if I could countenance the Court's decision to reach the merits of this case, I also think it has erred in rejecting the 1942 court's interpretation of the facts. That court rendered a very persuasive account of the congressional enactment. As the dissenting judges in the Court of Claims opinion under review pointedly stated: "The majority's view that the rations were not consideration for the Black Hills is untenable. What else was the money for?" 220 Ct. Cl. at 487, 601 F.2d at 1183. ***

I think the Court today rejects that conclusion largely on the basis of a view of the settlement of the American West which is not universally shared.

There were undoubtedly greed, cupidity, and other less-than-admirable tactics employed by the Government during the Black Hills episode in the settlement of the West, but the Indians did not lack their share of villainy either. It seems to me quite unfair to judge by the light of "revisionist" historians or the mores of another era actions that were taken under pressure of time more than a century ago. ***

NOTES AND QUESTIONS

1. *Revisiting* Lone Wolf. How much tension is there between *Lone Wolf* and *Sioux Nation*? To be sure, *Sioux Nation* repudiated the nonjusticiability language in *Lone Wolf*. But did *Sioux Nation* suggest any limit upon congressional authority to abrogate a treaty unilaterally?

2. *Compensation and Congress.* How likely was it in 1877 that anyone in Congress would anticipate that a court would order compensation for the Black Hills? Does that make any difference? Note that this temporal problem is common to federal Indian law: events of long ago, with whatever expectations that surrounded them, can have new meaning when they come under litigation in a new era. (A striking example is the *Menominee* case, where a Termination statute is extremely narrowly construed only fourteen years after enactment, by a court in a very different era of federal Indian policy.)

3. *Recognized title land versus fee simple land.* Note that the government has no defense to a claim for just compensation when it takes fee simple land on the ground that the government is somehow acting in good faith to the titleholder or is providing some sort of offsetting benefits (*e.g.*, by providing a beautiful new lake and fishing right next to the remainder of his or her land). What is the justification for the rule adopted that the Court borrows from *Fort Berthold*?

4. *Money for Paha Sapa?* The Supreme Court affirmed that the Sioux were entitled to over $17 million in compensation for the Black Hills, plus the interest that would have accrued on this sum since 1877, for a total of about $106 million. This might seem like a princely sum to offer the tribes, whose reservations comprise some of the poorest counties in the United States. Two weeks after the decision, however, the Black Hills Sioux Nation Council, the coordinating body for the tribes involved in the Black Hills litigation, affirmed their position that they would not accept money in exchange for the Black Hills. Called *Paha Sapa* in Lakota, the Black Hills have a sacred role in Sioux culture, and accepting money in exchange for them was seen as a rejection of that tradition. Recognizing the constitutive importance of land, Rosebud Sioux delegate Simon Broken Leg declared that money would eventually be spent, "then what you got tomorrow? You got no land; you got no future; you got no nothing." *Quoted in* Edward Lazarus, Black Hills/White Justice: The Sioux Nation Versus the United States, 1775 to the Present 404 (1991). Although some tribal members believed that accepting the money was the best they could get from the situation, over time all of the tribes involved enacted resolutions rejecting any award of money for the Black Hills. *Id.*

The Oglala Sioux Tribe also brought suit to reject the damage award and seek instead the return of the land, claiming that because the tribe had not authorized the attorneys in *Sioux Nation* to appeal on their behalf, they were not bound by the Supreme Court judgment. The suit was dismissed on the grounds that the Indian Claims Commission Act was the exclusive remedy to redress takings of the Black Hills. *Oglala Sioux Tribe v. United States,* 650 F.2d 140 (8th Cir. 1981), *cert denied* 455 U.S. 907 (1982). Various bills were also presented to Congress to provide for the return of at least the federal lands in the Black Hills; these too all failed. The award continues to collect interest; as of 2009, it was worth 900 million dollars. Chet Brokaw, *Lawsuit would let Sioux take money for Black Hills*, Rapid City Journal, April 21, 2009 (discussing class action by fourteen members of Sioux tribes to distribute funds despite tribal opposition). For a detailed history of the taking of the Black Hills, the litigation, and its aftermath, see Lazarus, Black Hills/White Justice, *supra.* For more critical accounts of the decision and litigation, see David E. Wilkins, American Indian Sovereignty and the U.S. Supreme Court: The Masking of Justice 215–234 (1997); John P. Lavelle, *Rescuing* Paha Sapa*: Achieving Environmental Justice By Restoring the Great Grasslands and Returning the Sacred Black Hills to the Great Sioux Nation*, 5 Great Plains Nat. Resources J. 40 (2001).

---

3. The Problem of Executive Order Reservations

Millions of acres of tribal land in the western United States resulted from the setting aside of land by federal executive order, not by treaty, statute, or agreement. In many instances, this is the result of nothing more than historical happenstance. Recall that Congress abandoned treatymaking with tribes in 1871. This was before many western tribes had anything approaching settled relationships with the federal government. Often, the Army would negotiate (or impose) some sort of settlement regarding land, which would be ratified by the War Department in Washington and sometimes would result in the President ratifying the arrangement by executive order. Eventually, in 1919, Congress forbade the future use of executive orders in this fashion. *See* 43 U.S.C. § 150. *Note also* 25 U.S.C. § 398d (requiring congressional authorization for altering the boundaries of executive order reservations).

In modern times, at least, courts have been willing to interpret these executive orders relatively generously, consistent with the Indian law canons of interpretation. For most purposes, executive order reservations are treated similarly to treaty-based reservations. But on the question of recognized title, an alarming difference occurs. Unless Congress at some point ratified the executive order or otherwise recognized the Indian title, the executive order reservation is not held by recognized title. *See, e.g., Sioux Tribe v. United States,* 316 U.S. 317 (1942) (a case potentially distinguishable from later cases on the ground that the land set aside by executive order was apparently intended to be Indian country only for a limited time). On one hand, the Constitution may suggest this rule, both under general conceptions of the separation of powers and the specific language of the Property Clause of Article IV. On the other hand, however, the rule could lead to incredible harshness, as it means that even today, Congress could abolish the executive order reservation, confiscate the lands, and owe nothing. Considering the longstanding reliance interests of tribes on executive order reservations, the rule that this title is not recognized title needs to be rethought. *See, e.g., Karuk Tribe v. Ammon*, 209 F.3d 1366, 1380–83 (Fed. Cir. 2000) (Newman, J., dissenting). *See also* Cohen's Handbook of Federal Indian Law at 1061 (2012) ("Congressional action and congressional acquiescence in tribal occupation for more than 100 years should suffice to fix vested property rights in tribes on executive order reservations.").

C. RELIEF FOR BREACH OF TRUST RESPONSIBILITY

Recall that in *Cherokee Nation*, the tribes and the United States were described as having a relationship similar to that of a ward to its guardian. Over the years, this has been understood as a "trust relationship." *See generally* Reid Peyton Chambers, *Judicial Enforcement of the Federal Trust Responsibility to Indians*, 27 Stan. L. Rev. 1213 (1975).

Some basics about trusts and fiduciary responsibilities. Generally speaking, in private law a trust arises when a person (the trustor or settlor) transfers legal title to property (the *res*) to a trustee, who manages the *res* for the benefit of one or more beneficiaries (who hold the equitable interest in the property). The trustee owes fiduciary duties to the beneficiaries, both of honest dealing (subjective good faith) and of reasonable competence as measured against good business standards.

Indian trust property. Many tribal and individual Indian assets are held in trust by the United States. American law conceptualizes an Indian reservation this way, as well as individual Indian allotments. Moreover, in many cases the federal government not only holds legal title, but manages the property, supposedly for the benefit of the tribe or the person. It is rare, however, to find a federal statute or regulation that expressly acknowledges that the government in such circumstances has full fiduciary duties, enforceable through injunctive relief and/or damages. Accordingly, a tribe seeking judicial enforcement of duties arising from that relationship must navigate complicated rules of sovereign immunity.

A reminder about sovereign immunity. As discussed in Part A above, to sue the government successfully, you need both a waiver of sovereign immunity *and* a viable cause of action that the waiver authorizes you to claim against the government. For example, the Federal Tort Claims Act, 28 U.S.C. §§ 1346(b), 2671–2680, waives the United States' sovereign immunity for negligence claims arising from actions of federal officials, using the "the law of the place where the act or omission occurred" for the substantive basis of the action. 28 U.S.C. § 1346(b)(1). Accordingly, if an Indian alleges a malpractice claim against an Indian Health Service doctor for services received in Phoenix, Arizona, she may recover against the federal government pursuant to the FTCA, but she must state a cause of action and prevail under the standards governed by Arizona law.†

Now, consider the following passage from a Supreme Court opinion:

†. What if the incident occurs at a hospital on the reservation? Should tribal law count as the "law of the place"? Courts have differed on this question. *LaFromboise v. Leavitt*, 439 F.3d 792, 796 (8th Cir. 2006) (holding that the "law of the place" was state law); *Cheromiah v. United States*, 55 F. Supp. 2d 1295, 1308 (D.N.M. 1999) (holding that the "law of the place" was Acoma tribal law); *see also* Katherine J. Florey, *Choosing Tribal Law: Why State Choice-of-Law Principles Should Apply to Disputes with Tribal Contacts*, 55 Am. U. L. Rev. 1627, 1667–1671 (2006).

> [T]his Court has recognized the distinctive obligation of trust incumbent upon the Government in its dealings with these dependent and sometimes exploited people. *** In carrying out its treaty obligations with the Indian tribes the Government is something more than a mere contracting party. Under a humane and self-imposed policy which has found expression in many acts of Congress and numerous decisions of this Court, it has charged itself with moral obligations of the highest responsibility and trust. Its conduct, as disclosed in the acts of those who represent it in dealings with the Indians, should therefore be judged by the most exacting fiduciary standards.

Seminole Nation v. United States 316 U.S. 286, 296–97 (1942). This quotation encourages the reader to consider the trust relationship in Indian law to be akin to, perhaps even the equivalent of, fiduciary relationships in private law. Indeed, the Court in *Seminole* actually cited sources on fiduciary obligations that are routinely associated with private law trusts: leading treatises on trusts by Bogert and Scott, and the American Law Institute's Restatement of the Law of Trusts. Yet the case cannot be understood without considering the backdrop of sovereign immunity. What was the waiver of sovereign immunity? What cause of action authorized by the waiver was stated and proved?

Arising as it did before 1946 (when the Indian Claims Commission Act and §§ 1491 and 1505 were enacted), *Seminole Nation* necessarily was litigated under a "special jurisdictional statute" that constituted a targeted waiver of sovereign immunity for particular claims by a particular tribe. In this case, the statute provided a very broad waiver of sovereign immunity:

> That jurisdiction be, and is hereby, conferred upon the Court of Claims, notwithstanding the lapse of time or statutes of limitation, to hear, examine, and adjudicate and render judgment in any and all legal and equitable claims arising under or growing out of any treaty or agreement between the United States and the Seminole Indian Nation or Tribe, or arising under or growing out of any act of Congress in relation to Indian Affairs, which said Seminole Nation or Tribe may have against the United States, which claims have not heretofore been determined and adjudicated on their merits by the Court of Claims or the Supreme Court of the United States.

43 Stat. 133 (1924).

Thus, Congress invited the federal courts to consider the tribe's claims without any special consideration of plenary power, federal sovereignty, and the like, which has sometimes led courts, like the Court in *Seminole Nation*, to bring private-law conceptions of fiduciary duty into Indian law. Many other cases have been litigated under much less generous waivers of sovereign immunity, however. The rule: do not generalize from one case to another unless the underlying statutory waiver of sovereign immunity is identical or at least similar.

Relief other than money damages. Most federal judicial review of federal agency action is governed by the Administrative Procedure Act, 5 U.S.C. § 551 *et seq*. The APA contains a broad waiver of sovereign immunity for prospective injunctive relief. *See* 5 U.S.C. § 702 ("A person suffering legal wrong because of agency action, or adversely affected or aggrieved by agency action within the meaning of a relevant statute, is entitled to judicial review thereof. An action in a court of the United States seeking relief other than money damages and stating a claim that an agency or an officer or employee thereof acted or failed to act in an official capacity or under color of legal authority shall not be dismissed nor relief therein be denied on the ground that it is against the United States or that the United States is an indispensable party. *** ") This has encouraged some lower courts to consider themselves invited to give substantive meaning to the Indian trust relationship when examining whether the executive branch has defaulted on its obligations to tribes. A classic illustration is *Pyramid Lake Paiute Tribe v. Morton*, 354 F. Supp. 252 (D.D.C. 1972) (Gesell, J), in which the Court chided the Secretary of the Interior for treating a tribe and a non-Indian reclamation district equivalently when they were competing for the same water that was under the Secretary's management. According to the court, the Secretary owed heightened duties to the tribe, which he violated by giving the tribe only half the water and the reclamation district the other half. Of course, the remedy was Secretarial reconsideration of water allocation, not money damages for the past mistakes in allocation.

Notice that in a case like *Pyramid Lake*, the tribe has a broad, obviously applicable waiver of sovereign immunity for prospective relief. Moreover, note that § 702 allows the claim to be based upon an act or a failure to act on the part of a government official without explicitly tying the action or failure to act to any specific written source of duty, such as a statute or administrative regulation. Thus, the tribe has (1) a waiver of sovereign immunity and (2) may well be able to state a claim that the Secretary's act in allocating the water violated the federal-tribal trust relationship, a creature of federal common law (and thus the tribe arguably did not have to show that the Secretary violated a specific statute, administrative regulation, the Constitution, or some other source of positive law). The Ninth Circuit has recently cast doubt on this expansive view of the trust relationship as a cause of action, however. In *Gros Ventre Tribe v. United States*, 469 F.3d 801 (9th Cir. 2006), the court rejected the tribe's argument that it had an enforceable right under the trust doctrine to equitable relief in the context of the Department of Interior's alleged failure to comply with land management and environmental statutes concerning an off-reservation cyanide heap-leach gold mine. Acid rock drainage from the mine had contaminated the tribe's on-reservation water resources, but the court concluded that, in this context, there was no applicable statute giving the tribe a right any more expansive than under the relevant environmental statutes. The court did note, however, that it was leaving open "the question of whether the United States is required to take special consideration of tribal interests when complying with applicable statutes[.]" *Id.* at 810 n.10. *See* Robert T. Anderson, *Indigenous Rights to Water and Environmental Protection*, 53 Harv. C.R. C.L. L. Rev. 337, 362-367 (2018) (critiqueing judicial reluctance to rely on the trust responsibility to prospective agency action).

Money damages. Tribes have much greater difficulty when they seek retrospective money damages—damages for past wrongdoing—than they do when they seek prospective equitable relief, as in *Pyramid Lake*. Unlike with § 702 of the APA, there is no broadly worded waiver of sovereign immunity for money damages. Usually, tribes are stuck with claims under § 1505, the Indian Tucker Act, which you should now reread. Notice how § 1505 is largely tied to positive law: a claim arising under a statute or administrative regulation, for example. Could the tribe in *Pyramid Lake* state a claim under § 1505 for retrospective monetary relief for damages caused by prior Secretarial allocations of water? Can you see how it will be harder under § 1505 than under § 702 to state a claim that seems more common law-like in nature? What language in § 1505 might lend itself to a more common-law-like claim? This problem was considered in the next two cases, which arose from claims that the federal government had mismanaged the timber resources on allotted lands held in trust for Indian allottees. The cases still form the core precedents in claims for damages for breach of trust.

1. *Mitchell I* and *II*: Damages for Breach of Fiduciary Duties in Allotment Management

Much land allotted to individual Indians under the 1887 General Allotment Act was not suitable for residential or agricultural purposes, but was instead primarily valuable for harvesting marketable timber. Over time, the Bureau of Indian Affairs came to exercise comprehensive control over timber management on lands it held in trust for Indian allottees. In the *United States v. Mitchell* litigation, individual Indians holding interests in allotments with valuable timber resources on the Quinault Indian Reservation, joined by the Quinault Tribe, alleged that the allotments had been mismanaged by the federal government in a variety of ways, including failing to get fair market value for timber sales and failing to manage the timber on a sustained-yield basis. They brought suit under § 1491 and under § 1505 seeking money damages from what they considered to be a breach of trust duties. The government raised two core objections to this claim:

1. *Is there a waiver of sovereign immunity?* Read § 1491. The government contended that it was only a jurisdictional statute and not a waiver of sovereign immunity. Under this argument, the Court of Claims would have jurisdiction to hear only those claims for which there is an independent waiver of sovereign immunity (such as in a different statute).

2. *Is there a substantive cause of action?* The government contended that even if § 1491 waived sovereign immunity for certain claims, it did so only where a substantive cause of action was "founded either upon the Constitution, or any Act of Congress or any regulation of an executive department, or upon any express or implied contract with the United States," 28 U.S.C. § 1491(a)(1), and there was no such substantive basis for the action here.

In *United States v. Mitchell*, 445 U.S. 535 (1980) (*Mitchell I*), the Court reversed and remanded on the second question. The Court held that even if §§ 1491 and 1505 waived sovereign immunity, they only granted jurisdiction where the claimant had a substantive cause of action founded in other law. The Court found that the General Allotment Act did not, in itself, create a substantive claim for breach of trust in mismanagement of timber resources. *Mitchell I*, 445 U.S. at 542. Although the Act provided that the federal government would "hold the land *** in trust for the sole use and benefit of the" allottee, the Court found that it "created only a limited trust relationship between the United States and the allottee that does not impose any duty upon the Government to manage timber resources. The Act does not unambiguously provide that the United States has undertaken full fiduciary responsibilities as to the management of allotted lands" because the legislative history and other sections of the Act indicated that "the Indian allottee, and not a representative of the United States, is responsible for using the land for agricultural or grazing purposes. *** Under this scheme, then, the allottee, and not the United States, was to manage the land." *Id.* at 541–543. Congress inserted the "trust" language "not because it wished the Government to control use of the land and be subject to money damages for breaches of fiduciary duty, but simply because it wished to prevent alienation of the land and to ensure that allottees would be immune from the state taxation." *Id.* at 544.

Justice White, joined by Justices Brennan and Stevens dissented. They were satisfied that all the elements of a trust at common law existed (legal title held by trustee for the benefit of the beneficiary, trustee had sole authority and capacity to manage the property and therefore had duties of good faith and good management under general trust law), and it was a trust squarely provided for by the plain language of the General Allotment Act. *See* 445 U.S. at 547–548 (White, J., joined by Brennan & Stevens, JJ., dissenting).

The majority remanded for determination of whether a "right of the respondents to recover money damages for Government mismanagement of timber resources" could "be found in some source other than" the GAA. *Id.* at 546. That issue returned to the Court in *Mitchell II.*

UNITED STATES V. MITCHELL

463 U.S. 206, 103 S. Ct. 2961, 77 L.Ed.2d 580 (1983)

JUSTICE MARSHALL delivered the opinion of the Court.

[The Court first held that the Tucker Act constituted a waiver of immunity for the included claims, repudiating language in *Mitchell I* and earlier cases that had created confusion on this point.]

It nonetheless remains true that the Tucker Act "does not create any substantive right enforceable against the United States for money damages." A substantive right must be found in some other source of law, such as "the Constitution, or any Act of Congress, or any regulation of an executive department." Not every claim invoking the Constitution, a federal statute, or a regulation is cognizable under the Tucker Act. The claim must be one for money damages against the United States, and the claimant must demonstrate that the source of substantive law he relies upon "'can fairly be interpreted as mandating compensation by the Federal Government for the damages sustained.'" [*United States v. Testan,* 424 U.S. 392, 400 (1976).] ***

Thus, for claims against the United States "founded either upon the Constitution, or any Act of Congress, or any regulation of an executive department," a court must inquire whether the source of substantive law can fairly be interpreted as mandating compensation by the Federal Government for the damages sustained. In undertaking this inquiry, a court need not find a separate waiver of sovereign immunity in the substantive provision, just as a court need not find consent to suit in "any express or implied contract with the United States." The Tucker Act itself provides the necessary consent.

In this case, the Tucker Act provides the United States' consent to suit for claims founded upon statutes or regulations that create substantive rights to money damages. If a claim falls within this category, the existence of a waiver of sovereign immunity is clear. The question in this case is thus analytically distinct: whether the statutes or regulations at issue can be interpreted as requiring compensation. Because the Tucker Act supplies a waiver of immunity for claims of this nature, the separate statutes and regulations need not provide a second waiver of sovereign immunity, nor need they be construed in the manner appropriate to waivers of sovereign immunity.

III

Respondents have based their money claims against the United States on various Acts of Congress and executive department regulations. ***

A

The Secretary of the Interior's pervasive role in the sales of timber from Indian lands began with the Act of June 25, 1910. [*See* 25 U.S.C. §§ 406, 407.] Prior to that time, Indians had no right to sell timber on reservation land. The 1910 Act empowered the Secretary to sell timber on unallotted lands and apply the proceeds of the sales for the benefit of the Indians, and authorized the Secretary to consent to sales by allottees, with the proceeds to be paid to the allottees or disposed of for their benefit. *** From the outset, the Interior Department recognized its obligation to supervise the cutting of Indian timber. In 1911, the Department's Office of Indian Affairs promulgated detailed regulations covering its responsibilities in "managing the Indian forests so as to obtain the greatest revenue for the Indians consistent with a proper protection and improvement of the forests." The regulations addressed virtually every aspect of forest management, including the size of sales, contract procedures, advertisements and methods of billing, deposits and bonding requirements, administrative fee deductions, procedures for sales by minors, allowable heights of stumps, tree marking and scaling rules, base and top diameters of trees for cutting, and the percentage of trees to be left as a seed source. The regulations applied to allotted as well as tribal lands, and the Secretary's approval of timber sales on allotted lands was explicitly conditioned upon compliance with the regulations.

Over time, deficiencies in the Interior Department's performance of its responsibilities became apparent. Accordingly, as part of the Indian Reorganization Act of 1934, Congress imposed even stricter duties upon the Government with respect to Indian timber management. In § 6 of the Act, Congress expressly directed that the Interior Department manage Indian forest resources "on the principle of sustained-yield management."

Regulations promulgated under the Act required the preservation of Indian forest lands in a perpetually productive state, forbade the clear-cutting of large contiguous areas, called for the development of long-term working plans for all major reservations, required adequate provision for new growth when mature timber was removed, and required the regulation of run-off and the minimization of erosion. The regulatory scheme was designed to assure that the Indians receive " 'the benefit of whatever profit [the forest] is capable of yielding.' " In 1964 Congress amended the timber provisions of the 1910 Act, again emphasizing the Secretary of the Interior's management duties. As to sales of timber on allotted lands, the Secretary was directed to consider "the needs and best interests of the Indian owner and his heirs."

The timber management statutes and the regulations promulgated thereunder establish the "comprehensive" responsibilities of the Federal Government in managing the harvesting of Indian timber. The Department of the Interior-through the Bureau of Indian Affairs—"exercises literally daily supervision over the harvesting and management of tribal timber." ***

B

In *Mitchell I* this Court recognized that the General Allotment Act creates a trust relationship between the United States and Indian allottees but concluded that the trust relationship was limited. We held that the Act could not be read "as establishing that the United States has a fiduciary responsibility for management of allotted forest lands." In contrast to the bare trust created by the General Allotment Act, the statutes and regulations now before us clearly give the Federal Government full responsibility to manage Indian resources and land for the benefit of the Indians. They thereby establish a fiduciary relationship and define the contours of the United States' fiduciary responsibilities.

The language of these statutory and regulatory provisions directly supports the existence of a fiduciary relationship. For example, § 8 of the 1910 Act, as amended, expressly mandates that sales of timber from Indian trust lands be based upon the Secretary's consideration of "the needs and best interests of the Indian owner and his heirs" and that proceeds from such sales be paid to owners "or disposed of for their benefit." Similarly, even in its earliest regulations, the Government recognized its duties in "managing the Indian forests so as to obtain the greatest revenue for the Indians consistent with a proper protection and improvement of the forests." Office of Indian Affairs, Regulations and Instructions for Officers in Charge of Forests on Indian Reservations 4 (1911). Thus, the Government has "expressed a firm desire that the Tribe should retain the benefits derived from the harvesting and sale of reservation timber."

Moreover, a fiduciary relationship necessarily arises when the Government assumes such elaborate control over forests and property belonging to Indians. All of the necessary elements of a common-law trust are present: a trustee (the United States), a beneficiary (the Indian allottees), and a trust corpus (Indian timber, lands, and funds). [Citing Restatement (Second) of Trusts.] "[W]here the Federal Government takes on or has control or supervision over tribal monies or properties, the fiduciary relationship normally exists with respect to such monies or properties (unless Congress has provided otherwise) even though nothing is said expressly in the authorizing or underlying statute (or other fundamental document) about a trust fund, or a trust or fiduciary connection." *Navajo Tribe of Indians v. United States*, 624 F.2d 981, 987 (Ct. Cl. 1980).

Our construction of these statutes and regulations is reinforced by the undisputed existence of a general trust relationship between the United States and the Indian people. This Court has previously emphasized "the distinctive obligation of trust incumbent upon the Government in its dealings with these dependent and sometimes exploited people." *Seminole Nation*. This principle has long dominated the Government's dealings with Indians.

Because the statutes and regulations at issue in this case clearly establish fiduciary obligations of the Government in the management and operation of

Indian lands and resources, they can fairly be interpreted as mandating compensation by the Federal Government for damages sustained. Given the existence of a trust relationship, it naturally follows that the Government should be liable in damages for the breach of its fiduciary duties. It is well established that a trustee is accountable in damages for breaches of trust. [Citing Restatement (Second) of Trusts; G. Bogert, Law of Trusts and Trustees; A. Scott, Law of Trusts.] This Court and several other federal courts have consistently recognized that the existence of a trust relationship between the United States and an Indian or Indian tribe includes as a fundamental incident the right of an injured beneficiary to sue the trustee for damages resulting from a breach of the trust. [Citing, *e.g., Seminole Nation.*]

The recognition of a damages remedy also furthers the purposes of the statutes and regulations, which clearly require that the Secretary manage Indian resources so as to generate proceeds for the Indians. It would be anomalous to conclude that these enactments create a right to the value of certain resources when the Secretary lives up to his duties, but no right to the value of the resources if the Secretary's duties are not performed. "Absent a retrospective damages remedy, there would be little to deter federal officials from violating their trust duties, at least until the allottees managed to obtain a judicial decree against future breaches of trust." *Mitchell I* (White, J., dissenting.)

The Government contends that violations of duties imposed by the various statutes may be cured by actions for declaratory, injunctive or mandamus relief against the Secretary[.] In this context, however, prospective equitable remedies are totally inadequate. To begin with, the Indian allottees are in no position to monitor federal management of their lands on a consistent basis. Many are poorly educated, most are absentee owners, and many do not even know the exact physical location of their allotments. Indeed, it was the very recognition of the inability of the Indians to oversee their interests that led to federal management in the first place. A trusteeship would mean little if the beneficiaries were required to supervise the day-to-day management of their estate by their trustee or else be precluded from recovery for mismanagement.

In addition, by the time government mismanagement becomes apparent, the damage to Indian resources may be so severe that a prospective remedy may be next to worthless. For example, if timber on an allotment has been destroyed through Government mismanagement, it will take many years for nature to restore the timber. ***

We thus conclude that the statutes and regulations at issue here can fairly be interpreted as mandating compensation by the Federal Government for violations of its fiduciary responsibilities in the management of Indian property. [*Affirmed.*]

[JUSTICE POWELL, joined by JUSTICE REHNQUIST and JUSTICE O'CONNOR, dissented, arguing that neither § 1491 nor § 1505 waived sovereign immunity, and that the timber management statutes created no claim for money damages against the government.]

NOTES AND QUESTIONS

1. *Three groups of Justices.* Three Justices (Rehnquist, Powell, Stewart in *Mitchell I* and his replacement, O'Connor in *Mitchell II*) would have taken the hard-nosed approach suggested by the clear statement rule concerning sovereign immunity waivers both to construing § 1491 and the federal timber statutes and regulations. For them, both cases were easy: nowhere in federal law is there an express waiver of sovereign immunity for money damages for mismanagement of Indian timber. Of this group, we might say that they saw no reason why Indian law should take a more generous attitude about sovereign immunity than other fields. Three other Justices (Brennan, White, Stevens) took a diametrically opposed approach. For them, both cases were easy the other way: Congress had created a property relationship in the General Allotment Act exactly like a private trust, and once a trust existed, it should follow, absent a statute saying something to the contrary, that the trustee (the executive branch) had the usual fiduciary duties and was responsible for the usual damages for breach of those duties. For these Justices, it seemed plain that the General Allotment Act could be fairly read as demanding compensation. We might say that these Justices seemed to deviate from usual sovereign immunity approaches in the Indian law context. The swing Justices (Marshall, Blackmun; Burger did not participate in *Mitchell I* and joined *Mitchell II*), in a portion of the opinion not included here, seem more inscrutable on this point.

Be aware that this is a general pattern in the Supreme Court over the years: some Justices consider Indian law novel, perhaps even unique; some consider it no different from other areas of public law; some try to find some middle ground. In this instance, the Justices motivated by novelty are most favorable to the tribal interest. But sometimes things cut the other direction. In *Lone Wolf* and *Tee Hit Ton*, for example, the majority opinions were clearly motivated by the understanding that Indian law is separate from and driven by very different notions than the general public law.

2. *What is the holding?* Is the holding in *Mitchell II* that the executive branch owes full fiduciary duties to the allottees, at least except where a federal statute or regulation expressly says something to the contrary? This notion would be that, once Congress and the executive branch created a *de facto* trust relationship by enacting various statutes and regulations that put the federal government into full management mode, full fiduciary obligations apply. Or is the holding that, where the federal timbering statutes and regulations place a particular duty upon the executive branch, the breach of that duty is compensable in damages? Find language in the opinion that is ambiguous on this score. What is the practical difference between the two approaches?

---

2. Post–*Mitchell* Trust Cases

In 2003 the Supreme Court twice returned to the issues in *Mitchell I* and *II*. In *United States v. White Mountain Apache Tribe*, 537 U.S. 465 (2003), by a 5–4 vote, the Court concluded that the tribe had a viable *Mitchell II* claim for the government's alleged failure to maintain and preserve trust property. The federal statute in question provided that the "former Fort Apache Military Reservation" is "held by the United States in trust for the White Mountain Apache

Tribe, subject to the right of the Secretary of the Interior to use any part of the land and improvements." The tribe contended that the government's use of this property was actionable for money damages because the government had breached a fiduciary duty to maintain, protect, repair, and preserve the trust property. Justice Souter's majority opinion understood the *Mitchell* cases as holding (1) that the Tucker Act (§ 1491) and the Indian Tucker Act (§ 1505) are waivers of sovereign immunity and (2) a substantive right to money damages must be traced to a different statute or combination of statutes. Justice Souter wrote:

> As we said in *Mitchell II*, a statute creates a right capable of grounding a claim with the waiver of sovereign immunity if, but only if, it "can fairly be interpreted as mandating compensation by the Federal Government for the damage sustained." This "fair interpretation" rule demands a showing demonstrably lower than the standard for the initial waiver of sovereign immunity. *** It is enough *** that the statute creating a Tucker Act right be reasonably amenable to the reading that it mandates a right of recovery in damages. While the premise to a Tucker Act claim will not be "lightly inferred," [quoting *Mitchell II*], a fair inference will do.

Id. at 466. Justice Souter tied this approach to the results in *Mitchell I* (the General Allotment Act was only a "trust in name," not a more conventional fiduciary relationship) and *Mitchell II* (the timber statutes and regulations "raised the fair implication that the substantive obligations imposed on the United States by those statutes and regulations were enforceable by damages"). He then concluded that the Fort Apache statute provided the government control over the trust property and that although the statute does not (as did the *Mitchell II* statutes) expressly impose duties on the government, "the fact that the property occupied by the United States is expressly subject to a trust supports a fair inference that an obligation to preserve the property improvements was incumbent on the United States as trustee. This is so because elementary trust law, after all, confirms the commonsense assumption that a fiduciary actually administering trust property may not allow it to fall into ruin on its watch." *Id.* at 467.

The dissenting opinion of Justice Thomas, joined by Chief Justice Rehnquist, Justice Scalia, and Justice Kennedy, complained that the majority had expanded *Mitchell II* by unduly allowing common-law trust principles to substitute for the requisite congressional intent—an intent, they thought, to establish only a bare trust along the lines of *Mitchell I*.

Conversely, in *United States v. Navajo Nation*, 537 U.S. 488 (2003), the Court denied the tribe's attempt to recover for what it claimed was misconduct by the Secretary of the Interior. The case involved the royalty rate the Peabody Coal Company paid for the valuable coal mined from Navajo lands. Pursuant to a twenty-year lease signed in 1964, the rate had been set at no more than 37.5 cents per ton. In March of 1984, as the twenty-year anniversary approached, the Navajo Nation asked the Secretary of the Interior to adjust the rate. The rate was clearly inequitable, and was far below the 12.5% minimum set by Congress in 1977 for coal mined on federal lands. In June 1984, after reviewing reports and recommendations by several federal agencies, the Area Director for the Bureau of Indian Affairs issued a final decision adjusting the rate to 20% per ton. Peabody appealed the decision, but both parties expected the Secretary of Interior to reject the appeal. In July of 1985, when an unfavorable decision seemed imminent, Peabody retained a former Department of Interior employee with close ties to Don Hodel, the new Secretary of the Interior. The former employee met privately with Secretary Hodel without ever notifying the Navajo Nation of the meeting. After the meeting, Secretary Hodel sent the Deputy Assistant Secretary for Indian Affairs a memo telling them that a decision on the appeal was not imminent, and urging them to reach an agreed upon solution in the matter.

Having learned that there was pressure from higher ups at Interior to delay a decision and force the parties to settle the matter, the Navajo Nation went back to the bargaining table. Facing extreme economic pressure (and still receiving a far below market 37.5 cents per ton on its coal) the Nation ultimately agreed to a 12.5% royalty rate. Secretary Hodel promptly approved the amendments. The tribe contended that the case was just like *Mitchell II*, in that under the relevant federal statutes and regulations the Secretary controlled the leasing of coal on Indian land. In rejecting this argument, the majority opinion of Justice Ginsburg concluded that the Indian Mineral Leasing Act and its regulations did not impose management obligations similar to the timbering statutes and regulations at issue in *Mitchell II* and did not even include any "trust language" at all. Indeed, imposing liability would be inconsistent with the purposes of the IMLA, which was designed to enhance tribal self-determination by giving tribes more power to decide how to develop their mineral resources. Justice Souter dissented, joined by Justices Stevens and O'Connor.

On remand in *Navajo Nation*, the federal circuit held that a "network" of other federal statutes and regulations imposed sufficient management authority to infer a damages remedy for breach of federal duties. *Navajo Nation v. United States*, 501 F.3d 1327, 1343 (Fed. Cir. 2007). The Supreme Court again granted certiorari to review the decision and again reversed, holding that none of the laws cited by the Federal Circuit on remand provided a sounder basis for finding a trust responsibility in the case. *United States v. Navajo Nation*, 129 S. Ct. 1547 (2009). Justice Souter, joined by Justice Stevens, filed the following two-sentence concurrence: "I am not through regretting that my position in *United States v. Navajo Nation* (dissenting opinion), did not carry the day. But it did not, and I agree that the precedent of that case calls for the result reached here." *Id.* at 1558. (Justice O'Connor, the third member of Group 1, had retired.)

The Supreme Court's most recent decision furthers the restrictions on the trust responsibility. In *United States v. Jicarilla Apache Tribe*, 131 S. Ct. 2313 (2011), the Court refused to order the disclosure of government documents containing legal advice pertaining to tribal trust fund management to the Jicarilla Apache Tribe, the trust beneficiary. The Tribe had sued the United States alleging a breach of trust in the management of the funds. The Court refused to apply the common law rule that would require a private trustee to disclose attorney client communications related to trust fund management to the trust beneficiary. The Court reasoned that "[t]he United States *** does not have the same common-law disclosure obligations as a private trustee. As we have previously said, common-law principles are relevant only when applied to a 'specific, applicable, trust-creating statute or regulation.' *** The common law of trusts does not override the specific trust-creating statute and regulations that apply here." *Id.* at 2329. In *Jicarilla*, unlike in *Mitchell II* and *White Mountain Apache*, the view that Indian trust law is exceptional hurt the tribal interest instead of helping it.

In *Menominee Indian Tribe of Wisconsin v. United States*, 136 S. Ct. 750 (2016) the Tribe presented contract support cost claims (for contract years 1995 through 2004) to the Indian Health Service on September 7, 2005. The IHS denied the Tribe's claims for its 1996, 1997, and 1998 contracts based on the Contract Dispute Act's 6-year statute of limitations. The Tribe challenged the denials in the United States District Court for the District of Columbia, arguing, based on theories of class-action and equitable tolling, that the limitations period should be tolled for time during which a related class action had been pending. That class action was not certified, and the Supreme Court ruled that the doctrine of equitable tolling was not satisfied because the Tribe had no excuse for failing to file its action except its mistaken belief that mere pendency of a class action tolled the statute of limitations. The Court stated that "the equitable tolling test is met only where the circumstances that caused a litigant's delay are both extraordinary *and* beyond its control." The Court also rejected the argument that the federal trust responsibility provided a basis for tolling the statute of limitations, reasoning that the " 'general trust relationship' does not override the clear language of those statutes [governing contract dispute claims]."

3. Litigation Regarding Individual Indian Money Accounts

Cobell v. Norton is a class-action lawsuit filed in 1996 to force the federal government to account for billions of dollars belonging to approximately 500,000 American Indians and their heirs, and held in trust since the late 19th century. Elouise Cobell, founder of the nation's first Indian-owned bank and a member of the Blackfeet tribe in Montana, is the lead plaintiff in this case, which has two goals: to force the government to account for the money, and to bring about permanent reform of the system.

The facts underlying the litigation involve a broad sweep of United States history. As you already know, although U.S. policy in the 1870s was to locate Indians on reservations, hunger for the land by non-Indians led to a break-up of most of the reservations starting in the 1880s. Thousands of individual Indians generally were allotted parcels of land in the break-up. As trustee, the government took legal title to the parcels, established an Individual Indian Money Trust, and assumed responsibility for management of the trust lands. That included the duty to collect and disburse to the Indians any revenues generated by mining, oil and gas extraction, timber operations, grazing or similar activities.

No one argues that the government fulfilled that duty. Many of the records necessary to reconcile the accounts have been destroyed by fire or floods or lost over the years; others were left in sheds where they have been scattered and gnawed by mice. A 1992 congressional report found "significant, habitual problems in the BIA's ability to fully and accurately account for trust fund moneys, to properly discharge its fiduciary responsibilities, and to prudently manage the trust funds." Committee on Government Operations, *Misplaced Trust: The Bureau of Indian Affairs' Mismanagement of the Indian Trust Fund*, H.R. Rep. No. 102–499 at 2 (1992). The congressional investigators concluded that top officials "have utterly failed to grasp the human impact of its financial management of the Indian trust fund." *Id.* at 5.

The following article gives some idea of the disarray in account records:

> 78–year–old Jim Little Bull *** tries to keep track of an allotment owned by his 98–year–old mother, Mary, who lives in a nursing home. Instead of government royalty checks, he keeps getting water bills for irrigation that's supposedly going on at the property. One bill from May claims his mother owes $1,583. Little Bull says he doesn't know where the land is. But he learned one thing when he went to the local Indian agency office and asked about the charges. "The land wasn't leased. It's not farming land, and there's no water on it," Little Bull says.
>
> Besides the slipshod record-keeping, thousands of government checks are returned to the Treasury because the intended recipients either have died or can't be found. A glacial probate system takes so long to wrap up deceased Indians' financial affairs that the ownership of allotments splinters into minute portions, sometimes leaving hundreds of heirs with an interest in a single parcel. Cobell says it took 14 years for her father's estate to go through probate. "These are stories you hear over and over again on every Indian reservation," Cobell says.

John Gibeaut, *Another Broken Trust*, 85 A.B.A.J. 40 (1999).

On December 21, 1999, after a six-week bench trial, D.C. District Court Judge Royce Lamberth ruled that the secretaries of Interior and Treasury had breached their trust obligations to the Indians, declaring that "[i]t would be difficult to find a more historically mismanaged federal program than the Individual Indian Money (IIM) trust." *Cobell v. Babbitt*, 91 F. Supp. 2d 1, 6 (D.D.C. 1999). The court retained judicial oversight of the system for a minimum of five years, to ensure that it is overhauled, ordered Interior to provide an historical accounting of all trust funds, and appointed a federal monitor to assess Interior's efforts to comply. In his first report to the court—19 months after Judge Lamberth's order—the federal monitor declared that Interior's stated efforts to provide an accounting in compliance with the order were a sham, and were "still at the starting gate," having been marked by "unrealistic responses and evasion."

In 2001, the U.S. Court of Appeals affirmed Judge Lamberth's Dec. 21, 1999 order. The opinion shows the application of the trust responsibility to a case for injunctive relief and the continuing force of the Indian canons of construction as applied to statutes.

COBELL V. NORTON

240 F.3d 1081 (D.C. Cir. 2001)

SENTELLE, CIRCUIT JUDGE:

[The plaintiffs filed suit against the Secretary of the Interior and various federal officials as representatives of a class of Individual Indian Money ("IIM") trust account beneficiaries. They sought an accounting of funds held by the defendants. After a six-week trial, the district court held that the defendants had a trust responsibility to provide an accurate accounting of all moneys held in IIM accounts, and that they were in breach of that responsibility. The court ordered the defendants to create a workable plan and institute procedures to provide and maintain accurate accounts and provide quarterly reports on their progress toward meeting their responsibilities. The defendants appeal on the grounds that the district court mischaracterized their trust responsibilities and exceeded its authority in ordering equitable relief for the plaintiffs.] *** We find that the district court had before it ample evidence to support its finding of ongoing material breaches of appellants' fiduciary obligations. The relief ordered was well within the district court's equitable powers. While we order the district court to modify the characterization of some of its findings, we generally affirm its judgment and order.

***

In the second half of the nineteenth century, *** the federal government began to divide Indian lands into individual parcels, taking lands that had been set aside for Indian tribes and allotting them to individual tribe members. *** Under the General Allotment Act, beneficial title of the allotted lands vested in the United States as trustee for individual Indians. *** Allotment of tribal lands ceased with enactment of the Indian Reorganization Act of 1934 ("IRA"), 48 Stat. 984. *** Rather than undo the assimilationist allotment polices, the 1934 Act extended the trust period for allotted lands indefinitely. *Id.* § 462. The federal government retained control of lands already allotted but not yet fee-patented, and thereby retained its fiduciary obligations to administer the trust lands and funds arising therefrom for the benefit of individual Indian beneficiaries. These lands form the basis for the Individual Indian Money ("IIM") accounts that are at the heart of this case. ***

*** Because the United States holds IIM lands in trust for individual Indian beneficiaries, it assumes the fiduciary obligations of a trustee. " '[W]here the Federal Government takes on or has control or supervision over tribal monies or properties, the fiduciary relationship normally exists with respect to such monies or properties (unless Congress has provided otherwise) even though nothing is said expressly in the authorizing or underlying statute (or other fundamental document) about a trust fund, or a trust or fiduciary connection.' " *United States v. Mitchell* ("*Mitchell II*"), 463 U.S. 206, 225 (1983). As a result of allotment, individual Indians became beneficiaries of the trust lands, but lost the right to sell, lease, or burden the property without the federal government's approval. The federal government also probates estates related to Indian trust lands and receives and distributes income from the lease of allotted lands. Income generated from the trust lands is to be paid to the individual beneficiaries.

*** The federal government does not know the precise number of IIM trust accounts that it is to administer and protect. At present, the Interior Department's system contains over 300,000 accounts covering an estimated 11 million acres, but the Department is unsure whether this is the proper number of accounts. *** Plaintiffs claim that the actual number of accounts is far higher, exceeding 500,000 trust accounts.

Not only does the Interior Department not know the proper number of accounts, it does not know the proper balances for each IIM account, nor does

Interior have sufficient records to determine the value of IIM accounts. As the district court found, "[a]lthough the United States freely gives out 'balances' to plaintiffs, it admits that currently these balances cannot be supported by adequate transactional documentation." *** As a result, the government regularly issues payments to trust beneficiaries "in erroneous amounts—from unreconciled accounts—some of which are known to have incorrect balances." *Cobell v. Babbitt* ("*Cobell V*"), 91 F. Supp. 2d 1, 6 (D.D.C. 1999). Thus, the district court concluded, and the government does not deny, that "[i]t is entirely possible that tens of thousands of IIM trust beneficiaries should be receiving different amounts of money—their own money—than they do today. Perhaps not. But no one can say. *** " *Id.*

*** Concern over federal mismanagement of the IIM trust funds is not new. The General Accounting Office, Interior Department Inspector General, and Office of Management and Budget, among others, have all condemned the mismanagement of the IIM trust accounts over the past twenty years. *** Time and again Interior Department officials pledged to address these concerns. Yet, as Interior officials readily acknowledge, there has been little progress at reforming the management of IIM trust accounts. ***

To address these concerns, Interior commissioned an independent study which determined that reconciling the IIM trust accounts could cost over $200 million. *Cobell V*, 91 F. Supp. 2d at 13. Yet "[e]ven that expenditure would have yielded only a 'reconciliation' of approximately eighty-five percent reliability." *Id.* Once again the Interior Department pledged reforms; once again there was little improvement.

In 1994, Congress enacted the Indian Trust Fund Management Reform Act ("1994 Act"), Pub. L. No. 103–412 (1994). This law recognized the federal government's preexisting trust responsibilities. It further identified *some* of the Interior Secretary's duties to ensure "proper discharge of the trust responsibilities of the United States," 25 U.S.C. § 262a(d) [including the duty to implement systems to provide an accurate accounting of the trust accounts, to periodically reconcile those accounts to ensure accuracy, and to provide trust beneficiaries with periodic statements of their balances.]

*** The crux of appellants' argument is that there was no material breach of their fiduciary obligations as defined by the 1994 Act. Specifically, appellants contend that the district court found obligations beyond those enumerated in the Act. *** The fundamental problem with appellants' claims is the premise that their duties are solely defined by the 1994 Act. The Indian Trust Fund Management Reform Act reaffirmed and clarified preexisting duties; it did not create them. ***

*** *Mitchell II* held that "a fiduciary relationship necessarily arises when the government assumes such elaborate control over *** property belonging to Indians"—in particular where, as here, "[a]ll of the necessary elements of a common-law trust are present." 463 U.S. at 225. The general "contours" of the government's obligations may be defined by statute, but the interstices must be filled in through reference to general trust law. While *Mitchell II* involved a claim for damages, nothing in that decision or other Indian cases would imply that appellants are not entitled to declaratory or injunctive relief. Such remedies are the traditional ones for violations of trust duties.

Appellants imply that the district court did not show sufficient deference to their roles as administrative officials charged with developing and implementing policies and procedures to ensure the discharge of the federal government's obligations. Appellants thus imply, but do not argue, that their interpretation of the 1994 Act, and the obligations that it imposes, is due deference under *Chevron U.S.A., Inc. v. NRDC*, 467 U.S. 837 (1984). Assuming that the 1994 Act is ambiguous, this does not enable the government to escape liability by interpreting away its fiduciary obligations. While ordinarily we defer to an agency's interpretations of ambiguous statutes entrusted to it for administration, *Chevron* deference is not applicable in this case. The governing canon of construction requires that "statutes are to be construed liberally in favor of the Indians, with ambiguous provisions interpreted to their benefit." *Montana v. Blackfeet Tribe of Indians*, 471 U.S. 759, 766 (1985). Therefore, even where the ambiguous statute is one entrusted to an agency, we give the agency's interpretation "careful consideration" but we "do not defer to it." *Muscogee (Creek) Nation v. Hodel*, 851 F.2d 1439, 1445 n.8 (D.C. Cir. 1988). This departure from the *Chevron* norm arises from the fact that the rule of liberally construing statutes to the benefit of the Indians arises not from ordinary exegesis, but "from principles of equitable obligations and normative rules of behavior," applicable to the trust relationship between the United States and the Native American people. ***

Appellants' challenge focuses on the district court's conclusion that the IIM trust beneficiaries are entitled to a complete historical accounting of their trust accounts. The government maintains that no such right is conferred by the 1994 Act. Rather, the Act delegates responsibility for determining the nature and scope of an accounting to the Interior Department. The accounting required by Section 102 of the Act is merely a prospective right and, according to appellants, "does not speak to the extent to which the Secretary must inquire into the correctness of past transactions." ***

Contrary to appellants' claims, Section 102 of the 1994 Act makes clear that the Interior Secretary owes IIM trust beneficiaries an accounting for "*all* funds held in trust by the United States for the benefit of an Indian tribe or an individual Indian which are deposited or invested pursuant to the Act of June 24, 1938." "All funds" means *all funds,* irrespective of when they were deposited (or at least so long as they were deposited after the Act of June 24, 1938). Therefore, the 1994 Act reaffirms the government's preexisting fiduciary duty to perform a complete historical accounting of trust fund assets. ***

Even were the language of the 1994 Act ambiguous, this would not redeem appellants' position, as we follow the same rules of construction with regard to Indian trust expectations discussed above. Courts "must be guided by that 'eminently sound and vital canon' that 'statutes passed for the benefit of Indian tribes *** are to be liberally construed, doubtful expressions being resolved in favor of the Indians.' " *Bryan v. Itasca County*, 426 U.S. 373, 392 (1976). ***

The Interior Department has failed to discharge the fiduciary duties it owes to IIM beneficiaries for decades. Despite passage of the 1994 Act, the Department is still unable to execute the most fundamental of trust duties—an accurate accounting. While the district court may have mischaracterized some of the government's specific obligations, its broader conclusion that government officials breached their obligations to IIM beneficiaries is in accordance with the law and well-supported by the evidentiary record. Therefore, we affirm the order of the district court and remand the case to that court for further proceedings.

NOTES AND QUESTIONS

1. *Conclusion of Cobell?* District Court Judge Lamberth had little patience with the repeated failures of Interior and the BIA to comply with his orders. A Reagan appointee and former government attorney himself, Lambert reportedly "was a master bureaucrat in the U.S. Attorney's Office. *** And as a judge, he hasn't forgotten anything. He doesn't just know where the bodies are buried, he knows how to bury the bodies." Jonathan Groner, *A Scramble for Cover in Indian Case: Officials tap private counsel to avoid district judge's wrath*, Legal Times (Nov. 20, 2001). Over the course of the litigation, he issued several contempt orders against the governments' attorneys as well as the Secretary of the Interior, Secretary of Treasury, and the Assistant Secretary of Indian Affairs.

In 2006, in response to escalating hostility between the court and the executive branch, the Court of Appeals reassigned the case to Judge James Robertson. In 2008, Judge Robertson found that the defendants had "unreasonably delayed" completion of the accounting but that "it is now clear that completion of the required accounting is an impossible task," because Congress would never provide billions believed necessary to complete it. *Cobell v. Kempthorne*, 532 F.Supp.2d 37, 39, 103 n.21 (D.D.C. 2008). Later that year, the court ordered the defendants to pay the plaintiffs 455 million dollars, which was within the range of what the government estimated was necessary to account for missing money in the trust fund. *Cobell v. Kempthorne*, 569 F. Supp. 2d 223, 226 (D.D.C. 2008). This figure did not include potential damages to the plaintiffs from the defendants' mishandling of the fund, or the government's own profit from improperly withholding funds. *Id.* Some of the government's documents, moreover, suggested that only 77% of the IIM funds had been distributed, resulting in shortfalls of about three billion dollars. *Id.* While the government denied that this was the import of the documents, it had insufficient records to determine what the accurate figure actually was. *Id.* at 227. In 2009, the Court of Appeals reversed the district court's judgment, holding that it failed to adequately require the United States to meet its trust responsibilities. *Cobell v. Salazar*, 573 F.3d 808 (D.C. Cir. 2009).

Finally, on December 8, 2009, the plaintiffs and new Secretary of the Interior Ken Salazar announced a settlement. The United States would distribute $1.4 billion among the over 300,000 plaintiffs to compensate them for mismanagement of their accounts, and provide an additional two billion dollars for voluntary sales of fractionated lands and consolidation of the lands in tribes, plus $60 million for higher education scholarships. Lead plaintiff Elaine Cobell cited the poverty and death of the aging original trust account holders as a key reason for accepting the settlement. "Indians did not receive the full financial Settlement they deserved, but we achieved the best Settlement we could. This is a bittersweet victory, at best, but it will mean a great deal to the tens of thousands of impoverished Indians entitled to share in its financial fruits, as well as to the Indian youth whose dreams for a better life including the possibility of one day attending college can now be realized."

Congress passed the *Cobell* settlement and the president signed it into law in December 2010. Pub. L. No. 111-291 (2010). Elouise Cobell, who had been tireless in seeking authorization for the settlement, was there to watch. President Obama singled her out by name:

> [This case] began when Elouise Cobell—who's here today—charged the Interior Department with failing to account for tens of billions of dollars that they were supposed to collect on behalf of more than 300,000 of her fellow Native Americans.
>
> Elouise's argument was simple: The government, as a trustee of Indian funds, should be able to account for how it handles that money. And now, after 14 years of litigation, it's finally time to address the way that Native Americans were treated by their government. It's finally time to make things right.

The federal courts have now approved the settlement, finding that it was fair to the plaintiff class. *Cobell v. Salazar*, 679 F.3d 909 (D.C. Cir. 2012). The Settlement is now final. Secretary of the Interior Ken Salazar appointed a five-member National Commission on Indian Trust Administration and Reform under the Federal Advisory Committee Act to advise the Administration on settlement implementation and broader trust reform issues. The Commission submitted its report in December of 2013. Final Report of the Commission on Indian Trust Administration and Reform, Department of the Interior, December 10, 2013, http://www.interior.gov/cobell/commission/upload/Report-of-the-Commission-on-Indian-Trust-Administration-and-Reform_FINAL_Approved-12-10-2013.pdf. Elouise Cobell will not get to witness implementation of the settlement. Six months after the signing ceremony, she went to the Mayo Clinic for an operation for cancer. She died On October 16, 2011. *See* Bethany R. Berger, *Elouise Cobell: Bringing the United States to Account*, *in* "Our Cause Will Ultimately Triumph": Profiles from the American Indian Sovereignty Movement (Tim Alan Garrison ed. Carolina Academic Press 2014) (discussing Cobell's life and death).

2. What light does the *Cobell* case shed on the nature and, some might suggest, perversity, of how the trust doctrine works in practice? Consider, for example that the government lawyers currently fighting tooth and nail are also those charged with enforcing the Indian trust doctrine.

3. *An Inherent Conflict of Interest?* In *Nevada v. United States*, 463 U.S. 110 (1983), the Supreme Court held that the United States was bound by claim preclusion principles from relitigating a decree allocating water rights in the Truckee River. The United States was attempting to reopen the decree in order to assert additional water rights for the Pyramid Lake Indian Reservation. In the previous litigation, the United States had represented both the Pyramid Lake Paiute Tribe and the large reclamation project, known as the Newlands Project, that was dependent on significant diversions from the Truckee. The Tribe, on the other hand, had an historical interest in and attachment to Pyramid Lake, which in the years following the initial decree, shrank to a mere puddle of its former self due to the diversions for the Newlands Project and other private interests. If the United States cannot rectify harms to its beneficiary, a tribe, by modifying inequitable decisions in subsequent legal actions,

should there be a heightened fiduciary standard applied to all initial resource allocation decisions? Who would be the watchdog for this heightened standard? Just as judges must take special care to ensure that criminal defendants knowingly waive their rights when they plead guilty, should courts carry out an aspect of the trust obligation by canvassing tribes specially when approving settlement agreements? Would that work, and even if it were workable, would it be sufficient to avoid the conflict? For more on federal conflicts of interest with Indian tribes, see Ann C. Juliano, *Conflicted Justice: The Department of Justice's Conflict of Interest in Representing Native American Tribes*, 37 Ga. L. Rev. 1307 (2003).

4. In *United States v. Tohono O'odham Nation*, 131 S. Ct. 1723 (2011), the Nation sued the United States for breach of trust, but filed dual suits, the first in a federal district court seeking an accounting of trust accounts managed by the United States, and the second in the Court of Federal Claims (CFC) seeking money damages for the alleged breach of trust. Because 28 U.S.C. § 1500 precludes the latter court from exercising jurisdiction when the plaintiff has another suit for or in respect to that claim pending against the United States or its agents, the United States moved to dismiss the CFC action. The Supreme Court agreed.

> The two actions both alleged that the United States holds the same assets in trust for the Nation's benefit. They describe almost identical breaches of fiduciary duty—that the United States engaged in self-dealing and imprudent investment, and failed to provide an accurate accounting of the assets held in trust, for example. Indeed, it appears that the Nation could have filed two identical complaints, save the caption and prayer for relief, without changing either suit in any significant respect.
>
> The holding here precludes the CFC from exercising jurisdiction over the Nation's suit while the District Court case is pending. Should the Nation choose to dismiss the latter action, or upon that action's completion, the Nation is free to file suit again in the CFC if the statute of limitations is no bar. In the meantime, and in light of the substantial overlap in operative facts between them, the two suits are "for or in respect to" the same claim under § 1500, and the CFC case must be dismissed.

Id. at 1731-1732. If the cases had been filed in the reverse order, the CFC case would not have been dismissed because under *Tecon Engineers, Inc. v. United States*, 343 F.2d 943 (Fed. Cir. 1965), dismissal is only required if a second suit is pending at the time the CFC action is filed.

Dozens of cases like the Tohono O'odham's were pending against the United States, and in 2012, the Tohono O'odham and 40 other tribes agreed to a settlement of claims for mismanagement of money and resources held in trust by the United States. The settlement provides for $1.023 billion dollars to be divided among the tribes according to the value of the property mismanaged. Office of Public Affairs, *Interior Department, Secretary Salazar and Attorney General Holder Announce $1 Billion Settlement of Tribal Trust Accounting and Management Lawsuits Filed by More than 40 Tribes*, April 11, 2012. The tribal trust cases were filed and litigated according to similar theories and facts about government mismanagement as the *Cobell* litigation, described above.

CHAPTER 5

TRIBES, INDIAN COUNTRY, AND CRIMINAL JURISDICTION

■ ■ ■

Two basic ideas, "tribe" and "Indian country," define much of the scope of federal Indian law and the special jurisdictional rules that it includes. Whether a group is legally recognized as a tribe determines whether the law will protect its powers of self-government, whether the group and its members are entitled to federal Indian services such as health care and educational assistance, and whether it will be able to protect its territory using the federal Nonintercourse Act. "Indian country" is an equally important concept, defining the tribal territory and the area within which special Indian law jurisdictional rules apply. The first two sections of this chapter describe the legal rules defining tribes and Indian country. The third section describes legal efforts by tribes to restore their territory when it has been taken in violation of the Nonintercourse Act. The final section, on federal criminal jurisdictional rules, is included here because disputes over criminal jurisdiction provided the earliest framework for analyzing jurisdiction in Indian country, and remain an important backdrop for modern jurisdictional rules.

I. WHAT IS A TRIBE?

Although "tribe" is a basic term of federal Indian law, determinations that a particular group counts as a tribe are often ad hoc and inconsistent. The legal definition may not correspond to any anthropological definition of the term or to the relevant indigenous group's concept of its governmental organization. Rather, in its most common legal sense, the term signifies an indigenous Indian group with which United States maintains a particular legal relationship. The definition most commonly used in federal statutes does not attempt a more precise definition: " 'Indian tribe' means any Indian tribe, band, nation, or other organized group or community *** which is recognized as eligible for the special programs and services provided by the United States to Indians because of their status as Indians." 25 U.S.C. § 450b(e). The Secretary of the Interior is required annually to "publish in the Federal Register a list of all Indian tribes which the Secretary recognizes to be eligible for the special programs and services provided by the United States to Indians because of their status as Indians." 25 U.S.C. § 479a–1. The most recent list is found at 84 Fed. Reg. 1200 (20195). The preamble to the list states: "The listed entities are acknowledged to have the immunities and privileges available to other federally acknowledged Indian tribes by virtue of their government-to-government relationship with the United States as well as the responsibilities, powers, limitations and obligations of such tribes." For a list of tribes by state, see National Conference of State Legislatures, Federal and State Recognized Tribes (2016), available at http://www.ncsl.org/research/state-tribal-institute/list-of-federal-and-state-recognized-tribes.aspx [https://perma.cc/R32K-RRCG].

Which groups fall within this definition is sometimes as much the product of federal fiat or outside pressure as anything else. The Cheyenne–Arapaho Tribes of Oklahoma are composed of the politically and ethnically distinct Cheyenne and Arapaho peoples but are treated by the federal government as a single tribe because they were placed together on a single reservation. Similarly the Confederated Tribes of the Colville Reservation, a single political entity, is composed of twelve distinct tribes placed together on a single reservation. Federal actions have also divided tribes along artificial lines. The various federally recognized Sioux tribes of the Dakotas, for example, represent the divisions created when the federal government took much of the territory of the Great Sioux Nation and divided its members onto smaller reservations according to where they were registered to receive annuities. In addition, after the Great Sioux War, some members from other plains tribes, including the Northern Cheyenne, joined the Lakota bands and became enrolled members of their tribes rather than suffer the Northern Cheyenne's fate of forced removal to Oklahoma. Other tribes, such as the Eastern Band of Cherokee Indians of North Carolina or the Seminole Nation of Florida, were formed from the members that remained behind when the rest of the tribe was removed across the Mississippi. The decision to recognize a group as a tribe at all might also be an accident of history. Because federal treaties were the most common way to establish tribal status, some groups that did not enter into battles with the United States or that ceded their land to the British colonies or other countries were not federally recognized as tribes. Other groups maintained their primary relationship with states rather than the federal government, and so are state-recognized tribes that cannot assert the special status that comes with federal recognition. Such unrecognized groups must either petition the Secretary of the Interior for federal recognition or seek recognition through an act of Congress. For more on the deeply political process of how American Indian nations became "federally recognized tribes," *see* Sarah Krakoff, *Inextricably Political: Race, Membership and Tribal Sovereignty*, Wash. L. Rev. 1041 (2012).

The following materials address the federal power to define a group as a tribe, and survey modern debates and legal definitions of tribal status.

A. CONGRESSIONAL POWER TO DEFINE A TRIBE

UNITED STATES V. SANDOVAL

231 U.S. 28, 34 S. Ct. 1, 58 L.Ed. 107 (1913)

JUSTICE VAN DEVANTER delivered the opinion of the court:

[Felipe Sandoval was prosecuted in federal court for bringing liquor onto the Santa Clara Pueblo in New Mexico in violation of federal law. The Act admitting New Mexico to the Union declared that lands owned and occupied by Pueblo Indians would be treated as Indian country for purposes of federal jurisdiction. The district court dismissed the indictment on the grounds that the exercise of federal jurisdiction usurped the police power of the state.]

The question to be considered, then, is whether the status of the Pueblo Indians and their lands is such that Congress competently can prohibit the introduction of intoxicating liquor into those lands notwithstanding the admission of New Mexico to statehood.

There are as many as twenty Indian pueblos scattered over the state, having an aggregate population of over 8,000. The lands belonging to the several pueblos vary in quantity, but usually embrace *** 17,000 acres, held in communal, fee-simple ownership under grants from the King of Spain, made during the Spanish sovereignty, and confirmed by Congress since the acquisition of that territory by the United States. ***

The people of the pueblos, although sedentary rather than nomadic in their inclinations, and disposed to peace and industry, are nevertheless Indians in race, customs, and domestic government. Always living in separate and isolated communities, adhering to primitive modes of life, largely influenced by superstition and fetishism, and chiefly governed according to the crude customs inherited from their ancestors, they are essentially a simple, uninformed, and inferior people. Upon the termination of the Spanish sovereignty they were given enlarged political and civil rights by Mexico, but it remains an open question whether they have become citizens of the United States. *** Be this as it may, they have been regarded and treated by the United States as requiring special consideration and protection, like other Indian communities. Thus, public moneys have been expended in presenting them with farming implements and utensils, and in their civilization and instruction; agents and superintendents have been provided to guard their interests; central training schools and day schools at the pueblos have been established and maintained for the education of their children; dams and irrigation works have been constructed to encourage and enable them to cultivate their lands and sustain themselves; public lands, as before indicated, have been reserved for their use and occupancy where their own lands were deemed inadequate; a special attorney has been employed since 1898, at an annual cost of $2,000, to represent them and maintain their rights; and when latterly the territory undertook to tax their lands and other property, Congress forbade such taxation. ***

With one accord the reports of the superintendents charged with guarding their interests show that they are dependent upon the fostering care and protection of the government, like reservation Indians in general; that, although industrially superior, they are intellectually and morally inferior to many of them; and that they are easy victims to the evils and debasing influence of intoxicants. We extract the following from published reports of the superintendents:

> Albuquerque, 1904: "While a few of these Pueblo Indians are ready for citizenship and have indicated the same by their energy and willingness to accept service from the railroad companies and elsewhere, and by accepting the benefits of schools and churches, a large per cent of them are unable, and not yet enough advanced along the lines of civilization, to take upon themselves the burden of citizenship. It is my opinion that in the event taxation is imposed, it will be but a short time before the masses of the New Mexico Pueblo Indians will become paupers. Their lands will be sold for taxes, the whites and Mexicans will have possession of their

ancient grants, and the government will be compelled to support them or witness their extermination."

Sante Fe, 1904: "The Pueblo have little or no money, and they cannot understand why they should be singled out from all other Indians and be compelled to bear burdens [territorial taxes] which they are not able to assume. *** They will not vote, nor are they sufficiently well informed to do so intelligently."

***

Sante Fe, 1905: "Until the old customs and Indian practices are broken among this people we cannot hope for a great amount of progress. The secret dance, from which all whites are excluded, is perhaps one of the greatest evils. What goes on at this time I will not attempt to say, but I firmly believe that it is little less than a ribald system of debauchery. The Catholic clergy is unable to put a stop to this evil and know as little of same as others. The United States mails are not permitted to pass through the streets of the pueblos when one of these dances is in session; travelers are met on the outskirts of the pueblo and escorted at a safe distance around. The time must come when the Pueblos must give up these old pagan customs and become citizens in fact."

***

During the Spanish dominion the Indians of the pueblos were treated as wards requiring special protection, were subjected to restraints and official supervision in the alienation of their property, and were the beneficiaries of a law declaring "that in the places and pueblos of the Indians no wine shall enter, nor shall it be sold to them." ***

But it is not necessary to dwell specially upon the legal status of this people under either Spanish or Mexican rule, for whether Indian communities within the limits of the United States may be subjected to its guardianship and protection as dependent wards turns upon other considerations. Not only does the Constitution expressly authorize Congress to regulate commerce with the Indian tribes, but long continued legislative and executive usage and an unbroken current of judicial decisions have attributed to the United States as a superior and civilized nation the power and the duty of exercising a fostering care and protection over all dependent Indian communities within its borders, whether within its original territory or territory subsequently acquired, and whether within or without the limits of a state. *** In *Tiger v. Western Investment Co.*, 221 U.S. 286, 315 (1911), prior decisions were carefully reviewed and it was further said: "Taking these decisions together, it may be taken as the settled doctrine of this court that Congress, in pursuance of the long-established policy of the government, has a right to determine for itself when the guardianship which has been maintained over the Indian shall cease. It is for that body, and not the courts, to determine when the true interests of the Indian require his release from such condition of tutelage."

Of course, if it is not meant by this that Congress may bring a community or body of people within the range of this power by arbitrarily calling them an Indian tribe, but only that in respect of distinctly Indian communities the questions whether, to what extent, and for what time they shall be recognized and dealt with as dependent tribes requiring the guardianship and protection of the United States are to be determined by Congress, and not by the courts. ***

As before indicated, by an uniform course of action beginning as early as 1854 and continued up to the present time, the legislative and executive branches of the government have regarded and treated the Pueblos of New Mexico as dependent communities entitled to its aid and protection, like other Indian tribes, and, considering their Indian lineage, isolated and communal life, primitive customs and limited civilization, this assertion of guardianship over them cannot be said to be arbitrary, but must be regarded as both authorized and controlling. ***

It is said that such legislation cannot be made to embrace the Pueblos, because they are citizens. As before stated, whether they are citizens is an open question, and we need not determine it now, because citizenship is not in itself an obstacle to the exercise by Congress of its power to enact laws for the benefit and protection of tribal Indians as a dependent people. ***

It also is said that such legislation cannot be made to include the lands of the Pueblos, because the Indians have a fee simple title. It is true that the Indians of each pueblo do have such a title to all the lands connected therewith, excepting such as are occupied under Executive orders, but it is a communal title, no individual owning any separate tract. In other words, the lands are public lands of the pueblo, and so the situation is essentially the same as it was with the Five Civilized Tribes, whose lands, although owned in fee under patents from the United States, were adjudged subject to the legislation of Congress enacted in the exercise of the government's guardianship over those tribes and their affairs. *** Considering the reasons which underlie the authority of Congress to prohibit the introduction of liquor into the Indian country at all, it seems plain that this authority is sufficiently comprehensive to enable Congress to apply the prohibition to the lands of the Pueblos. ***

NOTES AND QUESTIONS

1. What test does the Court announce for whether a group counts as a tribe subject to federal power? Are there any limits on whom Congress may treat as a tribe? The Rainbow Tribe is a group of thousands of individuals who share a New Age and "Native American" influenced religion and lifestyle who camp out together in national parks; may Congress declare them a tribe? What about an Indian neighborhood in Los Angeles whose residents are members of multiple tribes that moved to the city from across the United States as part of the Urban Relocation Program of the 1950s?

2. Another important early definition of a tribe comes from *Montoya v. United States*, 180 U.S. 261 (1901), which concerned a statute permitting United States citizens to bring an action in the Court of Claims for property "taken or destroyed by Indians belonging to any band, tribe, or nation, in amity with the United States." Indian Depredation Act, 26 Stat. 851 (1891). The Court stated, "By a 'tribe' we understand a body of Indians of the same or a similar race, united in a community under one leadership or government, and inhabiting a particular though sometimes ill-defined territory." 180 U.S. at 266. This definition, however, has been used to determine what groups are

included in statutory references to a "tribe," rather than to limit congressional power. *See United States v. Candelaria*, 271 U.S. 432, 442 (1926); *Joint Council of Passamaquoddy Tribe v. Morton*, 528 F.2d 370, 377 n.8 (1st Cir. 1975). Do *Sandoval* and *Montoya* together articulate a clear or coherent definition of a "tribe?" Does *Montoya*'s inclusion of the criteria that tribes inhabit "a particular though sometimes ill-defined territory," seem important?

3. In *United States v. Joseph*, 94 U.S. 614 (1876), the Supreme Court had held that the Pueblos were not "Indians," and so were not covered by the Nonintercourse Act, now codified at 25 U.S.C. § 177, which prohibits taking of Indian land without federal authorization. As a result, the federal government could not bring an ejectment action against a non-Indian occupying Pueblo land. The Trade and Intercourse laws were designed for, in the Court's words:

> the nomadic Apaches, Comanches, Navajoes, and other tribes whose incapacity for self-government required both for themselves and for the citizens of the country this guardian care of the general government. The pueblo Indians, if, indeed, they can be called Indians, had nothing in common with this class. The degree of civilization which they had attained centuries before, their willing submission to all the laws of the Mexican government, the full recognition by that government of all their civil rights, including that of voting and holding office, and their absorption into the general mass of the population (except that they held their lands in common), all forbid the idea that they should be classed with the Indian tribes for whom the intercourse acts were made.

94 U.S. at 617. *Sandoval* distinguished *Joseph* on the grounds that the Nonintercourse Act referred only to "Indians" and did not mention Pueblos, while New Mexico's Enabling Act specifically declared that Pueblo Indians and land were included in federal legislation regarding Indians. 36 Stat. 557 (1910). In addition, the *Joseph* decision relied on the findings in a New Mexico Territorial Court decision that Pueblos were not protected by the Nonintercourse Act because while normal Indians were "wandering savages, given to murder, robbery, and theft," the pueblos were "a peaceable, industrious, intelligent, honest, and virtuous people," who were "Indians only in features, complexion, and a few of their habits," *U.S. v. Lucero*, 1 N.M. 422 (1869). The *Sandoval* Court declared these findings "at variance with other recognized sources of information, now available." *Sandoval* at 49. What other differences might have contributed to the different results in *Joseph* and *Sandoval*?

4. *Sandoval* employs the concept of dependency to justify the conclusion that the Pueblo are a tribe. Is *Sandoval*'s version of dependency the same as Chief Justice Marshall's in *Cherokee Nation*? Are they both irretrievably paternalistic, if not racist? Or is there a distinction between the two? Consider Professor Clinton's discussion of this issue:

> The contrast between the dependence Marshall describes and that which animates the imagination of the late nineteenth century judges, during the height of America's colonial expansion, could not be greater. Marshall's dependence is akin to an agreement between nations to come to one another's defense when one of the nations has technologically superior weaponry, while the conception of *Sandoval*, for example, is much more like the dependence of small children upon adults when the children's

> knowledge is so limited that one does not think twice about imposing any variety of decisions and limitations upon them for their own good.

Robert N. Clinton, *The Dormant Indian Commerce Clause*, 27 Conn. L. Rev. 1055, 1167 n. 328 (1995).

5. In the wake of *Joseph* and *Lucero*, the United States was prohibited from intervening to prevent non-Indians from occupying Pueblo land. Finally, in *United States v. Candelaria*, 271 U.S. 432 (1926), the Court held that Pueblos were Indians for purposes of the Nonintercourse Act and permitted the United States to sue on their behalf. Many non-Indians had already been occupying the land in reliance on the Lucero decision. To address the uncertainty Sandoval created for these non-Indians, the 1924 Pueblo Lands Act created a board to investigate non-Indian claims and quiet title in favor of non-Indians that had possessed the land under color of title since 1902, or without color of title since 1889. 43 Stat. 636 (1924). Eventually, eighty percent of non-Indian claims, comprising about 50,000 acres, were approved. Cohen's Handbook of Federal Indian Law 317 (2012). For a detailed history of Pueblo land, see Malcolm Ebright, Rick Hendricks and Richard W. Hughes, Four Square Leagues: Pueblo Indian Land in New Mexico (2014).

B. MODERN DEBATES OVER TRIBAL STATUS

As the preceding note regarding the effort of the Pueblos to assert protection under the Nonintercourse Act suggests, federally recognized tribal status was not only a source of federal power but was also important for tribal assertions of federal protection and other privileges. While federal policy was focused on the destruction of the Indian tribes, there was usually little incentive to fight for tribal status. With the 1934 Indian Reorganization Act, the federal government faced new questions as to who was eligible for economic development and governmental assistance programs. Lacking legislative or regulatory guidelines, however, the Bureau of Indian Affairs continued to make decisions on an *ad hoc* basis, relying heavily on the tribe's current relationship with the federal government. A series of other cases and congressional actions built additional pressure for a systematic compilation of "recognized tribes" and a method for the recognition of those wrongly excluded from recognition.

Litigation to protect fishing rights reserved in nineteenth-century treaties created disputes about which groups were the political successors to the treaty tribes. In 1970, when the United States brought suit on behalf of seven tribes to enforce treaty fishing rights in Washington State, seven additional tribes intervened. *United States v. Washington*, 520 F.2d 676 (9th Cir. 1975). Although a number of these tribes were not formally recognized by the federal government, the district court held that

> Nonrecognition of the tribe by the federal government and the failure of the Secretary of the Interior to approve a tribe's enrollment may result in loss of statutory benefits, but can have no impact on vested treaty rights. Whether a group of citizens of Indian ancestry is descended from a treaty signatory and has maintained an organized tribal structure is a factual question which a district court is competent to determine.

The court in that case held that two of these groups, the Stillaguamish and Upper Skagit Tribes, had maintained their tribal organizations and retained their rights under the Treaty of Point Elliott. 520 F.2d at 692–693. Five others were found not to be tribes according to those criteria. *United States v. Washington*, 476 F. Supp. 1101 (W.D. Wash.1979) (*Washington II*), *aff'd*, 641 F.2d 1368 (9th Cir. 1981). Although some of these groups later secured recognition as tribes from the federal government, they have not been permitted to relitigate their treaty rights. *See United States v. Washington*, 593 F.3d 790 (9th Cir. 2010) (*en banc*) (subsequent recognition by BIA not sufficient reason to justify reopening judgment under FRAP 60(b)).

The efforts by the Passamaquoddy Tribe of Maine seeking return of land acquired by states in violation of the Nonintercourse Act also drew heightened attention to the status of unrecognized tribes. Since 1790, the Nonintercourse Act has, with only slight changes, provided that "[n]o purchase *** of lands *** from any Indian nation or tribe of Indians shall be of any validity *** unless same be made by treaty *** under the authority of the United States." 25 U.S.C. § 177. In 1972, the Passamaquoddy asked the United States to sue on its behalf for lands acquired in violation of the Nonintercourse Act. The United States refused, claiming that because it had never signed a treaty or entered into a political relationship with the tribe, the tribe could not assert any rights under the Act.

JOINT TRIBAL COUNCIL OF THE PASSAMAQUODDY TRIBE V. MORTON

528 F.2d 370 (1st Cir. 1975)

CAMPBELL, CIRCUIT JUDGE.

***

Since its admission as a state, Maine has enacted approximately 350 laws which relate specifically to the Passamaquoddy Tribe. This legislation includes 72 laws providing appropriations for or regulating Passamaquoddy agriculture; 33 laws making provision for the appropriation of necessities, such as blankets, food, fuel, and wood, for the Tribe; 85 laws relating to educational services and facilities for the Tribe; 13 laws making provision for the delivery of health care services and facilities to the Tribe; 22 laws making allowance for Passamaquoddy housing; 54 laws making special provision for Indian indigent relief; 54 laws relating to the improvement and protection of roads and water on the Passamaquoddy reservation; and 15 laws providing for the legal representation of the Tribe and its members.

In contrast, the federal government's dealings with the Tribe have been few. It has never, since 1789, entered into a treaty with the Tribe, nor has Congress ever enacted any legislation mentioning the Tribe. In 1824, the Department of War contributed funds to the Tribe, one-third toward the construction of a school, pursuant to an act for the civilization of Indian tribes. Act of March 3, 1819, 3 Stat. 516. It also gave money annually from 1824 to 1828 under the same act to Elijah Kellogg of the Society for the Propagation of the Gospel Among the Indians, to support a school for the Tribe. The funds were granted at the request of the State of Maine, were channeled through the State, and were subject to State controls. Kellogg, according to one nineteenth century source, was himself sent to the Tribe as a schoolmaster by the State of Maine, and as a missionary by the Missionary Society of Massachusetts. These funds were withheld during 1829 because of intra-tribal differences concerning the religion of the Superintendent of the school and, as a result, two principal men of the Tribe, Deacon Sockbason and Sabattis Neptune, went to Washington to meet with Thomas L. McKenney, Director of the Office of Indian Affairs, and John H. Eaton, Secretary of War, to seek reinstatement of the school funds and additional money to hire a priest and to purchase a parcel of land. Money was again appropriated for the school and the priest in 1830, although discontinued after 1831 on account of the same intra-tribal differences. However, despite a request from President Jackson, Congress failed to appropriate any money to purchase land for the Tribe. After the school funds were again suspended during 1831 because of the same sectarian strife, the Tribe requested that the funding be reinstated and used for the improvement of the Tribe's agriculture; this request was also denied and the funding was never resumed. During the period from 1899 to 1912, five members of the Tribe attended the Carlisle Indian School for short periods of time. A member of the Tribe also graduated from Haskel Indian College in 1970. Since 1965, various federal agencies other than the Department of the Interior have provided funds to the Tribe under federal assistance programs available to all citizens meeting the requirements of the program. Some of these funds were taken from special Indian allocations or were administered by special Indian desks within the various agencies. In 1966, the General Counsel to the Department of Housing and Urban Development, writing to the Commissioner of the Maine Department of Indian Affairs in regard to the establishment of public housing authorities by the governing councils of the Passamaquoddy and Penobscot Tribes, stated in part that "[i]t is our understanding that these tribes do not have any governmental powers in their own right or by virtue of any federal law ***."

II

The central issue in this action is whether the Secretary of the Interior was correct in finding that the United States has no "trust relationship" with the Tribe and, therefore, should play no role in the Tribe's dispute with Maine. Whether, even if there is a trust relationship with the Passamaquoddies, the United States has an affirmative duty to sue Maine on the Tribe's behalf is a separate issue that was not raised or decided below and which consequently we do not address. The district court held only that defendants "erred in denying plaintiffs' request for litigation on the sole ground that no trust relationship exists between the United States and the Passamaquoddy Tribe." It was left to the Secretary to translate the finding of a "trust relationship" into concrete duties.

Over the years, the federal government has recognized many Indian tribes, specifically naming them in treaties, agreements, or statutes. The general notion of a "trust relationship," often called a guardian-ward relationship, has been used to characterize the resulting relationship between the federal government and those tribes, *see Worcester v. Georgia*, 31 U.S. (6 Pet.) 515 (1832); *Cherokee Nation v. Georgia*, 30 U.S. (5 Pet.) 1 (1831); and the cases cited in the district court's opinion, 388 F.Supp. at 662–63. It is the defendants' and the intervenor's contention here that such a relationship may only be claimed by those specifically recognized tribes.

The Tribe, however, contends otherwise. It rests its claim of a trust relationship on the Nonintercourse Act, enacted in its original form by the First Congress in 1790 to protect the lands of "any *** tribe of Indians." Plaintiffs argue, and the district court found, that the unlimited reference to "any *** tribe" must be read to include the Passamaquoddy Tribe as well as tribes specially recognized under separate federal treaties, agreements or statutes. As the Act applies to them, plaintiffs urge that it is sufficient to evidence congressional acknowledgement of a trust relationship in their case at least as respects the Tribe's land claims.

Before turning to the district court's rulings, we must acknowledge a certain awkwardness in deciding whether the Act encompasses the Tribe without considering at the same time whether the Act encompasses the controverted land transactions with Maine. Whether the Tribe is a tribe within the Act would best be decided, under ordinary circumstances, along with the Tribe's specific land claims, for the Act only speaks of tribes in the context of their land dealings. If that approach were adopted here, however, the Tribe would be deprived of a decision in time to do any good on those matters cited by the Department of the Interior as reasons for withholding assistance in litigation against Maine.[†] And without United States participation, the Tribe may find it difficult or impossible ever to secure a judicial determination of the claims. Given, in addition, the federal government's protective role under the Nonintercourse Act, see below, it is appropriate that plaintiffs and the federal government learn how they stand on these core matters before adjudication of the Tribe's dispute with Maine.

Yet the resulting bifurcation of decision necessarily restricts the reach of the present rulings. In reviewing the district court's decision that the Tribe is a tribe within the Nonintercourse Act, we are not to be deemed as settling, by implication or otherwise, whether the Act affords relief from, or even extends to, the Tribe's land transactions with Maine. When and if the specific transactions are litigated, new facts and legal and equitable considerations may well appear, and Maine should be free in any such future litigation to defend broadly, even to the extent of arguing positions and theories which overlap considerably those treated here. ***

Intervenor and defendants contend that "any ... tribe of Indians" is ambiguous; that its proper meaning is a community of Indians which the federal government has at some time specifically recognized; and that the Passamaquoddy Tribe is, in that sense, not a tribe. ***

But while Congress' power to regulate commerce with the Indian tribes, U.S. Const. art. I, § 8, includes authority to decide when and to what extent it shall recognize a particular Indian community as a dependent tribe under its guardianship, [*United States v. Sandoval*], Congress is not prevented from

†. The Secretary of the Interior refused to aid the Tribe in litigation under the Nonintercourse Act on the ground that the United States had no trust relationship with the Passamaquoddy Tribe. If the court forced the tribe to litigate the trust relationship claim at the same time it litigated the Nonintercourse Act claim against Maine, the Tribe would have been forced to litigate the merits of its land claim without the assistance of the United States—the very assistance it was seeking to compel in this case.

legislating as to tribes generally; and this appears to be what it has done in successive versions of the Nonintercourse Act. There is nothing in the Act to suggest that "tribe" is to be read to exclude a bona fide tribe not otherwise federally recognized. Nor, as the district court found, is there evidence of congressional intent or legislative history squaring with appellants' interpretation. Rather we find an inclusive reading consonant with the policy and purpose of the Act. That policy has been said to be to protect the Indian tribes' right of occupancy, even when that right is unrecognized by any treaty, *** and the purpose to prevent the unfair, improvident, or improper disposition of Indian lands. *** Since Indian lands have, historically, been of great concern to Congress, see *Oneida Indian Nation v. County of Oneida*, 414 U.S. 661, 667 (1974), we have no difficulty in concluding that Congress intended to exercise its power fully.

This is not to say that if there were doubt about the tribal status of the Tribe, the judgments of officials in the federal executive branch might not be of great significance. The Supreme Court has said that, "it is the rule of this court to follow the executive and other political departments of the government, whose more special duty is to determine such affairs." *United States v. Sandoval*, 231 U.S. at 47. But the Passamaquoddies were a tribe before the nation's founding and have to this day been dealt with as a tribal unit by the State. *** No one in this proceeding has challenged the Tribe's identity as a tribe in the ordinary sense. Moreover, there is no evidence that the absence of federal dealings was or is based on doubts as to the genuineness of the Passamaquoddies' tribal status, apart, that is, from the simple lack of recognition. Under such circumstances, the absence of specific federal recognition in and of itself provides little basis for concluding that the Passamaquoddies are not a "tribe" within the Act.

***

[The court also agreed with the district court that the federal government had a trust relationship with the Passamaquoddy Tribe]. The purpose of the Act has been held to acknowledge and guarantee the Indian tribes' right of occupancy, *** and clearly there can be no meaningful guarantee without a corresponding federal duty to investigate and take such action as may be warranted in the circumstances.

We emphasize what is obvious, that the "trust relationship" we affirm has as its source the Nonintercourse Act, meaning that the trust relationship pertains to land transactions which are or may be covered by the Act, and is rooted in rights and duties encompassed or created by the Act. Congress or the executive branch may at a later time recognize the Tribe for other purposes within their powers, creating a broader set of federal responsibilities; and we of course do not rule out the possibility that there are statutes or legal theories not now before us which might create duties and rights of unforeseen, broader dimension. But on the present record, only the Nonintercourse Act is the source of the finding of a "trust relationship," and neither the decision below nor our own is to be read as requiring the Department of the Interior to look to objects outside the Act in defining its fiduciary obligations to the Tribe.

***

We affirm, on the basis set forth herein, the finding of a trust relationship and the finding that the federal government may not decline to litigate on the sole ground that there is no trust relationship.

Judgment affirmed.

Other tribes soon followed with attempts to establish their status and their land claims, among them the Mashpee Tribe of Massachusetts. The Mashpee case, like that of the Passamaquoddy and other eastern tribes, required an initial resolution of the question of federal recognition. The Mashpee's case was unique, however, due to their ethnic and economic integration as well as the absence of formal governmental apparatus. As James Clifford described:

> The Mashpee plaintiffs represented most of the nonwhite inhabitants of what, for over three centuries, had been knows as an "Indian town" on Cape Cod; but their institutions of tribal governance had long been elusive ***. Moreover, since about 1800 the Massachusetts language had ceased to be commonly spoken in Mashpee. *** Over the centuries inhabitants had intermarried with other Indian groups. *** The inhabitants of Mashpee were active in the economy and society of modern Massachusetts. They were businessmen, schoolteachers, fishermen, domestic workers, small contractors. Could these people of Indian ancestry file suit as the Mashpee Tribe that had, they claimed, been despoiled of collectively held lands during the mid-nineteenth century? This was the question a federal judge posed to a Boston jury. Only if they answered yes could the matter proceed to a land-claim trial.

James Clifford, *Identity in Mashpee, in* The Predicament of Culture: Twentieth–Century Ethnography, Literature and Art 278 (1988).

MASHPEE TRIBE V. TOWN OF MASHPEE

447 F. Supp. 940 (D. Mass. 1978)

SKINNER, DISTRICT JUDGE.

[The Mashpee Tribe brought suit to recover possession of tribal lands allegedly alienated in violation of the Indian Nonintercourse Act (25 U.S.C. § 177). The defendants questioned whether the plaintiff group was a tribe, and that issue was severed for a separate trial. After forty days of testimony, the court instructed the jury that to find the Mashpee to be a tribe, they had to find that they constituted a group of the same or similar race; that they had a territorial land base, and that they had a political organization or formal leadership of some sort. The court issued a series of interrogatories to the jury requiring them to answer yes or no to the question whether Mashpee was a tribe on several key dates. The jury's answers appeared illogical, in that they found, among other things, that the Mashpee were not a tribe on July 22, 1790, the date of the first Nonintercourse Act, but then that they were a tribe on March 31, 1834, the date on which the District of Mashpee was established. The court nonetheless ruled in favor of the defendants on the basis of the jury's conclusions.]

The dates chosen in the special interrogatories were those deemed significant by the parties with respect to their several legal theories. I am of the opinion that several of these dates are not significant, as shall hereinafter appear, but they were included to preserve the widest possible scope of review of the legal issues. ***

The case is now before me on the defendants' motion for judgment of dismissal on the merits based on the jury's answer. Plaintiff has filed an opposition thereto claiming that the jury's answers are fatally inconsistent and on their face violate the court's instructions. ***

The basic history of Mashpee is not disputed, and a review thereof is necessary to the resolution of the pending motions. For simplicity's sake, I shall refer to the people claiming to be a tribe and their Indian ancestors as Indians[1] and everybody else as non-Indians. ***

In 1665, Richard Bourne, a Christian missionary to the Indians, desired to gather a community of Christian Indians in the area surrounding the Indian village of Mashpee and comprising the present Town of Mashpee and parts of present Sandwich and Falmouth. Accordingly, a deed was executed from two Indian leaders named Weepquish and Tookenchosen to five other named persons for the benefit of the "South Sea Indians." The status of the grantors and their capacity to grant title is unknown. One of the expert witnesses gave an opinion that the grantees were a group of village headmen who constituted the ruling council of a tribe known as the Cotichesetts, inhabiting the area of Mashpee and eastward to present Hyannis. The area granted contained a group of small villages of ten or twenty families, the remnants of a once numerous and thriving agricultural community largely wiped out in 1617 by an unidentified epidemic. ***

In 1685, apparently at the instance of Shearjashub Bourne, the son of Richard, the General Court of the Plymouth Colony granted the area to the South Sea Indians and their children, subject to a restraint on alienation, namely, that no land should be sold to an Englishman without the consent of all the Indians and the permission of the General Court. ***

By 1723, Mashpee had been organized as a proprietary. As a result of the 1685 deed, Mashpee differed from other proprietaries in an essential respect. Mashpee was designed to be a permanent Indian plantation, in which the land was to be held in common, entailed, and with a restraint on alienation into the indefinite future. ***

In 1746, the General Court appointed guardians to control the finances of the plantation.

These guardians apparently used their position to exploit their wards, and the efforts of the Indians to obtain redress through the General Court were unavailing. By a remarkable feat of daring and resolve, one of the Indians (a Mohegan Indian from Connecticut, who had settled in Mashpee) carried a petition to the King of England. As a result, in 1763, the Mashpee Proprietors

1. I recognize that the plaintiff's claim of being Indian is contested by the defendants, and that the evidence indicates considerable racial mixture among this group.

were given a large measure of self-government, including the right to appoint constables to protect their woodlots from depredation by neighboring non-Indian settlers.

During the Revolutionary War, the Indian men of Mashpee fought against the British, and a very large number of them were killed. After the war, there were said to be 70 widows in Mashpee out of a population of a few hundred. As one might suppose, this situation encouraged a considerable influx of unattached non-Indian males, mostly black, but including four escaped Hessians and a Portuguese sailor.

This influx apparently had a disintegrating effect, as a result of which the General Court reimposed guardians, whose approval was required for all significant actions.

By 1833, as under the previous guardians, the Indians felt that the guardians were not protecting them, but exploiting them. The precipitating issue was the cutting of wood from Indian land by outsiders. There was some violence. The Indians hired a lawyer and filed a petition with the General Court for relief from the guardianship. At the same time, the Indians rejected the ministry of the Reverend Phineas Fish, who had been sent down from Harvard to carry on "the blessed work of converting the poor Indian," and established their own Baptist Church under an Indian preacher, "Blind Joe" Amos.

In response to this well organized effort, the General Court created the District of Mashpee in 1834. Under the district organization, Mashpee (or "Marshpee") was governed substantially in the manner of a Massachusetts town, with the exception that certain transactions affecting the common lands and the treasury were subject to the approval of a Commissioner appointed by the Governor. The Commissioner also served as Treasurer. By successive legislation, the Commissioner's power was reduced to that ordinarily exercised by a Town Treasurer and eventually the office was filled by election of the proprietors of the district.

The 1834 Act also confirmed the allotment of land to those proprietors who had occupied and improved it, and required the Commissioner to keep a record of the allotments, as well as a list of proprietors. All of the land in the district, whether held in common or in severalty, was exempt from execution, and the proprietors were exempt from state and county taxes.

From 1834 onward, records of the district show that the proprietors voted various ordinances, including regulation of herring fishing. There are no existing records showing such regulations prior to this time.

In 1842, the General Court passed another Act which substantially altered the land title within the district and defined who were to be deemed proprietors. Each proprietor was to be allotted a sufficient portion of the common land of the district to bring his holdings (including the acreage confirmed to his use by the 1834 Act) up to sixty acres. All the land not so allotted remained common land under the control of the Selectmen of the District. ***

In 1869, the Governor of the Commonwealth proposed legislation relieving all the Indians in Massachusetts of their legal disabilities and admitting them to full citizenship. A legislative committee held a hearing in Mashpee. The questions being considered were citizenship and removal of the restraints on alienation of the land. About 40 people appeared, including several non-Indian husbands of female Indian proprietors. Some of the Indians were in favor of citizenship and removal of the "entailments" on the land, because under existing restrictions there was no way that an Indian could acquire mortgage money for improvements, or liquidate his land holdings to go into commerce. The non-Indians also favored elimination of restraints on alienation because they wished to be able to vote and hold property in Mashpee in their own right. "Blind Joe" Amos, by then describing himself as among the oldest inhabitants, opposed the changes on the ground that the Indians were not yet ready to deal on an equal footing with outsiders and would imprudently sell off all their land. He was in favor of the removal of the restrictions, but not until the generation then in school should come of age. A vote was taken which was split 18 to 18 on the question of citizenship and 26 to 14 in opposition to the removal of the restrictions on the land. ***

Nevertheless, in 1869 the General Court passed an act granting citizenship to the Indians, removing their legal disabilities, and releasing the restraints on alienation of land imposed originally in the 1685 deed and carried forward in the 1842 Act. In 1870, Mashpee was incorporated as a Town. The common land of the District was transferred to the Town, and upon application the Superior Court was authorized to order the sale thereof by Commissioners appointed for the purpose. There were some three thousand acres of common land remaining after the allotments of 1842. Most of this land was sold, presumably to the then inhabitants of Mashpee. ***

At this point, the ancestors of the present Indians had complete control of substantially all of the land in Mashpee, and they retained it for the next seventy years. "Blind Joe" Amos' prediction did not come true. The Selectmen of the District became the Selectmen of the Town, and the Board was composed of Indians until 1968, and a majority were Indians until 1972.

In the early part of the 20th century, it appears that some small part of the Town was sold to outsiders and developed as summer property. Up through the 1930's and early 1940's, however, the area remained substantially as it had been from the 1870's on. Indian witnesses testified that when they were growing up in Mashpee the land was still open and unfenced by its Indian owners, and the upland and shores were readily accessible to everyone for hunting, shellfishing and recreation.

By the 1930's, however, agriculture in New England was in general decline, and so it was in Mashpee. Some land was taken from Indian owners by the Town for taxes, but at least some tax title property was purchased at tax title auction by other Indians.

In the early 1950's and thereafter, the building of super highways to Cape Cod and the pressure of population moving out from the cities encouraged land developers to buy land on Cape Cod and in Mashpee. Some of the Indians sold their land during this period, and some retained their land. While each land sale doubtless appeared profitable to the individual seller at the time, the Indians now find that the aggregate of these land sales has substantially altered the life of their community, leaving them in the minority. The free access to upland and shore that they so long enjoyed has disappeared.

It is principally these land sales by individual Indians to non-Indians which the plaintiff seeks to have declared null and void as in violation of the Nonintercourse Act.

There was virtually no evidence introduced concerning life in Mashpee between 1870 and 1920. There was evidence that several students at the Carlisle Indian School had given "Mashpee" as their tribal designation during this period, but also that the grandfather of one of the witnesses had deliberately refrained from teaching his children the Indian language, because he wanted them to use English.

In 1920, there was a revival of interest in Indian customs. From 1928 to the present, there has been a "Pow-wow" held at Mashpee, more or less annually. This is a three- or four-day celebration featuring Indian dances and songs. Most of these are borrowed from Plains Indians, however, as are many of the decorative symbols and styles of dress, because the ancient modes of east coast Indians have been lost. From the early 1920's through the early 1940's, there were individuals who were sometimes recognized as chiefs and medicine men of the Indian community in Mashpee. The method by which the individuals were selected and their leadership functions were not revealed by the evidence. In 1956 the Sachem of the Wampanoag Nation appointed Earl Mills Chief of the "Mashpee Tribe," on the petition of some of the Indians in Mashpee. Mr. Mills remains the Chief to this day. Mr. John Peters was similarly appointed as Medicine Man and filled that post up until the time of trial, when he was appointed Supreme Medicine Man of the Wampanoag Nation. At one time there was a Tribal Council which met from time to time, but it appears that this group's functions, if any, were primarily social. In 1974 the Mashpee–Wampanoag Indian Tribal Council, Inc., was incorporated. It has acted as representative for the Indians in Mashpee with respect to securing federal educational grants and Comprehensive Employment and Training Act projects, and has been designated as the official representative of the Mashpee Indians in an executive order of the Governor of the Commonwealth. It lobbied for the passage of the executive order, and also secured the title to fifty-five acres of land in Mashpee granted to it by the Town, to be used for tribal purposes.

The leadership functions of the Chief, the Medicine Man and the incorporated Tribal Council, and the extent to which these individuals and the corporation were recognized as significant leaders by the Indians, were the subject of extensive and conflicting testimony.

[The court held that 1842, when the lands were allotted in severalty to the town members; 1870, when the remaining 3,000 acres of common lands were transferred to the Town of Mashpee and sold; and 1976, the present date, are the relevant dates for tribal status.]

Plaintiff's attack on the jury's finding that it was not a tribe in August of 1976 is not based on the evidence adduced with respect to 1976, but on the assertion that the pattern of the jury's other answers fatally impeach that finding. ***

In my view, the evidence would support the jury's finding that between 1842, when the Indians in Mashpee were active in establishing self-determination and asserting their right to their own customs, and 1869 when the legislative hearing was held, the proprietors had reoriented their efforts toward assimilation into the general non-Indian community. *** The absence of any indication of Indian self-identification, or of the establishment of tribal common land in the years immediately following 1869, at a time when the Indians exercised virtually complete control of the area, may have had some bearing on the jury's response. From all of the circumstances, the jury was entitled to find that tribal identity had been abandoned at some time between 1842 and 1869.

*** [T]he answer of the jury that the plaintiff was not a tribe for purposes of the Nonintercourse Act[7] in 1976 was fully supported by the evidence of the circumstances of the plaintiff's existence in Mashpee at that time. ***

Accordingly, the answers of the jury to the special interrogatories shall stand. These answers require that this action be DISMISSED on the merits, the plaintiff not having established its standing to bring suit as an Indian tribe. ***

NOTES AND QUESTIONS

1. Is a jury trial the appropriate mechanism for determining tribal existence?

2. Given the enormous pressures exerted on tribes to assimilate, is it reasonable to assume the desire not to exist as a tribe from assimilationist actions during the latter half of the nineteenth century? Consider Professor Jo Carrillo's comments about the *Mashpee* case:

> The Mashpee Wampanoag Tribe turned to federal law to validate what it regarded as its superior rights to its ancestral land. What the Mashpee Tribe discovered was that federal law served as both resource and constraint; *** The law presumed Indian ways to be primitive, chaotic, timeless, simple; more troubling, it assumed than any tribal adaptation to colonial society was in fact an assimilative embrace of the mainstream. *** According to this view, if tribespeople conformed to the broader culture, they were said to be choosing to assimilate ***.

Jo Carillo, *Identity as Idiom*: Mashpee *Reconsidered*, 28 Indiana L. Rev. 511, 544 (1995). How might tribes overcome this kind of stereotyping, both in litigation and in the various courts of public opinion? Consider how Professor Carrillo's observation about *Mashpee* resonates with current views about Indian gaming, for example.

3. As discussed in the following section, most tribes seeking federal recognition today opt to go through the administrative process established by the Bureau of Indian Affairs in 1978. The Mashpee, like the Passamaquoddy, had their tribal status adjudicated in federal court only because it was a prerequisite to pursuing their land claims. After losing their case in the district court and the federal appellate court, the Mashpee petitioned the BIA for recognition pursuant to the administrative process. Nearly three decades after their loss in the federal district court, the Mashpee Tribe achieved federal recognition. *See* Final Determination for Federal Acknowledgement of the Mashpee Wampanoag Indian Tribal Council, 72 Fed. Reg. 8007 (Feb. 22, 2007). The

---

7. The standards of that Act, at least as I have interpreted it, require that a tribe demonstrate a definable organization before it can qualify for the extraordinary remedy of the total voiding of land titles acquired in good faith and without fraud. Nothing herein, or in the answers of the jury, should be taken as holding or implying that the Mashpee Indians are not a tribe for other purposes, including participation in other federal or state programs, concerning which I express no opinion.

decision was greeted with joy and tears by the Mashpee: " 'We've been waiting so long,' sobbed Doris Middleton, 89. 'I've lost so many members of the family who were waiting for this day. We've all been waiting.' " Megan Tench and Michael Kranish, *Mashpees Near Federal Recognition*, Boston Globe, Apr. 1, 2006 at A1.

C. FEDERAL REGULATIONS ON TRIBAL ACKNOWLEDGEMENT

The Indian Self–Determination Act of 1975, Pub. L. 93–638, gave any tribe "which is recognized as eligible for the special programs and services provided by the United States to Indians because of their status as Indians" the right to contract for the direct administration of federal programs. 25 U.S.C. § 450 *et seq*. While informal lists of recognized tribes were maintained by local offices of the Bureau of Indian Affairs, and a list had been compiled to assist in implementation of the IRA in 1934, there had never been a list of such "recognized" tribes. *See* William W. Quinn, Jr., *Federal Acknowledgement of American Indian Tribes*, 17 Am. Indian L. Rev. 37, 38 (1992). Clearly, the BIA needed some mechanism for determining eligibility for Self–Determination Act contracts and other statutory benefits.

Further pressure was provided by the congressional American Indian Policy Review Commission, led by Senator Abourezk of South Dakota. In its 1976 report, the Commission identified 133 unrecognized tribes, and declared that the "results of 'nonrecognition' upon Indian communities and individuals have been devastating." *Task Force Ten: Terminated and Nonfederally Recognized Indians, Report on Terminated and Nonfederally Recognized Indians: Final Report to the American Indian Policy Review Commission* 1695 (1976). Abourezk proposed legislation that would extend recognition to any group that had been viewed as a tribe by the federal government or by other tribes, or that could show it had a functioning tribal council, unless the Bureau of Indian Affairs could prove otherwise.

Fearing an explosion in claims on its limited budget, in 1978 the Bureau of Indian Affairs for the first time created procedures and criteria for federal recognition. *See* 25 C.F.R. Part 83 (Procedures for Establishing That an American Indian Group Exists as an Indian Tribe). The regulations require that tribes prove they meet the following criteria:

In 2015 the Bureau of Indian Affairs published a revised rule setting out the substance and procedures for acknowledgement as an Indian tribe. The following preamble and bullet points from the Executive Summary set out the BIA's view on the major changes in the rule.

FEDERAL ACKNOWLEDGMENT OF AMERICAN INDIAN TRIBES

80 Fed. Reg. 37862 (July 1, 2015)

SUMMARY: This rule revises regulations governing the process and criteria by which the Secretary acknowledges an Indian tribe. The revisions seek to make the process and criteria more transparent, promote consistent implementation, and increase timeliness and efficiency, while maintaining the integrity and substantive rigor of the process. For decades, the current process has been criticized as "broken" and in need of reform. Specifically, the process has been criticized as too slow (a petition can take decades to be decided), expensive, burdensome, inefficient, intrusive, less than transparent and unpredictable. This rule reforms the process by, among other things, institutionalizing a phased review that allows for faster decisions; reducing the documentary burden while maintaining the existing rigor of the process; allowing for a hearing on a negative proposed finding to promote transparency and integrity; enhancing notice to tribes and local governments and enhancing transparency by posting all publicly available petition documents on the Department's Web site; establishing the Assistant Secretary's final determination as final for the Department to promote efficiency; and codifying and improving upon past Departmental implementation of standards, where appropriate, to ensure consistency, transparency, predictability and fairness. * * *

The rule does not substantively change the Part 83 criteria, except in two instances.

- One instance is that the final rule retains the current criterion (a), requiring identification of the petitioner as an Indian entity, but does not limit the evidence in support of this criterion to observations by those external to the petitioner. In other words, the final rule allows the Department to accept any and all evidence, such as the petitioner's own contemporaneous records, as evidence that the petitioner has been an Indian entity since 1900.
- The other instance in which the criteria is changed is in the review of the number of marriages in support of criterion (b) (community)—past Departmental practice has been to count the number of marriages within a petitioner; this rule instead provides that the Department count the number of petitioner members who are married to others in the petitioning group. [Note: If 30 members married 30 members it used to count as 30 marriages; now it will count as 60 and increase the percentage of marriages within the petitioning group versus those marriage outside the group.]

MANDATORY CRITERIA FOR FEDERAL ACKNOWLEDGEMENT

25 C.F.R. § 83.11

The criteria for acknowledgment as a federally recognized Indian tribe are delineated in paragraphs (a) through (g) of this section.

(a) Indian entity identification. The petitioner has been identified as an American Indian entity on a substantially continuous basis since 1900. Evidence that the group's character as an Indian entity has from time to time been denied will not be considered to be conclusive evidence that this criterion has not been met. Evidence to be relied upon in determining a group's Indian identity may include one or a combination of the following, as well as other evidence of identification.

(1) Identification as an Indian entity by Federal authorities.

(2) Relationships with State governments based on identification of the group as Indian.

(3) Dealings with a county, parish, or other local government in a relationship based on the group's Indian identity.

(4) Identification as an Indian entity by anthropologists, historians, and/or other scholars.

(5) Identification as an Indian entity in newspapers and books.

(6) Identification as an Indian entity in relationships with Indian tribes or with national, regional, or state Indian organizations.

(7) Identification as an Indian entity by the petitioner itself.

(b) Community. The petitioner comprises a distinct community and demonstrates that it existed as a community from 1900 until the present. Distinct community means an entity with consistent interactions and significant social relationships within its membership and whose members are differentiated from and distinct from nonmembers. Distinct community must be understood flexibly in the context of the history, geography, culture, and social organization of the entity. The petitioner may demonstrate that it meets this criterion by providing evidence for known adult members or by providing evidence of relationships of a reliable, statistically significant sample of known adult members. * * *

(c) Political influence or authority. The petitioner has maintained political influence or authority over its members as an autonomous entity from 1900 until the present. Political influence or authority means the entity uses a council, leadership, internal process, or other mechanism as a means of influencing or controlling the behavior of its members in significant respects, making decisions for the entity which substantially affect its members, and/or representing the entity in dealing with outsiders in matters of consequence. This process is to be understood flexibly in the context of the history, culture, and social organization of the entity. * * *

(d) Governing document. The petitioner must provide: [a copy of the entity's present governing document, including its membership criteria; or in the absence of a governing document, a written statement describing in full its membership criteria and current governing procedures.] ***

(e) Descent. The petitioner's membership consists of individuals who descend from a historical Indian tribe (or from historical Indian tribes that combined and functioned as a single autonomous political entity). * * *

(f) Unique membership. The petitioner's membership is composed principally of persons who are not members of any federally recognized Indian tribe. * * *

(g) Congressional termination. Neither the petitioner nor its members are the subject of congressional legislation that has expressly terminated or forbidden the Federal relationship. The Department must determine whether the petitioner meets this criterion, and the petitioner is not required to submit evidence to meet it.

The BIA explained that the use of 1900 (instead of "historical times" as used in the past) for criteria (b) and (c) was appropriate because "based on its experience in nearly 40 years of implementing the regulations, every group that has proven its existence from 1900 forward has successfully proven its existence prior to that time as well, making 1900 to the present a reliable proxy for all of history but at less expense." Like the previous rule, the new regulations provide an abbreviated process for tribes that were acknowledged in the past (but not terminated by Congress). 25 C.F.R. 83.12.

The greatest difficulty in proving these criteria is that most of the relevant documentary evidence was written by non-Indians. Tribes maintaining political and social cohesion would often have found it necessary to hide these practices; even when they did not, outsiders would often have difficulty understanding or accurately reporting what they had witnessed (remember the nineteenth century decisions that the Pueblos were too civilized to be Indians). Genealogical records were also affected by non-Indian biases; in particular, members of tribes that intermarried with African Americans were often listed as "Negro" in nineteenth century censuses. (This assumption hasn't ended. In the *Mashpee* case, for example, the defense argued to the jury that "black intermarriage made the Mashpees' proper racial identification black instead of Indian." Gerald Torres & Kathryn Milun, *Translating* Yonnondio *by Precedent and Evidence: The Mashpee Indian Case,* 1990 Duke L. J. 625, 650.)

The explosion of revenues from Indian gaming in the early 1990s has also affected the process. Although most of the tribes with pending petitions have been seeking recognition for decades, the potential for recognized tribes to engage in gaming has heightened the stakes, bringing in business money to help tribes and even more state and local government money to oppose them. The initial petitions filed with the BIA's Branch of Acknowledgement and Research (now known as the Office of Federal Acknowledgement) were a few hundred pages long; today, they are hundreds of thousands of pages, and the Branch reports that much of its time is taken up responding to Freedom of Information Act requests for these documents.

Given these factors, it is perhaps not surprising that the recognition process is painfully slow and that both proponents and opponents of recognition claim its results are arbitrary. As of 2013, only seventeen tribes had been acknowledged through the Section 83 process, and thirty-four had been denied acknowledgment. For a discussion of the process, see Cohen's Handbook of Federal Indian Law 153-60 (2012).

NOTES AND QUESTIONS

1. How would you marshal evidence to meet the first three criteria set forth in the regulation?

2. What explains the delay? Imagine if the Securities and Exchange Commission took a similar amount of time to decide whether a private corporation could issue an Initial Public Offering. Is this a fair comparison? Why, or why not?

3. Sometimes federally recognized tribes will oppose the proposed recognition of another tribe. Why might this occur? Does it point to an underlying dysfunction in the nature of the federal relationship, or is it an incurable matter of scarce resources?

4. There have been repeated efforts to reform the administrative process and standards. In 1994, the regulations were amended to provide for an early review of factors (e) (descent from historical tribes), (f) (membership not part of other recognized tribes), and (g) (tribe not subject to federal law terminating or denying recognition to the tribe). Petitioners that cannot establish these factors will not be reviewed under the other factors. 25 C.F.R. § 83.10(e). For the latest reform proposal, see Proposed Rule—Federal Acknowledgement of Indian Tribes, 79 Fed. Reg. 30766 (2014). One of the proposal's most significant elements is to require petitioners to show community status and political authority from 1934 onward, rather than from historical times to the present. The BIA denies that gaming has any relationship to the number of tribes seeking acknowledgement.

> Some think that the acknowledgment process is strongly related to gaming. The facts do not bear this out. Many of the petitioning groups came forward a long time ago. As the late Senator Daniel K. Inouye observed, if gaming were the driving force, "we would have to attribute to many of the petitioning tribal groups a clairvoyance that they knew that one day in the distant future there was going to be a Supreme Court decision and thereafter the Congress was going to enact a law authorizing and regulating the conduct of gaming … ." S. Hrng 109-91 at 3. Of the 17 tribes that have been recognized since this process began 37 years ago, only 11 have obtained land in trust, a process regulated by an additional, separate set of regulations (25 C.F.R. part 151), and only nine of these currently engage in Indian gaming. Of course, Congress has enacted a detailed law establishing whether trust land is eligible for gaming. It is set forth in the Indian Gaming Regulatory Act of 1988 (IGRA) and the Department has promulgated separate regulations implementing IGRA (25 C.F.R. part 292). For those nine tribes that successfully navigated acknowledgment and obtained land in trust, it took, on average, nearly 10 years after acknowledgment to engage in Indian gaming.

80 Fed. Reg. at 37864. Land—into—trust issues are considered starting at p. 293, *infra*. What do you think of this recommended change?

5. Also controversial in the rulemaking process was whether to allow groups that had previously been denied federal recognition to re-petition under the new rules. The proposed rule would have allowed it, but the Final Rule rejected that approach. The BIA explained:

> The proposed rule would have provided for a limited opportunity for re-petitioning. After reviewing the comments both in support of and in opposition to allowing for any opportunity for re-petitioning, limiting re-petitioning by providing for third-party input, and other suggested approaches for re-petitioning, the Department has determined that allowing re-petitioning is not appropriate. The final rule promotes consistency, expressly providing that evidence or methodology that was sufficient to satisfy any particular criterion in a previous positive decision on that criterion will be sufficient to satisfy the criterion for a present petitioner. The Department has petitions pending that have never been reviewed. Allowing for re-petitioning by denied petitioners would be unfair to petitioners who have not yet had a review, and would hinder the goals of increasing efficiency and timeliness by imposing the additional workload associated with re-petitions on the Department, and OFA in particular. The Part 83 process is not currently an avenue for re-petitioning. 80 Fed. Reg. at 37875.

What alternatives are left for previously rejected petitioners?

II. INDIAN COUNTRY: THE BASIC JURISDICTIONAL CONCEPT

A. THE INDIAN COUNTRY STATUTE: 18 U.S.C. § 1151

The first question to ask in determining jurisdiction in federal Indian law is where the relevant activity occurred, in "Indian Country" or not. "Generally speaking, primary jurisdiction over land that is Indian country rests with the Federal Government and the Indian tribe inhabiting it, and not with the States." *Alaska v. Native Village of Venetie Tribal Government*, 522 U.S. 520, 527 n.1 (1998). Outside Indian country, however, few of the special jurisdictional rules at play in Indian law apply.

Distinct boundaries between Indian and non-Indian areas have always existed—sometimes marked out by treaty, other times by statute, executive order, continued tribal occupation (original Indian title, or aboriginal title), and the like. The various federal Trade and Intercourse Acts, for example, took somewhat different approaches to the definition of the term. The Supreme Court clarified that Indian reservations within states were Indian country even if the reservations had been established by federal executive order after statehood had been granted and after the original Indian title had been extinguished. *See Donnelly v. United States*, 228 U.S. 243 (1913). So are areas that are not formal reservations but are "dependent Indian communities," *i.e.*, lands occupied by Indians under federal supervision and protection. *United States v. McGowan*, 302 U.S. 535 (1938) (land in Nevada purchased by federal government for Reno Colony of Indians was Indian country); *United States v.*

Sandoval, supra (Pueblo Indian lands are Indian country even though held in fee simple and pueblos had no treaty with federal government). Restricted Indian allotments remained Indian country as well. *See United States v. Pelican*, 232 U.S. 442 (1914); *United States v. Ramsey*, 271 U.S. 467 (1926).

In 1948, Congress codified this case law in the current definition of Indian country found in the federal criminal statutes. 18 U.S.C. § 1151 provides:

> *** [T]he term "Indian country", as used in this chapter, means
>
> (a) all land within the limits of any Indian reservation under the jurisdiction of the United States Government, notwithstanding the issuance of any patent, and, including rights-of-way running through the reservation,
>
> (b) all dependent Indian communities within the borders of the United States whether within the original or subsequently acquired territory thereof, and whether within or without the limits of a state, and
>
> (c) all Indian allotments, the Indian titles to which have not been extinguished, including rights-of-way running through the same.

The Supreme Court has used this definition for civil as well as criminal cases. *See, e.g., California v. Cabazon Band of Mission Indians*, 480 U.S. 202, 208 n.5 (1987). The Court has also understood Congress to intend a liberal interpretation of "Indian country" so that the term applies to "all lands set aside by whatever means for the residence of tribal Indians under federal protection," *Oklahoma Tax Comm'n v. Sac & Fox Nation*, 508 U.S. 114, 125 (1993), including "formal and informal reservations," *id.* at 123.

Note that in § 1151, Congress expressly provided that fee lands and rights of way within reservations are Indian country. Thus, an Indian reservation is a jurisdictional, area-wide term that does not depend upon whether land title is in fee simple or trust status or is in Indian or non-Indian hands. Subsequent chapters discuss some important modern limitations on *tribal* jurisdiction on fee land within reservation boundaries, but for Indian country status, and generally for federal and state jurisdiction, it is reservation status, not land ownership, that counts. This is in accord with more general understandings of distinctions between property ownership and applicable law. Imagine, for example, a home owner with fee simple absolute title living in Colorado attempting to argue that Colorado law should not apply to her because she, not the state government, owns her land.

The diagram below shows different types of land ownership frequently encountered in and around Indian country. Take some time to consider the jurisdictional status of the different parcels represented.

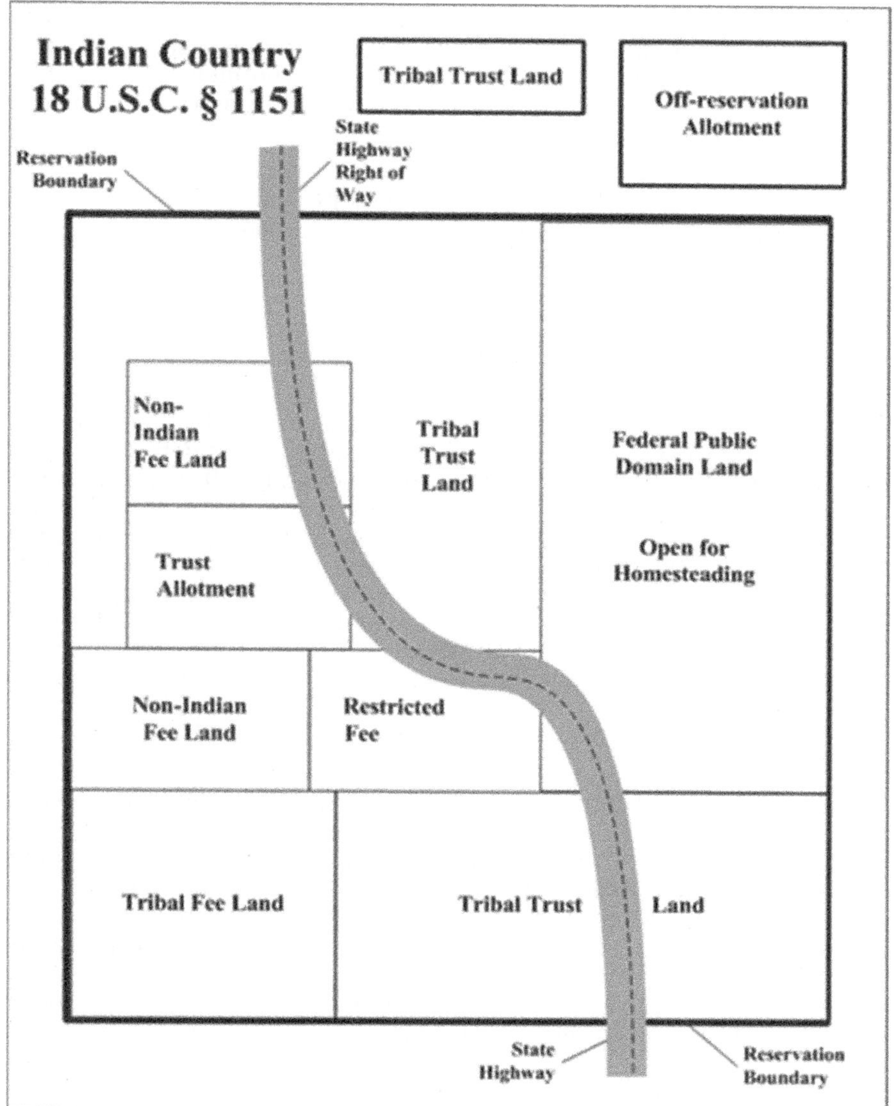

B. ALLOTMENT AND RESERVATION BOUNDARIES

Consider a common problem. Suppose that in a treaty a tribe reserved for itself certain lands as a reservation. Consistent with the plenary power doctrine as developed in *Lone Wolf*, Congress has the authority unilaterally to abrogate an Indian treaty and abolish the reservation status of an area at a later time. Congress, however, will not be assumed to have intended this result without clear evidence. Thus, without more, the mere opening of a reservation to non-Indians (through the allotment process or otherwise) has not been held to terminate reservation status. *See Seymour v. Superintendent*, 368 U.S. 351 (1962). When there is some evidence that Congress assumed, or intended, reservation status to evaporate upon allotment and non-Indian homesteading, however, a closer question arises. Consider the following cases, the principal recent precedents attempting to identify when the allotment process has "diminished" a reservation to exclude the area opened to settlement, or terminated or "disestablished" the reservation altogether.

SOLEM V. BARTLETT

465 U.S. 463, 104 S. Ct. 1161, 79 L.Ed.2d 443 (1984)

JUSTICE MARSHALL delivered the opinion of the Court.

[Bartlett, an enrolled member of the Cheyenne River Sioux Tribe, was tried and convicted in state court for a crime he committed on fee land within the boundaries of the Cheyenne River Sioux Reservation as defined in an 1889 federal statute. In his federal habeas corpus petition, he alleged that the state lacked jurisdiction because the crime had been committed by an Indian in Indian country (and thus was subject to federal jurisdiction). According to the state, however, a 1908 federal statute that opened up the reservation for non-Indian homesteading diminished the boundaries of the original reservation, leaving the area where the crime occurred outside the current boundaries (and thus outside Indian country) and therefore subject to state jurisdiction. The current boundaries of the reservation were the subject of great legal confusion, as the Eighth Circuit *en banc* (with two dissenters) held that the 1908 Act had worked no diminishment, while the Supreme Court of South Dakota had held that it did.]

In the latter half of the nineteenth century, large sections of the western States and Territories were set aside for Indian reservations. Towards the end of the century, however, Congress increasingly adhered to the view that the Indian tribes should abandon their nomadic lives on the communal reservations and settle into an agrarian economy on privately-owned parcels of land. This shift was fueled in part by the belief that individualized farming would speed the Indians' assimilation into American society and in part by the continuing demand for new lands for the waves of homesteaders moving West.[6] As a result of these combined pressures, Congress passed a series of surplus land acts at the turn of the century to force Indians onto individual allotments carved out of reservations and to open up unallotted lands for non-Indian settlement. Initially, Congress legislated its Indian allotment program on a national scale, but by the time of the Act of May 29, 1908, Congress was dealing with the surplus land question on a reservation-by-reservation basis, with each surplus land act employing its own statutory language, the product of a unique set of tribal negotiation and legislative compromise.

The modern legacy of the surplus land acts has been a spate of jurisdictional disputes between State and Federal officials as to which sovereign has authority over lands that were opened by the acts and have since passed out of

6. *** The amount of surplus lands freed up by moving Indians onto individual allotments was considerable. For instance, in 1908, the 2,626 members of the Cheyenne River Sioux Tribe had over 2.8 million acres of reservation land, or over 1,000 acres per Tribal member. Under the allotment program, the average allotment per member was under 500 acres. ***

Indian ownership.[8] As a doctrinal matter, the States have jurisdiction over unallotted opened lands if the applicable surplus land act freed that land of its reservation status and thereby diminished the reservation boundaries. On the other hand, Federal, State, and Tribal authorities share jurisdiction over these lands if the relevant surplus land act did not diminish the existing Indian reservation because the entire opened area is Indian country under 18 U.S.C. § 1151(a).

Unfortunately, the surplus land acts themselves seldom detail whether opened lands retained reservation status or were divested of all Indian interests. When the surplus land acts were passed, the distinction seemed unimportant. The notion that reservation status of Indian lands might not be coextensive with tribal ownership was unfamiliar at the turn of the century. Indian lands were judicially defined to include only those lands in which the Indians held some form of property interest: trust lands, individual allotments, and, to a more limited degree, opened lands that had not yet been claimed by non-Indians. Only in 1948 did Congress uncouple reservation status from Indian ownership, and statutorily define Indian country to include lands held in fee by non-Indians within reservation boundaries. *See* Act of June 25, 1948, ch. 645, § 1151, 62 Stat. 757 (codified at 18 U.S.C. § 1151).

Another reason why Congress did not concern itself with the effect of surplus land acts on reservation boundaries was the turn-of-the-century assumption that Indian reservations were a thing of the past. Consistent with prevailing wisdom, members of Congress voting on the surplus land acts believed to a man that within a short time-within a generation at most-the Indian tribes would enter traditional American society and the reservation system would cease to exist. Given this expectation, Congress naturally failed to be meticulous in clarifying whether a particular piece of legislation formally sliced a certain parcel of land off one reservation.

Although the Congresses that passed the surplus land acts anticipated the imminent demise of the reservation and, in fact, passed the acts partially to facilitate the process, we have never been willing to extrapolate from this expectation a specific congressional purpose of diminishing reservations with the passage of every surplus land act. Rather, it is settled law that some surplus land acts diminished reservations, *see, e.g., Rosebud Sioux Tribe v. Kneip*, 430 U.S. 584 (1977); *DeCoteau v. District County Court*, 420 U.S. 425 (1975), and other surplus land acts did not, *see, e.g., Mattz v. Arnett*, 412 U.S. 481 (1973); *Seymour v. Superintendent*, 368 U.S. 351 (1962). The effect of any given surplus land act depends on the language of the act and the circumstances underlying its passage.[10]

---

8. Regardless of whether the original reservation was diminished, Federal and tribal courts have exclusive jurisdiction over those portions of the opened lands that were and have remained Indian allotments. *See* 18 U.S.C. § 1151(c). In addition, opened lands that have been restored to reservation status by subsequent act of Congress *** fall within the exclusive criminal jurisdiction of federal and tribal courts[.]

10. At one extreme, for example, the Act of March 3, 1891, ch. 543, 26 Stat. 1035 *et seq.*, expressly stated that the Lake Traverse Indian Tribe agreed to "cede, sell, relinquish and convey" all interest in unalloted lands on the Lake Traverse Indian Reservation, and the Act further provided that the Tribe would receive full compensation in consideration for its loss. In *DeCoteau v. District County Court, supra,* we found that the Lake Traverse Act, with its express language of cession, diminished the Lake Traverse Indian Reservation. At the other extreme, the Act of March 22, 1906, ch. 1126, § 1, 34 Stat. 80, simply authorized the Secretary of Interior "to sell or dispose of"

Our precedents in the area have established a fairly clean analytical structure for distinguishing those surplus land acts that diminished reservations from those acts that simply offered non-Indians the opportunity to purchase land within established reservation boundaries. The first and governing principle is that only Congress can divest a reservation of its land and diminish its boundaries. Once a block of land is set aside for an Indian Reservation and no matter what happens to the title of individual plots within the area, the entire block retains its reservation status until Congress explicitly indicates otherwise.

Diminishment, moreover, will not be lightly inferred. Our analysis of surplus land acts requires that Congress clearly evince an "intent to change boundaries" before diminishment will be found. *Rosebud v. Kneip*. The most probative evidence of congressional intent is the statutory language used to open the Indian lands. Explicit reference to cession or other language evidencing the present and total surrender of all tribal interests strongly suggests that Congress meant to divest from the reservation all unallotted opened lands. *DeCoteau*; *Seymour*. When such language of cession is buttressed by an unconditional commitment from Congress to compensate the Indian tribe for its opened land, there is an almost insurmountable presumption that Congress meant for the tribe's reservation to be diminished. *See DeCoteau*.

As our opinion in *Rosebud Sioux Tribe* demonstrates, however, explicit language of cession and unconditional compensation are not prerequisites for a finding of diminishment. When events surrounding the passage of a surplus land act—particularly the manner in which the transaction was negotiated with the tribes involved and the tenor of legislative reports presented to Congress—unequivocally reveal a widely-held, contemporaneous understanding that the affected reservation would shrink as a result of the proposed legislation, we have been willing to infer that Congress shared the understanding that its action would diminish the reservation, notwithstanding the presence of statutory language that would otherwise suggest reservation boundaries remained unchanged. To a lesser extent, we have also looked to events that occurred after the passage of a surplus land act to decipher Congress's intentions. Congress's own treatment of the affected areas, particularly in the years

---

unalloted lands on a portion of the Colville Indian Reservation; under the Act, the Colville Tribe received whatever proceeds these sales generated, rather than a sum certain. *Id.*, § 9. 34 Stat., at 81. In *Seymour v. Superintendent, supra,* we held that, because the Colville Act lacked an unconditional divestiture of Indian interest in the lands, the Act simply opened a portion of the Colville Reservation to non-Indian settlers and did not diminish the Reservation.

Between these extremes was the case of the Rosebud Sioux Reservation. In 1901, the Rosebud Sioux Tribe voted in favor of an agreement to cede a portion of their land in Gregory County to the United States in exchange for a sum certain. Three years later, Congress passed the Act of April 23, 1904, ch. 1484, 33 Stat. 254–258, which incorporated the agreement's cession language, but replaced sum-certain payment with a provision guaranteeing the Tribe only the proceeds from the sale of the opened lands. Over the following years, Congress passed two more surplus land acts involving Rosebud Reservation land in other counties; each of the subsequent acts authorized the sale and disposal of additional lands and promised the tribes the proceeds of the sales. *See* Act of March 2, 1907, ch. 2536, 34 Stat. 1230–1232; Act of May 30, 1910, ch. 260, 36 Stat. 448–452. Although none of the Rosebud Acts clearly severed the Tribe from its interest in the unalloted opened lands and even though the last two Acts were strikingly similar to the 1906 Act found not to have diminished the Colville Reservation in *Seymour v. Superintendent, supra,* this Court held that the circumstances surrounding the passage of the three Rosebud Acts unequivocally demonstrated that Congress meant for each Act to diminish the Rosebud Reservation. *Rosebud Sioux Tribe v. Kneip, supra.*

immediately following the opening, has some evidentiary value, as does the manner in which the Bureau of Indian Affairs and local judicial authorities dealt with unalloted open lands.

On a more pragmatic level, we have recognized that who actually moved onto opened reservation lands is also relevant to deciding whether a surplus land act diminished a reservation. Where non-Indian settlers flooded into the opened portion of a reservation and the area has long since lost its Indian character, we have acknowledged that *de facto,* if not *de jure,* diminishment may have occurred. *See Rosebud*; *DeCoteau*. In addition to the obvious practical advantages of acquiescing to *de facto* diminishment,[12] we look to the subsequent demographic history of opened lands as one additional clue as to what Congress expected would happen once land on a particular reservation was opened to non-Indian settlers.[13]

There are, of course, limits to how far we will go to decipher Congress's intention in any particular surplus land act. When both an act and its legislative history fail to provide substantial and compelling evidence of a congressional intention to diminish Indian lands, we are bound by our traditional solicitude for the Indian tribes to rule that diminishment did not take place and that the old reservation boundaries survived the opening. *Mattz*; *Seymour*.

*** We begin with the [1908] Act's operative language, which reads:

> [T]he Secretary of the Interior *** is hereby [ ] authorized and directed, as hereinafter provided, to sell and dispose of all that portion of the Cheyenne River and Standing Rock Indian reservations in the States of South Dakota and North Dakota lying and being within the following described boundaries ***
>
> [F]rom the proceeds arising from the sale and disposition of the lands aforesaid, exclusive of the customary fees and commissions, there shall be deposited in the Treasury of the United States, to the credit of the Indians belonging and having tribal rights on the reservation aforesaid in the States of South Dakota and North Dakota the sums to which the respective tribes may be entitled *** Ch. 218, §§ 1, 6, 35 Stat. 460–461, 463.

These provisions stand in sharp contrast to the explicit language of cession employed in the Lake Traverse and 1904 Rosebud Acts discussed in our opinions in *DeCoteau* and *Rosebud Sioux Tribe*. *See* n. 10, *supra*. Rather than reciting an Indian agreement to "cede, sell, relinquish and convey" the opened lands, the Cheyenne River Act simply authorizes the Secretary to "sell and dispose" of certain lands. This reference to the sale of Indian lands, coupled with the creation of Indian accounts for proceeds, suggests that the Secretary of the Interior was simply being authorized to act as the Tribe's sales agent. Indeed, when faced with precisely the same language in *Seymour*, we

---

12. When an area is predominately populated by non-Indians with only a few surviving pockets of Indian allotments, finding that the land remains Indian country seriously burdens the administration of State and local governments. *See Rosebud; DeCoteau*. Conversely, problems of an imbalanced checkerboard jurisdiction arise if a largely Indian opened area is found to be outside Indian country. *See Seymour*.

13. Resort to subsequent demographic history is, of course, an unorthodox and potentially unreliable method of statutory interpretation. However, in the area of surplus land acts, where various factors kept Congress from focusing on the diminishment issue, the technique is a necessary expedient.

concluded that such provisions "did no more than to open the way for non-Indian settlers to own land on the reservation in a manner which the Federal Government, acting as guardian and trustee for the Indians, regarded as beneficial to the development of its wards."[15]

The balance of the Cheyenne River Act is largely consistent with the implication of the operative language that the Act opened but did not diminish the Cheyenne River Sioux Reservation. Nowhere else in the Act is there specific reference to the cession of Indian interests in the opened lands or any change in existing reservation boundaries. In fact, certain provisions of the Act strongly suggest that the unalloted opened lands would for the immediate future remain an integral part of the Cheyenne River Reservation. In § 1 of the Act, the Secretary was authorized to set aside portions of the opened lands "for agency, school, and religious purposes, to remain reserved as long as needed, and as long as agency, school, or religious institutions are maintained thereon for the benefit of said Indians." It is difficult to imagine why Congress would have reserved lands for such purposes if it did not anticipate that the opened area would remain part of the reservation. This interpretation is supported by § 2 of the Act, under which Cheyenne River Indians were given permission to continue to obtain individual allotments on the affected portion of the reservation before the land was officially opened to non-Indian settlers. Also in § 2, Congress instructed the Geological Survey to examine the opened area for "lands bearing coal" and exempted those sections from allotment or disposal, the apparent purpose being to reserve those mineral resources for the whole tribe.

This case is made more difficult, however, by the presence of some language in the Cheyenne River Act that indirectly supports petitioner's view that the Reservation was diminished. For instance, in a provision permitting Indians already holding allotments on the opened lands to obtain new allotments in the unopened territories, the Act refers to the unopened territories as "within the respective reservations thus diminished." C. 218, § 2, 35 Stat. 461. Elsewhere, the Act permits tribal members to harvest timber on certain parts of the opened lands, but conditions the grant for "only as long as the lands remain part of the public domain." On the assumption that Congress would refer to opened lands as being part of the public domain only if the lands had lost all vestiges of reservation status, petitioners and several amici point to the term "public domain" as well as the phrase "reservations thus diminished" as evidence that Congress understood the Cheyenne River Act to divest unalloted open lands of their reservation status. *** These isolated phrases, however, are hardly dispositive.[17] And, when balanced against the Cheyenne River Act's

15. As Petitioner stresses, the operative language of the Cheyenne River Act is also similar to language in the 1907 and 1908 Rosebud Acts, which this Court held diminished the Rosebud Sioux Reservation. Our analysis of Rosebud acts, however, was strongly colored by the existence of a 1904 Rosebud Act containing cession language "precisely suited" to disestablishment, and the admission of the Indians that the second two Rosebud acts must have diminished their reservation if the previous act did.

17. There is also considerable doubt as to what Congress meant in using these phrases. In 1908, "diminished" was not yet a term of art in Indian law. When Congress spoke of the "reservation thus diminished," it may well have been referring to diminishment in common lands and not diminishment of reservation boundaries. Similarly, even without diminishment, unallotted opened lands could be conceived of as being in the "public domain" inasmuch as they were available for settlement.

stated and limited goal of opening up reservation lands for sale to non-Indian settlers, these two phrases cannot carry the burden of establishing an express congressional purpose to diminish. ***

III. B.

The circumstances surrounding the passage of the Cheyenne River Act also fail to establish a clear congressional purpose to diminish the Reservation. In contrast to the Lake Traverse Act and 1904 Rosebud Act, the Cheyenne River Act did not begin with an agreement between the United States and the Indian Tribes, in which the Indians agreed to cede a portion of their territory to the Federal government. The Cheyenne River Act had its origins in "A bill to authorize the sale and disposition of a portion of the surplus and unalloted lands in the Cheyenne River and Standing Rock reservations," introduced by Senator Gamble of South Dakota on December 9, 1907. S.1385, 60th Cong., 1st Sess. (1907). Once the bill was under consideration, the Secretary of the Interior dispatched an Inspector McLaughlin to the two affected Reservations to consult with the Tribes about the bills.

During his meeting with members of the Cheyenne River Tribe, Inspector McLaughlin admittedly spoke in terms of cession and the relinquishment of Indian interests in the opened territories. However, it is impossible to say that the Tribe agreed to the terms that McLaughlin presented. Due to bad weather during McLaughlin's visit, only 63 members of the Tribe attended his meeting. At the close of McLaughlin's presentation, the president of the Cheyenne River Business Council said that he would have to discuss the matter with the entire Tribe before he could respond to the proposed bill. McLaughlin agreed to delay submission of his report to Congress until he had received word from the Tribe, but, when the Tribe's vote had not reached Washington 14 days later, McLaughlin sent his report to Congress with the conclusion: "The general sentiment of the Indians in council with me at the agency was in favor of the relinquishment [of the opened lands]." H.R. Rep. No. 1539, 60th Cong., 1st Sess., 7 (1908); *see id.*, at 23–24, 28. McLaughlin, however, also informed Congress of the low attendance at his meeting with the Cheyenne River Tribe and acknowledged that he had never received formal approval from the Tribe. *Id.* at 8.

With a full report of Inspector McLaughlin's meeting with the Cheyenne River Tribe before it, Congress considered the Cheyenne River Act in April and May of 1908. In neither floor debates or legislative reports is there a clear statement that Congress interpreted Inspector McLaughlin's report to establish an agreement on the part of the Cheyenne River Indians to cede the opened areas.[21] Indeed, the most explicit statement of Congress's view of the Indian's position was: "The Indians upon both reservations are satisfied to have the surplus and unalloted lands disposed of under the provisions of the bill as amended." S. Rep. 439, 60th Cong., 1st Sess., 4 (1908), quoted in H.R. Rep. 1539, 60th Cong., 1st Sess., 3 (1908). For the most part, the legislative debate of the Cheyenne River Act centered on how much money the Indians would be paid for certain sections of the opened area that the United States was going to buy for school lands, and no mention was made of the Act's effect on the

21. One reason why Congress may not have interpreted the McLaughlin report as evidence of Tribal agreement to cede the land is that a delegation from the Tribe followed McLaughlin back to Washington to urge Congress not to pass the proposed legislation. ***

reservation's boundaries or whether State or Federal officials would have jurisdiction over the opened areas.

To be sure, there are a few phrases scattered through the legislative history of the Cheyenne River Act that support petitioner's position. Both the Senate and House Reports refer to the "reduced reservation" and state that "lands reserved for the use of the Indians upon both reservations as diminished *** are ample *** for the present and future needs of the respective tribes." S. Rep. 439, *supra,* at 4, quoted and adopted in H.R. Rep. 1539, *supra,* at 3. However, it is unclear whether Congress was alluding to the reduction in Indian-owned lands that would occur once some of the opened lands were sold to settlers or to the reduction that a complete cession of tribal interests in the opened area would precipitate. *See also* n. 17, *supra.* Without evidence that Congress understood itself to be entering into an agreement under which the Tribe committed itself to cede and relinquish all interests in unallotted opened lands, and in the absence of some clear statement of congressional intent to alter reservation boundaries, it is impossible to infer from a few isolated and ambiguous phrases a congressional purpose to diminish the Cheyenne River Sioux Reservation.

The subsequent treatment of the Cheyenne River Sioux Reservation by Congress, courts, and the Executive is so rife with contradictions and inconsistencies as to be of no help to either side. For instance, two years after the Cheyenne River Act, Congress passed a bill to sell a portion of the opened lands and called the area "surplus and unalloted lands *in the Cheyenne River Indian Reservation,*" suggesting that the opened area was still part of the reservation. Act of June 23, 1910, ch. 369, 36 Stat. 602 (emphasis added). But, twelve years after that, Congress passed another piece of legislation referring to the opened lands as "the former" Cheyenne River Sioux Reservation and suggesting that the Reservation had been diminished. *See* Act of Apr. 25, 1922, ch. 140, 42 Stat. 499. Ample additional examples pointing in both directions leave one with the distinct impression that subsequent Congresses had no clear view whether the opened territories were or were not still part of the Cheyenne River Reservation. A similar state of confusion characterizes the Executive's treatment of the Cheyenne River Sioux Reservation's opened lands. Moreover, both parties have been able to cite instances in which State and Federal courts exerted criminal jurisdiction over the disputed area in the years following opening.[23] Neither sovereign dominated the jurisdictional history of the opened lands in the decades immediately following 1908.

What is clear, however, is what happened to the Cheyenne River Sioux Tribe after the Act of May 29, 1908, was passed. Most of the members of the Tribe obtained individual allotments on the lands opened by the Act. Because most of the tribe lived on the opened territories, tribal authorities and Bureau of Indian Affairs personnel took primary responsibility for policing and supplying social services to the opened lands during the years following 1908. The

23. According to one study, Federal, Tribal, and State courts shared jurisdiction over the opened areas in the decades following opening. Between 1910 and 1920, only two Indians were tried in state court for crimes committed on the opened lands. During this period, the Federal authorities were primarily responsible for Indian life on both opened and unopened portions of the reservation. In later years, however, the state courts came to assume that the opened areas fell within their general criminal jurisdiction. It was only in 1973 that the Eighth Circuit challenged this assumption in [a *habeas* case.]

strong Tribal presence in the opened area has continued until the present day. Now roughly two thirds of the Tribe's enrolled members live in the opened area. The seat of Tribal government is now located in a town in the opened area, where most important tribal activities take place.

Also clear is the historical fact that the opening of the Cheyenne River Sioux Reservation was a failure. Few homesteaders perfected claims on the lands, due perhaps in part to the price of the land but probably more importantly to the fact that the opened area was much less fertile than the lands in southern South Dakota opened by other surplus land acts. As a result of small number of homesteaders who settled on the opened lands and the high percentage of Tribal members who continue to live in the area, the population of the disputed area is now evenly divided between Indian and non-Indian residents. Under these circumstances, it is impossible to say that the opened areas of the Cheyenne River Sioux Reservation have lost their Indian character. ***

NOTES AND QUESTIONS

1. *The diminishment inquiry*. There seem to be two analytically plausible ways of resolving the diminishment question. The first would be to apply the plenary power/canons model: Congress may unilaterally abrogate the prior treaty by allotting the reservation; it even has the authority by virtue of its plenary power to abolish the legal status of the reservation; but merely opening the reservation to non-Indians is insufficient evidence of congressional intent to diminish or abolish reservation status. Note that in *Solem* the Court suggests that very few allotment statutes contained any mention of reservation status. Thus, under the plenary power/canons model, virtually all reservations would have remained intact despite allotment. The alternative approach would forsake the standard plenary power/canons model, perhaps in light of arguably reasonable expectations created in non-Indian homesteaders and others that their lands would be treated just like off-reservations lands (both subject to state and local, rather than tribal and federal, control). Under this approach, even if the statutory text and legislative history do not clearly reveal a congressional intent to change reservation status, the congressional purposes associated with allotment—assimilating the tribes, opening up land for non-Indian occupancy and use, settling theretofore Indian areas with non-Indians, and so on—are so obviously assimilationist that the reservation status should be understood as having been altered. What is clear is that the Court (at least as a formal matter) has not adopted either of these two plausible approaches, because the first would mean virtually all reservations survived allotment and the second would mean that virtually all of them would be deemed altered by allotment, and yet the cases go both ways. The Court's discussion in *Solem* may have a "have your cake and eat it, too" quality, as it attempts to reconcile the prior (analytically inconsistent) cases by focusing on the canons (approach 1) *and* the subsequent understandings of non-Indians, the state and local governments, and current demographics (approach 2).

2. *Is there a test for diminishment?* Note that in explaining the prior cases, *Solem* draws a distinction between allotment statutes in which the tribe supposedly agreed to cede, sell, relinquish, and convey land for a sum certain, versus other allotment statutes in which the tribe supposedly agreed to sell

and dispose of the land with piecemeal payments on a parcel-by-parcel basis. Does the former language indicate a stronger congressional intent and/or tribal agreement to diminish the reservation than the latter language? Isn't it crystal clear what Congress wanted in both situations—assimilation and the destruction of the reservation, over a generation? Does the presence of tribal understanding, or even consent, make any difference? Could anyone have predicted that the different words would have a radically different legal effect? If not, what is the Court doing in these cases?

3. *Solem* states that one of the relevant factors in the diminishment analysis is who actually lives on the land, whether the population is predominantly non-Indian or retains "its Indian character." How is this relevant to an inquiry about congressional intent?

Hagen v. Utah, 510 U.S. 399 (1994). In 1994, the Supreme Court considered whether allotment had diminished a portion of the Uintah reservation. Congress originally passed a law in 1902 providing that if the Uintah and White River tribes of Ute Indians consented, the reservation set aside for them by treaty would be allotted to them in severalty. Act of May 27, 1902, ch. 888, 32 Stat. 263. The 1902 Act also provided that when the deadline for allotments passed, "all the unallotted lands within said reservation *shall be restored to the public domain*" and subject to homesteading at $1.25 per acre, and the proceeds from the sales of the land would be used to benefit the Uintah and White River tribes. *Id.* (emphasis added).

The tribes refused to consent to allotment. In January of 1903, however, the Supreme Court decided *Lone Wolf v. Hitchcock*, holding that tribal consent was not needed to allot a reservation. In March of 1903, Congress passed a new law delaying the opening of the reservation, and directing the Secretary of the Interior to again seek consent of the tribes, but to allot the reservation even if consent could not be obtained. Congress delayed opening of the reservation again in 1904 and 1905. In May of 1905, Congress passed a law delaying the allotment under the 1904 Act, but providing that allotment would occur in 1905, and providing that unallotted land "shall be disposed of under the general provisions of the homestead and town-site laws of the United States, and shall be opened to settlement and entry by proclamation of the President." 33 Stat. 1069. The Government once again failed to obtain the consent of the Indians, and on July 14, 1905, President Roosevelt proclaimed the land "opened to entry, settlement and disposition under the general provisions of the homestead and townsite laws of the United States." 34 Stat. 3120.

The Court relied on language in the 1902 Act stating that the unallotted lands would be "restored to the public domain" to find that the reservation had been diminished:

> Statutes of the period indicate that Congress considered Indian reservations as separate from the public domain. *See, e.g.,* Act of June 25, 1910, § 6, 36 Stat. 857 (criminalizing forest fires started "upon the public domain, or upon any Indian reservation")[.] Likewise, in *DeCoteau* we emphasized the distinction between reservation and public domain lands: "That the lands ceded in the other agreements were *returned to the public domain, stripped of reservation status,* can hardly be questioned. *** The

> sponsors of the legislation stated repeatedly that the ratified agreements would return the ceded lands to the 'public domain.' "

Hagen at 413. The Court also noted that in *Seymour v. Superintendent of Wash. State Penitentiary*, 368 U.S. 351 (1962), it held that the south half of the Colville Reservation was not diminished, but had stated that the north half was diminished by an 1892 Act providing that "all the [north half] of the Colville Reservation *** is hereby, vacated and restored to the public domain, notwithstanding any executive order or other proceeding where the same was set apart as a reservation for any band of Indians." 27 Stat. 62, 63 (1892). The Court conceded that in *Solem* it had held that an allotment act "which authorized the Secretary of the Interior to 'sell and dispose of' unallotted reservation lands merely opened the reservation to non-Indian settlement and did not diminish it," even though "in the same statute, Congress had granted the Indians permission to harvest timber on the opened lands 'as long as the lands remain part of the public domain.' " *Hagen* at 413. But, the Court said, the "public domain" language in *Solem* was not in the "operative" portion of the statute and thus not controlling. The Court also rejected the plaintiff's argument that the 1905 Act had not preserved the language of the 1902 Act referring to restoration to the public domain.

The Court stated that its conclusion that the statutory language indicated diminishment was "not controverted by the subsequent demographics of the Uintah Valley area":

> We have recognized that "[w]hen an area is predominately populated by non-Indians with only a few surviving pockets of Indian allotments, finding that the land remains Indian country seriously burdens the administration of state and local governments." *Solem*. Of the original 2 million acres reserved for Indian occupation, approximately 400,000 were opened for non-Indian settlement in 1905. Almost all of the non-Indians live on the opened lands. The current population of the area is approximately 85 percent non-Indian. *** The population of the largest city in the area—Roosevelt City, named for the President who opened the reservation for settlement—is about 93 percent non-Indian. *Id.*, Table 3, p. 13.
>
> The seat of Ute tribal government is in Fort Duchesne, which is situated on Indian trust lands. By contrast, we found it significant in *Solem* that the seat of tribal government was located on opened lands. The State of Utah exercised jurisdiction over the opened lands from the time the reservation was opened until the Tenth Circuit's *Ute Indian Tribe* decision. That assumption of authority again stands in sharp contrast to the situation in *Solem*, where "tribal authorities and Bureau of Indian Affairs personnel took primary responsibility for policing *** the opened lands during the years following [the opening in] 1908." This "jurisdictional history," as well as the current population situation in the Uintah Valley, demonstrates a practical acknowledgment that the Reservation was diminished; a contrary conclusion would seriously disrupt the justifiable expectations of the people living in the area.

Hagen at 420–21.

JUSTICE BLACKMUN, joined by **JUSTICE SOUTER**, dissented, declaring:

> "Great nations, like great men, should keep their word," *FPC v. Tuscarora Indian Nation,* 362 U.S. 99, 142 (1960) (Black, J., dissenting), and we do not lightly find that Congress has broken its solemn promises to Indian tribes. The Court relies on a single, ambiguous phrase in an Act that never became effective, and which was deleted from the controlling statute, to conclude that Congress must have intended to diminish the Uintah Valley Reservation. I am unable to find a clear expression of such intent in either the operative statute or the surrounding circumstances and am compelled to conclude that the original Uintah Valley Reservation boundaries remain intact. ***

Hagen at 422. Note that in *Hagen*, the Court has arguably expanded the list of "magic language" so that returning land to the public domain also counts as an "intent" to diminish. Is this consistent with the past precedents?

South Dakota v. Yankton Sioux Tribe, 522 U.S. 329 (1998) arose from a dispute over environmental regulations regarding a solid waste dump. Several counties wanted to build a municipal landfill within the borders of the Yankton Sioux Tribe's 1858 reservation. The tribe protested that the proposed compacted clay liner was insufficient to prevent leakage from the site. They further argued that because the land was Indian country, the dump was subject to federal environmental regulations that required a composite liner. The case involved a law professor's dream hypothetical. On the one hand, Article I of the allotment agreement contained the "magic language" ("cede, sell, relinquish, and convey to the United States all their claim, right, title, and interest in and to all the unallotted lands within the reservation"), and Article II provided payment of a sum certain for the land. On the other hand, Article XVIII, the last article of the agreement, stated that "Nothing in this agreement shall be construed to abrogate the treaty of April 19th, 1858, between the Yankton tribe of Sioux Indians and the United States."

The unanimous Court, per Justice O'Connor, first acknowledged the Indian law canons, then noted that the presence of the "magic language" created a "nearly conclusive presumption of diminishment" (quoting *Solem*). The Court rejected the arguments of the Yankton Tribe and the United States that the savings clause of Article XVIII meant that "the parties intended to modify the 1858 Treaty only insofar as necessary to open the surplus lands for settlement, without fundamentally altering the Treaty's terms":

> Such a literal construction of the saving clause, as the South Dakota Supreme Court noted in *State v. Greger*, 559 N.W.2d 854, 863 (S.D. 1997), would "impugn the entire sale." The unconditional relinquishment of the Tribe's territory for settlement by non-Indian homesteaders can by no means be reconciled with the central provisions of the 1858 Treaty, which recognized the reservation as the Tribe's "permanent" home and prohibited white settlement there. *** Moreover, the Government's contention that the Tribe intended to cede some property but maintain the entire reservation as its territory contradicts the common understanding of the time: that tribal ownership was a critical component of reservation status. *See Solem*. We cannot ignore plain language that, viewed in historical

context and given a fair appraisal, clearly runs counter to a tribe's late claims. *Klamath.*

*** The most plausible interpretation of Article XVIII revolves around the annuities in the form of cash, guns, ammunition, food, and clothing that the Tribe was to receive in exchange for its aboriginal claims for 50 years after the 1858 Treaty. Along with the proposed sale price, these annuities and other unrealized Yankton claims dominated the 1892 negotiations between the Commissioners and the Tribe. The tribal historian testified, before the District Court, that the loss of their rations would have been "disastrous" to the Tribe, App. 589, and members of the Tribe clearly perceived a threat to the annuities. ***

The language in Article XVIII specifically ensuring that the "Yankton Indians shall continue to receive their annuities under the [1858 Treaty]" underscores the limited purpose and scope of the saving clause. It is true that the Court avoids interpreting statutes in a way that "renders some words altogether redundant." *** But in light of the fact that the record of the negotiations between the Commissioners and the Yankton Tribe contains no discussion of the preservation of the 1858 boundaries but many references to the Government's failure to fulfill earlier promises, *see, e.g.*, Council of the Yankton Indians (Dec. 3, 1892), transcribed in S. Exec. Doc. No. 27, at 54–55, it seems most likely that the parties inserted and understood Article XVIII, including both the general statement regarding the force of the 1858 Treaty and the particular provision that payments would continue as specified therein, to assuage the Tribes' concerns about their past claims and future entitlements.

***

Finally, the Tribe argues that, at a minimum, the saving clause renders the statute equivocal, and that confronted with that ambiguity we must adopt the reading that favors the Tribe. The principle according to which ambiguities are resolved to the benefit of Indian tribes is not, however, a license to disregard clear expressions of tribal and congressional intent. *DeCoteau*. In previous decisions, this Court has recognized that the precise cession and sum certain language contained in the 1894 Act plainly indicates diminishment, and a reasonable interpretation of the saving clause does not conflict with a like conclusion in this case.

As in *Hagen v. Utah*, subsequent references to the reservation were contradictory. Finally, in remarkably ambivalent language, the Court turned to the current demographics of the area:

This final consideration is the least compelling for a simple reason: Every surplus land Act necessarily resulted in a surge of non-Indian settlement and degraded the "Indian character" of the reservation, yet we have repeatedly stated that not every surplus land Act diminished the affected reservation. *See Solem* at 468–469. The fact that the Yankton population in the region promptly and drastically declined after the 1894 Act does, however, provide "one additional clue as to what Congress expected," *id.* at 472. Today, fewer than 10 percent of the 1858 reservation lands are in Indian hands, non-Indians constitute over two-thirds of the population within the 1858 boundaries, and several municipalities inside those boundaries have been incorporated under South Dakota law. The opening of the tribal casino in 1991 apparently reversed the population trend; the tribal presence in the area has steadily increased in recent years, and the advent of gaming has stimulated the local economy. In addition, some acreage within the 1858 boundaries has reverted to tribal or trust land. *** Nonetheless, the area remains "predominantly populated by non-Indians with only a few surviving pockets of Indian allotments," and those demographics signify a diminished reservation. *Solem* at 471, n.12.

***

The allotment era has long since ended, and its guiding philosophy has been repudiated. Tribal communities struggled but endured, preserved their cultural roots, and remained, for the most part, near their historic lands. But despite the present-day understanding of a "government-to-government relationship between the United States and each Indian tribe," *see, e.g.,* 25 U.S.C. § 3601, we must give effect to Congress' intent in passing the 1894 Act. Here, as in *DeCoteau*, we believe that Congress spoke clearly, and although "[s]ome might wish [it] had spoken differently, *** we cannot remake history." 420 U.S. at 449.

The U.S. Supreme Court's next opportunity to consider whether a tribe's reservation boundaries had been altered came in another context with challenging demographics. Nonetheless, the Court upheld the *Solem* framework and appeared even less tolerant of post-enactment history or present-day population as an indicator of congressional intent.

NEBRASKA V. PARKER

136 S. Ct. 1072 (2016)

JUSTICE THOMAS delivered the opinion of the Court.

The village of Pender, Nebraska sits a few miles west of an abandoned right-of-way once used by the Sioux City and Nebraska Railroad Company. We must decide whether Pender and surrounding Thurston County, Nebraska, are within the boundaries of the Omaha Indian Reservation or whether the passage of an 1882 Act empowering the United States Secretary of the Interior to sell the Tribe's land west of the right-of-way "diminished" the reservation's boundaries, thereby "free[ing]" the disputed land of "its reservation status." We hold that Congress did not diminish the reservation in 1882 and that the disputed land is within the reservation's boundaries.

I. A.

Centuries ago, the Omaha Tribe settled in present-day eastern Nebraska. By the mid–19th century, the Tribe was destitute and, in exchange for much-needed revenue, agreed to sell a large swath of its land to the United States. In 1854, the Tribe entered into a treaty with the United States to create a 300,000–acre reservation. Treaty with the Omahas (1854 Treaty), Mar. 16, 1854, 10 Stat. 1043. The Tribe agreed to "cede" and "forever relinquish all right and title to" its land west of the Mississippi River, excepting the reservation, in exchange for $840,000, to be paid over 40 years. *Id.*, at 1043–1044.

In 1865, after the displaced Wisconsin Winnebago Tribe moved west, the Omaha Tribe agreed to "cede, sell, and convey" an additional 98,000 acres on the north side of the reservation to the United States for the purpose of creating a reservation for the Winnebagoes. Treaty with the Omaha Indians (1865 Treaty), Mar. 6, 1865, 14 Stat. 667–668. The Tribe sold the land for a fixed sum of $50,000. *Id.*, at 667.

In 1872, the Tribe again expressed its wish to sell portions of the reservation, but Congress took a different tack than it had in the 1854 and 1865 Treaties. Instead of purchasing a portion of the reservation for a fixed sum, Congress authorized the Secretary of the Interior to survey, appraise, and sell up to 50,000 acres on the western side of the reservation "to be separated from the remaining portion of said reservation" by a north-south line agreed to by the Tribe and Congress. Act of June 10, 1872 (1872 Act), ch. 436, § 1, 17 Stat. 391. Under the 1872 Act, a nonmember could purchase "tracts not exceeding one hundred and sixty acres each" or "the entire body offered." *Ibid.* Proceeds from any sales would be "placed to the credit of said Indians on the books of the treasury of the United States." *Ibid.* But the proceeds were meager. The 1872 Act resulted in only two sales totaling 300.72 acres.

Then came the 1882 Act, central to the dispute between petitioners and respondents. In that Act, Congress again empowered the Secretary of the Interior "to cause to be surveyed, if necessary, and sold" more than 50,000 acres lying west of a right-of-way granted by the Tribe and approved by the Secretary of the Interior in 1880 for use by the Sioux City and Nebraska Railroad Company. Act of Aug. 7, 1882 (1882 Act), 22 Stat. 341. The land for sale under the terms of the 1882 Act overlapped substantially with the land Congress tried, but failed, to sell in 1872. Once the land was appraised "in tracts of forty acres each," the Secretary was "to issue [a] proclamation" that the "lands are open for settlement under such rules and regulations as he may prescribe." §§ 1, 2, *id.*, at 341. Within one year of that proclamation, a nonmember could purchase up to 160 acres of land (for no less than $2.50 per acre) in cash paid to the United States, so long as the settler "occup[ied]" it, made "valuable improvements thereon," and was "a citizen of the United States, or ... declared his intention to become such." § 2, *id.*, at 341. The proceeds from any land sales, "after paying all expenses incident to and necessary for carrying out the provisions of th[e] act," were to "be placed to the credit of said Indians in the Treasury of the United States." § 3, *id.*, at 341. Interest earned on the proceeds was to be "annually expended for the benefit of said Indians, under the direction of the Secretary of the Interior." *Ibid.*

The 1882 Act also included a provision, common in the late 19th century, that enabled members of the Tribe to select individual allotments as a means of encouraging them to depart from the communal lifestyle of the reservation. The 1882 Act provided that the United States would convey the land to a member or his heirs in fee simple after holding it in trust on behalf of the member and his heirs for 25 years. Members could select allotments on any part of the reservation, either east or west of the right-of-way.

After the members selected their allotments—only 10 to 15 of which were located west of the right-of-way—the Secretary proclaimed that the remaining

50,157 acres west of the right-of-way were open for settlement by nonmembers in April 1884. One of those settlers was W.E. Peebles, who "purchased a tract of 160 acres, on which he platted the townsite for Pender."

B.

The village of Pender today numbers 1,300 residents. Most are not associated with the Omaha Tribe. Less than 2% of Omaha tribal members have lived west of the right-of-way since the early 20th century.

Despite its longstanding absence, the Tribe sought to assert jurisdiction over Pender in 2006 by subjecting Pender retailers to its newly amended Beverage Control Ordinance. The ordinance requires those retailers to obtain a liquor license (costing $500, $1,000, or $1,500 depending upon the class of license) and imposes a 10% sales tax on liquor sales. Nonmembers who violate the ordinance are subject to a $10,000 fine.

The village of Pender and Pender retailers, including bars, a bowling alley, and social clubs, brought a federal suit against members of the Omaha Tribal Council in their official capacities to challenge the Tribe's power to impose the requirements of the Beverage Control Ordinance on nonmembers. Federal law permits the Tribe to regulate liquor sales on its reservation and in "Indian country" so long as the Tribe's regulations are (as they were here) "certified by the Secretary of the Interior, and published in the Federal Register." 18 U.S.C. § 1161. The challengers alleged that they were neither within the boundaries of the Omaha Indian Reservation nor in Indian country and, consequently, were not bound by the ordinance.

The State of Nebraska intervened on behalf of the plaintiffs, and the United States intervened on behalf of the Omaha Tribal Council members. The State's intervention was prompted, in part, by the Omaha Tribe's demand that Nebraska share with the Tribe revenue that the State received from fuel taxes imposed west of the right-of-way. In addition to the relief sought by Pender and the Pender retailers, Nebraska sought a permanent injunction prohibiting the Tribe from asserting tribal jurisdiction over the 50,157 acres west of the abandoned right-of-way.

After examining the text of the 1882 Act, as well as the contemporaneous and subsequent understanding of the 1882 Act's effect on the reservation boundaries, the District Court concluded that Congress did not diminish the Omaha Reservation in 1882. Accordingly, the District Court denied the plaintiffs' request for injunctive and declaratory relief barring the Tribe's enforcement of the Beverage Control Ordinance. The Eighth Circuit affirmed. We granted certiorari to resolve whether the 1882 Act diminished the Omaha Reservation.

II.

We must determine whether Congress "diminished" the Omaha Indian Reservation in 1882. If it did so, the State now has jurisdiction over the disputed land. If Congress, on the other hand, did not diminish the reservation and instead only enabled nonmembers to purchase land within the reservation, then federal, state, and tribal authorities share jurisdiction over these "opened" but undiminished reservation lands.

The framework we employ to determine whether an Indian reservation has been diminished is well settled. [The Court recited the test from Solem, *see* p. 276-77 of the textbook.]

A.

As with any other question of statutory interpretation, we begin with the text of the 1882 Act, the most "probative evidence" of diminishment. * * *

The 1882 Act bore none of these hallmarks of diminishment. The 1882 Act empowered the Secretary to survey and appraise the disputed land, which then could be purchased in 160–acre tracts by nonmembers. 22 Stat. 341. The 1882 Act states that the disputed lands would be "open for settlement under such rules and regulations as [the Secretary of the Interior] may prescribe." *Ibid.* And the parcels would be sold piecemeal in 160–acre tracts. *Ibid.* So rather than the Tribe's receiving a fixed sum for all of the disputed lands, the Tribe's profits were entirely dependent upon how many nonmembers purchased the appraised tracts of land.

From this text, it is clear that the 1882 Act falls into another category of surplus land Acts: those that "merely opened reservation land to settlement and provided that the uncertain future proceeds of settler purchases should be applied to the Indians' benefit." * * *

Our conclusion that Congress did not intend to diminish the reservation in 1882 is confirmed by the text of earlier treaties between the United States and the Tribe. In drafting the 1882 Act, Congress legislated against the backdrop of the 1854 and 1865 Treaties—both of which terminated the Tribe's jurisdiction over their land "in unequivocal terms." *Ibid.* Those treaties "ced[ed]" the lands and "reliquish[ed]" any claims to them in exchange for a fixed sum. 10 Stat. 1043–1044; see also 14 Stat. 667 ("The Omaha tribe of Indians do hereby *cede, sell, and convey* to the United States a tract of land from the north side of their present reservation ..." (emphasis added)). The 1882 Act speaks in much different terms, both in describing the way the individual parcels were to be sold to nonmembers and the way in which the Tribe would profit from those sales. That 1882 Act also closely tracks the 1872 Act, which petitioners do not contend diminished the reservation. The change in language in the 1882 Act undermines petitioners' claim that Congress intended to do the same with the reservation's boundaries in 1882 as it did in 1854 and 1865. Petitioners have failed at the first and most important step. They cannot establish that the text of the 1882 Act evinced an intent to diminish the reservation.

B.

We now turn to the history surrounding the passage of the 1882 Act. The mixed historical evidence relied upon by the parties cannot overcome the lack of clear textual signal that Congress intended to diminish the reservation. That historical evidence in no way "*unequivocally* reveal[s] a widely held, contemporaneous understanding that the affected reservation would shrink as a result of the proposed legislation."

Petitioners rely largely on isolated statements that some legislators made about the 1882 Act. Senator Henry Dawes of Massachusetts, for example, noted that he had been "assured that [the 1882 Act] would *leave an ample reservation*" for the Tribe. 13 Cong. Rec. 3032 (1882) (emphasis added). And Senator John Ingalls of Kansas observed "that this bill practically breaks up that portion at least of the reservation which is to be sold, and provides that it shall be disposed of to private purchasers." *Id.*, at 3028. Whatever value these contemporaneous floor statements might have, other such statements support the opposite conclusion—that Congress never intended to diminish the reservation. Senator Charles Jones of Florida, for example, spoke of "white men purchas[ing] titles to land *within* this reservation and settl[ing] down with the Indians on it." *Id.*, at 3078 (emphasis added). Such dueling remarks by individual legislators are far from the "clear and plain" evidence of diminishment required under this Court's precedent. *Yankton Sioux,* 522 U.S., at 343, 118 S. Ct. 789 (internal quotation marks omitted); see also *Solem,* 465 U.S., at 478, 104 S. Ct. 1161 (noting that it was unclear whether statements referring to a " 'reduced reservation' " alluded to the "reduction in Indian-owned lands that would occur once some of the opened lands were sold to settlers or to the reduction that a complete cession of tribal interests in the opened area would precipitate").

More illuminating than cherry-picked statements by individual legislators would be historical evidence of "the manner in which the transaction was negotiated" with the Omaha Tribe. *Id.*, at 471, In *Yankton Sioux,* for example, recorded negotiations between the Commissioner of Indian Affairs and leaders of the Yankton Sioux Tribe unambiguously "signaled [the Tribe's] understanding that the cession of the surplus lands dissolved tribal governance of the 1858 reservation." No such unambiguous evidence exists in the record of these negotiations. In particular, petitioners' reliance on the remarks of Representative Edward Valentine of Nebraska, who stated, "You cannot find one of those Indians that does not want the western portion sold," and that the Tribe wished to sell the land to those who would " 'reside upon it and cultivate it' " so that the Tribe members could "benefit of these improvements," 13 Cong. Rec. 6541, falls short. Nothing about this statement or other similar statements unequivocally supports a finding that the existing boundaries of the reservation would be diminished.

C.

Finally, we consider both the subsequent demographic history of opened lands, which serves as "one additional clue as to what Congress expected would happen once land on a particular reservation was opened to non-Indian settlers," as well as the United States' "treatment of the affected areas, particularly in the years immediately following the opening," which has "some evidentiary value." Our cases suggest that such evidence might "reinforc[e]" a finding of diminishment or nondiminishment based on the text. *Mattz,* 412 U.S., at 505, 93 S. Ct. 2245; see also, *e.g., Rosebud Sioux Tribe v. Kneip,* 430 U.S. 584, 604–605, 97 S. Ct. 1361, 51 L.Ed.2d 660 (1977) (invoking subsequent history to reject a petitioner's "strained" textual reading of a congressional Act). But this Court has never relied solely on this third consideration to find diminishment.

As petitioners have discussed at length, the Tribe was almost entirely absent from the disputed territory for more than 120 years. Brief for Petitioners 24–30. The Omaha Tribe does not enforce any of its regulations—including those governing businesses, fire protection, animal control, fireworks, and wildlife and parks—in Pender or in other locales west of the right-of-way. 996 F.Supp.2d, at 832. Nor does it maintain an office, provide social services, or host tribal celebrations or ceremonies west of the right-of-way.

This subsequent demographic history cannot overcome our conclusion that Congress did not intend to diminish the reservation in 1882. And it is not our role to "rewrite" the 1882 Act in light of this subsequent demographic history. After all, evidence of the changing demographics of disputed land is "the least compelling" evidence in our diminishment analysis, for "[e]very surplus land Act necessarily resulted in a surge of non-Indian settlement and degraded the 'Indian character' of the reservation, yet we have repeatedly stated that not every surplus land Act diminished the affected reservation."

Evidence of the subsequent treatment of the disputed land by Government officials likewise has "limited interpretive value." Petitioners highlight that, for more than a century and with few exceptions, reports from the Office of Indian Affairs and in opinion letters from Government officials treated the disputed land as Nebraska's. It was not until this litigation commenced that the Department of the Interior definitively changed its position, concluding that the reservation boundaries were in fact not diminished in 1882. For their part, respondents discuss late–19th–century statutes referring to the disputed land as part of the reservation, as well as inconsistencies in maps and statements by Government officials. This "mixed record" of subsequent treatment of the disputed land cannot overcome the statutory text, which is devoid of any language indicative of Congress' intent to diminish.

Petitioners' concerns about upsetting the "justifiable expectations" of the almost exclusively non-Indian settlers who live on the land are compelling, but these expectations alone, resulting from the Tribe's failure to assert jurisdiction, cannot diminish reservation boundaries. Only Congress has the power to diminish a reservation. And though petitioners wish that Congress would have "spoken differently" in 1882, "we cannot remake history." * * *

In light of the statutory text, we hold that the 1882 Act did not diminish the Omaha Indian Reservation. Because petitioners have raised only the single question of diminishment, we express no view about whether equitable considerations of laches and acquiescence may curtail the Tribe's power to tax the retailers of Pender in light of the Tribe's century-long absence from the disputed lands. *Cf. City of Sherrill v. Oneida Indian Nation of N.Y.*, 544 U.S. 197, 217–221, (2005).

The judgment of the Court of Appeals for the Eighth Circuit is affirmed.

NOTES AND QUESTIONS

1. The Court in *Yankton* recited the Indian law canons in the opinion but treated the "magic language" words as trumping the treaty savings clause. Do the cession and payment words provide the requisitely clear intent to do this?

2. *Demographics.* Until *Nebraska v. Parker*, some commentators argued the only way to explain the outcomes was to focus on demographics. Professor

Robert Laurence wrote: "[W]hen *Hagen* and *Solem* are viewed side-by-side, they present an odd, and for many, discouraging tableau of American Indian law. Together, they set forth a largely nonsensical role for modern demography to play in construction of decades-old statutes. *** The modern demography of the land on or near the reservation—precisely, the race of those who live there—seems to function for the Court as a judicial rheostat, which varies the potency of the reluctance to diminish." Robert Laurence, *The Dominant Society's Judicial Reluctance to Allow Tribal Civil Law to Apply to Non–Indians: Reservation Diminishment, Modern Demography and the Indian Civil Rights Act*, 30 U. Rich. L. Rev. 781, 795 (1996). Are demographics an appropriate consideration as a matter of policy if not law? Or is this a determination that Congress and not the court should make.

3. *Why did the Court take* Nebraska v. Parker? There was no conflict with any state court or circuit court decision. In its Reply to the Opposition Brief of the United States, Nebraska argued that: "For over 130 years, the individuals who have chosen to reside in the Pender, Nebraska area and build homes, schools, and churches, open businesses and raise families, have developed justifiable expectations that the area in which they are doing these things was under the jurisdiction of the State of Nebraska. The Eighth Circuit's decision needlessly alters the status quo by precluding meaningful consideration of the third [*Solem*] factor [de facto diminishment, or subsequent demographic history]". 2015 WL 5169182 (U.S.), 8. After *Parker*, when should lower courts consider subsequent demographic history?

4. The 10th Circuit Court of Appeals ruled that the Creek Nation's reservation was not disestablished in *Murphy v Royal*, No.s 07-7068 & 15-7041, 875 F.3d. 896, (10th Cir 2017), *petition for cert. granted*, No. 17-1107 (May 21, 2018). The opinion overturned a murder conviction and death sentence handed down by the Oklahoma State courts. The decision is likely to have significant implications for Oklahoma. One distinguished commentator reacted: "It's huge, especially for criminal jurisdiction," said University of Tulsa Professor Judith Royster. "The primary impact it's going to have is any crime committed by or against an Indian, not just a Creek citizen, but any Indian, in the boundaries of the Creek reservation can no longer be prosecuted by the state of Oklahoma." Cursit Killman, *Experts: Court Ruling Overturning Native American Man's Murder Conviction, Death Penalty Could have Huge Implications,* TULSA WORLD (Aug. 8, 2017), http://www.tulsaworld.com/news/courts/experts-court-ruling-overturning-native-american-man-s-murder-conviction/article_dd761b1d-2d9c-5542-8a50-771f2f92de85.html [https://perma.cc/ZLH3-KMXR]. The Supreme Court granted the State's petition for certiorari, heard oral argument during the 2018-19 term, but then held the case over for the 2019-20 term.

C. DEPENDENT INDIAN COMMUNITIES

As the previous cases show, the boundaries of a reservation are not always clear, but once they are established the Indian country determination is easy: all lands within the boundaries, however held, are Indian country. But what about dependent Indian communities? Section (a) of the Indian country statute covers all reservation land, and section (c) covers all Indian allotments, so section (b) must cover something else. Lower courts interpreting section (b) held that land simply purchased by a tribe within a predominantly non-Indian area was not a dependent Indian community, *Weddell v. Meierhenry*, 636 F.2d 211, 212–13 (8th Cir. 1980); *see Buzzard v. Oklahoma Tax Commission*, 992 F.2d 1073 (10th Cir. 1993), but that non-Indian owned land in an area where 47% of the land is held in trust for Indians, and part of a community that is predominantly tribal and treated as such by the federal government would be, *Pittsburgh & Midway Coal Co. v. Watchman*, 52 F.3d 1531 (10th Cir. 1995), as would trust land set aside for an Indian housing project. *United States v. Driver*, 945 F.2d 1410, 1415 (8th Cir. 1991) (housing project on trust land).

The first post–1948 Supreme Court case concerning dependent Indian communities arose from the distinctive status of Alaska Native land. By virtue of Alaska's late entry into the Union and the inhospitable nature of a land mass bisected by the Arctic Circle, the indigenous peoples of Alaska had never been militarily conquered or agreed to cede their lands to the United States. But in 1955, in *Tee–Hit–Ton Indians v. United States*, 348 U.S. 272 (1955), the Supreme Court held unless the Alaska Natives' title had been formally recognized by a federal treaty, statute, or agreement, the United States could take Alaska Native land without paying any compensation. In 1968, however, Alaska statehood and the subsequent discovery of oil in Alaska's Prudhoe Bay inspired oil companies to advocate for a settlement that would resolve the uncertainty surrounding Native claims and clear the way for oil development. The response was the 1971 Alaska Native Claims Settlement Act ("ANCSA"). 85 Stat. 688, *codified as amended at* 43 U.S.C. § 1601 *et seq.* ANCSA permitted the 221 Alaska Native villages to reserve 44 million acres of land in exchange for relinquishing all claims to the 272 million acres they had previously used and occupied. 43 U.S.C. § 1603. (For more on ANCSA, see Chapter 12, *infra.*) In 1998, the Supreme Court held that lands set aside under ANCSA were not Indian Country.

ALASKA V. NATIVE VILLAGE OF VENETIE TRIBAL GOVERNMENT

522 U.S. 520, 118 S. Ct. 948, 140 L. Ed. 2d 30 (1998)

JUSTICE THOMAS delivered the opinion of the Court.

In this case, we must decide whether approximately 1.8 million acres of land in northern Alaska, owned in fee simple by the Native Village of Venetie Tribal Government pursuant to the Alaska Native Claims Settlement Act, is "Indian country." We conclude that it is not, and we therefore reverse the judgment below.

*** The Village of Venetie, which is located in Alaska above the Arctic Circle, is home to the Neets'aii Gwich'in Indians. In 1943, the Secretary of the Interior created a reservation for the Neets'aii Gwich'in out of the land surrounding Venetie and another nearby tribal village, Arctic Village. *** This land, which is about the size of Delaware, remained a reservation until 1971, when Congress enacted the Alaska Native Claims Settlement Act (ANCSA). ***

In enacting ANCSA, Congress sought to end the sort of federal supervision over Indian affairs that had previously marked federal Indian policy. ANCSA's text states that the settlement of the land claims was to be accomplished:

> without litigation, with maximum participation by Natives in decisions affecting their rights and property, without establishing any permanent racially defined institutions, rights, privileges, or obligations, [and] *without creating a reservation system or lengthy wardship or trusteeship*."

43 U.S.C. § 1601(b) (emphasis added).

To this end, ANCSA revoked "the various reserves set aside *** for Native use" by legislative or Executive action, except for the Annette Island Reserve inhabited by the Metlakatla Indians, and completely extinguished all aboriginal claims to Alaska land. 43 U.S.C. §§ 1603, 1618(a). In return, Congress authorized the transfer of $962.5 million in state and federal funds and approximately 44 million acres of Alaska land to state-chartered private business corporations that were to be formed pursuant to the statute; all of the shareholders of these corporations were required to be Alaska Natives. §§ 1605, 1607, 1613. The ANCSA corporations received title to the transferred land in fee simple, and no federal restrictions applied to subsequent land transfers by them.

Pursuant to ANCSA, two Native corporations were established for the Neets'aii Gwich'in, one in Venetie, and one in Arctic Village. In 1973, those corporations elected to make use of a provision in ANCSA allowing Native corporations to take title to former reservation lands set aside for Indians prior to 1971, in return for forgoing the statute's monetary payments and transfers of nonreservation land. 43 U.S.C. § 1618(b). The United States conveyed fee simple title to the land constituting the former Venetie Reservation to the two corporations as tenants in common; thereafter, the corporations transferred title to the land to the Native Village of Venetie Tribal Government (Tribe).

In 1986, the State of Alaska entered into a joint venture agreement with a private contractor for the construction of a public school in Venetie, financed with state funds. In December 1986, the Tribe notified the contractor that it owed the Tribe approximately $161,000 in taxes for conducting business activities on the Tribe's land. When both the contractor and the State, which under the joint venture agreement was the party responsible for paying the tax, refused to pay, the Tribe attempted to collect the tax in tribal court from the State, the school district, and the contractor.

The State then filed suit in Federal District Court for the District of Alaska and sought to enjoin collection of the tax. [The State alleged that the tribe was not a tribe with powers of self-government and that the tribal lands were not Indian country. The District Court held that the tribe did exist as a factual and legal matter, but that the lands were not a dependent Indian community. The Court of Appeals for the Ninth Circuit reversed and held that the lands were Indian country.]

***

Because ANCSA revoked the Venetie Reservation, and because no Indian allotments are at issue, whether the Tribe's land is Indian country depends on whether it falls within the "dependent Indian communities" prong of the [Indian Country] statute, 18 U.S.C. § 1151(b). Since 18 U.S.C. § 1151 was enacted in 1948, we have not had an occasion to interpret the term "dependent Indian communities." We now hold that it refers to a limited category of Indian lands that are neither reservations nor allotments, and that satisfy two requirements—first, they must have been set aside by the Federal Government for the use of the Indians as Indian land; second, they must be under federal superintendence. ***

Before § 1151 was enacted, we held in three cases that Indian lands that were not reservations could be Indian country and that the Federal Government could therefore exercise jurisdiction over them. *See United States v. Sandoval*, 231 U.S. 28 (1913); *United States v. Pelican*, 232 U.S. 442 (1914); *United States v. McGowan*, 302 U.S. 535 (1938). [In *Sandoval*, we] rejected the contention that federal power could not extend to the Pueblo lands because, unlike Indians living on reservations, the Pueblos owned their lands in fee simple. *Id.* at 48. We indicated that the Pueblos' title was not fee simple title in the commonly understood sense of the term. Congress had recognized the Pueblos' title to their ancestral lands by statute, and Executive orders had reserved additional public lands "for the [Pueblos'] use and occupancy." *Id.* at 39. In addition, Congress had enacted legislation with respect to the lands "in the exercise of the Government's guardianship over th[e] [Indian] tribes and their affairs," *id.* at 48, including federal restrictions on the lands' alienation. Congress therefore could exercise jurisdiction over the Pueblo lands, under its general power over "all dependent Indian communities within its borders, whether within its original territory or territory subsequently acquired, and whether within or without the limits of a State." *Id.* at 46. ***

In *United States v. McGowan*, we held that the Reno Indian Colony in Reno, Nevada, was Indian country even though it was not a reservation. 302 U.S. at 539. We reasoned that, like Indian reservations generally, the colony had been " 'validly set apart for the use of the Indians *** under the superintendence of the Government.' " We noted that the Federal Government had created the colony by purchasing the land with "funds appropriated by Congress" and that the Federal Government held the colony's land in trust for the benefit of the Indians residing there. 302 U.S. at 537 and n.4. We also emphasized that the Federal Government possessed the authority to enact "regulations and protective laws respecting th[e] [colony's] territory," *id.* at 539, which it had exercised in retaining title to the land and permitting the Indians to live there. For these reasons, a federal statute requiring the forfeiture of automobiles carrying "intoxicants" into the Indian country applied to the colony; we noted that the law was an example of the protections that Congress had extended to all "dependent Indian communities" within the territory of the United States. *Id.* at 538.

In each of these cases, therefore, we relied upon a finding of both a federal set-aside and federal superintendence in concluding that the Indian lands in question constituted Indian country and that it was permissible for the Federal Government to exercise jurisdiction over them. Section 1151 does not purport to alter this definition of Indian country.[5] ***

5. In attempting to defend the Court of Appeals' judgment, the Tribe asks us to adopt a different conception of the term "dependent Indian communities." Borrowing from Chief Justice Marshall's seminal opinions in *Cherokee Nation v. Georgia*, 30 U.S. 1, 5 Pet. 1, 8 L.Ed. 25 (1831), and *Worcester v. Georgia*, 31 U.S. 515, 6 Pet. 515, 8 L.Ed. 483 (1832), the Tribe argues that the term refers to political dependence, and that Indian country exists wherever land is owned by a federally recognized tribe. Federally recognized tribes, the Tribe contends, are "domestic

We therefore must conclude that in enacting § 1151(b), Congress indicated that a federal set-aside *and* a federal superintendence requirement must be satisfied for a finding of a "dependent Indian community"—just as those requirements had to be met for a finding of Indian country before 18 U.S.C. § 1151 was enacted. *** The federal set-aside requirement ensures that the land in question is occupied by an "Indian community"; the federal superintendence requirement guarantees that the Indian community is sufficiently "dependent" on the Federal Government that the Federal Government and the Indians involved, rather than the States, are to exercise primary jurisdiction over the land in question. ***

The Tribe's ANCSA lands do not satisfy either of these requirements. ***

With respect to the federal set-aside requirement, it is significant that ANCSA, far from designating Alaskan lands for Indian use, revoked the existing Venetie Reservation, and indeed revoked all existing reservations in Alaska "*set aside* by legislation or by Executive or Secretarial Order *for Native use*," save one. 43 U.S.C. § 1618(a) (emphasis added). ***

The Tribe argues—and the Court of Appeals majority agreed—that the ANCSA lands were set apart for the use of the Neets'aii Gwich'in, "as such," because the Neets'aii Gwich'in acquired the lands pursuant to an ANCSA provision allowing Natives to take title to former reservation lands in return for forgoing all other ANCSA transfers. The difficulty with this contention is that ANCSA transferred reservation lands to private, state-chartered Native corporations, without any restraints on alienation or significant use restrictions, and with the goal of avoiding "any permanent racially defined institutions, rights, privileges, or obligations." § 1601(b). *** By ANCSA's very design, Native corporations can immediately convey former reservation lands to non-Natives, and such corporations are not restricted to using those lands for Indian purposes. Because Congress contemplated that non-Natives could own the former Venetie Reservation, and because the Tribe is free to use it for non-Indian purposes, we must conclude that the federal set-aside requirement is not met. ***

Equally clearly, ANCSA ended federal superintendence over the Tribe's lands. *** Congress stated explicitly that ANCSA's settlement provisions were intended to avoid a "lengthy wardship or trusteeship." § 1601(b). After ANCSA, federal protection of the Tribe's land is essentially limited to a statutory declaration that the land is exempt from adverse possession claims, real property taxes, and certain judgments as long as it has not been sold, leased, or developed. *See* § 1636(d). These protections, if they can be called that, simply do not approach the level of superintendence over the Indians' land that existed in our prior cases. In each of those cases, the Federal Government actively

---

dependent nations," *Cherokee Nation v. Georgia, supra,* at 17,and thus ipso facto under the superintendence of the Federal Government. See Brief for Respondents 23–24.

This argument ignores our Indian country precedents, which indicate both that the Federal Government must take some action setting apart the land for the use of the Indians "as such," and that it is the land in question, and not merely the Indian tribe inhabiting it, that must be under the superintendence of the Federal Government. See, e.g., *United States v. McGowan,* 302 U.S. 535, 539, 58 S. Ct. 286, 288, 82 L.Ed. 410 (1938) ("The Reno Colony has been validly set apart for the use of the Indians. It is under the superintendence of the Government. The Government retains title to the lands which it permits the Indians to occupy"); *United States v. Pelican,* 232 U.S. 442, 449, 34 S. Ct. 396, 399, 58 L.Ed. 676 (1914) (noting that the Federal Government retained "ultimate control" over the allotments in question).

controlled the lands in question, effectively acting as a guardian for the Indians. *** Finally, it is worth noting that Congress conveyed ANCSA lands to state-chartered and state-regulated private business corporations, hardly a choice that comports with a desire to retain *federal* superintendence over the land.

The Tribe contends that the requisite federal superintendence is present because the Federal Government provides "desperately needed health, social, welfare, and economic programs" to the Tribe. *** Our Indian country precedents, however, do not suggest that the mere provision of "desperately needed" social programs can support a finding of Indian country. Such health, education, and welfare benefits are merely forms of general federal aid; considered either alone or in tandem with ANCSA's minimal land-related protections, they are not indicia of active federal control over the Tribe's land sufficient to support a finding of federal superintendence.

The Tribe's federal superintendence argument, moreover, is severely undercut by its view of ANCSA's primary purposes, namely, to effect Native self-determination and to end paternalism in federal Indian relations. *** The broad federal superintendence requirement for Indian country cuts against these objectives, but we are not free to ignore that requirement as codified in 18 U.S.C. § 1151. Whether the concept of Indian country should be modified is a question entirely for Congress. ***

NOTES AND QUESTIONS

1. Alaska Native Villages have the same legal status as other tribes and are included on the Secretary of the Interior's list of federally recognized tribes. 84 Fed. Reg. 1200 (2019). They receive all the special federal health, education, and welfare services provided to native peoples. Since the self-determination era, all of these services have been directed toward increasing Native self-determination. Does this mean that no Indian community can be considered under "federal superintendence" as the two-prong dependent Indian community test requires? What would qualify as federal superintendence under the Court's reasoning?

2. What about the federal set-aside requirement? The Venetie lands were clearly set aside for the Gwich'in villages under a federal statute, ANCSA, which also exempts the lands from state or local taxation. Why did the Court hold that this was not a sufficient set-aside? *Sandoval* had declared lands held in fee simple to be Indian country. Is it simply the fact that the lands can be sold that distinguishes the Indian lands, or is it the distinctive purposes and language of ANCSA?

3. Part of the reason the Venetie villages may have sought to raise money through taxation is that in order to exercise the option to retain their former reservation lands, they had to give up the right to share in profits from Native corporation lands under 43 U.S.C. § 1606(i) and the right to a share in ANCSA settlement funds. *See* 43 U.S.C. § 1618(b).

4. The Supreme Court's apparently narrow definition of superintendence and set-aside in *Venetie* created questions about non-reservation lands outside of Alaska. In particular, it raises issues about the various pueblos of

New Mexico. The pueblo boundaries were established by Spanish land grants that gave the pueblos a communal right to the lands in fee simple; Congress confirmed these grants after the United States assumed sovereignty over the area. Act of December 22, 1858, 35th Cong., 11 Stat. 374 (1858). Today, much land within these pueblo boundaries is owned by non-Indians; indeed, the town of Taos is located within the Taos Pueblo. After *Venetie*, two cases arose in which the state sought to prosecute pueblo members for crimes committed on non-Indian fee lands within the boundaries of the Pojoaque and Taos Pueblos. The New Mexico Supreme Court held that the pueblos as a whole met the definition of a dependent Indian community. *State v. Romero*, 142 P.3d 887 (N.M. 2006). Although the state argued that dependent Indian communities encompassed only restricted lands actually owned by Indians, the court held that § 1151(b) created "a functional definition focusing on the federal purpose in recognizing or establishing a reasonably distinct location for the residence of tribal Indians under federal protection. This definition supplanted the earlier reliance on land title, which had become impractical owing to allotments, reservation openings and rights-of-way." 142 P.2d at 893. The court also distinguished *Venetie* on the ground that "Congress and the United States Supreme Court have established that pueblo lands are Indian country." *Id.* at 892. *Cf.*, *State v. Quintana*, 178 P.3d 820, 821 (N.M. 2008) (finding a state road serving as the border between Santo Domingo Pueblo and Cochiti Pueblo was not within the boundaries of either pueblo and thus not Indian country).

5. *Venetie* also left open the question of how to determine the relevant boundaries of a "community" for assessing whether an area is a "dependent Indian community." Should courts look only to the particular plot of land where the disputed activities occur? Or should "community" encompass a broader area, defined by political, social and cultural boundaries? *Venetie* itself did not address this question, but subsequent courts have wrestled with it. Those resisting a finding of Indian country opt for the narrower definition if the actions arise on non-Indian fee lands within a broader area that has an Indian character. Those supporting a finding of Indian country, not surprisingly, contend that § 1151(b)'s plain meaning requires the broader view. In *Hydro Res., Inc. v. U.S. E.P.A.*, 608 F.3d 1131, 1148 (10th Cir. 2010) the *en banc* court of appeals rejected the broad view and held that dependent Indian communities under § 1151(b) consist only of lands explicitly set aside for Indian use by Congress (or its designee), and which are also under federal superintendence. The court stated that "[t]he superintendence requirement means that the federal government currently must be actively controlling the lands in question, effectively acting as a guardian for the Indians."

6. Is there jurisdiction without Indian country? In *John v. Baker*, 982 P.2d 738 (Alaska 1999), the Alaska Supreme Court held that although Alaska Native villages lacked Indian country, they retained jurisdiction over certain matters. The court held that an Alaska Native village had the power to adjudicate a child custody dispute between a member of the village and a member of another tribe who voluntarily submitted herself to the jurisdiction of the tribal court. The court ruled that "in determining whether tribes retain their sovereign powers, the United States Supreme Court looks to the character of the power that the tribe seeks to exercise, not merely the location of the events," 982 P.2d at 752, and that the child custody dispute was at the "core of sovereignty—a tribe's inherent power to determine membership, to regulate

domestic relations among members, and to prescribe rules of inheritance for members." *Id.* at 758. Because the tribal court had jurisdiction over the dispute, the state court gave effect to the decision under the doctrine of comity. *John v. Baker*, 30 P.3d 68 (Alaska 2001); *see also Simmonds v. Parks*, 329 P.3d 995, 101 (Alaska 2014) ("[T]ribal court judgments in ICWA-defined child custody proceedings are entitled to full faith and credit to the same extent as a judgment of a sister state"); *McCrary v. Ivanof Bay Vill.*, 265 P.3d 337, 340 (Alaska 2011) ("Alaska Native tribes, by virtue of their sovereign powers, have concurrent tribal jurisdiction to adjudicate certain child custody disputes involving tribal members."); *In the Matter of C.R.H.*, 29 P.3d 849 (Alaska 2001) (Alaska Native villages may accept jurisdiction over Indian Child Welfare Act cases transferred from state court); *State v. Cent. Council of Tlingit & Haida Indian Tribes of Alaska*, 371 P.3d 255 (Alaska 2016) (upholding tribal jurisdiction to set non-member child support obligations).

D. FEDERAL EXPANSION OF INDIAN COUNTRY: 25 U.S.C. § 465

To reverse the effect of allotment on Indian land holdings, Section 5 of the Indian Reorganization Act authorized the Secretary of the Interior "in his discretion, to acquire, through purchase, relinquishment, gift, exchange, or assignment, any interest in lands, water rights, or surface rights to lands, within or without existing reservations, including trust or otherwise restricted allotments, whether the allottee be living or deceased, for the purpose of providing land for Indians. *** Title to any lands or rights acquired pursuant to this Act *** shall be taken in the name of the United States in trust for the Indian tribe or individual Indian for which the land is acquired, and such lands or rights shall be exempt from State and local taxation." 25 U.S.C. § 465.

Would such lands constitute Indian country under 18 U.S.C. § 1151? If so, under which provision? Consider the fact that 25 U.S.C. § 467 provides that "[t]he Secretary of the Interior is hereby authorized to proclaim new Indian reservations on lands acquired pursuant to any authority conferred by this Act [the IRA], or to add such lands to existing reservations[.]"

Today, land-into-trust applications generally begin with the petitioning tribe purchasing land and then requesting the Bureau of Indian Affairs to accept it into trust. Unless directed by another statute, regulations provide that the Secretary may only take land into trust "(1) When the property is located within the exterior boundaries of the tribe's reservation or adjacent thereto, or within a tribal consolidation area; or (2) When the tribe already owns an interest in the land; or (3) When the Secretary determines that the acquisition of the land is necessary to facilitate tribal self-determination, economic development, or Indian housing." 25 C.F.R. § 151.3. In addition, the Secretary must consider the need of the tribe for the land, the purposes for which it will be used, the impact on the state and local government of removal of the land from the tax rolls, and jurisdictional and land use conflicts the acquisition may cause. 25 C.F.R. § 151.10. Where the land is not within the tribe's existing reservation, the Secretary must also consider the distance from the reservation, giving greater scrutiny to the acquisition the greater the distance, and greater weight to state and local government statements regarding regulatory and taxation impacts of the acquisition. 25 C.F.R. § 151.11. The regulations as adopted did not apply to Alaska, but a district court held that limitation was invalid under the statute, and the Department of the Interior finalized a rule allowing trust land acquisitions in Alaska. *See* 79 Fed. Reg. 76,888 (Dec. 23, 2014). The court of appeals determined that the controversy between Akiachak and the Department of the Interior was moot and dismissed the State of Alaska's attempt to appeal as the State had brought no independent claim for relief when it intervened in the case. The court also vacated the lower court rulings. *Akiachak Native Comty. v. U.S. Dep't of the Interior*, 827 F.3d 100 (D.C. Cir. 2016). The state declined to appeal so the rule is now in effect, and land was taken in trust for the tribe located in Craig, Alaska. Land Acquisitions: Craig Tribal Association, 82 Fed. Reg. 4915 (2017) (1.08 acres). The Trump Administration announced a six-month review process of the regulation and its legality. *Withdrawal of Sol. Op. M-37043. "Authority to Acquire Land into Trust in Alaska," Pending Review*, Sol. Op. M-37053 (June 29, 2018).

In *Confederated Tribes of the Grand Ronde Community of Oregon v. Jewell*, 830 F3d. 552 (D.C. Cir. 2016) the court upheld a decision by the Secretary of the Interior to take into trust 152 acres of land for the Cowlitz Indian Tribe for gaming purposes. The Cowlitz Tribe had become federally recognized in 2002 so the Secretary was required to determine if the Tribe was "under Federal jurisdiction" in 1934 in order to meet the legal standard set out in *Carcieri*.

> The Secretary interpreted "now under Federal jurisdiction" to require a two-part inquiry. First, the Secretary considers:
>
>> whether there is a sufficient showing in the tribe's history, at or before 1934, that it was under federal jurisdiction, *i.e.*, whether the United States had in 1934 or at some point in the tribe's history prior to 1934, taken an action or series of actions—through a course of dealings or other relevant acts for or on behalf of the tribe or in some instance tribal members—that are sufficient to establish, or that generally reflect federal obligations, duties, responsibility for or authority over the tribe by the Federal Government.
>
> The second part of the test takes into account whether the Federal-jurisdiction status remained intact in 1934.
>
>> Applying this test, the Secretary detailed the government's course of dealings with the Cowlitz dating from failed treaty negotiations at the 1855 Chehalis River Treaty Council, to acknowledgment and communication with Cowlitz chiefs in the late 19th century, to government provision of services into the 1900s, to supervision in the 1920s by the local Taholah Agency, to organization and claims efforts leading up to the ICC award, to allotment activities. Another "important action by the Federal Government evidencing the Tribe was under federal jurisdiction in 1934" was Interior's approval of an attorney contract for the Tribe in 1932, pursuant to a statute that required contracts between Indian tribes and attorneys be approved by the Commissioner of Indian Affairs and Secretary. Furthermore, the Secretary explicitly rejected arguments relating to the 2005 NIGC Restored Lands Opinion, which discussed the lack of a government-

> to-government relationship with the Tribe, as conflating the modern, political concept of recognition with that used in the IRA, which was closer to an "ethnological and cognitive" concept. In any event, the Secretary explained, "recognition is not the inquiry before us. Rather, it is the concept of federal jurisdiction that is addressed."* * *

> The Secretary's two-part test is furthermore reasonable. It makes sense to take treaty negotiations into account, as one of several factors reflecting authority over a tribe, even if they did not ultimately produce agreement. This is all the more so given the context within which the particular negotiations at issue occurred. The Cowlitz refused to sign an 1855 land cession treaty proposed at the Chehalis River Treaty Council, whereby Governor Stevens of the Washington Territory and other federal agents sought to move the Cowlitz to a reservation on the Pacific Coast. The Cowlitz resisted relocation and refused the treaty, but years later the United States offered the Cowlitz's land for sale to settlers without compensation anyway. As the District Court explained, the fact that the government nevertheless took the Cowlitz land even after the tribe resisted the treaty corroborates that the government treated the Cowlitz as under its jurisdiction.

Land-into-trust decisions are often the target of extended litigation by states and other parties.[2] *See* Frank Pommersheim, *Land into Trust: An Inquiry into Law, Policy, and History*, 519 Idaho L. Rev. 519 (2013). In *Carcieri v. Salazar*, 555 U.S. 379 (2009) the Court considered a challenge by the Governor of Rhode Island to the Department of the Interior's decision to take land into trust for the Narragansett Tribe. The Court denied review on the nondelegation issue, but held that the Tribe, which was not federally recognized until 1983, was not eligible to have land taken into trust for it under the Indian Reorganization Act on the ground that the statute applied only to tribes "that were under the federal jurisdiction of the United States when the IRA was enacted in 1934." *Id.* at 395. Since the Narragansett Tribe had not disputed the assertion that they were neither recognized nor under federal jurisdiction in 1934, the Court held that the IRA did not authorize the trust land acquisition. The decision undermined the long-standing assumptions and practice of the Department of the Interior and has led to proposals for a congressional fix, but these have not yet been successful.

Match-E-Be-Nash-She-Wish Band of Pottawatomi Indians v. Patchak, 132 S. Ct. 2199 (2012), extends the potential impact of *Carcieri* to lands already in trust when the case was decided. Before *Match-E-Be-Nash-She-Wish-Band*, three courts of appeals had held that the limited waiver of federal sovereign immunity under the Quiet Title Act precluded judicial review of decisions to take land into trust after the title had actually been recorded in the name of the United States. *See Neighbors for Rational Development, Inc. v. Norton*, 379

---

2. There have been a number of challenges arguing that Section 465 is an unconstitutional delegation of congressional authority to the Secretary, but decisions in multiple circuits now reject this claim. *Carcieri v. Norton*, 423 F.3d 45, 58 (1st Cir. 2005), *rev'd on other grounds sub nom. Carcieri v. Salazar*, 555 U.S. 379 (2009); *South Dakota v. U.S. Dept. of the Interior*, 423 F.3d 790 (8th Cir. 2005); *United States v. Roberts*, 185 F.3d 1125, 1137 (10th Cir. 1999); *Mich. Gambling Opposition v. Kempthome*, 525 F.3d 23, 33 (D.C. Cir. 2008).

F.3d 956, 961-962 (10th Cir. 2004); *Metropolitan Water Dist. of Southern Cal. v. United States,* 830 F.2d 139, 143-144 (9th Cir. 1987) (*per curiam*); *Florida Dept. of Bus. Regulation v. Department of Interior,* 768 F.2d 1248, 1253-1255 (11th Cir. 1985). However, in *Match-E-Be-Nash-She-Wish Band,* the Supreme Court held that the Quiet Title Act did not apply to challenges where the plaintiffs did not claim title for themselves, so that neighbors could challenge land-into-trust decisions under the APA. Under the APA, individuals arguably have six years after the land was taken into trust to challenge the decision.

Part of the concern about land into trust decisions stems from fear of Indian gaming on off-reservation trust land. The Indian Gaming Regulatory Act, however, provides that land acquired by a tribe after 1988 cannot be used for Indian gaming unless the Secretary of the Interior first determines that gaming on the off-reservation land would be in the best interest of the tribe and not detrimental to the surrounding community. Second, gaming may not proceed unless the governor of the relevant state concurs in the Secretary's findings. Other exceptions to the off-reservation ban apply when the land is taken into trust (1) as part of a settlement of a land claim, (2) as the initial reservation for a newly recognized tribe, or (3) for a tribe restored to federal recognition. 25 U.S.C. § 2719(b)(1). *See, e.g., TOMAC v. Norton,* 433 F.3d 852, 865 (D.C. Cir. 2006) (finding that Pokagon Tribe was a "restored" tribe that could game on its land acquired after 1988).

III. ATTEMPTS TO RESTORE TRIBAL TERRITORY THROUGH LAND CLAIMS LITIGATION

In the *Passamaquoddy* and *Mashpee* decisions, the courts were determining tribal status as a prerequisite to considering whether the tribes could assert that their lands were taken from them in violation of federal law. Once the issue of tribal status is determined (and for many tribes this threshold question of federal status is obvious and need not be adjudicated), then the land claims cases can go forward. There are two strategies that tribes have pursued, both having their own hurdles and difficulties. One approach is to sue the federal government for its failure to enforce its laws prohibiting land sales to non-Indians, alleging treaty, trust, and statutory violations. These cases are exemplified by *Passamaquoddy Tribe v. Morton, supra*. The other approach is to sue the current land-owners, who are the beneficiaries of title that the tribes allege is invalid due to earlier violations of federal law. These cases, which arise predominately on the east coast where widespread violations of the Indian Nonintercourse Acts occurred, are fraught and sensitive in ways similar to the diminishment cases. The land claims cases raise, either directly or beneath the surface, concerns about non-Indian expectations and the extent to which courts are willing to right centuries-old wrongs.

COUNTY OF ONEIDA V. ONEIDA INDIAN NATION

470 U.S. 226, 105 S. Ct. 1245, 84 L.Ed.2d 169 (1985)

JUSTICE POWELL delivered the opinion of the Court.

These cases present the question whether three Tribes of the Oneida Indians may bring a suit for damages for the occupation and use of tribal land allegedly conveyed unlawfully in 1795.

I

The Oneida Indian Nation of New York, the Oneida Indian Nation of Wisconsin, and the Oneida of the Thames Band Council (the Oneidas) instituted this suit in 1970 against the Counties of Oneida and Madison, New York. The Oneidas alleged that their ancestors conveyed 100,000 acres to the State of New York under a 1795 agreement that violated the Trade and Intercourse Act of 1793 (Nonintercourse Act), 1 Stat. 329, and thus that the transaction was void. The Oneidas' complaint sought damages representing the fair rental value of that part of the land presently owned and occupied by the Counties of Oneida and Madison, for the period January 1, 1968, through December 31, 1969.

***

II

The respondents in these cases are the direct descendants of members of the Oneida Indian Nation, one of the six nations of the Iroquois, the most powerful Indian Tribe in the Northeast at the time of the American Revolution. From time immemorial to shortly after the Revolution, the Oneidas inhabited what is now central New York State. Their aboriginal land was approximately six million acres, extending from the Pennsylvania border to the St. Lawrence River, from the shores of Lake Ontario to the western foothills of the Adirondack Mountains.

Although most of the Iroquois sided with the British, the Oneidas actively supported the colonists in the Revolution. This assistance prevented the Iroquois from asserting a united effort against the colonists, and thus the Oneidas' support was of considerable aid. After the War, the United States recognized the importance of the Oneidas' role, and in the Treaty of Fort Stanwix, 7 Stat. 15 (Oct. 22, 1784), the National Government promised that the Oneidas would be secure "in the possession of the lands on which they are settled." Within a short period of time, the United States twice reaffirmed this promise, in the Treaties of Fort Harmer, 7 Stat. 33 (Jan. 9, 1789), and of Canandaigua, 7 Stat. 44 (Nov. 11, 1794).

During this period, the State of New York came under increasingly heavy pressure to open the Oneidas' land for settlement. Consequently, in 1788, the State entered into a "treaty" with the Indians, in which it purchased the vast majority of the Oneidas' land. The Oneidas retained a reservation of about 300,000 acres, an area that, the parties stipulated below, included the land involved in this suit.

In 1790, at the urging of President Washington and Secretary of War Knox, Congress passed the first Indian Trade and Intercourse Act, ch. 33, 1 Stat. 137. *See* 4 American State Papers, Indian Affairs, Vol. 1, p. 53 (1832); F. Prucha, American Indian Policy in the Formative Years 43–44 (1962). The Act prohibited the conveyance of Indian land except where such conveyances were entered pursuant to the treaty power of the United States. In 1793, Congress passed a stronger, more detailed version of the Act, providing that "no purchase or grant of lands, or of any title or claim thereto, from any Indians or nation or tribe of Indians, within the bounds of the United States, shall be of any validity in law or equity, unless the same be made by a treaty or convention entered into pursuant to the constitution *** [and] in the presence, and with the approbation of the commissioner or commissioners of the United States" appointed to supervise such transactions. 1 Stat. 330, § 8. Unlike the 1790 version, the new statute included criminal penalties for violation of its terms. [The statute is currently codified at 25 U.S.C. § 177.]

Despite Congress' clear policy that no person or entity should purchase Indian land without the acquiescence of the Federal Government, in 1795 the State of New York began negotiations to buy the remainder of the Oneidas' land. When this fact came to the attention of Secretary of War Pickering, he warned Governor Clinton, and later Governor Jay, that New York was required by the Nonintercourse Act to request the appointment of federal commissioners to supervise any land transaction with the Oneidas. The State ignored these warnings, and in the summer of 1795 entered into an agreement with the Oneidas whereby they conveyed virtually all of their remaining land to the State for annual cash payments. It is this transaction that is the basis of the Oneidas' complaint in this case.

The District Court found that the 1795 conveyance did not comply with the requirements of the Nonintercourse Act. In particular, the court stated that "[t]he only finding permitted by the record *** is that no United States Commissioner or other official of the federal government was present at the *** transaction." The petitioners did not dispute this finding on appeal. Rather, they argued that the Oneidas did not have a federal common-law cause of action for this violation. Even if such an action once existed, they contended that the Nonintercourse Act pre-empted it, and that the Oneidas could not maintain a private cause of action for violations of the Act. Additionally, they maintained that any such cause of action was time-barred or nonjusticiable, that any cause of action under the 1793 Act had abated, and that the United States had ratified the conveyance. The Court of Appeals, with one judge dissenting, rejected these arguments. Petitioners renew these claims here; we also reject them and affirm the court's finding of liability.

III

At the outset, we are faced with petitioner counties' contention that the Oneidas have no right of action for the violation of the 1793 Act. Both the District Court and the Court of Appeals rejected this claim, finding that the Oneidas had the right to sue on two theories: first, a common-law right of action for unlawful possession; and second, an implied statutory cause of action under the Nonintercourse Act of 1793. We need not reach the latter question as we think the Indians' common-law right to sue is firmly established.

A

Federal Common Law

By the time of the Revolutionary War, several well-defined principles had been established governing the nature of a tribe's interest in its property and how those interests could be conveyed. It was accepted that Indian nations held "aboriginal title" to lands they had inhabited from time immemorial. *See* Cohen, *Original Indian Title*, 32 Minn. L. Rev. 28 (1947). The "doctrine of discovery" provided, however, that discovering nations held fee title to these lands, subject to the Indians' right of occupancy and use. As a consequence, no one could purchase Indian land or otherwise terminate aboriginal title without the consent of the sovereign. *Oneida I*, 414 U.S. at 667.

With the adoption of the Constitution, Indian relations became the exclusive province of federal law. From the first Indian claims presented, this Court recognized the aboriginal rights of the Indians to their lands. The Court spoke of the "unquestioned right" of the Indians to the exclusive possession of their lands, *Cherokee Nation v. Georgia*, 5 Pet. 1, 17, and stated that the Indians' right of occupancy is "as sacred as the fee simple of the whites." *Mitchel v. United States*, 9 Pet. 711 (1835). This principle has been reaffirmed consistently. Thus, as we concluded in *Oneida I*, "the possessory right claimed [by the Oneidas] is a *federal* right to the lands at issue in this case." 414 U.S. at 671 (emphasis in original).

Numerous decisions of this Court prior to *Oneida I* recognized at least implicitly that Indians have a federal common-law right to sue to enforce their aboriginal land rights. In *Johnson v. McIntosh*, *supra*, the Court declared invalid two private purchases of Indian land that occurred in 1773 and 1775 without the Crown's consent. Subsequently in *Marsh v. Brooks*, 8 How. 223, 232 (1850), it was held: "That an action of ejectment could be maintained on an Indian right to occupancy and use, is not open to question. This is the result of the decision in *Johnson v. McIntosh*." More recently, the Court held that Indians have a common-law right of action for an accounting of "all rents, issues and profits" against trespassers on their land. *United States v. Santa Fe Pacific R. Co.*, 314 U.S. 339 (1941). Finally, the Court's opinion in *Oneida I* implicitly assumed that the Oneidas could bring a common-law action to vindicate their aboriginal rights. *Citing United States v. Santa Fe Pacific R. Co.*, *supra*, at 347, we noted that the Indians' right of occupancy need not be based on treaty, statute, or other formal Government action. We stated that "absent federal statutory guidance, the governing rule of decision would be fashioned by the federal court in the mode of the common law."

In keeping with these well-established principles, we hold that the Oneidas can maintain this action for violation of their possessory rights based on federal common law.

B

Pre-emption

Petitioners argue that the Nonintercourse Acts pre-empted whatever right of action the Oneidas may have had at common law ***. We find this view to be unpersuasive. In determining whether a federal statute pre-empts common-law causes of action, the relevant inquiry is whether the statute "[speaks] directly to [the] question" otherwise answered by federal common law. As we stated in *Milwaukee II*, federal common law is used as a "necessary expedient" when Congress has not "spoken to a particular issue." 451 U.S. 304, 315 (1981). The Nonintercourse Act of 1793 does not speak directly to the question of remedies for unlawful conveyances of Indian land. ***

We recognized in *Oneida I* that the Nonintercourse Acts simply "put in statutory form what was or came to be the accepted rule—that the extinguishment of Indian title required the consent of the United States." 414 U.S. at 678. Nothing in the statutory formulation of this rule suggests that the Indians' right to pursue common-law remedies was thereby pre-empted. Accordingly, we hold that the Oneidas' right of action under federal common law was not pre-empted by the passage of the Nonintercourse Acts.

IV

Having determined that the Oneidas have a cause of action under federal common law, we address the question whether there are defenses available to the counties. We conclude that none has merit.

A

Statute of Limitations

There is no federal statute of limitations governing federal common-law actions by Indians to enforce property rights. In the absence of a controlling federal limitations period, the general rule is that a state limitations period for an analogous cause of action is borrowed and applied to the federal claim, provided that the application of the state statute would not be inconsistent with underlying federal policies. We think the borrowing of a state limitations period in these cases would be inconsistent with federal policy. Indeed, on a number of occasions Congress has made this clear with respect to Indian land claims.

***

Congress recently reaffirmed this policy in addressing the question of the appropriate statute of limitations for certain claims brought by the United States on behalf of Indians. Originally enacted in 1966, this statute provided a special limitations period of 6 years and 90 days for contract and tort suits for damages brought by the United States on behalf of Indians. 28 U.S.C. §§ 2415(a), (b). The statute stipulated that claims that accrued prior to its date of enactment, July 18, 1966, were deemed to have accrued on that date. § 2415(g). Section 2415(c) excluded from the limitations period all actions "to establish the title to, or right of possession of, real or personal property."

In 1972 and again in 1977, 1980, and 1982, as the statute of limitations was about to expire for pre–1966 claims, Congress extended the time within which the United States could bring suits on behalf of the Indians. The legislative history of the 1972, 1977, and 1980 amendments demonstrates that Congress did not intend § 2415 to apply to suits brought by the Indians themselves, and that it assumed that the Indians' right to sue was not otherwise subject to any statute of limitations. Both proponents and opponents of the amendments shared these views. ***

With the enactment of the 1982 amendments, Congress for the first time imposed a statute of limitations on certain tort and contract claims for damages brought by individual Indians and Indian tribes. These amendments, enacted as the Indian Claims Limitation Act of 1982, Pub. L. 97–394, 96 Stat. 1976, note following 28 U.S.C. § 2415, established a system for the final resolution of pre–1966 claims cognizable under §§ 2415(a) and (b). The Act directed the Secretary of the Interior to compile and publish in the Federal Register a list of all Indian claims to which the statute of limitations provided in 28 U.S.C. § 2415 applied. The Act also directed that the Secretary notify those Indians who may have an interest in any such claims. The Indians were then given an opportunity to submit additional claims; these were to be compiled and published on a second list. Actions for claims subject to the limitations periods of § 2415 that appeared on neither list were barred unless commenced within 60 days of the publication of the second list.

The legislative history of the successive amendments to § 2415 is replete with evidence of Congress' concern that the United States had failed to live up to its responsibilities as trustee for the Indians, and that the Department of the Interior had not acted with appropriate dispatch in meeting the deadlines provided by § 2415. By providing a 1–year limitations period for claims that the Secretary decides not to pursue, Congress intended to give the Indians one last opportunity to file suits covered by § 2415(a) and (b) on their own behalf. Thus, we think the statutory framework adopted in 1982 presumes the existence of an Indian right of action not otherwise subject to any statute of limitations. It would be a violation of Congress' will were we to hold that a state statute of limitations period should be borrowed in these circumstances.

B

Laches

The dissent argues that we should apply the equitable doctrine of laches to hold that the Oneidas' claim is barred. Although it is far from clear that this defense is available in suits such as this one,[16] we do not reach this issue today. While petitioners argued at trial that the Oneidas were guilty of laches, the District Court ruled against them and they did not reassert this defense on appeal. As a result, the Court of Appeals did not rule on this claim, and we likewise decline to do so.

***

VI

The decisions of this Court emphasize "Congress' unique obligation toward the Indians." *Morton v. Mancari,* 417 U.S. 535, 555 (1974). The

16. We note, as Justice Stevens properly recognizes, that application of the equitable defense of laches in an action at law would be novel indeed. Moreover, the logic of the Court's holding in *Ewert v. Bluejacket,* 259 U.S. 129 (1922), seems applicable here: "the equitable doctrine of laches, developed and designed to protect good-faith transactions against those who have slept on their rights, with knowledge and ample opportunity to assert them, cannot properly have application to give vitality to a void deed and to bar the rights of Indian wards in lands subject to statutory restrictions." *Id.* at 138. Additionally, this Court has indicated that extinguishment of Indian title requires a sovereign act. *See, e.g., Oneida I,* 414 U.S. 661, 670 (1974); *United States v. Candelaria,* 271 U.S. 432, 439 (1926), quoting *United States v. Sandoval,* 231 U.S. 28, 45–47 (1913). In these circumstances, it is questionable whether laches properly could be applied. Furthermore, the statutory restraint on alienation of Indian tribal land adopted by the Nonintercourse Act of 1793 is still the law. *See* 25 U.S.C. § 177. This fact not only distinguishes the cases relied upon by the dissent, but also suggests that, as with the borrowing of state statutes of limitations, the application of laches would appear to be inconsistent with established federal policy. Although the issue of laches is not before us, we add these observations in response to the dissent.

Government, in an amicus curiae brief, urged the Court to affirm the Court of Appeals. The Government recognized, as we do, the potential consequences of affirmance. It was observed, however, that "Congress has enacted legislation to extinguish Indian title and claims related thereto in other eastern States, *** and it could be expected to do the same in New York should the occasion arise." *See* Rhode Island Indian Claims Settlement Act, 25 U.S.C. § 1701 *et seq.*; Maine Indian Claims Settlement Act, 25 U.S.C. § 1721 *et seq.* We agree that this litigation makes abundantly clear the necessity for congressional action.

One would have thought that claims dating back for more than a century and a half would have been barred long ago. As our opinion indicates, however, neither petitioners nor we have found any applicable statute of limitations or other relevant legal basis for holding that the Oneidas' claims are barred or otherwise have been satisfied. The judgment of the Court of Appeals is affirmed with respect to the finding of liability under federal common law,[27] and reversed with respect to the exercise of ancillary jurisdiction over the counties' cross-claim for indemnification. The cases are remanded to the Court of Appeals for further proceedings consistent with our decision.

***

It is so ordered.

JUSTICE STEVENS, with whom THE CHIEF JUSTICE [BURGER], JUSTICE WHITE, and JUSTICE REHNQUIST join, dissenting in No. 83–1065.

***

I believe that the equitable doctrine of laches, with its focus on legitimate reliance and inexcusable delay, best reflects the limitation principles that would have governed this ancient claim at common law—without requiring a historian's inquiry into the archaic limitation doctrines that would have governed the claims at any specific time in the preceding two centuries. Of course, the application of a traditional equitable defense in an action at law is something of a novelty. But this novel development in litigation involving Indian claims arose in order to benefit a special class of litigants, and it remains true that an equitable defense to the instant claim is less harsh than a straightforward application of the limitations rule dictated by our usual practice. At least equal to the maxim that equity follows the law is the truth that common-law real property principles were often tempered by equitable considerations—as the rules limiting a ward's power to avoid an unlawful conveyance demonstrate.

As the Court recognizes, the instant action arises under the federal common law, not under any congressional enactment, and in this context the Court would not risk frustrating the will of the Legislature by applying this familiar doctrine of equity. The merger of law and equity in one federal court is, of course, primarily procedural. Considering the hybrid nature of these claims and the evolving character of the common law, however, I believe that the

27. The question whether equitable considerations should limit the relief available to the present day Oneida Indians was not addressed by the Court of Appeals or presented to this Court by petitioners. Accordingly, we express no opinion as to whether other considerations may be relevant to the final disposition of this case should Congress not exercise its authority to resolve these far-reaching Indian claims.

application of laches as a limitation principle governing ancient Indian claims will promote uniformity of result in law and at equity, maintain the proper measure of flexibility to protect the legitimate interests of the tribes, while at the same time honoring the historic wisdom in the value of repose. ***

Given their burden of explaining nearly two centuries of delay in the prosecution of this claim, and considering the legitimate reliance interests of the counties and the other property owners whose title is derived from the 1795 conveyance, the Oneida have not adequately justified their delay.

Of course, the traditional rule was "that 'the conduct of Indians is not to be measured by the same standard which we apply to the conduct of other people.' But their very analogy to persons under guardianship suggests a limitation to their pupilage, since the utmost term of disability of an infant is but 21 years, and it is very rare that the relations of guardian and ward under any circumstances, even those of lunacy, are maintained for a longer period than this." *Felix v. Patrick*, 145 U.S., at 330–331 (quoting *The Kansas Indians,* 5 Wall. 737, 758 (1867)). In this case, the testimony at trial indicates that the Oneida people have independently held land derived from tribal allotments at least since the Dawes Act of 1887, and probably earlier in the State of New York. They have received formal schooling at least since 1796 in New York, and have gradually become literate in the English language. They have developed a sophisticated system of tribal government, and at various times in the past 175 years, have petitioned the Government for the redress of grievances, or sent commissions to confer with their brethren.

In all the years after the 1795 conveyance—until the years leading up to this litigation—the Oneida made few efforts to raise this specific grievance against the State of New York and the landowners holding under the State's title. Claims to lands in New York most often were only made in connection with generalized grievances concerning the Tribe's treatment at the hands of the United States Government. Although the Oneida plainly knew or should have known that they had conveyed their lands to the State of New York in violation of federal law, and that they might have some cause for redress, they inexplicably delayed filing a lawsuit on their claim until 175 years after the conveyance was made. Finally, "[t]here is no evidence that any of the plaintiffs or their predecessors ever refused or returned any of the payments received for the purported sale of land pursuant to the Treaty of 1795."

The Oneida have not met their formidable burden of disproving unjustifiable delay to the prejudice of others. In my opinion their cause of action is barred by the doctrine of laches. The remedy for the ancient wrong established at trial should be provided by Congress, not by judges seeking to rewrite history at this late date.

***

V

The Framers recognized that no one ought be condemned for his forefathers' misdeeds—even when the crime is a most grave offense against the Republic. The Court today ignores that principle in fashioning a common-law remedy for the Oneida Nation that allows the Tribe to avoid its 1795 conveyance 175 years after it was made. This decision upsets long-settled expectations in the ownership of real property in the Counties of Oneida and Madison,

New York, and the disruption it is sure to cause will confirm the common-law wisdom that ancient claims are best left in repose. The Court, no doubt, believes that it is undoing a grave historical injustice, but in doing so it has caused another, which only Congress may now rectify.

I respectfully dissent.

NOTES AND QUESTIONS

1. In the first round of litigation in the Oneida land claims case, the Supreme Court held that the tribes' claims were based in federal law, and therefore properly filed in federal court. *Oneida Indian Nation v. County of Oneida*, 414 U.S. 661 (1974) (*Oneida I*). The *Oneida I* Court stressed the relationship between the tribes and the federal government and the judicial recognition, extending back to *Johnson v. McIntosh*, that termination of tribal rights is "exclusively the province of federal law." *Id.* at 670.

2. Consider carefully the holding of the *Oneida II* decision. The Court upheld the district court's finding that the 1795 conveyance of Oneida lands violated the Nonintercourse Act, and then rejected each of the defendants' affirmative defenses. What was left for the lower court to do on remand? The district court eventually ordered recoveries of $15,994 from Oneida County and $18,970 from Madison County, plus prejudgment interest. *Oneida Indian Nation of N.Y. v. County of Oneida*, 217 F.Supp.2d 292, 310 (N.D. N.Y. 2002). Why was the Oneida Indian Nation requesting such narrow relief?

3. *Oneida I* and *Oneida II* cleared the way for Indian land claims cases to be brought in federal court, but the *Oneida II* majority and dissent also stressed that a congressional solution would be preferable. Many east coast tribes have succeeded in achieving legislative settlements of their land claims, often after initial rounds of litigation. *See, e.g.*, Rhode Island Indian Claims Settlement Act of 1978, 25 U.S.C. §§ 1701–1712; Maine Indian Claims Settlement Act, 25 U.S.C. §§ 1721–1735 (passed after the decision in the *Passamaquoddy* case, *supra*). Legislative solutions do not always end the jurisdictional disputes. The Narragansett Indian Tribe, for example, has engaged in repeated battles with Rhode Island concerning tribal versus state control over tribal lands. *See Narragansett Indian Tribe v. Rhode Island*, 449 F.3d 16 (1st Cir. 2006); *Carcieri v. Salazar*, 555 U.S. 379 (2009).

4. There is to date no legislative settlement of the claims of the Oneida Indian Nation or any of the other New York tribes. As a result, some New York tribes have pursued dual strategies of litigation and reacquisition of their former reservation lands through open market purchases. In terms of the litigation approach, armed with the *Oneida II* decision, tribes expanded their claims, requesting damages for a broader time frame as well as equitable relief. The lower courts, echoing Justice Stevens' dissent in *Oneida II*, often narrowed the forms of relief out of deference to expectations of current landowners who, albeit holders of illegitimate title, were not parties to the original wrongdoing. *See Cayuga Indian Nation of New York v. Village of Union Springs*, 390 F.Supp.2d 203 (N.D. N.Y. 2005) (recounting the litigation history, including dismissal of non-Indian landowners as defendants and narrowing of remedies to damages). Some damages claims were successful, but to achieve the goal of

restoring tribal territory, the land acquisition strategy seemed like a promising alternative. The Oneida Indian Nation pursued this approach and purchased parcels of land within its former reservation. As evident in the following case, even this approach ran into reluctance to revive what the Supreme Court viewed as old claims when they would upset current expectations.

In ***City of Sherrill v. Oneida Indian Nation of New York,*** 544 U.S. 197 (2005), the Court considered whether the City of Sherrill could impose property taxes on parcels of land purchased by the Oneida Indian Nation in 1997 and 1998. The parcels were within the tribe's original reservation boundaries, and the tribe argued that because *Oneida II* affirmed that the original transfers of these lands were void under the Nonintercourse Act, the tribe's sovereign authority over its territory was restored when it purchased the property and was restored to possession. As discussed in Chapter 7, *infra*, one of the bedrock principles of tribal sovereignty is that tribes are immune from state taxation within reservation boundaries. After the City brought eviction proceedings in state court against the Tribe for failure to pay property taxes, the Oneida Indian Nation brought suit in federal court for a declaration that tribal property was not subject to state taxation. The Court, in an opinion authored by Justice Ginsburg, held that the tribe could not assert "sovereign immunity" from taxes because too much time had passed since the wrong was committed:

> Our 1985 decision recognized that the Oneidas could maintain a federal common-law claim for damages for ancient wrongdoing in which both national and state governments were complicit. Today, we decline to project redress for the Tribe into the present and future, thereby disrupting the governance of central New York's counties and towns. Generations have passed during which non-Indians have owned and developed the area that once composed the Tribe's historic reservation. And at least since the middle years of the 19th century, most of the Oneidas have resided elsewhere. Given the longstanding, distinctly non-Indian character of the area and its inhabitants, the regulatory authority constantly exercised by New York State and its counties and towns, and the Oneidas' long delay in seeking judicial relief against parties other than the United States, we hold that the Tribe cannot unilaterally revive its ancient sovereignty, in whole or in part, over the parcels at issue. The Oneidas long ago relinquished the reins of government and cannot regain them through open-market purchases from current titleholders.

Interestingly, Justice Stevens, who in his *Oneida II* dissent had urged the Court to apply laches to the Oneida Indian Nation's land claims, dissented in *Sherrill*:

> [A]s a matter of equity I believe that the "principle that the passage of time can preclude relief," should be applied sensibly and with an even hand. It seems perverse to hold that the reliance interests of non-Indian New Yorkers that are predicated on almost two centuries of inaction by the Tribe do not foreclose the Tribe's enforcement of judicially created damages remedies for ancient wrongs, but do somehow mandate a forfeiture of a tribal immunity that has been consistently and uniformly

protected throughout our history. In this case, the Tribe reacquired reservation land in a peaceful and lawful manner that fully respected the interests of innocent landowners—it purchased the land on the open market. To now deny the Tribe its right to tax immunity—at once the most fundamental of tribal rights and the least disruptive to other sovereigns—is not only inequitable, but also irreconcilable with the principle that only Congress may abrogate or extinguish tribal sovereignty. I would not decide this case on the basis of speculation about what may happen in future litigation over other regulatory issues. For the answer to the question whether the City may require the Tribe to pay taxes on its own property within its own reservation is pellucidly clear. Under settled law, it may not.

NOTES AND QUESTIONS

1. Several commentators have criticized the Court's decision in *Sherrill*. Professor Joseph Singer has recounted the history of Indian tribes' ability to sue, and argued that, as a legal and practical matter, the Oneida Indian Nation and other tribes could not have brought their suits against the counties any sooner than the late 1960's, precisely when Oneida filed its first case. Joseph William Singer, *Nine–Tenths of the Law: Title, Possession & Sacred Obligations*, 38 Conn. L. Rev. 605 (2006); *see also* Curtis Berkey, City of Sherrill v. Oneida Indian Nation, 30 Am. Indian L. Rev. 373 (2005–2006) (noting that the Justices did not give the attorneys warning of their theory of the case until oral argument, preventing development of facts or doctrine regarding the laches test); Kathryn E. Fort, *The New Laches: Creating Title Where None Existed*, 16 Geo. Mason L. Rev. 357 (2009) (critiquing decision for failing to apply traditional laches doctrine). Others have pointed out that the Court may have felt constrained to apply laches as a way to dismiss the case, because neither Indian tax law nor reservation diminishment law could be readily deployed to rule in favor of the city. *See* Sarah Krakoff, City of Sherrill v. Oneida Indian Nation of New York: *A Regretful Postscript to the Taxation Chapter in Cohen's Handbook of Federal Indian Law*, 41 Tulsa L. Rev. 5 (2005). If these commentators are right, what explains the Court's decision here? Are non-Indian expectations and demographics, as in the diminishment cases, driving outcomes? If so, what role is there on the crowded, predominately non-Indian reservations of many east coast tribes for tribal territory and sovereignty? As a postscript, the Oneida Indian Nation is currently pursuing the only option left open to it by the *Sherrill* Court for asserting its sovereign immunity from taxation by seeking to have the land restored to federal trust status. In 2008, the federal government agreed to take 13,000 acres of Oneida land (including that at issue in *Sherrill*) into trust under 25 U.S.C. § 465. Although the counties and state immediately sued, they agreed to drop their objections as part of a settlement of a number of disputes in 2013. *See New York v. Jewell*, 6:08-CV-0644 LEK/DEP, 2014 WL 841764 (N.D.N.Y. Mar. 4, 2014).

2. The *Sherrill* Court stated that "the question of damages for the Tribe's ancient dispossession is not at issue in this case, and we therefore do not disturb our holding in *Oneida II*." *Sherrill*, 544 U.S. at 221. Despite the narrowness of its holding, *Sherrill* has had deeply unsettling effects on all of

the land claims cases. Lower courts have reversed findings of damages for tribes, drawing distinctions between damages rooted in equitable claims versus damages rooted in legal claims. *See Cayuga Indian Nation of New York v. Pataki,* 413 F.3d 266 (2nd Cir. 2005); *Oneida Indian Nation of New York v. New York,* 617 F.3d 114 (2nd Cir. 2010). In 2014, the Second Circuit dismissed the land claims of the Stockbridge-Munsee Indians, stating, "It is well-settled that claims by an Indian tribe alleging that it was unlawfully dispossessed of land early in America's history are barred by the equitable principles of laches, acquiescence, and impossibility." *Stockbridge-Munsee Cmty. v. New York,* 756 F.3d 163, 164 (2d Cir. 2014). Do you think that the Supreme Court foresaw this result? If not, what can it do at this point? Is there any possibility of a congressional solution to the problem of equitable defenses? Finally, with regard to the land claims cases in particular, is a legislative settlement for the New York tribes more or less likely after *Sherrill,* and how does your answer affect your view of the Court's decision?

3. On remand in *Sherrill,* the district court refused to allow the city to foreclose on the property based on the Nonintercourse Act and tribal sovereign immunity. *Oneida Indian Nation of New York v. Madison County,* 401 F.Supp.2d 219 (N.D. N.Y. 2005). Does this make any sense? Was the court making the best attempt at rough justice, given the convoluted doctrine? Now the situation is as follows: the Oneida Nation has aboriginal and legal title over the disputed parcels, but has lost its sovereignty to be free of city taxes, and the city has the power to tax, with no power to collect. The Second Circuit affirmed the district court decision on sovereign immunity grounds. 605 F.3d 149 (2d Cir. 2010). On October 12, 2010, the Supreme Court granted review on the sovereign immunity question, but before the case was heard the Oneida Indian Nation enacted a resolution agreeing to waive sovereign immunity with respect to tax foreclosures. The Supreme Court then vacated and remanded the Circuit Court decision with instructions to determine whether it should revisit its ruling in light of this factual development. *Madison County v. Oneida Indian Nation*, 131 S. Ct. 704 (2011). Why do you think the Oneida Indian Nation enacted this resolution, given that they had been defending the issue of their immunity from suit so strenuously in the courts?

After the Supreme Court remanded the case, the Second Circuit reversed the lower court's decision based on the Oneida Indian Nation's waiver of immunity, thereby allowing the County to foreclose on the properties in question. But the court rejected Madison County's argument that the entire Oneida Indian Nation's reservation had been disestablished, and it determined that the OIN would not owe penalties or interest on any taxes due before 2005. 665 F.3d 408 (2d Cir. 2011). Further foreclosure actions were dropped as part of the comprehensive 2013 settlement. *New York v. Jewell,* 6:08-CV-0644 LEK/DEP, 2014 WL 841764 (N.D.N.Y. Mar. 4, 2014).

Although those actions have settled, the Second Circuit held in 2014 that sovereign immunity prevented Seneca County from foreclosing on Cayuga property for failure to pay *ad valorem* taxes. *Cayuga Indian Nation of New York v. Seneca County*, 761 F.3d 218 (2d Cir. 2014). Where does that leave the county with respect to tax collection?

4. Land claims have created significant divisions between tribal and non-tribal communities. For tribes whose land was taken in violation of the

Nonintercourse Act, the claims represent a long overdue chance to correct a historic wrong. For current property owners, the claims unfairly punish them for decisions made long before their time. The sign pictured here, taken on a highway in upstate New York on Cayuga Lake outside Seneca Falls shows how frustration over land claims has led to backlash against tribal rights generally.

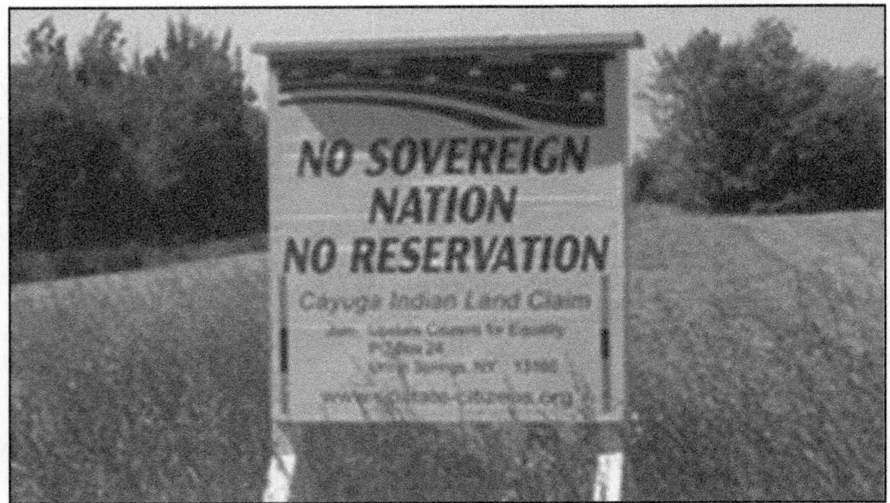

One of many signs that dotted the road along Cayuga Lake in June 2009 (photograph by Bethany Berger).

IV. FEDERAL ALLOCATION OF CRIMINAL JURISDICTION IN INDIAN COUNTRY

The allocation of federal jurisdiction provides one of the clearest examples of the pervasiveness of federal power in Indian country. The power to prosecute and punish crimes is often thought of as a fundamental expression of a community's notion of justice. Like other communities, tribal governments initially had complete control to express community norms in this manner. *See, e.g.*, Sidney Harring, Crow Dog's Case: American Indian Sovereignty, Tribal Law, and United States Law in the Nineteenth Century 104–105 (1994); Rennard Strickland, Fire and the Spirits: Cherokee Law from Clan to Court (1982), Karl N. Llewellyn & E. Adamson Hoebel, The Cheyenne Way (1941). Until the late 1800s, moreover, tribes retained exclusive jurisdiction to punish crimes between their members. Today, however, the federal government is the eight-hundred-pound gorilla of criminal jurisdiction in Indian country. As described by a law professor and former federal prosecutor:

> When a Navajo tribal member commits a serious felony against another Navajo on the remote Navajo Indian Reservation, the crime sets in motion not a tribal criminal investigation and tribal court proceeding, but a federal investigation and federal court proceeding under the federal Major Crimes Act. For trial, the Navajo defendant, the Navajo victim, and the witnesses (all of whom are also likely to be Navajo) will be summoned

> to a federal district court far away from the reservation and the specific community where the crime occurred. Unlike a felony involving only non-Indians, which would be routinely adjudicated at the local county or district courthouse, the Navajo felony will be tried in a distant federal court in Phoenix, Salt Lake City, or Albuquerque.
>
> The federal court operates in a language that is foreign to many Navajos; thus the Navajo defendants, victims, and witnesses may require interpreters to translate the proceedings. Neither the judge, the court reporter, the prosecutor, the court security officers, the deputy marshals, nor the defense attorney or investigator are likely to be Navajo or even understand or speak the Navajo language. Perhaps even more importantly, the federal jury that hears the evidence is unlikely to include a Navajo, or even an Indian, or any other member of the community where the crime occurred.

Kevin K. Washburn, *American Indians, Crime and the Law*, 104 Mich. L. Rev. 709, 710–11 (2006). This criminal justice system is not unique to Navajo but spans over a hundred reservations and involves thousands of felonies a year. *Id.* at 711.

The first federal laws regarding Indians specified federal punishments for non-Indians committing crimes in Indian country. Since the first Trade and Intercourse Act, Congress has specified punishments for non-Indians committing crimes against Indians. 1 Stat. 138 § 4 (1790). Since that time, new federal laws increasing federal jurisdiction over Indian people, combined with judicial decisions expanding state criminal jurisdiction and limiting tribal jurisdiction, have created what has been called a "jurisdictional maze" or "crazy-quilt" in Indian country. Robert N. Clinton, *Criminal Jurisdiction Over Indian Lands: A Journey Through a Jurisdictional Maze*, 18 Ariz. L. Rev. 503 (1976); Tim Vollmann, *Criminal Jurisdiction in Indian Country: Tribal Sovereignty and Defendants' Rights in Conflict*, 22 Kan. L. Rev. 387, 387 (1974).

The two federal statutes with the most influence on this jurisdictional maze are the Indian Country Crimes Act, 18 U.S.C. § 1152, and the Major Crimes Act, 18 U.S.C. § 1153. These statutes operate against two background presumptions: states have no criminal jurisdiction over Indians in Indian country, and tribes retain all aspects of their inherent sovereignty which Congress has not expressly taken away. These basic assumptions are limited by two developments, discussed further in later chapters and outlined briefly here. First, in Public Law 280, 18 U.S.C. § 1162, and other similar statutes, the federal government gave several states criminal jurisdiction over Indians in all or part of the Indian country found in those states. Second, in *Oliphant v. Suquamish Indian Tribe*, 435 U.S. 191 (1978), the Supreme Court held as a matter of federal common law that tribes could not exercise criminal jurisdiction over non-Indians. In *Duro v. Reina*, 495 U.S. 676 (1990), the Court held that tribes also lack criminal jurisdiction over Indians that were not their members, but Congress repudiated this holding in the so-called "*Duro* Fix," which affirms "the inherent power of Indian tribes *** to exercise criminal jurisdiction over all Indians" in their territory. 25 U.S.C. § 1301(2). Congress partially reversed the *Oliphant* decision in the Violence Against Women Reauthorization Act of 2013, which restores inherent tribal criminal jurisdiction over certain non-Indian perpetrators of domestic violence in Indian country. It is codified at 25 U.S.C. § 1304 and discussed below.

A. THE INDIAN COUNTRY CRIMES ACT, 18 U.S.C. § 1152

The Indian Country Crimes Act (also called the General Crimes Act) is a direct descendant of the initial Trade and Intercourse statutes. *See* 1 Stat. 137–138 (1790). These early laws were designed to control "lawless whites on the frontier" in order to fulfill treaty obligations and prevent retaliation between whites and Indians. Francis Paul Prucha, The Great Father: The United States Government and the American Indians 92 (1984). This effort was complemented by treaties acknowledging and facilitating tribal punishment of non-Indians. *See* Treaty with the Cherokees, Dec. 29, 1835, art. 5, 7 Stat. 478; Treaty with the Choctaw, October 18, 1820, art. 13, 7 Stat. 210; Treaty with the Wyandots, Delawares, Shawanoes, Ottawas, Chipewas, Putawatimes, Miamis, Eel-river, Weea's, Kickapoos, Piankashaws, and Kaskaskias, Aug. 3, 1795, art. 6, 7 Stat. 49; Treaty with the Chickasaws, Jan. 10, 1786, art. 5, 7 Stat. 24, 25. The laws did not initially address crimes committed by Indians within Indian country, and even crimes committed by Indians against non-Indians outside Indian country were handled diplomatically, by seeking compensation from the tribe to which the Indian offender belonged. *See* 2 Stat. 143–144 § 14 (1802). In 1817, however, the statute was amended to provide general federal jurisdiction over crimes by "any Indian, or other person or persons" in Indian country, excluding jurisdiction over crimes committed by one Indian against another and jurisdiction that would violate treaty stipulations. 3 Stat. 383 (1817). In 1854, another exception was provided for Indians who had been punished by the local law of the tribe. 10 Stat. 270. There have been few substantive changes since then to the law, which now provides that:

> Except as otherwise expressly provided by law, the general laws of the United States as to the punishment of offenses committed in any place within the sole and exclusive jurisdiction of the United States, except the District of Columbia, shall extend to the Indian country.
>
> This section shall not extend to offenses committed by one Indian against the person or property of another Indian, nor to any Indian committing any offense in the Indian country who has been punished by the local law of the tribe, or to any case where, by treaty stipulations, the exclusive jurisdiction over such offenses is or may be secured to the Indian tribes respectively.

Notice how this statute works: the federal criminal code adopted for areas of federal concern (*e.g.*, national parks, military bases) also applies in Indian country by virtue of the first paragraph of the statute, unless one of the exceptions in the second paragraph applies.

What do the text of the statute and the exceptions suggest about tribal legal systems? What is the extent of their jurisdiction? Does it reach non-Indians?

Notice that although crimes between Indians are excluded, there is no exception for crimes committed by one non-Indian against another. Following *Worcester v. Georgia*, which held that the state could not prosecute a non-Indian missionary for his activities on the Cherokee reservation, one would expect that states had no criminal jurisdiction over non-Indians in Indian country. This assumption had changed by the end of the 19th century, to the extent that the Court held that the federal government could not have criminal jurisdiction over crimes between non-Indians. In *United States v. McBratney*, 104 U.S. 621 (1881), the Court held that because the U.S. had admitted Colorado to statehood without reserving federal jurisdiction over reservations in the state's enabling act, it could not continue to exercise federal jurisdiction over a murder committed by one white man of another on the Ute Reservation. In *Draper v. United States*, 164 U.S. 240 (1896), the Court extended this holding to the state of Montana, whose enabling act renounced any title to Indian lands and declared that "said Indian lands shall remain under the absolute jurisdiction and control of the Congress of the United States." 164 U.S. at 244. Relying on the "equal footing doctrine," under which states are assumed to be admitted to the union on an equal footing with each other, the Court construed the enabling act not to preserve federal jurisdiction over crimes between non-Indians. 164 U.S. at 245. Although modern cases hold that the equal footing doctrine does not abrogate other principles of Indian law jurisdiction upon admission to statehood, *see Minnesota v. Mille Lacs Band of Chippewa Indians*, 526 U.S. 172, 204 (1999), the holdings of *McBratney* and *Draper* remain the law. *See New York ex rel Ray v. Martin*, 326 U.S. 496 (1946).

What if no federal law makes an act a crime? Federal statutory criminal law is fairly limited, as in most contexts states are the primary enforcers of criminal law. To fill in the gaps, Congress enacted the Assimilative Crimes Act (ACA) in 1825. The ACA applies to areas that are within (among other things) any waters subject to federal maritime or admiralty jurisdiction, as well as "[a]ny lands reserved or acquired for the use of the United States, and under the exclusive or concurrent jurisdiction thereof[.]" 18 U.S.C. § 7. It provides that whoever in these areas "is guilty of any act or omission which, although not made punishable by any enactment of Congress, would be punishable if committed or omitted within the jurisdiction of the State, Territory, Possession, or District in which such place is situated, by the laws thereof in force at the time of such act or omission, shall be guilty of a like offense and subject to a like punishment." 18 U.S.C. § 13. Although neither the ACA nor its legislative history mention Indian tribes, the Supreme Court assumed without analysis that the statute is applicable to Indian Country as one of the "general laws of the United States" referred to in the Indian Country Crimes Act. *See Williams v. U.S.*, 327 U.S. 711 (1946).

Williams involved the prosecution of a white married man for statutory rape of a 17–year–old girl on the Colorado River Indian reservation. *Id.* at 713. As there was no charge of lack of consent or force, there was no crime under federal criminal law; Arizona law, however, provided a minimum five-year sentence for anyone having sexual intercourse with a female under 18 years of age. *Id.* at 717. Although the Court stated that the Assimilative Crimes Act applied to Indian Country, it held that it did not permit application of the Arizona statute, because federal law defined the age of lawful consent at 16 years, and the act could not be used to reach a result inconsistent with federal law. *Id.* at 717–718. Since *Williams*, lower courts have applied the Assimilative Crimes Act to crimes in Indian country. *See, e.g., United States v. Billadeau*, 275 F.3d 692 (8th Cir. 2001) (using ACA to hold that federal officer had authority to stop non-Indian for driving while intoxicated on Fort Berthold Reservation).

More difficult questions arise when the Assimilative Crimes Act is used to prosecute so-called "victimless crimes" committed by Indians, which are arguably within the Indian versus Indian exception to the ICCA. It would seem that if the federal government lacks jurisdiction to prosecute "offenses committed by one Indian against the person or property of another Indian," 18 U.S.C. § 1152, it would equally lack jurisdiction to prosecute a crime committed by an Indian where no non-Indian was involved. *See* Cohen's Handbook of Federal Indian Law § 9.02[1][c] (2012). An early case took this view, rejecting an effort to prosecute two Sioux Indians for adultery:

> It is true that adultery is a voluntary act on the part of both participants, and, strictly speaking, not an offense against the person of either. But are the words of the exception to be taken so strictly? Murder and manslaughter are concededly offenses against the person, and much more serious than is adultery. Was it intended that a prosecution should lie for adultery, but not for murder or manslaughter? Rape also is concededly an offense against the person, and is generally regarded as among the most heinous, so much so that death is often prescribed as the punishment. Was it intended that a prosecution should lie for adultery, where the woman's participation is voluntary, but not for rape, where she is subjected to the same act forcibly and against her will? Is it not obvious that the words of the exception are used in a sense which is more consonant with reason? And are they not intended to be in accord with the policy reflected by the legislation of Congress and its administration for many years, that the relations of the Indians among themselves—the conduct of one toward another—is to be controlled by the customs and laws of the tribe, save when Congress expressly or clearly directs otherwise?

U.S. v. Quiver, 241 U.S. 602, 605–606 (1916). A more recent lower court case opined that *Quiver* should be limited to laws regarding domestic relations, an area of special tribal concern. *See United States v. Thunder Hawk*, 127 F.3d 705, 709 (8th Cir. 1997). Other cases have permitted prosecution of Indians for state crimes without a clear victim without fully considering the victimless crimes question. *See United States v. Marcyes*, 557 F.2d 1361, 1364–1365 (9th Cir. 1977) (prosecution for possession of fireworks); *United States v. Sosseur*, 181 F.2d 873 (7th Cir. 1950) (prosecution for operation of slot machines).

B. MAJOR CRIMES ACT, 18 U.S.C. § 1153

Until 1885, federal courts lacked any jurisdiction over crimes committed by one Indian against another. *See Ex Parte Crow Dog*, Ch. 3, *supra*. In reaction to the Court's *Crow Dog* decision, however, Congress enacted the Major Crimes Act, creating federal jurisdiction over certain serious felonies committed by Indians. The current version of the Major Crimes Act provides:

> (a) Any Indian who commits against the person or property of another Indian or other person any of the following offenses, namely, murder, manslaughter, kidnapping, maiming, [felony sexual abuse], incest, assault with intent to commit murder, assault with a dangerous weapon, assault resulting in serious bodily injury ***, an assault against an individual who has not attained the age of 16 years, arson, burglary, robbery,

and a [felony theft] within the Indian country, shall be subject to the same law and penalties as all other persons committing any of the above offenses, within the exclusive jurisdiction of the United States.

(b) Any offense referred to in subsection (a) of this section that is not defined and punished by Federal law in force within the exclusive jurisdiction of the United States shall be defined and punished in accordance with the laws of the State in which such offense was committed as are in force at the time of such offense.

Note that the Major Crimes Act applies only to Indian perpetrators but applies to crimes committed against either "another Indian or other person." The Ninth Circuit has held that a "person" cannot include a government agency, dismissing an indictment against a juvenile for burglarizing a BIA building. *United States v. Errol D., Jr.*, 292 F.3d 1159 (9th Cir. 2002).

One question that has arisen under the Major Crimes Act is whether it divests tribes of concurrent jurisdiction over the listed crimes, but there is little to support that position. First, consider what the language of the statute suggests. Compare it to the language of the ICCA. Consider also the purposes of the MCA: would Congress have wanted to prevent tribes from also exercising jurisdiction over these crimes? Which way do the Indian law canons of construction point? Now consider the (limited) legislative history: the language for the Major Crimes Act originally appeared in an 1885 bill that would have provided for trial in federal courts "and not otherwise." This phrase was deleted in an amendment because concurrent jurisdiction was believed to be sufficient. 16 Cong. Rec. 934–935 (1885). Finally, tribes continued to exercise criminal jurisdiction over felonies committed by tribal members well after the passage of the major crimes act. In *Talton v. Mayes*, 136 U.S. 376 (1896), discussed in Ch. 6., the Cherokee Nation prosecuted a tribal member for murder and neither the parties nor the Court raised any question about the tribe's jurisdiction over the crime.

While the Supreme Court has stated that concurrent tribal jurisdiction over Major Crimes is an "open question," *Duro v. Reina*, 495 U.S. 676, 680 n.1 (1990), the Ninth Circuit rejected a habeas petition challenging a tribal conviction for murder, holding that a tribal court is competent to try a tribal member for a crime covered by the Major Crimes Act. *Wetsit v. Stafne*, 44 F.3d 823, 825 (9th Cir. 1995).

The MCA provides for trial "in the same manner" as federal enclave and maritime prosecutions. 18 U.S.C. § 3242.

In *Keeble v. United States*, 412 U.S. 205 (1973), the Supreme Court ruled that an Indian charged with a major crime is entitled to a jury instruction on a lesser included offense.

C. BASIC CHART FOR FEDERAL CRIMINAL JURISDICTION

By reading the statutes closely, one can see that in non-Public Law 280 states where the crime is not one that falls within a federal statute of general application, federal criminal jurisdiction in Indian country looks like this:

If the perpetrator is a non-Indian:

— and the crime is one of the offenses specified in the Major Crimes Act, there is nonetheless no federal jurisdiction under that statute because it applies only to Indian perpetrators

— and the victim is non-Indian, there is exclusive state jurisdiction under McBratney.

— and the victim is Indian:

— if the crime violates either the federal criminal code or the criminal code of the state of occurrence, there is federal jurisdiction under the Indian Country Crimes Act.

— and there is no victim?

— unclear, but both states (under McBratney) and the federal government (under the ICCA) have exercised jurisdiction.

If the perpetrator is Indian:

— and the victim is Indian:

— if the crime is one of the enumerated major crimes, federal jurisdiction lies under the Major Crimes Act

— if the crime is not a "major crime," there is no jurisdiction under either the Major Crimes Act or the Indian Country Crimes Act (recall the first exception to the ICCA); hence, tribal criminal jurisdiction is exclusive

— and the victim is non-Indian:

— if it is a "major crime," there is federal jurisdiction under the Major Crimes Act

— if it is not a major crime there is federal jurisdiction under the Indian Country Crimes Act, unless the perpetrator has already been punished by the tribe.

D. WHO COUNTS AS AN "INDIAN"?

As you can see, determining Indian status is crucial in determining criminal jurisdiction. The term is defined differently in different areas of Federal Indian law. For purposes of criminal jurisdiction, there is a two-part test: (1) the person must have some Indian blood; and (2) the person must be "recognized" as an Indian by the tribe or the federal government. *See United States v. Maggi*, 598 F.3d 1073 (9th Cir. Mont. 2009); *United States v. Prentiss*, 273 F.3d 1277, 1280 (10th Cir. 2001). The first part of the test is a relic of the Supreme Court's 1846 decision that a white man who had been adopted as a citizen of the Cherokee Nation was not an Indian under the precursor to the Indian Country Crimes Act. *United States v. Rogers*, 45 U.S. 567 (1846); *see* Bethany R. Berger, *"Power Over this Unfortunate Race": Race, Politics and Indian Law in* United States v. Rogers, 45 Wm. & Mary L. Rev. 1957 (2004), for an extended history of the case.

The second part of the test requires affiliation with a federally recognized tribe; membership in a state recognized or terminated tribe is not sufficient. *See United States v. Maggi*, 598 F.3d 1073, at 1078 (9th Cir. Mont. 2009); *LaPier v. McCormick*, 986 F.2d 303, 305 (9th Cir. 1993); *State v. Sebastian*, 701 A.2d 13, 24–27 (Conn. 1997). Recent decisions have held that formal enrollment or even eligibility for enrollment is not necessary; instead, there must be evidence that the individual is recognized as politically, not merely racially, an Indian. *See United States v. Bruce*, 394 F.3d 1215 (9th Cir. 2005) (holding that a woman who was one-eighth Chippewa but not enrolled in tribe should have had her affirmative defense of Indian status submitted to the jury because she was born on a reservation and currently lived on one, participated in Indian religious ceremonies, had on several occasions been treated at Indian hospitals, and had previously been arrested by tribal authorities). Sometimes even fairly close cultural connections will not suffice, however. *United States v. Maggi*, 598 F.3d 1073 (9th Cir. Mont. 2009) (holding that man of 1/64 Blackfeet and 1/32 Cree descent whose mother was a member of the Blackfeet Tribe, who was ineligible for enrollment and had never lived on the reservation, but who as a "descendant member" was eligible for tribal health care, educational scholarships, and hunting and fishing rights, and who had been arrested and prosecuted by tribal officials several times, was not Indian); *In re Garvais*, 402 F.Supp.2d. 1219 (E.D. Wash. 2004) (holding that non-enrolled individual of tribal descent who grew up off-reservation, did not start holding himself out as Indian until his 20s, but had received Indian preference with the Bureau of Indian Affairs, possessed an eagle feather, and participated in sweats was not an Indian for purposes of criminal jurisdiction); *see also United States v. Antelope*, 430 U.S. 641, 647 n.7 (1977) (noting that "enrollment in an official tribe has not been held to be an absolute requirement for federal jurisdiction, at least where the Indian defendant lived on the reservation and 'maintained tribal relations with the Indians thereon,' " but not ruling on the question).

The Ninth Circuit, in a decision by the full *en banc* court, recently clarified its approach for determining who is an Indian for purposes of the federal criminal statutes. "We hold that proof of Indian status under the IMCA requires only two things: (1) proof of some quantum of Indian blood, whether or not that blood derives from a member of a federally recognized tribe, and (2) proof of membership in, or affiliation with, a federally recognized tribe." *United States v. Zepeda*, 792 F.3d 1103, 1113 (9th Cir. 2015), *cert. denied*, 136 S. Ct. 1712, (2016). The Court elaborated:

> On the first *Bruce* prong, the court should instruct the jury that it has to find beyond a reasonable doubt that the defendant has some quantum of Indian blood. On the second prong, the court should instruct the jury that it has to find beyond a reasonable doubt that the defendant was a member of, or affiliated with, a federally recognized tribe at the time of the offense. We described in our opinion in *Bruce* the criteria for such recognition. *Bruce,* 394 F.3d at 1224; *see also Cruz,* 554 F.3d at 846. We restate them here, emphasizing that each of these criteria requires a link to a federally recognized tribe. The criteria are, in declining order of importance: (1) enrollment in a federally recognized tribe; (2) government recognition formally and informally through receipt of assistance available only to individuals who are members, or are eligible to become members, of federally recognized tribes; (3) enjoyment of the benefits of affiliation with a federally recognized tribe; (4) social recognition as someone affiliated with a federally recognized tribe through residence on a reservation and participation in the social life of a federally recognized tribe. If the court has found that the tribe of which the government claims the defendant is a member, or with which the defendant is affiliated, is

federally recognized, it should inform the jury that the tribe is federally recognized as a matter of law.

United States v. Zepeda, 792 F.3d at 1114–15.

E. CRISIS OF CRIMINAL JUSTICE IN INDIAN COUNTRY

So how well does this jurisdictional crazy-quilt work? If statistics regarding victimization and incarceration provide any evidence, not very well. American Indians are two and a half times more likely to be the victims of violent crimes than the national average, and twice as likely as African Americans, the next most victimized group. The rate of rape is twice as high as it is for other groups, and one in three native women will be raped in her lifetime. The vast majority of crime is committed by people of the same race as the victim, yet about 70% of American Indian victims of violent crime reported that the offender was of a different race. (One problem with these figures, however, is that they do not distinguish Indian country crimes from those occurring outside of Indian jurisdictional boundaries.) *See* Steven W. Perry, U.S. Dep't of Justice, American Indians and Crime (2004), *available at* http://www.justice.gov/otj/pdf/american_indians_and_crime.pdf; Kevin K. Washburn, *Federal Criminal Law and Tribal Self–Determination*, 84 N.C.L. Rev. 779, 787 (2006); Sarah Deer, *Toward an Indigenous Jurisprudence of Rape*, 14 Kan. J. L. & Pub. Pol'y 121, 123 (2004). In a 2007 Report, Amnesty International called the difficulties faced by American Indian and Alaska Native victims of sexual violence in this system a human rights violation:

> Overall, Amnesty International's findings indicate that many American Indian and Alaska Native victims of sexual violence find access to legal redress, adequate medical attention and reparations difficult, if not impossible. Impunity for perpetrators and indifference towards survivors contribute to a climate where sexual violence is seen as normal and inescapable rather than criminal, and where women do not seek justice because they know they will be met with inaction.
>
> Sexual violence against women is not only a criminal or social issue, it is a human rights abuse. All women have the right to be safe and free from violence and the authorities have a responsibility to ensure that women can enjoy that right. This report shows that the US government is failing in its obligations under international law to ensure these rights.

Amnesty International, Maze of Injustice: The Failure to Protect Indigenous Women from Sexual Violence in the U.S. at 9–10 (2007), *available at* https://www.amnestyusa.org/wp-content/uploads/2017/05/mazeofinjustice.pdf [https://perma.cc/L6RT-RFWG].

Lack of federal prosecution may be one cause of the problems. Federal prosecutorial offices are not organized to do the bread and butter criminal justice work; they usually can count on states to do that and wait to prosecute the more notorious crimes and stronger cases. Reports of high rates of declining cases referred to federal officials have continued for decades. Because they are not based in the communities where the crimes occur, federal prosecutors may also be divorced from community concerns and priorities. In addition, the historic conflict with the federal government and the contemporary distance between tribes and federal prosecutors may reduce reliance on and cooperation with federal law enforcement. As Professor Washburn writes, federal officers may bring with them a sense that "the cavalry has arrived," and in Indian country that is not necessarily a good thing. Kevin K. Washburn, *Indians, Crime and the Law*, 104 Mich. L. Rev. 709, 735–737 (2006). Tribal liaisons have recently been established in some U.S. Attorneys' offices to address these problems.

Tribal governments often cannot fill the gap. The Indian Civil Rights Act limits tribal punishments for "any one offense" to up to one year in jail or a fine of $5000. 25 U.S.C. § 1302(7). Courts have disagreed as to whether tribes may impose consecutive one-year sentences for each violation of a criminal law in a single criminal episode. *Compare Miranda v. Anchondo*, 684 F.3d 844 (9th Cir. 2012) (tribes may impose sentences for multiple offenses that exceed one year) *with Spears v. Red Lake Band of Chippewa Indians*, 363 F. Supp. 2d 1176 (D. Minn. 2005) (ICRA precluded sentence of more than one year for conviction of six crimes in a single crime spree). Tribes also typically lack the facilities or resources to imprison offenders for lengthy periods. In addition, because tribal courts may be perceived as products of federal efforts to control tribal people, tribal legal systems face some of the same legitimacy challenges experienced by federal systems.

State jurisdiction may not address and may even exacerbate the problem. States have little interest in expending resources to police vast reservation territories. Indeed one study suggests that Public Law 280, by creating the illusion of state law enforcement, in fact exacerbates lawlessness in Indian country by discouraging tribal law enforcement efforts and federal support for them. *See* Duane Champagne & Carole Goldberg, Captured Justice: Native Nations and Public Law 280, at 200 (2012); Robert T. Anderson, *Negotiating Jurisdiction: Retroceding State Authority Over Indian Country Granted by Public Law 280*, 87 Wash. L. Rev. 915 (2012); Carole Goldberg–Ambrose, *Public Law 280 and the Problem of Lawlessness in California Indian Country*, 44 UCLA L. Rev. 1405 (1997). A positive development to address the gaps in law enforcement is the advent of cross-deputization agreements between tribes and states so that the law enforcement officers of each can arrest offenders subject to the jurisdiction of the other. *See, e.g.*, Ariz. Rev. Stat. § 13–3874; N.M. Stat. § 29–1–11; Mich. Comp. Law § 28.609(6); *State v. Manypenny*, 662 N.W.2d 183 (Minn. Ct. App. 2003); Neb. Op. Att'y Gen. No. 02009 (2002); 27 Okl. Op. Att'y Gen. 66 (1997); 22 Okl. Op. Att'y Gen. 71 (1991); Wash. AGLO 1978 No. 18 (1978). *See also* Rev. Code Wash. § 10.92.020 (providing that tribal police officers may be treated as state officers within Indian country). *Cf State v. Eriksen*, 259 P.3d 1079 (Wash. 2011) (holding that tribal police on the reservation may detain non-Indians who commit an on-reservation crime, but if a non-Indian drunk driver can speed off the reservation, tribal police may not stop and detain the non-Indian).

F. FIXING THE SYSTEM?

In the 2010 Tribal Law and Order Act and the 2013 reauthorization of the Violence Against Women Act, Congress made the first significant changes to the criminal jurisdiction system in decades. Congress spelled out some of the reasons for the changes in the findings of the Tribal Law and Order Act:

TRIBAL LAW AND ORDER ACT OF 2010

SEC. 202. FINDINGS; PURPOSES.

(a) **FINDINGS.**—Congress finds that—

(1) the United States has distinct legal, treaty, and trust obligations to provide for the public safety of Indian country;

(2) Congress and the President have acknowledged that—

(A) tribal law enforcement officers are often the first responders to crimes on Indian reservations; and

(B) tribal justice systems are often the most appropriate institutions for maintaining law and order in Indian country;

(3) less than 3,000 tribal and Federal law enforcement officers patrol more than 56,000,000 acres of Indian country, which reflects less than 1⁄2 of the law enforcement presence in comparable rural communities nationwide;

(4) the complicated jurisdictional scheme that exists in Indian country—

(A) has a significant negative impact on the ability to provide public safety to Indian communities;

(B) has been increasingly exploited by criminals; and

(C) requires a high degree of commitment and cooperation among tribal, Federal, and State law enforcement officials;

(5)(A) domestic and sexual violence against American Indian and Alaska Native women has reached epidemic proportions;

(B) 34 percent of American Indian and Alaska Native women will be raped in their lifetimes; and

(C) 39 percent of American Indian and Alaska Native women will be subject to domestic violence;

(6) Indian tribes have faced significant increases in instances of domestic violence, burglary, assault, and child abuse as a direct result of increased methamphetamine use on Indian reservations; and

(7) crime data is a fundamental tool of law enforcement, but for decades the Bureau of Indian Affairs and the Department of Justice have not been able to coordinate or consistently report crime and prosecution rates in tribal communities.

One of the most important elements of the act authorizes tribes to issue penalties of up to three years in jail and/or a $15,000 fine per offense under tribal law, or up to nine years in a single criminal proceeding. 25 U.S.C. § 1302(b). While the Act increases the potential authority of tribal governments, it places numerous conditions on this power by requiring counsel for indigent defendants, law training and licensing by any jurisdiction (including a tribe) for the judge, and requiring prisoners to serve their time either in a tribal facility approved by the Bureau of Indian Affairs, in the facility of a state, local, or federal government, or in a tribal rehabilitation center. *See* Ch.6, § II, *infra*.

The law also seeks to ensure more effective federal assistance in criminal enforcement and facilitate greater federal and state coordination with tribes. For example, the Act requires the Department of Justice to collect Indian-country-specific crime statistics, as well as data on federal decisions not to prosecute Indian country cases. It also addresses lackluster federal law enforcement by authorizing the appointment of tribal attorneys as special federal prosecutors to assist in prosecuting federal misdemeanors. To address enforcement gaps in mandatory Public Law 280 states, the Act allows tribes in these states to request concurrent federal jurisdiction under the Major Crimes Act and the Indian Country Crimes Act. Further, responding to a long-standing deficiency, the law also mandates that the Indian Health Service implement an effective protocol in sexual assault cases.

In a further attempt to address violence against Native women, the 2013 reauthorization of the Violence Against Women Act restored tribal jurisdiction over non-Indians in certain contexts. 25 U.S.C. § 1304(b)(1). The law applies to "dating violence" and "domestic violence" by a non-Indian against a current or former spouse or intimate partner. 25 U.S.C. §§ 1304(a) & (b). It applies only if the crime or conduct giving rise to the civil protection order takes place in the Indian country of the participating tribe, 25 U.S.C. § 1304(c)(2), and the defendant either resides in the tribe's territory, is employed in the tribe's territory, or is the spouse, intimate partner, or dating partner of a tribal member or a nonmember Indian residing in the tribe's territory. 25 U.S.C. § 1304(b)(4)(B). The Act does not apply to dating or domestic violence crimes in which neither the defendant nor the victim is Indian. 25 U.S.C. § 1304(b)(4)(A)(i).

If a prosecution under the act may result in a sentence of any length, the tribe must provide the individual with a jury that constitutes a fair cross section of the community as well as the right to counsel and other protections required before tribes may impose sentences of more than one year. 25 U.S.C. § 1304(d). A final catch-all provision guarantees "all other rights whose protection is necessary under the Constitution of the United States in order for Congress to recognize and affirm the inherent power of the participating tribe to exercise special domestic violence criminal jurisdiction over the defendant." *Id.*

As of 2019, eighteen tribes had begun exercising special domestic violence criminal jurisdiction (SDVJC) under VAWA. The National Congress of American Indians conducted an analysis of tribes' adoption and implementation of VAWA and concluded that it had "fundamentally changed the landscape of tribal criminal jurisdiction in the modern era." More specific conclusions from the report include the following:

> By exercising SDVCJ, many communities have increased safety and justice for victims who had previously seen little of either. SDVCJ has allowed tribes to "respond to long-time abusers who previously had evaded justice" and has given a ray of hope to victims and communities that safety can be restored.

Tribes are implementing SDVCJ with careful attention to the requirements of federal law and in a manner that upholds the rights of defendants .... Most of these implementing tribes have worked closely with a group of over 50 other tribes as part of an Inter-tribal Technical-Assistance Working Group (ITWG) on SDVCJ that has been an important forum for tribal governments to work collaboratively to develop best practices.

To date, the implementing tribes report 143 arrests of 128 non-Indian abusers. These arrests ultimately led to 74 convictions, 5 acquittals, and 24 cases currently pending. There has not been a single petition for habeas corpus review brought in federal court in an SDVCJ case. Although preliminary, the absence of habeas petitions suggests the fairness of tribal courts and the care with which tribes are implementing SDVCJ.

Implementation of SDVCJ has had other positive outcomes as well. For many tribes, it has led to much-needed community conversations about domestic violence. For others it has provided an impetus to more comprehensively update tribal criminal codes. Implementation of SDVCJ has also resulted in increased collaboration among tribes and between the local, state, federal, and tribal governments. It has revealed places where federal administrative policies and practices needed to be strengthened to enhance justice, and it has shown where the jurisdictional framework continues to leave victims—including children and law enforcement—vulnerable. Implementation thus far has also revealed that additional resources are necessary in order for the benefits of the law to expand to more reservations.

VAWA 2013's Special Domestic Violence Criminal Jurisdiction: Five-Year Report, The National Congress of American Indians (2018), *available at* http://www.ncai.org/resources/ncai-publications/SDVCJ_5_Year_Report.pdf [https://perma.cc/N7BA-8JRG].

In *United States v. Bryan*, 136 S. Ct. 1954 (2016), the Supreme Court considered whether tribal convictions for domestic violence crimes could count as predicates to a federal conviction for serial domestic violence in Indian country. The Court held that tribal convictions did qualify, and that the defendant's Sixth Amendment right to counsel was not violated by relying on them. *Bryan* involved a tribal member defendant but is nonetheless an important precedent affirming the validity of tribal court convictions that may prove relevant to later challenges to the VAWA provisions.

The Tribal Law and Order Act also established a bipartisan Tribal Law and Order Commission to evaluate and make recommendations regarding the criminal justice system in Indian country. The resulting report was sharply critical of the existing system:

American Indian and Alaska Native communities and lands are frequently less safe—and sometimes dramatically more dangerous—than most other places in our country. Ironically, the U.S. government, which has a trust responsibility for Indian Tribes, is fundamentally at fault for this public safety gap. Federal government policies have displaced and diminished the very institutions that are best positioned to provide trusted, accountable, accessible, and cost-effective justice in Tribal communities.

> *** This system was imposed on Indian nations without their consent in the late 19th century and is remarkably unchanged since that time. The system is complex, expensive, and simply cannot provide the criminal justice services that Native communities expect and deserve.

A Roadmap for Making Native America Safer, Report to the President and Congress of the United States (2015), *available at* http:// https:// www.aisc.ucla.edu/iloc/report/files/A_Roadmap_For_Making_Native_America_Safer-Full.pdf [https://perma.cc/QC8N-WHAM].

The Report makes many recommendations—too many to recount here. The first is the most sweeping. The Commission recommends that any tribe be permitted to opt-out of federal Indian country and state criminal jurisdiction and be able to exercise criminal jurisdiction over all persons within their territorial boundaries, without the sentencing limitations imposed by the Indian Civil Rights Act. Opt-out, however, would require a guarantee of civil rights protections equivalent to those of the constitution and full appellate review. To undertake this review, the United States would create a new circuit court, the Federal Indian Court of Appeals, to hear federal law questions arising from these cases. What do you think of the recommendation? What objections—from the federal government, states, tribes, or individuals within Indian communities, would you anticipate?

NOTES AND QUESTIONS

1. To test your knowledge of criminal jurisdiction in Indian country, fill in the following chart with the extent of jurisdiction under each of these variations.

Victim	**Defendant**	
	Indian	***Non–Indian***
Indian	Tribe:	Tribe:
	US:	US:
	State:	State:
Non–Indian	Tribe:	Tribe:
	US:	US:
	State:	State:

2. The following questions require you to put together your knowledge of criminal jurisdiction, your knowledge of Indian country, and your knowledge of equal protection jurisprudence in Indian law.

   a. Tom Jones, a member of the Cheyenne River Sioux Tribe, murders Sarah Taylor, his non-Indian wife, while on the Spirit Lake Reservation in North Dakota. The U.S. Attorney seeks to prosecute him for the crime.

Tom challenges federal jurisdiction over him. What result? What authority supports your answer?

b. Tom claims that because he is not a member of the Spirit Lake Tribe, and because a non-Indian would not be subject to federal jurisdiction for the crime, exercising jurisdiction over him violates his right to equal protection. What result? What authority supports your conclusion?

c. Rachel Greenberg, a non-Indian, and Jeremy Harris, a member of the Bay Mills Band of Chippewa Indians, are married and live together on the Bay Mills Reservation in Michigan. They have a son, George Harris–Greenberg. Although George meets tribal enrollment criteria, has lived on the reservation all his life, and receives services through the tribe's health care program, he has never been enrolled with the tribe. After receiving reports indicating that Rachel has been violently abusing her son, Michigan seeks to prosecute her for child abuse. Rachel challenges state jurisdiction. What result? Can the Bay Mills Band prosecute her? Can the federal government? What authority supports your answer?

d. Same fact scenario, except now they live off the reservation on the allotment originally allotted to Jeremy's grandparents.

e. Same fact scenario, except now the abuse occurred on off-reservation land that the tribe has purchased to build a housing development.

f. Same fact scenario, except now the abuse occurred on fee land within the reservation that Rachel inherited from her grandparents, non-Indian homesteaders who obtained the land when the Bay Mills reservation was opened to non-Indian settlement during the allotment era.

g. Sarah Taylor, a member of the San Carlos Apache Tribe, is charged with vandalizing the personal car (*i.e.*, a car that is not considered federal property) of a non-Indian FBI agent visiting the reservation. The tribe prosecutes her and punishes her by placing her in an alternative diversion program that emphasizes traditional healing. Dissatisfied with this punishment, the federal government seeks to prosecute Sarah as well. Sarah challenges federal jurisdiction. What result?

h. Al Mayhew, a non-Indian, lives in Seattle but is married to Jenny Franklin, a member of the Tulalip Tribe. Franklin alleges that Mayhew hit her and broke her nose while she was at her parents' home on the Tulalip Reservation. The Tulalip Tribe is exercising special domestic violence criminal jurisdiction under the Violence Against Women Act. Can the Tulalip Tribe prosecute Mayhew?

3. The criminal section of Public Law 280, codified at 18 U.S.C. § 1162, required six states to exercise criminal jurisdiction in Indian country, and permitted others to exercise such jurisdiction if they chose to do so. In the six mandatory states, federal jurisdiction under the MCA and the ICCA is supplanted by state jurisdiction. *See* Chapter 7, § II, *infra*.

CHAPTER 6

TRIBAL SOVEREIGNTY

■ ■ ■

I. THE NATURE AND SOURCE OF TRIBAL SOVEREIGNTY

In 1832, *Worcester v. Georgia* declared Indian tribes to be "distinct political communities, having territorial boundaries, within which their authority is exclusive, and having a right to all the lands within those boundaries, which is not only acknowledged, but guarantied by the United States." 31 U.S. 515, 557 (1832). But over the next fifty years, the United States made increasing intrusions onto Indian lands, passing laws that regulated wholly intratribal matters and selling large chunks of reservation lands to non-Indians. *United States v. Kagama*, 118 U.S. 375 (1886), claimed to rely on the Marshall era cases, but described Indian tribes as wholly dependent and helpless wards of the United States. Could the traditional notion of tribal sovereignty, on the one hand, be reconciled with congressional plenary power and wardship status, on the other? Consider the following enormously important case, decided a decade after *Kagama*.

TALTON V. MAYES

163 U.S. 376, 16 S. Ct. 986, 41 L. Ed. 196 (1896)

JUSTICE WHITE, after stating the case, delivered the opinion of the court.

[Bob Talton, a Cherokee citizen, was convicted by the Cherokee Nation courts of the murder of two other Cherokees and sentenced to death by hanging. He was imprisoned awaiting sentence in the national jail at Tahlequah, the Cherokee capital, by Washington Mayes, high sheriff of the Cherokee Nation. Talton filed a habeas corpus petition in federal district court seeking release on the grounds that his conviction violated the Fifth Amendment grand jury and due process clauses.]

[T]he appellant asserts, 1st, that the grand jury, consisting only of five persons, was not a grand jury within the contemplation of the fifth amendment to the constitution, which it is asserted is operative upon the Cherokee Nation in the exercise of its legislative authority as to purely local matters; 2d, that the indictment by a grand jury thus constituted was not due process of law within the intendment of the fourteenth amendment ***. A decision as to the merits of these contentions involves a consideration of the relation of the Cherokee Nation to the United States, and of the operation of the constitutional provisions relied on upon the purely local legislation of that Nation. ***

By treaties and statutes of the United States the right of the Cherokee Nation to exist as an autonomous body, subject always to the paramount authority of the United States, has been recognized. And from this fact there has consequently been conceded to exist in that Nation power to make laws defining offenses and providing for the trial and punishment of those who violate them when the offenses are committed by one member of the tribe against another one of its members within the territory of the Nation.

Thus, by the fifth article of the treaty of 1835 (7 Stat. 481), it is provided:

> The United States hereby covenant and agree that the lands ceded to the Cherokee Nation in the foregoing article shall, in no future time without their consent, be included within the territorial limits or jurisdiction of any state or territory. But they shall secure to the Cherokee Nation the right by their national councils to make and carry into effect all such laws as they may deem necessary for the government and protection of the persons and property within their own country belonging to their people or such persons as have connected themselves with them: provided always that they shall not be inconsistent with the constitution of the United States and such acts of congress as have been or may be passed regulating trade and intercourse with the Indians; and also, that they shall not be considered as extending to such citizens and army of the United States as may travel or reside in the Indian country by permission according to the laws and regulations established by the government of the same.

This guarantee of self-government was reaffirmed in the treaty of 1866 (14 Stat. 803), the thirteenth article of which reads as follows:

> Art. 13. The Cherokees also agree that a court or courts may be established by the United States in said territory, with such jurisdiction and organized in such manner as may be prescribed by law: provided, that the judicial tribunals of the Nation shall be allowed to retain exclusive jurisdiction in all civil and criminal cases arising within their country in which members of the Nation, by nativity or adoption, shall be the only parties, or where the cause of action shall arise in the Cherokee Nation, except as otherwise provided in this treaty.

So, also, in "An act to provide a temporary government for the territory of Oklahoma, to enlarge the jurisdiction of the United States court in the Indian Territory, and for other purposes," approved May 2, 1890 (26 Stat. 81), it was provided, in section [31] as follows ***:

> The constitution of the United States and all general laws of the United States which prohibit crimes and misdemeanors in any place within the sole and exclusive jurisdiction of the United States except in the District of Columbia, and all laws relating to national banking associations, shall have the same force and effect in the Indian Territory as elsewhere in the United States; but nothing in this act shall be so construed as to deprive any of the courts of the civilized nations of exclusive jurisdiction over all cases arising wherein members of said nations, whether by treaty, blood or adoption, are the sole parties, nor so as to interfere with the right and powers of said civilized nations to punish said members for violation of the statutes and laws enacted by their national councils where such laws are not contrary to the treaties and laws of the United States.

The crime of murder committed by one Cherokee Indian upon the person of another within the jurisdiction of the Cherokee Nation is, therefore, clearly not an offense against the United States, but an offense against the local laws of the Cherokee Nation. Necessarily, the statutes of the United States which provide for an indictment by a grand jury, and the number of persons who shall constitute such a body, have no application, for such statutes relate only, if not otherwise specially provided, to grand juries impaneled for the courts of and under the laws of the United States.

The question, therefore, is, does the fifth amendment to the constitution apply to the local legislation of the Cherokee Nation so as to require all prosecutions for offenses committed against the laws of that Nation to be initiated by a grand jury organized in accordance with the provisions of that amendment? The solution of this question involves an inquiry as to the nature and origin of the power of local government exercised by the Cherokee Nation, and recognized to exist in it by the treaties and statutes. *** [T]he fifth amendment to the constitution of the United States is a limitation only upon the powers of the general government; that is, that the amendment operates solely on the constitution itself by qualifying the powers of the national government which the constitution called into being. ***

The case, in this regard, therefore depends upon whether the powers of local government exercised by the Cherokee Nation are federal powers created by and springing from the constitution of the United States, and hence controlled by the fifth amendment to that constitution, or whether they are local powers not created by the constitution, although subject to its general provisions and the paramount authority of congress. The repeated adjudications of this court have long since answered the formed question in the negative. ***

It cannot be doubted, as said in *Worcester*, that prior to the formation of the constitution treaties were made with the Cherokee tribes by which their autonomous existence was recognized. And in that case Chief Justice Marshall also said: "The Indian nations had always been considered as distinct, independent political communities, retaining their original natural rights." ***

In reviewing the whole subject in *United States v. Kagama*, 118 U.S. 375, 381, this court said:

> [The Indians] were, and always have been, regarded as having a semi-independent position when they preserved their tribal relations; not as states, not as nations, not as possessed of the full attributes of sovereignty, but as a separate people, with the power of regulating their internal and social relations, and thus far not brought under the laws of the Union, or of the state within whose limits they resided.

*** True it is that in many adjudications of this court the fact has been fully recognized that, although possessed of these attributes of local self-government when exercising their tribal functions, all such rights are subject to the supreme legislative authority of the United States. But the existence of the right in congress to regulate the manner in which the local powers of the Cherokee Nation shall be exercised does not render such local powers federal powers arising from and created by the constitution of the United States. It follows that, as the powers of local self-government enjoyed by the Cherokee Nation existed prior to the constitution, they are not operated upon by the fifth amendment, which, as we have said, had for its sole object to control the powers conferred by the constitution on the national government. The fact that the Indian tribes are subject to the dominant authority of congress, and that their powers of local self-government are also operated upon and restrained by the general provisions of the constitution of the United States, completely answers the argument of inconvenience which was pressed in the discussion at bar. ***

NOTES AND QUESTIONS

1. *Inherent authority or authorized federal authority?* To what extent, if any, was it important in *Talton* that federal treaties and statutes recognized the Cherokee authority to prosecute its own members? The most accurate way to think about this question is to view the federal treaties and statutes as providing federal recognition of tribal status—the Cherokee are clearly a recognized federal Indian tribe. As such, the tribe should be viewed as having retained all of its pre-contact sovereignty (as defined by the Marshall trilogy to exclude external international relations) except where a federal treaty or statute has divested some of that authority. Thus, it should not matter whether federal treaties and statutes expressly provide that the Cherokee may prosecute its own members—all that matters is that no treaty or statute had taken away that power. This is yet another application of the favorable canons of construction: tribes should not be understood to have lost inherent authority by inference or innuendo or by a federal failure to recite that the tribe retains the authority.

2. *Divestment of inherent tribal authority?* Reread the references to the U.S. Constitution in the federal treaties and statutes quoted in *Talton*. Could these references support the argument that the tribe agreed (by treaty) or Congress imposed (by statute) the limitations of the Constitution upon the legislative and judicial authority of the tribe? Can the reference be understood to mean something else? Is this yet another example where the canons of construction are useful in providing an outcome-determinative approach, leaving for the future the question whether Congress should expressly impose restraints upon internal tribal sovereignty that are similar or identical to those the Constitution imposes upon the federal or state governments?

3. *Not delegated federal authority.* The Court clearly holds that, when the Cherokee are prosecuting one of their own members for a crime against another member within the tribe's geographical domain, the tribe is exercising its pre-contact, pre-constitutional, inherent, retained, never been ceded away by the tribe, never been divested by the federal government, sovereignty. (See if you can think of any more modifiers to add to this chain!) The fact that Congress has never divested the tribe of this authority does not mean that the tribe is authorized by the federal government to act such that the tribal action should be understood as federal action subject to the Constitution. Even more clearly, the Court rejects any notion that the tribe is acting not just with delegated federal permission, but with delegated federal authority (where application of the Constitution would presumably follow as a matter of course). Note that the Court reached this conclusion even in a setting in which it is clear that the tribe had westernized its institutions and procedures for criminal justice to the extent that a key portion of it—the process by which crimes are charged—had been converted to a grand jury system.

4. Talton *and concurrent tribal jurisdiction over major crimes.* The Major Crimes Act, discussed in the previous chapter, was passed ten years before *Talton* was decided. The Court assumed that the Cherokee Nation's inherent powers to prosecute felonies survived the passage of that statute. Does this add support to the argument that tribes retain concurrent jurisdiction to prosecute major crimes?

5. *What* Talton *means. Talton* concludes that, notwithstanding the ward-guardian analogy and the doctrine of congressional plenary power, tribes have not been incorporated into the federal government and thus remain separate sovereigns. Thus, the U.S. Constitution does not apply to tribal exercises of inherent, retained authority. This means that a government within the boundaries of the United States is allowed to prosecute and imprison people, and they have *no federal constitutional rights* in this process. Does that surprise or trouble you? Should this be as controversial as the notion that holding alleged foreign combatants at Guantanamo Bay supposedly cannot be reviewed by the federal courts under the Constitution? One major difference, which we will study soon, is that, in 1968, Congress exercised its plenary power and enacted the Indian Civil Rights Act. 25 U.S.C. §§ 1301–1303. That statute imposes upon tribes a number of limitations similar to those found in the U.S. Constitution and also provides that federal district courts have jurisdiction to issue writs of *habeas corpus* when tribes incarcerate someone in violation of the statute. Be clear that in this context it is federal statutory rights that are being violated, not the U.S. Constitution.

6. *Can (should) the* Talton *rule survive twentieth century developments?* In the twentieth century, the federal bureaucratic role in Indian country, played by the Bureau of Indian Affairs and other federal agencies, came in many circumstances to dominate tribal capacity to make decisions. Over that same span of time, the U.S. Supreme Court radically expanded the reach of the Constitution by applying almost all the limitations of the Bill of Rights, originally understood as reaching only federal action (as *Talton* stated), to the states as implied limitations agreed to by state acceptance of the Fourteenth Amendment. *See Duncan v. Louisiana*, 391 U.S. 145 (1968). Thus, by the 1970s, a criminal defendant in state court had essentially the same federally enforceable constitutional rights as a criminal defendant in federal court. (The Court has also never held that the right to a grand jury was incorporated against the states.) To some extent the same movement occurred in Indian law, as a result of the Indian Civil Rights Act. By the second half of the twentieth century, was there any continuing reason to see the tribes as sovereigns separate from the federal government, for purposes of the federal constitution? See the next case.

UNITED STATES V. WHEELER

435 U.S. 313, 98 S. Ct. 1079, 55 L. Ed. 2d 303 (1978)

JUSTICE STEWART delivered the opinion of the Court.

The question presented in this case is whether the Double Jeopardy Clause of the Fifth Amendment bars the prosecution of an Indian in a federal district court under the Major Crimes Act, 18 U.S.C. § 1153, when he has previously been convicted in a tribal court of a lesser included offense arising out of the same incident.

I

[Anthony Wheeler, a member of the Navajo Tribe, pleaded guilty in Navajo court to disorderly conduct and contributing to the delinquency of a minor in violation of the Navajo Tribal Code. He was sentenced to 15 days in jail or a fine of $30 on the first charge and to 60 days in jail (to be served concurrently with the other jail term) or a fine of $120 on the second. Over a year later, Wheeler was indicted for statutory rape for the same conduct in federal court. He moved to dismiss this indictment, claiming that since the tribal offense of contributing to the delinquency of a minor was a lesser included offense of statutory rape, the tribal proceedings barred the federal prosecution.]

II

In *Bartkus v. Illinois,* 359 U.S. 121 (1959), and *Abbate v. United States,* 359 U.S. 187 (1959), this Court reaffirmed the well-established principle that a federal prosecution does not bar a subsequent state prosecution of the same person for the same acts, and a state prosecution does not bar a federal one.* The basis for this doctrine is that prosecutions under the laws of separate sovereigns do not, in the language of the Fifth Amendment, "subject [the defendant] for the same offence to be twice put in jeopardy."

It was noted in *Abbate* that the "undesirable consequences" that would result from the imposition of a double jeopardy bar in such circumstances further support the "dual sovereignty" concept. Prosecution by one sovereign for a relatively minor offense might bar prosecution by the other for a much graver one, thus effectively depriving the latter of the right to enforce its own laws. While, the Court said, conflict might be eliminated by making federal jurisdiction exclusive where it exists, such a "marked change in the distribution of powers to administer criminal justice" would not be desirable. *Ibid.*

The "dual sovereignty" concept does not apply, however, in every instance where successive cases are brought by nominally different prosecuting entities. *Grafton v. United States*, 206 U.S. 333 (1907), held that a soldier who had been acquitted of murder by a federal court-martial could not be retried for the same offense by a territorial court in the Philippines. *** Similarly, in *Waller v. Florida*, 397 U.S. 387 (1970), we held that a city and the State of which it is a political subdivision could not bring successive prosecutions for unlawful conduct growing out of the same episode, despite the fact that state law treated the two as separate sovereignties.

---

* [Eds: This principle was reaffirmed in *Gamble v. United States*, 139 S. Ct. 1960 (2019).]

The respondent contends, and the Court of Appeals held, that the "dual sovereignty" concept should not apply to successive prosecutions by an Indian tribe and the United States because the Indian tribes are not themselves sovereigns, but derive their power to punish crimes from the Federal Government. This argument relies on the undisputed fact that Congress has plenary authority to legislate for the Indian tribes in all matters, including their form of government. *** Because of this all-encompassing federal power, the respondent argues that the tribes are merely "arms of the federal government" which, in the words of his brief, "owe their existence and vitality solely to the political department of the federal government."

*** It is true that Territories are subject to the ultimate control of Congress, and cities to the control of the State which created them. But that fact was not relied upon as the basis for the decisions in *Grafton, Shell Co.*, and *Waller*. What differentiated those cases from *Bartkus* and *Abbate* was not the extent of control exercised by one prosecuting authority over the other but rather the ultimate source of the power under which the respective prosecutions were undertaken.

Bartkus and *Abbate* rest on the basic structure of our federal system, in which States and the National Government are separate political communities. State and Federal Governments "[derive] power from different sources," each from the organic law that established it. *United States v. Lanza*, 260 U.S. 377, 382 (1922). Each has the power, inherent in any sovereign, independently to determine what shall be an offense against its authority and to punish such offenses, and in doing so each "is exercising its own sovereignty, not that of the other." *Ibid.* And while the States, as well as the Federal Government, are subject to the overriding requirements of the Federal Constitution, and the Supremacy Clause gives Congress within its sphere the power to enact laws superseding conflicting laws of the States, this degree of federal control over the exercise of state governmental power does not detract from the fact that it is a State's own sovereignty which is the origin of its power.

By contrast, cities are not sovereign entities. *** A city is nothing more than "an agency of the State." *** Any power it has to define and punish crimes exists only because such power has been granted by the State; the power "derive[s] *** from the source of [its] creation." *** Similarly, a territorial government is entirely the creation of Congress, "and its judicial tribunals exert all their powers by authority of the United States." ***

III

It is undisputed that Indian tribes have power to enforce their criminal laws against tribe members. Although physically within the territory of the United States and subject to ultimate federal control, they nonetheless remain "a separate people, with the power of regulating their internal and social relations." *United States v. Kagama*, 118 U.S. at 381–382; *Cherokee Nation v. Georgia*.[18] Their right of internal self-government includes the right to prescribe laws applicable to tribe members and to enforce those laws by criminal sanctions. *** [T]he controlling question in this case is the source of this power to punish tribal offenders: Is it a part of inherent tribal sovereignty, or an aspect

18. Thus, unless limited by treaty or statute, a tribe has the power to determine tribe membership, to regulate domestic relations among tribe members, and to prescribe rules for the inheritance of property. ***

of the sovereignty of the Federal Government which has been delegated to the tribes by Congress?

***

The powers of Indian tribes are, in general, "*inherent powers of a limited sovereignty which has never been extinguished*." F. Cohen, Handbook of Federal Indian Law 122 (1945) (emphasis in original). Before the coming of the Europeans, the tribes were self-governing sovereign political communities. *** Like all sovereign bodies, they then had the inherent power to prescribe laws for their members and to punish infractions of those laws.

Indian tribes are, of course, no longer "possessed of the full attributes of sovereignty." *United States v. Kagama*, 118 U.S. at 381. Their incorporation within the territory of the United States, and their acceptance of its protection, necessarily divested them of some aspects of the sovereignty which they had previously exercised. By specific treaty provision they yielded up other sovereign powers; by statute, in the exercise of its plenary control, Congress has removed still others.

But our cases recognize that the Indian tribes have not given up their full sovereignty. We have recently said that: "Indian tribes are unique aggregations possessing attributes of sovereignty over both their members and their territory *** [They] are a good deal more than 'private, voluntary organizations.'" *United States v. Mazurie*, 419 U.S. 544, 557 (1975). *** The sovereignty that the Indian tribes retain is of a unique and limited character. It exists only at the sufferance of Congress and is subject to complete defeasance. But until Congress acts, the tribes retain their existing sovereign powers. In sum, Indian tribes still possess those aspects of sovereignty not withdrawn by treaty or statute, or by implication as a necessary result of their dependent status. *See Oliphant v. Suquamish Indian Tribe*, 435 U.S. 191 (1978).

***

It is evident that the sovereign power to punish tribal offenders has never been given up by the Navajo Tribe and that tribal exercise of that power today is therefore the continued exercise of retained tribal sovereignty. ***

Moreover, the sovereign power of a tribe to prosecute its members for tribal offenses clearly does not fall within that part of sovereignty which the Indians implicitly lost by virtue of their dependent status. The areas in which such implicit divestiture of sovereignty has been held to have occurred are those involving the relations between an Indian tribe and nonmembers of the tribe. Thus, Indian tribes can no longer freely alienate to non-Indians the land they occupy. *Oneida Indian Nation v. County of Oneida*, 414 U.S. 661, 667–668 (1974); *Johnson v. M'Intosh*, 21 U.S. 543 (1823). They cannot enter into direct commercial or governmental relations with foreign nations. *Worcester v. Georgia*, 31 U.S. 515 (1832). *** And, as we have recently held, they cannot try nonmembers in tribal courts. *Oliphant v. Suquamish Indian Tribe.*

These limitations rest on the fact that the dependent status of Indian tribes within our territorial jurisdiction is necessarily inconsistent with their freedom independently to determine their external relations. But the powers of self-government, including the power to prescribe and enforce internal criminal laws, are of a different type. They involve only the relations among members of a tribe. Thus, they are not such powers as would necessarily be lost by virtue of a tribe's dependent status. ***

It is true that in the exercise of the powers of self-government, as in all other matters, the Navajo Tribe, like all Indian tribes, remains subject to ultimate federal control. Thus, before the Navajo Tribal Council created the present Tribal Code and tribal courts, the Bureau of Indian Affairs established a Code of Indian Tribal Offenses and a Court of Indian Offenses for the reservation. *See* 25 C.F.R. Part 11 (1977). *** And the Indian Civil Rights Act of 1968, 82 Stat. 77, 25 U.S.C. § 1302, made most of the provisions of the Bill of Rights applicable to the Indian tribes and limited the punishment tribal courts could impose to imprisonment for six months, or a fine of $500, or both.

But none of these laws *created* the Indians' power to govern themselves and their right to punish crimes committed by tribal offenders. *** That Congress has in certain ways regulated the manner and extent of the tribal power of self-government does not mean that Congress is the source of that power.

In sum, the power to punish offenses against tribal law committed by Tribe members, which was part of the Navajos' primeval sovereignty, has never been taken away from them, either explicitly or implicitly, and is attributable in no way to any delegation to them of federal authority. It follows that when the Navajo Tribe exercises this power, it does so as part of its retained sovereignty and not as an arm of the Federal Government.[28] ***

***

[T]ribal courts are important mechanisms for protecting significant tribal interests. Federal pre-emption of a tribe's jurisdiction to punish its members for infractions of tribal law would detract substantially from tribal self-government, just as federal pre-emption of state criminal jurisdiction would trench upon important state interests. Thus, just as in *Bartkus* and *Abbate,* there are persuasive reasons to reject the respondent's argument that we should arbitrarily ignore the settled "dual sovereignty" concept as it applies to successive tribal and federal prosecutions. ***

NOTES AND QUESTIONS

1. *Wheeler* affirms the *Talton* principle for the modern era: tribal sovereignty is inherent retained sovereignty, not the product of the Constitution or the Federal government. Therefore successive tribal and federal prosecutions, like successive state and federal prosecutions, do not violate the Double Jeopardy Clause. For a more recent affirmation of this principle, see *United States v. Lara*, 541 U.S. 193 (2004), Ch.8, § II.D.

2. Other aspects of the opinion are more ominous for tribes. The Court states that tribal sovereignty "exists only at the sufferance of Congress and is subject to complete defeasance." While this is not so different from the *Talton* formulation of inherent tribal sovereignty subject to "supreme" federal power,

---

28. By emphasizing that the Navajo Tribe never lost its sovereign power to try tribal criminals, we do not mean to imply that a tribe which was deprived of that right by statute or treaty and then regained it by Act of Congress would necessarily be an arm of the Federal Government. That interesting question is not before us, and we express no opinion thereon.

the Court adds something new, that certain powers are "implicitly lost by virtue of [tribal] dependent status" and these powers include jurisdiction over nonmembers. We will return to this concept of "implicit divestiture," loss of tribal sovereignty over nonmembers without express congressional action, in later chapters.

II. CONGRESSIONAL LIMITATION ON TRIBAL SOVEREIGNTY: THE INDIAN CIVIL RIGHTS ACT OF 1968

Even during the height of the Termination Era, lower courts affirmed the independence of tribal sovereigns from constitutional restrictions. In 1954, a federal district court held that tribal decisions alleged to discriminate against non-Indian religions were not actions under color of state or federal law. *Toledo v. Pueblo de Jemez*, 119 F. Supp. 429 (D. N.M. 1954) (only Catholic religion adherents permitted to be buried in tribal community cemetery; Protestants not allowed to build a church on Pueblo land, nor to use their homes for church purposes). In *Native American Church v. Navajo Tribal Council*, 272 F.2d 131 (10th Cir. 1959), the Court of Appeals affirmed this principle in a case challenging a Navajo law criminalizing the sale, possession, or use of peyote, a hallucinogen used in the rituals of the Native American church. The court acknowledged that the First Amendment applied to states, but found that tribes "have a status higher than that of states. They are subordinate and dependent nations possessed of all powers as such limited only to the extent that they have been expressly required to surrender them by the superior sovereign, the United States." *Id.* at 134. Other courts reached similar holdings in the context of the Fifth and Fourteenth Amendments. *Martinez v. Southern Ute Tribe*, 249 F.2d 915, 919 (10th Cir. 1957) (Fifth Amendment due process claim); *Barta v. Oglala Sioux Tribe*, 259 F.2d 553 (8th Cir. 1958) (Fourteenth Amendment). In one case, the Ninth Circuit held that the Gros Ventre tribal court was partly a federal agency because the Department of the Interior had organized and funded it, and therefore had to provide a tribal citizen with the right to counsel and confrontation of witnesses before sentencing her to five days imprisonment for refusing to remove her cattle from land leased by another. *Colliflower v. Garland*, 342 F.2d 369 (9th Cir. 1965). But this holding was against the trend of cases.

In 1968, Congress enacted the Indian Civil Rights Act to create federally enforceable quasi-constitutional rights against Indian tribes. 25 U.S.C. §§ 1301–03 ("ICRA"). The legislative hearings focused on concern for the rights of criminal defendants in tribal courts, *see* Note, *The Indian Bill of Rights and the Constitutional Status of Tribal Governments*, 82 Harv. L. Rev. 1343, 1356 (1969), but the Act includes most (but not all) other provisions of the Bill of Rights as well. The law is the product of the transition from the Termination Era to the Self–Determination Era. On the one hand, the statute was proposed in 1961 and its primary sponsor was Senator Sam Ervin, an advocate of the Termination policy. It also imposes a series of restrictions on tribal institutions against the protests of many tribal representatives. On the other hand, the law acknowledges the powers of self-government of Indian tribes, and the legislative history reflects congressional concern with imposing requirements that would overly burden tribal institutions or cultural autonomy. *Id.*, 82 Harv. L. Rev. at 1359. As amended, the statute provides as follows:

INDIAN CIVIL RIGHTS ACT

§ 1301. Definitions

For purposes of this title, the term—

(1) "Indian tribe" means any tribe, band, or other group of Indians subject to the jurisdiction of the United States and recognized as possessing powers of self-government;

(2) "powers of self-government" means and includes all governmental powers possessed by an Indian tribe, executive, legislative, and judicial, and all offices, bodies, and tribunals by and through which they are executed, including courts of Indian offenses; [and means the inherent power of Indian tribes, hereby recognized and affirmed, to exercise criminal jurisdiction over all Indians];

(3) "Indian court" means any Indian tribal court or court of Indian offense; and

(4) "Indian" means any person who would be subject to the jurisdiction of the United States as an Indian under section 1153, title 18, United States Code, if that person were to commit an offense listed in that section in Indian country to which that section applies. [Subsection (4) and material in brackets in subsection (2) above were added in 1990 by the so-called *Duro* fix, discussed in Chapter 8.]

§ 1302. Constitutional rights

(a) In general

No Indian tribe in exercising powers of self-government shall—

(1) make or enforce any law prohibiting the free exercise of religion, or abridging the freedom of speech, or of the press, or the right of the people peaceably to assemble and to petition for a redress of grievances;

(2) violate the right of the people to be secure in their persons, houses, papers, and effects against unreasonable search and seizures, nor issue warrants, but upon probable cause, supported by oath or affirmation, and particularly describing the place to be searched and the person or thing to be seized;

(3) subject any person for the same offense to be twice put in jeopardy;

(4) compel any person in any criminal case to be a witness against himself;

(5) take any private property for a public use without just compensation;

(6) deny to any person in a criminal proceeding the right to a speedy and public trial, to be informed of the nature and cause of the accusation, to be confronted with the witnesses against him, to have compulsory process for obtaining witnesses in his favor, and at his own

expense to have the assistance of counsel for his defense (except as provided in subsection (b));

(7)(A) require excessive bail, impose excessive fines, or inflict cruel and unusual punishments; [Material in italics below was added by the Tribal Law and Order Act in 2010. ICRA originally limited punishments for any one offense to six months and/or $500; this was increased to one year and/or $5,000 in 1986.]

(B) except as provided in subparagraph (C), impose for conviction of any 1 offense any penalty or punishment greater than imprisonment for a term of 1 year or a fine of $5,000, or both;

(C) subject to subsection (b), impose for conviction of any 1 offense any penalty or punishment greater than imprisonment for a term of 3 years or a fine of $15,000, or both; or

(D) impose on a person in a criminal proceeding a total penalty or punishment greater than imprisonment for a term of 9 years;

(8) deny to any person within its jurisdiction the equal protection of its laws or deprive any person of liberty or property without due process of law;

(9) pass any bill of attainder or ex post facto law; or

(10) deny to any person accused of an offense punishable by imprisonment the right, upon request, to a trial by jury of not less than six persons.

(b) Offenses subject to greater than 1-year imprisonment or a fine greater than $5,000

A tribal court may subject a defendant to a term of imprisonment greater than 1 year but not to exceed 3 years for any 1 offense, or a fine greater than $5,000 but not to exceed $15,000, or both, if the defendant

(1) has been previously convicted of the same or a comparable offense by any jurisdiction in the United States; or

(2) is being prosecuted for an offense comparable to an offense that would be punishable by more than 1 year of imprisonment if prosecuted by the United States or any of the States.

(c) Rights of defendants

In a criminal proceeding in which an Indian tribe, in exercising powers of self-government, imposes a total term of imprisonment of more than 1 year on a defendant, the Indian tribe shall—

(1) provide to the defendant the right to effective assistance of counsel at least equal to that guaranteed by the United States Constitution; and

(2) at the expense of the tribal government, provide an indigent defendant the assistance of a defense attorney licensed to practice law by any jurisdiction in the United States that applies appropriate professional licensing standards and effectively ensures the competence and professional responsibility of its licensed attorneys;

(3) require that the judge presiding over the criminal proceeding—

(A) has sufficient legal training to preside over criminal proceedings; and

(B) is licensed to practice law by any jurisdiction in the United States;

(4) prior to charging the defendant, make publicly available the criminal laws (including regulations and interpretative documents), rules of evidence, and rules of criminal procedure (including rules governing the recusal of judges in appropriate circumstances) of the tribal government; and

(5) maintain a record of the criminal proceeding, including an audio or other recording of the trial proceeding.

(d) Sentences

In the case of a defendant sentenced in accordance with subsections (b) and (c), a tribal court may require the defendant--

(1) to serve the sentence--

(A) in a tribal correctional center that has been approved by the Bureau of Indian Affairs for long-term incarceration, in accordance with guidelines to be developed by the Bureau of Indian Affairs (in consultation with Indian tribes) not later than 180 days after July 29, 2010;

(B) in the nearest appropriate Federal facility, at the expense of the United States pursuant to the Bureau of Prisons tribal prisoner pilot program described in section 304(c) of the Tribal Law and Order Act of 2010;

(C) in a State or local government-approved detention or correctional center pursuant to an agreement between the Indian tribe and the State or local government; or

(D) in an alternative rehabilitation center of an Indian tribe; or

(2) to serve another alternative form of punishment, as determined by the tribal court judge pursuant to tribal law.

§ 1303. Habeas corpus

The privilege of the writ of habeas corpus shall be available to any person, in a court of the United States, to test the legality of his detention by order of an Indian tribe.

§ 1304. Tribal Jurisdiction over Crimes of Domestic Violence

Section 1304, added by the VAWA reauthorization of 2013, authorizes tribes to exercise criminal jurisdiction over non-Indians committing domestic violence against Indians in Indian country. Domestic violence is defined as "violence committed by a current or former spouse or intimate partner of the victim, by a person with whom the victim shares a child in common, by a person who is cohabitating with or has cohabitated with the victim as a spouse or intimate partner, or by a person similarly situated to a spouse of the victim under the domestic- or family- violence laws of an Indian tribe that has jurisdiction over the Indian country where the violence occurs." Defendants must be granted all of the protections of § 1302(b) (extended sentences). In addition defendants have:

1. all rights described in section 1302(c) if a term of imprisonment of any length may be imposed,;

2. a right to a trial by a jury that includes a "fair cross-section of the community" and does not systematically exclude any group, including non-Indians; and

3. all other rights whose protection is necessary under the Constitution of the United States in order for Congress to recognize and affirm the inherent power of the participating tribe to exercise special domestic violence criminal jurisdiction over the non-Indian defendant. § 1304(d)(4),

In addition, a convicted defendant may seek a stay of detention as part of a habeas corpus petition filed under § 1303. § 1304(e).

NOTES AND QUESTIONS

1. *ICRA as a fundamental constitutive framework?* Compare § 1302 to the U.S. Constitution's Bill of Rights. Just as the Bill of Rights limits federal exercises of sovereignty (and the Fourteenth Amendment limits state exercises of sovereignty), ICRA purports to limit tribal exercises of sovereignty. Should ICRA be understood as quasi-constitutional: fundamental to our scheme of rights and limited government and subject to expansive judicial elaboration and evolution over time, as the Bill of Rights and Fourteenth Amendment have been understood to be? What would be the right answer to this question according to the Cohen formulation of Indian law principles? If federal courts should treat the ICRA differently than the Bill of Rights, what reasons are there for the distinction?

2. *ICRA rights and constitutional rights.* As compared to the Bill of Rights and the Fourteenth Amendment, what rights are "missing" from ICRA?

3. The VAWA jurisdiction over non-Indians, 25 U.S.C. § 1304, contains elevated due process requirements if a tribe wishes to exercise criminal jurisdiction over non-Indian domestic abusers. A recent study summarized the Act's implementation.

> To date, 18 tribes are known to be exercising [VAWA jurisdiction] (throughout this report these tribes are referred to collectively as "implementing tribes"). Tribes are implementing [VAWA] with careful attention to the requirements of federal law and in a manner that upholds the rights of defendants. In order to exercise [VAWA jurisdiction], tribes must comply with a series of federal statutory requirements that include, among other things, providing certain due process protections to non-Indian defendants. Most of these implementing tribes have worked closely with a group of over 50 other tribes as part of an Inter-tribal Technical-Assistance Working Group on [VAWA jurisdiction] that has been an important forum for tribal governments to work collaboratively to develop best practices.

National Congress of American Indians, "VAWA 2013's Special Domestic Violence Criminal Jurisdiction: Five-Year Report." (2018).

Why do you think Congress provided the elevated protections for non-Indians accused of committing domestic violence? Why do you think only 18 tribes are implementing the statute so far?

4. *Federal judicial enforcement.* It is obvious, under § 1303, that a person being held in detention by a tribal government may apply for federal judicial relief. In the decade after the enactment of ICRA, however, the lower courts almost uniformly held that federal jurisdiction over ICRA claims was not limited to habeas review. These decisions included review of claims as essential to tribal self-government as impeachment of tribal officers, *Stands Over Bull v. Bureau of Indian Affairs*, 442 F. Supp. 360 (D. Mont. 1977); tribal membership requirements, *Slattery v. Arapahoe Tribal Council*, 453 F.2d 278, 282 (10th Cir. 1971) (upholding one quarter Indian blood requirement); *Daly v. United States*, 483 F.2d 700, 705 (8th Cir. 1973) (upholding one quarter Indian blood requirement for membership and one half degree for office holding); and a vast array of cases examining tribal election procedures. *See, e.g.*, *Two Hawk v. Rosebud Sioux Tribe*, 534 F.2d 101 (8th Cir. 1976); *St. Marks v. Chippewa–Cree Tribe of Rocky Boy Reservation, Montana*, 545 F.2d 1188 (9th Cir. 1976); *Means v. Wilson*, 522 F.2d 833 (8th Cir. 1975); *Wounded Head v. Tribal Council of Oglala Sioux Tribe of Pine Ridge Reservation*, 507 F.2d 1079 (8th Cir. 1975); *Brown v. United States*, 486 F.2d 658 (8th Cir. 1973); *White Eagle v. One Feather*, 478 F.2d 1311 (8th Cir. 1973); *Pomani v. Crow Creek Sioux Tribe*, 418 F. Supp. 166 (D.S.D. 1976); *Williams v. Sisseton–Wahpeton Sioux Tribal Council*, 387 F. Supp. 1194 (D.S.D. 1975). *But see Pinnow v. Shoshone Tribal Council*, 314 F. Supp. 1157 (D. Wyo. 1970) (holding that federal court could not exercise jurisdiction over claim challenging tribal enrollment procedures). Although the courts more often than not held that the tribes had not violated the ICRA, federal scrutiny of such claims-imposed costs on tribal governments and likely affected their ability to manage tribal affairs. In the next case, the Court addressed the jurisdiction created by the Indian Civil Rights Act.

SANTA CLARA PUEBLO V. MARTINEZ

436 U.S. 49, 98 S. Ct. 1670, 56 L. Ed. 2d 106 (1978)

JUSTICE MARSHALL delivered the opinion of the Court.

This case requires us to decide whether a federal court may pass on the validity of an Indian tribe's ordinance denying membership to the children of certain female tribal members.

Petitioner Santa Clara Pueblo is an Indian tribe that has been in existence for over 600 years. Respondents, a female member of the tribe and her daughter, brought suit in federal court against the tribe and its Governor *** seeking declaratory and injunctive relief against enforcement of a tribal ordinance denying membership in the tribe to children of female members who marry outside the tribe, while extending membership to children of male members who marry outside the tribe. Respondents claimed that this rule discriminates on the basis of both sex and ancestry in violation of Title I of the Indian Civil Rights Act of 1968 (ICRA), which provides in relevant part that "[n]o Indian tribe in exercising powers of self-government shall *** deny to any person within its jurisdiction the equal protection of its laws." [25 U.S.C. § 1302(8).]

*** ICRA does not expressly authorize the bringing of civil actions for declaratory or injunctive relief to enforce its substantive provisions. The threshold issue in this case is thus whether the Act may be interpreted to impliedly authorize such actions, against a tribe or its officers in the federal courts. For the reasons set forth below, we hold that the Act cannot be so read.

I.

Respondent Julia Martinez is a fullblooded member of the Santa Clara Pueblo, and resides on the Santa Clara Reservation in Northern New Mexico. In 1941 she married a Navajo Indian with whom she has since had several children, including respondent Audrey Martinez. Two years before this marriage, the Pueblo passed the membership ordinance here at issue, which bars admission of the Martinez children to the tribe because their father is not a Santa Claran.[2] Although the children were raised on the reservation and continue to reside there now that they are adults, as a result of their exclusion from membership they may not vote in tribal elections or hold secular office in the tribe; moreover, they have no right to remain on the reservation in the event of their mother's death, or to inherit their mother's home or her possessory interests in the communal lands.

After unsuccessful efforts to persuade the tribe to change the membership rule, respondents filed this lawsuit in the United States District Court for the District of New Mexico, on behalf of themselves and others similarly situated. Petitioners moved to dismiss the complaint on the ground that the court lacked jurisdiction to decide intratribal controversies affecting matters of tribal self-government and sovereignty. The District Court rejected petitioners' contention, finding that jurisdiction was conferred by 28 U.S.C. § 1343(4)[4] and 25 U.S.C. § 1302(8). The court apparently concluded, first, that the substantive provisions of [ICRA] impliedly authorized civil actions for declaratory and injunctive relief, and second, that the tribe was not immune from such suit.

---

2. The ordinance, enacted by the Santa Clara Pueblo Council pursuant to its legislative authority under the Constitution of the Pueblo, establishes the following membership rules:

1. All children born of marriages between members of the Santa Clara Pueblo shall be members of the Santa Clara Pueblo.

2.*** [C]hildren born of marriages between male members of the Santa Clara Pueblo and non-members shall be members of the Santa Clara Pueblo.

3. Children born of marriages between female members of the Santa Clara Pueblo and non-members shall not be members of the Santa Clara Pueblo.

4. Persons shall not be naturalized as members of the Santa Clara Pueblo under any circumstances.

Respondents challenged only subparagraphs 2 and 3. By virtue of subparagraph 4, Julia Martinez' husband is precluded from joining the Pueblo and thereby assuring the children's membership pursuant to subparagraph 1.

4. [28 U.S.C. § 1343(4) provides that the federal "district courts shall have original jurisdiction of any civil action authorized by law to be commenced by any person *** [t]o recover damages or to secure equitable or other relief under any Act of Congress providing for the protection of civil rights, including the right to vote."].

Following a full trial, the District Court found for petitioners on the merits. While acknowledging the relatively recent origin of the disputed rule, the District Court nevertheless found it to reflect traditional values of patriarchy still significant in tribal life. The court recognized the vital importance of respondents' interests,[5] but also determined that membership rules were "no more or less than a mechanism of social *** self-definition," and as such were basic to the tribe's survival as a cultural and economic entity. In sustaining the ordinance's validity under the "equal protection clause" of the ICRA, § 1302(8), the District Court concluded that the balance to be struck between these competing interests was better left to the judgment of the Pueblo.

On respondents' appeal, the Court of Appeals for the Tenth Circuit upheld the District Court's determination that 28 U.S.C. § 1343(4) provides a jurisdictional basis for actions under Title I of the ICRA. It found that "since [the ICRA] was designed to provide protection against tribal authority, the intention of Congress to allow suits against the tribe was an essential aspect [of the ICRA]. Otherwise, it would constitute a mere unenforceable declaration of principles." The Court of Appeals disagreed, however, with the District Court's ruling on the merits. While recognizing that standards of analysis developed under the Fourteenth Amendment's Equal Protection Clause were not necessarily controlling in the interpretation of this statute, the Court of Appeals apparently concluded that because the classification was one based upon sex it was presumptively invidious and could be sustained only if justified by a compelling tribal interest. Because of the ordinance's recent vintage, and because in the court's view the rule did not rationally identify those persons who were emotionally and culturally Santa Clarans, the court held that the tribe's interest in the ordinance was not substantial enough to justify its discriminatory effect. ***

II.

Indian tribes are "distinct, independent political communities, retaining their original natural rights" in matters of local self-government. *Worcester*; F. Cohen, Handbook of Federal Indian Law 122–123 (1945). ***

As separate sovereigns pre-existing the Constitution, tribes have historically been regarded as unconstrained by those constitutional provisions framed specifically as limitations on federal or state authority. [*See Talton.*] In ensuing years the lower federal courts have extended the holding of *Talton* to other provisions of the Bill of Rights, as well as to the Fourteenth Amendment. ***

As the Court in *Talton* recognized, however, Congress has plenary authority to limit, modify or eliminate the powers of local self-government which the tribes otherwise possess. [ICRA] represents an exercise of that authority. In [§ 1302], Congress acted to modify the effect of *Talton* and its progeny by imposing certain restrictions upon tribal governments similar, but not identical, to those contained in the Bill of Rights and the Fourteenth Amendment. In [§ 1303], the only remedial provision expressly supplied by Congress, the "privilege of the writ of habeas corpus" is made "available to any person, in a court of the United States, to test the legality of his detention by order of an Indian tribe."

---

5. The court found that "Audrey Martinez and many other children similarly situated have been brought up on the Pueblo, speak the Tewa language, participate in its life, and are, culturally, for all practical purposes, Santa Claran Indians." 402 F. Supp. at 18.

Petitioners concede that § 1302 modifies the substantive law applicable to the tribe; they urge, however, that Congress did not intend to authorize federal courts to review violations of its provisions except as they might arise on habeas corpus. They argue, further, that Congress did not waive the tribe's sovereign immunity from suit. Respondents, on the other hand, contend that § 1302 not only modifies the substantive law applicable to the exercise of sovereign tribal powers, but also authorizes civil suits for equitable relief against the tribe and its officers in federal courts. We consider these contentions first with respect to the tribe.

III.

Indian tribes have long been recognized as possessing the common-law immunity from suit traditionally enjoyed by sovereign powers. This aspect of tribal sovereignty, like all others, is subject to the superior and plenary control of Congress. But "without congressional authorization," the "Indian Nations are exempt from suit."

It is settled that a waiver of sovereign immunity " 'cannot be implied but must be unequivocally expressed.' " Nothing on the face of Title I of the ICRA purports to subject tribes to the jurisdiction of the federal courts in civil actions for injunctive or declaratory relief. Moreover, since the respondent in a habeas corpus action is the individual custodian of the prisoner, the provisions of § 1303 can hardly be read as a general waiver of the tribe's sovereign immunity. In the absence here of any unequivocal expression of contrary legislative intent, we conclude that suits against the tribe under the ICRA are barred by its sovereign immunity from suit.

IV.

As an officer of the Pueblo, petitioner Lucario Padilla is not protected by the tribe's immunity from suit. *See Puyallup Tribe, Inc. v. Washington Department of Game*, 433 U.S. 165, 171 (1977); *** *cf. Ex parte Young*, 209 U.S. 123 (1908). We must therefore determine whether the cause of action for declaratory and injunctive relief asserted here by respondents, though not expressly authorized by the statute, is nonetheless implicit in its terms.

In addressing this inquiry, we must bear in mind that providing a federal forum for issues arising under § 1302 constitutes an interference with tribal autonomy and self-government beyond that created by the change in substantive law itself. Even in matters involving commercial and domestic relations, we have recognized that "subject[ing] a dispute arising on the reservation among reservation Indians to a forum other than the one they have established for themselves," *Fisher v. District Court*, 424 U.S. 382 (1976), may "undermine the authority of the tribal cour[t] *** and hence *** infringe on the right of the Indians to govern themselves." *A fortiori*, resolution in a foreign forum of intratribal disputes of a more "public" character, such as the one in this case, cannot help but unsettle a tribal government's ability to maintain authority. Although Congress clearly has power to authorize civil actions against tribal officers, and has done so with respect to habeas corpus relief in § 1303, a proper respect both for tribal sovereignty itself and for the plenary authority of Congress in this area cautions that we tread lightly in the absence of clear indications of legislative intent.

*** [W]e turn now to those factors of more general relevance in determining whether a cause of action is implicit in a statute not expressly providing one. *See Cort v. Ash*, 422 U.S. 66 (1975).[10] We note at the outset that a central purpose of the ICRA and in particular of Title I was to "secur[e] for the American Indian the broad constitutional rights afforded to other Americans," and thereby to "protect individual Indians from arbitrary and unjust actions of tribal governments." S. Rep. No. 841, 90th Cong., 1st Sess., 5–6 (1967). There is thus no doubt that respondents, American Indians living on the Santa Clara Reservation, are among the class for whose especial benefit this legislation was enacted. Moreover, we have frequently recognized the propriety of inferring a federal cause of action for the enforcement of civil rights, even when Congress has spoken in purely declarative terms. *** These precedents, however, are simply not dispositive here. Not only are we unpersuaded that a judicially sanctioned intrusion into tribal sovereignty is required to fulfill the purposes of the ICRA, but to the contrary, the structure of the statutory scheme and the legislative history of Title I suggest that Congress' failure to provide remedies other than habeas corpus was a deliberate one.

A.

Two distinct and competing purposes are manifest in the provisions of the ICRA: In addition to its objective of strengthening the position of individual tribal members vis-à-vis the tribe, Congress also intended to promote the well-established federal "policy of furthering Indian self-government." *Mancari*. This commitment to the goal of tribal self-determination is demonstrated by the provisions of Title I itself. Section 1302, rather than providing in wholesale fashion for the extension of constitutional requirements to tribal governments, as had been initially proposed, selectively incorporated and in some instances modified the safeguards of the Bill of Rights to fit the unique political, cultural, and economic needs of tribal governments. Thus, for example, the statute does not prohibit the establishment of religion, nor does it require jury trials in civil cases, or appointment of counsel for indigents in criminal cases.

The other Titles of the ICRA also manifest a congressional purpose to protect tribal sovereignty from undue interference. For instance, Title III, 25 U.S.C. §§ 1321–26, hailed by some of the ICRA's supporters as the most important part of the Act, provides that States may not assume civil or criminal jurisdiction over "Indian country" [under Public Law 280] without the prior consent of the tribe, thereby abrogating prior law to the contrary. Other Titles of the ICRA provide for strengthening certain tribal courts through training of Indian judges, and for minimizing interference by the Federal Bureau of Indian Affairs in tribal litigation.

Where Congress seeks to promote dual objectives in a single statute, courts must be more than usually hesitant to infer from its silence a cause of action that, while serving one legislative purpose, will disserve the other. Creation of a federal cause of action for the enforcement of rights created in Title I, however useful it might be in securing compliance with § 1302, plainly would be at odds with the congressional goal of protecting tribal self-government. Not

10. "First, is the plaintiff 'one of the class for whose *especial* benefit the statute was enacted'—that is, does the statute create a federal right in favor of the plaintiff? Second, is there any indication of legislative intent, explicit or implicit, either to create such a remedy or to deny one? Third, is it consistent with the underlying purposes of the legislative scheme to imply such a remedy for the plaintiff? And finally, is the cause of action one traditionally relegated to state [or tribal] law, in an area basically the concern of the States [or tribes], so that it would be inappropriate to infer a cause of action based solely on federal law?" [*Cort*.]

only would it undermine the authority of tribal forums, but it would also impose serious financial burdens on already "financially disadvantaged" tribes.

Moreover, contrary to the reasoning of the court below, implication of a federal remedy in addition to habeas corpus is not plainly required to give effect to Congress' objective of extending constitutional norms to tribal self-government. Tribal forums are available to vindicate rights created by the ICRA, and § 1302 has the substantial and intended effect of changing the law which these forums are obliged to apply. Tribal courts have repeatedly been recognized as appropriate forums for the exclusive adjudication of disputes affecting important personal and property interests of both Indians and non-Indians. Nonjudicial tribal institutions have also been recognized as competent law-applying bodies. *See United States v. Mazurie*, 419 U.S. 544 (1975).[22] Under these circumstances, we are reluctant to disturb the balance between the dual statutory objectives which Congress apparently struck in providing only for habeas corpus relief.

B.

Our reluctance is strongly reinforced by the specific legislative history underlying 25 U.S.C. § 1303. This history, extending over more than three years, indicates that Congress' provision for habeas corpus relief, and nothing more, reflected a considered accommodation of the competing goals of "preventing injustices perpetrated by tribal governments, on the one hand, and, on the other, avoiding undue or precipitous interference in the affairs of the Indian people."

In settling on habeas corpus as the exclusive means for federal-court review of tribal criminal proceedings, Congress opted for a less intrusive review mechanism than had been initially proposed. Originally, the legislation would have authorized *de novo* review in federal court of all convictions obtained in tribal courts. At hearings held on the proposed legislation in 1965, however, it became clear that even those in agreement with the general thrust of the review provision—to provide some form of judicial review of criminal proceedings in tribal courts—believed that *de novo* review would impose unmanageable financial burdens on tribal governments and needlessly displace tribal courts. Moreover, tribal representatives argued that *de novo* review would "deprive the tribal court of all jurisdiction in the event of an appeal, thus having a harmful effect upon law enforcement within the reservation," and urged instead that "decisions of tribal courts *** be reviewed in the U.S. district courts upon petition for a writ of *habeas corpus*." After considering numerous alternatives for review of tribal convictions, Congress apparently decided that review by way of *habeas corpus* would adequately protect the individual interests at stake while avoiding unnecessary intrusions on tribal governments.

Similarly, and of more direct import to the issue in this case, Congress considered and rejected proposals for federal review of alleged violations of the

---

22. By the terms of its Constitution, adopted in 1935 and approved by the Secretary of the Interior in accordance with the Indian Reorganization Act of 1934, 25 U.S.C. § 476, judicial authority in the Santa Clara Pueblo is vested in its tribal council.

Many tribal constitutions adopted pursuant to 25 U.S.C. § 476, though not that of the Santa Clara Pueblo, include provisions requiring that tribal ordinances not be given effect until the Department of Interior gives its approval. *** In these instances, persons aggrieved by tribal laws may, in addition to pursuing tribal remedies, be able to seek relief from the Department of the Interior.

Act arising in a civil context. As initially introduced, the Act would have required the Attorney General to "receive and investigate" complaints relating to deprivations of an Indian's statutory or constitutional rights, and to bring "such criminal or other action as he deems appropriate to vindicate and secure such right to such Indian." Notwithstanding the screening effect this proposal would have had on frivolous or vexatious lawsuits, it was bitterly opposed by several tribes. *** In response, this provision for suit by the Attorney General was completely eliminated from the ICRA. At the same time, Congress rejected a substitute proposed by the Interior Department that would have authorized the Department to adjudicate civil complaints concerning tribal actions, with review in the district courts available from final decisions of the agency.

Given this history, it is highly unlikely that Congress would have intended a private cause of action for injunctive and declaratory relief to be available in the federal courts to secure enforcement of § 1302. Although the only Committee Report on the ICRA in its final form, S. Rep. No. 841, 90th Cong., 1st Sess. (1967), sheds little additional light on this question, it would hardly support a contrary conclusion. Indeed its description of the purpose of Title I, as well as the floor debates on the bill, indicates that the ICRA was generally understood to authorize federal judicial review of tribal actions only through the habeas corpus provisions of § 1303. These factors, together with Congress' rejection of proposals that clearly would have authorized causes of action other than habeas corpus, persuade us that Congress, aware of the intrusive effect of federal judicial review upon tribal self-government, intended to create only a limited mechanism for such review, namely, that provided for expressly in § 1303.

V.

As the bill's chief sponsor, Senator Ervin, commented in urging its passage, the ICRA "should not be considered as the final solution to the many serious constitutional problems confronting the American Indian." Although Congress explored the extent to which tribes were adhering to constitutional norms in both civil and criminal contexts, its legislative investigation revealed that the most serious abuses of tribal power had occurred in the administration of criminal justice. In light of this finding, and given Congress' desire not to intrude needlessly on tribal self-government, it is not surprising that Congress chose at this stage to provide for federal review only in habeas corpus proceedings.

By not exposing tribal officials to the full array of federal remedies available to redress actions of federal and state officials, Congress may also have considered that resolution of statutory issues under § 1302, and particularly those issues likely to arise in a civil context, will frequently depend on questions of tribal tradition and custom which tribal forums may be in a better position to evaluate than federal courts. *** As is suggested by the District Court's opinion in this case, efforts by the federal judiciary to apply the statutory prohibitions of § 1302 in a civil context may substantially interfere with a tribe's ability to maintain itself as a culturally and politically distinct entity.[32]

32. A tribe's right to define its own membership for tribal purposes has long been recognized as central to its existence as an independent political community. *** Given the often vast gulf between tribal traditions and those with which federal courts are more intimately familiar, the judiciary should not rush to create causes of action that would intrude on these delicate matters.

As we have repeatedly emphasized, Congress' authority over Indian matters is extraordinarily broad, and the role of courts in adjusting relations between and among tribes and their members correspondingly restrained. *See Lone Wolf.* Congress retains authority expressly to authorize civil actions for injunctive or other relief to redress violations of § 1302, in the event that the tribes themselves prove deficient in applying and enforcing its substantive provisions. But unless and until Congress makes clear its intention to permit the additional intrusion on tribal sovereignty that adjudication of such actions in a federal forum would represent, we are constrained to find that § 1302 does not impliedly authorize actions for declaratory or injunctive relief against either the tribe or its officers.

[Reversed.]

[**JUSTICE REHNQUIST** joined Parts I, II, IV, and V of this opinion; **JUSTICE BLACKMUN** did not participate.]

JUSTICE WHITE, dissenting.

*** The ICRA itself gives no indication that the constitutional rights it extends to American Indians are to be enforced only by means of federal habeas corpus actions. On the contrary, since several of the specified rights are most frequently invoked in noncustodial situations, the natural assumption is that some remedy other than habeas corpus must be contemplated. *** While I believe that the uniqueness of the Indian culture must be taken into consideration in applying the constitutional rights granted in § 1302, I do not think that it requires insulation of official tribal actions from federal-court scrutiny. Nor do I find any indication that Congress so intended.

***

[T]he Senate Report states that the purpose of the ICRA "is to insure that the American Indian is afforded the broad constitutional rights secured to other Americans." Not only is a private cause of action consistent with that purpose, it is necessary for its achievement. The legislative history indicates that Congress was concerned, not only about the Indian's lack of substantive rights, but also about the lack of remedies to enforce whatever rights the Indian might have. During its consideration of this legislation, the Senate Subcommittee pointed out that "[t]hough protected against abridgment of his rights by State or Federal action, the individual Indian is *** without redress against his tribal authorities." Summary Report 3.

***

I agree with the majority that the legislative history demonstrates that Congress was also concerned with furthering Indian self-government. I do not agree, however, that this concern on the part of Congress precludes our recognition of a federal cause of action to enforce the terms of the Act. The major intrusion upon the tribe's right to govern itself occurred when Congress enacted the ICRA and mandated that the tribe "in exercising powers of self-government" observe the rights enumerated in § 1302. The extension of constitutional rights to individual citizens is *intended* to intrude upon the authority of government. And once it has been decided that an individual does possess certain rights vis-à-vis his government, it necessarily follows that he has some way to enforce those rights. Although creating a federal cause of action may "constitut[e] an interference with tribal autonomy and self-government beyond that created by the change in substantive law itself," in my mind it is a further step that must be taken; otherwise, the change in the law may be meaningless. ***

NOTES AND QUESTIONS

1. *Federal courts versus tribal institutions.*

   a. *Members.* Does the majority of the Court conclude that Ms. Martinez is without any ICRA remedy in any forum? Or does it assume that tribal institutions (tribal court, tribal council) are required by ICRA to accommodate her statutory rights? If tribal institutions default on this obligation, does Ms. Martinez have any avenue of federal review or relief?

   b. *Nonmembers.* If a tribe imposes discriminatory taxes on a non-Indian doing business on tribal land, what avenue(s) of relief would the non-Indian have after *Santa Clara Pueblo*? Note that members and nonmembers seem similarly situated for purposes of how ICRA applies to them. Should nonmembers have greater opportunities to invoke ICRA outside the context of criminal jurisdiction (where of course ICRA provides habeas corpus relief)? Is there a danger that this arrangement will make nonmembers more reluctant to do business in Indian country, harming tribes and tribal members economically? Professor Robert Laurence has suggested that *Santa Clara Pueblo*, which leaves non-members with no direct federal court review of allegedly discriminatory tribal decisions, has contributed to other forms of judicial intermeddling in tribal jurisdiction over nonmembers. *See* Robert Laurence, Martinez, Oliphant, *and Federal Court Review of Tribal Acts under the Indian Civil Rights Act*, 10 Campbell L. Rev. 411 (1988). His point is that the decision, while respectful of tribal sovereignty, established a regime in which later federal courts would be unable to resist taking away categories of tribal jurisdiction over non-Indians. Assume that Professor Laurence is correct about this; should the Court in any event have decided *Martinez* the way it did? Why or why not?

2. *Revisiting the Cohen Formulation after* Santa Clara Pueblo *and* Wheeler. Recall Cohen's formulation of federal Indian law from Chapter 3: "An Indian tribe possesses, in the first instance, all the powers of any sovereign state. *** These powers are subject to qualification by treaties and by express legislation by Congress, but save as thus expressly qualified, full powers of internal sovereignty are vested in the Indian tribes and in their duly constituted organs of government." Notice the ways that *Wheeler* and the majority opinion in *Santa Clara Pueblo* fit this formulation. In *Wheeler*, tribal power to prosecute tribal members is the product of inherent sovereignty; while it may be regulated by the federal government, it is not the product of federal delegation. In *Santa Clara Pueblo*, the Court finds that although Congress may subject tribal governments to federal judicial review, and has done so with respect

to *habeas* actions, ICRA did not expressly create a broader cause of action, leaving tribal sovereigns themselves to adjudicate alleged violations of ICRA rights.

Tribal Rights, Women's Rights, and the Debate over *Santa Clara Pueblo v. Martinez*

Although *Santa Clara Pueblo v. Martinez* has far-reaching implications for Indian tribes, in the broader legal community attention to the decision has focused on whether tribes systematically disadvantage women. As with many other prominent cases in federal Indian law, the dominant community knows so little about the tribal context that it becomes almost irresistible to generalize one tribe's approach to all tribes. Beyond the question of membership, the hundreds of federally recognized Indian tribes have enormous differences across them in the way gender lines have historically been used. Increasingly, women serve as tribal leaders; several women have, for example, served as the top elected official of Indian tribes, well before any woman had a meaningful chance of serving as president of the United States. In terms of formal legal equality for women, the Navajo Nation passed its equivalent of an Equal Rights Amendment without controversy, something that has yet to be achieved in the United States. *See* Sarah Krakoff, *A Narrative of Sovereignty: Illuminating the Paradox of the Domestic Dependent Nation*, 83 Or. L. Rev. 1109, 1138 (2004). At the same time, domestic violence and sexual abuse are serious problems on reservations. For an interesting overview, see Gloria Valencia–Weber and Christine P. Zuni, *Domestic Violence and Tribal Protection of Indigenous Women in the United States*, 69 St. John's L. Rev. 69 (1995).

Despite the range of women's experiences in Indian country, by far the most common reference to American Indian women in legal scholarship concerns *Santa Clara Pueblo*. A 2003 article, for example, discusses the way that the reluctance of western legal institutions to intervene in cases involving religion or traditional culture is actually a decision to prefer the claims of certain community members over others: "Thus far, law has used its power to authorize fundamentalist control over women and individuals, forcefully helping to preserve tradition against modernity." Madhavi Sunder, *Piercing the Veil*, 112 Yale L. J. 1399, 1407 (2003). Professor Sunder points to *Santa Clara Pueblo* as an example of this phenomenon, arguing that the Court failed to acknowledge that the tribe itself was conflicted and instead "deferred to tribal leaders at the expense of the Pueblo woman's effort to seek equal justice for women within the tribe." *Id.* at 1430.

Judith Resnik, in *Dependent Sovereigns: Indian Tribes, States, and Federal Courts*, 56 U. Chi. L. Rev. 671 (1989), focuses on the history of the membership rule. She notes that historians of the Pueblo before 1935 do not mention the impact of parentage on membership, and the evidence conflicted as to whether the tribe was "matrilineal" (tracing identity through the maternal line) or "patrilineal" (tracing identity through the paternal line). In its initial 1935 constitution, Santa Clara did not make gender distinctions, but instead provided that all children of two Santa Clara parents would be members, that children of mixed marriages could be admitted with the approval of tribal council, and that all persons could be naturalized as members of the Pueblo. In

1939, however, the Pueblo created the discriminatory rule and eliminated the naturalization rule. The Secretary of the Interior approved the ordinance, as required under the Pueblo Constitution. Professor Resnik interrogates the origins of the ordinance:

> In 1935, the Department made a "declaration" of its views on "Membership in Indian Tribes"; a circular addressed to all "engaged in Indian Reorganization Act" stated that "Congress [has] a definite policy to limit the application of Indian benefits ***." To implement that policy, the Department planned "to urge and insist that any constitutional provision conferring automatic tribal membership upon children hereafter born, should limit such membership to persons who reasonably can be expected to participate in tribal relations and affairs." Suggested tests for such membership included having both parents be recognized tribal members or be residents of the reservation or that an individual possess a "certain degree of Indian blood." *** That policy statement is dated November 18, 1935; Santa Clara Pueblo's original constitution, with its inclusive membership rules, was approved just a month later. Four years later, the more restrictive rules were put into place. ***
>
> *** I cannot share the ease with which the Supreme Court in *Santa Clara Pueblo* assumed the 1939 Ordinance to be an artifact of Santa Clara sovereignty. The emergence of a codified, written, non-discretionary, gender-based membership rule is linked to the Pueblo's decision to organize under guidance of the Department of the Interior, is linked to the Pueblo as a recipient of federal funds, and is linked to the Pueblo as situated in a United States culture that has made patrilineal and patriarchal rules so familiar that, to some, they seem uncontroversial.

Id. at 715–715. Does it make a difference whether contemporary tribal choices are the products of traditional practices adhered to before contact or of non-Indian influence? On the one hand, isn't it in some sense notions of tribal difference and uniqueness that lead to public desire to recognize tribal autonomy? On the other, can it be that tribal sovereignty will only be protected when tribes act as they did before non-Indian contact and the vast changes that came with it?

Professor Resnik wrote that "the case was an 'easy' one for the Supreme Court to proclaim its commitment to tribal sovereignty because it accorded with federal norms about the treatment of women." *Dependent Sovereigns*, 56 U. Chi. L. Rev. at 727. In a 2004 symposium on *Santa Clara Pueblo*, Bethany Berger disagrees, arguing that:

> [*Santa Clara Pueblo*] was a particularly hard case—and not because the justices were such committed feminists. Rather, the case was a tough one for the Supreme Court and for non-Indian policy makers because the federal government and the colonial governments before it had always used the needs of Indian women as an excuse for erosion of Indian sovereignty. Indian women, by the common account, needed the federal government to come save them from drudgery, from sexual slavery, from oppression. *** [T]he women whose plight called out for European and American protection were not real women—instead they were imagined by the colonizers, tailored to their ideas of gender and culture and their needs in justifying the colonial project.

Indian Policy and the Imagined Indian Woman, 14 Kan. J. L. & Pub. Pol'y 103, (2004). Professor Berger suggests that the heightened scholarly attention given to *Santa Clara Pueblo* is part of this pattern:

> While Julia Martinez was a real woman who sought to change the membership ordinance that excluded her children before her lawyers ever got involved, *** similar factors may be at work in reactions to the *Martinez* case.
>
> First, *** the position of the Martinezes has been understood largely according to western priorities. The Martinez children participated fully in the religious and cultural life of the Santa Clara Pueblo, which perhaps even more than for most tribes, has long been the most important kind of membership in a Pueblo community. Both Julia Martinez and her Navajo husband Myles remained affiliated with the Santa Clara Pueblo until their deaths in 2000 and 2001 respectively, and several of their children still live there. While today increased tribal revenue with the advent of casino gaming may exacerbate the differences between those formally enrolled and those not, the most severe hardship faced by the Martinez children came not at the hands of the tribal government but from the Indian Health Service, which denied the children medical care for lack of tribal enrollment. This problem, however, was resolved in 1968, long before the case was filed, when the Bureau of Indian Affairs gave the Martinezes Indian census numbers. But the indicia of membership that were familiar and valued in Anglo–American society, voting and citizenship rights in the government established at federal urging in 1935, were far more visible and important to the non-Pueblo judges.
>
> Another similarity is the vehement reaction of non-Indians to the case. There is some evidence that the case got to the Supreme Court only because it involved protection of women. Several previous cases [decided before *Morton v. Mancari*] had challenged membership ordinances that relied on percentage of Indian blood. If the equal protection provisions of the Indian Civil Rights Act were enforced in the same way as those in the U.S. Constitution, these ordinances would be far more offensive, as racial classifications are entitled to strict scrutiny, while gender-based ones receive only heightened scrutiny. But the Circuit courts, even the Tenth Circuit that struck down the Santa Clara Pueblo ordinance, had little trouble upholding these membership requirements. Before the passage of ICRA, moreover, the New York State courts had, with little hand wringing, repeatedly upheld Iroquois laws providing that children could only inherit tribal membership through their mothers. In fact, it appears that among Indian Reorganization Act membership laws, ordinances that exclude the children of male tribal members with non-members, while admitting all children of female members, are more common than those like the Santa Clara ordinance. None of these ordinances, however, generates publicity or concern similar to that attending the Santa Clara Pueblo law. It takes a case that calls upon the courts in their role as protectors of Indian women to do that.

Id. at 111–112. The most powerful statement about the case comes from Rina Swentzell, a member of the Santa Clara Pueblo, many of whose children and grandchildren cannot enroll in the tribe:

I am a woman from Santa Clara Pueblo. I was born there. I lived with my great-grandmother on the main plaza next to the Winter kiva until she died when I was thirteen years old. *** I was 39 years old when the Supreme Court ruled on the *Santa Clara v. Martinez* case. Even then, I wanted the courts to rule in favor of the tribe—to rule for tribal sovereignty. My desire was not because I was not concerned about my children who would not be considered members of the Pueblo, because I am a woman married to a non-Santa Clara person. It was not because I did not know that my cousin would have his children considered members because he is a man, though he was not born in the Pueblo, did not grow up there, and was married to a non-Santa Clara person. Of course, I also knew that it did not make sense; that it was not just or fair. I knew that what was happening in the community was blatant gender discrimination.

***

At Santa Clara Pueblo, the social order was not traditionally either/or, not matriarchical or patriarchical. It was both. Even today, every child is born as a Winter person or a Summer person with the option to become the other if the sensibilities are of the other. To know and acknowledge both is encouraged, because ultimately, the goal is to embrace the whole—to be a part of the larger context, to be a part of society. *** It is believed that every person has feminine and masculine, warm and cold, dark and light qualities. ***

At Santa Clara, the ideal person was and still is the gia. Earth, who gave the people birth is called gia, so is the biological woman who gives birth, and so are the community women who nurture and take care of many extended families. They give ceremonial or political advice, physical shelter and food, if needed, and housing. Most unusual is that men in the community who behave as nurturing, embracing people in the political and ceremonial realms are also called, gias, that is, mothers. The best way to behave in that world is as a mother, because we are emulating the earth on whom we daily walk and move, but we are still obliged to acknowledge the father embodied in the sun without whom there would be no children to mother.

***

I thought long and hard about the Martinez case. I wanted my children to be members of Santa Clara, although I had married a non-Indian who I met in college. If the case favored the Martinez family, who I assumed had been encouraged by non-Native people to initiate the lawsuit, I felt that Santa Clara would lose any remnants of itself as a vital, self-determining community. I was relieved to hear the decision. Santa Clara was to retain the on-going conversation about who is a recognized member of the community. But, more importantly, the Western world was acknowledging a way of life which traditionally honored nurturing and feminine qualities.

Two of my children live at Santa Clara today. One is a full member of Santa Clara, because he was born out of wedlock, and the tribe will "adopt" illegitimate children of women no matter who is the father. This has led to a group of women who will not marry the fathers of their children because of loss of tribal membership. The other child is the daughter of my non-Indian husband. She has lived in Santa Clara for almost twenty years where she raised two children. She participates in community activities. She has been on the Community Membership Committee. ***

*** When American lawyers became involved with the writing of the 1936 Santa Clara Constitution, which was written mostly by non-pueblo people, a different mentality and approach to life came into the forefront. Opposites in the American world are adversarial. It is one or the other, not both. It is a cultural approach that also acknowledges that the world is in tension, but in the Western world, only one side wins.

As I have talked with all three of my daughters (34 to 42 years old) and three granddaughters (17, 19 and 20 years old) who are affected by the Martinez decision, I hear their pain of being excluded—to some point. My middle daughter, mentioned above, built her house at Santa Clara, participates in Pueblo activities and is honored by the Winter group to which she belongs and at this point, even more than my son who is a full member. She moves through the hills and Pueblo as if she belongs. She assumes that the Pueblo is home and that if there are problems about her being there, they will most certainly come from one member of our extended family who claims the family allotment of land on which she lives. But, this has nothing to do with the tribe. In fact, the rest of the family knows that if the issue goes to Tribal Council, the Council would protect my daughter's right to stay in her house. ***

As I talk to this middle daughter who lives at Santa Clara about the Martinez case issues, she prefers to have decision-making about tribal membership stay within the community. She was on the tribal membership committee when an amendment to base membership on other than gender was proposed some eight years ago. She recalls that the amendment was tabled not because of disagreement over issues but because of an interpersonal conflict between a councilperson and an angry female. The conversation has been quieted but awaits an impetus to awaken and continue, she says. She feels that the pain of non-acceptance and inequality is still held in the hearts of those affected and will surface again when the time is right.

The other two daughters do not live in Santa Clara and did not grow up in the community. The eldest has always felt discriminated against because of the light color of her skin. She was refused participation in dances because "she didn't look right." Now, this daughter feels distant and refuses to accept Santa Clara as her community in a counter-rejection move. In spite of her angers for being rejected, she upholds Santa Clara's right to retain its sovereign status and decision-making capability, because in many ways "it remains a place that embodies good human ideals to be emulated by all people."

My third daughter also does not live in Santa Clara but "looks right," or looks Indian. She feels that the reason the Martinez decision has not worked as a vehicle for community justice and hence, community coherence is that men in the community had been for several decades deprived of their traditional roles as farmers, hunters, and providers. The Santa Clara Constitution, with its premise of patrilineal rule, gives the men of

Santa Clara much needed meaning and authority, albeit through repression of their wives, sisters, and children. They are not so willing to give up their new-found sense of power. She, like the other two daughters, maintains hope that the old teachings and traditions, which talk about all the people being children of the community, will be remembered and used to restructure the social order. Outsiders will only diminish that further, she feels. And, she needs to know that her identity with that community, which gives her a sense of place, a sense of home, remains a vital, self-determining unit.

The next generation of women in my family with whom I talked are the 17 to 20 year olds. They are also affected differently by the tribal stance that explicit or formal written membership and property ownership follows the male line. The eldest is the furthest removed, again because of the color of her skin. She maintains a distance and offered a shrug of her shoulders for her opinion. The middle granddaughter grew up in Santa Clara, speaks Tewa and because she considers Santa Clara her home, feels that she belongs there. Although, she doubts that the Council reciprocates with her sense of belonging. She definitely feels that tribal sovereignty must be acknowledged over the pain of personal discrimination. Her solution for the membership issue is that membership be determined by residence and participation. The seventeen-year-old is a full member because her father, my illegitimate son, is a recognized member of the tribe. She realizes that she has to be careful about whom she marries, but her brothers do not. That angers her, and she also expresses that something needs to be done by the community but not by outsiders or by the American court system.

***

What has been introduced by outside thinking is that we have to choose between uncompromising opposites, between male and female dominance, between individual rights or community wellbeing. *** We are even tempted to think that American law can bring equality by written mandates, making us forget that we are capable of remembering a system in which focus on relationships might lead us to different solutions. ***

Rina Swentzell, *Testimony of a Santa Clara Woman*, 14 Kan. J. L. & Pub. Pol'y 97, 97–101 (2004).

It is not true that Julia Martinez's actions were the product of non-Indian instigation; she had been actively seeking to address this issue outside of court for years before contacting attorneys:

Julia Martinez first attempted to have Audrey recognized as a member of the Pueblo in 1946, shortly after Audrey was born. Since 1963 her efforts have been vigorous and constant. Julia Martinez has met with her representative to the Council, to request that he present the request that Audrey be enrolled to the council. When her representative refused to bring the matter up in Council, she obtained special permission from the Governor to address the Council herself. She and other women in her situation have formed a committee which as a group petitioned representatives and, with special permission, the Council. Julia Martinez, individually and with the committee, succeeded in having a special meeting of the entire Pueblo convened to discuss the situation. Julia Martinez,

> individually and with the committee of similarly situated women attended meetings with various BIA officials, and with the All–Pueblo Agency in Albuquerque. She and her husband Myles attempted to have Myles Martinez naturalized as a member of the Pueblo, in which case their children would have automatically been recognized as members. Mrs. Martinez also met with her State Representative concerning the recognition of her children as members of Santa Clara. Finally Mrs. Martinez attended hearings held by the Subcommittee on Constitutional Rights of the United States Senate Committee on the Judiciary, where she sought the help of then Senator Sam Ervin, Jr. In most instances there has been more than one attempt to resolve the matter through a particular channel; in particular, meetings with the Council representatives, the Governor and the Council have occurred four or five times over the last ten years. Finally, in 1971, Julia and Audrey Martinez sought legal advice. This suit was filed only after attempts by their lawyer to gain recognition for Audrey had failed. Plaintiffs have exhausted all available remedies within the Pueblo.

Martinez v. Santa Clara Pueblo, 402 F. Supp. 5, 11 (D.N.M. 1975). Do you agree with Rina Swentzell that even when tribal remedies are so clearly unavailing, change must be sought through the community and not from outsiders or the federal court system?

ICRA Review After *Santa Clara Pueblo v. Martinez*

The Supreme Court established in *Santa Clara Pueblo* that the only avenue to challenge tribal actions in federal court under the ICRA is through a writ of *habeas corpus*. Habeas review is thus clearly available to test criminal detention or a meaningful threat of criminal detention. *Means v. Navajo Nation*, 432 F.3d 924, 929 (9th Cir. 2005) (holding that court had habeas jurisdiction where individual was on pretrial release and tribe intended to continue its prosecution). It may not be available to test sanctions which do not constitute meaningful restrictions on liberty or remote threats of deprivation of liberty. *Moore v. Nelson*, 270 F.3d 789 (9th Cir. 2001) (no ICRA jurisdiction to test legality of a fine although failure to pay fine could result in detention).

Although one decision suggested ICRA created jurisdiction to challenge child custody proceedings resulting in removal of a child, the Supreme Court has rejected such jurisdiction under other federal habeas statutes, and most cases reject such jurisdiction under ICRA. *Compare Lehman v. Lycoming County Children's Servs. Agency*, 458 U.S. 502, 508-12 (1982) (no jurisdiction to challenge termination of parental rights under 28 U.S.C. § 2254), *Azure-Lonefight v. Cain*, 317 F.Supp.2d 1148 (D.N.D. 2004) (no ICRA review of child custody decision), *and Sandman v. Dakota*, 816 F. Supp. 448, 451 (W.D. Mich. 1992), *aff'd mem.* 7 F.3d 234 (6th Cir. 1993) (same), *with DeMent v. Oglala Sioux Tribal Court*, 874 F.2d 510 (8th Cir. 1989) (permitting ICRA review in custody case where non-Indian father challenged jurisdiction of tribal court); *see also Boozer v. Wilder*, 381 F.3d 931, 934 n. 2 (9th Cir.2004) (suggesting challenges to tribal court custody jurisdiction over non-Indians should be heard under 28 U.S.C. § 1331 rather than ICRA).

More recently, courts have struggled with whether *habeas* review is available to individuals banished from the reservation. *Compare Poodry v. Tonawanda Band of Seneca Indians* 85 F.3d 874 (2d Cir. 1996) (finding habeas jurisdiction to challenge criminal banishment from reservation) *and Sweet v. Hinzman*, 634 F. Supp. 2d 1196 (W.D. Wash. 2008) (same), *with Alire v. Jackson*, 65 F.Supp.2d 1124 (D. Or. 1999) (no habeas jurisdiction to challenge exclusion from reservation). *See also Jeffredo v. Macarro*, 599 F.3d 913 (9th Cir. 2009) (although banishment could create habeas jurisdiction, disenrollment from tribe did not, even though those disenrolled could not access certain tribal facilities). The next case carefully considers and rejects the possibility of habeas corpus relief for temporary banishment.

TAVARES V. WHITEHOUSE

851 F.3d 863 (9th Cir. 2017)

MCKEOWN, CIRCUIT JUDGE:

This appeal tests the limits of federal court jurisdiction to hear a habeas petition brought under the Indian Civil Rights Act ("ICRA"), 25 U.S.C. §§ 1301–1303, where the underlying claim arises not from an actual detention or imprisonment, but instead from a tribe's temporary exclusion of its own members. * * *

The ICRA created a new federal habeas remedy "to test the legality of ... detention by order of an Indian tribe." 25 U.S.C. § 1303. Because § 1303 provides the exclusive federal remedy for tribal violations of the ICRA, unless a petitioner is in "detention by order of an Indian tribe," the federal courts lack jurisdiction over an ICRA challenge and the complaint must be brought in tribal court. The question here is whether a temporary exclusion from tribal land, but not the entire reservation, constitutes a detention under the ICRA. Reading the ICRA's habeas provision in light of the Indian canons of construction and Congress's plenary authority to limit tribal sovereignty, we hold that the district court lacked jurisdiction under § 1303 of the ICRA to review this temporary exclusion claim.

BACKGROUND

Before the first Europeans arrived in California, as many as 350,000 Indians lived within the state's borders, speaking up to eighty different languages. S. Rep. No. 103-340, at 1 (1994). By the time Mexico ceded California to the United States in 1848, the indigenous population had dropped to approximately 150,000 people; by 1900, it had plummeted to about 15,000. *Id.* at 1–2. This decline was not, of course, unique to California, but instead mirrored the effects of disease, war, and removal policies on tribes across the country.

One of the indigenous groups still in California at the turn of the century was the Auburn Band, "a small, cohesive band of Indians" that lived about forty miles outside of Sacramento. *Id.* at 4. By 1953, the federal government had acquired forty acres of land (the "Auburn Rancheria" or "Rancheria") in trust on the Band's behalf. *Id.* But by the mid-1950s, Congress adopted a policy of "assimilation through termination," Cohen's § 1.06, at 85, and the Auburn Rancheria was ultimately terminated in 1967. S. Rep. No. 103-340, at 5. As a result, "[R]ancheria lands formerly held in tribal or community ownership" were divided and distributed. H.R. Rep. No. 103-812, at 22 (1994).*** [Congress restored the Band's federal recognition in 1994 and today it owns about a dozen parcels of land on its historic Rancheria along with an off-reservation casino.]

In keeping with the goals of current federal Indian policy, the Tribe is self-governing. It is run by an elected five-member Tribal Council, which enacts legislation and takes executive action. The Council also disciplines tribal members for civil violations of the Tribe's constitution and ordinances. Like many tribes today, the UAIC does not have a criminal code and does not exercise criminal jurisdiction over its members.

The Tribe adopted a constitution and bylaws, three of which are particularly implicated by this appeal. Ordinance 2004-001 III(B) imposes a duty on all tribal members "to refrain from damaging or harming tribal programs or filing of false information in connection with a tribal program." Ordinance 2004-001 III(I) requires members to "refrain from defaming the reputation of the Tribe, its officials, its employees or agents outside of a tribal forum[.]" And the Enrollment Ordinance provides that a Tribe member can be punished—up to and including disenrollment—for making misrepresentations against the Tribe.

This appeal arises out of actions taken by the Tribal Council in 2011. Petitioners Jessica Tavares, Dolly Suehead, Donna Caesar, and Barbara Suehead (collectively, "the petitioners") disagreed with how the Council was governing internal tribal affairs and, on November 7, 2011, they submitted a recall petition to the Tribe's Election Committee. The recall petition raised a litany of allegations against the members of the Council: financial mismanagement, retaliation, electoral irregularity, denial of due process, denial of access to an audit, and restrictions on access to Tribe members' mailing addresses. The Election Committee rejected the recall petition after determining that it did not have signatures from forty percent of tribal members, some of the signatures were not notarized, and some signatories did not provide a date and address, as required by a tribal ordinance.

Around the same time, the petitioners circulated to mass media outlets two press releases detailing their complaints. The first press release stated that the Council had engaged in "questionable financial practices" and "cover-ups of financial misdealings," that the Council had "fraudulently" refused to conduct a financial audit of the Tribe's resources, and that the Tribe's elections were "dishonest and rigged." After the Election Committee denied the recall petition, the petitioners circulated the second press release, which alleged that the Council had "scuttle[d]" the petition.

Four days after the recall petition was rejected, the Council sent each petitioner a Notice of Discipline and Proposed Withholding of Per Capita. The Notices stated that the petitioners' press releases "contained numerous inaccurate, false and defamatory statements" that wound up being published in non-tribal news outlets like the *Sacramento Bee*. The Notices informed the petitioners that, through the press releases, the petitioners had "[r]epeatedly libel[ed] and slander[ed] the Tribe and its agents maliciously and in disregard of the truth in non-tribal forums" and had taken "[h]armful and damaging actions to tribal programs, specifically our tribal businesses and government, and provid[ed] outsiders with false information about tribal programs," in violation of tribal law. The Notices also stated that the Council had voted to withhold the petitioners' per capita distributions and to ban them temporarily from tribal lands and facilities.

The exclusion orders were effective immediately. The petitioners were barred from tribal events, properties, offices, schools, health and wellness facilities, a park, and the casino. During their terms of exclusions, the petitioners could not run for tribal office, but they could vote in tribal elections through absentee ballots. They were not excluded from the twenty-one privately owned parcels of land, including their own homes and land owned by other members of the Tribe, and they retained their tribal health care benefits. Tavares was excluded for ten years, while the others were excluded for two years. None of the petitioners had a right to a hearing or an appeal on the exclusion orders.

The Notices also stated that the Council intended to withhold the petitioners' "per capita distributions and all other financial benefits and membership privileges," excluding health care benefits, for four years (as to Tavares) and six months (as to the others). Unlike the exclusion orders, the withholding orders were not effective immediately. Instead, the petitioners were entitled to a hearing before the Council and to an appeal. The Council confirmed the proposed suspension of the petitioners' per capita distributions after a hearing.

On appeal, the Appeals Board affirmed the Council's findings and actions in a thirty-page thoroughly-reasoned decision. ***

The petitioners filed a petition for a writ of habeas corpus in federal court under 25 U.S.C. § 1303 of the ICRA against the members of the Council. The district court dismissed the petition for lack of subject matter jurisdiction, concluding that the petitioners' punishment was not a "detention" sufficient to invoke federal habeas jurisdiction.

ANALYSIS

I. Principles Animating Habeas Jurisdiction Under §1303 of the Indian Civil Rights Act.

***

Because Indian tribes have sovereignty that predates the Constitution, they are not subject to the constitutional restraints that bind the federal government and the states. *See Talton v. Mayes*, 163 U.S. 376, 382–84, 16 S. Ct. 986, 41 L.Ed. 196 (1896). Congress can, however, impose such restraints by statute as part of its plenary authority over tribal affairs. In 1968, Congress exercised this authority and enacted the ICRA, which extends much of the Bill of Rights to tribes by statute. The ICRA also contains an explicit federal habeas remedy: "The privilege of the writ of habeas corpus shall be available to any person, in a court of the United States, to test the legality of his detention by order of an Indian tribe." 25 U.S.C. § 1303.

II. Per Capita Withholding Orders

[The court concurred with other decisions holding that federal habeas jurisdiction does not operate to remedy economic restraints, *e.g.*, denial of per capita payments.]

III. Temporary Exclusion Orders

We now turn to the crux of this appeal—whether the petitioners, who were temporarily excluded from tribal lands, were in "detention" under § 1303 for purposes of federal habeas jurisdiction.

We start with the words Congress used in § 1303, focusing on a difference between the language used in that provision and the language used in the general federal habeas statutes. When Congress enacted the ICRA in 1968, it was legislating against a well-established habeas framework: the federal courts have habeas jurisdiction whenever a petitioner is "in custody." [citations omitted] Yet Congress chose not to incorporate this language into the ICRA. Instead, under § 1303, habeas corpus is available only to a person who wishes to "test the legality of his detention by order of an Indian tribe." *** [W]e think Congress's use of "detention" instead of "custody" when it created habeas jurisdiction over tribal actions is significant in multiple respects.

At the time Congress enacted the ICRA, "detention" was generally understood to have a meaning distinct from and, indeed, narrower than "custody." Specifically, "detention" was commonly defined to require physical confinement. *See, e.g.*, *Preiser v. Rodriguez*, 411 U.S. 475, 484–85, 93 S. Ct. 1827, 36 L.Ed.2d 439 (1973) (equating "detention" and "physical confinement"); *** By contrast, "custody" had a more fluid definition: while it meant "physical control of the person," it did not require physical confinement or imprisonment. Instead, a person was in custody for habeas purposes if there was "restraint of [that] person by another [such] that the latter can produce the body of the former at a hearing as directed by writ or order." In other words, at the time of the ICRA's enactment, detention was understood as a subset of custody.***

Under English common law, and for much of our history, physical custody, confinement, or detention was required as a prerequisite to habeas relief. holding that petitioner was in custody when he was released on personal recognizance pending execution of his sentence).

By the time Congress enacted the ICRA in 1968, this expansion of "custody" was well under way. The Supreme Court had already explained that "custody" should not be construed unduly narrowly because habeas "is not now and never has been a static, narrow, formalistic remedy; its scope has grown to achieve its grand purpose—the protection of individuals against erosion of their right to be free from wrongful restraints upon their liberty." *Jones*, 371 U.S. at 243, 83 S. Ct. 373. Congress could have used the parallel "in custody" language or indicated that ICRA's habeas provision was to be read in light of that jurisprudence by using "custody" rather than "detention," but it did not do so.

Three cases that involve the limits of detention under § 1303 inform our analysis. We begin with *Poodry v. Tonawanda Band*, the first case to address this issue. 85 F.3d 874. The petitioners, members of the Tonawanda Band, were convicted of treason after they accused the tribal council of misconduct. *Id.* at 877–78. As punishment, the tribe disenrolled them and permanently banished them from the whole of the tribe's 7,500 acre reservation. *Id.* at 878. The disenrollment and banishment orders were served on the petitioners at their homes by up to twenty-five people, who attempted to take the petitioners "into custody and eject them from the reservation." *Id.* Although the initial ejection attempts failed, the respondents "continued to harass and assault the petitioners and their family members," attacking one petitioner on Main Street and "stoning" a second petitioner. *Id.* The tribe also denied the petitioners home electrical services and health services and medications. *Id.*

The Second Circuit held that the ICRA created federal habeas jurisdiction over the tribal actions. Construing ICRA's "detention" requirement as "no broader" than the "custody" requirement of other federal habeas statutes, the Second Circuit concluded that the facts alleged—including the manner in which the banishment orders were served, the attempts at removal, the threats and assaults, and the denial of electrical services—constituted "severe restraints on [individual] liberty" under *Hensley* 's custody test. *Id.* at 893–95.

The Second Circuit did not clearly distinguish between whether it was the disenrollment or banishment of the petitioners that constituted the severe restraint on liberty, although it focused on the disenrollment. ***

Two years later, in *Shenandoah*, the Second Circuit revisited jurisdiction under the ICRA. 159 F.3d 708. The petitioners in *Shenandoah*, like the petitioners in *Poodry*, were members of a tribe who challenged tribal leadership. The petitioners alleged that, because of these activities, they lost their jobs, their "voice[s]" in tribal governance, their health insurance, their access to the tribe's health center, and their quarterly per capita distributions; were banished from tribal businesses and recreational facilities; were stricken from tribal membership rolls; were prohibited from speaking with some tribe members; and were not sent tribal mailings. *Id.* at 714.

Significantly, the Second Circuit stepped back from *Poodry* and limited its reach. It clarified that *Poodry* had only recognized federal habeas jurisdiction for cases involving permanent banishment. *Id.* at 714 (citing *Poodry* in support of the proposition that "[h]abeas relief does address more than actual physical custody, and includes parole, probation, release on one's own recognizance pending sentencing or trial, and permanent banishment"). The Second Circuit then concluded that the tribe's misconduct at issue in *Shenandoah*, while "serious," was not a sufficiently severe restraint on liberty to create habeas jurisdiction."

***

Looking at the statute and these cases, several principles emerge. First, we do not need to decide whether to adopt *Poodry*'s conclusion that tribal banishment orders amount to "detention" under § 1303, because even under *Poodry*'s logic, the Second Circuit limited habeas jurisdiction only to permanent banishment orders, not temporary exclusion orders like those in this case.. In addition, we have already rejected *Poodry*'s assertion of federal habeas jurisdiction over tribal membership disputes. We also have taken issue with *Poodry*'s assertion that a tribe's interference with "an individual's social, cultural, and political affiliations" can create custody. ***

Second, the federal courts lack jurisdiction to review direct appeals of tribal membership decisions because they fall within the scope of tribes' inherent sovereignty. In many cases, a tribe's decision to temporarily exclude a member will be another expression of its sovereign authority to determine the makeup of the community. Because exclusion orders are often intimately tied to community relations and membership decisions, we cannot import an exclusion-as-custody analysis from the ordinary habeas context. ***

Third, tribes have the authority to exclude non-members from tribal land. *See Merrion v. Jicarilla Apache Tribe*, 455 U.S. 130, 142, 102 S. Ct. 894, 71 L.Ed.2d 21 (1982) (recognizing tribes' authority to exclude non-members); If tribal exclusion orders were sufficient to invoke habeas jurisdiction for tribal members, there would be a significant risk of undercutting the tribes' power because "any person," members and nonmembers alike, would be able to challenge exclusion orders through § 1303. Thus, tribal sovereignty vis-à-vis exclusion of non-members would collide with habeas jurisdiction.

With this framework in mind, we return to the principles animating habeas jurisdiction under § 1303 of the ICRA. We view Congress's choice of "detention" rather than "custody" in § 1303 as a meaningful restriction on the scope of habeas jurisdiction under the ICRA. A temporary exclusion is not tantamount to a detention. And recognizing the temporary exclusion orders at issue here as beyond the scope of "detention" under the ICRA bolsters tribes' sovereign authority to determine the makeup of their communities and best preserves the rule that federal courts should not entangle themselves in such disputes.***

Thus, we conclude that the district court lacked jurisdiction under § 1303 of the ICRA to review the challenge to the temporary exclusion orders. In so holding, we in no way minimize the significance of petitioners' allegations or the personal impact of the exclusion orders. The petitioners raise free speech and due process claims that implicate the substantive protections Congress saw fit to grant Indians with respect to their tribes through the ICRA. But the petitioners' remedy is with the Tribe, not in the federal courts. *Cf. Fisher v. Dist. Court*, 424 U.S. 382, 390–91, 96 S. Ct. 943, 47 L.Ed.2d 106 (1976) ("[E]ven if a jurisdictional holding occasionally results in denying an Indian plaintiff a forum to which a non-Indian has access, such disparate treatment of the Indian is justified because it is intended to benefit the class of which he is a member by furthering the congressional policy of Indian self-government.").

WARDLAW, CIRCUIT JUDGE, [dissented and would hold that any banishment is "detention" that would give rise to federal habeas jurisdiction].

NOTES AND QUESTIONS

1. Do you think the court's result would be different if the Auburn Band had imposed a permanent exclusion order? What if the banished member owned property within the reservation?

2. It seems clear in the Ninth Circuit that stripping members of tribal citizenship does not give rise to federal habeas jurisdiction. *Jeffredo v. Macarro*, 599 F.3d 913, 918–19 (9th Cir. 2010) (rejecting claim that loss of tribal membership, resulting in loss of access to senior center, tribal health clinic, and tribal school, resulted in "detention" for *habeas* review). In many of the banishment and disenrollment cases, the claim is that the tribal action is motivated by politics or greed. Should federal courts be involved in these cases? Should Congress provide relief? Remember that tribal courts are normally available to provide review. What if such decisions are not reviewable in tribal court?

3. Courts agree that *habeas* review is only available where the petitioner has exhausted all tribal remedies, including appeals. *See Selam v. Warm Springs Tribal Correction Facility*, 134 F.3d 948, 953–954 (9th Cir. 1998) (affirming denial of habeas relief where petitioner failed to exhaust tribal appeals process or demonstrate that exhaustion would be futile). Courts that have considered the matter also agree that the ICRA's provisions need not be interpreted identically to their constitutional counterparts. Instead tribal courts are free to apply the ICRA to provide an "essential fairness" consistent with tribal traditions and circumstances. Cohen's Handbook of Federal Indian Law 987 n.63 (2012).

4. In the absence of general federal court review, tribal institutions are the primary fora for ICRA claims. Despite fears that this limitation would effectively mean no review at all, reports have generally concluded that tribal courts have taken this responsibility seriously, overturning tribal actions that violated ICRA and developing a robust tribal jurisprudence of protection of rights and fairness in the process. *See* Christian Freitag, *Putting* Martinez *to the Test: Tribal Court Disposition of Due Process*, 72 Ind. L. J. 831, 864–67 (1997); Robert J. McCarthy, *Civil Rights in Tribal Courts: The Indian Bill of Rights at Thirty Years*, 34 Idaho L. Rev. 465 (1998); Mark D. Rosen, *Multiple Authoritative Interpreters of Quasi–Constitutional Federal Law: Of Tribal Courts and the Indian Civil Rights Act*, 69 Fordham L. Rev. 479 (2000); *see also* Bethany R. Berger, *Justice and the Outsider: Jurisdiction Over Nonmembers in Tribal Legal Systems*, 37 Ariz. St. L. J. 1047 (2005). A dozen years after *Santa Clara Pueblo v. Martinez*, the U.S. Civil Rights Commission released a report on tribal court implementation of the ICRA. The investigation was based on information gathered over several years and included testimony from numerous witnesses in several states. The Commission found that while there were some problems in tribal courts, they were primarily due to insufficient funds and the problems of any new court system in establishing its role and the scope of its authority. Far from recommending further restrictions on tribal courts, the Commission recommended more federal funding for their development, and expressed its "hopes that the current trend towards the narrowing of tribal jurisdiction will be reversed[.]" The Indian Civil Rights Act: A Report of the United States Commission on Civil Rights 74 (June 1991). In response, Congress adopted the Indian Tribal Justice Support Act of 1993, finding that "tribal justice systems are an essential part of tribal governments and serve as important forums for ensuring public health and safety and the political integrity of tribal governments;" and "traditional tribal justice practices are essential to the maintenance of the culture and identity of Indian tribes," but that "tribal justice systems are inadequately funded, and the lack of adequate funding impairs their operation." 25 U.S.C. § 3601; *see* Cohen's Handbook of Federal Indian Law 1450 (2012).

5. *Other avenues to challenge membership ordinances?* One of the most severe impacts of lack of membership was the denial of federal health benefits, and that Julia Martinez was ultimately able to get benefits from the Indian Health Service through the intervention of her lawyers. Today, formal enrollment is not necessary for eligibility for health services; instead the Indian Health Service provides health care to those who are of Indian descent and are part of a tribal community whether through residence on the reservation, participation in tribal affairs, or other indicia of membership. 42 C.F.R. § 136.12(a)(1). May an individual bring an action directly against the federal

government for refusing to provide services because the individual may not enroll due to a discriminatory membership ordinance?

Suits to Challenge Exclusion of "Freedmen" Citizens

Recent high profile membership disputes involve the descendants of the so-called "freedmen" of the Seminole and Cherokee Tribes. Litigation arising from these disputes raises complicated questions of history, tribal sovereign immunity, and federal authority.

Many African Americans incorporated with the Choctaw, Chickasaw, Creek, Cherokee and Seminole tribes in the years before the Civil War. In some tribes, most were slaves held by tribal members; in others, they were incorporated as citizens and even leaders within their tribes. In the wake of the Civil War, these tribes signed treaties with the U.S. agreeing to admit former slaves as citizens under certain conditions. Both before and after the Civil War, tribal members married and had children with African Americans. In creating rolls of those eligible to receive land under the Dawes Allotment Act, however, the United States placed individuals of African American appearance on "Freedmen" rolls and those of Indian appearance on rolls as citizens "by blood." Over the years, these tribes have sought to exclude descendants from these freedmen rolls. For summaries of these controversies and their history, see Ariela Gross, What Blood Won't Tell: A History of Race on Trial in America (2008); Kevin Mulroy, The Seminole Freedmen: A History (2007); Kevin Maillard, *Redwashing History: Tribal Anachronisms in the Seminole Nation Cases*, The Freedom Center J. 96 (2008); Circe Sturm, *Blood Politics, Racial Classification, and Cherokee National Identity: The Trials and Tribulations of the Cherokee Freedmen, in* Confounding the Color Line: The Indian–Black Experience in North America (James F. Brooks, ed. 2002).

The federal government sometimes participates in and sometimes rejects tribal exclusion of freedmen descendants. For example, the BIA refused to issue Certificates of Degree of Indian Blood (CDIBs) to descendants from the Seminole Freedmen rolls, with the result that they could not receive certain health and social services benefits. Although freedmen descendants challenged the refusal in federal court, the court dismissed the suit because sovereign immunity prevented joining the Seminole Nation of Oklahoma. *See, e.g.*, *Davis v. United States*, 343 F.3d 1282 (10th Cir. 2003). Later, however, when the Seminole Nation voted to amend its constitution to limit Seminole citizenship to "blood" descendants, then Assistant Secretary for Indian Affairs Kevin Gover refused to recognize the amendments or the newly elected Seminole government because freedmen descendants were not permitted to vote. When the Seminole Nation challenged this, the federal court largely upheld the Secretary's decision:

> The Court acknowledges and appreciates the importance of the Nation's right, as a sovereign body, to self-determination and self-government. However, as a sovereign, the Nation has the duty and the responsibility to respect the rights of all of its members, including the rights of its minority members, as guaranteed by the Nation's Constitution. *** Where the Nation will not protect the Constitutional rights of its minority

> members, the BIA has the responsibility and indeed, the duty, to intervene and attempt to protect those rights through appropriate remedies.

Seminole Nation of Oklahoma v. Norton, 223 F.Supp.2d 122, 146–147 (D.D.C. 2002). In 2003, the United States began issuing CDIBs to Seminole freedmen descendants, and the tribe reluctantly recognized their membership, but they retain an uneasy status within the Seminole Nation.

A more recent dispute involves the Cherokee Nation of Oklahoma. In 2003, the Cherokee Nation voted to remove the requirement that the Secretary of Interior approve constitutional amendments. Although the Cherokees freedmen descendants claimed that they were not permitted to participate in the election, Assistant Secretary for Indian Affairs Neal McCaleb approved the amendment. When freedmen descendants sued, the United States again argued that the suit could not proceed without joining the Cherokee Nation. After years of litigation, the D.C. Circuit concluded that although sovereign immunity barred any action against the Cherokee Nation itself, the Cherokee Nation Principal Chief and other tribal officials could be joined under the *Ex Parte Young* doctrine, and the litigation could proceed. *Vann v. U.S. Dept. of Interior*, 701 F.3d 927 (D.C. Cir. 2012).

While the federal litigation was pending, the disenfranchised Cherokees sought relief in the Cherokee courts. Lucy Allen argued that a Cherokee law limiting membership to those descended from the blood rolls violated the Cherokee Constitution and the 1866 Treaty. In March 2006, the Nation's highest court upheld her claim. *Allen v. Cherokee Nation Tribal Council*, JAT–04–09 (Cher. Jud. App. Trib. 2006). Although the Court rested its opinion on the plain language of the Cherokee Constitution, it also emphasized the importance of the Cherokee Treaty of 1866: "When the Cherokee Nation enters into treaties with other nations, we expect the other sovereign to live up to the promises they make. It is rightly expected that we will also keep the promises we make." *Id.* at 17–18. As a result of the decision, over two thousand descendants of those on the freedmen rolls enrolled with the tribe.

In 2007, however, the Cherokees voted to amend their constitution to limit citizenship to descendants of those listed on the "blood" rolls, thus excluding those whose ancestors were listed only on the Freedmen or Intermarried White rolls. Although the Cherokee District Court held that the constitutional amendment was invalid because it violated the 1866 Treaty, the Cherokee Nation Supreme Court reversed, finding that Cherokee Nation courts could not question the validity of the constitution itself. *Cherokee Nation Registrar v. Nash*, Case No. SC-2011-02 (Cher. S. Ct. 2011). The court also held that the Treaty of 1866 reserved the right to the Cherokee Nation to change its citizenship laws. *Id.*

As a result of the decision, Cherokee freedmen were declared ineligible to vote in a September 2011 run-off election for Cherokee Principal Chief between incumbent Chad Smith and challenger Bill John Baker. Most freedmen descendants were expected to vote for Baker, as Smith had strongly supported exclusion. The Obama administration reacted to the Cherokee decision by withholding a 33 million dollar HUD payment to the tribe and declaring it would not recognize the government under the winner of the run-off election until the federal litigation was resolved. At a September 20, 2011 hearing in the federal litigation, the Cherokee Nation agreed to permit the already enrolled freedmen descendants to vote, and accord them full rights as citizens pending final resolution of the case.

In 2017, the federal district court ruled on the merits in a 46 page opinion that is rich in history.

CHEROKEE NATION V. NASH

267 F.Supp.3d 86 (D.D.C. 2017)

Although it is a grievous axiom of American history that the Cherokee Nation's narrative is steeped in sorrow as a result of United States governmental policies that marginalized Native American Indians and removed them from their lands, it is, perhaps, lesser known that both nations' chronicles share the shameful taint of African slavery. This lawsuit harkens back a century-and-a-half ago to a treaty entered into between the United States and the Cherokee Nation in the aftermath of the Civil War. In that treaty, the Cherokee Nation promised that "never here-after shall either slavery or involuntary servitude exist in their nation" and "all freedmen who have been liberated by voluntary act of their former owners or by law, as well as all free colored persons who were in the country at the commencement of the rebellion, and are now residents therein, or who may return within six months, and their descendants, shall have all the rights of native Cherokees... ." Treaty With The Cherokee, 1866, U.S.–Cherokee Nation of Indians, art. 9, July 19, 1866, 14 Stat. 799 [hereinafter 1866 Treaty].

The parties to this lawsuit have called upon the Court to make a judicial determination resolving what they believe to be the "core" issue in this case, which is whether the 1866 Treaty guarantees a continuing right to Cherokee Nation citizenship for the extant descendants of freedmen listed on the Final Roll of Cherokee Freedmen compiled by the United States Commission to the Five Civilized Tribes, also known as the "Dawes Commission."

***

As indicated, each of the parties have moved for full or partial summary judgment in their favor on the principal issue of whether the 1866 Treaty provides a lasting right to Cherokee Nation citizenship for the descendants of freedmen who were listed on the Dawes Commission's Final Roll of Cherokee Freedmen.

***

There is no dispute that Article 9 of the 1866 Treaty states that the Cherokee Nation:

> [F]urther agree that all freedmen who have been liberated by voluntary act of their former owners or by law, as well as all free colored persons who were in the country at the commencement of the rebellion, and are now residents therein, or who may return within six months, and their descendants, shall have all the rights of native Cherokees... .

***

There appears to be no dispute that the Cherokee Freedmen are descendants of freedmen who were held as slaves by Cherokees and ultimately listed on the Dawes Freedmen Roll. Article 9 of the Treaty of 1866 entitles them to "all the rights of native Cherokees," 14 Stat. at 801, which means they have a right to citizenship so long as native Cherokees have that right. Nothing in the 1866 Treaty qualified that right by subjecting it to a condition antecedent that would terminate it, including the extinction of Indian Territory upon Oklahoma statehood. Although the Cherokee Nation Constitution defines citizenship, Article 9 of the 1866 Treaty guarantees that the Cherokee Freedmen shall have the right to it for as long as native Cherokees have that right. The history, negotiations, and practical construction of the 1866 Treaty suggest no other result. Consequently, the Cherokee Freedmen's right to citizenship in the Cherokee Nation is directly proportional to native Cherokees' right to citizenship, and the Five Tribes Act has no effect on that right.*** [T]he Cherokee Freedmen have a present right to citizenship in the Cherokee Nation that is coextensive with the rights of native Cherokees.

III. TRIBAL SOVEREIGN IMMUNITY

MICHIGAN V. BAY MILLS INDIAN COMMUNITY

572 U.S. 782, 134 S. Ct. 2024, 188 L.Ed.2d 1071 (2014)

JUSTICE KAGAN delivered the opinion of the Court.

The question in this case is whether tribal sovereign immunity bars Michigan's suit against the Bay Mills Indian Community for opening a casino outside Indian lands. We hold that immunity protects Bay Mills from this legal action. Congress has not abrogated tribal sovereign immunity from a State's suit to enjoin gaming off a reservation or other Indian lands. And we decline to revisit our prior decisions holding that, absent such an abrogation (or a waiver), Indian tribes have immunity even when a suit arises from off-reservation commercial activity. Michigan must therefore resort to other mechanisms, including legal actions against the responsible individuals, to resolve this dispute.

I

The Indian Gaming Regulatory Act (IGRA or Act), 102 Stat. 2467, 25 U.S.C. § 2701 *et seq.*, creates a framework for regulating gaming activity on Indian lands.[1] The Act divides gaming into three classes. Class III gaming, the most closely regulated and the kind involved here, includes casino games, slot machines, and horse racing. *See* § 2703(8). A tribe may conduct such gaming

1. The Act defines "Indian lands" as "(A) all lands within the limits of any Indian reservation; and (B) any lands title to which is either held in trust by the United States for the benefit of any Indian tribe or individual[,] or held by any Indian tribe or individual subject to restriction by the United States against alienation and over which an Indian tribe exercises governmental power." § 2703(4).

on Indian lands only pursuant to, and in compliance with, a compact it has negotiated with the surrounding State. *** Notable here, IGRA itself authorizes a State to bring suit against a tribe for certain conduct violating a compact: Specifically, § 2710(d)(7)(A)(ii) allows a State to sue in federal court to "enjoin a class III gaming activity located on Indian lands and conducted in violation of any Tribal–State compact ... that is in effect."

Pursuant to the Act, Michigan and Bay Mills, a federally recognized Indian Tribe, entered into a compact in 1993. The compact empowers Bay Mills to conduct class III gaming on "Indian lands"; conversely, it prohibits the Tribe from doing so outside that territory. The compact also contains a dispute resolution mechanism, which sends to arbitration any contractual differences the parties cannot settle on their own. A provision within that arbitration section states that "[n]othing in this Compact shall be deemed a waiver" of either the Tribe's or the State's sovereign immunity. Since entering into the compact, Bay Mills has operated class III gaming, as authorized, on its reservation in Michigan's Upper Peninsula.

In 2010, Bay Mills opened another class III gaming facility in Vanderbilt, a small village in Michigan's Lower Peninsula about 125 miles from the Tribe's reservation. [Bay Mills argued that because the land was purchased with interest from a federal fund to compensate for takings of its ancestral lands, the land was "Indian land" under the terms of the federal award.]

Michigan disagreed: The State sued Bay Mills in federal court to enjoin operation of the new casino, alleging that the facility violated IGRA and the compact because it was located outside Indian lands. The same day Michigan filed suit, the federal Department of the Interior issued an opinion concluding (as the State's complaint said) that the Tribe's use of Land Trust earnings to purchase the Vanderbilt property did not convert it into Indian territory. The District Court entered a preliminary injunction against Bay Mills, which promptly shut down the new casino and took an interlocutory appeal. [The Court of Appeals for the Sixth Circuit vacated the injunction, holding that tribal sovereign immunity barred Michigan's suit against Bay Mills unless Congress provided otherwise.]

[W]e now affirm the Court of Appeals' judgment.

II

Indian tribes are "domestic dependent nations" that exercise "inherent sovereign authority." *Oklahoma Tax Comm'n v. Citizen Band Potawatomi Tribe of Okla.*, 498 U.S. 505, 509 (1991) (*Potawatomi*). As dependents, the tribes are subject to plenary control by Congress. *See United States v. Lara*, 541 U.S. 193, 200 (2004). And yet they remain "separate sovereigns pre-existing the Constitution." *Santa Clara Pueblo v. Martinez*, 436 U.S. 49, 56 (1978). Thus, unless and "until Congress acts, the tribes retain" their historic sovereign authority. *United States v. Wheeler*, 435 U.S. 313, 323 (1978).

Among the core aspects of sovereignty that tribes possess—subject, again, to congressional action—is the "common-law immunity from suit traditionally enjoyed by sovereign powers." *Santa Clara Pueblo*. That immunity, we have explained, is "a necessary corollary to Indian sovereignty and self-governance." *Three Affiliated Tribes of Fort Berthold Reservation v. Wold Engineering, P.C.*, 476 U.S. 877, 890 (1986). And the qualified nature of Indian sovereignty modifies that principle only by placing a tribe's immunity, like its other governmental powers and attributes, in Congress's hands. Thus, we have time and again treated the "doctrine of tribal immunity [as] settled law" and dismissed any suit against a tribe absent congressional authorization (or a waiver).

In doing so, we have held that tribal immunity applies no less to suits brought by States (including in their own courts) than to those by individuals. *** Or as we elsewhere explained: While each State at the Constitutional Convention surrendered its immunity from suit by sister States, "it would be absurd to suggest that the tribes"—at a conference "to which they were not even parties"—similarly ceded their immunity against state-initiated suits. *Blatchford v. Native Village of Noatak*, 501 U.S. 775, 782 (1991).

Equally important here, we declined in *Kiowa* to make any exception for suits arising from a tribe's commercial activities, even when they take place off Indian lands. In that case, a private party sued a tribe in state court for defaulting on a promissory note. The plaintiff asked this Court to confine tribal immunity to suits involving conduct on "reservations or to noncommercial activities." We said no. *** "[O]ur precedents," we *** concluded, have not previously "drawn the[ ] distinctions" the plaintiff pressed in the case. They had established a broad principle, from which we thought it improper suddenly to start carving out exceptions. Rather, we opted to "defer" to Congress about whether to abrogate tribal immunity for off-reservation commercial conduct.

Our decisions establish as well that such a congressional decision must be clear. The baseline position, we have often held, is tribal immunity; and "[t]o abrogate [such] immunity, Congress must 'unequivocally' express that purpose." *C & L Enterprises, Inc. v. Citizen Band Potawatomi Tribe of Okla.*, 532 U.S. 411, 418 (2001) (quoting *Santa Clara Pueblo*). That rule of construction reflects an enduring principle of Indian law: Although Congress has plenary authority over tribes, courts will not lightly assume that Congress in fact intends to undermine Indian self-government.

The upshot is this: Unless Congress has authorized Michigan's suit, our precedents demand that it be dismissed. And so Michigan, naturally enough, makes two arguments: first, that IGRA indeed abrogates the Tribe's immunity from the State's suit; and second, that if it does not, we should revisit—and reverse—our decision in *Kiowa*, so that tribal immunity no longer applies to claims arising from commercial activity outside Indian lands. We consider—and reject—each contention in turn.

III

IGRA partially abrogates tribal sovereign immunity in § 2710(d)(7)(A)(ii)—but this case, viewed most naturally, falls outside that term's ambit. The provision, as noted above, authorizes a State to sue a tribe to "enjoin a class III gaming activity located on Indian lands and conducted in violation of any Tribal–State compact." A key phrase in that abrogation is "on Indian lands"—three words reflecting IGRA's overall scope (and repeated some two dozen times in the statute). A State's suit to enjoin gaming activity *on* Indian lands (assuming other requirements are met, see n. 6, *infra*) falls within § 2710(d)(7)(A)(ii); a similar suit to stop gaming activity *off* Indian lands does not. And that creates a fundamental problem for Michigan. After all, the very premise of this suit—the reason Michigan thinks Bay Mills is acting unlawfully—is that the Vanderbilt casino is *outside* Indian lands. By dint of that theory, a suit to enjoin gaming in Vanderbilt is correspondingly outside § 2710(d)(7)(A)(ii)'s abrogation of immunity.

Michigan first attempts to fit this suit within § 2710(d)(7)(A)(ii) by relocating the "class III gaming activity" to which it is objecting. True enough, Michigan states, the Vanderbilt casino lies outside Indian lands. But Bay Mills "authorized, licensed, and operated" that casino from within its own reservation. Brief for Michigan 20. According to the State, that necessary administrative action—no less than, say, dealing craps—is "class III gaming activity," and because it occurred on Indian land, this suit to enjoin it can go forward.

But that argument comes up snake eyes, because numerous provisions of IGRA show that "class III gaming activity" means just what it sounds like—the stuff involved in playing class III games. ***

Stymied under § 2710(d)(7)(A)(ii), Michigan next urges us to adopt a "holistic method" of interpreting IGRA that would allow a State to sue a tribe for illegal gaming off, no less than on, Indian lands. *** But this Court does not revise legislation, as Michigan proposes, just because the text as written creates an apparent anomaly as to some subject it does not address.

*** True enough, a State lacks the ability to sue a tribe for illegal gaming when that activity occurs off the reservation. But a State, on its own lands, has many other powers over tribal gaming that it does not possess (absent consent) in Indian territory. Unless federal law provides differently, "Indians going beyond reservation boundaries" are subject to any generally applicable state law. So, for example, Michigan could, in the first instance, deny a license to Bay Mills for an off-reservation casino. And if Bay Mills went ahead anyway, Michigan could bring suit against tribal officials or employees (rather than the Tribe itself) seeking an injunction for, say, gambling without a license. As this Court has stated before, analogizing to *Ex parte Young,* 209 U.S. 123 (1908), tribal immunity does not bar such a suit for injunctive relief against *individuals,* including tribal officers, responsible for unlawful conduct. *Santa Clara Pueblo.* And to the extent civil remedies proved inadequate, Michigan could resort to its criminal law, prosecuting anyone who maintains—or even frequents—an unlawful gambling establishment. In short (and contrary to the dissent's unsupported assertion, see *post,* at 2051), the panoply of tools Michigan can use to enforce its law on its own lands—no less than the suit it could bring on Indian lands under § 2710(d)(7)(A)(ii)—can shutter, quickly and permanently, an illegal casino.

Finally, if a State really wants to sue a tribe for gaming outside Indian lands, the State need only bargain for a waiver of immunity. *** And many States have taken that path. To be sure, Michigan did not: As noted earlier, the compact at issue here, instead of authorizing judicial remedies, sends disputes to arbitration and expressly retains each party's sovereign immunity. But Michigan—like any State—could have insisted on a different deal (and indeed may do so now for the future, because the current compact has expired and remains in effect only until the parties negotiate a new one. And in that event, the limitation Congress placed on IGRA's abrogation of tribal immunity—whether or not anomalous as an abstract matter—would have made no earthly difference.

IV

Because IGRA's plain terms do not abrogate Bay Mills' immunity from this suit, Michigan (and the dissent) must make a more dramatic argument: that this Court should "revisit[ ] *Kiowa*'s holding" and rule that tribes "have no immunity for illegal commercial activity outside their sovereign territory." Michigan argues that tribes increasingly participate in off-reservation gaming and other commercial activity, and operate in that capacity less as governments than as private businesses. Further, Michigan contends, tribes have broader immunity from suits arising from such conduct than other sovereigns—most notably, because Congress enacted legislation limiting foreign nations' immunity for commercial activity in the United States. 28 U.S.C. § 1605(a)(2). It is time, Michigan concludes, to "level[ ] the playing field."

But this Court does not overturn its precedents lightly. *Stare decisis,* we have stated, "is the preferred course because it promotes the evenhanded, predictable, and consistent development of legal principles, fosters reliance on judicial decisions, and contributes to the actual and perceived integrity of the judicial process." ***

And that is more than usually so in the circumstances here. First, *Kiowa* itself was no one-off: Rather, in rejecting the identical argument Michigan makes, our decision reaffirmed a long line of precedents, concluding that "the doctrine of tribal immunity"—without any exceptions for commercial or off-reservation conduct—"is settled law and controls this case. Second, we have relied on *Kiowa* subsequently: In another case involving a tribe's off-reservation commercial conduct, we began our analysis with *Kiowa*'s holding that tribal immunity applies to such activity (and then found that the Tribe had waived its protection). See *C & L Enterprises*. Third, tribes across the country, as well as entities and individuals doing business with them, have for many years relied on *Kiowa* (along with its forebears and progeny), negotiating their contracts and structuring their transactions against a backdrop of tribal immunity. As in other cases involving contract and property rights, concerns of *stare decisis* are thus "at their acme." ***

But instead, all the State musters are retreads of assertions we have rejected before. *** *Kiowa* did more, in fact, than acknowledge those arguments; it expressed a fair bit of sympathy toward them. *See id.* (noting "reasons to doubt the wisdom of perpetuating the doctrine" as to off-reservation commercial conduct). Yet the decision could not have been any clearer: "We decline to draw [any] distinction" that would "confine [immunity] to reservations or to noncommercial activities." *Ibid.*

We ruled that way for a single, simple reason: because it is fundamentally Congress's job, not ours, to determine whether or how to limit tribal immunity. The special brand of sovereignty the tribes retain—both its nature and its extent—rests in the hands of Congress. *See Lara*; *Wheeler*. *Kiowa* chose to respect that congressional responsibility (as *Potawatomi* had a decade earlier) when it rejected the precursor to Michigan's argument: Whatever our view of the merits, we explained, "we defer to the role Congress may wish to exercise in this important judgment." Congress, we said—drawing an analogy to its role in shaping foreign sovereign immunity—has the greater capacity "to weigh and accommodate the competing policy concerns and reliance interests" involved in the issue. And Congress repeatedly had done just that: It had restricted tribal immunity "in limited circumstances" (including, we noted, in

§ 2710(d)(7)(A)(ii)), while "in other statutes" declaring an "intention not to alter" the doctrine.

All that we said in *Kiowa* applies today, with yet one more thing: Congress has now reflected on *Kiowa* and made an initial (though of course not irrevocable) decision to retain that form of tribal immunity. Following *Kiowa,* Congress considered several bills to substantially modify tribal immunity in the commercial context. *** But instead of adopting those reversals of *Kiowa*, Congress chose to enact a far more modest alternative requiring tribes either to disclose or to waive their immunity in contracts needing the Secretary of the Interior's approval. *See* Indian Tribal Economic Development and Contract Encouragement Act of 2000, § 2, 114 Stat. 46 (codified at 25 U.S.C. § 81(d)(2)); *see also* F. Cohen, Handbook of Federal Indian Law § 7.05[1][b], p. 643 (2012). Since then, Congress has continued to exercise its plenary authority over tribal immunity, specifically preserving immunity in some contexts and abrogating it in others, but never adopting the change Michigan wants. So rather than confronting, as we did in *Kiowa*, a legislative vacuum as to the precise issue presented, we act today against the backdrop of a congressional choice: to retain tribal immunity (at least for now) in a case like this one.

Reversing *Kiowa* in these circumstances would scale the heights of presumption: Beyond upending "long-established principle[s] of tribal sovereign immunity," that action would replace Congress's considered judgment with our contrary opinion. As *Kiowa* recognized, a fundamental commitment of Indian law is judicial respect for Congress's primary role in defining the contours of tribal sovereignty. That commitment gains only added force when Congress has already reflected on an issue of tribal sovereignty, including immunity from suit, and declined to change settled law. And that force must grow greater still when Congress considered that issue partly at our urging. *** As in *Kiowa*—except still more so—"we decline to revisit our case law[,] and choose" instead "to defer to Congress."

[*Affirmed and remanded.*]

JUSTICE SOTOMAYOR, concurring.

*** The majority compellingly explains why *stare decisis* and deference to Congress' careful regulatory scheme require affirming the decision below. I write separately to further detail why both history and comity counsel against limiting Tribes' sovereign immunity in the manner the principal dissent advances.

*** Principles of comity strongly counsel in favor of continued recognition of tribal sovereign immunity, including for off-reservation commercial conduct. *** We have held that Tribes may not sue States in federal court, *Blatchford v. Native Village of Noatak*, 501 U.S. 775 (1991), including for commercial conduct that chiefly impacts Indian reservations, *Seminole Tribe of Fla. v. Florida*, 517 U.S. 44, (1996). *** As the principal dissent observes, "comity is about one sovereign respecting the dignity of another." This Court would hardly foster respect for the dignity of Tribes by allowing States to sue Tribes for commercial activity on State lands, while prohibiting Tribes from suing States for commercial activity on Indian lands. ***

The principal dissent contends that Tribes have emerged as particularly "substantial and successful" commercial actors. The dissent expresses concern that, although tribal leaders can be sued for prospective relief, Tribes' purportedly growing coffers remain unexposed to broad damages liability. These observations suffer from two flaws.

First, not all Tribes are engaged in highly lucrative commercial activity. Nearly half of federally recognized Tribes in the United States do not operate gaming facilities at all. A. Meister, Casino City's Indian Gaming Industry Report 28 (2009–2010 ed.) (noting that "only 237, or 42 percent, of the 564 federally recognized Native American tribes in the U.S. operate gaming"). And even among the Tribes that do, gaming revenue is far from uniform. As of 2009, fewer than 20% of Indian gaming facilities accounted for roughly 70% of the revenues from such facilities. *Ibid.* One must therefore temper any impression that Tribes across the country have suddenly and uniformly found their treasuries filled with gaming revenue.

*** Second, even if all Tribes were equally successful in generating commercial revenues, that would not justify the commercial-activity exception urged by the principal dissent. For tribal gaming operations cannot be understood as mere profit-making ventures that are wholly separate from the Tribes' core governmental functions. A key goal of the Federal Government is to render Tribes more self-sufficient, and better positioned to fund their own sovereign functions, rather than relying on federal funding. *** And tribal business operations are critical to the goals of tribal self-sufficiency because such enterprises in some cases "may be the only means by which a tribe can raise revenues," Struve, 36 Ariz. St. L. J., at 169. This is due in large part to the insuperable (and often state-imposed) barriers Tribes face in raising revenue through more traditional means.

For example, States have the power to tax certain individuals and companies based on Indian reservations, making it difficult for Tribes to raise revenue from those sources. *** As commentators have observed, if Tribes were to impose their own taxes on these same sources, the resulting double taxation would discourage economic growth. Fletcher, *In Pursuit of Tribal Economic Development as a Substitute for Reservation Tax Revenue*, 80 N. D. L. Rev. 759, 771 (2004). ***

To be sure, poverty has decreased over the past few decades on reservations that have gaming activity. *** But even reservations that have gaming continue to experience significant poverty, especially relative to the national average. The same is true of Indian reservations more generally.

Both history and proper respect for tribal sovereignty—or comity—counsel against creating a special "commercial activity" exception to tribal sovereign immunity. For these reasons, and for the important reasons of *stare decisis* and deference to Congress outlined in the majority opinion, I concur.

JUSTICE SCALIA, dissenting.

*** For the reasons given today in Justice Thomas's dissenting opinion, which I join, I am now convinced that *Kiowa* was wrongly decided; that, in the intervening 16 years, its error has grown more glaringly obvious; and that *stare decisis* does not recommend its retention. Rather than insist that Congress clean up a mess that I helped make, I would overrule *Kiowa* and reverse the judgment below.

JUSTICE THOMAS, with whom JUSTICES SCALIA, GINSBURG, and ALITO join, dissenting.

In *Kiowa Tribe of Okla. v. Manufacturing Technologies, Inc.*, 523 U.S. 751 (1998), this Court extended the judge-made doctrine of tribal sovereign immunity to bar suits arising out of an Indian tribe's commercial activities conducted outside its territory. That was error. Such an expansion of tribal immunity is unsupported by any rationale for that doctrine, inconsistent with the limits on tribal sovereignty, and an affront to state sovereignty.

That decision, wrong to begin with, has only worsened with the passage of time. *** As the commercial activity of tribes has proliferated, the conflict and inequities brought on by blanket tribal immunity have also increased. Tribal immunity significantly limits, and often extinguishes, the States' ability to protect their citizens and enforce the law against tribal businesses. This case is but one example. *** The problem repeats itself every time a tribe fails to pay state taxes, harms a tort victim, breaches a contract, or otherwise violates state laws, and tribal immunity bars the only feasible legal remedy.

In the wake of Kiowa, tribal immunity has also been exploited in new areas that are often heavily regulated by States. For instance, payday lenders (companies that lend consumers short-term advances on paychecks at interest rates that can reach upwards of 1,000 percent per annum) often arrange to share fees or profits with tribes so they can use tribal immunity as a shield for conduct of questionable legality. Martin & Schwartz, *The Alliance Between Payday Lenders and Tribes: Are Both Tribal Sovereignty and Consumer Protection at Risk?*, 69 Wash. & Lee L. Rev. 751, 758–759, 777 (2012). ***

In sum, any number of Indian tribes across the country have emerged as substantial and successful competitors in interstate and international commerce, both within and beyond Indian lands. As long as tribal immunity remains out of sync with this reality, it will continue to invite problems, including de facto deregulation of highly regulated activities; unfairness to tort victims; and increasingly fractious relations with States and individuals alike. The growing harms wrought by *Kiowa*'s unjustifiable rule fully justify overruling it.

JUSTICE GINSBURG, dissenting.

I join Justice Thomas' dissenting opinion with one reservation. *** I also believe that the Court has carried beyond the pale the immunity possessed by States of the United States. *** Neither brand of immoderate, judicially confirmed immunity, I anticipate, will have staying power.

NOTES AND QUESTIONS

1. What are the justifications for tribal sovereign immunity? What is the argument that those justifications do not apply to tribal commercial activities and activities off reservation? What is the argument that they do? For an excavation of the history of the doctrine, see William Wood, *It Wasn't An Accident: The Tribal Sovereign Immunity Story*, 62 Am. U.L. Rev. 1587 (2013).

2. Tribal sovereign immunity may be waived either by clear congressional action or by the tribe itself. As the Court notes, Congress has created explicit waivers for suits by states against tribes for failure to comply with state-tribal gaming compacts. 25 U.S.C. § 2710(d)(7)(A)(ii). Congress also requires liability insurance for tribal self-governance activities, such as

federally-funded police, health, and educational activities, and requires that the insurer waive tribal sovereign immunity defenses for suits arising from these activities. 25 U.S.C. § 450f(c).

Clear action by a tribe will also waive sovereign immunity. *C & L Enterprises v. Citizen Band Potawatomi Indian Tribe*, 532 U.S. 411, 418 (2001). In *C & L Enterprises*, the Court found the requisite clear waiver in a binding arbitration clause providing that "arbitral awards may be reduced to judgment in accordance with applicable proceedings in any court having jurisdiction thereof." *Id.* at 419. Putting aside the question of whether this is indeed a clear waiver, many tribes do explicitly waive sovereign immunity in commercial contracts. Why would a tribe choose to do this? Consider, for example, that tribes often enter into financing arrangements and other commercial transactions with banks and other entities, and that those entities require some form of recourse. Tribal council members often struggle with a lawyer's advice to waive sovereign immunity in this context. How might you advise a tribal legislative body faced with a decision about waiving immunity from suit in these situations? Given the requirement of a clear waiver, how might you draft the language if you were representing the non-Indian party to the transaction? Recall, too, that the tribal entity agreeing to the waiver must be authorized to do so under tribal law. *Attorney's Process & Investigation Serv. v. Sac & Fox Tribe*, 609 F.3d 927 (8th Cir. 2010) (holding that authority of ousted tribal chairman to waive sovereign immunity was a question of tribal law not subject to federal review); *cf. Wells Fargo Bank v. Lake of the Torches Econ. Dev. Corp.*, 658 F.3d 684 (7th Cir. 2011) (holding that waiver of immunity invalid because it was part of gaming management contract requiring approval by the Secretary of the Interior).

3. *Tribal court or foreign court?* Tribes often agree to broader waivers of sovereign immunity in tribal court than in federal or state courts. Tribes commonly, for example, waive their immunity from damages suits in tribal courts. Like similar state waivers of immunity, these waivers are often limited, whether to the extent of liability insurance, Navajo Sovereign Immunity Act, 1 N.N.C. § 554(F), Yavapai–Prescott Tribal Code § 17.3(c)(1)(iii), to the exclusion of claims for punitive damages, XII Mashantucket Pequot Tribal Laws Ch.1, § 5(c)(2), or up to a certain amount. Coushatta Judicial Code, Title I, ch. I, § 9 (waiver for tort claims up to $500,000). Sovereign immunity is often justified as protecting not only sovereign monetary assets but the dignitary interests of the sovereign; as the Supreme Court declared in holding that a state could not be forced to respond to a claim of violation of federal shipping laws at a federal administrative tribunal, "[t]he preeminent purpose of state sovereign immunity is to accord States the dignity that is consistent with their status as sovereign entities." *Fed. Mar. Comm'n v. S.C. State Ports Auth.*, 535 U.S. 743, 760 (2002). How does the dignity consideration apply to the choice between suit in tribal versus federal or state courts? For more on tribal sovereign immunity and tribal courts, *see* Catherine T. Struve, *Tribal Immunity and Tribal Courts*, 36 Ariz. St. L. J. 137 (2004).

4. *Damages or injunctive relief?* Sovereign immunity applies primarily to claims for money damages or property. Under *Ex Parte Young*, 209 U.S. 123 (1908), state officials may be sued in their official capacity for prospective relief—injunctions or declarations of illegality—without implicating sovereign immunity. The *Young* doctrine rests on the fiction that a suit against an official (rather than the government itself) to stop future violations of the law is not a

suit against the government or its property. *Santa Clara Pueblo v. Martinez* applied this doctrine to tribal officials, finding that the Pueblo's sovereign immunity did not bar a suit for declaratory and injunctive relief against Lucario Padilla, the Governor of the Pueblo. 436 U.S. at 59. *Cf. Fletcher v. United States,* 116 F.3d 1315 (10th Cir. 1997) (order of creation of new constitutional commission and a referendum regarding new constitution barred by tribal sovereign immunity). The Court held that ICRA did not, however, create a federal cause of action in federal courts, holding that tribal fora were the appropriate place to hear ICRA claims. Many tribes have, either by statute or judicial decision, held that tribal sovereign immunity does not bar ICRA claims for injunctive or declaratory relief in tribal court. *See Halona v. MacDonald,* 1 Nav. R. 189 (Navajo Ct. App. 1978); *Healy v. Mashantucket Pequot Gaming Enterprise,* 1 Mash. Pequ. R. 63 (Mashantucket Pequot Ct. App. 1999); Robert J. McCarthy, *Civil Rights in Tribal Courts: The Indian Bill of Rights at Thirty Years,* 34 Idaho L. Rev. 465, 480–483 (1998). What does *Michigan v. Bay Mills* add to the question of injunctive relief against tribal officials?

5. *Tribal Employees Sued in Individual Capacity.* In *Lewis v. Clarke,* — U.S. —, 137 S. Ct. 1285, 197 L.Ed.2d 631 (2017), the Court held that a tribe's sovereign immunity does not bar a lawsuit brought in state court against a tribal member in his individual capacity. Brian and Michelle Lewis were driving on a highway in Connecticut when William Clarke, an employee of the Mohegan Tribe's Gaming Authority, hit their car from behind. Clarke was acting in the scope of his employment at the time, driving Mohegan Sun Casino patrons to their homes. The Court held that because Clarke, not the Tribe, was the real party in interest, and Clarke was sued in his individual capacity, the Tribe's sovereign immunity was not implicated. Further, the Court held that an indemnification clause, requiring the Gaming Authority to indemnify Clarke for any adverse judgment, did not affect its conclusion. "The critical inquiry is who may be legally bound by the court's adverse judgment, not who will pick up the tab." *Id.* at 1292-93.

6. *Adverse Possession, Sovereign Immunity & Rule 19. Upper Skagit Indian Tribe v. Lundgren,* — U.S. —, 138 S. Ct. 1649, 200 L.Ed.2d 931 (2018). The Tribe purchased a parcel of fee land on the open market. A post-purchase survey revealed that a fence built by the adjacent property owners, the Lundgrens, was actually on the Tribe's newly acquired land. The fence enclosed about one acre of land that the survey showed to belong to the Tribe. The Washington Supreme Court agreed with the Lundgrens' claim of ownership by adverse possession of the one-acre strip in a quiet title action brought as an *in rem* action against the land. The court rejected the Tribe's argument that sovereign immunity prevented state courts from exercising jurisdiction over the property because the tribe had record title and could not be joined due to tribal immunity. The U.S. Supreme Court reversed the holding that *in rem* proceedings could be used as an end-run around tribal immunity:

> Like some courts before it, the Washington Supreme Court read [*County of Yakima v. Confederated Tribes and Bands of Yakima Nation,* 502 U.S. 251(1992)] as distinguishing *in rem* from *in personam* lawsuits and "establish[ing] the principle that ... courts have subject matter jurisdiction over *in rem* proceedings in certain situations where claims of sovereign immunity are asserted." 187 Wash.2d, at 868, 389 P.3d, at 574. That was error. *Yakima* did not address the scope of tribal sovereign immunity. Instead, it involved only a much

> more prosaic question of statutory interpretation concerning the Indian General Allotment Act of 1887. *See* 24 Stat. 388.

Upper Skagit Indian Tribe v. Lundgren, 138 S. Ct. 1649, 1652 (2018). The Court remanded the case for consideration of alternative theories as to how the action might proceed. The case was settled before any further proceedings in the state courts. The Tribe purchased the disputed land.

7. *Payday Lending.* Corporations created and managed by tribes for tribal purposes—so called arms-of-the-tribe—share tribal sovereign immunity. Recently, a number of payday lenders (lenders making small, short term loans) have partnered with tribes in order to continue charging rates and engaging in other practices that violate state usury laws. Tribes, many of whom have few other sources of economic development or jobs, create new lending businesses as arms of the tribe, so that the business benefits from sovereign immunity. *People v. Miami Nation Enterprises*, 223 Cal.App.4th 21 (2014) (holding Ameriloan, United Cash Loans, U.S. Fast Cash, Preferred Cash and One Click Cash were arms of two Indian tribes and shielded from prosecution by sovereign immunity). In *Williams v. Big Picture Loans*, LLC, 929 F.3d 170, 174 (4th Cir. 2019), a class action suit, which alleged that a tribal payday lending company charged interest rates that were more than fifty times higher than Virginia state law allowed, was dismissed on the ground that the tribal payday lending company was an arm of the tribe and thus entitled to sovereign immunity. *See* Adam Crepelle, *Tribal Lending and Tribal Sovereignty*, 66 Drake L. Rev. 1, 2 (2018) (collecting most of the sovereign immunity cases and noting that "there are more payday lending stores in the United States than McDonald's"); and Nathalie Martina & Joshua Schwartz, *The Alliance between Payday Lenders and Tribes: Are Both Tribal Sovereignty and Consumer Protection At Risk?*, 69 Wash. & Lee L. Rev. 751 (2012).

Other courts have allowed suits to proceed against tribal officials on an *Ex parte Young* theory. *Gingras v. Think Finance, Inc.*, 922 F.3d 112 (2d Cir 2019) ("Tribes and their officers are not free to operate outside of Indian lands without conforming their conduct in these areas to federal and state law."). Some states are now seeking to stop illegal payday lenders by acting against the banks that process the electronic transactions to and from the borrowers. *See Otoe-Missouria Tribe of Indians v. New York State Dept. of Financial Services*, 769 F.3d 105 (2d Cir. 2014) (rejecting claims that cease and desist letters to off-reservation banks violated federal Indian law). If you were the attorney for a tribe approached by a payday lender, what would you suggest they consider?

8. *No Immunity from Suits by the United States.* While Indian tribes and the States are immune from suits brought by each other, their immunity does not protect against suits brought by the United States, or federal agencies authorized to sue in their own right. *EEOC v. Karuk Tribe Hous. Auth.*, 260 F.3d 1071, 1075 (9th Cir. 2001) ("Indian tribes do not, however, enjoy sovereign immunity from suits brought by the federal government."); *United States v. Red Lake Band of Chippewa Indians*, 827 F.2d 380, 383 (8th Cir. 1987) ("We conclude that just as a state may not assert sovereign immunity as against the federal government, [*United States v.*] *Mississippi*, 380 U.S. [128] at 140–41, neither may an Indian tribe, as a dependent nation, do so.").

9. *Patent Litigation.* The Saint Regis Mohawk Tribe acquired several drug patents from the pharmaceutical company, Allergan, which was involved in administrative litigation over the validity of the patents. The Tribe received $13,500,000 and a promise of substantial future royalties when it leased the patents back to Allergan. As the new title holder of the patents, the Tribe asserted sovereign immunity in the Patent Trial and Appeal Board's administrative proceeding reviewing the validity of the patents. The Federal Circuit ruled that tribal sovereign immunity could not be asserted by the tribe because the proceeding was more like an agency enforcement action than a civil suit, and tribes lack immunity against the United States. *Saint Regis Mohawk Tribe v. Mylan Pharmaceuticals Inc.*, 896 F.3d 1322, 1325 (Fed. Cir. 2018). *See* Katrina Grace Geddes, *Sovereign Immunity for Rent: How the Commodification of Tribal Sovereign Immunity Reflects the Failures of the U.S. Patent System*, 29 Fordham Intell. Prop. Media & Ent. L.J. 767 (2019).

IV. TRIBAL SOVEREIGN INSTITUTIONS

What are tribes doing with their sovereignty? What does tribal sovereignty mean to tribes and to others? What kinds of institutions—courts, legislatures, and businesses—are tribes developing? While the materials in the subsequent chapters illustrate the ways Federal Indian Law has responded to specific tribal struggles to exercise and protect sovereignty in the modern era, the following materials focus on tribal concerns and actions. First, they address the reciprocal relationship between economic development and tribal sovereignty. They then turn to tribal courts, one of the key institutions involved in the day-to-day construction and use of tribal sovereignty.

A. SOVEREIGN INSTITUTIONS AND ECONOMIC DEVELOPMENT

Even before the advent of Indian gaming, tribes had begun to manage natural resources and other commercial activities on their reservations. This has only increased since tribes began gaming on their reservations in the 1980s. Tribes now manage significant businesses, from commercial fisheries to pharmaceutical companies. In 2006, the Seminole Nation of Florida made national headlines when it purchased the Hard Rock Café. Seminole council representative Max Osceola declared at the press conference, "Our ancestors sold Manhattan for trinkets. We're going to buy Manhattan back, one burger at a time." Michael J. de la Merced, *Florida's Seminole Tribe Buys Hard Rock Cafés and Casinos*, New York Times, Dec. 8, 2006, at C3.

Despite this, poverty and unemployment remain significant issues for Indian nations. The vast majority of Indian gaming profits go to a few well situated tribes; most gaming facilities provide some needed governmental revenue but not enough to fill community needs. As of the 2010 census, 27% of Indian people remain below the poverty line, compared to 14.3% of the general population; poverty rates are far higher for those living on reservations or in Indian country. Economic development is therefore a pressing concern for almost all Indian tribes. The following excerpt argues that concern for economic development is not an isolated "jobs and businesses" matter, but touches all aspects of tribal institution building.

STEPHEN CORNELL, *SOVEREIGNTY, POLICY, AND PROSPERITY IN INDIAN COUNTRY TODAY*

(Community Reinvestment, Fed. Res. Bk. Ks. City, Winter 1997)

A "nation-building" concept of economic development has a goal of building viable, sovereign nations. Its purpose is to build an environment that encourages investors to invest, that helps businesses last, and that allows investments to flourish and pay off. Key elements of that environment are the governing infrastructure, the legal infrastructure, and the rules and procedures by which the society is run.

A "jobs and income" approach seldom leads to economic prosperity. We've learned through our research that we need to think differently about economic development. The solution has to be much more comprehensive and ambitious than just starting businesses. The solution is to build a nation in which business can flourish. It involves creating an environment in which the governing infrastructure and the legal infrastructure—the rules and procedures by which the society is run—support prosperity.

I. Sovereignty

The first key to economic development is sovereignty. "De facto" sovereignty, meaning genuine decision-making control over affairs, is a necessary prerequisite for economic development. Who is really deciding the economic strategy? Who is deciding how many trees will be cut? Who is deciding whether the joint venture agreement with an outside investor will go forward? Who is deciding how the housing money will be spent? In Indian Country, when the answer to these questions is "the tribe", we have de facto sovereignty—sovereignty in fact and in practice.

While sovereignty as a legal phenomenon waxes and wanes with federal court decisions and legislation, today the potential for de facto sovereignty is substantial. An assertive and capable tribe can take effective control of many economic decisions away from other contenders for that control, such as the Bureau of Indian Affairs and other federal agencies.

In virtually every case that we have seen of sustained economic development on American Indian reservations, the primary economic decisions are being made by the tribe, not by outsiders. In every case, the tribe is in the driver's seat. In every case, the role of the Bureau of Indian Affairs (BIA) and other outsider agencies has shifted from decision-maker to resource, from the controlling influence in decisions to advisor or provider of technical assistance.

***

As long as the decision makers don't pay the price of bad decisions, there's no incentive for them to make better decisions. Making the feds bear responsibility for making things better on Indian reservations may be good political rhetoric but it is bad economic strategy. The research shows that when tribes take responsibility for what happens economically, they have started down the path to improving economic conditions. Assertions of sovereignty can have very concrete payoffs.

For example, a Harvard Project study analyzed the performance in the marketplace of 75 tribes with significant forestry operations. In the late 1980s, 49 of those tribes shifted some portion of their forest product industry control from BIA to tribal control. For every highly skilled position transferred from BIA to tribal control, both production and revenue to the tribe increased, and did so on a sustained-yield basis. Tribal control typically resulted not only in better forest management but in better marketing as well. The bottom line was increased prices for forest products and increased revenue to the tribe. In other words, the effective exercise of sovereignty has concrete, bottom line results.

This illustrates another finding that emerges from our research. It often has been asserted that if tribes wish to be sovereign, they must first establish sound economies. We think this is backwards. What the research indicates is that if you want a sound economy, you need first to be sovereign. There are three reasons for this.

- First, sovereignty brings with it accountability. Those whose resources and well being are at stake are the ones calling the shots.
- Second, the sovereign status of tribes offers distinct legal and economic market opportunities, from reduced tax and regulatory burdens for industry to unique niches for gaming and the commercial use of wildlife.
- And third, sovereignty secures the bases of development itself: control of one's own affairs and resources.

It is no coincidence that after tribal self-determination became federal policy in the 1970s, a significant number of tribes have begun to break the relentless pattern of reservation poverty and dependence. Before self-determination, there was very little in the way of sustained economic development on Indian reservations.

There is a major policy lesson in this. The lesson is that sovereignty is one of the primary development resources a tribe can have. ***

II. Institutions

Institutions are the second key to economic development. Any nation—Indian or not—that wants to be economically successful over the long haul must have capable institutions of self-governance, from commercial codes to effective and independent judicial systems, to controls on opportunistic politicians. Our research strongly indicates that sovereignty without the ability to exercise it effectively is a poor basis for economic development.

We work with one tribe that is among the wealthiest tribes in the country in terms of natural resources, but the reservation economy is a shambles. Unemployment is sky high, there are almost no viable enterprises on the reservation, and the tribe is dependent on federal money to keep many of its activities going. Social problems such as alcohol and suicide are major concerns. The political struggles have at times threatened to turn violent. This sovereign Indian nation has a long history of battling in the courts to affirm its sovereignty. It has won the right to control its own destiny. It is resource-rich and people-rich, but it remains poor.

The problem is the inability of this tribe to exercise its power effectively. Its constitution provides a system of government in which it is extremely difficult to get anything done. Its governmental system encourages recurrent factional battles that sap the energies of the tribe's leaders and distract them from the real tasks of government.

The instability in tribal government means that massive personnel changes occur overnight following the changes in administration. Few good records are kept; skilled people get hired and soon throw up their hands and quit. It's difficult to keep track of the money. Tribal plans change from one day to the next; leases made by the last administration are canceled by the next. Enterprises fail because of government interference.

This is hardly a promising environment for economic development. Outside investors won't invest—they don't like the risks such an environment creates. Equally important, inside investors—tribal members who might not have a lot of money but who do have ideas or energy or skills—won't invest either. Why should they invest their energy in the tribal future when the environment is one of uncertainty, political favoritism, and instability? ***

One of the unfortunate consequences of a century of federal control of Indian nations is a legacy of institutional dependency, a situation in which tribes have had to rely on someone else's institutions, someone else's rules, someone else's models, to get things done. On many reservations, tribal government has become little more than a grants-and-programs funnel attached to the federal apparatus. On others, tribes have simply adopted the institutions of the larger society without considering whether those institutions in fact are appropriate to their situations. Such dependency and blind imitation are the antithesis of self-determination, and the challenge is to break these patterns.

To do so, a tribe must create laws, rules, and procedures that are appropriate to its situation and its heritage and that can get things done in the real world that tribes confront. ***

Separation of politics and business. The first institutional factor in the effective exercise of tribal sovereignty is the separation of politics from day-to-day business management. On many reservations the tribal government—typically the tribal council or the tribal president—controls tribal businesses. Business decisions are made by the council, administrative and personnel disputes are referred to the council, and the council or president intervenes in the day-to-day running of the enterprise.

***

In an ongoing survey of tribally-owned businesses, our research indicates that chances of being profitable rise 400 percent if the business is isolated from political interference in day-to-day operations, with management by a board of directors and a corporate charter that are beyond the direct control of council members or the tribal president. For sustainable enterprises on reservations, tribal leadership needs to take the crucial step of setting strategic direction, then put the day-to-day decisions in the hands of others. ***

Separation of government powers. The second institutional factor in the effective exercise of tribal sovereignty is the separation of powers. Basically, this means having a strong and independent judiciary. It means assuring people that their claims and disputes—including disputes with the tribe itself—will be fairly adjudicated.

***

Again, the data are persuasive. We have examined 67 tribes for which comparable information is available, and have found that those tribes that have strong, genuinely independent judicial systems economically outperform those that don't. The measure we used was unemployment, and after eliminating other factors, we found that simply having an independent judicial system reduces unemployment, on average 5 percent. If you're a tribal council member and you're looking for ways to reduce long-term unemployment on your reservation, one of the best things you can do is establish a strong, genuinely independent, effective judiciary that can fairly settle disputes and adjudicate claims.

With a jobs and income strategy, the focus is on starting a business. With a nation-building strategy, the focus is on creating a system that reassures investors, levels the playing field, and gives businesses the opportunity to flourish. Governing power is used not to personally make judicial decisions, but to build an institutional foundation for real sovereignty and lasting prosperity.

Effective bureaucracy. The third institutional factor in the effective exercise of tribal sovereignty is an effective bureaucracy. A tribe—or any other community—has to be able to get things done, consistently, fairly, and predictably. A civil service, established administrative procedures that are consistently observed, solid record-keeping, independent audits, and a commercial code are essential. ***

The business world is an uncertain world at best. It tends to be especially uncertain on reservations. To keep investors involved, and to keep tribal members investing in the future of their community, the uncertainties they deal with need to be reduced. An effective, dependable bureaucracy is a crucial part of doing that. Without effective institutions of self-governance, sovereignty is hollow. The question of where to get those institutions brings us to the last of the three keys to economic development.

III. Cultural match

The legitimacy of governing institutions depends on a match with the values and culture of the people they govern. That doesn't necessarily mean reviving all traditional governments. We live in a very different world today, and government has to be designed to work within that world. But the government has to have the support of the people if it is going to work.

For example, two of the tribes we work with at the Harvard Project on American Indian Economic Development are the White Mountain Apache Tribe of the Fort Apache Reservation in Arizona and the Oglala Sioux Tribe of the Pine Ridge Reservation in South Dakota. Both of these tribes have governments organized under the provisions of the Indian Reorganization Act (IRA) of 1934, which many tribes established in the aftermath of that act. The two government structures are almost identical, with boilerplate IRA government provisions: centralized power, strong executives, no independent judiciary, executive oversight of business operations. But while the institutions of governance are essentially the same, the performances of these two tribes are radically different.

Economically, the White Mountain Apaches are one of the most successful tribes in the country. They run a number of economic enterprises that are consistently in the black. Their timber company outperforms non-Indian timber operations throughout the West. Their ski resort is one of the economic engines of that region of Arizona.

The Pine Ridge Reservation, on the other hand, is possibly the poorest reservation in the country. It has a history of repeated failure in tribal enterprises. It has some of the highest rates of unemployment and related social problems in Indian Country.

Resource differences cannot explain the very different record in the performance of tribal enterprises. ***

We think the difference is in the cultural fit of the governments. If we look at both tribes in the middle of the nineteenth century, before either tribe had come under the effective control of the United States, we see some important differences.

In the Apache tribe, enormous power was given to single, charismatic leaders. Those leaders selected the tribal council to whom they looked for advice. There was no independent judiciary; the leader resolved the disputes. The leader made most of the economic decisions as well.

That looks a lot like the contemporary IRA government at Fort Apache. When they adopted the IRA constitution suggested by the United States government, they got a government that in many ways resembled their traditional government. As a result, people tend to believe in and support that government. It fits with their concept of how authority ought to be organized and exercised.

At Pine Ridge, however, traditional Sioux government looked radically different from their IRA constitution. There, decisions were traditionally made by the "Big Bellies"—all the men over forty—with very little power in the hands of single individuals. That council chose four executives, called the Shirt Wearers. It also selected a police force from among the warrior societies, called the akicita, who enforced the law and settled disputes. The akicita were remarkably independent. There are cases on record of the akicita physically beating Shirt Wearers—chief executives—for failing to observe the law.

There was a clear separation between strategic decisions and day-to-day business management. The council might decide where to move to, or when to gather for the buffalo hunt, but when it came time to actually move, or camp, or hunt, or go to war, the council chose individuals known to be superbly skilled in those activities, and those individuals took charge of the activities themselves. Once the hunt began, skilled and knowledgeable hunt leaders were in charge, and you did what they said, not what the leaders of the nation said. This was a very sophisticated system of government, with a separation of powers, checks and balances, and clear lines of authority. And it worked.

Today, the IRA government is the opposite of how the Sioux, under conditions of freedom, chose to govern themselves. It places power in the hands of single leaders, has no separation of powers, muddies the lines of authority, fails to place checks on the behavior of leaders, and offers no independent, impartial means for settling disputes. As a result, few people really believe in it, and where people don't think the institutions are much good, they're unlikely to invest. Those who do invest eventually get burned, resources are squandered, and the chances of long-term prosperity disappear.

What's at stake is the legitimacy of governing institutions with the community itself. The institutions of governance at Fort Apache have legitimacy with the people. The institutions of governance at Pine Ridge, which on paper are virtually the same as Fort Apache, have little legitimacy with the people. They don't match the culture.

Conclusion

So the keys to economic development are sovereignty, institutions, and legitimacy. *** Indian nations need to know that the connection between sovereignty and economic development runs through institutions of self-governance. Those tribes that build governing institutions capable of the effective exercise of sovereignty are the ones that are most likely to achieve long-term, self-determined economic prosperity. The name of the game, in other words, is nation-building. ***

NOTES AND QUESTIONS

1. Professor Cornell uses the term "de facto sovereignty." What does he mean by this? What is the relationship between de facto sovereignty and the residual inherent sovereignty that tribes possess as a legal matter according to *Talton* and *Wheeler*?

2. *Building legitimate governmental institutions.* How are tribes to achieve governmental institutions that can achieve legitimacy and cultural match? What if institutions that feel culturally appropriate to tribal members seem foreign or unfair to investors and other nonmembers? How are tribes to manage divisions between more and less traditional members of the tribe? Many tribes find themselves in a double bind in this regard, as existing tribal institutions may be perceived as tainted both by their difference from pre-colonial institutions and by their difference from non-tribal institutions. Frank Pommersheim eloquently lays out this dilemma with regard to tribal courts, but his words could apply to many tribal governmental structures:

> Identifiable segments of most tribes have at times refused to consider tribal courts legitimate. In this regard, many tribal courts are vilified as "white men's" creations flowing from the IRA and an entire history directed to assimilation. The courts are seen as instruments of outside forces and values that are not traditional and therefore not legitimate.
>
> By contrast, some segments of most tribal populations (and local non-Indian populations) view tribal courts as illegitimate because they fall, or appear to fall, far below recognized state and federal standards in such matters ranging from the institutional separation of powers to the provision of civil due process and enforcement of judgments.

Frank Pommersheim, Braid of Feathers: American Indian Law and Contemporary Tribal Life 67–68 (1995). This problem exists with tribal constitutions and government structures as well; recall the materials on tribal constitution drafting during the Indian New Deal Era. How are tribes to address these problems? For an interesting article on one tribe's effort to draft a constitution that would be both perceived as legitimate and respond to contemporary tribal issues, see Eric Lemont, *Overcoming the Politics of Reform: The Story of the*

Cherokee Nation of Oklahoma Constitutional Convention, 28 Am. Indian L. Rev. 1 (2003/2004). For more on tribal constitution drafting, see American Indian Constitutional Reform and the Rebuilding of Native Nations (Eric D. Lemont ed. 2006).

As the materials on Santa Clara Pueblo and the Cherokee and Seminole Freedmen suggest, one of the most controversial issues faced in developing tribal governments is determining who legally should be a member of the community. Although few citizenship criteria raise gender or racial issues so clearly, all tribes face difficult questions. Should the benefits of membership be limited to those who have maintained cultural or geographic contact with the tribe, or should it include those who do not, perhaps because of economic or assimilationist pressures? Should citizenship depend on a particular tribal blood quantum or more broadly on descent from those included on old federal census rolls? What rights can or should be accorded to those without tribal heritage who live in the tribal territory, or have married tribal members? How should tribes handle the reality that limitation of citizenship to those with Indian "blood" often leads to cries of racism, but that according membership to those with significant non-Indian heritage results in the opposite claim that the tribes aren't really Indian, and therefore are not entitled to sovereignty? For a thoughtful exploration of these issues, see Carole Goldberg, *Members Only? Designing Citizenship Requirements for Indian Nations*, 50 U. Kan. L. Rev. 437 (2002). *See also* Kirsty Gover, *Membership as Continuity: Explaining the Growing Tribal Preference for Descent Rules in Membership Governance in the United* States, 33 Am. Ind. L. Rev. 243 (2008–2009) (surveying trends in tribal membership provisions and explaining modern preference for descent requirements as an effort to maintain historic continuity in the face of growing geographic dispersal); Angela R. Riley, *(Tribal) Sovereignty and Illiberalism*, 95 Cal. L. Rev. 799 (2007) (applying political theoretical approach to membership and other contested issues).

B. TRIBAL JUDICIAL SYSTEMS

As Stephen Cornell suggests, a vital tribal court system has far-ranging benefits for tribal governments. Indian peoples, like other societies, have always had dispute resolution mechanisms. Within the Iroquois Confederacy, for example, dispute resolution powers appear to have been divided between a council of fifty war chiefs and the clan mothers, the female heads of the clans, and individual leaders designated as "peacemakers." Impeachments were debated in three sessions of the war chiefs, but ultimately carried out by the clan mothers. Probate, or the descent of property and rights of the deceased, was decided by the clan mothers of the respective clans at a Dead Feast held ten days after death. The pre-contact Cherokee people divided dispute resolution among several specialized legal bodies, including a general court, a war court, and a women's court. In addition, debts not recovered and crimes older than a year could be expiated at an annual religious ceremony. Among the Navajo, the community *nataani*, a person selected for his wisdom, oratorical ability, and ability to recite the Beauty Way ceremony, was charged with resolving disputes, often at a public meeting at which the two disputants or their representatives would speak, and then interested community members would provide their evidence or opinions. The *nataani* was then responsible for articulating a resolution that would gain the acceptance of the disputants and the community.

With European–American contact, new demands and pressures were placed on tribal justice systems. The first western-style tribal court system was developed by the Cherokee Nation in the early 1800s. The system included a series of district courts and an appellate Supreme Court. Much of the business of the courts concerned commercial disputes involving mixed-blood Cherokees. *See* Rennard Strickland, Fire and the Spirits: Cherokee Law from Clan to Court 75 (1975). Anglo court systems staffed by tribal members came to many other reservations toward the end of the nineteenth century, first as experiments by federal agents to enhance reservation control. In 1883, the Indian Office formalized these "Courts of Indian Offenses," promulgating regulations prohibiting practices seen as obstacles to tribal assimilation: religious dances, polygamy, use of medicine men, and the custom of abandoning and destroying the homes of the dead. In 1888, the District Court of Oregon called these courts "mere educational and disciplinary instrumentalities, by which the government of the United States is endeavoring to improve and elevate the condition of these dependent tribes to whom it sustains the relation of guardian." *United States v. Clapox*, 35 F. 575, 577 (D. Or. 1888). Many contemporary tribal courts have their origins in the Courts of Indian Offenses.

In the twentieth century, tribes began taking control of their courts and developing tribal codes and common law which more fully reflect tribal legal traditions and needs. To some extent, the development of tribal judicial systems came about as a defensive measure in response to the Termination Era. On the Navajo Nation, for example, the tribe adopted its own court system in part to fend off any efforts Arizona might make to assume jurisdiction under Public Law 280. *See* Stephen Conn, *Mid–Passage: The Navajo Tribe and Its First Legal Revolution*, 6 Am. Indian L. Rev. 329, 343–46 (1978). These steps by Navajo also proved crucial for the development of federal law recognizing tribal judicial jurisdiction, in that they contributed to the Supreme Court's decision in *Williams v. Lee*, 358 U.S. 217 (1959). *Williams*, which is presented in full in the following chapter, ousted state court jurisdiction over a case by a non-Indian plaintiff against tribal member defendants. The Court referred explicitly to the Navajo Nation's court system as a basis for upholding exclusive tribal jurisdiction over the matter. *See* Bethany R. Berger, Williams v. Lee *and the Debate Over Indian Equality*, 109 Mich. L. Rev. 1514, 1463, 1517-18 (2011) (recounting discussion of Navajo courts in oral argument and opinion).

Today there are approximately 275 functioning tribal courts; about 22 tribes continue to rely on the Courts of Indian Offenses. Tribal courts often employ less formal procedural rules than state or federal courts. Yavapai–Prescott law, for example, states regarding procedure that "the Tribal Judge shall conduct the trial in such a manner as to do substantial justice between the parties according to the rules of substantive law." Yavapai–Prescott Tribal Code, § 2.16. Other courts, particularly those with many non-Indian litigants, adopt state or federal rules. The Mashantucket Pequot Tribal Court, for example, which hears many claims by non-Indian patrons and employees of its casino, follows the Federal Rules of Evidence. Mashantucket Pequot Rules of Evidence § 101–1105. Some courts have formal bar exams for admission, but many do not. In order to encourage tribal language and custom in tribal courts, many courts permit tribal members to qualify to appear before the court as advocates without graduation from law school.

Many tribes are simultaneously developing their courts to be more adept at handling disputes with nonmembers as well as to incorporate indigenous practices and norms. Thus tribal courts are adopting traditional substantive and procedural laws and using them where appropriate to resolve contemporary disputes. This traditional law, often called tribal common law, is "comprised of customs and long-used ways of doing things" that gain the status of law, like the Anglo common law catalogued by Blackstone. Tom Tso, *The Process of Decision Making in Tribal Courts*, 31 Ariz. L. Rev. 225, 230 (1989); *In re Estate of Belone* (*Dawes v. Yazzie*), 5 Navajo Rptr. 161 (1987); *see* Raymond D. Austin, Navajo Courts and Navajo Common Law: A Tradition of Tribal Self-Governance (2009) (providing in-depth examination of Navajo common law); Matthew L.M. Fletcher, *Rethinking Customary Law in Tribal Jurisprudence*, 13 Mich. J. Race & Law 57 (2007) (critiquing use of customary law); Pat Sekaquaptewa, *Key Concepts in the Finding, Definition and Consideration of Custom Law in Tribal Lawmaking*, 32 Am. Indian L. Rev. 319 (2007) (setting out a theoretical framework to ascertain customary law); Pat Sekaquaptewa, *Evolving the Hopi Common Law*, 9 Kan. J. L. & Pub. Pol'y 761 (2000) (discussing questions that arise in incorporation of customary law); Justin B. Richland, *"What Are You Going to Do with the Village's Knowledge?" Talking Tradition, Talking Law in Hopi Tribal Court*, 39 L. & Soc'y Rev. 235 (2005) (discussing contested understandings of common law among tribal court judges and litigants). Tribes are also developing alternative dispute resolution mechanisms along the lines of traditional problem solving entities. Some of the same courts are also putting more money into training their judges, developing their written codes, and ensuring judicial independence from political branches.

While many tribes have their own appellate courts, in some more traditional tribes appeal may be to the tribal council. Other tribes share resources by bringing appeals to an intertribal appellate court. The Northwest Intertribal Court System serves a number of tribes in the Oregon, Washington, Alaska, Idaho and Northern California. The various Sioux tribes are working to develop a general Sioux Supreme Court. Many tribes also have specialized administrative courts to deal with workers compensation, taxation, domestic violence, and other issues.

There is a developing literature on tribal court systems. For an excellent compilation and introduction to this literature, see Justin B. Richland & Sarah Deer, Introduction to Tribal Legal Studies (2010). The following articles present a range of perspectives on contemporary tribal courts. The first three emphasize the importance of customary law and procedures, but each takes a different perspective on their modern incorporation. The fourth provides the perspective of a long-time Navajo Nation judge on the distinct concerns that federal law and policy create for the modern tribal judge.

SANDRA DAY O'CONNOR, *LESSONS FROM THE THIRD SOVEREIGN: INDIAN TRIBAL COURTS*

33 Tulsa L. J. 1 (1997)

Today, in the United States, we have three types of sovereign entities—the Federal government, the States, and the Indian tribes. Each of the three sovereigns has its own judicial system, and each plays an important role in the administration of justice in this country. ***

[M]any tribes today attempt to incorporate traditional tribal values, symbols, and customs into their courtrooms and decisions. Some tribal courts, in proceedings that otherwise differ little from what would be seen in State or Federal court, have incorporated traditional features of Indian dispute-resolution to try to infuse the proceedings with values of consensus and community. For example, the placement of litigants and court personnel in a circle aspires to minimize the appearance of hierarchy and highlight the participation and needs of the entire group in place of any one individual.

The tribal courts, while relatively young, are developing in leaps and bounds. For example, many tribes are working to revise their tribal constitutions and to codify their civil, regulatory, and criminal laws to provide greater guidance and predictability in tribal justice. At the same time, tribes have expanded the use of traditional law. Many tribal codes now combine unique tribal law with adapted State and Federal law principles. The number of law-trained Native Americans has increased. Both State and Federal courts continue to recognize the tribal courts as important fora for resolution of reservation-based claims involving both Indians and non-Indians.

Tribal courts today face significant challenges. They must work to satisfy the sometimes-competing demands of those inside and outside the tribal communities. But while the challenges are great, the effective operation of tribal courts [is] essential to promote the sovereignty and self-governance of the Indian tribes. As the Supreme Court has recognized, "Tribal courts play a vital role in tribal self-government, and the Federal Government has consistently encouraged their development." *Iowa Mut. Ins. Co. v. LaPlante*, 480 U.S. 9, 14–15 (1987).

To fulfill their role as an essential branch of tribal government, the tribal courts must provide a forum that commands the respect of both the tribal community and the non-tribal community including courts, governments, and litigants. To do so, tribal courts need to be perceived as both fair and principled. And at the same time the courts seek to satisfy these conditions, they must strive to embody tribal values—values that at times suggest the use of different methods than those used in the Anglo–American, adversarial, common-law tradition. ***

In addressing the matters that come before them, the decision-making process by tribal courts need not, and sometimes do not, replicate the process undertaken in State and Federal courts. Tribal courts often act more quickly, and more informally, than do their counterparts. The factors considered to reach a decision, the procedures used, and the punishment or resolution arrived at, may differ in reflection of tribal values. Tribal court judges frequently are tribal members who seek to infuse cultural values into the process.

While tribal customs and beliefs vary of course from tribe to tribe, some general patterns emerge. In contrast with the Anglo–American system's emphasis on punishment and deterrence, with a "win-lose" approach that often drives parties to adopt extreme adversarial positions, some tribal judicial systems seek to achieve a restorative justice, placing emphasis on restitution rather than retribution and on keeping harmonious relations among the members of the community. To further these traditional Native American values, tribal courts may employ inclusive discussion and creative problem-solving. The focus on traditional values in contemporary circumstances has permitted tribal courts to conceive of alternatives to conventional adversarial processes.

The development of different methods of solving disputes in tribal legal systems provides the tribal courts with a way both to incorporate traditional values and to hold up an example to the nation about the possibilities of alternative dispute resolution. New methods have much to offer to the tribal communities, and much to teach the other court systems operating in the United States. For about the last fifteen years, in recognition of the plain fact that the adversarial process is often not the best means to a fair outcome, both the State and Federal systems have turned with increasing interest to the possibilities offered by mediation, arbitration, and other forms of alternate dispute resolution. In many situations, alternative methods offer a quicker, more personal, and more efficient way of arriving at an answer for the parties' difficulties. ***

Many tribal courts have already developed methods that meet the needs of their communities while at the same time using to the extent possible the tribe's underlying traditions and values. A good example is the Navajo Peacemaker Court, formed in 1982 by the Judicial Conference of the Navajo Nation to provide a forum for traditional mediation. The Navajo Peacemaker Court is now an active, modern legal institution which incorporates traditional Navajo concepts into a judicial process for dispute resolution. The process is directed by a mediator, who acts to guide and encourage parties to resolve their dispute. The process relies on parties' participation and their commitment to reaching a solution, rather than on the imposition of a judgment by an impersonal decisionmaker in order to reach a successful conclusion. In this way the Navajo Peacemaker Court successfully blends beneficial aspects of both Anglo–American and Indian traditions.

The Northwest Intertribal Court System, a consortium of fifteen tribes in the Pacific Northwest, was established in 1979 to provide court services and personnel to the individual tribal courts of member tribes. Several of the member tribes have supplemented their formal tribal court system with Peacemaker programs that are based on traditional values of consensus and respectful attention to individuals. ***

While tribal courts seek to incorporate the best elements of their own customs into the courts' procedures and decisions, the tribal courts have also sought to include useful aspects of the Anglo–American tradition. For example, more and more tribal judicial systems have established mechanisms to ensure the effective appealability of decisions to higher courts. In addition, some tribes have sought to provide tribal judiciaries with the authority to conduct review of regulations and ordinances promulgated by the tribal council. And one of the most important initiatives is the move to ensure judicial independence for tribal judges. Tribal courts are often subject to the complete control of the tribal councils, whose powers often include the ability to select and remove judges. Therefore, the courts may be perceived as a subordinate arm of the councils rather than as a separate and equal branch of government. The existence of such control is not conducive to neutral adjudication on the merits and can threaten the integrity of the tribal judiciary. Some tribes, like the Cheyenne River Sioux Tribe in South Dakota, have amended their constitutions to provide for formal separation of powers.

The growing number of law-trained, well-prepared people participating in the system, both as lawyers and judges is a vital improvement of the tribal judicial systems. Many tribal judges have taken steps to craft ethical guidelines and to institute tribal bar requirements for the lawyers who practice before them, and have participated themselves in further training for the task of judging. Both lawyers and judges must be knowledgeable and principled if the tribal judicial systems are to engender confidence in the fairness and integrity of their courts. Whether in tribal court, state court, or federal court, the exercise of a court's jurisdiction is a serious matter, and all persons—Indian and non-Indian—who come before a court are entitled to just and reasoned proceedings.

The judicial systems of the three sovereigns—the Indian tribes, the Federal government, and the States—have much to teach one another. While each system will develop along different lines, each can take the best from the others. Just as a "single courageous State may, if its citizens choose, serve as a laboratory *** " for the development of laws, the experiments and examples provided by the various Indian tribes and their courts may offer models for the entire nation to follow. ***

ROBERT B. PORTER, *STRENGTHENING TRIBAL SOVEREIGNTY THROUGH PEACEMAKING: HOW THE ANGLO-AMERICAN LEGAL TRADITION DESTROYS INDIGENOUS SOCIETIES*

28 Colum. Hum. Rts. L. Rev. 235 (1997)

*** Until March 25, 1995, the Seneca Nation of Indians had existed for almost 150 years as a constitutional republic without one of its members being killed in a domestic political dispute. Recently, however, the Seneca Nation has been paralyzed by internal conflict, including several months of open civil warfare, that not only has resulted in a loss of life but has nearly destroyed the Seneca government. This "civil war," which began as a dispute between the newly-elected President and two tribal Council members in 1994, was spawned by years of festering disagreements over politics and money that grew to envelop the entire political, social, and economic fabric of the Seneca Nation. While the risk of further internal violence since has decreased, the underlying issues that led to the conflict have not been resolved, and the dispute continues to the present day.

The Seneca Civil War is worthy of study because it demonstrates the extremes to which some people will go to effectuate their personal political agendas. It was clearly the case that the disputing parties were willing to take reckless actions that could lead to a loss of life. It is also clear that they were willing to escalate the tragedy by taking the dispute to a foreign court system and thereby sacrifice Seneca sovereignty.

Unfortunately, it cannot be said that the Seneca Civil War and its resultant impact on Seneca sovereignty is a unique occurrence within Indian country. In recent years, there has been a significant increase in intratribal violence and deadly internal political disputes. In some cases, like that of the Senecas, the disputing parties in these disputes have sought to resolve their disagreements by destroying the very sovereignty that they purport to protect.

*** Despite the richness of the traditional native peacemaking process, most Indians today resolve disputes by litigation conducted in formal judicial systems. While each Indian nation may have its own particular court structure and practice rules, all modern tribal court systems have the same common denominator—they are direct descendants of the Anglo–American legal tradition. ***

The American legal system, and Anglo–American society, is based upon the primacy of the individual and his or her rights. In contrast, peacemaking is heavily dependent upon serving the justice needs of the community, not the individual. This difference in approach requires Indians to make radical changes in their behavior in order to make litigation work for them. Because litigation is heavily, if not fatally, distorted by reliance upon individual self-interest, parties to a lawsuit simply do not care about whether the "system" as a whole works or not or whether there are any negative side-effects on the greater community. They care only about themselves and their pursuit of victory. ***

The concept of involving uninterested third parties to impose a solution on the parties if they fail to reach a settlement is another aspect of the American legal system that tears at the fabric of tribal societies. Given the size and degree of interconnectedness of Indian communities, it is hard to believe that a person appointed or elected a tribal judge from that community does not bring to the bench a lifetime of personal experiences that will influence his or her decision making process. ***

The failure of decision making for native people is heightened by the reliance upon fixed procedural and substantive law. The existence of such rules perpetuates a destructive belief in the mind of the parties (and maybe even the judge) that technical correctness is more important than justice. ***

[I]n every significant aspect, the American legal system is in conflict with the manner in which native people have traditionally resolved disputes. As a result, tribes that have embraced litigation subject their citizens to a dispute resolution process that precipitates and requires a radical change in their behavior in order to obtain justice from the system. While behaving like an American may not seem problematic (especially for Americans), the resulting effect is that native people end up relinquishing traditional cultural values, particularly those relating to community and relationship. As native people lose their connectedness to one another, the fragmentation of their societies soon follows. ***

The Honorable Robert Yazzie, the author of the next two excerpts, served first as a Navajo Nation trial court judge, and then as the Chief Justice of the Navajo Nation Supreme Court from 1992 to 2003.

THE HONORABLE ROBERT YAZZIE, *"LIFE COMES FROM IT": NAVAJO JUSTICE CONCEPTS*

24 N.M. L. Rev. 175 (1994)

*** Law, in Anglo definitions and practice, is written rules which are enforced by authority figures. It is man-made. Its essence is power and force. ***

The Navajo word for "law" is *beehaz'aanii*. It means something fundamental, and something that is absolute and exists from the beginning of time. Navajos believe that the Holy People "put it there for us from the time of beginning" for better thinking, planning, and guidance. It is the source of a healthy, meaningful life, and thus "life comes from it." Navajos say that "life comes from *beehaz'aanii*," because it is the essence of life. The precepts of *beehaz'aanii* are stated in prayers and ceremonies which tell us of *hozho*—"the perfect state." Through these prayers and ceremonies we are taught what ought to be and what ought not to be.

Our religious leaders and elders say that man-made law is not true "law." Law comes from the Holy People who gave the Navajo people the ceremonies, songs, prayers, and teachings to know it. If we lose our prayers and ceremonies, we will lose the foundations of life. Our religious leaders also say that if we lose those teachings, we will have broken the law.

***

I draw upon two sources as I attempt to reconcile Navajo justice thinking with Anglo–European thought. I am a product of a Bureau of Indian Affairs (BIA) boarding school education which was so destructive of the Navajo culture. When I got out of boarding school, I was given a ticket to California to learn a manual skill in an electronics school. They told me I could not go to college, so I went to college. I was fascinated with the power, authority and (as I thought then) the money that went with being a lawyer so I went to law school. When I got my law degree, I put it to use as a trial judge in the Courts of the Navajo Nation. That returned me to another school—the school of the Navajo life. Now, I seek to reconcile my paper knowledge with the vast knowledge that is held by my Elders—"the keepers of the tribal encyclopedia."

Sometimes I get impatient when I consider how traditional wisdom has so much value that has been forgotten. Sometimes I get angry about how Anglo law has overcome Navajo law, to the harm of Navajos. I read an evaluation of my talk on Navajo common law after a conference with state judges and lawyers which said, "Yazzie is bashing Anglo justice systems again." That is not my intent. ***

To me, and to many other Navajos, law is something that "just is." To explain it in my own mind and to you, I need a basis for comparison. That basis is the shortcoming of modern American adjudication, and I am not alone in decrying its destructive elements. I share a fondness for centuries of English–American common law traditions, but changing circumstances now require us to take a new look at that undefinable quality we call justice. As we of the Navajo Nation discuss the traditional knowledge that gives us power to survive in modern times, I find a property that is immensely valuable. I want to share it with you out of respect and to honor Navajo distributive justice. You, who have taken an interest to read this, are like a relative. This relationship will help us grow together in a good way because life comes from it.

HONORABLE ROBERT YAZZIE, "*WATCH YOUR SIX*": *AN INDIAN NATION JUDGE'S VIEW OF 25 YEARS OF INDIAN LAW, WHERE WE ARE AND WHERE WE ARE GOING*

23 Am. Indian L. Rev. 497 (1998/1999)

A friend from Rutgers University writes us and often concludes a letter with this advice: "Watch your six." That is police slang for watching out at six o'clock in military directions. In other words, "Watch your tail—cover your behind." That is the lesson for Indian nation judges for 25 years of the decline of Indian law. Now, I want to review the dangers we face, given recent defeats in the courts and legislature. I also want to identify some of the bright spots and possibilities for the future which can come from a few positive developments.

***

A few years ago, when Navajo Nation Chief Justice Tom Tso went to Washington to work on Indian court enhancement legislation, he was invited to a meeting of Capitol Hill lawyers on the "*Duro*-fix" legislation. During the meeting, one Indian Affairs Committee staffer called down to the Justice Department to get its views on the bill. She laughed when she got off the phone, saying, "They had their usual position: all Indian legislation is unconstitutional because it is race-based." When asked whom she spoke with in the Justice Department, she replied that it was someone in the Office of the General Counsel. That is the most powerful and influential division of Justice; it is the "lawyer for the lawyers." What is even more interesting is the fact that Chief Justice Rehnquist and Associate Justice Scalia were both assistant attorneys general in charge of the Office of the General Counsel.

***

Until the appointment of Justice Rehnquist to the U.S. Supreme Court, there was a general principle that the states had no authority in Indian Country. However, the Rehnquist Court pulled a rabbit out of the hat. This rabbit was the new trick that somehow the Supreme Court can "imply" that Indian nations have lost certain powers. That is, Indian nations have no "inherent" jurisdiction over non-Indians or nonmember Indians because somehow that is "implied." Isn't it strange that if Congress is the primary source of Indian affairs policy (and we know that these days, Congress can do no wrong), then the courts, and not Congress, get to "imply" that Indian nations lost their power?

***

So here we are: Every time I sit on a jurisdiction case, I've got to watch my six.

*** It is not all gloom and doom. On March 12 and 13, something very nice happened. Chief Justice Zlacket of the Arizona Supreme Court invited me, Chief Justice Francini of the New Mexico Supreme Court, and Chief Justice

Zimmerman of the Utah Supreme Court to sit down and talk informally about mutual concerns and interests. I was delighted to find that the justices were interested in the Navajo Nation courts, traditional Navajo law, peacemaking, who we are and what we do. I told the justices a story which applies to this discussion.

In 1994, the Navajo Nation Supreme Court sat at the Stanford University Law School in California. After the oral argument, there was a reception. One of the members of the law school faculty talked about how complex Indian jurisdiction law is and asked how we dealt with such problems. A member of our group said, "Simple—we make friends!" The professor did not quite know how to take that, but it is true. At one point, a litigant before the Arizona Supreme Court was bashing me and my decisions, and a justice told him to stop it, saying, "I know Judge Yazzie personally."

The lesson for me is that if I am to do a good job watching my six, I need friends. I find that most state judges do not know what an Indian court looks like. They do not know how we operate. They do not know us. Recently, we have been meeting with the state judges in northern Arizona and we find that as we make friends with them, we are getting things done. We find that state judges share our desire to solve problems, to stop family violence, to collect child support, to teach each other, and to share resources. ***

*** I am going to try to play the cards as they are dealt to me. I am also going to try to make friends, use my Nation's original law, and get the word out that the justices, judges, and courts of the Navajo Nation are competent and legitimate organs of government. I am going to thumb my nose at the anti-Indian hate mob and try to point out that Indian governments and courts do serve legitimate interests that should be honored. While doing that, I am going to watch my six.

***

The following opinions, one by the Navajo Nation Court of Appeals (now called the Navajo Nation Supreme Court), one by the Hopi Court of Appeals, and one by the Mashantucket Pequot Court of Appeals, reflect tribal responses to three common problems faced by tribal courts: first, judicial review of tribal council decisions; second, resolution of probate disputes among members; and third, recognition of foreign judgments by state courts. How well do they reflect or address the concerns described in the excerpts above? Are they consistent with the concerns about tribal institutions that Professor Cornell raised in the excerpt about economic development and de facto sovereignty?

HALONA V. MACDONALD

1 Nav. R. 189 (Navajo Ct. App. 1978)

Before **BLUEHOUSE, ACTING CHIEF JUSTICE** and **LINCOLN (RETIRED CHIEF JUSTICE** sitting by special designation) and **NESWOOD, ASSOCIATE JUSTICES.**
Per Curiam

This case comes on appeal from a decision of the Shiprock District Court issued May 18, 1977, enjoining the defendants from expending any funds appropriated by the Navajo Tribal Council for the legal expenses of [Navajo Nation Chairman] Peter MacDonald and declaring the appropriation illegal for failure to comply with certain tribal procedures and for being violative of certain substantive rights of the Plaintiffs. ***

The issues presented on appeal may be summarized as follows:

1. Whether venue as to Peter MacDonald and Eldon Hansen was properly found to lie in the Shiprock district. ***

5. Whether actions of the Navajo Tribal Council are reviewable by courts of the Navajo Nation. ***

8. Whether the expenditure of Navajo Tribal funds in this instance was for a public or a private purpose and, if for a private purpose, whether Navajo law prohibits such an expenditure.

III.

We find that the Shiprock District Court did not err in determining that venue was proper in that district as to Peter MacDonald and Eldon Hansen. ***

Rule 26 (Venue) of the Navajo Rules of Civil Procedure says "an action shall be filed in the district in which any defendant resides or in which the cause of action arises ***." The Shiprock District Court entertained the suit against Peter MacDonald on the grounds that he is registered as a voter in Teec Nos Pos, which is within the Shiprock district, and that this was sufficient indication of domicile to bring the suit within the proper scope of the rule. *** We agree fully with the District Court's analysis.

There is another consideration to this issue besides the purely technical analysis. That is the court's concern for fairness. It is a fact that, for all practical purposes, Appellant MacDonald lives in Window Rock, not Teec Nos Pos. But for Navajos, domicile is not as clear or fixed as it might be for non-Indians, if indeed the matter is really all that clear for our non-Indian brothers.

By custom, Navajos consider themselves to be from the same area their mothers are from. Thus, wherever they may be, they return home frequently for religious ceremonies and family functions, as well as to vote. By custom, Navajos are allowed to register and vote in the area where they are from, rather than where they live. Even the Navajo Tribal Code's election law is silent on this point. Perhaps this custom may have to be breached in the future, but for the present, Navajos may be considered to be domiciled where they maintain their traditional and legal ties, regardless of where they actually live.

Given the resources available to the Chairman and the Controller to defend against this suit and the underlying tradition concerning residence, we agree with the District Court that it would have been grossly unfair to have required plaintiffs below to file their action in the Window Rock District Court. This is not to say that we sanction in our opinion here "nationwide" venue as to suits against tribal officials. We do not. We here rule only that the circumstances of this particular suit justified a finding of venue in the Shiprock district by the District Judge there. ***

VII.

The right and power of the Navajo courts to authoritatively review actions of the Navajo Tribal Council has been called into question before, not only in our courts, but also in federal courts. ***

There is no question in our minds about the existence of such authority. When the Navajo Tribal Council adopted Title 7, Section 133 of the Tribal Code, it did not exclude review of Council actions from its broad grant of power to the courts.

Indeed, in our opinion, [the Indian Civil Rights Act] precludes such an exclusion of judicial review of legislative actions because that law is a mandate for Indian governments which necessarily assumes and requires judicial review of any allegedly illegal action by a tribal government.

In particular, 25 U.S.C. § 1302 (8) prohibits the denial of equal protection of the laws and deprivation of liberty or property without due process of law. We cannot imagine how any legislative body accused of violating these primary rights could be the judge of its own actions and at the same time comply with the federal law. Of course, this is not possible.

Judicial review must, therefore, necessarily follow. If the courts established by Indian tribes cannot exercise this power, then the only alternative is review in every case by federal courts.

It is inconceivable to us that the Navajo Tribal Council would prefer review of its actions by far-away federal courts unfamiliar with Navajo customs and laws to review by Navajo courts.

***

Our right to pass upon the legality or meaning of these actions has been questioned in certain places but never by the Council or its Chairman. That is because they have a traditional and abiding respect for the impartial adjudicatory process. When all have been heard and the decision is made, it is respected. This has been the Navajo way since before the time of the present judicial system. The Navajo People did not learn this principle from the white man. They have carried it with them through history.

The style and the form of problem-solving and dispensing justice has changed over the years but not the principle. Those appointed by the People to resolve their disputes were and are unquestioned in their power to do so. Whereas once the clan was the primary forum (and still is a powerful and respected instrument of justice), now the People through their Council have delegated the ultimate responsibility for this to their courts. That is why 7 N.T.C. 133 is so broadly written.

***

VIII.

In analyzing the propriety of Council Resolution CAP–32–77, we must look first to the existing applicable law and then we must determine what effect is to be given to Resolution CAP–32–77, given that it is inconsistent with the codified law. ***

Council Resolution CF–18–77, adopted by the Council February 28, 1977, sets forth the duties and powers of the Budget and Finance Committee of the

Navajo Tribal Council. Among the procedures set forth in that statute for the control of the budgetary process of the Navajo Nation's government is the requirement that requests for interim budget revisions be submitted to the Committee for its approval or disapproval prior to their submission to the full Council, if submission to the Council is required at all.

[The statute] makes no exception for any kind of interim budget revisions. ***

We cannot understand how any court could assume without clear legislative direction that the legislature intended to override in a particular, hastily-drawn and approved resolution the fiscal and legislative system that they had so carefully considered and approved only two months before. If any later minor legislation not passed in accordance with the procedures established by the Council itself can automatically override such procedures, one would rightfully wonder what the point of having procedures would be. What the courts would be left with is chaos. No one could ever be sure whether the procedures established by the Council really had to be complied with. Due process of law would be a joke, available when useful to certain people, something to be ignored when not so useful.

***

We are reminded at this point that the Navajo Nation possesses no constitution. It is for this reason that the Navajo courts must be so careful to preserve the concepts of due process of law embodied in the Indian Civil Rights Act. Analyzing legislation so as to guarantee that the process by which the legislature gives us the laws which we must interpret and enforce is consistent and fair to all is absolutely essential to the preservation of Navajo sovereignty and to the avoidance of actions which might otherwise be in violation of federal law. Had CAP–32–77 expressly repealed all prior inconsistent resolutions (as did CO–65–77) or at least had it expressly suspended CF–18–77, then we would have no problem upholding CAP–32–77. But unfortunately, the drafters of that act were hasty and consequently deficient in their work. As a result, we must rule that CAP–32–77 is invalid. ***

X.

The final issue is whether the expenditure was for a public or a private purpose and, if for a private purpose, whether Navajo law prohibits such an expenditure.

This question can only be answered by reference to Navajo tradition and by an analysis of Navajo history, especially as that history related to the land which produces all Navajo income. The Navajo People are supreme and all residual power lies with the People. In the end, all monies spent by the Navajo Tribal Council are monies of the Navajo People.

Because we cannot adequately explain our ruling on this point in English, we have chosen to announce this part of our decision from the bench in Navajo. This part of our opinion will then be transcribed into Navajo at the earliest possible date and issued as a supplemental part of this decision.

For the reasons we have already stated above in English, the decision of the Shiprock District Court of the Navajo Nation is hereby *AFFIRMED.*

NUTONGLA SANCHEZ V. GARCIA

(Hopi App. Ct. 1999)

Before SEKAQUAPTEWA, CHIEF JUSTICE and LOMAYESVA and ABBEY, JUSTICES.

This case involves a dispute over the inheritance of certain property of Madge Nutongla Garcia (the Decedent), a member of the village of Hotevilla, who died on March 20, 1991. Included in the Decedent's estate are several physical structures located within the Village of Hotevilla, including: a rock house (hereinafter: "Rock House"), an addition to the rock house ("Addition"), and an orchard storage house ("Orchard House"). After the Decedent passed away, her children were unable to agree how this property should be distributed.

Initially, the Decedent's children attempted to settle their dispute by bringing the matter to a clan relative, Homer Koiyayumptewa. Mr. Koiyayumptewa, after considering what all interested parties had to say, determined that the Decedent died leaving an oral will, and distributed the property in issue in accordance with what he found to be the terms of her will. Under this distribution, the Rock House went to Marilyn Nutongla Sanchez (Appellant), the Addition to Walter Garcia (Respondent), and the Orchard House to Dell Garcia (Respondent). All of the parties involved in the distribution settlement initially expressed satisfaction with how Mr. Koiyayumptewa distributed the estate. However, at a later date, Appellant informed the other parties to the settlement that she no longer agreed with Mr. Koiyayumptewa's distribution. When the other parties to the settlement refused to alter the distribution to meet the Appellant's new demands, Appellant brought the matter before the Hotevilla Village Board of Directors. For a variety of reasons, the Board was unable to resolve the case.

Ultimately, it waived its authority under the Hopi Constitution to determine the inheritance of the Decedent's property pursuant to Article III, § 2. After the village waived its jurisdiction, Appellant petitioned the Tribal Court for distribution of the Decedent's estate.

Appellant, in her Petition for Distribution, asserted that the Decedent had died intestate. She argued that under traditional Hopi laws of intestacy the eldest daughter of a decedent is entitled to receive all of the decedent's houses located within the decedent's village. Since the Decedent in this case was a member of the Village of Hotevilla, and Appellant is her eldest daughter, Appellant claims that she is entitled to receive the Rock House, the Addition, and the Orchard House. ***

The Tribal Court found that the Decedent died leaving a valid oral will and ordered [distribution] in accordance with what it found to be the terms of the will. *** This distribution was identical to Mr. Koiyayumptewa's original distribution. ***

This court will not reach the issue whether the trial court erred in distributing the property according to the oral will, because we hold that the trial court erred at the outset by allowing the parties to re-litigate an issue in the Tribal Court that had already been resolved at the village level. Homer

Koiyayumptewa, the disputants' clan relative, resolved this dispute before it was brought to the Tribal Court, and his previous decision binds the parties before this court. ***

Article III, Section 2 of the Hopi Constitution reserves four subject matter areas to the Hopi villages. Section 2(c) reserves to the villages the power to "regulate the inheritance of property of the members of the villages." The language of this subsection gives rise to an interpretive issue because it provides that inheritance disputes are reserved to "the villages," but speaks no further on the matter. It does not specify what governmental entity or entities within the village possess the constitutional power to resolve disputes falling under Section 2(c).

The answer to this question is not obvious, because the respective villages at Hopi vary significantly in terms of their governmental structures: some are "traditional" villages, where the preeminent village authority is the *kikmongwi*; some are "modern" villages, with a formal constitution allocating governmental powers within the village; and most are "hybrid" villages, where the division of power between traditional leaders and popularly elected village board members remains somewhat uncertain.

In a hybrid village, legal authority is not concentrated in any one governmental entity. Because Hotevilla is a hybrid village, it cannot be assumed that the language of section 2(c) vests the power to resolve inheritance disputes in the Hotevilla Village Board exclusively. Outside of the Hotevilla Village Board, other Hotevilla village members possess legal authority within the village. The basis of this legal authority is tradition and custom. Traditional legal authorities, as well as the Village Board, may possess the power to resolve inheritance disputes and distribute property pursuant to the Hopi Constitution.

A village member is a traditional legal authority in the area of inheritance law where there is a long standing custom within the village recognizing his or her power to resolve inheritance disputes. *** [I]t is a common practice at Hopi for the heirs of a decedent to take any inheritance dispute that may arise among them to the appropriate clan relative, who determines how the decedent's estate should be distributed. ***

Clan relative settlement is an effective means to resolve intra-village inheritance disputes in a traditional Hopi manner and in a traditional Hopi legal forum. For the Tribal Courts to disregard this method of dispute resolution would be to show disrespect for traditional Hopi law and traditional legal authorities within the villages. Perhaps more to the point, the Hopi Constitution mandates that the Tribal Court give deference to the villages in inheritance matters. Because the villages have exclusive jurisdiction over intra-village inheritance disputes under Article III, Section 2(c), the Hopi courts cannot overrule a village decision in this area.

*** The remaining question to address is whether Mr. Koiyayumptewa rendered a "final decision" that binds the parties and should have precluded relitigation in the Tribal Court.

***

Mediation is a fundamentally non-coercive process, whereby all parties must agree upon a proposed resolution or decision before it is given legal effect. However, for mediation to serve any useful purpose, it is necessary that once the parties reach an agreement, the courts recognize that agreement as final and binding. *** Having voluntarily submitted to the clan relative dispute resolution process, Appellant was not entitled to take her lawsuit to a different forum merely because she ultimately came to disagree with the result reached by Mr. Koiyayumptewa. ***

***

A trial court has the authority to certify village orders in matters reserved to the villages. Certification allows the trial court a means by which to formally recognize a village decision and to proceed to the enforcement of such village decisions. A trial court, however, must hold an evidentiary hearing to determine whether all interested parties have been provided with a fundamentally fair opportunity to participate in the village decision making process before the court can recognize and certify the village decision. Fundamental fairness requires, at a minimum, that all interested parties were provided with adequate notice and a meaningful opportunity to be heard at the village level. ***

After hearing extensive testimony over the course of two separate hearings, the trial court in this case made the two findings that are crucial to establish the fundamental fairness of a clan relative's distribution settlement. First, it found that Appellant agreed to have Homer Koiyayumptewa resolve this inheritance dispute. Second, it found that Appellant initially expressed satisfaction with Mr. Koiyayumptewa's distribution of the property, and that it was not until "a later date [that Appellant] informed the parties she no longer agreed with the distribution ***."

These findings are more than sufficient to demonstrate the presence of fundamental fairness in the village decision-making process. Since the Appellant agreed to have Homer Koiyayumptewa resolve the dispute, there is no question that she had "adequate notice." And, the fact that she expressed satisfaction with Mr. Koiyayumptewa's decision proves that she had a "meaningful opportunity to be heard." ***

HUSBAND V. WIFE

(Mashantucket Pequot Ct. App. 2003)

Before **HARPER, BIGLER AND TOMPKINS, APPELLATE COURT JUDGES**, sitting *en banc.*

JUDGE KEITH HARPER.

The defendant-appellant, Husband, appeals from the decision and judgment of the Mashantucket Pequot Family Court ("Family Court") adopting the judgment of the Connecticut Superior Court *** on Plaintiff–Appellee, Wife's, action for dissolution of marriage as a judgment of the Family Court in accordance with VI M.P.T.L. ch. 8, § 2(b). *** We hold that (1) Mashantucket law requires that the adoption of the Husband and Wife's dissolution judgments is to be evaluated pursuant to principles of comity; (2) the Superior Court judgment does not contravene public policy; and (3) the Family Court may adopt a

Connecticut dissolution judgment even where the dissolution involves a resident of the Reservation. ***

The pertinent facts are not in dispute. Husband and Wife were married under the laws of the State of Connecticut. Wife is a non-Indian and a resident of the State of Rhode Island. On November 1, 1995, Wife filed an action for dissolution of marriage in Superior Court. Husband is a member of the Mashantucket Pequot Indian Tribe and is a resident of the Reservation and, furthermore, had been a resident of the Reservation for at least twelve months immediately preceding the date Wife initiated her dissolution action.

Wife's Superior Court action was brought pursuant to Connecticut General Statutes § 46b–44, which provides in pertinent part ***

> (c) A decree dissolving a marriage or granting a legal separation may be entered if: (1) One of the parties to the marriage has been a resident of this state for at least the twelve months next preceding the date of the filing of the complaint or next preceding the date of the decree.

[The Connecticut Superior Court entered an order dissolving the marriage and Wife filed papers to enforce the judgment in ***Mashantucket Pequot Family Court. Husband objected that Connecticut lacked subject matter jurisdiction over this dissolution because he, as a resident of the Reservation, is not a resident of Connecticut under § 46b–44(c)(1). The trial court rejected Husband's argument and adopted the Connecticut judgment. Husband appealed.]

***

*** Wife seeks to enforce the dissolution judgment *** pursuant to the "Recognition and Enforcement of Foreign Judgment" provisions of the Mashantucket Pequot Tribal Nation's Family Relations Law.

[The Family Relations Law] VI M.P.T.L. ch. 8, § 2(b) provides:

> [A family relations judgment of a competent court of a state or another tribe] shall become a judgment of the Tribal Court and shall be enforceable provided that such judgment does not contravene the public policy of the Mashantucket Pequot Tribe. ***

As a preliminary matter, we must decide whether the intent of ch. 8, § 2(b) is that the tribal court give "full faith and credit" to appropriate "foreign judgments" or merely that the tribal court adopt such judgments in appropriate circumstances on the basis of "comity." ***

The term "Full Faith and Credit" as understood in American jurisprudence is a concept rooted in the United States Constitution. *** And it is well settled that where full faith and credit applies, an enforcing court is prohibited from exercising discretion. *** The elimination of the recognizing jurisdiction's discretion was a means to achieve unification of the American Republic and realize federal supremacy over the theretofore sovereign several states; as the Court stated in *General Motors Corp. v. Baker*:

> The animating purpose of the full faith and credit command *** "was to alter the status of the several states as independent foreign sovereignties, each free to ignore obligations created under the laws or by the judicial proceedings of the others, and to make them integral parts of a single nation throughout which a remedy upon a just obligation might be demanded as of right, irrespective of the state of its origin."

522 U.S. at 232. ***

Thus, by both definition and design, application of full faith and credit in the constitutional sense is antithetical to permitting any evaluation of whether the "public policy" of the enforcing jurisdiction is offended. ***

In stark contrast to the Full Faith and Credit Clause as revealed in case law, VI M.P.T.L. ch. 8, § 2(b) requires the tribal court, prior to enforcement of a foreign judgment, to determine whether "such judgment *** contravene[s] the public policy of the Mashantucket Pequot Tribe." It therefore would be wholly at odds with the language of ch. 8, § 2(b) to conclude that it intends to require application of "full faith and credit"—as that term is understood under settled constitutional law—to foreign marriage dissolution judgments.

Instead, we believe, Mashantucket Law requires that foreign judgments be evaluated, and where appropriate, recognized through the far more flexible construct of "comity," where consideration of public policy considerations is permissible. ***

***

[A]pplication of comity pursuant to VI M.P.T.L. ch. 8, § 2(b) requires us to decide two other issues. *** First, we must determine if the judgment somehow "contravenes the public policy of the Mashantucket Pequot Tribe." Second, pursuant to VI M.P.T.L. ch. 8, § 1(e), we must rule whether the Superior Court is "a Court of competent jurisdiction of [a] state," and therefore an appropriate judgment to enforce as a tribal judgment.

On the issue of public policy, we agree with the Tribe that, as a general matter, enforcement of lawful dissolution of marriage judgment from the State of Connecticut does not contravene Mashantucket public policy. [T]he "Purpose" section of the Family Relations Law, which is perhaps the clearest indication of Mashantucket policy on this issue, recognizes that:

> [F]amilies thrive when they receive appropriate emotional and financial support, and that the lives of children and families improve by strengthening parental responsibility for family and child support. The Tribe encourages the development of Tribal law and policies and procedures that protect and preserve the continuity of family and promote a uniform, efficient and equitable recognition and implementation of these responsibilities.

Plainly, this provision accords substantial weight to judgments which adjudicate dissolution claims and properly and fairly place "financial support" on parents of children. This view of Mashantucket policy is confirmed by the Child Welfare Law as well:

> The Mashantucket Pequot Tribe finds that there is no resource more vital to its continued existence and integrity than its children. *** The Tribe hereby declares that it is the policy of this Nation to protect the health and welfare of children and families within the Mashantucket Pequot community ***.

Here, tribal children are among the main beneficiaries of the judgment under consideration, which requires the payment of child support. Their welfare—obviously a paramount consideration of the Tribe—militates strongly for adoption of the judgment. Moreover, in this case, there is no indication—and

Husband does not contend—that the division of parental financial responsibility is inequitable. Under these circumstances, we have no trouble concluding that Mashantucket policy, in general, supports recognition of a lawful Connecticut dissolution judgment, particularly since child support is involved.

Husband raises one additional issue specific to his case (*i.e.*, not to enforcement of dissolution judgments generally) regarding public policy that is worthy of consideration: Whether it violates Mashantucket policy to recognize a judgment which subjects a tribal member living on the reservation to jurisdiction in a state court proceeding. ***

*** To find that Husband was a resident of Connecticut, the Connecticut Supreme Court held that his domicile on the Reservation meant he was a domicile of Connecticut. *** Importantly, their decision is largely an interpretation of the meaning of state law. *** As such, we need not agree with every jot and tittle of the rationale employed by the Connecticut courts in reaching their conclusive reading of state statutes for our limited collateral review under comity principles. *** Our task is merely to ensure that the state assertion of authority over the Husband and Wife's dissolution (1) is not a naked *ultra vires* act, and (2) does not undermine the Tribe's right to exercise its own authority over matters arising on the Reservation. ***

***

*** It is a matter of record that the Husband and Wife's marriage was created under Connecticut law. *** In addition, as a Reservation resident, Husband is eligible to participate in state and federal elections, like all other citizens of the State of Connecticut. While this factor is not sufficient to permit an assertion of state jurisdiction over an Indian on a reservation, it does show that Husband has a "relationship" to the state distinct from say a resident of the Pine Ridge Reservation in South Dakota. ***

It is undoubtedly true that in most circumstances the assertion of state adjudicatory jurisdiction over Indians has a devastating impact on the sovereign rights of tribes (and has been and remains a prime point of contention between states and Indian tribes). ***

With regard to the dissolution, Husband points to no facts—other than his residence—to support a conclusion that the marriage or dissolution thereof "aris[es] out of conduct on an Indian reservation." Instead, all significant acts—the marriage household, Wife's residence, the residence of their children, the loci of the marriage contract—all occurred off "an Indian reservation." Accordingly, absent federal or tribal law suggesting a contrary conclusion, we do not see how the enforcement of the Connecticut judgment could possibly "infringe[] on the right of the [Mashantucket Tribe] to make their own laws and be ruled by them." *Williams*, 358 U.S. 223. In short, since Connecticut's assertion of jurisdiction over the dissolution in no way infringes on Mashantucket jurisdictional authority and its underlying decision is an interpretation of a state law statute, we have no reason to disturb through a collateral action the lawful Connecticut judgment. ***

NOTES AND QUESTIONS

1. How do these opinions differ from what you might expect of analogous state court decisions? How are they similar? Consider how these differences and similarities relate to questions about the meaning of sovereignty.

2. What distinctive challenges do the tribal courts face in these opinions?

3. Assuming that these opinions are fair representations of the range of tribal judicial decision-making, would you be comfortable representing clients in these fora? Why or why not? If you would require additional information to come to a conclusion about this, what more would you want to know?

CHAPTER 7

STATE–TRIBAL STRUGGLES OVER JURISDICTION

■ ■ ■

Struggles between states and tribes over jurisdiction form some of the most bitter battles in Indian law. In 2003, Rhode Island state troopers stormed the tiny Narragansett Reservation and brought down tribal council members with German shepherds to enforce taxes on cigarette sales. In 1995, Seneca tribal members blocked state highways in upstate New York to prevent imposition of cigarette and Todagas taxes, provoking a violent confrontation with police. Tribal-state conflicts no longer threaten to bring down the "ship of state," as they did in the Cherokee–Georgia conflict in the 1830s, but they still rouse passions and are the subject of most of the Indian law cases before the modern Supreme Court.

Under the foundational principles we have studied, three rules of law might be expected concerning these conflicts:

> First, a state has no inherent sovereign authority in Indian country. That is the holding of *Worcester*.
>
> Second, outside Indian country, a tribe and its members are generally subject to state law just like anyone else.
>
> Third, by virtue of its plenary authority, Congress may change the first two rules as it sees fit.

Perhaps surprisingly, only the second of these rules can be discussed in short order. As the rule specifies, generally speaking, Indian country is the dividing line between state authority on the one hand and tribal and federal authority on the other. That is to say, the usual Indian law canons "flip" when the location is outside Indian country: unless a federal statute or treaty provides to the contrary, state law governs. *See Mescalero Apache Tribe v. Jones*, 411 U.S. 145, 148–49 (1973). Despite the existence of state jurisdiction, however, tribes are immune from suit even for off-reservation tribal economic activity, *Bay Mills, supra,* and some tribes have reserved off-reservation treaty rights to hunt, fish and gather free of state regulation.

Section 1 of this chapter begins with the three cases that establish the continuing limitations on state authority in Indian country in the modern era. Section 2 examines Public Law 280, the primary instance in which Congress, pursuant to the third rule, has authorized states to exercise authority in Indian country. Section 3 examines the modern cases concerning when states may regulate nonmembers in Indian country, as well as the Indian Gaming Regulatory Act, passed in reaction to a decision affirming exclusive tribal authority. Section 4 considers the Indian Child Welfare Act, through which Congress confirmed exclusive tribal authority over custody cases involving children within

Indian country, and expanded tribal jurisdiction in such cases outside Indian country.

I. THE FOUNDATIONAL MODERN PRECEDENTS

As federal Indian policy began to move away from the notion of termination of tribal status in the late 1950s, the Supreme Court encountered a case in which the courts of Arizona held they had jurisdiction over a dispute between a non-Indian plaintiff and Indian defendants involving the collection of a debt. The holding in that case marks the beginning of what Professor Charles Wilkinson has called the "modern era" of Indian law. Charles F. Wilkinson, American Indians, Time and the Law 1 (1987). The case both affirms the traditional barriers to state authority in Indian country and acknowledges the extent to which tribes retain inherent powers over reservation affairs.

WILLIAMS V. LEE

358 U.S. 217, 79 S. Ct. 269, 3 L. Ed. 2d 251 (1959)

JUSTICE BLACK delivered the opinion of the Court.

Respondent, who is not an Indian, operates a general store in Arizona on the Navajo Indian Reservation under a license required by federal statute. [25 U.S.C. § 262.] He brought this action in the Superior Court of Arizona against petitioners, a Navajo Indian and his wife who live on the Reservation, to collect for goods sold them there on credit. Over petitioners' motion to dismiss on the ground that jurisdiction lay in the tribal court rather than in the state court, judgment was entered in favor of respondent. The Supreme Court of Arizona affirmed, holding that since no Act of Congress expressly forbids their doing so Arizona courts are free to exercise jurisdiction over civil suits by non-Indians against Indians though the action arises on an Indian reservation. *** Because this was a doubtful determination of the important question of state power over Indian affairs, we granted certiorari. ***

Originally the Indian tribes were separate nations within what is now the United States. Through conquest and treaties they were induced to give up complete independence and the right to go to war in exchange for federal protection, aid, and grants of land. When the lands granted lay within States these governments sometimes sought to impose their laws and courts on the Indians. Around 1830 the Georgia Legislature extended its laws to the Cherokee Reservation despite federal treaties with the Indians which set aside this land for them. The Georgia statutes forbade the Cherokees from enacting laws or holding courts and prohibited outsiders from being on the Reservation except with permission of the State Governor. The constitutionality of these laws was tested in *Worcester*, when the State sought to punish a white man, licensed by the Federal Government to practice as a missionary among the Cherokees, for his refusal to leave the Reservation. Rendering one of his most courageous and eloquent opinions, Chief Justice Marshall held that Georgia's assertion of power was invalid. ***

Despite bitter criticism and the defiance of Georgia which refused to obey this Court's mandate in *Worcester* the broad principles of that decision came to be accepted as law. Over the years this Court has modified these principles in cases where essential tribal relations were not involved and where the rights of Indians would not be jeopardized, but the basic policy of *Worcester* has remained. Thus, suits by Indians against outsiders in state courts have been sanctioned. *See Felix v. Patrick*, 145 U.S. 317 (1892); *United States v. Candelaria*, 271 U.S. 432 (1926); *see also Harrison v. Laveen*, 196 P.2d 456 (Ariz. 1948). And state courts have been allowed to try non-Indians who committed crimes against each other on a reservation. *E.g., New York ex rel. Ray v. Martin*, 326 U.S. 496 (1946). But if the crime was by or against an Indian, tribal jurisdiction or that expressly conferred on other courts by Congress has remained exclusive. *Donnelly v. United States*, 228 U.S. 243, 269–272 (1913); *Williams v. United States*, 327 U.S. 711 (1946). Essentially, absent governing Acts of Congress, the question has always been whether the state action infringed on the right of reservation Indians to make their own laws and be ruled by them. *Cf. Utah & Northern Railway Co. v. Fisher*, 116 U.S. 28 (1886).

Congress has also acted consistently upon the assumption that the States have no power to regulate the affairs of Indians on a reservation. To assure adequate government of the Indian tribes it enacted comprehensive statutes in 1834 regulating trade with Indians and organizing a Department of Indian Affairs. 4 Stat. 729, 735. Not satisfied solely with centralized government of Indians, it encouraged tribal governments and courts to become stronger and more highly organized. [Citing Indian Reorganization Act of 1934.] Congress has followed a policy calculated eventually to make all Indians full-fledged participants in American society. This policy contemplates criminal and civil jurisdiction over Indians by any State ready to assume the burdens that go with it as soon as the educational and economic status of the Indians permits the change without disadvantage to them. [Citing legislative history of Public Law 280.] Significantly, when Congress has wished the States to exercise this power it has expressly granted them the jurisdiction which *Worcester* had denied. [Citing Public Law 280 and an earlier, similar statute authorizing New York to assume jurisdiction in Indian country.]

No departure from the policies which have been applied to other Indians is apparent in the relationship between the United States and the Navajos. On June 1, 1868, a treaty was signed between General William T. Sherman, for the United States, and numerous chiefs and headmen of the "Navajo nation or tribe of Indians." At the time this document was signed the Navajos were an exiled people, forced by the United States to live crowded together on a small piece of land on the Pecos River in eastern New Mexico, some 300 miles east of the area they had occupied before the coming of the white man. In return for their promises to keep peace, this treaty "set apart" for "their permanent home" a portion of what had been their native country, and provided that no one, except United States Government personnel, was to enter the reserved area. Implicit in these treaty terms, as it was in the treaties with the Cherokees involved in *Worcester*, was the understanding that the internal affairs of the Indians remained exclusively within the jurisdiction of whatever tribal government existed. Since then, Congress and the Bureau of Indian Affairs have assisted in strengthening the Navajo tribal government and its courts. The Tribe itself has in recent years greatly improved its legal system through increased expenditures and better-trained personnel. Today the Navajo Courts of Indian Offenses exercise broad criminal and civil jurisdiction which covers suits by outsiders against Indian defendants. No Federal Act has given state courts jurisdiction over such controversies. In [Public Law 280] Congress did express its willingness to have any State assume jurisdiction over reservation Indians if the State Legislature or the people vote affirmatively to accept such responsibility. To date, Arizona has not accepted jurisdiction, possibly because the people of the State anticipate that the burdens accompanying such power might be considerable.

There can be no doubt that to allow the exercise of state jurisdiction here would undermine the authority of the tribal courts over Reservation affairs and hence would infringe on the right of the Indians to govern themselves. It is immaterial that respondent is not an Indian. He was on the Reservation and the transaction with an Indian took place there. The cases in this Court have consistently guarded the authority of Indian governments over their reservations. Congress recognized this authority in the Navajos in the Treaty of 1868, and has done so ever since. If this power is to be taken away from them, it is for Congress to do it. *Lone Wolf.*

Reversed.

NOTES AND QUESTIONS

1. *Williams v. Lee* is an extraordinary case. In the Termination Era, one might have expected the Court to authorize state court jurisdiction. Indeed, lower court decisions in the first half of the twentieth century sometimes ratified state power in Indian country, reasoning either that tribal sovereignty was a dated notion or that express federal action was required to oust state jurisdiction. As Professor Wilkinson has noted, "[t]he view that tribalism was a thing of the past in the United States was also well represented in the academic literature. One scholar concluded in 1959 that Indian tribal sovereignty 'has been pure legal fiction for decades.'" Charles F. Wilkinson, American Indians, Time and the Law 27 (1987) (citation omitted.) That scholar's timing was particularly poor, given that the Supreme Court decided *Williams* the very same year.

2. To appreciate the Court's recognition of tribal sovereignty, consider the facts of *Williams* carefully. Both plaintiff and defendants were citizens of Arizona. The cause of action arose in Arizona. The subject matter of the dispute was a run-of-the-mill contract action. In other circumstances, the Arizona state court would have had personal jurisdiction over the Williamses. State courts, because they are courts of general jurisdiction, also typically have subject matter jurisdiction over these kinds of cases. So what ousts the state of jurisdiction here?

3. Missing from the Court's opinion is why the case mattered to Paul and Lorena Williams and their family. Hugh Lee filed a writ of attachment along with his Arizona court action and had the county sheriff seize part of the family sheep herd to secure the expected judgment. Sheep were the main source of support for Mr. and Mrs. Williams and their eight children; they supported themselves by trading wool for goods at the trading post in the fall, and lambs in the spring. As for most traditional Navajo families, raising and caring for sheep played a central role in Navajo family life and culture. There is a Navajo saying, "*Dibé Diné bí íína,*" sheep is the life of the people. At 99 years old, Mrs. Williams recalled the seizure and eventual sale of her sheep, without

notice or explanation, as among the most painful events in her life. Even after the Supreme Court vindicated their position, the family was never compensated for the loss of their sheep or the money they had spent on ceremonies to secure success in the lawsuit. Forty-nine years after the Supreme Court decision, however, the Navajo Nation honored Mrs. Williams and her family for their contributions to Navajo sovereignty. *See* Bethany R. Berger, Williams v. Lee *and the Debate over Indian Equality*, 109 Mich. L. Rev. 1463 (2011).

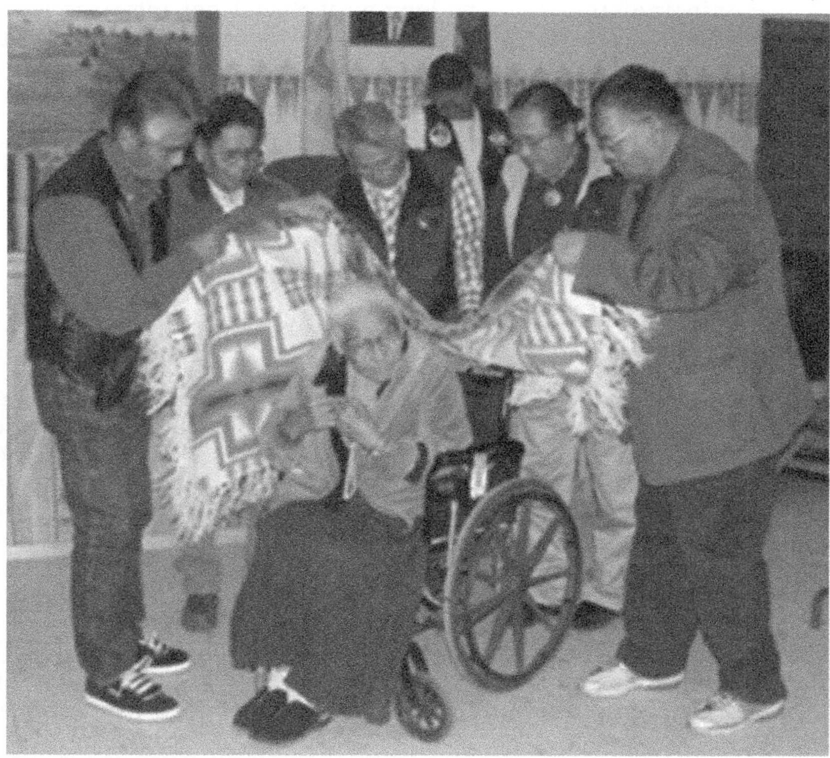

Navajo Nation President Joe Shirley, Chief Justice Robert Yazzie, and others present Mrs. Williams with an honoring blanket (April 27, 2008), reprinted with permission of the Navajo Nation Office of President and Vice–President.

The Court in *Williams* emphasized two important notions. First the Court acknowledged that the holding in *Worcester* had been diluted by *McBratney*, which provides that states have jurisdiction over crimes committed by non-Indians against non-Indians in Indian country. The Court nonetheless treated *Worcester* as the most important precedent in federal Indian law. It tried to make sense of *Worcester* in the modern era by developing a test: the state may not assert authority in Indian country if that would infringe on the right of reservation Indians to make their own laws and be governed by them. The Court found that state court jurisdiction over reservation affairs would do this by undermining the authority of the tribe's lawmaking institutions, its legislative and adjudicatory bodies. Second, the Court noted that, in Public Law 280, Congress had provided Arizona a way to obtain state court jurisdiction over civil cases arising in Indian country, and Arizona had not elected to do so.

A problem is that the Court did not explain the relationship between these two approaches. The second approach would seem to imply that Public Law 280 and similarly explicit authorizations of state jurisdiction should be understood as providing the only way a state can have authority in Indian country (except that, because of *stare decisis*, the anomalous result in *McBratney* would still stand). But if that is the basis for the result in *Williams*, there would have been no reason to talk about the first approach. Under *Williams*, could a state have authority in Indian country so long as it would not interfere with the tribe's ability to make its laws? What if the state sought jurisdiction over those who are not members of the tribe? Consider the next case.

WARREN TRADING POST CO. V. ARIZONA STATE TAX COMMISSION

380 U.S. 685, 85 S. Ct. 1242, 14 L. Ed. 2d 165 (1965)

JUSTICE BLACK delivered the opinion of the Court.

Arizona has levied a tax of 2% on the "gross proceeds of sales, or gross income" of appellant Warren Trading Post Company, which does a retail trading business with Indians on the Arizona part of the Navajo Indian Reservation under a license granted by the United States Commissioner of Indian Affairs pursuant to 19 Stat. 200, 25 U.S.C. § 261 (1958 ed.).[1] Appellant claimed that as applied to its income from trading with reservation Indians on the reservation the state tax was invalid as (1) in violation of Art. I, § 8, cl. 3 of the United States Constitution, which provides that "Congress shall have Power *** To regulate Commerce *** with the Indian Tribes"; (2) inconsistent with the comprehensive congressional plan, enacted under authority of Art. I, § 8, to regulate Indian trade and traders and to have Indian tribes on reservations govern themselves. The State Supreme Court rejected these contentions and upheld the tax, one Justice dissenting. 387 P.2d 809. *** Since we hold that this state tax cannot be imposed consistently with federal statutes applicable to the Indians on the Navajo Reservation, we find it unnecessary to consider whether the tax is also barred by that part of the Commerce Clause giving Congress power to regulate commerce with the Indian tribes.

The Navajo Reservation was set apart as a "permanent home" for the Navajos in a treaty made with the "Navajo nation or tribe of Indians" on June 1, 1868. Long before that, in fact from the very first days of our Government, the Federal Government had been permitting the Indians largely to govern themselves, free from state interference,[3] and had exercised through statutes and

---

1. *** The tax is applicable to "every person engaging or continuing within this state in the business of selling any tangible personal property whatever at retail," with stated exceptions. Ariz. Rev. Stat. § 42–1312. Appellant's challenge to these statutes is limited to the State's attempt to apply them to gross income from sales made on the reservation to reservation Indians.

3. Arizona was admitted to the Union on its agreement that

> the people inhabiting said proposed State do agree and declare that they forever disclaim all right and title to *** all lands lying within said boundaries owned or held by any Indian or Indian tribes, the right or title to which shall have been acquired through or from the United States or any prior sovereignty, and that until the title of such Indian or Indian

treaties a sweeping and dominant control over persons who wished to trade with Indians and Indian tribes. As Chief Justice John Marshall recognized in *Worcester v. Georgia*, "From the commencement of our government, congress has passed acts to regulate trade and intercourse with the Indians; which treat them as nations, respect their rights, and manifest a firm purpose to afford that protection which treaties stipulate." He went on to say that: "The treaties and laws of the United States contemplate the Indian territory as completely separated from that of the states; and provide that all intercourse with them shall be carried on exclusively by the government of the union." *Id.* at 557.

In the very first volume of the federal statutes is found an Act, passed in 1790 by the first Congress, "to regulate trade and intercourse with the Indian tribes," requiring that Indian traders obtain a license from a federal official, and specifying in detail the conditions on which such licenses would be granted. ***

Such comprehensive federal regulation of Indian traders has continued from that day to this. Existing statutes make specific restrictions on trade with the Indians, and one of them, passed in 1876 and tracing back to comprehensive enactments of 1802 and 1834, provides that the Commissioner of Indian Affairs shall have "the sole power and authority to appoint traders to the Indian tribes" and to specify "the kind and quantity of goods and the prices at which such goods shall be sold to the Indians." [25 U.S.C. § 261.] Acting under authority of this statute and one added in 1901, the Commissioner has promulgated detailed regulations prescribing in the most minute fashion who may qualify to be a trader and how he shall be licensed; penalties for acting as a trader without a license; conditions under which government employees may trade with Indians; articles that cannot be sold to Indians; and conduct forbidden on a licensed trader's premises. He has ordered that detailed business records be kept and that government officials be allowed to inspect these records to make sure that prices charged are fair and reasonable; that traders pay Indians in money; that bonds be executed by proposed licensees; and that the governing body of an Indian reservation may assess from a trader "such fees, etc., as it may deem appropriate." [25 C.F.R. Parts 140 and 141.] It was under these comprehensive statutes and regulations that the Commissioner of Indian Affairs licensed appellant to trade with the Indians on the Navajo Reservation. These apparently all-inclusive regulations and the statutes authorizing them would seem in themselves sufficient to show that Congress has taken the business of Indian trading on reservations so fully in hand that no room remains for state laws imposing additional burdens upon traders. ***

Congress has, since the creation of the Navajo Reservation nearly a century ago, left the Indians on it largely free to run the reservation and its affairs without state control, a policy which has automatically relieved Arizona of all burdens for carrying on those same responsibilities. And in compliance with its treaty obligations the Federal Government has provided for roads, education and other services needed by the Indians. We think the assessment and

---

> tribes shall have been extinguished the same shall be and remain subject to the disposition and under the absolute jurisdiction and control of the Congress of the United States ***. Act of June 20, 1910, 36 Stat. 557, 569. ***

Certain state laws have been permitted to apply to activities on Indian reservations, where those laws are specifically authorized by acts of Congress, or where they clearly do not interfere with federal policies concerning the reservations. ***

collection of this tax would to a substantial extent frustrate the evident congressional purpose of ensuring that no burden shall be imposed upon Indian traders for trading with Indians on reservations except as authorized by Acts of Congress or by valid regulations promulgated under those Acts. This state tax on gross income would put financial burdens on appellant or the Indians with whom it deals in addition to those Congress or the tribes have prescribed, and could thereby disturb and disarrange the statutory plan Congress set up in order to protect Indians against prices deemed unfair or unreasonable by the Indian Commissioner. And since federal legislation has left the State with no duties or responsibilities respecting the reservation Indians, we cannot believe that Congress intended to leave to the State the privilege of levying this tax.[18] Insofar as they are applied to this federally licensed Indian trader with respect to sales made to reservation Indians on the reservation, these state laws imposing taxes cannot stand. *Cf. Rice v. Santa Fe Elevator Corp.*, 331 U.S. 218 (1947). The judgment of the Supreme Court of Arizona is reversed and the cause remanded for further proceedings not inconsistent with this opinion.

NOTES AND QUESTIONS

1. *Preemption as a barrier to state authority. Warren Trading Post* adds federal preemption of conflicting state laws to the ways that state authority can be excluded from Indian country. But how could the Court conclude that state taxes conflicted with federal laws that neither prohibited state taxes nor provided for special federal taxes? Outside Indian law, where federal and state power overlap, the courts have developed an elaborate approach to the question whether a federal statute or regulation "preempts" state law. Under the Constitution's Supremacy Clause, of course, federal law is the supreme law of the land. Preemption analysis is easy to do in two circumstances: when the federal statute expressly provides that state law is preempted, or when the federal statute expressly provides that state law is not preempted. In both instances, Congress's explicit instructions govern. When Congress has not seen fit to legislate expressly on the preemption issue, however, the Supreme Court has generally approached preemption as a federalism problem and guarded state authority from preemption except in limited circumstances. Thus, there is a canon of statutory interpretation presuming that Congress does not intend to preempt state power, so that in ambiguous circumstances the state law generally survives. *See, e.g., Cipollone v. Liggett Group, Inc.*, 505 U.S. 504 (1992). Of course, if federal and state law conflict, the federal law prevails even if there is no express preemption provision in it. *See, e.g., Florida Lime & Avocado Growers, Inc., v. Paul*, 373 U.S. 132 (1963). In a small number of circumstances, the Supreme Court has found "field preemption": that the federal

---

18. The Buck Act, now 4 U.S.C. § 105–110 (1964 ed.), in which Congress permitted States to levy sales or use taxes within certain federal areas, has been interpreted by what appears to be the only court to consider the question before this case, and by the Interior Department, as not applying to Indian reservations. *Your Food Stores, Inc. v. Village of Espanola*, 361 P.2d 950, 955–956 (1961), excepting taxes on Indians from the scope of the Act. We think that interpretation was correct. *** Moreover, we hold that Indian traders trading on a reservation with reservation Indians are immune from a state tax like Arizona's, not simply because those activities take place on a reservation, but rather because Congress in the exercise of its power granted in Art. I, § 8, has undertaken to regulate reservation trading in such a comprehensive way that there is no room for the States to legislate on the subject. ***

statutory and regulatory scheme is so pervasive that there is no room left for state law to apply. *See, e.g., Rice v. Santa Fe Elevator Corp.*, 331 U.S. 218 (1947) (Federal Warehouse Act).

Although *Warren Trading Post* cited *Rice* to support its finding that state taxation was preempted because Congress "has undertaken to regulate reservation trading in such a comprehensive way that there is no room for the States to legislate on the subject," federal laws and policies had not in fact regulated Indian traders besides requiring them to obtain federal licenses and preventing them from selling alcohol. In fact, the lack of federal intervention had allegedly created a "system of unregulated trading post monopolies" on the Navajo Nation, leading to a class action demanding that the Secretary of the Interior exercise his authority to promulgate regulations governing the traders. *Rockbridge v. Lincoln*, 449 F.2d 567, 568 (9th Cir. 1971).

Understanding this, it becomes clearer that the historical exclusion of state authority from reservations and the special federal-tribal relationship does significant work in *Warren*. As you will see, the Court's application of the preemption analysis in Indian law does not follow the presumptions that apply when Congress legislated "in a field which the States have traditionally occupied," in which the courts "start with the assumption that the historic police powers of the States were not to be superseded by the Federal Act unless that was the clear and manifest purpose of Congress." *Rice*, 331 U.S. at 230. Rather the Indian preemption analysis has more in common with the analysis applied if "the Act of Congress may touch a field in which the federal interest is so dominant that the federal system will be assumed to preclude enforcement of state laws on the same subject." *Id.* In some areas, such as foreign relations and immigration, regulation is traditionally left to the federal government, and far less interference with federal purposes will suffice to preempt state authority. *See Arizona v. United States*, 567 U.S. 387, 416 (2012)("Arizona may have understandable frustrations with the problems caused by illegal immigration . . . but the State may not pursue policies that undermine federal law."); *Hines v. Davidowitz*, 312 U.S. 52 (1941) (striking down Pennsylvania law requiring immigrants to register with the state); *National Foreign Trade Council v. Natsios*, 181 F.3d 38, 68 (1st Cir. 1999) (holding that Massachusetts law prohibiting state government from purchasing goods made in Burma was unconstitutional because it interfered with the nation's ability to speak with one voice on foreign relations), *aff'd on other grounds, Crosby v. National Foreign Trade Council*, 530 U.S. 363 (2000). Similarly, in Indian country, states traditionally have no authority, and federal and tribal authority is exclusive, making preemption without explicit statement more likely.

But what if there is no federal scheme regulating the area in question? The next case arose from a challenge brought by Rosalind McClanahan, then an 18-year-old teller for a local bank. Richard Pomp, *The Unfilled Promise of the Indian Commerce Clause and State Taxation*, 63 Tax Law. 897 (2011). McClanahan was represented by DNA–People's Legal Services, which was established in 1969 to provide free legal services to the people of the Navajo Nation. For many years she was the fiscal manager for DNA, which was praised throughout her tenure for its sound financial management.

MCCLANAHAN V. STATE TAX COMMISSION OF ARIZONA

411 U.S. 164, 93 S. Ct. 1257, 36 L. Ed. 2d 129 (1973)

JUSTICE MARSHALL delivered the opinion of the Court.

*** Appellant is an enrolled member of the Navajo tribe who lives on that portion of the Navajo Reservation located within the State of Arizona. Her complaint alleges that all her income earned during 1967 was derived from within the Navajo Reservation. Pursuant to Ariz. Rev. Stat. Ann. § 43–188(f) (Supp.1972–1973), $16.20 was withheld from her wages for that year to cover her state income tax liability. At the conclusion of the tax year, appellant filed a protest against the collection of any taxes on her income and a claim for a refund of the entire amount withheld from her wages. When no action was taken on her claim, she instituted this action in Arizona Superior Court on behalf of herself and those similarly situated, demanding a return of the money withheld and a declaration that the state tax was unlawful as applied to reservation Indians.

The trial court dismissed the action for failure to state a claim, and the Arizona Court of Appeals affirmed. Citing this Court's decision in *Williams v. Lee*, 358 U.S. 217 (1959), the Court of Appeals held that the test "is not whether the Arizona state income tax infringes on plaintiff's rights as an individual Navajo Indian, but whether such a tax infringes on the rights of the Navajo tribe of Indians to be self-governing." 14 Ariz. App. at 454, 484 P.2d at 223. The court thus distinguished cases dealing with state taxes on Indian real property on the ground that these taxes, unlike the personal income tax, infringed tribal autonomy. ***

The Arizona Supreme Court denied a petition for review of this decision, and the case came here on appeal. ***

II.

*** [T]his case involves the narrow question whether the State may tax a reservation Indian for income earned exclusively on the reservation.

The principles governing the resolution of this question are not new. On the contrary, "[t]he policy of leaving Indians free from state jurisdiction and control is deeply rooted in the Nation's history." *Rice v. Olson*, 324 U.S. 786, 789 (1945). This policy was first articulated by this Court 141 years ago when Mr. Chief Justice Marshall held that Indian nations were "distinct political communities, having territorial boundaries, within which their authority is exclusive, and having a right to all the lands within those boundaries, which is not only acknowledged, but guarantied by the United States." *Worcester v. Georgia*, 6 Pet. 515, 557 (1832). It followed from this concept of Indian reservations as separate, although dependent nations, that state law could have no role to play within the reservation boundaries. ***

[I]t would vastly oversimplify the problem to say that nothing remains of the notion that reservation Indians are a separate people to whom state jurisdiction, and therefore state tax legislation, may not extend. Thus, only a few years ago, this Court struck down Arizona's attempt to tax the proceeds of a trading company doing business within the confines of the very reservation involved in this case. *See Warren Trading Post Co. v. Arizona Tax Comm'n,* 380 U.S. 685 (1965). The tax in no way interfered with federal land or with the National Government's proprietary interests. But it was invalidated nonetheless because "from the very first days of our Government, the Federal Government had been permitting the Indians largely to govern themselves, free from state interference." *Id.* at 686–687.[6] ***

This is not to say that the Indian sovereignty doctrine, with its concomitant jurisdictional limit on the reach of state law, has remained static during the 141 years since *Worcester* was decided. Not surprisingly, the doctrine has undergone considerable evolution in response to changed circumstances. As noted above, the doctrine has not been rigidly applied in cases where Indians have left the reservation and become assimilated into the general community. *** Similarly, notions of Indian sovereignty have been adjusted to take account of the State's legitimate interests in regulating the affairs of non-Indians. *** This line of cases was summarized in this Court's landmark decision in *Williams v. Lee*: "Over the years this Court has modified [the *Worcester* principle] in cases where essential tribal relations were not involved and where the rights of Indians would not be jeopardized. *** Thus, suits by Indians against outsiders in state courts have been sanctioned. *** And state courts have been allowed to try non-Indians who committed crimes against each other on a reservation. *** But if the crime was by or against an Indian, tribal jurisdiction or that expressly conferred on other courts by Congress has remained exclusive. *** Essentially, absent governing Acts of Congress, the question has always been whether the state action infringed on the right of reservation Indians to make their own laws and be ruled by them." ***

Finally, the trend has been away from the idea of inherent Indian sovereignty as a bar to state jurisdiction and toward reliance on federal pre-emption. *See Mescalero Apache Tribe v. Jones,* 411 U.S. 145 (1973). The modern cases thus tend to avoid reliance on platonic notions of Indian sovereignty and to look instead to the applicable treaties and statutes which define the limits of state power. *Compare, e.g., United States v. Kagama,* 118 U.S. 375 (1886), *with Kennerly v. District Court,* 400 U.S. 423 (1971).

The Indian sovereignty doctrine is relevant, then, not because it provides a definitive resolution of the issues in this suit, but because it provides a backdrop against which the applicable treaties and federal statutes must be read. It must always be remembered that the various Indian tribes were once independent and sovereign nations, and that their claim to sovereignty long predates that of our own Government. Indians today are American citizens. They have the right to vote, to use state courts, and they receive some state services.[12] But it is nonetheless still true, as it was in the last century, that "[t]he

---

6. The court below distinguished *Warren Trading Post* as limited to cases where the Federal Government has pre-empted state law by regulating Indian traders in a manner inconsistent with state taxation. 484 P.2d 221, 224. But although the Court was, no doubt, influenced by the federal licensing requirements, the reasoning of *Warren Trading Post* cannot be so restricted. ***

12. The court below pointed out that Arizona was expending tax monies for education and welfare within the confines of the Navajo Reservation. It should be noted, however, that the Federal Government defrays 80% of Arizona's ordinary social security payments to reservation Indians, and has authorized the expenditure of more than $88 million for rehabilitation programs for Navajos and Hopis living on reservations. *** Moreover, "[c]onferring rights and privileges on these Indians cannot affect their situation, which can only be changed by treaty stipulation, or a voluntary abandonment of their tribal organization." *The Kansas Indians,* 72 U.S. 737, 757 (1866).

relation of the Indian tribes living within the borders of the United States *** [is] an anomalous one and of a complex character. *** They were, and always have been, regarded as having a semi-independent position when they preserved their tribal relations; not as States, not as nations, not as possessed of the full attributes of sovereignty, but as a separate people, with the power of regulating their internal and social relations, and thus far not brought under the laws of the Union or of the State within whose limits they resided." *United States v. Kagama*, 118 U.S. at 381–381.

III.

When the relevant treaty and statutes are read with this tradition of sovereignty in mind, we think it clear that Arizona has exceeded its lawful authority by attempting to tax appellant. The beginning of our analysis must be with the treaty which the United States Government entered with the Navajo Nation in 1868. The agreement provided, in relevant part, that a prescribed reservation would be set aside "for the use and occupation of the Navajo tribe of Indians" and that "no persons except those herein so authorized to do, and except such officers, soldiers, agents, and employees of the government, or of the Indians, as may be authorized to enter upon Indian reservations in discharge of duties imposed by law, or the orders of the President, shall ever be permitted to pass over, settle upon, or reside in, the territory described in this article." 15 Stat. 668.

The treaty nowhere explicitly states that the Navajos were to be free from state law or exempt from state taxes. But the document is not to be read as an ordinary contract agreed upon by parties dealing at arm's length with equal bargaining positions. We have had occasion in the past to describe the circumstances under which the agreement was reached. "At the time this document was signed the Navajos were an exiled people, forced by the United States to live crowded together on a small piece of land on the Pecos River in eastern New Mexico, some 300 miles east of the area they had occupied before the coming of the white man. In return for their promises to keep peace, this treaty 'set apart' for 'their permanent home' a portion of what had been their native country." *Williams v. Lee.*

It is circumstances such as these which have led this Court in interpreting Indian treaties, to adopt the general rule that "[d]oubtful expressions are to be resolved in favor of the weak and defenseless people who are the wards of the nation, dependent upon its protection and good faith." *Carpenter v. Shaw*, 280 U.S. 363, 367 (1930). When this canon of construction is taken together with the tradition of Indian independence described above, it cannot be doubted that the reservation of certain lands for the exclusive use and occupancy of the Navajos and the exclusion of non-Navajos from the prescribed area was meant to establish the lands as within the exclusive sovereignty of the Navajos under general federal supervision. It is thus unsurprising that this Court has interpreted the Navajo treaty to preclude extension of state law—including state tax law—to Indians on the Navajo Reservation. *See Warren Trading Post; Williams v. Lee.*

Moreover, since the signing of the Navajo treaty, Congress has consistently acted upon the assumption that the States lacked jurisdiction over Navajos living on the reservation. Thus, when Arizona entered the Union, its entry was expressly conditioned on the promise that the State would "forever disclaim all right and title to *** all lands lying within said boundaries owned or held by any Indian or Indian tribes, the right or title to which shall have been acquired through or from the United States or any prior sovereignty, and that until the title of such Indian or Indian tribes shall have been extinguished the same shall be and remain subject to the disposition and under the absolute jurisdiction and control of the Congress of the United States." Arizona Enabling Act, 36 Stat. 569.

Nor is the Arizona Enabling Act silent on the specific question of tax immunity. The Act expressly provides that "nothing herein, or in the ordinance herein provided for, shall preclude the said State from taxing as other lands and other property are taxed any lands and other property *outside of an Indian reservation* owned or held by any Indian." *Id.* at 570 (emphasis added). It is true, of course, that exemptions from tax laws should, as a general rule, be clearly expressed. But we have in the past construed language far more ambiguous than this as providing a tax exemption for Indians, *see, e.g., Squire v. Capoeman*, 35 U.S. 1 (1956), and we see no reason to give this language an especially crabbed or restrictive meaning.

Indeed, Congress' intent to maintain the tax-exempt status of reservation Indians is especially clear in light of the Buck Act, 4 U.S.C. § 104 *et seq.*, which provides comprehensive federal guidance for state taxation of those living within federal areas. Section 106(a) of Title 4 U.S.C. grants to the States general authority to impose an income tax on residents of federal areas, but § 109 expressly provides that "[n]othing in sections 105 and 106 of this title shall be deemed to authorize the levy or collection of any tax on or from any Indian not otherwise taxed." To be sure, the language of the statute itself does not make clear whether the reference to "any Indian not otherwise taxed" was intended to apply to reservation Indians earning their income on the reservation. But the legislative history makes plain that this proviso was meant to except reservation Indians from coverage of the Buck Act, *see* S. Rep. No. 1625, 76th Cong., 3d Sess., 2, 4 (1940); 84 Cong. Rec. 10685, and this Court has so interpreted it. While the Buck Act itself cannot be read as an affirmative grant of tax-exempt status to reservation Indians, it should be obvious that Congress would not have jealously protected the immunity of reservation Indians from state income taxes had it thought that the States had residual power to impose such taxes in any event. Similarly, narrower statutes authorizing States to assert tax jurisdiction over reservations in special situations are explicable only if Congress assumed that the States lacked the power to impose the taxes without special authorization. [25 U.S.C. § 398 (congressional authorization for States to tax mineral production on unallotted tribal lands).] ***

IV.

When Arizona's contentions are measured against these statutory imperatives, they are simply untenable. The State relies primarily upon language in *Williams v. Lee* stating that the test for determining the validity of state action is "whether [it] infringed on the right of reservation Indians to make their own laws and be ruled by them." Since Arizona has attempted to tax individual Indians and not the tribe or reservation as such, it argues that it has not infringed on Indian rights of self-government.

In fact, we are far from convinced that when a State imposes taxes upon reservation members without their consent, its action can be reconciled with tribal self-determination. But even if the State's premise were accepted, we reject the suggestion that the *Williams* test was meant to apply in this situation. It must be remembered that cases applying the *Williams* test have dealt principally with situations involving non-Indians. In these situations, both the tribe and the State could fairly claim an interest in asserting their respective jurisdictions. The *Williams* test was designed to resolve this conflict by providing that the State could protect its interest up to the point where tribal self-government would be affected.

The problem posed by this case is completely different. Since appellant is an Indian and since her income is derived wholly from reservation sources, her activity is totally within the sphere which the relevant treaty and statutes leave for the Federal Government and for the Indians themselves. Appellee cites us to no cases holding that this legislation may be ignored simply because tribal self-government has not been infringed. On the contrary, this Court expressly rejected such a position only two years ago. In *Kennerly v. District Court*, 400 U.S. 423 (1971), the Blackfoot Indian Tribe had voted to make state jurisdiction concurrent within the reservation, [but the Court held the state could not assume jurisdiction without complying with the requirements of Public Law 280, even though the tribal action suggested that jurisdiction would not interfere with tribal self-government.]

Finally, we cannot accept the notion that it is irrelevant "whether the *** state income tax infringes on (appellant's) rights as an individual Navajo Indian," as the State Court of Appeals maintained. To be sure, when Congress has legislated on Indian matters, it has, most often, dealt with the tribes as collective entities. But those entities are, after all, composed of individual Indians, and the legislation confers individual rights. This Court has therefore held that "the question has always been whether the state action infringed on the right of *reservation Indians* to make their own laws and be ruled by them." *Williams v. Lee, supra* (emphasis added). In this case, appellant's rights as a reservation Indian were violated when the state collected a tax from her which it had no jurisdiction to impose. Accordingly, the judgment of the court below must be reversed.

NOTES AND QUESTIONS

1. The argument for the state is straightforward. No federal statute or treaty expressly immunizes a member of the Navajo tribe from state income taxation. Thus, there is no federal preemption of state power. Nor does state taxation of the income of an individual member infringe on the right of the Navajo to make their own laws and be governed by them (the *Williams* infringement test). For example, the Navajo remain free to adopt their own income tax and apply it to members. Just as federal employees are subject to state income tax, so should reservation-residing Indians. If Congress does not approve of this result, it can change it by ordinary legislation, by virtue of its plenary power.

Why does the Court in *McClanahan* reject these arguments? Near the beginning of the opinion, the Court states that *Worcester*'s categorical exclusion of state authority has been diluted over the years and that the current test is not based on "platonic notions of Indian sovereignty" but instead requires a focus on federal treaties and statutes. This sounds like a standard federal preemption test, in which, as discussed above, the general presumption is that

Congress does not intend to preempt state law. If this approach were applied in *McClanahan*, one would think that the state should have won. Go through the positive pieces of federal law—treaty and statutes. Do any of them expressly preempt state taxation in this context?

Only by having a presumption that the state may not tax, putting the burden of argument on the state to demonstrate tribal (in the treaty) or federal (in some statute) permission to tax, does the decision make sense. In fact, despite its general discussion to the contrary, in the latter portions of the opinion the Court seems to approach the treaty and the statutes with this framing of the issue in mind. In particular, the Court's statement that the "Indian sovereignty doctrine is relevant *** because it provides a backdrop against which the applicable treaties and federal statutes must be read," suggests that Indian law preemption does not work the same way as garden-variety federal preemption does. How does it work then? Does the tribal sovereignty backdrop account for the flip in the usual presumptions about state law preemption?

Although the Indian interest prevailed in *McClanahan*, these analytical problems may have contributed to the tensions in the cases that follow. In each case, the state can plausibly argue that its attempt to regulate in Indian country does not interfere with tribal capacity to make laws that govern tribal members (the *Williams* infringement test) and is not preempted by federal treaties or statutes (the *McClanahan* preemption test). Had *Williams* and *McClanahan* simply said, "a state that seeks to regulate in Indian country must demonstrate that a treaty or statute authorizes the regulation," it would have been unnecessary to litigate any of the rest of the cases in this Chapter. Why might the Court, or at least enough members to detract from a majority, have been reluctant to take such a broad approach?

2. One of the possible confusions flowing from *McClanahan* was whether its preemption analysis required litigation on a case-by-case basis about state authority to tax Indians who live in and earn their income in Indian country. After all, the case seemed to indicate that a particularized focus upon the various treaties and statutes applicable to a particular tribe and its reservation was required, and it did not seem to decide the case on the simple ground that no treaty or statute plainly authorized Arizona to tax. Nonetheless, just three years later, in *Bryan v. Itasca County*, 426 U.S. 373 (1976) the Court understood *McClanahan* as announcing a flat rule against state taxation of Indians residing in and earning their income in Indian country unless a treaty or statute clearly provided to the contrary:

> *McClanahan* held that Arizona was disabled in the absence of congressional consent from imposing a state income tax on the income of a reservation Indian earned solely on the reservation. On the authority of *McClanahan*, *Moe v. Salish & Kootenai Tribes*, 425 U.S. 463 (1976), held this Term that in the absence of congressional consent the State was disabled from imposing a personal property tax on motor vehicles owned by tribal members living on the reservation, or a vendor license fee applied to a reservation Indian conducting a business for the tribe on reservation land, or a sales tax as applied to on-reservation sales by Indians to Indians.
>
> Thus *McClanahan* and *Moe* preclude any authority in respondent county to levy a personal property tax upon petitioner's mobile home in the absence of congressional consent. ***

426 U.S. at 376–377. Nine years later, the Court stated this approach in particularly strong rule-like language and developed a specific canon of clear statement to implement it. In *Montana v. Blackfeet Tribe*, 471 U.S. 759 (1985), the question was whether the state could tax the tribe's royalty interests in oil and gas leases under which non-Indian lessees were extracting minerals from tribal lands. Such leases are heavily regulated by federal statutes and regulations. A 1924 statute explicitly authorized states to tax royalties from leases entered into under the Act, but a 1938 statute revising the leasing system contained no such authorization. The Blackfeet Tribe challenged state taxation of their royalties from leases issued pursuant to the 1938 statute. Consider the way in which the Court understood how to approach the question whether the state could tax Indians in Indian country:

> The Constitution vests the Federal Government with exclusive authority over relations with Indian tribes. Art. I, § 8, cl. 3; [*Worcester*.] As a corollary of this authority, and in recognition of the sovereignty retained by Indian tribes even after formation of the United States, Indian tribes and individuals generally are exempt from state taxation within their own territory. In *The Kansas Indians*, 5 Wall. 737 (1867), for example, the Court ruled that lands held by Indians in common as well as those held in severalty were exempt from state taxation. It explained that "[i]f the tribal organization *** is preserved intact, and recognized by the political department of the government as existing, then they are a 'people distinct from others,' *** separated from the jurisdiction of [the State], and to be governed exclusively by the government of the Union." Likewise, in *The New York Indians*, 5 Wall. 761 (1867), the Court characterized the State's attempt to tax Indian reservation land as extraordinary, an "illegal" exercise of state power, and "an unwarrantable interference, inconsistent with the original title of the Indians, and offensive to their tribal relations." As the Government points out, this Court has never wavered from the views expressed in these cases. *See, e.g., Bryan; Moe; Mescalero Apache Tribe v. Jones.*
>
> In keeping with its plenary authority over Indian affairs, Congress can authorize the imposition of state taxes on Indian tribes and individual Indians. It has not done so often, and *the* Court *consistently has held that it will find the Indians' exemption from state taxes lifted only when Congress has made its intention to do so unmistakably clear. E.g., Bryan.* The 1924 [federal mineral leasing] Act contains such an explicit authorization. As a result, in *British–American Oil Producing Co. v. Board of Equalization of Montana*, 299 U.S. 159 (1936), the Court held that the State of Montana could tax oil and gas produced under leases executed under the 1924 Act.
>
> The State urges us that the taxing authorization provided in the 1924 Act applies to leases executed under the 1938 Act as well. It argues that nothing in the 1938 Act is inconsistent with the 1924 taxing provision and thus that the provision was not repealed by the 1938 Act. It cites decisions of this Court that a clause repealing only inconsistent Acts "implies very strongly that there may be acts on the same subject which are not thereby repealed," and that such a clause indicates Congress' intent "to leave in force some portions of former acts relative to the same subject-matter." The State also notes that there is a strong presumption against repeals by implication, especially an implied repeal of a specific statute by a general

one, *Morton v. Mancari*. Thus, in the State's view, sound principles of statutory construction lead to the conclusion that its taxing authority under the 1924 Act remains intact.

> *The State fails to appreciate, however, that the standard principles of statutory construction do not have their usual force in cases involving Indian law.* As we said earlier this Term, "[t]he canons of construction applicable in Indian law are rooted in the unique trust relationship between the United States and the Indians." *Oneida County v. Oneida Indian Nation*, 470 U.S. 226, 247 (1985). Two such canons are directly applicable in this case: first, the States may tax Indians only when Congress has manifested clearly its consent to such taxation, *e.g., Bryan*; second, statutes are to be construed liberally in favor of the Indians, with ambiguous provisions interpreted to their benefit, *e.g., McClanahan*. When the 1924 and 1938 Acts are considered in light of these principles, it is clear that the 1924 Act does not authorize Montana to enforce its tax statutes with respect to leases issued under the 1938 Act.

471 U.S. at 764–766 (emphasis added). The Court has drawn a sharp line, however, between the on- and off-reservation application of this rule. It rejected the Chickasaw Nation's attempt to bar state taxes from being imposed on tribal members who worked on-reservation for the tribe but resided off-reservation: "the Tribe gains no support from the rule that Indians and Indian tribes are generally immune from state taxation [citing *McClanahan*] as this principle does not operate outside Indian country." *Oklahoma Tax Com'n v. Chickasaw Nation*, 515 U.S. 450, 464 (1995).

There is a tension between the adoption of (flat) rules and more context-specific standards in all law, but this tension may be even more vivid in federal Indian law. What might explain the path from *McClanahan*'s somewhat unclear explication of the implied preemptive effect of various treaties and statutes to *Blackfeet Tribe*'s flat rule prohibiting state taxation unless Congress's consent to taxation is unmistakably clear? (Note well, by the way, that any attorney representing Indians should be able to retrieve from memory the italicized language above that "the standard principles of statutory construction do not have their usual force in cases involving Indian law.") As a preview to the materials in Section 3 below, the near-categorical rule in *Blackfeet Tribe* has evolved into a general prohibition on state taxation of tribes and tribal members in Indian country. The rules regarding state taxation of nonmembers in Indian country have gone in a different direction, evolving from the fairly pro-tribal version of preemption in *Warren* and *McClanahan* to a balancing test approach that sanctions many forms of state taxation and accompanying regulation. When you read the cases in Section 3, occasionally take a look back at the text of *Williams* and *McClanahan* and consider what has happened to the Supreme Court's background assumptions about sovereignty.

II. CONGRESSIONAL AUTHORIZATION OF STATE JURISDICTION IN INDIAN COUNTRY

The primary instance in which Congress has authorized states to exercise jurisdiction in Indian country is Public Law 280, Act of Aug. 15, 1953, 67 Stat.

588–90. Professor Carole Goldberg, the foremost authority on the law, provides the following brief history of the Act:†

> During the first half of this century, Congress enacted laws instituting state jurisdiction on several individual reservations in different states and over all the reservations in New York. The affected tribes neither solicited these legislative actions nor consented to them. Congress was responding to state initiatives and seeking to lighten the federal government's jurisdictional burden.
>
> Then in 1953, at the height of its post-World War II assimilationist impulse, Congress established a more comprehensive regime for empowering states on reservations. The new law, known as Public Law 280, withdrew federal criminal jurisdiction on reservations in six designated states, including California, and authorized those same states to assume criminal jurisdiction and to hear civil cases against Indians arising in Indian country. For all other states, Public Law 280 established a mechanism for future assumption of the same type of criminal and civil jurisdiction. This second group of states had to enact affirmative legislation accepting authority over reservation Indians; and in states that had disclaimers of Indian jurisdiction in their constitutions, constitutional amendments were provided for as well. As was the case with the pre–1953 laws, tribes neither requested nor approved of states' Public Law 280 jurisdiction; it was imposed upon them in order to relieve federal financial obligations and to address perceived "lawlessness" on reservations.
>
> From the very beginning, the absence of a tribal consent provision in Public Law 280 raised moral concerns, and not only among the affected tribes. Many tribes actively opposed passage of the law, at least to the extent their meager funds could support travel to congressional hearings. And in signing the bill into law, President Eisenhower indicated that the lack of such a provision left him with "grave doubts." ***
>
> Fifteen years and many expressions of outrage after the enactment of Public Law 280, Congress finally amended the law to require tribal consent, via referendum, before states could assume jurisdiction. By that time, nine states (in addition to the six named in the statute) had claimed some or all of the jurisdiction that Public Law 280 allowed. Remarkably, the 1968 amendments did not apply to the areas of Indian country that had already become subject to state jurisdiction under the original act. Only future extensions of state jurisdiction were covered. To no one's surprise, not a single tribe has consented to state jurisdiction since 1968. But what of the tribes in the six "mandatory" states and the others that had already been forced to bear the weight of state jurisdiction? The 1968 amendments offered no mechanism for tribes to initiate "retrocessions" of jurisdiction back to the federal government—a striking lack of parallelism with the provisions allowing states to initiate such a process.

Carole Goldberg–Ambrose, *Public Law 280 and the Problem of Lawlessness in Indian Country*, 44 UCLA L. Rev. 1405, 1405–1408 (1997).

---

†. *See also* Carole E. Goldberg, *Public Law 280: The Limits of State Jurisdiction over Reservation Indians*, 22 UCLA L. Rev. 535 (1975).

Public Law 280

Begin by reading the basic jurisdictional provisions of Public Law 280, which specify the nature of the jurisdiction as well as identify the so-called "mandatory states."

18 U.S.C. § 1162. State jurisdiction over offenses committed by or against Indians in the Indian country

(a) Each of the States or Territories listed in the following table shall have jurisdiction over offenses committed by or against Indians in the areas of Indian country listed opposite the name of the State or Territory to the same extent that such State or Territory has jurisdiction over offenses committed elsewhere within the State or Territory, and the criminal laws of such State or Territory shall have the same force and effect within such Indian country as they have elsewhere within the State or Territory:

State or Territory	Indian Country Affected
Alaska	All Indian country within the State, except that on the Annette Islands, the Metlakatla Indian community may exercise jurisdiction over offenses committed by Indians in the state in the same manner in which such jurisdiction may be exercised by Indian tribes in Indian country over which State jurisdiction has not been extended
California	All Indian country within the State
Minnesota	All Indian country within the State except the Red Lake Reservation
Nebraska	All Indian country within the State
Oregon	All Indian country within the State except the Warm Springs Reservation
Wisconsin	All Indian country within the State

(b) Nothing in this section shall authorize the alienation, encumbrance, or taxation of any real or personal property, including water rights, belonging to any Indian or any Indian tribe, band, or community that is held in trust by the United States or is subject to a restriction against alienation imposed by the United States; or shall authorize regulation of the use of such property in a manner inconsistent with any Federal treaty, agreement, or statute or with any regulation made pursuant thereto; or shall deprive any Indian or any Indian tribe, band, or community of any right, privilege, or immunity afforded under Federal treaty, agreement, or statute with respect to hunting, trapping, or fishing or the control, licensing, or regulation thereof.

(c) The provisions of sections 1152 and 1153 of this chapter [eds.: the Indian Country Crimes Act and the Major Crimes Act] shall not be applicable within the areas of Indian country listed in subsection (a) of this section as areas over which the several States have exclusive jurisdiction.

(d) Notwithstanding subsection (c), at the request of an Indian tribe, and after consultation with and consent by the Attorney General—

(1) sections 1152 and 1153 shall apply in the areas of the Indian country of the Indian tribe; and

(2) jurisdiction over those areas shall be concurrent among the Federal Government, State governments, and, where applicable, tribal governments. [This subsection was added by the Tribal Law and Order Act of 2010 with implementing regulations at 28 C.F.R. 50.25. eds.]

28 U.S.C. § 1360. State civil jurisdiction in actions to which Indians are parties

(a) Each of the States listed in the following table shall have jurisdiction over civil causes of action between Indians or to which Indians are parties which arise in the areas of Indian country listed opposite the name of the State to the same extent that such State has jurisdiction over other civil causes of action, and those civil laws of such State that are of general application to private persons or private property shall have the same force and effect within such Indian country as they have elsewhere within the State:

State of	Indian country affected
Alaska	All Indian country within the State
California	All Indian country within the State
Minnesota	All Indian country within the State, except the Red Lake Reservation
Nebraska	All Indian country within the State
Oregon	All Indian country within the State, except the Warm Springs Reservation
Wisconsin	All Indian country within the State

(b) Nothing in this section shall authorize the alienation, encumbrance, or taxation of any real or personal property, including water rights, belonging to any Indian or any Indian tribe, band, or community that is held in trust by the United States or is subject to a restriction against alienation imposed by the United States; or shall authorize regulation of the use of such property in a manner inconsistent with any Federal treaty, agreement, or statute or with any regulation made pursuant thereto; or shall confer jurisdiction upon the State to adjudicate, in probate proceedings or otherwise, the ownership or right to possession of such property or any interest therein.

(c) Any tribal ordinance or custom heretofore or hereafter adopted by an Indian tribe, band, or community in the exercise of any authority which it may possess shall, if not inconsistent with any applicable civil law of the State, be given full force and effect in the determination of civil causes of action pursuant to this section.

Public Law 280 fundamentally reworks bedrock assumptions of federal Indian law, allowing the states—which as *Kagama* famously said, historically have been viewed as the tribes' "deadliest enemies"—to assume jurisdiction in Indian country. As such, one might expect the Indian law canons of interpretation to counsel courts to interpret the statute quite narrowly. On the other hand, Public Law 280 was adopted during the heart of the Termination Era. The Congress that adopted Public Law 280 embraced a federal policy of essentially destroying the jurisdictional line drawn by Indian country where it was deemed feasible (by terminating the federal relationship with some tribes) and significantly diluting the effect of jurisdictional lines otherwise (by requiring certain states, and authorizing others, to assume jurisdiction in Indian country). If a court saw its interpretive responsibility as being the faithful agent of the intent of the enacting Congress, it might well interpret Public Law 280 broadly to authorize state jurisdiction even in ambiguous circumstances. In addition, states, which were not provided with any federal funds to carry out the extensive policing and judicial services now thrust on them, may well have expected that new taxing power would accompany these new jurisdictional responsibilities. Consider this interpretive conundrum in the context of the next case.

BRYAN V. ITASCA COUNTY

426 U.S. 373, 96 S. Ct. 2102, 48 L. Ed. 2d 710 (1976)

JUSTICE BRENNAN delivered the opinion of the Court.

This case presents the question *** whether the grant of civil jurisdiction to the States conferred by *** 28 U.S.C. § 1360 is a congressional grant of power to the States to tax reservation Indians except insofar as taxation is expressly excluded by the terms of the statute.

Petitioner Russell Bryan, an enrolled member of the Minnesota Chippewa Tribe, resides in a mobile home on land held in trust by the United States for the Chippewa Tribe on the Leech Lake Reservation in Minnesota. In June 1972, petitioner received notices from the auditor of respondent Itasca County, Minn., that he had been assessed personal property tax liability on the mobile home totaling $147.95.† Thereafter, in September 1972, petitioner brought this suit in the Minnesota District Court seeking a declaratory judgment that the

---

†. [Eds. While a house is generally considered part of the real property and therefore part of the property held in trust, a mobile home such as that owned by Bryan may be considered personal property and thus is not trust property. Although affixing the mobile home to the land may transform it into real property, the attorneys in *Bryan* decided not to litigate this issue. Kevin K. Washburn, *The Legacy of* Bryan v. Itasca County*: How an Erroneous $147 County Tax Notice Helped Bring Tribes $200 Million in Gaming Revenue*, 92 Minn. L. Rev. 919, 925 (2008).]

State and county were without authority to levy such a tax on personal property of a reservation Indian on the reservation and that imposition of such a tax was contrary to federal law. The Minnesota District Court rejected the contention and entered judgment for respondent county. The Minnesota Supreme Court affirmed. We granted certiorari and now reverse.

I.

*** *McClanahan* and *Moe* preclude any authority in respondent County to levy a personal property tax upon petitioner's mobile home in the absence of congressional consent. Our task therefore is to determine whether § 4 of Pub. L. 280, 28 U.S.C. § 1360, constitutes such consent.

Section 4(a), 28 U.S.C. § 1360(a) provides:

> Each of the States listed *** shall have jurisdiction over civil causes of action between Indians or to which Indians are parties which arise in the areas of Indian country listed *** to the same extent that such State has jurisdiction over other civil causes of action, and those civil laws of such State that are of general application to private persons or private property shall have the same force and effect within such Indian country as they have elsewhere within the State. ***
>
> Minnesota *** All Indian country within the State, except the Red Lake Reservation.

The statute does not in terms provide that the tax laws of a State are among "civil laws *** of general application to private persons or private property." The Minnesota Supreme Court concluded, however, that they were, finding in § 4(b) of the statute a negative implication of inclusion in § 4(a) of a general power of tax.

Section 4(b), 28 U.S.C. § 1360(b), provides:

> Nothing in this section shall authorize the alienation, encumbrance, or taxation of any real or personal property, including water rights, belonging to any Indian or any Indian tribe, band, or community that is held in trust by the United States or is subject to a restriction against alienation imposed by the United States. ***

The Minnesota Supreme Court reasoned that "unless paragraph (a) is interpreted as a general grant of the power to tax, then the exceptions contained in paragraph (b) are limitations on a nonexistent power." Therefore, the state court held: "Public Law 280 is a clear grant of the power to tax." We disagree. That conclusion is foreclosed by the legislative history of Pub. L. 280 and the application of canons of construction applicable to congressional statutes claimed to terminate Indian immunities.

II.

The primary concern of Congress in enacting Pub. L. 280 that emerges from its sparse legislative history was with the problem of lawlessness on certain Indian reservations, and the absence of adequate tribal institutions for law enforcement. *See* Carole Goldberg, *Public Law 280: The Limits of State Jurisdiction over Reservation Indians*, 22 UCLA L. Rev. 535, 541–542 (1975). The House Report states:

> These States lack jurisdiction to prosecute Indians for most offenses committed on Indian reservations or other Indian country, with limited exceptions. The applicability of Federal criminal laws in States having Indian reservations is also limited. ***
>
> As a practical matter, the enforcement of law and order among the Indians in the Indian country has been left largely to the Indian groups themselves. In many States, tribes are not adequately organized to perform that function; consequently, there has been created a hiatus in law-enforcement authority that could best be remedied by conferring criminal jurisdiction on States indicating an ability and willingness to accept such responsibility. H.R. Rep. No. 848, 83d Cong., 1st Sess., 5–6 (1953).

Thus, provision for state criminal jurisdiction over offenses committed by or against Indians on the reservations was the central focus of Pub. L. 280 and is embodied in § 2 of the Act, 18 U.S.C. § 1162.

In marked contrast in the legislative history is the virtual absence of expression of congressional policy or intent respecting § 4's grant of civil jurisdiction to the States. Of special significance for our purposes, however, is the total absence of mention or discussion regarding a congressional intent to confer upon the States an authority to tax Indians or Indian property on reservations. Neither the Committee Reports nor the floor discussion in either House mentions such authority. This omission has significance in the application of the canons of construction applicable to statutes affecting Indian immunities, as some mention would normally be expected if such a sweeping change in the status of tribal government and reservation Indians had been contemplated by Congress. The only mention of taxation authority is in a colloquy between Mr. Sellery, Chief Counsel of the Bureau of Indian Affairs, and Congressman Young during House committee hearings on Pub. L. 280. That colloquy strongly suggests that Congress did not mean to grant tax authority to the States:

> Mr. Young. Does your bill limit the provision for Federal assistance to States in defraying the increased expenses of the courts in connection with the widening of the jurisdiction that the bill encompasses?
>
> Mr. Sellery. No; it does not.
>
> Mr. Young. Do you think it would be necessary to provide for some payment, inasmuch as the great portion of Indian lands are not subject to taxation?
>
> Mr. Sellery. *** Generally, the Department's views are that if we started in the processes of Federal financial assistance or subsidization of law enforcement activities among the Indians, it might turn out to be a rather costly program, and it is a problem which the States should deal with and accept without Federal financial assistance; otherwise there will be some tendency, the Department believes, for the Indian to be thought of and perhaps to think of himself because of the financial assistance which comes from the Federal Government as still somewhat a member of a race or group which is set apart from other citizens of the State. And it is desired to give him and the other citizens of the State the feeling of a conviction that he is in the same status and has access to the same services, including the courts, as other citizens of the State who are not Indians.

Mr. Young. That would not quite be true, though; would it? Because for the most part he does not pay any taxes.

Mr. Sellery. No. There is that difference.

Mr. Young. A rather sizable difference in not paying for the courts or paying for the increased expenses for judicial proceedings.

Mr. Sellery. The Indians, of course, do pay other forms of taxes. I do not know how the courts of Nevada are supported financially, but the Indians do pay the sales tax and other taxes.

Mr. Young. But no income tax or corporation tax or profits tax. You understand a large portion of the land is held in trust and therefore is not subject to tax.

Mr. Sellery. That is correct.

Mr. Young. So far as my State is concerned, it would be a large burden on existing costs of judicial procedure. I think it is only right that the Federal Government should make some contribution for that. You seem to differentiate. I think there is a differentiation, too, in that they are not paying taxes.

Mr. Sellery. I will concede your point that they are not paying taxes. The Department has recommended, nevertheless, that no financial assistance be afforded to the States.

[Transcript of Hearings on H.R. 1063 before the Subcommittee on Indian Affairs of the House Committee on Interior and Insular Affairs, 83d Cong., 1st Sess. (1953).]

Piecing together as best we can the sparse legislative history of § 4, subsection (a) seems to have been primarily intended to redress the lack of adequate Indian forums for resolving private legal disputes between reservation Indians, and between Indians and other private citizens, by permitting the courts of the States to decide such disputes; this is definitely the import of the statutory wording conferring upon a State "jurisdiction over civil causes of action between Indians or to which Indians are parties which arise in *** Indian country *** to the same extent that such State *** has jurisdiction over other civil causes of action." With this as the primary focus of § 4(a), the wording that follows in § 4(a) "and those civil laws of such state *** that are of general application to private persons or private property shall have the same force and effect within such Indian country as they have elsewhere within the State" authorizes application by the state courts of their rules of decision to decide such disputes. This construction finds support in the consistent and uncontradicted references in the legislative history to "permitting" "State courts to *adjudicate* civil controversies" arising on Indian reservations, H.R. Rep. No. 848, pp. 5, 6 (emphasis added), and the absence of anything remotely resembling an intention to confer general state civil regulatory control over Indian reservations.[11] In short, the consistent and exclusive use of the terms "civil causes of

11. Moreover, this interpretation is consistent with the title of Pub. L. 280, H.R. Rep. No. 848, p. 3: "A bill to confer jurisdiction on the States ***, with respect to criminal offenses and civil causes of action committed or arising on Indian reservations within such States, and for other purposes" (the other purposes being § 8's withdrawal from the affected areas of the operation of the Federal Indian Liquor Laws, and §§ 6–7's provision of a method whereby additional States could assume civil and criminal jurisdiction over Indian reservations). ***

action," "aris[ing] on," "civil laws *** of general application to private persons or private property," and "adjudicate[ion]," in both the Act and its legislative history virtually compels our conclusion that the primary intent of § 4 was to grant jurisdiction over private civil litigation involving reservation Indians in state court. ***

Our construction is also more consistent with Title IV of the Civil Rights Act of 1968, 82 Stat. 78, 25 U.S.C. §§ 1321–26. Title IV repeals § 7 of Pub. L. 280 and requires tribal consent as a condition to further state assumptions of the jurisdiction provided in 18 U.S.C. § 1162 and 28 U.S.C. § 1360. *** Section 406 of Title IV, 25 U.S.C. § 1326, which provides for Indian consent, refers to "State jurisdiction acquired pursuant to this subchapter with respect to criminal offenses or civil causes of action. *** " It is true, of course, that the primary interpretation of § 4 must have reference to the legislative history of the Congress that enacted it rather than to the history of Acts of a later Congress. Nevertheless, Title IV of the 1968 Act is intimately related to § 4, as it provides the method for further state assumptions of the jurisdiction conferred by § 4, and we previously have construed the effect of legislation affecting reservation Indians in light of "intervening" legislative enactments. *Moe v. Confederated Salish & Kootenai Tribes*. It would be difficult to suppose that Congress in 1968 intended the meaning of § 4 to vary depending upon the time and method by which particular States acquired jurisdiction. And certainly the legislative history of Title IV makes it difficult to construe § 4 jurisdiction acquired pursuant to Title IV as extending general state civil regulatory authority, including taxing power, to govern Indian reservations. Senator Ervin, who offered and principally sponsored Title IV, referred to § 1360 civil jurisdiction as follows:

> Certain representatives of municipalities have charged that the repeal of [§ 7 of] Public Law 280 would hamper air and water pollution controls and provide a haven for undesirable, unrestricted business establishments within tribal land borders. Not only does this assertion show the lack of faith that certain cities have in the ability and desire of Indian tribes to better themselves and their environment, but, *most importantly, it is irrelevant, since Public Law 280 relates primarily to the application of state civil and criminal law in court proceedings*, and has no bearing on programs set up by the States to assist economic and environmental development in Indian territory. (Emphasis added.)

[Subcommittee Hearing transcript.]

III.

Other considerations also support our construction. Today's congressional policy toward reservation Indians may less clearly than in 1953 favor their assimilation, but Pub. L. 280 was plainly not meant to effect total assimilation. Pub. L. 280 was only one of many types of assimilationist legislation under active consideration in 1953. And nothing in its legislative history remotely suggests that Congress meant the Act's extension of civil jurisdiction to the States should result in the undermining or destruction of such tribal governments as did exist and a conversion of the affected tribes into little more than " 'private, voluntary organizations,' " *United States v. Mazurie*, a possible result if tribal governments and reservation Indians were subordinated to the full panoply of civil regulatory powers, including taxation, of state and local governments.[14] The Act itself refutes such an inference: there is notably absent any conferral of state jurisdiction over the tribes themselves, and § 4(c), 28 U.S.C. § 1360(c), providing for the "full force and effect" of any tribal ordinances or customs "heretofore or hereafter adopted by an Indian tribe *** if not inconsistent with any applicable civil law of the State," contemplates the continuing vitality of tribal government.

Moreover, the same Congress that enacted Pub. L. 280 also enacted several termination Acts—legislation which is cogent proof that Congress knew well how to express its intent directly when that intent was to subject reservation Indians to the full sweep of state laws and state taxation. These termination enactments provide expressly for subjecting distributed property "and any income derived therefrom by the individual, corporation, or other legal entity *** to the same taxes, State and Federal, as in the case of non-Indians," 25 U.S.C., §§ 564j, 749, 898, and provide that "all statutes of the United States which affect Indians because of their status as Indians shall no longer be applicable to the members of the tribe, and the laws of the several States shall apply to the tribe and its members in the same manner as they apply to other citizens or persons within their jurisdiction." *** These contemporaneous termination Acts are *in pari materia* with Pub. L. 280. *** Reading this express language respecting state taxation and application of the full range of state laws to tribal members of these contemporaneous termination Acts, the negative inference is that Congress did not mean in § 4(a) to subject reservation Indians to state taxation. Thus, rather than inferring a negative implication of a grant of general taxing power in § 4(a) from the exclusion of certain taxation in § 4(b), we conclude that construing Pub. L. 280 *in pari materia* with these Acts shows that if Congress in enacting Pub. L. 280 had intended to confer upon the States general civil regulatory powers, including taxation, over reservation Indians, it would have expressly said so.

IV.

Additionally, we note that § 4(b), excluding "taxation of any real or personal property *** belonging to any Indian or any Indian tribe *** that is held in trust by the United States or is subject to a restriction against alienation imposed by the United States," is not obviously the narrow exclusion of state taxation that the Minnesota Supreme Court read it to be. On its face the statute is not clear whether the exclusion is applicable only to taxes levied directly on the trust property specifically, or whether it also excludes taxation on activities taking place in conjunction with such property and income deriving from its use. And even if read narrowly to apply only to taxation levied against trust

---

14. Much has been written on the subject of a devastating impact on tribal governments that might result from an interpretation of § 4 as conferring upon state and local governments general civil regulatory control over reservation Indians. *** The suggestion is that since tribal governments are disabled under many state laws from incorporating as local units of government, general regulatory control might relegate tribal governments to a level below that of counties and municipalities, thus essentially destroying them, particularly if they might raise revenue only after the tax base had been filtered through many governmental layers of taxation. Present federal policy appears to be returning to a focus upon strengthening tribal self-government, [Indian Financing Act of 1974; Indian Self–Determination and Education Assistance Act of 1975], and the Court of Appeals for the Ninth Circuit has expressed the view that courts "are not obliged in ambiguous instances to strain to implement [an assimilationist] policy Congress has now rejected, particularly where to do so will interfere with the present congressional approach to what is, after all, an ongoing relationship." *Santa Rosa Band of Indians v. Kings County*, 532 F.2d 655, 663 (9th Cir. 1975).

property directly, § 4(b) certainly does not expressly authorize all other state taxation of reservation Indians.

Moreover, the express prohibition of any "alienation, encumbrance, or taxation" of any trust property can be read as prohibiting state courts, acquiring jurisdiction over civil controversies involving reservation Indians pursuant to § 4 from applying state laws or enforcing judgments in ways that would effectively result in the "alienation, encumbrance, or taxation" of trust property. Indeed any other reading of this provision of § 4(b) is difficult to square with the identical prohibition contained in § 2(b) of the Act, which applies the same restrictions upon States exercising criminal jurisdiction over reservation Indians. It would simply make no sense to infer from the identical language of § 2(b) a general power in § 2(a) to tax Indians in all other respects since § 2(a) deals only with criminal jurisdiction.

Indeed, § 4(b) in its entirety may be read as simply a reaffirmation of the existing reservation Indian–Federal Government relationship in all respects save the conferral of state-court jurisdiction to adjudicate private civil causes of action involving Indians. ***

Finally, in construing this "admittedly ambiguous" statute, *Board of Comm'rs v. Seber*, 318 U.S. at 713, we must be guided by that "eminently sound and vital canon," *Northern Cheyenne Tribe v. Hollowbreast*, 425 U.S. 649, 655 n.7 (1976), that "statutes passed for the benefit of dependent Indian tribes *** are to be liberally construed, doubtful expressions being resolved in favor of the Indians." *** This principle of statutory construction has particular force in the face of claims that ambiguous statutes abolish by implication Indian tax immunities. *** "This is so because *** Indians stand in a special relation to the federal government from which the states are excluded unless the Congress has manifested a clear purpose to terminate [a tax] immunity and allow states to treat Indians as part of the general community." What we recently said of a claim that Congress had terminated an Indian reservation by means of an ambiguous statute is equally applicable here to the respondent's claim that § 4(a) of Pub. L. 280 is a clear grant of power to tax, and hence a termination of traditional Indian immunity from state taxation:

> Congress was fully aware of the means by which termination could be effected. But clear termination language was not employed in the *** Act. This being so, we are not inclined to infer an intent to terminate. *** A congressional determination to terminate must be expressed on the face of the Act or be clear from the surrounding circumstances and legislative history.

Mattz v. Arnett, 412 U.S. 481, 504–505 (1973).

[*Reversed.*]

NOTES AND QUESTIONS

1. What may get lost in the opinion is precisely what Public Law 280 says. Reread the basic jurisdictional provisions. The text provides a strong basis for a state assertion of taxation power—both through the plain language of § 1360(a) and the implications that flow from § 1360(b). Increasingly since the late 1980s, the Supreme Court has been prone to follow the ordinary meaning

of statutory text and allow legislative history only a limited role in interpretation. *See, e.g.*, William N. Eskridge, Jr., *The New Textualism*, 37 UCLA L. Rev. 621 (1990). What arguments did the Court in *Bryan* develop—or can you develop—to undercut the clarity of the text? Assuming that the Court should look at the legislative history, how clearly does it undercut the textual meaning?

Now, move beyond static sources of interpretive authority—statutory text and documents in the legislative history, frozen in form in 1953—to other potential sources of interpretive guidance. Should later developments—for example, the 1968 amendments to Public Law 280 or the federal change of policy, beginning in the 1960s, away from termination and returning to the notion of the appropriateness of tribal self-governance—influence the interpretation of Public Law 280 provisions that have themselves not been amended? Should the Indian law canons of interpretation influence the inquiry, and if so, how? For the argument that *Bryan* is a good context in which to consider how the Indian law canons should guide federal courts to resolve issues in Indian law, see Philip P. Frickey, *Marshalling Past and Present: Colonialism, Constitutionalism, and Interpretation in Federal Indian Law*, 107 Harv. L. Rev. 381, 429–32 (1993).

2. Note that, from the perspective of the states, Public Law 280 is a poor deal. As understood in *Bryan*, the state and its subdivisions cannot raise revenue through taxation in Indian country to offset the increased expenditures needed to provide the jurisdiction mandated by the statute (police protection, prosecution of crimes by state prosecutors before state judges, state judicial jurisdiction to hear civil cases arising in Indian country). As *Bryan* discusses, Congress also did not provide any federal money to the states for these purposes. Public Law 280 thus is an unfunded federal mandate.

3. The lack of funding, the beliefs of some local and state governments that tribal members on reservations were not their responsibility, and the poor relations that sometimes exist between states and tribes often result in ineffective law enforcement under Public Law 280. In mandatory states, moreover, Public Law 280 preempts federal criminal jurisdiction in Indian country. Although the law has been held not to preempt tribal criminal or civil jurisdiction, tribes in Public Law 280 states were not given federal funding available to other tribes to enhance their tribal legal systems and had less incentive to participate in the widespread development of tribal courts that began in the 1960s and 1970s. In a review of the impact of these factors, Carole Goldberg concluded: "Even if one accepts the claim that many reservations were lawless at the time Public Law 280 was enacted, a tragic irony is inescapable. Taking account of the direct and indirect effects described above, Public Law 280 has itself become a source of lawlessness on reservations." Carole Goldberg–Ambrose, *Public Law 280 and the Problem of Lawlessness in Indian Country*, 44 UCLA L. Rev. 1405, 1418 (1997); *see also* Carole Goldberg & Duane Champagne, *Is Public Law 280 Fit for the Twenty–First Century? Some Data at Last*, 30 Conn. L. Rev. 697, 711 (2007) (reporting based on study of seventeen reservations that "[r]eservation residents on Public Law 280 reservations are significantly less satisfied with the availability and quality of law enforcement than reservation residents on non-Public Law 280 reservations."); Carole Goldberg & Duane Champagne, *Law Enforcement and Criminal Justice Under Public Law 280* (2007) *available at* https://www.law.ucla.edu/centers/social-policy/native-nations-law-and-policy-center/publications/law-enforcement-

criminal-justice-public-law-280/ [https://perma.cc/7L4P-M4DJ] (reporting extensive findings of study).

4. *The Trust Property Exception.* Public Law 280 specifically provides that "[n]othing in this section shall authorize the alienation, encumbrance, or taxation of any real or personal property *** that is held in trust by the United States or is subject to a restriction against alienation imposed by the United States." The Court rejected a good statutory construction argument based on the principle "*inclusio unius est exclusio alterius*" (to include one is to exclude others not mentioned) that this specific exemption did not mean that non-trust property was subject to taxation. (Recall that the mobile home owned by the Bryans was treated as personal property, not real property, and therefore was not considered to be held in trust.) So what does this provision mean? It means that even in cases where a court has adjudicatory jurisdiction, it does not have jurisdiction to affect trust property. So in a divorce case, for example, a state court cannot affect ownership of a house or land that is part of trust property; similarly, in a contract case, the court cannot execute the judgment by attaching the trust property of the defendant.

5. *Authorization of jurisdiction in non-mandatory states.* In addition to the mandatory states, ten other states accepted some degree of jurisdiction under the Act's provisions. *See* Cohen's Handbook of Federal Indian Law 537-38 (2012) (describing actions of Arizona, Florida, Idaho, Iowa, Montana, Nevada, North Dakota, South Dakota, Utah, and Washington). Florida accepted full jurisdiction and Iowa, which already had significant criminal jurisdiction over the Sac and Fox Reservation pursuant to Public L. 848 (1948), assumed civil jurisdiction over the reservation as well. The other states accepted jurisdiction on a piecemeal or conditional basis. Washington State established the most complicated scheme, accepting full jurisdiction over Indians and non-Indians on all fee lands within reservations, and over non-Indians on trust and allotted lands within reservations. It also accepted jurisdiction over Indians on on-reservation trust, or restricted lands in eight subject matter areas (compulsory school attendance, public assistance, domestic relations, mental illness, juvenile delinquency, adoption proceedings, dependent children, and motor vehicles), and other subjects with tribal consent. Finally it asserted full jurisdiction over Indians on off-reservation allotments and other off-reservation trust lands. In *Washington v. Confederated Bands of Yakima Indian Nation*, 439 U.S. 463 (1979), the Supreme Court held this partial acceptance of jurisdiction permissible under the statute and rejected an equal protection challenge to Washington's actions in accepting greater jurisdiction over cases involving non-Indians than Indians. *See* Robert T. Anderson, *Negotiating Jurisdiction: Retroceding State Authority Over Indian Country Granted by Public Law 280*, 87 Wash. L. Rev. 915 (2012) (discussing Washington's scheme and state law providing for retrocession of state jurisdiction).

Some partial acceptances of jurisdiction may be problematic. Arizona accepted jurisdiction over air and water pollution only. What might be the problem with this after *Bryan*? South Dakota assumed jurisdiction only over criminal offenses and civil causes of action arising on highways, and conditioned acceptance of full Public Law 280 jurisdiction on federal government reimbursement of the state for the cost of the additional jurisdiction assumed. The Eighth Circuit later held that the state could not accept jurisdiction over only the most financially lucrative form of state jurisdiction. *Rosebud Sioux Tribe v. South Dakota*, 900 F.2d 1164, 1170 (8th Cir. 1990).

Several statutes that provide for federal recognition or settlement of land claims for particular tribes also provide for state criminal and/or civil jurisdiction over the lands for those tribes. *See, e.g.*, Act of Aug. 18, 1987, 101 Stat. 670 (codified at 25 U.S.C. § 1300g et seq. and 25 U.S.C. §§ 731–37) (providing Texas with jurisdiction over Ysleta del Sur Pueblo and Alabama and Coushatta reservations); 25 U.S.C. § 1755 (providing Connecticut with civil and criminal jurisdiction over actions arising on the Mashantucket Pequot Reservation); 25 U.S.C. § 1775d (providing Connecticut with criminal jurisdiction over the Mohegan Reservation). Although most of these acts specifically refer to Public Law 280 and are interpreted similarly, controversial decisions have interpreted the somewhat different language of the Rhode Island Indian Claims Settlement Act and the Maine Indian Claims Settlement Act to provide significant regulatory jurisdiction as well as a waiver of tribal sovereign immunity. *Narragansett Indian Tribe v. Rhode Island*, 449 F.3d 16, 25–26 (1st Cir. 2006) (waiver of immunity in Rhode Island Act); *Great Northern Paper, Inc. v. Penobscot Nation*, 770 A.2d 574, 586 (Me. 2001) (holding that Maine settlement laws subjected tribes to general municipal laws and waived sovereign immunity).

6. *What can a tribe do if it prefers not to be subject to state jurisdiction?* In 1968 Congress amended Public Law 280 to provide that the "United States is authorized to accept a retrocession by any State of all or any measure of the criminal or civil jurisdiction, or both, acquired by such State pursuant to [Public Law 280.]" Nevada originally accepted full Public Law 280 jurisdiction, but in 1975 retroceded jurisdiction except for those tribes who consented to continue under the Act. Jurisdiction now has been retroceded for most reservations in Nevada and for some tribes in several other states. Notice, however, that the tribes have no official role in the process. A state may retrocede, and the Secretary is "authorized to accept" the retrocession. *See* Robert T. Anderson, *Negotiating Jurisdiction: Retroceding State Authority Over Indian Country Granted by Public Law 280*, 87 Wash. L. Rev. 915 (2012) (discussing the process).

The 1968 amendments also required tribal consent to future assumptions of jurisdiction. 25 U.S.C. § 1326. Only one state, Utah, sought jurisdiction after the 1968 amendments required tribal consent for future acquisitions. No tribe has consented to state jurisdiction.

7. *The Bewildering Criminal/Prohibitory v. Civil/Regulatory Distinction. Bryan* narrowly construed the civil jurisdiction provisions of Public Law 280. Note, however, that the criminal jurisdiction provisions, if given their plain meaning, might overwhelm any positive effects of *Bryan* upon tribal sovereignty. For example, it is clear that, under *Bryan*, a state or county civil regulatory law does not apply in Indian country. Thus, a county law requiring that electricians be licensed would not apply—except that, what is the answer if the county law provides a criminal penalty for unlicensed electrical work? Does that come within the criminal jurisdiction that Public Law 280 states are authorized to exercise? If it does, any regulatory law that has a criminal penalty would apply in Indian country, radically undercutting the attempt in *Bryan* to keep state regulation out of Indian country in Public Law 280 contexts.

The Supreme Court addressed this puzzle in the following case.

***California v. Cabazon Band of Mission Indians*, 480 U.S. 202 (1987).**

In *Cabazon*, two California tribes operated bingo games open to the public and one of the two also ran poker and other card games. California attempted to apply two penal code provisions to the tribes, neither of which prohibited bingo entirely, but which imposed various restrictions on how such games must be run. In addition, Riverside County sought to apply its local gaming ordinances to the tribes. The tribes filed suit in federal court objecting to the county's regulations and California intervened. The Supreme Court held that Public Law 280 did not make the state and county laws applicable to the tribes:

> *** In § 2 [of Public Law 280], California was granted broad criminal jurisdiction over offenses committed by or against Indians within all Indian country within the State. Section 4's grant of civil jurisdiction was more limited. *** Congress' primary concern in enacting Pub. L. 280 was combating lawlessness on reservations. The Act plainly was not intended to effect total assimilation of Indian tribes into mainstream American society. [In *Bryan*] we recognized that a grant to States of general civil regulatory power over Indian reservations would result in the destruction of tribal institutions and values. Accordingly, when a State seeks to enforce a law within an Indian reservation under the authority of Pub. L. 280, it must be determined whether the law is criminal in nature, and thus fully applicable to the reservation under § 2, or civil in nature, and applicable only as it may be relevant to private civil litigation in state court.
>
> The Minnesota personal property tax at issue in *Bryan* was unquestionably civil in nature. The California bingo statute is not so easily categorized. California law permits bingo games to be conducted only by charitable and other specified organizations, and then only by their members who may not receive any wage or profit for doing so; prizes are limited, and receipts are to be segregated and used only for charitable purposes. Violation of any of these provisions is a misdemeanor. California insists that these are criminal laws which Pub. L. 280 permits it to enforce on the reservations.
>
> *** In [an earlier case] applying what it thought to be the civil/criminal dichotomy drawn in *Bryan v. Itasca County*, the Court of Appeals drew a distinction between state "criminal/prohibitory" laws and state "civil/regulatory" laws: if the intent of a state law is generally to prohibit certain conduct, it falls within Pub. L. 280's grant of criminal jurisdiction, but if the state law generally permits the conduct at issue, subject to regulation, it must be classified as civil/regulatory and Pub. L. 280 does not authorize its enforcement on an Indian reservation. The shorthand test is whether the conduct at issue violates the State's public policy. Inquiring into the nature of § 326.5, the Court of Appeals held that it was regulatory rather than prohibitory. ***
>
> We are persuaded that the prohibitory/regulatory distinction is consistent with *Bryan*'s construction of Pub. L. 280. It is not a bright-line rule, however; and as the Ninth Circuit itself observed, an argument of some weight may be made that the bingo statute is prohibitory rather than regulatory. But in the present case, *** we are reluctant to disagree with that court's view of the nature and intent of the state law at issue here.

There is surely a fair basis for its conclusion. California does not prohibit all forms of gambling. California itself operates a state lottery and daily encourages its citizens to participate in this state-run gambling. California also permits parimutuel horse-race betting. Although certain enumerated gambling games are prohibited under [state law], games not enumerated, including the card games played in the Cabazon card club, are permissible. The Tribes assert that more than 400 card rooms similar to the Cabazon card club flourish in California, and the State does not dispute this fact. *** In light of the fact that California permits a substantial amount of gambling activity, including bingo, and actually promotes gambling through its state lottery, we must conclude that California regulates rather than prohibits gambling in general and bingo in particular.

California argues, however, that high stakes, unregulated bingo, the conduct which attracts organized crime, is a misdemeanor in California and may be prohibited on Indian reservations. But that an otherwise regulatory law is enforceable by criminal as well as civil means does not necessarily convert it into a criminal law within the meaning of Pub. L. 280. Otherwise, the distinction between § 2 and § 4 of that law could easily be avoided and total assimilation permitted. *** Accordingly, we conclude that Pub. L. 280 does not authorize California to enforce Cal. Penal Code Ann. § 326.5 within the Cabazon and Morongo Reservations.[11]

***

[The remainder of the opinion, which concerns whether California can enforce its laws even without any congressional authorization to do so, *i.e.*, whether federal law preempts state law, is included later in this chapter, along with a discussion of the Indian Gaming Regulatory Act enacted in the wake of *Cabazon*.]

[The dissenting opinion of **JUSTICE STEVENS**, joined by **JUSTICES O'CONNOR** and **SCALIA**, is omitted. Stevens argued that the plain language of Public Law 280 authorized the state to apply its criminal laws concerning gaming.]

NOTES AND QUESTIONS

1. *Cabazon* establishes that simply criminalizing certain conduct does not mean that state laws can be applied under Public Law 280's grant of criminal jurisdiction. One can see why this is necessary to preserve the adjudicatory/regulatory distinction established in *Bryan*: a state personal property tax,

---

11. Nor does Pub. L. 280 authorize the county to apply its gambling ordinances to the reservations. We note initially that it is doubtful that Pub. L. 280 authorizes the application of any local laws to Indian reservations. Section 2 of Pub. L. 280 provides that the criminal laws of the "State" shall have the same force and effect within Indian country as they have elsewhere. This language seems clearly to exclude local laws. We need not decide this issue, however, because even if Pub. L. 280 does make local criminal/prohibitory laws applicable on Indian reservations, the ordinances in question here do not apply. Consistent with our analysis *** above, we conclude that Ordinance No. 558, the bingo ordinance, is regulatory in nature. Although Ordinance No. 331 prohibits gambling on all card games, including the games played in the Cabazon card club, the county does not prohibit municipalities within the county from enacting municipal ordinances permitting these card games, and two municipalities have in fact done so. It is clear, therefore, that Ordinance No. 331 does not prohibit these card games for purposes of Pub. L. 280.

like that in *Bryan*, could be enforced simply by declaring that failure to pay the tax was a crime. But how does one draw the line between statutes which are truly criminal-prohibitory and those that are simply regulatory? *Cabazon* states that the test is as follows: "[I]f the intent of a state law is generally to prohibit certain conduct, it falls within Public Law 280's grant of criminal jurisdiction, but if the state law generally permits the conduct at issue, subject to regulation, it must be classified as civil/regulatory and Public Law 280 does not authorize its enforcement on an Indian reservation."

The courts in Public Law 280 states have had a difficult time with the prohibitory/regulatory distinction. *Compare St. Germaine v. Circuit Court for Vilas County*, 938 F.2d 75 (7th Cir. 1991) (Wisconsin prohibition on operating a motor vehicle with a suspended license is criminal) *with State v. Johnson*, 598 N.W.2d 680 (Minn. 1999) (Minnesota law prohibiting driving after license revocation is regulatory), and *State v. Losh*, 755 N.W.2d. 736 (Minn. 2008) (Minnesota law prohibiting driving after license revocation is criminal when premise of revocation was conviction for driving while intoxicated). Cohen's Handbook of Federal Indian Law (2012) suggests that courts should "focus on the nature of the regulated conduct in relation to other forms of unregulated conduct. If the subset of outlawed conduct is small relative to the entire class of activity, the law is regulatory in nature." *Id.* at 545. Does the Cohen suggestion, or any other formulation you can think of, help courts to define the relevant category of activity? In the case of driving without a license, for example, is the appropriate category driving, which is generally allowed, with the license requirement being simply a regulation of that right? Or is the appropriate category driving without a license, which is wholly prohibited? How about speeding? *Compare Confederated Tribes of the Colville Reservation v. Washington*, 938 F.2d 146 (9th Cir. 1991) (holding that state speeding rule was civil-regulatory) *with Rosebud Sioux Tribe v. South Dakota*, 709 F. Supp. 1502 (D. S.D. 1989), *vacated on other grounds by* 900 F.2d 1164 (8th Cir. 1990) (holding that state speeding law was criminal-prohibitory). If you determine that such laws are regulatory, can you make a distinction for a law criminalizing reckless driving, which is driving with criminal disregard for human life or safety? Similarly, can you think of a logical way to justify the intuition that a law prohibiting growing marijuana belongs in the generally prohibited category of manufacture of drugs rather than the generally permitted but regulated category of farming?

2. *The Public Policy Shorthand*? *Cabazon* states that the "shorthand" for the regulatory/prohibitory test described is "whether the conduct at issue violates the State's public policy." Does this "shorthand" add anything? Aren't all state laws a representation of state public policy? Nevertheless, some courts rely on this test, although one commentator claims that the public policy test "is often used as an excuse for courts that don't want the tribe to have exclusive authority [because of] the criminal or regulatory importance of the law to the state ***." Arthur F. Foerster, *Divisiveness and Delusion: Public Law 280 and the Elusive Criminal/Regulatory Distinction*, 46 UCLA L. Rev. 1333, 1358 (1999).

3. As noted earlier, Washington accepted full jurisdiction over eight subject matter areas within Indian reservations: (1) compulsory school attendance; (2) public assistance; (3) domestic relations; (4) mental illness; (5) juvenile delinquency; (6) adoption proceedings; (7) dependent children; and (8) operation of motor vehicles upon the public streets, alleys, roads and highways.

Can Washington enforce a law requiring children to attend school if the only punishment for failure to comply is a fine, or incarceration for up to seven days to compel attendance?

III. STATE AUTHORITY IN INDIAN COUNTRY WITHOUT CONGRESSIONAL AUTHORIZATION

One might expect that a Supreme Court that had worked as hard as it did in *Bryan* and *Cabazon* to cabin congressional authorization of state jurisdiction in Indian country would be especially loathe to allow states to assert such authority in the absence of any congressional approval. *Worcester v. Georgia* held that a state had no jurisdiction over a non-Indian missionary on Cherokee land. Even in the modern era, *Warren Trading Post*, section 1, *supra*, held that a state had no jurisdiction to tax a non-Indian federally licensed Indian trader doing business on the reservation. The Court expanded upon *Warren Trading Post* in *Central Machinery Co. v. Arizona State Tax Commission*, 448 U.S. 160 (1980). In that case, a tribe purchased agricultural equipment from a local dealer. The dealer's place of business was off the reservation, and the dealer was not a federally licensed Indian trader, but the contract was entered into and delivery of the tractors also took place on the reservation. By a 5–4 vote, the Court held that these distinctions were irrelevant, and the state could not impose its gross receipts tax on the transaction, which was to be paid by the non-Indian seller. In a number of modern decisions, however, the Supreme Court has held that states have certain jurisdiction over non-Indians and non-members engaging in activities on reservations. Consider the following cases.

WASHINGTON V. CONFEDERATED TRIBES OF THE COLVILLE RESERVATION

447 U.S. 134, 100 S. Ct. 2069, 65 L. Ed. 2d 10 (1980)

JUSTICE WHITE delivered the opinion of the Court.

***

II.

The State of Washington levies a cigarette excise tax of $1.60 per carton on the "sale, use, consumption, handling, possession or distribution" of cigarettes within the State. The tax is enforced with tax stamps; and dealers are required to sell only cigarettes to which such stamps have been affixed. Indian tribes are permitted to possess unstamped cigarettes for purposes of resale to members of the tribe, but are required by regulation to collect the tax with respect to sales to non-members. The District Court found, on the basis of its examination of state authorities, that the legal incidence of the tax is on the purchaser in transactions between an Indian seller and a non-Indian buyer.[9]

---

9. Essentially, the court accepted the State's contention that the tax falls upon the first event which may constitutionally be subjected to it. In the case of sales by non-Indians to non-Indians, this means the incidence of the tax is on the seller, or perhaps on someone even further up the chain of distribution, because that person is the one who first sells, uses, consumes, handles,

The State has sought to enforce its cigarette tax by seizing as contraband unstamped cigarettes bound for various tribal reservations. It claims that it is entitled to make such seizures whenever the cigarettes are destined to be sold to non-Indians without affixation of stamps or collection of the tax.

Washington also imposes a sales tax on sales of personal property, including cigarettes. This tax, which was 5% during the relevant period, is collected from the purchaser by the retailer. It does not apply to on-reservation sales to reservation Indians.

The state motor vehicle excise tax is imposed on "the privilege of using in the state any motor vehicle." *** The tax is assessed annually, and during the relevant period the amount was 2% of the fair market value of the vehicle in question. In addition, the State imposes an annual tax in the amount of 1% of fair market value on the privilege of using campers and trailers in the State.

Each of the Tribes involved in this litigation is recognized by the United States as a sovereign Indian tribe. *** The Colville Tribe has some 5,800 members, of whom about 3,200 live on the Colville Indian Reservation. Enrolled members of the Tribe constitute just under half of the reservation's population. The Lummi Tribe has approximately 2,000 members. Roughly 1,250 of them live on the reservation. The Makah Tribe has about 1,000 members. Some 900 live on the reservation. The Colville, Lummi, and Makah Reservations are isolated and underdeveloped. Many members reside in mobile homes. Most own at least one automobile which is used both on and off the reservation.

The Yakima Tribe has more than 6,000 members, of whom about 5,000 live on the reservation. Enrolled members, however, constitute less than one-fifth of the reservation's population. The balance is made up of approximately 1,500 Indians who are not members of the Tribes and more than 20,000 non-Indians.

The Colville, Lummi, and Makah tribes have nearly identical cigarette sales and taxing schemes. Each Tribe has enacted ordinances pursuant to which it has authorized one or more on-reservation tobacco outlets. These ordinances have been approved by the Secretary of the Interior; and the dealer at each tobacco outlet is a federally licensed Indian trader. All three Tribes use federally restricted tribal funds to purchase cigarettes from out-of-state dealers. The Tribes distribute the cigarettes to the tobacco outlets and collect from the operators of those outlets both the wholesale distribution price and a tax of 40 to 50 cents per carton. The cigarettes remain the property of the Tribe until sale. The taxing ordinances specify that the tax is to be passed on to the ultimate consumer of the cigarettes. From 1972 through 1976, the Colville Tribe realized approximately $266,000 from its cigarette tax; the Lummi Tribe realized $54,000 and the Makah Tribe realized $13,000.

While the Colville, Lummi, and Makah Tribes function as retailers, retaining possession of the cigarettes until their sale to consumers, the Yakima Tribe acts as a wholesaler. It purchases cigarettes from out-of-state dealers and then sells them to its licensed retailers. The Tribe receives a markup over the wholesale price from those retailers as well as a tax of 22.5 cents per carton.

---

possesses, or distributes the products. But where the wholesaler or retailer is an Indian on whom the tax cannot be imposed under *McClanahan*, the first taxable event is the use, consumption, or possession by the non-Indian purchaser. Hence, the District Court concluded, the tax falls on that purchaser. We accept this conclusion.

There is no requirement that this tax be added to the selling price. In 1975, the Yakima Tribe derived $278,000 from its cigarette business.

Indian tobacco dealers make a large majority of their sales to non-Indians—residents of nearby communities who journey to the reservation especially to take advantage of the claimed tribal exemption from the state cigarette and sales taxes. The purchaser saves more than a dollar on each carton, and that makes the trip worthwhile. All parties agree that if the State were able to tax sales by Indian smokeshops and eliminate that $1 saving, the stream of non-Indian bargain hunters would dry up. In short, the Indian retailer's business is to a substantial degree dependent upon his tax-exempt status, and if he loses that status his sales will fall off sharply. ***

IV.

A.

In *Moe v. Salish & Kootenai Tribes*, 425 U.S. 463 (1976), we considered a state taxing scheme remarkably similar to the cigarette and sales taxes at issue in the present cases. Montana there sought to impose a cigarette tax on sales by smokeshops operated by tribal members and located on leased trust lands within the reservation, and sought to require the smokeshop operators to collect the tax. We upheld the tax, insofar as sales to non-Indians were concerned, because its legal incidence fell on the non-Indian purchaser. Hence, "the competitive advantage which the Indian seller doing business on tribal land enjoys over all other cigarette retailers, within and without the reservation, is dependent on the extent to which the non-Indian purchaser is willing to flout *his* legal obligation to pay the tax." ([E]mphasis in original.) We upheld the collection requirement, as applied to purchases by non-Indians, on the ground that it was a "minimal burden" designed to aid the State in collecting an otherwise valid tax.

Moe establishes several principles relevant to the present cases. The State may sometimes impose a nondiscriminatory tax on non-Indian customers of Indian retailers doing business on the reservation. Such a tax may be valid even if it seriously disadvantages or eliminates the Indian retailer's business with non-Indians. And the State may impose at least "minimal" burdens on the Indian retailer to aid in enforcing and collecting the tax. There is no automatic bar, therefore, to Washington's extending its tax and collection and recordkeeping requirements onto the reservation in the present cases.

Although it narrows the issues in the present cases, *Moe* does not definitively resolve several important questions. First, unlike in *Moe*, each of the Tribes imposes its own tax on cigarette sales, and obtains further revenues by participating in the cigarette enterprise at the wholesale or retail level. Second, Washington requires the Indian retailer to keep detailed records of exempt and nonexempt sales in addition to simply precollecting the tax. *Moe* expressed no opinion regarding the "complicated problems" of enforcement that distinctions between exempt and nonexempt purchasers might entail. Third, *Moe* left unresolved the question of whether a State can tax purchases by on-reservation Indians not members of the governing tribe, as Washington seeks to do in the present cases. Finally, unlike in *Moe*, Washington has seized, and threatens to continue seizing, shipments of unstamped cigarettes en route to the reservations from wholesalers outside the State. We address each of these questions.

B.

(1)

At the outset, the State argues that the Colville, Makah, and Lummi Tribes have no power to impose their cigarette taxes on nontribal purchasers. We disagree. The power to tax transactions occurring on trust lands and significantly involving a tribe or its members is a fundamental attribute of sovereignty which the tribes retain unless divested of it by federal law or necessary implication of their dependent status. ***

(2)

The Tribes contend that their involvement in the operation and taxation of cigarette marketing on the reservation ousts the State from any power to exact its sales and cigarette taxes from nonmembers purchasing cigarettes at tribal smokeshops. The primary argument is economic. It is asserted that smokeshop cigarette sales generate substantial revenues for the Tribes which they expend for essential governmental services, including programs to combat severe poverty and underdevelopment at the reservations. Most cigarette purchasers are outsiders attracted onto the reservations by the bargain prices the smokeshops charge by virtue of their claimed exemption from state taxation. If the State is permitted to impose its taxes, the Tribes will no longer enjoy any competitive advantage vis-á-vis businesses in surrounding areas. Indeed, because the Tribes themselves impose a tax on the transaction, if the state tax is also collected the price charged will necessarily be higher and the Tribes will be placed at a competitive disadvantage as compared to businesses elsewhere. Tribal smokeshops will lose a large percentage of their cigarette sales and the Tribes will forfeit substantial revenues. Because of this economic impact, it is argued, the state taxes are (1) pre-empted by federal statutes regulating Indian affairs; (2) inconsistent with the principle of tribal self-government; and (3) invalid under "negative implications" of the Indian Commerce Clause.

It is painfully apparent that the value marketed by the smokeshops to persons coming from outside is not generated on the reservations by activities in which the Tribes have a significant interest. What the smokeshops offer these customers, and what is not available elsewhere, is solely an exemption from state taxation. The Tribes assert the power to create such exemptions by imposing their own taxes or otherwise earning revenues by participating in the reservation enterprises. If this assertion were accepted, the Tribes could impose a nominal tax and open chains of discount stores at reservation borders, selling goods of all descriptions at deep discounts and drawing customers from surrounding areas. We do not believe that principles of federal Indian law, whether stated in terms of pre-emption, tribal self-government, or otherwise, authorize Indian tribes thus to market an exemption from state taxation to persons who would normally do their business elsewhere.

The federal statutes cited to us, even when given the broadest reading to which they are fairly susceptible, cannot be said to pre-empt Washington's sales and cigarette taxes. The Indian Reorganization Act of 1934, 48 Stat. 984, 25 U.S.C. § 461 *et seq.*, the Indian Financing Act of 1974, 88 Stat. 77, 25 U.S.C. § 1451 *et seq.*, and the Indian Self–Determination and Education Assistance Act of 1975, 88 Stat. 2203, 25 U.S.C. § 450 *et seq.*, evidence to varying degrees a congressional concern with fostering tribal self-government and economic development, but none goes so far as to grant tribal enterprises selling goods to nonmembers an artificial competitive advantage over all other businesses in a State. The Indian traders statutes, 25 U.S.C. § 261 *et seq.*, incorporate a congressional desire comprehensively to regulate businesses selling goods to reservation Indians for cash or exchange, *see Warren Trading Post*, but no similar intent is evident with respect to sales by Indians to nonmembers of the Tribe. The Washington Enabling Act, 25 Stat. 676, reflects an intent that the State not tax reservation lands or income derived therefrom, but the present taxes are assessed against nonmembers of the Tribes and concern transactions in personalty with no substantial connection to reservation lands. The relevant treaties, Treaty of Point Elliott, 12 Stat. 927 (1855) (Lummi Tribe); Treaty with the Makah Tribe, 12 Stat. 939 (1855); Treaty with the Yakimas, 12 Stat. 951 (1855), can be read to recognize inherent tribal power to exclude non-Indians or impose conditions on those permitted to enter; but purchasers entering the reservation are not the State's agents and any agreements which they might make cannot bind it. Finally, although the Tribes themselves could perhaps pre-empt state taxation through the exercise of properly delegated federal power to do so, we do not infer from the mere fact of federal approval of the Indian taxing ordinances, or from the fact that the Tribes exercise congressionally sanctioned powers of self-government, that Congress has delegated the far-reaching authority to pre-empt valid state sales and cigarette taxes otherwise collectible from nonmembers of the Tribe.

Washington does not infringe the right of reservation Indians to "make their own laws and be ruled by them," *Williams v. Lee*, merely because the result of imposing its taxes will be to deprive the Tribes of revenues which they currently are receiving. The principle of tribal self-government, grounded in notions of inherent sovereignty and in congressional policies, seeks an accommodation between the interests of the Tribes and the Federal Government, on the one hand, and those of the State, on the other. *McClanahan*. While the Tribes do have an interest in raising revenues for essential governmental programs, that interest is strongest when the revenues are derived from value generated on the reservation by activities involving the Tribes and when the taxpayer is the recipient of tribal services. The State also has a legitimate governmental interest in raising revenues, and that interest is likewise strongest when the tax is directed at off-reservation value and when the taxpayer is the recipient of state services. As we have already noted, Washington's taxes are reasonably designed to prevent the Tribes from marketing their tax exemption to nonmembers who do not receive significant tribal services and who would otherwise purchase their cigarettes outside the reservations.

It can no longer be seriously argued that the Indian Commerce Clause, of its own force, automatically bars all state taxation of matters significantly touching the political and economic interests of the Tribes. *See Moe*. That Clause may have a more limited role to play in preventing undue discrimination against, or burdens on, Indian commerce. But Washington's taxes are applied in a nondiscriminatory manner to all transactions within the State. And although the result of these taxes will be to lessen or eliminate tribal commerce with nonmembers, that market existed in the first place only because of a claimed exemption from these very taxes. The taxes under consideration do not burden commerce that would exist on the reservations without respect to the tax exemption.

We cannot fault the State for not giving credit on the amount of tribal taxes paid. It is argued that if a credit is not given, the tribal retailers will actually be placed at a competitive disadvantage, as compared to retailers elsewhere, due to the overlapping impact of tribal and state taxation. While this argument is not without force, we find that the Tribes have failed to demonstrate that business at the smokeshops would be significantly reduced by a state tax without a credit as compared to a state tax with a credit. With a credit, prices at the smokeshops would presumably be roughly the same as those off the reservation, assuming that the Indian enterprises are operated at an efficiency similar to that of businesses elsewhere; without a credit, prices at smokeshops would exceed those off the reservation by the amount of the tribal taxes, about 40 to 50 cents per carton for the Lummi, Makah, and Colville Tribes, and 22.5 cents per carton for the Yakima Tribe. It is evident that even if credit were given, the bulk of the smokeshops' present business would still be eliminated, since nonresidents of the reservation could purchase cigarettes at the same price and with greater convenience nearer their homes and would have no incentive to travel to the smokeshops for bargain purchases as they do now. Members of the Tribes, of course, would be indifferent to whether a credit were given because under *Moe* they are immune from any state tax, whether credited or not. Some nonmembers of the Tribes living on the reservations would possibly travel elsewhere to purchase cigarettes if a state credit were not given, and smokeshop business would to this extent be decreased as compared to the situation under a credited tax. But the Tribes have not shown whether or to what extent this would be the case, and we cannot infer on the present record that by failing to give a credit Washington impermissibly taxes reservation value by deterring sales that, if credit were given, would occur on the reservation because of its location and because of the efforts of the Tribes in importing and marketing the cigarettes.

A second asserted ground for the invalidity of the state taxes is that they somehow conflict with the Tribes' cigarette ordinances and thereby are subject to pre-emption or contravene the principle of tribal self-government. This argument need not detain us. There is no direct conflict between the state and tribal schemes, since each government is free to impose its taxes without ousting the other. Although taxes can be used for distributive or regulatory purposes, as well as for raising revenue, we see no nonrevenue purposes to the tribal taxes at issue in these cases, and, as already noted, we perceive no intent on the part of Congress to authorize the Tribes to pre-empt otherwise valid state taxes. Other provisions of the tribal ordinances do comprehensively regulate the marketing of cigarettes by the tribal enterprises; but the State does not interfere with the Tribes' power to regulate tribal enterprises when it simply imposes its tax on sales to nonmembers. Hence, we perceive no conflict between state and tribal law warranting invalidation of the State's taxes.

C.

We recognized in *Moe* that if a State's tax is valid, the State may impose at least minimal burdens on Indian businesses to aid in collecting and enforcing that tax. The simple collection burden imposed by Washington's cigarette tax on tribal smokeshops is legally indistinguishable from the collection burden upheld in *Moe*, and we therefore hold that the State may validly require the tribal smokeshops to affix tax stamps purchased from the State to individual packages of cigarettes prior to the time of sale to nonmembers of the Tribe.

The state sales tax scheme requires smokeshop operators to keep detailed records of both taxable and nontaxable transactions. The operator must record the number and dollar volume of taxable sales to nonmembers of the Tribe. With respect to nontaxable sales, the operator must record and retain for state inspection the names of all Indian purchasers, their tribal affiliations, the Indian reservations within which sales are made, and the dollar amount and dates of sales. In addition, unless the Indian purchaser is personally known to the operator he must present a tribal identification card.

*** [W]e find the State's recordkeeping requirements valid in toto. The Tribes bear the burden of showing that the recordkeeping requirements which they are challenging are invalid. The District Court made the factual finding, which we accept, that there was no evidence of record on this question. Applying the correct burden of proof to the District Court's finding, we hold that the Tribes have failed to demonstrate that the State's recordkeeping requirements for exempt sales are not reasonably necessary as a means of preventing fraudulent transactions.

D.

The State asserts the power to apply its sales and cigarette taxes to Indians resident on the reservation but not enrolled in the governing Tribe. ***

Federal statutes, even given the broadest reading to which they are reasonably susceptible, cannot be said to pre-empt Washington's power to impose its taxes on Indians not members of the Tribe. We do not so read the Major Crimes Act, 18 U.S.C. § 1153, which at most provides for federal-court jurisdiction over crimes committed by Indians on another Tribe's reservation. Similarly, the mere fact that nonmembers resident on the reservation come within the definition of "Indian" for purposes of the Indian Reorganization Act of 1934, 48 Stat. 988, 25 U.S.C. § 479, does not demonstrate a congressional intent to exempt such Indians from state taxation.

Nor would the imposition of Washington's tax on these purchasers contravene the principle of tribal self-government, for the simple reason that nonmembers are not constituents of the governing Tribe. For most practical purposes those Indians stand on the same footing as non-Indians resident on the reservation. There is no evidence that nonmembers have a say in tribal affairs or significantly share in tribal disbursements. We find, therefore, that the State's interest in taxing these purchasers outweighs any tribal interest that may exist in preventing the State from imposing its taxes.

E.

Finally, the State contends that it has the power to seize unstamped cigarettes as contraband if the Tribes do not cooperate in collecting the State's taxes. The State in fact seized shipments traveling to the reservations from out-of-state wholesalers before being enjoined from doing so by the District Court, and it has declared its intention to continue such seizures if successful in this litigation. The Tribes contest this power, noting that because sales by wholesalers to the tribal businesses are concededly exempt from state taxation, no state tax is due while the cigarettes are in transit.

We find that Washington's interest in enforcing its valid taxes is sufficient to justify these seizures. Although the cigarettes in transit are as yet exempt from state taxation, they are not immune from seizure when the Tribes, as here, have refused to fulfill collection and remittance obligations which the State has validly imposed. It is significant that these seizures take place outside the reservation, in locations where state power over Indian affairs is considerably more expansive than it is within reservation boundaries. By seizing cigarettes en route to the reservation, the State polices against wholesale evasion of its own valid taxes without unnecessarily intruding on core tribal interests.

Washington further contends that it may enter onto the reservations, seize stocks of cigarettes which are intended for sale to nonmembers, and sell these stocks in order to obtain payment of the taxes due. However, this question, which obviously is considerably different from the preceding one, is not properly before us. *** We therefore express no opinion on the matter.

V.

The next issue concerns the challenge in the Colville case to the Washington motor vehicle and mobile home, camper and travel trailer taxes. Although not identical, these taxes are quite similar. Each is denominated an excise tax for the "privilege" of using the covered vehicle in the State, each is assessed annually at a certain percentage of fair market value, and each is sought to be imposed upon vehicles owned by the Tribe or its members and used both on and off the reservation.

Once again, our departure point is *Moe*. There we held that Montana's personal property tax could not validly be applied to motor vehicles owned by tribal members who resided on the reservation. The vehicles Montana attempted to tax were apparently used both on and off the reservation, and the tax was assessed annually at a percentage of market value of the vehicles in question. Thus, the only difference between the taxes now before us and the one struck down in *Moe* is that these are called excise taxes and imposed for the privilege of using the vehicle in the State, while the Montana tax was labeled a personal property tax. The State asserts that this difference mandates a different result. In *Moe*, it argues, the District Court concluded that the taxable event was "the ownership of a motor vehicle as of January 1 of each year," [based on the language of the relevant state statute], and that event took place on the reservation. Accordingly, under *McClanahan*, Montana was without authority to impose its tax. In the present case, the State continues, the taxable event is the use within the State of the vehicle in question. Thus, we are told, the *McClanahan* principle is inapplicable and the tax should be upheld under *Mescalero Apache Tribe v. Jones*.

We do not think *Moe* and *McClanahan* can be this easily circumvented. While Washington may well be free to levy a tax on the use outside the reservation of Indian-owned vehicles, it may not under that rubric accomplish what *Moe* held was prohibited. Had Washington tailored its tax to the amount of actual off-reservation use, or otherwise varied something more than mere nomenclature, this might be a different case. But it has not done so, and we decline to treat the case as if it had.

JUSTICE BRENNAN, with whom **JUSTICE MARSHALL** joins, concurring in part and dissenting in part.

*** In my view, the State of Washington's cigarette taxing scheme should be invalidated both because it undermines the Tribes' sovereign authority to regulate and tax the distribution of cigarettes on trust lands and because it conflicts with tribal activities and functions that have been expressly approved by the Federal Government.

*** As the Court points out, *Moe* does suggest a number of limits upon Indian sovereignty in general and the federal interests in tribal self-government and economic growth in particular: It permits state law to come on the reservation in the form of a tax and collection requirement, and it upholds the imposition of a tax that will undoubtedly hurt Indian retailing activities by depriving tribal smokeshops of a competitive edge.

But while in *Moe* the cigarette business was largely a private operation, the Tribes involved in these cases have adopted comprehensive ordinances regulating and taxing the distribution of cigarettes by on-reservation shops. Phrased differently, these Tribes are acting in federally sanctioned and encouraged ways—they are raising governmental revenues, establishing commercial enterprises, and struggling to escape from "a century of oppression and paternalism." *** H.R. Rep. No. 1804, 73d Cong., 2d Sess., 6 (1934). As I see it, that difference has three important consequences. First, it means that in this case the sharp drop in cigarette sales that would result from imposition of the state tax will reduce revenues not only of individual Indian retailers, but also of the Tribes themselves as governmental units. Second, it means that a decision permitting application of the state tax would place Indian goods at an actual competitive *disadvantage* as compared to non-Indian ones because the former would have to bear two tax burdens while the latter bore but one. And third, it leads to an actual conflict of jurisdiction and sovereignty because imposition of the Washington tax would inject state law into an on-reservation transaction which the Indians have chosen to subject to their own laws.

*** [T]hese three consequences bring the Washington taxes into sharp conflict with important federal policies. ***

The conflict with federal law is particularly evident on the present facts because the Secretary of the Interior—acting pursuant to lawful regulations—has approved the tribal taxing and regulatory schemes at issue here. That approval, and the federal policies which underlie it, both enhances tribal authority and ousts inconsistent state law. ***

JUSTICE STEWART, concurring in part and dissenting in part.

I join all but Part IV–B(2) and Part V of the Court's opinion. My disagreement with Part V is for the reasons stated in Part III of Mr. Justice Rehnquist's separate opinion [that the state could impose motor vehicle taxes on tribal members who use their vehicles off reservation]. My disagreement with Part IV–B(2) stems from the belief that the State of Washington cannot impose the full combined measure of its cigarette and sales taxes on purchases by nontribal members of cigarettes from tobacco outlets on the Colville, Lummi, and Makah Reservations.

*** It seems clear to me that the appellee Tribes enjoy a power at least equal to that of the State to tax the on-reservation sales of cigarettes to nontribal members. Those sales are entered into and consummated in places and circumstances subject to the Tribes' protection and control. Furthermore, the taxation of such transactions effectuates recognized federal policies by providing funds for the maintenance and operation of tribal self-government. *See generally* Indian Reorganization Act of 1934; *McClanahan*; *Williams v. Lee.*

Consequently, when a State and an Indian tribe tax in a functionally identical manner the same on-reservation sales to nontribal members, it is my view that congressional policy conjoined with the Indian Commerce Clause requires the State to credit against its own tax the amount of the tribe's tax. This solution fully effectuates the State's goal of assuring that its citizens who are not tribal members do not cash in on the exemption from state taxation that the tribe and its members enjoy. On the other hand, it permits the tribe to share with the State in the tax revenues from cigarette sales, without at the same time placing the tribe's federally encouraged enterprises at a competitive disadvantage compared to similarly situated off-reservation businesses. ***

[**JUSTICE REHNQUIST** dissented on the grounds that a balancing test was inappropriate, and strict preemption should apply, and that it was irrelevant that the state had not tailored its motor vehicle tax to the amount of off-reservation use.]

NOTES AND QUESTIONS

1. Colville *in Context: Battles over Tribal Revival in the Pacific Northwest.* There was great interest in the *Colville* case in the Pacific Northwest. Tribes were asserting their treaty rights to fish and passing laws and regulations to allow for economic development. Many high profile people in the region, including Washington Attorney General Slade Gorton, saw every case involving tribal rights, whether the power to tax, to impose criminal jurisdiction, or to fish at off-reservation sites, as a threat to states' rights. *The Indian Voice*, a regional tribal newspaper, described the many cases in the region under the colorful title "Courtroom wars," and described Gorton as "a bitter foe of Indians," who vowed to fight the tribal taxes all the way to the Supreme Court. *See* Sarah Krakoff, *The Story of* Oliphant v. Suquamish Indian Tribe, *in* Indian Law Stories (Goldberg, Washburn, & Frickey, eds., 2011).

2. *Preemption versus Balancing Tribal, State and Federal Interests.* In *Warren Trading Post* and *Central Machinery*, the Court held that state taxes on non-Indians selling goods to Indians were preempted simply because of the federal authority to license and regulate Indian traders. In *Colville*, however, the Court finds that state taxes on purchases by non-Indians are permitted even though the sellers are (1) federally licensed Indian traders, (2) working for the tribes, (3) selling cigarettes purchased by the tribes with federal funds and federal encouragement in order to achieve tribal economic development. The Indian traders are required not only to collect a tax on sales, but to demand ID cards with proof of tribal membership from purchasers, and to keep detailed records of who purchased cigarettes. Why was state jurisdiction an invalid burden on a comprehensive federal scheme in *Warren Trading Post* and *Central Machinery*, but not *Colville*?

The answer seems to be that the Court added a balancing of interest test to the preemption test of *McClanahan* and *Warren Trading Post*. Because the states had an interest in the non-Indian customers coming from off-reservation, and because the value of the cigarettes was created off-reservation, the significant tribal and federal interests in economic development, and their expression in federal laws and tribal laws enacted with federal approval, were undermined. On the one hand, one might argue that the involvement of off-reservation state interests made the traditional Indian country preemption analysis inappropriate. On the other hand, because management of the smokeshops was so clearly a matter of federal policy and law, it would seem to be at the core of the federal role in regulating commerce with Indian tribes, and exercise of state authority that would wholly terminate that commerce (as the parties agreed that state taxation would) should be preempted. Logical or not, the Court has reaffirmed and even extended *Colville*, upholding even more onerous burdens on federal Indian traders and tribes selling cigarettes to non-Indians in *Department of Taxation and Finance v. Milhelm Attea & Bros., Inc.*, 512 U.S. 61 (1994).

3. *Marketing a Tax Exemption?* At the heart of the majority's unease with the case is the notion that the tribes are "marketing a tax exemption," that the only reason non-Indians want to buy cigarettes on the reservation is because the sales taxes are lower. This does suggest two ways in which state interests were affected by the on-reservation sales. Because demand for cigarettes is fairly inelastic (people buy the same number of cigarettes with little regard for their price), and smokers are not a sympathetic constituency, states use cigarette taxes to raise revenue much more freely than they do other forms of taxes; tax-free tribal sales would deprive them of a portion of this revenue. At the same time, because cigarettes are the same everywhere, smokers will spurn off-reservation convenience stores if they can buy cigarettes more cheaply on-reservation, reducing business to the off-reservation stores. Notice, however, that the tribes are simply exercising the same power that state and local governments do by adjusting the tax burden to attract business there rather than to other locations. In addition, while off-reservation stores may suffer some loss of business, most on-reservation stores will have almost no business without these tax advantages. Note also that the Court condemns the non-Indian purchaser for willingness to "flout *his* legal obligation to pay" the state tax. Yet isn't this circular reasoning, given that the customer had no legal obligation to pay the tax until the Supreme Court affirmed it? To compare, is the New York resident "flouting" her legal obligation to pay New York sales taxes when she crosses the state line into New Jersey to shop, sales-tax free, at one of the many malls? Do we typically think of our shopping habits in this way, or do we think of ourselves as simply looking for the best buy? Similarly, do we judge states poorly for marketing their tax exemptions in precisely this way? Perhaps the difficulty with this comparison, and the struggles the Court has with this topic, derive in part from the overlapping geographic boundaries between states and tribes. This gets back to a more fundamental question. If there is friction between the competing and at times overlapping sovereignty that states and tribes have, should the Court weigh in to make the correction? Is there a structural argument either in favor of or against the Court playing this role?

4. *Infringement of the Tribal Right of Self–Government? Williams v. Lee* held that state adjudicatory jurisdiction over a dispute between a non-Indian and two Navajos regarding a contract dispute arising on a reservation would impermissibly infringe on tribal self-government. *Colville* held that imposition of state authority on sales between tribal enterprises and non-Indians did not impermissibly infringe on tribal self-government. Why not? What remains of the infringement test after *Colville*?

5. *Economic versus Legal Burden: The Legal Incidence Test.* Although the tax imposed a very heavy economic burden on the tribes, the Court found it important that the legal responsibility to pay the tax (the "legal incidence") fell not on the tribe but on the non-Indian purchaser. *See Colville* at 142 n.9.

The legal incidence test has become crucial in questions of taxation in Indian country:

> The initial and frequently dispositive question in Indian tax cases *** is who bears the legal incidence of a tax. If the legal incidence of an excise tax rests on a tribe or on tribal members for sales made inside Indian country, the tax cannot be enforced absent clear congressional authorization. But if the legal incidence of the tax rests on non-Indians, no categorical bar prevents enforcement of the tax; if the balance of federal, state, and tribal interests favors the State, and federal law is not to the contrary, the State may impose its levy. ***

Oklahoma Tax Comm'n v. Chickasaw Nation, 515 U.S. 450, 458–59 (1995). Note that this test is largely formalistic: a state may shift the legal incidence, and often the validity, of the tax simply by shifting who has the legal responsibility to pay the tax. Recently, the Supreme Court further entrenched this formalistic approach, upholding a state motor fuel tax imposed on non-Indian distributors who sell the fuel to on-reservation tribal retailers. *See Wagnon v. Prairie Band Potawatomi Nation*, 546 U.S. 95 (2005).

WHITE MOUNTAIN APACHE TRIBE V. BRACKER

448 U.S. 136, 100 S. Ct. 2578, 65 L. Ed. 2d 665 (1980)

JUSTICE MARSHALL delivered the opinion of the Court.

***

I.

The 6,500 members of petitioner White Mountain Apache Tribe reside on the Fort Apache Reservation in a mountainous and forested region of northeastern Arizona. *** The revenue used to fund the Tribe's governmental programs is derived almost exclusively from tribal enterprises. Of these enterprises, timber operations have proved by far the most important, accounting for over 90% of the Tribe's total annual profits.

*** Under federal law, timber on reservation land is owned by the United States for the benefit of the Tribe and cannot be harvested for sale without the consent of Congress. Acting under the authority of 25 CFR § 141.6 (1979) and the tribal constitution, and with the specific approval of the Secretary of the Interior, the Tribe in 1964 organized the Fort Apache Timber Co. (FATCO), a tribal enterprise that manages, harvests, processes, and sells timber. FATCO, which conducts all of its activities on the reservation, was created with the aid of federal funds. It employs about 300 tribal members.

The United States has entered into contracts with FATCO, authorizing it to harvest timber pursuant to regulations of the Bureau of Indian Affairs. FATCO has itself contracted with six logging companies, including Pinetop, which perform certain operations that FATCO could not carry out as economically on its own. Since it first entered into agreements with FATCO in 1969, Pinetop has been required to fell trees, cut them to the correct size, and transport them to FATCO's sawmill in return for a contractually specified fee. Pinetop employs approximately 50 tribal members. Its activities, performed solely on the Fort Apache Reservation, are subject to extensive federal control.

In 1971 [Arizona] sought to impose on Pinetop the two state taxes at issue here. The first, a motor carrier license tax, is assessed on "[e]very common motor carrier of property and every contract motor carrier of property." Pinetop is a "contract motor carrier of property" since it is engaged in "the transportation by motor vehicle of property, for compensation, on any public highway." The motor carrier license tax amounts to 2.5% of the carrier's gross receipts. The second tax at issue is an excise or use fuel tax designed "[f]or the purpose of partially compensating the state for the use of its highways." The tax amounts to eight cents per gallon of fuel used "in the propulsion of a motor vehicle on any highway within this state." The use fuel tax was assessed on Pinetop because it uses diesel fuel to propel its vehicles on the state highways within the Fort Apache Reservation.

Pinetop paid the taxes under protest, and then brought suit in state court, asserting that under federal law the taxes could not lawfully be imposed on logging activities conducted exclusively within the reservation or on hauling activities on Bureau of Indian Affairs and tribal roads.[6] The Tribe agreed to reimburse Pinetop for any tax liability incurred as a result of its on-reservation business activities, and the Tribe intervened in the action as a plaintiff. [The state courts held that the state could impose the disputed taxes.]

II.

*** [O]ur decisions establish several basic principles with respect to the boundaries between state regulatory authority and tribal self-government. Long ago the Court departed from Mr. Chief Justice Marshall's view that "the laws of [a State] can have no force" within reservation boundaries, *Worcester*. At the same time we have recognized that the Indian tribes retain "attributes of sovereignty over both their members and their territory." As a result, there is no rigid rule by which to resolve the question whether a particular state law may be applied to an Indian reservation or to tribal members. ***

Congress has broad power to regulate tribal affairs under the Indian Commerce Clause. This congressional authority and the "semi-independent position" of Indian tribes have given rise to two independent but related barriers to the assertion of state regulatory authority over tribal reservations and members. First, the exercise of such authority may be pre-empted by federal law. *See, e.g., Warren Trading Post*; *McClanahan*. Second, it may unlawfully infringe "on the right of reservation Indians to make their own laws and be ruled by them." *Williams v. Lee*. The two barriers are independent because either, standing alone, can be a sufficient basis for holding state law inapplicable to activity undertaken on the reservation or by tribal members. They are related, however, in two important ways. The right of tribal self-government is ultimately dependent on and subject to the broad power of Congress. Even so, traditional notions of Indian self-government are so deeply engrained in our

6. For purposes of this action petitioners have conceded Pinetop's liability for both motor carrier license and use fuel taxes attributable to travel on state highways within the reservation. Pinetop has maintained records of fuel attributable to travel on those highways, and computations would evidently be made in order to allocate a portion of the gross receipts taxable under the motor carrier license tax to state highways.

jurisprudence that they have provided an important "backdrop," *McClanahan*, against which vague or ambiguous federal enactments must always be measured.

The unique historical origins of tribal sovereignty make it generally unhelpful to apply to federal enactments regulating Indian tribes those standards of pre-emption that have emerged in other areas of the law. Tribal reservations are not States, and the differences in the form and nature of their sovereignty make it treacherous to import to one notions of pre-emption that are properly applied to the other. The tradition of Indian sovereignty over the reservation and tribal members must inform the determination whether the exercise of state authority has been pre-empted by operation of federal law. As we have repeatedly recognized, this tradition is reflected and encouraged in a number of congressional enactments demonstrating a firm federal policy of promoting tribal self-sufficiency and economic development. Ambiguities in federal law have been construed generously in order to comport with these traditional notions of sovereignty and with the federal policy of encouraging tribal independence. We have thus rejected the proposition that in order to find a particular state law to have been preempted by operation of federal law, an express congressional statement to that effect is required. *Warren Trading Post*. At the same time any applicable regulatory interest of the State must be given weight, and "automatic exemptions 'as a matter of constitutional law' " are unusual. *Moe*.

When on-reservation conduct involving only Indians is at issue, state law is generally inapplicable, for the State's regulatory interest is likely to be minimal and the federal interest in encouraging tribal self-government is at its strongest. *McClanahan*. More difficult questions arise where, as here, a State asserts authority over the conduct of non-Indians engaging in activity on the reservation. In such cases we have examined the language of the relevant federal treaties and statutes in terms of both the broad policies that underlie them and the notions of sovereignty that have developed from historical traditions of tribal independence. This inquiry is not dependent on mechanical or absolute conceptions of state or tribal sovereignty, but has called for a particularized inquiry into the nature of the state, federal, and tribal interests at stake, an inquiry designed to determine whether, in the specific context, the exercise of state authority would violate federal law. *Compare Warren Trading Post and Williams v. Lee with Moe.*

III.

With these principles in mind, we turn to the respondents' claim that they may, consistent with federal law, impose the contested motor vehicle license and use fuel taxes on the logging and hauling operations of petitioner Pinetop. At the outset we observe that the Federal Government's regulation of the harvesting of Indian timber is comprehensive. That regulation takes the form of Acts of Congress, detailed regulations promulgated by the Secretary of the Interior, and day-to-day supervision by the Bureau of Indian Affairs. Under 25 U.S.C. §§ 405–407, the Secretary of the Interior is granted broad authority over the sale of timber on the reservation. Timber on Indian land may be sold only with the consent of the Secretary, and the proceeds from any such sales, less administrative expenses incurred by the Federal Government, are to be used for the benefit of the Indians or transferred to the Indian owner. Sales of timber must "be based upon a consideration of the needs and best interests of the

Indian owner and his heirs." 25 U.S.C. § 406(a). The statute specifies the factors which the Secretary must consider in making that determination. In order to assure the continued productivity of timber-producing land on tribal reservations, timber on unallotted lands "may be sold in accordance with the principles of sustained yield." 25 U.S.C. § 407. The Secretary is granted power to determine the disposition of the proceeds from timber sales. He is authorized to promulgate regulations for the operation and management of Indian forestry units.

Acting pursuant to this authority, the Secretary has promulgated a detailed set of regulations to govern the harvesting and sale of tribal timber. Among the stated objectives of the regulations is the "development of Indian forests by the Indian people for the purpose of promoting self-sustaining communities, to the end that the Indians may receive from their own property not only the stumpage value, but also the benefit of whatever profit it is capable of yielding and whatever labor the Indians are qualified to perform." 25 CFR § 141.3(a)(3) (1979). The regulations cover a wide variety of matters: for example, they restrict clear-cutting, § 141.5; establish comprehensive guidelines for the sale of timber, § 141.7; regulate the advertising of timber sales, §§ 141.8, 141.9; specify the manner in which bids may be accepted and rejected, § 141.11; describe the circumstances in which contracts may be entered into, §§ 141.12, 141.13; require the approval of all contracts by the Secretary, § 141.13; call for timber-cutting permits to be approved by the Secretary, § 141.19; specify fire protective measures, § 141.21; and provide a board of administrative appeals, § 141.23. Tribes are expressly authorized to establish commercial enterprises for the harvesting and logging of tribal timber. § 141.6.

Under these regulations, the Bureau of Indian Affairs exercises literally daily supervision over the harvesting and management of tribal timber. In the present case, contracts between FATCO and Pinetop must be approved by the Bureau; indeed, the record shows that some of those contracts were drafted by employees of the Federal Government. Bureau employees regulate the cutting, hauling, and marking of timber by FATCO and Pinetop. The Bureau decides such matters as how much timber will be cut, which trees will be felled, which roads are to be used, which hauling equipment Pinetop should employ, the speeds at which logging equipment may travel, and the width, length, height, and weight of loads.

The Secretary has also promulgated detailed regulations governing the roads developed by the Bureau of Indian Affairs. 25 C.F.R. Part 162 (1979). Bureau roads are open to "[f]ree public use." § 162.8. Their administration and maintenance are funded by the Federal Government, with contributions from the Indian tribes. §§ 162.6–162.6a. On the Fort Apache Reservation the Forestry Department of the Bureau has required FATCO and its contractors, including Pinetop, to repair and maintain existing Bureau and tribal roads and in some cases to construct new logging roads. Substantial sums have been spent for these purposes. In its federally approved contract with FATCO, Pinetop has agreed to construct new roads and to repair existing ones. A high percentage of Pinetop's receipts are expended for those purposes, and it has maintained separate personnel and equipment to carry out a variety of tasks relating to road maintenance.

In these circumstances we agree with petitioners that the federal regulatory scheme is so pervasive as to preclude the additional burdens sought to be imposed in this case. Respondents seek to apply their motor vehicle license and use fuel taxes on Pinetop for operations that are conducted solely on Bureau and tribal roads within the reservation. There is no room for these taxes in the comprehensive federal regulatory scheme. In a variety of ways, the assessment of state taxes would obstruct federal policies. And equally important, respondents have been unable to identify any regulatory function or service performed by the State that would justify the assessment of taxes for activities on Bureau and tribal roads within the reservation.

At the most general level, the taxes would threaten the overriding federal objective of guaranteeing Indians that they will "receive *** the benefit of whatever profit [the forest] is capable of yielding. *** " 25 CFR § 141.3(a)(3) (1979). Underlying the federal regulatory program rests a policy of assuring that the profits derived from timber sales will inure to the benefit of the Tribe, subject only to administrative expenses incurred by the Federal Government. That objective is part of the general federal policy of encouraging tribes "to revitalize their self-government" and to assume control over their "business and economic affairs." The imposition of the taxes at issue would undermine that policy in a context in which the Federal Government has undertaken to regulate the most minute details of timber production and expressed a firm desire that the Tribe should retain the benefits derived from the harvesting and sale of reservation timber.

In addition, the taxes would undermine the Secretary's ability to make the wide range of determinations committed to his authority concerning the setting of fees and rates with respect to the harvesting and sale of tribal timber. The Secretary reviews and approves the terms of the Tribe's agreements with its contractors, sets fees for services rendered to the Tribe by the Federal Government, and determines stumpage rates for timber to be paid to the Tribe. Most notably in reviewing or writing the terms of the contracts between FATCO and its contractors, federal agents must predict the amount and determine the proper allocation of all business expenses, including fuel costs. The assessment of state taxes would throw additional factors into the federal calculus, reducing tribal revenues and diminishing the profitability of the enterprise for potential contractors.

Finally, the imposition of state taxes would adversely affect the Tribe's ability to comply with the sustained-yield management policies imposed by federal law. Substantial expenditures are paid out by the Federal Government, the Tribe, and its contractors in order to undertake a wide variety of measures to ensure the continued productivity of the forest. *** The expenditures are largely paid for out of tribal revenues, which are in turn derived almost exclusively from the sale of timber. The imposition of state taxes on FATCO's contractors would effectively diminish the amount of those revenues and thus leave the Tribe and its contractors with reduced sums with which to pay out federally required expenses.

As noted above, this is not a case in which the State seeks to assess taxes in return for governmental functions it performs for those on whom the taxes fall. Nor have respondents been able to identify a legitimate regulatory interest served by the taxes they seek to impose. They refer to a general desire to raise revenue, but we are unable to discern a responsibility or service that justifies the assertion of taxes imposed for on-reservation operations conducted solely on tribal and Bureau of Indian Affairs roads. Pinetop's business in Arizona is conducted solely on the Fort Apache Reservation. Though at least the use fuel tax purports to "compensat[e] the state for the use of its highways," Ariz. Rev. Stat. Ann. § 28–1552 (Supp. 1979), no such compensatory purpose is present here. The roads at issue have been built, maintained, and policed exclusively by the Federal Government, the Tribe, and its contractors. We do not believe that respondents' generalized interest in raising revenue is in this context sufficient to permit its proposed intrusion into the federal regulatory scheme with respect to the harvesting and sale of tribal timber.

Respondents' argument is reduced to a claim that they may assess taxes on non-Indians engaged in commerce on the reservation whenever there is no express congressional statement to the contrary. That is simply not the law. In a number of cases we have held that state authority over non-Indians acting on tribal reservations is pre-empted even though Congress has offered no explicit statement on the subject. *See Warren Trading Post*; *Williams v. Lee*. The Court has repeatedly emphasized that there is a significant geographical component to tribal sovereignty, a component which remains highly relevant to the pre-emption inquiry; though the reservation boundary is not absolute, it remains an important factor to weigh in determining whether state authority has exceeded the permissible limits. *** Moreover, it is undisputed that the economic burden of the asserted taxes will ultimately fall on the Tribe. Where, as here, the Federal Government has undertaken comprehensive regulation of the harvesting and sale of tribal timber, where a number of the policies underlying the federal regulatory scheme are threatened by the taxes respondents seek to impose, and where respondents are unable to justify the taxes except in terms of a generalized interest in raising revenue, we believe that the proposed exercise of state authority is impermissible.

*** *Reversed.*

JUSTICE STEVENS, with whom **JUSTICE STEWART** and **REHNQUIST** join, dissenting.

*** As the Court points out, the Federal Government has imposed a detailed scheme of regulation on the tribal logging business. *** The Court reasons that, because the imposition of state taxes on non-Indian contractors is likely to increase the price of their services to the tribe and thus decrease the profitability of the tribal enterprise, the taxes would substantially interfere with this scheme. ***

From a practical standpoint, the Court's prediction of massive interference with federal forest-management programs seems overdrawn, to say the least. The logging operations involved in this case produced a profit of $1,508,713 for the Indian tribal enterprise in 1973. As noted above, the maximum annual taxes Pinetop would be required to pay would be $5,000–$6,000 or less than 1% of the total annual profits. *** It is difficult to believe that these relatively trivial taxes could impose an economic burden that would threaten to "obstruct federal policies."

Under these circumstances I find the Court's reliance on the indirect financial burden imposed on the Indian Tribe by state taxation of its contractors disturbing. As a general rule, a tax is not invalid simply because a nonexempt taxpayer may be expected to pass all or part of the cost of the tax through to a person who is exempt from tax. *** *Cf. Washington v. Confederated Tribes of the Colville Indian Reservation.* *** In *Warren Trading Post* the Court found an exception to this rule where Congress had chosen to regulate the relationship between an Indian tribe and a non-Indian trader to such an extent that there was no room for the additional burden of state taxation. In this case, since the state tax is unlikely to have a serious adverse impact on the tribal business, I would not infer the same congressional intent to confer a tax immunity. ***

NOTES AND QUESTIONS

1. The dissent in *White Mountain Apache* has a point. In *Colville*, non-Indians purchasing cigarettes from federally licensed Indian traders (who the Court had already held were extensively regulated in *Warren Trading Post*) were forced to pay state taxes even though the economic burden of those taxes would be devastating to the tribal enterprise the traders were participating in. In *White Mountain Apache*, a non-Indian contractor with an extensively regulated tribal enterprise was held exempt from state taxes even though the effect of those taxes on the tribal enterprise was speculative at best. What makes the difference between the two cases? It appears to be two things: first, the enterprise in *White Mountain Apache* depends on value generated by the tribe or from reservation resources, and second, the state has little to do with contributing to that enterprise. (One might, of course, question whether Washington State contributed much to the value of cigarettes that were in all likelihood manufactured out of state).

2. *What kinds of state interests suffice?* States are always interested in raising money through taxes; that's why they impose them. In *White Mountain Apache*, however, the Court declared that a "generalized interest in raising revenue" was not sufficient to justify state taxation of on-reservation activity. What about state contribution to the value taxed? One might claim that a non-Indian contractor like Pinetop who resides and has its business headquarters off-reservation is receiving substantial state support for that business. The Court in *Colville* suggested a similar argument, stating that the argument for state taxation was stronger when the "taxpayer is the recipient of state services." In 1982, in *Ramah Navajo School Board v. New Mexico*, the Supreme Court firmly rejected this suggestion, holding that the state could not tax a non-Indian business headquartered off reservation on his contract with a tribal entity to build an on-reservation school. 458 U.S. 832, 844 (1982). Rather, the state must have a "specific, legitimate regulatory interest" in the on-reservation activity to justify the taxation. *Id.* at 843.

3. Consider footnote 6 of the *White Mountain Apache* opinion. The tribe was well advised to exclude the taxes assessed for driving on state highways from its challenge because the state interest in taxing that activity would be higher. Yet this highlights the problem of geographic overlap that was noted in the notes following *Colville*, *supra*. States do not own and operate the highways and roads of other states, so this type of sovereignty conflict does not arise in that context. Does it make sense to approach taxing authority on a highway-by-highway basis? Is there any way to avoid doing so given the tests the Court has established?

4. As stated in the notes after *Colville*, *supra*, states can avoid the categorical prohibition against taxing tribes or tribal members for activity in

Indian country by placing the legal incidence of a tax on nonmembers. In *Wagnon v. Prairie Band Potawatomi Nation*, 546 US. 95 (2005), the Supreme Court extended this formalist approach. The Court determined that the legal incidence of a state motor fuel tax fell on non-Indian distributors, not tribal retailers, and also refused to apply *White Mountain Apache*'s balancing approach because the tax was first triggered by the off-reservation receipt of the fuel by the distributors, not the on-reservation sale by the tribal retailers. Justice Ginsburg, joined by Justice Kennedy, dissented:

> The Prairie Band Potawatomi Nation (hereinafter Nation) maintains a casino and related facilities on its reservation. On nearby tribal land, as an adjunct to its casino, the Nation built, owns, and operates a gas station known as the Nation Station. Some 73% of the Nation Station's customers are casino patrons or employees. The Nation imposes its own tax on fuel sold at the Nation Station, pennies per gallon less than Kansas' tax. Both the Nation and the State have authority to tax fuel sales at the Nation Station. *** As a practical matter, however, the two tolls cannot coexist. If the Nation imposes its tax on top of Kansas' tax, then unless the Nation operates the Nation Station at a substantial loss, scarcely anyone will fill up at its pumps. Effectively double-taxed, the Nation Station must operate as an unprofitable venture, or not at all. In these circumstances, which tax is paramount?

Id. at 116 (Ginsburg, J., dissenting). Justice Ginsburg applied the *White Mountain Apache* balancing test and determined that on these facts, the answer was the tribal tax. Taking issue with the majority's refusal to engage in the balancing approach, Justice Ginsburg preceded her analysis with the following observations:

> Balancing tests have been criticized as rudderless, affording insufficient guidance to decisionmakers. *See Colville*, 447 U.S., at 176, (Rehnquist, J. concurring in part, concurring in result in part, and dissenting in part) (criticizing the "case-by-case litigation which has plagued this area of the law"). Pointed as the criticism may be, one must ask, as in life's choices generally, what is the alternative. "The principle of tribal self-government, grounded in notions of inherent sovereignty and in congressional policies, seeks an accommodation between the interests of the Tribes and the Federal Government, on the one hand, and those of the State, on the other." *Colville*, 447 U.S., at 156. No "bright-line" test is capable of achieving such an accommodation with respect to state taxes formally imposed on non-Indians, but impacting on-reservation ventures. The one the Court adopts inevitably means, so long as the State officially places the burden on the non-Indian distributor in cases of this order, the Tribe loses. ***

Id. at 124–125.

Do you agree with Justice Ginsburg that, after *Wagnon*, states will always win so long as they place the legal incidence on non-Indian activity that occurs off the reservation, even if the effects on tribes are extreme? Even before *Wagnon*, the Court only upheld one case in which economic burden alone preempted a state tax. There, the Court summarily affirmed an appellate decision that Montana's unusually high coal severance taxes, which had a negative effect on the marketability of coal mined from Crow land, were preempted by the

economic burden on the Crow Tribe. *Montana v. Crow Tribe*, 484 U.S. 997 (1988), *summarily aff'g* 819 F.2d 895 (9th Cir. 1987).

5. *Tension between federal regulation and self-determination.* If extensive federal regulation is necessary to preempt state authority, this undermines the basic goal of modern federal Indian policy of encouraging tribal self-determination. Even in the area of timber management discussed in *White Mountain Apache*, this kind of elaborate federal supervision has been found inimical to self-determination and efficient management. But as the federal government seeks to turn management of reservation services over to tribes, won't that undercut the argument that the federal scheme was comprehensive enough to preempt state authority? *Ramah Navajo,* which concerned a tribal school being constructed under the Indian Self–Determination and Education Assistance Act (ISDEAA) dealt with this question to some degree. Although the Court found federal regulation of school construction and financing to be as comprehensive as the timber management scheme in *White Mountain Apache*, the Court also identified a preemptive effect in the ISDEAA's "express federal policy of encouraging tribal self-sufficiency," a policy which would be undermined by imposition of state authority. *Ramah Navajo Sch. Bd. v. New Mexico Bureau of Revenue*, 458 U.S. 832, 845 (1982). In the following case as well, tribal sovereign activities were held to preempt conflicting state laws.

NEW MEXICO V. MESCALERO APACHE TRIBE

462 U.S. 324, 103 S. Ct. 2378, 76 L. Ed. 2d 611 (1983)

JUSTICE MARSHALL delivered the opinion of the court.

We are called upon to decide in this case whether a State may restrict an Indian Tribe's regulation of hunting and fishing on its reservation. With extensive federal assistance and supervision, the Mescalero Apache Tribe has established a comprehensive scheme for managing the reservation's fish and wildlife resources. Federally approved Tribal ordinances regulate in detail the conditions under which both members of the Tribe and nonmembers may hunt and fish. New Mexico seeks to apply its own laws to hunting and fishing by nonmembers on the reservation. We hold that this application of New Mexico's hunting and fishing laws is preempted by the operation of federal law.

I.

*** The Tribe has constructed a resort complex financed principally by federal funds, and has undertaken a substantial development of the reservation's hunting and fishing resources. These efforts provide employment opportunities for members of the Tribe, and the sale of hunting and fishing licenses and related services generates income which is used to maintain the Tribal government and provide services to Tribe members.

Development of the reservation's fish and wildlife resources has involved a sustained, cooperative effort by the Tribe and the Federal Government. Indeed, the reservation's fishing resources are wholly attributable to these recent efforts. Using federal funds, the Tribe has established eight artificial lakes which, together with the reservation's streams, are stocked by the Bureau of Sport Fisheries and Wildlife of the U.S. Fish and Wildlife Service, Department of the Interior, which operates a federal hatchery located on the reservation. None of the waters are stocked by the State.[5] The United States has also contributed substantially to the creation of the reservation's game resources. Prior to 1966 there were only 13 elk in the vicinity of the reservation. In 1966 and 1967 the National Park Service donated a herd of 162 elk which was released on the reservation. Through its management and range development the Tribe has dramatically increased the elk population, which by 1977 numbered approximately 1,200. New Mexico has not contributed significantly to the development of the elk herd or the other game on the reservation, which includes antelope, bear and deer.[7]

The Tribe and the Federal Government jointly conduct a comprehensive fish and game management program. Pursuant to its Constitution and to an agreement with the Bureau of Sport Fisheries and Wildlife, the Tribal Council adopts hunting and fishing ordinances each year. The tribal ordinances, which establish bag limits and seasons and provide for licensing of hunting and fishing, are subject to approval by the Secretary under the Tribal Constitution and have been so approved. The Tribal Council adopts the game ordinances on the basis of recommendations submitted by a Bureau of Indian Affairs range conservationist who is assisted by full-time conservation officers employed by the Tribe. The recommendations are made in light of the conservation needs of the reservation, which are determined on the basis of annual game counts and surveys. Through the Bureau of Fish and Wildlife, the Secretary also determines the stocking of the reservation's waters based upon periodic surveys of the reservation.

Numerous conflicts exist between State and tribal hunting regulations. For instance, tribal seasons and bag limits for both hunting and fishing often do not coincide with those imposed by the State. *** The Tribe permits a hunter to kill both a buck and a doe; the State permits only buck to be killed. Unlike the State, the Tribe permits a person to purchase an elk license in two consecutive years. Moreover, since 1977, the Tribe's ordinances have specified that State hunting and fishing licenses are not required for Indians or non-Indians who hunt or fish on the reservation. The New Mexico Department of Game and Fish has enforced the State's regulations by arresting non-Indian hunters for illegal possession of game killed on the reservation in accordance with tribal ordinances but not in accordance with State hunting regulations.

In 1977 the Tribe filed suit against the State and the Director of its Fish and Game Department *** seeking to prevent the State from regulating on-reservation hunting or fishing by members or nonmembers. [The district court and court of appeals] ruled in favor of the Tribe. *** We granted certiorari, and we now affirm.

II.

New Mexico concedes that on the reservation the Tribe exercises exclusive jurisdiction over hunting and fishing by members of the Tribe and may also

5. The State has not stocked any waters on the reservation since 1976.

7. The New Mexico Department of Game and Fish issued a permit for the importation of the elk from Wyoming into New Mexico. The Department has provided the Tribe with any management assistance which the Tribe has requested; such requests have been limited.

regulate the hunting and fishing by nonmembers. New Mexico contends, however, that it may exercise concurrent jurisdiction over nonmembers and that therefore its regulations governing hunting and fishing throughout the State should also apply to hunting and fishing by nonmembers on the reservation. ***

*** State jurisdiction is preempted by the operation of federal law if it interferes or is incompatible with federal and tribal interests reflected in federal law, unless the State interests at stake are sufficient to justify the assertion of State authority. *White Mountain Apache v. Bracker*. ***

*** The exercise of State authority which imposes additional burdens on a tribal enterprise must ordinarily be justified by functions or services performed by the State in connection with the on-reservation activity. *Ramah Navajo School Board*. Thus a State seeking to impose a tax on a transaction between a Tribe and nonmembers must point to more than its general interest in raising revenues. *** A State's regulatory interest will be particularly substantial if the State can point to off-reservation effects that necessitate State intervention. ***

III.

With these principles in mind, we turn to New Mexico's claim that it may superimpose its own hunting and fishing regulations on the Mescalero Apache Tribe's regulatory scheme.

A.

It is beyond doubt that the Mescalero Apache Tribe lawfully exercises substantial control over the lands and resources of its reservation, including its wildlife. ***

[T]his aspect of tribal sovereignty has been expressly confirmed by numerous federal statutes. *** This authority is afforded the protection of the federal criminal law by 18 U.S.C. § 1165, which makes it a violation of federal law to enter Indian land to hunt, trap or fish without the consent of the tribe. The 1981 amendments to the Lacey Act, 16 U.S.C. § 3371 *et seq.*, further accord tribal hunting and fishing regulations the force of federal law by making it a federal offense "to import, export, transport, sell, receive, acquire, or purchase any fish or wildlife *** taken or possessed in violation of any *** Indian tribal law."

B.

Several considerations strongly support the Court of Appeals' conclusion that the Tribe's authority to regulate hunting and fishing preempts State jurisdiction. It is important to emphasize that concurrent jurisdiction would effectively nullify the Tribe's authority to control hunting and fishing on the reservation. Concurrent jurisdiction would empower New Mexico wholly to supplant tribal regulations. The State would be able to dictate the terms on which nonmembers are permitted to utilize the reservation's resources. The Tribe would thus exercise its authority over the reservation only at the sufferance of the State. The tribal authority to regulate hunting and fishing by nonmembers, which has been repeatedly confirmed by federal treaties and laws and which we explicitly recognized in *Montana v. United States, supra,* would have a rather hollow ring if tribal authority amounted to no more than this.

Furthermore, the exercise of concurrent State jurisdiction in this case would completely "disturb and disarrange," *Warren Trading Post.*, the comprehensive scheme of federal and tribal management established pursuant to federal law. [F]ederal law requires the Secretary to review each of the Tribe's hunting and fishing ordinances. Those ordinances are based on the recommendations made by a federal range conservationist employed by the Bureau of Indian Affairs. Moreover, the Bureau of Sport Fisheries and Wildlife stocks the reservation's waters based on its own determinations concerning the availability of fish, biological requirements, and the fishing pressure created by on-reservation fishing. ***

Concurrent State jurisdiction would supplant this regulatory scheme with an inconsistent dual system: members would be governed by Tribal ordinances, while nonmembers would be regulated by general State hunting and fishing laws. This could severely hinder the ability of the Tribe to conduct a sound management program. Tribal ordinances reflect the specific needs of the reservation by establishing the optimal level of hunting and fishing that should occur, not simply a maximum level that should not be exceeded. State laws in contrast are based on considerations not necessarily relevant to, and possibly hostile to, the needs of the reservation. For instance, the ordinance permitting a hunter to kill a buck and a doe was designed to curb excessive growth of the deer population on the reservation. Enforcement of the State regulation permitting only buck to be killed would frustrate that objective. *** Permitting the State to enforce different restrictions simply because they have been determined to be appropriate for the State as a whole would impose on the Tribe the possibly insurmountable task of ensuring that the patchwork application of State and Tribal regulations remains consistent with sound management of the reservation's resources.

Federal law commits to the Secretary and the Tribal Council the responsibility to manage the reservation's resources. It is most unlikely that Congress would have authorized, and the Secretary would have established, financed, and participated in Tribal management if it were thought that New Mexico was free to nullify the entire arrangement. ***

The assertion of concurrent jurisdiction by New Mexico not only would threaten to disrupt the federal and tribal regulatory scheme, but would also threaten Congress' overriding objective of encouraging tribal self-government and economic development. The Tribe has engaged in a concerted and sustained undertaking to develop and manage the reservation's wildlife and land resources specifically for the benefit of its members. The project generates funds for essential tribal services and provides employment for members who reside on the reservation. This case is thus far removed from those situations, such as on-reservation sales outlets which market to nonmembers goods not manufactured by the tribe or its members, in which the tribal contribution to an enterprise is *de minimis. See Washington v. Confederated Tribes of the Colville Reservation.* The Tribal enterprise in this case clearly involves "value generated on the reservation by activities involving the Trib[e]." *Id.* ***

C.

The State has failed to "identify any regulatory function or service *** that would justify" the assertion of concurrent regulatory authority. *White Mountain Apache v. Bracker.* The hunting and fishing permitted by the Tribe occur entirely on the reservation. The fish and wildlife resources are either native to the reservation or were created by the joint efforts of the Tribe and the Federal Government. New Mexico does not contribute in any significant respect to the maintenance of these resources, and can point to no other "governmental functions it provides," *Ramah Navajo School Board,* in connection with hunting and fishing on the reservation by nonmembers that would justify the assertion of its authority.

The State also cannot point to any off-reservation effects that warrant State intervention. Some species of game never leave tribal lands, and the State points to no specific interest concerning those that occasionally do. Unlike *Puyallup Tribe v. Washington Game Dept.,* this is not a case in which a Treaty expressly subjects a tribe's hunting and fishing rights to the common rights of nonmembers and in which a State's interest in conserving a scarce, common supply justifies State intervention. The State concedes that the Tribe's management has "not had an adverse impact on fish and wildlife outside the reservation." ***

We recognize that New Mexico may be deprived of the sale of state licenses to nonmembers who hunt and fish on the reservation, as well as some federal matching funds calculated in part on the basis of the number of State licenses sold. However, any financial interest the State might have in this case is simply insufficient to justify the assertion of concurrent jurisdiction. The loss of revenues to the State is likely to be insubstantial given the small numbers of persons who purchase tribal hunting licenses. Moreover, unlike *Confederated Tribes, supra,* the activity involved here concerns value generated on the reservation by the tribe. Finally, *** the State has pointed to no services it has performed in connection with hunting and fishing by nonmembers which justify imposing a tax in the form of a hunting and fishing license, *Ramah Navajo School Board,* and its general desire to obtain revenues is simply inadequate to justify the assertion of concurrent jurisdiction in this case. ***

IV.

*** Given the strong interests favoring exclusive tribal jurisdiction and the absence of State interests which justify the assertion of concurrent authority, we conclude that the application of the State's hunting and fishing laws to the reservation is preempted. ***

Affirmed.

NOTES AND QUESTIONS

1. Note that although reservation hunting and fishing were extensively regulated, the source of the regulation was largely tribal ordinances developed with federal encouragement rather than federal law itself. Although the Supreme Court in *Colville* rejected an argument that federal approval of tribal ordinances and taxes on cigarettes sales had a significant preemptive effect, *Mescalero Apache* is a rare unanimous decision rejecting state jurisdiction over non-members. What explains this unanimity? Are overlapping hunting and fishing regulations more overtly unworkable than overlapping taxes? Or is the context of tribally managed natural resources more sympathetic than that of tribal marketing of cigarettes?

2. The White Mountain Apache Tribe has lucrative timber resources. The Mescalero Apache Tribe has an area ripe for development as a tourist resort, not only for hunting and fishing, but also for golf, skiing, and other recreation. What options are there for tribes that do not have natural resources from which to generate on-reservation value for economic development? See the next case.

CALIFORNIA V. CABAZON BAND OF MISSION INDIANS

480 U.S. 202, 107 S. Ct. 1083, 94 L. Ed. 2d 244 (1987)

JUSTICE WHITE delivered the opinion of the Court.

The Cabazon and Morongo Bands of Mission Indians, federally recognized Indian Tribes, occupy reservations in Riverside County, California. Each Band, pursuant to an ordinance approved by the Secretary of the Interior, conducts bingo games on its reservation. The Cabazon Band has also opened a card club at which draw poker and other card games are played. The games are open to the public and are played predominantly by non-Indians coming onto the reservations. The games are a major source of employment for tribal members, and the profits are the Tribes' sole source of income. The State of California seeks to apply to the two Tribes Cal. Penal Code Ann. § 326.5 (West Supp. 1987). That statute does not entirely prohibit the playing of bingo but permits it when the games are operated and staffed by members of designated charitable organizations who may not be paid for their services. Profits must be kept in special accounts and used only for charitable purposes; prizes may not exceed $250 per game. Asserting that the bingo games on the two reservations violated each of these restrictions, California insisted that the Tribes comply with state law. ***

[In a portion of the opinion reprinted earlier in this Chapter, the Court held that Public Law 280 did not authorize California or its counties to apply their gaming laws to tribal gaming operations because the state regulated, rather than prohibited, gambling.]

Because the state and county laws at issue here are imposed directly on the Tribes that operate the games, and are not expressly permitted by Congress, the Tribes argue that the judgment below should be affirmed without more. They rely on the statement in *McClanahan* that " '[s]tate laws generally are not applicable to tribal Indians on an Indian reservation except where Congress has expressly provided that State laws shall apply' " (quoting United States Dept. of the Interior, Federal Indian Law 845 (1958)). Our cases, however, have not established an inflexible *per se* rule precluding state jurisdiction over tribes and tribal members in the absence of express congressional consent.[17] "[U]nder certain circumstances a State may validly assert authority

---

17. In the special area of state taxation of Indian tribes and tribal members, we have adopted a *per se* rule. In *Blackfeet Tribe*, we held that Montana could not tax the Tribe's royalty interests in oil and gas leases issued to non-Indian lessees under the Indian Mineral Leasing Act of 1938. We stated: "In keeping with its plenary authority over Indian affairs, Congress can authorize the imposition of state taxes on Indian tribes and individual Indians. It has not done so often, and the

over the activities of nonmembers on a reservation, and *** in exceptional circumstances a State may assert jurisdiction over the on-reservation activities of tribal members." *Mescalero Apache Tribe*. Both *Moe* and *Colville* are illustrative. In those decisions we held that, in the absence of express congressional permission, a State could require tribal smokeshops on Indian reservations to collect state sales tax from their non-Indian customers. Both cases involved nonmembers entering and purchasing tobacco products on the reservations involved. The State's interest in assuring the collection of sales taxes from non-Indians enjoying the off-reservation services of the State was sufficient to warrant the minimal burden imposed on the tribal smokeshop operators.

This case also involves a state burden on tribal Indians in the context of their dealings with non-Indians since the question is whether the State may prevent the Tribes from making available high stakes bingo games to non-Indians coming from outside the reservations. Decision in this case turns on whether state authority is pre-empted by the operation of federal law; and "[s]tate jurisdiction is pre-empted *** if it interferes or is incompatible with federal and tribal interests reflected in federal law, unless the state interests at stake are sufficient to justify the assertion of state authority." *Mescalero Apache Tribe*. The inquiry is to proceed in light of traditional notions of Indian sovereignty and the congressional goal of Indian self-government, including its "overriding goal" of encouraging tribal self-sufficiency and economic development. *Id.*

These are important federal interests. They were reaffirmed by the President's 1983 Statement on Indian Policy. More specifically, the Department of the Interior, which has the primary responsibility for carrying out the Federal Government's trust obligations to Indian tribes, has sought to implement these policies by promoting tribal bingo enterprises. Under the Indian Financing Act of 1974, 25 U.S.C. § 1451 *et seq.* (1982 ed. and Supp. III), the Secretary of the Interior has made grants and has guaranteed loans for the purpose of constructing bingo facilities. The Department of Housing and Urban Development and the Department of Health and Human Services have also provided financial assistance to develop tribal gaming enterprises. Here, the Secretary of the Interior has approved tribal ordinances establishing and regulating the gaming activities involved. The Secretary has also exercised his authority to review tribal bingo management contracts under 25 U.S.C. § 81, and has issued detailed guidelines governing that review.

These policies and actions, which demonstrate the Government's approval and active promotion of tribal bingo enterprises, are of particular relevance in this case. The Cabazon and Morongo Reservations contain no natural resources which can be exploited. The tribal games at present provide the sole source of revenues for the operation of the tribal governments and the provision of tribal services. They are also the major sources of employment on the reservations. Self-determination and economic development are not within reach if the Tribes cannot raise revenues and provide employment for their members. The Tribes' interests obviously parallel the federal interests.

California seeks to diminish the weight of these seemingly important tribal interests by asserting that the Tribes are merely marketing an

Court consistently has held that it will find the Indians' exemption from state taxes lifted only when Congress has made its intention to do so unmistakably clear." ***

exemption from state gambling laws. In *Colville*, we held that the State could tax cigarettes sold by tribal smokeshops to non-Indians, even though it would eliminate their competitive advantage and substantially reduce revenues used to provide tribal services, because the Tribes had no right "to market an exemption from state taxation to persons who would normally do their business elsewhere." We stated that "[i]t is painfully apparent that the value marketed by the smokeshops to persons coming from outside is not generated on the reservations by activities in which the Tribes have a significant interest." Here, however, the Tribes are not merely importing a product onto the reservations for immediate resale to non-Indians. They have built modern facilities which provide recreational opportunities and ancillary services to their patrons, who do not simply drive onto the reservations, make purchases and depart, but spend extended periods of time there enjoying the services the Tribes provide. The Tribes have a strong incentive to provide comfortable, clean, and attractive facilities and well-run games in order to increase attendance at the games. The tribal bingo enterprises are similar to the resort complex, featuring hunting and fishing, that the Mescalero Apache Tribe operates on its reservation through the "concerted and sustained" management of reservation land and wildlife resources. *Mescalero Apache Tribe.* *** We there rejected the notion that the Tribe is merely marketing an exemption from state hunting and fishing regulations and concluded that New Mexico could not regulate on-reservation fishing and hunting by non-Indians. Similarly, the Cabazon and Morongo Bands are generating value on the reservations through activities in which they have a substantial interest. ***

The sole interest asserted by the State to justify the imposition of its bingo laws on the Tribes is in preventing the infiltration of the tribal games by organized crime. To the extent that the State seeks to prevent any and all bingo games from being played on tribal lands while permitting regulated, off-reservation games, this asserted interest is irrelevant and the state and county laws are pre-empted. Even to the extent that the State and county seek to regulate short of prohibition, the laws are pre-empted. The State insists that the high stakes offered at tribal games are attractive to organized crime, whereas the controlled games authorized under California law are not. This is surely a legitimate concern, but we are unconvinced that it is sufficient to escape the preemptive force of federal and tribal interests apparent in this case. California does not allege any present criminal involvement in the Cabazon and Morongo enterprises, and the Ninth Circuit discerned none. An official of the Department of Justice has expressed some concern about tribal bingo operations, but far from any action being taken evidencing this concern—and surely the Federal Government has the authority to forbid Indian gambling enterprises—the prevailing federal policy continues to support these tribal enterprises, including those of the Tribes involved in this case.

We conclude that the State's interest in preventing the infiltration of the tribal bingo enterprises by organized crime does not justify state regulation of the tribal bingo enterprises in light of the compelling federal and tribal interests supporting them. State regulation would impermissibly infringe on tribal government, and this conclusion applies equally to the county's attempted regulation of the Cabazon card club. [*Affirmed.*]

JUSTICE STEVENS, joined by JUSTICES O'CONNOR and SCALIA, dissenting.

Unless and until Congress exempts Indian-managed gambling from state law and subjects it to federal supervision, I believe that a State may enforce its laws prohibiting high-stakes gambling on Indian reservations within its borders. Congress has not pre-empted California's prohibition against high-stakes bingo games and the Secretary of the Interior plainly has no authority to do so. While gambling provides needed employment and income for Indian tribes, these benefits do not, in my opinion, justify tribal operation of currently unlawful commercial activities. Accepting the majority's reasoning would require exemptions for cockfighting, tattoo parlors, nude dancing, houses of prostitution, and other illegal but profitable enterprises. As the law now stands, I believe tribal entrepreneurs, like others who might derive profits from catering to non-Indian customers, must obey applicable state laws. ***

NOTES AND QUESTIONS

1. *Distinguishing Colville and Cabazon.* In many ways, the smokeshops in *Colville* and the bingo halls in *Cabazon* are similar: both are federally encouraged tribal enterprises marketing an exemption from state law to non-members to provide desperately needed income to their tribes. Tribal and federal interests are thus largely equivalent in both cases. Why are the state taxes permitted in *Colville*, but the state regulations rejected in *Cabazon*? The comments below discuss some ways suggested in the opinion.

   a. *Added Value.* The Court in *Cabazon Band* thought the bingo enterprise derived its value from the reservation and therefore the case was more like *Mescalero Apache Tribe* than like *Colville*. Does the construction and staffing of a bingo hall add more value than the construction and staffing of a tribal smokeshop? Or is it that one involves sales of goods created off-reservation, while the other involves sales of services generated on reservation? Following *Cabazon*, could a tribe that rolled its own cigarettes on reservation sell them tax free? The Winnebago Tribe of Nebraska is now doing just that. *See* http://www.hcidistribution.com (website for tribe's Ho–Chunk Industries local industries).

   b. *State interest.* In *Colville*, the Court found that the state's concern that the sale of the cigarettes on the reservation free of state tax would unfairly undercut the market for off-reservation cigarette sellers was a sufficient state interest to permit the state to tax on-reservation sales. Why isn't the concern about organized crime sufficient to justify California's gambling laws in *Cabazon*? Or is the basic difference that there were no substantial off-reservation gambling businesses threatened by the tribal operations, or that, if there were, the Court was not as concerned about them as the mom and pop convenience stores selling cigarettes imagined in *Colville*?

   c. *Regulation of members versus non-members.* The Court suggests that another difference between the two cases may be that the tax in *Colville* was imposed on non-members of the tribe, while the state gambling laws would have been imposed on the tribe itself. Is that distinction persuasive? In *Colville*, the tribal enterprises had to collect the tax from non-members and comply with relatively complicated reporting requirements in doing so. In *Cabazon*, similarly, application of state law would not have required the tribes to impose the pot limits on their own members, but rather required them to enforce the laws against nonmembers.

d. *Cigarettes versus gambling.* While there are valid differences between the cases, it is hard to avoid the impression that in *Cabazon,* the Court took seriously federal and tribal interests, while in *Colville,* it did not. The ironic result is that economic development through cigarette sales were doomed, but economic development through gaming enterprises (surely more troubling to many states) was not.

2. In *Rice v. Rehner, infra,* the Court permitted state regulation of a tribal member's liquor store within Indian country and California argued that the same reasoning applied in *Cabazon.* The Court rejected the argument, stating that "Congress had never recognized any sovereign tribal interest in regulating liquor traffic and that Congress, historically, had plainly anticipated that the States would exercise concurrent authority to regulate the use and distribution of liquor on Indian reservations. There is no such traditional federal view governing the outcome of this case, since, as we have explained, the current federal policy is to promote precisely what California seeks to prevent." *Cabazon,* 480 U.S. at 220.

3. *Indian Gaming Regulatory Act: Statutory Response to* Cabazon. When *Cabazon* was decided, Congress had already been debating legislation to regulate Indian gaming for years. S. Rep. 100–446 (1988). State pressure in the wake of the decision created the impetus to pass the Indian Gaming Regulatory Act in 1988. Pub. L. 100–497, Oct. 17, 1988, 102 Stat 2467, codified at 25 U.S.C. § 2701 *et seq.* The law divides gaming into three categories, class I, traditional games for minimal value, class II, largely bingo and card games not played against the house, and class III, all other forms of gaming. Class III includes the most profitable forms of gaming, including slot machines, blackjack, roulette, and pari-mutuel horse racing. Tribes may engage in class I gaming on their lands without state or federal regulation. If the state allows class II gaming by any entity within the state, the tribe may engage in class II gaming without state regulation, but with regulation by the federal National Indian Gaming Commission. If the state allows class III gaming by any entity within the state, the state must negotiate a class III gaming compact with the tribe to agree upon the terms on which the tribe can conduct class III gaming on its land. IGRA's rules apply in non-Public Law 280 states as well as Public Law 280 states. Does IGRA's codification of tribal authority to game as stated in *Cabazon* increase tribal authority or increase state authority? *See* § IV, *infra,* for more material on Indian gaming.

***Rice v. Rehner*, 463 U.S. 713, 103 S. Ct. 3291, 77 L. Ed. 2d 961 (1983)**

McClanahan v. Arizona Tax Commission suggested that the relevant "backdrop" in the preemption test was tribal sovereignty and the presumed exclusion of state authority generally, not the history with respect to the particular state activity. *Mescalero Apache* (in which the tribe had acquiesced in state regulation of hunting and fishing until 1977) and *Cabazon* (in which the tribe had not previously engaged in bingo on its lands) confirmed this suggestion. *Rice v. Rehner* took a different approach which, while rare, has troubling implications. Federal statutes provide that liquor may be sold in Indian country so long as the "act or transaction is in conformity both with the laws of the State *** and with an ordinance adopted by the tribe." 18 U.S.C. § 1161. *Rice* concerned whether a liquor vendor in Indian country need only comply with the substantive state liquor laws (*e.g.*, age of purchaser), or must also comply with the state licensing requirements. (Such licenses often are quite expensive; some localities place a ceiling on the number of licenses available, which can make it impossible for a new vendor to be licensed at least unless she purchases an existing license, sometimes at a monopoly price.). The majority of the Court in *Rice* held that a member of a tribe who has a tribal license to sell liquor on her reservation must also have a state license. The opinion could have turned on the meaning to be attributed to § 1161 alone. A portion of the opinion, however, purported to apply Indian law preemption analysis to this problem. After stating that "[t]he role of tribal sovereignty in pre-emption analysis varies in accordance with the particular 'notions of sovereignty that have developed from historical traditions of tribal independence,' " 463 U.S. at 719, the Court found that the " 'backdrop' of tribal sovereignty that will inform our pre-emption analysis" was limited to "the licensing and distribution of alcoholic beverages." *Id.* at 720. The Court found there was no backdrop of sovereignty for this particular activity: congressional actions since 1832 regulated liquor sales in Indian country, and permitting states to prohibit such sales, effectively deflated what would otherwise be the argument for Indian independence from state law. This "bursting bubble" notion of tribal sovereignty has not generally been adopted by other courts but might be one way to explain the decision below.

COTTON PETROLEUM CORPORATION V. NEW MEXICO

490 U.S. 163, 109 S. Ct. 1698, 104 L. Ed. 2d 209 (1989)

JUSTICE STEVENS delivered the opinion of the Court.

This case is a sequel to *Merrion v. Jicarilla Apache Tribe*, 455 U.S. 130 (1982), in which we held that the Jicarilla Apache Tribe (Tribe) has the power to impose a severance tax on the production of oil and gas by non-Indian lessees of wells located on the Tribe's reservation. We must now decide whether the State of New Mexico can continue to impose its severance taxes on the same production of oil and gas.

*** The Indian Mineral Leasing Act of 1938 (1938 Act) grants the Tribe authority, subject to the approval of the Secretary of the Interior (Secretary), to execute mineral leases. *** Mineral leases now encompass a substantial portion of the reservation and constitute the primary source of the Tribe's general operating revenues. [In 1972, the Tribe enacted and the Secretary of the Interior approved an ordinance imposing a severance tax on "any oil and natural gas severed, saved and removed from Tribal lands." In *Merrion*, the Court upheld the tax.] ***

[Cotton Petroleum is a non-Indian company that extracts and markets oil and gas under leases with the tribe entered pursuant to the 1938 Act.] Cotton pays the Tribe's oil and gas severance and privilege taxes, which amount to approximately 6 percent of the value of its production. ***

Prior to 1982, Cotton paid, without objection, five different oil and gas production taxes to the State of New Mexico. The state taxes amount to about 8 percent of the value of Cotton's production. The same 8 percent is collected from producers throughout the State. Thus, on wells outside the reservation, the total tax burden is only 8 percent, while Cotton's reservation wells are taxed at a total rate of 14 percent (8 percent by the State and 6 percent by the Tribe).

[After *Merrion* was issued, Cotton challenged the state taxes.] *** Cotton contended that state taxes imposed on reservation activity are only valid if related to actual expenditures by the State in relation to the activity being taxed. *** In support of this theory, Cotton presented evidence at trial tending to prove that the amount of tax it paid to the State far exceeded the value of services that the State provided to it and that the taxes paid by all nonmember oil producers far exceeded the value of services provided to the reservation as a whole.[6] Cotton did not, however, attempt to prove that the state taxes imposed any burden on the Tribe.

After trial, the Tribe sought, and was granted, leave to file a brief *amicus curiae.* *** The Tribe argued that a decision upholding the state taxes would substantially interfere with the Tribe's ability to raise its own tax rates and would diminish the desirability of on-reservation oil and gas leases. *** [The New Mexico District Court and Court of Appeals upheld the state taxes, and the New Mexico Supreme Court denied certiorari.] We now affirm the judgment of the New Mexico Court of Appeals.

III.

Although determining whether federal legislation has pre-empted state taxation of lessees of Indian land is primarily an exercise in examining congressional intent, the history of tribal sovereignty serves as a necessary "backdrop" to that process. *** As a result, questions of pre-emption in this area are not resolved by reference to standards of pre-emption that have developed in other areas of the law, and are not controlled by "mechanical or absolute conceptions of state or tribal sovereignty." *White Mountain Apache Tribe v. Bracker*. Instead, we have applied a flexible pre-emption analysis sensitive to the particular facts and legislation involved. Each case "requires a particularized examination of the relevant state, federal, and tribal interests." *Ramah Navajo School Board v. Bureau of Revenue of New Mexico*. Moreover, in examining the pre-emptive force of the relevant federal legislation, we are cognizant of both the broad policies that underlie the legislation and the history of tribal independence in the field at issue. It bears emphasis that although congressional silence no longer entails a broad-based immunity from taxation for private parties doing business with Indian tribes, federal pre-emption is not limited to cases in which Congress has expressly—as compared to impliedly—pre-empted the state activity. Finally, we note that although state interests must

6. Cotton's evidence tended to prove that for the tax years 1981–1985 it paid New Mexico $2,293,953, while only receiving the equivalent of $89,384 in services to its operations in return. *See* 745 P.2d at 1173. Cotton's evidence further suggested that over the same period the State received total tax revenues of $47,483,306 from the on-reservation, nonmember oil and gas producers, while only providing $10,704,748 in services to the reservation as a whole. *See ibid.*

be given weight and courts should be careful not to make legislative decisions in the absence of congressional action, ambiguities in federal law are, as a rule, resolved in favor of tribal independence.

Against this background, Cotton argues that the New Mexico taxes are pre-empted by the "federal laws and policies which protect tribal self-government and strengthen impoverished reservation economies." *** Most significantly, Cotton contends that the 1938 Act exhibits a strong federal interest in guaranteeing Indian tribes the maximum return on their oil and gas leases. ***

The 1938 Act neither expressly permits state taxation nor expressly precludes it, but rather simply provides that "unallotted lands within any Indian reservation or lands owned by any tribe *** may, with the approval of the Secretary of the Interior, be leased for mining purposes, by authority of the tribal council *** for terms not to exceed ten years and as long thereafter as minerals are produced in paying quantities." 25 U.S.C. § 396(a). The Senate and House Reports that accompanied the Act, moreover—even when considered in their broadest possible terms—shed little light on congressional intent concerning state taxation of oil and gas produced on leased lands. *** Both Reports reflect that the proposed legislation was suggested by the Secretary and *** simply rely on the Secretary's letter of transmittal to describe the purpose of the Act. That letter contains the following passage:

> *It is not believed that the present law is adequate to give the Indians the greatest return from their property.* As stated, present law provides for locating and taking mineral leases in the same manner as mining locations are made on the public lands of the United States; but there are disadvantages in following this procedure on Indian lands that are not present in applying for a claim on the public domain. [This Act removes those disadvantages.]

Relying on the first sentence in this paragraph, Cotton argues that the 1938 Act embodies a broad congressional policy of maximizing revenues for Indian tribes. Cotton finds support for this proposition in *Montana v. Blackfeet Tribe*, 471 U.S. 759 (1985). That case raised the question whether the 1938 Act authorizes state taxation of a tribe's royalty interests under oil and gas leases issued to nonmembers. Applying the settled rule that a tribe may only be directly taxed by a State if "Congress has made its intention to [lift the tribe's exemption] unmistakably clear," *id.* at 765, we concluded that "the State may not tax Indian royalty income from leases issued pursuant to the 1938 Act," *id.* at 768. In a footnote we added the observation that direct state taxation of Indian revenues would frustrate the 1938 Act's purpose of "ensur[ing] that Indians receive 'the greatest return from their property,'" *Id.* at 767 n.5.

*** We thus agree that a purpose of the 1938 Act is to provide Indian tribes with badly needed revenue, but find no evidence for the further supposition that Congress intended to remove all barriers to profit maximization. ***

More significantly for purposes of this case, when Congress first authorized oil and gas leasing on Executive Order reservations in the 1927 Act, it expressly waived immunity from state taxation of oil and gas lessees operating in those reservations. See 44 Stat. (part 2) 1347, 25 U.S.C. § 398c. *** [Although the 1938 Act, under which Cotton Petroleum's leases were created, did not include this authorization of state taxes, this change is best explained by a change in the case law. Before *Helvering v. Mountain Producers Corp.*, 303 U.S. 376 (1938), the Court had held that states could not tax federal property or tribal property held in trust by the federal government without violating federal rights. In *Helvering*, this approach was overruled, so Congress did not need to expressly authorize state taxation in the 1938 Act.] Thus, at least as to Executive Order reservations, state taxation of nonmember oil and gas lessees was the norm from the very start. There is, accordingly, simply no history of tribal independence from state taxation of these lessees to form a "backdrop" against which the 1938 Act must be read. ***

Cotton nonetheless maintains that our decisions in *White Mountain Apache* and *Ramah Navajo School Bd.*, compel the conclusion that the New Mexico taxes are preempted by federal law. ***

The factual findings of the New Mexico District Court clearly distinguish this case. *** After conducting a trial, that court found that "New Mexico provides substantial services to both the Jicarilla Tribe and Cotton," costing the State approximately $3 million per year. Indeed, Cotton concedes that from 1981 through 1985 New Mexico provided its operations with services costing $89,384, but argues that the cost of these services is disproportionate to the $2,293,953 in taxes the State collected from Cotton. Neither *[White Mountain Apache]* nor *Ramah Navajo School Bd.*, however, imposes such a proportionality requirement on the States. Rather, both cases involved complete abdication or noninvolvement of the State in the on-reservation activity. The present case is also unlike *[White Mountain Apache* and *Ramah Navajo School Bd.*, in that the District Court found that "[n]o economic burden falls on the tribe by virtue of the state taxes," App. to Juris. Statement 15, and that the Tribe could, in fact, increase its taxes without adversely affecting on-reservation oil and gas development, *Id. at* 17. Finally, the District Court found that the State regulates the spacing and mechanical integrity of wells located on the reservation. *Id. at* 16. Thus, although the federal and tribal regulations in this case are extensive, they are not exclusive, as were the regulations in *[White Mountain Apache]* and *Ramah Navajo School Bd.*

We thus conclude that federal law, even when given the most generous construction, does not pre-empt New Mexico's oil and gas severance taxes. This is not a case in which the State has had nothing to do with the on-reservation activity, save tax it. Nor is this a case in which an unusually large state tax has imposed a substantial burden on the Tribe. It is, of course, reasonable to infer that the New Mexico taxes have at least a marginal effect on the demand for on-reservation leases, the value to the Tribe of those leases, and the ability of the Tribe to increase its tax rate. Any impairment to the federal policy favoring the exploitation of on-reservation oil and gas resources by Indian tribes that might be caused by these effects, however, is simply too indirect and too insubstantial to support Cotton's claim of pre-emption. ***

JUSTICE BLACKMUN, with whom **JUSTICE BRENNAN** and **JUSTICE MARSHALL** join, dissenting.

*** The [Indian Mineral Leasing Act of 1938] is silent on the question of state taxation. But, as interpreted by this Court in *Montana v. Blackfeet Tribe*, the silence of the 1938 Act is eloquent and argues forcefully against the result reached by the majority.

In *Montana,* the State sought to tax the Blackfeet Tribe's royalty interests under oil and gas leases held, pursuant to the 1938 Act, by non-Indian lessees operating on the reservation. The State sought to do so despite the fact that the 1938 Act contains no express authorization for *any* state tax on such leases. The State based its claim of taxation authority on a 1924 statute enacted to permit oil and gas leasing on Indian reservations created by treaty. [25 U.S.C. § 398.] The 1924 Act contained a proviso that "the production of oil and gas and other minerals on such lands may be taxed by the State in which said lands are located in all respects the same as production on unrestricted lands, and the Secretary of the Interior is authorized and directed to cause to be paid the tax so assessed against the royalty interests on said lands." The State took the position that the 1938 Congress could not be presumed by mere silence to have abrogated the law permitting state taxation.

In *Montana,* we squarely *rejected* the State's argument. After noting that the 1938 Act was "comprehensive legislation," containing a general repealer of all statutory provisions " 'inconsistent herewith,' " we held that, under the canons of construction applicable to laws governing Indians, the general repealer clause could not be taken as implicitly incorporating consistent provisions of earlier laws. Rather, in the Indian context, clear congressional consent to state taxation was required and, on that point, we found no "indication that Congress intended to incorporate implicitly in the 1938 Act the taxing authority of the 1924 Act." Interpreting the 1938 Act as preserving the taxing authority of the 1924 Act, we held, would not "satisfy the rule requiring that statutes be construed liberally in favor of the Indians." In addition, we observed that such an interpretation would undermine the purposes of the 1938 Act as reflected in its legislative history: to achieve uniformity in tribal leasing, to harmonize tribal leasing with the goals of the [Indian Reorganization Act], and "to ensure that Indians receive 'the greatest return from their property.' "

[T]he clear import of our decision in *Montana* is that Congress' silence in 1938 expressed an intent substantially to narrow state taxing authority.

[The majority now takes the position that the failure to authorize state taxation in the 1938 statute is explained by the change in the jurisprudence regarding taxation of federal property.] The argument that the 1938 congressional silence regarding lessee taxation is consistent with an intent to permit such taxation cannot, for two reasons, withstand close scrutiny. First, even if the majority is correct in seeking the meaning of Congress' silence in changes in this Court's intergovernmental tax immunity jurisprudence, the facts defeat the majority's theory. Second, and fundamentally, the majority's court-centered approach fails to give due weight to a far more significant intervening event: the major change in federal Indian policy embodied in the IRA.

[The bill that became the 1938 Act was first developed in 1935 and 1936, and reached its final form in 1937, well before *Helvering v. Mountain Producers* was decided.] It defies historical sense to make *Mountain Producers* the centerpiece of the interpretation of a statute which reached final form before *Mountain Producers* was decided.

The Court in *Montana* put forward a more sensible explanation of the absence of state taxation authority in the 1938 Act. As the relevant House and Senate Reports explain, the 1938 Act was crafted, proposed, and enacted in light of the recently enacted IRA. The IRA worked a fundamental change in federal Indian law marked by two principal goals: " 'to rehabilitate the Indian's economic life and to give him a chance to develop the initiative destroyed by a century of oppression and paternalism.' " *** H.R. Rep. No. 1804, 73d Cong., 2d Sess., 6 (1934). *** It would be a mistake to impute the political compromises of the allotment period into legislation enacted soon after the passage of the IRA, legislation expressly tailored to bring Indian mineral policy into line with a radically altered set of assumptions about the political and economic future of the Indians. ***

II.

Even if we did not have such direct evidence of Congress' intent to preclude state taxation of non-Indian oil production on Indian lands, that conclusion would be amply supported by a routine application of the traditional tools of Indian pre-emption analysis. ***

Federal regulation of leasing of Indian oil lands "is both comprehensive and pervasive." *Ramah Navajo*. Provisions of the 1938 Act regulate all stages of the process of oil and gas leasing and production on Indian reservations. The auction or bidding process through which leases are acquired is supervised by the Department of the Interior. 25 U.S.C. § 396b. Successful lessees must furnish a bond to secure compliance with lease terms, § 396c, and each lessee's operations are in all respects subject to federal rules and regulations, § 396d. Longstanding regulations promulgated pursuant to the 1938 Act govern the minute details of the bidding process, 25 CFR § 211.3, and give the Secretary of the Interior the power to reject bids that are not in the best interest of the Indian lessor, § 211.3(b). Federal law sets acreage limitations, § 211.9, the term of each lease, § 211.10, and royalty rates, methods, and times of payment, §§ 211.13 and 211.16. Turning to the regulation of the lessee's operations, federal law controls when operations may start, § 211.20, and federal supervisory personnel are empowered to ensure the conservation of resources and prevention of waste, §§ 211.19–211.21. Additional restrictions are placed on lessees by the Federal Oil and Gas Royalty Management Act of 1982. ***

In addition, the Jicarilla Apache, as expressly authorized by their Constitution, have enacted regulations of their own to supplement federal guidelines, and have created a tribal Oil and Gas Administration to exercise tribal authority in this area.[8] ***

The majority acknowledges that federal and tribal regulations in this case are extensive. But because the District Court found that the State regulates spacing and the mechanical integrity of wells, and that federal and tribal regulations are therefore not "exclusive," the majority concludes without further ado that there is sufficient state activity to support the State's claimed authority to tax.[9] The majority's reliance on the proposition that "[t]his is not a case in which the State has had nothing to do with the on-reservation activity, save tax it," *ante*, at 1713, reflects a mechanical and absolutist approach to the delicate issue of pre-emption that this Court expressly has repudiated. *White*

8. Tribal regulation is expressly contemplated by regulations promulgated under the 1938 Act, which specify that certain statutory and regulatory provisions "may be superseded by the provisions" of tribal law enacted pursuant to the IRA. 25 CFR § 211.29.

9. The manner in which a State exercises a regulatory role in the area of well spacing indeed underscores the comprehensiveness of *federal* law in this area: state law applies not of its own force, but only if its application is approved by the Bureau of Land Management. *** *See* 43 CFR §§ 3162.3–1(a) and (b) (1987).

Mountain Apache. "[C]omplete abdication or noninvolvement," *ante,* at 1712, has never been the applicable standard.

*** Just as the majority errs by adopting a standard of "exclusivity," it places undue significance on the fact that the State made some expenditures that benefited Cotton Petroleum's on-reservation activities. Concededly, the State did spend some money on the reservation for purposes directly and indirectly related to oil and gas production. It is clear on this record, however, that the infrastructure which supports oil and gas production on the Jicarilla Apache Reservation is provided almost completely by the federal and tribal governments rather than by the State. Indeed, the majority appears to accept the fact that the state taxes are vastly disproportionate, *ante,* at 1712, as well it must: $89,384 in services, as compared with $2,293,953 in taxes, speaks for itself.[11] *** Under the majority's analysis, insignificant state expenditures, reflecting minimal state interests, are sufficient to support state interference with significant federal and tribal interests. The exclusion of all sense of proportion has led to a result that is antithetical to the concerns that animate our Indian pre-emption jurisprudence.

Finally, the majority sorely underestimates the degree to which state taxation of oil and gas production adversely affects the interests of the Jicarilla Apache. Assuming that the Tribe continues to tax oil and gas production at present levels, on-reservation taxes will remain 75% higher (14% as opposed to 8% of gross value) than off-reservation taxes within the State. *** Therefore, Cotton Petroleum's willingness to drill infill wells does not reflect its willingness to develop new lands. Federal and tribal interests legitimately include long-term planning for development of lease revenues on new lands, where there is greater economic risk, see Tr. 450, and a greater probability that difference in tax rates will have an adverse effect on a producer's willingness to drill new wells and on the competitiveness of Jicarilla leases. ***

I respectfully dissent.

NOTES AND QUESTIONS

1. *Cotton Petroleum* remains the Court's last general word on preemption analysis and state authority to regulate non-Indians in Indian country. Although *Cotton Petroleum* recites the test enunciated by *White Mountain Apache,* does it apply it the way that *White Mountain Apache* or *Cabazon* did? Compare the decision to *Warren Trading Post*—in which case is there a better argument for federal occupation of the field? Does the existence of the 1924 statute authorizing state taxation make the crucial difference? If not, what does?

2. After *Cotton Petroleum,* courts have generally upheld state taxation of non-Indian businesses within Indian country if the state can show any interest in the transactions aside from raising revenue. *See, e.g., Gila River Indian Community v. Waddell,* 91 F.3d 1232, 1238 (9th Cir. 1996) (upholding state taxes on non-Indian concessionaire operating raceway and amphitheater

---

11. The distribution of responsibility is even clearly reflected in the relevant oil-and-gas-related expenditures during the 5–year period at issue in this case: federal expenditures were $1,206,800; tribal expenditures were $736,358; the State spent, at most, $89,384. ***

on tribal lands; state provides a number of governmental functions, *e.g.* police and fire protection, traffic control, critical to the success of entertainment events); *Ute Mountain Ute Tribe v. Rodriguez*, 660 F.3d 1177 (10th Cir. 2011) (upholding New Mexico's tax on non-Indians' severance of oil and gas on Ute Mountain Ute Reservation in New Mexico); *Mashantucket Pequot Tribe v. Town of Ledyard*, 722 F.3d 457, 476 (2d Cir. 2013) (upholding personal property tax on non-Indian lessors of slot machines to tribal casino).

In an effort to tip the balance in favor of federal preemption of state taxation, the Bureau of Indian Affairs promulgated a regulation in the tribal leasing context that provides:

> (a) Subject only to applicable Federal law, permanent improvements on the leased land, without regard to ownership of those improvements, are not subject to any fee, tax, assessment, levy, or other charge imposed by any State or political subdivision of a State. Improvements may be subject to taxation by the Indian tribe with jurisdiction.
>
> (b) Subject only to applicable Federal law, activities under a lease conducted on the leased premises are not subject to any fee, tax, assessment, levy, or other charge (e.g., business use, privilege, public utility, excise, gross revenue taxes) imposed by any State or political subdivision of a State. Activities may be subject to taxation by the Indian tribe with jurisdiction.
>
> (c) Subject only to applicable Federal law, the leasehold or possessory interest is not subject to any fee, tax, assessment, levy, or other charge imposed by any State or political subdivision of a State. Leasehold or possessory interests may be subject to taxation by the Indian tribe with jurisdiction.

25 C.F.R. § 162.017 (2012).

The sweeping language in the new regulation could be read as evincing agency intent to preempt state taxes completely in the covered circumstances. That is not the case. In recent Ninth Circuit litigation the Department of the Interior denied that the regulation has any binding, preemptive effect. The case involved a challenge brought by a water agency that delivers and charges fees for water deliveries to non-Indian lessors of tribal land.

> The only thing § 162.017 does, according to Interior, is to state publicly the agency's interpretation of existing law (namely, *Bracker* [*White Mountain Apache*]), and to clarify its opinion that under *Bracker* [*White Mountain Apache*], the federal and tribal interests at stake are strong enough to have a preemptive effect in the generality of cases. But on the ultimate question of whether any *specific* state tax or charge is preempted under *Bracker* [*White Mountain Apache*], Interior is agnostic; courts must answer such questions in the same way they always have, by applying the *Bracker* [*White Mountain Apache*] test de novo. Interior's views as set out in § 162.017 may well influence courts when they gauge the federal and tribal interests under *Bracker* [*White Mountain Apache*], but Interior does not contend that § 162.017 has any independent legal effect.

Desert Water Agency v. United States Department of the Interior, 849 F.3d 1250, 1254 (9th Cir. 2017).

3. In a portion of the *Cotton* opinion not included above, the Court discussed whether the Commerce Clause prohibited dual state and tribal taxation of the oil and gas severance. Similar double taxation by two states is avoided because, under the Interstate Commerce Clause, state taxes must be apportioned so as to tax only that activity with a substantial nexus to the state. *See Complete Auto Transit, Inc. v. Brady*, 430 U.S. 274, 279 (1977). Even where two states have concurrent jurisdiction to tax an activity, one state will credit the taxes paid to another state to avoid dual taxation, although it has not yet been determined whether this is constitutionally required. So if an individual works in one state but resides in another, both states may legally tax her income, but the home state will generally give credit for income taxes paid to the sister state to avoid an undue burden on interstate commerce.

In *Cotton Petroleum*, however, the Court declined to require states to provide a credit for tribal taxes, holding that it was "treacherous" to import principles from Interstate Commerce jurisprudence into interpretation of the Indian Commerce Clause. 490 U.S. at 192–93. Even if such concepts were applied, the Court opined, the state taxes might not be invalid because the activity took place entirely within both tribal and state borders. To facilitate tax collection and avoid litigation over dual taxation, a number of states and tribes have reached agreements in which some credit is provided for tribal taxes, but dual taxation remains a burden on tribal economic development. *Id.* As one commentator has noted, these sovereign-to-sovereign agreements have been one way in which tribes have advanced their inherent powers despite the limiting backdrop of Supreme Court decisions. *See* Sarah Krakoff, *A Narrative of Sovereignty: Illuminating the Paradox of the Domestic Dependent Nation*, 83 Or. L. Rev. 1109, 1173–74 (2004).

IV. INDIAN GAMING

After the victory in *California v. Cabazon Band of Mission Indians*, *supra*, one might have expected Indian tribes to resist federal legislation that would provide states with a role in regulating Indian gaming. The Johnson Act, 15 U.S.C. § 1175, criminalized possession, manufacture, sale or use of illegal gambling devices in Indian country, so that while tribal casino-style gaming might be immune from state regulation, federal law prohibited the most lucrative types of gaming. Pressure from the states and concerns about the possible influence of organized crime, combined with the need for tribal relief from the Johnson Act, prompted passage of the Indian Gaming Regulatory Act. Congress stated the purposes of the statute:

> **(1)** to provide a statutory basis for the operation of gaming by Indian tribes as a means of promoting tribal economic development, self-sufficiency, and strong tribal governments;
>
> **(2)** to provide a statutory basis for the regulation of gaming by an Indian tribe adequate to shield it from organized crime and other corrupting influences, to ensure that the Indian tribe is the primary beneficiary of the gaming operation, and to assure that gaming is conducted fairly and honestly by both the operator and players; and
>
> **(3)** to declare that the establishment of independent Federal regulatory authority for gaming on Indian lands, the establishment of Federal

> standards for gaming on Indian lands, and the establishment of a National Indian Gaming Commission are necessary to meet congressional concerns regarding gaming and to protect such gaming as a means of generating tribal revenue.

25 U.S.C. § 2702. To effect these purposes Congress adopted a framework that calls for significant federal oversight of tribal gaming, and requires tribal-state compacts for certain tribal gaming activities:

> After lengthy hearings, negotiations and discussions, the Committee concluded that the use of compacts between tribes and states is the best mechanism to assure that the interests of both sovereign entities are met with respect to the regulation of complex gaming enterprises such as pari-mutuel horse and dog racing, casino gaming, jai alai and so forth. The Committee notes the strong concerns of states that state laws and regulations relating to sophisticated forms of class III gaming be respected on Indian lands where, with few exceptions, such laws and regulations do not now apply. The Committee balanced these concerns against the strong tribal opposition to any imposition of State jurisdiction over activities on Indian lands. The Committee concluded that the compact process is a viable mechanism for sett[l]ing various matters between two equal sovereigns.

S. Rep. 100–446 at 13. For tribes that have such compacts, IGRA waives application of the Johnson Act, 15 U.S.C. § 1175. Tribal gaming that does not conform to IGRA's dictates remains illegal "gambling," and may be prosecuted under federal law. 18 U.S.C. § 1166.

For the history of the litigation leading to IGRA's passage and its legislative history, see Kevin K. Washburn, *The Legacy of Bryan v. Itasca County: How an Erroneous $147 County Tax Notice Helped Bring Tribes $200 Billion in Indian Gaming Revenue*, 92 Minn. L. Rev. 919 (2008); and Franklin Ducheneaux, *The Indian Gaming Regulatory Act: Background and Legislative History*, 42 Ariz. St. L. J. (2010) (The entire issue of the law review contains articles regarding Indian gaming issues.).

IGRA divides gaming into three classes, each subject to different levels of tribal, federal, and state regulation. Class I games, which are social games for minimal value and traditional games of chance, are subject to exclusive tribal control. 25 U.S.C. §§ 2703(6) & 2710(a)(1). Class II includes bingo, games like bingo, pull tabs and lotto. 25 U.S.C. § 2703(7)(A)(i). It also includes card games allowed under state law, except games which, like black jack and baccarat, are played against the house. § 2703(A)(ii) & B(i). Class II excludes electronic games of chance and slot machines. § 2703(7)(B)(ii). If a state allows "such gaming for any purpose by any person, organization or entity," tribes may conduct Class II games on their land subject only to regulation by the tribe and the federal National Indian Gaming Commission. 25 U.S.C. § 2710(b).

All other forms of gaming fall into Class III. 25 U.S.C. § 2703(8). A tribe may only engage in Class III gaming in a state if (1) it has eligible trust lands in the state, (2) the state "permits such gaming for any purpose by any person, organization, or entity," 25 U.S.C. § 2710(d)(1)(B), and (3) the gaming is conducted in conformance with a compact with the state. 25 U.S.C. § 2710(d)(1)(B). States, in turn, must "negotiate in good faith" with tribes that request compacts. 25 U.S.C. § 2710(d)(3)(A).

Disputes over interpretation and enforcement of IGRA have led one court to dub the statute a "litigation-spawning juggernaut." *Florida v. Seminole Tribe of Florida*, 181 F.3d 1237, 1239 n.1 (11th Cir. 1999). Some of the important questions under the Act include (1) the scope of gaming requiring state negotiation; (2) what constitutes negotiation and enforcement of the good faith negotiation requirement; and (3) the role of the National Indian Gaming Commission. While some litigation continues, the level has dropped in recent years as more issues have become settled.

A. SCOPE OF GAMING

IGRA states that "Class III gaming activities shall be lawful on Indian lands only if such activities are *** located in a State that permits such gaming for any purpose by any person, organization, or entity." 25 U.S.C. § 2710(d)(1)(B). States typically argue that "such gaming" means the particular kind of Class III game; thus a state that allows roulette or horse racing need not negotiate regarding slot machines. Tribes, on the other hand, argue that because IGRA was influenced by *Cabazon*, which permitted tribes to conduct high stakes bingo and card games in part because the state allowed horse racing and lotteries, a state which permits any Class III games must permit all Class III games.

The Eighth and Ninth Circuits have adopted the narrower definition of the scope of gaming. *See Cheyenne River Sioux Tribe v. South Dakota*, 3 F.3d 273, 277 (8th Cir. 1993) (holding that a state that only permitted video keno need not negotiate regarding regular keno); *Rumsey Indian Rancheria v. Wilson*, 64 F.3d 1250, 1258 (9th Cir. 1994) ("IGRA does not require a state to negotiate over one form of Class III gaming activity simply because it has legalized another, albeit similar form of gaming."). The Second Circuit suggested a less restrictive interpretation, stating that "[t]he compact process is therefore to be invoked unless, applying the *Cabazon* test, it is determined that the state, 'as a matter of criminal law and public policy, prohibit[s] [class III] gaming activity.'" *Mashantucket Pequot Tribe v. Connecticut*, 913 F.2d 1024, 1030 (2d Cir. 1990). Similarly the district court of Wisconsin held that "[t]he initial question in determining whether Wisconsin 'permits' the gaming activities at issue is not whether the state has given express approval to the playing of a particular game, but whether Wisconsin's public policy toward class III gaming is prohibitory or regulatory." *Lac du Flambeau Band of Lake Superior Chippewa Indians v. Wisconsin*, 770 F. Supp. 480, 486 (W.D. Wisc. 1991).

In *Mashantucket Pequot*, the court concluded that the state was required to negotiate regarding Class III gaming because Connecticut law allowed charities to conduct "Las Vegas Nights," and permitted "other forms of gambling such as state-operated lottery, bingo, jai alai and other forms of pari-mutuel betting." *Mashantucket Pequot Tribe*, 913 F.2d at 1031–1032; *see also Northern Arapaho Tribe v. Wyoming*, 389 F.3d 1308, 1310 (10th Cir. 2004), *precedential value restricted by* 429 F.3d 934 (10th Cir. 2005) (a state which permits the full range of casino style games for social and charitable purposes must negotiate regarding all Class III gaming). Connecticut subsequently entered into compacts with the Mashantucket Pequot and Mohegan tribes. In 2003, seeking to avoid an obligation to negotiate compacts with tribes then petitioning for federal acknowledgment, the state repealed the authorization for charities to conduct Las Vegas nights. 2003 Conn. Pub. Acts (Jan. 6 Spec. Sess.) 03–1. Read the relevant language in IGRA; what problems arise if Connecticut seeks to use the repeal to avoid negotiations with tribes acknowledged in the future?

The Department of the Interior, which has responsibility for enforcing the obligation to negotiate when states refuse to negotiate in good faith and assert immunity from suit, *see* 25 C.F. R. § 291, has taken a middle ground, stating that "[t]he relevant question" in determining a "scope of gaming" issue "would be whether, in light of traditional understandings and the text and legislative history of IGRA, the State has reasonably characterized the relevant State laws as completely prohibiting a distinct form of gaming. If the State has not reasonably so characterized its laws, it would have a duty to negotiate with respect to the gaming." 63 Fed. Reg. 3289, 3293 (Jan. 22, 1998). The federal position is closely aligned with that of the Ninth Circuit as set forth in *Rumsey, supra*. Consider the views of Judge William Canby, Jr., who dissented from the court's denial of rehearing *en banc*.

RUMSEY INDIAN RANCHERIA OF WINTUN INDIANS V. WILSON

64 F.3d 1250 (9th Cir. 1994)

O' SCANNLAIN, CIRCUIT JUDGE.

***

IGRA does not require a state to negotiate over one form of Class III gaming activity simply because it has legalized another, albeit similar form of gaming. Instead, the statute says only that, if a state allows a gaming activity "for any purpose by any person, organization, or entity," then it also must allow Indian tribes to engage in that same activity. 25 U.S.C. § 2710(d)(1)(B). In other words, a state need only allow Indian tribes to operate games that others can operate, but need not give tribes what others cannot have.

***

CANBY, CIRCUIT JUDGE, joined by **PREGERSON, REINHARDT**, and **HAWKINS, CIRCUIT JUDGES**, dissenting from the denial of rehearing *en banc*:

This is a case of major significance in the administration of the Indian Gaming Regulatory Act ("IGRA") and it has been decided incorrectly, in a manner that conflicts with the Second Circuit's interpretation of the same statutory language. The result is to frustrate the scheme of state-tribal negotiation that Congress established in IGRA. We should have granted rehearing *en banc* to prevent the near-nullification of IGRA in a circuit that encompasses a great portion of the nation's Indian country. Our failure to do so may close the only route open to many tribes to escape a century of poverty.

Rumsey holds that California, which permits several varieties of Class III gambling, has no duty under IGRA to negotiate with the tribes over the tribes' ability to conduct any game that is illegal under California law. This ruling effectively frustrates IGRA's entire plan governing Class III Indian gaming. The primary purpose of IGRA, as set forth in the Act, is "to provide a statutory basis for the operation of gaming by Indian tribes as a means of promoting tribal economic development, self-sufficiency, and strong tribal governments." 25 U.S.C. § 2702(1). IGRA's otherwise drastic extension of state gaming law to Indian country (to be enforced only by the federal government) was modified by IGRA's process by which the states and tribes could arrive at compacts specifying what games might be allowed and who might have jurisdiction to enforce gaming laws. *See* 25 U.S.C. § 2710(d)(3); 18 U.S.C. § 1166(c)(2) (exempting Class III gaming conducted pursuant to a tribal-state compact from the application of state gaming laws extended into Indian country by § 1166(a)). The whole idea was to foster these compacts. That goal is defeated if the details of the state's regulatory schemes, allowing some games and prohibiting others, apply if the state does nothing. Thus the Second Circuit, in arriving at a conclusion precisely opposite to that of *Rumsey,* stated:

> Under the State's approach, *** even where a state does not prohibit class III gaming as a matter of criminal law and public policy, an Indian tribe could nonetheless conduct such gaming only in accord with, and by acceptance of, the entire state corpus of laws and regulations governing such gaming. The compact process that Congress established as the centerpiece of the IGRA's regulation of class III gaming would thus become a dead letter; there would be nothing to negotiate, and no meaningful compact would be possible.

Mashantucket Pequot Tribe v. Connecticut, 913 F.2d 1024, 1030–31 (2d Cir. 1990).

The Second Circuit's fears of turning IGRA's compact process into a dead letter are well-founded. It is well to keep in mind that the issue here is not whether California must allow every game the tribes want to conduct; it is merely whether California has a duty to negotiate with the tribes to determine what games should be conducted, on what scale, and who has jurisdiction to enforce gaming laws. In passing IGRA, Congress knew that states and tribes both had important interests at stake. If a state has a genuine prohibitory public policy against all Class III gaming, as some states do, it can rest on that policy and not entertain the possibility of Indian Class III gaming within its borders. States like California that have no such wholesale public policy against Class III gaming must, under IGRA, reach an accommodation between their interests and the strong interests of the tribes in conducting such gaming. IGRA's method of reaching such an accommodation is by negotiation between the two affected groups. IGRA imposes on the states a duty to negotiate compacts in good faith. That duty is enforceable in federal court with the aid, if necessary, of a court appointed mediator to arrive at a compact and the Secretary of the Interior to dictate a compact if the parties do not accept the mediator's ruling. 25 U.S.C. § 2710(d)(7). But under *Rumsey,* this whole process is nipped in the bud if the tribe seeks to operate games that state law, criminal *or* regulatory, happens to prohibit. The state has no duty to begin negotiations, even though under IGRA a compact may permit the tribe to operate games that state law otherwise prohibits. 18 U.S.C. § 1166(c)(2). The State thus has no incentive to negotiate, and there is no system to require negotiation. IGRA is rendered toothless.

Such a nullifying interpretation of IGRA might be understandable if it were required by the plain words of the statute, but it is not. *Rumsey* defeats the congressional plan for Class III gaming by a manifestly flawed interpretation of the statutory language. ***

The only natural reading of section 2710(d)(1)(B) is that, when Congress says "Class III gaming activities shall be lawful *** if located in a State that permits such gaming," then "such gaming" refers back to the category of "Class

III gaming," which is the next prior use of the word "gaming." *Rumsey* interprets the statutory language as if it said: "A Class III game shall be lawful *** if located in a State that permits that game." But that is not what Congress said, and it is not a natural reading of the statutory language. The plain language cuts directly against *Rumsey;* Congress allows a tribe to conduct Class III gaming activities (pursuant to a compact) if the State allows Class III gaming by anyone.

Furthermore, Class II gaming is governed by virtually identical language in section 2710(b)(1)(A). A tribe may conduct and regulate "*Class II gaming* *** if such Indian gaming is located within a State that *permits such gaming* for any purpose by any person, organization or entity ***." 25 U.S.C. § 2710(b)(1)(A) (emphasis added). We have held that the state cannot allow or disallow Class II Indian gaming game-by-game. *Sycuan Band of Mission Indians v. Miller,* 54 F.3d 535 (9th Cir. 1995) (amended opinion). Our decision in *Sycuan Band* followed the reasoning of the Supreme Court in *California v. Cabazon Band of Mission Indians,* 480 U.S. 202 (1987), the seminal Indian gaming case that ultimately led to the passage of IGRA. In deciding for purposes of Public Law 280 whether California's prohibition of high-stakes bingo could be enforced against the Band, the Supreme Court noted that "[t]he shorthand test is whether the conduct at issue violates the State's public policy." After reviewing California's treatment of gambling, the Court stated:

> In light of the fact that California permits a substantial amount of gambling activity, including bingo, and actually promotes gambling through its state lottery, we must conclude that California regulates rather than prohibits *gambling in general* and bingo in particular.

Id. at 211 (emphasis added). Thus, *Cabazon Band* ascertained California's public policy at a level of generality far above that of the individual game in issue, and concluded that the Band could conduct high-stakes bingo even though California made that activity a misdemeanor. We applied a similarly broad and categorical approach to Class II gaming in *Sycuan Band.*

The *Rumsey* opinion refuses to apply the reasoning of *Cabazon Band* and *Sycuan Band,* and instead holds that a class-wide, categorical approach is precluded by the "unambiguous" plain words of section 2710(d)(1)(B), even though identical words in section 2710(b)(1)(A) require a contrary result for Class II gaming. The majority in *Rumsey* justifies its interpretation by referring to the Senate Committee Report on IGRA, which approves the approach of *Cabazon Band* for Class II gaming but says nothing about *Cabazon Band*'s applicability to Class III gaming. *See* Sen. Rep. No. 100–446, 1988 U.S.C.C.A.N. 3071, 3076. But we should not read a congressional negative into a committee report's failure to mention *Cabazon Band* in regard to Class III gaming. *Cabazon Band* dealt with games that IGRA placed in Class II, and that is explanation enough why the discussion of *Cabazon Band* in the Committee's report arose only in connection with Class II gaming. The fact remains that Congress wrote provisions of essentially identical wording and structure to govern both Class II and Class III gaming. We should give them both the same categorical meaning.

NOTES AND QUESTIONS

1. *The Tribal Response in California.* As a result of the *Rumsey* decision, California was not obliged to negotiate with Indian tribes over the most lucrative types of Class III gaming. After a proposition requiring the State to enter into Tribal–State compacts authorizing slot machine and banking and percentage card games was held unconstitutional, California voters ratified Proposition 1A, amending the California Constitution to provide:

> Notwithstanding *** any other provision of state law, the Governor is authorized to negotiate and conclude compacts, subject to ratification by the Legislature, for the operation of slot machines and for the conduct of lottery games and banking and percentage card games by federally recognized Indian tribes on Indian lands in California in accordance with federal law. Accordingly, slot machines, lottery games, and banking and percentage card games are hereby permitted to be conducted and operated on tribal lands subject to those compacts.

Cal. Const. art. IV, § 19(f). The monopoly thus provided for Indian gaming was upheld over a federal equal protection challenge in *Artichoke Joe's California Grand Casino v. Norton*, 353 F.3d 712 (9th Cir. 2003).

2. *Negotiation and Approval of Compacts.* The California Constitution expressly provides that the Governor may negotiate compacts, but subject to ratification by the legislature. What if state law is unclear as to the role of the legislature, but the Governor unilaterally asserts the authority to negotiate compacts without legislative approval? IGRA simply provides that the Secretary of the Interior "is authorized to approve any Tribal–State compact entered into between an Indian tribe and a State governing gaming on Indian lands of such Indian tribe." 25 U.S.C. § 2710(d)(8)(a).

The Governor of New Mexico in 1995 negotiated and signed fourteen compacts with New Mexico Pueblos and Tribes, which were approved by the Secretary of the Interior. The New Mexico Supreme Court subsequently declared that the Governor did not have the authority to enter into binding compacts without legislative authorization. *State ex. rel. Clark v. Johnson,* 904 P.2d 11 (N.M. 1995). The Tribes brought an action in federal court seeking a declaration that once the Secretary approved the compacts they became effective as a matter of federal law and remained as such notwithstanding the Supreme Court's ruling. In *Pueblo of Santa Ana v. Kelly*, 104 F.3d 1546 (10th Cir. 1997), the court ruled that state law governed the determination of authority to enter into a compact and the Secretary's approval could not make the compacts effective. *See also Florida House of Representatives v. Crist*, 990 So.2d 1035 (Fla. 2008) holding that governor lacked the authority to execute a gaming compact without state legislative action). Other cases have held that the governor had authority to enter into compacts without full legislative approval. *See Dewberry v. Kulongoski*, 406 F.Supp.2d 1136 (D. Or. 2005) (holding that governor had authority to enter into compacts based on provision authorizing governor to "transact all necessary business" on behalf of the state); *Langley v. Edwards,* 872 F. Supp. 1531, 1535 (W.D. La.1995) ("Compact approval by the Secretary cannot be invalidated on the basis of a governor's *ultra vires* action, because a contrary rule would compel the Secretary to consider state law before approving any compact."), *aff'd on other grounds,* 77 F.3d 479 (5th Cir. 1996); *Taxpayers of Michigan Against Casinos v. State,* 471 Mich. 306, 316–317, 685 N.W.2d

221, 225–226 (2004) (holding that gaming compacts did not comprise state legislation, but were instead compacts between sovereigns imposing obligations on tribes and amending application of federal law, and so did not need to be enacted through the regular legislative process).

B. NEGOTIATION IN GOOD FAITH

Simply refusing to negotiate with an eligible tribe would clearly violate the obligation to negotiate in good faith. *Mashantucket Pequot Tribe*, 913 F.2d at 1032. But what if a state demands that the compact include terms that the tribe refuses? The threshold question in analyzing a breakdown of negotiations is whether the state's proposed compact terms are authorized by IGRA. IGRA provides that

> (3)(C) Any Tribal–State compact negotiated under subparagraph (A) may include provisions relating to—
>
> (i) the application of the criminal and civil laws and regulations of the Indian tribe or the State that are directly related to, and necessary for, the licensing and regulation of such activity;
>
> (ii) the allocation of criminal and civil jurisdiction between the State and the Indian tribe necessary for the enforcement of such laws and regulations;
>
> (iii) the assessment by the State of such activities in such amounts as are necessary to defray the costs of regulating such activity;
>
> (iv) taxation by the Indian tribe of such activity in amounts comparable to amounts assessed by the State for comparable activities;
>
> (v) remedies for breach of contract;
>
> (vi) standards for the operation of such activity and maintenance of the gaming facility, including licensing; and
>
> (vii) any other subjects that are directly related to the operation of gaming activities.
>
> (4) Except for any assessments that may be agreed to under paragraph (3)(C)(iii) of this subsection, nothing in this section shall be interpreted as conferring upon a State or any of its political subdivisions authority to impose any tax, fee, charge, or other assessment upon an Indian tribe or upon any other person or entity authorized by an Indian tribe to engage in a class III activity. No State may refuse to enter into the negotiations described in paragraph (3)(A) based upon the lack of authority in such State, or its political subdivisions, to impose such a tax, fee, charge, or other assessment.

25 U.S.C. § 2710(3)(C)–2710(4).

Tribal-state compacts typically agree on such things as standards for liquor sales, kinds of games authorized, licensing of dealers, inspection and testing of gaming machines, and allocation of tribal and state authority to enforce these standards. They also often agree on payments to the state and local governments to cover their costs in regulating the activity. Questions have arisen regarding what other subjects are "directly related to the operation of gaming activities." One court has upheld durational limits in tribal-state compacts, finding them to be within the permissible range of items included in a compact. *Chemehuevi Indian Tribe v. Newsom*, 919 F.3d 1148, 1154 (9th Cir. 2019) ("[T]he State is correct that IGRA's plain language permits durational limits on compacts under the catch-all provision of 25 U.S.C. § 2710(d)(3)(C)(vii).").

IN RE INDIAN GAMING RELATED CASES

331 F.3d 1094 (9th Cir. 2003)

WILLIAM A. FLETCHER, CIRCUIT JUDGE.

The Coyote Valley Band of Pomo Indians ("Coyote Valley") contends that the State of California ("the State") has refused to negotiate in good faith with the tribe to conclude a Tribal–State compact, as required by the Indian Gaming Regulatory Act ("IGRA"), 25 U.S.C. § 2710(d)(3)(A), and moved in the district court for an order that would require it to do so, 25 U.S.C. § 2710(d)(7)(B)(iii). In a carefully considered decision, the district court denied the motion and entered judgment for the State. We agree with the district court that the State has negotiated in good faith within the meaning of IGRA. We therefore *AFFIRM*.

***

IGRA makes class III gaming lawful on Indian lands only if such activities are: (1) authorized by an ordinance or resolution adopted by the governing body of the Indian tribe and the Chairman of the National Indian Gaming Commission;[5] (2) located in a State that permits such gaming for any purpose by any person, organization, or entity; and (3) conducted in conformance with a Tribal–State compact entered into by the Indian tribe and the State and approved by the Secretary of the Interior. 25 U.S.C. § 2710(d)(1), (3)(B). *** [The court recounted the tortured history of Indian gaming in California, which culminated with the adoption of a model compact agreed to by 57 tribes, but not the Coyote Band of Pomo Indians.]

The core of the negotiated compact (the "Davis Compact") is that the State granted the tribes the exclusive right to conduct lucrative Las Vegas-style class III gaming, free from non-tribal competition in the State. In return, the tribes agreed to a number of restrictions and obligations concerning their gaming enterprises. Specifically, the tribes agreed to three provisions that Coyote Valley contends in this suit are impermissible and whose inclusion in the ultimate compact demonstrates the bad faith of the State. These challenged provisions are: (1) the Revenue Sharing Trust Fund provision; (2) the Special Distribution Fund provision; and (3) the Labor Relations provision.

The Revenue Sharing Trust Fund: The preamble to the Davis Compact recites that the "State has an interest in promoting the purposes of IGRA for all federally-recognized Indian tribes in California, whether gaming or non-

---

5. The Commission is a federal regulatory agency created by IGRA that oversees the business of Indian gaming in order to ensure its lasting integrity. It performs a variety of functions, such as the review of management contracts that tribes enter with outside parties to run tribal casinos. *See* 25 U.S.C. § 2704.

gaming." In furtherance of this interest, Section 4.3.2.1 of the compact creates a Revenue Sharing Trust Fund (the "RSTF") that grants a maximum of $1.1 million dollars to each of the State's non-gaming tribes each year. [The RSTF is funded by fees imposed per slot machine operated by gaming tribes above a certain number.] *** According to the State, the purpose of the progressive fee structure is to ensure that tribes with the largest, and therefore most lucrative, gaming establishments will pay a relatively greater share in supporting other California tribes in return for the right to operate additional licensed machines. The progressive fee structure also assists in achieving the State's objective of limiting the expansion of gaming facilities.

The Special Distribution Fund: The preamble to the compact also recites that the

> exclusive rights that Indian tribes in California[ ] will enjoy under this Compact create a unique opportunity for the Tribe to operate its Gaming Facility in an economic environment free of competition from the Class III gaming referred to in Section 4.0 of this Compact on non-Indian lands in California. The parties are mindful that this unique environment is of great economic value to the Tribe and the fact that income from Gaming Devices represents a substantial portion of the tribes' gaming revenues. In consideration for the exclusive rights enjoyed by the tribes, and in further consideration for the State's willingness to enter into this Compact, the tribes have agreed to provide the State, on a sovereign-to-sovereign basis, a portion of its revenue from Gaming Devices.

Pursuant to this part of the preamble, the compact provides in Section 5 for the creation of a Special Distribution Fund ("SDF"), to be financed out of the tribes' net win from the operation of their gaming devices. ***

The Labor Relations Provision: Section 10.7 of the compact provides that it

> shall be null and void if, on or before October 13, 1999, the Tribe has not provided an agreement or other procedure acceptable to the State for addressing organizational and representational rights of Class III Gaming Employees and other employees associated with the Tribe's Class III gaming enterprise, such as food and beverage, housekeeping, cleaning, bell and door services, and laundry employees at the Gaming Facility or any related facility, the only significant purpose of which is to facilitate patronage at the Gaming Facility.

Between late July and September 1999, California tribes conducted independent negotiations with labor representatives and agreed on a model Tribal Labor Relations Ordinance (the "TLRO") that meets the requirements of Section 10.7. The TLRO provides limited organizational rights to workers at tribal gaming establishments and related facilities that employ 250 or more employees. These rights include union access to eligible employees in break rooms and locker rooms during non-work time, as well as the right to engage in collective bargaining if the union becomes the exclusive collective bargaining representative by winning an election. The TLRO also contains several provisions that protect tribal interests. For example, it guarantees tribal gaming establishments the right to grant employment preferences to Native Americans, places strict limits upon a union's right to strike, and completely prohibits picketing on Indian lands.

Coyote Valley initially signed a letter of intent stating that it accepted the Davis Compact, including the three just described provisions it now challenges. However, when the time came actually to execute the compact, Coyote Valley refused. In a letter dated October 13, 1999, Coyote Valley informed the State that before it would agree to sign, it needed to meet with State representatives to discuss "various issues and concerns" regarding certain provisions in the Davis Compact. The State replied in a letter dated October 18, 1999. The State did not respond to the tribe's request for a meeting, but instead emphasized the numerous negotiating opportunities the tribe had had, and highlighted the fact that the tribe had already signed a letter of intent to enter the Davis Compact. The tribe responded by letter on October 20, again requesting a meeting with the State on an individual tribal basis to discuss its concerns. The State replied on October 25, asking that Coyote Valley submit in writing any proposed changes or modifications to the Davis Compact for consideration.

Coyote Valley submitted its proposed changes to the State on November 12. In addition to several other modifications, the tribe sought: (1) the complete elimination of the RSTF provision; (2) a limitation of its obligation to contribute to the SDF to only those amounts necessary to reimburse the costs to the State of regulating activities at Coyote Valley's gaming facility; and (3) the complete elimination of the Labor Relations provision. In an accompanying cover letter, Coyote Valley indicated that it was only proposing changes "to the provisions of the Compact that it views as irreconcilable with IGRA." The tribe also indicated that it was putting into place its own "Tribal Employees Rights Ordinance" (rather than the TLRO) to address the rights of its class III gaming employees, and that it would forward the document to the State shortly.

The State replied on December 8, rejecting all of Coyote Valley's proposed modifications. The State specifically indicated that the tribe must adopt a labor ordinance identical to the TLRO in order for that ordinance to be acceptable to the State under Section 10.7 of the Davis Compact. The State indicated that it would be willing to meet with the tribe's representative to discuss the State's position and to allow the tribe an opportunity to discuss its position. No such meeting ever occurred.

***

II. Discussion

A

IGRA provides that, in determining whether a State has negotiated in good faith, a court:

> (I) may take into account the public interest, public safety, criminality, financial integrity, and adverse economic impacts on existing gaming activities, and
>
> (II) shall consider any demand by the State for direct taxation of the Indian tribe or of any Indian lands as evidence that the State has not negotiated in good faith.

25 U.S.C. § 2710(d)(7)(B)(iii). "[U]pon the introduction of evidence by an Indian tribe that *** the State *** did not respond to [the request of the Indian tribe to negotiate a compact] in good faith, the burden of proof shall be upon the State to prove that the State has negotiated with the Indian tribe in good faith

to conclude a Tribal–State compact governing the conduct of gaming activities." 25 U.S.C. § 2710(d)(7)(B)(ii). ***

B

Coyote Valley makes two kinds of arguments. The first is procedural. The tribe contends that the State's conduct during negotiations—specifically its dilatory tactics over the course of a seven-year period—constitutes bad faith. The second is substantive. The tribe contends that the RSTF, SDF, and Labor Relations provisions of the Davis Compact fall outside the list of appropriate topics for Tribal–State compacts set forth in 25 U.S.C. § 2710(d)(3)(C), and that the State therefore acted with "*per se* bad faith" when it demanded that these provisions be included in any compact it entered with the tribe. The tribe also contends that the State's insistence on the RSTF and SDF provisions constitutes a "demand by the State for direct taxation of the Indian tribe," giving rise to a statutory presumption that the State has not negotiated in good faith. 25 U.S.C. § 2710(d)(7)(B)(iii)(II).

1. Procedural Objections

We cannot conclude from the history of negotiations recounted above that, as a procedural matter, the State has refused to negotiate in good faith. ***

On the record before us, it appears that the Davis Administration has actively negotiated with Indians tribes, including Coyote Valley, concerning class III gaming, and that it has negotiated despite the absence of any legal obligation to do so. Until Proposition 1A was ratified in March of 2000, the State had no obligation to negotiate with Coyote Valley over the types of class III games covered in the Davis Compact. *See Rumsey,* 64 F.3d 1250 (holding that the phrase "such gaming" in IGRA does not include all class III gaming). Moreover, at the time Coyote Valley filed its amended complaint with the district court, alleging bad faith by the Wilson and Davis Administrations, the State remained willing to meet with the tribe for further discussions. To the extent that Coyote Valley may have a valid objection to negotiations by the Davis Administration, it is not an objection to the timing and procedures of those negotiations. It is, rather, an objection to the substance of the three provisions of the Davis Compact to which Coyote Valley specifically objects.

2. Substantive Objections

We do not believe that the three challenged provisions are categorically forbidden by the terms of IGRA. Nor do we believe on the facts of this case that the State's insistence on their inclusion in the compact demonstrates a lack of good faith.

a. The Revenue Sharing Trust Fund

Coyote Valley first argues that the Revenue Sharing Trust Fund, which requires that gaming tribes share gaming revenues with non-gaming tribes, is impermissible under IGRA. Coyote Valley takes the position that except for "assessment[s] by the State [ ] in such amounts as are necessary to defray the costs of regulating" tribal gaming activities, 25 U.S.C. § 2710(d)(3)(C)(iii), a provision in a Tribal–State compact requiring that the tribe pay a "tax, fee, charge, or other assessment" to the State or a third party is categorically prohibited, *id.* § 2710(d)(4). The tribe relies on § 2710(d)(4) and § 2710(d)(7)(B)(iii)(II), and emphasizes Congress's concern that States would use the negotiation process as a means of extracting forbidden taxes from tribes. *See Oklahoma Tax Comm'n v. Chickasaw Nation,* 515 U.S. 450, 458, 115 S. Ct. 2214, 132 L.Ed.2d 400 (1995) (explaining that absent express Congressional permission, a State is without power to tax reservation lands and reservation Indians). Because the RSTF provision requires payments from compacting tribes that go beyond amounts necessary to defray the costs incurred by the State in regulating class III gaming, Coyote Valley contends that the provision cannot properly be included in a Tribal–State compact. By insisting that this forbidden provision be included in the compact, the tribe argues, the State failed to negotiate in good faith.

As explained more fully below, we hold that § 2710(d)(3)(C)(vii) authorizes the RSTF provision and that the State did not lack good faith when it insisted that Coyote Valley adopt it as a precondition to entering a Tribal–State compact. In so holding, we do not interpret IGRA as "conferring upon a State or any of its political subdivisions *authority to impose* any tax, fee, charge or other assessment upon an Indian tribe." 25 U.S.C. § 2710(d)(4) (emphasis added). Given that the State offered meaningful concessions in return for its demands, it did not "impose" the RSTF within the meaning of § 2710(d)(4). To the extent that the State's insistence on the RSTF provision constitutes a "demand by the State for direct taxation of the Indian tribe," *id.* § 2710(d)(7)(B)(iii)(II), which we do not decide, the State has successfully rebutted any inference of bad faith created thereby.

Section 2710(d)(3)(C)(vii) explicitly provides that a "Tribal–State compact *** may include provisions relating to *** subjects that are directly related to the operation of gaming activities." It is clear that the RSTF provision falls within the scope of paragraph (3)(C)(vii). Congress sought through IGRA to "promot[e] tribal economic development, self-sufficiency, and strong tribal governments." *Id.* § 2702(1). The RSTF provision advances this Congressional goal by creating a mechanism whereby *all* of California's tribes—not just those fortunate enough to have land located in populous or accessible areas—can benefit from class III gaming activities in the State. *See* Washburn, 1 Wyo. L. Rev. at 435 ("Not surprisingly, the most successful gaming operations are located in close proximity to large urban areas. A handful of tribes blessed by geography and demographics have been fabulously successful. The poorest of tribes have remained the poorest communities in the United States."). Moreover, the provision accomplishes this in a manner directly related to the operation of gaming activities.

Coyote Valley asks us to read § 2710(d)(3)(C)(vii) narrowly and to hold that it does not encompass a provision like the RSTF. The tribe invokes the Senate Committee's statement that we should "interpret any ambiguities on these issues in a manner that will be most favorable to tribal interests." S. Rep. No. 100–446, at 15 (1988), *reprinted in* 1988 U.S.C.C.A.N. 3071, 3085. Even with the assistance of this language from the legislative history, we do not agree with Coyote Valley's reading of paragraph (3)(C)(vii). First, we believe that the paragraph is not ambiguous and that the RSTF provision clearly falls within its scope. Second, we do not believe that Coyote Valley's preferred reading of paragraph (3)(C)(vii) as forbidding revenue-sharing with non-gaming tribes is the interpretation "most favorable to tribal interests." *See* Koenig, 36 U.S.F. L. Rev. at 1035 ("For tribes that have not elected to take part in gaming, or whose lands are too far from urban centers to make gaming feasible, revenue sharing agreements have reduced dependence on welfare, and produced critical income to ensure basic provisions for tribal members."). Third, it is clear from the legislative history that by limiting the proper topics for compact negotiations to those that bear a direct relationship to the operation of gaming activities, Congress intended to prevent compacts from being used as subterfuge for imposing State jurisdiction on tribes concerning issues unrelated to gaming. *See* S. Rep. No. 100–446, at 14 (1988), *reprinted in* 1988 U.S.C.C.A.N. 3071, 3084. In advocating the inclusion of the RSTF, the State has not sought to engage in such a subterfuge.

***

We do not hold that the State could have, *without offering anything in return,* taken the position that it would conclude a Tribal–State compact with Coyote Valley only if the tribe agreed to pay into the RSTF. Where, as here, however, a State offers meaningful concessions in return for fee demands, it does not exercise "authority to impose" anything. Instead, it exercises its authority to negotiate, which IGRA clearly permits. *See* S. Rep. No. 100–446, at 13 (1988), *reprinted in* 1988 U.S.C.C.A.N. 3071, 3083 (describing the compacting process as a "viable mechanism for setting various matters between two equal sovereigns"). Depending on the nature of both the fees demanded and the concessions offered in return, such demands might, of course, amount to an attempt to "impose" a fee, and therefore amount to bad faith on the part of a State. If, however, offered concessions by a State are real, § 2710(d)(4) does not categorically prohibit fee demands. Instead, courts should consider the totality of that State's actions when engaging in the fact-specific good-faith inquiry IGRA generally requires. *See* 25 U.S.C. § 2710(d)(7)(B)(iii).

In this case, Coyote Valley cannot seriously contend that the State offered no real concessions in return for its insistence on the RSTF provision. Under our holding in *Rumsey,* the State had no obligation to enter any negotiations at all with Coyote Valley concerning most forms of class III gaming. Nor did the State have any obligation to amend its constitution to grant a monopoly to tribal gaming establishments or to offer tribes the right to operate Las Vegas-style slot machines and house-banked blackjack. As part of its negotiations with the tribes, the State offered to do both things. We therefore reject the tribe's challenge to the RSTF premised on § 2710(d)(4).

***

Given that the State offered significant concessions to tribes during the course of negotiations in return for the RSTF provision, that the provision originated in proposals by the tribes and now has strong support among the tribes, and that Coyote Valley was not excluded from the negotiations that shaped the RSTF provision, we hold that the State did not act in bad faith by refusing to enter a compact with Coyote Valley that did not include this provision.

b. The Special Distribution Fund

Unlike contributions to the RSTF, money that goes into the Special Distribution Fund *does* go into the pocket of the State. But it does not go into just any pocket. Although at the outset of compact negotiations with the UTCSC the State sought unrestricted access to a percentage of the tribes' net win from gaming devices, the SDF provision ultimately incorporated into the Davis Compact is much more restrictive. It provides that money from the SDF may be appropriated by the Legislature for only the following purposes:

(a) grants for programs designed to address gambling addiction;

(b) grants for the support of state and local government agencies impacted by tribal gaming;

(c) compensation for regulatory costs incurred by the State Gaming Agency and the state Department of Justice in connection with the implementation and administration of the compact;

(d) payment of shortfalls that may occur in the RSTF; and

(e) any other purposes specified by the legislature.

The district court interpreted subsection (e) under the *ejusdem generis* principle to be "limited to purposes that, like the first four enumerated purposes, are *directly related* to gaming." (Emphasis added.) *See United States v. Lacy,* 119 F.3d 742, 748 (9th Cir. 1997) ("[A] general term following more specific terms means that the things embraced in the general term are of the same kind as those denoted by the specific terms." (internal quotation marks omitted)). The State does not contest that construction on appeal, and we adopt it here.

***

We conclude that for the State to demand that Coyote Valley, in exchange for these exclusive gaming rights, accede to the limited revenue sharing required in the SDF provision does not constitute bad faith. The tribes who drafted and placed Proposition 5 on the ballot thought such an exchange was fair. The Proposition 5 model compact required that tribes, in exchange for exclusive rights to conduct certain class III games in the State, contribute funds to counties in California to supplement emergency medical care and programs on addictive gambling and to address the needs of the cities or counties within the boundaries of which tribal gaming facilities are located. The former Secretary of the Interior also appears to believe such an exchange is fair, given that he approved the Davis Compact in May 2000. *See* 65 Fed. Reg. 31189 (May 16, 2000). *See also* 25 U.S.C. § 2710(d)(8)(B) (providing that the Secretary may disapprove compacts that violate IGRA or the trust obligations of the United States to Indians).

c. The Labor Relations Provision

Finally, Coyote Valley contends that the Labor Relations provision is improper, arguing that labor relations are too far afield from tribal gaming to be an appropriate topic for Tribal–State compact negotiations. The State counters that because thousands of its citizens are employed at tribal casinos, it is proper for the State to insist on some minimal level of protection for those workers as a precondition to entering a Tribal–State compact. We hold that the provision falls within the scope of § 2710(d)(3)(C)(vii) and that, under the circumstances of this case, the State did not act in bad faith in requiring that Coyote Valley adopt it or forgo entering a compact.

During the negotiation of the Davis Compact, the State did not demand that tribes adopt a specific set of legal rules governing general employment practices on tribal lands. Instead, it demanded that tribes meet with labor unions to negotiate independently a labor ordinance addressing only organizational and representational rights and applicable only to employees *at tribal casinos and related facilities.* This demand became Section 10.7 of the Davis Compact:

> Notwithstanding any other provision of this Compact, this Compact shall be null and void if, on or before October 13, 1999, the Tribe has not provided an agreement or other procedure acceptable to the State for addressing organizational and representational rights of Class III Gaming Employees and other employees associated with the Tribe's Class III gaming enterprise, such as food and beverage, housekeeping, cleaning, bell and door services, and laundry employees at the Gaming Facility or any related facility, the only significant purpose of which is to facilitate patronage at the Gaming Facility.

We hold that this provision is "directly related to the operation of gaming activities" and thus permissible pursuant to 25 U.S.C. § 2710(d)(3)(C)(vii). Without the "operation of gaming activities," the jobs this provision covers would not exist; nor, conversely, could Indian gaming activities operate without someone performing these jobs. We therefore reject Coyote Valley's argument that IGRA categorically forbids its inclusion in the Davis Compact.

***

NOTES AND QUESTIONS

1. *Labor Relations.* Was the court correct to effectively require the tribe to negotiate over union organization? In one sense, working conditions of casino employees are logically related to casino operations. In another, state regulation of labor was probably not the kind of state concern Congress sought to address in the IGRA compact provision. The NLRB has been successful in its effort to assert jurisdiction, to the exclusion of tribal law, over union organization at Indian gaming facilities. *San Manuel Indian Bingo and Casino v. NLRB*, 475 F.3d 1306 (D.C. Cir. 2007). *NLRB v. Little River Band of Ottawa Indians Tribal Government*, 788 F.3d 537 (6th Cir. 2015); *Soaring Eagle Casino & Resort v. N.L.R.B.*, 791 F.3d 648 (6th Cir. 2015), *cert. denied*, 136 S. Ct. 2509 (2016). *See* Alex T. Skibine, *Practical Reasoning and the Application of General Federal Regulatory Laws to Indian Nations*, 22 Wash. & Lee J. Civil Rts. & Soc. Just. 123, 138-54 (2016) (discussing the approach proposed by the *Soaring Eagle* panel and offering alternatives). *See* Ch. 4 § I.B, *supra*. While the NLRB clearly has the upper hand in the litigation, there is still room for tribal law. The United Auto Workers and the Mashantucket Pequot Tribe negotiated the first union organization effort at an Indian casino under tribal law. *See* Nat'l Pub. Radio, UAW Brokers First Union Contract Under Tribal Law (March 14, 2010), *available at* https://www.npr. org/templates/story/story.php?storyId=124625523 [https://perma.cc/V3YQ-HH8J].

2. *Revenue Sharing.* Many compacts provide that tribes will share a certain percentage of their revenues with states. Do you see the statutory problem with demanding such revenue sharing in a compact? The Secretary of the Interior has agreed to approve compacts that include revenue sharing provisions on the condition that something of sufficient economic value, generally the right to exclusively operate in the state, is given in exchange. *See* Cohen's Handbook of Federal Indian Law § 12.05[2] (2012); *Sault St. Marie Tribe of Chippewa Indians v. Engler*, 271 F.3d 235, 238–39 (6th Cir. 2001) (holding that tribes that had agreed to pay 8% of slot revenue in exchange for exclusive right to operate slot machines had no obligation to pay after state permitted several

other tribes to operate slots). The Ninth Circuit, however, held that California engaged in bad faith by demanding new revenue sharing from the Rincon Band of Luiseno Mission Indians in exchange for exclusivity, where the tribe was already entitled to exclusivity under its prior revenue sharing agreements. *Rincon Band of Luiseno Mission Indians of Rincon Reservation v. Schwarzenegger*, 602 F.3d 1019, 1042 (9th Cir. 2010). The court held that "giving a party something to which he already has an absolute right" could not be the "meaningful concession" required to support the new revenue sharing demand. *Id.* at 1037. One study reported that "revenue sharing flows have in certain places been substantial, for example: $1 billion in 11 years to Arizona (Arizona Department of Gaming 2014), and $6.7 billion in 22 years to Connecticut (Connecticut Department of Consumer Protection 2014). In 2012, nationwide Indian gaming revenue sharing with states was estimated to be $1.5 billion. K. Q. Akee, Katherine A. Spilde and Jonathan B. Taylor, *The Indian Gaming Regulatory Act and Its Effects on American Indian Economic Development*, Vol. 29 (3) J. of Econ. Persp. 201 (Summer 2015).

3. *What is the standard to determine "good faith?"* Beyond the subjects of negotiation, what other standards determine whether negotiation is in good faith? The only court to discuss the issue took guidance from the duty to negotiate under the National Labor Relations Act, which courts had held " 'requires more than a willingness to enter upon a sterile discussion of' the parties' differences," and required parties to " 'enter into discussions with an open and fair mind and a sincere purpose to find a basis for agreement.' " *In re Indian Gaming Related Cases*, 147 F.Supp.2d 1011, 1020–21 (N.D. Cal. 2001). Did Judge Fletcher use this standard in affirming the district court decision?

4. *Enforcement of IGRA.* IGRA specifically authorizes federal courts to hear any cause of action to enjoin class III gaming conducted in violation of a Tribal–State compact, thus waiving tribal sovereign immunity in these actions. 25 U.S.C. § 2710(d)(7)(A)(ii). A companion provision authorizes courts to hear actions against states alleging violation of the obligation to negotiate in good faith. 25 U.S.C. § 2710(d)(7)(A)(i). In 1996, however, the Supreme Court held that this provision violated the Eleventh Amendment by subjecting states to suit by "private parties" in federal court against their will. *Seminole Tribe of Florida v. Florida*, 517 U.S. 44, 72 (1996). The decision had wide-ranging implications beyond Indian law, overruling past precedent to hold that Congress could not, except when it acted under the Fourteenth Amendment, abrogate state sovereign immunity. *See id.* at 65. The impact on IGRA, however, has not been as great as might be expected. First, states may waive sovereign immunity to clarify their obligations under the Act. Second, the Department of the Interior enacted regulations in the wake of *Seminole* authorizing the Secretary of the Interior to issue gaming procedures itself if negotiations break down and the state refuses to waive its sovereign immunity. 25 C.F.R. Part 291. The Fifth and Tenth Circuits, however, have found that these rules exceeded the authority Congress delegated to the agency. *New Mexico v. Department of Interior*, 854 F.3d 1207, 1226 (10th Cir. 2017) ("We find implausible the Secretary's assertion of implicit power to create an alternative to the explicit and detailed remedial scheme that IGRA prescribes."); *Texas v. United States*, 497 F.3d 491, 508 (5th Cir. 2007) (same). For discussion of a potential congressional fix, *see* Matthew M. Fletcher, *Bringing Balance to Indian Gaming*, 44 Harv. J. on Legis. 39 (2007).

What happened to the Seminole Tribe of Florida itself? The state continued to refuse to negotiate, but the tribe went ahead and began conducting Class III gaming on its lands. The U.S. Attorney declined to prosecute the tribe for this activity. Florida then filed suit against the tribe to enjoin the gaming activity. IGRA, however, only waives tribal sovereign immunity for violations of an existing Tribal–State compact; because Florida had never agreed to a compact with the tribe, the waiver of sovereign immunity did not apply. Declaring that the case "demonstrates the continuing vitality of the venerable maxim that turnabout is fair play," the Eleventh Circuit affirmed the district court's dismissal of the case. *Florida v. Seminole Tribe of Florida*, 181 F.3d 1237, 1239 (11th Cir. 1999). Many states waive their immunity in compacts, or do not assert it as a bar to negotiating compacts. *See, e.g., Pauma Band of Luiseno Mission Indians of Pauma & Yuima Reservation v. California*, 813 F.3d 1155, 1170 (9th Cir. 2015) (state waiver of immunity in compact does not allow for money damages but includes authorization for tribe to seek the remedy of rescission and restitution based on state's misrepresentation in negotiations).

5. *Impact of IGRA*. Although anti-gaming state interests were a significant catalyst for IGRA, Indian gaming has exploded under the act. In 1988, tribal revenues from Indian gaming were about 500 million a year. By 2006, the National Indian Gaming Commission reported that there were over 400 tribal gaming facilities generating 25.7 billion dollars of revenue a year. In 2019, the NIGC reported 2018 Indian Gaming Revenues of $33.7 billion—a 4.1% increase over 2017. There are 249 tribes operating 520 facilities in 29 states. About 70% of tribes in the lower 48 states now engage in Class II or Class III gaming. The wealth is not distributed evenly; about half of gaming revenue goes to a small number of tribes. In addition, as one would expect, fabulous gaming profits are earned only by tribes in very populous areas. One study revealed that of "367 facilities in operation in 2004, the 15 largest accounted for more than 37 percent of total Indian gaming revenues and the 55 largest accounted for close to 70 percent of total sector revenue." Joseph P. Kalt, et al., The State of Native Nations 149 (2008). Still, about 90% of tribal gaming facilities are profitable, and this money has been a tremendous benefit to tribes.

All gaming profits must be used for tribal governmental programs, tribal welfare, charitable donations, or donations to local governments. 25 U.S.C. § 2710(b)(2)(B). Per capita payments to tribal members are only permitted if the tribe has an approved plan for allocation of the revenues to tribal government and welfare and other authorized purposes, and the Secretary of the Interior approves the per capita payment plan. 25 U.S.C. § 2710(b)(3). Tribes have used their gaming revenue to finance tribal health care, law enforcement, and education, to purchase tribal lands and build housing for their members, to preserve their culture and environment, and to diversify into other businesses.

Indian household income, poverty, welfare dependence, unemployment, housing, and education status have all improved significantly between the 1990 and 2000 census. Although both gaming and non-gaming tribes have experienced these gains, with the exception of two out of twelve factors (the two were housing overcrowding and lack of complete plumbing), the gains were greater for gaming than for non-gaming tribes. Jonathan B. Taylor & Joseph P. Kalt, Cabazon, *The Indian Gaming Regulatory Act, and the Socioeconomic Consequences of American Indian Governmental Gaming, A Ten Year Review* xi (Harvard Project on American Indian Economic Development 2005). Despite these gains, Indian people remain at the bottom of the socio-economic ladder in the United States. For example, the average per capita income for reservation-based Indians in gaming areas was only about 45% of the national average; for Indians in non-gaming areas it was 35%. *Id.* at 8. Similarly, unemployment rates were 22% for Indians in reservation areas without gaming, 15% in areas with gaming, and 6% for all races nationally. *Id.* at 29. Indian gaming has thus brought about significant improvements in the status of Indian people, but not come close to closing the gap between Indians and others.

What about the impact on non-Indian communities? A 2000 study evaluating 30 social and economic indicators found that the economic impact on communities within 50 miles of Indian gaming was largely positive. Jonathan B. Taylor, Matthew B. Krepps, and Patrick Wang, *The National Evidence on Socioeconomic Impacts of American Indian Gaming on Non–Indian Communities*, American Behavioral Scientist (2000). Non–Indian income rose, unemployment and welfare dependence fell, and, in most areas, robbery and auto theft actually fell as well. *Id.* at 28–29. The authors believed these results could be explained by the fact that most reservation casinos were located in remote, economically depressed areas, so the employment provided by and business attracted by the casino benefited the region as a whole. The study did, however, find more negative crime effects for three "large market" casinos in more populous areas. And yet a different group of researches observe that "[a] more recent study found that local effects were more often positive. *** [R]eservation economic activity requires goods and services from off-reservation communities, which incur local and state taxes on sales and income." K. Q. Akee, Katherine A. Spilde and Jonathan B. Taylor, *The Indian Gaming Regulatory Act and Its Effects on American Indian Economic Development*, 29(3) J. Econ. Persp. 201 (Summer 2015).

Indian gaming is undoubtedly highly successful. It not only provides income and jobs for tribal members and non-Indians in nearby communities, it has also been a means by which tribes increased their sovereign capacity to govern, and to operate successful businesses. Of course, there are examples of failed gaming enterprises, but they are few in comparison to the successful ventures. Tribes located near large markets naturally have the largest revenue streams, but the smaller and more rural casinos still provide important revenues and job opportunities. Kevin Washburn, who became the Assistant Secretary of Indian Affairs in the Obama Administration, said in 2008 that "Indian gaming is simply the most successful economic venture ever to occur consistently across a wide range of American Indian reservations." Those words ring true today.

C. THE ROLE OF THE NATIONAL INDIAN GAMING COMMISSION

COLORADO RIVER INDIAN TRIBES V. NATIONAL INDIAN GAMING COMMISSION

466 F.3d 134 (D.C. Cir. 2006)

RANDOLPH, CIRCUIT JUDGE.

This is an appeal from an order of the district court, Bates, J., granting summary judgment in favor of the Colorado River Indian Tribes and against the National Indian Gaming Commission, the Commission's Chairman, and two of its members. The issue is whether the Indian Gaming Regulatory Act, 25 U.S.C. §§ 2701–2721, gives the Commission authority to promulgate regulations establishing mandatory operating procedures for certain kinds of gambling in tribal casinos.

Congress enacted the Indian Gaming Regulatory Act in the wake of the Supreme Court's decision that state gaming laws could not be enforced on Indian reservations within states otherwise permitting gaming. The Act established the Commission as an agency within the Department of the Interior. 25 U.S.C. § 2704(a). The Commission has the authority to investigate and audit certain types of Indian gaming, to enforce the collection of civil fines, and to "promulgate such regulations and guidelines as it deems appropriate to implement the provisions" of the Act. *Id.* § 2706; *see Cabazon Band of Mission Indians v. Nat'l Indian Gaming Comm'n,* 14 F.3d 633, 634 (D.C. Cir. 1994).

The Tribe operates the BlueWater Resort and Casino on Indian lands in Parker, Arizona. The casino offers what the Act defines as "class II" and "class III" gaming. Class II gaming includes bingo; "non-banking" card games; and pull-tabs, lotto, and other games similar to bingo, if played in the same location. 25 U.S.C. § 2703(7)(A), (B). Class III gaming includes most conventional forms of casino gaming such as slot machines, roulette, and blackjack. *Id.* § 2703(8); 25 C.F.R. § 502.4. Class I gaming consists of social gaming for minimal prizes and traditional forms of Indian gaming in connection with tribal ceremonies. 25 U.S.C. § 2703(6).

The Act treats each gaming class differently. "Class I gaming on Indian lands is within the exclusive jurisdiction of the Indian tribes," and is not subject to the Act. *Id.* § 2710(a)(1). As to class II gaming, the Commission and the tribes share regulatory authority: the tribes must enact a gaming ordinance applying the Act's minimum regulatory requirements; and the Commission's Chairman must approve the tribal ordinance before gaming may occur. *Id.* § 2710(a)(2), (b). The Act regulates how tribes engaging in class II gaming may make payments to tribal members, *id.* § 2710(b)(3), and it requires an annual outside audit of the gaming and various contracts, *id.* § 2710(b)(2)(C), (D).

Like class II gaming, class III gaming is lawful only if it takes place on Indian land "in a State that permits such gaming for any purpose by any person, organization, or entity. *** " *Id.* § 2710(d)(1)(B). But unlike class II gaming, a tribe conducts class III gaming pursuant to a compact with the state. *Id.*

§ 2710(d)(1)(C). The Secretary of the Interior must approve any such compact before it may become effective. *Id.* § 2710(d)(3)(B). Thereafter, the "Tribal–State compact govern[s] the conduct of gaming activities," *id.* § 2710(d)(3)(A), and the tribe's class III gaming operations must be "conducted in conformance" with the compact, *id.* § 2710(d)(1)(C). Tribal-state compacts may contain provisions related to "standards for the operation of such activity" and "any other subjects that are directly related to the operation of gaming activities." *Id.* § 2710(d)(3)(C)(vi), (vii). The Commission must approve any tribal ordinances for regulating and conducting class III gaming and any contracts the tribe enters into for the management of its class III gaming. *Id.* § 2710(d)(1)(A)(iii), (d)(9).

The Colorado River Indian Tribes regulates gaming at its BlueWater casino pursuant to a tribal ordinance and rules contained in a tribal-state class III gaming compact with the State of Arizona. *See* Gaming Ordinance of the Colo. River Indian Tribes, Ord. No. 94–1 (Aug. 31, 1994); Colo. River Indian Tribes and State of Ariz. Gaming Compact (Jan. 31, 2003) (*Gaming Compact*). Both the ordinance and the compact contain their own internal control standards. The most recent version of the compact requires the Tribe's gaming agency to create standards governing operating procedures that are at least as stringent as those contained in the rules the Commission promulgated in 1999. *Gaming Compact* § 3(b)(3)(B). The State of Arizona monitors the Tribe's compliance with the standards, for which the Tribe reimburses the state about $250,000 per year. The Tribe's gaming agency employs twenty-nine employees and has an annual budget of $1.2 million.

In 1999 the Commission promulgated regulations, which it termed "Minimum Internal Control Standards," governing class II and class III gaming. *See* 64 Fed. Reg. 590 (Jan. 5, 1999) (codified as amended at 25 C.F.R. pt. 542). The regulations take up more than eighty pages in the Code of Federal Regulations. No operational detail is overlooked. The rules establish standards for individual games, *see, e.g.,* 25 C.F.R. § 542.7, .8, .10, customer credit, *id.* § 542.15, information technology, *id.* § 542.16, complimentary services, *id.* § 542.17, and many other aspects of gaming. To illustrate, tribes must establish "a reasonable time period" not to exceed seven days for removing playing cards from play, but "if a gaming operation uses plastic cards (not plastic-coated cards), the cards may be used for up to three (3) months if the plastic cards are routinely inspected, and washed or cleaned in a manner and time frame approved by the Tribal gaming regulatory authority." *Id.* § 542.9(d), (e). To take another example the district court mentioned, coin drops are regulated differently according to the size of the gaming facility. *See id.* § 542.21, .31, .41. There are rules prescribing the number and type of employees who must be involved in the removal of the coin drop, *id.* § 542.21(g)(1), the timing of the removal of the coin drop, *id.* § 542.21(g)(2), the tagging and transportation of the coin drop, *id.* § 542.21(g)(4), the manner in which the coin drop must be housed while in the machine, *id.* § 542.21(g)(5), and the purposes for which a coin drop may be used, *id.* § 542.21(g)(6).

In January 2001, the Commission sought to audit the Tribe's class III gaming at the BlueWater casino in order to determine whether the Tribe was complying with the regulations. The Tribe protested on the ground that the rules exceeded the Commission's authority under the Act. The auditors departed and the Commission issued a notice of violation. After administrative hearings, the Commission fined the Tribe $2,000 for terminating the audit.

Colo. River, 383 F.Supp.2d at 130. The Commission denied the Tribe's objection, citing its authority to "promulgate such regulations and guidelines as it deems appropriate to implement the provisions" of the Act, 25 U.S.C. § 2706(b)(10), among which is the provision stating that one of the Act's purposes is to protect the integrity of gaming revenue, *id.* § 2702. *In re Colo. River Indian Tribes,* NOV/CFA 01–01, 5–6 (Nat'l Indian Gaming Comm'n May 30, 2002) (*NIGC Final Order*). The Commission located its power to audit the casino in § 2706(b)(4), which authorizes the Commission to "audit all papers, books, and records respecting gross revenues of class II gaming conducted on Indian lands and any other matters necessary to carry out the duties of the Commission under this chapter. *** " *See NIGC Final Order* at 7. The Tribe brought an action in federal district court challenging the decision and the Commission's statutory authority to regulate class III gaming. The district court reached the "inescapable conclusion" that Congress did not intend to give such broad authority to the Commission, and therefore vacated the Commission's decision and declared the regulations unlawful as applied to class III gaming. *Colo. River,* 383 F.Supp.2d at 132.

There was a time when the Commission agreed with the district court's view of the Act. The first Chairman of the Commission notified the Inspector General of the Department of the Interior in 1993 that "the regulation of class III gaming was not assigned to the Commission but was left to the tribes and the states. *** " Memorandum from Anthony J. Hope, Chairman, Nat'l Indian Gaming Comm'n to the Assistant Inspector General for Audits, Dep't of the Interior 2 (Oct. 18, 1993). He explained that this was why the Commission had not imposed "gaming control standards" on class III gaming: "the Act assigns those responsibilities to the tribes and/or the states." *Id.* The Commission's Chairman took the same position when he testified before Congress the following year. *See Manner in which Gaming Activities Are Regulated by the Several States and the Role of the Federal Government in the Regulation of Indian Gaming Activities: Hearing Before the S. Comm. on Indian Affairs,* 103d Cong. 7–8 (1994) (testimony of Chairman Hope, Nat'l Indian Gaming Comm'n). Despite many legislative efforts since then, all of which are cited in Judge Bates's careful opinion, 383 F.Supp.2d at 142 n. 13, Congress has never amended the Act to confer any such express power on the Commission.

Even now the Commission concedes that no provision of the Act explicitly grants it the power to impose operational standards on class III gaming. Section 2706 grants the Commission authority over several aspects of class II regulation. Thus, the Commission "shall monitor class II gaming," and "inspect and examine all premises located on Indian lands on which class II gaming is conducted. *** " 25 U.S.C. § 2706(b)(1), (2). It "may demand access to and inspect, examine, photocopy, and audit all papers, books, and records respecting gross revenues of class II gaming conducted on Indian lands and any other matters necessary to carry out the duties of the Commission under this chapter. *** " *Id.* § 2706(b)(4). While the statute grants the Commission audit authority over "any other matters necessary to carry out [its] duties," the statute does not indicate that these duties extend to class III regulation. Instead, the main provision dealing with the regulation of class III gaming—§ 2710(d)—contemplates joint tribal-state regulation. The Act describes tribal-state compacts as agreements "governing the conduct of [class III] gaming activities." *Id.* § 2710(d)(3)(A). A compact may contain provisions relating to "the application of the criminal and civil laws and regulations of the Indian tribe or the State that are directly related to, and necessary for, the licensing and regulation of" class III gaming, *id.* § 2710(d)(3)(C)(i), "standards for the operation of such activity," *id.* § 2710(d)(3)(C)(vi), and "any other subjects that are directly related to the operation of [class III] gaming activities," *id.* § 2710(d)(3)(C)(vii). That the Act sets up concurrent tribal-state regulation of class III gaming, not tribal-state-Commission regulation, is evident from § 2710(d)(5): "Nothing in this subsection shall impair the right of an Indian tribe to regulate class III gaming on its Indian lands concurrently with the State, except to the extent that such regulation is inconsistent with, or less stringent than"—not Commission regulations, but—"the State laws and regulations made applicable by any Tribal–State compact entered into by the Indian tribe under paragraph (3) that is in effect." Contrast this provision with § 542.4(c) of the regulations, which states that if a standard in the Commission's regulations is more stringent than a standard in a tribal-state compact, the Commission's regulation "shall prevail." 25 C.F.R. § 542.4(c). There are other indications that Congress intended to leave the regulation of class III gaming to the tribes and the states, including the fact that the Secretary of the Interior—rather than the Commission—approves (or disapproves) tribal-state compacts regulating class III gaming. 25 U.S.C. § 2710(d)(3)(B). ***

As against this, the Commission offers three main arguments. One is that the Commission has "oversight" authority over class III gaming, that the dictionary defines "oversight" to mean "supervision," and that the Commission's regulation of class III gaming falls within that definition. The trouble is that the Act does not use the word "oversight." The Commission relies not on statutory language, but on a sentence from the Senate committee report on the Act: "The Commission will have a regulatory role for class II gaming and an oversight role with respect to class III gaming." S. Rep. No. 100–446, at 1 (1988), *reprinted in* 1988 U.S.C.C.A.N. 3071, 3071. But just two sentences before the "oversight" passage, the report states that the Senate bill "provides for a system for joint regulation by tribes and the Federal Government of class II gaming on Indian lands and a system for compacts between tribes and States for regulation of class III gaming." *Id.* One might wonder why the Committee would rely on tribal-state compacts to regulate class III gaming. The report gives this explanation: "the Committee notes that there is no adequate Federal regulatory system in place for class III gaming, nor do tribes have such systems for the regulation of class III gaming currently in place. Thus a logical choice is to make use of existing State regulatory systems, although the adoption of State law is not tantamount to an accession to State jurisdiction. The use of State regulatory systems can be accomplished through negotiated compacts but this is not to say that tribal governments can have no role to play in regulation of class III gaming—many can and will." *Id.* at 13, 1988 U.S.C.C.A.N. at 3083–84. In addition to the point that a committee report is not law, it is perfectly clear that whatever the Senate committee thought "oversight" might entail, the committee did not foresee the Commission regulating class III gaming.

The Commission's other arguments proceed from the text of the Act. The Commission is funded by a percentage of each tribe's gross gaming revenues from class II and class III gaming. 25 U.S.C. § 2717(a). To this end, tribes must submit annual "outside audits" to the Commission of their class II and class III gaming operations. *Id.* § 2710(b)(2)(C), (d)(1)(A)(ii). From this the Commission infers that it has the authority to regulate the handling and accounting of gaming receipts in order to ensure the integrity of audits. We cannot see how the right to receive an outside audit, presumably conducted in accordance with Generally Accepted Auditing Standards, translates into a power to control gaming operations. Under the Securities Exchange Act of 1934, public companies must file reports necessary to the protection of investors. *See* 15 U.S.C. § 78m(a). If the public company happened to be in the casino business, such as Harrah's Entertainment, Inc., the Commission's logic here would entitle the SEC to dictate the details of how Harrah's conducts its casino operations because the SEC receives reports from the company. The SEC obviously has no such authority, and neither does the Commission.

This brings us to the Commission's third argument-namely, that its regulations are valid in light of its authority to "promulgate such regulations and guidelines as it deems proper to implement the provisions of [the Act]." 25 U.S.C. § 2706(b)(10). *** The Commission is correct that Congress wanted to ensure the integrity of Indian gaming, but it is equally clear that Congress wanted to do this in a particular way. The declared policy is therefore not simply to shield Indian tribes "from organized crime and other corrupting influences" and "to assure that gaming is conducted fairly and honestly by both the operator and players," 25 U.S.C. § 2702(2), but to accomplish this through the "statutory basis for the regulation of gaming" provided in the Act, *id.* This leads us back to the opening question-what is the statutory basis empowering the Commission to regulate class III gaming operations? Finding none, we affirm.

NOTES AND QUESTIONS

1. *Should Congress authorize greater federal regulation?* Why was the Commission seeking to regulate Class III tribal gaming activity without the explicit statutory authorization it had in the case of Class II gaming? Is it simply a modern example of federal paternalism, or is it from a genuine desire to protect the integrity of Indian gaming from corruption? While acknowledging that "[c]rime and corruption has, for the most part, been carefully kept in check in Indian gaming," Kevin Washburn (then Dean of the university of New Mexico Law School who later served as Assistant Secretary in the Department of Interior (in charge of the Bureau of Indian Affairs) under President Obama) called on Congress to provide the NIGC with clear statutory authority to impose standards like those at issue in *Colorado River Indian Tribes*. Testimony on the Regulation of Indian Gaming, Oversight Hearing on Indian Gaming, before the United States Senate, Committee on Indian Affairs, 109th Congress, 1st Sess. (September 21, 2005).

2. In response to the NIGC's effort to obtain express authorization to adopt the regulations struck down in *Colorado River Indian Tribes*, Chairman Ron Allen of the Jamestown S'Klallam Tribe had the following to say: "[I]t is completely unnecessary. NIGC has substantial existing authority: IGRA authorizes the NIGC to review and approve tribal gaming regulatory laws, review tribal background checks and gaming licenses, receive independent annual audits of tribal gaming facilities, approve management contracts, and work with tribal gaming regulatory agencies to promote tribal implementation of tribal gaming regulatory ordinances." Sen. Hearing 110–143, Discussion Draft Legislation Regarding Regulation of Class III Gaming, p. 56 (June 28, 2007). Who has the better argument as a matter of policy?

3. *Management contract approval.* When a tribe uses an outside management entity to operate its Class II or Class III gaming facilities, IGRA requires that the NIGC approve the contract. 25 U.S.C. §§ 2711 & 2710(d)(9). There are detailed requirements that include detailed background checks as well as limits in the amount of compensation allowed (30% of revenues, or 40% in exceptional circumstances). Today, however, many tribes have taken over management of their casinos in order to capture the revenues that would otherwise go to outside contractors. For a concise discussion of this area, *see* Cohen's Handbook of Federal Indian Law § 12.08 (2012).

D. LANDS ON WHICH TRIBES MAY CONDUCT GAMING

Under IGRA, tribes may only engage in gaming on "Indian lands," within the tribe's jurisdiction. 25 U.S.C. § 2710. Indian lands are defined as

> **(A)** all lands within the limits of any Indian reservation; and
>
> **(B)** any lands title to which is either held in trust by the United States for the benefit of any Indian tribe or individual or held by any Indian tribe or individual subject to restriction by the United States against alienation and over which an Indian tribe exercises governmental power.

25 U.S.C. § 2703[4]

In addition, IGRA generally prohibits gaming on land acquired by the Secretary in trust for a tribe after the effective date of the Act, October 17, 1988. There are several exceptions. First, it does not apply to lands acquired in trust that are within or contiguous to the boundaries of the tribe's reservation on the effective date of the Act. Second is an exception for tribes without a reservation in 1988, which allows gaming on lands within such a tribe's last recognized reservation. 25 U.S.C. § 2719(a).

The prohibition on post–1988 gaming also is lifted when

> **(A)** the Secretary, after consultation with the Indian tribe and appropriate State and local officials, including officials of other nearby Indian tribes, determines that a gaming establishment on newly acquired lands would be [1] in the best interest of the Indian tribe and its members, and [2] would not be detrimental to the surrounding community, but only if the Governor of the State in which the gaming activity is to be conducted concurs in the Secretary's determination; or
>
> **(B)** lands are taken into trust as part of—
>
> > **(i)** a settlement of a land claim,
> >
> > **(ii)** the initial reservation of an Indian tribe acknowledged by the Secretary under the Federal acknowledgment process, or
> >
> > **(iii)** the restoration of lands for an Indian tribe that is restored to Federal recognition.

25 U.S.C. § 2719(b)(1). Tribes have complained bitterly about the fact that gubernatorial consent is required in addition to Secretarial approval under subsection **(A)**, *supra*, but the statute is clear and courts have rejected constitutional challenges to the process. *Lac Courte Oreilles Band v. United States*, 367

F.3d 650 (2004) (upholding gubernatorial consent provision over tribal objections based on appointments clause, Tenth Amendment and separation of powers). As of 2008, there had been only four occasions when a governor concurred in positive Secretarial findings, but 30 applications were pending. For litigation regarding the other exceptions to the post–1988 ban see *TOMAC v. Norton*, 433 F.3d 852 (D.C. Cir. 2006) (administratively terminated tribe whose recognition was "affirmed" by Congress could be considered a restored tribe); *Citizens Exposing Truth About Casinos v. Kempthorne*, 492 F.3d 460 (D.C. Cir. 2007) (deferring to Secretary's determination of initial reservation). There has been a great deal of administrative decision-making regarding these exceptions and the NIGC maintains a comprehensive database on its website. https://www.nigc.gov/general-counsel/commission-regulations [https://perma.cc/LYB7-TKC2].

V. THE INDIAN CHILD WELFARE ACT

The Indian Child Welfare Act of 1978 is unusual among federal Indian statutes: it expands tribal jurisdiction outside Indian country in some circumstances and fundamentally affects the way state courts deal with cases involving Indian children. The factors that led Congress to take this step are described in the House Report below.

HOUSE REPORT NO. 95–1386

July 24, 1978

" *** I can remember (the welfare worker) coming and taking some of my cousins and friends. I didn't know why and I didn't question it. It was just done and had always been done. *** "[2]

The wholesale separation of Indian children from their families is perhaps the most tragic and destructive aspect of American Indian life today.

Surveys of American states with large Indian populations conducted by the Association of American Indian Affairs (AAIA) in 1969 and again in 1974 indicate that approximately 25–35 percent of all Indian children are separated from their families and placed in foster homes, adoptive homes, or institutions. In some states, the problem is getting worse. In Minnesota, one in every eight Indian children under 18 years of age is living in an adoptive home; and, in 1971–72, nearly one in every four Indian children under 1 year of age was adopted.

The disparity in placement rates for Indians and non-Indians is shocking. In Minnesota, Indian children are placed in foster care or in adoptive homes at a per capita rate five times greater than non-Indian children. In Montana, the ratio of Indian foster-care placement is at least 13 times greater. In South Dakota, 40 percent of all adoptions made by the State's Department of Public Welfare since 1967–68 are of Indian children, yet Indians make up only 7 percent of the juvenile population. The number of South Dakota Indian children

---

2. Testimony of Valancia Thacker before Task Force 4 of the American Indian Policy Review Commission.

living in foster homes is, per capita, nearly 16 times greater than the non-Indian rate. In the State of Washington, the Indian adoption rate is 19 times greater and the foster care rate 10 times greater. In Wisconsin, the risk run by Indian children of being separated from their parents is nearly 1,600 percent greater than it is for non-Indian children. ***

The federal boarding school and dormitory programs also contribute to the destruction of Indian family and community life. The Bureau of Indian Affairs (BIA) in its school census for 1971, indicates that 34,538 children live in its institutional facilities rather than at home. This represents more than 17 percent of the Indian school age population of federally recognized reservations. *** On the Navajo reservation, about 20,000 children or 90 percent of the BIA school population in grades k–12, live at boarding schools. ***

In addition to the trauma of separation from their families, most Indian children in placement or in institutions have to cope with the problems of adjusting to a social and cultural environment much different than their own. In 16 states surveyed in 1969, approximately 85 percent of all Indian children in foster care were living in non-Indian homes. In Minnesota today, according to state figures, more than 90 percent of nonrelated adoptions of Indian children are made by non-Indian couples.

***

The Indian child welfare crisis will continue until the standards for defining mistreatment are revised. Very few Indian children are removed from their families on the grounds of physical abuse. One study of a North Dakota reservation showed that these grounds were advanced in only 1 percent of the cases. Another study of a tribe in the northwest showed the same incidence. The remaining 99 percent of the cases were argued on such vague grounds as "neglect" or "social deprivation." ***

In judging the fitness of a particular family, many social workers, ignorant of Indian cultural values and social norms, make decisions that are wholly inappropriate in the context of Indian family life and so they frequently discover neglect or abandonment where none exists.

For example, the dynamics of Indian extended families are largely misunderstood. An Indian child may have scores of, perhaps more than a hundred, relatives who are counted as close, responsible members of the family. Many social workers, untutored in the ways of Indian family life or assuming them to be socially irresponsible, consider leaving the child with persons outside the nuclear family as neglect and thus as grounds for terminating parental rights.

***

The question then is: "Is the regulation of child custody proceedings and the imposition of minimum federal standards an appropriate exercise of Congress' plenary power over Indian affairs?" *** [As the Maryland Court of Appeals stated in *Wakefield v. Little Light*, 276 Md. 333, 347 A.2d 228 (1975)]:

> *** [T]here can be no greater threat to "essential tribal relations" and no greater infringement on the right of the tribe to govern themselves than to interfere with tribal control over the custody of their children. ***

Even this state court recognized that a tribe's children are vital to its integrity and future. Since the United States has the responsibility to protect the integrity of the tribes, we can say with the *Kagama* Court, " *** there arises the duty of protection, and with it the power."

***

Congress sought to address the situation in four ways:

First, by transferring jurisdiction of child custody cases to tribal courts where possible, and involving tribes in child custody cases where not.

Second, by providing parents with added procedural protections and raising substantive standards before involuntarily removing a child.

Third, by creating placement preferences for children who are removed to encourage placement with the child's extended family, tribe, and other Indian families.

And fourth, by providing assistance to tribes to manage their own child welfare services and facilitating cooperation between tribes and states.

The first three aspects of ICWA are covered in the following excerpts from the statute.

THE INDIAN CHILD WELFARE ACT

(25 U.S.C. § 1901 *et seq.*)

---

25 U.S.C. § 1901. Congressional findings

Recognizing the special relationship between the United States and the Indian tribes and their members and the Federal responsibility to Indian people, the Congress finds—

(1) that clause 3, section 8, article I of the United States Constitution provides that "The Congress shall have Power *** To regulate Commerce *** with Indian tribes" and, through this and other constitutional authority, Congress has plenary power over Indian affairs;

(2) that Congress, through statutes, treaties, and the general course of dealing with Indian tribes, has assumed the responsibility for the protection and preservation of Indian tribes and their resources;

(3) that there is no resource that is more vital to the continued existence and integrity of Indian tribes than their children and that the United States has a direct interest, as trustee, in protecting Indian children who are members of or are eligible for membership in an Indian tribe;

(4) that an alarmingly high percentage of Indian families are broken up by the removal, often unwarranted, of their children from them by nontribal public and private agencies and that an alarmingly high percentage of such children are placed in non-Indian foster and adoptive homes and institutions; and

(5) that the States, exercising their recognized jurisdiction over Indian child custody proceedings through administrative and judicial bodies, have

often failed to recognize the essential tribal relations of Indian people and the cultural and social standards prevailing in Indian communities and families.

25 U.S.C. § 1902. Congressional declaration of policy.

The Congress hereby declares that it is the policy of this Nation to protect the best interests of Indian children and to promote the stability and security of Indian tribes and families by the establishment of minimum Federal standards for the removal of Indian children from their families and the placement of such children in foster or adoptive homes which will reflect the unique values of Indian culture, and by providing for assistance to Indian tribes in the operation of child and family service programs.

25 U.S.C. § 1903. Definitions.

For the purposes of this chapter, except as may be specifically provided otherwise, the term—

(1) "child custody proceeding" shall mean and include—

(i) "foster care placement" which shall mean any action removing an Indian child from its parent or Indian custodian for temporary placement in a foster home or institution or the home of a guardian or conservator where the parent or Indian custodian cannot have the child returned upon demand, but where parental rights have not been terminated;

(ii) "termination of parental rights" which shall mean any action resulting in the termination of the parent-child relationship;

(iii) "preadoptive placement" which shall mean the temporary placement of an Indian child in a foster home or institution after the termination of parental rights, but prior to or in lieu of adoptive placement; and

(iv) "adoptive placement" which shall mean the permanent placement of an Indian child for adoption, including any action resulting in a final decree of adoption.

Such term or terms shall not include a placement based upon an act which, if committed by an adult, would be deemed a crime or upon an award, in a divorce proceeding, of custody to one of the parents.

(2) "extended family member" shall be as defined by the law or custom of the Indian child's tribe or, in the absence of such law or custom, shall be a person who has reached the age of eighteen and who is the Indian child's grandparent, aunt or uncle, brother or sister, brother-in-law or sister-in-law, niece or nephew, first or second cousin, or stepparent;

(3) "Indian" means any person who is a member of an Indian tribe, or who is an Alaska Native and a member of a Regional Corporation as defined in section 1606 of title 43 [the Alaska Native Claims Settlement Act];

(4) "Indian child" means any unmarried person who is under age eighteen and is either (a) a member of an Indian tribe or (b) is eligible for membership in an Indian tribe and is the biological child of a member of an Indian tribe;

***

(6) "Indian custodian" means any Indian person who has legal custody of an Indian child under tribal law or custom or under State law or to whom temporary physical care, custody, and control has been transferred by the parent of such child;

***

(9) "parent" means any biological parent or parents of an Indian child or any Indian person who has lawfully adopted an Indian child, including adoptions under tribal law or custom. It does not include the unwed father where paternity has not been acknowledged or established;

(10) "reservation" means Indian country as defined in section 1151 of title 18, United States Code and any lands, not covered under such section, title to which is either held by the United States in trust for the benefit of any Indian tribe or individual or held by any Indian tribe or individual subject to a restriction by the United States against alienation;

***

25 U.S.C. § 1911. Indian tribe jurisdiction over Indian child custody proceedings.

(a) Exclusive jurisdiction.

An Indian tribe shall have jurisdiction exclusive as to any State over any child custody proceeding involving an Indian child who resides or is domiciled within the reservation of such tribe, except where such jurisdiction is otherwise vested in the State by existing Federal law. Where an Indian child is a ward of a tribal court, the Indian tribe shall retain exclusive jurisdiction, notwithstanding the residence or domicile of the child.

(b) Transfer of proceedings; declination by tribal court.

In any State court proceeding for the foster care placement of, or termination of parental rights to, an Indian child not domiciled or residing within the reservation of the Indian child's tribe, the court, in the absence of good cause to the contrary, shall transfer such proceeding to the jurisdiction of the tribe, absent objection by either parent, upon the petition of either parent or the Indian custodian or the Indian child's tribe: Provided, That such transfer shall be subject to declination by the tribal court of such tribe.

(c) State court proceedings; intervention.

In any State court proceeding for the foster care placement of, or termination of parental rights to, an Indian child, the Indian custodian of the child and the Indian child's tribe shall have a right to intervene at any point in the proceeding.

(d) Full faith and credit to public acts, records, and judicial proceedings of Indian tribes.

The United States, every State, every territory or possession of the United States, and every Indian tribe shall give full faith and credit to the public acts, records, and judicial proceedings of any Indian tribe applicable to Indian child custody proceedings to the same extent that such entities give full faith and credit to the public acts, records, and judicial proceedings of any other entity.

25 U.S.C. § 1912. Pending court proceedings.

(a) In any involuntary proceeding in a State court, where the court knows or has reason to know that an Indian child is involved, the party seeking the foster care placement of, or termination of parental rights to, an Indian child shall notify the parent or Indian custodian and the Indian child's tribe, by registered mail with return receipt requested, of the pending proceedings and of their right of intervention. If the identity or location of the parent or Indian custodian and the tribe cannot be determined, such notice shall be given to the Secretary in like manner, who shall have fifteen days after receipt to provide the requisite notice to the parent or Indian custodian and the tribe. No foster care placement or termination of parental rights proceeding shall be held until at least ten days after receipt of notice by the parent or Indian custodian and the tribe or the Secretary: Provided, That the parent or Indian custodian or the tribe shall, upon request, be granted up to twenty additional days to prepare for such proceeding.

(b) In any case in which the court determines indigency, the parent or Indian custodian shall have the right to court-appointed counsel in any removal, placement, or termination proceeding. The court may, in its discretion, appoint counsel for the child upon a finding that such appointment is in the best interest of the child. Where State law makes no provision for appointment of counsel in such proceedings, the court shall promptly notify the Secretary upon appointment of counsel, and the Secretary, upon certification of the presiding judge, shall pay reasonable fees and expenses out of funds which may be appropriated pursuant to the Act of November 2, 1921 (42 Stat. 208; 25 U.S.C. § 13).

(c) Each party to a foster care placement or termination of parental rights proceeding under State law involving an Indian child shall have the right to examine all reports or other documents filed with the court upon which any decision with respect to such action may be based.

(d) Any party seeking to effect a foster care placement of, or termination of parental rights to, an Indian child under State law shall satisfy the court that active efforts have been made to provide remedial services and rehabilitative programs designed to prevent the breakup of the Indian family and that these efforts have proved unsuccessful.

(e) No foster care placement may be ordered in such proceeding in the absence of a determination, supported by clear and convincing evidence, including testimony of qualified expert witnesses, that the continued custody of the child by the parent or Indian custodian is likely to result in serious emotional or physical damage to the child.

(f) No termination of parental rights may be ordered in such proceeding in the absence of a determination, supported by evidence beyond a reasonable doubt, including testimony of qualified expert witnesses, that the continued custody of the child by the parent or Indian custodian is likely to result in serious emotional or physical damage to the child.

25 U.S.C. § 1913. Parental rights; voluntary termination.

(a) Where any parent or Indian custodian voluntarily consents to a foster care placement or to termination of parental rights, such consent shall not be valid unless executed in writing and recorded before a judge of a court of competent jurisdiction and accompanied by the presiding judge's certificate that the terms and consequences of the consent were fully explained in detail and were fully understood by the parent or Indian custodian. The court shall also certify that either the parent or Indian custodian fully understood the explanation in English or that it was interpreted into a language that the parent or Indian custodian understood. Any consent given prior to, or within ten days after, birth of the Indian child shall not be valid.

(b) Any parent or Indian custodian may withdraw consent to a foster care placement under State law at any time and, upon such withdrawal, the child shall be returned to the parent or Indian custodian.

(c) In any voluntary proceeding for termination of parental rights to, or adoptive placement of, an Indian child, the consent of the parent may be withdrawn for any reason at any time prior to the entry of a final decree of termination or adoption, as the case may be, and the child shall be returned to the parent.

(d) After the entry of a final decree of adoption of an Indian child in any State court, the parent may withdraw consent thereto upon the grounds that consent was obtained through fraud or duress and may petition the court to vacate such decree. Upon a finding that such consent was obtained through fraud or duress, the court shall vacate such decree and return the child to the parent. No adoption which has been effective for at least two years may be invalidated under the provisions of this subsection unless otherwise permitted under State law.

25 U.S.C. § 1914. Petition to court of competent jurisdiction to invalidate action upon showing of certain violations

Any Indian child who is the subject of any action for foster care placement or termination of parental rights under State law, any parent or Indian custodian from whose custody such child was removed, and the Indian child's tribe may petition any court of competent jurisdiction to invalidate such action upon a showing that such action violated any provision of sections 1911, 1912, and 1913 of this Act.

25 U.S.C. § 1915. Placement of Indian children.

(a) Adoptive placements; preferences.

In any adoptive placement of an Indian child under State law, a preference shall be given, in the absence of good cause to the contrary, to a placement with (1) a member of the child's extended family; (2) other members of the Indian child's tribe; or (3) other Indian families.

(b) Foster care placements; preferences.

Any child accepted for foster care or preadoptive placement shall be placed in the least restrictive setting which most approximates a family and in which his special needs, if any, may be met. The child shall also be placed within reasonable proximity to his or her home, taking into account any special needs of the child. In any foster care or preadoptive placement, a preference shall be given, in the absence of good cause to the contrary, to a placement with—,

(i) a member of the Indian child's extended family;

(ii) a foster home licensed, approved, or specified by the Indian child's tribe;

(iii) an Indian foster home licensed or approved by an authorized non-Indian licensing authority; or

(iv) an institution for children approved by an Indian tribe or operated by an Indian organization which has a program suitable to meet the Indian child's needs.

(c) Tribal resolution for different order of preference; personal preference considered; anonymity in application of preferences

In the case of a placement under subsection (a) or (b) of this section, if the Indian child's tribe shall establish a different order of preference by resolution, the agency or court effecting the placement shall follow such order so long as the placement is the least restrictive setting appropriate to the particular needs of the child, as provided in subsection (b) of this section. Where appropriate, the preference of the Indian child or parent shall be considered: Provided, That where a consenting parent evidences a desire for anonymity, the court or agency shall give weight to such desire in applying the preferences.

(d) Social and cultural standards applicable

The standards to be applied in meeting the preference requirements of this section shall be the prevailing social and cultural standards of the Indian community in which the parent or extended family resides or with which the parent or extended family members maintain social and cultural ties.

***

25 U.S.C. § 1918. Reassumption of jurisdiction over child custody proceedings.

(a) Any Indian tribe which became subject to State jurisdiction pursuant to the provisions of the Act of August 15, 1953 (67 Stat. 588), as amended by title IV of the Act of April 11, 1968 (82 Stat. 73, 78), or pursuant to any other Federal law, may reassume jurisdiction over child custody proceedings. Before any Indian tribe may reassume jurisdiction over Indian child custody proceedings, such tribe shall present to the Secretary for approval a petition to reassume such jurisdiction which includes a suitable plan to exercise such jurisdiction.

***

NOTES AND QUESTIONS

1. *"Child custody proceeding."* Does ICWA apply if a parent voluntarily gives his child up for adoption or foster care? What if two parents are seeking a divorce and fighting over custody of their child? What if the parents fighting over custody were never married?

2. *"Indian child."* Use the language of the statute to answer the following hypotheticals.

a. Sarah is the daughter of Alex, a member of the Navajo Nation. She is eligible for membership but has never enrolled or lived on the reservation. Is she an "Indian child" under ICWA?

b. Jacob has no Indian ancestry but has been adopted by a Cheyenne River Sioux couple and been enrolled as a member of the tribe. Is he an "Indian child" under ICWA? *See Matter of Dependency & Neglect of A.L.*, 442 N.W.2d 233 (S.D. 1989).

c. Lucy is the daughter of Carol, both of whom have grown up on the White Mountain Apache Reservation, and both of whom are full blood Apache and eligible for membership, but neither of whom have officially enrolled. Is Lucy an "Indian child" under ICWA?

d. A tribe and a state disagree regarding whether a child is eligible for membership under the tribe's membership laws. Whose interpretation controls?

Questions were raised about ICWA's application to children who were not enrolled in their tribes. The 1978 House Report addressed these questions:

> If the courts have found that Congress has the power to act with respect to nonenrolled Indians [in cases of federal criminal jurisdiction], how much more is its power to act to protect the valuable rights of a minor Indian who is eligible for enrollment in a tribe? This minor, perhaps infant, Indian does not have the capacity to initiate the formal, mechanical procedure necessary to become enrolled in his tribe to take advantage of the very valuable cultural and property benefits flowing therefrom. Obviously, Congress has power to act for their protection. The constitutional and plenary power of Congress over Indians and Indian tribes and affairs cannot be made to hinge upon the cranking into operation of a mechanical process established under tribal law, particularly with respect to Indian children who, because of their minority, cannot make a reasoned decision about their tribal and Indian identity.

H.R. Rep. 95–1386 at 17. Did Congress appropriately draw the line to protect the interests of such children?

3. *BIA Regulations*. In 2016 the BIA issued binding regulations to implement the statute. The Summary to the rule states: "This final rule adds a new subpart to the Department of the Interior's (Department) regulations implementing the Indian Child Welfare Act (ICWA), to improve ICWA implementation. The final rule addresses requirements for State courts in ensuring implementation of ICWA in Indian child-welfare proceedings and requirements for States to maintain records under ICWA." Indian Child Welfare Act Proceedings, 81 Fed. Reg. 38778 (June 16, 2016), *codified at* 25 C.F.R. part 23. The rule became effective December 12, 2016. *Id.* The BIA also published notice of new Guidelines for Implementing the Indian Child Welfare Act, 81 Fed. Reg. 96,476 (Dec. 30, 2016).

Immediately after the rule was published, "a coalition of adoption organizations, including the National Council for Adoption, Catholic Charities and others, argued the regulations 'may well be harmful to children,' and are beyond the scope of the federal government's authority under the law." Erica Martinson, *New Federal Rule Aims to Keep Children in Native Families*, Alaska Dispatch News (June 14, 2016; updated July 14, 2016) http://www.adn.com/politics/2016/06/14/new-federal-rule-aims-to-keep-native-children-up-for-adoption-in-tribal-communities/ [https://perma.cc/4UJT-USUS].

In *Brackeen v. Bernhardt*, 937 F.3d 406 (5th Cir. 2019) the court rejected a facial constitutional challenge to the statute as well as constitutional and statutory challenges to the regulations. In relevant part, the court stated

> The district court concluded that ICWA's "Indian Child" definition was a race-based classification. We conclude that this was error. Congress has exercised plenary power "over the tribal relations of the Indians ... from the beginning, and the power has always been deemed a political one, not subject to be controlled by the judicial department of the government." *Lone Wolf v. Hitchcock*, 187 U.S. 553, 565 (1903). The Supreme Court's decisions "leave no doubt that federal legislation with respect to Indian tribes ... is not based upon impermissible racial classifications." *United States v. Antelope*, 430 U.S. 641, 645 (1977). *** ICWA's definition of "Indian child" is not based solely on tribal ancestry or race. ICWA defines an "Indian child" as "any unmarried person who is under age eighteen and is either (a) a member of an Indian tribe or (b) is eligible for membership in an Indian tribe and is the biological child of a member of an Indian tribe." 25 U.S.C. § 1903(4). As Defendants explain, under some tribal membership laws, eligibility extends to children without Indian blood, such as the descendants of former slaves of tribes who became members after they were freed, or the descendants of adopted white persons. Accordingly, a child may fall under ICWA's membership eligibility standard because his or her biological parent became a member of a tribe, despite not being racially Indian. Additionally, many racially Indian children, such as those belonging to non-federally recognized tribes, do not fall within ICWA's definition of "Indian child." Conditioning a child's eligibility for membership, in part, on whether a biological parent is a member of the tribe is therefore not a proxy for race, as the district court concluded, but rather for not-yet-formalized tribal affiliation, particularly where the child is too young to formally apply for membership in a tribe.
>
> [The court then rejected the argument that ICWA violates the Tenth Amendment's anticommandeering doctrine by setting standards for state courts and state agencies to follow in child custody proceedings. The court also found that the provision allowing tribes to change the statutory child placement preferences did not violate the non-delegation doctrine. Finally, the court held that the BIA did not exceed its broad authority under the ICWA and that the BIA regulations were not otherwise unconstitutional. A petition for rehearing *en banc* is pending.]

4. *Tribal jurisdiction over children domiciled outside of Indian country.* Section 1911(b) deals with child custody cases involving Indian children who are domiciled outside of Indian country. To see how this provision works, consider a hypothetical. Alex, a member of the Laguna Pueblo tribe, and Lisa, a non-Indian, are married and live in Albuquerque. After Alex is killed in a car crash, Lisa seeks to have her adult niece (Joanna's cousin) adopt their infant daughter Joanna. Joanna is eligible for membership in the Laguna Pueblo.

a. The tribe intervenes and seeks to have the case transferred to the Laguna Pueblo court. Lisa does not want the case transferred. Will the court transfer the case?

b. Assume the court does not transfer the case. The state social worker says that there is an unrelated Laguna Pueblo family interested in adopting Joanna. Assuming both homes are found suitable, should the court place the child with Joanna's cousin or with the Laguna Pueblo family? What if Lisa wants Joanna adopted by an unrelated family?

5. *Tribal jurisdiction over children domiciled in Indian country.* ICWA's provisions regarding jurisdiction over children domiciled in Indian country reflect earlier case law. *Fisher v. District Court*, 424 U.S. 382 (1976), held that the Northern Cheyenne Tribe had exclusive jurisdiction over a case involving custody of a tribal member where the parties resided on the reservation. Earlier cases had held that tribes also had exclusive jurisdiction over cases involving Indian children who were domiciled on, but temporarily residing off, the reservation. *See, e.g., Wisconsin Potawatomies of Hannahville Indian Community v. Houston*, 393 F. Supp. 719 (W.D. Mich. 1973) (holding that orphaned children who had been domiciled on reservation until mother brought them with her temporarily before moving to Milwaukee were domiciled on the reservation at time of parents' death and therefore subject to tribal jurisdiction). The following case discusses the meaning of § 1911(a) and the interpretation of ICWA generally.

MISSISSIPPI BAND OF CHOCTAW INDIANS V. HOLYFIELD

490 U.S. 30, 109 S. Ct. 1597, 104 L. Ed. 2d 29 (1989)

JUSTICE BRENNAN delivered the opinion of the Court.

This appeal requires us to construe the provisions of the Indian Child Welfare Act that establish exclusive tribal jurisdiction over child custody proceedings involving Indian children domiciled on the tribe's reservation.

***

At the heart of the ICWA are its provisions concerning jurisdiction over Indian child custody proceedings. Section 1911 lays out a dual jurisdictional scheme. Section 1911(a) establishes exclusive jurisdiction in the tribal courts for proceedings concerning an Indian child "who resides or is domiciled within the reservation of such tribe," as well as for wards of tribal courts regardless of domicile. Section 1911(b), on the other hand, creates concurrent but presumptively tribal jurisdiction in the case of children not domiciled on the reservation: on petition of either parent or the tribe, state-court proceedings for foster care placement or termination of parental rights are to be transferred to the tribal court, except in cases of "good cause," objection by either parent, or declination of jurisdiction by the tribal court. ***

This case involves the status of twin babies, known for our purposes as B.B. and G.B., who were born out of wedlock on December 29, 1985. Their mother, J.B., and father, W.J., were both enrolled members of appellant Mississippi Band of Choctaw Indians (Tribe), and were residents and domiciliaries of the Choctaw Reservation in Neshoba County, Mississippi. J.B. gave birth to the twins in Gulfport, Harrison County, Mississippi, some 200 miles from the reservation. On January 10, 1986, J.B. executed a consent-to-adoption form before the Chancery Court of Harrison County. W.J. signed a similar form. On January 16, appellees Orrey and Vivian Holyfield filed a petition for adoption in the same court, and the chancellor issued a Final Decree of Adoption on January 28. Despite the court's apparent awareness of the ICWA, the adoption decree contained no reference to it, nor to the infants' Indian background.

Two months later the Tribe moved in the Chancery Court to vacate the adoption decree on the ground that under the ICWA exclusive jurisdiction was vested in the tribal court. On July 14, 1986, the court overruled the motion, holding that the Tribe "never obtained exclusive jurisdiction over the children involved herein." *** The court's one-page opinion relied on two facts in reaching that conclusion. The court noted first that the twins' mother "went to some efforts to see that they were born outside the confines of the Choctaw Indian Reservation" and that the parents had promptly arranged for the adoption by the Holyfields. Second, the court stated: "At no time from the birth of these children to the present date have either of them resided on or physically been on the Choctaw Indian Reservation." The Supreme Court of Mississippi affirmed. ***

II

*** In enacting the ICWA Congress confirmed that, in child custody proceedings involving Indian children domiciled on the reservation, tribal jurisdiction was exclusive as to the States.

*** The sole issue in this case is, as the Supreme Court of Mississippi recognized, whether the twins were "domiciled" on the reservation.

A.

The meaning of "domicile" in the ICWA is, of course, a matter of Congress' intent. The ICWA itself does not define it. The initial question we must confront is whether there is any reason to believe that Congress intended the ICWA definition of "domicile" to be a matter of state law. *** We start, however, with the general assumption that "in the absence of a plain indication to the contrary, *** Congress when it enacts a statute is not making the application of the federal act dependent on state law." *Jerome v. United States*, 318 U.S. 101, 104 (1943). ***

For the two principal reasons that follow, we believe that [this presumption] applies equally well to the ICWA.

First, and most fundamentally, the purpose of the ICWA gives no reason to believe that Congress intended to rely on state law for the definition of a critical term; quite the contrary. It is clear from the very text of the ICWA, not to mention its legislative history and the hearings that led to its enactment, that Congress was concerned with the rights of Indian families and Indian communities vis-á-vis state authorities. More specifically, its purpose was, in part, to make clear that in certain situations the state courts did *not* have jurisdiction over child custody proceedings. Indeed, the congressional findings that are a part of the statute demonstrate that Congress perceived the States and their courts as partly responsible for the problem it intended to correct. *See* 25 U.S.C. § 1901(5). *** Under these circumstances it is most improbable that Congress would have intended to leave the scope of the statute's key jurisdictional provision subject to definition by state courts as a matter of state law.

Second, Congress could hardly have intended the lack of nationwide uniformity that would result from state-law definitions of domicile. *** Even if we could conceive of a federal statute under which the rules of domicile (and thus of jurisdiction) applied differently to different Indian children, a statute under which different rules apply from time to time to the same child, simply as a result of his or her transport from one State to another, cannot be what Congress had in mind. ***

B.

It remains to give content to the term "domicile" in the circumstances of the present case. ***

We therefore look both to the generally accepted meaning of the term "domicile" and to the purpose of the statute.

*** "Domicile" is not necessarily synonymous with "residence," and one can reside in one place but be domiciled in another. For adults, domicile is established by physical presence in a place in connection with a certain state of mind concerning one's intent to remain there. One acquires a "domicile of origin" at birth, and that domicile continues until a new one (a "domicile of choice") is acquired. Since most minors are legally incapable of forming the requisite intent to establish a domicile, their domicile is determined by that of their parents. In the case of an illegitimate child, that has traditionally meant the domicile of its mother. [Citations omitted.] Restatement 2d Conflict of Laws § 14(2), § 22, Comment *c;* 25 Am. Jur. 2d, Domicile § 69 (1966). Under these principles, it is entirely logical that "[o]n occasion, a child's domicile of origin will be in a place where the child has never been." Restatement § 14, Comment *b.*

It is undisputed in this case that the domicile of the mother (as well as the father) has been, at all relevant times, on the Choctaw Reservation. Thus, it is clear that at their birth the twin babies were also domiciled on the reservation, even though they themselves had never been there. The statement of the Supreme Court of Mississippi that "[a]t no point in time can it be said the twins *** were domiciled within the territory set aside for the reservation," 511 So.2d at 921, may be a correct statement of that State's law of domicile, but it is inconsistent with generally accepted doctrine in this country and cannot be what Congress had in mind when it used the term in the ICWA.

Nor can the result be any different simply because the twins were "voluntarily surrendered" by their mother. Tribal jurisdiction under § 1911(a) was not meant to be defeated by the actions of individual members of the tribe, for Congress was concerned not solely about the interests of Indian children and families, but also about the impact on the tribes themselves of the large numbers of Indian children adopted by non-Indians. *See* 25 U.S.C. §§ 1901(3) ("[T]here is no resource that is more vital to the continued existence and integrity of Indian tribes than their children"), 1902 ("promote the stability and security of Indian tribes"). The numerous prerogatives accorded the tribes through the ICWA's substantive provisions, *e.g.,* §§ 1911(a) (exclusive jurisdiction over reservation domiciliaries), 1911(b) (presumptive jurisdiction over nondomiciliaries), 1911(c) (right of intervention), 1912(a) (notice), 1914 (right to petition for invalidation of state-court action), 1915(c) (right to alter presumptive placement priorities applicable to state-court actions), 1915(e) (right to obtain records), 1919 (authority to conclude agreements with States), must, accordingly, be seen as a means of protecting not only the interests of individual Indian children and families, but also of the tribes themselves.

In addition, it is clear that Congress' concern over the placement of Indian children in non-Indian homes was based in part on evidence of the detrimental impact on the children themselves of such placements outside their culture. Congress determined to subject such placements to the ICWA's jurisdictional and other provisions, even in cases where the parents consented to an adoption, because of concerns going beyond the wishes of individual parents. As the 1977 Final Report of the congressionally established American Indian Policy Review Commission stated, in summarizing these two concerns, "[r]emoval of Indian children from their cultural setting seriously impacts a long-term tribal survival and has damaging social and psychological impact on many individual Indian children." Senate Report, at 52.

These congressional objectives make clear that a rule of domicile that would permit individual Indian parents to defeat the ICWA's jurisdictional scheme is inconsistent with what Congress intended. *** The appellees in this case argue strenuously that the twins' mother went to great lengths to give birth off the reservation so that her children could be adopted by the Holyfields. But that was precisely part of Congress' concern. Permitting individual members of the tribe to avoid tribal exclusive jurisdiction by the simple expedient of giving birth off the reservation would, to a large extent, nullify the purpose the ICWA was intended to accomplish. The Supreme Court of Utah expressed this well in its scholarly and sensitive opinion in what has become a leading case on the ICWA:

> To the extent that [state] abandonment law operates to permit [the child's] mother to change [the child's] domicile as part of a scheme to facilitate his adoption by non-Indians while she remains a domiciliary of the reservation, it conflicts with and undermines the operative scheme established by subsections [1911(a)] and [1913(a)] to deal with children of domiciliaries of the reservation and weakens considerably the tribe's ability to assert its interest in its children. The protection of this tribal interest is at the core of the ICWA, which recognizes that the tribe has an interest in the child which is distinct from but on a parity with the interest of the parents. This relationship between Indian tribes and Indian children domiciled on the reservation finds no parallel in other ethnic cultures found in the United States. It is a relationship that many non-Indians find difficult to understand and that non-Indian courts are slow to recognize. It is precisely in recognition of this relationship, however, that the ICWA designates the tribal court as the exclusive forum for the determination of custody and adoption matters for reservation-domiciled Indian children, and the preferred forum for nondomiciliary Indian children. [State] abandonment law cannot be used to frustrate the federal legislative judgment expressed in the ICWA that the interests of the tribe in custodial decisions made with respect to Indian children are as entitled to respect as the interests of the parents. *In re Adoption of Halloway*, 732 P.2d 962, 969–970 (1986).

We agree with the Supreme Court of Utah that the law of domicile Congress used in the ICWA cannot be one that permits individual reservation-domiciled tribal members to defeat the tribe's exclusive jurisdiction by the simple expedient of giving birth and placing the child for adoption off the reservation. Since, for purposes of the ICWA, the twin babies in this case were domiciled on the reservation when adoption proceedings were begun, the Choctaw tribal court possessed exclusive jurisdiction pursuant to 25 U.S.C. § 1911(a). The

Chancery Court of Harrison County was, accordingly, without jurisdiction to enter a decree of adoption; under ICWA § 104, 25 U.S.C. § 1914, its decree of January 28, 1986, must be vacated.

III

We are not unaware that over three years have passed since the twin babies were born and placed in the Holyfield home, and that a court deciding their fate today is not writing on a blank slate in the same way it would have in January 1986. Three years' development of family ties cannot be undone, and a separation at this point would doubtless cause considerable pain.

Whatever feelings we might have as to where the twins should live, however, it is not for us to decide that question. We have been asked to decide the legal question of *who* should make the custody determination concerning these children—not what the outcome of that determination should be. The law places that decision in the hands of the Choctaw tribal court. Had the mandate of the ICWA been followed in 1986, of course, much potential anguish might have been avoided, and in any case the law cannot be applied so as automatically to "reward those who obtain custody, whether lawfully or otherwise, and maintain it during any ensuing (and protracted) litigation." *Halloway*, 732 P.2d at 972. It is not ours to say whether the trauma that might result from removing these children from their adoptive family should outweigh the interest of the Tribe—and perhaps the children themselves—in having them raised as part of the Choctaw community. Rather, "we must defer to the experience, wisdom, and compassion of the [Choctaw] tribal courts to fashion an appropriate remedy." ***

Reversed.

JUSTICE STEVENS, with whom THE CHIEF JUSTICE and JUSTICE KENNEDY join, dissenting.

Although parents of Indian children are shielded from the exercise of state jurisdiction when they are temporarily off the reservation, the Act also reflects a recognition that allowing the tribe to defeat the parents' deliberate choice of jurisdiction would be conducive neither to the best interests of the child nor to the stability and security of Indian tribes and families. Section 1911(b), providing for the exercise of concurrent jurisdiction by state and tribal courts when the Indian child is not domiciled on the reservation, gives the Indian parents a veto to prevent the transfer of a state-court action to tribal court. ***

If J.B. and W.J. had established a domicile off the reservation, the state courts would have been required to give effect to their choice of jurisdiction; there should not be a different result when the parents have not changed their own domicile, but have expressed an unequivocal intent to establish a domicile for their children off the reservation. *** The interpretation of domicile adopted by the Court requires the custodian of an Indian child who is off the reservation to haul the child to a potentially distant tribal court unfamiliar with the child's present living conditions and best interests. Moreover, it renders any custody decision made by a state court forever suspect, susceptible to challenge at any time as void for having been entered in the absence of jurisdiction. Finally, it forces parents of Indian children who desire to invoke state-court jurisdiction to establish a domicile off the reservation. Only if the custodial parent has the wealth and ability to establish a domicile off the reservation will the parent be able to use the processes of state court. I fail to see how such a requirement serves the paramount congressional purpose of "promot[ing] the stability and security of Indian tribes and families." 25 U.S.C. § 1902. ***

NOTES AND QUESTIONS

1. The usual touchstone for child custody determinations is the best interests of the child. As interpreted by *Holyfield*, does ICWA displace that standard, redefine it, or both?

2. *Holyfield* is a dramatic example of § 1914 of ICWA, which provides for invalidation of any placement made in violation of the Act's jurisdictional provisions. Notice that violation of the Act's placement provisions (that is, assuming the proper assertion of state jurisdiction) is not subject to this extraordinary remedy. Why might Congress' concerns in enacting ICWA have led it to place so much emphasis on tribal jurisdiction?

3. *Aftermath of* Holyfield. Notice that *Holyfield* does not decide the ultimate placement issue, but instead which court will decide. On remand, the Mississippi Choctaw Tribal Court decided that it was in the best interests of the children to remain with their adoptive mother and granted the adoption but ordered that the children have contact with their Choctaw relatives. *See* Solangel Maldonado, *The Story of the Holyfield Twins:* Mississippi Band of Choctaw Indians v. Holyfield, *in* Family Law Stories 113 (2007). Although Orrey Holyfield died when the twins were three (one of the reasons the couple could not adopt through normal channels was that Orrey was 60 years old and had both heart disease and diabetes), the Choctaw Court found that Vivian Holyfield had provided the children with a good home, and it would be wrong to separate them from the only mother they had known. The children have maintained contact with their half-siblings and extended family members. *Id.*

In *Matter of Adoption of Halloway*, 732 P.2d 962 (Utah 1986), the state court decision relied on by *Holyfield*, the Navajo Nation courts similarly affirmed the non-Indian parents' custody. Thomas B. Rosenstiel, *Utah Couple Wins Guardianship of Navajo Boy*, L.A. Times, Oct. 30, 1987; *see also* Betty Reid, *Dispute in the Past, Baby K Back Home*, Arizona Republic, July 6, 2005 (discussing Allyssa Keetso–Pitts, for whom the Navajo court affirmed the original adoption, who chose to return to Navajo and live with her grandmother after graduating from high school).

4. *Good cause not to transfer*. Section 1911(b) provides that state courts "shall transfer" child custody cases involving children domiciled off-reservation absent parental veto, tribal declination, or "good cause to the contrary." What constitutes good cause? The new BIA regulations provide:

> (c) In determining whether good cause exists, the court must not consider:
>
> > (1) Whether the foster-care or termination-of-parental-rights proceeding is at an advanced stage if the Indian child's parent, Indian custodian, or Tribe did not receive notice of the child-custody proceeding until an advanced stage;
> >
> > (2) Whether there have been prior proceedings involving the child for which no petition to transfer was filed;

(3) Whether transfer could affect the placement of the child;

(4) The Indian child's cultural connections with the Tribe or its reservation; or

(5) Socioeconomic conditions or any negative perception of Tribal or BIA social services or judicial systems.

25 C.F.R. § 23.118.

Consider this guidance and the purposes of ICWA in answering the following hypotheticals:

(a) The state court judge believes living on the reservation is not in the best interests of the child. Good cause to deny transfer?

(b) The state court believes that the tribal court is biased against child's non-Indian relatives, who are potential foster parents for child. Is there good cause to deny transfer?

(c) The mother, child, and the child's extended family have always lived in New York City, and the tribe is located in Idaho, and cannot afford to pay the travel costs of witnesses. Is there good cause to deny transfer? If you find that there is, what might be other options for the tribe or the court?

5. *Placement preferences.* States hearing ICWA cases must, in deciding on a placement for a child, follow certain placement preferences again "absent good cause to the contrary." The adoption preferences direct placement with the child's extended family, then members of the child's tribe, then other Indian families, while the foster care preferences direct placement with the child's extended family, then a foster care home licensed or approved by the tribe, then an Indian foster care home approved by a non-Indian agency, then an Indian organization or an organization approved by the tribe. Consider the following questions on what constitutes "good cause" to depart from the placement preferences.

(a) Should "good cause" be interpreted in the same way as a generalized "best interests of the child" standard?

(b) What if the child has been living with a non-Indian foster family for four years but an Indian foster family is now available?

What if the choice is between an Indian foster home and non-Indian adoptive family? (NB: This is a trick question.)

The new BIA regulations provide that:

(c) A court's determination of good cause to depart from the placement preferences must be made on the record or in writing and should be based on one or more of the following considerations:

(1) The request of one or both of the Indian child's parents, if they attest that they have reviewed the placement options, if any, that comply with the order of preference;

(2) The request of the child, if the child is of sufficient age and capacity to understand the decision that is being made;

(3) The presence of a sibling attachment that can be maintained only through a particular placement;

(4) The extraordinary physical, mental, or emotional needs of the Indian child, such as specialized treatment services that may be unavailable in the community where families who meet the placement preferences live;

(5) The unavailability of a suitable placement after a determination by the court that a diligent search was conducted to find suitable placements meeting the preference criteria, but none has been located. For purposes of this analysis, the standards for determining whether a placement is unavailable must conform to the prevailing social and cultural standards of the Indian community in which the Indian child's parent or extended family resides or with which the Indian child's parent or extended family members maintain social and cultural ties.

(d) A placement may not depart from the preferences based on the socioeconomic status of any placement relative to another placement.

(e) A placement may not depart from the preferences based solely on ordinary bonding or attachment that flowed from time spent in a non-preferred placement that was made in violation of ICWA.

25 C.F.R. § 23.132.

The placement preferences are one of the most controversial aspects of ICWA. Randall Kennedy, for example, condemns them as "the last stand of open race matching in America," and argues (without evidence) that they "decrease the likelihood that needy children will find adoptive homes, popularize hurtful superstitions, and reinforce claims that unfairly stigmatize substantial numbers of non-Indian adoptive parents." Interracial Intimacies: Sex, Marriage, Identity and Adoption 480, 518 (2003). *But see* Carole Goldberg, *Descent into Race*, 49 UCLA L. Rev. 1373, 1386 (2002). A 2005 General Accounting Office report evaluated the concern that the preferences would lengthen the period that children remained without permanent placements. The report did not find evidence to support the concern: children subject to ICWA did not remain without permanent placements longer or experience more changes in placements than other children in foster care. *See* General Accounting Office, GAO–05–290, *Indian Child Welfare Act: Existing Information on Implementation Issues Could be Used to Target Assistance to States* 4 (2005).

6. *The Existing Indian Family Exception.* Some courts have declined to apply ICWA by claiming that the statute does not apply where there is not an "existing Indian family" involved. By this, the courts mean that although the child is an "Indian child" as defined by the statute, the family has insufficient social or cultural ties with an Indian community, so that removing the child from the family does not disrupt the kind of "Indian families" that ICWA was intended to protect. The doctrine was first created by the Kansas courts in *In*

re Adoption of Baby Boy L., in which a non-Indian mother sought to have a non-Indian family adopt her infant son over the objections of her son's Kiowa father and the Kiowa tribe. The court declared:

> A careful study of the legislative history behind the Act and the Act itself discloses that the overriding concern of Congress and the proponents of the Act was the maintenance of the family and tribal relationships existing in Indian homes. *** It was not to dictate that an illegitimate infant who has never been a member of an Indian home or culture, and probably never would be, should be removed from its primary cultural heritage and placed in an Indian environment over the express objections of its non-Indian mother.

643 P.2d 168, 175 (Kan. 1982). Today, six states follow the doctrine: Alabama, Indiana, Louisiana, Missouri, Nevada, and Tennessee. *See S.A. v. E.J.P.*, 571 So.2d 1187 (Ala. Civ. App. 1990); *In re Adoption of T.R.M.*, 525 N.E.2d 298 (Ind. 1988); *Hampton v. J.A.L.*, 658 So.2d 331 (La. Ct. App. 1995); *In re S.A.M.*, 703 S.W.2d 603 (Mo. Ct. App. 1986); *Dawn M. v. Nev. State Div. of Child & Family Servs. (In re N.J.),* 125 Nev. 835 (Nev. 2009); *In re Morgan*, 1997 WL 716880 (Tenn. Ct. App. 1997). California's intermediate courts are split regarding the doctrine. *Compare Adoption of Hannah S.*, 48 Cal. Rptr. 3d 605 (Ct. App. 3d Dist. 2006) (rejecting the doctrine) *and In re Alicia S.*, 65 Cal. App. 4th 79 (Cal. Ct. App. 5th Dist. 1998) (rejecting the doctrine) *with In re Santos Y.*, 92 Cal. App. 4th 1274 (Cal. Ct. App. 2d Dist. 2001) (accepting the doctrine on constitutional grounds).

The new regulations do not declare that there is no "Existing Indian Family" exception to ICWA, but the rules do provide: "In determining whether ICWA applies to a proceeding, the State court may not consider factors such as the participation of the parents or the Indian child in Tribal cultural, social, religious, or political activities, the relationship between the Indian child and his or her parents, whether the parent ever had custody of the child, or the Indian child's blood quantum." 25 C.F.R. § 23.103. Will this effectively eliminate the exception in the states that follow the doctrine? Can the regulations bind state courts?

Fifteen states have rejected the doctrine by decision or statute, including some states, such as Oklahoma and Kansas, which initially adopted it. The states are Alaska, Arizona, Colorado, Idaho, Illinois, Iowa, Kansas, Michigan, Minnesota, Montana, New Jersey, Oklahoma, South Dakota, North Dakota, Utah and Washington. *See In re Adoption of T.N.F.*, 781 P.2d 973 (Alaska 1989); *Michael J., Jr. v. Michael J., Sr.*, 198 Ariz. 154 (Ct. App. 2000); *In re Baby Boy Doe*, 123 Idaho 464 (1993); *In re Adoption of S.S.*, 167 Ill.2d 250 (Ill. 1995); *In re R.E.K.F.*, 698 N.W.2d 147 (Ia. 2005); *In re A.J.S.*, 204 P.3d 543 (Kan. 2009); *In re Elliott*, 554 N.W. 2d 32 (Mich. 1996); *In re Welfare of S.N.R.*, 617 N.W.2d 77 (Minn. Ct. App. 2000); *In re Adoption of Riffle*, 922 P.2d 510 (Mont. 1996); *In re Adoption of a Child of Indian Heritage*, 111 N.J. 155 (N.J. 1988); *Hoots v. K.B.*, 663 N.W.2d 625, 636 (N.D. 2003); *In re Adoption of Baade*, 462 N.W.2d 485 (S.D. 1990); *In the Matter of Baby Boy L.*, 103 P.3d 1099 (Okla. 2004); *In re D.A.C.*, 933 P.2d 993 (Utah Ct. App. 1997); *In re N.B.*, 199 P.3d 16 (Colo. Ct. App. 2007); *Matter of Adoption of T.A.W.*, 383 P.3d 492, 505 (Wash. 2016) (recognizing and endorsing legislative reversal of prior case applying exception). One of New York's appellate divisions has also rejected the doctrine. *In re Baby Boy C.*, 805 N.Y.S.2d 313 (N.Y. App. Div. 2005).

The Second District of the California Appellate Court adopted the exception on constitutional grounds, holding that where there is little contact with an Indian community besides eligibility for enrollment, application of ICWA violates the Fifth, Tenth, and Fourteenth Amendments to the United States Constitution because it treats children differently because of their race and deprives states of authority over custody of children within state borders. Consider the facts of the two cases taking this approach. *In re Bridget R.*, 41 Cal. App. 4th 1483 (Cal. Ct. App. 1996), concerned twin girls surrendered by their parents for adoption at birth. The parents, themselves 20 and 21 at the time, were living in a shelter and believed they could not care for the twins in addition to their two other children. The girls' mother Cindy was descended from the Yaqui tribe of Mexico but had no contact with the Yaqui tribe of the United States. The girls' father Richard was a member of the Dry Creek Rancheria of the Pomo Indians but lived in Los Angeles, several hundred miles from the tribe's reservation in Sonoma County. Although Richard originally recorded his ethnicity as one-quarter Indian on the relevant adoption forms, the attorney facilitating the adoption told him that this would delay the adoption, so Richard filled in new forms recording his ethnicity as white. Shortly after their birth the twins were taken to Ohio with their new foster parents. A few months later Richard told his mother about the relinquishment, and with her assistance and the assistance of the tribe sought to rescind the adoption so that the children could be adopted by an extended family member. There was no question that the relinquishment and adoption had not satisfied the procedural requirements of ICWA. The court decided that applying ICWA under these facts would be unconstitutional. The court declared:

> We have no quarrel with the proposition that preserving American Indian culture is a legitimate, even compelling, governmental interest. At the same time, however, we agree with those courts which have held that this purpose will not be served by applying the provisions of ICWA which are at issue in this case to children whose biological parents do not have a significant social, cultural or political relationship with an Indian community. It is almost too obvious to require articulation that "the unique values of Indian culture" (25 U.S.C. § 1902) will not be preserved in the homes of parents who have become fully assimilated into non-Indian culture. This being so, it is questionable whether a rational basis, far less a compelling need, exists for applying the requirements of the Act where fully assimilated Indian parents seek to voluntarily relinquish children for adoption.

41 Cal. App. 4th at 1507. *See also In re Santos Y.*, 92 Cal. App. 4th 1274 (Cal. Ct. App. 2001) (applying existing Indian family exception to adoption proceeding where tribal member mother lived in Los Angeles most of her life and had no contact with her tribe).

Why are the state courts unwilling to apply ICWA in these cases? Do you see how the facts of these cases might trouble tribes about the possibility of having state courts decide who is "Indian enough" for ICWA to apply? Was declaring ICWA unconstitutional as applied necessary to avoid the results the courts didn't want in these cases? *See* Barbara Atwood, *Flashpoints Under the Existing Indian Family Exception: Toward a New Understanding of State Court Resistance*, 51 Emory L. J. 587 (2002) (discussing the concerns leading to the existing family exception, but arguing that ICWA properly construed can address these concerns without the escape hatch of the existing Indian family doctrine) *and* Lorie M. Graham, *The Past Never Vanishes: A Contextual Critique of the Existing Indian Family Doctrine*, 23 Am. Ind. L. Rev. 1 (1998) (arguing that the exception is both bad policy and bad law).

How would you evaluate the constitutional challenges to the existing Indian family doctrine? Review *Mancari* and the discussion of equal protection analysis in the context of federally recognized tribes. Does *Bridget R* tackle the equal protection issues according to existing law? Is the doctrine a reasonable interpretation of the statute itself?

In the following case, the Supreme Court does not apply the existing Indian family doctrine, but instead interprets provisions of ICWA narrowly to avoid applying it to an adoption case. Are some of the same concerns at play in this case as in the California cases? Are the concerns justified?

ADOPTIVE COUPLE V. BABY GIRL

570 U.S. 637, 133 S. Ct. 2552, 186 L.Ed.2d 729 (2013)

JUSTICE ALITO delivered the opinion of the Court.

This case is about a little girl (Baby Girl) who is classified as an Indian because she is 1.2% (3/256) Cherokee. Because Baby Girl is classified in this way, the South Carolina Supreme Court held that certain provisions of the federal Indian Child Welfare Act of 1978 required her to be taken, at the age of 27 months, from the only parents she had ever known and handed over to her biological father, who had attempted to relinquish his parental rights and who had no prior contact with the child. The provisions of the federal statute at issue here do not demand this result.

Contrary to the State Supreme Court's ruling, we hold that 25 U.S.C. § 1912(f)—which bars involuntary termination of a parent's rights in the absence of a heightened showing that serious harm to the Indian child is likely to result from the parent's "continued custody" of the child—does not apply when, as here, the relevant parent never had custody of the child. We further hold that § 1912(d)—which conditions involuntary termination of parental rights with respect to an Indian child on a showing that remedial efforts have been made to prevent the "breakup of the Indian family"—is inapplicable when, as here, the parent abandoned the Indian child before birth and never had custody of the child. Finally, we clarify that § 1915(a), which provides placement preferences for the adoption of Indian children, does not bar a non-Indian family like Adoptive Couple from adopting an Indian child when no other eligible candidates have sought to adopt the child. We accordingly reverse the South Carolina Supreme Court's judgment and remand for further proceedings.

***

Three provisions of the ICWA are especially relevant to this case. First, "[a]ny party seeking" an involuntary termination of parental rights to an Indian child under state law must demonstrate that "active efforts have been made to provide remedial services and rehabilitative programs designed to prevent the breakup of the Indian family and that these efforts have proved unsuccessful." § 1912(d). Second, a state court may not involuntarily terminate parental rights to an Indian child "in the absence of a determination, supported by evidence beyond a reasonable doubt, including testimony of qualified expert witnesses, that the continued custody of the child by the parent or Indian custodian is likely to result in serious emotional or physical damage to the child." § 1912(f). Third, with respect to adoptive placements for an Indian child under state law, "a preference shall be given, in the absence of good cause to the contrary, to a placement with (1) a member of the child's extended family; (2) other members of the Indian child's tribe; or (3) other Indian families." § 1915(a).

In this case, Birth Mother (who is predominantly Hispanic) and Biological Father (who is a member of the Cherokee Nation) became engaged in December 2008. One month later, Birth Mother informed Biological Father, who lived about four hours away, that she was pregnant. After learning of the pregnancy, Biological Father asked Birth Mother to move up the date of the wedding. He also refused to provide any financial support until after the two had married. The couple's relationship deteriorated, and Birth Mother broke off the engagement in May 2009. In June, Birth Mother sent Biological Father a text message asking if he would rather pay child support or relinquish his parental rights. Biological Father responded via text message that he relinquished his rights.

Birth Mother then decided to put Baby Girl up for adoption. Because Birth Mother believed that Biological Father had Cherokee Indian heritage, her attorney contacted the Cherokee Nation to determine whether Biological Father was formally enrolled. The inquiry letter misspelled Biological Father's first name and incorrectly stated his birthday, and the Cherokee Nation responded that, based on the information provided, it could not verify Biological Father's membership in the tribal records.

Working through a private adoption agency, Birth Mother selected Adoptive Couple, non-Indians living in South Carolina, to adopt Baby Girl. Adoptive Couple supported Birth Mother both emotionally and financially throughout her pregnancy. Adoptive Couple was present at Baby Girl's birth in Oklahoma on September 15, 2009, and Adoptive Father even cut the umbilical cord. The next morning, Birth Mother signed forms relinquishing her parental rights and consenting to the adoption. Adoptive Couple initiated adoption proceedings in South Carolina a few days later, and returned there with Baby Girl. After returning to South Carolina, Adoptive Couple allowed Birth Mother to visit and communicate with Baby Girl.

It is undisputed that, for the duration of the pregnancy and the first four months after Baby Girl's birth, Biological Father provided no financial assistance to Birth Mother or Baby Girl, even though he had the ability to do so. Indeed, Biological Father "made no meaningful attempts to assume his responsibility of parenthood" during this period.

Approximately four months after Baby Girl's birth, Adoptive Couple served Biological Father with notice of the pending adoption. (This was the first notification that they had provided to Biological Father regarding the adoption proceeding.) Biological Father signed papers stating that he accepted service and that he was "not contesting the adoption." But Biological Father later testified that, at the time he signed the papers, he thought that he was relinquishing his rights to Birth Mother, not to Adoptive Couple.

Biological Father contacted a lawyer the day after signing the papers, and subsequently requested a stay of the adoption proceedings.[2] In the adoption proceedings, Biological Father sought custody and stated that he did not consent to Baby Girl's adoption. Moreover, Biological Father took a paternity test, which verified that he was Baby Girl's biological father.

A trial took place in the South Carolina Family Court in September 2011, by which time Baby Girl was two years old. The Family Court concluded that Adoptive Couple had not carried the heightened burden under § 1912(f) of proving that Baby Girl would suffer serious emotional or physical damage if Biological Father had custody. The Family Court therefore denied Adoptive Couple's petition for adoption and awarded custody to Biological Father. On December 31, 2011, at the age of 27 months, Baby Girl was handed over to Biological Father, whom she had never met.

The South Carolina Supreme Court affirmed the Family Court's denial of the adoption and the award of custody to Biological Father.

III

It is undisputed that, had Baby Girl not been 3/256 Cherokee, Biological Father would have had no right to object to her adoption under South Carolina law. The South Carolina Supreme Court held, however, that Biological Father is a "parent" under the ICWA and that two statutory provisions— namely, § 1912(f) and § 1912(d)—bar the termination of his parental rights. We need not—and therefore do not—decide whether Biological Father is a "parent." See § 1903(9) (defining "parent"). Rather, assuming for the sake of argument that he is a "parent," we hold that neither § 1912(f) nor § 1912(d) bars the termination of his parental rights.

A

Section 1912(f) addresses the involuntary termination of parental rights with respect to an Indian child. Specifically, § 1912(f) provides that "[n]o termination of parental rights may be ordered in such proceeding in the absence of a determination, supported by evidence beyond a reasonable doubt, ... that the *continued custody* of the child by the parent or Indian custodian is likely to result in serious emotional or physical damage to the child." (Emphasis added.) The South Carolina Supreme Court held that Adoptive Couple failed to satisfy § 1912(f) because they did not make a heightened showing that Biological Father's "*prospective* legal and physical custody" would likely result in serious damage to the child. 731 S.E.2d, at 564 (emphasis added). That holding was error.

Section 1912(f) conditions the involuntary termination of parental rights on a showing regarding the merits of "*continued* custody of the child by the parent." (Emphasis added.) The adjective "continued" plainly refers to a pre-existing state. As Justice Sotomayor concedes, (hereinafter the dissent), "continued" means "[c]arried on or kept up without cessation" or "[e]xtended in space without interruption or breach of conne[ct]ion." Compact Edition of the Oxford English Dictionary 909 (1981 reprint of 1971 ed.) (Compact OED) . . . . The term "continued" also can mean "resumed after interruption." Webster's

2. Around the same time, the Cherokee Nation identified Biological Father as a registered member and concluded that Baby Girl was an "Indian child" as defined in the ICWA. The Cherokee Nation intervened in the litigation approximately three months later.

Third 493. The phrase "continued custody" therefore refers to custody that a parent already has (or at least had at some point in the past). As a result, § 1912(f) does not apply in cases where the Indian parent never had custody of the Indian child.

B

Our reading of § 1912(f) comports with the statutory text demonstrating that the primary mischief the ICWA was designed to counteract was the unwarranted removal of Indian children from Indian families due to the cultural insensitivity and biases of social workers and state courts. The statutory text expressly highlights the primary problem that the statute was intended to solve: "an alarmingly high percentage of Indian families [were being] broken up by the *removal*, often unwarranted, of their children from them by nontribal public and private agencies." § 1901(4) (emphasis added); see also § 1902 (explaining that the ICWA establishes "minimum Federal standards for the *removal* of Indian children from their families" (emphasis added)); *Holyfield*, 490 U.S., at 32–34. And if the legislative history of the ICWA is thought to be relevant, it further underscores that the Act was primarily intended to stem the unwarranted removal of Indian children from intact Indian families. In sum, when, as here, the adoption of an Indian child is voluntarily and lawfully initiated by a non-Indian parent with sole custodial rights, the ICWA's primary goal of preventing the unwarranted removal of Indian children and the dissolution of Indian families is not implicated.

Under our reading of § 1912(f), Biological Father should not have been able to invoke § 1912(f) in this case, because he had never had legal or physical custody of Baby Girl as of the time of the adoption proceedings. As an initial matter, it is undisputed that Biological Father never had physical custody of Baby Girl. And as a matter of both South Carolina and Oklahoma law, Biological Father never had legal custody either. ***

In sum, the South Carolina Supreme Court erred in finding that § 1912(f) barred termination of Biological Father's parental rights.

C

Section 1912(d) provides that "[a]ny party" seeking to terminate parental rights to an Indian child under state law "shall satisfy the court that active efforts have been made to provide remedial services and rehabilitative programs designed *to prevent the breakup of the Indian family* and that these efforts have proved unsuccessful." (Emphasis added.) The South Carolina Supreme Court found that Biological Father's parental rights could not be terminated because Adoptive Couple had not demonstrated that Biological Father had been provided remedial services in accordance with § 1912(d). We disagree.

Consistent with the statutory text, we hold that § 1912(d) applies only in cases where an Indian family's "breakup" would be precipitated by the termination of the parent's rights. The term "breakup" refers in this context to "[t]he discontinuance of a relationship," American Heritage Dictionary 235 (3d ed. 1992), or "an ending as an effective entity," Webster's 273 (defining "breakup" as "a disruption or dissolution into component parts: an ending as an effective entity") ***. But when an Indian parent abandons an Indian child prior to birth and that child has never been in the Indian parent's legal or physical custody, there is no "relationship" that would be "discontinu[ed]"—and no "effective entity" that would be "end[ed]"—by the termination of the Indian parent's rights. In such a situation, the "breakup of the Indian family" has long since occurred, and § 1912(d) is inapplicable.

Our interpretation of § 1912(d) is, like our interpretation of § 1912(f), consistent with the explicit congressional purpose of providing certain "standards for the *removal* of Indian children from their families." § 1902 (emphasis added). ***

Our interpretation of § 1912(d) is also confirmed by the provision's placement next to § 1912(e) and § 1912(f), both of which condition the outcome of proceedings on the merits of an Indian child's "continued custody" with his parent. That these three provisions appear adjacent to each other strongly suggests that the phrase "breakup of the Indian family" should be read in harmony with the "continued custody" requirement ***. None of these three provisions *creates* parental rights for unwed fathers where no such rights would otherwise exist. Instead, Indian parents who are already part of an "Indian family" are provided with access to "remedial services and rehabilitative programs" under § 1912(d) so that their "custody" might be "continued" in a way that avoids foster-care placement under § 1912(e) or termination of parental rights under § 1912(f). In other words, the provision of "remedial services and rehabilitative programs" under § 1912(d) supports the "continued custody" that is protected by § 1912(e) and § 1912(f).[8]

Section 1912(d) is a sensible requirement when applied to state social workers who might otherwise be too quick to remove Indian children from their Indian families. It would, however, be unusual to apply § 1912(d) in the context of an Indian parent who abandoned a child prior to birth and who never had custody of the child. [T]his would *** unnecessarily place vulnerable Indian children at a unique disadvantage in finding a permanent and loving home, even in cases where neither an Indian parent nor the relevant tribe objects to the adoption.

In sum, the South Carolina Supreme Court erred in finding that § 1912(d) barred termination of Biological Father's parental rights. IV In the decision below, the South Carolina Supreme Court suggested that if it had terminated Biological Father's rights, then § 1915(a)'s preferences for the adoptive placement of an Indian child would have been applicable. In so doing, however, the court failed to recognize a critical limitation on the scope of § 1915(a).

Section 1915(a) provides that "[i]n any adoptive placement of an Indian child under State law, a preference shall be given, in the absence of good cause to the contrary, to a placement with (1) a member of the child's extended family; (2) other members of the Indian child's tribe; or (3) other Indian families." Contrary to the South Carolina Supreme Court's suggestion, § 1915(a)'s

8. The dissent claims that our reasoning "necessarily extends to all Indian parents who have never had custody of their children," even if those parents have visitation rights. As an initial matter, the dissent's concern about the effect of our decision on individuals with visitation rights will be implicated, at most, in a relatively small class of cases. For example, our interpretation of § 1912(d) would implicate the dissent's concern only in the case of a parent who abandoned his or her child prior to birth and never had physical or legal custody, but did have some sort of visitation rights. Moreover, in cases where this concern is implicated, such parents might receive "comparable" protections under state law. And in any event, it is the dissent's interpretation that would have far-reaching consequences: Under the dissent's reading, any biological parent—even a sperm donor—would enjoy the heightened protections of § 1912(d) and § 1912(f), even if he abandoned the mother and the child immediately after conception.

preferences are inapplicable in cases where no alternative party has formally sought to adopt the child. This is because there simply is no "preference" to apply if no alternative party that is eligible to be preferred under § 1915(a) has come forward.

In this case, Adoptive Couple was the only party that sought to adopt Baby Girl in the Family Court or the South Carolina Supreme Court. Biological Father is not covered by § 1915(a) because he did not seek to adopt Baby Girl; instead, he argued that his parental rights should not be terminated in the first place. Moreover, Baby Girl's paternal grandparents never sought custody of Baby Girl. Nor did other members of the Cherokee Nation or "other Indian families" seek to adopt Baby Girl, even though the Cherokee Nation had notice of—and intervened in—the adoption proceedings.[12]

The Indian Child Welfare Act was enacted to help preserve the cultural identity and heritage of Indian tribes, but under the State Supreme Court's reading, the Act would put certain vulnerable children at a great disadvantage solely because an ancestor—even a remote one—was an Indian. As the State Supreme Court read §§ 1912(d) and (f), a biological Indian father could abandon his child *in utero* and refuse any support for the birth mother—perhaps contributing to the mother's decision to put the child up for adoption—and then could play his ICWA trump card at the eleventh hour to override the mother's decision and the child's best interests. If this were possible, many prospective adoptive parents would surely pause before adopting any child who might possibly qualify as an Indian under the ICWA. Such an interpretation would raise equal protection concerns, but the plain text of §§ 1912(f) and (d) makes clear that neither provision applies in the present context. Nor do § 1915(a)'s rebuttable adoption preferences apply when no alternative party has formally sought to adopt the child. We therefore reverse the judgment of the South Carolina Supreme Court and remand the case for further proceedings not inconsistent with this opinion.

JUSTICE THOMAS, concurring.

*** Each party in this case has put forward a plausible interpretation of the relevant sections of the Indian Child Welfare Act (ICWA). However, the interpretations offered by respondent Birth Father and the United States raise significant constitutional problems as applied to this case. Because the Court's decision avoids those problems, I concur in its interpretation.

This case arises out of a contested state-court adoption proceeding. Adoption proceedings are adjudicated in state family courts across the country every day, and "domestic relations" is "an area that has long been regarded as a virtually exclusive province of the States." *Sosna v. Iowa*, 419 U.S. 393, 404 (1975). ***

*** Congress may regulate areas of traditional state concern only if the Constitution grants it such power. The threshold question, then, is whether

---

12. To be sure, an employee of the Cherokee Nation testified that the Cherokee Nation certifies families to be adoptive parents and that there are approximately 100 such families "that are ready to take children that want to be adopted." Record 446. However, this testimony was only a general statement regarding the Cherokee Nation's practices; it did not demonstrate that a specific Indian family was willing to adopt Baby Girl, let alone that such a family formally sought such adoption in the South Carolina courts.

the Constitution grants Congress power to override state custody law whenever an Indian is involved.

The ICWA asserts that the Indian Commerce Clause, Art. I, § 8, cl. 3, and "other constitutional authority" provides Congress with "plenary power over Indian affairs." § 1901(1). The reference to "other constitutional authority" is not illuminating, and I am aware of no other enumerated power that could even arguably support Congress' intrusion into this area of traditional state authority. *** Although this Court has said that the "central function of the Indian Commerce Clause is to provide Congress with plenary power to legislate in the field of Indian affairs," *Cotton Petroleum Corp. v. New Mexico*, 490 U.S. 163 (1989), neither the text nor the original understanding of the Clause supports Congress' claim to such "plenary" power.

A

The Indian Commerce Clause gives Congress authority "[t]o regulate *Commerce* ... with the Indian tribes." Art. I, § 8, cl. 3 (emphasis added). "At the time the original Constitution was ratified, 'commerce' consisted of selling, buying, and bartering, as well as transporting for these purposes." *United States v. Lopez*, 514 U.S. 549 (1995) (Thomas, J., concurring). *** Furthermore, the term "commerce with Indian tribes" was invariably used during the time of the founding to mean "'trade with Indians.'" ***

The Indian Commerce Clause contains an additional textual limitation relevant to this case: Congress is given the power to regulate Commerce "with the Indian *tribes*." The Clause does not give Congress the power to regulate commerce with all Indian *persons* any more than the Foreign Commerce Clause gives Congress the power to regulate commerce with all foreign nationals traveling within the United States. A straightforward reading of the text, thus, confirms that Congress may only regulate commercial interactions—"commerce"—taking place with established Indian communities—"tribes." That power is far from "plenary."

B

Congress' assertion of "plenary power" over Indian affairs is also inconsistent with the history of the Indian Commerce Clause. At the time of the founding, the Clause was understood to reserve to the States general police powers with respect to Indians who were citizens of the several States. The Clause instead conferred on Congress the much narrower power to regulate trade with Indian tribes—that is, Indians who had not been incorporated into the body-politic of any State.

***

In light of the original understanding of the Indian Commerce Clause, the constitutional problems that would be created by application of the ICWA here are evident. First, the statute deals with "child custody proceedings," § 1903(1), not "commerce." ***

Second, the portions of the ICWA at issue here do not regulate Indian tribes as tribes. Sections 1912(d) and (f), and § 1915(a) apply to all child custody proceedings involving an Indian child, regardless of whether an Indian tribe is involved. This case thus does not directly implicate Congress' power to "legislate in respect to Indian *tribes*." *United States v. Lara*, 541 U.S. 193, 200 (2004) (emphasis added). *** Nothing in the Indian Commerce Clause permits

Congress to enact special laws applicable to Birth Father merely because of his status as an Indian.

Because adoption proceedings like this one involve neither "commerce" nor "Indian tribes," there is simply no constitutional basis for Congress' assertion of authority over such proceedings. *** Because the Court's plausible interpretation of the relevant sections of the ICWA avoids these constitutional problems, I concur.

JUSTICE BREYER, concurring.

*** [W]e should decide here no more than is necessary. Thus, this case does not involve a father with visitation rights or a father who has paid "all of his child support obligations." Neither does it involve special circumstances such as a father who was deceived about the existence of the child or a father who was prevented from supporting his child. The Court need not, and in my view does not, now decide whether or how §§ 1912(d) and (f) apply where those circumstances are present. ***

[O]ther statutory provisions not now before us may nonetheless prove relevant in cases of this kind. Section 1915(a) grants an adoptive "preference" to "(1) a member of the child's extended family; (2) other members of the Indian child's tribe; or (3) other Indian families ... in the absence of good cause to the contrary." Further, § 1915(c) allows the "Indian child's tribe" to "establish a different order of preference by resolution." Could these provisions allow an absentee father to reenter the special statutory order of preference with support from the tribe, and subject to a court's consideration of "good cause?" I raise, but do not here try to answer, the question.

JUSTICE SCALIA, dissenting.

I join Justice Sotomayor's dissent except as to one detail. I reject the conclusion that the Court draws from the words "continued custody" in 25 U.S.C. § 1912(f) not because "literalness may strangle meaning," *see post*, at 2577, but because there is no reason that "continued" must refer to custody in the past rather than custody in the future. I read the provision as requiring the court to satisfy itself (beyond a reasonable doubt) not merely that initial or temporary custody is not "likely to result in serious emotional or physical damage to the child," but that continued custody is not likely to do so. *See* Webster's New International Dictionary 577 (2d ed. 1950) (defining "continued" as "[p]rotracted in time or space, esp. without interruption; constant"). For the reasons set forth in Justice Sotomayor's dissent, that connotation is much more in accord with the rest of the statute.

While I am at it, I will add one thought. The Court's opinion, it seems to me, needlessly demeans the rights of parenthood. It has been the constant practice of the common law to respect the entitlement of those who bring a child into the world to raise that child. We do not inquire whether leaving a child with his parents is "in the best interest of the child." It sometimes is not; he would be better off raised by someone else. But parents have their rights, no less than children do. This father wants to raise his daughter, and the statute amply protects his right to do so. There is no reason in law or policy to dilute that protection.

JUSTICE SOTOMAYOR, with whom **JUSTICE GINSBURG** and **JUSTICE KAGAN** join, and with whom **JUSTICE SCALIA** joins in part, dissenting.

A casual reader of the Court's opinion could be forgiven for thinking this an easy case, one in which the text of the applicable statute clearly points the way to the only sensible result. In truth, however, the path from the text of the Indian Child Welfare Act of 1978 (ICWA) to the result the Court reaches is anything but clear, and its result anything but right.

***

Beginning its reading with the last clause of § 1912(f), the majority concludes that a single phrase appearing there—"continued custody"—means that the entirety of the subsection is inapplicable to any parent, however committed, who has not previously had physical or legal custody of his child. Working back to front, the majority then concludes that § 1912(d), tainted by its association with § 1912(f), is also inapplicable; in the majority's view, a family bond that does not take custodial form is not a family bond worth preserving from "breakup." Because there are apparently no limits on the contaminating power of this single phrase, the majority does not stop there. Under its reading, § 1903(9), which makes biological fathers "parent[s]" under this federal statute (and where, again, the phrase "continued custody" does not appear), has substantive force only when a birth father has physical or state-recognized legal custody of his daughter.

When it excludes noncustodial biological fathers from the Act's substantive protections, this textually backward reading misapprehends ICWA's structure and scope. Moreover, notwithstanding the majority's focus on the perceived parental shortcomings of Birth Father, its reasoning necessarily extends to all Indian parents who have never had custody of their children, no matter how fully those parents have embraced the financial and emotional responsibilities of parenting. The majority thereby transforms a statute that was intended to provide uniform federal standards for child custody proceedings involving Indian children and their biological parents into an illogical piecemeal scheme.

A

Better to start at the beginning and consider the operation of the statute as a whole. ***

ICWA commences with express findings. Congress recognized that "there is no resource that is more vital to the continued existence and integrity of Indian tribes than their children," 25 U.S.C. § 1901(3), and it found that this resource was threatened. *** As § 1901(4) makes clear, and as this Court recognized in *Mississippi Band of Choctaw Indians v. Holyfield*, 490 U.S. 30, 33, 109 S. Ct. 1597, 104 L.Ed.2d 29 (1989), adoptive placements of Indian children with non-Indian families contributed significantly to the overall problem.

*** Section 1903 then goes on to establish the reach of these protections through its definitional provisions. For present purposes, two of these definitions are crucial to understanding the statute's full scope.

First, ICWA defines the term "parent" broadly to mean "any biological parent ... of an Indian child or any Indian person who has lawfully adopted an Indian child." § 1903(9). It is undisputed that Baby Girl is an "Indian child" within the meaning of the statute, see § 1903(4); and Birth Father consequently qualifies as a "parent" under the Act. The statutory definition of parent "does not include the unwed father where paternity has not been acknowledged or established," § 1903(9), but Birth Father's biological paternity has never been questioned by any party and was confirmed by a DNA test during the state court proceedings.

***

Second, the Act's comprehensive definition of "child custody proceeding" includes not only " 'adoptive placement[s],' " " 'preadoptive placement[s],' " and " 'foster care placement[s],' " but also " 'termination of parental rights' " proceedings. § 1903(1). This last category encompasses "any action resulting in the termination of the *parent-child relationship*," § 1903(1)(ii) (emphasis added). So far, then, it is clear that Birth Father has a federally recognized status as Baby Girl's "parent" and that his "parent-child relationship" with her is subject to the protections of the Act. ***

Section 1912(a) requires that any party seeking "*termination of parental rights* t[o] an Indian child" provide notice to both the child's "parent or Indian custodian" and the child's tribe "of the pending proceedings and of their right of intervention." Section 1912(b) mandates that counsel be provided for an indigent "parent or Indian custodian" in any "termination proceeding." Section 1912(c) also gives all "part[ies]" to a termination proceeding—which, thanks to §§ 1912(a) and (b), will always include a biological father if he desires to be present—the right to inspect all material "reports or other documents filed with the court." By providing notice, counsel, and access to relevant documents, the statute ensures a biological father's meaningful participation in an adoption proceeding where the termination of his parental rights is at issue.

*** Having assumed a uniform federal definition of "parent" that confers certain procedural rights, the majority then illogically concludes that ICWA's substantive protections are available only to a subset of "parent[s]": those who have previously had physical or state- recognized legal custody of his or her child. The statute does not support this departure.

Section 1912(d) provides that "Any party seeking to effect a foster care placement of, or *termination of parental rights* to, an Indian child under State law shall satisfy the court that active efforts have been made to provide remedial services and rehabilitative programs designed to prevent the breakup of the Indian family and that these efforts have proved unsuccessful." (Emphasis added.)

In other words, subsection (d) requires that an attempt be made to cure familial deficiencies before the drastic measures of foster care placement or termination of parental rights can be taken.

The majority would hold that the use of the phrase "breakup of the Indian family" in this subsection means that it does not apply where a birth father has not previously had custody of his child. But there is nothing about this capacious phrase that licenses such a narrowing construction. As the majority notes, "breakup" means "'[t]he discontinuance of a relationship.'" *Ante*, at 2562 (quoting American Heritage Dictionary 235 (3d ed. 1992)). So far, all of § 1912's provisions expressly apply in actions aimed at terminating the "parent-child relationship" that exists between a birth father and his child, and they extend to it meaningful protections. *** Nothing in the text of subsection (d) indicates that this blood relationship should be excluded from the category of familial "relationships" that the provision aims to save from "discontinuance."

The majority, reaching the contrary conclusion, asserts baldly that "when an Indian parent abandons an Indian child prior to birth and that child has never been in the Indian parent's legal or physical custody, there is no 'relationship' that would be 'discontinu[ed]' ... by the termination of the Indian parent's rights." Says who? Certainly not the statute. Section 1903 recognizes Birth Father as Baby Girl's "parent," and, in conjunction with ICWA's other provisions, it further establishes that their "parent-child relationship" is protected under federal law. In the face of these broad definitions, the majority has no warrant to substitute its own policy views for Congress' by saying that "no 'relationship'" exists between Birth Father and Baby Girl simply because, based on the hotly contested facts of this case, it views their family bond as insufficiently substantial to deserve protection. ***

Section 1912(f) is paired with § 1912(e), and as the majority notes, both come on the heels of the requirement of rehabilitative efforts just reviewed. *** Nothing in subsections (a) through (d) suggests a limitation on the types of parental relationships that are protected by any of the provisions of § 1912, and there is nothing in the structure of § 1912 that would lead a reader to expect subsection (e) or (f) to introduce any such qualification. Indeed, both subsections, in their opening lines, refer back to the prior provisions of § 1912 with the phrase "in such proceeding." This language indicates, quite logically, that in actions where subsections (a), (b), (c), and (d) apply, (e) and (f) apply too.

All this, and still the most telling textual evidence is yet to come: The text of the subsection begins by announcing, "[n]o termination of parental rights may be ordered" unless the specified evidentiary showing is made. To repeat, a "termination of parental rights" includes "*any* action resulting in the termination of the parent-child relationship," 25 U.S.C. § 1903(1)(ii) (emphasis added), including the relationship Birth Father, as an ICWA "parent," has with Baby Girl. The majority's reading disregards the Act's sweeping definition of "termination of parental rights," which is not limited to terminations of custodial relationships.

The entire foundation of the majority's argument that subsection (f) does not apply is the lonely phrase "continued custody." It simply cannot bear the interpretive weight the majority would place on it. *** In keeping with § 1903(1) and the structure and language of § 1912 overall, the phrase "continued custody" is most sensibly read to refer generally to the continuation of the parent-child relationship that an ICWA "parent" has with his or her child. A court applying § 1912(f) where the parent does not have pre-existing custody should, as Birth Father argues, determine whether the party seeking termination of parental rights has established that the continuation of the parent-child relationship will result in "serious emotional or physical damage to the child."

B

The majority also does not acknowledge the full implications of its assumption that there are some ICWA "parent[s]" to whom §§ 1912(d) and (f) do not apply. *** Consider an Indian father who, though he has never had custody of his biological child, visits her and pays all of his child support obligations. Suppose that, due to deficiencies in the care the child received from her custodial parent, the State placed the child with a foster family and proposed her ultimate adoption by them. Clearly, the father's parental rights would have to be terminated before the adoption could go forward. On the majority's view, notwithstanding the fact that this father would be a "parent" under ICWA, he would not receive the benefit of either § 1912(d) or § 1912(f). Presumably the court considering the adoption petition would have to apply some standard to determine whether termination of his parental rights was appropriate. But from whence would that standard come?

Not from the statute Congress drafted, according to the majority. The majority suggests that it might come from state law. But it is incongruous to suppose that Congress intended a patchwork of federal and state law to apply in termination of parental rights proceedings. *** While some States might provide protections comparable to § 1912(d)'s required remedial efforts and § 1912(f)'s heightened standard for termination of parental rights, many will provide less. There is no reason to believe Congress wished to leave protection of the parental rights of a subset of ICWA "parent[s]" dependent on the happenstance of where a particular "child custody proceeding" takes place. I would apply, as the statute construed in its totality commands, the standards Congress provided in §§ 1912(d) and (f) to the termination of all ICWA "parent[s']" parent-child relationships.

II

The majority's textually strained and illogical reading of the statute might be explicable, if not justified, if there were reason to believe that it avoided anomalous results or furthered a clear congressional policy. But neither of these conditions is present here.

There is nothing "bizarre," about placing on the party seeking to terminate a father's parental rights the burden of showing that the step is necessary as well as justified. "For ... natural parents, ... the consequence of an erroneous termination [of parental rights] is the unnecessary destruction of their natural family." *Santosky*, 455 U.S., at 766. In any event, the question is a nonissue in this case given the family court's finding that Birth Father is "a fit and proper person to have custody of his child" who "has demonstrated [his] ability to parent effectively" and who possesses "unwavering love for this child." Petitioners cannot show that rehabilitative efforts have "proved unsuccessful," 25 U.S.C. § 1912(d), because Birth Father is not in need of rehabilitation.

***

C

The majority also protests that a contrary result to the one it reaches would interfere with the adoption of Indian children. This claim is the most perplexing of all. A central purpose of ICWA is to "promote the stability and security of Indian ... families," 25 U.S.C. § 1902, in part by countering the trend of placing "an alarmingly high percentage of [Indian] children ... in non-Indian foster and adoptive homes and institutions." § 1901(4). *** The majority may consider this scheme unwise. But no principle of construction licenses a court to interpret a statute with a view to averting the very consequences Congress expressly stated it was trying to bring about. ***

D

The majority does not rely on the theory pressed by petitioners and the guardian ad litem that the canon of constitutional avoidance compels the conclusion that ICWA is inapplicable here. It states instead that it finds the statute clear. But the majority nevertheless offers the suggestion that a contrary result would create an equal protection problem.

It is difficult to make sense of this suggestion in light of our precedents, which squarely hold that classifications based on Indian tribal membership are not impermissible racial classifications. *See United States v. Antelope*, 430 U.S. 641, 645–647 (1977); *Morton v. Mancari*, 417 U.S. 535, 553–554 (1974). The majority's repeated, analytically unnecessary references to the fact that Baby Girl is 3/256 Cherokee by ancestry do nothing to elucidate its intimation that the statute may violate the Equal Protection Clause as applied here. I see no ground for this Court to second-guess the membership requirements of federally recognized Indian tribes, which are independent political entities. *See Santa Clara Pueblo v. Martinez*, 436 U.S. 49, 72, n. 32 (1978). I am particularly averse to doing so when the Federal Government requires Indian tribes, as a prerequisite for official recognition, to make "descen[t] from a historical Indian tribe" a condition of membership. 25 CFR § 83.7(e) (2012).

III

***

The majority casts Birth Father as responsible for the painful circumstances in this case, suggesting that he intervened "at the eleventh hour to override the mother's decision and the child's best interests." I have no wish to minimize the trauma of removing a 27-month-old child from her adoptive family. It bears remembering, however, that Birth Father took action to assert his parental rights when Baby Girl was four months old, as soon as he learned of the impending adoption. As the South Carolina Supreme Court recognized, "'[h]ad the mandate of … ICWA been followed [in 2010], … much potential anguish might have been avoided[;] and in any case the law cannot be applied so as automatically to "reward those who obtain custody, whether lawfully or otherwise, and maintain it during any ensuing (and protracted) litigation." 731 S.E.2d, at 564 (quoting *Holyfield*, 490 U.S., at 53-54).

The majority's hollow literalism distorts the statute and ignores Congress' purpose in order to rectify a perceived wrong that, while heartbreaking at the time, was a correct application of federal law and that in any case cannot be undone. Baby Girl has now resided with her father for 18 months. However difficult it must have been for her to leave Adoptive Couple's home when she was just over 2 years old, it will be equally devastating now if, at the age of 3-1/2, she is again removed from her home and sent to live halfway across the country. Such a fate is not foreordained, of course. But it can be said with certainty that the anguish this case has caused will only be compounded by today's decision.

NOTES AND QUESTIONS

1. *Aftermath.* As Justice Sotomayor noted, at the time of the decision the child involved (who became known in the media as Baby Veronica) had lived with her birth father for eighteen months. She was apparently a happy, well-adjusted girl who had bonded with her birth father and his wife. On July 17, 2013, however, the South Carolina Supreme Court refused to remand the case for a factual finding on her best interests and instead ordered the father's

parental rights terminated and the adoption finalized in the adoptive couple. *Adoptive Couple v. Baby Girl*, App. No. 2011-205166 (July 17, 2013). The birth father challenged the decision, and the Native American Rights Fund and other national organizations filed a federal civil rights complaint on Veronica's behalf, alleging that the South Carolina courts deprived Veronica of her civil rights by refusing to hold a best-interests hearing. Finally, on September 23, 2013, the birth father relinquished his daughter to the adoptive parents. Soon after, he ended all appeals in the case, saying tearfully, "I cannot bear to continue it any longer ... I love her too much to continue to have her in the spotlight." *See* Bethany R. Berger, *In the Name of the Child: Race, Gender, and Economics in Adoptive Couple v. Baby Girl*, 60 Fla. L. Rev. 295 (2015).

2. *Placement preferences.* The South Carolina Supreme Court refused to consider the § 1915 placement preferences on remand, because at the time the couple sought to institute adoption proceedings, they were the only ones to formally seek to adopt her. Although the birth father's parents, Baby Veronica's grandparents, had formally petitioned to adopt her by that point, the court held that § 1915 could not "be invoked at the midnight hour to further delay the resolution of this case. We find the clear import of the Supreme Court's majority opinion to foreclose successive § 1915 petitions, for litigation must have finality, and it is the role of this court to ensure 'the sanctity of the adoption process' under state law is 'jealously guarded.' " *Adoptive Couple v. Baby Girl*, App. No. 2011-205166 *2 (July 17, 2013) (quoting *Garner v. Baby Edward,* 342 S.E.2d 601, 603 (S.C. 1986)). Was this result necessary under the Supreme Court's opinion?

The Alaska Supreme Court applied *Adoptive Couple* to a dependency/neglect case involving the post-termination placement of a child who was a member of the Native Village of Tununak. *See Native Village of Tununak v. Dept. of Health & Social Svs.*, 334 P.3d 165 (Alaska 2014.). Despite the fact that the tribe had been a party to the proceedings all along, and had proposed the child's grandmother as an appropriate placement, the court refused to apply ICWA's placement preferences because the grandmother had not formally petitioned for adoption in the trial court: "[T]he court interprets the Supreme Court as requiring that 'with respect to adoptive placements for an Indian child *under state law*,' a formal state court adoption petition or a formal 'proxy,' must be filed before a person will be considered for adoptive placement preference under § 1915(a)." *Id.* at *179-80 (emphasis in original.) Did *Adoptive Couple* command this highly technical interpretation? Assume you are representing a tribe in an ICWA case. What steps would you advise the tribe to take to ensure the placement preferences will be applied?

Note that the new BIA Regulations on ICWA suggest that one basis for finding good cause not to follow the placement preferences is "the unavailability of a suitable placement after a determination by the court that a diligent search was conducted to find suitable placements meeting the preference criteria, but none has been located." Are *Adoptive Couple* and *Native Village of Tununak* consistent with this guideline?

3. *Statutory construction.* Read the relevant portions of ICWA carefully. Whose interpretation do you find most consistent with the statute, the majority's or the dissent's? Does the statutory text clearly point one way or the other? If not, do the statute's structure and purpose illuminate the best reading? If there are strong arguments to be made based on all of these sources of

interpretation and you remain uncertain as to whether Congress contemplated this precise situation, what should guide your decision about how to fill Congress's gap?

4. *Rights of birth fathers.* The right of noncustodial birth fathers to contest adoptions of their children was an evolving constitutional and state law issue between the 1970s and 1990s. As Justice Sotomayor noted in her dissent, at the time of ICWA's passage, 15 states recognized the rights of all unwed, noncustodial fathers in adoption proceedings, and today three states (Arizona, Washington, and Nevada) still do. When ICWA was adopted, the Supreme Court had resolved that a father's interest in the "companionship, care, custody, and management" of his children is "cognizable and substantial," and a child could not be taken from a custodial unwed father absent a hearing on his fitness, *Stanley v. Illinois*, 405 U.S. 645 (1972), but that a father who had no involvement with his eleven year old son had no standing to object to his adoption by his stepfather. *Quilloin v. Walcott*, 434 U.S. 246 (1978). Since then state statutes have created different regimes. Many states, like South Carolina, deny unwed fathers rights to notice or opportunity to contest adoptions of their young children unless they lived with or provided child support to their child or the child's mother over the last six months; others grant standing to fathers who have registered on an unmarried father's registry; while others provide fathers who do not live with their children more of an opportunity to prove that they were thwarted in their desire to be involved in their children's lives. Under most state regimes, however, the significant majority of noncustodial unmarried fathers would have no rights to contest an adoption, and therefore, under the Supreme Court's ruling, no right to contest termination of their parental rights. Did ICWA adopt a different regime, one more similar to Arizona and Washington's? The majority did not think so, but the dissent did.

5. *Constitutional claims.* The Petitioners and the Guardian *ad Litem*, represented by star Supreme Court practitioners Lisa Blatt and Paul Clement (who is also a previous Solicitor General), argued that ICWA was unconstitutional if applied to allow the birth father to block the adoption. The Supreme Court did not discuss these arguments but mentioned briefly that an interpretation of ICWA that would make it more difficult to adopt Indian children "would raise equal protection concerns." Further, Justice Alito's opinion makes several references to the fractional nature of Veronica's and her father's Cherokee lineage. The dissent addressed this argument more directly, stating that classifications based on tribal membership have repeatedly been upheld against equal protection challenges. In *Brackeen v. Bernhardt*, 937 F.3d 406 (5th Cir. 2019) the Fifth Circuit upheld ICWA against an equal protection challenge, consistent with the dissent's approach. What role did anxiety about race and race-matching play in *Adoptive Couple*? Recall that during the same term, two important cases addressing the continuing relevance of race—*Fisher v. University of Texas*, 570 U.S. 297 (2013), and *Shelby County v. Holder*, 570 U.S. 529 (2013), were decided in ways that elevated the Court's scrutiny over any forms of racial classifications.

Justice Thomas concurred in the opinion, but largely because he thinks ICWA is not constitutionally authorized under the Indian Commerce Clause. What do you think of his argument? Review the materials earlier in the casebook about the transition from the Articles of Confederation to the Constitution. Chapter 2, § II.B. How does Justice Thomas's interpretation comport with other generally accepted understandings of the consolidation of federal power over Indian affairs? Under Justice Thomas's view, what other statutes and regulations would be constitutionally suspect? The Indian Citizenship Act of 1924? Any and all employment, education, and health care preferences for American Indians? Given the definitions of tribes and Indians, is it useful, practical, and perhaps even constitutional to distinguish between legislation affecting "tribes" and legislation affecting "Indians?" For a response to Thomas, arguing that he got his history wrong, see Gregory Ablavsky, *Beyond the Indian Commerce Clause*, 124Yale L. J. 1012 (forthcoming 2015).

CHAPTER 8

TRIBAL JURISDICTION OVER NONMEMBERS

■ ■ ■

I. EARLY LAW REGARDING TRIBAL JURISDICTION OVER NONMEMBERS

Few nineteenth-century tribes had legal systems recognized as such by non-Indian observers, and few early cases considered the scope of tribal jurisdiction over non-Indians. Several early treaties, however, mention tribal criminal jurisdiction over non-Indians. The 1786 treaties with the Five Civilized Tribes, for example, state that if non-Indians settled within the tribes' treaty boundaries without permission, "the [tribe] may punish him or not as they please." Treaty with the Chickasaws, art. 4, Jan. 10, 1786, 7 Stat. 24; Treaty with the Cherokees at Hopewell, art. 5, 7 Stat. 18, Nov. 28, 1785; *see also* Treaty with the Wyandots, Delawares, Shawanoes, Ottawas, Chipewas, Putawatimes, Miamis, Eel-river, Weea's, Kickapoos, Piankashaws, and Kaskaskias, art. 6, Aug. 3, 1795, 7 Stat. 49; *see also* Russel L. Barsh & James Y. Henderson, *The Betrayal:* Oliphant v. Suquamish Indian Tribe *and the Hunting of the Snark*, 63 Minn. L. Rev. 609, app. (1978–1979) (collecting treaties providing tribal jurisdiction over non-Indians). A few treaties promised federal assistance to tribes in exercising such jurisdiction. *See* Treaty with the Cherokees, Dec. 29, 1835, art. 5, 7 Stat. 478 ("The United States hereby covenant and agree that *** they shall secure to the Cherokee Nation the right by their national councils to make and carry into effect all such laws as they may deem necessary for the government and protection of the persons and property within their own country belonging to their people or such persons as have connected themselves with them ***."). An 1820 treaty even provided federal monies to the Choctaw police force, the Lighthorse, "so that good order may be maintained, and that all men, both white and red, may be compelled to pay their just debts." Treaty with the Choctaw, October 18, 1820, art. 13, 7 Stat. 210.

Federal authorities generally assumed that tribes retained whatever jurisdiction federal statutes and treaties had not removed. For example, an 1834 House Report on a bill to regulate jurisdiction in the Indian Territory stated that absent the proposed federal restrictions a tribe had "jurisdiction over all persons and property within its limits." H. Rep. No. 23–474 at 18, 23d Cong., 1st Sess. (1834). While Congress proposed removing jurisdiction over federal employees and those passing through the territory, and giving the federal government the power to review sentences of death imposed on non-Indians, the report declared that "[a]s to those persons not required to reside in the Indian country, who voluntarily go there to reside, they must be considered as voluntarily submitting themselves to the laws of the tribes." *Id.* Authorities often assumed, however, that laws, such as the Non-Intercourse Acts, which created federal jurisdiction over crimes committed by Indians preempted tribal criminal jurisdiction. *See, e.g.*, 7 Op. Atty. Gen. 174, 177–178 (1855); *Ex Parte Kenyon*, 14 F.Cas. 353 (W.D. Ark. 1878); *see also* 2 Op. Atty. Gen. 693, 694 (1834) (treaty providing that Choctaws had jurisdiction over "the Choctaw nation of red people and their descendants" limited criminal jurisdiction to Choctaws).

In the later nineteenth century, federal Indian agents began to appoint Indian police to administer justice. Many of the enforcement actions involved ejecting non-Indian trespassers and apprehending thieves, murderers and bootleggers. *See* William T. Hagan, Indian Police and Judges: Experiments in Acculturation and Control 52–53 (1966).

In 1941, Felix Cohen opined that originally a tribe "might punish aliens within its jurisdiction according to its own laws and customs," and that "[s]uch jurisdiction continues to this day, save as it has been expressly limited by the acts of a superior government." Felix S. Cohen, Handbook of Federal Indian Law 146 (1941).

Authorities generally agreed that tribes retained civil jurisdiction over activity within their reservations. In a question concerning Choctaw jurisdiction over a property claim involving a non-Indian, for example, the U.S. Attorney General opined, "By all possible rules of construction the inference is clear that jurisdiction is left to the Choctaws themselves of civil controversies arising strictly within the Choctaw nation. *** Justice and policy alike demand that, so long as they are allowed to remain a separate people, they should be protected and encouraged by us in their laudable attempts to maintain local order[.] *** " 7 Op. Atty. Gen. 174, 180–181, 185 (1855). Similarly, at the turn of the twentieth century, the Supreme Court and Eighth Circuit sustained tribal taxes imposed on non-Indians engaging in business on reservations. *Morris v. Hitchcock*, 194 U.S. 384 (1904) (sustaining a tribal tax imposed on non-Indians grazing cattle on land they owned within tribal territory); *Buster v. Wright*, 135 F. 947, 950 (8th Cir. 1905) (upholding tribal tax on non-Indian activity on fee lands within reservation and stating that the "authority of the [tribe] to prescribe the terms upon which noncitizens may transact business within its borders [is] one of the inherent and essential attributes of its original sovereignty [which remains] until by the agreement of the nation itself or by the superior power of the republic it is taken from it").

Most of these cases concerned non-Indians acting on lands they had come to own through allotment. Solicitor Nathan Margold in his opinion on the *Powers of Indian Tribes* for the Department of the Interior, summarized the general rule:

> Over tribal lands, the tribe has the rights of a landowner as well as the rights of a local government, dominion as well as sovereignty. But over all the lands of the reservation, whether owned by the tribe, by members thereof, or by outsiders, the tribe has the sovereign power of determining the conditions upon which persons shall be permitted to enter its domain, to reside therein, and to do business, provided only such determination is consistent with applicable Federal laws and does not infringe any vested rights of persons now occupying reservation lands under lawful authority.

55 I.D. 14, 31 (1934).

The Bureau of Indian Affairs created the Courts of Indian Offenses in 1883 to provide for the administration of justice and education of Indians as part of the assimilation agenda. The Courts were created pursuant to an order of the Secretary of the Interior and were often staffed out of the ranks of the Indian police. Indian Police and Judges, *supra*, at 104–112. In 1889, the Commissioner of Indian Affairs called the courts "a tentative and somewhat crude attempt to break up superstitious practices, brutalizing dances, plural marriages and kindred evils, and to provide an Indian tribunal which, under the guidance of the agent, could take cognizance of crimes, misdemeanors and disputes among Indians, and by which they could be taught to respect law and obtain some rudimentary knowledge of legal processes." Annual Report of the Commissioner of Indian Affairs for 1889. *See also United States v. Clapox*, 35 F. 575 (D. Or. 1888). The courts exist on some reservations to this day under regulations first promulgated in 1935 and amended in 1968. Their current purpose is to provide adequate machinery for the administration of justice in those areas where tribes retain jurisdiction over Indians that is exclusive of state jurisdiction, but where tribal courts have not been established to exercise that jurisdiction. 25 C.F.R. § 11.100. Perhaps because of the limited purpose of these courts, the regulations provide the courts with limited jurisdiction: criminal jurisdiction only over Indians, and civil jurisdiction only over disputes between tribal members and disputes between members and nonmembers that were before the court on the stipulation of both parties. 25 C.F.R. §§ 11.102 & 11.103.

As tribes began to develop their own western-influenced court systems, many adopted these limitations into their tribal codes. By the 1950s, however, tribes began removing these limitations, and exercising both judicial and regulatory jurisdiction over all persons acting on their reservations.

In the early modern era, two Supreme Court decisions, *Williams v. Lee* and *U.S. v. Mazurie*, supported these exercises of jurisdiction.

Williams v. Lee, 358 U.S. 217 (1959) (*see also* Ch. 7, § I). A non-Indian merchant who operated a store on the Navajo reservation brought an action in state court against a Navajo couple to collect a debt for goods purchased on credit at the store. The Supreme Court unanimously held that state court jurisdiction was forbidden because it would infringe on the right of reservation Indians to make their own laws and be governed by them. The Court declared,

> There can be no doubt that to allow the exercise of state jurisdiction here would undermine the authority of the tribal courts over Reservation affairs and hence would infringe on the right of the Indians to govern themselves. It is immaterial that respondent is not an Indian. He was on the Reservation and the transaction with an Indian took place there. *** The cases in this Court have consistently guarded the authority of Indian governments over their reservations. Congress recognized this authority in the Navajos in the Treaty of 1868, and has done so ever since. If this power is to be taken away from them, it is for Congress to do it.

Williams v. Lee at 223. Because there was no indication that the nonmember merchant had overtly consented to tribal court jurisdiction, and no federal statute or treaty purported to confer jurisdiction on the tribal court, the case stands for the proposition that inherent tribal sovereignty includes jurisdiction over such causes of action. The Navajo Nation, in reliance on *Williams*, eventually enacted legislation expanding the jurisdiction of its tribal courts to include " 'civil actions in which the defendant is a resident of Navajo Indian country, or has caused an action to occur in Navajo Indian country.' " Sarah Krakoff, *A Narrative of Sovereignty: Illuminating the Paradox of the Domestic Dependent Nation*, 83 Or. L. Rev. 1109, 1139 (quoting Res. of the Navajo Tribal Council, CF–19–80 (1980)). Does the Navajo statute go beyond the jurisdiction authorized by *Williams*? If so, is it still defensible according to the articulation of tribal powers in the Solicitor's opinion above?

United States v. Mazurie, 419 U.S. 544 (1975). Federal statutes provide that liquor can be sold in Indian country only if consistent both with the law of the state and the law of the tribe; violating these requirements is a federal crime. When the Wind River Shoshone and Arapahoe Tribes refused to renew the liquor license of a bar on its reservation that was on fee simple land and operated by non-Indians, the owners continued to operate the bar anyway. When the U.S. attorney brought criminal charges against them, the defendants contended that the federal statute in question was unconstitutional because it delegated federal lawmaking authority to a private, voluntary association (a tribe). The court of appeals agreed with this contention. The Supreme Court reversed in a unanimous opinion authored by Justice Rehnquist, stating:

> This Court has recognized limits on the authority of Congress to delegate its legislative power. *Panama Refining Co. v. Ryan*, 293 U.S. 388 (1935). Those limitations are, however, less stringent in cases where the entity exercising the delegated authority itself possesses independent authority over the subject matter. *United States v. Curtiss–Wright Export Corp.*, 299 U.S. 304, 319–322 (1936). Thus it is an important aspect of this case that Indian tribes are unique aggregations possessing attributes of sovereignty over both their members and their territory, *Worcester*; they are "a separate people" possessing "the power of regulating their internal and social relations. *** " *Kagama*.
>
> Cases such as *Worcester* and *Kagama* surely establish the proposition that Indian tribes within "Indian country" are a good deal more than "private, voluntary organizations," and they thus undermine the rationale of the Court of Appeals' decision. These same cases, in addition, make clear that when Congress delegated its authority to control the introduction of alcoholic beverages into Indian country, it did so to entities which possess a certain degree of independent authority over matters that affect the internal and social relations of tribal life. Clearly the distribution and use of intoxicants is just such a matter. We need not decide whether this independent authority is itself sufficient for the tribes to impose [the tribal liquor ordinance]. It is necessary only to state that the independent tribal authority is quite sufficient to protect Congress' decision to vest in tribal councils this portion of its own authority "to regulate Commerce *** with the Indian tribes."

United States v. Mazurie, 419 U.S. 544, 556–7 (1975).

Theoretical basis for a general inherent tribal authority: In Solicitor Nathan Margold's opinion for the Department of the Interior, *Powers of Indian Tribes*, 55 I.D. 14 (1934), and in the first edition of Felix Cohen's Handbook of Federal Indian Law (1941), Felix Cohen, who was the Associate Solicitor of the Interior, provided the most coherent conceptualization of inherent tribal authority ever to work its way into American case law.

Cohen's argument proceeded in three steps. First, consistent with the Marshall trilogy, prior to European contact, a tribe possessed "all the powers of any sovereign state." Handbook at p. 123. Second, also following from the Marshall trilogy, Cohen wrote that the European colonial process, which he labeled "[c]onquest,"

> renders the tribe subject to the legislative power of the United States and, in substance, terminates the external powers of sovereignty of the tribe, *e.g.*, its power to enter into treaties with foreign nations, but does not by itself affect the internal sovereignty of the tribe, *i.e.*, its powers of local self-government.

Id. Third, tribes therefore retain internal sovereignty "subject to qualification by treaties and by express legislation of Congress." *Id.* Cohen summarized his approach by stating that tribal powers are not "delegated powers granted by express acts of Congress," but instead are "inherent powers of a limited sovereignty which has never been extinguished." Handbook at p. 122. The Supreme Court quoted this page of the Cohen Handbook in both *U.S. v. Wheeler*, 435 U.S. 313 (1978), and *Santa Clara Pueblo v. Martinez*, 436 U.S. 49 (1978), both covered in Ch. 6. See if the Cohen formulation fits the next case, and note a puzzle: *Wheeler*, affirming that tribal power to prosecute tribal members was inherent and thus not limited by the Double Jeopardy Clause; *Santa Clara Pueblo*, relying on tribal sovereignty to hold that federal courts had no jurisdiction over non-habeas Indian Civil Rights Act claims; and *Oliphant* were all decided the same Supreme Court Term (*Oliphant* on March 6, 1978; *Wheeler* on March 22, 1978; and *Santa Clara Pueblo* on May 15, 1978).

II. MODERN JUDICIAL DIMINISHMENT OF TRIBAL SOVEREIGNTY

A. Criminal Jurisdiction Over Non-Indians

OLIPHANT V. SUQUAMISH INDIAN TRIBE

435 U.S. 191, 98 S. Ct. 1011, 55 L.Ed.2d 209 (1978)

JUSTICE REHNQUIST delivered the opinion of the Court.

Two hundred years ago, the area bordering Puget Sound consisted of a large number of politically autonomous Indian villages, each occupied by from a few dozen to over 100 Indians. These loosely related villages were aggregated into a series of Indian tribes, one of which, the Suquamish, has become the focal point of this litigation. By the 1855 Treaty of Point Elliott, 12 Stat. 927, the Suquamish Indian Tribe relinquished all rights that it might have had in the lands of the State of Washington and agreed to settle on a 7,276–acre reservation near Port Madison, Wash. Located on Puget Sound across from the city of Seattle, the Port Madison Reservation is a checkerboard of tribal community land, allotted Indian lands, property held in fee simple by non-Indians, and various roads and public highways maintained by Kitsap County.[1]

The Suquamish Indians are governed by a tribal government which in 1973 adopted a Law and Order Code. The Code, which covers a variety of offenses from theft to rape, purports to extend the Tribe's criminal jurisdiction over both Indians and non-Indians.[2] Proceedings are held in the Suquamish Indian Provisional Court. Pursuant to the Indian Civil Rights Act of 1968, defendants are entitled to many of the due process protections accorded to defendants in federal or state criminal proceedings. However, the guarantees are not identical. Non–Indians, for example, are excluded from Suquamish tribal court juries.[4]

Both petitioners are non-Indian residents of the Port Madison Reservation. Petitioner Mark David Oliphant was arrested by tribal authorities during the Suquamish's annual Chief Seattle Days celebration and charged with assaulting a tribal officer and resisting arrest. *** Petitioner Daniel B. Belgarde was arrested by tribal authorities after an alleged high-speed race along the Reservation highways that only ended when Belgarde collided with a tribal police vehicle. *** Tribal court proceedings against both petitioners have been stayed pending a decision in this case. [Both petitioners applied for writs of habeas corpus, which the federal district court denied.]

I.

Respondents do not contend that their exercise of criminal jurisdiction over non-Indians stems from affirmative congressional authorization or treaty provision.[6] Instead, respondents urge that such jurisdiction flows

---

1. According to the District Court's findings of fact "[The] Port Madison Indian Reservation consists of approximately 7276 acres of which approximately 63% thereof is owned in fee simple absolute by non-Indians and the remainder 37% is Indian-owned lands subject to the trust status of the United States, consisting mostly of unimproved acreage upon which no persons reside. Residing on the reservation is an estimated population of approximately 2928 non-Indians living in 976 dwelling units. There lives on the reservation approximately 50 members of the Suquamish Indian Tribe. Within the reservation are numerous public highways of the State of Washington, public schools, public utilities and other facilities in which neither the Suquamish Indian Tribe nor the United States has any ownership or interest." App. 75. The Suquamish Indian Tribe, unlike many other Indian tribes, did not consent to non-Indian homesteading of unallotted or "surplus" lands within their reservation ***. Instead, the substantial non-Indian population on the Port Madison Reservation is primarily the result of the sale of Indian allotments to non-Indians by the Secretary of the Interior. Congressional legislation has allowed such sales where the allotments were in heirship, fell to "incompetents," or were surrendered in lieu of other selections. The substantial non-Indian landholdings on the Reservation are also a result of the lifting of various trust restrictions, a factor which has enabled individual Indians to sell their allotments.

2. Notices were placed in prominent places at the entrances to the Port Madison Reservation informing the public that entry onto the Reservation would be deemed implied consent to the criminal jurisdiction of the Suquamish tribal court.

4. [ICRA] provides for "a trial by jury of not less than six persons," § 1302(10), but the tribal court is not explicitly prohibited from excluding non-Indians from the jury even where a non-Indian is being tried. In 1977, the Suquamish Tribe amended its Law and Order Code to provide that only Suquamish tribal members shall serve as jurors in tribal court.

6. Respondents do contend that Congress has "confirmed" the power of Indian tribes to try and to punish non-Indians through the Indian Reorganization Act of 1934 and the Indian Civil Rights Act of 1968. Neither Act, however, addresses, let alone "confirms," tribal criminal jurisdiction over non-Indians. The Indian Reorganization Act merely gives each Indian Tribe the right "to organize for its common welfare" and to "adopt an appropriate constitution and bylaws." With certain specific additions not relevant here, the tribal council is to have such powers as are vested

automatically from the "Tribe's retained inherent powers of government over the Port Madison Indian Reservation." Seizing on language in our opinions describing Indian tribes as "quasi-sovereign entities," *Mancari*, the Court of Appeals agreed and held that Indian tribes, "though conquered and dependent, retain those powers of autonomous states that are neither inconsistent with their status nor expressly terminated by Congress." According to the Court of Appeals, criminal jurisdiction over anyone committing an offense on the reservation is a "sine qua non" of such powers.

The Suquamish Indian Tribe does not stand alone today in its assumption of criminal jurisdiction over non-Indians. Of the 127 reservation court systems that currently exercise criminal jurisdiction in the United States, 33 purport to extend that jurisdiction to non-Indians. Twelve other Indian tribes have enacted ordinances which would permit the assumption of criminal jurisdiction over non-Indians. Like the Suquamish these tribes claim authority to try non-Indians not on the basis of congressional statute or treaty provision but by reason of their retained national sovereignty.

The effort by Indian tribal courts to exercise criminal jurisdiction over non-Indians, however, is a relatively new phenomenon. And where the effort has been made in the past, it has been held that the jurisdiction did not exist. Until the middle of this century, few Indian tribes maintained any semblance of a formal court system. Offenses by one Indian against another were usually handled by social and religious pressure and not by formal judicial processes; emphasis was on restitution rather than on punishment. In 1834 the Commissioner of Indian Affairs described the then status of Indian criminal systems: "With the exception of two or three tribes, who have within a few years past attempted to establish some few laws and regulations among themselves, the Indian tribes are without laws, and the chiefs without much authority to exercise any restraint."

It is therefore not surprising to find no specific discussion of the problem before us in the volumes of the United States Reports. But the problem did not lie entirely dormant for two centuries. A few tribes during the 19th century did have formal criminal systems. From the earliest treaties with these tribes, it was apparently assumed that the tribes did not have criminal jurisdiction over non-Indians absent a congressional statute or treaty provision to that effect. For example, the 1830 Treaty with the Choctaw Indian Tribe, which had one of the most sophisticated of tribal structures, guaranteed to the Tribe "the jurisdiction and government of all the persons and property that may be within their limits." Despite the broad terms of this governmental guarantee, however, the Choctaws at the conclusion of this treaty provision "express *a wish*

"by existing law." The Indian Civil Rights Act merely extends to "any person" within the tribe's jurisdiction certain enumerated guarantees of the Bill of Rights of the Federal Constitution.

As respondents note, an early version of the Indian Civil Rights Act extended its guarantees only to "American Indians," rather than to "any person." The purpose of the later modification was to extend the Act's guarantees to "all persons who may be subject to the jurisdiction of tribal governments, whether Indians or non-Indians." Summary Report on the Constitutional Rights of American Indians, Subcommittee on Constitutional Rights of the Senate Committee on the Judiciary, 89th Cong., 2d Sess., 10 (1966). But this change was certainly not intended to give Indian tribes criminal jurisdiction over non-Indians. Nor can it be read to "confirm" respondents' argument that Indian tribes have inherent criminal jurisdiction over non-Indians. Instead, the modification merely demonstrates Congress' desire to extend the Act's guarantees to non-Indians if and where they come under a tribe's criminal or civil jurisdiction by either treaty provision or Act of Congress.

that Congress *may grant* to the Choctaws the right of punishing by their own laws any white man who shall come into their nation, and infringe any of their national regulations."[8] Such a request for affirmative congressional authority is inconsistent with respondents' belief that criminal jurisdiction over non-Indians is inherent in tribal sovereignty. Faced by attempts of the Choctaw Tribe to try non-Indian offenders in the early 1800's, the United States Attorneys General also concluded that the Choctaws did not have criminal jurisdiction over non-Indians absent congressional authority. *See* 2 Op.Atty.Gen. 693 (1834); 7 Op.Atty.Gen. 174 (1855). According to the Attorney General in 1834, tribal criminal jurisdiction over non-Indians, is *inter alia,* inconsistent with treaty provisions recognizing the sovereignty of the United States over the territory assigned to the Indian nation and the dependence of the Indians on the United States.

---

8. The history of Indian treaties in the United States is consistent with the principle that Indian tribes may not assume criminal jurisdiction over non-Indians without the permission of Congress. The earliest treaties typically expressly provided that "any citizen of the United States, who shall do an injury to any Indian of the [tribal] nation, or to any other Indian or Indians residing in their towns, and under their protection, shall be punished according to the laws of the United States." *See, e. g.,* Treaty with the Shawnees, Art. III, 7 Stat. 26 (1786). While, as elaborated further below, these provisions were not necessary to remove criminal jurisdiction over non-Indians from the Indian tribes, they would naturally have served an important function in the developing stage of United States–Indian relations by clarifying jurisdictional limits of the Indian tribes. The same treaties generally provided that "[i]f any citizen of the United States *** shall attempt to settle on any of the lands hereby allotted to the Indians to live and hunt on, such person shall forfeit the protection of the United States of America, and the Indians may punish him or not as they please." *See, e.g.,* Treaty with the Choctaws, Art. IV, 7 Stat. 22 (1786). Far from representing a recognition of any inherent Indian criminal jurisdiction over non-Indians settling on tribal lands, these provisions were instead intended as a means of discouraging non-Indian settlements on Indian territory, in contravention of treaty provisions to the contrary. *See* 5 Annals of Cong. 903–904 (1796). Later treaties dropped this provision and provided instead that non-Indian settlers would be removed by the United States upon complaint being lodged by the tribe. *See, e.g.,* Treaty with the Sacs and Foxes, 7 Stat. 84 (1804).

As the relationship between Indian tribes and the United States developed through the passage of time, specific provisions for the punishment of non-Indians by the United States, rather than by the tribes, slowly disappeared from the treaties. Thus, for example, none of the treaties signed by Washington Indians in the 1850's explicitly proscribed criminal prosecution and punishment of non-Indians by the Indian tribes. As discussed below, however, several of the treaty provisions can be read as recognizing that criminal jurisdiction over non-Indians would be in the United States rather than in the tribes. The disappearance of provisions explicitly providing for the punishment of non-Indians by the United States, rather than by the Indian tribes, coincides with and is at least partly explained by the extension of federal enclave law over non-Indians in the Trade and Intercourse Acts and the general recognition by Attorneys General and lower federal courts that Indians did not have jurisdiction to try non-Indians. See *infra,* at 1016–1017. When it was felt necessary to expressly spell out respective jurisdictions, later treaties still provided that criminal jurisdiction over non-Indians would be in the United States. *See, e.g.,* Treaty with the Utah–Tabeguache Band, Art. 6, 13 Stat. 674 (1863).

Only one treaty signed by the United States has ever provided for any form of tribal criminal jurisdiction over non-Indians (other than in the illegal-settler context noted above). The first treaty signed by the United States with an Indian tribe, the 1778 Treaty with the Delawares, provided that neither party to the treaty could "proceed to the infliction of punishments on the citizens of the other, otherwise than by securing the offender or offenders by imprisonment, or any other competent means, till a fair and impartial trial can be had by judges or juries *of both parties,* as near as can be to the laws, customs and usages of the contracting parties and natural justice: *The mode of such tryals to be hereafter fixed by the wise men of the United States in Congress assembled,* with the assistance of ***deputies of the Delaware nation ***." Treaty with the Delawares, Art. IV, 7 Stat. 14 (emphasis added). While providing for Delaware participation in the trial of non-Indians, this treaty section established that non-Indians could only be tried under the auspices of the United States and in a manner fixed by the Continental Congress.

At least one court has previously considered the power of Indian courts to try non-Indians and it also held against jurisdiction.[9] In *Ex parte Kenyon*, 14 F. Cas. 353 (No. 7,720) (W.D. Ark. 1878), Judge Isaac C. Parker, who as District Court Judge for the Western District of Arkansas was constantly exposed to the legal relationships between Indians and non-Indians, held that to give an Indian tribal court "jurisdiction of the person of an offender, such offender must be an Indian." *Id.* at 355. The conclusion of Judge Parker was reaffirmed only recently in a 1970 opinion of the Solicitor of the Department of the Interior. *See Criminal Jurisdiction of Indian Tribes over Non–Indians,* 77 I.D. 113.[11]

While Congress was concerned almost from its beginning with the special problems of law enforcement on the Indian reservations, it did not initially address itself to the problem of tribal jurisdiction over non-Indians. For the reasons previously stated, there was little reason to be concerned with assertions of tribal court jurisdiction over non-Indians because of the absence of formal tribal judicial systems. Instead, Congress' concern was with providing effective protection for the Indians "from the violence of the lawless part of our frontier inhabitants." Seventh Annual Address of President George Washington, 1 Messages and Papers of the Presidents, 1789–1897, pp. 181, 185 (J. Richardson, ed., 1897). Without such protection, it was felt that "all the exertions of the Government to prevent destructive retaliations by the Indians will prove fruitless and all our present agreeable prospects illusory." *Ibid.* Beginning with the Trade and Intercourse Act of 1790, 1 Stat. 137, therefore, Congress assumed federal jurisdiction over offenses by non-Indians against Indians which "would be punishable by the laws of [the] state or district *** if the offense had been committed against a citizen or white inhabitant thereof." In 1817, Congress went one step further and extended federal enclave law to the Indian country; the only exception was for "any offence committed by one Indian against another."

It was in 1834 that Congress was first directly faced with the prospect of Indians trying non-Indians. In the Western Territory bill, Congress proposed to create an Indian territory beyond the western-directed destination of the settlers; the territory was to be governed by a confederation of Indian tribes and was expected ultimately to become a State of the Union. While the bill would have created a political territory with broad governing powers, Congress was careful not to give the tribes of the territory criminal jurisdiction over United States officials and citizens traveling through the area. The reasons were quite practical:

> Officers, and persons in the service of the United States, and persons required to reside in the Indian country by treaty stipulations, must necessarily be placed under the protection, and subject to the laws of the United States. To persons merely travelling in the Indian country the same protection is extended. The want of fixed laws, of competent tribunals of justice, which must for some time continue in the Indian country,

9. According to Felix Cohen's Handbook of Federal Indian Law 148 (U.S. Dept. of the Interior 1941) "attempts of tribes to exercise jurisdiction over non-Indians *** have been generally condemned by the federal courts since the end of the treaty-making period, and the writ of *habeas corpus* has been used to discharge white defendants from tribal custody."

11. The 1970 opinion of the Solicitor was withdrawn in 1974 but has not been replaced. No reason was given for the withdrawal.

> absolutely requires for the peace of both sides that this protection should be extended. H.R. Rep. No. 474, 23d Cong., 1st Sess., 18 (1834).

Congress' concern over criminal jurisdiction in this proposed Indian Territory contrasts markedly with its total failure to address criminal jurisdiction over non-Indians on other reservations, which frequently bordered non-Indian settlements. The contrast suggests that Congress shared the view of the Executive Branch and lower federal courts that Indian tribal courts were without jurisdiction to try non-Indians.

This unspoken assumption was also evident in other congressional actions during the 19th century. In 1854, for example, Congress amended the Trade and Intercourse Act to proscribe the prosecution in federal court of an Indian who has already been tried in tribal court. No similar provision, such as would have been required by parallel logic if tribal courts had jurisdiction over non-Indians, was enacted barring retrial of non-Indians. Similarly, in the Major Crimes Act of 1885, Congress placed under the jurisdiction of federal courts Indian offenders who commit certain specified major offenses. If tribal courts may try non-Indians, however, as respondents contend, those tribal courts are free to try non-Indians even for such major offenses as Congress may well have given the federal courts *exclusive* jurisdiction to try members of their own tribe committing the exact same offenses.

In 1891, this Court recognized that Congress' various actions and inactions in regulating criminal jurisdiction on Indian reservations demonstrated an intent to reserve jurisdiction over non-Indians for the federal courts. In *In re Mayfield*, 141 U.S. 107 (1891), the Court noted that the policy of Congress had been to allow the inhabitants of the Indian country "such power of self-government as was thought to be consistent with the safety of the white population with which they may have come in contact, and to encourage them as far as possible in raising themselves to our standard of civilization." The "general object" of the congressional statutes was to allow Indian nations criminal "jurisdiction of all controversies between Indians, or where a member of the nation is the only party to the proceeding, and to reserve to the courts of the United States jurisdiction of all actions to which its own citizens are parties on either side." While Congress never expressly forbade Indian tribes to impose criminal penalties on non-Indians, we now make express our implicit conclusion of nearly a century ago that Congress consistently believed this to be the necessary result of its repeated legislative actions.

In a 1960 Senate Report, that body expressly confirmed its assumption that Indian tribal courts are without inherent jurisdiction to try non-Indians, and must depend on the Federal Government for protection from intruders.[15] In considering a statute that would prohibit unauthorized entry upon Indian land for the purpose of hunting or fishing, the Senate Report noted:

> The problem confronting Indian tribes with sizable reservations is that the United States provides no protection against trespassers

15. In 1977, a congressional Policy Review Commission, citing the lower court decisions in *Oliphant* and *Belgarde*, concluded that "[t]here is an established legal basis for tribes to exercise jurisdiction over non-Indians." 1 Final Report of the American Indian Policy Review Commission 114, 117, 152–154 (1977). However, the Commission's report does not deny that for almost 200 years before the lower courts decided *Oliphant* and *Belgarde*, the three branches of the Federal Government were in apparent agreement that Indian tribes do not have jurisdiction over non-Indians. ***

> comparable to the protection it gives to Federal property as exemplified by title 18, United States Code, section 1863 [trespass on national forest lands]. Indian property owners should have the same protection as other property owners. For example, a private hunting club may keep nonmembers off its game lands or it may issue a permit for a fee. One who comes on such lands without permission may be prosecuted under State law but a non-Indian trespasser on an Indian reservation enjoys immunity. *This is by reason of the fact that Indian tribal law is enforceable against Indians only; not against non-Indians.*
>
> ***
>
> Non–Indians are not subject to the jurisdiction of Indian courts and cannot be tried in Indian courts on trespass charges. Further, there are no Federal laws which can be invoked against trespassers.
>
> ***
>
> The committee has considered this bill and believes that the legislation is meritorious. The legislation will give to the Indian tribes and to individual Indian owners certain rights that now exist as to others, and fills a gap in the present law for the protection of their property.

S. Rep. No. 1686, 86th Cong., 2d Sess., 2–3 (1960) (emphasis added).

II.

While not conclusive on the issue before us, the commonly shared presumption of Congress, the Executive Branch, and lower federal courts that tribal courts do not have the power to try non-Indians carries considerable weight. "Indian law" draws principally upon the treaties drawn and executed by the Executive Branch and legislation passed by Congress. These instruments, which beyond their actual text form the backdrop for the intricate web of judicially made Indian law, cannot be interpreted in isolation but must be read in light of the common notions of the day and the assumptions of those who drafted them.

While in isolation the Treaty of Point Elliott would appear to be silent as to tribal criminal jurisdiction over non-Indians, the addition of historical perspective casts substantial doubt upon the existence of such jurisdiction. In the Ninth Article, for example, the Suquamish "acknowledge their dependence on the government of the United States." As Mr. Chief Justice Marshall explained in *Worcester*, such an acknowledgment is not a mere abstract recognition of the United States' sovereignty. "The Indian nations were, from their situation, necessarily dependent on [the United States] *** for their protection from lawless and injurious intrusions into their country." By acknowledging their dependence on the United States, in the Treaty of Point Elliott, the Suquamish were in all probability recognizing that the United States would arrest and try non-Indian intruders who came within their Reservation. Other provisions of the Treaty also point to the absence of tribal jurisdiction. Thus the Tribe "agree[s] not to shelter or conceal offenders against the laws of the United States, but to deliver them up to the authorities for trial." Read in conjunction with 18 U.S.C. § 1152, which extends federal enclave law to non-Indian offenses on Indian reservations, this provision implies that the Suquamish are to promptly deliver up any non-Indian offender, rather than try and punish him themselves.

By themselves, these treaty provisions would probably not be sufficient to remove criminal jurisdiction over non-Indians if the Tribe otherwise retained such jurisdiction. But an examination of our earlier precedents satisfies us that, even ignoring treaty provisions and congressional policy, Indians do not have criminal jurisdiction over non-Indians absent affirmative delegation of such power by Congress. Indian tribes do retain elements of "quasi-sovereign" authority after ceding their lands to the United States and announcing their dependence on the Federal Government. *Cherokee Nation*. But the tribes' retained powers are not such that they are limited only by specific restrictions in treaties or congressional enactments. As the Court of Appeals recognized, Indian tribes are prohibited from exercising both those powers of autonomous states that are expressly terminated by Congress *and* those powers "*inconsistent with their status.*"

Indian reservations are "a part of the territory of the United States." Indian tribes "hold and occupy [the reservations] with the assent of the United States, and under their authority." [*United States v. Rogers*, 4 How. 567, 571 (1846).] Upon incorporation into the territory of the United States, the Indian tribes thereby come under the territorial sovereignty of the United States and their exercise of separate power is constrained so as not to conflict with the interests of this overriding sovereignty. "[T]heir rights to complete sovereignty, as independent nations, [are] necessarily diminished." *Johnson v. McIntosh.*

We have already described some of the inherent limitations on tribal powers that stem from their incorporation into the United States. In *Johnson v. McIntosh,* we noted that the Indian tribes' "power to dispose of the soil at their own will, to whomsoever they pleased," was inherently lost to the overriding sovereignty of the United States. And in *Cherokee Nation*, the Chief Justice observed that since Indian tribes are "completely under the sovereignty and dominion of the United States, *** any attempt [by foreign nations] to acquire their lands, or to form a political connexion with them, would be considered by all as an invasion of our territory, and an act of hostility."

*** Protection of territory within its external political boundaries is, of course, as central to the sovereign interests of the United States as it is to any other sovereign nation. But from the formation of the Union and the adoption of the Bill of Rights, the United States has manifested an equally great solicitude that its citizens be protected by the United States from unwarranted intrusions on their personal liberty. *** By submitting to the overriding sovereignty of the United States, Indian tribes therefore necessarily give up their power to try non-Indian citizens of the United States except in a manner acceptable to Congress. This principle would have been obvious a century ago when most Indian tribes were characterized by a "want of fixed laws [and] of competent tribunals of justice." H.R. Rep. No. 474, 23d Cong., 1st Sess., 18 (1834). It should be no less obvious today, even though present-day Indian tribal courts embody dramatic advances over their historical antecedents.

In *Crow Dog*, the Court was faced with almost the inverse of the issue before us here—whether, prior to the passage of the Major Crimes Act, federal courts had jurisdiction to try Indians who had offended against fellow Indians on reservation land. In concluding that criminal jurisdiction was exclusively in the tribe, it found particular guidance in the "nature and circumstances of the case." The United States was seeking to extend United States

> law, by argument and inference only, *** over aliens and strangers; over the members of a community separated by race [and] tradition, *** from the authority and power which seeks to impose upon them the restraints of an external and unknown code ***; which judges them by a standard made by others and not for them. *** It tries them, not by their peers, nor by the customs of their people, nor the law of their land, but by *** a different race, according to the law of a social state of which they have an imperfect conception. ***

These considerations, applied here to the non-Indian rather than Indian offender, speak equally strongly against the validity of respondents' contention that Indian tribes, although fully subordinated to the sovereignty of the United States, retain the power to try non-Indians according to their own customs and procedure.

As previously noted, Congress extended the jurisdiction of federal courts, in the Trade and Intercourse Act of 1790, to offenses committed by non-Indians against Indians within Indian Country. In doing so, Congress was careful to extend to the non-Indian offender the basic criminal rights that would attach in non-Indian related cases. Under respondents' theory, however, Indian tribes would have been free to try the same non-Indians without these careful proceedings unless Congress affirmatively legislated to the contrary. Such an exercise of jurisdiction over non-Indian citizens of the United States would belie the tribes' forfeiture of full sovereignty in return for the protection of the United States.

In summary, respondents' position ignores that

> Indians are within the geographical limits of the United States. The soil and people within these limits are under the political control of the Government of the United States, or of the States of the Union. There exists in the broad domain of sovereignty but these two. There may be cities, counties, and other organized bodies with limited legislative functions, but they *** exist in subordination to one or the other of these. *Kagama.*

We recognize that some Indian tribal court systems have become increasingly sophisticated and resemble in many respects their state counterparts. We also acknowledge that with the passage of the Indian Civil Rights Act of 1968, which extends certain basic procedural rights to *anyone* tried in Indian tribal court, many of the dangers that might have accompanied the exercise by tribal courts of criminal jurisdiction over non-Indians only a few decades ago have disappeared. Finally, we are not unaware of the prevalence of non-Indian crime on today's reservations which the tribes forcefully argue requires the ability to try non-Indians. But these are considerations for Congress to weigh in deciding whether Indian tribes should finally be authorized to try non-Indians. They have little relevance to the principles which lead us to conclude that Indian tribes do not have inherent jurisdiction to try and to punish non-Indians. *Reversed.*

[**JUSTICE BRENNAN** did not participate.]

JUSTICE MARSHALL, with whom **THE CHIEF JUSTICE** joins, dissenting.

I agree with the court below that the "power to preserve order on the reservation *** is a *sine qua non* of the sovereignty that the Suquamish originally possessed." In the absence of affirmative withdrawal by treaty or statute, I am of the view that Indian tribes enjoy as a necessary aspect of their retained sovereignty the right to try and punish all persons who commit offenses against tribal law within the reservation. Accordingly, I dissent.

NOTES AND QUESTIONS

1. *Cohen's formulation.* How does the Court in *Oliphant* fail to follow Cohen's formulation? Does the Court acknowledge that it is deviating from a heretofore established method of deciding Indian law cases? Return to the three-part categorization of tribal power, based on Cohen's formulation, found in the notes immediately before *Oliphant*. In what category does the opinion in *Oliphant* belong? How would the title to that category have to be amended?

2. *Role of Congress and the Courts.* The previous cases we have read, from *Lone Wolf* to *Santa Clara Pueblo*, relied on congressional plenary power to limit tribal sovereignty, with the Court playing a limited role in reviewing those congressional actions. Does the Court hold that Congress or the Executive removed tribal jurisdiction over non-members? How does the Court's role in *Oliphant* compare to its role in earlier cases?

3. *Role of history.* What role does history, the "shared assumptions" of the federal branches, play in the opinion? Examine Justice Rehnquist's evidence carefully. At what particular point in time did the tribes, or this tribe, lose inherent criminal jurisdiction over all persons within their territories? On the opinion's use of history, see Russel Lawrence Barsh & James Youngblood Henderson, *The Betrayal:* Oliphant v. Suquamish Indian Tribe *and the Hunting of the Snark*, 63 Minn. L. Rev. 609 (1978–1979). In particular, Barsh and Henderson note that Justice Rehnquist's quotation from the "Western Territory Bill" omits a part of the Committee Report stating ["A]s to those persons *not required* to reside in Indian country, who voluntarily go there to reside, they must be considered as *voluntarily submitting to the laws* of the tribes." *Id.* at 625–26 (emphasis added).

4. Professor Alexandra (Sasha) Harmon, a lawyer and historian at the University of Washington, recounts Suquamish history in her recent book. With regard to the *Oliphant* case, she concludes:

> In sum, when Mark Oliphant and his lawyer chose to resist Suquamish tribal prosecution on federal Indian law grounds—tribe leaders despite a history of US policies that saddled them with a reservation populated by non-Indians—put their fate and perhaps their faith in non-Indian judges and lawyers. The strategy recommended itself in large part because of past Indian victories in federal courts, some in the early years of the republic, some very recent, and some close to home. But the Supreme Court betrayed the Indians' faith (if faith it was).*** Ignoring a trend in the US government of respecting tribes' aspirations for meaningful power, six justices decided that Indian tribes could not be allowed to judge non-Indians' guilt. To them, it seems, Indian societies were still too alien to ensure fairness for non-Indian defendants but no longer independent enough to define their own powers.

Alexandra Harmon, Reclaiming the Reservation: Histories of Indian Sovereignty Suppressed and Renewed 294 (2019).

5. *A manner acceptable to Congress.* The Court states that "[b]y submitting to the overriding sovereignty of the United States, Indian tribes therefore necessarily give up their power to try non-Indian citizens of the United States except in a manner acceptable to Congress." Hasn't Congress spoken regarding tribal courts and intrusions on personal liberty in the ICRA, or has the Court identified evidence of another congressional concern? If so, is the Court or Congress better placed to address this concern?

6. *Bad facts make bad law?* Read footnote 1 and the end of footnote 4. In some ways, *Oliphant* was a terrible test case from the tribal perspective. Vine Deloria, Jr., one of the leading American Indian intellectuals of the twentieth century, had this to say about the facts:

> The facts of the situation make the Indian argument not only moot but demonstrate that it was based on an idea of sovereignty having little relation to actual reality. *** Surely, here was an instance of a doctrine run amok. When attorneys and scholars come to believe that doctrines have a greater reality than the data from which they are derived, all aspects of the judicial process suffer accordingly.

Vine Deloria, Jr., *Laws Founded in Justice and Humanity: Reflections on the Content and Character of Federal Indian Law*, 31 Ariz. L. Rev. 203, 215 (1989). Does the Court explicitly rely upon the demographics? How important might they have been to the outcome? Note that the Court imposes a flat rule: a tribe does not have inherent criminal jurisdiction over non-Indians anywhere, although few reservations have demographics like the Suquamish. Could the Court have crafted a narrower decision, divesting the Suquamish Tribe of jurisdiction but reserving the question of other tribes' jurisdiction? Can lawyers for tribes take away any strategic lessons from the "bad facts" problem in *Oliphant*?

7. *Good facts make bad law?* Other facts provide a different perspective. First, there were facts about the absence of state or local law enforcement. Mark Oliphant was arrested during the Suquamish Tribe's Chief Seattle Days celebration for disorderly conduct and resisting arrest stemming from a drunken fight. As the Ninth Circuit panel noted, quoting from the Suquamish Tribe's brief, " 'When the Suquamish Indian Tribe planned its annual Chief Seattle Days celebration, the Tribe knew that thousands of people would be congregating in a small area near the tribal traditional encampment grounds for the celebration.' " *Oliphant v. Schlie*, 544 F.2d 1007, 1013 (9th Cir. 1976). The Tribe had therefore sought law enforcement assistance from Kitsap County and the Bureau of Indian Affairs. The County provided just one deputy for one 8–hour period during the entire weekend of the celebration, and the BIA provided no assistance at all. *Id.* Oliphant was arrested at approximately 4:30 a.m., and the only law enforcement officers available were tribal deputies. "Without the exercise of jurisdiction by the Tribe and its courts, there could have been no law enforcement whatsoever on the Reservation during this major gathering which clearly created a potentially dangerous situation with regard to law enforcement." *Id.* The law enforcement situation on the Port Madison Reservation was not an anomaly. As the panel decision further observed:

> Federal law is not designed to cover the range of conduct normally regulated by local governments. Minor offenses committed by non-Indians within Indian reservations frequently go unpunished and thus unregulated ***. Prosecutors in counties adjoining Indian reservations are

> reluctant to prosecute non-Indians for minor offenses where limitations on state process within Indian country may make witnesses difficult to obtain, where the jurisdictional division between federal, state, and tribal governments over the offense is not clear, and where the peace and dignity of the government affected is not his own but that of the Indian tribe. Traffic offenses, trespasses, violations of tribal hunting and fishing regulations, disorderly conduct and even petty larcenies and simple assaults committed by non-Indians go unpunished. The dignity of the tribal government suffers in the eyes of Indian and non-Indian alike, and a tendency towards lawless behavior necessarily follows.

Id. at 1013–1014.

In addition, the Tribe had no non-criminal options for dealing with Oliphant. In two previous Ninth Circuit cases, the courts affirmed the tribal power to exclude non-Indians as an approach to the problem of lawlessness on reservations. *See Ortiz–Barraza v. United States*, 512 F.2d 1176 (9th Cir. 1975); *Quechan Tribe of Indians v. Rowe*, 531 F.2d 408 (9th Cir. 1976). But Mark Oliphant was one of the 2,928 non-Indians living on the Port Madison Reservation. He could not be excluded. The Tribe's only meaningful option was to charge and punish him criminally. Daniel Belgarde, arrested several months after Oliphant for leading tribal officers on a high-speed chase that ended when Belgarde crashed into a tribal police car, also lived on the reservation. Highlighting the problem of non-Indian lawlessness due to disrespect for tribal institutions, a passenger along for Mr. Belgarde's wild ride was his friend, Mark Oliphant. For more context and backstory on the *Oliphant* case, *see* Sarah Krakoff, *Mark the Plumber v. Tribal Empire, or Non-Indian Anxiety v. Tribal Sovereignty?: The Story of* Oliphant v. Suquamish Indian Tribe, in Indian Law Stories (Goldberg, Washburn & Frickey, eds., 2011).

Further, Oliphant and Belgarde were not the only ones causing trouble on reservations. "State and federal police, spread thin in rural areas, could not or would not provide adequate patrols or respond reliably to criminal activity on reservations. *** Non-Indian troublemakers knew they could defy the law with impunity." Harmon, *supra*, at 297.Are these facts relevant? Why do you think they did not make an impression on the *Oliphant* majority? Professor Harmon writes that at oral argument it did not appear that such facts mattered to the Court, and the Tribe's attorney did not explain the situation from the tribal perspective. *Id.* at 273.

Suquamish Tribal Police Car; Photo by Robert Anderson.

8. *The new implicit divestiture approach.* The Court in *Oliphant* reaches all the way back to *Johnson v. McIntosh* for support for the notion that tribes have been implicitly divested of some aspects of sovereignty due to their incorporation into the United States. What does *McIntosh* have to do with criminal jurisdiction over non-Indians? Notice that even in *McIntosh*, the Court had federal and British statutes saying that non-Indians could not purchase tribal land without federal consent.

In *United States v. Wheeler*, decided 16 days after *Oliphant*, the Court sought to harmonize the decision with its earlier cases:

> *** Indian tribes still possess those aspects of sovereignty not withdrawn by treaty or statute, or by implication as a necessary result of their dependent status. *See Oliphant*. ***
>
> [T]he sovereign power of a tribe to prosecute its members for tribal offenses clearly does not fall within that part of sovereignty which the Indians implicitly lost by virtue of their dependent status. The areas in which such implicit divestiture of sovereignty has been held to have occurred are those involving the relations between an Indian tribe and nonmembers of the tribe. Thus, Indian tribes can no longer freely alienate to non-Indians the land they occupy. *Johnson v. M'Intosh*. They cannot enter into direct commercial or governmental relations with foreign nations. *Worcester*; *Cherokee Nation*. And, as we have recently held, they cannot try nonmembers in tribal courts. *Oliphant*.
>
> These limitations rest on the fact that the dependent status of Indian tribes within our territorial jurisdiction is necessarily inconsistent with their freedom independently to determine their external relations. But the powers of self-government, including the power to prescribe and enforce internal criminal laws, are of a different type. They involve only the relations among members of a tribe. Thus, they are not such powers as would necessarily be lost by virtue of a tribe's dependent status. "[T]he settled doctrine of the law of nations is, that a weaker power does not surrender its independence—its right to self government, by associating with a stronger, and taking its protection." *Worcester*.

Wheeler, 435 U.S. at 323, 326 (1978)

How is prosecuting crimes committed within one's own territory a part of a sovereign's "external relations"? If you as an American citizen travel to France, France considers it part of its internal sovereignty to prosecute you for any crimes you commit there. To be sure, its external relations with the United States may affect its internal exercises of sovereignty with respect to U.S. citizens—but that would be the result of a treaty France joined or, perhaps, because of customary international law. Why is Indian law different? Can this notion of "external relations" be made consistent with the result in *Williams v. Lee, supra*?

9. *Congressional authorization of tribal criminal jurisdiction over non-Indians.* Note that the Court in *Oliphant* acknowledged that Congress could authorize tribes to exercise criminal jurisdiction over non-Indians. Congress took up the invitation in the Violence Against Women Reauthorization Act of 2013, 25 U.S.C. § 1304(b)(1). The Act, discussed in detail in Chapter 5, allows tribes to exercise criminal jurisdiction over all persons, including non-Indians, for crimes involving domestic or dating violence. Review the provision, reprinted in Chapter 5, again. Is this a delegation of federal power, or a recognition of inherent sovereignty? Could a non-Indian criminal defendant challenge the statute on constitutional grounds? We will reconsider this question later after review of *United States v. Lara, infra.*

B. Tribal Civil Regulatory Authority Over Nonmembers: 1981–1989

Oliphant seemed to reflect the distinctive history of criminal jurisdiction, in which the federal courts have always asserted jurisdiction over non-Indians committing crimes in Indian country. As discussed in section A, while authorities sometimes assumed this federal jurisdiction was exclusive, they usually reached the opposite conclusion regarding civil and regulatory jurisdiction. The first case regarding regulatory jurisdiction in the wake of *Oliphant* supported this assumption.

Washington v. Confederated Tribes of Colville Indian Reservation, 447 U.S. 134 (1980). The portion of the opinion concerning whether states could tax cigarette sales to nonmembers is excerpted in Chapter 7. The case also considered whether a tribe could impose a tax on the on-reservation sale of cigarettes to nonmembers. The Court unanimously upheld the tribe's taxing authority:

> The power to tax transactions occurring on trust lands and significantly involving a tribe or its members is a fundamental attribute of sovereignty which the tribes retain unless divested of it by federal law or necessary implication of their dependent status. *Cf. Wheeler.*
>
> The widely held understanding within the Federal Government has always been that federal law to date has not worked a divestiture of Indian taxing power. Executive branch officials have consistently recognized that Indian tribes possess a broad measure of civil jurisdiction over the activities of non-Indians on Indian reservation lands in which the tribes have a significant interest. *** *Powers of Indian Tribes*, 55 I.D. 14, 46 (1934). According to the Solicitor of the Department of the Interior: "Chief among the powers of sovereignty recognized as pertaining to an Indian

> tribe is the power of taxation. Except where Congress has provided otherwise, this power may be exercised over members of the tribe *and over nonmembers*, so far as such nonmembers may accept privileges of trade, residence, etc., to which taxes may be attached as conditions." [*Id.*] (emphasis added).
>
> Federal courts also have acknowledged tribal power to tax non-Indians entering the reservation to engage in economic activity. No federal statute cited to us shows any congressional departure from this view. To the contrary, authority to tax the activities or property of non-Indians taking place or situated on Indian lands, in cases where the tribe has a significant interest in the subject matter, was very probably one of the tribal powers under "existing law" confirmed by § 16 of the Indian Reorganization Act of 1934, 48 Stat. 987, 25 U.S.C. § 476. In these respects the present cases differ sharply from *Oliphant*, in which we stressed the shared assumptions of the Executive, Judicial, and Legislative Departments that Indian tribes could not exercise criminal jurisdiction over non-Indians.
>
> Tribal powers are not implicitly divested by virtue of the tribes' dependent status. This Court has found such a divestiture in cases where the exercise of tribal sovereignty would be inconsistent with the overriding interests of the National Government, as when the tribes seek to engage in foreign relations, alienate their lands to non-Indians without federal consent, or prosecute non-Indians in tribal courts which do not accord the full protections of the Bill of Rights. In the present cases, we can see no overriding federal interest that would necessarily be frustrated by tribal taxation. ***

Washington, 447 U.S. at 152–154.

The next case, however, partially extended *Oliphant* to tribal regulatory jurisdiction on nonmember fee land.

MONTANA V. UNITED STATES

450 U.S. 544, 101 S. Ct. 1245, 67 L.Ed.2d 493 (1981)

JUSTICE STEWART delivered the opinion of the Court.

This case concerns the sources and scope of the power of an Indian tribe to regulate hunting and fishing by non-Indians on lands within its reservation owned in fee simple by non-Indians. ***

The Crow Indians originated in Canada, but some three centuries ago they migrated to what is now southern Montana. In the 19th century, warfare between the Crows and several other tribes led the tribes and the United States to sign the First Treaty of Fort Laramie of 1851, in which the signatory tribes acknowledged various designated lands as their respective territories. *** The treaty identified approximately 38.5 million acres as Crow territory and, in Article 5, specified that, by making the treaty, the tribes did not "surrender the privilege of hunting, fishing, or passing over" any of the lands in dispute. In 1868, the Second Treaty of Fort Laramie established a Crow Reservation of roughly 8 million acres, including land through which the Big Horn River flows. ***

Several subsequent Acts of Congress reduced the reservation to slightly fewer than 2.3 million acres. *** In addition, the General Allotment Act of 1887, ch. 119, 24 Stat. 388, and the Crow Allotment Act of 1920, 41 Stat. 751, authorized the issuance of patents in fee to individual Indian allottees within the reservation. Under these Acts, an allottee could alienate his land to a non-Indian after holding it for 25 years. Today, roughly 52 percent of the reservation is allotted to members of the Tribe and held by the United States in trust for them, 17 percent is held in trust for the Tribe itself, and approximately 28 percent is held in fee by non-Indians. The State of Montana owns in fee simple 2 percent of the reservation, the United States less than 1 percent.

Since the 1920's, the State of Montana has stocked the waters of the reservation with fish, and the construction of a dam by the United States made trout fishing in the Big Horn River possible. The reservation also contains game, some of it stocked by the State. Since the 1950's, the Crow Tribal Council has passed several resolutions respecting hunting and fishing on the reservation, including Resolution No. 74–05, the occasion for this lawsuit. That resolution prohibits hunting and fishing within the reservation by anyone who is not a member of the Tribe. The State of Montana, however, has continued to assert its authority to regulate hunting and fishing by non-Indians within the reservation.

On October 9, 1975, proceeding in its own right and as fiduciary for the Tribe, the United States endeavored to resolve the conflict between the Tribe and the State by filing the present lawsuit. The plaintiff sought (1) a declaratory judgment quieting title to the bed of the Big Horn River in the United States as trustee for the Tribe, (2) a declaratory judgment establishing that the Tribe and the United States have sole authority to regulate hunting and fishing within the reservation, and (3) an injunction requiring Montana to secure the permission of the Tribe before issuing hunting or fishing licenses for use within the reservation. ***

[In the first part of the opinion, reprinted in Ch. 9, *infra*, the Court held that although the tribe's treaty lands encompassed the Big Horn River, title to the riverbed passed to the state under the Equal Footing doctrine, under which states obtain title to land under navigable waters when they enter the Union. Therefore the Court concluded that the state, not the tribe, owned the riverbed.]

III.

*** The Court of Appeals held that the Tribe may prohibit nonmembers from hunting or fishing on land belonging to the Tribe or held by the United States in trust for the Tribe, and with this holding we can readily agree. We also agree with the Court of Appeals that if the Tribe permits nonmembers to fish or hunt on such lands, it may condition their entry by charging a fee or establishing bag and creel limits. What remains is the question of the power of the Tribe to regulate non-Indian fishing and hunting on reservation land owned in fee by nonmembers of the Tribe. The Court of Appeals held that, with respect to fee-patented lands, the Tribe may regulate, but may not prohibit, hunting and fishing by non-member resident owners or by those, such as tenants or employees, whose occupancy is authorized by the owners. The court further held that the Tribe may totally prohibit hunting and fishing on lands within the reservation owned by non-Indians who do not occupy that land.

The Court of Appeals found two sources for this tribal regulatory power: the Crow treaties *** and "inherent" Indian sovereignty. We believe that neither source supports the court's conclusion.

A.

The purposes of the 1851 treaty were to assure safe passage for settlers across the lands of various Indian Tribes; to compensate the Tribes for the loss of buffalo, other game animals, timber, and forage; to delineate tribal boundaries; to promote intertribal peace; and to establish a way of identifying Indians who committed depredations against non-Indians. *** [T]he treaty did not even create a reservation, although it did designate tribal lands. Only Article 5 of that Treaty referred to hunting and fishing, and it merely provided that the eight signatory tribes "do not surrender the privilege of hunting, fishing, or passing over any of the tracts of country heretofore described." The treaty nowhere suggested that Congress intended to grant authority to the Crow Tribe to regulate hunting and fishing by nonmembers on nonmember lands. Indeed, the Court of Appeals acknowledged that after the treaty was signed non-Indians, as well as members of other Indian tribes, undoubtedly hunted and fished within the treaty-designated territory of the Crows.

The 1868 Fort Laramie Treaty reduced the size of the Crow territory designated by the 1851 treaty. Article II of the treaty established a reservation for the Crow Tribe, and provided that it be "set apart for the *absolute and undisturbed use and occupation* of the Indians herein named, and for such other friendly tribes or individual Indians as from time to time they may be willing, with the consent of the United States, to admit amongst them ***," (emphasis added) and that "the United States now solemnly agrees that no persons, except those herein designated and authorized so to do *** shall ever be permitted to pass over, settle upon, or reside in the territory described in this article for the use of said Indians. *** " The treaty, therefore, obligated the United States to prohibit most non-Indians from residing on or passing through reservation lands used and occupied by the Tribe, and, thereby, arguably conferred upon the Tribe the authority to control fishing and hunting on those lands. But that authority could only extend to land on which the Tribe exercises "absolute and undisturbed use and occupation." And it is clear that the quantity of such land was substantially reduced by the allotment and alienation of tribal lands as a result of the passage of the General Allotment Act of 1887 and the Crow Allotment Act of 1920. If the 1868 treaty created tribal power to restrict or prohibit non-Indian hunting and fishing on the reservation, that power cannot apply to lands held in fee by non-Indians.[9]

---

9. The Court of Appeals discussed the effect of the Allotment Acts as follows:

> While neither of these Acts, nor any other to which our attention has been called, explicitly qualifies the Tribe's rights over hunting and fishing, it defies reason to suppose that Congress intended that non-members who reside on fee patent lands could hunt and fish thereon only by consent of the Tribe. So far as the record of this case reveals, no efforts to exclude completely non-members of the Crow Tribe from hunting and fishing within the reservation were being made by the Crow Tribe at the time of enactment of the Allotment Acts.

But nothing in the Allotment Acts supports the view of the Court of Appeals that the Tribe could nevertheless bar hunting and fishing by non-resident fee owners. The policy of the Acts was the

*** [T]reaty rights with respect to reservation lands must be read in light of the subsequent alienation of those lands. Accordingly, the language of the 1868 treaty provides no support for tribal authority to regulate hunting and fishing on land owned by non-Indians.

B.

*** "[I]nherent sovereignty" is not so broad as to support the application of Resolution No. 74–05 to non-Indian lands.

This Court most recently reviewed the principles of inherent sovereignty in *Wheeler*. *** [T]he Court was careful to note that, through their original incorporation into the United States as well as through specific treaties and statutes, the Indian tribes have lost many of the attributes of sovereignty. The Court distinguished between those inherent powers retained by the tribes and those divested:

> The areas in which such implicit divestiture of sovereignty has been held to have occurred are those involving *the relations between an Indian tribe and nonmembers of the tribe* ***.
>
> These limitations rest on the fact that the dependent status of Indian tribes within our territorial jurisdiction is necessarily inconsistent with their freedom independently *to determine their external relations*. But the powers of self-government, including the power to prescribe and enforce internal criminal laws, are of a different type. They involve *only the relations among members of a tribe*. Thus, they are not such powers as would necessarily be lost by virtue of a tribe's dependent status. (Emphasis added.)

Thus, in addition to the power to punish tribal offenders, the Indian tribes retain their inherent power to determine tribal membership, to regulate domestic relations among members, and to prescribe rules of inheritance for members. But exercise of tribal power beyond what is necessary to protect tribal self-government or to control internal relations is inconsistent with the dependent status of the tribes, and so cannot survive without express congressional delegation. Since regulation of hunting and fishing by nonmembers of a tribe on lands no longer owned by the tribe bears no clear relationship to tribal

---

eventual assimilation of the Indian population and the "gradual extinction of Indian reservations and Indian titles." The Secretary of the Interior and the Commissioner of Indian Affairs repeatedly emphasized that the allotment policy was designed to eventually eliminate tribal relations. *** And throughout the congressional debates on the subject of allotment, it was assumed that the "civilization" of the Indian population was to be accomplished, in part, by the dissolution of tribal relations.

There is simply no suggestion in the legislative history that Congress intended that the non-Indians who would settle upon alienated allotted lands would be subject to tribal regulatory authority. Indeed, throughout the congressional debates, allotment of Indian land was consistently equated with the dissolution of tribal affairs and jurisdiction. ***It defies common sense to suppose that Congress would intend that non-Indians purchasing allotted lands would become subject to tribal jurisdiction when an avowed purpose of the allotment policy was the ultimate destruction of tribal government. And it is hardly likely that Congress could have imagined that the purpose of peaceful assimilation could be advanced if fee-holders could be excluded from fishing or hunting on their acquired property.

The policy of allotment and sale of surplus reservation land was, of course, repudiated in 1934 by the Indian Reorganization Act. But what is relevant in this case is the effect of the land alienation occasioned by that policy on Indian treaty rights tied to Indian use and occupation of reservation land.

self-government or internal relations,[13] the general principles of retained inherent sovereignty did not authorize the Crow Tribe to adopt Resolution No. 74–05.

*** Though *Oliphant* only determined inherent tribal authority in criminal matters,[14] the principles on which it relied support the general proposition that the inherent sovereign powers of an Indian tribe do not extend to the activities of nonmembers of the tribe. To be sure, Indian tribes retain inherent sovereign power to exercise some forms of civil jurisdiction over non-Indians on their reservations, even on non-Indian fee lands. A tribe may regulate, through taxation, licensing, or other means, the activities of nonmembers who enter consensual relationships with the tribe or its members, through commercial dealing, contracts, leases, or other arrangements. [*Williams v. Lee; Morris v. Hitchcock; Buster v. Wright; Washington v. Confederated Tribes of the Colville Reservation.*] A tribe may also retain inherent power to exercise civil authority over the conduct of non-Indians on fee lands within its reservation when that conduct threatens or has some direct effect on the political integrity, the economic security, or the health or welfare of the tribe. [*Fisher v. District Court; Williams v. Lee.*]

No such circumstances, however, are involved in this case. Non–Indian hunters and fishermen on non-Indian fee land do not enter any agreements or dealings with the Crow Tribe so as to subject themselves to tribal civil jurisdiction. And nothing in this case suggests that such non-Indian hunting and fishing so threaten the Tribe's political or economic security as to justify tribal regulation. The complaint in the District Court did not allege that non-Indian hunting and fishing on fee lands imperil the subsistence or welfare of the Tribe.[16] Furthermore, the District Court made express findings, left unaltered by the Court of Appeals, that the Crow Tribe has traditionally accommodated itself to the State's "near exclusive" regulation of hunting and fishing on fee lands within the reservation. 457 F.Supp. at 609–610. And the District Court found that Montana's statutory and regulatory scheme does not prevent the Crow Tribe from limiting or forbidding non-Indian hunting and fishing on lands still owned by or held in trust for the Tribe or its members. *Id.* at 609.

[**JUSTICE STEVENS** filed a concurring opinion, and **JUSTICE BLACKMUN** filed an opinion dissenting in part, in which **JUSTICE BRENNAN** and **JUSTICE MARSHALL** joined.]

---

13. Any argument that Resolution No. 74–05 is necessary to Crow tribal self-government is refuted by the findings of the District Court that the State of Montana has traditionally exercised "near exclusive" jurisdiction over hunting and fishing on fee lands within the reservation, and that the parties to this case had accommodated themselves to the state regulation. The Court of Appeals left these findings unaltered and indeed implicitly reaffirmed them, adding that the record reveals no attempts by the Tribe at the time of the Crow Allotment Act to forbid non-Indian hunting and fishing on reservation lands.

14. By denying the Suquamish Tribe criminal jurisdiction over non-Indians, however, the *Oliphant* case would seriously restrict the ability of a tribe to enforce any purported regulation of non-Indian hunters and fishermen. ***

16. Similarly, the complaint did not allege that the State has abdicated or abused its responsibility for protecting and managing wildlife, has established its season, bag, or creel limits in such a way as to impair the Crow Indians' treaty rights to fish or hunt, or has imposed less stringent hunting and fishing regulations within the reservation than in other parts of the State. ***

NOTES AND QUESTIONS

1. *Regulatory jurisdiction on tribally owned and trust land.* The Court states that tribes may regulate nonmembers on land to which they may also prohibit entry, by conditioning entry on acceptance of regulations. Is that the basis of jurisdiction for other sovereigns? Why is it for tribes?

2. *Loss of full regulatory jurisdiction on non-Indian fee land.* What deprives tribes of full regulatory powers on fee land? Is it a long-standing historical assumption as in *Oliphant*? Is it a logical extension of the decision in that case—is all tribal jurisdiction over non-members "inconsistent with their dependent status," and so must be justified by property ownership, consent, or a fundamental effect on self-government? Or is it an expression of congressional intent in the allotment acts? If so, how does this compare with the interpretation of the allotment acts we saw in the diminishment cases, *Solem v. Bartlett*, *Hagen v. Utah*, and *Yankton Sioux*?

3. *Interpretation of the 1851 and 1868 treaties.* The Court finds that while the treaties "arguably" give the tribes the right to regulate non-Indian hunting and fishing on lands they still own, they do not include regulatory authority over nonmember owned lands. Thus, although the 1851 treaty specifically protected Crow hunting and fishing rights, "The treaty nowhere suggested that Congress intended to grant authority to the Crow Tribe to regulate hunting and fishing by nonmembers on nonmember lands." Compare this to the way the Court interpreted treaties in the other cases we have read.

4. *Retained jurisdiction on nonmember fee land.* The Court states that tribes may regulate the activities of nonmembers who "enter consensual relationships with the tribe," or whose conduct "threatens or has some direct effect on the political integrity, the economic security, or the health or welfare of the tribe." This second situation appeared at first glance quite broad; it is comparable to the general police powers of a state to legislate for the "health, safety or welfare" of its people. The 1982 Cohen Handbook, for example, stated that *Montana* stood for nothing more than the proposition that tribes could not regulate nonmembers on fee lands when they had no significant interest in the activity. Consider the reasons the Court found that regulation of nonmember hunting and fishing did not fit into this second *Montana* prong. Do you find more troubling reasoning for tribes there? Should it be significant that the tribe has traditionally accommodated itself to state jurisdiction over non-Indian hunting and fishing?

5. *Searching for the relevant precedent:* Oliphant *or* Williams v. Lee? *Montana* was not filed as a case about tribal jurisdiction; rather, it was filed by the United States on behalf of the tribe as a case challenging state jurisdiction and arguing that the tribe had exclusive regulatory authority over hunting and fishing on the reservation. The plaintiffs would have found support for this position from *Williams v. Lee*, which held that not only did tribal courts have jurisdiction over a transaction between a non-Indian and Navajo, but the states lacked any, saying "The cases in this Court have consistently guarded the authority of Indian governments over their reservations. Congress recognized this authority in the Navajos in the Treaty of 1868, and has done so ever since. If this power is to be taken away from them, it is for Congress to do it." Instead, the Court flipped the question considered, assuming that the states had jurisdiction, and holding that the tribe lacked any jurisdiction over hunting and

fishing on fee land. *Montana* relied on *Oliphant* as the central precedent, limiting *Williams* to an affirmation of jurisdiction in situations where the non-Indian has entered into a consensual relationship with a tribal member.

6. *What's left of inherent sovereignty?* An extreme reading of *Montana* might be that tribes have no inherent sovereignty over nonmembers, and that any regulatory rights they had derived either from the right to exclude, consent of the nonmember, or direct infringement on tribal health, welfare or self-government. This suggestion was rebutted in *Merrion*, which was initially argued before *Montana* was decided, but reargued in light of that decision.

MERRION V. JICARILLA APACHE TRIBE

455 U.S. 130, 102 S. Ct. 894, 71 L.Ed.2d 21 (1982)

JUSTICE MARSHALL delivered the opinion of the Court.

Pursuant to long-term leases with the Jicarilla Apache Tribe, petitioners, 21 lessees, extract and produce oil and gas from the Tribe's reservation lands. In these two consolidated cases, petitioners challenge an ordinance enacted by the Tribe imposing a severance tax on "any oil and natural gas severed, saved and removed from Tribal lands." *See* Oil and Gas Severance Tax No. 77–0–02, App. 38. We granted certiorari to determine whether the Tribe has the authority to impose this tax, and, if so, whether the tax imposed by the Tribe violates the Commerce Clause.

I.

The Jicarilla Apache Tribe resides on a reservation in northwestern New Mexico. Established by Executive Order in 1887,[1] the reservation contains 742,315 acres, all of which are held as tribal trust property. ***

The Tribe is organized under the Indian Reorganization Act of 1934, which authorizes any tribe residing on a reservation to adopt a constitution and bylaws, subject to the approval of the Secretary of the Interior (Secretary). The Tribe's first Constitution, approved by the Secretary on August 4, 1937, preserved all powers conferred by § 16 of the Indian Reorganization Act of 1934, ch. 576, 48 Stat. 987, 25 U.S.C. § 476. In 1968, the Tribe revised its Constitution to specify:

> The inherent powers of the Jicarilla Apache Tribe, including those conferred by Section 16 of the Act of June 18, 1934 (48 Stat. 984), as amended, shall vest in the tribal council and shall be exercised thereby subject only to limitations imposed by the Constitution of the United States, applicable Federal statutes and regulations of the Department of the Interior, and the restrictions established by this revised constitution.

Revised Constitution of the Jicarilla Apache Tribe, Art. XI, § 1.

---

1. *** The fact that the Jicarilla Apache Reservation was established by Executive Order rather than by treaty or statute does not affect our analysis; the Tribe's sovereign power is not affected by the manner in which its reservation was created. *E.g., Washington v. Confederated Tribes.*

The Revised Constitution provides that "[t]he tribal council may enact ordinances to govern the development of tribal lands and other resources," Art. XI, § 1(a)(3). It further provides that "[t]he tribal council may levy and collect taxes and fees on tribal members, and may enact ordinances, subject to approval by the Secretary of the Interior, to impose taxes and fees on non-members of the tribe doing business on the reservation," Art. XI, § 1(e). The Revised Constitution was approved by the Secretary on February 13, 1969.

To develop tribal lands, the Tribe has executed mineral leases encompassing some 69% of the reservation land. Beginning in 1953, the petitioners entered into leases with the Tribe. The Commissioner of Indian Affairs, on behalf of the Secretary, approved these leases, as required by [the federal Mineral Leasing Act of 1938.] In exchange for a cash bonus, royalties, and rents, the typical lease grants the lessee "the exclusive right and privilege to drill for, mine, extract, remove, and dispose of all the oil and natural gas deposits in or under" the leased land for as long as the minerals are produced in paying quantities. *** Petitioners' activities on the leased land have been subject to taxes imposed by the State of New Mexico on oil and gas severance and on oil and gas production equipment.

Pursuant to its Revised Constitution, the Tribal Council adopted an ordinance imposing a severance tax on oil and gas production on tribal land. The ordinance was approved by the Secretary, through the Acting Director of the Bureau of Indian Affairs, on December 23, 1976. The tax applies to "any oil and natural gas severed, saved and removed from Tribal lands. *** " *Ibid.* *** Oil and gas consumed by the lessees to develop their leases or received by the Tribe as in-kind royalty payments are exempted from the tax.

In two separate actions, petitioners sought to enjoin enforcement of the tax by either the tribal authorities or the Secretary. [The District Court ruled against the Tribe, but the Court of Appeals reversed, holding that the tax fell within the tribe's inherent sovereign powers that had not been divested by any treaty or statute.]

II.

Petitioners argue, and the dissent agrees, that an Indian tribe's authority to tax non-Indians who do business on the reservation stems exclusively from its power to exclude such persons from tribal lands. Because the Tribe did not initially condition the leases upon the payment of a severance tax, petitioners assert that the Tribe is without authority to impose such a tax at a later time. We disagree with the premise that the power to tax derives only from the power to exclude. Even if that premise is accepted, however, we disagree with the conclusion that the Tribe lacks the power to impose the severance tax.

A.

In *Washington v. Confederated Tribes of the Colville Reservation*, 447 U.S. 134 (1980), we addressed the Indian tribes' authority to impose taxes on non-Indians doing business on the reservation. We held that "[t]he power to tax transactions occurring on trust lands and significantly involving a tribe or its members is a fundamental attribute of sovereignty which the tribes retain unless divested of it by federal law or necessary implication of their dependent status." 455 U.S. at 137 (quoting *Colville*). The power to tax is an essential attribute of Indian sovereignty because it is a necessary instrument of self-government and territorial management. This power enables a tribal government to raise revenues for its essential services. The power does not derive solely from the Indian tribe's power to exclude non-Indians from tribal lands. Instead, it derives from the tribe's general authority, as sovereign, to control economic activity within its jurisdiction, and to defray the cost of providing governmental services by requiring contributions from persons or enterprises engaged in economic activities within that jurisdiction.

The petitioners avail themselves of the "substantial privilege of carrying on business" on the reservation. *** They benefit from the provision of police protection and other governmental services, as well as from " 'the advantages of a civilized society' " that are assured by the existence of tribal government. *Exxon Corp. v. Wisconsin Dept. of Revenue*, 447 U.S. 207, 228 (1980). Numerous other governmental entities levy a general revenue tax similar to that imposed by the Jicarilla Tribe when they provide comparable services. Under these circumstances, there is nothing exceptional in requiring petitioners to contribute through taxes to the general cost of tribal government.[5] *Cf. Commonwealth Edison Co. v. Montana*, 453 U.S. 609, 624–629 (1981).

As we observed in *Colville*, the tribe's interest in levying taxes on nonmembers to raise "revenues for essential governmental programs *** is strongest when the revenues are derived from value generated on the reservation by activities involving the Tribes and when the taxpayer is the recipient of tribal services." This surely is the case here. The mere fact that the government imposing the tax also enjoys rents and royalties as the lessor of the mineral lands does not undermine the government's authority to impose the tax. The royalty payments from the mineral leases are paid to the Tribe in its role as partner in petitioners' commercial venture. The severance tax, in contrast, is petitioners' contribution "to the general cost of providing governmental services." State governments commonly receive both royalty payments and severance taxes from lessees of mineral lands within their borders.

Viewing the taxing power of Indian tribes as an essential instrument of self-government and territorial management has been a shared assumption of all three branches of the Federal Government. In *Colville*, the Court relied in part on a 1934 opinion of the Solicitor for the Department of the Interior. In this opinion, the Solicitor recognized that, in the absence of congressional action to the contrary, the tribes' sovereign power to tax " 'may be exercised over members of the tribe and over nonmembers, so far as such nonmembers may accept privileges of trade, residence, etc., to which taxes may be attached as conditions.' " [*Powers of Indian Tribes*, 55 I.D. 14, 46 (1934).] *Colville* further noted that official executive pronouncements have repeatedly recognized that "Indian tribes possess a broad measure of civil jurisdiction over the activities of non-Indians on Indian reservation lands in which the tribes have a significant interest ***, including jurisdiction to tax." [23 Op. Atty. Gen. 214 (1900); 17 Op. Atty. Gen. 134 (1881); 7 Op. Atty. Gen. 174 (1855)].[6]

5. ***We agree with Judge McKay's observation that "[i]t simply does not make sense to expect the tribes to carry out municipal functions approved and mandated by Congress without being able to exercise at least minimal taxing powers, whether they take the form of real estate taxes, leasehold taxes or severance taxes." 617 F.2d at 550 (McKay, J., concurring).

6. Moreover, in its revision of the classic treatise on Indian Law, the Department of the Interior advances the view that the Indian tribes' power to tax is not limited by the power to exclude. *See* U.S. Solicitor for Dept. of Interior, Federal Indian Law 438 (1958) ("The power to tax does not depend upon the power to remove and has been upheld where there was no power in the tribe to remove the taxpayer from the tribal jurisdiction") (footnote omitted). *See also* F. Cohen, Handbook

Similarly, Congress has acknowledged that the tribal power to tax is one of the tools necessary to self-government and territorial control. As early as 1879, the Senate Judiciary Committee acknowledged the validity of a tax imposed by the Chickasaw Nation on non-Indians legitimately within its territory:

> We have considered [Indian tribes] as invested with the right of self-government and jurisdiction over the persons and property within the limits of the territory they occupy, except so far as that jurisdiction has been restrained and abridged by treaty or act of Congress. Subject to the supervisory control of the Federal Government, they may enact the requisite legislation to maintain peace and good order, improve their condition, establish school systems, and aid their people in their efforts to acquire the arts of civilized life; and *they undoubtedly possess the inherent right to resort to taxation to raise the necessary revenue for the accomplishment of these vitally important objects*—a right not in any sense derived from the Government of the United States." S. Rep. No. 698, 45th Cong., 3d Sess., 1–2 (1879) (emphasis added).

Thus, the views of the three federal branches of government, as well as general principles of taxation, confirm that Indian tribes enjoy authority to finance their governmental services through taxation of non-Indians who benefit from those services. Indeed, the conception of Indian sovereignty that this Court has consistently reaffirmed permits no other conclusion. [*U.S. v. Mazurie*; *Worcester v. Georgia*; Cohen, *The Spanish Origin of Indian Rights in the Law of the United States*, *in* The Legal Conscience 230, 234 (L. Cohen ed. 1960).] Adhering to this understanding, we conclude that the Tribe's authority to tax non-Indians who conduct business on the reservation does not simply derive from the Tribe's power to exclude such persons, but is an inherent power necessary to tribal self-government and territorial management.

Of course, the Tribe's authority to tax nonmembers is subject to constraints not imposed on other governmental entities: the Federal Government can take away this power, and the Tribe must obtain the approval of the Secretary before any tax on nonmembers can take effect. These additional constraints minimize potential concern that Indian tribes will exercise the power to tax in an unfair or unprincipled manner, and ensure that any exercise of the tribal power to tax will be consistent with national policies.

B.

Alternatively, if we accept the argument *** that the Tribe's authority to tax derives solely from its power to exclude non-Indians from the reservation, we conclude that the Tribe has the authority to impose the severance tax challenged here. Nonmembers who lawfully enter tribal lands remain subject to the tribe's power to exclude them. This power necessarily includes the lesser power to place conditions on entry, on continued presence, or on reservation conduct, such as a tax on business activities conducted on the reservation. When a tribe grants a non-Indian the right to be on Indian land, the tribe agrees not to exercise its ultimate power to oust the non-Indian as long as the

---

of Federal Indian Law 142 (1942) ("One of the powers essential to the maintenance of any government is the power to levy taxes. That this power is an inherent attribute of tribal sovereignty which continues unless withdrawn or limited by treaty or by act of Congress is a proposition which has never been successfully disputed.") (footnote omitted).

non-Indian complies with the initial conditions of entry. However, it does not follow that the lawful property right to be on Indian land also immunizes the non-Indian from the tribe's exercise of its lesser-included power to tax or to place other conditions on the non-Indian's conduct or continued presence on the reservation. A nonmember who enters the jurisdiction of the tribe remains subject to the risk that the tribe will later exercise its sovereign power. The fact that the tribe chooses not to exercise its power to tax when it initially grants a non-Indian entry onto the reservation does not permanently divest the tribe of its authority to impose such a tax.

Petitioners argue that their leaseholds entitle them to enter the reservation and exempt them from further exercises of the Tribe's sovereign authority. Similarly, the dissent asserts that the Tribe has lost the power to tax petitioners' mining activities because it has leased to them the use of the mineral lands and such rights of access to the reservation as might be necessary to enjoy the leases. ***

*** [P]etitioners and the dissent confuse the Tribe's role as commercial partner with its role as sovereign. This confusion relegates the powers of sovereignty to the bargaining process undertaken in each of the sovereign's commercial agreements. It is one thing to find that the Tribe has agreed to sell the right to use the land and take from it valuable minerals; it is quite another to find that the Tribe has abandoned its sovereign powers simply because it has not expressly reserved them through a contract.

Confusing these two results denigrates Indian sovereignty. Indeed, the dissent apparently views the tribal power to exclude, as well as the derivative authority to tax, as merely the power possessed by any individual landowner or any social group to attach conditions, including a "tax" or fee, to the entry by a stranger onto private land or into the social group, and not as a sovereign power. *** [I]n arguing that the Tribe somehow "lost" its power to tax petitioners by not including a taxing provision in the original leases or otherwise notifying petitioners that the Tribe retained and might later exercise its sovereign right to tax them, the dissent attaches little significance to the sovereign nature of the tribal authority to tax, and it obviously views tribal authority as little more than a landowner's contractual right.

Moreover, the dissent implies that the power to tax depends on the consent of the taxed as well as on the Tribe's power to exclude non-Indians. Whatever place consent may have in contractual matters and in the creation of democratic governments, it has little if any role in measuring the validity of an exercise of legitimate sovereign authority. Requiring the consent of the entrant deposits in the hands of the excludable non-Indian the source of the tribe's power, when the power instead derives from sovereignty itself. Only the Federal Government may limit a tribe's exercise of its sovereign authority. *Wheeler*.[13] Indian sovereignty is not conditioned on the assent of a nonmember; to the contrary, the nonmember's presence and conduct on Indian lands are conditioned by the limitations the tribe may choose to impose.

Viewed in this light, the absence of a reference to the tax in the leases themselves hardly impairs the Tribe's authority to impose the tax. Contractual

13. *** Federal limitations on tribal sovereignty can also occur when the exercise of tribal sovereignty would be inconsistent with overriding national interests. *See Colville*. This concern is not presented here. *See* [*id.*].

arrangements remain subject to subsequent legislation by the presiding sovereign. Even where the contract at issue requires payment of a royalty for a license or franchise issued by the governmental entity, the government's power to tax remains unless it "has been specifically surrendered in terms which admit of no other reasonable interpretation." *St. Louis v. United R. Co.*, 210 U.S. 266, 280 (1908). [The Court refused to distinguish tribal sovereignty from federal or state sovereignty with respect to this rule.]

No claim is asserted in this litigation, nor could one be, that petitioners' leases contain the clear and unmistakable surrender of taxing power required for its extinction. We could find a waiver of the Tribe's taxing power only if we inferred it from silence in the leases. To presume that a sovereign forever waives the right to exercise one of its sovereign powers unless it expressly reserves the right to exercise that power in a commercial agreement turns the concept of sovereignty on its head, and we do not adopt this analysis.

Finding no defect in the Tribe's exercise of its taxing power, we now address petitioners' contention that the severance tax violates the "negative implications" of the Commerce Clause because it taxes an activity that is an integral part of the flow of commerce, discriminates against interstate commerce, and imposes a multiple burden on interstate commerce. ***

To date *** this Court has relied on the Indian Commerce Clause as a shield to protect Indian tribes from state and local interference, and has not relied on the Clause to authorize tribal regulation of commerce without any constitutional restraints. We see no need to break new ground in this area today: even if we assume that tribal action is subject to the limitations of the Interstate Commerce Clause, this tax does not violate the "negative implications" of that Clause.

*** Judicial review of state taxes under the Interstate Commerce Clause is intended to ensure that States do not disrupt or burden interstate commerce when Congress' power remains unexercised: it protects the free flow of commerce, and thereby safeguards Congress' latent power from encroachment by the several States.

*** However, we only engage in this review when Congress has not acted or purported to act. *** Here, Congress has affirmatively acted by providing a series of federal checkpoints that must be cleared before a tribal tax can take effect. Under the Indian Reorganization Act, 25 U.S.C. §§ 476, 477, a tribe must obtain approval from the Secretary before it adopts or revises its constitution to announce its intention to tax nonmembers. Further, before the ordinance imposing the severance tax challenged here could take effect, the Tribe was required again to obtain approval from the Secretary. *See* Revised Constitution of the Jicarilla Tribe, Art. XI, §§ 1(e), 2. ***

*** [I]t is not our function nor our prerogative to strike down a tax that has traveled through the precise channels established by Congress, and has obtained the specific approval of the Secretary.

B.

The tax challenged here would survive judicial scrutiny under the Interstate Commerce Clause, even if such scrutiny were necessary. In *Complete Auto Transit, Inc. v. Brady*, 430 U.S. at 279, we held that a state tax on activities connected to interstate commerce is sustainable if it "is applied to an activity with a substantial nexus with the taxing State, is fairly apportioned, does not discriminate against interstate commerce, and is fairly related to the services provided by the State." ***

[P]etitioners focus their attack on the third factor, and argue that the tax discriminates against interstate commerce. In essence, petitioners argue that the language "sold or transported off the reservation" exempts from taxation minerals sold on the reservation, kept on the reservation for use by individual members of the Tribe, and minerals taken by the Tribe on the reservation as in-kind royalty. *** We do not accept petitioners' arguments; instead, we agree with the Tribe, the Solicitor General, and the Court of Appeals that the tax is imposed on minerals sold on the reservation or transported off the reservation before sale. *** Under this interpretation, the tax does not treat minerals transported away from the reservation differently than it treats minerals that might be sold on the reservation. ***[26]

JUSTICE STEVENS, joined by **CHIEF JUSTICE BURGER** and **JUSTICE REHNQUIST**, dissenting.

*** Over its own members, an Indian tribe's sovereign powers are virtually unlimited; the incorporation of the tribe into the United States has done little to change internal tribal relations. In becoming part of the United States, however, the tribes yielded their status as independent nations; Indians and non-Indians alike answered to the authority of a new Nation, organized under a new Constitution based on democratic principles of representative government. In that new system of government, Indian tribes were afforded no general powers over citizens of the United States. ***

This difference is consistent with the fundamental principle that "[i]n this Nation each sovereign governs only with the consent of the governed." *Nevada v. Hall*, 440 U.S. 410 (1979). Since nonmembers are excluded from participation in tribal government, the powers that may be exercised over them are appropriately limited. Certainly, tribal authority over nonmembers—including the power to tax—is not unprecedented. An examination of cases that have upheld this power, however, demonstrates that the power to impose such a tax derives solely from the tribes' power to exclude nonmembers entirely from territory that has been reserved for the tribe. This "power to exclude" logically has been held to include the lesser power to attach conditions on a right of entry

---

26. Petitioners contend that because New Mexico may tax the same mining activity at full value, the Indian tax imposes a multiple tax burden on interstate commerce in violation of the Commerce Clause. The multiple taxation issue arises where two or more taxing jurisdictions point to some contact with an enterprise to support a tax on the entire value of its multistate activities, which is more than the contact would justify. *E.g., Standard Oil Co. v. Peck*, 342 U.S. 382, 384–385 (1952). This Court has required an apportionment of the tax based on the portion of the activity properly viewed as occurring within each relevant State. *** This rule has no bearing here, however, for there can be no claim that the Tribe seeks to tax any more of petitioners' mining activity than the portion occurring within Tribal jurisdiction. Indeed, petitioners do not even argue that the Tribe is seeking to seize more tax revenues than would be fairly related to the services provided by the Tribe. In the absence of such an assertion, and when the activity taxed by the Tribe occurs entirely on tribal lands, the multiple taxation issue would arise only if a *State* attempted to levy a tax on the same activity, which is more than the *State's* contact with the activity would justify. In such a circumstance, any challenge asserting that tribal and state taxes create a multiple burden on interstate commerce should be directed at the state tax, which, in the absence of congressional ratification, might be invalidated under the Commerce Clause. These cases, of course, do not involve a challenge to state taxation, and we intimate no opinion on the possibility of such a challenge.

granted by the tribe to a nonmember to engage in particular activities within the reservation. ***

*** Tribal powers over nonmembers are appropriately limited because nonmembers are foreclosed from participation in tribal government. If the power to tax is limited to situations in which the tribe has the power to exclude, then the nonmember is subjected to the tribe's jurisdiction only if he accepts the conditions of entry imposed by the tribe. The limited source of the power to tax nonmembers—the power to exclude intruders—is thus consistent with this Court's recognition of the limited character of the power of Indian tribes over nonmembers in general. ***

This conclusion is consistent with [*Colville.*] *** The tax in *Colville*, which was applied to nonmembers who entered the reservation and sought to purchase cigarettes, is clearly valid under the rationale that the tribes' power to tax derives from the right to exclude nonmembers from the reservation and the lesser right to attach conditions on the entry of such nonmembers seeking to do business there.[43] ***

But [here] the Tribe did not impose any tax prior to petitioners' entry or as a condition attached to the privileges granted by the leases in 1953. As a result, the tax imposed in 1976 is not valid unless the Tribe retained its power either to exclude petitioners from the reservation or to prohibit them from continuing to extract oil and gas from reservation lands.

*** In my opinion it is clear that the parties negotiated the leases in question with absolutely no expectation that a severance tax could later be imposed; in the contemplation of the parties, the conditions governing petitioners' right to extract oil and gas were not subject to change during the terms of the agreements. ***

Petitioners were granted authority by the Tribe to extract oil and gas from reservation lands. The Tribe now seeks to change retroactively the conditions of that authority. These petitioners happen to be prosperous oil companies. Moreover, it may be sound policy to find additional sources of revenue to better the economic conditions of many Indian tribes. If this retroactive imposition of a tax on oil companies is permissible, however, an Indian tribe may with equal legitimacy contract with outsiders for the construction of a school or a hospital, or for the rendition of medical or technical services, and then—after the contract is partially performed—change the terms of the bargain by imposing a gross receipts tax on the outsider. If the Court is willing to ignore the risk of such unfair treatment of a local contractor or a local doctor because the Secretary of the Interior has the power to veto a tribal tax, it must equate the unbridled discretion of a political appointee with the protection afforded by rules of law. That equation is unacceptable to me. Neither wealth, political opportunity, nor past transgressions can justify denying any person the protection of the law.

---

43. A nonmember can avoid the tax by declining to do business on the reservation; the "sanction" imposed for refusal to pay the tax is denial of permission to buy cigarettes.

NOTES AND QUESTIONS

1. Montana *and* Merrion. How can *Montana* and *Merrion* be reconciled? One way is that in *Montana* the nonmember activity occurred on nonmember fee land; in *Merrion* the nonmember activity occurred on tribal land. How much does the Court rely on this distinction? Another possibility is that the Court viewed the power to tax differently from the general power to regulate. Is there language in *Merrion* to support that argument? Don't taxes often serve a regulatory function?

2. *Analogy to state severance taxes.* The majority concludes that, because states may impose severance taxes upon state public land from which minerals are being extracted under pre-existing mineral leases, tribes should be able to do so as well. To be sure, in both situations the sovereign (the state, the tribe) holds a royalty interest. But there may be two critical differences. First, in the usual scenario, a state will have a general mineral severance tax that applies on state and private land alike. Because raising the tax decreases not only the oil companies' income but also the income of the private royalty holders, there is a certainty that those who oppose the tax are represented in the state legislature. In contrast, in *Merrion*, the only "losers" are the oil companies; the universe of royalty holders (the tribe) wins by the imposition of the tax. Second, in the usual state scenario, the state cannot avoid the political fallout of private royalty holder objection to tax increases by selectively raising the severance tax only on the public lands, because state constitutions generally have a "uniformity of tax" requirement that may oblige the severance tax to be the same on public and private lands. In *Merrion*, in contrast, the oil companies look like sitting ducks for this tax—what should stop the tribe from imposing a tax right up to the limits of the companies' profit margin, taking into account the costs of walking away from the deal, which would involve extraordinary costs of pulling pipe and equipment from the ground? These kinds of concerns seemingly motivated Justice Stevens's dissenting concern that the tax was not appropriate because it lacked the legitimacy of the consent of the governed. Would the analysis change if a substantial number of oil producing allotted lands were covered by the tribal tax?

3. *Sovereignty and negotiation.* The whole case would have gone away if the leases had expressly provided that the tribe could, or could not, impose a severance tax. Upon which party—the tribe or the oil companies—should the consequences of the silence in the leases fall? Another way to put it is, which party had the obligation *ex ante* to raise and negotiate about the issue? Note how the answer depends upon sovereignty or property conceptions. As the majority opinion in *Merrion* states, a sovereign is assumed not to have waived any of its sovereign powers unless it has done so expressly. A private party, of course, is subject to far less favorable baseline assumptions flowing from the principle of freedom of contract and the imposition of default rules for contracts based on commercial statutes and the common law. Is there any question that, if the lease had been between two private parties, one party could not rewrite the deal (as the oil companies think the tribe did here)? Should there be any question that, if the lease is given by a sovereign, the sovereign gets the benefit of the doubt? Why might the 1953 leases not have provided for imposition of the tax?

4. *Role of secretarial approval.* Another response to the complaint about the tax being unsupported by the consent of the governed is to note that the

Secretary of the Interior had approved it. In dissent, Justice Stevens found that argument unpersuasive, as it substitutes the protections of the legal process with the unreviewable discretion of a bureaucrat (indeed, one who might be delighted to approve measures increasing tribal revenue at the expense of private companies, perhaps offsetting federal aid to the tribe). In any event, the argument evaporated three years later. In *Kerr–McGee v. Navajo Tribe*, 471 U.S. 195 (1985), the Court had a case identical in all respects to *Merrion* except that the Navajo severance tax in question had been adopted without secretarial approval. (Most tribal constitutions that were adopted pursuant to the Indian Reorganization Act have a requirement of secretarial approval of some or all tribal ordinances; the Navajo have no such constitution or requirement.) The unanimous Court in *Kerr–McGee* (with one Justice not participating) upheld the validity of the tribal tax for the simple, Felix Cohen-like reason that nothing in federal law prohibited it:

> [We do not] agree that Congress intended to recognize as legitimate only those tribal taxes authorized by constitutions written under the IRA. Long before the IRA was enacted, the Senate Judiciary Committee acknowledged the validity of a tax imposed by the Chickasaw Nation on non-Indians. *See* S. Rep. No. 698, 45th Cong., 3d Sess., 1–2 (1879).
>
> *** As we noted in *New Mexico v. Mescalero Apache Tribe*, 462 U.S. 324 (1983), the Federal Government is "firmly committed to the goal of promoting tribal self-government." The power to tax members and non-Indians alike is surely an essential attribute of such self-government; the Navajos can gain independence from the Federal Government only by financing their own police force, schools, and social programs. *See* President's Statement on Indian Policy, 19 Weekly Comp.Pres.Doc. 98, 99 (Jan. 24, 1983). ***
>
> The Navajo Government has been called "probably the most elaborate" among tribes. H.R. Rep. No. 78, 91st Cong., 1st Sess., 8 (1969). The legitimacy of the Navajo Tribal Council, the freely elected governing body of the Navajos, is beyond question. *** We agree with the Court of Appeals that neither Congress nor the Navajos have found it necessary to subject the Tribal Council's tax laws to review by the Secretary of the Interior; accordingly, the judgment is *Affirmed.*

Kerr–McGee, 471 U.S. at 198–201. *Kerr–McGee* is overshadowed by *Merrion*, which is typically cited as the major precedent in support of tribal taxation of non-Indians. Yet *Kerr–McGee* might be considered an even stronger statement in support of inherent sovereignty, given the lack of Secretarial approval and the absence, therefore, of any justification rooted in federal delegation. To the Navajo Nation, *Kerr–McGee* is certainly momentous; the Tribal Council designated a tribal holiday, "Navajo Nation Sovereignty Day," in honor of the decision. *See* Sarah Krakoff, *A Narrative of Sovereignty: Illuminating the Paradox of the Domestic Dependent Nation*, 83 Or. L. Rev. 1109, 1166 (2004).

5. *Consistency across the cases?* The Court in *Merrion* stated: "The power to tax is an essential attribute of Indian sovereignty because it is a necessary instrument of self-government and territorial management." Would not the same be true for criminal jurisdiction? Regulation of hunting and fishing?

***Brendale v. Confederated Tribes and Bands of the Yakima Indian Reservation*, 492 U.S. 408 (1989).**

Brendale concerned tribal zoning of nonmember fee land on the Yakima reservation. The case fractured the Court into three non-majority factions.

By virtue of allotment, about 20% of the land on the Yakima Reservation was held in fee by both Indians and non-Indians. Most of the fee lands were in one corner of the reservation, but the rest was scattered throughout the reservation. The reservation had a "closed" area, a mostly forested region, and an "open area," where most Reservation residents lived. Less than 4% of the land in the closed area was held in fee. The tribe limited access to the closed area to members and nonmembers who owned land there.

Both the tribe and Yakima County asserted authority to zone fee land on the reservation. Three Justices—Justice Blackmun, joined by Justices Brennan and Marshall—took the Felix–Cohen-like view that, because no federal treaty or statute provided to the contrary, the tribe should have the power to zone all property on the reservation. Four Justices—Justice White, joined by Chief Justice Rehnquist, Justice Scalia, and Justice Kennedy—concluded in contrast that the tribe should have no authority to zone fee land owned by nonmembers, regardless of the location of the land. The remaining two Justices—Justice Stevens, joined by Justice O'Connor—controlled the outcome in the case. They joined the "White Four" on the conclusion that the tribe could not zone nonmember fee land in the open area, but also joined the "Blackmun Three" on the conclusion that the tribe could zone nonmember fee land in the closed area.

These two holdings remain of precedential power on their facts, but because of the confusing division of Justices and the fact that only two Justices joined these holdings in full, later courts have not given much precedential weight to any of the alternative rationales put forward in the three *Brendale* opinions. For our purposes, probably the most interesting thing to be gleaned from the case is the struggle all three groups of Justices had in attempting to make sense of *Montana*.

For the "White Four," *Montana* established a "governing principle" that a "tribe has no authority itself, by way of tribal ordinance or actions in the tribal courts, to regulate the use of fee land." Instead, tribes had "an interest under federal law, defined in terms of the impact of the challenged uses on the political integrity, economic security, or the health or welfare of the tribe." This interest, however, "does not entitle the tribe to complain or obtain relief against every use of fee land that has some adverse effect on the tribe"; rather, "[t]he impact must be demonstrably serious and must imperil the political integrity, the economic security, or the health and welfare of the tribe." White would have reformulated *Montana* as a rule about tribal property rights rather than a rule about tribal sovereignty. In this view, the second exception established that Indian property owners have a federally protected property right, akin to the law of nuisance, to obtain relief when non-Indian neighbors engage in land use damaging the interests recognized in the exception. Because the county would have the zoning authority over the non-Indian land, the practical result would be that the tribe would have to complain to the county zoning authorities about violation of these federal property rights.

The "Blackmun Three" argued that *Montana* did not establish a "general rule that tribes lacked jurisdiction" over nonmembers. To be consistent with the Court's decisions before and after *Montana*, the case "must be read to recognize the inherent authority of tribes to exercise civil jurisdiction over non-Indian activities on tribal reservations where those activities, as they do in the case of land use, implicate a significant tribal interest," arguing that "a tribe's inability to zone substantial tracts of fee land within its own reservation—tracts that are inextricably intermingled with reservation trust lands—would destroy the tribe's ability to engage in the systematic and coordinated utilization of land that is the very essence of zoning authority[.]" Thus, the Blackmun Three would have allowed the tribe to zone all land within the reservation and excluded the county from any role.

Rather than seeking much guidance from *Montana*, Justices Stevens and O'Connor would have held that so long as tribes generally retained a power to exclude nonmembers from an area (albeit not from the parcels the nonmembers owned) they retained the power to zone so as to maintain the "essential character" of an area. Stevens pinned his legal conclusion on an assumption about congressional intent concerning the allotment process: "Although it is inconceivable that Congress would have intended that the sale of a few lots would divest the Tribe of the power to determine the character of the tribal community, it is equally improbable that Congress envisioned that the Tribe would retain its interest in regulating the use of vast ranges of land sold in fee to nonmembers who lack any voice in setting tribal policy." Justice Stevens argued that the tribe should be able to zone fee land in the closed area, stressing that the tribe had largely maintained the area as a "unique tribal asset": "By maintaining the power to exclude nonmembers from entering all but a small portion of the closed area, the Tribe has preserved the power to define the essential character of that area. In fact, the Tribe has exercised this power, taking care that the closed area remains an undeveloped refuge of cultural and religious significance, a place where tribal members 'may camp, hunt, fish, and gather roots and berries in the tradition of their culture.' " *Id.* at 441. With respect to the open area, however, time had "produced an integrated community that is not economically or culturally delimited by reservation boundaries. Because the Tribe no longer has the power to exclude nonmembers from a large portion of this area, it also lacks the power to define the essential character of the territory." *Id.* at 444–445.[†]

What are the different visions of tribal sovereignty reflected in the three opinions? All the members of the Blackmun Three retired within five years after *Brendale*. We shall see that the outcome in favor of tribal authority has been denigrated in two later Supreme Court cases.

---

†. Justice Blackmun responded sharply to this analysis: "In my view, even under Justice Stevens' analysis, it must not be the case that tribes can retain the 'essential character' of their reservations (necessary to the exercise of zoning authority) only if they forgo economic development and maintain those reservations according to a single, perhaps quaint, view of what is characteristically 'Indian' today." *Id.* at 465.

C. Tribal Adjudicative Authority Over Nonmembers: 1985–1997

By the end of the 1980's, the Court had posited several conflicting ideas of tribal civil *regulatory* authority over nonmembers. What about tribal civil *adjudicative* authority over nonmembers? Recall *Williams v. Lee* and consider the following cases. The first, like *Montana*, arose on the Crow Indian Reservation.

Crow Indian Reservation, Montana, by Jimmy Emerson, Creative Commons License.

NATIONAL FARMERS UNION INSURANCE COMPANIES V. CROW TRIBE OF INDIANS

471 U.S. 845, 105 S. Ct. 2447, 85 L.Ed.2d 818 (1985)

JUSTICE STEVENS delivered the opinion of the Court.

*** On May 27, 1982, Leroy Sage, a Crow Indian minor, was struck by a motorcycle in the Lodge Grass Elementary School parking lot while returning from a school activity. The school has a student body that is 85% Crow Indian. It is located on land owned by the State within the boundaries of the Crow Indian Reservation. Through his guardian, Flora Not Afraid, Sage initiated a lawsuit in the Crow Tribal Court against the School District, a political subdivision of the State, alleging damages of $153,000, including medical expenses of $3,000 and pain and suffering of $150,000.

On September 28, 1982, process was served by Dexter Falls Down on Wesley Falls Down, the Chairman of the School Board. For reasons that have not been explained, Wesley Falls Down failed to notify anyone that a suit had been filed. On October 19, 1982, a default judgment was entered pursuant to the rules of the Tribal Court, and on October 25, 1982, Judge Roundface entered findings of fact, conclusions of law, and a judgment for $153,000 against the

School District. *Sage v. Lodge Grass School District,* 10 Indian L. Rep. 6019 (1982). A copy of that judgment was hand-delivered by Wesley Falls Down to the school Principal who, in turn, forwarded it to National on October 29, 1982.

On November 3, 1982, National and the School District (petitioners) filed a verified complaint and a motion for a temporary restraining order in the District Court for the District of Montana. ***

[T]he petitioners [invoked] 28 U.S.C. § 1331 as a basis for federal jurisdiction. *** On December 29, 1982, the District Court granted the plaintiffs a permanent injunction against any execution of the Tribal Court judgment, [holding that] "the Crow Tribal Court lacked subject-matter jurisdiction over the tort that was the basis of the default judgment." 560 F. Supp. 213, 214.

A divided panel of the Court of Appeals for the Ninth Circuit reversed. 736 F.2d 1320 (1984). Without reaching the merits of petitioners' challenge to the jurisdiction of the Tribal Court, the majority concluded that the District Court's exercise of jurisdiction could not be supported on any constitutional, statutory, or common-law ground.[4] ***

I.

Section 1331 of the Judicial Code provides that a federal district court "shall have original jurisdiction of all civil actions arising under the Constitution, laws, or treaties of the United States." 28 U.S.C. § 1331. It is well settled that this statutory grant of "jurisdiction will support claims founded upon federal common law as well as those of a statutory origin." Federal common law as articulated in rules that are fashioned by court decisions are "laws" as that term is used in § 1331.

Thus, in order to invoke a federal district court's jurisdiction under § 1331, it was not essential that the petitioners base their claim on a federal statute or a provision of the Constitution. It was, however, necessary to assert a claim "arising under" federal law. As Justice Holmes wrote for the Court, a "suit arises under the law that creates the cause of action." Petitioners contend that the right which they assert—a right to be protected against an unlawful exercise of Tribal Court judicial power—has its source in federal law because federal law defines the outer boundaries of an Indian tribe's power over non-Indians.

As we have often noted, Indian tribes occupy a unique status under our law. At one time they exercised virtually unlimited power over their own members as well as those who were permitted to join their communities. Today, however, the power of the Federal Government over the Indian tribes is plenary. Federal law, implemented by statute, by treaty, by administrative regulations, and by judicial decisions, provides significant protection for the individual, territorial, and political rights of the Indian tribes. The tribes also

4. After the District Court's injunction was vacated, tribal officials issued a writ of execution on August 1, 1984, and seized computer terminals, other computer equipment, and a truck from the School District. A sale of the property was scheduled for August 22, 1984. On that date, the School District appeared in the Tribal Court, attempting to enjoin the sale and to set aside the default judgment. App. to Brief in Opposition 1a–9a. The Tribal Court stated that it could not address the default-judgment issue "without a full hearing, research, and briefs by counsel," *id.*, at 4a; that it would consider a proper motion to set aside the default judgment; and that the sale should be postponed. *** On September 19, the Tribal Court entered an order postponing a ruling on the motion to set aside the default judgment until after final review by this Court. ***

retain some of the inherent powers of the self-governing political communities that were formed long before Europeans first settled in North America.

This Court has frequently been required to decide questions concerning the extent to which Indian tribes have retained the power to regulate the affairs of non-Indians. We have also been confronted with a series of questions concerning the extent to which a tribe's power to engage in commerce has included an immunity from state taxation. In all of these cases, the governing rule of decision has been provided by federal law. In this case the petitioners contend that the Tribal Court has no power to enter a judgment against them. Assuming that the power to resolve disputes arising within the territory governed by the Tribe was once an attribute of inherent tribal sovereignty, the petitioners, in essence, contend that the Tribe has to some extent been divested of this aspect of sovereignty. More particularly, when they invoke the jurisdiction of a federal court under § 1331, they must contend that federal law has curtailed the powers of the Tribe, and thus afforded them the basis for the relief they seek in a federal forum.

The question whether an Indian tribe retains the power to compel a non-Indian property owner to submit to the civil jurisdiction of a tribal court is one that must be answered by reference to federal law and is a "federal question" under § 1331. Because petitioners contend that federal law has divested the Tribe of this aspect of sovereignty, it is federal law on which they rely as a basis for the asserted right of freedom from Tribal Court interference. They have, therefore, filed an action "arising under" federal law within the meaning of § 1331. The District Court correctly concluded that a federal court may determine under § 1331 whether a tribal court has exceeded the lawful limits of its jurisdiction.

II.

Respondents' contend that, even though the District Court's jurisdiction was properly invoked under § 1331, the Court of Appeals was correct in ordering that the complaint be dismissed because the petitioners failed to exhaust their remedies in the tribal judicial system. They further assert that the underlying tort action "has turned into a procedural and jurisdictional nightmare" because petitioners did not pursue their readily available Tribal Court remedies. Petitioners, in response, relying in part on *Oliphant v. Suquamish Indian Tribe*, 435 U.S. 191 (1978), assert that resort to exhaustion as a matter of comity "is manifestly inappropriate."

In *Oliphant* we held that the Suquamish Indian Tribal Court did not have criminal jurisdiction to try and to punish non-Indians for offenses committed on the reservation. That holding adopted the reasoning of early opinions of two United States Attorneys General, [2 Op. Atty. Gen. 693 (1834); 7 Op. Atty. Gen. 174 (1855)] and concluded that federal legislation conferring jurisdiction on the federal courts to try non-Indians for offenses committed in Indian Country had implicitly pre-empted tribal jurisdiction. We wrote:

> "While Congress never expressly forbade Indian tribes to impose criminal penalties on non-Indians, we now make express our implicit conclusion of nearly a century ago that Congress consistently believed this to be the necessary result of its repeated legislative actions." *Id.* at 204.

If we were to apply the *Oliphant* rule here, it is plain that any exhaustion requirement would be completely foreclosed because federal courts would *always* be the only forums for civil actions against non-Indians. For several reasons, however, the reasoning of *Oliphant* does not apply to this case. First, although Congress' decision to extend the criminal jurisdiction of the federal courts to offenses committed by non-Indians against Indians within Indian Country supported the holding in *Oliphant,* there is no comparable legislation granting the federal courts jurisdiction over civil disputes between Indians and non-Indians that arise on an Indian reservation.[16] Moreover, the opinion of one Attorney General on which we relied in *Oliphant* specifically noted the difference between civil and criminal jurisdiction. Speaking of civil jurisdiction, Attorney General Cushing wrote:

> But there is no provision of treaty, and no statute, which takes away from the Choctaws jurisdiction of a case like this, a question of property strictly internal to the Choctaw nation; nor is there any written law which confers jurisdiction of such a case in any court of the United States. ***
>
> The conclusion seems to me irresistible, not that such questions are justiciable nowhere, but that they remain subject to the local jurisdiction of the Choctaws. ***
>
> Now, it is admitted on all hands *** that Congress has "paramount right" to legislate in regard to this question, in all its relations. *It has legislated, in so far as it saw fit, by taking jurisdiction in criminal matters, and omitting to take jurisdiction in civil matters. *** By all possible rules of construction the inference is clear that jurisdiction is left to the Choctaws themselves of civil controversies arising strictly within the Choctaw Nation.*

7 Op. Atty. Gen. 175, 179–181 (1855) (emphasis added).

Thus, we conclude that the answer to the question whether a tribal court has the power to exercise civil subject-matter jurisdiction over non-Indians in a case of this kind is not automatically foreclosed, as an extension of *Oliphant* would require. Rather, the existence and extent of a tribal court's jurisdiction will require a careful examination of tribal sovereignty, the extent to which that sovereignty has been altered, divested, or diminished, as well as a detailed study of relevant statutes, Executive Branch policy as embodied in treaties and elsewhere, and administrative or judicial decisions.

We believe that examination should be conducted in the first instance in the Tribal Court itself. Our cases have often recognized that Congress is committed to a policy of supporting tribal self-government and self-determination. That policy favors a rule that will provide the forum whose jurisdiction is being challenged the first opportunity to evaluate the factual and legal bases for the challenge.[21] Moreover the orderly administration of justice in the federal court will be served by allowing a full record to be developed in the Tribal Court before either the merits or any question concerning appropriate relief is

---

16. F. Cohen, Handbook of Federal Indian Law 253 (1982) ("The development of principles governing civil jurisdiction in Indian Country has been markedly different from the development of rules dealing with criminal jurisdiction").

21. We do not suggest that exhaustion would be required where an assertion of tribal jurisdiction "is motivated by a desire to harass or is conducted in bad faith," *cf. Judice v. Vail,* 430 U.S. 327, 338 (1977), or where the action is patently violative of express jurisdictional prohibitions, or where exhaustion would be futile because of the lack of an adequate opportunity to challenge the court's jurisdiction.

addressed.[22] The risks of the kind of "procedural nightmare" that has allegedly developed in this case will be minimized if the federal court stays its hand until after the Tribal Court has had a full opportunity to determine its own jurisdiction and to rectify any errors it may have made. Exhaustion of tribal court remedies, moreover, will encourage tribal courts to explain to the parties the precise basis for accepting jurisdiction, and will also provide other courts with the benefit of their expertise in such matters in the event of further judicial review.[25]

III.

Our conclusions that § 1331 encompasses the federal question whether a tribal court has exceeded the lawful limits of its jurisdiction, and that exhaustion is required before such a claim may be entertained by a federal court, require that we reverse the judgment of the Court of Appeals. Until petitioners have exhausted the remedies available to them in the Tribal Court system, n. 4, *supra*, it would be premature for a federal court to consider any relief. ***

NOTES AND QUESTIONS

1. *Federal question jurisdiction.* The first question addressed in *National Farmers* was whether the federal courts even had jurisdiction to hear the case. Federal courts are courts of limited jurisdiction; they may hear cases only when Congress has authorized jurisdiction. One of the main authorizations is 28 U.S.C. § 1331, which provides jurisdiction over cases arising from a federal question. Section 1331 has been interpreted to authorize jurisdiction only when federal law creates the cause of action, not when it simply forms a defense to the action. The Court of Appeals correctly held that neither the Indian Civil Rights Act nor the Fourteenth Amendment provided a cause of action to the petitioners (do you remember why?). It also held that ICRA claims were the exclusive way to challenge violations of tribal adjudicatory authority. The Supreme Court reversed on this last point, holding that any limitations on tribal jurisdiction over nonmembers (other than those created by the tribe itself) must come from federal law; therefore any claim that a tribe did not have jurisdiction over a nonmember must be based on an assertion that federal law had removed that jurisdiction. In so holding, the Court also explained that *Oliphant* and *Montana* were based on federal common law, or the law that courts create to resolve matters within federal authority "when the substance of that rule is not clearly suggested by federal enactments." Martha A. Field, *Sources of Law: The Scope of Federal Common Law*, 99 Harv. L. Rev. 883, 890 (1986). Because any claim that a tribe did not have jurisdiction over a nonmember must be founded in an argument that federal law, whether statute, treaty, or federal common law, removed such jurisdiction, there was federal question jurisdiction over such a claim.

---

22. Four days after receiving notice of the default judgment, petitioners requested that the District Court enter an injunction. Crow Tribal Court Rule of Civil Procedure 17(d) provides that a party in a default may move to set aside the default judgment at any time within 30 days. App. 17. Petitioners did not utilize this legal remedy. It is a fundamental principle of long standing that a request for an injunction will not be granted as long as an adequate remedy at law is available.

25. *Ibid.; see, e.g., North Dakota ex rel. Wefald v. Kelly,* 10 Indian L.Rep. 6059 (1983); *Crow Creek Sioux Tribe v. Buum,* 10 Indian L.Rep. 6031 (1983).

2. *Tribal exhaustion.* Although the Court held that the federal courts had jurisdiction over a claim that a tribe lacked jurisdiction, it held that any such claims must first be exhausted in tribal court. There are three bases for this holding: first, the federal policy of encouraging tribal self-government and self-determination; second, the desire to achieve orderly administration of justice and avoid the "procedural nightmare" that had occurred; and third, to allow the federal courts to benefit from tribal expertise regarding their own jurisdiction. How does the exhaustion requirement further each of these goals? The Court outlines some exceptions to the exhaustion requirement in note 21. These exceptions roughly track those available in other exhaustion contexts, such as administrative and federal employment law. Do these strike a fair balance between the doctrine's goals and fairness to litigants?

3. *Tribal adjudicatory jurisdiction.* Because the Court held that tribal exhaustion was required, it did not decide whether the tribe had jurisdiction over the case, which involved a nonmember defendant. But the decision has important implications for the scope of tribal civil adjudicatory jurisdiction: if tribes as a general matter lacked such jurisdiction over nonmembers, the exhaustion requirement would be a waste of time. What does the Court suggest about such jurisdiction? Why is this jurisdiction different from the criminal jurisdiction in *Oliphant*? Note also that the accident occurred on non-Indian (state) owned fee land. What does this suggest about the impact of *Montana* on adjudicatory jurisdiction?

4. *What happened next?* The school and its insurance company began the federal court action to prevent the tribe from seizing school equipment to execute the default judgment entered because the school board chairman failed to notify them of the complaint. The Supreme Court decided that the tribal courts had jurisdiction in the first instance over the challenge to jurisdiction. Rule 17(d) of the Crow Rules of Civil Procedure provides that parties have 30 days to challenge a default judgment. After the first Ninth Circuit decision, the defendants filed a motion to set aside the default judgment, but then failed to file any briefs or attend the hearing on the motion, and the motion was denied. Thirty-five days after the Supreme Court issued its decision, the defendants had taken no further action in the tribal court, and the court issued an order refusing to set aside the default judgment. On July 15, the defendants appealed the order to the Crow Court of Appeals. The Crow Court of Appeals first held that the tribal court had jurisdiction over the suit under either of the *Montana* tests, but also held that the original default judgment should be set aside:

> Tribal Courts, in both their present form and their "traditional" predecessors, *** have been centrally concerned with the overall concept of justice and have often times managed to be free of the obsession with technicalities that has so often plagued non-tribal court systems. In light of this, this Appeals Court must consider alternative reasonable readings of Rule 17(d) and correspondingly reasonable methods for counting the days elapsed so as to serve the interests of "justice". It appears from the documents which have been filed with this Court that Defendant School District counted the elapsed time from the entry of the Default Judgment differently than that counted by the Trial Judge. *** Defendants could reasonably have interpreted the Crow Rules of Civil Procedure to have found that only 29 days elapsed before the filing of their Motion to Set Aside the Default Judgment. This Court must scrutinize the issue presented here in keeping with its traditional concern for justice and fairness,

> and in the interest, when appropriate, of deciding important cases on their merits rather than o[n] mere technicalities. We conclude, therefore, that the Default Judgment should have been set aside by the Tribal Judge in the interest of justice and in accordance with Rule 17(d) of the Crow Rules of Civil Procedure.
>
> *** This ruling should not be interpreted to abolish or denigrate the time periods established in the Crow Rules of Civil Procedure, but rather should be found to support the interests of justice when a reasonable reading of the rules allows more than one interpretation. ***

Sage v. Lodge Grass School Dist. No. 27, (Crow Ct. App. 1986). *National Farmers* was written by Justice Stevens, who in the opinions we have read elsewhere expressed significant concern about nonmembers being subject to tribal court jurisdiction. Might the availability of opinions like these reduce those kinds of fairness concerns? Footnote 25 of the opinion cites to the Indian Law Reporter, the first general printed source of tribal court opinions; it is the only reference to tribal court opinions (other than for procedural history) that we have seen in a Supreme Court opinion.

5. *National Farmers* concerned a case in which the federal courts had very limited jurisdiction—solely to determine the jurisdiction of the tribal court. Would the exhaustion rule apply when another court had jurisdiction over not simply the procedural questions, but the entire subject matter of the dispute, as federal courts do in diversity cases? The Court answered this question two years later in *Iowa Mutual Insurance Co. v. LaPlante.*

IOWA MUTUAL INSURANCE CO. V. LAPLANTE

480 U.S. 9, 107 S. Ct. 971, 94 L.Ed.2d 10 (1987)

JUSTICE MARSHALL delivered the opinion of the Court.

[Edward LaPlante, a member of the Blackfeet Tribe, filed suit in Blackfeet Tribal Court against his employer, the non-Indian Wellman Ranch, for injuries suffered when his truck jackknifed when he was driving it on land owned by the Wellmans within the Blackfeet Reservation, and against their insurance company, Iowa Mutual, for bad faith in their resolution of the claim. While the lawsuit was pending, Iowa Mutual brought an action in federal court seeking a declaration that the injury was not covered by its insurance policy with the Wellman Ranch, and that the tribal court lacked jurisdiction over the claim. It asserted diversity jurisdiction under 28 U.S.C. § 1332, on the grounds that Wellman and LaPlante were citizens of Montana, and it was not. The district court, Ninth Circuit, and Supreme Court rejected a claim that the exhaustion requirement did not apply in diversity cases.]

Tribal courts play a vital role in tribal self-government, cf. *United States v. Wheeler*, and the Federal Government has consistently encouraged their development. Although the criminal jurisdiction of the tribal courts is subject to substantial federal limitation, *see Oliphant v. Suquamish Indian Tribe*, their civil jurisdiction is not similarly restricted. *See National Farmers Union*, nn.

16 and 17. If state-court jurisdiction over Indians or activities on Indian lands would interfere with tribal sovereignty and self-government, the state courts are generally divested of jurisdiction as a matter of federal law. *Fisher v. District Court*; *Williams v. Lee, supra.*

A federal court's exercise of jurisdiction over matters relating to reservation affairs can also impair the authority of tribal courts, as we recognized in *National Farmers Union.* ***

Although petitioner alleges that federal jurisdiction in this case is based on diversity of citizenship, rather than the existence of a federal question, the exhaustion rule announced in *National Farmers Union* applies here as well. Regardless of the basis for jurisdiction, the federal policy supporting tribal self-government directs a federal court to stay its hand in order to give the tribal court a "full opportunity to determine its own jurisdiction." *Ibid.* In diversity cases, as well as federal-question cases, unconditional access to the federal forum would place it in direct competition with the tribal courts, thereby impairing the latter's authority over reservation affairs. *** Adjudication of such matters by any nontribal court also infringes upon tribal law-making authority, because tribal courts are best qualified to interpret and apply tribal law.

As *National Farmers Union* indicates, proper respect for tribal legal institutions requires that they be given a "full opportunity" to consider the issues before them and "to rectify any errors." 471 U.S. at 857. The federal policy of promoting tribal self-government encompasses the development of the entire tribal court system, including appellate courts. At a minimum, exhaustion of tribal remedies means that tribal appellate courts must have the opportunity to review the determinations of the lower tribal courts. In this case, the Tribal Court has made an initial determination that it has jurisdiction over the insurance dispute, but Iowa Mutual has not yet obtained appellate review, as provided by the Tribal Code, ch. 1, § 5. Until appellate review is complete, the Blackfeet Tribal Courts have not had a full opportunity to evaluate the claim and federal courts should not intervene.

Petitioner argues that the statutory grant of diversity jurisdiction overrides the federal policy of deference to tribal courts. We do not agree. Although Congress undoubtedly has the power to limit tribal court jurisdiction, we do not read the general grant of diversity jurisdiction to have implemented such a significant intrusion on tribal sovereignty. ***

Tribal authority over the activities of non-Indians on reservation lands is an important part of tribal sovereignty. *See Montana v. United States*; *Washington v. Confederated Tribes of the Colville Reservation*; *Fisher v. District Court.* Civil jurisdiction over such activities presumptively lies in the tribal courts unless affirmatively limited by a specific treaty provision or federal statute. "Because the Tribe retains all inherent attributes of sovereignty that have not been divested by the Federal Government, the proper inference from silence *** is that the sovereign power *** remains intact." *Merrion v. Jicarilla Apache Tribe*; *see also Santa Clara Pueblo v. Martinez.*

Petitioner also contends that the policies underlying the grant of diversity jurisdiction—protection against local bias and incompetence—justify the exercise of federal jurisdiction in this case. We have rejected similar attacks on tribal court jurisdiction in the past. *See, e.g., Santa Clara Pueblo v. Martinez,* n.21. The alleged incompetence of tribal courts is not among the exceptions to the exhaustion requirement established in *National Farmers Union*, 471 U.S. at 856 n.21, and would be contrary to the congressional policy promoting the development of tribal courts. ***

Although petitioner must exhaust available tribal remedies before instituting suit in federal court, the Blackfeet Tribal Courts' determination of tribal jurisdiction is ultimately subject to review. If the Tribal Appeals Court upholds the lower court's determination that the tribal courts have jurisdiction, petitioner may challenge that ruling in the District Court. *National Farmers Union*. Unless a federal court determines that the Tribal Court lacked jurisdiction, however, proper deference to the tribal court system precludes relitigation of issues raised by the LaPlantes' bad-faith claim and resolved in the Tribal Courts. ***

[JUSTICE STEVENS dissented, arguing that the reasons for staying consideration of tribal determinations of jurisdiction did not justify staying and deferring to tribal determinations of substantive questions.]

NOTES AND QUESTIONS

1. *Extension of exhaustion requirement.* Following the reasoning of *Iowa Mutual*, a number of courts have held that exhaustion is required whatever the source of jurisdiction. *See Stock West Corp. v. Taylor*, 964 F.2d 912, 919–920 (9th Cir. 1992). Some state courts have thus applied the exhaustion requirement to cases involving general grants of state jurisdiction like Public Law 280. *See, e.g., Cohen v. Little Six, Inc.*, 543 N.W.2d 376, 381 n.3 (Minn. Ct. App. 1996), *aff'd*, 561 N.W.2d 889 (Minn. 1997); *Drumm v. Brown*, 716 A.2d 50 (Conn. 1998). The state decisions have generally been issued in contexts where tribes were involved in the claims. One state court, however, rejected an argument that exhaustion should apply in a personal injury action between a tribal member and a "descendant" of the tribe that arose from a traffic accident on a state highway within the reservation. *McCrea v. Denison*, 885 P.2d 856 (Wash. Ct. App. 1994).

2. *Procedure for exhaustion. Iowa Mutual* helps to clarify the procedures after exhaustion. All tribal court remedies, including appeals, must be exhausted. After exhaustion, the reviewing court initially reviews only the tribe's jurisdictional determination. In this review, the court must defer to tribal determinations of tribal law, as well as tribal determinations of fact unless clearly erroneous. *See Duncan Energy Co. v. Three Affiliated Tribes of the Fort Berthold Reservation*, 27 F.3d 1294, 1300 (8th Cir. 1994). If the court determines that the tribe had jurisdiction, it must dismiss the action; the tribal judgment is conclusive. Only if the court holds that the tribe lacked jurisdiction may it review the substantive dispute, if it otherwise has jurisdiction.

3. *Exceptions to exhaustion.* As noted above, the Court in *National Farmers* listed three exceptions to the exhaustion requirement: first, where the assertion of jurisdiction " 'is motivated by a desire to harass or is conducted in bad faith,' " second, "where the action is patently violative of express jurisdictional prohibitions," and third, "where exhaustion would be futile because of the lack of an adequate opportunity to challenge the court's jurisdiction." What would satisfy these exceptions?

Iowa Mutual states that an accusation of tribal court bias does not excuse exhaustion. *See also Burrell v. Armijo*, 456 F.3d 1159, 1168 (10th Cir. 2006) ("Allegations of local bias and tribal court incompetence *** are not exceptions to the exhaustion requirement."). Do you see why this makes sense given the reasons for the exhaustion requirement? Courts have, however, held that exhaustion is excused if the tribe lacks a functioning tribal court. *See Comstock Oil & Gas, Inc. v. Ala. & Coushatta Indian Tribes*, 261 F.3d 567, 572–73 (5th Cir. 2001). An excessive delay in ruling on a matter may also excuse exhaustion. *See Astorga v. Wing*, 118 P.3d 1103, 1109 (Ariz. Ct. App. 2005) (holding that exhaustion was not required in part because the Navajo court had not yet ruled on its jurisdiction after a two-year delay).

Exhaustion may not be required if federal law provides for exclusive jurisdiction in non-tribal courts, and tribal claims are not otherwise distinguishable from those preempted by the federal scheme. *See El Paso Natural Gas Co. v. Neztsosie*, 526 U.S. 473 (1999) (Price–Anderson Act made federal court exclusive forum to decide claims from injury due to incidents from nuclear power). Some courts have extended this exception to situations where a contract includes a choice of forum clause providing for jurisdiction in non-tribal courts, *see Altheimer & Gray v. Sioux Mfg. Corp.*, 983 F.2d 803, 812–815 (7th Cir. 1993)(choice of forum clause in contract specifying exclusive jurisdiction in state court abrogated exhaustion requirement); *FGS Constructors, Inc. v. Carlow*, 64 F.3d 1230, 1233 (8th Cir. 1995) (clause providing disputes would be litigated in tribal court or any other court of competent jurisdiction avoided need to exhaust), whereas others have held that tribal courts should be given the first opportunity to construe contractual provisions to determine whether tribal jurisdiction was unambiguously excluded. *See Ninigret Dev. Corp. v. Narragansett Indian Wetuomuck Housing Authority*, 207 F.3d 21, 33 (1st Cir. 2000) (exhaustion required for tribal court to review forum selection clause); *Basil Cook Enterprises, Inc. v. St. Regis Mohawk Tribe*, 117 F.3d 61, 69 (2d Cir. 1997) (exhaustion required to interpret arbitration clause).

What if there is no pending tribal court proceeding? How do the policies underlying the exhaustion requirement apply in a situation where no tribal action was filed before the suit in state or federal court? Some courts have held that exhaustion is not required in this situation. *See, e.g., Garcia v. Akwesasne Hous. Auth.*, 268 F.3d 76, 80 (2d Cir. 2001) ("[C]omity and deference owed to a tribal court that is adjudicating an intra-tribal dispute under tribal law does not compel abstention by a federal court where a non-member asserts state and federal claims and nothing is pending in tribal court."). Most courts, however, have found that tribal sovereignty requires that tribal courts be given a chance to hear cases over which they have jurisdiction. *See_Duncan Energy v. Three Affiliated Tribes*, 27 F.3d 1294 (8th Cir. 1994); *Marceau v. Blackfeet Hous. Auth.*, 540 F.3d 916 (9th Cir. 2008); *United States v. Tsosie*, 92 F.3d 1037 (10th Cir. 1996).

The Supreme Court next considered the question of tribal court civil jurisdiction ten years later in *Strate v. A–1 Contractors*.

STRATE V. A–1 CONTRACTORS

520 U.S. 438, 117 S. Ct. 1404, 137 L. Ed. 2d 661 (1997)

JUSTICE GINSBURG delivered the opinion of the Court.

This case concerns the adjudicatory authority of tribal courts over personal injury actions against defendants who are not tribal members. Specifically, we confront this question: When an accident occurs on a portion of a public highway maintained by the State under a federally granted right-of-way over Indian reservation land, may tribal courts entertain a civil action against an allegedly negligent driver and the driver's employer, neither of whom is a member of the tribe?

Such cases, we hold, fall within state or federal regulatory and adjudicatory governance; tribal courts may not entertain claims against nonmembers arising out of accidents on state highways, absent a statute or treaty authorizing the tribe to govern the conduct of nonmembers on the highway in question. We express no view on the governing law or proper forum when an accident occurs on a tribal road within a reservation.

I.

In November 1990, petitioner Gisela Fredericks and respondent Lyle Stockert were involved in a traffic accident on a portion of a North Dakota state highway running through the Fort Berthold Indian Reservation. The highway strip crossing the reservation is a 6.59–mile stretch of road, open to the public, affording access to a federal water resource project. North Dakota maintains the road under a right-of-way granted by the United States to the State's Highway Department; the right-of-way lies on land held by the United States in trust for the Three Affiliated Tribes (Mandan, Hidatsa, and Arikara) and their members.

The accident occurred when Fredericks' automobile collided with a gravel truck driven by Stockert and owned by respondent A–1 Contractors, Stockert's employer. A–1 Contractors, a non-Indian-owned enterprise with its principal place of business outside the reservation, was at the time under a subcontract with LCM Corporation, a corporation wholly owned by the Tribes, to do landscaping work related to the construction of a tribal community building. *** The record does not show whether Stockert was engaged in subcontract work at the time of the accident. Neither Stockert nor Fredericks is a member of the Three Affiliated Tribes or an Indian. Fredericks, however, is the widow of a deceased member of the Tribes and has five adult children who are tribal members.

Fredericks sustained serious injuries in the accident and was hospitalized for 24 days. In May 1991, she sued respondents A–1 Contractors and Stockert, as well as A–1 Contractors' insurer, in the Tribal Court ***. In the same lawsuit, Fredericks' five adult children filed a loss-of-consortium claim. ***

Respondents and the insurer made a special appearance in the Tribal Court to contest that court's personal and subject-matter jurisdiction. The Tribal Court ruled that it had authority to adjudicate Gisela Fredericks' case, and therefore denied respondents' motion to dismiss the action.[3] Respondents appealed the Tribal Court's jurisdictional ruling to the Northern Plains Intertribal Court of Appeals, which affirmed. ***

Before Tribal Court proceedings resumed, respondents commenced this action in the United States District Court for the District of North Dakota [seeking] a declaratory judgment that, as a matter of federal law, the Tribal Court lacked jurisdiction to adjudicate Fredericks' claims. The respondents also sought an injunction against further proceedings in the Tribal Court. [Relying on *National Farmers* and *Iowa Mutual*, the federal district court held that the tribal court had jurisdiction. The Eighth Circuit, *en banc*, in an 8–4 decision, reversed, concluding that *Montana* was the controlling precedent and under it, the tribal court lacked subject-matter jurisdiction.][4]

II.

Our case law establishes that, absent express authorization by federal statute or treaty, tribal jurisdiction over the conduct of nonmembers exists only in limited circumstances. In *Oliphant*, the Court held that Indian tribes lack criminal jurisdiction over non-Indians. *Montana*, decided three years later, is the pathmarking case concerning tribal civil authority over nonmembers. *** The Court said in *Montana* that the restriction on tribal criminal jurisdiction recognized in *Oliphant* rested on principles that support a more "general proposition." In the main, the Court explained, "the inherent sovereign powers of an Indian tribe"—those powers a tribe enjoys apart from express provision by treaty or statute—"do not extend to the activities of nonmembers of the tribe." The *Montana* opinion added, however, that in certain circumstances, even where Congress has not expressly authorized it, tribal civil jurisdiction may encompass nonmembers:

> To be sure, Indian tribes retain inherent sovereign power to exercise some forms of civil jurisdiction over non-Indians on their reservations, even on non-Indian fee lands. A tribe may regulate, through taxation, licensing, or other means, the activities of nonmembers who enter consensual relationships with the tribe or its members, through commercial dealing, contracts, leases, or other arrangements. A tribe may also retain inherent power to exercise civil authority over the conduct of non-Indians on fee lands within its reservation when that conduct threatens or has some direct effect on the political integrity, the economic security, or the health or welfare of the tribe

Petitioners and the United States as *amicus curiae* urge that *Montana* does not control this case. They maintain that the guiding precedents are *National Farmers* and *Iowa Mutual*, and that those decisions establish a rule converse to *Montana*'s. Whatever *Montana* may instruct regarding *regulatory* authority, they insist, tribal courts retain *adjudicatory* authority in disputes over

---

3. Satisfied that it could adjudicate Gisela Fredericks' claims, the Tribal Court declined to address her adult children's consortium claim, App. 25; thus, no ruling on that claim is here at issue.

4. Petitioner Fredericks has commenced a similar lawsuit in a North Dakota state court "to protect her rights against the running of the State's six-year statute of limitations." Reply Brief 6, n. 2. Respondents assert that they have answered the complaint and "are prepared to proceed in that forum." Brief for Respondents 8, n. 6. Respondents also note, without contradiction, that the state forum "is physically much closer by road to the accident scene *** than [is] the tribal courthouse." *Ibid.*

occurrences inside a reservation, even when the episode-in-suit involves nonmembers, unless a treaty or federal statute directs otherwise. Petitioners, further supported by the United States, argue, alternately, that *Montana* does not cover lands owned by, or held in trust for, a tribe or its members. *Montana* holds sway, petitioners say, only with respect to alienated reservation land owned in fee simple by non-Indians. We address these arguments in turn.

A.

We begin with petitioners' contention that *National Farmers* and *Iowa Mutual* broadly confirm tribal-court civil jurisdiction over claims against nonmembers arising from occurrences on any land within a reservation. We read our precedent differently. *National Farmers* and *Iowa Mutual,* we conclude, are not at odds with, and do not displace, *Montana.* Both decisions describe an exhaustion rule allowing tribal courts initially to respond to an invocation of their jurisdiction; neither establishes tribal-court adjudicatory authority, even over the lawsuits involved in those cases. ***

Petitioners underscore the principal reason we gave in *National Farmers* for the exhaustion requirement there stated. Tribal-court jurisdiction over non-Indians in criminal cases is categorically restricted under *Oliphant,* we observed, while in civil matters "the existence and extent of a tribal court's jurisdiction will require a careful examination of tribal sovereignty, the extent to which that sovereignty has been altered, divested, or diminished, as well as a detailed study of relevant statutes, Executive Branch policy as embodied in treaties and elsewhere, and administrative or judicial decisions."

The Court's recognition in *National Farmers* that tribal courts have more extensive jurisdiction in civil cases than in criminal proceedings, and of the need to inspect relevant statutes, treaties, and other materials, does not limit *Montana*'s instruction. As the Court made plain in *Montana,* the general rule and exceptions there announced govern only in the absence of a delegation of tribal authority by treaty or statute. *** [W]e do not extract from *National Farmers* anything more than a prudential exhaustion rule, in deference to the capacity of tribal courts "to explain to the parties the precise basis for accepting [or rejecting] jurisdiction."

*** The Court recognized in *Iowa Mutual* that the exhaustion rule *** was "prudential," not jurisdictional. *** Respect for tribal self-government made it appropriate "to give the tribal court a 'full opportunity to determine its own jurisdiction.' " *** Elaborating on the point, the Court stated:

> Tribal authority over the activities of non-Indians on reservation lands is an important part of tribal sovereignty. *See Montana* ***. Civil jurisdiction over such activities presumptively lies in the tribal courts unless affirmatively limited by a specific treaty provision or federal statute. *** In the absence of any indication that Congress intended the diversity statute to limit the jurisdiction of the tribal courts, we decline petitioner's invitation to hold that tribal sovereignty can be impaired in this fashion.

Petitioners and the United States fasten upon the Court's statement that "[c]ivil jurisdiction over such activities presumptively lies in the tribal courts." Read in context, however, this language scarcely supports the view that the *Montana* rule does not bear on tribal-court adjudicatory authority in cases involving nonmember defendants.

The statement stressed by petitioners and the United States was made in refutation of the argument that "Congress intended the diversity statute to limit the jurisdiction of the tribal courts." The statement is preceded by [the] informative citation *** to the passage in *Montana* in which the Court advanced "the general proposition that the inherent sovereign powers of an Indian tribe do not extend to the activities of nonmembers of the tribe," with two prime exceptions[.] In light of the citation of *Montana,* the *Iowa Mutual* statement emphasized by petitioners does not limit the *Montana* rule. In keeping with the precedent to which *Iowa Mutual* refers, the statement stands for nothing more than the unremarkable proposition that, where tribes possess authority to regulate the activities of nonmembers, "[c]ivil jurisdiction over [disputes arising out of] such activities presumptively lies in the tribal courts."

Recognizing that our precedent has been variously interpreted, we reiterate that *National Farmers* and *Iowa Mutual* enunciate only an exhaustion requirement, a "prudential rule," based on comity. These decisions do not expand or stand apart from *Montana*'s instruction on "the inherent sovereign powers of an Indian tribe." While *Montana* immediately involved regulatory authority, the Court broadly addressed the concept of "inherent sovereignty." Regarding activity on non-Indian fee land within a reservation, *Montana* delineated—in a main rule and exceptions—the bounds of the power tribes retain to exercise "forms of civil jurisdiction over non-Indians." As to nonmembers, we hold, a tribe's adjudicative jurisdiction does not exceed its legislative jurisdiction. Absent congressional direction enlarging tribal-court jurisdiction, we adhere to that understanding. Subject to controlling provisions in treaties and statutes, and the two exceptions identified in *Montana,* the civil authority of Indian tribes and their courts with respect to non-Indian fee lands generally "do[es] not extend to the activities of nonmembers of the tribe."

B.

We consider next the argument that *Montana* does not govern this case because the land underlying the scene of the accident is held in trust for the Three Affiliated Tribes and their members. Petitioners and the United States point out that in *Montana* *** the challenged tribal authority related to nonmember activity on alienated, non-Indian reservation land. We "can readily agree," in accord with *Montana,* that tribes retain considerable control over nonmember conduct on tribal land. On the particular matter before us, however, we agree with respondents: The right-of-way North Dakota acquired for the State's highway renders the 6.59–mile stretch equivalent, for nonmember governance purposes, to alienated, non-Indian land. ***

Congress authorized grants of rights-of-way over Indian lands in 1948 legislation. Act of Feb. 5, 1948, ch. 45, 62 Stat. 17, 25 U.S.C. §§ 323–328. A grant over land belonging to a tribe requires "consent of the proper tribal officials," § 324, and the payment of just compensation, § 325. The grant involved in this case was made, pursuant to the federal statute, in 1970. ***

In the granting instrument, the United States conveyed to North Dakota "an easement for a right-of-way for the realignment and improvement of North Dakota State Highway No. 8 over, across and upon [specified] lands." App. to Brief for Respondents 1. The grant provides that the State's "easement is subject to any valid existing right or adverse claim and is without limitation as to tenure, so long as said easement shall be actually used for the purpose *** specified." *Id.* at 3. *** [T]he Three Affiliated Tribes expressly reserved no right to exercise dominion or control over the right-of-way.

Forming part of the State's highway, the right-of-way is open to the public, and traffic on it is subject to the State's control.[11] The Tribes have consented to, and received payment for, the State's use of the 6.59–mile stretch for a public highway. They have retained no gatekeeping right. So long as the stretch is maintained as part of the State's highway, the Tribes cannot assert a landowner's right to occupy and exclude. We therefore align the right-of-way, for the purpose at hand, with land alienated to non-Indians. Our decision in *Montana,* accordingly, governs this case.

III.

Petitioners and the United States refer to no treaty or statute authorizing the Three Affiliated Tribes to entertain highway-accident tort suits of the kind Fredericks commenced against A–1 Contractors and Stockert. Rather, petitioners and the United States ground their defense of tribal-court jurisdiction exclusively on the concept of retained or inherent sovereignty. *** To prevail here, petitioners must show that Fredericks' tribal-court action against nonmembers qualifies under one of *Montana's* two exceptions.

The first exception to the *Montana* rule covers "activities of nonmembers who enter consensual relationships with the tribe or its members, through commercial dealing, contracts, leases, or other arrangements." The tortious conduct alleged in Fredericks' complaint does not fit that description. The dispute, as the Court of Appeals said, is "distinctly non-tribal in nature." It "arose between two non-Indians involved in [a] run-of-the-mill [highway] accident." Although A–1 was engaged in subcontract work on the Fort Berthold Reservation, and therefore had a "consensual relationship" with the Tribes, "Gisela Fredericks was not a party to the subcontract, and the [T]ribes were strangers to the accident." 76 F.3d at 940.

Montana's list of cases fitting within the first exception indicates the type of activities the Court had in mind: *Williams v. Lee* (declaring tribal jurisdiction exclusive over lawsuit arising out of on-reservation sales transaction between nonmember plaintiff and member defendants); *Morris v. Hitchcock,* 194 U.S. 384 (1904) (upholding tribal permit tax on nonmember-owned livestock within boundaries of the Chickasaw Nation); *Buster v. Wright,* 135 F. 947 (CA8 1905) (upholding Tribe's permit tax on nonmembers for the privilege of conducting business within Tribe's borders; court characterized as "inherent" the Tribe's "authority *** to prescribe the terms upon which noncitizens may transact business within its borders"); *Colville* (tribal authority to tax on-reservation cigarette sales to nonmembers "is a fundamental attribute of sovereignty which the tribes retain unless divested of it by federal law or necessary implication of their dependent status"). Measured against these cases, the Fredericks–Stockert highway accident presents no "consensual relationship" of the qualifying kind.

The second exception to *Montana's* general rule concerns conduct that "threatens or has some direct effect on the political integrity, the economic security, or the health or welfare of the tribe." Undoubtedly, those who drive

11. We do not here question the authority of tribal police to patrol roads within a reservation, including rights-of-way made part of a state highway, and to detain and turn over to state officers nonmembers stopped on the highway for conduct violating state law. ***

carelessly on a public highway running through a reservation endanger all in the vicinity, and surely jeopardize the safety of tribal members. But if *Montana*'s second exception requires no more, the exception would severely shrink the rule. Again, cases cited in *Montana* indicate the character of the tribal interest the Court envisioned.

***

Read in isolation, the *Montana* rule's second exception can be misperceived. Key to its proper application, however, is the Court's preface: "Indian tribes retain their inherent power [to punish tribal offenders,] to determine tribal membership, to regulate domestic relations among members, and to prescribe rules of inheritance for members. *** But [a tribe's inherent power does not reach] beyond what is necessary to protect tribal self-government or to control internal relations." Neither regulatory nor adjudicatory authority over the state highway accident at issue is needed to preserve "the right of reservation Indians to make their own laws and be ruled by them." [*Williams v. Lee*.] The *Montana* rule, therefore, and not its exceptions, applies to this case.

Gisela Fredericks may pursue her case against A–1 Contractors and Stockert in the state forum open to all who sustain injuries on North Dakota's highway. Opening the Tribal Court for her optional use is not necessary to protect tribal self-government; and requiring A–1 and Stockert to defend against this commonplace state highway accident claim in an unfamiliar court[13] is not crucial to "the political integrity, the economic security, or the health or welfare of the [Three Affiliated Tribes]."[14]

[*Affirmed.*]

NOTES AND QUESTIONS

1. *Adjudicatory versus regulatory jurisdiction. National Farmers* and *Iowa Mutual* seemed to reconcile *Williams v. Lee* with *Montana* by stating that even on fee land tribal adjudicatory jurisdiction over nonmembers in civil causes of action was so important to tribal sovereignty that it existed unless it was "affirmatively limited by a specific treaty provision or federal statute." Was this language a reasonable interpretation of *Montana*? *Strate* interpreted this language to mean that tribal courts only presumptively had adjudicatory jurisdiction if they also had regulatory jurisdiction, and they presumptively did not have regulatory jurisdiction on fee land. Was this a reasonable interpretation of *National Farmers* and *Iowa Mutual*? What about *Williams v. Lee*?

Whatever its consistency with past precedent, *Strate* is now the law: "As to nonmembers *** a tribe's adjudicative jurisdiction does not exceed its legislative jurisdiction." Note that this is not the case in other contexts: a state

---

13. Within the federal system, when nonresidents are the sole defendants in a suit filed in state court, the defendants ordinarily may remove the case to federal court. *See* 28 U.S.C. § 1441.

14. When, as in this case, it is plain that no federal grant provides for tribal governance of nonmembers' conduct on land covered by *Montana*'s main rule, it will be equally evident that tribal courts lack adjudicatory authority over disputes arising from such conduct. As in criminal proceedings, state or federal courts will be the only forums competent to adjudicate those disputes. *See National Farmers*. Therefore, when tribal-court jurisdiction over an action such as this one is challenged in federal court, the otherwise applicable exhaustion requirement must give way, for it would serve no purpose other than delay.

typically may not regulate the actions of persons residing and acting out of state, but it may adjudicate actions against them if it gains personal jurisdiction over them, either by serving them in the state, *see Burnham v. Superior Court*, 495 U.S. 604 (1990), or because they otherwise have sufficient "minimum" contacts with the state, *see International Shoe Co. v. Washington*, 326 U.S. 310 (1945). The standards governing whether states may subject non-resident defendants to jurisdiction in their courts are grounded in the Due Process Clause, which does not apply to tribes directly. The ICRA, however, imposes due process requirements on tribal governments. The *Strate* Court chose to adopt the categorical, status-based rules from *Montana*, but could it instead have adopted a flexible due-process like standard to determine whether it would be fair, in the context of the particular case, to subject the nonmember defendant to suit there? If the Court had done so, would A–1 Contractors be subject to suit in the Fort Berthold tribal court? When answering this, consider that A–1 was on the reservation to do work for the tribe, and would not have been driving on the highway but for its contract with the tribe. Further, note that the highway is a road that dead-ends at a reservoir, which is a park used largely by tribal members. *See* Sarah Krakoff, *Undoing Indian Law One Case at a Time: Judicial Minimalism and Tribal Sovereignty*, 50 Am. U. L. Rev. 1177, 1257–60 (2001).

2. *Land covered by* Montana's *"main rule."* The Court held that by granting the state an easement over trust land without reserving a "gatekeeping" right, the land had become the legal equivalent of the allotted land in *Montana*. Because the tribe had lost the right to exclude, it could not exercise the general powers of a sovereign on this land. Was this consistent with *Merrion*? Was it consistent with *Montana*'s concern about congressional intent in allotment and the expectations of non-Indians purchasing tribal land?

3. *Preserving the gatekeeping right.* In reaction to *Strate*, tribes have sought to preserve their gatekeeping right by including consent to jurisdiction in leases and rights of way regarding tribal land. Interviews with Navajo Nation officials reveal the difficulty with this strategy:

> [T]he Navajo Nation has adopted a policy of requiring consent to tribal jurisdiction in every lease, contract, or other consensual agreement. But every negotiation with a non-Indian business is now conducted in a context in which non-Indian perceptions of the uncertainty and strangeness of tribal law are bolstered by their sense that these laws need not apply to them. Obtaining consent to tribal law and jurisdiction in these circumstances is awkward if not impossible. [These difficulties] are interfering with the Navajo Nation's ability to enter into agreements concerning rights of way for electric utilities, pipelines, and business site leases. Before *Strate*, consent to tribal jurisdiction did not raise nearly as much opposition or concern. Post–*Strate*, the Navajo Nation will not give up on the consent term, and increasingly the non-Indian businesses refuse to include it. The Court's jurisprudence has altered jurisdictional expectations in a way that creates barriers to transactions, and therefore potentially interferes with tribal economic development.

Sarah Krakoff, *A Narrative of Sovereignty: Illuminating the Paradox of the Domestic Dependent Nation*, 83 Or. L. Rev. 1109, 1161 (2004).

4. *Elevating* Montana *and restricting the "exceptions." Strate* transformed *Montana* into a "general rule" against tribal jurisdiction over

nonmembers on land on which tribes had lost the right to exclude. It also importantly restricted the "exceptions" to this rule. Note that A–1 had a number of consensual relationships with the tribe. How does the Court limit the consensual relationship exception so that these relationships are irrelevant?

The Court also limits the direct effect exception. The Court admits that driving carelessly on highways endangers the health and safety of tribal members as well as nonmembers. In addition, this accident, by severely injuring the mother of five tribal members, had a very direct effect on one tribal family. Notice how the Court limits the second exception so that it does not encompass these effects. Would the tribe have had jurisdiction if Fredericks herself was a tribal member? *See Wilson v. Marchington*, 127 F.3d 805 (9th Cir. 1997) (holding that Blackfeet court lacked jurisdiction over action by tribal member against nonmember arising from accident on state highway); *but see McDonald v. Means*, 309 F.3d 530 (9th Cir. 2002) (upholding tribal court jurisdiction over tribal member's tort claim against nonmember for accident occurring on tribal road).

After *Strate*, may a tribe impose civil penalties on nonmembers speeding on state highways within the reservation? How would you distinguish such an attempt from the personal injury case in *Strate*?

5. *Restricting the exhaustion requirement.* Read footnote 14, *supra*. What exception does it add to the exhaustion requirement? Recall the facts of *National Farmers* and *Iowa Mutual*. Is the new exception justified given those facts?

6. *Commonplace claims in unfamiliar courts.* Some authors believe the key to *Strate* lies in this phrase: "Requiring A–1 and Stockert to defend against this commonplace state highway accident claim in an unfamiliar court is not crucial to 'the political integrity, the economic security, or the health or welfare of the [Three Affiliated Tribes].'" How did the Supreme Court determine what is "crucial" to the Tribes? What is meant by the phrase "unfamiliar court"?

D. Further Limitations on Tribal Civil Authority Over Nonmembers, 1997–Present

Strate makes *Montana* the major precedent governing both tribal civil regulatory and tribal civil adjudicatory jurisdiction. Two cases following *Strate* concerned tribal taxation authority over nonmembers and tribal adjudicatory authority over a tort action brought by a member against state officers for conduct in Indian country. These cases are considered in turn.

ATKINSON TRADING CO. V. SHIRLEY

532 U.S. 645, 121 S. Ct. 1825, 149 L.Ed.2d 889 (2001)

CHIEF JUSTICE REHNQUIST delivered the opinion of the Court.

In *Montana*, we held that, with limited exceptions, Indian tribes lack civil authority over the conduct of nonmembers on non-Indian fee land within a reservation. The question with which we are presented is whether this general rule applies to tribal attempts to tax nonmember activity occurring on non-Indian fee land. We hold that it does and that neither of *Montana*'s exceptions obtains here.

In 1916, Hubert Richardson, lured by the possibility of trading with wealthy Gray Mountain Navajo cattlemen, built the Cameron Trading Post just south of the Little Colorado River near Cameron, Arizona. Richardson purchased the land directly from the United States, but the Navajo Nation Reservation, which had been established in 1868, was later extended eight miles south so that the Cameron Trading Post fell within its exterior boundaries. *See* Act of June 14, 1934, ch. 521, 48 Stat. 960–962. This 1934 enlargement of the Navajo Reservation—which today stretches across northeast Arizona, northwest New Mexico, and southeast Utah—did not alter the status of the property: It is, like millions of acres throughout the United States, non-Indian fee land within a tribal reservation.

Richardson's "drafty, wooden store building and four small, one-room-shack cabins overlooking the bare river canyon," have since evolved into a business complex consisting of a hotel, restaurant, cafeteria, gallery, curio shop, retail store, and recreational vehicle facility. The current owner, petitioner Atkinson Trading Company, Inc., benefits from the Cameron Trading Post's location near the intersection of Arizona Highway 64 (which leads west to the Grand Canyon) and United States Highway 89 (which connects Flagstaff on the south with Glen Canyon Dam to the north). A significant portion of petitioner's hotel business stems from tourists on their way to or from the Grand Canyon National Park.

In 1992, the Navajo Nation enacted a hotel occupancy tax, which imposes an 8 percent tax upon any hotel room located within the exterior boundaries of the Navajo Nation Reservation. Although the legal incidence of the tax falls directly upon the guests, the owner or operator of the hotel must collect and remit it to *** the Navajo Tax Commission. The nonmember guests at the Cameron Trading Post pay approximately $84,000 in taxes to respondents annually. [The Navajo Tax Commission, the Navajo Supreme Court, and the federal trial and appellate courts upheld the validity of the tax.]

Although the Court of Appeals agreed with petitioner that our cases in this area "did make an issue of the fee status of the land in question," it nonetheless concluded that the status of the land as "fee land or tribal land is simply one of the factors a court should consider" when determining whether civil jurisdiction exists. Relying in part upon [*Merrion*], the court "complement[ed]" *Montana*'s framework with a "case-by-case approach" that balanced the non-Indian fee status of the land with "the nature of the inherent sovereign powers the tribe is attempting to exercise, its interests, and the impact that the exercise of the tribe's powers has upon the nonmember interests involved." The Court of Appeals then likened the Navajo hotel occupancy tax to similar taxes imposed by New Mexico and Arizona, concluding that the tax fell under *Montana*'s first exception because a "consensual relationship exists in that the nonmember guests could refrain from the privilege of lodging within the confines of the Navajo Reservation and therefore remain free from liability for the [tax]." The dissenting judge would have applied *Montana* without "any language or 'factors' derived from *Merrion*" and concluded that, based upon her view of the record, none of the *Montana* exceptions applied.

We granted certiorari and now reverse.

Tribal jurisdiction is limited: For powers not expressly conferred upon them by federal statute or treaty, Indian tribes must rely upon their retained or inherent sovereignty. In *Montana*, the most exhaustively reasoned of our modern cases addressing this latter authority, we observed that Indian tribe power over nonmembers on non-Indian fee land is sharply circumscribed. At issue in *Montana* was the Crow Tribe's attempt to regulate nonmember fishing and hunting on non-Indian fee land within the reservation. Although we "readily agree[d]" that the 1868 Fort Laramie Treaty authorized the Crow Tribe to prohibit nonmembers from hunting or fishing on tribal land, we held that such "power cannot apply to lands held in fee by non-Indians." This delineation of members and nonmembers, tribal land and non-Indian fee land, stemmed from the dependent nature of tribal sovereignty. Surveying our cases in this area[, we] noted that "through their original incorporation into the United States as well as through specific treaties and statutes, Indian tribes have lost many of the attributes of sovereignty." We concluded that the inherent sovereignty of Indian tribes was limited to "their members and their territory": "[E]xercise of tribal power beyond what is necessary to protect tribal self-government or to control internal relations is inconsistent with the dependent status of the tribes."

Although we extracted from our precedents "the general proposition that the inherent sovereign powers of an Indian tribe do not extend to the activities of nonmembers of the tribe," we nonetheless noted in *Montana* two possible bases for tribal jurisdiction over non-Indian fee land. First, "[a] tribe may regulate, through taxation, licensing, or other means, the activities of nonmembers who enter consensual relationships with the tribe or its members, through commercial dealings, contracts, leases, or other arrangements." *Ibid.* Second, "[a] tribe may *** exercise civil authority over the conduct of non-Indians on fee lands within its reservation when that *** conduct threatens or has some direct effect on the political integrity, the economic security, or the health or welfare of the tribe." ***

The framework set forth in *Montana* "broadly addressed the concept of 'inherent sovereignty.'" *Strate.* ***

Citing our decision in *Merrion*, respondents submit that *Montana* and *Strate* do not restrict an Indian tribe's power to impose revenue-raising taxes. In *Merrion*, just one year after our decision in *Montana*, we upheld a severance tax imposed by the Jicarilla Apache Tribe upon non-Indian lessees authorized to extract oil and gas from tribal land. In so doing, we noted that the power to tax derives not solely from an Indian tribe's power to exclude non-Indians from tribal land, but also from an Indian tribe's "general authority, as sovereign, to control economic activity within its jurisdiction." Such authority, we held, was incident to the benefits conferred upon nonmembers: "They benefit from the provision of police protection and other governmental services, as well as from " 'the advantages of a civilized society' " that are assured by the existence of tribal government."

Merrion, however, was careful to note that an Indian tribe's inherent power to tax only extended to "'transactions occurring on *trust lands* and significantly involving a tribe or its members.'" There are undoubtedly parts of the *Merrion* opinion that suggest a broader scope for tribal taxing authority than the quoted language above. But *Merrion* involved a tax that only applied to activity occurring on the reservation, and its holding is therefore easily reconcilable with the *Montana–Strate* line of authority, which we deem to be controlling. *See Merrion* ("[A] tribe has no authority over a nonmember until the nonmember enters tribal lands or conducts business with the tribe"). An Indian tribe's sovereign power to tax—whatever its derivation—reaches no further than tribal land.[5]

We therefore do not read *Merrion* to exempt taxation from *Montana*'s general rule that Indian tribes lack civil authority over nonmembers on non-Indian fee land. Accordingly, as in *Strate*, we apply *Montana* straight up. Because Congress has not authorized the Navajo Nation's hotel occupancy tax through treaty or statute, and because the incidence of the tax falls upon nonmembers on non-Indian fee land, it is incumbent upon the Navajo Nation to establish the existence of one of *Montana*'s exceptions.

Respondents argue that both petitioner and its hotel guests have entered into a consensual relationship with the Navajo Nation justifying the imposition of the hotel occupancy tax. [R]espondents note that the Cameron Trading Post benefits from the numerous services provided by the Navajo Nation. The record reflects that the Arizona State Police and the Navajo Tribal Police patrol the portions of United States Highway 89 and Arizona Highway 64 traversing the reservation; that the Navajo Tribal Police and the Navajo Tribal Emergency Medical Services Department will respond to an emergency call from the Cameron Trading Post; and that local Arizona Fire Departments and the Navajo Tribal Fire Department provide fire protection to the area. Although we do not question the Navajo Nation's ability to charge an appropriate fee for a particular service actually rendered, we think the generalized availability of tribal services patently insufficient to sustain the Tribe's civil authority over nonmembers on non-Indian fee land.

The consensual relationship must stem from "commercial dealing, contracts, leases, or other arrangements," *Montana*, and a nonmember's actual or potential receipt of tribal police, fire, and medical services does not create the requisite connection. If it did, the exception would swallow the rule: All non-Indian fee lands within a reservation benefit, to some extent, from the "advantages of a civilized society" offered by the Indian tribe. Such a result does not square with our precedents; indeed, we implicitly rejected this argument in *Strate* where we held that the nonmembers had not consented to the Tribes' adjudicatory authority by availing themselves of the benefit of tribal police protection while traveling within the reservation. We therefore reject respondents' broad reading of *Montana*'s first exception, which ignores the dependent status of Indian tribes and subverts the territorial restriction upon tribal power.

Respondents and their principal *amicus*, the United States, also argue that petitioner consented to the tax by becoming an "Indian trader." Congress has authorized the Commissioner of Indian Affairs "to appoint traders to the Indian tribes and to make such rules and regulations as he may deem just and proper specifying the kind and quantity of goods and the prices at which such

5. ***At least in the context of non-Indian fee land, we [find] inapt the Court of Appeals' analogy to state taxing authority. Our reference in *Merrion* to a State's ability to tax activities with which it has a substantial nexus was made in the context of describing an Indian tribe's authority over *tribal land*. Only full territorial sovereigns enjoy the "power to enforce laws against all who come within the sovereign's territory, whether citizens or aliens," and Indian tribes "can no longer be described as sovereigns in this sense." *Duro v. Reina*, 495 U.S. 676, 685 (1990).

goods shall be sold to the Indians." 25 U.S.C. § 261. Petitioner has acquired the requisite license to transact business with the Navajo Nation and therefore is subject to the regulatory strictures promulgated by the Indian Affairs Commissioner.[10] But whether or not the Navajo Nation could impose a tax on activities arising out of this relationship, an issue not before us, it is clear that petitioner's "Indian trader" status by itself cannot support the imposition of the hotel occupancy tax.

Montana's consensual relationship exception requires that the tax or regulation imposed by the Indian tribe have a nexus to the consensual relationship itself. In *Strate*, for example, even though respondent A–1 Contractors was on the reservation to perform landscaping work for the Three Affiliated Tribes at the time of the accident, we nonetheless held that the Tribes lacked adjudicatory authority because the other nonmember "was not a party to the subcontract, and the [T]ribes were strangers to the accident." A nonmember's consensual relationship in one area thus does not trigger tribal civil authority in another ***. The hotel occupancy tax at issue here is grounded in petitioner's relationship with its nonmember hotel guests, who can reach the Cameron Trading Post on United States Highway 89 and Arizona Highway 64, non-Indian public rights-of-way. Petitioner cannot be said to have consented to such a tax by virtue of its status as an "Indian trader."

[B]oth respondents and the United States argue that the hotel occupancy tax is warranted in light of the direct effects the Cameron Trading Post has upon the Navajo Nation. Again noting the Navajo Nation's provision of tribal services and petitioner's status as an "Indian trader," respondents emphasize that petitioner employs almost 100 Navajo Indians; that the Cameron Trading Post derives business from tourists visiting the reservation; and that large amounts of tribal land surround petitioner's isolated property.[11] Although we have no cause to doubt respondents' assertion that the Cameron Chapter of the Navajo Nation possesses an "overwhelming Indian character," we fail to see how petitioner's operation of a hotel on non-Indian fee land "threatens or has some direct effect on the political integrity, the economic security, or the health or welfare of the tribe."[12]

We find unpersuasive respondents' attempt to augment this claim by reference to *Brendale* [, where,] per the reasoning of two Justices, we held that the Yakima Nation had the authority to zone a small, non-Indian parcel located

---

10. Although the regulations do not "preclude" the Navajo Nation from imposing upon "Indian traders" such "fees or taxes [it] may deem appropriate," the regulations do not contemplate or authorize the hotel occupancy tax at issue here. 25 C.F.R. § 141.11 (2000).

11. *** 96.3 percent of the Navajo Nation's 16,224,896 acres is tribally owned, with allotted land comprising 762,749 acres, or 4.7 percent, of the reservation. *** The 1990 Census reports that that 96.6 percent of residents on the Navajo Nation are Indian. The Cameron Chapter of the Navajo Nation, in which petitioner's land lies, has a non-Indian population of 2.3 percent.

12. Although language in *Merrion* referred to taxation as "necessary to tribal self-government and territorial management," it did not address assertions of tribal jurisdiction over non-Indian fee land. Just as with *Montana*'s first exception, incorporating *Merrion*'s reasoning here would be tantamount to rejecting *Montana*'s general rule. In *Strate*, we stated that *Montana*'s second exception "can be misperceived." The exception is only triggered by *nonmember conduct* that threatens the Indian tribe; it does not broadly permit the exercise of civil authority wherever it might be considered "necessary" to self-government. Thus, unless the drain of the nonmember's conduct upon tribal services and resources is so severe that it actually "imperil[s]" the political integrity of the Indian tribe, there can be no assertion of civil authority beyond tribal lands. Petitioner's hotel has no such adverse effect upon the Navajo Nation.

"in the heart" of over 800,000 acres of closed and largely uninhabited tribal land. Respondents extrapolate from this holding that Indian tribes enjoy broad authority over nonmembers wherever the acreage of non-Indian fee land is minuscule in relation to the surrounding tribal land. But we think it plain that the judgment in *Brendale* turned on both the closed nature of the non-Indian fee land and the fact that its development would place the entire area "in jeopardy." Irrespective of the percentage of non-Indian fee land within a reservation, *Montana*'s second exception grants Indian tribes nothing " 'beyond what is necessary to protect tribal self-government or to control internal relations.' " *Strate* (quoting *Montana*). Whatever effect petitioner's operation of the Cameron Trading Post might have upon surrounding Navajo land, it does not endanger the Navajo Nation's political integrity. ***

[*Reversed.*]

JUSTICE SOUTER, with whom **JUSTICES KENNEDY** and **THOMAS** join, concurring.

If we are to see coherence in the various manifestations of the general law of tribal jurisdiction over non-Indians, the source of doctrine must be *Montana*, and it is in light of that case that I join the Court's opinion. Under *Montana*, the status of territory within a reservation's boundaries as tribal or fee land may have much to do (as it does here) with the likelihood (or not) that facts will exist that are relevant under the exceptions to Montana's "general proposition" that "the inherent sovereign powers of an Indian tribe do not extend to the activities of nonmembers of the tribe." That general proposition is, however, the first principle, regardless of whether the land at issue is fee land, or land owned by or held in trust for an Indian tribe.

NOTES AND QUESTIONS

1. The Court correctly distinguishes *Merrion* on its facts. Does it do so on its reasoning? Note that the non-Indian leases of the lands in *Merrion* were made pursuant to federal law, with federal approval and tribal compensation, and without retaining a gatekeeping right, the same facts that led *Strate* to hold that the state right of way was the legal equivalent of the fee land covered by *Montana*'s "main rule."

2. Look at the Court's concluding sentence: "Whatever effect petitioner's operation of the Cameron Trading Post might have upon surrounding Navajo land, it does not endanger the Navajo Nation's political integrity." Suppose the operation of the Trading Post is adversely affecting surrounding Navajo land; what is the Nation's recourse and where may it be sought?

3. What about trust land that tribes had never alienated? Language in *Montana* suggested such land was subject to different considerations:

> The Court of Appeals held that the Tribe may prohibit nonmembers from hunting or fishing on land belonging to the Tribe or held by the United States in trust for the Tribe, and with this holding we can readily agree. We also agree with the Court of Appeals that if the Tribe permits nonmembers to fish or hunt on such lands, it may condition their entry by charging a fee or establishing bag and creel limits.

Strate reaffirmed this, stating that "We 'can readily agree,' in accord with *Montana*, that tribes retain considerable control over nonmember conduct on tribal land." One could make the argument that if trust and non-Indian lands are *not* treated differently, the portion of the *Montana* opinion that held that the state owned the bed of the Bighorn River was irrelevant to the jurisdictional question. But other language in *Montana* suggested that the limitations on tribal jurisdiction were more general. A few weeks after *Atkinson*, the Supreme Court considered the question in the next case.

NEVADA V. HICKS

533 U.S. 353, 121 S. Ct. 2304, 150 L.Ed.2d 398 (2001)

JUSTICE SCALIA delivered the opinion of the Court.

This case presents the question whether a tribal court may assert jurisdiction over civil claims against state officials who entered tribal land to execute a search warrant against a tribe member suspected of having violated state law outside the reservation.

I.

Respondent Hicks is one of about 900 members of the Fallon Paiute–Shoshone Tribes of western Nevada. He resides on the Tribes' reservation of approximately 8,000 acres, established by federal statute in 1908, ch. 53, 35 Stat. 85. In 1990 Hicks came under suspicion of having killed, off the reservation, a California bighorn sheep, a gross misdemeanor under Nevada law. A state game warden obtained from state court a search warrant "SUBJECT TO OBTAINING APPROVAL FROM THE FALLON TRIBAL COURT IN AND FOR THE FALLON PAIUTE–SHOSHONE TRIBES." According to the issuing judge, this tribal-court authorization was necessary because "[t]his Court has no jurisdiction on the Fallon Paiute–Shoshone Indian Reservation." A search warrant was obtained from the tribal court, and the warden, accompanied by a tribal police officer, searched respondent's yard, uncovering only the head of a Rocky Mountain bighorn, a different (and unprotected) species of sheep.

Approximately one year later, a tribal police officer reported to the warden that he had observed two mounted bighorn sheep heads in respondent's home. The warden again obtained a search warrant from state court; though this warrant did not explicitly require permission from the Tribes, a tribal-court warrant was nonetheless secured, and respondent's home was again (unsuccessfully) searched by three wardens and additional tribal officers.

Respondent, claiming that his sheep heads had been damaged, and that the second search exceeded the bounds of the warrant, brought suit against the Tribal Judge, the tribal officers, the state wardens in their individual and official capacities, and the State of Nevada in the Tribal Court in and for the Fallon Paiute–Shoshone Tribes. (His claims against all defendants except the state wardens and the State of Nevada were dismissed by directed verdict and are not at issue here.) Respondent's causes of action included trespass to land and chattels, abuse of process, and violation of civil rights—specifically, denial of equal protection, denial of due process, and unreasonable search and seizure, each remediable under 42 U.S.C. § 1983. Respondent later voluntarily dismissed his case against the State and against the state officials in their official capacities, leaving only his suit against those officials in their individual capacities.

The Tribal Court held that it had jurisdiction over the claims, a holding affirmed by the Tribal Appeals Court. The state officials and Nevada then filed an action in Federal District Court seeking a declaratory judgment that the Tribal Court lacked jurisdiction. The District Court granted summary judgment to respondent on the issue of jurisdiction, and also held that the state officials would have to exhaust any claims of qualified immunity in the tribal court. The Ninth Circuit affirmed, concluding that the fact that respondent's home is located on tribe-owned land within the reservation is sufficient to support tribal jurisdiction over civil claims against nonmembers arising from their activities on that land.

II.

In this case, which involves claims brought under both tribal and federal law, it is necessary to determine, as to the former, whether the Tribal Court in and for the Fallon Paiute–Shoshone Tribes has jurisdiction to adjudicate the alleged tortious conduct of state wardens executing a search warrant for evidence of an off-reservation crime; and, as to the latter, whether the Tribal Court has jurisdiction over claims brought under § 1983. We address the former question first.

A.

The principle of Indian law central to this aspect of the case is our holding in *Strate*: "As to nonmembers *** a tribe's adjudicative jurisdiction does not exceed its legislative jurisdiction ***." That formulation leaves open the question whether a tribe's adjudicative jurisdiction over nonmember defendants *equals* its legislative jurisdiction.[2] We will not have to answer that open question if we determine that the Tribes in any event lack legislative jurisdiction in this case. We first inquire, therefore, whether the Fallon Paiute–Shoshone Tribes—either as an exercise of their inherent sovereignty, or under grant of federal authority—can regulate state wardens executing a search warrant for evidence of an off-reservation crime.

Indian tribes' regulatory authority over nonmembers is governed by the principles set forth in *Montana*, which we have called the "pathmarking case" on the subject. [*Strate*.] *** Where nonmembers are concerned, the "exercise of tribal power *beyond what is necessary to protect tribal self-government or to control internal relations* is inconsistent with the dependent status of the

2. In *National Farmers* we avoided the question whether tribes may generally adjudicate against nonmembers claims arising from on-reservation transactions, and we have never held that a tribal court had jurisdiction over a nonmember defendant. Typically, our cases have involved claims brought against tribal defendants. *See*, e.g. *Williams v. Lee*. In *Strate*, however, we assumed that "where tribes possess authority to regulate the activities of nonmembers, civil jurisdiction over disputes arising out of such activities presumably lies in the tribal courts," without distinguishing between nonmember plaintiffs and nonmember defendants. *See also Iowa Mutual Ins. Co. v. LaPlante*. Our holding in this case is limited to the question of tribal-court jurisdiction over state officers enforcing state law. We leave open the question of tribal-court jurisdiction over nonmember defendants in general.

tribes, and so cannot survive without express congressional delegation." *Montana*.[3]

Both *Montana* and *Strate* rejected tribal authority to regulate nonmembers' activities on land over which the tribe could not "assert a landowner's right to occupy and exclude." Respondents and the United States argue that since Hicks's home and yard *are* on tribe-owned land within the reservation, the Tribe may make its exercise of regulatory authority over nonmembers a condition of nonmembers' entry. Not necessarily. While it is certainly true that the non-Indian ownership status of the land was central to the analysis in both *Montana* and *Strate,* the reason that was so was *not* that Indian ownership suspends the "general proposition" derived from *Oliphant* that "the inherent sovereign powers of an Indian tribe do not extend to the activities of nonmembers of the tribe" except to the extent "necessary to protect tribal self-government or to control internal relations." *Montana*. *Oliphant* itself drew no distinctions based on the status of land. And *Montana*, after announcing the general rule of no jurisdiction over nonmembers, cautioned that "[t]o be sure, Indian tribes retain inherent sovereign power to exercise some forms of civil jurisdiction over non-Indians on their reservations, even on non-Indian fee lands"—clearly implying that the general rule of *Montana* applies to both Indian and non-Indian land. The ownership status of land, in other words, is only one factor to consider in determining whether regulation of the activities of nonmembers is "necessary to protect tribal self-government or to control internal relations." It may sometimes be a dispositive factor. Hitherto, the absence of tribal ownership has been virtually conclusive of the absence of tribal civil jurisdiction; with one minor exception, we have never upheld under *Montana* the extension of tribal civil authority over nonmembers on non-Indian land. [*Brendale*]. But the existence of tribal ownership is not alone enough to support regulatory jurisdiction over nonmembers.

We proceed to consider, successively, the following questions: whether regulatory jurisdiction over state officers in the present context is "necessary to protect tribal self-government or to control internal relations," and, if not, whether such regulatory jurisdiction has been congressionally conferred.

B.

In *Strate,* we explained that what is necessary to protect tribal self-government and control internal relations can be understood by looking at the examples of tribal power to which *Montana* referred: tribes have authority "[to punish tribal offenders,] to determine tribal membership, to regulate domestic relations among members, and to prescribe rules of inheritance for members." These examples show, we said, that Indians have " 'the right *** to make their own laws and be ruled by them.' " *Strate* (quoting *Williams v. Lee*). Tribal assertion of regulatory authority over nonmembers must be connected to that right of the Indians to make their own laws and be governed by them.

---

3. *Montana* recognized an exception to this rule for tribal regulation of "the activities of nonmembers who enter consensual relationships with the tribe or its members, through commercial dealing, contracts, leases, or other arrangements." Though the wardens in this case "consensually" obtained a warrant from the Tribal Court before searching respondent's home and yard, we do not think this qualifies as an "other arrangement" within the meaning of this passage. Read in context, an "other arrangement" is clearly another *private consensual* relationship, from which the official actions at issue in this case are far removed.

Our cases make clear that the Indians' right to make their own laws and be governed by them does not exclude all state regulatory authority on the reservation. State sovereignty does not end at a reservation's border. Though tribes are often referred to as "sovereign" entities, it was "long ago" that "the Court departed from Chief Justice Marshall's view [in *Worcester*] that 'the laws of [a State] can have no force' within reservation boundaries." *White Mountain Apache Tribe v. Bracker*, 448 U.S. 136, 141 (1980).[4] "Ordinarily," it is now clear, "an Indian reservation is considered part of the territory of the State." U.S. Dept. of Interior, *Federal Indian Law* 510, and n.1 (1958)[.]

That is not to say that States may exert the same degree of regulatory authority within a reservation as they do without. To the contrary, the principle that Indians have the right to make their own laws and be governed by them requires "an accommodation between the interests of the Tribes and the Federal Government, on the one hand, and those of the State, on the other." *Confederated Tribes*. "When on-reservation conduct involving only Indians is at issue, state law is generally inapplicable, for the State's regulatory interest is likely to be minimal and the federal interest in encouraging tribal self-government is at its strongest." *Bracker*. When, however, state interests outside the reservation are implicated, States may regulate the activities even of tribe members on tribal land as exemplified by our decision in *Colville* ***. It is also well established in our precedent that States have criminal jurisdiction over reservation Indians for crimes committed (as was the alleged poaching in this case) off the reservation. ***

While it is not entirely clear from our precedent whether the last mentioned authority entails the corollary right to enter a reservation (including Indian-fee lands) for enforcement purposes, several of our opinions point in that direction. *** [W]e considered, in *United States v. Kagama*, 118 U.S. 375 (1886), whether Congress could enact a law giving federal courts jurisdiction over various common-law, violent crimes committed by Indians on a reservation within a State. We expressed skepticism that the Indian Commerce Clause could justify this assertion of authority in derogation of state jurisdiction, but ultimately accepted the argument that the law

> does not interfere with the process of the State courts within the reservation, nor with the operation of State laws upon white people found there. Its effect is confined to the acts of an Indian of some tribe, of a criminal character, committed within the limits of the reservation. ***

The Court's references to "process" in *** *Kagama* and the Court's concern in *Kagama* over possible federal encroachment on state prerogatives, suggest state authority to issue search warrants in cases such as the one before us. ***

We conclude today, in accordance with these prior statements, that tribal authority to regulate state officers in executing process related to the violation, off reservation, of state laws is not essential to tribal self-government or internal relations—to "the right to make laws and be ruled by them." The State's interest in execution of process is considerable, and even when it relates to Indian-fee lands it no more impairs the tribe's self-government than federal enforcement of federal law impairs state government.

---

4. Our holding in *Worcester* must be considered in light of the fact that "[t]he 1828 treaty with the Cherokee Nation ***guaranteed the Indians their lands would never be subjected to the jurisdiction of any State or Territory." *Organized Village of Kake v. Egan*, 369 U.S. 60, 71 (1962).

III.

We turn next to the contention of respondent and the Government that the tribal court, as a court of general jurisdiction, has authority to entertain federal claims under § 1983. It is certainly true that state courts of "general jurisdiction" can adjudicate cases invoking federal statutes, such as § 1983, absent congressional specification to the contrary. *** Indeed, that state courts could enforce federal law is presumed by Article III of the Constitution, which leaves to Congress the decision whether to create lower federal courts at all. This historical and constitutional assumption of concurrent state-court jurisdiction over federal-law cases is completely missing with respect to tribal courts.

Respondents' contention that tribal courts are courts of "general jurisdiction" is also quite wrong. A state court's jurisdiction is general, in that it "lays hold of all subjects of litigation between parties within its jurisdiction, though the causes of dispute are relative to the laws of the most distant part of the globe." Tribal courts, it should be clear, cannot be courts of general jurisdiction in this sense, for a tribe's inherent adjudicative jurisdiction over nonmembers is at most only as broad as its legislative jurisdiction. ***

Furthermore, tribal-court jurisdiction would create serious anomalies, as the Government recognizes, because the general federal-question removal statute refers only to removal from *state* court, see 28 U.S.C. § 1441. Were § 1983 claims cognizable in tribal court, defendants would inexplicably lack the right available to state-court § 1983 defendants to seek a federal forum. ***

IV.

The last question before us is whether petitioners were required to exhaust their jurisdictional claims in Tribal Court before bringing them in Federal District Court. In *National Farmers Union* we recognized exceptions to the exhaustion requirement, where "an assertion of tribal jurisdiction is motivated by a desire to harass or is conducted in bad faith, *** or where the action is patently violative of express jurisdictional prohibitions, or where exhaustion would be futile because of the lack of an adequate opportunity to challenge the court's jurisdiction." None of these exceptions seems applicable to this case, but we added a broader exception in *Strate*: "[w]hen *** it is plain that no federal grant provides for tribal governance of nonmembers' conduct on land covered by *Montana*'s main rule," so the exhaustion requirement "would serve no purpose other than delay." Though this exception too is technically inapplicable, the reasoning behind it is not. Since it is clear, as we have discussed, that tribal courts lack jurisdiction over state officials for causes of action relating to their performance of official duties, adherence to the tribal exhaustion requirement in such cases "would serve no purpose other than delay," and is therefore unnecessary.

***

[*Reversed.*]

JUSTICE SOUTER, joined by **JUSTICES KENNEDY** and **THOMAS**, concurring.

I agree that the Fallon Paiute–Shoshone Tribal Court had no jurisdiction to entertain Hicks's claims against the petitioning state officers here, and I join the Court's opinion. While I agree with the Court's analysis as well as its conclusion, I would reach that point by a different route. *** I would *** make it explicit that land status within a reservation is not a primary jurisdictional fact, but is relevant only insofar as it bears on the application of one of *Montana*'s exceptions to a particular case. ***

The ability of nonmembers to know where tribal jurisdiction begins and ends, it should be stressed, is a matter of real, practical consequence given "[t]he special nature of [Indian] tribunals," *Duro v. Reina*, which differ from traditional American courts in a number of significant respects. To start with the most obvious one, it has been understood for more than a century that the Bill of Rights and the Fourteenth Amendment do not of their own force apply to Indian tribes. *See Talton v. Mayes*. Although the Indian Civil Rights Act of 1968 (ICRA) makes a handful of analogous safeguards enforceable in tribal courts, "the guarantees are not identical," *Oliphant*, and there is a "definite trend by tribal courts" toward the view that they "ha[ve] leeway in interpreting" the ICRA's due process and equal protection clauses and "need not follow the U.S. Supreme Court precedents 'jot-for-jot,'" Newton, *Tribal Court Praxis: One Year in the Life of Twenty Indian Tribal Courts*, 22 Am. Indian L. Rev. 285, 344 n. 238 (1998). In any event, a presumption against tribal-court civil jurisdiction squares with one of the principal policy considerations underlying *Oliphant*, namely, an overriding concern that citizens who are not tribal members be "protected *** from unwarranted intrusions on their personal liberty."

Tribal courts also differ from other American courts (and often from one another) in their structure, in the substantive law they apply, and in the independence of their judges. Although some modern tribal courts "mirror American courts" and "are guided by written codes, rules, procedures, and guidelines," tribal law is still frequently unwritten, being based instead "on the values, mores, and norms of a tribe and expressed in its customs, traditions, and practices," and is often "handed down orally or by example from one generation to another." Melton, *Indigenous Justice Systems and Tribal Society*, 79 Judicature 126, 130–131 (1995). The resulting law applicable in tribal courts is a complex "mix of tribal codes and federal, state, and traditional law," National American Indian Court Judges Assn., Indian Courts and the Future 43 (1978), which would be unusually difficult for an outsider to sort out. ***

JUSTICE GINSBURG, concurring.

I join the Court's opinion. As the Court plainly states, and as Justice Souter recognizes, the "holding in this case is limited to the question of tribal-court jurisdiction over state officers enforcing state law." The Court's decision explicitly "leave[s] open the question of tribal-court jurisdiction over nonmember defendants in general," including state officials engaged on tribal land in a venture or frolic of their own (a state officer's conduct on tribal land "unrelated to [performance of his law-enforcement duties] is potentially subject to tribal control").

I write separately only to emphasize that *Strate v. A–1 Contractors* similarly deferred larger issues. *Strate* *** "express[ed] no view on the governing law or proper forum" for cases arising out of nonmember conduct on tribal land. The Court's opinion, as I understand it, does not reach out definitively to answer the jurisdictional questions left open in *Strate*.

JUSTICE O'CONNOR, with whom **JUSTICE STEVENS** and **JUSTICE BREYER** join, concurring in part and concurring in the judgment.

The Court holds that a tribe has no power to regulate the activities of state officials enforcing state law on land owned and controlled by the tribe. The majority's sweeping opinion, without cause, undermines the authority of tribes to " 'make their own laws and be ruled by them.' " *Strate v. A–1 Contractors* (quoting *Williams v. Lee*). I write separately because Part II of the Court's decision is unmoored from our precedents.

*** Today, the Court finally resolves that *Montana v. United States* governs a tribe's civil jurisdiction over nonmembers regardless of land ownership. This is done with little fanfare, but the holding is significant because we have equivocated on this question in the past. ***

[T]he majority is quite right that *Montana* should govern our analysis of a tribe's civil jurisdiction over nonmembers both on and off tribal land. I part company with the majority, however, because its reasoning is not faithful to *Montana* or its progeny. ***

Under the first *Montana* exception, a tribe may exercise regulatory jurisdiction where a nonmember enters into a consensual relationship with the tribe. The majority in this case dismisses the applicability of this exception in a footnote, concluding that any consensual relationship between tribes and nonmembers "clearly" must be a "private" consensual relationship "from which the official actions at issue in this case are far removed." The majority provides no support for this assertion. ***

State governments may enter into consensual relationships with tribes, such as contracts for services or shared authority over public resources. Depending upon the nature of the agreement, such relationships could provide official consent to tribal regulatory jurisdiction. Some States have formally sanctioned the creation of state-tribal agreements. *** In addition, there are a host of cooperative agreements between tribes and state authorities to share control over tribal lands, to manage public services, and to provide law enforcement. ***

Without a full understanding of the applicable relationships among tribal, state, and federal entities, there is no need to create a *per se* rule that forecloses future debate as to whether cooperative agreements, or other forms of official consent, could ever be a basis for tribal jurisdiction. ***

The second *Montana* exception states that a tribe may regulate nonmember conduct where that conduct "threatens or has some direct effect on the political integrity, the economic security, or the health or welfare of the tribe." 450 U.S. at 566. The majority concentrates on this aspect of *Montana* asking whether "regulatory jurisdiction over state officers in the present context is 'necessary to protect tribal self-government or to control internal relations,' " and concludes that it is not.

At the outset, the Court recites relatively uncontroversial propositions. A tribe's right to make its own laws and be governed by them "does not exclude all state regulatory authority on the reservation"; a reservation " 'is considered part of the territory of the State' "; "States may regulate the activities even of tribe members on tribal land"; and the " 'process of [state] courts may run into [a] *** reservation.' "

None of "these prior statements," however, "accord[s]" with the majority's conclusion that "tribal authority to regulate state officers in executing process related to [an off-reservation violation of state law] is not essential to tribal self-government or internal relations." Our prior decisions are informed by the understanding that tribal, Federal, and State Governments *share* authority over tribal lands. [*Cotton Petroleum Corp. v. New Mexico*; *Rice v. Rehner*; *Washington v. Confederated Tribes of the Colville Reservation*.] *** Saying that tribal jurisdiction must "accommodat[e]" various sovereign interests does not mean that tribal interests are to be nullified through a *per se* rule. ***

This case involves state officials acting on tribal land. The Tribes' sovereign interests with respect to nonmember activities on its land are not extinguished simply because the nonmembers in this case are state officials enforcing state law. *** The actions of state officials on tribal land in some instances may affect tribal sovereign interests to a greater, not lesser, degree than the actions of private parties. In this case, for example, it is alleged that state officers, who gained access to Hicks' property by virtue of their authority as state actors, exceeded the scope of the search warrants and damaged Hicks' personal property. ***

*** The Court's sweeping analysis gives the impression that this case involves a conflict of great magnitude between the State of Nevada and the Fallon Paiute–Shoshone Tribes. That is not so. At no point did the Tribes attempt to exclude the State from the reservation. At no point did the Tribes attempt to obstruct state officials' efforts to secure or execute the search warrants. Quite the contrary, the record demonstrates that judicial and law enforcement officials from the State and the Tribes acted in full cooperation to investigate an off-reservation crime. ***

[I] would resolve this case by applying basic principles of official and qualified immunity.

The doctrines of official immunity, *Westfall v. Erwin*, 484 U.S. 292 (1988) and qualified immunity, *see, e.g., Harlow v. Fitzgerald*, 457 U.S. 800 (1982), are designed to protect state and federal officials from civil liability for conduct that was within the scope of their duties or conduct that did not violate clearly established law. These doctrines short-circuit civil litigation for officials who meet these standards so that these officials are not subjected to the costs of trial or the burdens of discovery. ***

I would hold that *Montana* governs a tribe's civil jurisdiction over nonmembers, and that in order to protect government officials, immunity claims should be considered in reviewing tribal court jurisdiction. ***

[JUSTICE STEVENS, joined by JUSTICE BREYER, joined in JUSTICE O'CONNOR's opinion and issued a separate opinion arguing that tribes should have jurisdiction over Section 1983 claims.]

NOTES AND QUESTIONS

1. *Legal realism about* Hicks. Focus on the question before the Court: may the tribal court hear a civil suit against state law enforcement officers in their individual capacities (*i.e.*, in which they are being sued personally and if liable, might have to pay damages from their own pockets) for allegedly violating the rights of a member suspected of committing an off-reservation violation of state law when they searched his home on Indian land on the reservation?

Put that way, the answer is predictable, triggering both the Scalia majority's concern for state law enforcement and the Souter concurrence's concern about "intrusions on personal liberty." Yet both lower federal courts to consider the question held that the tribal court *did* have jurisdiction. Reconsider the concerns about the state and personal liberty. Did the state assumption that they needed tribal consent for on reservation warrants interfere with state law enforcement activity? And wasn't Mr. Hicks simply seeking a local forum (in which he sued tribal as well as state officers) complaining about an intrusion on his personal liberty when law enforcement agents entered his home and damaged his property? How should the Court have resolved these conflicting concerns?

2. *Courts of general jurisdiction?* In the portion of the majority opinion holding that tribal courts do not have jurisdiction over § 1983 claims, Justice Scalia expresses concern regarding defendants' inability to remove such claims from tribal court to federal court. Does this provide another clue as to any non-doctrinally based reasons for the *Hicks* outcome? In fashioning a legislative response to *Hicks* and the other post-*Montana* cases, should federal judicial review of tribal court decisions be part of the package? Given *Strate*'s addition to the exceptions to tribal court exhaustion, how would direct federal court review differ from the current situation?

3. *What is decided in* Hicks? Each of the opinions emphasized that *Hicks* was limited to its particular facts: tribal court jurisdiction over state law enforcement officers for actions taken in their official capacity. Some argue that as a result of *Hicks, Montana*'s limitation on tribal jurisdiction applies on trust and Indian-owned land. If that were the case, however, why would Justice Ginsburg (the author of the majority opinion in *Strate*) concur in order to make clear her understanding that *Montana's* application to tribal land remains an open question? And why would Justice Souter write a concurring opinion complaining that the majority should have made "it explicit that land status within a reservation is not a primary jurisdictional fact, but is relevant only as it bears on the application of one of Montana's exceptions to a particular case"?

4. *What about Justice Souter's suggestions about potential unfairness to non-members in tribal court?* There are many anecdotes but few comprehensive studies of tribal courts or their treatment of non-members. In 1991, however, the U.S. Civil Rights Commission conducted a study investigating tribal court implementation of ICRA. While the Commission found some problems in tribal courts, it attributed them largely to inadequate funding and growing pains of any developing court system. The Commission supported permanent legislation ensuring tribal jurisdiction over nonmember Indians, and expressed its "hopes that the current trend towards the narrowing of tribal jurisdiction will be reversed." U.S. Comm'n on Civil Rights, The Indian Civil Rights Act 73, 74 (1991). A more recent study looked at all available decisions by the Navajo courts involving non-Indians and non-member Indians between 1969 and 2004. Bethany R. Berger, *Justice and the Outsider: Jurisdiction over Non-Members in Tribal Legal Systems*, 37 Ariz. St. L.J. 1037 (2005). The study found that non-members won about half of all cases against tribal members, even though the Navajo Nation is one of the pioneers in the use of tribal customary law, a particular concern of Justice Souter's. *See also* Mark D. Rosen, *Multiple Authoritative Interpreters of Quasi-Constitutional Federal Law: Of Tribal Courts and the Indian Civil Rights Act*, 69 Fordham L. Rev. 479, 578 (2000) (concluding in context of more limited sample that "there is no

indication that tribal courts have succumbed to the temptation to favor the insider at the expense of outsiders.").

5. *State service of process to tribal members on reservation?* One of the things that *Hicks* did not decide is whether states do in fact have jurisdiction to enforce warrants against tribal members without tribal authorization. (Notice the weakness of its suggestion that states might have some such power. The Court relies significantly on the *Kagama* decision; do you remember what *Kagama* said about state jurisdiction over Indians? If not, take a moment to review that aspect of the opinion.) In 2004, the South Dakota Supreme Court held that without a tribal warrant or permission state police could not pursue a tribal member onto the reservation for a traffic violation. *South Dakota v. Cummings*, 679 N.W.2d 484 (S.D. 2004):

> [I]n *Hicks*, the Tribe was attempting to extend its jurisdiction over state officials by subjecting them to claims in tribal court. Here, the State is attempting to extend its jurisdiction into the boundaries of the Tribe's Reservation without consent of the Tribe of a tribal-state compact allowing such jurisdiction. *** This is significant because historically, the Federal Government has been highly protective of the Tribe's right to be free from harm and interference by states.

Id. at 487. In contrast, the Washington Supreme Court recently relied on *Hicks* to hold that a state could execute a state-issued warrant on tribal trust land for an on-reservation crime over which it had jurisdiction without tribal consent. *State v. Clark*, 308 P.3d 590 (Wash. 2013) (*en banc*). The court rejected arguments that the statements in *Hicks* about state jurisdiction over criminal process on reservation were dictum: "Because the *Hicks* Court relied on its discussion of tribal sovereignty and federal preemption to reach its holding, this portion of *Hicks* is binding law." 308 P.3d at 595. Other courts have held that states have jurisdiction to enter reservations to execute process or make arrests for off-reservation crimes so long as such process did not violate governing tribal law or procedure. *See State v. Harrison*, 238 P.3d 869 (N.M. 2010); *State v. Mathews*, 986 P.2d 323 (Idaho 1999).

The U.S. Supreme Court next addressed tribal jurisdiction over nonmembers in a case arising from loan transactions between a non-Indian bank and a family business engaged in ranching on the Cheyenne River Sioux Reservation. Ronnie Long and his wife Lila, both tribal members, owned 51% of the business. The company was a majority tribal-member-owned business, and the bank's loans to the company were therefore protected by Bureau of Indian Affairs guarantees. The Long company had done business with the bank for 29 years, but after many of its cattle died in blizzards in the harsh winter of 1996, the company defaulted on its loans, and the bank seized 2,230 acres of land on the reservation that Kenneth Long had put up as collateral. The bank gave the Long Company an option to repurchase the land, but it could not do so and the bank eventually sold the property to non-Indians. The bank originally discussed more favorable terms with the Long Company for reacquisition of the land, but later withdrew those terms in a letter "citing 'possible jurisdictional problems' posed by the Long Company's status as an 'Indian owned entity on the reservation.' " 491 F.3d 878, 882 (8th Cir. 2007). The Long Company sued the bank in Cheyenne River Sioux tribal court, alleging breach of contract, violation of good faith, discrimination in the terms of the option to purchase, and violation of self-help remedies. A jury found for the Long Company on the contract, good faith, and discrimination claims, and the trial court awarded the plaintiffs $750,000 in compensatory damages. The court later issued a supplemental order providing the Long Company with the option to repurchase the land. The Cheyenne River Sioux Court of Appeals affirmed the decision on the discrimination claim, and did not reach the contract and good faith claims. Plains Commerce Bank challenged the tribal court's jurisdiction in federal court. Both the district court and Eighth Circuit upheld jurisdiction. 491 F.3d 878 (8th Cir. 2007); 440 F.Supp.2d 1070 (D.S.D. 2006). The Supreme Court granted certiorari and reversed.

PLAINS COMMERCE BANK V. LONG FAMILY LAND AND CATTLE CO.

554 U.S. 316, 128 S. Ct. 2709, 171 L.Ed.2d 457 (2008)

CHIEF JUSTICE ROBERT delivered the opinion of the Court.

***

III.

A.

For nearly two centuries now, we have recognized Indian tribes as "distinct, independent political communities," *Worcester* v. *Georgia*, 6 Pet. 515, 559 (1832), qualified to exercise many of the powers and prerogatives of self-government, see *United States* v. *Wheeler*, 435 U. S. 313, 322–323 (1978). We have frequently noted, however, that the "sovereignty that the Indian tribes retain is of a unique and limited character." *Id.*, at 323. It centers on the land held by the tribe and on tribal members within the reservation. ***

As part of their residual sovereignty, tribes retain power to legislate and to tax activities on the reservation, including certain activities by nonmembers, to determine tribal membership, and to regulate domestic relations among members. They may also exclude outsiders from entering tribal land. But tribes do not, as a general matter, possess authority over non-Indians who come within their borders.*** As we explained in *Oliphant* v. *Suquamish Tribe*, 435 U. S. 191 (1978), the tribes have, by virtue of their incorporation into the American republic, lost "the right of governing ... person[s] within their limits except themselves." *Id.*, at 209.

This general rule restricts tribal authority over nonmember activities taking place on the reservation, and is particularly strong when the nonmember's activity occurs on land owned in fee simple by non-Indians—what we have called "non-Indian fee land." Thanks to the Indian General Allotment Act of 1887, 24 Stat. 388, as amended, 25 U. S. C. §331 *et seq.*, there are millions of acres of non-Indian fee land located within the contiguous borders of Indian tribes. *** [T]he effect of the Act was to convert millions of acres of formerly tribal land into fee simple parcels, "fully alienable," *id.*, at 264, and "free of all charge or encumbrance whatsoever," 25 U. S. C. §348.

Our cases have made clear that once tribal land is converted into fee simple, the tribe loses plenary jurisdiction over it.*** Among the powers lost is the authority to prevent the land's sale,—not surprisingly, as "free alienability" by the holder is a core attribute of the fee simple. Moreover, when the tribe or tribal members convey a parcel of fee land "*to non-Indians*, [the tribe] loses any former right of absolute and exclusive use and occupation of the conveyed lands." *South Dakota* v. *Bourland*, 508 U. S. 679, 689 (1993) (emphasis added). This necessarily entails "the loss of regulatory jurisdiction over the use of the land by others." *Ibid.****

We have recognized two exceptions to this principle, circumstances in which tribes may exercise "civil jurisdiction over non-Indians on their reservations, even on non-Indian fee lands." *Montana*, 450 U. S., at 565. First, "[a] tribe may regulate, through taxation, licensing, or other means, the activities of nonmembers who enter consensual relationships with the tribe or its members, through commercial dealing, contracts, leases, or other arrangements." *Ibid.* Second, a tribe may exercise "civil authority over the conduct of non-Indians on fee lands within the reservation when that conduct threatens or has some direct effect on the political integrity, the economic security, or the health or welfare of the tribe." *Id.*, at 566. These rules have become known as the *Montana* exceptions, after the case that elaborated them. By their terms, the exceptions concern regulation of "the *activities* of nonmembers" or "the *conduct* of non-Indians on fee land."

Given *Montana*'s " 'general proposition that the inherent sovereign powers of an Indian tribe do not extend to the activities of nonmembers of the tribe,' " efforts by a tribe to regulate nonmembers, especially on non-Indian fee land, are "presumptively invalid." The burden rests on the tribe to establish one of the exceptions to *Montana*'s general rule that would allow an extension of tribal authority to regulate nonmembers on non-Indian fee land. These exceptions are "limited" ones, and cannot be construed in a manner that would "swallow the rule," or "severely shrink" it, *Strate*, 520 U. S., at 458. ***

B

According to our precedents, "a tribe's adjudicative jurisdiction does not exceed its legislative jurisdiction." *Id.*, at 453. We reaffirm that principle today and hold that the Tribal Court lacks jurisdiction to hear the Longs' discrimination claim because the Tribe lacks the civil authority to regulate the Bank's sale of its fee land.

The Longs' discrimination claim challenges a non-Indian's sale of non-Indian fee land. Despite the Longs' attempt to recharacterize their claim as turning on the Bank's alleged "failure to pay to respondents loans promised for cattle-raising on tribal trust land," in fact the Longs brought their discrimination claim "seeking to have the land sales set aside on the ground that the sale to nonmembers 'on terms more favorable' than the bank had extended to the Longs" violated tribal tort law, 491 F.3d, at 882. That discrimination claim thus concerned the sale of a 2,230-acre fee parcel that the Bank had acquired from the estate of a non-Indian.

The status of the land is relevant "insofar as it bears on the application of ... *Montana*'s exceptions to [this] case." *Hicks*, 533 U. S., at 376 (Souter, J., concurring). The acres at issue here were alienated from the Cheyenne River Sioux's tribal trust and converted into fee simple parcels as part of the Act of

May 27, 1908, 35 Stat. 312, commonly called the 1908 Allotment Act.*** The 1908 Act released particular Indian owners from these restrictions ahead of schedule, vesting in them full fee ownership. In 1934, Congress passed the Indian Reorganization Act, 48 Stat. 984, which "pu[t] an end to further allotment of reservation land," but did not "return allotted land to pre-General Allotment status, leaving it fully alienable by the allottees, their heirs, and assigns." *County of Yakima*, 502 U. S., at 264.

The tribal tort law the Longs are attempting to enforce, however, operates as a restraint on alienation. *** It regulates the substantive terms on which the Bank is able to offer its fee land for sale. ***

Montana does not permit Indian tribes to regulate the sale of non-Indian fee land. *Montana* and its progeny permit tribal regulation of nonmember *conduct* inside the reservation that implicates the tribe's sovereign interests. *Montana* expressly limits its first exception to the "activities of nonmembers," 450 U. S., at 565, allowing these to be regulated to the extent necessary "to protect tribal self-government [and] to control internal relations," *id.*, at 564. ***

Tellingly, with only "one minor exception, we have never upheld under *Montana* the extension of tribal civil authority over nonmembers *on non-Indian land*." *Hicks, supra,* at 360 (emphasis added). The exception is *Brendale* v. *Confederated Tribes and Bands of Yakima Nation*, 492 U. S. 408, and even it fits the general rubric noted above: In that case, we permitted a tribe to restrain particular *uses* of non-Indian fee land through zoning regulations.***

But again, whether or not we have permitted regulation of nonmember activity on non-Indian fee land in a given case, in no case have we found that *Montana* authorized a tribe to regulate the sale of such land. Rather, our *Montana* cases have always concerned nonmember conduct on the land.

The distinction between sale of the land and conduct on it is well-established in our precedent, *** and entirely logical given the limited nature of tribal sovereignty and the liberty interests of nonmembers. By virtue of their incorporation into the United States, the tribe's sovereign interests are now confined to managing tribal land, see *Worcester*, 6 Pet., at 561 (persons are allowed to enter Indian land only "with the assent of the [tribal members] themselves"), "protect[ing] tribal self-government," and "control[ling] internal relations," see *Montana, supra*, at 564. The logic of *Montana* is that certain activities on non-Indian fee land (say, a business enterprise employing tribal members) or certain uses (say, commercial development) may intrude on the internal relations of the tribe or threaten tribal self-rule. To the extent they do, such activities or land uses may be regulated. Put another way, certain forms of nonmember behavior, even on non-Indian fee land, may sufficiently affect the tribe as to justify tribal oversight. While tribes generally have no interest in regulating the conduct of nonmembers, then, they may regulate nonmember behavior that implicates tribal governance and internal relations.

The regulations we have approved under *Montana* all flow directly from these limited sovereign interests. The tribe's "traditional and undisputed power to exclude persons" from tribal land, *Duro*, 495 U. S., at 696, for example, gives it the power to set conditions on entry to that land via licensing requirements and hunting regulations. Much taxation can be justified on a similar basis.***

***By definition, fee land owned by nonmembers has already been removed from the tribe's immediate control. See *Strate*, 520 U. S., at 456 (tribes lack power to "assert [over non-Indian fee land] a landowner's right to occupy and exclude"). It has already been alienated from the tribal trust. The tribe cannot justify regulation of such land's sale by reference to its power to superintend tribal land, then, because non-Indian fee parcels have ceased to *be* tribal land.

Nor can regulation of fee land sales be justified by the tribe's interests in protecting internal relations and self-government. Any direct harm to its political integrity that the tribe sustains as a result of fee land sale is sustained at the point the land passes from Indian to non-Indian hands. It is at that point the tribe and its members lose the ability to use the land for their purposes. Once the land has been sold in fee simple to non-Indians and passed beyond the tribe's immediate control, the mere resale of that land works no additional intrusion on tribal relations or self-government. Resale, by itself, causes no additional damage.

This is not to suggest that the sale of the land will have no impact on the tribe. The *uses* to which the land is put may very well change from owner to owner, and those uses may well affect the tribe and its members. As our cases bear out, the tribe may quite legitimately seek to protect its members from noxious uses that threaten tribal welfare or security, or from nonmember conduct on the land that does the same. But the key point is that any threat to the tribe's sovereign interests flows from changed uses or nonmember activities, rather than from the mere fact of resale. The tribe is able fully to vindicate its sovereign interests in protecting its members and preserving tribal self-government by regulating nonmember *activity* on the land, within the limits set forth in our cases. The tribe has no independent interest in restraining alienation of the land itself, and thus, no authority to do so.

***

Montana provides that, in certain circumstances, tribes may exercise authority over the conduct of nonmembers, even if that conduct takes place on non-Indian fee land. But conduct taking place on the land and the sale of the land are two very different things. The Cheyenne River Sioux Tribe lost the authority to restrain the sale of fee simple parcels inside their borders when the land was sold as part of the 1908 Allotment Act. Nothing in *Montana* gives it back.

C

Neither the District Court nor the Court of Appeals relied for its decision on the second *Montana* exception. *** The second *Montana* exception stems from the same sovereign interests that give rise to the first, interests that do not reach to regulating the sale of non-Indian fee land.

The second exception authorizes the tribe to exercise civil jurisdiction when non-Indians' "conduct" menaces the "political integrity, the economic security, or the health or welfare of the tribe." *Montana*, 450 U. S., at 566. The conduct must do more than injure the tribe, it must "imperil the subsistence" of the tribal community. *Ibid.****

*** The land in question here has been owned by a non-Indian party for at least 50 years, during which time the project of tribal self-government has proceeded without interruption. The land's resale to another non-Indian hardly "imperil[s] the subsistence or welfare of the tribe." *Montana, supra*, at 566. Accordingly, we hold the second *Montana* exception inapplicable in this case. ***

The judgment of the Court of Appeals for the Eighth Circuit is reversed.

JUSTICE GINSBURG, with whom **JUSTICE STEVENS**, **JUSTICE SOUTER**, and **JUSTICE BREYER** join, concurring in part, concurring in the judgment in part, and dissenting in part.

I dissent from the Court's decision to the extent that it overturns the Tribal Court's principal judgment awarding the Longs damages in the amount of $750,000 plus interest. That judgment did not disturb the Bank's sale of fee land to non-Indians. It simply responded to the claim that the Bank, in its on-reservation commercial dealings with the Longs, treated them disadvantageously because of their tribal affiliation and racial identity. A claim of that genre, I would hold, is one the Tribal Court is competent to adjudicate.***

As the basis for their discrimination claim, the Longs essentially asserted that the Bank offered them terms and conditions on land-financing transactions less favorable than the terms and conditions offered to non-Indians. Although the Tribal Court could not reinstate the Longs as owners of the ranch lands that had been in their family for decades, that court could hold the Bank answerable in damages, the law's traditional remedy for the tortious injury the Longs experienced.

I

In the pathmarking case, *Montana* v. *United States,* this Court restated that, absent a treaty or statute, Indian tribes generally lack authority to regulate the activities of nonmembers. While stating the general rule, *Montana* also identified two exceptions.*** These two exceptions, *Montana* explained, recognize that "Indian tribes retain inherent sovereign power to exercise some forms of civil jurisdiction over non-Indians on their reservations, *even on non-Indian fee lands*." *Id.*, at 565 (emphasis added).

Montana specifically addressed the regulatory jurisdiction of tribes. *See id.,* at 557. This Court has since clarified that when a tribe has authority to regulate the activity of nonmembers, tribal courts presumably have adjudicatory authority over disputes arising out of that activity. In my view, this is a clear case for application of *Montana's* first or "consensual relationships" exception.

***

This case, it bears emphasis, involves no unwitting outsider forced to litigate under unfamiliar rules and procedures in tribal court. Hardly a stranger to the tribal court system, the Bank regularly filed suit in that forum. The Bank enlisted tribal-court aid to serve notice to quit on the Longs in connection with state-court eviction proceedings. The Bank later filed a counterclaim for eviction and motion for summary judgment in the case the Longs commenced in the Tribal Court. In its summary judgment motion, the Bank stated, without qualification, that the Tribal Court "ha[d] jurisdiction over the subject matter of this action." Had the Bank wanted to avoid responding in tribal court or the application of tribal law, the means were readily at hand: The Bank could have included forum selection, choice-of-law, or arbitration clauses in its agreements with the Longs, which the Bank drafted.

II.

Resolving this case on a ground neither argued nor addressed below, the Court holds that a tribe may not impose any regulation—not even a nondiscrimination requirement—on a bank's dealings with tribal members regarding on-reservation fee lands. I do not read *Montana* or any other case so to instruct, and find the Court's position perplexing.

***

III.

As earlier observed, I agree that the Tribal Court had no authority to grant the Longs an option to purchase the 960-acre parcel the Bank had contracted to sell to individuals unaffiliated with the Tribe.*** Although the Tribal Court overstepped in its supplemental judgment ordering the Bank to give the Longs an option to purchase land third parties had contracted to buy, it scarcely follows that the Tribal Court lacked jurisdiction to adjudicate the Longs' discrimination claim, and to order in its principal judgment, monetary relief.

*** The Federal Government and every State, county, and municipality can make nondiscrimination the law governing contracts generally, and real property transactions in particular. *See, e.g.,* 42 U. S. C. §§1981, 1982. Why should the Tribe lack comparable authority to shield its members against discrimination by those engaging in on-reservation commercial relationships—including land-secured lending—with them?

A.

***In their complaint, the Longs alleged that the Bank allowed the non-Indians "ten years to pay for the land, but the bank would not permit [the] Longs even 60 days to pay for their land," and that "[s]uch unfair discrimination by the bank prevented the Longs and the [Long] Company from buying back their land from the bank." Although the allegations about the Bank's contracts to sell to nonmembers were central to the Longs' lawsuit, those transactions with third parties were not the wrong about which the Longs complained. Rather, as the tribal trial court observed, the contracts with nonmembers simply supplied "*evidence* that the Bank denied the Longs the privilege of contracting for a deed because of their status as tribal members."

***

B.

The Longs requested a remedy the Tribal Court did not have authority to grant—namely, an option to repurchase land the Bank had already contracted to sell to nonmember third parties. That limitation, however, does not affect the court's jurisdiction to hear the Longs' discrimination claim and to award damages on that claim. ***

***

For the reasons stated, I would leave undisturbed the Tribal Court's initial judgment awarding the Longs damages, prejudgment interest, and costs as redress for the Bank's breach of contract, bad faith, and discrimination. Accordingly, I would affirm in large part the judgment of the Court of Appeals.

NOTES AND QUESTIONS

1. *An easy case made hard?* The Eighth Circuit and the four dissenting Justices viewed this case as clearly within the tribal court's jurisdiction. The bank's longstanding relationship with the Longs, its own resort to the tribal court, and its power, had it exercised it, to include a forum selection clause to avoid tribal court, made it an easy case for *Montana*'s consensual relationship exception. Some think the majority recast the case as one solely involving the sale of fee land from one non-Indian to another non-Indian in order to void the tribal victory. What do you think? Is there a less cynical explanation, or not? After re-casting the case as one about ownership of non-Indian feel land, is the *Plains Commerce* majority correct in concluding that the allotment statutes require tribes to lose all regulatory authority over ownership of fee land within their boundaries? Do the allotment statutes say this specifically? If not, what interpretive approach is the majority relying on to reach that conclusion?

2. *What's left of civil jurisdiction over cases involving nonmembers?* Despite the trend in the Supreme Court, tribal courts continue to hear numerous cases involving nonmembers. Recall that under *Williams v. Lee*, tribal courts have *exclusive* jurisdiction over cases where members are defendants that arise on reservations. Similarly, under *Michigan v. Bay Mills Indian Community*, 134 S. Ct. 2024 (2014) and its predecessors, tribal courts are the exclusive fora for suits against tribes themselves, absent a tribal or federal waiver of sovereign immunity. In addition, because tribes and their members are increasingly entering into business relationships with nonmembers, tribal courts will presumably have jurisdiction under *Montana*'s consensual relationship prong over suits against nonmembers arising from those relationships. Thus, although the Navajo Nation did not have taxing jurisdiction over hotel guests at the Atkinson Trading Post, its courts should have such jurisdiction over employment actions brought by tribal member employees against Atkinson. As Professor Krakoff has observed:

> [W]hat appears to be a relentless march toward elimination of all forms of tribal authority over nonmembers in fact has left tribes and reviewing federal courts room to approve tribal civil jurisdiction in certain well-defined contexts. Those contexts include (1) claims arising directly from a nonmember's consensual relationship with the tribe or tribal members, and (2) claims involving nonmember conduct on tribal lands that either harms the land itself or challenges the tribe's ability to provide for the peace and security of tribal members.

Sarah Krakoff, *Tribal Civil Judicial Jurisdiction Over Nonmembers: A Practical Guide for Judges*, 81 Colo. L. Rev. 1187, 1191 (2010).

For recent cases approving tribal court jurisdiction or exhaustion of tribal remedies, see *Attorney's Process & Investigation Serv. v. Sac & Fox Tribe*, 609 F.3d 927 (8th Cir. 2010) (upholding jurisdiction over non-Indian contractor that raided governmental offices and remanding regarding jurisdiction over funds provided to contractor); *Smith v. Confederated Salish & Kootenai College*, 434 F.3d 1127 (9th Cir. 2006) (*en banc*) (holding that tribal court had jurisdiction over counterclaims brought by nonmember plaintiff against tribal defendant arising out of an accident on a U.S. highway within reservation); *Elliott v. White Mountain Apache Tribal Court*, 566 F.3d 842 (9th Cir. 2009) (holding tribal court had colorable claim of jurisdiction over action against nonmember for allegedly trespassing, setting a fire, and destroying natural resources on tribal lands); *Ford Motor Co. v. Todecheene*, 488 F.3d 1215 (9th Cir. 2007) (vacating and remanding for tribal exhaustion products liability action against off-reservation car manufacturer for accident on reservation).[6] For cases concluding that the tribal court lacked jurisdiction, see *Phillip Morris USA, Inc. v. King Mountain Tobacco, Inc.*, 569 F.3d 932 (9th Cir. 2009) (Yakama Tribal Court does not have colorable jurisdiction to decide whether off-reservation cigarette sales by tribal member defendants infringe the Marlboro trademark); *MacArthur v. San Juan County*, 497 F.3d 1057 (10th Cir. 2007) (holding that tribe lacked jurisdiction over employment relationship between tribal member and employer who was a political subdivision of the state); *McDonald v. Means*, 309 F.3d 530 (9th Cir. 2002) (holding that tribal court had jurisdiction over tribal member's tort claim against nonmember for accident occurring on tribal road and refusing to apply the *Montana* analysis).

3. *The Role of Land Status.* In terms of the question about land status left open by *Strate*, *Atkinson*, and *Hicks*, the Ninth Circuit has held that tribes retain presumptive jurisdiction over non-Indians for actions occurring on and affecting tribal lands. *See Water Wheel Camp Recreational Area, Inc. v. LaRance*, 642 F.3d 802, 814 (9th Cir. 2011) (*per curiam*). The court upheld tribal court jurisdiction over an eviction action brought against a non-Indian lessee of the tribe's land. Water Wheel had a long-term lease with the tribe, but refused to pay rent after renegotiations failed. The tribe brought an eviction action in tribal court and Water Wheel contested jurisdiction under the *Montana* line of cases. The court reasoned that *Montana* did not apply under these circumstances:

> In this instance, where the non-Indian activity in question occurred on tribal land, the activity interfered directly with the tribe's inherent powers to exclude and manage its own lands, and there are no competing state interests at play, the tribe's status as landowner is enough to support regulatory jurisdiction without considering *Montana*. Finding otherwise would contradict Supreme Court precedent establishing that land ownership may sometimes be dispositive and would improperly limit tribal sovereignty without clear direction from Congress.

The Supreme Court declined to review the case. Do you agree with the Ninth Circuit's approach?

4. Knighton v. Cedarville Rancheria *case*. The Ninth Circuit expanded on the *Water Wheel* holding in a recent case involving alleged fraudulent conduct by a non-Indian tribal employee.

> Among the tribe's many claims are allegations that Knighton invested the Tribe's money without appropriate authority, concealed investment documents and audit reports from the Tribe, and attempted to enter financial agreements without the appropriate authorization or waiver of tribal

6. On remand in *Todacheene* the Navajo Supreme Court held that it had jurisdiction over the claim on the ground that the Montana presumption did not apply, and if it did, both exceptions were satisfied, *Ford Motor Co. v. Kayenta Dist. Ct.*, 7 American Tribal Law Rep. 652 (Navajo 2008).

> sovereign immunity. The Tribe also alleges that Knighton made unreasonably risky investments that led to investment losses in excess of $ 1.2 million, excess transaction fees, and state and federal tax exposure, and that she breached her fiduciary duty and deceived the Tribe, causing it to pay $ 300,000, $ 150,000 above market value, for [a] building purchase. Finally, the Tribe alleges that when she resigned her employment with the Tribe, Knighton took all files, including files belonging to the Tribe, room furnishings, and a computer, representing to the Tribe that the property removed belonged to [another entity]... We conclude that this conduct threatened the Tribe's very subsistence ... .

Knighton v. Cedarville Rancheria of Northern Paiute Indians, 922 F.3d 892, 905 (9th Cir. 2019).

The court held that the tribe had authority to regulate the nonmember employee's conduct pursuant to its inherent power to exclude nonmembers from tribal lands. Alternatively, the court ruled that the tribe had regulatory authority over the nonmember employee's conduct under both *Montana* exceptions. *Knighton v. Cedarville Rancheria*, 922 F.3d at 895.

5. *The Meaning of Threats to Tribal Self-Rule after* Plains Commerce. The Fifth Circuit, which hears very few Indian law cases, upheld tribal court jurisdiction in a civil case involving allegations of sexual abuse of a minor tribal member by an employee of a non-Indian corporation. *See Dolgencorp, Inc. v. Mississippi Band of Choctaw Indians*, 746 F.3d 167 (5th Cir. 2014). The employee worked at a Dollar General Store operated by Dolgen on tribal trust land, and the minor was participating in an internship program supervised by Dolgen's employee. The court held that the tribe had jurisdiction under *Montana*'s consensual relationship exception, declining to interpret *Plains Commerce* as requiring that the consensual relationship itself "threaten self-rule." *Id.* at 175.

> It is hard to imagine how a single employment relationship between a tribe member and a business could ever have such an impact. On the other hand, at a higher level of generality, the ability to regulate the working conditions (particularly as pertains to health and safety) of tribe members employed on reservation land is plainly central to the tribe's power of self-government. Nothing in *Plains Commerce* requires a focus on the highly specific rather than the general.

Id. Do you agree with the court's approach to the consensual relationship exception? Is there a "direct effects" argument to support tribal court jurisdiction as well?

The Supreme Court affirmed the Fifth Circuit decision on a 4-4 vote, with no opinion. *Dollar General Corp. v. Mississippi Choctaw Tribe*, 13-1496, 136 S. Ct. 2159 (2016).

E. Judicial Divestiture Meets Congressional Plenary Power: Criminal Jurisdiction Over Nonmember Indians

Section D traced the federal judicial divestiture of tribal civil authority over nonmembers in roughly chronological sequence. In this Section, we return to tribal criminal jurisdiction. The Court started the implicit divestiture ball rolling by deciding in *Oliphant* that tribes lack inherent jurisdiction to prosecute crimes by non-Indians in Indian country. In *Duro v. Reina*, the Court encountered whether the same rule applied to tribal prosecution of nonmember Indians (*e.g.*, if a Yankton Sioux commits a crime on the Jemez Pueblo reservation). Following the Court's rejection of this tribal authority, Congress responded by enacting legislation—the so-called "*Duro* fix"—that authorizes tribes to act in this manner. In the second case in this section, *United States v. Lara*, the Court confronted the questions of the legal effect and the constitutionality of this legislation.

DURO V. REINA

495 U.S. 676, 110 S. Ct. 2053, 109 L.Ed.2d 693 (1990)

JUSTICE KENNEDY delivered the opinion of the Court.

We address in this case whether an Indian tribe may assert criminal jurisdiction over a defendant who is an Indian but not a tribal member. We hold that the retained sovereignty of the tribe as a political and social organization to govern its own affairs does not include the authority to impose criminal sanctions against a citizen outside its own membership.

I.

The events giving rise to this jurisdictional dispute occurred on the Salt River Indian Reservation. *** The reservation is the home of the Salt River Pima–Maricopa Indian Community, a recognized Tribe with an enrolled membership. Petitioner in this case, Albert Duro, is an enrolled member of another Indian Tribe, the Torres–Martinez Band of Cahuilla Mission Indians. Petitioner is not eligible for membership in the Pima–Maricopa Tribe. As a nonmember, he is not entitled to vote in Pima–Maricopa elections, to hold tribal office, or to serve on tribal juries. ***.

*** Between March and June 1984, [Duro] resided on the Salt River Reservation with a Pima–Maricopa woman friend. He worked for the PiCopa Construction Company, which is owned by the Tribe.

On June 15, 1984, petitioner allegedly shot and killed a 14–year–old boy within the Salt River Reservation boundaries. The victim was a member of the Gila River Indian Tribe of Arizona, a separate Tribe that occupies a separate reservation. A complaint was filed in United States District Court charging petitioner with murder [under the Major Crimes Act] and aiding and abetting murder[.] Federal agents arrested petitioner in California, but the federal indictment was later dismissed without prejudice on the motion of the United States Attorney.

Petitioner then was placed in the custody of Pima–Maricopa officers, and he was taken to stand trial in the Pima–Maricopa Indian Community Court. The tribal court's powers are regulated by [ICRA], which at that time limited tribal criminal penalties to six months' imprisonment and a $500 fine. The tribal criminal code is therefore confined to misdemeanors. Petitioner was charged with the illegal firing of a weapon on the reservation. After the tribal court denied petitioner's motion to dismiss the prosecution for lack of jurisdiction, he filed a petition for a writ of *habeas corpus* in the United States District Court for the District of Arizona, naming the tribal chief judge and police chief as respondents. [The district court granted the writ, but the Ninth Circuit reversed.]

We think the rationale of our decisions in *Oliphant* and *Wheeler,* as well as subsequent cases, compels the conclusion that Indian tribes lack jurisdiction over persons who are not tribe members. ***

[T]he double jeopardy question in *Wheeler* demanded an examination of the nature of retained tribal power. *** Our finding that the tribal prosecution of the defendant in *Wheeler* was by a sovereign other than the United States rested on the premise that the prosecution was a part of the tribe's *internal* self-governance. Had the prosecution been a manifestation of external relations between the Tribe and outsiders, such power would have been inconsistent with the Tribe's dependent status, and could only have come to the Tribe by delegation from Congress, subject to the constraints of the Constitution. ***

It is true that our decisions recognize broader retained tribal powers outside the criminal context. *** In the area of criminal enforcement, however, tribal power does not extend beyond internal relations among members. Petitioner is not a member of the Pima–Maricopa Tribe, and is not now eligible to become one. Neither he nor other members of his Tribe may vote, hold office, or serve on a jury under Pima–Maricopa authority. For purposes of criminal jurisdiction, petitioner's relations with this Tribe are the same as the non-Indian's in *Oliphant.* We hold that the Tribe's powers over him are subject to the same limitations.

III.

*** The historical record in this case is somewhat less illuminating than in *Oliphant,* but tends to support the conclusion we reach. ***

Respondents rely for their historical argument upon evidence that definitions of "Indian" in federal statutes and programs apply to all Indians without respect to membership in a particular tribe. For example, the federal jurisdictional statutes applicable to Indian country use the general term "Indian." [*e.g.*, 18 U.S.C. §§ 1151 (Indian Country); 1152 (Indian Country Crimes Act); 1153 (Major Crimes Act).] Respondents also emphasize that courts of Indian offenses, which were established by regulation in 1883 by the Department of the Interior and continue to operate today on reservations without tribal courts, possess jurisdiction over *all* Indian offenders within the relevant reservation. *See* 25 C.F.R. § 11.2(a) (1989).

This evidence does not stand for the proposition respondents advance. Congressional and administrative provisions such as those cited above reflect the Government's treatment of Indians as a single large class with respect to *federal* jurisdiction and programs. Those references are not dispositive of a question of *tribal* power to treat Indians by the same broad classification. ***

Whatever might be said of the historical record, we must view it in light of petitioner's status as a citizen of the United States. *** That Indians are citizens does not alter the Federal Government's broad authority to legislate with respect to enrolled Indians as a class, whether to impose burdens or benefits. *See Mancari.* In the absence of such legislation, however, Indians like other citizens are embraced within our Nation's "great solicitude that its citizens be protected *** from unwarranted intrusions on their personal liberty." *Oliphant.*

Criminal trial and punishment is so serious an intrusion on personal liberty that its exercise over non-Indian citizens was a power necessarily surrendered by the tribes in their submission to the overriding sovereignty of the United States. [*Oliphant.*] We hesitate to adopt a view of tribal sovereignty that would single out another group of citizens, nonmember Indians, for trial by political bodies that do not include them. As full citizens, Indians share in the territorial and political sovereignty of the United States. The retained sovereignty of the tribe is but a recognition of certain additional authority the tribes maintain over Indians who consent to be tribal members. Indians like all other citizens share allegiance to the overriding sovereign, the United States. A tribe's additional authority comes from the consent of its members, and so in the criminal sphere membership marks the bounds of tribal authority.

The special nature of the tribunals at issue makes a focus on consent and the protections of citizenship most appropriate. While modern tribal courts include many familiar features of the judicial process, they are influenced by the unique customs, languages, and usages of the tribes they serve. Tribal courts are often "subordinate to the political branches of tribal governments," and their legal methods may depend on "unspoken practices and norms." [1982 Cohen Handbook.] It is significant that the Bill of Rights does not apply to Indian tribal governments. *Talton.* The Indian Civil Rights Act of 1968 provides some statutory guarantees of fair procedure, but these guarantees are not equivalent to their constitutional counterparts. There is, for example, no right under the Act to appointed counsel for those unable to afford a lawyer. ***

Tribal authority over members, who are also citizens, is not subject to these objections. Retained criminal jurisdiction over members is accepted by our precedents and justified by the voluntary character of tribal membership and the concomitant right of participation in a tribal government, the authority of which rests on consent. ***

With respect to such internal laws and usages, the tribes are left with broad freedom not enjoyed by any other governmental authority in this country. *See, e.g., Martinez* (noting that Bill of Rights is inapplicable to tribes, and holding that the Indian Civil Rights Act of 1968 does not give rise to a federal cause of action against the tribe for violations of its provisions). This is all the more reason to reject an extension of tribal authority over those who have not given the consent of the governed that provides a fundamental basis for power within our constitutional system. ***

V.

Respondents and *amici* contend that without tribal jurisdiction over minor offenses committed by nonmember Indians, no authority will have jurisdiction over such offenders. ***

State authorities may lack the power, resources, or inclination to deal with reservation crime. Arizona, for example, specifically disclaims jurisdiction over Indian country crimes. Ariz. Const., Art. 20, ¶ 4. And federal authority over minor crime, otherwise provided by the Indian Country Crimes Act, 18 U.S.C. § 1152, may be lacking altogether in the case of crime committed by a nonmember Indian against another Indian, since § 1152 states that general federal jurisdiction over Indian country crime "shall not extend to offenses committed by one Indian against the person or property of another Indian."

Our decision today does not imply endorsement of the theory of a jurisdictional void presented by respondents and the court below. States may, with the consent of the tribes, assist in maintaining order on the reservation by punishing minor crime. Congress has provided a mechanism by which the States now without jurisdiction in Indian country may assume criminal jurisdiction through Pub. L. 280. ***

If the present jurisdictional scheme proves insufficient to meet the practical needs of reservation law enforcement, then the proper body to address the problem is Congress, which has the ultimate authority over Indian affairs. ***

[**JUSTICE BRENNAN**, joined by **JUSTICE MARSHALL**, dissented.]

NOTES AND QUESTIONS

1. *Analogies to* Oliphant? Recall that the Court's opinion in *Oliphant* made two basic points: the supposed shared assumptions of the federal branches were that tribes lacked criminal jurisdiction over non-Indians, and there would be serious civil rights concerns if tribes had criminal jurisdiction over persons who could not be tribal members and could not participate in tribal affairs (such as vote and serve on juries). Are nonmember Indians similarly situated to non-Indians in both these respects?

2. *Political process deficits.* As just mentioned, in both *Oliphant* and *Duro* the Court was concerned about unfairness. *Duro* goes to great lengths to say that tribal members are subject to tribal jurisdiction because they have given the consent of the governed to their tribes. But ordinarily, a court of general jurisdiction can hear criminal cases arising out of its territorial sovereignty regardless of whether the defendant is a resident or citizen of that jurisdiction. A French citizen who commits a crime in Oregon, for example, is certainly subject to the criminal jurisdiction of Oregon courts. Why treat tribal courts differently for criminal jurisdiction purposes?

3. *Revisiting "consent."* The Court has not had a stable, understandable conception of what it means to consent to tribal authority. How did *Montana* and its progeny understand consent? How does *Duro*? Given the flux in the Court's conceptions of consent, is it a viable argument that nonmember Indians can always back out of being subject to the criminal jurisdiction of another tribe by withdrawing membership from their own tribe? In other words, being a tribal member remains a consensual matter, not an immutable characteristic.

4. *The jurisdictional void.* The Court in *Duro* papered over a serious practical problem with its holding, which clearly differentiated the case from *Oliphant*. When a non-Indian allegedly commits a crime against an Indian in Indian country, there is federal criminal jurisdiction to handle the matter under the Indian Country Crimes Act. To be sure, the United

States Attorney may decline to prosecute, but at least there is the theoretical possibility of prosecuting such wrongdoers even in the absence of tribal jurisdiction. When a non-member Indian, such as Albert Duro, allegedly commits a crime against an Indian in Indian Country, the jurisdictional circumstances are different. If the offense is an enumerated crime in the Major Crimes Act, federal jurisdiction is present. But if the offense is not, there is no federal jurisdiction (recall that the Indian Country Crimes Act contains an "Indian versus Indian" exception). With tribal jurisdiction precluded by the holding in *Duro*, what other option is there? The Court helpfully suggests that tribes consent to the state opting into Public Law 280 jurisdiction. How likely is it that a tribe would see this as a good option? Indeed, how likely is it that the state would, either?

5. *Federal common law, Court/Congress relations, and the "Duro fix."* *Duro* is a federal common law decision—at least, it certainly does not seem to be based on the federal Constitution or federal statute or administrative regulation, but on judge-made, case-by-case law. Typically, when common law precedents lead to an arguably anomalous result, judges either modify or overrule them, or if for some reason that seems imprudent, suggest that the legislature should address the matter through statutory reform. At the end of the *Duro* opinion, Justice Kennedy suggests that Congress might want to revisit the matter. What sort of federal statutory revisions do you suppose Kennedy envisioned?

Tribes and their advocates reacted quickly to the decision. Within ten days, he National Congress of American Indians ("NCAI") had convened a meeting of tribal, Bureau of Indian Affairs, and congressional representatives to discuss the implications of the case and possible legislative responses. Over the summer, the legislation was re-shaped and Indian communities were mobilized behind the proposal. On November 5, 1990, just six months after the decision, Congress enacted the *Duro* Fix as part of a Defense Appropriations Bill. As Professor Berger describes,

> [A]dvocates from within the Indian community were not only the engine of the *Duro* fix but also fundamentally shaped its form. *** In its previous cases, including *Duro*, the Supreme Court had referred only to congressional "delegations" of jurisdiction to Indian tribes. The initial proposals for the *Duro* fix were that it too "delegate" power to the tribes. But when these proposals got to the American Indian Law Center ("AILC") in Albuquerque that summer, the proposal changed. *** [Sam] Deloria, Director of the AILC, expressed concern that truly delegated power would be subject to constitutional restrictions not normally applicable to tribal governments, and that perhaps Congress could instead correct the Court's understanding of tribal inherent jurisdiction. *** In the next month, Nell Jessup Newton, a professor of Constitutional and American Indian law, who was teaching in the AILC Pre–Law Summer Institute for native students entering law school, corresponded with Virginia Boylan of the Senate Committee on Indian Affairs to argue for the approach and propose the language that would ultimately become the *Duro* fix. *** The ultimate proposal that went to Congress made clear that the law "recognized and affirmed" the "inherent power of Indian tribes *** to exercise criminal jurisdiction over all Indians."

To placate Senator Slade Gorton, the law included a sunset provision that it would expire on September 30, 1991. When a bill was proposed to make the law permanent, the Utah Attorney General, on behalf of the Attorneys General from Utah, Montana, Nevada, North Dakota, South Dakota, and Washington, the Citizens Equal Rights Alliance and several western county attorneys, all opposed the law. But Indian country had mobilized non-Indian support as well.

The Conference of Western Governors, several western state legislatures, the Bureau of Indian Affairs, the U.S. Commission on Civil Rights, and the International Association of Chiefs of Police, and others all submitted statements of support. When opponents raised concerns about denying constitutional rights to non-member Indians, numerous representatives from Indian country testified to their preference to tribal rather than state or federal jurisdiction, as well as to the kind of political influence non-member Indians had in Indian communities. The NCAI also presented a survey of the high number of non-member Indians on reservations and their integration in tribal communities. "There could be no question," Professor Berger concludes, "that the people that actually knew what was good for the Indians agreed that the bill was in their interests." Bethany R. Berger, United States v. Lara *as a Story of Native Agency*, 40 Tulsa L. Rev. 5, 11–17 (2004).

The *Duro* Fix itself consists of only a handful of words amending the Indian Civil Rights Act. The new words are those underlined below:

§ 1301. Definitions

For purposes of this title, the term—

> *** (2) "powers of self-government" means and includes all governmental powers possessed by an Indian tribe, executive, legislative, and judicial, and all offices, bodies, and tribunals by and through which they are executed, including courts of Indian offenses; <u>and means the inherent power of Indian tribes, hereby recognized and affirmed, to exercise criminal jurisdiction over all Indians</u>;
>
> ***
>
> (4) "Indian" means any person who would be subject to the jurisdiction of the United States as an Indian under section 1153, title 18, United States Code, if that person were to commit an offense listed in that section in Indian country to which that section applies.

Separation of Powers, the Constitution, and the *Duro* Fix

United States v. Wheeler held that because tribal power to prosecute tribal members was a product of tribal sovereignty, the Double Jeopardy Clause did not prohibit a subsequent federal prosecution for the same offense. The intent of the *Duro* Fix language was to affirm that tribal power to charge nonmember Indians was also the product of inherent sovereignty. *See* Philip S. Deloria & Nell Jessup Newton, *The Criminal Jurisdiction of Tribal Courts over Non–Member Indians: An Examination of the Basic Framework of Inherent Tribal Sovereignty Before and After* Duro v. Reina, 38 Fed. B. News & J. 70 (Mar. 1991).

Lower courts struggled with the question of whether Congress had the power to do this. There were at least three possibilities: *Duro* was a federal common law decision based on the Court's interpretation of congressional intent, so Congress had complete discretion to express a different intent; *Duro* was a federal common law decision but Congress could only affirm tribal inherent power if the Court was wrong in interpreting history to find that tribes had lost that power; and finally that *Duro* was a constitutional decision, in which case Congress had no power to undermine the Supreme Court's decision.

Fractured decisions within the Eighth and Ninth Circuits adopted each of these positions. *See United States v. Weaselhead*, 36 F.Supp.2d 908 (D. Neb. 1997) (*Duro* was a common law decision and "if a judicial body errs in determining congressional intent, Congress can permissibly legislate a correction."), *rev'd by Weaselhead v. United States*, 156 F.3d 818, 824 (8th Cir. 1998). ("[A]scertainment of first principles regarding the position of Indian tribes within our constitutional structure of government is a matter ultimately entrusted to the Court and thus beyond the scope of Congress's authority to alter retroactively to legislative fiat."), *vacated by equally divided court, United States v. Weaselhead*, 165 F.3d 1209 (8th Cir. 1999) (*en banc*), *cert. denied*, 528 U.S. 829 (1999); *United States v. Enas*, 255 F.3d 662, 673–675 (9th Cir. 2001) (*en banc*) (*Duro* decision was based on federal common law rooted in an interpretation of history, and Congress had the power to correct the Court's interpretation of history to affirm inherent power); *United States v. Enas*, 255 F.3d at 279 & 279 n.4 (Pregerson J., concurring) (opining that whether a sovereign power is inherent does not depend on history; "there is nothing new about the idea that the federal government may authorize a new power that is "inherent" in another sovereign. ... although Congress may authorize the tribes to act, the tribes nonetheless act in their own sovereign capacity."), *cert. denied,* 534 U.S. 1115 (2002).

Finally, the Court granted certiorari in *United States v. Lara*. Billy Jo Lara was a prime example of the tribal need for jurisdiction over nonmembers. Although a member of the Turtle Mountain Band of Chippewa Indians, Lara was married to a Spirit Lake Sioux woman and lived on the Spirit Lake Reservation. Since 1999, Lara had been repeatedly prosecuted for domestic abuse, public intoxication, and resisting arrest. His wife had fled the reservation and sought safety in an out-of-state-shelter to escape him. After the federal government refused to prosecute him, the tribal government passed a resolution excluding him from the reservation on September 22, 2000. Lara violated the order, and on June 13, 2001, tribal and BIA police were called to address a complaint of public intoxication against him. During the arrest, Lara struck both officers, knocking one unconscious. Lara pled guilty in tribal court, and was sentenced to six months detention. The United States subsequently indicted Lara for striking a federal officer. The Eighth Circuit held *en banc* that the federal prosecution violated the Double Jeopardy Clause: "Once the federal sovereign divests a tribe of a particular power, it is no longer an inherent power and it may only be restored by delegation of Congress's power." *United States v. Lara*, 324 F.3d 635, 639 (8th Cir. 2003) (*en banc*). The Supreme Court granted certiorari, and reversed.

UNITED STATES V. LARA

541 U.S. 193, 124 S. Ct. 1628, 158 L.Ed.2d 420 (2004)

JUSTICE BREYER delivered the opinion of the Court.

This case concerns a congressional statute "recogniz[ing] and affirm[ing]" the "inherent" authority of a tribe to bring a criminal misdemeanor prosecution against an Indian who is not a member of that tribe—authority that this Court previously held a tribe did not possess. *Compare* 25 U.S.C. § 1301(2) *with Duro.* We must decide whether Congress has the constitutional power to relax restrictions that the political branches have, over time, placed on the exercise of a tribe's inherent legal authority. We conclude that Congress does possess this power.

I.

Respondent Billy Jo Lara is an enrolled member of the Turtle Mountain Band of Chippewa Indians in north-central North Dakota. He married a member of a different tribe, the Spirit Lake Tribe, and lived with his wife and children on the Spirit Lake Reservation, also located in North Dakota. After several incidents of serious misconduct, the Spirit Lake Tribe issued an order excluding him from the reservation. Lara ignored the order; federal officers stopped him; and he struck one of the arresting officers.

The Spirit Lake Tribe subsequently prosecuted Lara in the Spirit Lake Tribal Court for "violence to a policeman." Lara pleaded guilty and, in respect to that crime, served 90 days in jail.

After Lara's tribal conviction, the Federal Government charged Lara in the Federal District Court for the District of North Dakota with the federal crime of assaulting a federal officer. Key elements of this federal crime mirror elements of the tribal crime of "violence to a policeman." And this similarity between the two crimes would *ordinarily* have brought Lara within the protective reach of the Double Jeopardy Clause. U.S. Const., Amdt. 5. But the Government, responding to Lara's claim of double jeopardy, pointed out that the Double Jeopardy Clause does not bar successive prosecutions brought by *separate sovereigns*, and it argued that this "dual sovereignty" doctrine determined the outcome here. ***

[T]his Court has held that an Indian tribe acts as a separate sovereign when it prosecutes its *own members. United States v. Wheeler* (a tribe's "*sovereign* power to punish *tribal* offenders," while subject to congressional "defeasance," remains among those " 'inherent powers of a limited sovereignty which has never been extinguished' "). The Government recognized, of course, that Lara is not one of the Spirit Lake Tribe's *own* members; it also recognized that, in *Duro* this Court had held that a tribe no longer possessed *inherent or sovereign authority* to prosecute a "nonmember Indian." But it pointed out that, soon after this Court decided *Duro,* Congress enacted new legislation specifically authorizing a tribe to prosecute Indian members of a different tribe. That new statute, in permitting a tribe to bring certain tribal prosecutions against nonmember Indians, does not purport to delegate the Federal Government's own *federal* power. Rather, it enlarges the *tribes'* own " 'powers of self-government' " to include "the inherent power of Indian tribes, hereby recognized and affirmed, to exercise criminal jurisdiction over *all* Indians," including nonmembers.

In the Government's view, given this statute, the Tribe, in prosecuting Lara, had exercised its own inherent *tribal* authority, not delegated *federal* authority; hence the "dual sovereignty" doctrine applies, and since the two prosecutions were brought by two different sovereigns, the second, federal, prosecution does not violate the Double Jeopardy Clause. [A federal magistrate agreed with this argument, an Eighth Circuit panel affirmed, but the Eighth Circuit *en banc* reversed by a vote of 7 to 4, concluding that the tribal prosecution was an exercise of federal rather than tribal authority and hence double jeopardy barred the later federal prosecution.]

II.

We assume, as do the parties, that Lara's double jeopardy claim turns on the answer to the "dual sovereignty" question. What is "the source of [the] power to punish" nonmember Indian offenders, "inherent *tribal* sovereignty" or delegated *federal* authority?

We also believe that Congress intended the former answer. The statute says that it "recognize[s] and affirm[s]" in each tribe the "*inherent*" *tribal* power (not delegated federal power) to prosecute nonmember Indians for misdemeanors. And the statute's legislative history confirms that such was Congress' intent. *See, e.g.*, H.R. Conf. Rep. No. 102–261, pp 3–4 (1991) ("The Committee of the Conference notes that *** this legislation is not a delegation of this jurisdiction but a clarification of the status of tribes as domestic dependent nations"); accord, H.R. Rep. No. 102–61, p 7 (1991); *see also* S. Rep. No. 102–168, p 4 (1991) ***; 137 Cong. Rec. 9446, 10712–10714 (1991) (statement of Rep. Miller, House manager of the bill) (the statute "is not a delegation of authority but an affirmation that tribes retain all rights not expressly taken away" and the bill "recognizes an inherent tribal right which always existed"). ***

Thus the statute seeks to adjust the tribes' status. It relaxes the restrictions, recognized in *Duro*, that the political branches had imposed on the tribes' exercise of inherent prosecutorial power. The question before us is whether the Constitution authorizes Congress to do so. Several considerations lead us to the conclusion that Congress does possess the constitutional power to lift the restrictions on the tribes' criminal jurisdiction over nonmember Indians as the statute seeks to do.

First, the Constitution grants Congress broad general powers to legislate in respect to Indian tribes, powers that we have consistently described as "plenary and exclusive." This Court has traditionally identified the Indian Commerce Clause and the Treaty Clause as sources of that power. *E.g. Morton v. Mancari*, 417 U.S. 535, 552 (1974). The "central function of the Indian Commerce Clause," we have said, "is to provide Congress with plenary power to legislate in the field of Indian affairs." *Cotton Petroleum Corp. v New Mexico*, 490 U.S. 163, 192 (1989).

*** Moreover, "at least during the first century of America's national existence *** Indian affairs were more an aspect of military and foreign policy than a subject of domestic or municipal law." [1982 Cohen Handbook of Federal Indian Law.] Insofar as that is so, Congress' legislative authority would rest in part, not upon "affirmative grants of the Constitution," but upon the Constitution's adoption of preconstitutional powers necessarily inherent in any Federal

Government, namely powers that this Court has described as "necessary concomitants of nationality." *United States v. Curtiss–Wright Export Corp.*, 299 U.S. 304, 315–322 (1936); *** *Worcester* ("The treaties and laws of the United States contemplate *** that all intercourse with [Indians] shall be carried on exclusively by the government of the union").

Second, Congress, with this Court's approval, has interpreted the Constitution's "plenary" grants of power as authorizing it to enact legislation that both restricts and, in turn, relaxes those restrictions on tribal sovereign authority. From the Nation's beginning Congress' need for such legislative power would have seemed obvious. After all, the Government's Indian policies, applicable to numerous tribes with diverse cultures, affecting billions of acres of land, of necessity would fluctuate dramatically as the needs of the Nation and those of the tribes changed over time. And Congress has in fact authorized at different times very different Indian policies (some with beneficial results but many with tragic consequences). ***

Such major policy changes inevitably involve major changes in the metes and bounds of tribal sovereignty. The 1871 statute, for example, changed the status of an Indian tribe from a "powe[r] *** capable of making treaties" to a "power with whom the United States may [not] contract by treaty." *Compare Worcester* with 25 U.S.C. § 71.

One can readily find examples in congressional decisions to recognize, or to terminate, the existence of individual tribes. Indeed, Congress has restored previously extinguished tribal status—by re-recognizing a Tribe whose tribal existence it previously had terminated. 25 U.S.C. §§ 903–903f (restoring the Menominee Tribe); *cf. United States v. Long*, 324 F.3d 475 (CA7) (upholding against double jeopardy challenge successive prosecutions by the restored Menominee Tribe and the Federal Government), *cert. denied*, 540 U.S. ___ (2003). Congress has advanced policies of integration by conferring United States citizenship upon all Indians. 8 U.S.C. § 1401(b). Congress has also granted tribes greater autonomy in their inherent law enforcement authority (in respect to tribal members) by increasing the maximum criminal penalties tribal courts may impose. § 4217, 100 Stat 3207–146, codified at 25 U.S.C. § 1302(7) (raising the maximum from "a term of six months and a fine of $500" to "a term of one year and a fine of $5,000").

Third, Congress' statutory goal—to modify the degree of autonomy enjoyed by a dependent sovereign that is not a State—is not an unusual legislative objective. The political branches, drawing upon analogous constitutional authority, have made adjustments to the autonomous status of other such dependent entities—sometimes making far more radical adjustments than those at issue here. *See, e.g.*, Hawaii—*Hawaii v. Mankichi*, 190 U.S. 197, 209–210 (1903) (describing annexation of Hawaii by joint resolution of Congress and the maintenance of a "Republic of Hawaii" until formal incorporation by Congress); Northern Mariana Islands—note following 48 U.S.C. § 1801 ("in accordance with the [United Nations] trusteeship agreement *** [establishing] a self-governing commonwealth *** in political union with and under the sovereignty of the United States"); the Philippines—22 U.S.C. § 1394 (congressional authorization for the president to "withdraw and surrender all right of *** sovereignty" and to "recognize the independence of the Philippine Islands as a separate and self-governing nation"); Presidential Proclamation No. 2695, 60 Stat 1352 (so proclaiming); Puerto Rico—Act of July 3, 1950, 64 Stat 319 ("[T]his

Act is now adopted in the nature of a compact so that people of Puerto Rico may organize a government pursuant to a constitution of their own adoption") ***.

Fourth, Lara points to no explicit language in the Constitution suggesting a limitation on Congress' institutional authority to relax restrictions on tribal sovereignty previously imposed by the political branches. *But cf.* Part III, *infra.*

Fifth, the change at issue here is a limited one. It concerns a power similar in some respects to the power to prosecute a tribe's own members—a power that this Court has called "inherent." *Wheeler*. In large part it concerns a tribe's authority to control events that occur upon the tribe's own land. *See Mazurie* ("Indian tribes are unique aggregations possessing attributes of sovereignty over both their members and *their territory*" (emphasis added)); *see also, e.g.*, S. Rep. No. 102–168, at 21. And the tribes' possession of this additional criminal jurisdiction is consistent with our traditional understanding of the tribes' status as "domestic dependent nations." Consequently, we are not now faced with a question dealing with potential constitutional limits on congressional efforts to legislate far more radical changes in tribal status. In particular, this case involves no interference with the power or authority of any State. Nor do we now consider the question whether the Constitution's Due Process or Equal Protection Clauses prohibit tribes from prosecuting a nonmember citizen of the United States. *See* Part III, *infra.*

Sixth, our conclusion that Congress has the power to relax the restrictions imposed by the political branches on the tribes' inherent prosecutorial authority is consistent with our earlier cases. True, the Court held in those cases that the power to prosecute nonmembers was an aspect of the tribes' external relations and hence part of the tribal sovereignty that was divested by treaties and by Congress. *Wheeler; Oliphant*; *Duro*. But these holdings reflect the Court's view of the tribes' retained sovereign status *as of the time* the Court made them. They did not set forth constitutional limits that prohibit Congress from changing the relevant legal circumstances, *i.e.*, from taking actions that modify or adjust the tribes' status.

To the contrary, *Oliphant* and *Duro* make clear that the Constitution does not dictate the metes and bounds of tribal autonomy, nor do they suggest that the Court should second-guess the political branches' own determinations. In *Oliphant*, the Court rested its conclusion about inherent tribal authority to prosecute tribe members in large part upon "the commonly shared presumption of Congress, the Executive Branch, and lower federal courts," a presumption which, "[w]hile not conclusive ***[,] carries considerable weight." The Court pointed out that " 'Indian law' draws principally upon the treaties drawn and executed by the Executive Branch and *legislation passed by Congress*." It added that those "instruments *** form the backdrop for the intricate web of *judicially made* Indian law."

Similarly, in *Duro*, the Court drew upon a host of different sources in order to reach its conclusion that a tribe does not possess the inherent power to prosecute a nonmember. The Court referred to historic practices, the views of experts, the experience of forerunners of modern tribal courts, and the published opinions of the Solicitor of the Department of the Interior. *See also, e.g., Hicks* ("Our holding in *Worcester* must be considered in light of *** the 1828 treaty"); *South Dakota v. Bourland*, 508 U.S. 679, 695 (1993) ("Having concluded that Congress clearly abrogated the Tribe's pre-existing regulatory control over non-Indian hunting and fishing, we find no evidence *in the relevant treaties or statutes* that Congress intended to allow the Tribes to assert regulatory jurisdiction over these lands pursuant to *inherent sovereignty*"); *National Farmers Union Ins. Cos.* ("[T]he existence and extent of a tribal court's jurisdiction will require *[inter alia]* a detailed study of relevant statutes, Executive Branch policy as embodied in treaties and elsewhere, and administrative or judicial decisions"); *Kagama* (characterizing *Ex parte Crow Dog* as resting on extant treaties and statutes and recognizing congressional overruling of *Crow Dog*).

Thus, the Court in these cases based its descriptions of inherent tribal authority upon the sources as they existed at the time the Court issued its decisions. Congressional legislation constituted one such important source. And that source was subject to change. Indeed *Duro* itself anticipated change by inviting interested parties to "address the problem [to] Congress."

We concede that *Duro,* like several other cases, referred only to the need to obtain a congressional statute that "*delegated*" power to the tribes. *See id.* at 686, *Bourland*; *Montana*; *Mazurie*. But in so stating, *Duro* (like the other cases) simply did not consider whether a statute, like the present one, could constitutionally achieve the same end by removing restrictions on the tribes' inherent authority. Consequently we do not read any of these cases as holding that the Constitution forbids Congress to change "judicially made" federal Indian law through this kind of legislation. *Oliphant*; *cf. County of Oneida v. Oneida Indian Nation of N.Y.*, 470 U.S. 226, 233–237 (1985) (recognizing the "federal common law" component of Indian rights, which "common law" federal courts develop as "a 'necessary expedient' when Congress has not 'spoken to a *particular* issue' "); *id.*, at 313 ("[F]ederal common law is 'subject to the paramount authority of Congress' "). ***

Wheeler, Oliphant, and *Duro,* then, are not determinative because Congress has enacted a new statute, relaxing restrictions on the bounds of the inherent tribal authority that the United States recognizes. And that fact makes all the difference.

III.

Lara makes several additional arguments. First, he points out that the Indian Civil Rights Act of 1968 lacks certain constitutional protections for criminal defendants, in particular the right of an indigent defendant to counsel. And he argues that the Due Process Clause forbids Congress to permit a tribe to prosecute a nonmember Indian citizen of the United States in a forum that lacks this protection. *See Argersinger v. Hamlin*, 407 U.S. 25 (1972) (Constitution guarantees indigents counsel where imprisonment possible).

Lara's due process argument, however, suffers from a critical structural defect. To explain the defect, we contrast this argument with Lara's "lack of constitutional power" argument discussed in Part II, *supra*. Insofar as that "constitutional power" argument might help Lara win his double jeopardy claim, it must proceed in four steps:

Step One: Congress does not possess the constitutional power to enact a statute that modifies tribal power by "recogniz[ing] and affirm[ing]" the tribes' "inherent" authority to prosecute nonmember Indians.

Step Two: Consequently, the word "inherent" in the statute's phrase "inherent power" is void.

Step Three: The word "inherent" is severable from the rest of the statute (as are related words). The remainder of the statute is valid without those words, but it then delegates *federal* power to the tribe to conduct the prosecution.

Step Four: Consequently, the Tribe's prosecution of Lara was federal. The current, second, prosecution is also federal. Hence Lara wins his Double Jeopardy Clause claim, the subject of the present proceeding.

Although the Eighth Circuit accepted this argument, 324 F.3d at 640, we reject Step One of the argument, Part II, *supra*. That rejection, without more, invalidates the argument.

Lara's due process argument, however, is significantly different. That argument (if valid) would show that *any* prosecution of a nonmember Indian under the statute is invalid; so Lara's tribal prosecution would be invalid, too. Showing Lara's tribal prosecution was invalid, however, does not show that the *source* of that tribal prosecution was *federal power* (showing that a state prosecution violated the Due Process Clause does not make that prosecution *federal*). But without that "federal power" showing, Lara cannot win his double jeopardy claim here. Hence, we need not, and we shall not, consider the merits of Lara's due process claim. Other defendants in tribal proceedings remain free to raise that claim should they wish to do so. *See* 25 U.S.C. § 1303 (vesting district courts with jurisdiction over habeas writs from tribal courts).

Second, Lara argues that Congress' use of the words "all Indians," in the statutory phrase "inherent power *** to exercise criminal jurisdiction over all Indians," violates the Equal Protection Clause. He says that insofar as the words include nonmember Indians within the statute's scope (while excluding all non-Indians) the statute is race-based and without justification. Like the due process argument, however, this equal protection argument is simply beside the point, therefore we do not address it. At best for Lara, the argument (if valid) would show, not that Lara's first conviction was federal, but that it was constitutionally defective. And that showing cannot help Lara win his double jeopardy claim.

Third, Lara points out that the *Duro* Court found the absence of certain constitutional safeguards, for example, the guarantee of an indigent's right to counsel, as an important reason for concluding that tribes lacked the "inherent power" to try a "group of citizens" (namely nonmember Indians) who were not "include[d]" in those "political bodies." In fact, *Duro* says the following: "We hesitate to adopt a view of tribal sovereignty that would single out another group of citizens, nonmember Indians, for trial by political bodies that do not include them." But this argument simply repeats the due process and equal protection arguments rejected above in a somewhat different form. Since precisely the same problem would exist were we to treat the congressional statute as delegating *federal* power, this argument helps Lara no more than the others.

IV.

For these reasons, we hold, with the reservations set forth in Part III, *supra*, that the Constitution authorizes Congress to permit tribes, as an exercise of their inherent tribal authority, to prosecute nonmember Indians. We hold that Congress exercised that authority in writing this statute. That being so, the Spirit Lake Tribe's prosecution of Lara did not amount to an exercise of federal power, and the Tribe acted in its capacity of a separate sovereign.

Consequently, the Double Jeopardy Clause does not prohibit the Federal Government from proceeding with the present prosecution for a discrete *federal* offense. [*Reversed.*]

JUSTICE STEVENS, concurring.

While I join the Court's opinion without reservation, the additional writing by my colleagues prompts this comment. The inherent sovereignty of the Indian tribes has a historical basis that merits special mention. They governed territory on this continent long before Columbus arrived. In contrast, most of the States were never actually independent sovereigns, and those that were enjoyed that independent status for only a few years. Given the fact that Congress can authorize the States to exercise—as *their own*—inherent powers that the Constitution has otherwise placed off limits, *see, e.g., Prudential Ins. Co. v. Benjamin*, 328 U.S. 408, 437–438 (1946), I find nothing exceptional in the conclusion that it can also relax restrictions on an ancient inherent tribal power.

JUSTICE KENNEDY, concurring in the judgment.

The amendment to the Indian Civil Rights Act of 1968 (ICRA) enacted after the Court's decision in *Duro* demonstrates Congress' clear intention to restore to the tribes an inherent sovereign power to prosecute nonmember Indians. Congress was careful to rely on the theory of inherent sovereignty, and not on a delegation. *** Under that view, the first prosecution of Lara was not a delegated federal prosecution, and his double jeopardy argument must fail. That is all we need say to resolve this case.

The Court's analysis goes beyond this narrower rationale and culminates in a surprising holding: "For these reasons, we hold *** that the Constitution authorizes Congress to permit tribes, as an exercise of their inherent tribal authority, to prosecute nonmember Indians." The Court's holding is on a point of major significance to our understanding and interpretation of the Constitution; and, in my respectful view, it is most doubtful.

Were we called upon to decide whether Congress has this power, it would be a difficult question. Our decision in *Wheeler*, which the Court cites today but discusses very little, is replete with references to the inherent authority of the tribe over its own members. As I read that case, it is the historic possession of inherent power over "the relations among members of a tribe" that is the whole justification for the limited tribal sovereignty the Court there recognized. It is a most troubling proposition to say that Congress can relax the restrictions on inherent tribal sovereignty in a way that extends that sovereignty beyond those historical limits. *Cf., e.g. Strate* ("In the main *** 'the inherent sovereign powers of an Indian tribe'—those powers a tribe enjoys apart from express provision by treaty or statute—'do not extend to the activities of nonmembers of the tribe' " (quoting *Montana*)). To conclude that a tribe's inherent sovereignty allows it to exercise jurisdiction over a nonmember in a criminal case is to enlarge the "unique and limited character" of the inherent sovereignty that *Wheeler* recognized.

Lara, after all, is a citizen of the United States. To hold that Congress can subject him, within our domestic borders, to a sovereignty outside the basic structure of the Constitution is a serious step. The Constitution is based on a theory of original, and continuing, consent of the governed. Their consent depends on the understanding that the Constitution has established the federal structure, which grants the citizen the protection of two governments, the

Nation and the State. Each sovereign must respect the proper sphere of the other, for the citizen has rights and duties as to both. Here, contrary to this design, the National Government seeks to subject a citizen to the criminal jurisdiction of a third entity to be tried for conduct occurring wholly within the territorial borders of the Nation and one of the States. This is unprecedented. There is a historical exception for Indian tribes, but only to the limited extent that a member of a tribe consents to be subjected to the jurisdiction of his own tribe. *See Duro*. The majority today reaches beyond that limited exception.

The Court resolves, or perhaps avoids, the basic question of the power of the Government to yield authority inside the domestic borders over citizens to a third sovereign by using the euphemistic formulation that in amending the ICRA Congress merely relaxed restrictions on the tribes. There is no language in the statute, or the legislative history, that justifies this unusual phrase, *compare* 25 U.S.C. § 1301(2) (referring to "the inherent power of Indian tribes, hereby recognized and affirmed, to exercise criminal jurisdiction over all Indians"); and, in my respectful view, it obscures what is actually at stake in this case. The terms of the statute are best understood as a grant or cession from Congress to the tribes, and it should not be doubted that what Congress has attempted to do is subject American citizens to the authority of an extraconstitutional sovereign to which they had not previously been subject.***

In addition to trying to evade the important structural question by relying on the verbal formula of relaxation, the Court also tries to bolster its position by noting that due process and equal protection claims are still reserved. That is true, but it ignores the elementary principle that the Constitutional structure was in place before the Fifth and Fourteenth Amendments were adopted. To demean the constitutional structure and the consent upon which it rests by implying they are wholly dependent for their vindication on the Due Process and Equal Protection Clauses is a further, unreasoned holding of serious import. The political freedom guaranteed to citizens by the federal structure is a liberty both distinct from and every bit as important as those freedoms guaranteed by the Bill of Rights. The individual citizen has an enforceable right to those structural guarantees of liberty, a right which the majority ignores. Perhaps the Court's holding could be justified by an argument that by enrolling in one tribe Lara consented to the criminal jurisdiction of other tribes, but the Court does not mention the point. And, in all events, we should be cautious about adopting that fiction.

The present case, however, does not require us to address these difficult questions of constitutional dimension. Congress made it clear that its intent was to recognize and affirm tribal authority to try Indian nonmembers as inherent in tribal status. The proper occasion to test the legitimacy of the tribe's authority, that is, whether Congress had the power to do what it sought to do, was in the first, tribal proceeding. There, however, Lara made no objection to the tribe's authority to try him. In the second, federal proceeding, because the express rationale for the tribe's authority to try Lara—whether legitimate or not—was inherent sovereignty, not delegated federal power, there can be no double jeopardy violation. For that reason, I concur in the judgment.

JUSTICE THOMAS, concurring in the judgment.

As this case should make clear, the time has come to reexamine the premises and logic of our tribal sovereignty cases. It seems to me that much of the confusion reflected in our precedent arises from two largely incompatible and doubtful assumptions. First, Congress (rather than some other part of the Federal Government) can regulate virtually every aspect of the tribes without rendering tribal sovereignty a nullity. Second, the Indian tribes retain inherent sovereignty to enforce their criminal laws against their own members. These assumptions, which I must accept as the case comes to us, dictate the outcome in this case, and I therefore concur in the judgment.

I write separately principally because the Court fails to confront these tensions, a result that flows from the Court's inadequate constitutional analysis. I cannot agree with the Court, for instance, that the Constitution grants to Congress plenary power to calibrate the "metes and bounds of tribal sovereignty." Unlike the Court, I cannot locate such congressional authority in the Treaty Clause, U.S. Const., Art. II, § 2, cl. 2, or the Indian Commerce Clause, Art. I, § 8, cl. 3. Additionally, I would ascribe much more significance to legislation such as the Act of Mar. 3, 1871, Rev Stat § 2079, 16 Stat 566, codified at 25 U.S.C. § 71, that purports to terminate the practice of dealing with Indian tribes by treaty. The making of treaties, after all, is the one mechanism that the Constitution clearly provides for the Federal Government to interact with sovereigns other than the States. Yet, if I accept that Congress does have this authority, I believe that the result in *Wheeler* is questionable. In my view, the tribes either are or are not separate sovereigns, and our federal Indian law cases untenably hold both positions simultaneously.

I.

[In the *Duro* fix, Congress clearly recognized inherent tribal power rather than delegated federal authority to the tribes.] But even if the statute were less clear, I would not interpret it as a delegation of federal power. The power to bring federal prosecutions, which is part of the putative delegated power, is manifestly and quintessentially executive power. Congress cannot transfer federal executive power to individuals who are beyond "meaningful Presidential control." And this means that, at a minimum, the President must have some measure of "the power to appoint and remove" those exercising that power.

*** That is, reading the "*Duro* fix" as a delegation of federal power (without also divining some adequate method of Presidential control) would create grave constitutional difficulties. Accordingly, the Court has only two options: Either the "*Duro* fix" changed the result in *Duro* or it did nothing at all.

II.

In *Wheeler*, the Court explained that, prior to colonization, "the tribes were self-governing sovereign political communities." The Court acknowledged, however, that, after "[t]heir incorporation within the territory of the United States," the tribes could exercise their inherent sovereignty only as consistent with federal policy embodied in treaties, statutes, and Executive Orders. Examining these sources for potential conflict, the Court concluded that the tribes retained the ability to exercise their inherent sovereignty to punish their own members.

Although *Wheeler* seems to be a sensible example of federal common lawmaking, I am not convinced that it was correctly decided. To be sure, it makes sense to conceptualize the tribes as sovereigns that, due to their unique situation, cannot exercise the full measure of their sovereign powers. *Wheeler*, at times, seems to analyze the problem in just this way.

But I do not see how this is consistent with the apparently "undisputed fact that Congress has plenary authority to legislate for the Indian tribes in all matters, including their form of government." *Wheeler*. The sovereign is, by definition, the entity "in which independent and supreme authority is vested." Black's Law Dictionary 1395 (6th ed. 1990). It is quite arguably the essence of sovereignty not to exist merely at the whim of an external government.

Further, federal policy itself could be thought to be inconsistent with this residual-sovereignty theory. In 1871, Congress enacted a statute that purported to prohibit entering into treaties with the "Indian nation[s] or tribe[s]." 16 Stat 566, codified at 25 U.S.C. § 71. Although this Act is constitutionally suspect (the Constitution vests in the President both the power to make treaties, Art. II, § 2, cl. 2, and to recognize foreign governments, Art. II, § 3), it nevertheless reflects the view of the political branches that the tribes had become a purely domestic matter.

To be sure, this does not quite suffice to demonstrate that the tribes had lost their sovereignty. After all, States retain sovereignty despite the fact that Congress can regulate States *qua* States in certain limited circumstances. But the States (unlike the tribes) are part of a constitutional framework that allocates sovereignty between the State and Federal Governments and specifically grants Congress authority to legislate with respect to them, *see* U.S. Const., Amdt. 14, § 5. And even so, we have explained that "the Framers explicitly chose a Constitution that confers upon Congress the power to regulate individuals, not States."

The tribes, by contrast, are not part of this constitutional order, and their sovereignty is not guaranteed by it. *** Chief Justice Marshall *** described the tribes as "independent political communities, retaining their original natural rights," and specifically noted that the tribes possessed the power to "mak[e] treaties." *Worcester*. Although the tribes never fit comfortably within the category of foreign nations, the 1871 Act tends to show that the political branches no longer considered the tribes to be anything like foreign nations. And it is at least arguable that the United States no longer considered the tribes to be sovereigns. Federal Indian policy is, to say the least, schizophrenic. And this confusion continues to infuse federal Indian law and our cases.

Nevertheless, if I accept *Wheeler*, I also must accept that the tribes do retain inherent sovereignty (at least to enforce their criminal laws against their own members) and the logical consequences of this fact. In *Heath v. Alabama*, 474 U.S. 82, 88 (1985), the Court elaborated the dual sovereignty doctrine and explained that a single act that violates the " 'peace and dignity' of two sovereigns by breaking the laws of each" constitutes two separate offenses. This, of course, is the reason that the Double Jeopardy Clause does not bar successive prosecutions by separate sovereigns. But whether an act violates the "peace and dignity" of a sovereign depends not in the least on whether the perpetrator is a member (in the case of the tribes) or a citizen (in the case of the States and the Nation) of the sovereign.

Heath also instructs, relying on *Wheeler*, that the separate-sovereign inquiry "turns on whether the two entities draw their authority to punish the offender from distinct sources of power." But *Wheeler* makes clear that the tribes and the Federal Government do draw their authority to punish from distinct sources and that they are separate sovereigns. Otherwise, the subsequent federal prosecution in *Wheeler* would have violated the Double Jeopardy

Clause.[3] It follows from our case law that Indian tribes possess inherent sovereignty to punish *anyone* who violates their laws.

In *Duro*, the Court held that the Indian tribes could no longer enforce their criminal laws against nonmember Indians. Despite the obvious tension, *Duro* and *Wheeler* are not necessarily inconsistent. Although *Wheeler* and *Heath*, taken together, necessarily imply that the tribes retain inherent sovereignty to try anyone who violates their criminal laws, *Wheeler* and *Duro* make clear that conflict with federal policy can operate to prohibit the exercise of this sovereignty. *Duro*, then, is not a case about "inherent sovereignty" (a term that we have used too imprecisely); rather, it is a case about whether a specific exercise of tribal sovereignty conflicts with federal policy.

Indeed, the Court in *Duro* relied primarily on *Oliphant*, which held that tribes could not enforce their criminal laws against non-Indians. In reaching that conclusion, the Court in *Oliphant* carefully examined the views of Congress and the Executive Branch[, discussing treaties, statutes, and views of the Executive Branch, Attorney General opinions, and concluding that tribal exercise of criminal jurisdiction over non-Indians was inconsistent with various treaties.] *Duro* at least rehearsed the same analysis. Thus, although *Duro* is sprinkled with references to various constitutional concerns, *Duro, Oliphant*, and *Wheeler* are classic federal-common-law decisions.

I acknowledge that our cases have distinguished between "tribal power [that] is necessary to protect tribal self-government or to control internal relations" and tribal power as it relates to the external world. [*Montana*; *Hicks*; *Duro*; *Wheeler*.] This distinction makes perfect sense as a matter of federal common law: Purely "internal" matters are by definition unlikely to implicate any federal policy. But, critically, our cases have never drawn this line as a constitutional matter. That is why we have analyzed extant federal law (embodied in treaties, statutes, and Executive Orders) before concluding that particular tribal assertions of power were incompatible with the position of the tribes. *See* *** *Oliphant* ("While Congress never expressly forbade Indian tribes to impose criminal penalties on non-Indians, we now make express our implicit conclusion of nearly a century ago [referring to *In re Mayfield*, 141 U.S. 107 (1891)] that Congress consistently believed this to be the necessary result of its repeated legislative actions").

As noted, in response to *Duro*, Congress amended ICRA. Specifically, Congress "recognized and affirmed" the existence of "inherent power *** to exercise criminal jurisdiction over all Indians." 25 U.S.C. § 1301(2). President Bush signed this legislation into law. Further, as this litigation demonstrates, it is the position of the Executive Branch that the tribes possess inherent authority to prosecute nonmember Indians.

In my view, these authoritative pronouncements of the political branches make clear that the exercise of this aspect of sovereignty is not inconsistent with federal policy and therefore with the position of the tribes. Thus, while *Duro* may have been a correct federal-common-law decision at the time, the political branches have subsequently made clear that the tribes' exercise of criminal jurisdiction against nonmember Indians is consistent with federal

3. I acknowledge that *Wheeler* focused specifically on the tribes' authority to try their own members. But, as I discuss below, the distinction between the tribes' external and internal powers is not constitutionally required.

policy. The potential conflicts on which *Duro* must have been premised, according to the political branches, do not exist. I therefore agree that, as the case comes to us, the tribe acted as a separate sovereign when it prosecuted respondent. Accordingly, the Double Jeopardy Clause does not bar the subsequent federal prosecution.

III.

I believe that we must examine more critically our tribal sovereignty case law. Both the Court and the dissent, however, compound the confusion by failing to undertake the necessary rigorous constitutional analysis. I would begin by carefully following our assumptions to their logical conclusions and by identifying the potential sources of federal power to modify tribal sovereignty.

The dissent admits that "[t]reaties and statutes delineating the tribal-federal relationship are properly viewed as an independent elaboration by the political branches of the fine details of the tribes' dependent position, which strips the tribes of any power to exercise criminal jurisdiction over those outside their own membership." To the extent that this is a description of the federal-common-law process, I agree. But I do not understand how the dissent can then conclude that "the jurisdictional implications [arising from this analysis are] constitutional in nature." ***

I do, however, agree that this case raises important constitutional questions that the Court does not begin to answer. The Court utterly fails to find any provision of the Constitution that gives Congress enumerated power to alter tribal sovereignty. The Court cites the Indian Commerce Clause and the treaty power. I cannot agree that the Indian Commerce Clause " 'provide[s] Congress with plenary power to legislate in the field of Indian affairs.' " [Majority opinion, quoting *Cotton Petroleum Corp. v. New Mexico*, 490 U.S. 163, 192 (1989).] At one time, the implausibility of this assertion at least troubled the Court, *see, e.g., Kagama* (considering such a construction of the Indian Commerce Clause to be "very strained"), and I would be willing to revisit the question.

Next, the Court acknowledges that "[t]he treaty power does not literally authorize Congress to act legislatively, for it is an Article II power authorizing the President, not Congress, 'to make Treaties.' " This, of course, suffices to show that it provides *no* power to *Congress*, at least in the absence of a specific treaty. The treaty power does not, as the Court seems to believe, provide Congress with free-floating power to legislate as it sees fit on topics that could potentially implicate some unspecified treaty. Such an assertion is especially ironic in light of Congress' enacted prohibition on Indian treaties.

***

The Court should admit that it has failed in its quest to find a source of congressional power to adjust tribal sovereignty. Such an acknowledgement might allow the Court to ask the logically antecedent question *whether* Congress (as opposed to the President) has this power. A cogent answer would serve as the foundation for the analysis of the sovereignty issues posed by this case. We might find that the Federal Government cannot regulate the tribes through ordinary domestic legislation and simultaneously maintain that the tribes are sovereigns in any meaningful sense. But until we begin to analyze these questions honestly and rigorously, the confusion that I have identified will continue to haunt our cases.

JUSTICE SOUTER, with whom **JUSTICE SCALIA** joins, dissenting.

It is as true today as it was in 1886 that the relationship of Indian tribes to the National Government is "an anomalous one and of a complex character." *Kagama*. Questions of tribal jurisdiction, whether legislative or judicial, do not get much help from the general proposition that tribes are "domestic dependent nations" or "wards of the [American] nation." Our cases deciding specific questions, however, demonstrate that the tribes do retain jurisdiction necessary to protect tribal self-government or control internal tribal relations, *Montana*, including the right to prosecute tribal members for crimes, *Wheeler*, a sovereign right that is "inherent," but neither exclusive, *Kagama* (federal criminal jurisdiction), nor immune to abrogation by Congress, *Wheeler* ("the sufferance of Congress"). Furthermore, except as provided by Congress, tribes lack criminal jurisdiction over non-Indians, *Oliphant*, and over nonmember Indians, *Duro*.

Of particular relevance today, we held in *Duro* that because tribes have lost their inherent criminal jurisdiction over nonmember Indians, any subsequent exercise of such jurisdiction "could only have come to the Tribe" (if at all) "by delegation from Congress." [Quoting *Duro*.] *** Our precedent, then, is that any tribal exercise of criminal jurisdiction over nonmembers necessarily rests on a "delegation" of federal power and is not akin to a State's congressionally permitted exercise of some authority that would otherwise be barred by the dormant Commerce Clause. It is more like the delegation of lawmaking power to an administrative agency, whose jurisdiction would not even exist absent congressional authorization.

It is of no moment that we have given ostensibly alternating explanations for this conclusion. We have sometimes indicated that the tribes' lack of inherent criminal jurisdiction over nonmembers is a necessary legal consequence of the basic fact that the tribes are dependent on the Federal Government. *** *Oliphant* ("By submitting to the overriding sovereignty of the United States, Indian tribes therefore necessarily give up their power to try non-Indian citizens of the United States ***."). At other times, our language has suggested that the jurisdictional limit stems from congressional and treaty limitations on tribal powers. *See Oliphant* ("Congress' various actions and inactions in regulating criminal jurisdiction on Indian reservations demonstrated an intent to reserve jurisdiction over non-Indians for the federal courts")***. What has never been explicitly stated, but should come as no surprise, is that these two accounts are not inconsistent. Treaties and statutes delineating the tribal-federal relationship are properly viewed as an independent elaboration by the political branches of the fine details of the tribes' dependent position, which strips the tribes of any power to exercise criminal jurisdiction over those outside their own memberships.

What should also be clear, and what I would hold today, is that our previous understanding of the jurisdictional implications of dependent sovereignty was constitutional in nature, certainly so far as its significance under the Double Jeopardy Clause is concerned. Our discussions of Indian sovereignty have naturally focused on the scope of tribes' inherent legislative or judicial jurisdiction. And application of the double jeopardy doctrine of dual sovereignty, under which one independent sovereign's exercise of criminal jurisdiction does not bar another sovereign's subsequent prosecution of the same defendant, turns on just this question of how far a prosecuting entity's inherent jurisdiction extends. When we enquire "whether the two [prosecuting] entities draw their authority to punish the offender from distinct sources of power," *Heath v. Alabama*, in other words, we are undertaking a constitutional analysis based on legal categories of constitutional dimension (*i.e.*, is this entity an independent or dependent sovereign?). Thus, our application of the doctrines of independent and dependent sovereignty to Indian tribes in response to a double jeopardy claim must itself have had constitutional status.

That means that there are only two ways that a tribe's inherent sovereignty could be restored so as to alter application of the dual sovereignty rule: either Congress could grant the same independence to the tribes that it did to the Philippines, or this Court could repudiate its existing doctrine of dependent sovereignty. The first alternative has obviously not been attempted, and I see no reason for us to venture down a path toward the second. To begin with, the theory we followed before today has the virtue of fitting the facts: no one could possibly deny that the tribes are subordinate to the National Government. Furthermore, while this is not the place to reexamine the concept of dual sovereignty itself, there is certainly no reason to adopt a canon of broad construction calling for maximum application of the doctrine. Finally, and perhaps most importantly, principles of *stare decisis* are particularly compelling in the law of tribal jurisdiction, an area peculiarly susceptible to confusion. And confusion, I fear, will be the legacy of today's decision, for our failure to stand by what we have previously said reveals that our conceptualizations of sovereignty and dependent sovereignty are largely rhetorical.

I would therefore stand by our explanations in *Oliphant* and *Duro* and hold that Congress cannot reinvest tribal courts with inherent criminal jurisdiction over nonmember Indians. It is not that I fail to appreciate Congress's express wish that the jurisdiction conveyed by statute be treated as inherent, but Congress cannot control the interpretation of the statute in a way that is at odds with the constitutional consequences of the tribes' continuing dependent status. What may be given controlling effect, however, is the principal object of the 1990 amendments to the Indian Civil Rights Act of 1968, 25 U.S.C. § 1301 *et seq.*, which was to close "the jurisdictional void" created by *Duro* by recognizing (and empowering) the tribal court as "the best forum to handle misdemeanor cases over non-member Indians," H.R. Rep. No. 102–61, p 7 (1991). I would therefore honor the drafters' substantive intent by reading the Act as a delegation of federal prosecutorial power that eliminates the jurisdictional gap. Finally, I would hold that a tribe's exercise of this delegated power bars subsequent federal prosecution for the same offense.

NOTES AND QUESTIONS

1. *The erosion of congressional plenary power?* In an area in which Congress supposedly has "plenary power," the result in *Lara* should have been straightforward: Congress can do as it chooses in allocating sovereign authority over Indian country, so the *Duro* fix is valid. But only a bare majority of Justices reach anything like this result. There are at least two reasons for this. First, the separate opinion of Justice Thomas questions the origins and coherence of the plenary-power. Does the majority have an effective answer to his challenge? Second, Justices Kennedy, Souter, and Scalia seem most reluctant to cede to Congress the ultimate authority over sovereign arrangements in

Indian country. Why are they so resistant to the notion that a tribe can have authority to prosecute nonmember Indians? Did either Kennedy or Souter find some legally cognizable (as opposed to policy) argument in support of their concerns? Are they in effect attempting to substitute the Court for the Congress as the federal entity holding plenary power over Indian affairs? What, if anything, supports Kennedy's wide-ranging vision of constitutional citizenship or Souter's notion that *Oliphant* and *Duro* are constitutional, rather than common law, decisions?

2. *The erosion of the "common law of colonialism"?* Note that, by suggesting that judicial federal common lawmaking power is limited and should be closely tied to the federal constitution, statutes, treaties, and other sources of positive law, Justice Thomas implicitly, but powerfully, questioned the basis for the Court's common law holdings beginning in *Oliphant*. Is it conceivable that the Court will reconsider its role in federal Indian law and perhaps return to the old congressional plenary power paradigm (where Congress, not the Court, is to develop colonial policies, which work to the disadvantage of tribes only if Congress is sufficiently explicit in the statute to satisfy the canons of interpretation)? With the plenary power doctrine under similar attack from Thomas, where else could the Court go?

3. *The erosion of tribal status as sovereign.* Justice Thomas contended that tribes are either sovereign or they are not, and in trying to have it both ways, Indian law flunks the requirement of legal rationality. This issue has been around at least since Chief Justice Marshall in *Cherokee Nation* labeled tribes "domestic dependent sovereigns," a term that may well seem oxymoronic. But does sovereignty have to be an all-or-nothing concept? The trends in some other parts of the world, most notably the European Union, are away from a country being fully sovereign unto itself and toward a group of allied countries confederating into sovereign alliances where some aspects of sovereignty are shared. Is there anything in American law or logic that must condemn the longstanding hybrid status of tribes? Is there anything in American positive law that supports the hybrid status? Recall Marshall's constitutional analysis in *Cherokee Nation*. *See also* Sarah Krakoff, *The Virtues and Vices of Sovereignty*, 38 Conn. L. Rev. 797 (2006).

4. *Issues left open.* The Court pointedly did not decide whether Congress violated the equal protection component of the Fifth Amendment in subjecting nonmember Indians, but not non-Indians, to tribal criminal jurisdiction. (How would *Morton v. Mancari* and *United States v. Antelope* apply to such a claim?) It also did not decide whether the Due Process component prevented Congress from affirming jurisdiction in courts not subject to the full panoply of constitutional requirements.

While *Lara* was being decided, these issues were being considered in the Navajo courts and the Ninth Circuit. *Means v. Chinle District Court*, 26 Ind. L. Rep. 6083 (Nav. S. Ct. 1999); *Means v. Navajo Nation*, 432 F.3d 924 (9th Cir. 2005). Russell Means, a well-known Oglala Lakota activist and actor, had married a Navajo woman and lived on the Navajo Nation for many years. In 1997, the Navajo Nation prosecuted Means for battery of his father in law, a member of the Omaha tribe, and his brother in law, a member of the Navajo tribe. Means claimed that the prosecution violated the equal protection provisions of the Indian Civil Rights Act and the Navajo Nation Bill of Rights, and that the *Duro* Fix violated the Fifth Amendment of the United States Constitution. In considering this challenge, the Navajo Supreme Court first emphasized the tribe's need to address serious crime and domestic violence problems on the nation:

> [A]t least 9,327 "other" or nonmember Indians resided within the Navajo Nation in 1990. They are involved in some of the 27,000 plus criminal charges in our system and in the 3,435 plus domestic violence cases. The questions are whether nonmember Indians should have de facto immunity from criminal prosecution, given the failure of federal officials to effectively address crime in the Navajo Nation, and whether this Court should rule that thousands of innocent victims, Navajo and non-Navajo, should be permitted to suffer. We must sadly take judicial notice of the fact that, with a few exceptions, non-Indians and nonmember Indians who commit crimes within the Navajo Nation escape punishment for the crimes they commit. The social health of the Navajo Nation is at risk in addressing the petitioner's personal issues, as is the actual health and well-being of thousands of people.

The court then rejected both the ICRA and constitutional arguments. The court also rejected the argument that the *Duro* Fix was the sole source of criminal jurisdiction over Means, finding that the 1868 Treaty as understood by the Navajos who negotiated it provided the tribe with jurisdiction over nonmember Indians:

> Article II of the Treaty, 15 Stats. at 668, begins with a boundary description and then says that "this reservation" is "set apart for the use and occupation of the Navajo tribe of Indians, and for such other friendly tribes or individual Indians as from time to time they may be willing, with the consent of the United States, to admit among them ... ." ***
>
> The plain language of Article II indicates that the Navajo Reservation exists for the exclusive use of not only Navajos, but other Indians, either as tribes or as individuals, where both the Navajo Nation and the United States agree to their admission. ***

The court drew on historical discussions regarding the status of the Paiutes and the Utes on Navajo land to find that this provision included Navajo jurisdiction over nonmember Indians the tribe consented to admit among them. The Court also found that under Navajo common law, by marrying into the tribe, Means had become a member of the tribe and was subject to Navajo jurisdiction:

> While there is a formal process to obtain membership as a Navajo, see 1 N.N.C. §§ 751–759 (1995), that is not the only kind of "membership" under Navajo Nation law. An individual who marries or has an intimate relationship with a Navajo is a hadane (in-law). The Navajo People have adoone'e or clans, and many of them are based upon the intermarriage of original Navajo clan members with people of other nations. The primary clan relation is traced through the mother, and some of the "foreign nation" clans include the "Flat Foot–Pima clan," the "Ute people clan," the "Zuni clan," the "Mexican clan," and the "Mescalero Apache clan." *See*, Saad Ahaah Sinil, Dual Language: A Navajo–English Dictionary, 3–4 (1986). The list of clans based upon other peoples is not exhaustive. A hadane or in-law assumes a clan relation to a Navajo when an intimate relationship forms, and when that relationship is conducted within the

> Navajo Nation, there are reciprocal obligations to and from family and clan members under Navajo common law. Among those obligations is the duty to avoid threatening or assaulting a relative by marriage (or any other person).
>
> We find that the petitioner, by reason of his marriage to a Navajo, longtime residence within the Navajo Nation, his activities here, and his status as a hadane, consented to Navajo Nation criminal jurisdiction. This is not done by "adoption" in any formal or customary sense, but by assuming tribal relations and establishing familial and community relationships under Navajo common law.

Means v. Chinle District Court, 26 Ind. L. Rep. 6083 (Nav. S. Ct. 1999). Means then brought a habeas petition challenging jurisdiction. The federal district court denied the petition. The Ninth Circuit affirmed, focusing on the challenges to the *Duro* Fix:

> Means's equal protection argument has real force. He argues that, although the 1990 Amendments permit the Navajo tribe to criminally prosecute its own members and members of other Indian tribes, the Navajo tribe cannot constitutionally prosecute whites, blacks, Asians, or any other non-Navajos who are accused of crimes on the reservation. This makes Means's case different from, say, an Alaskan who threatens and batters his father-in-law in Los Angeles, and then is prosecuted by the State of California. Not only can an Alaskan become a Californian, but the State of California, although "sovereign," nonetheless is bound by the Due Process and Equal Protection Clauses of the Fourteenth Amendment. Although he is an Indian, Means is nonetheless a citizen of the United States, entitled to the full protection of the United States Constitution. But unlike states, when Indian tribes exercise their sovereign authority they do not have to comply with the United States Constitution. As an Oglala–Sioux, Means can never become a member of the Navajo political community, no matter how long he makes the Navajo reservation his home.
>
> Despite the force of Means's argument, we nonetheless conclude that the weight of established law requires us to reject Means's equal protection claim. ***
>
> [*Morton v. Mancari* held that] "[l]egislation that singles out Indians for particular and special treatment" is in a special category because of the historical relationship of the United States with the Indians and the Indian Commerce Clause, and "[a]s long as the special treatment can be tied rationally to the fulfillment of Congress' unique obligation toward the Indians, such legislative judgments will not be disturbed." ***
>
> We conclude that a law subjecting nonmember Indians to tribal criminal jurisdiction in "Indian country" passes the "rational tie" standard of *Mancari*. First, recognizing criminal jurisdiction of tribal courts over nonmember Indians furthers Indian self-government. The Navajo reservation, larger than many states and countries, has to be able to maintain order within its boundaries. The 1990 Amendments to the Indian Civil Rights Act were meant to protect Indians and others who reside in or visit Indian country against lawlessness by nonmember Indians who might not otherwise be subject to any criminal jurisdiction. As the Navajo Supreme Court notes, there are a significant number of Indians who are not

> Navajos but live on the Navajo reservation because of intermarriage. It is a matter of ordinary experience that many people are not at their best when their marriages break up, so misdemeanor jurisdiction over nonmember Indians is rationally related to Indian self-government in an area where rapid and effective tribal responses may be needed. ***
>
> Second, the reason Congress can recognize the power of a tribe to exercise criminal jurisdiction over a nonmember Indian like Means—but not over a nonmember, non-Indian who like Means might become involved in a domestic dispute—is the same reason given by the Supreme Court for the employment preference in *Mancari:* Indian tribal identity is political rather than racial, and the only Indians subjected to tribal court jurisdiction are enrolled or *de facto* members of tribes, not all ethnic Indians. ***
>
> Because the criminal proceedings against Means in the Navajo trial court have been stayed pending the outcome of his jurisdictional challenge, an "as applied" due process challenge to the Navajo trial proceedings would be premature. Means's facial due process challenge to the 1990 Amendments has no force. Although the U.S. Constitution does not bind the Navajo tribe in the exercise of its own sovereign powers, the Indian Civil Rights Act confers all the criminal protections on Means that he would receive under the Federal Constitution, except for the right to grand jury indictment and the right to appointed counsel if he cannot afford an attorney. The right to grand jury indictment would not pertain regardless, because Means is charged with a misdemeanor. The right to appointed counsel is conferred by the Navajo Bill of Rights to any person within its jurisdiction. Thus as a facial matter, Means will not be deprived of any constitutionally protected rights despite being tried by a sovereign not bound by the Constitution.

Means v. Navajo Nation, 432 F.3d 924, 932–935 (9th Cir. 2005). The Supreme Court denied certiorari in *Means* case, but may consider the question in the future. How should the Court decide? As a matter of law? As a matter of policy?

The Violence Against Women Act Reauthorization and a Partial *Oliphant* Fix

Many Indian law observers thought the day would never come when Congress restored any criminal authority to tribes over non-Indians. Yet in 2013, the Violence Against Women Reauthorization Act, Pub. L. 113-4, Title IX, § 904, 127 Stat. 120, discussed in Chapter 5, partially reversed the Supreme Court's decision in *Oliphant v. Suquamish Tribe*. Congress provided that

> Notwithstanding any other provision of law, in addition to all powers of self-government recognized and affirmed by [the Indian Civil Rights Act, 25 U.S.C. §§ 1301 & 1303] the powers of self-government of a participating tribe include the inherent power of that tribe, which is hereby recognized and affirmed, to exercise special domestic violence criminal jurisdiction over all persons.

25 U.S.C. § 1304(b)(1).

The statute applies to "dating violence" and "domestic violence" as defined in the Act, but only if either the defendant or victim is an Indian and the crime or conduct takes place in Indian country. 25 U.S.C. § 1304(c). If a prosecution under the act may result in a prison sentence of any length, the tribe must provide the defendant with a jury that constitutes a fair cross section of the community as well as the right to counsel and other protections required before tribes may impose sentences of more than one year. 25 U.S.C. § 1304(d). A final catch-all provision guarantees "all other rights whose protection is necessary under the Constitution of the United States in order for Congress to recognize and affirm the inherent power of the participating tribe to exercise special domestic violence criminal jurisdiction over the defendant." *Id.* On February 6, 2014, the Pascua Yaqui, Umatilla, and Tulalip Tribes were certified to begin exercising expanded jurisdiction under a pilot program; all tribes will be able to exercise expanded jurisdiction beginning March 2015. The statute works as an opt-in assumption of sovereignty, so if tribes do not want to provide the additional procedural protections and rights to defendants, they do not have to and will forego the partial restoration of their inherent powers.

A coalition of Native domestic violence advocates, federal and state prosecutors, tribes, and tribal supporters paved the way for the VAWA Reauthorization's passage. In addition, renowned Ojibwe author Louise Erdrich published a powerful novel, The Round House, that brought home to millions of readers the pain and anguish of tribes' inability to impose criminal laws to protect their members from violent acts.

As described above, the partial *Oliphant* fix requires tribes to provide virtually the same rights to criminal defendants that federal and state governments do. If a non-Indian is prosecuted by the Tulalip Tribe for a crime of domestic violence and sentenced to a prison term, how procedurally will he challenge his conviction? What arguments will he raise? If such a case reaches the Supreme Court, how do you think the Court will resolve the questions concerning congressional power and individual constitutional rights?

Attorney Advocacy and the Federal Judicial Role

Consider the way in which the evolution of federal Indian law beginning in *Oliphant* and ending in *Lara* arguably has warped both the appropriate federal judicial role and the role of counsel:

PHILIP P. FRICKEY, *(NATIVE) AMERICAN EXCEPTIONALISM IN FEDERAL PUBLIC LAW*

119 Harv. L. Rev. 431, 483–85 (2005)

*** Under the old plenary power/canons model, the tribes were trapped in a paradigm that fed on itself. In briefs before the Supreme Court, counsel for tribes would necessarily have to confess that, under current law, Congress possessed a plenary power over Indian affairs. Counsel would then attempt to make a silk purse out of this sow's ear. The common argument took one of two related forms, reflecting the twin aspects of this paradigm. First, if the entity that had formulated the antitribal policy was not Congress—in other words, if it was a state or the executive branch—then tribal counsel would argue that the entity had clearly acted *ultra vires*. If Congress was the culprit, then counsel would contend that the statute lacked sufficient clarity to satisfy the Indian law canons. These dual strategies won many important cases for tribes. In these cases, however, the Court would often pick up on this dualist quality and go out of its way to acknowledge congressional plenary power while still awarding the win to the tribe.[271] Every victory was bittersweet from the broader perspective of promoting more tribal self-governance in the longer term, for each ratified the tribes' subordination to Congress.

The plenary power/canons paradigm forced tribes to be pragmatic. Winning in the Supreme Court meant that the burden of legislative inertia fell on tribal opponents. As tribes became sophisticated lobbyists, they could often prevent reactive federal legislation, as of course it is much easier to kill legislation than to pass it. In this way, the paradigm *** had some of the features of the camel: ugly and mean-spirited, but nonetheless somewhat functional.

The rise of the common law of colonialism posed a huge problem for tribal advocates. It upset the simplicity of the standard argument: even if Congress had not clearly authorized the invasion of tribal authority, the Court might use federal common law to reduce tribal sovereignty. No longer could counsel for tribes say to the Justices, in effect, "Don't worry about functionality or fairness; those are issues for Congress." Instead, counsel was required to attempt to educate nine non-Indian Justices about such particularistic questions as how a non-Indian would be treated if criminally prosecuted in a tribal court (as if all tribal courts were fungible), how hunting by non-Indian fee simple landowners on the reservation might undermine legitimate tribal interests (as if all reservations or non-Indians were fungible), or how authorizing a county rather than a tribe to zone non-Indian fee land on the reservation might conflict with important tribal cultural and religious values (as if all such values were similar). Often the Court has taken one factual situation and spun a general common law rule out of it—either not recognizing or not caring that a one-size-fits-all solution should not be imposed on communities as radically varied as those composing America's Indian country.

In addition, the common law mentality has led to a dramatic shift toward historical inquiries—for example, how tribes had exercised criminal authority over nonmembers, or how the opening of a reservation to non-Indian settlement had affected the delivery of public services. It also has encouraged the Court to undertake abstract inquiries about contemporary values—for example, whether Indian citizenship somehow conflicts with tribal court jurisdiction over nonmember Indians. In effect, the Supreme Court has become the site of an ongoing mini-constitutional convention for evaluating the essentially insolvable conundrums of the place of tribes in the American constitutional system. Cases come to the Court with their own complicated facts and background, much of which is novel rather than a good basis for generalization, and yet they become the battleground for the application of [the] American values of liberty, egalitarianism, individualism, populism, and laissez-faire. Native American exceptionalism in federal public law has collided with American exceptionalism in a case-by-case agony of happenstance.

---

271. *See, e.g., Martinez* ("Congress has plenary authority to limit, modify, or eliminate the powers of local self-government which the tribes otherwise possess.").

Now, in addition to the common law power providing for judicial intrusion upon tribal authority when Congress has failed or refused to intrude, several Justices have suggested that the Court, not Congress, sometimes has the last word on tribal authority. If the mentality of Justices Kennedy or Souter were to prevail, the Court would have the final say in an area in which, of all the institutions involved, it surely knows the least and is least able to provide a forum for wide-ranging dialogue and jurisgenerativity. A bare majority of Justices, at least for the time being, have avoided this arrogation of authority by continuing to follow the doctrine of congressional plenary authority. At the same time, the candor of Justice Thomas points in two starkly opposing directions: a reduction of federal power over tribes, without a sense for whether a corresponding expansion of state authority would be the other shoe to drop, or a judicial termination of tribal sovereignty. The only certainty is that, of all the political entities involved, the tribes will have the least influence on whatever direction federal Indian law will take.

The behind-the-scenes history of *Lara* may create a somewhat more hopeful vision of tribal influence on federal Indian law:

BETHANY BERGER, UNITED STATES V. LARA *AS A STORY OF NATIVE AGENCY*

40 Tulsa L. Rev. 5, 19–23 (2004)

*** [A]s documented by Professor David Getches, tribal interests lost in 77 percent of Supreme Court decisions between 1986 (when William Rehnquist became Chief Justice) and 2000, down from a 58 percent win rate between 1969 and 1986, when Warren Burger was Chief Justice. To respond to this trend, Indian people are again unifying to share their knowledge and strategic resources, this time in the courts. In *Lara*, we see the first significant results of this effort.

In 2002, the Native American Rights Fund and the National Congress of American Indians created the Tribal Supreme Court Project ("Project") to respond to the crisis in the Court with the same kind of organizational links and pooling of expertise that have proved so effective in Congress. The Project has built a Supreme Court Project Working Group of hundreds of attorneys and academics to share legal information and experience. An Advisory Board of Tribal leaders adds political expertise and a tribal perspective to these legal resources.

The Project sometimes calls upon tribes to sacrifice their individual interests when necessary to pursue the collective goals of the project. In particular, because one of the goals of the project is to keep cases unlikely to result in success (most cases in the current Court) out of the Supreme Court, tribes may be asked not to appeal cases in which they have lost, or settle, where possible, cases they have won. ***

When certiorari is granted in a case involving tribal rights, the Project offers the litigants the resources of the Working Group to try to ensure that the best possible argument is presented to the Court. ***

[When certiorari was granted in *Lara*, the] Working Group fired up, holding dozens of conference calls about who should write *amicus* briefs and what arguments they should make. The result was just two briefs, one on behalf of the NCAI, which would make the constitutional arguments in support of construing the *Duro* fix as a valid affirmation of inherent tribal authority, and the other on behalf of eighteen tribes, including the Spirit Lake Sioux Nation where Billy Jo Lara resided, presenting the tribal perspective and the policy arguments in favor of upholding the *Duro* fix as written.

The choices made in these briefs clearly reflect a tribal perspective on both the tribal-federal relationship and the lived realities of reservation communities. In arguing for tribal inherent jurisdiction under the *Duro* fix, the U.S. Attorney in [an earlier case] had stated that, "Tribal sovereignty is a vessel that Congress may fill or drain at its pleasure," 255 F.3d at 680, a metaphor which, while it supported congressional power to affirm inherent sovereignty, presented that sovereignty as an insignificant thing, the toy of Congress. The NCAI briefs did not rely on such demeaning metaphors. Instead, *** they argued that plenary power over tribes was like that over states under the Commerce Clause, and just as states exercised inherent, not delegated, authority when Congress relaxed common law restrictions on state authority, so did tribes under the *Duro* fix. In addition, the brief stated, although Congress had usually used its plenary power to diminish tribal sovereignty, there was nothing to suggest that "Congress's authority in this area is a one-way ratchet, permitting diminution of tribal sovereignty but never the recognition or affirmation of it." The arguments centered not on the boundless nature of congressional power, but on its relationship to tribal sovereignty: "It is precisely because a Tribe is a sovereign governmental authority that Congress may authorize the Tribe qua sovereign to exercise sovereign powers, rather than to act as a federal agency." ***

The members of the Working Group also encouraged sympathetic states to submit an amicus brief of their own, with the result that Washington, Arizona, California, Colorado, Michigan, Montana, New Mexico, and Oregon—most of the states with the largest Indian communities in the Nation—filed a brief fully supporting the United States. The brief was an effective counterweight to the far less supportive brief filed by six other states. ***

*** [T]he [NCAI] brief did not dwell on whether the Supreme Court got its history wrong in suggesting that tribes had lost inherent criminal jurisdiction over non-members. *** The historical argument was left for the brief by the tribes, part of the policy argument for upholding the affirmation, rather than justification for congressional power to do so. The tribes' brief also emphasized the reality of non-member Indians in Indian country, and the tribes' need for reversal of the *Duro* decision "to keep the peace in their communities." ***

The decision in *Lara* reflected the influence of both of these briefs, citing the tribes' brief for the status of Lara in the Spirit Lake Sioux community, and relying, both in oral argument, and in the decision, on the notion that congressional power over tribal sovereignty was not a one-way ratchet. The briefs also appear to have influenced the Court's description of congressional plenary power,*** [describing it as] part of an ongoing relationship with a sovereign community, rather than the creature of tribal dependence and helplessness ***. Although early in his career Justice Stevens had expressed concern about subjection of non-members to tribal jurisdiction, in *Lara* he concurred specifically to reiterate the tribal position that, "[g]iven the fact that Congress can authorize the States to exercise—as *their own*—inherent powers that the Constitution has otherwise placed off limits, I find nothing exceptional in the conclusion that it can also relax restrictions on an ancient inherent tribal power." *** Coordinated legal advocacy may finally be having the effect of educating the Court, at least on a case-by-case basis.

After the Tribal Supreme Court Project was founded in 2002, the tribal record in the Rehnquist Court was closer to a 50–50 ratio, with wins in *Lara*; *United States v. White Mountain Apache Tribe*, 537 U.S. 465 (2003); and *Cherokee Nation of Oklahoma v. Leavitt*, 543 U.S. 631 (2005), losses in *City of Sherrill v. Oneida Indian Nation*, 544 U.S. 197 (2005); *United States v. Navajo Nation*, 537 U.S. 488 (2003); and a nominal loss that was more of a punt in *Inyo County v. Paiute–Shoshone Indians of the Bishop Community*, 538 U.S. 701 (2003). Taking into account the significance of these cases and the extent to which they altered the legal landscape, *Sherrill*, a loss, was extremely significant, while *Lara* was extremely significant on the win side.

The first ten years of the Roberts Court seemed to be a step backwards for tribal interests. By 2013, the Court had decided eleven Indian law cases and ruled against the tribal parties in nine of those. For more on Indian law in the first decade of the Roberts Court, see Richard A. Guest, *Motherhood and Apple Pie: Judicial Termination and the Roberts Court*, 56 APR Fed. Lawyer 52 (March/April 2009). From the 2012/13 term forward, however, the Court has upheld foundational principles in several key opinions and decided in favor of tribal interests in eight out of nine cases for a tribal win/loss record of nine out of ten since 2005. Justices Kagan, Sotomayor, and Gorsuch have proven to be reliable proponents of the Indian law principles of interpretation as well as strong defenders of tribal treaties. Why, despite the different political and interpretive commitments of these Justices, do you think they all tend to view at least some Indian law cases similarly?

Supreme Court Case	Outcome for Tribal Interests	Brief Summary
Wagnon v. Prairie Band Pottawatomie Nation, 546 U.S. 95 (2005)	L	State can tax gas sold by non-Indian distributor to tribal gas station providing fuel largely to customers at tribal casino.
Plains Commerce Bank v. Long Family Land & Cattle Co., 554 U.S. 316 (2008)	L	Tribal court lacks jurisdiction over suit by tribal members against non-Indian bank .
Carcieri v. Salazar, 555 U.S. 379 (2009)	L	Secretary of Interior cannot put land into trust for tribes not under federal jurisdiction in 1934.
Hawaii v. Office of Hawaiian Affairs, 556 U.S. 163 (2009)	L	State cannot prevent further encumbrance of land seized from Kingdom of Hawai'i despite congressional resolution

Supreme Court Case	Outcome for Tribal Interests	Brief Summary
		acknowledging overthrow of Hawai'ian government.
United States v. Navajo Nation, 556 U.S. 287 (2009)	L	Tribe does not have trust claim against U.S. under federal statutes governing coal and mineral leasing.
Madison County v. Oneida Indian Nation, 562 U.S. 42 (2011)	V	Dispute between county and tribe over taxation of tribal property vacated after tribe's voluntary waiver of sovereign immunity.
United States v. Tohono O'odham Nation, 131 S. Ct. 1723 (2011) and *United States v. Eastern Shawnee Tribe*, 131 S. Ct. 2872 (2011)	L/V	*Tohono O'odham*: No jurisdiction over trust claim against U.S. while court of claims cases pending; *Eastern Shawnee* vacated following *Tohono O'odham*.
United States v. Jicarilla Apache Nation, 131 S. Ct. 2313 (2011)	L	U.S. can assert attorney-client privilege and refuse to disclose documents to tribe relevant to trust claims.
Salazar v. Ramah Navajo Nation, 132 S. Ct. 2181 (2012)	W	U.S. must pay contract support costs to tribe under self-government contracts.
Match-E-Be-Nash-She-Wish Band of Pottawatomi Indians v. Patchak, 132 S. Ct. 2199 (2012)	L	Non-tribal party has standing to challenge Secretary's land-into-trust decision.
Adoptive Couple v. Baby Girl, 133 S. Ct. 2552 (2013)	L	Indian Child Welfare Act does not require showing of harm to child before terminating parental rights of tribal member father who never had physical custody of child placed for adoption by non-Indian mother.
Michigan v. Bay Mills Indian Community, 134 S. Ct. 2024 (2014)	W	Tribal sovereign immunity bars state's lawsuit against tribe for operating casino on off-reservation land acquired by tribe with congressional trust funds.
Menominee Indian Tribe of Wisconsin v. United States, 136 S. Ct. 750 (2016)	L	Tribe's failure to file cost recovery claim from the Indian Health Service within administrative deadline is not overcome by the government's trust obligation or other equitable tolling provisions.
Nebraska v. Parker, 136 S. Ct. 1072 (2016)	W	Tribe's reservation is not diminished by allotment statutes.
United States v. Bryant, 136 S. Ct. 1954 (2016)	W	No Sixth Amendment violation when tribal court domestic violence convictions are counted as predicates to a federal crime.

Supreme Court Case	Outcome for Tribal Interests	Brief Summary
Dollar General Corp. v. Mississippi Band of Choctaw Indians, 136 S. Ct. 2159 (2016)	[W]	Equally divided Court affirms Fifth Circuit in holding that non-Indian corporation is subject to tribal court jurisdiction.
Upper Skagit Indian Tribe v. Lundgren, 138 S. Ct. 1649 (2018)	W	Tribal sovereign immunity from suit is not foreclosed in an action about ownership of non-Indian real property.
Washington v. United States, 138 S. Ct. 1832 (2018)	[W]	Equally divided Court affirms Ninth Circuit decision requiring state to dismantle culverts that block fish passage in violation of tribal treaty rights.
Washington State Dep't of Licensing v. Cougar Den, Inc., 139 S. Ct. 1000 (2019)	W	Tribal treaty provision preempts state fuel tax from applying to tribal enterprise's importation of fuel for sale on-reservation.
Herrera v. Wyoming, 139 S. Ct. 1686 (2019)	W	Tribal off-reservation treaty hunting rights were not abrogated by state's admission to the union or establishment of national forest.

NOTES AND QUESTIONS

Before turning to specialized topics in the remaining chapters of this book, it is worth your time to consider the material examined so far as a topic for extended deliberation. Consider, for example, whether there is a fundamental contradiction in founding a country that has evolved into a democracy based on universal suffrage, popular and open elections, and the protection of individual freedoms and private property, through the process of colonization, involuntary displacement, and subordination of indigenous persons and their pre-existing institutions. How well has the United States done in balancing the felt necessities of the colonial project with its commitment to democracy and human rights within our borders? Where has the United States fallen particularly short? In contrast, where has the United States done better? For example, even a century ago, it was probably unimaginable to non-Indian political leaders that tribes would have vibrant self-government in the twenty-first century. And yet it is clear that today, despite the vision of tribal self-governance that emerges from some recent Supreme Court cases, American Indian nations are here to stay, and in many ways are striving to meet the cultural, political, and economic needs of their communities. No doubt this is almost entirely the result of Indian resolve, but are there features of U.S. law that have provided mechanisms that have assisted the tribes?

It is sometimes said that federal Indian law is a strange and anachronistic enterprise, concerned with internal colonial administration. Other times, it is said that the most conspicuous feature of this area of law is its profound incoherence, the unsteady and unpredictable path of the case law. But is federal Indian law truly less coherent than other bodies of law you have studied? Is federal Indian law less coherent than, for example, the *Erie* doctrine? If not, why do you think people might nonetheless notice the incoherence in federal

Indian law more than in other fields? Finally, it might be said that, although the United States has often fallen short of its ideals in this area, there are aspects of this body of law that represent a great country attempting to mitigate its historic wrongs. What do you think?

CHAPTER 9

NATURAL RESOURCES, HUNTING, FISHING AND GATHERING RIGHTS

■ ■ ■

Indian tribes and individuals own approximately 56 million acres of land held in trust by the United States for the benefit of the Indians or subject to federal restrictions on alienation. Approximately 45 million more acres are held in fee simple by Alaska Native corporations pursuant to the Alaska Native Claims Settlement Act and are free of restrictions on alienation. *See* Chapter 12. Lands held in fee simple within the boundaries of Indian country may also be subject to special tribal and federal jurisdictional rules, but Alaska Native corporation lands are not Indian country. In addition, tribes and their members may have rights of access to other property outside Indian country for hunting, fishing or gathering of natural resources. These property interests are subject to a complex web of federal regulations, controls and protections. Section I of this chapter covers the nature of tribal ownership of land; special statutory schemes governing tribal development of their resources; regulation of water and air; and ownership of submerged lands. Section II covers hunting, fishing and gathering rights retained by tribes both on and off of their reservations. Indian water rights are covered in the next chapter.

I. LAND OWNERSHIP AND ENVIRONMENTAL REGULATION

Early American law characterized Indian possessory rights as aboriginal title, or original Indian title. In *Mitchel v. United States*, 34 U.S. 711, 746 (1835) the Court reviewed the nature of aboriginal title:

> Indian possession or occupation was considered with reference to their habits and modes of life; their hunting grounds were as much in their actual possession as the cleared fields of the whites; and their rights to its exclusive enjoyment in their own way and for their own purposes were as much respected, until they abandoned them, made a cession to the government, or an authorized sale to individuals. *** The merits of this case do not make it necessary to inquire whether the Indians within the United States had any other rights of soil or jurisdiction; it is enough to consider it as a settled principle, that their right of occupancy is considered as sacred as the fee simple of the whites.

The rights of occupancy and possession included in aboriginal title can only be extinguished by the United States. *Id.; see also Johnson v. M'Intosh,* 21 U.S. 543 (1823), ch. 2, *supra.*

Despite the statements that aboriginal title was sacred and entitled to respect and protection, in *Tee–Hit–Ton Indians* the Court held that the federal government could extinguish aboriginal title without paying the compensation otherwise required by the Fifth Amendment's Takings Clause. *Tee–Hit–Ton Indians v. United States*, 348 U.S. 272 (1955), ch. 4, § II, *supra*. Tribal rights to much of the remaining unextinguished aboriginal land, however, have been formally acknowledged in federal treaties, statutes, or executive orders. Thus, while most treaties entered into with tribes provided for the cession of vast amounts of land to the United States government, the treaties also reserved lands "for the exclusive use and benefit" of the signatory tribe or tribes. For example, the Treaty with the Nez Perce, art 2, 12 Stat. 957 (1855) provides: "There is, however, Reserved, from the lands above ceded for the use and occupation of the said tribe, and as a general reservation for other friendly tribes and bands of Indians in Washington Territory, *** the tract of land included within the following boundaries ***." Other tribes had their title confirmed through agreements ratified by Congress after the end of treaty-making in 1871. In *Sioux Nation v. United States*, 448 U.S. 371 (1980), the Court limited the scope of *Tee–Hit–Ton* by affirming that "federally recognized" aboriginal title was protected by the Takings Clause. *See* ch. 4, § II., 1, *supra*.

This summary does not resolve many complex questions regarding tribal property rights. Do they include timber, mineral rights, and other natural resources on tribal lands? How are these resources to be managed? Who—the federal government, the states, or the tribes—has authority over environmental regulation in Indian country? These matters are discussed below. Finally, the materials in this chapter address the conflicting precedents concerning who has the right to lands submerged beneath navigable waters in Indian country. For a more detailed examination of the intersection between Natural Resources and Federal Indian Law, see Judith V. Royster, Michael C. Blumm & Elizabeth A. Kronk Warner, Native American Natural Resources Law: Cases and Materials (4th Ed. 2018).

A. OWNERSHIP AND MANAGEMENT OF NATURAL RESOURCES ON TRIBAL LANDS

Indian reservations and trust lands outside of Alaska encompass an estimated four percent of known U.S. oil and gas, 40 percent of uranium deposits, and 30 percent of western coal reserves. Cohen's Handbook of Federal Indian Law § 17.04, 995 (2012). They also contain over 6 million acres of commercial timberlands. *Id.* Although the common law rule in other contexts is that ownership of a tract of land includes the rights "*Cujus est solum ejus est usque ad coelum*," from the heavens to the center of the earth, the government challenged whether such rights would be included in tribal ownership. This question was resolved in the following case.

UNITED STATES V. SHOSHONE TRIBE

304 U.S. 111, 58 S. Ct. 794, 82 L.Ed. 1213 (1938)

JUSTICE BUTLER delivered the opinion of the Court.

The Shoshone Tribe brought this suit to recover the value of part of its reservation taken by the United States by putting upon it without the tribe's consent, a band of Arapahoe Indians. ***

The sole question for decision is whether, as the United States contends, the Court of Claims erred in holding that the right of the tribe included the timber and mineral resources within the reservation.

The findings show: The United States, by the treaty of July 2, 1863, 18 Stat. 685, set apart for the Shoshone Tribe a reservation of 44,672,000 acres located in Colorado, Utah, Idaho, and Wyoming. By the treaty of July 3, 1868, 15 Stat. 673, the tribe ceded that reservation to the United States. And by it the United States agreed that the "district of country" 3,054,182 acres definitely described "shall be and the same is set apart for the absolute and undisturbed use and occupation of the Shoshone Indians ***, and the United States now solemnly agrees that no persons," with exceptions not important here, "shall ever be permitted to pass over, settle upon, or reside in" that territory. ***

The treaty emphasized the importance of education; the United States agreed to provide a school house and teacher for every thirty children, and the tribe promised to send the children to school. The United States also agreed to provide instruction by a farmer for members cultivating the soil, clothing for members of the tribe, and a physician, carpenter, miller, engineer, and blacksmith. It stipulated that no treaty for the cession of any portion of the reservation held in common should be valid as against the Indians, unless signed by at least a majority of all interested male adults; and that no cession by the tribe should be construed to deprive any member of his right to any tract of land selected by him.

When the treaty of 1868 was made, the tribe consisted of full-blood blanket Indians, unable to read, write, or speak English. Upon consummation of the treaty, the tribe went, and has since remained, upon the reservation. It was known to contain valuable mineral deposits—gold, oil, coal, and gypsum. It included more than 400,000 acres of timber, extensive well-grassed bench lands and fertile river valleys conveniently irrigable. It was well protected by mountain ranges and a divide, and was the choicest and best-watered portion of Wyoming. [In March of 1878 the United States escorted most of the Northern Arapahoe Tribe to the Shoshone Reservation and forced them to remain there. *Shoshone Tribe v. United States*, 82 Ct. Cl. 23, para. 10 (Ct. Cl. 1935). Thereafter the two tribes were treated as tenants in common.]

In 1904 the Shoshones and Arapahoes ceded to the United States 1,480,000 acres to be held by it in trust for the sale of such timber lands, timber, and other products, and for the making of leases for various purposes. The net proceeds were to be credited to the Indians. From 1907 to 1919 there were allotted to members of the tribes 245,058 acres.

The court's finding of the ultimate fact is: "The fair and reasonable value of a one-half undivided interest of the Shoshone or Wind River Reservation of a total of 2,343,540† acres, which was taken by the United States on March 19, 1878, from the Shoshone Tribe of Indians for the Northern Arapahoe Tribe, was, on March 19, 1878, $1,581,889.50." That is $1.35 per acre for 1,171,770 acres, one-half of the reservation in 1878, at the time of taking. The United States does not challenge the principle or basis upon which the court determined the amount to be added to constitute just compensation.

The substance of the government's point is that in fixing the value of the tribe's right, the lower court included as belonging to the tribe substantial elements of value, ascribable to mineral and timber resources, which in fact belonged to the United States.

It contends that the Shoshones' right to use and occupy the lands of the reservation did not include the ownership of the timber and minerals and that the opinion of the court below departs from the general principles of law regarding Indian land tenure and the uniform policy of the government in dealing with Indian tribes. It asks for reversal with directions to "determine the value of the Indians' right of use and occupancy but to exclude therefrom 'the net value of the lands' and 'the net value of any timber or minerals.' "

***

In this case we have held, 299 U.S. 476, 484, that the tribe had the right of occupancy with all its beneficial incidents; that, the right of occupancy being the primary one and as sacred as the fee, division by the United States of the Shoshones' right with the Arapahoes was an appropriation of the land *pro tanto*; that although the United States always had legal title to the land and power to control and manage the affairs of the Indians, it did not have power to give to others or to appropriate to its own use any part of the land without rendering, or assuming the obligation to pay, just compensation to the tribe, for that would be not the exercise of guardianship or management, but confiscation.

It was not then necessary to consider, but we are now called upon to decide, whether, by the treaty, the tribe acquired beneficial ownership of the minerals and timber on the reservation. The phrase "absolute and undisturbed use and occupation" is to be read, with other parts of the document, having regard to the purpose of the arrangement made, the relation between the parties, and the settled policy of the United States fairly to deal with Indian tribes. In treaties made with them the United States seeks no advantage for itself; friendly and dependent Indians are likely to accept without discriminating scrutiny the terms proposed. They are not to be interpreted narrowly, as sometimes may be writings expressed in words of art employed by conveyancers, but are to be construed in the sense in which naturally the Indians would understand them. ***

The principal purpose of the treaty was that the Shoshones should have, and permanently dwell in, the defined district of country. To that end the United States granted and assured to the tribe peaceable and unqualified possession of the land in perpetuity. Minerals and standing timber are constituent

†. The reservation had been reduced to 2,343,000 acres by the Shoshone's cession to the United States of 700,642 acres in 1874. Eds.

elements of the land itself. *** For all practical purposes, the tribe owned the land. Grants of land subject to the Indian title by the United States, which had only the naked fee, would transfer no beneficial interest. *Leavenworth, L. & G.R.R. v. United States*, 92 U.S. 733, 742, 743; *Beecher v. Wetherby*, 95 U.S. 517, 525. The right of perpetual and exclusive occupancy of the land is not less valuable than full title in fee. ***

The treaty, though made with knowledge that there were mineral deposits and standing timber in the reservation, contains nothing to suggest that the United States intended to retain for itself any beneficial interest in them. The words of the grant, coupled with the government's agreement to exclude strangers, negative the idea that the United States retained beneficial ownership. The grant of right to members of the tribe severally to select and hold tracts on which to establish homes for themselves and families, and the restraint upon cession of land held in common or individually, suggest beneficial ownership in the tribe. As transactions between a guardian and his wards are to be construed favorably to the latter, doubts, if there were any, as to ownership of lands, minerals, or timber would be resolved in favor of the tribe. The cession in 1904 by the tribe to the United States in trust reflects a construction by the parties that supports the tribe's claim, for if it did not own, creation of a trust to sell or lease for its benefit would have been unnecessary and inconsistent with the rights of the parties.

Although the United States retained the fee, and the tribe's right of occupancy was incapable of alienation or of being held otherwise than in common, that right is as sacred and as securely safeguarded as is fee simple absolute title. *Cherokee Nation v. State of Georgia*, 5 Pet. 1, 48; *Worcester v. State of Georgia*, *supra*, 6 Pet. 515, 580, 8 L.Ed. 483. Subject to the conditions imposed by the treaty, the Shoshone Tribe had the right that has always been understood to belong to Indians, undisturbed possessors of the soil from time immemorial. Provisions in aid of teaching children and of adult education in farming, and to secure for the tribe medical and mechanical service, to safeguard tribal and individual titles, when taken with other parts of the treaty, plainly evidence purpose on the part of the United States to help to create an independent permanent farming community upon the reservation. Ownership of the land would further that purpose. In the absence of definite expression of intention so to do, the United States will not be held to have kept it from them. The authority of the United States to prescribe title by which individual Indians may hold tracts selected by them within the reservation, to pass laws regulating alienation and descent and for the government of the tribe and its people upon the reservation detracts nothing from the tribe's ownership, but was reserved for the more convenient discharge of the duties of the United States as guardian and sovereign. ***

The lower court did not err in holding that the right of the Shoshone Tribe included the timber and minerals within the reservation.

NOTES AND QUESTIONS

1. In cases like *United States v. Winans* and *Worcester v. Georgia* discussed in earlier chapters, treaties were construed under the expansive

"reserved right" theory, *i.e.*, that treaties were a grant of rights from the Indians, not to them, with a reservation of all rights not explicitly ceded to the United States. What possible rationale is there for the narrow position argued by the government in *Shoshone*? What is the meaning of the Court's statement that the United States retains only the "naked fee" in the land?

2. Does it matter whether the tribe was located within its aboriginal territory, or whether the tribe had been removed to a different and distant location?

Management of Tribal Timber, Agricultural Lands and Minerals

Shoshone and similar cases establish that tribes retain ownership of natural resources on tribal lands, but not who has the authority to manage such resources and how. Historically, the federal government dominated management of such surface resources. Although today federal laws and policies do more to encourage tribal management of such resources, development is still governed by the Nonintercourse Act, 25 U.S.C. § 177, and a host of other federal laws, including some that require federal approval of any leases of tribal property. Cohen's Handbook of Federal Indian Law § 17.011129-30 (2012). The principal statutory authorization for the lease of Indian lands provides:

> Any restricted Indian lands, whether tribally, or individually owned, may be leased by the Indian owners, with the approval of the Secretary of the Interior, for public, religious, educational, recreational, residential, or business purposes, including the development or utilization of natural resources in connection with operations under such leases, for grazing purposes, and for those farming purposes which require the making of a substantial investment in the improvement of the land for the production of specialized crops as determined by said Secretary. All leases so granted shall be for a term of not to exceed twenty-five years, except leases of land located [within particular enumerated reservations].

25 U.S.C. § 415(a). Some tribes are exempt from Secretarial approval under the statute and others have longer lease terms in certain contexts. *See* 25 U.S.C. §§ b-g (exempting Tulalip and other tribes from requirement of Secretarial approval and recognizing longer terms for Navajo, Gila River, and the Assiniboine and Sioux Tribes). Federal leases of tribal land also require consent of the affected tribe. 25 U.S.C. § 5123(e). A major amendment to the statute was passed in 2012 to permit greater tribal autonomy with regard to surface leases. Helping Expedite and Advance Responsible Tribal Home Ownership Act (HEARTH Act of 2012), Pub. L. No. 112-151. The amendments provide that tribes may lease such land for 25 years without secretarial approval, and may provide for two renewals of up to 25 years each. 25 U.S.C. § 415(h). Leases for public, religious, educational, recreational, or residential purposes, may have a term of 75 years. *Id.* The leases must be issued pursuant to tribal code provisions approved by the Secretary, and must include an environmental review process. The act does not apply to mineral leases, timber contracts, grazing permits, rights of way, or water rights except when associated with use of the land itself.

The American Indian Agricultural Resources Management Act of 1990, 25 U.S.C. §§ 3701–3745, was adopted in part to "carry out the trust responsibility of the United States and promote the self-determination of Indian tribes by providing for the management of Indian agricultural lands and related renewable resources in a manner consistent with identified tribal goals and priorities for conservation, multiple use, and sustained yield." 25 U.S.C. § 3702. The statute applies to farmland and rangeland and explicitly excludes forest land. The Act authorizes Indian tribes to develop their own "10–year Indian agriculture resource management and monitoring plan ***." Substantive elements of the plans are mandated by Congress and include assessment and identification of resources, and resource management goals, along with the requirement that a public process be followed for development of the plan. 25 U.S.C. § 3711(b). Secretarial approval of individual or tribal leases is provided for in 25 U.S.C. § 3715.

Another major regulatory program covers timberlands, also known as forested land. The federal government's role in Indian forest management is pervasive, *see United States v. Mitchell*, 463 U.S. 206 (1983), although the National Indian Forest Resource Management Act, 25 U.S.C. §§ 3101–3120, provides for greater tribal involvement and control if desired by the tribe. The Act provides that, "The Secretary shall undertake forest land management activities on Indian forest land, either directly or through contracts, cooperative agreements, or grants under the Indian Self–Determination Act [25 U.S.C. § 450f, *et seq.*]." 25 U.S.C. § 3104. Congress also supplied management objectives for the approximately 18 million acres of Indian forest lands:

> (1) the development, maintenance, and enhancement of Indian forest land in a perpetually productive state in accordance with the principles of sustained yield and with the standards and objectives set forth in forest management plans by providing effective management and protection through the application of sound silvicultural and economic principles to—
>
> (A) the harvesting of forest products,
>
> (B) forestation,
>
> (C) timber stand improvement, and
>
> (D) other forestry practices;
>
> (2) the regulation of Indian forest lands through the development and implementation, with the full and active consultation and participation of the appropriate Indian tribe, of forest management plans which are supported by written tribal objectives and forest marketing programs;
>
> (3) the regulation of Indian forest lands in a manner that will ensure the use of good method and order in harvesting so as to make possible, on a sustained yield basis, continuous productivity and a perpetual forest business;
>
> (4) the development of Indian forest lands and associated value-added industries by Indians and Indian tribes to promote self-sustaining communities, so that Indians may receive from their Indian forest land not only stumpage value, but also the benefit of all the labor and profit that such Indian forest land is capable of yielding;

(5) the retention of Indian forest land in its natural state when an Indian tribe determines that the recreational, cultural, aesthetic, or traditional values of the Indian forest land represents the highest and best use of the land;

(6) the management and protection of forest resources to retain the beneficial effects to Indian forest lands of regulating water run-off and minimizing soil erosion; and

(7) the maintenance and improvement of timber productivity, grazing, wildlife, fisheries, recreation, aesthetic, cultural and other traditional values.

25 U.S.C. § 3104(b).

The statutes governing tribal agricultural and timber resources contemplate either tribal or federal management of the resources. One study of 75 tribal timber industries showed that each position transferred from BIA to tribal control increased both sustained-yield harvests and the price received for tribal timber. Matthew B. Krepps & Richard E. Caves, *Bureaucrats and Indians: Principal–Agent Relations and Efficient Management of Tribal Forest Resources*, 24 J. Econ. Behavior & Org. 133 (1994). Why would an Indian tribe elect to have its resources managed by the Secretary of the Interior through the Bureau of Indian Affairs?

Leasing Indian land for mineral development is governed chiefly by the Indian Mineral Leasing Act of 1938 (IMLA), the Indian Mineral Development Act of 1982, and the Indian Tribal Energy Development and Self–Determination Act of 2005. *See* Cohen's Handbook of Federal Indian Law, *supra*, § 17.02, 1120-41. In *United States v. Navajo Nation*, 537 U.S. 488 (2003), the Supreme Court described the operation of the IMLA in a case involving breach of trust claims brought by the Navajo Nation after the Secretary of the Interior refused to approve recommended increases in coal production royalties.

UNITED STATES V. NAVAJO NATION

537 U.S. 488, 123 S. Ct. 1079, 155 L.Ed.2d 60 (2003)

The IMLA, which governs aspects of mineral leasing on Indian tribal lands, states that "unallotted lands within any Indian reservation," or otherwise under federal jurisdiction, "may, with the approval of the Secretary ***, be leased for mining purposes, by authority of the tribal council or other authorized spokesmen for such Indians, for terms not to exceed ten years and as long thereafter as minerals are produced in paying quantities." § 396a. In addition "to provid[ing] Indian tribes with a profitable source of revenue," *Cotton Petroleum Corp. v. New Mexico,* 490 U.S. 163, 179 (1989), the IMLA aimed to foster tribal self-determination by "giv[ing] Indians a greater say in the use and disposition of the resources found on Indian lands," *BHP Minerals Int'l Inc.,* 139 I.B.L.A. 269, 311 (1997).

Prior to enactment of the IMLA, decisions whether to grant mineral leases on Indian land generally rested with the Government. *See, e.g.,* Act of June 30, 1919, ch. 4, § 26, 41 Stat. 31, as amended, 25 U.S.C. § 399; *see also infra,* at

1092–1093 (describing § 99). Indian consent was not required, and leases were sometimes granted over tribal objections. *See* H.R. Rep. No. 1872, 75th Cong., 3d Sess., 2 (1938); S. Rep. No. 985, 75th Cong., 1st Sess., 2 (1937); 46 Fed. Cl. 217, 230 (2000). The IMLA, designed to advance tribal independence, empowers Tribes to negotiate mining leases themselves, and, as to coal leasing, assigns primarily an approval role to the Secretary.

Although the IMLA covers mineral leasing generally, in a number of discrete provisions it deals particularly with oil and gas leases. *See* 25 U.S.C. § 396b (requirements for public auctions of oil and gas leases); § 396d (oil and gas leases are "subject to the terms of any reasonable cooperative unit or other plan approved or prescribed by [the] Secretary"); § 396g ("[T]o avoid waste or to promote the conservation of natural resources or the welfare of the Indians," the Secretary may approve leases of Indian lands "for the subsurface storage of oil and gas."). The IMLA contains no similarly specific prescriptions for coal leases; it simply remits coal leases, in common with all mineral leases, to the governance of rules and regulations promulgated by the Secretary. § 396d.

During all times relevant here, the IMLA regulations provided that "Indian tribes *** may, with the approval of the Secretary *** or his authorized representative, lease their land for mining purposes." 25 C.F.R. § 211.2 (1985). In line with the IMLA itself, the regulations treated oil and gas leases in more detail than coal leases. The regulations regarding royalties, for example, specified procedures applicable to oil and gas leases, including criteria for the Secretary to employ in setting royalty rates. §§ 211.13, 211.16, 211.17. As to coal royalties, in contrast, the regulations required only that the rate be "not less than 10 cents per ton." § 211.15(c). No other limitation was placed on the Tribe's negotiating capacity or the Secretary's approval authority.

Although the courts below found that the Secretary of the Interior improperly used its approval authority to act in the interests of the Peabody Coal Company by concealing its approval of a higher royalty rate, the Supreme Court ruled in *Navajo Nation* that the United States was not liable for a breach of trust because the IMLA no longer gave the federal government detailed management responsibilities for coal on Indian lands. On remand the Federal Circuit identified additional laws and regulations that it held gave rise to a breach of trust claim, but the Supreme Court again reversed. *United States v. Navajo Nation*, 556 U.S. 287, 129 S. Ct. 1547 (2009); *see* ch. 4, § II. B., *supra*. *See also*, Alan Ramo & Deborah Behles, *Transitioning a Community Away from Fossil-Fuel Generation to a Green Economy: An Approach Using State Utility Commission Authority*, 15 Minn. J.L. Sci. & Tech. 505, 510-13 (2014) (noting that the Navajo Nation was only receiving a 2% royalty under the old lease).

THE INDIAN TRIBAL ENERGY DEVELOPMENT AND SELF–DETERMINATION ACT (ITESDA)

25 U.S.C. §§ 3501–3506

This classic self-determination era statute allows tribes to enter into agreements with the Secretary of the Interior to remove the Secretary of the Interior's responsibility of approving tribal leases for energy development. It was passed in 2005 but had provisions that made tribes wary of taking advantage of it. Amendments in 2018 were intended to make it more user-friendly. In tandem with the HEARTH Act of 2012, it provides tribes with the opportunity to remove a good deal of the paternalism bound up with federal restrictions on encumbrance of tribal lands. The Act provides, in part, as follows:

25 U.S.C. § 3504 (a) Leases and business agreements

In accordance with this section—

(1) an Indian tribe may, at the discretion of the Indian tribe, enter into a lease or business agreement for the purpose of energy resource development on tribal land, including a lease or business agreement for—

(A) exploration for, extraction of, processing of, or other development of the energy mineral resources of the Indian tribe located on tribal land;

(B) construction or operation of—

(i) an electric production, generation, transmission, or distribution facility (including a facility that produces electricity from renewable energy resources) located on tribal land; or

(ii) a facility to process or refine energy resources, at least a portion of which have been developed on or produced from tribal land; or

(C) pooling, unitization, or communitization of the energy mineral resources of the Indian tribe located on tribal land

*** [The Tribe does not need Secretarial approval for any such lease of business agreement if it first has in place a tribal energy resource agreement as provided in the next section.]

(e) Tribal energy resource agreements

(2)(A)(i) In general

On the date that is 271 days after the date on which the Secretary receives a tribal energy resource agreement from a qualified Indian tribe under paragraph (1), the tribal energy resource agreement shall take effect, unless the Secretary disapproves the tribal energy resource agreement under subparagraph (B).

(B) Disapproval

The Secretary shall disapprove a tribal energy resource agreement submitted pursuant to paragraph (1) or (4)(B) only if—

(i) a provision of the tribal energy resource agreement violates applicable Federal law (including regulations) or a treaty applicable to the Indian tribe;

(C) Tribal energy resource agreements submitted under paragraph (1) shall establish, and include provisions to ensure compliance with, an environmental review process that, with respect to a lease, business agreement, or right-of-way under this section, provides for, at a minimum--

(i) a process for ensuring that—

(I) the public is informed of, and has reasonable opportunity to comment on, any significant environmental impacts of the proposed action; and

(II) the Indian tribe provides responses to relevant and substantive public comments on any impacts described in subclause (I) before the Indian tribe approves the lease, business agreement, or right-of-way;

***

Energy resource agreements must also contain provisions providing: for periodic review of the tribal program by the Secretary. Regulations implementing the statute can be found at 25 C.F.R. part 224.

NOTES AND QUESTIONS

1. *Removing the federal government from the equation?* ITEDSA's effect is to reduce the role of the federal government in tribal leasing and development decisions, and replace the multiple laws governing different energy and mineral resources with a single legal regime. To take advantage of the statute, however, the Secretary of the Interior must first approve a detailed tribal energy resource agreement (TERA) with the tribe. Because of the numerous requirements for such agreements, many beyond the capacity of most tribes, few if any tribes had been able to access ITEDSA's benefits. *See* Judith V. Royster, *Tribal Energy Development: Renewables and the Problem of the Current Statutory Structures*, 31 Stan. Envtl. L.J. 91 (2012); *see also* Elizabeth Ann Kronk Warner, *Tribal Renewable Energy Development Under the Hearth Act: An Independently Rational but Collectively Deficient Option*, 55 Ariz. L. Rev. 1031 (2013) (critiquing HEARTH Act and ITEDSA). The significant amendments in 2018 are predicted to substantially improve the process. *See* Michael Maruca, *From Exploitation to Equity: Building Native-Owned Renewable Energy Generation in Indian Country*, 43 Wm. & Mary Envtl. L. & Pol'y Rev. 391 (2019)) discussome some of the issues with TERA and how the 2018 changes to the act are supposed to help).

The approval process requires federal compliance with the National Environmental Policy Act (NEPA). *See* 25 C.F.R. § 224.70. Can you think of any benefits of asserting greater tribal control under the 2005 Energy Act amendments? Would there be any detriment to a tribe that asserted such control? Remember that federal approval of tribal actions can trigger NEPA and/or the Endangered Species Act.

2. *Self–Determination and federal control.* Why should the federal government, through the Secretary of the Interior, exercise such pervasive control over the leasing of tribal resources? Is this just a relic of the past that will not go away, or is there a substantive reason for the continued role of the Secretary?

3. *Self-determination by federal regulation?* The Department of Interior in 2012 revised the regulations governing leasing on Indian land for housing, economic development, and other purposes. 25 C.F.R. § 162.001. The regulations provide that "activities under a lease conducted on the leased premises are not subject to any fee, tax, assessment, levy, or other charge (e.g., business use, privilege, public utility, excise, gross revenue taxes) imposed by any State or political subdivision of a State." 25 C.F.R. § 162.017. What is the source of authority for the Secretary to preclude state and local taxation, and regulation? One court held that a state rental tax imposed on a non-Indian lessee was invalid but conducted its own preemption analysis rather than simply deferring to the Secretary's interpretation. *See Seminole Tribe of Florida v. Stranburg*, 799 F.3d 1324, 1335 (11th Cir. 2015), *cert. denied sub nom. Seminole Tribe of Florida v. Biegalski*, 136 S. Ct. 2480 (2016) (applying the *White Mountain Apache Tribe v. Bracker* test to a state rental tax assessed against a non-Indian tribal lessee). *See* Ch. 7, § 3 (covering federal preemption of state law).

B. ENVIRONMENTAL REGULATION

In the modern era, Congress has passed several environmental statutes that provide national baselines for environmental protection. Some of these laws include tribes, along with states, as eligible to administer the regulatory programs within their jurisdiction. Since states generally lack regulatory authority over tribal members and tribes within Indian country, the Environmental Protection Agency (EPA) has sometimes enforced general federal environmental laws within Indian country. *Compare Phillips Petroleum Co. v. EPA*, 803 F.2d 545 (10th Cir. 1986) (affirming EPA's authority under Safe Drinking Water Act to regulate oil and gas development to protect groundwater sources) *and Washington Dept. of Ecology v. EPA*, 752 F.2d 1465 (9th Cir. 1985) (denying state jurisdiction to regulate Indians and non-Indians within Indian country under Resource Conservation and Recovery Act, since Congress had not authorized state regulation). While tribes have inherent power to regulate their members and territories, the Supreme Court has sharply curtailed tribal authority over nonmembers acting on nonmember owned land in Indian country. *See*, ch. 8, *supra*. Under some federal environmental laws, however, tribes have assumed federal authority to regulate environmental conditions in their territory, and thus achieved jurisdiction over non-Indians regardless of land status. Most of the litigation has involved the Clean Water Act and Clean Air Act. The next case, *City of Albuquerque v. Browner*, concerns tribal regulation under the Clean Water Act, and the following case, *Arizona Public Service Company v. EPA*, concerns the Clean Air Act. The cases highlight different approaches to environmental regulation—or do they?

CITY OF ALBUQUERQUE V. BROWNER

97 F.3d 415 (10th Cir. 1996)

MCKAY, CIRCUIT JUDGE.

The City of Albuquerque [Albuquerque] filed a complaint challenging the U.S. Environmental Protection Agency's [EPA] approval of the Pueblo of Isleta's [Isleta Pueblo] water quality standards on numerous grounds. After denying Albuquerque a temporary restraining order and a preliminary injunction, the district court denied its motion for summary judgment while granting the Defendant EPA's motion for summary judgment. Albuquerque now appeals the district court's judgment.

I. Background

In 1987, Congress amended the Clean Water Act to authorize the Defendant EPA to treat Indian tribes as states under certain circumstances for purposes of the Clean Water Act. Through the amendment Congress merged two of the four critical elements necessary for tribal sovereignty—water rights and government jurisdiction—by granting tribes jurisdiction to regulate their water resources in the same manner as states. Congress's authorization for the EPA to treat Indian tribes as states preserves the right of tribes to govern their water resources within the comprehensive statutory framework of the Clean Water Act. This case involves the first challenge to water quality standards adopted by an Indian tribe under the Clean Water Act amendment.[4]

The Rio Grande River flows south through New Mexico before turning southeast to form the border between Texas and Mexico. Plaintiff City of Albuquerque operates a waste treatment facility which dumps into the river approximately five miles north of the Isleta Pueblo Indian Reservation. The EPA recognized Isleta Pueblo as a state for purposes of the Clean Water Act on October 12, 1992. The Isleta Pueblo adopted water quality standards for Rio

---

4. The Clean Water Act provides two measures of water quality. One measure is an "effluent limitations guideline." Effluent limitations guidelines are uniform, technology-based standards promulgated by the EPA, which restrict the quantities, rates and concentrations of specified substances discharged from point sources. *See* 33 U.S.C. §§ 1311, 1314. The other measure of water quality is a "water quality standard." Unlike the technology-based effluent limitations guidelines, water quality standards are not based on pollution control technologies, but express the desired condition or use of a particular waterway. Water quality standards supplement technology-based effluent limitations guidelines "so that numerous point sources, despite individual compliance with effluent limitations, may be further regulated to prevent water quality from falling below acceptable levels." *EPA v. California ex rel. State Water Resources Control Bd.*, 426 U.S. 200, 205 n. 12 (1976). In this case, the water quality standards of the Isleta Pueblo are at issue.

There are three elements of water quality standards under the Clean Water Act: (1) one or more designated "uses" of each waterway (*e.g.*, public water supply, recreation, or agriculture) consistent with the goals of the Act as articulated in 33 U.S.C. § 1251; (2) "criteria" expressed in numerical concentration levels or narrative statements specifying the amount of various pollutants that may be present in the water and still protect the designate uses; and (3) an anti-degradation provision. 33 U.S.C. § 1313(c)(2)(A); 40 C.F.R. § 131 (1995).

Grande water flowing through the tribal reservation, which were approved by the EPA on December 24, 1992.[5] The Isleta Pueblo's water quality standards are more stringent than the State of New Mexico's standards.

The Albuquerque waste treatment facility discharges into the Rio Grande under a National Pollution Discharge Elimination System [NPDES] permit issued by the EPA. The EPA sets permit discharge limits for waste treatment facilities so they meet state water quality standards. Albuquerque filed this action as the EPA was in the process of revising Albuquerque's NPDES permit to meet the Isleta Pueblo's water quality standards.

In its complaint, Albuquerque challenged the EPA's approval of Isleta Pueblo's water quality standards on numerous grounds. The district court denied Albuquerque's request for a temporary restraining order and a preliminary injunction. Then, the district court denied Plaintiff's motion for summary judgment while granting the Defendant EPA's motion for summary judgment.

***

III. Tribal Sovereignty Under the Clean Water Act

Albuquerque acknowledges that the 1987 amendment to the Clean Water Act authorizes the EPA to treat tribes as states. Act of Feb. 4, 1987, Pub. L. No. 100–4, tit. V, § 506, 101 Stat. 76 (codified as amended at 33 U.S.C. § 1377). Albuquerque contends, however, that 33 U.S.C. § 1377 does not allow tribes to establish water quality standards more stringent than federal standards and does not permit tribal standards to be enforced beyond tribal reservation boundaries.

In *Chevron, USA, Inc. v. Natural Resources Defense Council,* 467 U.S. 837, 842–43 (1984), the Supreme Court established a two-step approach to judicial review of agency interpretations of acts of Congress. First, the reviewing court must determine whether there is a clear and unambiguous congressional intent concerning the precise question at issue. If congressional intent is clear and unambiguous, then that intent is the law and must be given effect. A reviewing court proceeds to the second step "if the statute is silent or ambiguous with respect to the specific issue." *Id.* at 843. Then, "the question for the court is whether the agency's answer is based on a permissible construction of the statute." *Id.* The EPA, however, is entitled to considerable deference in its interpretation of the Clean Water Act because it is charged with administering the Act. *See Chevron,* 467 U.S. at 844; *see also Arkansas v. Oklahoma,* 503 U.S. 91, 112 (1992) (criticizing this Court for failing to afford the EPA's interpretation of the Clean Water Act "an appropriate level of deference").

---

5. The EPA provides states with substantial guidance in drafting water quality standards. States must adopt criteria that protect the designated uses. 40 C.F.R. § 131.11 (1995). The Clean Water Act requires the EPA to develop criteria for water quality that reflect the latest scientific knowledge, and to provide those criteria to the states as guidance. 33 U.S.C. § 1314(a). States can draw upon the EPA's recommended water quality criteria or use other criteria for which they have sound scientific support. *See* 40 C.F.R. § 131.11 (1995).

Prior to adopting or revising any water quality standard, the state must provide notice and an opportunity for a public hearing. 40 C.F.R. § 131.10(e) (1995). The criteria may be based on EPA guidance, EPA guidance modified to reflect conditions at the site, or on other scientifically defensible methods. *Id.* After adoption, the states must submit the water quality standards to the EPA for review and approval. 33 U.S.C. § 1313(c)(2). The EPA reviews the state's water quality standards to ensure that they are consistent with the Act's requirements. *Id.* at § 1313(c)(3).

In regard to the first question at issue, we reach the second step of *Chevron* because congressional intent is unclear and ambiguous. Under Albuquerque's interpretation of § 1377, tribes could devise water quality standards which are neither more nor less stringent than federal standards. Albuquerque's statutory construction is based on a negative implication inferred from Congress's failure to incorporate all provisions of the Clean Water Act in § 1377(e). We find that Congress's intent is unclear and ambiguous in regard to § 1377(e) but that the EPA's construction of the 1987 amendment to the Clean Water Act is reasonable and permissible.

Congress's objective in the Clean Water Act is to "restore and maintain the chemical, physical, and biological integrity of the Nation's waters" through the elimination of pollutant discharge into those waters. 33 U.S.C. § 1251(a). Through the Act, Congress designed a comprehensive regulatory scheme that recognized and preserved a primary role for the states in eliminating pollution from our waterways. 33 U.S.C. § 1251(b). The power of states under the Act is underlined by their ability to force the development of technology by setting stringent water quality standards that the EPA can enforce against upstream polluters. *See* 33 U.S.C. §§ 1311(k), 1341, 1342, 1370; *Arkansas,* 503 U.S. at 106 (holding that the EPA's requirement that NPDES dischargers must comply with downstream States' water quality standards was a reasonable exercise of the agency's statutory discretion pursuant to §§ 1341, 1342). In the Clean Water Act, Congress provided the EPA "substantial statutory discretion." *Arkansas,* 503 U.S. at 107. Pursuant to the 1987 amendment of the Clean Water Act, the EPA can treat Indian tribes as states under the Act, provided that the tribes meet certain criteria listed in 33 U.S.C. § 1377(e) and 40 C.F.R. § 131.8(a).[8] ***

In its letter approving the Isleta Pueblo's standards, the EPA cites 33 U.S.C. § 1370 as the basis for Isleta Pueblo's authority to set water quality standards that are more stringent than those recommended by the EPA under the Clean Water Act. Albuquerque argues that tribes cannot adopt discharge limits more stringent than those of the EPA because § 1377 does not make reference to § 1370. Section 1370 prohibits states from imposing standards which are less stringent than those imposed by the federal government, while acknowledging states' inherent right to impose standards or limits that are more stringent than those imposed by the federal government. 33 U.S.C. § 1370. Congress's intent in excluding § 1370 from § 1377(e) is unclear and

8. To qualify as a state under the Act, an Indian tribe must submit an application to the EPA which includes: a statement that the tribe is recognized by the Secretary of the Interior; a descriptive statement demonstrating that the tribal governing body is currently carrying out substantial government functions over a defined area; a description of the tribe's authority to regulate water quality over certain waters; a description of the tribe's capability to administer an effective water quality standards program; and any additional documentation which the Administrator deems necessary to support a tribal application. 40 C.F.R. § 131.8 (1995).

Upon receipt of the application, the Regional Administrator will notify appropriate government entities of the tribe's application and the basis of the tribe's authority to regulate water quality. The Administrator provides a thirty-day period to receive comments on the tribe's assertion of authority. If comments challenge the tribe's authority, the Regional Administrator, after consulting with the Secretary of the Interior, shall determine whether the tribe meets the requirements of 40 C.F.R. § 131.8(a)(3) (1995). Once recognized as a state for purposes of the Act, a tribe may submit proposed water quality standards to EPA.

ambiguous. We decline to read § 1377 as incorporating § 1370 because it was not explicitly included in § 1377(e), as other sections are.

The EPA, however, also construes § 1370 as a savings clause that merely recognizes powers already held by the states. 56 Fed. Reg. 64,886 (1991). Thus, Congress's failure to incorporate § 1370 into § 1377 does not prevent Indian tribes from exercising their inherent sovereign power to impose standards or limits that are more stringent than those imposed by the federal government. Indian tribes have residual sovereign powers that already guarantee the powers enumerated in § 1370, absent an express statutory elimination of those powers.[12] In *Arkansas,* the Court explained that § 1370 "only concerns *state* authority and does not constrain the *EPA's* authority," 503 U.S. at 107; likewise, we do not view § 1370 as implicitly constraining tribes' sovereign authority. We conclude that the EPA's construction of the 1987 amendment to the Clean Water Act—that tribes may establish water quality standards that are more stringent than those imposed by the federal government—is permissible because it is in accord with powers inherent in Indian tribal sovereignty.

In the second question at issue, Albuquerque argues that § 1377 does not expressly permit Indian tribes to enforce effluent limitations or standards under § 1311 to upstream point source dischargers outside of tribal boundaries. Albuquerque misconstrues the Clean Water Act by selectively reading isolated sections; the Clean Water Act is a comprehensive regulatory scheme, and it must be read as such. The express incorporation in § 1377(e) of §§ 1341 and 1342 gives the EPA the authority to issue NPDES permits in compliance with a tribe's water quality standards. Section 1341 authorizes states to establish NPDES programs with the EPA, and § 1342 authorizes the EPA to issue NPDES permits in compliance with downstream state's water quality standards. *See Arkansas,* 503 U.S. at 102, 107 (construing §§ 1341 and 1342 as giving the EPA authority to require an upstream NPDES discharger to comply with downstream state water quality standards). Under the statutory and regulatory scheme, tribes are not applying or enforcing their water quality standards beyond reservation boundaries.[14] Instead, it is the EPA which is exercising its own authority in issuing NPDES permits in compliance with downstream state and tribal water quality standards. In regard to this question, therefore, the 1987 amendment to the Clean Water Act clearly and unambiguously provides tribes the authority to establish NPDES programs in conjunction with the EPA. Under §§ 1311, 1341, 1342 and 1377, the EPA has the authority to require upstream NPDES dischargers, such as Albuquerque, to comply with downstream tribal standards. ***

---

12. *See, e.g., United States v. Wheeler,* 435 U.S. 313, 323, 98 S. Ct. 1079, 1086, 55 L.Ed.2d 303 (1978). For example, Indian tribes could use their water rights, which are an element of tribal sovereignty, to assert an action against upstream polluters or to recover damages for groundwater contamination. *See* Comment, *Indian Reserved Water Rights Doctrine and the Groundwater Question,* 19 Am. Indian L. Rev. 403, 441 n. 297 (1994).

14. Although, Indian tribes could have inherent jurisdiction over non-Indian conduct or non-Indian resources if there is "some direct effect on the political integrity, the economic security, or the health or welfare of the tribe." *Montana v. United States,* 450 U.S. 544, 566, (1981) (citations omitted).

NOTES AND QUESTIONS

1. *Regulating non-member fee land.* We learned from the *Montana* line of cases, *supra* Ch. 8, that tribal authority over non-members on fee land is more limited than tribal authority over activities on Indian lands. EPA spoke to this issue when it promulgated its regulations implementing the treatment as a state amendment to the Clean Water Act.

> The CWA establishes a policy of "recogniz[ing], preserv[ing], and protect[ing] the primary responsibilities and rights of States to prevent, reduce, and eliminate pollution, [and] to plan the development and use (including restoration, preservation, and enhancement) of land and water resources" section 101(b). By extension, the treatment of Indian Tribes as States means that Tribes are to be primarily responsible for the protection of reservation water resources. As Senator Burdick, floor manager of the 1987 CWA Amendments, explained, the purpose of section 518 was to "provide clean water for the people of this Nation." 133 Cong. Rec. S1018 (daily ed. Jan 21, 1987). This goal was to be accomplished, he asserted, by giving "tribes *** the primary authority to set water quality standards to assure fishable and swimmable water and to satisfy all beneficial uses." *Id.* ***
>
> The Agency also believes that the effects on tribal health and welfare necessary to support Tribal regulation of non-Indian activities on the reservation may be easier to establish in the context of water quality management than with regard to zoning, which was at issue in *Brendale*.
>
> ***
>
> Operationally, EPA's generalized findings regarding the relationship of water quality to tribal health and welfare will affect the legal analysis of a tribal submission by, in effect, supplementing the factual showing a tribe makes in applying for treatment as a State. Thus, a tribal submission meeting the requirements of § 131.8 of this regulation will need to make a relatively simple showing of facts that there are waters within the reservation used by the Tribe or tribal members, (and thus that the Tribe or tribal members could be subject to exposure to pollutants present in, or introduced into, those waters) and that the waters and critical habitat are subject to protection under the Clean Water Act. The Tribe must also explicitly assert that impairment of such waters by the activities of non-Indians, would have a serious and substantial effect on the health and welfare of the Tribe. Once the Tribe meets this initial burden, EPA will, in light of the facts presented by the tribe and the generalized statutory and factual findings regarding the importance of reservation water quality discussed above, presume that there has been an adequate showing of tribal jurisdiction of fee lands, unless an appropriate governmental entity (*e.g.*, an adjacent Tribe or State) demonstrates a lack of jurisdiction on the part of the Tribe.

Amendments to the Water Quality Standards Regulation That Pertain to Standards on Indian Reservations Final Rule, 56 Fed. Reg. 64876, 64878–9 (1991).

EPA in 2016 changed its position on the interpretation of the Clean Water Act's delegation issue. In an interpretive rule the agency announced that it would no longer require tribal applicants to demonstrate authority over non-Indians under the *Montana* line of cases because it now views the CWA as a delegation of federal authority. EPA explained in its summary that:

> [S]ince 1991, EPA has followed a cautious interpretation that has required tribes, as a condition of receiving TAS regulatory authority under section 518, to demonstrate inherent authority to regulate waters and activities on their reservations under principles of federal Indian common law. The Agency has consistently stated, however, that its approach was subject to change in the event of further congressional or judicial guidance addressing tribal authority under CWA section 518. Based on such guidance, EPA in the interpretive rule we are finalizing today concludes definitively that section 518 includes an express delegation of authority by Congress to Indian tribes to administer regulatory programs over their entire reservations, subject to the eligibility requirements in section 518. This reinterpretation streamlines the process for applying for TAS, eliminating the need for applicant tribes to demonstrate inherent authority to regulate under the Act and allowing eligible tribes to implement the congressional delegation of authority. The reinterpretation also brings EPA's treatment of tribes under the CWA in line with EPA's treatment of tribes under the Clean Air Act, which has similar statutory language addressing tribal regulation of Indian reservation areas. This interpretive rule ... does not revise any regulatory text. Regulatory provisions remain in effect requiring tribes to identify the boundaries of the reservation areas over which they seek to exercise authority and allowing the adjacent state(s) to comment to EPA on an applicant tribe's assertion of authority. This rule will reduce burdens on applicants associated with the existing TAS process and has no significant cost.

Revised Interpretation of Clean Water Act Tribal Provision, 81 Fed. Reg. 30183 (May 16, 2016).

2. *EPA's presumption of effects on water.* In *Montana v. EPA*, 137 F.3d 1135 (9th Cir. 1998), the court of appeals upheld EPA's approval of an application of the Confederated Salish and Kootenai Tribes of the Flathead Reservation. The court rejected EPA's claim that it should be given deference on the legal question of tribal inherent power over non-members, but agreed with EPA's conclusion that non-member pollution would have a direct effect on the health, safety and welfare of the tribe, and that tribal authority was therefore consistent with *Montana*'s second exception. 137 F.3d at 1140–41. *See also Wisconsin v. EPA*, 266 F.3d 741 (7th Cir. 2001) (state's ownership of lake's waterbed did not preclude federally-approved regulation of the quality of lake water by tribe). *See* Elizabeth Kronk Warner, *Tribes As Innovative Environmental "Laboratories,"* 86 U. Colo. L. Rev. 789, 797-809 (2015)(discussing cases).

ARIZONA PUBLIC SERVICE COMPANY V. ENVIRONMENTAL PROTECTION AGENCY

211 F.3d 1280 (D.C. Cir. 2001)

HARRY T. EDWARDS, CHIEF JUDGE:

In 1990, Congress passed a compendium of amendments to the Clean Air Act ("CAA" or "the Act"). This case concerns those amendments that specifically address the power of Native American nations (or "tribes") to implement air quality regulations under the Act. Petitioners challenge the Environmental Protection Agency's ("EPA" or "the Agency") regulations, promulgated in 1998, implementing the 1990 Amendments. *See* Indian Tribes: Air Quality Planning and Management, 63 Fed. Reg. 7254 (1998) (to be codified at 40 C.F.R. pts. 9, 35, 49, 50, and 81) ("Tribal Authority Rule). Petitioners' principal contention is that EPA has granted too much authority to tribes.

Petitioners' primary challenges focus on two issues. The first is whether Congress expressly delegated to Native American nations authority to regulate air quality on all land within reservations, including fee land held by private landowners who are not tribe members. The second is whether EPA has properly construed "reservation" to include trust lands and Pueblos.

***

We find petitioners' challenges to be mostly meritless. We hold that the Agency did not err in finding delegated authority to Native American nations to regulate all land within reservations, including fee land owned by nonmembers. We also uphold EPA's construction of "reservation" to include trust lands and Pueblos.

***

I. BACKGROUND

A. Statutory Background

The Act establishes a framework for a federal-state partnership to regulate air quality. The provisions of the 1990 Amendments under review, fairly read, constitute an attempt by Congress to increase the role of Native American nations in this partnership. There are three areas of regulation under the Act particularly relevant to this case.

First, the Act grants states primary responsibility for assuring that air quality meets national standards. *See* 42 U.S.C. § 7407(a) (1994). States meet this burden by submitting state implementation plans ("SIPs") that "provide for implementation, maintenance, and enforcement" of these standards. *Id.* § 7410(a)(1) (1994). SIPs must be approved by the Agency before they may be federally enforced. In 1990, § 7410 was amended to authorize Native American nations to submit tribal implementation plans ("TIPs") "applicable to all areas *** located within the exterior boundaries of the reservation." *Id.* § 7410(o).

Second, the Act permits states and Native American nations to "redesignate" lands pursuant to the Act's Prevention of Significant Deterioration ("PSD") program. *See id.* § 7474(a), (c) (1994). Under the PSD program, land is classified as Class I, II, or III. The land's classification determines the maximum allowable increase over the baseline by which concentrations of sulfur dioxide and other particulate matter shall not be exceeded. *See id.* § 7473 (1994). Land may, under certain circumstances, be redesignated as Class I, II, or III. *See id.* § 7474(a). Since 1977, Native American nations have had authority to redesignate land "within the exterior boundaries of reservations." *Id.* § 7474(c).

Finally, under Title V of the Act, states must develop a comprehensive permitting program applicable to major air pollution sources. *See id.* § 7661a (1994). The Agency must approve the permitting program; if none is approved, EPA must promulgate a permitting program that will be federally enforceable. *See id.* § 7661a(d)(3). One of the requirements for approval is that the program provide for judicial review of permitting actions. *See id.* § 7661a(b)(6), (7). Petitioners claim that the Agency has improperly interpreted the 1990 Amendments to give Native American nations the possibility of exemption from some portions of the judicial review requirements.

Importantly, the 1990 Amendments added language to the Act granting EPA the "author[ity] to treat Indian tribes as States under this chapter," *id.* § 7601(d)(1)(A) (1994), provided tribes meet the following requirements:

> (A) the Indian tribe has a governing body carrying out substantial governmental duties and powers;
>
> (B) the functions to be exercised by the Indian tribe pertain to the management and protection of air resources within the exterior boundaries of the reservation or other areas within the tribe's jurisdiction; and
>
> (C) the Indian tribe is reasonably expected to be capable, in the judgment of the Administrator, of carrying out the functions to be exercised in a manner consistent with the terms and purposes of this chapter and all applicable regulations.

Id. § 7601(d)(2).

The 1990 Amendments also directed EPA to promulgate regulations "specifying those provisions of this chapter for which it is appropriate to treat Indian tribes as States." *Id.* If the Agency "determines that the treatment of Indian tribes as identical to States is inappropriate or administratively infeasible," EPA may announce other ways for the Agency to administer the program "so as to achieve the appropriate purpose." *Id.* § 7601(d)(4).

B. The Challenged Rule

On August 25, 1994, EPA proposed rules to implement the 1990 Amendments. *See* Proposed Tribal Authority Rule, 59 Fed. Reg. 43,956 (1994) (proposed Aug. 25, 1994). On February 12, 1998, after receiving and responding to public comments, EPA issued the final Tribal Authority Rule. *See* Tribal Authority Rule, 63 Fed. Reg. at 7254. The Agency first found that the 1990 Amendments constitute a delegation of federal authority to regulate air quality to Native American nations within the boundaries of reservations, regardless of whether the land is owned by the tribes. *See id.* The Agency read the statute to support this "territorial view of tribal jurisdiction," authorizing a "tribal role for all air resources within the exterior boundaries of Indian reservations without distinguishing among various categories of on reservation land." *Id.* EPA believed that this "territorial approach *** best advances rational, sound, air quality management." *Id.* at 7255. Thus, the Agency determined that Congress delegated to tribes the authority to regulate air quality in areas within the exterior boundaries of a reservation.

The Act does not define "reservation" for the purposes of tribal regulation. EPA interpreted "reservation" to include "trust lands that have been validly set apart for the use of a tribe even though the land has not been formally designated as a reservation." *Id.* at 7258. The Agency explained that this interpretation was consistent with the Supreme Court's definition of "reservation" in *Oklahoma Tax Commission v. Citizen Band Potawatomi Indian Tribe of Oklahoma,* 498 U.S. 505 (1991). EPA held that it would decide on a case-by-case basis whether other types of land may be considered "reservations" under the Act. *See* Tribal Authority Rule, 63 Fed. Reg. at 7258.

For areas not within a "reservation," the Agency determined that a tribe would be allowed to regulate such areas if the tribe could demonstrate inherent jurisdiction over the particular non-reservation area under general principles of federal Indian law. *See id.* at 7259. This means that tribes may propose air quality regulations in "allotted land" and "dependent Indian communities" provided they can otherwise demonstrate inherent jurisdiction over these areas. ***

II. ANALYSIS

Petitioners raise several challenges to EPA's final rule. First, petitioners claim that the 1990 Amendments cannot be interpreted to constitute an express delegation of authority to Native American nations to regulate privately owned fee land located within a reservation. Second, petitioners argue that EPA impermissibly interpreted the word "reservation" to include lands held in trust and Pueblos. ***

We analyze EPA's interpretation of the Act under familiar principles. "Where congressional intent is ambiguous, *** an agency's interpretation of a statute entrusted to its administration is entitled to deference, so long as it is reasonable." Our primary concern under *Chevron* is to ensure that an agency acts within the bounds of congressional delegation. "[A]s long as the agency stays within [Congress'] delegation, it is free to make policy choices in interpreting the statute, and such interpretations are entitled to deference." *Arent v. Shalala,* 70 F.3d 610, 615 (D.C. Cir. 1995). ***

A. Express Delegation of Authority to Native American Nations

It is undisputed that Native American nations retain significant sovereign power. Native American nations have inherent power to determine forms of tribal government, to determine tribal membership, to make substantive criminal and civil laws governing internal matters, to administer tribal judicial systems, to exclude others from tribal lands, and, to some extent, to exercise civil jurisdiction over nonmembers, including non-Indians. *See* Cohen, Handbook of Federal Indian Law, at 247–53; *Montana v. United States,* 450 U.S. 544, 564 (1981). It is this last category of power that is at issue in the instant case, because petitioners claim that the 1990 Amendments to the Act do not authorize tribes to administer the Act over fee land within a reservation that is owned by nonmembers. As the Supreme Court has held,

> exercise of tribal power beyond what is necessary to protect tribal self-government or to control internal relations is inconsistent with the dependent status of the tribes, and so cannot survive without express congressional delegation.

Montana, 450 U.S. at 564.

There is no doubt that tribes hold "inherent sovereign power to exercise some forms of civil jurisdiction over non-Indians on their reservations, even on non-Indian fee lands." *Id.* at 565. For instance, if the behavior of non-Indians on fee lands within the reservation "threatens or has some direct effect on the political integrity, the economic security, or the health or welfare of the tribe," the tribe may regulate that activity. *Id.* at 566. To satisfy this standard, however, a tribe must show, on a case-by-case basis, that the disputed activity constitutes a "demonstrably serious" impact that "imperil[s] the political integrity, the economic security, or the health and welfare of the tribe." *Brendale v. Confederated Tribes and Bands of the Yakima Indian Nation,* 492 U.S. 408, 431 (1989) (plurality opinion). EPA suggests, not implausibly, that "inherent sovereign power" may apply to tribal regulation under the Act of fee lands within a reservation, *see* Proposed Tribal Authority Rule, 59 Fed. Reg. at 43,598 n.5, but the Agency does not press this argument on appeal. Rather, EPA contends that the 1990 Amendments constitute an express congressional delegation to the tribes of the authority to regulate air quality on fee lands located within the exterior boundaries of a reservation.

"There are few examples of congressional delegation of authority to tribes." Cohen, Handbook of Federal Indian Law, at 253. However, as is the case in any situation in which we are called upon to find congressional intent in construing a contested statute, we start with traditional sources of statutory interpretation, including the statute's text, structure, purpose, and legislative history. *** Our review of the CAA indicates that EPA's interpretation comports with congressional intent.

Section 7601(d), in pertinent part, authorizes EPA to treat otherwise eligible tribes as states if "the functions to be exercised by the Indian tribe pertain to the management and protection of air resources within the exterior boundaries of the reservation or other areas within the tribe's jurisdiction." 42 U.S.C. § 7601(d)(2)(B). The statute's clear distinction between areas "within the exterior boundaries of the reservation" and "other areas within the tribe's jurisdiction" carries with it the implication that Congress considered the areas within the exterior boundaries of a tribe's reservation to be *per se* within the tribe's jurisdiction. Thus, EPA correctly interpreted § 7601(d) to express congressional intent to grant tribal jurisdiction over nonmember owned fee land within a reservation without the need to determine, on a case-specific basis, whether a tribe possesses "inherent sovereign power" under *Montana.*

Petitioners do not dispute that an important purpose of the Act is to ensure *effective* enforcement of clean air standards. Obviously, this is best done by allowing states and tribes to establish uniform standards within their boundaries. As EPA explained in its proposed rule,

> [a]ir pollutants disperse over areas several and sometimes even hundreds of miles from their source of origin, as dictated by the physical and chemical properties of the pollutants at issue and the prevailing winds and other meteorological conditions. The high mobility of air pollutants,

> resulting areawide effects and the seriousness of such impacts, underscores the undesirability of fragmented air quality management within reservations.

Proposed Tribal Authority Rule, 59 Fed. Reg. at 43,959.

Accepting petitioners' interpretation of the 1990 Amendments would result in a "checkerboard" pattern of regulation within a reservation's boundaries that would be inconsistent with the purpose and provisions of the Act. ***

Finally, petitioners note that the Agency declined to find an express delegation of power to regulate fee lands under §§ 518(e) and (h) of the Clean Water Act; this is noteworthy to petitioners, because they can glean no difference between the cited provisions under the Clean Water Act and the disputed provisions in this case under the Clean Air Act. We find no merit in this argument. The Clean Water Act states that "[t]he Administrator is authorized to treat an Indian tribe as a State *** if *** the functions to be exercised by the Indian tribe pertain to the management and protection of water resources which are held by an Indian tribe *** within the borders of an Indian reservation." 33 U.S.C. § 1377(e)(2) (1994). "Reservation" is defined as "all land within the limits of any Indian reservation under the jurisdiction of the United States Government, notwithstanding the issuance of any patent, and including rights-of-way running through the reservation." *Id.* § 1377(h)(1). In construing these provisions, EPA concluded that because the legislative history was "ambiguous and inconclusive," it would not find that the Clean Water Act expanded or limited the scope of tribal authority beyond that inherent in the tribe. Amendments to the Water Quality Standards Regulation That Pertain to Standards on Indian Reservations, 56 Fed. Reg. 64,876, 64,880 (1991) (codified at 40 C.F.R. pt. 131).

The situation here is quite different from what EPA found with respect to the Clean Water Act. Although the disputed language in the Clean Air Act and the Clean Water Act is somewhat similar, it is far from identical. As noted above, EPA correctly relied on the CAA's clear distinction between areas "within the exterior boundaries of the reservation" and "other areas within the tribe's jurisdiction" to find a congressional intention to define the areas within the exterior boundaries of a tribe's reservation to be *per se* within the tribe's jurisdiction. Furthermore, as we have already indicated, the legislative history of the 1990 Amendments plainly supports EPA's interpretation. Thus, the legislative history underlying the Clean Air Act is not "ambiguous and inconclusive," as was found to be the case with respect to the Clean Water Act.

It is also of some significance that EPA's interpretation of the Clean Water Act never has been subject to judicial review on the question of the presence or absence of an express delegation to tribes to regulate fee lands within the bounds of reservations. One federal court has observed, in *dicta,* that "the statutory language [in the Clean Water Act] seems to indicate plainly that Congress did intend to delegate *** authority to tribes." *State of Montana v. EPA,* 941 F. Supp. 945, 951 (D. Mont. 1996). The court noted, however, that in construing the provisions of the Clean Water Act, "EPA determined that it would take the more cautious view, that Congress did not expressly delegate jurisdiction to tribes over non-Indians and that tribes would have to prove on a case-by-case basis that they possess such jurisdiction." *Id.* at 952. There was no reason for EPA to take a similarly "cautious view" with respect to the Clean

Air Act, because the language and legislative history of the 1990 Amendments differ from that of the Clean Water Act.

B. EPA's Interpretation of "Reservation"

Given that EPA correctly interpreted § 7601(d) to expressly delegate jurisdiction to otherwise eligible tribes over all land within the exterior boundaries of reservations, including fee land, the next question is what areas are covered by a "reservation." EPA interprets "reservation" as used in three different statutory provisions (42 U.S.C. §§ 7410(o), 7474(c), 7601(d)(2)(B)) to mean formally designated reservations as well as "trust lands that have been validly set apart for the use of a tribe even though the land has not been formally designated as a reservation." Tribal Authority Rule, 63 Fed. Reg. at 7258. This includes what EPA terms "Pueblos" and tribal trust land. Pueblos are villages, primarily located in New Mexico, held by tribes in communal fee-simple ownership, originally acquired under grants from Spain and Mexico, and confirmed by Congress in the late 1800s. *See United States v. Sandoval,* 231 U.S. 28, 38–39 (1913). Petitioners ignore the status of Pueblos and concentrate their attack on EPA's interpretation of "reservation" to include tribal trust land.

The Secretary of the Interior is authorized to acquire land in trust for a tribe under 25 U.S.C. § 465 (1994), and such land can only formally be designated a reservation via the process provided by 25 U.S.C. § 467 (1994). Petitioners claim that EPA's interpretation contravenes the Act's plain language and renders 25 U.S.C. § 467 superfluous by ignoring the distinction between "trust lands" and "reservations." EPA counters that the statute is ambiguous, and that its reasonable interpretation is entitled to *Chevron* deference. ***

[The] varying definitions of "reservation" lay to waste petitioners' argument. Petitioners appear to assert that, in the absence of any specific definition, "reservation" as used in the 1990 Amendments to the Act can only mean the formal reservation contemplated by 25 U.S.C. § 467. This is a specious contention. First, § 467 does not purport to offer an exclusive definition of "reservation"; it simply defines the terms under which federal land is formally designated a reservation. Second, if Congress had wanted to limit the term "reservation" as petitioners suggest, Congress could have done so. Indeed, Congress on many occasions has defined "reservation" in terms of other statutes. *See* 12 U.S.C. § 4702(11) (1994) (defining "reservation" according to 25 U.S.C. § 1903(10)); 22 U.S.C. § 2124c(m)(1) (1994) (defining "Indian reservation" with reference to 25 U.S.C. § 1452(d)); 25 U.S.C. § 1903(10) (defining "reservation" with reference to 18 U.S.C. § 1151, as well as trust land); 26 U.S.C. § 168(j)(6) (1994 & Supp. III 1997) (defining "Indian reservation" with reference to 25 U.S.C. § 1452(d) and 25 U.S.C. § 1903(10)); 42 U.S.C. § 10101(19) (1994) (defining "reservation" to include communities referred to in 18 U.S.C. § 1151(a), (b)); *id.* § 11332(a) (1994) (defining "reservation" according to 25 U.S.C. § 1452(d)). Moreover, given the varying definitions of the term used throughout the Code, it would be a curious result indeed for this court to insist that the absence of a definition requires EPA to advance the most restrictive definition as put forth by petitioners.

Aside from the statute's plain meaning and its context, other sources of statutory interpretation offer no insight into congressional intent with respect to the meaning of "reservation." The Report of the Senate Committee on

Environment and Public Works refers to the authority of Indian tribes to "administer and enforce the Clean Air Act in Indian lands," as well as enforcement of the Act in "Indian country." S. Rep. No. 101–228, at 79, 80 (1989), *reprinted in* Legislative History of the Clean Air Act Amendments of 1990, at 8419–20. These terms are arguably broader than the definition of "reservation" urged by petitioners, and simply confirm the term's ambiguity as used by Congress.

Accordingly, we turn to step two of the *Chevron* inquiry. That is, did the Agency reasonably interpret the term "reservation" to include formal reservations, Pueblos, and trust lands? EPA supported its interpretation of "reservation" by looking to relevant case law, in particular Supreme Court precedent holding that there is no relevant distinction between tribal trust land and reservations for the purpose of tribal sovereign immunity. *See Oklahoma Tax Comm'n,* 498 U.S. at 511. This view is consonant with other federal court holdings that an Indian reservation includes trust lands. *See United States v. John,* 437 U.S. 634, 649 (1978) (finding "no apparent reason" why lands held in trust should not be considered a "reservation" under § 1151(a)); *HRI, Inc. v. EPA,* 198 F.3d 1224, 1249–54 (10th Cir. 2000) (same); *United States v. Azure,* 801 F.2d 336, 339 (8th Cir.1986) (considering tribal trust land to be Indian country under either § 1151(a) as a "*de facto*" reservation or § 1151(b) as a dependent Indian community); *United States v. Sohappy,* 770 F.2d 816, 822–23 (9th Cir. 1985) (holding that trust land is a "reservation" under § 1151(a)). ***

Petitioners note that, for several years, EPA has defined reservation, for the purposes of the PSD program, to be "any federally recognized reservation established by Treaty, Agreement, executive order, or act of Congress." 40 C.F.R. 52.21(b)(27) (1999). Given the Agency's reasoned justification for a broader definition of "reservation" in the Tribal Authority Rule, and its proposal to amend the PSD definition to ensure consistency with the Tribal Authority Rule, EPA's departure from the PSD definition does not preclude this court from upholding EPA's new definition. In light of the ample precedent treating trust land as reservation land in other contexts, and the canon of statutory interpretation calling for statutes to be interpreted favorably towards Native American nations, we cannot condemn as unreasonable EPA's interpretation of "reservations" to include Pueblos and tribal trust land. ***

GINSBURG, CIRCUIT JUDGE, dissented in part [on the ground that Congress did not intend to delegate authority over non-Indian fee lands]. ***

NOTES AND QUESTIONS

1. *Delegation of federal power versus tribal inherent power?* Is there a functional difference between the end results in these two cases? Would a tribe have less authority if the Clean Water Act were treated as a delegation of federal power, rather than a recognition of a tribe's "inherent authority?" *See* Robert T. Anderson, *Water Rights, Water Quality, and Regulatory Jurisdiction in Indian Country*, 34 Stan. Envtl. L.J. 195, 232 (2015) (discussing EPA's new rule just prior to its being finalized).

2. For a review of air pollution issues in Indian country, *see* Arnold W. Reitze, Jr., *The Control of Air Pollution on Indian Reservations*, 46 Envtl L.

893, 918 (2016) ("As of October 2015, there were forty-nine tribes—some with multiple approvals—that had TAS status for various CAA provisions.")

3. *Other delegations of regulatory authority.* In *Bugenig v. Hoopa Valley Tribe*, 266 F.3d 1201, 1215 (9th Cir. 2001) (*en banc*) the court of appeals found that when Congress passed a statute that "ratified and confirmed" the Hoopa Valley Tribe's constitution, it delegated regulatory authority over non-member fee land since the tribal constitution provides the tribal council with the power "to safeguard and promote the peace, safety, morals, and general welfare of the Hoopa Valley Indians by *regulating* the conduct of trade and *the use* and disposition *of property upon the reservation, provided that any ordinance directly affecting non-members* of the Hoopa Valley Tribe shall be subject to the approval of the Commissioner of Indian Affairs. ..." How does this holding compare to those in *Arizona Public Service Company* or *City of Albuquerque v. Browner*?

C. SUBMERGED LANDS

Distinct questions of ownership arise regarding lands submerged beneath navigable waters in Indian country. Although lands beneath nonnavigable waters are owned by the adjacent property owner, there is a presumption that lands beneath navigable waters are owned by the sovereign in trust for the public. In the United States, any such lands not within the boundary of a state are owned by the federal government. Upon statehood, however, such ownership devolves to the state unless it is specifically reserved by the federal government. *See Shively v. Bowlby*, 152 U.S. 1, 48 (1894) ("We cannot doubt, therefore, that congress has the power to make grants of lands below high-water mark of navigable waters in any territory of the United States, whenever it becomes necessary to do so in order to perform international obligations, or to effect the improvement of such lands for the promotion and convenience of commerce with foreign nations and among the several states, or to carry out other public purposes appropriate to the objects for which the United States hold the territory.").

When such navigable waters are located within federally recognized Indian lands, this presumption conflicts with the Indian law canon that tribes retain all property rights not explicitly ceded to the federal government. Courts have reached different results in resolving this conflict. *Compare Choctaw Nation v. Oklahoma*, 397 U.S. 620, 634 (1970) (holding that the Choctaw Nation retained treaty rights to lands under the Arkansas River in light of the "countervailing rule of construction that well-founded doubt should be resolved in [the Choctaw Nation's] favor") and *United States v. Holt State Bank,* 270 U.S. 49 (1926) (treaties setting aside lands for "permanent homes" for the Chippewa did not reserve rights to lands under Mud Lake). The following cases represent more contrasting views on this question.

MONTANA V. UNITED STATES

450 U.S. 544, 101 S. Ct. 1245, 67 L.Ed.2d 493 (1981)

JUSTICE STEWART delivered the opinion of the Court.

*** The Crow Indians originated in Canada, but some three centuries ago they migrated to what is now southern Montana. In the 19th century, warfare between the Crows and several other tribes led the tribes and the United States to sign the First Treaty of Fort Laramie of 1851, in which the signatory tribes acknowledged various designated lands as their respective territories. *See* 11 Stat. 749 and 2 C. Kappler, Indian Affairs: Laws and Treaties 594 (1904) (hereinafter Kappler). The treaty identified approximately 38.5 million acres as Crow territory and, in Article 5, specified that, by making the treaty, the tribes did not "surrender the privilege of hunting, fishing, or passing over" any of the lands in dispute. In 1868, the Second Treaty of Fort Laramie established a Crow Reservation of roughly 8 million acres, including land through which the Big Horn River flows. 15 Stat. 649. By Article II of the treaty, the United States agreed that the reservation "shall be *** set apart for the absolute and undisturbed use and occupation" of the Crow Tribe, and that no non-Indians except agents of the Government "shall ever be permitted to pass over, settle upon, or reside in" the reservation.

Several subsequent Acts of Congress reduced the reservation to slightly fewer than 2.3 million acres and the Crow Allotment Act of 1920, 41 Stat. 751, authorized the issuance of patents in fee to individual Indian allottees within the reservation. Under these Acts, an allottee could alienate his land to a non-Indian after holding it for 25 years. Today, roughly 52 percent of the reservation is allotted to members of the Tribe and held by the United States in trust for them, 17 percent is held in trust for the Tribe itself, and approximately 28 percent is held in fee by non-Indians. The State of Montana owns in fee simple 2 percent of the reservation, the United States less than 1 percent.

Since the 1920's, the State of Montana has stocked the waters of the reservation with fish, and the construction of a dam by the United States made trout fishing in the Big Horn River possible. The reservation also contains game, some of it stocked by the State. Since the 1950's, the Crow Tribal Council has passed several resolutions respecting hunting and fishing on the reservation, including Resolution No. 74–05, the occasion for this lawsuit. That resolution prohibits hunting and fishing within the reservation by anyone who is not a member of the Tribe. The State of Montana, however, has continued to assert its authority to regulate hunting and fishing by non-Indians within the reservation.

On October 9, 1975, proceeding in its own right and as fiduciary for the Tribe, the United States endeavored to resolve the conflict between the Tribe and the State by filing the present lawsuit. The plaintiff sought (1) a declaratory judgment quieting title to the bed of the Big Horn River in the United States as trustee for the Tribe, (2) a declaratory judgment establishing that the Tribe and the United States have sole authority to regulate hunting and fishing within the reservation, and (3) an injunction requiring Montana to secure the permission of the Tribe before issuing hunting or fishing licenses for use within the reservation. ***

II

The respondents seek to establish a substantial part of their claim of power to control hunting and fishing on the reservation by asking us to recognize their title to the bed of the Big Horn River.[1] The question is whether the United States conveyed beneficial ownership of the riverbed to the Crow Tribe by the treaties of 1851 or 1868, and therefore continues to hold the land in trust for the use and benefit of the Tribe, or whether the United States retained ownership of the riverbed as public land which then passed to the State of Montana upon its admission to the Union. *Choctaw Nation v. Oklahoma*, 397 U.S. 620, 627–628, 90 S. Ct. 1328, 1332–1333, 25 L.Ed.2d 615.

Though the owners of land riparian to *nonnavigable* streams may own the adjacent riverbed, conveyance by the United States of land riparian to a *navigable* river carries no interest in the riverbed. Rather, the ownership of land under navigable waters is an incident of sovereignty. As a general principle, the Federal Government holds such lands in trust for future States, to be granted to such States when they enter the Union and assume sovereignty on an "equal footing" with the established States. *Pollard's Lessee v. Hagan*, 3 How. 212, 222–223, 229. After a State enters the Union, title to the land is governed by state law. The State's power over the beds of navigable waters remains subject to only one limitation: the paramount power of the United States to ensure that such waters remain free to interstate and foreign commerce. *United States v. Oregon*, 295 U.S. 1, 14. It is now established, however, that Congress may sometimes convey lands below the high-water mark of a navigable water,

> [and so defeat the title of a new State,] in order to perform international obligations, or to effect the improvement of such lands for the promotion and convenience of commerce with foreign nations and among the several States, or to carry out other public purposes appropriate to the objects for which the United States hold the Territory. *Shively v. Bowlby*, 152 U.S. 1, 48.

But because control over the property underlying navigable waters is so strongly identified with the sovereign power of government, *United States v. Oregon, supra*, at 14, 55 S. Ct., at 615, it will not be held that the United States has conveyed such land except because of "some international duty or public exigency." *United States v. Holt State Bank*, 270 U.S., at 55. *See also Shively v. Bowlby, supra*, at 48. ***

In *United States v. Holt State Bank, supra*, this Court applied these principles to reject an Indian Tribe's claim of title to the bed of a navigable lake. The lake lay wholly within the boundaries of the Red Lake Indian Reservation,

---

1. According to the respondents, the Crow Tribe's interest in restricting hunting and fishing on the reservation focuses almost entirely on sports fishing and duck hunting in the waters and on the surface of the Big Horn River. The parties, the District Court, and the Court of Appeals have all assumed that ownership of the riverbed will largely determine the power to control these activities. Moreover, although the complaint in this case sought to quiet title only to the bed of the Big Horn River, we note the concession of the United States that if the bed of the river passed to Montana upon its admission to the Union, the State at the same time acquired ownership of the banks of the river as well.

which had been created by treaties entered into before Minnesota joined the Union. In these treaties the United States promised to "set apart and withhold from sale, for the use of" the Chippewas, a large tract of land, Treaty of Sept. 30, 1854, 10 Stat. 1109, and to convey "a sufficient quantity of land for the permanent homes" of the Indians, Treaty of Feb. 22, 1855, 10 Stat. 1165. ***

The Crow treaties in this case, like the Chippewa treaties in *Holt State Bank*, fail to overcome the established presumption that the beds of navigable waters remain in trust for future States and pass to the new States when they assume sovereignty. The 1851 treaty did not by its terms formally convey any land to the Indians at all, but instead chiefly represented a covenant among several tribes which recognized specific boundaries for their respective territories. Treaty of Fort Laramie, 1851, Art. 5, 2 Kappler 594–595. It referred to hunting and fishing only insofar as it said that the Crow Indians "do not surrender the privilege of hunting, fishing, or passing over any of the tracts of country heretofore described," a statement that had no bearing on ownership of the riverbed. ***

Whatever property rights the language of the 1868 treaty created, however, its language is not strong enough to overcome the presumption against the sovereign's conveyance of the riverbed ***.[5]

Moreover, even though the establishment of an Indian reservation can be an "appropriate public purpose" within the meaning of *Shively v. Bowlby*, 152

5. In one recent case, *Choctaw Nation v. Oklahoma*, 397 U.S. 620, this Court did construe a reservation grant as including the bed of a navigable water, and the respondents argue that this case resembles *Choctaw Nation* more than it resembles the established line of cases to which *Choctaw Nation* is a singular exception. But the finding of a conveyance of the riverbed in *Choctaw Nation* was based on very peculiar circumstances not present in this case.

Those circumstances arose from the unusual history of the treaties there at issue, a history which formed an important basis of the decision. *Id.* at 622–628. Immediately after the Revolutionary War, the United States had signed treaties of peace and protection with the Cherokee and Choctaw Tribes, reserving them lands in Georgia and Mississippi. In succeeding years the United States bought large areas of land from the Indians to make room for white settlers who were encroaching on tribal lands, but the Government signed new treaties guaranteeing that the Indians could live in peace on those lands not ceded. The United States soon betrayed that promise. It proposed that the Tribes be relocated in a newly acquired part of the Arkansas Territory, but the new territory was soon overrun by white settlers, and through a series of new cession agreements the Indians were forced to relocate farther and farther west. Ultimately, most of the Tribe's members refused to leave their eastern lands, doubting the reliability of the Government's promises of the new western land, but Georgia and Mississippi, anxious for the relocation westward so they could assert jurisdiction over the Indian lands, purported to abolish the Tribes and distribute the tribal lands. The Choctaws and Cherokees finally signed new treaties with the United States aimed at rectifying their past suffering at the hands of the Federal Government and the States.

Under the Choctaw treaty, the United States promised to convey new lands west of the Arkansas Territory in fee simple, and also pledged that "no Territory or State shall ever have a right to pass laws for the government of the Choctaw Nation *** and that no part of the land granted to them shall ever be embraced in any Territory or State." Treaty of Dancing Rabbit Creek, Sept. 27, 1830, 7 Stat. 333–334, quoted in *Choctaw Nation v. Oklahoma*, 397 U.S., at 625. In 1835, the Cherokees signed a treaty containing similar provisions granting reservation lands in fee simple and promising that the tribal lands would not become part of any State or Territory. *Id.* at 626. In concluding that the United States had intended to convey the riverbed to the Tribes before the admission of Oklahoma to the Union, the *Choctaw* Court relied on these circumstances surrounding the treaties and placed special emphasis on the Government's promise that the reserved lands would never become part of any State. *Id.* at 634–635. Neither the special historical origins of the Choctaw and Cherokee treaties nor the crucial provisions granting Indian lands in fee simple and promising freedom from state jurisdiction in those treaties have any counterparts in the terms and circumstances of the Crow treaties of 1851 and 1868.

U.S., at 48, justifying a congressional conveyance of a riverbed, the situation of the Crow Indians at the time of the treaties presented no "public exigency" which would have required Congress to depart from its policy of reserving ownership of beds under navigable waters for the future States. As the record in this case shows, at the time of the treaty the Crows were a nomadic tribe dependent chiefly on buffalo, and fishing was not important to their diet or way of life. 1 App. 74. *Cf., Alaska Pacific Fisheries v. United States, supra,* at 88; *Skokomish Indian Tribe v. France,* 320 F.2d 205, 212 (9th Cir. 1963).

For these reasons, we conclude that title to the bed of the Big Horn River passed to the State of Montana upon its admission into the Union, and that the Court of Appeals was in error in holding otherwise.

[In the second part of the opinion, reprinted in Chapter 8, *supra,* the Court held that the Crow Tribe had no jurisdiction to regulate fishing on this state owned land.]

[**JUSTICES BLACKMUN**, joined by **JUSTICES MARSHALL** and **BRENNAN**, dissented, arguing that the Indian law canons of construction and *Choctaw Nation* controlled.]

IDAHO V. UNITED STATES

533 U.S. 262, 21 S. Ct. 2135, 150 L.Ed.2d 326 (2001)

JUSTICE SOUTER delivered the opinion of the Court.

The United States brought this quiet title action against the State of Idaho. The question is whether the National Government holds title, in trust for the Coeur d'Alene Tribe, to lands underlying portions of Lake Coeur d'Alene and the St. Joe River. We hold that it does.

I

The Coeur d'Alene Tribe once inhabited more than 3.5 million acres in what is now northern Idaho and northeastern Washington, including the area of Lake Coeur d'Alene and the St. Joe River. *** Tribal members traditionally used the lake and its related waterways for food, fiber, transportation, recreation, and cultural activities. The Tribe depended on submerged lands for everything from water potatoes harvested from the lake to fish weirs and traps anchored in riverbeds and banks.

Under an 1846 treaty with Great Britain, the United States acquired title to the region of Lake Coeur d'Alene, see Treaty in Regard to Limits Westward of the Rocky Mountains, 9 Stat. 869, subject to the aboriginal right of possession held by resident tribes[.] In 1867, in the face of immigration into the Tribe's aboriginal territory, President Johnson issued an Executive Order setting aside a reservation of comparatively modest size, although the Tribe was apparently unaware of this action until at least 1871, when it petitioned the Government to set aside a reservation. The Tribe found the 1867 boundaries unsatisfactory, due in part to their failure to make adequate provision for fishing and other uses of important waterways. When the Tribe petitioned the Commissioner of Indian Affairs a second time, it insisted on a reservation that included key river valleys because "we are not as yet quite up to living on farming" and "for a while yet we need have some hunting and fishing."

Following further negotiations, the Tribe in 1873 agreed to relinquish (for compensation) all claims to its aboriginal lands outside the bounds of a more substantial reservation that negotiators for the United States agreed to "set apart and secure" "for the exclusive use of the Coeur d'Alene Indians, and to protect *** from settlement or occupancy by other persons." The reservation boundaries described in the agreement covered part of the St. Joe River (then called the St. Joseph), and all of Lake Coeur d'Alene except a sliver cut off by the northern boundary.

Although by its own terms the agreement was not binding without congressional approval, later in 1873 President Grant issued an Executive Order directing that the reservation specified in the agreement be "withdrawn from sale and set apart as a reservation for the Coeur d'Alene Indians." Exec. Order of Nov. 8, 1873, reprinted in 1 C. Kappler, Indian Affairs: Laws and Treaties 837 (1904). The 1873 Executive Order set the northern boundary of the reservation directly across Lake Coeur d'Alene, which, the District Court found, was contrary "to the usual practice of meandering a survey line along the mean high water mark." An 1883 Government survey fixed the reservation's total area at 598,499.85 acres, which the District Court found necessarily "included submerged lands within the reservation boundaries."

As of 1885, Congress had neither ratified the 1873 agreement nor compensated the Tribe. This inaction prompted the Tribe to petition the Government again, to "make with us a proper treaty of peace and friendship *** by which your petitioners may be properly and fully compensated for such portion of their lands not now reserved to them; [and] that their present reserve may be confirmed to them." In response, Congress authorized new negotiations to obtain the Tribe's agreement to cede land outside the borders of the 1873 reservation. Act of May 15, 1886, ch. 333, 24 Stat. 44. In 1887, the Tribe agreed to cede "all right, title, and claim which they now have, or ever had, to all lands in said Territories [Washington, Idaho, and Montana] and elsewhere, except the portion of land within the boundaries of their present reservation in the Territory of Idaho, known as the Coeur d'Alene Reservation."

The Government, in return, promised to compensate the Tribe, and agreed that "[i]n consideration of the foregoing cession and agreements *** the Coeur d'Alene Reservation shall be held forever as Indian land and as homes for the Coeur d'Alene Indians *** and no part of said reservation shall ever be sold, occupied, open to white settlement, or otherwise disposed of without the consent of the Indians residing on said reservation." As before, the agreement was not binding on either party until ratified by Congress.

In January 1888, not having as yet ratified any agreement with the Tribe, the Senate expressed uncertainty about the extent of the Tribe's reservation and adopted a resolution directing the Secretary of the Interior to "inform the Senate as to the extent of the present area and boundaries of the Coeur d'Alene Indian Reservation in the Territory of Idaho," and specifically, "whether such area includes any portion, and if so, about how much of the navigable waters of Lake Coeur d'Alene, and of Coeur d'Alene and St. Joseph Rivers." "The

Secretary responded in February 1888 with a report of the Commissioner of Indian Affairs, stating that "the reservation appears to embrace all the navigable waters of Lake Coeur d'Alene, except a very small fragment cut off by the north boundary of the reservation," and that "[t]he St. Joseph River also flows through the reservation." Based largely, it appears, on this report, Idaho conceded in the Court of Appeals (as it does here) that the 1873 Executive Order reservation included submerged lands. ***

In May 1888, shortly after receiving the Secretary's report, Congress passed an Act granting a right-of-way to the Washington and Idaho Railroad Company "for the extension of its railroad through the lands in Idaho Territory set apart for the use of the Coeur d'Alene Indians by executive order, commonly known as the Coeur d'Alene Indian Reservation." Act of May 30, 1888, ch. 336, § 1, 25 Stat. 160. Notably, the Act directed that the Tribe's consent be obtained and that the Tribe alone (no one else being mentioned) be compensated for the right-of-way, a part of which crossed over navigable waters within the reservation.

Congress was not prepared to ratify the 1887 agreement, however, owing to a growing desire to obtain for the public not only any interest of the Tribe in land outside the 1873 reservation, but certain portions of the reservation itself. The House Committee on Indian Affairs later recalled that the 1887 agreement was not promptly ratified for

> sundry reasons, among which was a desire on the part of the United States to acquire an additional area, to wit, a certain valuable portion of the reservation specially dedicated to the exclusive use of said Indians under an Executive order of 1873, and which portions of said lands, situate[d] on the northern end of said reservation, is valuable and necessary to the citizens of the United States for sundry reasons. It contains numerous, extensive, and valuable mineral ledges. It contains large bodies of valuable timber ***. It contains a magnificent sheet of water, the Coeur d'Alene Lake ***. H.R. Rep. No. 1109, 51st Cong., 1st Sess., 4 (1890).

But Congress did not simply alter the 1873 boundaries unilaterally. Instead, the Tribe was understood to be entitled beneficially to the reservation as then defined, and the 1889 Indian Appropriations Act included a provision directing the Secretary of the Interior "to negotiate with the Coeur d'Alene tribe of Indians," and, specifically, to negotiate "for the purchase and release by said tribe of such portions of its reservation not agricultural and valuable chiefly for minerals and timber as such tribe shall consent to sell." Later that year, the Tribe and Government negotiators reached a new agreement under which the Tribe would cede the northern portion of the reservation, including approximately two-thirds of Lake Coeur d'Alene, in exchange for $500,000. The new boundary line, like the old one, ran across the lake, and General Simpson, a negotiator for the United States, reassured the Tribe that "you still have the St. Joseph River and the lower part of the lake." And, again, the agreement was not to be binding on either party until both it and the 1887 agreement were ratified by Congress.

On June 7, 1890, the Senate passed a bill ratifying both the 1887 and 1889 agreements. On June 10, the Senate bill was referred to the House, where a parallel bill had already been reported by the House Committee on Indian Affairs. H. R. Rep. No. 1109, 51st Cong., 1st Sess. (1890)

On July 3, 1890, while the Senate bill was under consideration by the House Committee on Indian Affairs, Congress passed the Idaho Statehood Act, admitting Idaho into the Union "on an equal footing with the original States," Act of July 3, 1890, ch. 656, 26 Stat. 215. The Statehood Act "accepted, ratified, and confirmed" the Idaho Constitution, *ibid.*, which "forever disclaim[ed] all right and title to *** all lands lying within [Idaho] owned or held by any Indians or Indian tribe" and provided that "until the title thereto shall have been extinguished by the United States, the same shall be subject to the disposition of the United States, and said Indian lands shall remain under the absolute jurisdiction and control of the congress of the United States," Idaho Const., Art. XXI, § 19 (1890).

*** On March 3, 1891, Congress "accepted, ratified, and confirmed" both the 1887 and 1889 agreements with the Tribe. The Act also directed the Secretary of the Interior to convey to one Frederick Post a "portion of [the] reservation" that the Tribe had purported to sell to Post in 1871. The property, located on the Spokane River and known as Post Falls, was described as "all three of the river channels and islands, with enough land on the north and south shores for water-power and improvements." *Ibid.*

***

The United States, acting in its own capacity and as trustee for the Tribe, initiated this action against the State of Idaho to quiet title (in the United States, to be held for the use and benefit of the Tribe) to the submerged lands within the exterior boundaries of the Tribe's current reservation, which encompass the lower third of Lake Coeur d'Alene and part of the St. Joe River.[4] The Tribe intervened to assert its interest in the submerged lands, and Idaho counterclaimed, seeking to quiet title in its own favor. Following a 9–day trial, the District Court quieted title "in favor of the United States, as trustee, and the Coeur d'Alene Tribe of Idaho, as the beneficially interested party of the trusteeship, to the bed and banks of the Coeur d'Alene Lake and the St. Joe River lying within the current boundaries of the Coeur d'Alene Indian Reservation." The Court of Appeals for the Ninth Circuit affirmed. 210 F.3d 1067 (2000). ***

II

Due to the public importance of navigable waterways, ownership of the land underlying such waters is "strongly identified with the sovereign power of government." In order to allow new States to enter the Union on an "equal footing" with the original States with regard to this important interest, "the United States early adopted and constantly has adhered to the policy of regarding lands under navigable waters in acquired territory *** as held for the ultimate benefit of future States." *United States v. Holt State Bank,* 270 U.S. 49 (1926); *see also Shively v. Bowlby,* 152 U.S. 1 (1894). Therefore, in contrast to the law governing surface land held by the United States, the default rule is that title to land under navigable waters passes from the United States to a newly admitted State. Specifically, although Congress has the power before

4. Because this action was brought by the United States, it does not implicate the Eleventh Amendment bar raised when the Tribe pressed its own claim to the submerged lands in *Idaho v. Coeur d'Alene Tribe of Idaho,* 521 U.S. 261 (1997). The United States' complaint was apparently motivated by Idaho's issuance of permits for the construction of "docks, piers, floats, pilings, breakwaters, boat ramps and other such aids to navigation within the southern one-third of Coeur d'Alene Lake."

statehood to convey land beneath navigable waters, and to reserve such land for the United States, " '[a] court deciding a question of title to the bed of navigable water must *** begin with a strong presumption against defeat of a State's title."

Armed with that presumption, we have looked to Congress's declarations and intent when we have had to resolve conflicts over submerged lands claimed to have been reserved or conveyed by the United States before statehood. ***

The issue of congressional intent is refined somewhat when submerged lands are located within a tract that the National Government has dealt with in some special way before statehood, as by reserving lands for a particular national purpose such as a wildlife refuge or, as here, an Indian reservation. Because reserving submerged lands does not necessarily imply the intent "to defeat a future State's title to the land," we undertake a two-step enquiry in reservation cases. We ask whether Congress intended to include land under navigable waters within the federal reservation and, if so, whether Congress intended to defeat the future State's title to the submerged lands.

Our most recent case of this sort, *United States v. Alaska,* [521 U.S. 1 (1997)] addressed two parcels of land initially reserved not by Congress but, as here, by the Executive Branch. We explained that the two-step test of congressional intent is satisfied when an Executive reservation clearly includes submerged lands, and Congress recognizes the reservation in a way that demonstrates an intent to defeat state title. We considered whether Congress was on notice that the Executive reservation included submerged lands, and whether the purpose of the reservation would have been compromised if the submerged lands had passed to the State. Where the purpose would have been undermined, we explained, "[i]t is simply not plausible that the United States sought to reserve only the upland portions of the area."

Here, Idaho has conceded that "the executive branch had intended, or by 1888 had interpreted, the 1873 Executive Order Reservation to include submerged lands." The concession is a sound one. A right to control the lakebed and adjacent waters was traditionally important to the Tribe, which emphasized in its petition to the Government that it continued to depend on fishing. *Cf. Montana* [, 450 U.S. 544 (1981)] (finding no intent to include submerged lands within a reservation where the tribe did not depend on fishing or use of navigable water). The District Court found that the acreage determination of the reserved area in 1883 necessarily included the area of the lakebed within the unusual boundary line crossing the lake from east to west. In light of those findings and Idaho's concession, the parties here concentrate on the second question, of Congress's intent to defeat Idaho's title to the submerged lands.[5]

---

5. The District Court and Court of Appeals accepted the United States's position that it had reserved the submerged lands, and that Congress intended that reservation to defeat Idaho's title. They did not reach the Tribe's alternative theory that, notwithstanding the scope of any reservation, the Tribe retained aboriginal title to the submerged lands, which cannot be extinguished without explicit action by Congress, *see Oneida Indian Nation,* 414 U.S., at 667–668, 94 S. Ct. 772; *cf. United States v. Winans,* 198 U.S. 371, 381, 25 S. Ct. 662, 49 L.Ed. 1089 (1905) (explaining that a treaty ceding some aboriginal lands to the United States and setting apart other lands as a reservation "was not a grant of rights to the Indians, but a grant of rights from them—a reservation of those not granted"). The Tribe does not press its unextinguished-aboriginal-title argument here.

In the Court of Appeals, Idaho also conceded one point covered in this second part of the enquiry. It agreed that after the Secretary of the Interior's 1888 report that the reservation embraced nearly "all the navigable water of Lake Coeur d'Alene," S. Exec. Doc. No. 76, 50th Cong., 1st Sess., at 3, Congress was on notice that the Executive Order reservation included submerged lands. Opening Brief for Appellant in No. 98–35831(CA9), at 11 ("[Congress was] informed that the Coeur d'Alene Reservation embraced submerged lands"). Again, Idaho's concession was prudent in light of the District Court's findings of facts. ("The evidence shows that prior to Idaho's statehood, Congress was on notice that the Executive Order of 1873 reserved for the benefit of the Tribe the submerged lands within the boundaries of the Coeur d'Alene Reservation").

*** And the District Court made the following findings about the period preceding negotiations authorized by Congress:

> The facts demonstrate that an influx of non-Indians into the Tribe's aboriginal territory prompted the Federal Government to negotiate with the Coeur d'Alenes in an attempt to confine the Tribe to a reservation and to obtain the Tribe's release of its aboriginal lands for settlement. Before it would agree to these conditions, however, the Tribe demanded an enlarged reservation that included the Lake and rivers. Thus, the Federal Government could only achieve its goals of promoting settlement, avoiding hostilities and extinguishing aboriginal title by agreeing to a reservation that included the submerged lands.
>
> ***

The manner in which Congress then proceeded to deal with the Tribe shows clearly that preservation of the land within the reservation, absent contrary agreement with the Tribe, was central to Congress's complementary objectives of dealing with pressures of white settlement and establishing the reservation by permanent legislation. The Tribe had shown its readiness to fight to preserve its land rights when in 1858 it defeated a force of the United States military, which it misunderstood as intending to take aboriginal lands. The concern with hostility arose again in 1873 before the reservation boundaries were established, when a surveyor on the scene had warned the Surveyor General that "[s]hould the fisheries be excluded there will in my opinion be trouble with these Indians."

Hence, although the goal of extinguishing aboriginal title could have been achieved by congressional fiat, *see Tee–Hit–Ton Indians v. United States,* and Congress was free to define the reservation boundaries however it saw fit, the goal of avoiding hostility seemingly could not have been attained without the agreement of the Tribe. Congress in any event made it expressly plain that its object was to obtain tribal interests only by tribal consent. When in 1886 Congress took steps toward extinguishing aboriginal title to all lands outside the 1873 boundaries, it did so by authorizing negotiation of agreements ceding title for compensation. Soon after that, when Congress decided to seek a reduction in the size of the 1873 reservation itself, the Secretary of the Interior advised the Senate against fiddling with the scope of the reservation without the Tribe's agreement. The report of February 1888 likewise urged that any move to diminish the reservation "should be done, if done at all, with the full and free consent of the Indians, and they should, of course, receive proper compensation for any land so taken." Accordingly, after receiving the Secretary's report, Congress undertook in the 1889 Act to authorize negotiation with the Tribe for the consensual, compensated cession of such portions of the Tribe's reservation "as such tribe shall consent to sell," Act of Mar. 2, 1889, ch. 412, § 4, 25 Stat. 1002. In the meantime it honored the reservation's recently clarified boundaries by requiring that the Tribe be compensated for the Washington and Idaho Railroad Company right-of-way, Act of May 30, 1888, ch. 336, § 1, 25 Stat. 160.

The facts, including the provisions of Acts of Congress in 1886, 1888, and 1889, thus demonstrate that Congress understood its objective as turning on the Tribe's agreement to the abrogation of any land claim it might have and to any reduction of the 1873 reservation's boundaries. The explicit statutory provisions requiring agreement of the Tribe were unchanged right through to the point of Congress's final 1891 ratification of the reservation, in an Act that of course contained no cession by the Tribe of submerged lands within the reservation's outer boundaries. Nor, it should be added, is there any hint in the evidence that delay in final passage of the ratifying Act was meant to pull a fast one by allowing the reservation's submerged lands to pass to Idaho under a legal presumption, by virtue of the Statehood Act approved eight months before Congress took final action on the reservation. There is no evidence that the Act confirming the reservation was delayed for any reason but comparison of the respective House and Senate bills, to assure that they were identical prior to the House's passage of the Senate version.

*** Congress did know that the reservation included submerged lands, and that it authorized the reservation's modification solely by agreement. The intent, in other words, was that anything not consensually ceded by the Tribe would remain for the Tribe's benefit, an objective flatly at odds with Idaho's view that Congress meant to transfer the balance of submerged lands to the State in what would have amounted to an act of bad faith accomplished by unspoken operation of law. Indeed, the implausibility of the State's current position is underscored by the fact that it made a contrary argument in the Court of Appeals, where it emphasized the District Court's finding that the 1889 Act was an authorization "to negotiate with the Tribe for a release of the submerged lands," and recognized that "[Congress was] informed that the Coeur d'Alene Reservation embraced submerged lands."

Idaho's position is at odds not only with evidence of congressional intent before statehood, but also with later congressional understanding that statehood had not affected the submerged lands in question. Eight months after passing the Statehood Act, Congress ratified the 1887 and 1889 agreements in their entireties (including language in the 1887 agreement that "the Coeur d'Alene Reservation shall be held forever as Indian land"), with no signal that some of the land over which the parties to those agreements had negotiated had passed in the interim to Idaho. The ratification Act suggested in a further way Congress's understanding that the 1873 reservation's submerged lands had not passed to the State, by including a provision confirming the Tribe's sale of river channels to Frederick Post. Confirmation would have been beyond Congress's power if title to the submerged riverbed had already passed to the State. ***[9]

---

9. Here, we agree with the dissent, that Congress cannot, after statehood, reserve or convey submerged lands that "ha[ve] already been bestowed" upon a State. Our point in mentioning

In sum, Congress undertook to negotiate with the Coeur d'Alene Tribe for reduction in the territory of an Executive Order reservation that Idaho concedes included the submerged lands at issue here. Congress was aware that the submerged lands were included and clearly intended to redefine the area of the reservation that covered them only by consensual transfer, in exchange for the guarantee that the Tribe would retain the remainder. There is no indication that Congress ever modified its objective of negotiated consensual transfer, which would have been defeated if Congress had let parts of the reservation pass to the State before the agreements with the Tribe were final. Any imputation to Congress either of bad faith or of secrecy in dropping its express objective of consensual dealing with the Tribe is at odds with the evidence. We therefore think the negotiating history, not to mention subsequent events, "ma[k]e [it] very plain," that Congress recognized the full extent of the Executive Order reservation lying within the stated boundaries it ultimately confirmed, and intended to bar passage to Idaho of title to the submerged lands at issue here.

The judgment of the Court of Appeals is affirmed.

CHIEF JUSTICE REHNQUIST, with whom **JUSTICE SCALIA**, **JUSTICE KENNEDY**, and **JUSTICE THOMAS** join, dissenting.

The Court makes out a plausible case for the proposition that, on the day Idaho was admitted to the Union, the Executive Branch of the Federal Government had intended to retain in trust for the Coeur d'Alene Indian Tribe the submerged lands under a portion of Lake Coeur d'Alene. But the existence of such intent on the part of the Executive Branch is simply not enough to defeat an incoming State's title to submerged lands within its borders. Decisions of this Court going back more than 150 years establish this proposition beyond a shadow of a doubt.

*** Congress itself did authorize negotiations with the Tribe in 1886 and 1889, but those Acts expressly provided that any resulting agreements were not binding "until ratified by Congress." Act of May 15, 1886, 24 Stat. 44, App. 51; Act of Mar. 2, 1889, 25 Stat. 1002, App. 144. And it is undisputed that ratification did not occur before Idaho gained admission. The Court, however, is willing to divine congressional intent to withhold submerged lands from the State from what are best described as inchoate prestatehood proceedings. In the Court's view it is sufficient that one House of Congress had acted to approve the agreements and that the other was in the process of considering similar legislation. *See ante,* at 2145. The Court thus speaks of the "final" ratification of the 1887 and 1889 negotiations as if the official approval of both Houses of Congress was but a mere formality. *Ibid. But see* U.S. Const., Art. I, § 7, cl. 2. But the indisputable fact remains that, as of July 3, 1890, "Congress" had passed the Idaho Statehood Act but had not ratified the 1887 and 1889 agreements.

***

Congress's actions after statehood is merely to confirm what Congress's prestatehood actions already make clear: that the lands at issue here were not bestowed upon Idaho at statehood, because Congress intended that they remain tribal reservation lands barring agreement to the contrary.

NOTES AND QUESTIONS

1. *Aboriginal title and tribal ownership.* Why did the tribe not press the aboriginal title argument in *Idaho v. United States*? Could the Court have relied on the reserved rights rule set out in *United States v. Winans*?

2. *Congressional intent to reserve submerged lands.* What act of Congress provided the clear evidence of intent to reserve title to the submerged lands to Lake Coeur d'Alene in the United States for the benefit of the tribes? What made this intent clearer than that in the 1868 Crow Treaty discussed in *Montana*? Was it clear that Congress could have extinguished the tribe's aboriginal title by "legislative fiat" without payment of compensation?

3. *Lower court treatment.* Note the different discussions in *Montana* and *United States v. Idaho* of the Crow and Coeur D'Alene historic reliance on the waterways. Determinations of the tribe's historic dependence on economic and cultural connections with navigable waterways often dictate lower court cases as well. *Compare Puyallup Indian Tribe v. Port of Tacoma*, 717 F.2d 1251, 1258 (9th Cir. 1983) ("[W]here a grant of real property to an Indian tribe includes within its boundaries a navigable water and the grant is made to a tribe dependent on the fishery resource in that water for survival, the grant must be construed to include the submerged lands if the Government was plainly aware of the vital importance of the submerged lands and the water resource to the tribe at the time of the grant."); *Confederated Salish and Kootenai Tribes v. Namen*, 665 F.2d 951 (9th Cir. 1982) (tribes own bed and banks of portion of lake within reservation); *United States v. Stotts*, 49 F.2d 619 (9th Cir. 1930) (Lummi Nation owns tidelands to low water mark), with *Skokomish Indian Tribe v. France*, 320 F.2d 205, 212 (9th Cir. 1963) ("tidelands were not essential to the livelihood of the Indians at the time of the treaty and the executive order providing for the reservation" and thus not owned by tribe); *United States v. Pend Oreille Public Utility Dist. No. 1*, 926 F.2d 1502 (9th Cir. 1991) (tribe's dependence on river did not rebut presumption against Government's conveyance of title to riverbed). *See* Cohen's Handbook of Federal Indian Law §15.05[3], 1019-24 (2012) (discussing cases and contradictions). *See also United States v. Milner,* 583 F.3d 1174 (9th Cir. 2009) (when erosion caused upland owners' shore defense structures to be surrounded by tribal tidelands, tribe and United States had common-law trespass claim against upland owner).

4. *Tribal management.* Does ownership of the bed and banks of a navigable body of water automatically give a government owner jurisdiction for all purposes? As a consequence of *Idaho v. United States*, the Coeur d'Alene Tribe exercises jurisdiction over encroachments on the water above tribal submerged lands. The material below describes the tribe's regulatory program for shorelands.

Shoreline Protection

Overview†

An encroachment for regulatory purposes is defined as any structure on, in or above submerged lands or waters of the Coeur d'Alene Reservation. Among the nearly 535 encroachments within the Reservation boundary some you may see on Coeur d'Alene Lake, Black Lake and the St. Joseph River include structures such as docks, piers, float homes, boat garages, jetties, floats, pilings, breakwaters, boat ramps, channels, basins, fills, dikes, power lines, and sea walls. A dock is one that for many carries special importance and is a very valued piece of waterfront living. It is more than just a place to park the boat, it is also a place for fishing, swimming, sunbathing, family gathering and relaxing and just a few of the reasons many are drawn to a waterfront lifestyle.

In recognition of these realities, the Coeur d'Alene Tribe extends the privilege of keeping a dock on Tribal Waters to our neighbors who own waterfront property. This privilege is also granted to secondary lot owners who are members of previously established homeowner associations. This use, including all structures, of Tribal Waters and submerged lands within the Reservation Boundary must be permitted through the Coeur d'Alene Tribe Shoreline Protection Program. ***

Encroachment Standards

A significant goal of the Encroachment Standards is to protect reasonable access to navigable waters for both dock owners and other users alike. We want a standard that allows dock construction but does not infringe upon the use and enjoyment of Tribal Waters by other people interested in boating, fishing and other recreational activities. In addition recreational users on Coeur d'Alene Lake are encouraged to familiarize themselves with Tribal Law and Order Code regulating boating on Tribal Waters. Any

†. Picture and text from web site with permission of Coeur d'Alene Indian Tribe. Brown, Jason. Shoreline Protection. Program Overview. Coeur d'Alene Tribe (2006). https://www.cdatribe-nsn.gov/lake-management/challenges/.

person using the waters within the Coeur d'Alene Reservation is deemed to have consented to the jurisdiction and laws of the Coeur d'Alene Tribe.

II. HUNTING, FISHING AND GATHERING RIGHTS

Recall the Supreme Court's description of Indian fishing rights in *United States v. Winans, supra* Ch. 3: "The right to resort to the fishing places in controversy was a part of larger rights possessed by the Indians, upon the exercise of which there was not a shadow of impediment, and which were not much less necessary to the existence of the Indians than the atmosphere they breathed." The Court spoke to the right of access to fish—not to ownership of fish and wildlife, which have been treated differently than real property and associated resources discussed in the foregoing section. While there was a period during which states claimed ownership of fish and wildlife within their boundaries, *Geer v. Connecticut*, 161 U.S. 519 (1896), this principle was overruled in *Hughes v. Oklahoma*, 441 U.S. 322 (1979), which involved an Oklahoma statute precluding transport of Oklahoma minnows out of state. The Court stated that "it is pure fantasy to talk of 'owning' wild fish, birds, or animals." *Id.* at 334 (quoting the dissent from *Geer*); *see* Eric T. Freyfogle and Dale D. Goble, Wildlife Law 25-29 (2009).

With the legal fiction of state ownership cast aside, the contest between states and tribes over fish, wildlife and plant resources typically involves the scope of Indian reserved rights and relative bounds of state and tribal jurisdiction over tribal members and non-members. It is generally accepted that federal laws setting aside tribal territories implicitly include the right to hunt, fish, and gather free of state regulation. In *Menominee Tribe of Indians v. United States*, 391 U.S. 404 (1968), Ch. 4, *supra*, for example, the Court considered the Treaty of Wolf River in 1854, which set aside the Wolf River Reservation "for a home, to be held as Indian lands are held." 10 Stat. 1064. The Court declared:

> Nothing was said in the 1854 treaty about hunting and fishing rights. Yet we agree with the Court of Claims that the language "to be held as Indian lands are held" includes the right to fish and to hunt. The record shows that the lands covered by the Wolf River Treaty of 1854 were selected precisely because they had an abundance of game. *See Menominee Tribe of Indians v. United States*, 95 Ct.Cl. 232, 240–241 (1941). The essence of the Treaty of Wolf River was that the Indians were authorized to maintain on the new lands ceded to them as a reservation their way of life which included hunting and fishing.

Id. at 406. As discussed further in Chapter 4, *supra*, the Court in *Menominee* held that these rights survived even the termination of the federal government's relationship with the tribe. Although there remain questions about the extent of federal regulation of tribal fishing, hunting, and gathering rights in Indian country, *see United States v. Dion*, 476 U.S. 734 (1986), Ch. 4, *supra*, and tribal regulation of nonmember hunting and fishing rights there, *compare Montana v. United States*, 450 U.S. 544 (1981) *with New Mexico v. Mescalero Apache*, 462 U.S. 324 (1983), Ch. 8, *supra*, most complicated questions arise regarding reserved tribal hunting, fishing, and gathering rights outside Indian country. The following case establishes important principles regarding the nature and extent of reserved off-reservation fishing rights.

WASHINGTON V. WASHINGTON STATE COMMERCIAL PASSENGER FISHING VESSEL ASSOCIATION

443 U.S. 658, 99 S. Ct. 3055, 61 L.Ed.2d 823 (1979)

JUSTICE STEVENS delivered the opinion of the Court.

To extinguish the last group of conflicting claims to lands lying west of the Cascade Mountains and north of the Columbia River in what is now the State of Washington,[1] the United States entered into a series of treaties with Indian tribes in 1854 and 1855. The Indians relinquished their interest in most of the Territory in exchange for monetary payments. In addition, certain relatively small parcels of land were reserved for their exclusive use, and they were afforded other guarantees, including protection of their "right of taking fish, at all usual and accustomed grounds and stations *** in common with all citizens of the Territory." 10 Stat. 1133.

The principal question presented by this litigation concerns the character of that treaty right to take fish. ***

I

Anadromous fish hatch in fresh water, migrate to the ocean where they are reared and reach mature size, and eventually complete their life cycle by returning to the fresh-water place of their origin to spawn. Different species have different life cycles, some spending several years and traveling great distances in the ocean before returning to spawn and some even returning to spawn on more than one occasion before dying. The regular habits of these fish make their "runs" predictable; this predictability in turn makes it possible for both fishermen and regulators to forecast and to control the number of fish that will be caught or "harvested." Indeed, as the terminology associated with it suggests, the management of anadromous fisheries is in many ways more akin to the cultivation of "crops"—with its relatively high degree of predictability and productive stability, subject mainly to sudden changes in climatic patterns—than is the management of most other commercial and sport fisheries.

Regulation of the anadromous fisheries of the Northwest is nonetheless complicated by the different habits of the various species of salmon and trout involved, by the variety of methods of taking the fish, and by the fact that a run of fish may pass through a series of different jurisdictions. Another complexity arises from the fact that the State of Washington has attempted to reserve one species, steelhead trout, for sport fishing and therefore conferred regulatory jurisdiction over that species upon its Department of Game, whereas

---

1. By three earlier treaties the United States had extinguished the conflicting claims of Spain in 1820 and Russia in 1824, 8 Stat. 252, 302, and Great Britain in 1846, 9 Stat. 869. In 1848, Congress established the Oregon Territory, 9 Stat. 323; that statute provided that nothing contained therein "shall be construed to impair the rights of person or property now pertaining to the Indians in said Territory, so long as such rights shall remain unextinguished by treaty between the United States and such Indians." In 1850, Congress authorized the negotiation of treaties to extinguish the Indian claims to land lying west of the Cascade Mountains, 9 Stat. 437. In 1853, the Washington Territory, which includes the present State of Washington, was organized out of the Oregon Territory. Ch. 90, 10 Stat. 172.

the various species of salmon are primarily harvested by commercial fishermen and are managed by the State's Department of Fisheries. Moreover, adequate regulation not only must take into account the potentially conflicting interests of sport and commercial fishermen, as well as those of Indian and nontreaty fishermen, but also must recognize that the fish runs may be harmed by harvesting either too many or too few of the fish returning to spawn.

The anadromous fish constitute a natural resource of great economic value to the State of Washington. Millions of salmon, with an average weight of from 4 or 5 to about 20 pounds, depending on the species, are harvested each year. Over 6,600 nontreaty fishermen and about 800 Indians make their livelihood by commercial fishing; moreover, some 280,000 individuals are licensed to engage in sport fishing in the State.[4]

II

One hundred and twenty-five years ago when the relevant treaties were signed, anadromous fish were even more important to most of the population of western Washington than they are today. At that time, about three-fourths of the approximately 10,000 inhabitants of the area were Indians. Although in some respects the cultures of the different tribes varied—some bands of Indians, for example, had little or no tribal organization[5] while others, such as the Makah and the Yakima, were highly organized—all of them shared a vital and unifying dependence on anadromous fish.

Religious rites were intended to insure the continual return of the salmon and the trout; the seasonal and geographic variations in the runs of the different species determined the movements of the largely nomadic tribes. Fish constituted a major part of the Indian diet, was used for commercial purposes, and indeed was traded in substantial volume. The Indians developed food-preservation techniques that enabled them to store fish throughout the year and to transport it over great distances. They used a wide variety of methods to catch fish, including the precursors of all modern netting techniques. Their usual and accustomed fishing places were numerous and were scattered throughout the area, and included marine as well as fresh-water areas.

All of the treaties were negotiated by Isaac Stevens, the first Governor and first Superintendent of Indian Affairs of the Washington Territory, and a small group of advisers. Contemporaneous documents make it clear that these people recognized the vital importance of the fisheries to the Indians and wanted to protect them from the risk that non-Indian settlers might seek to monopolize their fisheries. There is no evidence of the precise understanding the Indians had of any of the specific English terms and phrases in the treaty.[10] It is perfectly clear, however, that the Indians were vitally interested in

---

4. Although in terms of the number and weight of the fish involved, the commercial salmon catch is far more substantial than the recreational steelhead catch, the latter apparently provides the State with more revenue than the former, involves more people, and has accordingly been a more controversial political issue within the State. *See* [384 F. Supp.] at 399.

5. Indeed, the record shows that the territorial officials who negotiated the treaties on behalf of the United States took the initiative in aggregating certain loose bands into designated tribes and even appointed many of the chiefs who signed the treaties.

10. Indeed, the translation of the English words was difficult because the interpreter used a "Chinook jargon" to explain treaty terms, and that jargon not only was imperfectly (and often not) understood by many of the Indians but also was composed of a simple 300–word commercial vocabulary that did not include words corresponding to many of the treaty terms.

protecting their right to take fish at usual and accustomed places, whether on or off the reservations, [384 F.Supp]. at 355, and that they were invited by the white negotiators to rely and in fact did rely heavily on the good faith of the United States to protect that right.

Referring to the negotiations with the Yakima Nation, by far the largest of the Indian tribes, the District Court found:

> At the treaty council the United States negotiators promised, and the Indians understood, that the Yakimas would forever be able to continue the same off-reservation food gathering and fishing practices as to time, place, method, species and extent as they had or were exercising. The Yakimas relied on these promises and they formed a material and basic part of the treaty and of the Indians' understanding of the meaning of the treaty.

The Indians understood that non-Indians would also have the right to fish at their off-reservation fishing sites. But this was not understood as a significant limitation on their right to take fish.[12] Because of the great abundance of fish and the limited population of the area, it simply was not contemplated that either party would interfere with the other's fishing rights. The parties accordingly did not see the need and did not intend to regulate the taking of fish by either Indians or non-Indians, nor was future regulation foreseen.

Indeed, for several decades after the treaties were signed, Indians continued to harvest most of the fish taken from the waters of Washington, and they moved freely about the Territory and later the State in search of that resource. The size of the fishery resource continued to obviate the need during the period to regulate the taking of fish by either Indians or non-Indians. Not until major economic developments in canning and processing occurred in the last few years of the 19th century did a significant non-Indian fishery develop.[13] It was as a consequence of these developments, rather than of the treaty, that non-Indians began to dominate the fisheries and eventually to exclude most Indians from participating in it—a trend that was encouraged by the onset of often discriminatory state regulation in the early decades of the 20th century.[14]

In sum, it is fair to conclude that when the treaties were negotiated, neither party realized or intended that their agreement would determine whether, and if so how, a resource that had always been thought inexhaustible would be

---

12. "There is nothing in the written records of the treaty councils or other accounts of discussions with the Indians to indicate that the Indians were told that their existing fishing activities or tribal control over them would in any way be restricted or impaired by the treaty. The most that could be implied from the treaty context is that the Indians may have been told or understood that non-Indians would be allowed to take fish at the Indian fishing locations along with the Indians."

13. "The non-Indian commercial fishing industry did not fully develop in the case area until after the invention and perfection of the canning process. The first salmon cannery in Puget Sound began in 1877 with a small operation at Mukilteo. Large-scale development of the commercial fisheries did not commence in Puget Sound until the mid–1890's. The large-scale development of the commercial fishing industry in the last decades of the Nineteenth Century brought about the need for regulation of fish harvests." [384 F. Supp.] at 352.

14. The impact of illegal regulation, *see Tulee v. Washington*, 315 U.S. 681 (1942), and of illegal exclusionary tactics by non-Indians, *see United States v. Winans*, 198 U.S. 371 (1905), in large measure accounts for the decline of the Indian fisheries during this century and renders that decline irrelevant to a determination of the fishing rights the Indians assumed they were securing by initialing the treaties in the middle of the last century.

allocated between the native Indians and the incoming settlers when it later became scarce.

III

Unfortunately, that resource has now become scarce, and the meaning of the Indians' treaty right to take fish has accordingly become critical. The United States Court of Appeals for the Ninth Circuit and the Supreme Court of the State of Washington have issued conflicting decisions on its meaning. In addition, their holdings raise important ancillary questions that will appear from a brief review of this extensive litigation.

The federal litigation was commenced in the United States District Court for the Western District of Washington in 1970. The United States, on its own behalf and as trustee for seven Indian tribes, brought suit against the State of Washington seeking an interpretation of the treaties and an injunction requiring the State to protect the Indians' share of the anadromous fish runs. Additional Indian tribes, the State's Fisheries and Game Departments, and one commercial fishing group, were joined as parties at various stages of the proceedings, while various other agencies and groups, including all of the commercial fishing associations that are parties here, participated as *amici curiae*.

During the extensive pretrial proceedings, four different interpretations of the critical treaty language were advanced. Of those, three proceeded from the assumption that the language required some allocation to the Indians of a share of the runs of fish passing through their traditional fishing areas each year. The tribes themselves contended that the treaties had reserved a preexisting right to as many fish as their commercial and subsistence needs dictated. The United States argued that the Indians were entitled either to a 50% share of the "harvestable" fish that originated in and returned to the "case area" and passed through their fishing places,[15] or to their needs, whichever was less. The Department of Fisheries agreed that the Indians were entitled to "a fair and equitable share" stated in terms of a percentage of the harvestable salmon in the area; ultimately it proposed a share of "one-third."

Only the Game Department thought the treaties provided no assurance to the Indians that they could take some portion of each run of fish. That agency instead argued that the treaties gave the Indians no fishing rights not enjoyed by non-treaty fishermen except the two rights previously recognized by decisions of this Court—the right of access over private lands to their usual and accustomed fishing grounds, *see Seufert Bros. Co. v. United States*, 249 U.S. 194 [1919]; *United States v. Winans*, 198 U.S. 371 [1905], and an exemption from the payment of license fees. *See Tulee v. Washington*, 315 U.S. 681 [1942].

The District Court agreed with the parties who advocated an allocation to the Indians, and it essentially agreed with the United States as to what that allocation should be. It held that the Indians were then entitled to a 45% to 50% share of the harvestable fish that will at some point pass through recognized tribal fishing grounds in the case area. The share was to be calculated on a river-by-river, run-by-run basis, subject to certain adjustments.

15. The "harvestable" amount of fish is determined by subtracting from the total number of fish in each run the number that must be allowed to escape for conservation purposes. ***

The injunction entered by the District Court required the Department of Fisheries (Fisheries) to adopt regulations protecting the Indians' treaty rights. 384 F. Supp., at 416–417. After the new regulations were promulgated, however, they were immediately challenged by private citizens in suits commenced in the Washington state courts. The State Supreme Court, in two cases that are here in consolidated form in No. 77–983, ultimately held that Fisheries could not comply with the federal injunction. *Puget Sound Gillnetters Assn. v. Moos*, 565 P.2d 1151 (1977); *Fishing Vessel Assn. v. Tollefson*, 571 P.2d 1373 (1977).

As a matter of federal law, the state court first accepted the Game Department's and rejected the District Court's interpretation of the treaties and held that it did not give the Indians a right to a share of the fish runs, and second concluded that recognizing special rights for the Indians would violate the Equal Protection Clause of the Fourteenth Amendment. The opinions might also be read to hold, as a matter of state law, that Fisheries had no authority to issue the regulations because they had a purpose other than conservation of the resource. In this Court, however, the Attorney General of the State disclaims the adequacy and independence of the state-law ground and argues that the state-law authority of Fisheries is dependent on the answers to the two federal-law questions discussed above. We defer to that interpretation, subject, of course, to later clarification by the State Supreme Court. Because we are also satisfied that the constitutional holding is without merit,[20] our review of the state court's judgment will be limited to the treaty issue.

When Fisheries was ordered by the state courts to abandon its attempt to promulgate and enforce regulations in compliance with the federal court's decree—and when the Game Department simply refused to comply—the District Court entered a series of orders enabling it, with the aid of the United States Attorney for the Western District of Washington and various federal law enforcement agencies, directly to supervise those aspects of the State's fisheries necessary to the preservation of treaty fishing rights. 459 F. Supp. 1020. The District Court's power to take such direct action and, in doing so, to enjoin persons who were not parties to the proceeding was affirmed by the United States Court of Appeals for the Ninth Circuit. 573 F.2d 1123. ***

Because of the widespread defiance of the District Court's orders, this litigation has assumed unusual significance. We granted certiorari in the state and federal cases to interpret this important treaty provision and thereby to resolve the conflict between the state and federal courts regarding what, if any, right the Indians have to a share of the fish, to address the implications of international regulation of the fisheries in the area, and to remove any doubts about the federal court's power to enforce its orders.

---

20. The Washington Supreme Court held that the treaties would violate equal protection principles if they provided fishing rights to Indians that were not also available to non-Indians. The simplest answer to this argument is that this Court has already held that these treaties confer enforceable special benefits on signatory Indian tribes, *e.g., Tulee v. Washington*, 315 U.S. 681; *United States v. Winans*, 198 U.S. 371, and has repeatedly held that the peculiar semisovereign and constitutionally recognized status of Indians justifies special treatment on their behalf when rationally related to the Government's "unique obligation toward the Indians." *Morton v. Mancari*, 417 U.S. 535, 555 [1973].

IV

The treaties secure a "right of taking fish." The pertinent articles provide:

> The right of taking fish, at all usual and accustomed grounds and stations, is further secured to said Indians, in common with all citizens of the Territory, and of erecting temporary houses for the purpose of curing, together with the privilege of hunting, gathering roots and berries, and pasturing their horses on open and unclaimed lands: *Provided, however,* That they shall not take shell fish from any beds staked or cultivated by citizens.
>
> ***

A treaty, including one between the United States and an Indian tribe, is essentially a contract between two sovereign nations. *E.g., Lone Wolf v. Hitchcock,* 187 U.S. 553. When the signatory nations have not been at war and neither is the vanquished, it is reasonable to assume that they negotiated as equals at arm's length. There is no reason to doubt that this assumption applies to the treaties at issue here.

Accordingly, it is the intention of the parties, and not solely that of the superior side, that must control any attempt to interpret the treaties. When Indians are involved, this Court has long given special meaning to this rule. It has held that the United States, as the party with the presumptively superior negotiating skills and superior knowledge of the language in which the treaty is recorded, has a responsibility to avoid taking advantage of the other side. "[T]he treaty must therefore be construed, not according to the technical meaning of its words to learned lawyers, but in the sense in which they would naturally be understood by the Indians." *Jones v. Meehan,* 175 U.S. 1 [1899]. ***

Governor Stevens and his associates were well aware of the "sense" in which the Indians were likely to view assurances regarding their fishing rights. During the negotiations, the vital importance of the fish to the Indians was repeatedly emphasized by both sides, and the Governor's promises that the treaties would protect that source of food and commerce were crucial in obtaining the Indians' assent. It is absolutely clear, as Governor Stevens himself said, that neither he nor the Indians intended that the latter "should be excluded from their ancient fisheries," and it is accordingly inconceivable that either party deliberately agreed to authorize future settlers to crowd the Indians out of any meaningful use of their accustomed places to fish. That each individual Indian would share an "equal opportunity" with thousands of newly arrived individual settlers is totally foreign to the spirit of the negotiations.[22]

22. The State characterizes its interpretation of the treaty language as assuring Indians and non-Indians an "equal opportunity" to take fish from the State's waters. This appellation is misleading. In the first place, even the State recognizes that the treaties provide Indians with certain rights—*i.e.,* the right to fish without a license and to cross private lands—that non-Indians do not have. *See Tulee v. Washington,* 315 U.S. 681; *Seufert Bros. Co. v. United States,* 249 U.S. 194; *United States v. Winans,* 198 U.S. 371. *See also Puyallup Tribe v. Washington Dept. of Game,* 433 U.S. 165. Whatever opportunities the treaties assure Indians with respect to fish are admittedly not "equal" to, but are to some extent greater than, those afforded other citizens. It is therefore simply erroneous to suggest that the treaty language "confers upon non-Indians precisely the same right to fish that it confers upon Indians." Powell, J., dissenting, *post,* at 3081.

Moreover, in light of the far superior numbers, capital resources, and technology of the non-Indians, the concept of the Indians' "equal *opportunity*" to take advantage of a scarce resource is likely in practice to mean that the Indians' "right of taking fish" will net them virtually no catch

Such a "right," along with the $207,500 paid the Indians, would hardly have been sufficient to compensate them for the millions of acres they ceded to the Territory.

It is true that the words "in common with" may be read either as nothing more than a guarantee that individual Indians would have the same right as individual non-Indians or as securing an interest in the fish runs themselves. If we were to construe these words by reference to 19th-century property concepts, we might accept the former interpretation, although even "learned lawyers" of the day would probably have offered differing interpretations of the three words.[23] But we think greater importance should be given to the Indians' likely understanding of the other words in the treaties and especially the reference to the "right of *taking* fish"—a right that had no special meaning at common law but that must have had obvious significance to the tribes relinquishing a portion of their pre-existing rights to the United States in return for this promise. This language is particularly meaningful in the context of anadromous fisheries—which were not the focus of the common law—because of the relative predictability of the "harvest." In this context, it makes sense to say that a party has a right to "take"—rather than merely the "opportunity" to try to catch—some of the large quantities of fish that will almost certainly be *available at* a given place at a given time.

***

In our view, the purpose and language of the treaties are unambiguous; they secure the Indian's right to take a share of each run of fish that passes through tribal fishing areas. But our prior decisions provide an even more persuasive reason why this interpretation is not open to question. For notwithstanding the bitterness that this litigation has engendered, the principal issue

---

at all. For the "opportunity" is at best theoretical. Indeed, in 1974, before the District Court's injunction took effect, and while the Indians were still operating under the "equal opportunity" doctrine, their take amounted to approximately 2% of the total harvest of salmon and trout in the treaty area. 459 F. Supp. at 1032.

23. The State argues that at common law a "common fishery" was merely a nonexclusive right of access, *see* 3 J. Kent, Commentaries 412 (5th ed. 1844), and that the right of a fishery was appurtenant to specific parcels of real property. The State does not suggest, however, that these concepts were understood by, or explained to, the Indians. Indeed, there is no evidence that Governor Stevens understood them, although one of his advisers, George Gibbs, was a lawyer.

But even if we indulge in the highly dubious assumption that Gibbs was learned in the intricacies of water law, that he incorporated them in the treaties, and that he explained them fully to the Indians, the treaty language would still be subject to the different interpretations presented by the parties to this litigation. For in addition to "common fisheries," the "in common with" language was used in two other relevant senses during the period. First, a "common *of* fishery" meant a limited right, acquired from the previously exclusive owner of certain fishing rights (in this case the Indians), "of taking fish *in common with* certain others in waters flowing through [the grantor's] land." J. Gould, Laws of Waters § 183 (3d ed. 1900) (emphasis added); *see* 3 Kent, *supra*, at 410. Under that understanding of the language, it would hardly make sense that the Indians effectively relinquished all of their fishing rights by granting a merely nonexclusive right.

Even more to the point, the United States had previously used the "in common with" language in two treaties with Britain, including one signed in 1854, that dealt with fishing rights in certain waters adjoining the United States and Canada. Treaty of Oct. 20, 1818, 8 Stat. 248; Treaty of June 5, 1854, 10 Stat. 1089. As interpreted by the Department of State during the 19th century, these treaties gave each signatory country an "equal" and apportionable "share" of the take of fish in the treaty areas. *See* H.R. Ex. Doc. No. 84, 46th Cong., 2d Sess., 7 (1880); 5 American State Papers (For. Rel.) 528–529 (1823); J. Q. Adams, The Duplicate Letters, The Fisheries and the Mississippi, 184–185 (1822).

involved is virtually a "matter decided" by our previous holdings [in *United States v. Winans,* 198 U.S. 371 (1905); *Seufert Bros. Co. v. United States,* 249 U.S. 194 (1919); *Tulee v. Washington,* 315 U.S. 681 (1942); *Puyallup Tribe v. Washington Game Dept.,* 391 U.S. 392 (1968) (*Puyallup I*); *Washington Game Dept. v. Puyallup Tribe,* 414 U.S. 44 (1973) (*Puyallup II*); and *Puyallup Tribe v. Washington Game Dept.,* 433 U.S. 165 (1977) (*Puyallup III*).] ***

The purport of our cases is clear. Nontreaty fishermen may not rely on property law concepts, devices such as the fish wheel, license fees, or general regulations to deprive the Indians of a fair share of the relevant runs of anadromous fish in the case area. Nor may treaty fishermen rely on their exclusive right of access to the reservations to destroy the rights of other "citizens of the Territory." Both sides have a right, secured by treaty, to take a fair share of the available fish. That, we think, is what the parties to the treaty intended when they secured to the Indians the right of taking fish in common with other citizens.

V

We also agree with the Government that an equitable measure of the common right should initially divide the harvestable portion of each run that passes through a "usual and accustomed" place into approximately equal treaty and nontreaty shares, and should then reduce the treaty share if tribal needs may be satisfied by a lesser amount. ***

It bears repeating, however, that the 50% figure imposes a maximum but not a minimum allocation. As in *Arizona v. California* and its predecessor cases, the central principle here must be that Indian treaty rights to a natural resource that once was thoroughly and exclusively exploited by the Indians secures so much as, but no more than, is necessary to provide the Indians with a livelihood—that is to say, a moderate living. Accordingly, while the maximum possible allocation to the Indians is fixed at 50%,[27] the minimum is not; the latter will, upon proper submissions to the District Court, be modified in response to changing circumstances. If, for example, a tribe should dwindle to just a few members, or if it should find other sources of support that lead it to abandon its fisheries, a 45% or 50% allocation of an entire run that passes through its customary fishing grounds would be manifestly inappropriate because the livelihood of the tribe under those circumstances could not reasonably require an allotment of a large number of fish.

Although the District Court's exercise of its discretion, as slightly modified by the Court of Appeals, *** is in most respects unobjectionable, we are not satisfied that all of the adjustments it made to its division are consistent with the preceding analysis.

***

27. Because the 50% figure is only a ceiling, it is not correct to characterize our holding "as guaranteeing the Indians a specified percentage" of the fish. *See* Powell, J., dissenting, *post,* at 3080.

The logic of the 50% ceiling is manifest. For an equal division—especially between parties who presumptively treated with each other as equals—is suggested, if not necessarily dictated, by the word "common" as it appears in the treaties. Since the days of Solomon, such a division has been accepted as a fair apportionment of a common asset, and Anglo-American common law has presumed that division when, as here, no other percentage is suggested by the language of the agreement or the surrounding circumstances.

Accordingly, any fish (1) taken in Washington waters or in United States waters off the coast of Washington, (2) taken from runs of fish that pass through the Indian's usual and accustomed fishing grounds, and (3) taken by either members of the Indian tribes that are parties to this litigation, on the one hand, or by non-Indian citizens of Washington, on the other hand, shall count against that party's respective share of the fish.

***

VII

In addition to their challenges to the District Court's basic construction of the treaties, and to the scope of its allocation of fish to treaty fishermen, the State and the commercial fishing associations have advanced two objections to various remedial orders entered by the District Court.[32] It is claimed that the District Court has ordered a state agency to take action that it has no authority to take as a matter of state law and that its own assumption of the authority to manage the fisheries in the State after the state agencies refused or were unable to do so was unlawful.[33]

These objections are difficult to evaluate in view of the representations to this Court by the Attorney General of the State that definitive resolution of the basic federal question of construction of the treaties will both remove any state-law impediment to enforcement of the State's obligations under the treaties, and enable the State and Fisheries to carry out those obligations. Once the

32. The associations advance a third objection as well—that the District Court had no power to enjoin individual nontreaty fishermen, who were not parties to its decisions, from violating the allocations that it has ordered. The reason this issue has arisen is that state officials were either unwilling or unable to enforce the District Court's orders against nontreaty fishermen by way of state regulations and state law enforcement efforts. Accordingly, nontreaty fishermen were openly violating Indian fishing rights, and, in order to give federal law enforcement officials the power via contempt to end those violations, the District Court was forced to enjoin them. 459 F. Supp. at 1043, 1098–1099, 1113–1117. The commercial fishing organizations, on behalf of their individual members, argue that they should not be bound by these orders because they were not parties to (although the associations all did participate as *amici curiae* in) the proceedings that led to their issuance.

If all state officials stand by the Attorney General's representations that the State will implement the decision of this Court, this issue will be rendered moot because the District Court no longer will be forced to enforce its own decisions. Nonetheless, the issue is still live since state implementation efforts are now at a standstill and the orders are still in effect. Accordingly, we must decide it.

In our view, the commercial fishing associations and their members are probably subject to injunction under either the rule that nonparties who interfere with the implementation of court orders establishing public rights may be enjoined, or the rule that a court possessed of the res in a proceeding *in rem*, such as one to apportion a fishery, may enjoin those who would interfere with that custody. But in any case, these individuals and groups are citizens of the State of Washington, which was a party to the relevant proceedings, and "they, in their common public rights as citizens of the State, were represented by the State in those proceedings, and, like it, were bound by the judgment." Moreover, a court clearly may order them to obey that judgment.

33. The State has also argued that absent congressional legislation the treaties involved here are not enforceable. This argument flies directly in the face of Art. XIII of the treaties which states that they "shall be obligatory on the contracting parties as soon as [they are] ratified by the President and Senate of the United States." Moreover, the argument was implicitly rejected in *Winans* and our ensuing decisions regarding these treaties, all of which assumed that the treaties are self-enforcing. *E g., Puyallup I,* 391 U.S., at 397–398.

Significantly, Congress thrice rejected efforts in the early 1960's to terminate the Indians' fishing rights under these treaties. *See* S.J. Res. 170 and 171, 88th Cong., 2d Sess. (1964); H.J. Res. 48, 88th Cong., 1st Sess. (1963); H.J. Res. 698, 87th Cong., 2d Sess. (1962).

state agencies comply, of course, there would be no issue relating to federal authority to order them to do so or any need for the District Court to continue its own direct supervision of enforcement efforts.

The representations of the Attorney General are not binding on the courts and legislature of the State, although we assume they are authoritative within its executive branch. Moreover, the State continues to argue that the District Court exceeded its authority when it assumed control of the fisheries in the State, and the commercial fishing groups continue to argue that the District Court may not order the state agencies to comply with its orders when they have no state-law authority to do so. Accordingly, although adherence to the Attorney General's representations by the executive, legislative, and judicial officials in the State would moot these two issues, a brief discussion should foreclose the possibility that they will not be respected. State-law prohibition against compliance with the District Court's decree cannot survive the command of the Supremacy Clause of the United States Constitution. *Cooper v. Aaron*, 358 U.S. 1. It is also clear that Game and Fisheries, as parties to this litigation, may be ordered to prepare a set of rules that will implement the Court's interpretation of the rights of the parties even if state law withholds from them the power to do so. *E.g., North Carolina Board of Education v. Swann*, 402 U.S. 43 (1971). Once again the answer to a question raised by this litigation is largely dictated by our *Puyallup* trilogy. There, this Court mandated that state officers make precisely the same type of allocation of fish as the District Court ordered in this case. *See Puyallup III*, 433 U.S., at 177.

Whether Game and Fisheries may be ordered actually to promulgate regulations having effect as a matter of state law may well be doubtful. But the District Court may prescind that problem by assuming direct supervision of the fisheries if state recalcitrance or state-law barriers should be continued. It is therefore absurd to argue, as do the fishing associations, both that the state agencies may not be ordered to implement the decree and also that the District Court may not itself issue detailed remedial orders as a substitute for state supervision. The federal court unquestionably has the power to enter the various orders that state official and private parties have chosen to ignore, and even to displace local enforcement of those orders if necessary to remedy the violations of federal law found by the court. Even if those orders may have been erroneous in some respects, all parties have an unequivocal obligation to obey them while they remain in effect.

In short, we trust that the spirit of cooperation motivating the Attorney General's representation will be confirmed by the conduct of state officials. But if it is not, the District Court has the power to undertake the necessary remedial steps and to enlist the aid of the appropriate federal law enforcement agents in carrying out those steps. Moreover, the comments by the Court of Appeals strongly imply that it is prepared to uphold the use of stern measures to require respect for federal-court orders.[36]

---

36. "The state's extraordinary machinations in resisting the [1974] decree have forced the district court to take over a large share of the management of the state's fishery in order to enforce its decrees. Except for some desegregation cases ***, the district court has faced the most concerted official and private efforts to frustrate a decree of a federal court witnessed in this century. The challenged orders in this appeal must be reviewed by this court in the context of events forced by litigants who offered the court no reasonable choice." 573 F.2d 1123, 1126 (9th Cir. 1978).

JUSTICE POWELL, joined by JUSTICES STEWART and REHNQUIST, dissenting.

*** In my view, the District Court below—and now this Court—has formulated an apportionment doctrine that cannot be squared with the language or history of the treaties, or indeed with the prior decisions of this Court. The application of this doctrine, and particularly the construction of the term "in common" as requiring a basic 50-50 apportionment, is likely to result in an extraordinary economic windfall to Indian fishermen in the commercial fish market by giving them a substantial position in the market wholly protected from competition from non-Indian fishermen. Indeed, non-Indian fishermen apparently will be required from time to time to stay out of fishing areas completely while Indians catch their court-decreed allotment. In sum, the District Court's decision will discriminate quite unfairly against non-Indians. ***

I would hold that the treaties give to the Indians several significant rights that should be respected. As made clear in *Winans*, the purpose of the treaties was to assure to Indians the right of access over private lands so that they could continue to fish at their usual and accustomed fishing grounds. Indians also have the exclusive right to fish on their reservations, and are guaranteed enough fish to satisfy their ceremonial and subsistence needs. Moreover, as subsequently construed, the treaties exempt Indians from state regulation (including the payment of license fees) except as necessary for conservation in the interest of all fishermen. Finally, under *Puyallup II*, it is settled that even a facially neutral conservation regulation is invalid if its effect is to discriminate against Indian fishermen. These rights, privileges, and exemptions—possessed only by Indians—are quite substantial. I find no basis for according them additional advantages.

NOTES AND QUESTIONS

1. *State recalcitrance meets tribal determination.* Assertions of off-reservation treaty fishing rights in the 1960s and 1970s led to passionate disputes between Indian and non-Indian communities. For tribal communities, the dispute was central to tribal identity. In the words of Sue Masten, chair of the Yurok Tribe of Northern California, "We are salmon people. We couldn't let anyone take that from us." Charles Wilkinson, Blood Struggle: The Rise of Modern Indian Nations 150 (2005). For tribes across the United States, the fight to preserve treaty rights became a focal point of the struggle for tribal survival, and a source of resurgence of pride in tribal culture and community. For non-Indian communities, the claims of tribal fishermen to fish free of state regulation were perceived as claims for special rights that would deplete fish populations and interfere with livelihoods dependent on the fish. Tribal fishermen faced jeering crowds carrying signs reading "Save a Salmon: Can an Indian" in the Northwest, or "Spear an Indian: Save a Walleye" in the Great Lakes. For more on this history, see Wilkinson, Blood Struggle, *supra*, at 150–173, and Larry Nesper, The Walleye War: The Struggle for Ojibwe Spearfishing and Treaty Rights (2002). *Lac du Flambeau Band v. Stop Treaty Abuse Wisconsin*, 843 F. Supp. 1284 (W.D. Wis. 1994), considering a claim of racial discrimination made against such protesters, is reprinted in Chapter 3, *supra*.

Washington State Officials Arresting Tribal Leader Billy Frank for Exercising Treaty Fishing Rights in the 1960s.†

2. *What is a moderate standard of living?* What did the Court mean when it said the tribes are entitled to enough fish to provide a "moderate living?" None of the parties to the litigation had suggested such a qualification to the treaty right.

The late Professor and Dean David H. Getches of the University of Colorado School of Law reviewed the late Justice Marshall's papers and discerned the following history of the decision. "In the third draft of [Justice Stevens'] opinion, he added language to stress that the right of tribes stopped when they reached a "moderate" living standard, an idea not offered by any party or suggested in any of the briefs. He also elaborated on the reduced percentages of the fishery the tribes were likely to take, though the calculations he added to the opinion to garner support had to be modified on a motion by the State which pointed out there was no evidence on the record to support the figures. [Stevens had predicted that the Indian fishery would take no more than 20% of the runs.] Chief Justice Burger characterized Stevens' approach as "an 'arbitration' holding," and thus Stevens secured a majority vote." David H. Getches, *Conquering the Cultural Frontier: The New Subjectivisim of the Supreme Court in Indian Law*, 84 Cal. L. Rev. 1573, 1638–39 (1996).

In a ruling on shellfish allocation in the next generation of *United States v. Washington,* a district court elaborated on the moderate standard of living requirement:

> The Court finds that no persuasive evidence has been presented to the Court by the State and the intervenors showing that a substantial

†. Photograph courtesy of Northwest Indian Fisheries Commission.

change in circumstances has occurred, so that the Tribes could maintain a moderate living without the exercise of their fishing rights, or that the Tribes have voluntarily abandoned their fisheries. Therefore, the Court declines to apply the Moderate Living Doctrine to these facts.

The State of Washington and the intervenors argued at trial that the Court should engage in an economic discussion about the income levels of the tribal members in order to prove that the circumstances of the Tribes have changed to such a degree so as to warrant a reduction in the Tribes' share of shellfish.

The State's and intervenors' expert, Dr. Thomas, however, admitted that "moderate living" is not a term of art used by economists. The defendant and intervenors, through the income driven analysis of their expert, seek to prove that the Tribes already derive income from a variety of sources; thus the Tribes do not require a 50% share of the shellfish in order to maintain their "moderate living." Dr. Thomas relied solely on what he called "tribal household income" and compared it to a moderate living standard by reference to the Bureau of the Census income data for non-Indian households.

Dr. Thomas' argument is flawed because it relied only on income, namely it was a single-indicator analysis. A more appropriate analysis, such as the analysis of the Tribes' expert Dr. Meyer, focuses on several relevant factors in order to determine if the circumstances of the Tribes have changed to such a degree so that a reduction in the tribal share of shellfish is warranted. The uncontroverted evidence presented at trial is that the Tribes lag significantly behind other residents of the State of Washington in their overall standard of living. For example, approximately one in three Tribal members live below the poverty level; Indians in the State of Washington endure health circumstances characterized by the State as "very poor;" tribal members have per capita incomes that are less than one-half the per capita income of non-tribal residents of the State; and tribal members suffer from unemployment rates at least three times greater than that of all non-tribal residents of the State of Washington.

Therefore, the Court declines to apply the Moderate Living Doctrine to reduce the Tribes' share of harvestable fish on the basis that they already derive a sufficient income and standard of living from other sources.

United States v. Washington, 873 F. Supp. 1422, 1445–46 (W.D. Wash. 1994). On appeal the Ninth Circuit affirmed this finding and stated in a footnote: "Even if we were to consider Tribal income from casino operations as the Appellants ask us to do—we would not be left with a 'definite and firm conviction' that the district court's findings were erroneous." *United States v. Washington*, 157 F.3d 630, 652 n.11 (9th Cir. 1998).

3. *What methods may tribes use to exercise their treaty rights?* Fishing methods have changed substantially since the nineteenth century when the treaties reserving off-reservation rights were signed. Should tribes be limited to the methods used then, forbidding the use or more efficient motor boats, modern commercial fishing vessels, or manufactured fishing equipment? Courts to consider this issue have generally recognized that fishing methods

should not be fixed in the nineteenth century. In the litigation over Chippewa and Ottawa fishing rights in Michigan, for example, the court held that

> The Indians' right to fish, like the aboriginal use of the fishery on which it is based, is not a static right. The reserved fishing right is not affected by the passage of time or changing conditions. The right is not limited as to species of fish, origin of fish, the purpose of use or the time or manner of taking. The right may be exercised utilizing improvements in fishing techniques, methods and gear. It may expand with the commercial market which it serves, and supply the species of fish which that market demands, whatever the origin of the fish.

United States v. Michigan, 471 F. Supp. 192, 260 (W.D. Mich. 1979); *see also Mille Lacs Band of Chippewa Indians v. Minnesota*, 861 F. Supp. 784, 838 (D.Minn.1994) (Chippewa 1837 treaty right of "hunting, fishing, and gathering the wild rice" on ceded lands "was not limited to use of any particular techniques, methods, devices, or gear" and included right to use modern techniques for commercial purposes); *Lac Courte Oreilles Band of Lake Superior Chippewa Indians v. Wisconsin*, 653 F. Supp. 1420, 1430 (W.D.Wis.1987) ("Plaintiffs are not confined to the hunting and fishing methods their ancestors relied upon at treaty time."). In *United States v. Gotchnik*, 222 F.3d 506 (8th Cir. 2000), however, the court held that the right to fish using modern methods did not include the right to use modern methods to get to fishing places in light of the Boundary Waters Canoe Area Wilderness Act prohibiting use of motor vehicles in a federally protected area. The court stated that "although the use of evolving hunting and fishing implements may have been within the understanding of the signatory Bands, the same cannot reasonably be said of the use of modern modes of transportation to reach desired hunting and fishing areas." *Id.* at 510. Is this a meaningful distinction? Is it supportable in light of the Supreme Court's holding in *United States v. Winans* that the right to fish in usual and accustomed places included a right of access to such places, even if this required traversing lands protected by other property rights? *See Winans*, 198 U.S. 371, 381 (1905). Or is the decision better understood as a roundabout way of holding that the treaty rights had been abrogated by clear congressional intent? *See Gotchnik*, 222 F.3d at 510.

State Authority to Regulate for Conservation and Public Safety.

In earlier cases construing treaty fishing rights in Washington, the Supreme Court limited state rights of regulation to what has become known as the "conservation necessity" standard: "The right to fish 'at all usual and accustomed' places may, of course, not be qualified by the State ***. But the manner of fishing, the size of the take, the restriction of commercial fishing, and the like may be regulated by the State in the interest of conservation, provided the regulation meets appropriate standards and does not discriminate against the Indians." *Puyallup Tribe v. Dep't of Game*, 391 U.S. 392, 398 (1968); *Puyallup Tribe v. Dep't of Game*, 433 U.S. 165, 177 (1977). Lower courts have narrowly interpreted state authority. "Direct regulation of treaty Indian fishing in the interests of conservation is permissible only after the state has proved unable to preserve a run by forbidding the catching of fish by other citizens under its ordinary police power jurisdiction." *United States v.*

Washington, 520 F.2d 676 (9th Cir. 1975). In *United States v. Michigan*, 653 F.2d 277, 279 (6th Cir. 1981), the court articulated the following requirements:

> [A]ny such state regulations *** must be a necessary conservation measure [and] must be the least restrictive alternative method available for preserving fisheries in the Great Lakes from irreparable harm ***. Thus if Indian fishing is not likely to cause irreparable harm to fisheries within the territorial jurisdiction of the State of Michigan, the state may not regulate it. The state bears the burden of persuasion to show by clear and convincing evidence that it is highly probable that irreparable harm will occur and that the need for regulation exists.

The late Professor Ralph Johnson, one of the early contemporary leaders in the field, expressed a different view, arguing that state jurisdiction is not permissible as a matter of federal law unless authorized by a tribe's treaty, or Act of Congress. *See* Ralph W. Johnson, *The State Versus Off-Reservation Fishing, A United States Supreme Court Error*, 47 Wash. L. Rev. 207 (1972). If the Court had found that states had no "conservation authority" where would such authority exist?

The next case considers state authority to regulate Indian hunting to protect public safety.

LAC COURTE OREILLES BAND OF LAKE SUPERIOR CHIPPEWA INDIANS OF WISCONSIN V. STATE OF WISCONSIN

769 F.3d 543 (7th Cir. 2014)

POSNER, CIRCUIT JUDGE.

The plaintiffs, Wisconsin Indian tribes, moved the district court under Fed.R.Civ.P. 60(b)(5) to relieve them from a final judgment on the ground that its continued enforcement would be, in the language of the rule, "no longer equitable." There is no deadline for moving for relief under this provision, though a party must move within a reasonable time. See Fed.R.Civ.P. 60(c)(1). The district court denied the motion, precipitating this appeal.

The judgment in question, entered in 1991 and not appealed, upheld a state statute prohibiting members of the tribes from hunting deer at night outside the tribes' reservations. *Lac Courte Oreilles Band of Lake Superior Chippewa Indians v. Wisconsin,* 775 F. Supp. 321, 324 (W.D.Wis.1991). Wisconsin Indians had hunted deer at night since before they had electricity. Hunting deer at night is efficient because deer are more active at night, and because a bright light in a deer's visual field freezes the animal, making him a large stationary target. According to proposed findings of fact submitted by the plaintiffs, "tribal members need to hunt for subsistence purposes. Between 25% and 93% of Tribal members are unemployed. Many Tribal members that are employed still live below the poverty level." (Twenty-eight percent of the state's Indian population have incomes below the poverty level. Suzanne Macartney et al., "Poverty Rates for Selected Detailed Race and Hispanic Groups by State and Place: 2007–2011" 14 (Feb. 2013), www.census.gov/prod/2013pubs/acsbr11–17.pdf [https://perma.cc/5PRB-HY8Q] (visited Oct. 8, 2014, as were the other websites cited in this opinion).) Deer meat also is lean and therefore healthful (obesity is far more prevalent among Indians than among whites, see American Heart Association, *American Indian/Alaska Natives & Cardiovascular Diseases* (2013), www.heart.org/idc/groups/heart-public/@wcm/@sop/@smd/documents/downloadable/ucm—319569.pdf [https://perma.cc/Y5SV-VHN8]). According to the plaintiffs "a disproportionate number of Tribal members have chronic diseases such as heart disease and diabetes. Cheap, high fat hamburger meat purchased with food stamps cannot replace healthy venison in tribal populations experiencing chronic health problems," and in addition "tribal members need to hunt at night for cultural and religious reasons. Fresh deer meet [*sic*] may be needed for a ceremony, and the only opportunity to obtain it may be at night."

As shown in the map below, reservation lands in Wisconsin are limited and scattered. But much of the northern third of Wisconsin that is not reservation land (the solid black regions of the map) is territory ceded by the Indian tribes to the United States in the nineteenth century (as marked by the shaded region of the map). The treaties that governed the terms of the cession reserved the Indians' rights to hunt in the ceded territory. For example, a treaty of 1842 provided that "the Indians stipulate for the right of hunting on the ceded territory, with the other usual privileges of occupancy, until required to remove by the President of the United States." See *Lac Courte Oreilles Band of Lake Superior Chippewa Indians v. Voigt,* 700 F.2d 341, 345 (7th Cir. 1983).

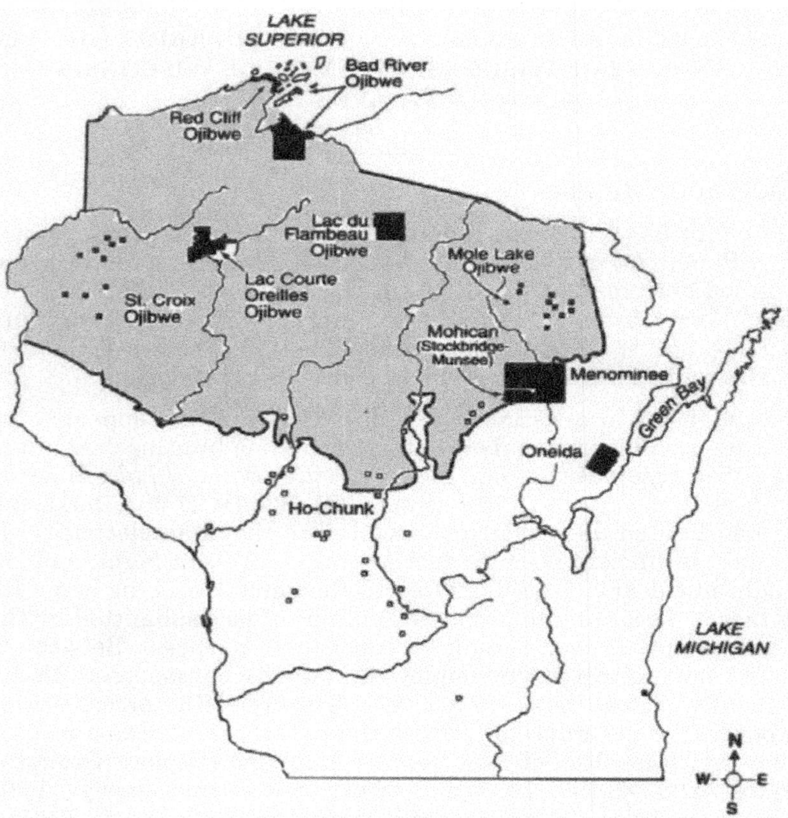

Though the treaties do not mention the states, states are allowed to regulate Indian activities in ceded territory so far as necessary "to protect [the state's] natural resources and its citizens." *Reich v. Great Lakes Indian Fish & Wildlife Commission,* 4 F.3d 490, 501 (7th Cir. 1993). State jurisdiction over Indians is limited but includes the right to take measures necessary to protect public safety, *id.,* and safety concerns were the justification given by Wisconsin for wanting to prohibit Indians from hunting deer at night outside their reservations. But the state must justify, not merely assert, a public-safety need to restrict Indian rights recognized by treaty with the federal government. It must show, first, "that a substantial detriment or hazard to public health or safety exists or is imminent. Second, ... that the particular regulation sought to be imposed is necessary to the prevention or amelioration of the public health or safety hazard. And third, ... that application of the particular regulation to the tribes is necessary to effectuate the particular public health or safety interest. Moreover, the state must show that its regulation is the least restrictive alternative available to accomplish its health and safety purposes." *Lac Courte Oreilles Band of Lake Superior Chippewa Indians v. Wisconsin,* 668 F. Supp. 1233, 1239 (W.D. Wis. 1987); see also *Mille Lacs Band of Chippewa Indians v. Minnesota,* 952 F. Supp. 1362, 1381–82 (D. Minn. 1997).

In and before 1989, which was when the evidence was presented on which the 1991 judgment was based, there had been very little night hunting of deer other than on Indian reservations. Occasionally law enforcement officers or employees of the state's department of natural resources would shoot deer at night, but this was rare, the reason being that night hunting was considered dangerous, although there appears to have been no evidence supporting that fear.

The tribes' motion to reopen the 1991 judgment is based largely on the fact that beginning in the late 1990s the number of deer killed at night, mainly by state employees though also by some private state contractors, increased markedly because of an explosion of the deer population and the advent of chronic wasting disease, a fatal disease common among deer. Night hunting was meant to reduce the deer population in general (one reason being that deer are frequent causes of serious traffic accidents) and to eradicate chronic wasting disease in particular. The tribes' argument is that the state's greater experience with night hunting of deer since the 1991 judgment shows that it is safer than had been believed—so safe indeed that, given sensible regulations governing such hunting, there is no reason to prohibit the tribes' members from engaging in such hunting on ceded territory. Hunting accidents in general have plummeted in Wisconsin in recent years: from just over 100 in 1989 to 28 in 2012. The latter number is particularly striking since Wisconsin's population in 2012 was 5.7 million and hunting is popular in that largely rural state.

The district judge rejected the tribes' argument on several grounds. One was that most of the increased night hunting has been by employees or contractors of the state government. But there is no evidence that the safety regulations that the tribes intend to impose on off-reservation night hunting are laxer than the regulations governing night hunting by the state's hunters. (In fact the opposite is true, as we'll see.) The safety record of deer hunting on reservations is outstanding. According to an uncontradicted expert witness's report, though there are no regulations specific to night hunting on the reservations (where night hunting is lawful) there have been only two reported incidents of a person being shot by a deer hunter, either day or night. Furthermore, there's no evidence that the state agents who hunt deer at night are experienced or well-trained. Apparently many are neither. In 2006 the state's department of natural resources noted that "shooters are coming to this program [eradication of chronic wasting disease by night hunting] ill prepared ... . Too many do not know the basic rules of firearms safety ... . Our trainees come from within the ranks of the department [of natural resources] and the vast majority are not seasoned shooters ... ." In contrast, those Indians who hunt deer tend to be experienced hunters, because on their reservations they are allowed to hunt both during the day and at night. Moreover, to be licensed to hunt they are required to pass a marksmanship test—at night. Their safety record is sterling: since 1989 there have been only two or three recorded hunting accidents involving Indians in ceded territory. According to another expert witness's report, the tribes' proposed permit requirements for nighttime deer hunting are far more stringent than those the state imposes on its hunters.

The judge remarked that "the chronic wasting disease initiative is some evidence that night hunting with lights can be engaged in safely but it is not conclusive in that regard. I cannot say that it shows that the judgment in this case has become 'an instrument of wrong.' " It's not clear what evidence would demonstrate "conclusively," in advance of permitting the hunting of deer at night by members of the plaintiff tribes, that such hunting was safe. All that can be said is that on the present record there is scant reason to think that safety concerns justify forbidding Indians to hunt deer at night in the thinly populated (by human beings) northern part of Wisconsin that consists of territory that the tribes ceded to the United States long ago. There are of course hunting accidents, but they are mainly to members of the shooting party—often they are self-inflicted wounds—rather than to bystanders. Between 2007 and 2011 there were 133 hunting-related injuries of which 48 were self-inflicted. Of the remaining 85 accidents, only 4 were to non-hunters—either bystanders or non-hunting members of the hunting party.

The night hunter doesn't shoot until the deer is a brightly lit stationary object—a perfect target. Hunting deer during the day is likely to be more dangerous because there are more people about and the hunter will often be shooting at a moving animal, which a shooter is more likely to miss than a stationary one. It's true that at night the hunter may well have greater difficulty seeing a person in the woods behind the deer that he's aiming at—and bullets fired from the high-powered rifles used to hunt deer carry a long way if they happen to miss the targeted deer. But in recognition of this danger the hunting regulations proposed by the tribes require the night-hunting Indians to lay out lines of sight in the daytime and submit a shooting plan for approval. Unless a hunter plans to fire from an elevated position (when because of the angle the bullet is likely to hit the ground within a safe distance), a member of the tribal conservation department or the tribe's internal regulatory agency must travel to the site and confirm that the shooting plan complies with safety standards. Further mitigating the danger is that one of the plaintiff's expert witnesses reports that there are very few people out and about at night in the ceded territory during the night deer-hunting season, which runs from November 1 until the first Monday in January, with a break during the state's regular nine-day hunting season when there are likely to be more people out both day and night.

According to data compiled by Wisconsin state agencies, between 2008 and 2011 there was a total of 1851 injuries and deaths in collisions between motor vehicles and deer, and only 37 injuries and deaths from all accidents—day and night—arising from the hunting of deer with guns, an average of 9 a year. Whether any of them were deaths from night hunting is unknown. But it is plausible—no stronger term is possible, given a dearth of evidence-that the more deer that Indians kill, the fewer deer-related accidents to humans there will be, since according to the statistics we quoted 98 percent of deer-related injuries arise from motor vehicle collisions with deer. Not that the effect will necessarily be large, though in 2013 Wisconsin hunters killed about 342,000 deer out of a population (before the hunting season) estimated at 1.4 million—24 percent of the deer population. A further point concerning safety is that the very small Indian population (1 percent of Wisconsin's total population) imposes a natural limit on the potential risk of Indian night hunting to public safety.

The judge said that the fact "that plaintiffs waited ten years after the chronic wasting disease reduction program started and four years after it ended before moving to reopen the judgment ... in itself might be good cause for denying their motion." Not so. The longer the wait, the more evidence is accumulated bearing on the safety of night hunting of deer. The plaintiffs filed their motion to reopen and modify the judgment in 2012; had they filed earlier they would have had a thinner statistical basis for their position. And it's not as if the state is harmed by delay in reopening the judgment.

A motion to modify a judgment under Fed.R.Civ.P. 60(b)(5) must, like any motion, be made in a reasonable time, since the rules specify no deadline. But what is reasonable depends on the circumstances. If reasonable reliance on a judgment is likely to grow over time, a motion to modify it should be made sooner rather than later. But in the case of regulatory decrees, such as the judgment in this case forbidding night hunting of deer, often the passage of time renders them obsolete, so that the case for modification or rescission actually grows with time, as in *Horne v. Flores,* 557 U.S. 433, 447–48, 129 S. Ct. 2579, 174 L.Ed.2d 406 (2009), *People Who Care v. Rockford Board of Education,* 246 F.3d 1073, 1075–76 (7th Cir.2001), and *Alliance to End Repression v. City of Chicago,* 237 F.3d 799, 801 (7th Cir.2001). That's what seems to have happened in this case. Based on almost no experience with night deer hunting in the 1980s, the district court at the beginning of the next decade upheld on safety grounds Wisconsin's ban on off-reservation night deer hunting by Indians. Greater experience with deer hunting suggests that a total ban is no longer (if it ever was) necessary to ensure public safety. And as noted in *Reich v. Great Lakes Indian Fish & Wildlife Commission, supra,* 4 F.3d at 501, it is only safety (and conservation, which however is not an issue in this case) that can justify a state's forbidding a normal Indian activity, authorized to the tribes on land ceded by them to the United States.

At least four states allow Indians to hunt deer at night—Oregon, Washington, Minnesota, and Michigan. Neither the tribes nor the state has presented evidence of the accident rate in any of those states. We do not know whether such statistics are obtainable. They would prove to be of little value were there substantial differences among these states or between them and Wisconsin in such potentially relevant domains as terrain, climate, deer population, location and size of ceded territory, the length and time of year of the night deer hunting season, safety regulations, Indian population as a percentage of total state population, population density, Indian cultural and dietary practices relating to deer hunting, poverty, and unemployment. But so far as we are able to determine there are few relevant differences among Minnesota, Michigan, and Wisconsin in these respects, though considerable differences between those three Midwestern states and Oregon and Washington. *See, e.g.*, U.S. Department of the Interior, Bureau of Indian Affairs, *2013 American Indian Population and Labor Force Report* (Jan. 16, 2014), www.bia.gov/cs/groups/public///–024782.pdf [https://perma.cc/3VCC-RW98]. For example, tribal hunting in the ceded territories in Wisconsin, Minnesota, and Michigan is managed by the same organization, the Great Lakes Indian Fish and Wildlife Commission. And in developing their proposed regulations the Wisconsin tribes looked to Michigan and Minnesota, both states that have allowed night hunting for at least a decade, for guidance—although the proposed Wisconsin regulations are far more stringent than those of the other states. The Wisconsin tribes' night hunting safety course and certification program are identical to those of the Minnesota tribes. Moreover, the ceded territories in each of the three states (the upper peninsula of Michigan, the northern third of Wisconsin, and the east-central portion of Minnesota) are comparable in population density, elevation, biomass (*i.e.* tree concentration), and average temperature during the hunting season. So it seems reasonable that Minnesota's and Michigan's experiences with night hunting of deer by Indians might have a bearing on our case.

We'll leave it to the district court to decide whether to invite the parties to submit such comparative evidence. The burden of production should be placed on the state, for as the record stands the evidence presented by the tribes that night hunting for deer in the ceded territory is unlikely to create a serious safety problem provides a compelling reason for vacating the 1991 judgment that prohibited Indians from hunting deer at night in that territory.

The judgment is reversed and the case remanded to the district court for further proceedings consistent with this opinion.

NOTE AND QUESTIONS

Why should the state have any conservation or public safety authority if the tribe has its own regulations in place already? The treaty is between the United States and the Lac Courte Oreilles. Is the answer that the courts assume that states have residual authority over treaty-based hunting? The federal government has traditionally left fish and game management to the states, but tribes have traditionally been free of state jurisdiction. This tension may explain why states have some authority but are subject to a heavy burden to justify conservation or safety-based regulation. Wisconsin's hunting season (with guns) generally runs for about 8 days in November, so hundreds of thousands of hunters are in the woods with high-powered rifles. The state archery season runs from mid-September to January 1. Wouldn't it be safer to spread the rifle season out longer? According to the Wisconsin Department of Natural Resources nearly 500,000 individual licenses were sold in 2017 for the season when rifles were allowed. *See* Trent Tetzlaff, *Wisconsin Department of Natural Resources Reports Deer License Sales Drop*, Post Cresent, Nov. 19, 2018, 6:33

pm, https://www.postcrescent.com/story/news/2018/11/19/wisconsin-dnr-reports-deer-license-sales-drop/2052874002/ [https://perma.cc/6MGJ-RGW9]. How safe would you feel going for a causal walk in the woods during that season? Some might think the State of Wisconsin has no place telling the tribes what their safety regulations ought to be.

Note on Tribal–State Cooperative Management

Both tribes and states have an interest in conserving the fisheries they share. This interest may often best be achieved through cooperative agreements. Typically many tribes have treaty rights to fish in the same waters; these tribes and the state must cooperate with each other to allocate the catch, dictate sustainable fishing methods, and implement and enforce these regulations. The successful assertion of treaty hunting and fishing rights have led to a number of intertribal consortia that work with states to achieve these common goals. *Reich v. Great Lakes Indian Fish and Wildlife Commission,* 4 F.3d 490 (7th Cir. 1993), reprinted in Chapter 4, *supra*, concerns one such consortium, composed of the thirteen tribes with hunting, fishing and gathering rights in the states abutting the Great Lakes. The consortium "fixes hunting, fishing, and gathering seasons for the various species of animal and plant covered by the usufructuary rights, sets limits on the amounts and type of catch permitted, and polices compliance with its regulations," both by enforcing the regulations against tribal hunters and, as cross-deputized state law enforcement officers, ensuring that non-Indians do not interfere with tribal exercise of treaty rights. *Id.* at 492. In the Northwest, a consortium of over twenty tribes works through the Northwest Indian Fisheries Commission to cooperatively manage sustainable fisheries. The Constitution of the Commission announces its purpose:

> We, the Indians of the Pacific Northwest, recognize that our fisheries are a basic and important natural resource and of vital concern to the Indians of this state, and that the conservation of this natural resource is dependent upon effective and progressive management. We further believe that by unity of action, we can best accomplish these things, not only for the benefit of our own people but for all of the people of the Pacific Northwest.

Overview of the NWIFC, Northwest Indian Fisheries Commission, http://nwifc.org/about-us/. The tribes regulate fishing by their members, while the state regulates non-Indian fishing activity. The primary co-management effort takes place in a lengthy meeting at a location near the Washington-Oregon border known as "North of Falcon." Northwest Indian Fisheries Commission Chair, Lorraine Loomis (Swinomish), had this to say in a recent column.

> It has taken more than 40 years for the tribes and state to build the working relationship needed to jointly manage the salmon resource. Like all relationships, ours has its ups and downs, but at the end of the day we all want the same thing: healthy, sustainable salmon populations that can support harvest. Even with an early start it won't be easy for the co-managers to reach agreement again this year. As salmon continue to decline, every management action we take requires increasingly careful

consideration. One thing that's certain is that fisheries management is better when we work together.

Lorriane Loomis, *Being Frank: North Of Falcon Underway Earlier*, Northwest Indian Fisheries (Feb. 7, 2017) https://nwtreatytribes org/frank-north-falcon-underway-earlier/ [https://perma.cc/wuq6-rtgk]. The case proceeds under the continuing jurisdiction of the federal district court that heard the original case in 1970.

Another consortium, the Chippewa Ottawa Resource Authority, works with the Michigan Department of Natural Resources to manage fishing rights in the Great Lakes assured by the Treaty with the Ottawa and Chippewa Nation of 1836. After a series of state and federal cases established that the Michigan could not regulate the exercise of treaty fishing rights by the signatory tribes, *see United States v. Michigan,* 712 F.2d 242 (6th Cir. 1983); *United States v. Michigan,* 471 F. Supp. 192 (W.D.Mich.1979), *modified in part,* 653 F.2d 277 (6th Cir. 1981); *People v. LeBlanc,* 248 N.W.2d 199 (Mich. 1976), the tribes, states and United States entered into consent decree agreeing to a cooperative system of regulation. Under the consent decree, the intertribal Chippewa Ottawa Resource Authority and the Michigan Department of Natural Resources work together to adopt management and allocation rules for fishing within Lake Huron, Lake Michigan, and Lake Superior. *See* Consent Decree, *United States v. Michigan,* Case No. 2:73 CV 26 (Aug. 7, 2000), *available at* http://www.michigan.gov/documents/dnr/consent_decree_2000_197687_7.pdf. (The initial decree was agreed on in 1985 and was to last for 15 years; when the decree expired in 2000, the parties entered into a new decree set to expire in 2020.) The agreement provides for elaborate regulations of permissible catches of each species of fish, when and how they can be taken. Consent Decree § IV, VII, VIII, X. Tribes adopt the regulations in their tribal codes, and tribal justice systems enforce the rules against their own members. *Id.* at §§ XVIII. Michigan Department of Natural Resources officers are deputized, however, to refer violators to the tribal systems. *Id.* at XVIII(B)(3). The tribal and state parties are mandated to share information and cooperate on both law enforcement and fishery management. *Id.* at §§ XVIII(B)(2) (law enforcement), XV (conservation information sharing). Reports suggest that while there are some violations by both state and tribal fishermen, their governments are working cooperatively to preserve the fisheries, and generally meeting or exceeding their conservation goals. *See* Michigan Department of Natural Resources, Implementation "Tribal Coordination" web page, https://www.michigan.gov/dnr/0,4570,7-350-79136_79236_84834---,00.html [https://perma.cc/M9EJ-4ZYJ].

Treaty–Based Protection of Fish and Wildlife Habitat

In *United States v. Washington,* 759 F.2d 1353 (9th Cir. 1985) (Phase II), the Ninth Circuit Court of Appeals vacated a district court's declaratory judgment that "the right to take fish necessarily includes the right to have those fish protected from man-made despoliation, so that the treaties impose upon the State [of Washington] a corresponding duty to refrain from degrading or authorizing the degradation of the fish habitat to an extent that would deprive the treaty Indians of their moderate living needs." 759 F.2d at 1355. The Ninth Circuit found that the "legal standards that will govern the State's precise obligations and duties under the treaty with respect to the myriad State actions that may affect the environment of the treaty area will depend for their definition and articulation upon concrete facts which underlie a dispute in a particular case." *Id.* at 1357.

UNITED STATES V. WASHINGTON

853 F.3d 946 (9th Cir. 2017), *aff'd by an equally divided court*, 138 S. Ct. 1832 (2018).

In 2001, pursuant to an injunction previously entered in this long-running litigation, twenty-one Indian tribes ("Tribes"), joined by the United States, filed a "Request for Determination"—in effect, a complaint—in the federal district court for the Western District of Washington. * * * The Tribes contended that Washington State had violated, and was continuing to violate, the Treaties by building and maintaining culverts that prevented mature salmon from returning from the sea to their spawning grounds; prevented smolt (juvenile salmon) from moving downstream and out to sea; and prevented very young salmon from moving freely to seek food and escape predators. * * *

The United States joined the Tribes' Request, seeking a declaration from the court that:

> The right of taking fish secured to the plaintiff tribes in the Stevens Treaties imposes a duty upon the State of Washington to refrain from degrading the fishery resource through the construction or maintenance of culverts under State owned roads and highways in a way that deprives the Tribes of a moderate living from the fishery.
>
> The State has violated and continues to violate the duty owed to the plaintiff tribes under the Stevens Treaties through the operation and maintenance of culverts which reduce the number of fish that would otherwise return to or pass through the Tribes' usual and accustomed fishing grounds and stations to such a degree as would deprive the Tribes of the ability to earn a moderate living from the fishery.

The United States sought a permanent injunction that would require Washington "within five years of the date of judgment (or such other time period as the Court deems necessary and just)" to "repair, retrofit, maintain, or replace" culverts that "degrade appreciably" the passage of fish.

Washington and the defendant state agencies (collectively "Washington" or "the State") answered by declaring that there is "no treaty-based right or duty of fish habitat protection as described" in the Request. In the alternative, Washington emphasized that some of its barrier culverts pass under highways funded in part by the United States, and that these highways were "designed according to standards set or approved" by the Federal Highway Administration, leading Washington to believe that its culverts complied with the Treaties. Further, Washington asserted that the United States and the Tribes have built and maintained barrier culverts on their own lands within the Case Area. Washington asserted that the United States "has a duty to take action on its own lands so as not to place on the State of Washington an unfair burden of complying with any such treaty-based duty."

Washington also made a "cross-request"—in effect, a counterclaim—against the United States seeking a declaration that the United States has violated its own duty to the Tribes under the Treaties, and seeking an injunction that would require the United States to modify or replace its own barrier culverts. The district court dismissed the cross-request on the ground that the United States had not waived its sovereign immunity. * * *

The fishing clause of the Stevens Treaties guarantees to the Tribes a right to engage in off-reservation fishing. It provides, in its entirety:

> The right of taking fish, at all usual and accustomed grounds and stations, is further secured to said Indians, in common with all citizens of the Territory, and of erecting temporary houses for the purpose of curing, together with the privilege of hunting, gathering roots and berries, and pasturing their horses on open and unclaimed lands: *Provided, however*, That they shall not take shell fish from any beds staked or cultivated by citizens.

Fishing Vessel, 443 U.S. at 674 (emphasis in original). Washington concedes that the clause guarantees to the Tribes the right to take up to fifty percent of the fish available for harvest, but it contends that the clause imposes no obligation on the State to ensure that any fish will, in fact, be available.

In its brief to us, Washington denies any treaty-based duty to avoid blocking salmon-bearing streams:

> [T]he Tribes here argue for a treaty right that finds no basis in the plain language or historical interpretation of the treaties. On its face, the right of taking fish in common with all citizens does not include a right to prevent the State from making land use decisions that could incidentally impact fish. Rather, such an interpretation is contrary to the treaties' principal purpose of opening up the region to settlement.

Brief at 27–28.

At oral argument, Washington even more forthrightly denied any treaty-based duty. Washington contended that it has the right, consistent with the Treaties, to block every salmon-bearing stream feeding into Puget Sound:

> The Court: Would the State have the right, consistent with the treaty, to dam every salmon stream into Puget Sound?
>
> Answer: Your honor, we would never and could never do that... .
>
> The Court: ... I'm asking a different question. Would you have the right to do that under the treaty?
>
> Answer: Your honor, the treaty would not prohibit that[.]
>
> The Court: So, let me make sure I understand your answer. You're saying, consistent with the treaties that Governor Stevens entered into with the Tribes, you could block every salmon stream in the Sound?
>
> Answer: Your honor, the treaties would not prohibit that[.]

Oral Argument at 1:07–1:45, October 16, 2015. * * *

Washington has a remarkably one-sided view of the Treaties. In its brief, Washington characterizes the "treaties' principal purpose" as "opening up the region to settlement." Brief at 29. Opening up the Northwest for white settlement was indeed the principal purpose of the United States. But it was most certainly not the principal purpose of the Indians. Their principal purpose was to secure a means of supporting themselves once the Treaties took effect.

Salmon were a central concern. An adequate supply of salmon was "not much less necessary to the existence of the Indians than the atmosphere they breathed." *Winans*, 198 U.S. at 381, 25 S. Ct. 662. Richard White, an expert on the history of the American West and Professor of American History at Stanford University, wrote in a declaration filed in the district court that, during the negotiations for the Point–No–Point Treaty, a Skokomish Indian worried aloud about "how they were to feed themselves once they ceded so much land to the whites." Professor White wrote, to the same effect, that during negotiations at Neah Bay, Makah Indians "raised questions about the role that fisheries were to play in their future." In response to these concerns, Governor Stevens repeatedly assured the Indians that there always would be an adequate supply of fish. Professor White wrote that Stevens told the Indians during negotiations for the Point Elliott Treaty, "I want that you shall not have simply food and drink now but that you may have them forever." During negotiations for the Point–No–Point Treaty, Stevens said, "This paper is such as a man would give to his children and I will tell you why. This paper gives you a home. Does not a father give his children a home? ... This paper secures your fish. Does not a father give food to his children?" *Fishing Vessel*, 443 U.S. at 667 n. 11, 99 S. Ct. 3055 (ellipsis in original).

The Indians did not understand the Treaties to promise that they would have access to their usual and accustomed fishing places, but with a qualification that would allow the government to diminish or destroy the fish runs. Governor Stevens did not make, and the Indians did not understand him to make, such a cynical and disingenuous promise. The Indians reasonably understood Governor Stevens to promise not only that they would have access to their usual and accustomed fishing places, but also that there would be fish sufficient to sustain them. They reasonably understood that they would have, in Stevens' words, "food and drink ... forever." * * *

The facts presented in the district court establish that Washington has acted affirmatively to build and maintain barrier culverts under its roads. The State's barrier culverts within the Case Area block approximately 1,000 linear miles of streams suitable for salmon habitat, comprising almost 5 million square meters. If these culverts were replaced or modified to allow free passage of fish, several hundred thousand additional mature salmon would be produced every year. Many of these mature salmon would be available to the Tribes for harvest.

Salmon now available for harvest are not sufficient to provide a "moderate living" to the Tribes. *Fishing Vessel*, 443 U.S. at 686. The district court found that "[t]he reduced abundance of salmon and the consequent reduction in tribal harvests has damaged tribal economies, has left individual tribal members unable to earn a living by fishing, and has caused cultural and social harm to the Tribes in addition to the economic harm." The court found, further, that "[m]any members of the Tribes would engage in more commercial and subsistence salmon fisheries if more fish were available."

We therefore conclude that in building and maintaining barrier culverts within the Case Area, Washington has violated, and is continuing to violate, its obligation to the Tribes under the Treaties. * * *

The district court issued a permanent injunction in 2013, on the same day it issued its Memorandum and Decision. The court ordered the State, in consultation with the Tribes and the United States, to prepare within six months a current list of all state-owned barrier culverts within the Case Area. * * * Washington declined to participate in the formulation of the injunction on the ground that it had not violated the Treaties and that, therefore, no remedy was appropriate. Washington now objects on several grounds to the injunction that was formulated without its participation. Washington specifically objects (1) that the injunction is too "broad," Brief at 50; (2) that the district court did not "defer to the State's expertise," *id.* at 54; (3) that the court did not properly consider costs and equitable principles, *id.* at 57; (4) and that the injunction "impermissibly and significantly intrudes into state government operations." *Id.* at 63. Finally, Washington objects that its four specific objections support a contention that the court's injunction is inconsistent with "federalism principles." *Id.* at 47, 65. We consider the State's objections in turn. [The court rejected all of the state objections]. * * *

In sum, we disagree with Washington's contention that the Tribes "presented no evidence," and that there was a "complete failure of proof," that state-owned barrier culverts have a substantial adverse effect on salmon. The record contains extensive evidence, much of it from the State itself, that the State's barrier culverts have such an effect. We also disagree with Washington's contention that the court ordered correction of "nearly every state-owned barrier culvert" without "any specific showing" that such correction will "meaningfully improve runs." The State's own evidence shows that hundreds of thousands of adult salmon will be produced by opening up the salmon habitat that is currently blocked by the State's barrier culverts. Finally, we disagree with Washington's contention that the court's injunction indiscriminately orders correction of "nearly every state-owned barrier culvert" in the Case Area. The court's order carefully distinguishes between high- and low-priority culverts based on the amount of upstream habitat culvert correction will open up. The order then allows for a further distinction, to be drawn by WSDOT in consultation with the United States and the Tribes, between those high-priority culverts that must be corrected within seventeen years and those that may be corrected on the more lenient schedule applicable to the low-priority culverts. * * *

6. Modification of the Injunction

It is possible that changing or newly revealed facts or circumstances will affect the fairness or efficacy of an injunction. In the case before us, the district court has ordered that many of WSDOT's high-priority barrier culverts be corrected over the course of seventeen years, and that the remainder be corrected only at the end of the culvert's natural life or when road work undertaken for independent reasons would in any event require replacement of the culvert. It is possible that, during this extended period, changed or newly revealed facts or circumstances will justify a modification of the injunction. The district court should not hesitate to modify its injunction if this proves to be the case. As the

Supreme Court wrote in *System Federation No. 91 v. Wright*, 364 U.S. 642, 647, 81 S. Ct. 368, 5 L.Ed.2d 349 (1961), "a sound judicial discretion may call for the modification of the terms of an injunctive decree if the circumstances, whether of law or fact, obtaining at the time of its issuance have changed, or new ones have since arisen." *See also Rufo v. Inmates of Suffolk Cnty. Jail*, 502 U.S. 367, 380–81, 112 S. Ct. 748, 116 L.Ed.2d 867 (1992). In affirming the judgment entered by the district court in this case, we emphasize that the flexibility inherent in equity jurisdiction allows the court, if changed or newly revealed facts or circumstances warrant, to modify its injunction accordingly.

Conclusion

In sum, we conclude that in building and maintaining barrier culverts Washington has violated, and continues to violate, its obligation to the Tribes under the fishing clause of the Treaties. The United States has not waived the rights of the Tribes under the Treaties, and has not waived its own sovereign immunity by bringing suit on behalf of the Tribes. The district court did not abuse its discretion in enjoining Washington to correct most of its high-priority barrier culverts within seventeen years, and to correct the remainder at the end of their natural life or in the course of a road construction project undertaken for independent reasons.

The Supreme Court affirmed the 9th circuit decision by an equally divided vote. *Washington v. United States*, 138 S Ct. 1832 (2018).

NOTES AND QUESTIONS

1. *How far does the ruling go?* What if it costs hundreds of millions of dollars to fix the culverts at issue in this case? Can the court order the state to appropriate funds? Suppose a developer has plans to fill wetlands for a housing development on private property. Can a tribe prevent the filling of the land if it can show some incremental harm to treaty fisheries? How much harm would it have to show? The decision is on appeal to the Ninth Circuit.

2. *Effect on federal action.* Protection of Indian treaty rights may preclude other federal action that could adversely affect treaty rights by harming the fish or game or the habitat necessary to support it. *See, e.g., Muckleshoot Indian Tribe v. Hall*, 698 F. Supp. 1504 (W.D. Wash. 1988) (court enjoins United States Army Corps of Engineers from permitting construction of marina that would interfere with treaty fishing rights); *Northwest Sea Farms v. Army Corp. of Engineers*, 931 F. Supp. 1515 (W.D. Wash. 1996) (salmon farming permit properly denied by Army Corps of Engineers as infringing upon the Lummi Nation's treaty right of access).

3. *What about damages?* Are the plaintiff Tribes entitled to damages for the past harm caused by the culverts? In *Skokomish Indian Tribe v. United States*, 410 F.3d 506 (9th Cir. 2005) (*en banc*) the court of appeals ruled that the Skokomish Tribe was not entitled to damages against the City of Tacoma for destroying a tribal fishery in the North Fork of the Skokomish River through construction and operation of a dam and hydroelectric facility. For

criticism of the decision *see* Willliam H. Rodgers, Jr., *Judicial Regrets and the Case of Cushman Dam*, 35 Envtl. L. 397 (2005).

4. *The Endangered Species Act.* The Endangered Species Act, 16 U.S.C. §§ 1531–1544, sometimes operates for the protection of tribal treaty rights. In *Klamath Water Users Protective Association v. Patterson*, 204 F.3d 1206 (9th Cir. 2000), Bureau of Reclamation water project irrigators argued that they were being unlawfully harmed by Reclamation's operational directives. The directives were imposed on a power company that by contract operated the dam on the Klamath River system, which controlled lake levels, instream flows and irrigation diversions. The United States defended on technical contract grounds (that the irrigators lacked standing to challenge the contractual arrangements between Reclamation and its contractor) and also on the ground that the federal government was obligated to operate the Project consistent with the requirements of senior tribal water rights and the Endangered Species Act. The court ruled:

> Because Reclamation retains authority to manage the Dam, and because it remains the owner in fee simple of the Dam, it has responsibilities under the ESA as a federal agency. These responsibilities include taking control of the Dam when necessary to meet the requirements of the ESA, requirements that override the water rights of the Irrigators.
>
> Similar to its duties under the ESA, the United States, as a trustee for the Tribes, has a responsibility to protect their rights and resources. *See, e.g., United States v. Adair*, 723 F.2d 1394, 1408–11, 1415 (9th Cir.1983) (holding that the Klamath Basin Tribes hold implied water rights to support hunting and fishing rights guaranteed by treaties between Tribes in Oregon and California and United States). Only Congress can abrogate Indian treaty rights, *see United States v. Dion*, 476 U.S. 734, 738 (1986), and it has not done so here.
>
> We have held that water rights for the Klamath Basin Tribes "carry a priority date of time immemorial." *Adair*, 723 F.2d at 1414. Because Reclamation maintains control of the Dam, it has a responsibility to divert the water and resources needed to fulfill the Tribes' rights, rights that take precedence over any alleged rights of the Irrigators.

204 F.3d at 1213–1214. The same result was reached in *Kandra v. United States*, 145 F.Supp.2d 1192 (N.D. Cal. 2001), where the court upheld agency action that had the effect of limiting deliveries of water to the Klamath Irrigation Project in order to fulfill requirements of the ESA and senior Indian reserved water rights. In *Baley v. United States*, 134 Fed.Cl. 619 (2017) the United States successfully defended a Fifth Amendment takings claim by irrigators who did not receive contract water from a Bureau of Reclamation project. The water was needed to support senior Indian reserved rights for fisheries habitat, so the junior state irrigation rights were not entitled to deliveries. The case is on appeal to the Federal Circuit.

Sometimes, however, ESA enforcement can cause conflict with tribes. The issue arises when tribes attempt to undertake development activities on lands that might be habitat for listed species. It can also arise when tribes seek to exercise senior reserved water rights for out-of-stream uses from waters where fish stocks are listed as threatened or endangered. Secretary of the Interior Bruce Babbitt and Secretary of Commerce William Daley signed an Order in

1997, directing both the National Marine Fisheries Service and the U.S. Fish and Wildlife Service to engage in government-to-government negotiations with affected Indian tribes when exercising authority under the ESA. Secretarial Order No. 3206, *American Indian Tribal Rights, Federal–Tribal Trust Responsibilities and the Endangered Species Act* (June 5, 1997). In addition, an appendix to the Secretarial Order spells out federal obligations to include tribes in the initial listing process and any section 7 consultations that follow. The Secretarial Order is explicit acknowledgement of the trust relationship between the United States and Indian tribes. *See* Charles F. Wilkinson, *The Role of Bilateralism in Fulfilling the Federal–Tribal Relationship: The Tribal Rights–Endangered Species Secretarial Order*, 72 Wash. L. Rev. 1063, 1071–1072 (1997) (Order and appendix reprinted as attachments to article); and Timothy Vollmann, *The Endangered Species Act and Indian Water Rights* at 39–43, Natural Resources and the Environment, Vol. 11, No. 2 (Fall 1996).

Reserved rights include more than fishing rights. Many tribes also have treaty rights to hunt and gather on "ceded lands," "open and unclaimed lands," or "unoccupied lands of the United States." As you read the next cases, consider the differences between the fishing rights at issue in *United States v. Washington* and the hunting and gathering rights. One difference reflected in the cases is the more frequent claim that hunting and gathering rights were temporary, and so were extinguished by statehood or other actions.

MINNESOTA V. MILLE LACS BAND OF CHIPPEWA INDIANS

526 U.S. 172, 119 S. Ct. 1187, 143 L.Ed.2d 270 (1999)

JUSTICE O'CONNOR delivered the opinion of the Court.

In 1837, the United States entered into a Treaty with several Bands of Chippewa Indians. Under the terms of this Treaty, the Indians ceded land in present-day Wisconsin and Minnesota to the United States, and the United States guaranteed to the Indians certain hunting, fishing, and gathering rights on the ceded land. We must decide whether the Chippewa Indians retain these usufructuary rights today. The State of Minnesota argues that the Indians lost these rights through an Executive Order in 1850, an 1855 Treaty, and the admission of Minnesota into the Union in 1858. After an examination of the historical record, we conclude that the Chippewa retain the usufructuary rights guaranteed to them under the 1837 Treaty.

I

A

In 1837, several Chippewa Bands, including the respondent Bands here, were summoned to Fort Snelling (near present-day St. Paul, Minnesota) for the negotiation of a treaty with the United States. The United States representative at the negotiations, Wisconsin Territorial Governor Henry Dodge, told the assembled Indians that the United States wanted to purchase certain Chippewa lands east of the Mississippi River, lands located in present-day Wisconsin and Minnesota. The Chippewa agreed to sell the land to the United States, but they insisted on preserving their right to hunt, fish, and gather in the ceded territory. In response to this request, Governor Dodge stated that he would "make known to your Great Father, your request to be permitted to make sugar, on the lands; and you will be allowed, during his pleasure, to hunt and fish on them." To these ends, the parties signed a treaty on July 29, 1837. In the first two articles of the 1837 Treaty, the Chippewa ceded land to the United States in return for 20 annual payments of money and goods. The United States also, in the fifth article of the Treaty, guaranteed to the Chippewa the right to hunt, fish, and gather on the ceded lands:

> The privilege of hunting, fishing, and gathering the wild rice, upon the lands, the rivers and the lakes included in the territory ceded, is guarantied [sic] to the Indians, during the pleasure of the President of the United States. 1837 Treaty with the Chippewa, 7 Stat. 537.

In 1842, many of the same Chippewa Bands entered into another Treaty with the United States, again ceding additional lands to the Federal Government in return for annuity payments of goods and money, while reserving usufructuary rights on the ceded lands. 1842 Treaty with the Chippewa, 7 Stat. 591. This Treaty, however, also contained a provision providing that the Indians would be "subject to removal therefrom at the pleasure of the President of the United States." Art. 6, *id.* at 592.

In the late 1840's, pressure mounted to remove the Chippewa to their unceded lands in the Minnesota Territory. On September 4, 1849, Minnesota Territorial Governor Alexander Ramsey urged the Territorial Legislature to ask the President to remove the Chippewa from the ceded land. *** President Taylor responded to this pressure by issuing an Executive Order on February 6, 1850. The order provided:

> The privileges granted temporarily to the Chippewa Indians of the Mississippi, by the Fifth Article of the Treaty made with them on the 29th of July 1837, "of hunting, fishing and gathering the wild rice, upon the lands, the rivers and the lakes included in the territory ceded" by that treaty to the United States; and the right granted to the Chippewa Indians of the Mississippi and Lake Superior, by the Second Article of the treaty with them of October 4th 1842, of hunting on the territory which they ceded by that treaty, "with the other usual privileges of occupancy until required to remove by the President of the United States," are hereby revoked; and all of the said Indians remaining on the lands ceded as aforesaid, are required to remove to their unceded lands.

The officials charged with implementing this order understood it primarily as a removal order, and they proceeded to implement it accordingly. [In the face of failure of the removal attempts and resulting protests by both Chippewa and non-Indian residents, the federal government abandoned the removal within a few years.] ***

Although the United States abandoned its removal policy, it did not abandon its attempts to acquire more Chippewa land. To this end, in the spring of 1854, Congress began considering legislation to authorize additional treaties for the purchase of Chippewa lands. The House of Representatives debated a bill "to provide for the extinguishment of the title of the Chippewa Indians to the lands owned and claimed by them in the Territory of Minnesota and State of Wisconsin." Cong. Globe, 33d Cong., 1st Sess., 1032 (1854). This bill did not require the removal of the Indians, but instead provided for the establishment of reservations within the ceded territories on which the Indians could remain.

The treaty authorization bill stalled in the Senate during 1854, but Commissioner of Indian Affairs George Manypenny began to implement it nonetheless. On August 11, he instructed Indian Agent Henry Gilbert to begin treaty negotiations to acquire more land from the Chippewa. Specifically, he instructed Gilbert to acquire "all the country" the Chippewa own or claim in the Minnesota Territory and the State of Wisconsin, except for some land that would be set aside for reservations. App. 264. Gilbert negotiated such a Treaty with several Chippewa Bands, 1854 Treaty with the Chippewa, 10 Stat. 1109, although for reasons now lost to history, the Mille Lacs Band of Chippewa was not a party to this Treaty. The signatory Chippewa Bands ceded additional land to the United States, and certain lands were set aside as reservations for the Bands. *Id.* Art. 2. In addition, the 1854 Treaty established new hunting and fishing rights in the territory ceded by the Treaty. *Id.* Art. 11.

When the Senate finally passed the authorizing legislation in December 1854, Minnesota's territorial delegate to Congress recommended to Commissioner Manypenny that he negotiate a treaty with the Mississippi, Pillager, and Lake Winnibigoshish Bands of Chippewa Indians. App. 286–287 (letter from Rice to Manypenny, Dec. 17, 1854). Commissioner Manypenny summoned representatives of those Bands to Washington, D.C., for the treaty negotiations, which were held in February 1855. *See id.* at 288 (letter from Manypenny to Gorman, Jan. 4, 1855). The purpose and result of these negotiations was the sale of Chippewa lands to the United States. To this end, the first article of the 1855 Treaty contains two sentences:

> The Mississippi, Pillager, and Lake Winnibigoshish bands of Chippewa Indians hereby cede, sell, and convey to the United States all their right, title, and interest in, and to, the lands now owned and claimed by them, in the Territory of Minnesota, and included within the following boundaries, viz: [describing territorial boundaries]. And the said Indians do further fully and entirely relinquish and convey to the United States, any and all right, title, and interest, of whatsoever nature the same may be, which they may now have in, and to any other lands in the Territory of Minnesota or elsewhere.

10 Stat. 1165–1166.

Article 2 set aside lands in the area as reservations for the signatory tribes. *Id.* at 1166–1167. The Treaty, however, makes no mention of hunting and fishing rights, whether to reserve new usufructuary rights or to abolish rights guaranteed by previous treaties. The Treaty Journal also reveals no discussion of hunting and fishing rights. App. 297–356 (Documents Relating to the Negotiation of the Treaty of Feb. 22, 1855) (hereinafter 1855 Treaty Journal).

A little over three years after the 1855 Treaty was signed, Minnesota was admitted to the Union. *See* Act of May 11, 1858, 11 Stat. 285. The admission Act is silent with respect to Indian treaty rights.

B

In 1990, the Mille Lacs Band of Chippewa Indians and several of its members filed suit in the Federal District Court for the District of Minnesota against the State of Minnesota, the Minnesota Department of Natural Resources, and various state officers (collectively State) seeking, among other things, a declaratory judgment that they retained their usufructuary rights under the 1837 Treaty and an injunction to prevent the State's interference with those rights. The United States intervened as a plaintiff in the suit; nine counties and six private landowners intervened as defendants. *** [The district court and court of appeals held that the tribal rights had not been extinguished.]

II

We are first asked to decide whether President Taylor's Executive Order of February 6, 1850, terminated Chippewa hunting, fishing, and gathering rights under the 1837 Treaty. [The Court agreed with the court of appeals that the 1830 Removal Act, which only authorized removal upon consent of the affected tribe, did not provide the President with authority to remove tribes like the Chippewa, which had not consented to removal.]

*** [T]he landowners argue for an alternative source of authority; they argue that the President's removal order was authorized by the 1837 Treaty itself. *** There is no support for this proposition, however. The Treaty makes no mention of removal, and there was no discussion of removal during the Treaty negotiations. Although the United States could have negotiated a treaty in 1837 providing for removal of the Chippewa—and it negotiated several such removal treaties with Indian tribes in 1837—the 1837 Treaty with the Chippewa did not contain any provisions authorizing a removal order. The silence in the Treaty, in fact, is consistent with the United States' objectives in negotiating it. Commissioner of Indian Affairs Harris explained the United States' goals for the 1837 Treaty in a letter to Governor Dodge on May 13, 1837. App. 42. In this letter, Harris explained that through this Treaty, the United States wanted to purchase Chippewa land for the pinewoods located on it; the letter contains no reference to removal of the Chippewa. Because the parties have pointed to no colorable source of authority for the President's removal order, we agree with the Court of Appeals' conclusion that the 1850 removal order was unauthorized. ***

The State argues that even if the removal portion of the order was invalid, the 1837 Treaty privileges were nevertheless revoked because the invalid removal order was severable from the portion of the order revoking Chippewa usufructuary rights. ***

The inquiry into whether a statute [and presumably an executive order] is severable is essentially an inquiry into legislative intent. *** Translated to the present context, we must determine whether the President would not have revoked the 1837 Treaty privileges if he could not issue the removal order.

We think it is clear that President Taylor intended the 1850 order to stand or fall as a whole. The 1850 order embodied a single, coherent policy, the predominant purpose of which was removal of the Chippewa from the lands that they had ceded to the United States. The federal officials charged with implementing the order certainly understood it as such. As soon as the

Commissioner of Indian Affairs received a copy of the order, he sent it to Governor Ramsey and placed him in charge of its implementation. The Commissioner's letter to Ramsey noted in passing that the order revoked the Chippewa's usufructuary privileges, but it did not discuss implementation of that part of the order. Rather, the letter addressed the mechanics of implementing the removal order. ***

When the 1850 order is understood as announcing a removal policy, the portion of the order revoking Chippewa usufructuary rights is seen to perform an integral function in this policy. The order tells the Indians to "go," and also tells them not to return to the ceded lands to hunt and fish. ***

We conclude that President Taylor's 1850 Executive Order was ineffective to terminate Chippewa usufructuary rights under the 1837 Treaty. The State has pointed to no statutory or constitutional authority for the President's removal order, and the Executive Order, embodying as it did one coherent policy, is inseverable. We do not mean to suggest that a President, now or in the future, cannot revoke the Chippewa usufructuary rights in accordance with the terms of the 1837 Treaty. All we conclude today is that the President's 1850 Executive Order was insufficient to accomplish this revocation because it was not severable from the invalid removal order.

III

The State argues that the Mille Lacs Band of Chippewa Indians relinquished its usufructuary rights under the 1855 Treaty with the Chippewa. Specifically, the State argues that the Band unambiguously relinquished its usufructuary rights by agreeing to the second sentence of Article 1 in that Treaty:

> And the said Indians do further fully and entirely relinquish and convey to the United States, any and all right, title, and interest, of whatsoever nature the same may be, which they may now have in, and to any other lands in the Territory of Minnesota or elsewhere.

10 Stat. 1166.

This sentence, however, does not mention the 1837 Treaty, and it does not mention hunting, fishing, and gathering rights. The entire 1855 Treaty, in fact, is devoid of any language expressly mentioning—much less abrogating—usufructuary rights. Similarly, the Treaty contains no language providing money for the abrogation of previously held rights. These omissions are telling because the United States treaty drafters had the sophistication and experience to use express language for the abrogation of treaty rights. In fact, just a few months after Commissioner Manypenny completed the 1855 Treaty, he negotiated a Treaty with the Chippewa of Sault Ste. Marie that expressly revoked fishing rights that had been reserved in an earlier Treaty. *See* Treaty with the Chippewa of Sault Ste. Marie, Art. 1, 11 Stat. 631 ("The said Chippewa Indians surrender to the United States the right of fishing at the falls of St. Mary's *** secured to them by the treaty of June 16, 1820").

The State argues that despite any explicit reference to the 1837 Treaty rights, or to usufructuary rights more generally, the second sentence of Article 1 nevertheless abrogates those rights. But to determine whether this language abrogates Chippewa Treaty rights, we look beyond the written words to the larger context that frames the Treaty, including "the history of the treaty, the negotiations, and the practical construction adopted by the parties." *Choctaw*

Nation v. United States, 318 U.S. 423, 432. In this case, an examination of the historical record provides insight into how the parties to the Treaty understood the terms of the agreement. This insight is especially helpful to the extent that it sheds light on how the Chippewa signatories to the Treaty understood the agreement because we interpret Indian treaties to give effect to the terms as the Indians themselves would have understood them.

The 1855 Treaty was designed primarily to transfer Chippewa land to the United States, not to terminate Chippewa usufructuary rights. It was negotiated under the authority of the Act of December 19, 1854. This Act authorized treaty negotiations with the Chippewa "for the extinguishment of their title to all the lands owned and claimed by them in the Territory of Minnesota and State of Wisconsin." The Act is silent with respect to authorizing agreements to terminate Indian usufructuary privileges, and this silence was likely not accidental. During Senate debate on the Act, Senator Sebastian, the chairman of the Committee on Indian Affairs, stated that the treaties to be negotiated under the Act would "reserv[e] to them [*i.e.*, the Chippewa] those rights which are secured by former treaties." Cong. Globe, 33d Cong., 1st Sess., 1404 (1854). ***

Indeed all of the participants in the negotiations, including the Indians, understood that the purpose of the negotiations was to transfer Indian land to the United States. The Chief of the Pillager Band of Chippewa stated: "It appears to me that I understand what you want, and your views from the few words I have heard you speak. You want land." *Id.*, at 309 (1855 Treaty Journal) (statement of Flat Mouth). Commissioner Manypenny confirmed that the chief correctly understood the purpose of the negotiations:

> He appears to understand the object of the interview. His people had more land than they wanted or could use, and stood in need of money; and I have more money than I need, but want more land.

Ibid. See also id. at 304 (statement of Hole-in-the-Day, the principal negotiator for the Chippewa: "Your words strike us in this way. They are very short. 'I want to buy your land.' These words are very expressive—very curt").

***

One final part of the historical record also suggests that the 1855 Treaty was a land purchase treaty and not a treaty that also terminated usufructuary rights: the 1854 Treaty with the Chippewa. Most of the Chippewa Bands that resided within the territory ceded by the 1837 Treaty were signatories to the 1854 Treaty; only the Mille Lacs Band was a party to the 1855 Treaty. If the United States had intended to abrogate Chippewa usufructuary rights under the 1837 Treaty, it almost certainly would have included a provision to that effect in the 1854 Treaty, yet that Treaty contains no such provision. To the contrary, it expressly secures new usufructuary rights to the signatory Bands on the newly ceded territory. The State proposes no explanation—compelling or otherwise—for why the United States would have wanted to abrogate the Mille Lacs Band's hunting and fishing rights, while leaving intact the other Bands' rights to hunt and fish on the same territory.

To summarize, the historical record provides no support for the theory that the second sentence of Article 1 was designed to abrogate the usufructuary privileges guaranteed under the 1837 Treaty, but it does support the theory that the Treaty, and Article 1 in particular, was designed to transfer Chippewa land to the United States. At the very least, the historical record refutes the State's assertion that the 1855 Treaty "unambiguously" abrogated the 1837 hunting, fishing, and gathering privileges. Given this plausible ambiguity, we cannot agree with the State that the 1855 Treaty abrogated Chippewa usufructuary rights. ***

IV

Finally, the State argues that the Chippewa's usufructuary rights under the 1837 Treaty were extinguished when Minnesota was admitted to the Union in 1858. In making this argument, the State faces an uphill battle. Congress may abrogate Indian treaty rights, but it must clearly express its intent to do so. *United States v. Dion*, 476 U.S. 734, 738–740 (1986). There must be "clear evidence that Congress actually considered the conflict between its intended action on the one hand and Indian treaty rights on the other, and chose to resolve that conflict by abrogating the treaty." *United States v. Dion, supra*, at 740. There is no such "clear evidence" of congressional intent to abrogate the Chippewa Treaty rights here. The relevant statute—Minnesota's enabling Act—provides in relevant part:

> [T]he State of Minnesota shall be one, and is hereby declared to be one, of the United States of America, and admitted into the Union on an equal footing with the original States in all respects whatever.

Act of May 11, 1858, 11 Stat. 285.

This language, like the rest of the Act, makes no mention of Indian treaty rights; it provides no clue that Congress considered the reserved rights of the Chippewa and decided to abrogate those rights when it passed the Act. The State concedes that the Act is silent in this regard, Brief for Petitioners 36, and the State does not point to any legislative history describing the effect of the Act on Indian treaty rights.

With no direct support for its argument, the State relies principally on this Court's decision in *Ward v. Race Horse*, 163 U.S. 504 (1896). In *Race Horse*, we held that a Treaty reserving to a Tribe " 'the right to hunt on the unoccupied lands of the United States, so long as game may be found thereon, and so long as peace subsists among the whites and Indians on the borders of the hunting districts' " terminated when Wyoming became a State in 1890. *Id.* at 507, 16 S. Ct. 1076 (quoting Art. 4 of the Treaty). This case does not bear the weight the State places on it, however, because it has been qualified by later decisions of this Court.

The first part of the holding in *Race Horse* was based on the "equal footing doctrine," the constitutional principle that all States are admitted to the Union with the same attributes of sovereignty (*i.e.*, on equal footing) as the original 13 States. As relevant here, it prevents the Federal Government from impairing fundamental attributes of state sovereignty when it admits new States into the Union. According to the *Race Horse* Court, because the Treaty rights conflicted irreconcilably with state regulation of natural resources—"an essential attribute of its governmental existence," *Race Horse, supra*, at 516, 16 S. Ct. 1076—the Treaty rights were held an invalid impairment of Wyoming's sovereignty. Thus, those rights could not survive Wyoming's admission to the Union on "equal footing" with the original States.

But *Race Horse* rested on a false premise. As this Court's subsequent cases have made clear, an Indian tribe's treaty rights to hunt, fish, and gather on state land are not irreconcilable with a State's sovereignty over the natural resources in the State. *See, e.g., Washington v. Washington State Commercial Passenger Fishing Vessel Assn.*, 443 U.S. 658. Rather, Indian treaty rights can coexist with state management of natural resources. Although States have important interests in regulating wildlife and natural resources within their borders, this authority is shared with the Federal Government when the Federal Government exercises one of its enumerated constitutional powers, such as treaty making. U.S. Const., Art. VI, cl. 2. *** Thus, because treaty rights are reconcilable with state sovereignty over natural resources, statehood by itself is insufficient to extinguish Indian treaty rights to hunt, fish, and gather on land within state boundaries.

*** The 1837 Treaty itself defines the circumstances under which the rights would terminate: when the exercise of those rights was no longer the "pleasure of the President." There is no suggestion in the Treaty that the President would have to conclude that the privileges should end when a State was established in the area. Moreover, unlike the rights at issue in *Race Horse*, there is no fixed termination point to the 1837 Treaty rights. The Treaty in *Race Horse* contemplated that the rights would continue only so long as the hunting grounds remained unoccupied and owned by the United States; the happening of these conditions was "clearly contemplated" when the Treaty was ratified. *Id.* at 509. By contrast, the 1837 Treaty does not tie the duration of the rights to the occurrence of some clearly contemplated event. Finally, we note that there is nothing inherent in the nature of reserved treaty rights to suggest that they can be extinguished by implication at statehood. Treaty rights are not impliedly terminated upon statehood. The *Race Horse* Court's decision to the contrary—that Indian treaty rights were impliedly repealed by Wyoming's statehood Act—was informed by that Court's conclusion that the Indian treaty rights were inconsistent with state sovereignty over natural resources and thus that Congress (the Senate) could not have intended the rights to survive statehood. But as we described above, Indian treaty-based usufructuary rights are not inconsistent with state sovereignty over natural resources. Thus, contrary to the State's contentions, *Race Horse* does not compel the conclusion that Minnesota's admission to the Union extinguished Chippewa usufructuary rights guaranteed by the 1837 Treaty.

Accordingly, the judgment of the United States Court of Appeals for the Eighth Circuit is affirmed.

It is so ordered.

CHIEF JUSTICE REHNQUIST, with whom **JUSTICE SCALIA**, **JUSTICE KENNEDY** and **JUSTICE THOMAS** join, dissenting.

The Court holds that the various Bands of Chippewa Indians retain a usufructuary right granted to them in an 1837 Treaty. To reach this result, the Court must successively conclude that: (1) an 1850 Executive Order explicitly revoking the privilege as authorized by the 1837 Treaty was unlawful; (2) an 1855 Treaty under which certain Chippewa Bands ceded "all" interests to the land does not include the treaty right to come onto the land and hunt; and (3) the admission of Minnesota into the Union in 1858 did not terminate the discretionary hunting privilege, despite established precedent of this Court to the contrary. Because I believe that each one of these three conclusions is demonstrably wrong, I dissent.

***

II

In 1850, President Taylor expressly terminated the 1837 Treaty privilege by Executive Order. *** The Court's first proposition is the seemingly innocuous statement that a President's Executive Order must be authorized by law in order to have any legal effect. *** [T]he Executive Order in this case was issued pursuant to a Treaty ratified by the advice and consent of the Senate, and thus became the supreme law of the land. *See* U.S. Const., Art. VI. ***. The Court's contrary conclusion is simply wrong.

The Court's second assumption is that the Executive Order was a "removal order"—that its primary purpose was the removal of the Chippewa. This assumption rests upon scattered historical evidence that, in the Court's view, "[t]he officials charged with implementing this order understood it primarily as a removal order, and they proceeded to implement it accordingly." *** Regardless of what the President's remote frontier agents may have thought, the plain meaning of the text of President Taylor's order can only support the opposite conclusion. The structure of the Executive Order is not that of a removal order, with the revocation of the hunting privileges added merely as an afterthought. Instead, the first part of the order (not to mention the bulk of its text) deals with the extinguishment of the Indians' privilege to enter onto the lands ceded to the United States and hunt. Only then (and then only in its final five words) does the Executive Order require the Indians to "remove to their unceded lands." App. to Pet. for Cert. 565 (Exec. Order, Feb. 6, 1850).

***

The Court's third finding is that the removal portion of the order is invalid because President Taylor had no authority to order removal. *** After the Treaty was executed and ratified, the ceded lands belonged to the United States, and the only real property interest in the land remaining to the Indians was the privilege to come onto it and hunt during the pleasure of the President. When the President terminated that privilege (a legal act that the Court appears to concede he had a right to make, *ante*, at 1199), he terminated the Indians' right to come onto the ceded lands and hunt. The Indians had no legal right to remain on the ceded lands for that purpose, and the removal portion of the order should be viewed in this context. Indeed, the Indians then had no legal rights at all with respect to the ceded lands, in which all title was vested in the United States. And this Court has long held that the President has the implied power to administer the public lands.

***

But even if I were to assume that the President were without authority to order removal, I would conclude that the removal provision is severable from that terminating the treaty privileges. *** Given the deference we are to accord this valid action made pursuant to a treaty, the order's termination of the treaty privileges should be sustained unless the Chippewa are able to clearly demonstrate that President Taylor would not have terminated them without a removal order. But there is no such evidence ***. Accordingly, I would conclude, if necessary, that the termination portion of the Executive Order is severable.

III

[The dissenters also argued that the plain language of the 1855 Treaty, by providing that the Chippewa Bands "fully and entirely relinquish and convey to the United States, any and all right, title, and interest, of whatsoever nature the same may be, which they now have in, and to any other lands in the Territory of Minnesota or elsewhere," under any "reasonable interpretation" terminated the tribes' off-reservation rights.]

IV

Finally, I note my disagreement with the Court's treatment of the equal footing doctrine, and its apparent overruling *sub silentio* of a precedent of 103 years' vintage. In *Ward v. Race Horse*, 163 U.S. 504, 16 S. Ct. 1076, 41 L.Ed. 244 (1896), we held that a Treaty granting the Indians "the right to hunt on the unoccupied lands of the United States, so long as game may be found thereon, and so long as peace subsists among the whites and the Indians on the borders of the hunting districts," did not survive the admission of Wyoming to the Union since the treaty right was "temporary and precarious." *Id.*, at 515, 16 S. Ct. 1076.

But the Court, in a feat of jurisprudential legerdemain, effectively overrules *Race Horse sub silentio.* *** *Race Horse* held merely that treaty rights which were only "temporary and precarious," as opposed to those which were "of such a nature as to imply their perpetuity," do not survive statehood. *** Here, the hunting privileges were clearly, like those invalidated in *Race Horse*, temporary and precarious: The privilege was only guaranteed "during the pleasure of the President"; the legally enforceable annuity payments themselves were to terminate after 20 years; and the Indians were on actual notice that the President might end the rights in the future, App. 78 (1837 Journal of Treaty Negotiations). ***

V

The Court today invalidates for no principled reason a 149–year–old Executive Order, ignores the plain meaning of a 144–year–old treaty provision, and overrules *sub silentio* a 103–year–old precedent of this Court. I dissent.

[**JUSTICE THOMAS** joined in the Chief Justice's dissent, but wrote separately to argue that even if the 1837 Treaty rights were preserved, this would not prevent the state from regulating Chippewa hunting and fishing rights on the same terms on which it regulated others fishing in the state.] ***

Ceded Territory in Northern Minnesota; Now Designated as Wilderness but Subject to Treaty Hunting, Fishing and Gathering Rights. Photo by Robert Anderson.

NOTES AND QUESTIONS

1. *Revocation of rights.* Under what conditions could the President revoke the hunting, fishing and gathering rights of the tribes? In roughly parallel litigation in Wisconsin, the Seventh Circuit addressed the issue:

> The second dispute between the parties concerns the meaning of the limiting language. "During the pleasure of the President" and "until required to remove by the President" would appear to confer unbridled discretion on the Government to extinguish the usufructuary rights. As the district court recognized, however, Indian treaties must ordinarily be construed as they were understood by the Indians.
>
> The judge below found that the Chippewas understood the treaties to mean that they enjoyed the use of their lands for an unlimited time *unless they misbehaved by harassing white settlers.* In reaching this conclusion, the district judge relied on the Indians' statements during the negotiations preceding the Treaty of 1837 indicating that they wished to continue hunting and fishing on the ceded lands and that they envisioned their grandchildren negotiating for further annuities in sixty-years time. He also noted that both Indians and non-Indians present at the 1842 treaty negotiations later wrote that the Indians had been assured they would not have to remove unless they misbehaved.

Lac Courte Oreilles Band of Lake Superior Chippewa Indians v. Voigt, 700 F.2d 341, 356 (7th Cir. 1983); *see* Charles F. Wilkinson, *To Feel the Summer in Spring: The Treaty Fishing Rights of the Wisconsin Chippewa*, 1991 Wis. L. Rev. 375 for a review of the long-running Wisconsin litigation.

2. *Effect of statehood.* In *Antoine v. Washington*, 420 U.S. 194 (1975), the Supreme Court rejected Washington's argument that its admission to the United States in 1889 precluded Congress from preserving tribal hunting and fishing rights on land ceded in 1891 from the Confederated Tribes of the Colville Reservation to the United States. The Washington Supreme Court had drawn a distinction between tribal rights confirmed by treaty, and the congressionally ratified agreement with the tribes of the Colville Reservation on the ground that the latter were only binding on the United States. The Court answered: "The fallacy in that proposition is that a legislated ratification of an agreement between the Executive Branch and an Indian tribe is a [Law] of the United States *** made in Pursuance of the Constitution and, therefore, like 'all Treaties made,' is made binding upon affected States by the Supremacy Clause." *Id.* at 201.

3. *The Demise of Ward v. Race Horse?* The Supreme Court recently reversed the Wyoming Supreme Court's ruling that statehood abrogated Crow Treaty rights to hunt on "unoccupied lands of the United States."

> In sum, *Mille Lacs* upended both lines of reasoning in *Race Horse*. The case established that the crucial inquiry for treaty termination analysis is whether Congress has expressly abrogated an Indian treaty right or whether a termination point identified in the treaty itself has been satisfied. Statehood is irrelevant to this analysis unless a statehood Act otherwise demonstrates Congress' clear intent to abrogate a treaty, or statehood appears as a termination point in the treaty. See 526 U.S. at 207, 119 S. Ct. 1187. "[T]here is nothing inherent in the nature of reserved treaty rights to suggest that they can be extinguished by *implication* at statehood." *Ibid.*
>
> ***
>
> Just as in *Mille Lacs*, there is no suggestion in the text of the 1868 Treaty with the Crow Tribe that the parties intended the hunting right to expire at statehood. The treaty identifies four situations that would terminate the right: (1) the lands are no longer "unoccupied"; (2) the lands no longer belong to the United States; (3) game can no longer "be found thereon"; and (4) the Tribe and non-Indians are no longer at "peace ... on the borders of the hunting districts." Art. IV, 15 Stat. 650. Wyoming's statehood does not appear in this list. Nor is there any hint in the treaty that any of these conditions would necessarily be satisfied at statehood. See *Mille Lacs*, 526 U.S. at 207, 119 S. Ct. 1187.

Herrera v. Wyoming, 139 S. Ct. 1686, 1696–97 (2019)

STATE V. BUCHANAN

978 P.2d 1070 (Wash. 1999)

*** [Defendants were prosecuted for shooting an elk out of season.] Defendant Buchanan's defense to the criminal charges brought against him is that he is not subject to State hunting laws because he has a treaty right to hunt on any open and unclaimed lands in "Washington Territory," and that this treaty right is superior to the right of the State to regulate hunting.

The State makes essentially three arguments. First, it argues that any treaty hunting right that exists in the Nooksack Tribe should be interpreted to permit hunting only on open and unclaimed land within the area ceded to the United States by the tribe, or upon land which the tribe has traditionally hunted. Second, the State argues that even if the treaty affords a right to hunt outside the ceded area, the Oak Creek Wildlife Area is not "open and unclaimed" land. Finally, it urges this court to hold that no treaty right to hunt or fish in violation of State regulations survived Washington's admission to the Union on "equal footing" with the original states.

Our initial inquiry is to determine the geographic scope of the Nooksack Tribe's treaty hunting right.

In 1854 and 1855 Isaac Stevens, who was the first Governor and Superintendent of Indian Affairs for Washington Territory, negotiated several treaties between the United States and the various tribes and bands of Indians who lived in the Territory.[5]

At the time the treaties were negotiated, approximately three-fourths of Western Washington's 10,000 or so inhabitants were Indians. The natural resources appeared to the parties to be inexhaustible.

In the treaties, the Indians relinquished their interest in most of the Territory in exchange for monetary payments. Additionally, certain relatively small parcels of land were reserved for the exclusive use of particular tribes or bands, and the Indians were afforded other guarantees, such as certain rights of fishing and hunting. *Fishing Vessel,* 443 U.S. at 662, 99 S. Ct. 3055.

The Treaty of Point Elliott was made in January 1855 and ratified March 8, 1859. As noted above, the Nooksack Indian Tribe was judicially determined to be a party to the treaty in *United States v. Washington,* 459 F. Supp. 1020. The first article of the treaty includes a description of lands ceded to the United States by the Indians. The treaty provides, in article 1, that the "said tribes and bands of Indians hereby cede, relinquish, and convey to the United States all their right, title, and interest in and to the lands and country occupied by them, bounded and described as follows: Commencing at [the inlets and bays of western Washington Territory] to the summit of the Cascade range of mountains." Treaty of Point Elliott at 927.

Article 5 of the treaty provides:

> The right of taking fish at usual and accustomed grounds and stations is further secured to said Indians in common with all citizens of the Territory, and of erecting temporary houses for the purpose of curing, together with the privilege of hunting and gathering roots and berries on open and unclaimed lands. Provided, however, that they shall not take shell-fish from any beds staked or cultivated by citizens.

---

5. In addition to what is now Washington State, Washington Territory included parts of Idaho and Montana. *See* Charles F. Wilkinson, *Indian Tribal Rights and the National Forests: The Case of the Aboriginal Lands of the Nez Perce Tribe,* 34 Idaho L. Rev. 435, 436–37 (1998).

Treaty of Point Elliott at 928.

***

Like any treaty between the United States and another sovereign nation, a treaty with Indians is the supreme law of the land and is binding on the State until Congress limits or abrogates the treaty. ***

The State argues that the hunting right reserved by the treaty was limited to the right previously exercised—that is to the ceded lands or to lands upon which the Nooksack Tribe traditionally hunted. We agree.

The scope of a tribe's off-reservation hunting rights is generally found in an Indian tribe's aboriginal use of or title to land and its reservation of the right in a treaty, or by agreement, executive order or statute. *See generally* Felix S. Cohen's Handbook of Federal Indian Law 41–46 (Rennard Strickland & Charles F. Wilkinson eds., 1982). Mr. Nye explains the origin of the right as follows:

> Though hunting rights can arise from various sources, most existing off-reservation hunting rights in the Pacific Northwest were reserved by tribes in treaties signed with the federal government between 1853 and 1871. Treaties were the primary means by which the federal government sought to provide for the orderly westward expansion of non-native society. In the typical treaty, the signatory Indians relinquished their rights to aboriginal lands in exchange for money and confinement to a reservation with distinct boundaries.
>
> The reservation system, in addition to minimizing confrontations between encroaching settlers and the resident Indians, was also intended to transform Indians into "a pastoral and civilized people." As a result, game populations were not one of the primary factors considered in the federal government's choice of reservation lands, and many tribes were removed to reservations located far from their traditional hunting grounds. In response to a strong desire on the part of tribes to retain access to these areas, treaties with Northwest Indians provided for *** "the privilege of hunting *** on open and unclaimed lands[.]" In essence, these treaty provisions preserved a portion of the aboriginal rights exercised by the signatory tribes. ***

Bradley I. Nye, *Where Do the Buffalo Roam? Determining the Scope of American Indian Off–Reservation Hunting Rights in the Pacific Northwest*, 67 Wash. L. Rev. 175, 177–78 (1992).

To determine the existence of original Indian title to land, and the right to hunt and fish following from that title, courts have generally required a showing of actual use and occupancy over an extended period of time. In *Mitchel v. United States* [34 U.S. (9 Pet.) 711 (1835)] the United States Supreme Court said:

> Indian possession or occupation was considered with reference to their habits and modes of life; their hunting grounds were as much in their actual possession as the cleared fields of the whites; and their rights to its exclusive enjoyment in their own way and for their own purposes were as much respected, until they abandoned them, made a cession to the government, or an authorized sale to individuals.

In claims against the United States based upon original title, a requirement of exclusive use and occupancy has been satisfied by a showing that two or more tribes jointly or amicably hunted in the same area to the exclusion of others ***.

> The existence of aboriginal hunting and fishing rights, however, does not necessarily turn upon the existence of original title to lands and is not dependent upon recognition in a treaty or act of Congress. Aboriginal rights remain in the Indians unless granted to the United States by treaty, abandoned, or extinguished by statute. When a treaty has been signed, aboriginal use may still be important to determine the extent of the rights reserved under the treaty.

Cohen, *supra,* at 442–43 (footnotes omitted).

There is no evidence in the record on appeal to support a finding that the Nooksack Tribe actually occupied or used, over an extended period of time, the Oak Creek Wildlife Area for hunting. The only area which the record shows the Tribe clearly used for hunting lies within the lands ceded to the United States in the treaty.

Defendant Buchanan argues that the Tribe's right to hunt does not depend on proof of aboriginal title or preexisting hunting practices and grounds. Instead, he claims the hunting right is based not on aboriginal title but on the treaty. In support of this argument, Buchanan points to fishing rights cases which interpret the phrase "usual and accustomed grounds and stations." These cases, he argues demonstrate that the treaty right to hunt or fish does not depend on aboriginal title or use. Buchanan additionally argues that the treaty fishing right is a limited one that permits fishing only at the usual and accustomed places, but that the hunting right is limited only to "open and unclaimed lands."

The treaty fishing right which was reserved by the Indians in the Stevens Treaties has been interpreted to provide a broad right to treaty tribes to fish outside of their ceded lands in all usual and accustomed fishing areas, without regard to whether these areas were part of the usual habitat of the tribe and without regard to whether there had been consistent and exclusive use of the areas. The treaty fishing right has been interpreted as insuring tribes a right to a fixed percentage of the number of harvestable fish, *United States v. Washington,* 384 F. Supp. at 343, and, further, interpreting the right as a permanent one, unless abrogated by Congress. *United States v. Washington,* 384 F. Supp. at 331–32.

In contrast, the treaty hunting right, by its terms, is of a temporary and self-limiting nature. The right was intended to diminish as lands became settled, without the need of congressional action. *See, e.g., Hicks,* 587 F. Supp. at 1165. The treaty hunting clause contained in the Stevens Treaties has not received the extent of analysis to which the fishing clause has been subjected and, although *State v. Chambers,* 506 P.2d 311, noted that the defendant, a Yakama tribal member, killed a deer on privately-owned property at least 40 miles from the nearest territory ceded to the United States by the Yakamas in their treaty, the issue now before us has not previously been squarely addressed by this court. *See also Hicks,* 587 F. Supp. at 1164.

The Supreme Courts of Idaho and Montana, interpreting Stevens Treaties, have held the treaty right is a reserved right "to hunt upon open and unclaimed land *** at any time of the year in any of the lands ceded to the federal government though such lands are outside the boundary of their reservation." *Arthur,* 261 P.2d 135; *see also State v. Coffee,* 556 P.2d 1185 (1976); *State v. Stasso,* 563 P.2d 562 (1977) (relying on the Idaho cases). ***

The geographic scope of the hunting right cannot be resolved from the language of the treaty alone. We hold that application of the reservation of rights doctrine is the more legally sound approach to interpreting the hunting rights provision of the Treaty of Point Elliott. Under such an analysis, open and unclaimed lands within the aboriginal hunting grounds of the Nooksack Tribe are reserved under the treaty for hunting by tribal members, so long as the lands remain open and unclaimed. The geographic area available for hunting would certainly include the territory ceded to the United States and described in article I of the Treaty of Point Elliott, and may include other areas if those areas are proven to have been actually used for hunting and occupied by the Nooksack Tribe over an extended period of time. Because the trial court did not so limit the geographic scope of the Nooksack's treaty, we reverse the dismissal of the charges against defendant Buchanan. However, we hold that, on remand, the defendant should have the opportunity to prove that the Nooksack Tribe's aboriginal hunting grounds include the land within the Oak Creek Wildlife Area.

We next consider whether the Oak Creek Wildlife Area is "open and unclaimed land" under the meaning of the Treaty of Point Elliott.

Under article 5 of the treaty, the Nooksack Tribe has a right to hunt on open and unclaimed lands. The United States Supreme Court has held that the treaty right to hunt, like the treaty right to fish, may only be regulated by the state "in the interest of conservation, provided the regulation meets appropriate standards and does not discriminate against the Indians." *Antoine,* 420 U.S. at 207. The "appropriate standards" requirement obligates the state to prove that its regulation is a "reasonable and necessary conservation measure, *and* that its application to the Indians is necessary in the interest of conservation." *Antoine,* 420 U.S at 207. ***

We limit our inquiry to whether the Oak Creek Wildlife Area is open and unclaimed land within the meaning of the Treaty of Point Elliott.

This court has previously interpreted the meaning of "open and unclaimed lands" as that term is used in Stevens Treaties in two decisions. Under both decisions, publicly-owned lands are considered "open and unclaimed." In *Miller,* 689 P.2d 81, the court held that national forest land is "open and unclaimed" land within the meaning of the treaty. In *Chambers,* 506 P.2d 311, this court approved a jury instruction defining "open and unclaimed lands" as "lands which are not in private ownership." These decisions are consistent with those of other jurisdictions interpreting Stevens Treaties. *See Stasso,* 563 P.2d 562 (national forest service lands that have not been patented to a private person are open and unclaimed lands within the meaning of a Stevens Treaty); *Arthur,* 261 P.2d 135 (the term "open and unclaimed" land as used in a Stevens Treaty was intended to include and embrace such lands as were not settled and occupied by the whites under possessory rights or patent or otherwise appropriated to private ownership and may include national forest reserve lands); *Coffee,* 556 P.2d 1185 (privately-owned land is not open and unclaimed within the meaning of a Stevens Treaty); *Confederated Tribes of Umatilla Indian Reservation v. Maison,* 262 F. Supp. 871 (D.Ore.1966) (national forests lands considered open and unclaimed under the terms of a Stevens Treaty), *aff'd sub nom. Holcomb v. Confederated Tribes of Umatilla Indian Reservation,* 382 F.2d 1013 (9th Cir.1967). *See also Hicks,* 587 F. Supp. at 1165 (trial court opined that the construction of "open and unclaimed lands" that best accommodates Indian hunting as settlement occurs and matures is that "open and unclaimed lands" include public lands put to uses consistent with an Indian hunting privilege).

The State, relying on *Hicks,* argues that once the hunting regulations with respect to elk went into effect, the use of the Oak Creek Wildlife Area for hunting was not a compatible use and, therefore, the lands were not open and unclaimed. Our acceptance of this argument would permit the State to avoid its burden of proving that regulations imposed on Indian treaty hunters are necessary for conservation purposes. *See Miller,* 689 P.2d 81. The State has designated the Oak Creek Wildlife Area for use for hunting, fishing and recreation. Limits on these activities in the Oak Creek Wildlife Area are by State regulation. The regulations must comply with standards developed by this court and the United States Supreme Court, and be necessary for conservation if the regulations are restrictive of treaty rights. The trial court's unchallenged finding in this case is that the State has not met its burden in this regard.[8]

The State also relies on *State v. Cutler,* 708 P.2d 853 (1985), to support its argument that lands which are located in a State-owned wildlife area which is operated as a wintering range for elk and deer are not "open and unclaimed." The treaty interpreted in *Cutler* was not a Stevens Treaty and the pertinent language of the treaty provided the Indians had the right to hunt on "unoccupied lands of the United States." The *Cutler* court held that the state wildlife area, which was converted from a privately-owned ranch, was "occupied" by the State of Idaho and that sufficient indicia of occupancy existed (fences, signs, cattle guards, cultivated fields, machinery, roads, campgrounds and buildings) to put the Indian hunters on notice that the land was not "unoccupied lands of the United States." *Cutler,* 708 P.2d 853. The State offered no evidence in this case that would bring it within the rationale of *Cutler.*

From the rulings in the various cases which discuss the issue, and in light of the treaty language, we discern that a general statement of the rule is that publicly-owned lands, which are not obviously occupied and which are put to a use which is compatible with hunting, are "open and unclaimed lands" under the terms of the Stevens Treaties. Treaty hunters have a right to hunt on such lands, unrestricted by State regulation, unless the regulations are necessary for conservation purposes. *Miller,* 689 P.2d 81. In this case, the Oak Creek Wildlife Area is publicly owned, is obviously unoccupied, and its purposes are compatible with and, in fact, include hunting. The trial court and Court of

---

8. Amicus Department of Fish and Wildlife additionally argues that the status of the land changes as regulations of the State change to close, control, restrict or otherwise put land to uses inconsistent with hunting. In essence, the Department argues that the land is open and unclaimed for elk hunting during the State's elk hunting season, but changes its status when State regulation closes the season in that particular area. This argument ignores established law governing when a State, by hunting regulations, can restrict treaty rights. *See Antoine v. Washington,* 420 U.S. 194, 206 (1975); *State v. McCormack,* 812 P.2d 483 (1991).

Appeals correctly determined that the Oak Creek Wildlife Area is open and unclaimed land. [The court also rejected the State's claim that the equal footing doctrine abrogated the treaty right.]

NOTES AND QUESTIONS

1. *Public versus private ownership.* Suppose that the Forest Service trades substantial amounts of land to a timber company in exchange for scattered parcels held by the company within a National Forest slated to be classified as a National Monument under the Antiquities Act. Is the land acquired by the timber company "open and unclaimed" land within the meaning of the treaty? Can the timber company open the land for hunting only in accordance with state law and thereby preclude the exercise of treaty rights?

2. *Treaty rights in National Parks.* The Blackfeet Indian Tribe ceded certain lands to the United States in 1896 pursuant to an agreement which provided "[t]hat said Indians hereby reserve and retain the right to hunt upon said lands and to fish in the streams thereof." 29 Stat. 321, 354 (1996). The land was subsequently included in Glacier National Park with a disclaimer: "All persons who shall locate or settle upon or occupy the same, or any part thereof, except as hereinafter provided, shall be considered trespassers and removed therefrom. Nothing herein contained shall affect any valid claim, location, or entry existing under the land laws of the United States before May 11, 1910, or the rights of any such claimant, locator, or entryman to the full use and enjoyment of his land." 16 U.S.C. § 161. Do Blackfeet Tribe members need to follow Park regulations? *See United States v. Kipp*, 369 F. Supp. 774 (D.C. Mont. 1974) (no, as to admission fee); *United States v. Momberg*, 378 F. Supp. 1152 (D.C. Mont. 1974) ("I find that the defendant, a Blackfeet Indian, cut a piece of dead wood from a live tree in Glacier National Park in violation of 36 C.F.R. § 2.20(a.1). He did this for the purpose of testing the Indian rights in that part of Glacier Park lying east of the Rocky Mountains. The wood so cut was obviously not cut for any of the purposes mentioned in the agreement of September 26, 1895, ratified June 10, 1896 (29 Stat. 353) and hence the defendant has no defense based upon that agreement.") How would you advise a Blackfeet Tribe member who wanted to fish in the Park without complying with Park Service regulations? *See United States v. Peterson*, 121 F.Supp.2d 1309 (D. Mont. 2000) (Blackfeet hunting rights within Park abrogated). Many other national park designations coincided with ouster of Indian tribes, and the Park Service has worked hard, if imperfectly, in the modern era to make up for these historic exclusions by accommodating indigenous rights and interests. For more on the history of the relationship between tribes and the Park Service, see Robert H. Keller & Michael F. Turek, American Indians and National Parks. (1999).

3. In *Herrera v. Wyoming*, 139 S. Ct. 1686, 1700-1701 (2019), the court also considered whether the creation of a national forest meant the forest land was no longer "unoccupied" within the meaning of the Crow Treaty. "We turn next to the question whether the 1868 Treaty right, even if still valid after Wyoming's statehood, does not protect hunting in Bighorn National Forest because the forest lands are 'occupied.' We agree with Herrera and the United States that Bighorn National Forest did not become categorically "occupied"

within the meaning of the 1868 Treaty when the national forest was created. *** Treaty analysis begins with the text, and treaty terms are construed as " 'they would naturally be understood by the Indians.' " *Fishing Vessel Assn.*, 443 U.S. at 676, 99 S. Ct. 3055. Here it is clear that the Crow Tribe would have understood the word 'unoccupied' to denote an area free of residence or settlement by non-Indians."

CHAPTER 10

WATER RIGHTS

■ ■ ■

The importance of water to life is obvious, and almost equally apparent is the fact that water is scarce in the western states where most Indian tribes are found. All of the western states in the continental United States follow some form of the prior appropriation doctrine. Under the traditional prior appropriation doctrine, one acquires a right to water by diverting it from its natural source and applying it to some beneficial use out of stream. Traditional beneficial uses included irrigated agriculture, mining, stock watering, domestic uses and power production. Continued beneficial use of the water is required in order to maintain the right. In periods of shortage, priority among rights is determined according to the date of initial diversion. *Colo. River Water Conservation Dist. v. United States*, 424 U.S. 800, 805 (1976). In other words, the first users are the last to be cut off from the supply of water, so that one who is "first in time is first in right" in prior appropriation jurisdictions. *See generally* 1 Waters and Water Rights, §§ 11.01 & 12.02 (Amy E. Kelley, ed., 3rd Ed. 2014) (listing 18 western states that follow the law of prior appropriation).

Suppose that a group of non-Indian farmers has appropriated nearly all the water from a particular stream for irrigation and domestic purposes and that the appropriations were made between 1890 and 1895. Now suppose as well, that an Indian reservation was established adjacent to same river in 1865, with the intent on the part of the United States that the tribe members should become farmers. In the typical case, the Indians were slow to put water to use for agricultural purposes—sometimes because they preferred other means of livelihood and more often because they had no resources to commence agricultural pursuits. What happens when the tribe is ready to commence agriculture, but there is no water left for appropriation under state law? Consider the following cases.

I. FOUNDATIONS OF INDIAN RESERVED RIGHTS

WINTERS V. UNITED STATES

207 U.S. 564, 28 S. Ct. 207, 52 L.Ed. 340 (1908)

*** The allegations of the bill *** are as follows: On the first day of May, 1888, a tract of land, the property of the United States, was reserved and set apart "as an Indian reservation as and for a permanent home and abiding place of the Gros Ventre and Assiniboine bands or tribes of Indians in the state (then Territory) of Montana, designated and known as the Fort Belknap Indian Reservation." The tract has ever since been used as an Indian reservation and as the home and abiding place of the Indians. *** It is alleged with detail that all of the waters of the river are necessary for all those purposes and the purposes for which the reservation was created, and that in furthering and advancing the civilization and improvement of the Indians, and to encourage habits of industry and thrift among them, it is essential and necessary that all of the waters of the river flow down the channel uninterruptedly and undiminished in quantity and undeteriorated in quality. ***

The allegations of the answer *** are as follows: ***

That the defendants, prior to the 5th day of July, 1898, and before any appropriation, diversion, or use of the waters of the river or its tributaries was made by the United States or the Indians on the Fort Belknap Reservation, except a pumping plant of the capacity of about 250 miners' inches,[†] without having notice of any claim made by the United States or the Indians that there was any reservation made of the waters of the river or its tributaries for use on said reservation, and believing that all the waters on the lands open for settlement as aforesaid were subject to appropriation under the laws of the United States and the laws, decisions, rulings, and customs of the state of Montana, in like manner as water on other portions of the public domain, entered upon the public lands in the vicinity of the river, made entry thereof at the United States land office, and thereafter settled upon, improved, reclaimed, and cultivated the same and performed all things required to acquire a title under the homestead and desert land laws, made due proof thereof, and received patents conveying to them, respectively, the lands in fee simple.

That all of said lands are situated within the watershed of the river, are riparian upon the river and its tributaries, but are arid and must be irrigated by artificial means to make them inhabitable and capable of growing crops.

That for the purpose of reclaiming the lands, and acting under the laws of the United States and the laws of Montana, the defendants [acquired rights to 5,000 miners' inches under state law] ***. If defendants are deprived of the waters their lands cannot be successfully cultivated, and they will become useless and homes cannot be maintained thereon.

JUSTICE MCKENNA delivered the opinion of the court:

*** The case, as we view it, turns on the agreement of May, 1888, resulting in the creation of Fort Belknap Reservation. In the construction of this agreement there are certain elements to be considered that are prominent and significant. The reservation was a part of a very much larger tract which the Indians had the right to occupy and use, and which was adequate for the habits and wants of a nomadic and uncivilized people. It was the policy of the government, it was the desire of the Indians, to change those habits and to become a pastoral and civilized people. If they should become such, the original tract was too extensive; but a smaller tract would be inadequate without a change of conditions. The lands were arid, and, without irrigation, were practically valueless. And yet, it is contended, the means of irrigation were deliberately given up by the Indians and deliberately accepted by the government. The lands ceded were, it is true, also arid; and some argument may be urged, and is urged, that with their cession there was the cession of the waters, without which they would be

†. A miner's inch in Montana equals 1/40 of a cubic foot per second (cfs). The miner's inch formulation differed from state to state and now has largely been abandoned as a unit of measure. Eds.

valueless, and "civilized communities could not be established thereon." And this, it is further contended, the Indians knew, and yet made no reservation of the waters. We realize that there is a conflict of implications, but that which makes for the retention of the waters is of greater force than that which makes for their cession. The Indians had command of the lands and the waters,—command of all their beneficial use, whether kept for hunting, "and grazing roving herds of stock," or turned to agriculture and the arts of civilization. Did they give up all this? Did they reduce the area of their occupation and give up the waters which made it valuable or adequate? *** By a rule of interpretation of agreements and treaties with the Indians, ambiguities occurring will be resolved from the standpoint of the Indians. And the rule should certainly be applied to determine between two inferences, one of which would support the purpose of the agreement and the other impair or defeat it. On account of their relations to the government, it cannot be supposed that the Indians were alert to exclude by formal words every inference which might militate against or defeat the declared purpose of themselves and the government, even if it could be supposed that they had the intelligence to foresee the "double sense" which might sometime be urged against them.

Another contention of appellants is that if it be conceded that there was a reservation of the waters of Milk river by the agreement of 1888, yet the reservation was repealed by the admission of Montana into the Union, February 22, 1889, "upon an equal footing with the original states." The language of counsel is that "any reservation in the agreement with the Indians, expressed or implied, whereby the waters of Milk river were not to be subject of appropriation by the citizens and inhabitants of said state, was repealed by the act of admission." But to establish the repeal counsel rely substantially upon the same argument that they advance against the intention of the agreement to reserve the waters. The power of the government to reserve the waters and exempt them from appropriation under the state laws is not denied, and could not be. *United States v. Rio Grande Dam & Irrig. Co.* 174 U. S. 702; *United States v. Winans*, 198 U. S. 371. That the government did reserve them we have decided, and for a use which would be necessarily continued through years. This was done May 1, 1888, and it would be extreme to believe that within a year Congress destroyed the reservation and took from the Indians the consideration of their grant, leaving them a barren waste—took from them the means of continuing their old habits, yet did not leave them the power to change to new ones.

Appellants' argument upon the incidental repeal of the agreement by the admission of Montana into the Union, and the power over the waters of Milk river which the state thereby acquired to dispose of them under its laws, is elaborate and able, but our construction of the agreement and its effect make it unnecessary to answer the argument in detail.

NOTES AND QUESTIONS

1. *Federal or tribal water rights?* In *Winters*, who reserved the water? Was it the tribe or the United States? How does the reserved rights theory of treaty interpretation in *United* States *v. Winans* affect the answer? *See* John Shurts, Indian Reserved Water Rights: The Winters Doctrine in its Social and

Legal Context, 1880s–1930s (2000); David H. Getches, *The Unsettling of the West: How Indians Got the Best Water Rights*, 99 Mich. L. Rev. 1473, 1481-83 (2001) (explaining that despite remnants of riparianism in the West, the prior appropriation doctrine was the overwhelming rule in the western states by 1908). The tribes of the Fort Belknap Indian Reservation still do not have a fully quantified water right for future uses. Montana commenced a state-wide general stream adjudication under the McCarran Amendment (*see* § III, *infra*) to determine all state, federal and tribal water rights in the state. Several tribes negotiated settlements with the state, federal government, and private water users. Fort Belknap reached a settlement with the state, but they have not been able to get congressional ratification.

2. *Canons of construction.* Why do the Indians win with respect to the conflict of implications in *Winters*? Is there any answer to non-Indians' claim that Congress could not have intended that their homesteaded lands be valueless due to a lack of water?

3. *Federal deference to state law.* In the Desert Land Act, 19 Stat. 377 (1877), and other nineteenth century statutes, Congress effectively made state law applicable to ownership of waters on unreserved federal lands, subject, however, to federal power to reserve use of such waters for federal purposes or in the aid of navigation. In *United States v. Rio Grande Dam & Irrigation Co.*, 174 U.S. 690, 706–707 (1899), the Court stated: "To hold that Congress, by these acts, meant to confer upon any state the right to appropriate all the waters of the tributary streams which unite into a navigable water course, and so destroy the navigability of that water course in derogation of the interests of all the people of the United States, is a construction which cannot be tolerated. It ignores the spirit of the legislation, and carries the statute to the verge of the letter, and far beyond what, under the circumstances of the case, must be held to have been the intent of Congress."

4. *Preemption of state law not necessarily tied to reservations of land.* In an exhaustive analysis of federal water rights, the United States Department of Justice's Office of Legal Counsel determined that the power to reserve waters for federal use does not require a federal set-aside of land, but that "the Supremacy Clause provides Congress with ample power, when coupled with the commerce power, the Property Clause, or other grants of federal power, to supersede state law." Federal "Non–Reserved" Water Rights, 6 Op. Off. Legal Counsel 328, 363 (1982). The opinion "still expresses executive branch policy." John D. Leshy, *Water Rights for New Federal Land Conservation Programs: A Turn-of-the-Century Evaluation*, 4 U. Denv. Water L. Rev. 271, 288 (2001).

5. *Senior diverters protected?* What result if the non-Indian state law appropriations had occurred before the reservation was established by the ratified agreement?

6. *Groundwater.* Do Indian reserved rights attach to groundwater? Most courts say yes. The Ninth Circuit ruled that Indian water rights extend to groundwater in *Agua Caliente Band of Cahuilla Indians v. Coachella Valley Water District*, 849 F.3d 1262 (9th 2017), *cert. denie*d, 138 S. Ct. 469 (2017). The *Agua Caliente* court held that the tribe's implied reserved water right included appurtenant groundwater underlying its reservation, not just appurtenant surface water. Surface water was minimal or non-existent for most of the year, and survival of the reservation therefore depended on access to groundwater. In a questionable ruling on remand, the district court denied the Agua

Caliente Band's right to a quantification because it produced no "evidence that the Tribe is unable, or may imminently become unable, to use sufficient water to fulfill the purposes of the reservation." *Agua Caliente Band of Cahuilla Indians v. Coachella Valley Water District*, 2019 WL 2610965, at *10 (C.D. Cal. 2019).

The Montana Supreme Court and the Arizona Supreme Court have held that the federal reserved water rights doctrine applies to groundwater. *Confederated Salish and Kootenai Tribes of the Flathead Reservation v. Stults*, 59 P.3d 1093, 1099 (Mont. 2002); *In re All Rights to Use Water in the Gila River System*, 989 P.2d 739 (Ariz. 1999), *cert. denied, sub. nom., Phelps Dodge Corp. v. United States*, 530 U.S. 1250 (2000). Earlier, the Wyoming Supreme Court had agreed that it made sense to apply the doctrine to groundwater, but declined to do so on the ground that no other court had done so. *In re All Rights to Use Water in the Big Horn River System*, 753 P.2d 76 (Wyo. 1988), *aff'd by equally divided court sub nom., Wyoming v. United States*, 492 U.S. 406 (1989). Should a court award groundwater to a tribe if surface water, albeit of lesser quality, can be used without injury to non-Indian water users?

7. *Pueblo Water Rights.* The Pueblo Indians of the southwest own land from several different sources. *See* Cohen's Handbook of Federal Indian Law 313-20 (2012). For land acquired under United States law, such as an Executive Order, the Pueblos have federal reserved rights under the *Winters* Doctrine. *New Mexico ex rel. Martinez v. Aamodt*, 618 F. Supp. 993, 1010 (D. N.M. 1985). Pueblos also hold land pursuant to Spanish land grants confirmed under the Pueblos Lands Act. As to these lands, the Pueblos have an aboriginal priority date. "The Pueblo aboriginal water right, as modified by Spanish and Mexican law, included the right to irrigate new land in response to need. Acreage brought under irrigation between 1846 and 1924 was thus also protected by federal law." *Id; see also* Cohen, *supra*, at 321-24.

8. *Average use and units of measure.* The nomenclature regarding measurement of water rights in the cases varies from jurisdiction to jurisdiction and can be confusing. Estimates of average water use for a family of four vary from one-half to about one acre foot per year for domestic purposes. The most common measurement equivalents are set out below and should help you understand the cases.

Water Equivalents Table

1 acre foot	325,851 gallons
1 cubic foot per second (CFS)	7.48 gallons per second
1 CFS	646,272 gallons per day (GPD)
1 million gallons per day	1.55 CFS

II. HOW MUCH WATER IS RESERVED? PRACTICABLY IRRIGABLE ACREAGE AND OTHER STANDARDS

The fact that tribal territories include reserved water rights does not answer a much more complicated question: how much water was reserved? In both Indian and non-Indian contexts, allocating water sources traversing more than one sovereign's territory creates litigation that lasts generations. The following materials address the standards courts have applied in determining the scope of Indian water rights.

ROBERT T. ANDERSON, *INDIAN WATER RIGHTS AND THE FEDERAL TRUST RESPONSIBILITY*

46 Nat. Resources J. 399 (2006)

*** In the few cases after *Winters* and before 1963, lower courts generally adhered to the practice endorsed in *Winters* of enjoining interference with extant tribal uses while leaving the door left open for expansion of the reserved right as tribal needs increased. For example, in *Conrad Investment Co. v. United States*[102] the court of appeals considered a dispute very similar to that in *Winters*, but went further than simply enjoining non-Indian interference with current tribal uses on the Blackfeet Indian Reservation. Instead, the court quantified the Indian rights at the level of existing use and explicitly provided the tribe with leave to seek additional quantities should the tribe's needs increase:

> [W]henever the needs and requirements of the complainant [the United States on behalf of the tribe] for the use of the waters of Birch creek for irrigating and other useful purposes upon the reservation exceed the amount of water reserved by the decree for that purpose, the complainant may apply to the court for a modification of the decree. This is entirely in accord with complainant's rights as adjudged by the decree. Having determined that the Indians on the reservation have a paramount right to the waters of Birch creek, it follows that the permission given to the defendant to have the excess over the amount of water specified in the decree should be subject to modification, should the conditions on the reservation at any time require such modification.[103]

In *United States v. Ahtanum Irrigation Dist.*,[104] the court concluded that the Treaty with the Yakama[105] included a reservation of water "not limited to the use of the Indians at any given date but *** to the ultimate needs of the Indians as those needs and requirements should grow to keep pace with the development of Indian agriculture upon the reservation."[106] The United States brought suit on behalf of an individual allotment owner in *Skeem v. United*

---

102. *Conrad Inv. Co. v. United States*, 161 F. 829 (9th Cir. 1908). The complaint in *Conrad* was actually filed six months before the *Winters* case. ***

103. *Conrad Inv. Co.*, 161 F. at 835.

104. *United States v. Ahtanum Irrigation Dist.*, 236 F.2d 321 (9th Cir. 1956), *cert. denied*, 352 U.S. 988 (1957).

105. Treaty between the United States and the Yakama Nation of Indians, 12 Stat. 951 (June 9, 1855).

106. *United States v. Ahtanum Irrigation Dist.*, 236 F.2d at 327.

States,[107] which involved a treaty with an explicit provision protecting actual Indian use at the time the treaty was signed.[108] The court agreed with the United States that reserved rights should be implied for future uses in addition to the actual uses expressly protected by the treaty.[109] In *United States ex rel Ray v. Hibner*, the court described claims made on behalf of individual Indians in the following terms:[110]

> The contention of the government as guardian for the Indian wards of the land allotted to them, is that, under the treaties and acts relating to the reservation, its wards have a superior right to the stream, which does not depend upon occupancy or possession of their lands, and which the defendants could not defeat or impair by first appropriating the water and actually applying it to their beneficial use, and that the Indian lands are entitled to a continuous flow through the entire year of a sufficient amount of water from Toponce creek for domestic and irrigation purposes for such portion of their lands as are susceptible to irrigation, regardless of whether or not they have placed under cultivation and actually irrigated all of such lands.[111]

Thus, by the middle of the Twentieth Century it was clear that Indian reservations with an agricultural purpose included water rights sufficient for irrigation and that the amount of water with a date of reservation priority would increase as tribal needs increased.[112] This made perfect sense, since one could not ascertain the future needs of the tribes with certainty at any given time.

The problem, of course, was that others who might invest in water use could not know with any certainty whether senior tribal reserved claims might later trump their junior priority uses. In 1963, the Supreme Court announced a method for determining the full allocation for the reservations and tribes involved in a comprehensive adjudication of the Colorado River.

ARIZONA V. CALIFORNIA

373 U.S. 546, 83 S. Ct. 1468, 10 L.Ed.2d 542 (1963)

JUSTICE BLACK delivered the opinion of the Court.

In 1952 the State of Arizona invoked the original jurisdiction of this Court by filing a complaint against the State of California and seven of its public agencies. Later, Nevada, New Mexico, Utah, and the United States were added

---

107. 273 F. 93 (9th Cir. 1921).

108. 31 Stat. 672, art. 8 (1898).

109. 273 F. at 94–95.

110. 27 F.2d 909 (D. Idaho 1928).

111. *Id.* at 910–11.

112. The same policy was followed with respect to lands allotted to individuals under the Dawes Act. *United States v. Powers*, 305 U.S. 527, 532 (1939) (when allotments of land were made, "the right to use some portion of tribal waters essential for cultivation passed to the owners"); *Skeem*, 273 F. 93, 96 (9th Cir. 1921) (water rights not lost when allotments leased to third parties).

as parties either voluntarily or on motion. The basic controversy in the case is over how much water each State has a legal right to use out of the waters of the Colorado River and its tributaries. ***

The Colorado River itself rises in the mountains of Colorado and flows generally in a southwesterly direction for about 1,300 miles through Colorado, Utah, and Arizona and along the Arizona–Nevada and Arizona–California boundaries, after which it passes into Mexico and empties into the Mexican waters of the Gulf of California. On its way to the sea it receives tributary waters from Wyoming, Colorado, Utah, Nevada, New Mexico, and Arizona. The river and its tributaries flow in a natural basin almost surrounded by large mountain ranges and drain 242,000 square miles, an area about 900 miles long from north to south and 300 to 500 miles wide from east to west—practically one-twelfth the area of the continental United States excluding Alaska. Much of this large basin is so arid that it is, as it always has been, largely dependent upon managed use of the waters of the Colorado River System to make it productive and inhabitable. The Master refers to archaeological evidence that as long as 2,000 years ago the ancient Hohokam tribe built and maintained irrigation canals near what is now Phoenix, Arizona, and that American Indians were practicing irrigation in that region at the time white men first explored it. ***

Congress decided that a fair division of the first 7,500,000 acre-feet of such mainstream waters would give 4,400,000 acre-feet to California, 2,800,000 to Arizona, and 300,000 to Nevada; Arizona and California would each get one-half of any surplus. *** [Determination of the tribal and federal claims remains.]

V. CLAIMS OF THE UNITED STATES

In these proceedings, the United States has asserted claims to waters in the main river and in some of the tributaries for use on Indian Reservations, National Forests, Recreational and Wildlife Areas and other government lands and works. *** We shall discuss only the claims of the United States on behalf of the Indian Reservations.

The Government, on behalf of five Indian Reservations in Arizona, California, and Nevada, asserted rights to water in the mainstream of the Colorado River. The Colorado River Reservation, located partly in Arizona and partly in California, is the largest. It was originally created by an Act of Congress in 1865, but its area was later increased by Executive Order. Other reservations were created by Executive Orders and amendments to them ranging in dates from 1870 to 1907. The Master found both as a matter of fact and law that when the United States created these reservations or added to them, it reserved not only land but also the use of enough water from the Colorado to irrigate the irrigable portions of the reserved lands. The aggregate quantity of water which the Master held was reserved for all the reservations is about 1,000,000 acre-feet, to be used on around 135,000 irrigable acres of land. Here, as before the Master, Arizona argues that the United States had no power to make a reservation of navigable waters after Arizona became a State; that navigable waters could not be reserved by Executive Orders; that the United States did not intend to reserve water for the Indian Reservations; that the amount of water reserved should be measured by the reasonably foreseeable needs of the Indians living on the reservation rather than by the number of irrigable acres; and, finally, that the judicial doctrine of equitable apportionment should be used to divide the water between the Indians and the other people in the State of Arizona.

The last argument is easily answered. The doctrine of equitable apportionment is a method of resolving water disputes between States. It was created by this Court in the exercise of its original jurisdiction over controversies in which States are parties. An Indian Reservation is not a State. And while Congress has sometimes left Indian Reservations considerable power to manage their own affairs, we are not convinced by Arizona's argument that each reservation is so much like a State that its rights to water should be determined by the doctrine of equitable apportionment. Moreover, even were we to treat an Indian Reservation like a State, equitable apportionment would still not control since, under our view, the Indian claims here are governed by the statutes and Executive Orders creating the reservations.

Arizona's contention that the Federal Government had no power, after Arizona became a State, to reserve waters for the use and benefit of federally reserved lands rests largely upon statements in *Pollard's Lessee v. Hagan*, 3 How. 212 (1845), and *Shively v. Bowlby*, 152 U.S. 1 (1894). Those cases and others that followed them gave rise to the doctrine that lands underlying navigable waters within territory acquired by the Government are held in trust for future States and that title to such lands is automatically vested in the States upon admission to the Union. But those cases involved only the shores of and lands beneath navigable waters. They do not determine the problem before us and cannot be accepted as limiting the broad powers of the United States to regulate navigable waters under the Commerce Clause and to regulate government lands under Art. IV, § 3, of the Constitution. We have no doubt about the power of the United States under these clauses to reserve water rights for its reservations and its property.

Arizona also argues that, in any event, water rights cannot be reserved by Executive Order. Some of the reservations of Indian lands here involved were made almost 100 years ago, and all of them were made over 45 years ago. In our view, these reservations, like those created directly by Congress, were not limited to land, but included waters as well. Congress and the Executive have ever since recognized these as Indian Reservations. Numerous appropriations, including appropriations for irrigation projects, have been made by Congress. They have been uniformly and universally treated as reservations by map makers, surveyors, and the public. We can give but short shrift at this late date to the argument that the reservations either of land or water are invalid because they were originally set apart by the Executive. *See United States v. Midwest Oil Co.*, 236 U.S. 459, 469–475 (1915).

Arizona also challenges the Master's holding as to the Indian Reservations on two other grounds: first, that there is a lack of evidence showing that the United States in establishing the reservations intended to reserve water for them; second, that even if water was meant to be reserved the Master has awarded too much water. We reject both of these contentions. Most of the land in these reservations is and always has been arid. If the water necessary to sustain life is to be had, it must come from the Colorado River or its tributaries. It can be said without overstatement that when the Indians were put on these reservations they were not considered to be located in the most desirable area of the Nation. It is impossible to believe that when Congress created the great Colorado River Indian Reservation and when the Executive Department of this

Nation created the other reservations they were unaware that most of the lands were of the desert kind—hot, scorching sands—and that water from the river would be essential to the life of the Indian people and to the animals they hunted and the crops they raised. In the debate leading to approval of the first congressional appropriation for irrigation of the Colorado River Indian Reservation, the delegate from the Territory of Arizona made this statement:

> Irrigating canals are essential to the prosperity of these Indians. Without water there can be no production, no life; and all they ask of you is to give them a few agricultural implements to enable them to dig an irrigating canal by which their lands may be watered and their fields irrigated, so that they may enjoy the means of existence. You must provide these Indians with the means of subsistence or they will take by robbery from those who have. During the last year I have seen a number of these Indians starved to death for want of food. Cong. Globe, 38th Cong., 2d Sess. 1321 (1865).

The question of the Government's implied reservation of water rights upon the creation of an Indian Reservation was before this Court in *Winters v. United States*, 207 U.S. 564 decided in 1908. Much the same argument made to us was made in *Winters* to persuade the Court to hold that Congress had created an Indian Reservation without intending to reserve waters necessary to make the reservation livable. The Court rejected all of the arguments. ***

The Court in *Winters* concluded that the Government, when it created that Indian Reservation, intended to deal fairly with the Indians by reserving for them the waters without which their lands would have been useless. *Winters* has been followed by this Court as recently as 1939 in *United States v. Powers*, 305 U.S. 527. We follow it now and agree that the United States did reserve the water rights for the Indians effective as of the time the Indian Reservations were created. This means, as the Master held, that these water rights, having vested before the Act became effective on June 25, 1929, are "present perfected rights" and as such are entitled to priority under the Act.

We also agree with the Master's conclusion as to the quantity of water intended to be reserved. He found that the water was intended to satisfy the future as well as the present needs of the Indian Reservations and ruled that enough water was reserved to irrigate all the practicably irrigable acreage on the reservations. Arizona, on the other hand, contends that the quantity of water reserved should be measured by the Indians' "reasonably foreseeable needs," which, in fact, means by the number of Indians. How many Indians there will be and what their future needs will be can only be guessed. We have concluded, as did the Master, that the only feasible and fair way by which reserved water for the reservations can be measured is irrigable acreage. The various acreages of irrigable land which the Master found to be on the different reservations we find to be reasonable. ***

NOTES AND QUESTIONS

1. *Federal record in protecting Indian water rights?* Although the federal government, as trustee of tribal lands and the water that makes them livable, might be expected to act to protect Indian water rights, it has more often diverted that water for other projects, including dams and non-Indian

irrigation and reservoirs. The National Water Commission in 1973 concluded that "[i]n the history of the United States Government's treatment of Indian tribes, its failure to protect Indian water rights for use on the reservations it set aside for them is one of the sorrier chapters." Nat'l Water Comm'n., Water Policies for the Future—Final Report to the President and the Congress of the United States 475 (GPO, 1973). The Commission recognized the United States' trust responsibility to tribes with respect to water and went on to recommend that the United States quantify Indian water rights in federal court. *Id.* at 477–79. The Commission also recommended that some accommodation be made to non-Indians who the United States encouraged to use water owned by Indian tribes. *Id.* at 482–83. *See* Daniel C. McCool, Native Waters 36 (2002) (stating that "the Bureau of Reclamation operates 348 reservoirs that provide water for ten million acres of farmland and 31 million people *** [b]ut the BIA has never finished an [Indian] irrigation project.").

2. In *Arizona v. California* II, 460 U.S. 605 (1983), the Court considered motions to intervene by the five Indian tribes whose water rights were before the Court in the 1963 proceeding. After granting the motions, the Court rejected their claims that the decree should be reopened and additional water rights awarded for land that was not claimed as practicably irrigable in the earlier proceeding:

> Our decision to rely upon the amount of practicably irrigable acreage contained within the Reservation constituted a rejection of Arizona's proposal that the quantity of water reserved should be measured by the Indians' "reasonably foreseeable needs," *i.e.*, by the number of Indians. The practicably irrigable acreage standard was preferable because how many Indians there will be and what their future needs will be could "only be guessed," 373 U.S., at 601. By contrast, the irrigable acreage standard allowed a present water allocation that would be appropriate for future water needs. 373 U.S., at 600–601. Therefore, with respect to the question of reserved rights for the Reservations, and the measurement of those rights, the Indians, as represented by the United States, won what can be described only as a complete victory. A victory, it should be stressed, that was in part attributable to the Court's interest in a fixed calculation of future water needs. Applying the irrigable acreage standard, we found that the Master's determination as to the amount of practicably irrigable acreage, an issue also subject to adversary proceedings, was reasonable. *** We also fear that the urge to relitigate, once loosed, will not be easily cabined. The States have already indicated, if the issue were reopened, that the irrigable acreage standard itself should be reconsidered in light of our decisions in *United States v. New Mexico,* 438 U.S. 696 (1978) and *Washington v. Washington State Commercial Passenger Fishing Vessel Assn.,* 443 U.S. 658 (1979), and we are not persuaded that a defensible line can be drawn between the reasons for reopening this litigation advanced by the Tribes and the United States on the one hand and the States on the other. It would be counter to the interests of all parties to this case to open what may become a Pandora's Box, upsetting the certainty of all aspects of the decree. These considerations, combined with the practice in our original cases and the strong *res judicata* interests involved, lead us to conclude that the irrigable acreage question should not be relitigated.

460 U.S. at 617–626.

The tribes did eventually realize more irrigable acreage, however, as a result of the Court's ruling that the 1963 decision contemplated subsequent resolution of questions concerning the tribes' boundary disputes. The Supreme Court issued its final consolidated decree in *Arizona v. California*, 547 U.S. 150 (2006).

Irrigation Canal on the Colorado River Indian Reservation (1972), by Charles O'Rear, U.S. National Archives.

How should courts determine the "present and future needs" of the Indians on a reservation where agriculture is not the dominant feature of the local economy? Should reserved water rights include only sufficient water for the purposes for which the reservation was originally created, or do they include water to sustain changing reservation economies? The following cases consider these questions.

UNITED STATES V. ADAIR

723 F.2d 1394 (9th Cir. 1983)

FLETCHER, CIRCUIT JUDGE.

In 1975 the United States filed suit in district court, pursuant to 28 U.S.C. § 1345 (1976), for a declaration of water rights within an area whose boundaries roughly coincide with the former Klamath Indian Reservation. The suit named as defendants some 600 individual owners of land within the former reservation. The Klamath Tribe intervened as a plaintiff and the State of Oregon as a defendant. ***

I. BACKGROUND.

A. History of the Litigation Area.

This suit concerns water rights in a portion of the Williamson River watershed. The Williamson River is part of the larger Klamath River watershed of Southern Oregon and Northern California. That part of the Williamson River watershed involved in this litigation drains an area of low, forested mountains, flat, grassy valleys and marshes east of the Cascade Range in south-central Oregon. The average rainfall in the area is low; summers are dry and winters are severe.

The major feature of the subject area is a large flat valley historically known as the Klamath Marsh. As the Williamson flows into the north end of this valley, it spreads out and soaks into the porous, pumice soil. During the wet months of the year, open water and aquatic vegetation cover the lower portion of the valley, the water to a depth of a few feet. The remainder of the valley is grassland. During dry summer months, as the water recedes, the grassland in the valley increases. This fluctuating marsh has been an important feeding and resting area for migratory ducks, geese and other waterfowl for thousands of years. In addition, the Marsh has always supported a variety of other indigenous wildlife. More recently, large parts of the Klamath Marsh have been used for grazing cattle.

The Klamath Indians have hunted, fished, and foraged in the area of the Klamath Marsh and upper Williamson River for over a thousand years. In 1864 the Klamath Tribe entered into a treaty with the United States whereby it relinquished its aboriginal claim to some 12 million acres of land in return for a reservation of approximately 800,000 acres in south-central Oregon. This reservation included all of the Klamath Marsh as well as large forested tracts of the Williamson River watershed. Treaty between the United States of America and the Klamath and Moadoc Tribes and Yahooskin Band of Snake Indians, Oct. 14, 1864, 16 Stat. 707. Article I of the treaty gave the Klamath the exclusive right to hunt, fish, and gather on their reservation. Article II provided funds to help the Klamath adopt an agricultural way of life. 16 Stat. 708.

For 20 years, until 1887, the Klamath lived on their reservation under the terms of the 1864 treaty. In 1887 Congress passed the General Allotment Act, ch. 119, 24 Stat. 388 (1887), which fundamentally changed the nature of land ownership on the Klamath Reservation. Prior to the Act, the tribe held the reservation land in communal ownership. Pursuant to the terms of the Allotment Act, however, parcels of tribal land were granted to individual Indians in fee. Under the allotment system, approximately 25% of the original Klamath Reservation passed from tribal to individual Indian ownership. Over time, many of these individual allotments passed into non-Indian ownership.

The next major change in the pattern of land ownership on the Klamath Reservation occurred in 1954 when Congress approved the Klamath Termination Act. Act of Aug. 13, 1954, c. 732, § 1, 68 Stat. 718. Under this Act, tribe members could give up their interest in tribal property for cash. A large majority of the tribe chose to do this. In order to meet the cash obligation, in 1961, the United States purchased much of the former Klamath Reservation. The balance of the reservation was placed in a private trust for the remaining tribe members. In 1973, to complete implementation of the Klamath Termination Act, the United States condemned most of the tribal land held in trust. Payments from the condemnation proceeding and sale of the remaining trust land went to Indians still enrolled in the tribe. This final distribution of assets essentially extinguished the original Klamath Reservation as a source of tribal property.

Even though the Klamath Tribe no longer holds any of its former reservation, the United States still holds title to much of the former reservation lands. In 1958 the Government purchased approximately 15,000 acres of the Klamath Marsh, the heart of the former reservation, to establish a migratory bird refuge under the jurisdiction of the United States Fish and Wildlife Service. Pub. L. No. 85–731, 72 Stat. 816 (1958) (codified as amended at 25 U.S.C. § 564w–1 (1976)). In 1961 and again in 1973, the Government purchased large forested portions of the former Klamath Reservation. This forest land became part of the Winema National Forest under the jurisdiction of the United States Forest Service. 25 U.S.C. §§ 564w–1(d), 564w–2 (1976). By these two purchases, the Government became the owner of approximately 70% of the former reservation lands. The balance of the reservation is in private, Indian and non-Indian, ownership either through allotment or sale of reservation lands at the time of termination. ***

***

III. WATER RIGHTS

***

A. A Reservation of Water to Accompany the Tribe's Treaty Right to Hunt, Fish, and Gather.

Article I of the 1864 treaty with the Klamath Tribe reserved to the Tribe the exclusive right to hunt, fish, and gather on its reservation. 16 Stat. 707, 708; *Kimball I,* 493 F.2d at 566. This right survived the Klamath Termination Act, 25 U.S.C. §§ 564–564w (1976). *See Kimball v. Callahan,* 590 F.2d 768, 775 (9th Cir.), *cert. denied,* 444 U.S. 826 (1979) (*Kimball II*); *Kimball I,* 493 F.2d at 569. The issue presented for decision in this case is whether, as the district court held, these hunting and fishing rights carry with them an implied reservation of water rights.

1. Reservation of Water in the 1864 Treaty.

In *Winters v. United States,* 207 U.S. 564, 576–77 (1908), the Supreme Court held that the treaty creating the Fort Belknap Indian Reservation contained an implied reservation of water to irrigate the arid Indian lands. More recently, in *Cappaert v. United States,* 426 U.S. 128 (1976), and *United States v. New Mexico,* 438 U.S. 696 (1978), the Supreme Court addressed the scope and nature of *Winters* doctrine water rights on federal lands other than Indian reservations. In *Cappaert,* the Court upheld a lower court determination that, in setting aside the Devil's Hole National Monument, the United States had reserved a quantity of water sufficient to meet the purposes for which the Monument was established. The Court stated:

> In determining whether there is a federally reserved water right implicit in a federal reservation of public land, the issue is whether the Government intended to reserve unappropriated and thus available water. Intent

> is inferred if the previously unappropriated waters are necessary to accomplish the purposes for which the reservation was created.

426 U.S. at 139. In *New Mexico,* the Supreme Court clarified the scope of the reserved water rights doctrine in the course of determining whether the United States had reserved water for use on the Gila National Forest in New Mexico. The Court indicated that water may be reserved under the *Winters* doctrine only for the primary purposes of a federal reservation. 438 U.S. at 702. Hence, even though the Supreme Court agreed that hunting, fishing, and recreation are among the purposes for which the National Forest System is maintained, it determined that these purposes are secondary to the purposes of "securing favorable conditions of water flows," and furnishing "a continuous supply of timber." Accordingly, only the latter purposes carried with them an implied reservation of water rights. 438 U.S. at 713–15. *New Mexico* and *Cappaert,* while not directly applicable to *Winters* doctrine rights on Indian reservations, *see* F. Cohen, Handbook of Federal Indian Law 581–85 (1982 ed.),[13] establish several useful guidelines. First, water rights may be implied only "[w]here water is necessary to fulfill the very purposes for which a federal reservation was created," and not where it is merely "valuable for a secondary use of the reservation." *New Mexico,* 438 U.S. at 702. Second, the scope of the implied right is circumscribed by the necessity that calls for its creation. The doctrine "reserves only that amount of water necessary to fulfill the purpose of the reservation, no more." *Cappaert,* 426 U.S. at 141.

The question, therefore, is whether securing to the Indians the right to hunt, fish, and gather was a primary purpose of the Klamath Reservation. Resolution of this question, in turn, depends on an analysis of the intent of the parties to the 1864 Klamath Treaty as reflected in its text and the surrounding circumstances. *See Washington v. Fishing Vessel Ass'n,* 443 U.S. 658, 675–76 (1979); *United States v. Winters,* 207 U.S. at 575–76. The State and individual appellants argue that the intent of the 1864 Treaty was to convert the Indians to an agricultural way of life. The Government and the Tribe argue that an equally important purpose of the treaty was to guarantee continuity of the Indians' hunting and gathering lifestyle. Under the guidelines established in *Cappaert* and *New Mexico,* we find that both objectives qualify as primary purposes of the 1864 Treaty and accompanying reservation of land. ***

Neither *Cappaert* nor *New Mexico* requires us to choose between these activities or to identify a single essential purpose which the parties to the 1864 Treaty intended the Klamath Reservation to serve. *** In fact, in *Colville Confederated Tribes v. Walton,* 647 F.2d 42 (9th Cir.1981), this court found that provision of a "homeland for the Indians to maintain their agrarian society," as well as "preservation of the tribe's access to fishing grounds," were dual purposes behind establishment of the Colville Reservation. Consequently the court found an implied reservation of water to support both of these activities. President Grant established the Colville Reservation in a one-paragraph Executive Order that stated only that the land would be "set apart as a reservation for

---

13. *See also* W. Canby, American Indian Law 245–46 (1981) ("While the purpose for which the federal government reserves other types of lands may be strictly construed, *United States v. New Mexico,* 438 U.S. 696 (1979) (national forest), the purposes of Indian reservations are necessarily entitled to broader interpretation if the goal of Indian self-sufficiency is to be attained"). Additionally, where interpretation of an Indian treaty is involved, not only the intent of the Government, but also the intent of the tribe must be discerned. *See Washington v. Fishing Vessel Ass'n,* 443 U.S. 658, 675–76 (1979).

said Indians." Thus the court in *Colville* discovered the purposes of the reservation and implied water rights from a much less explicit text than that provided by the 1864 Klamath Treaty, Articles I through V. *See Colville,* 647 F.2d at 47 n. 8. We therefore have no difficulty in upholding the district court's finding that at the time the Klamath Reservation was established, the Government and the Tribe intended to reserve a quantity of the water flowing through the reservation not only for the purpose of supporting Klamath agriculture, but also for the purpose of maintaining the Tribe's treaty right to hunt and fish on reservation lands. ***

3. Priority of the Water Right Reserved to Accompany the Tribe's Treaty Right to Hunt and Fish.

***

In 1864, at the time the Klamath entered into a treaty with the United States, the Tribe had lived in Central Oregon and Northern California for more than a thousand years. This ancestral homeland encompassed some 12 million acres. Within its domain, the Tribe used the waters that flowed over its land for domestic purposes and to support its hunting, fishing, and gathering lifestyle. This uninterrupted use and occupation of land and water created in the Tribe aboriginal or "Indian title" to all of its vast holdings. *** The Tribe's title also included aboriginal hunting and fishing rights, *** and by the same reasoning, an aboriginal right to the water used by the Tribe as it flowed through its homeland. ***

With this background in mind, we examine the priority date attaching to the Klamath Tribe's reservation of water to support its hunting and fishing rights. *** There is no indication in the treaty, express or implied, that the Tribe intended to cede any of its interest in those lands it reserved for itself. *See United States v. Winans,* 198 U.S. at 381. *** Nor is it possible that the Tribe would have understood such a reservation of land to include a relinquishment of its right to use the water as it had always used it on the land it had reserved as a permanent home. *** Further, we find no language in the treaty to indicate that the United States intended or understood the agreement to diminish the Tribe's rights in that part of its aboriginal holding reserved for its permanent occupancy and use. Accordingly, we agree with the district court that within the 1864 Treaty is a recognition of the Tribe's aboriginal water rights and a confirmation to the Tribe of a continued water right to support its hunting and fishing lifestyle on the Klamath Reservation.

*** Such water rights necessarily carry a priority date of time immemorial. The rights were not created by the 1864 Treaty, rather, the treaty confirmed the continued existence of these rights. *See Washington v. Fishing Vessel Ass'n,* 443 U.S. at 678–81. To assign the Tribe's hunting and fishing water rights the later, 1864, priority date argued for by the State and individual appellants would ignore one of the fundamental principles of prior appropriations law—that priority for a particular water right dates from the time of first use. Furthermore, an 1864 priority date might limit the scope of the Tribe's hunting and fishing water rights by reduction for any pre–1864 appropriations of water. This could extinguish rights the Tribe held before 1864 and intended to reserve to itself thereafter. Thus, we are compelled to conclude that where, as here, a tribe shows its aboriginal use of water to support a hunting and fishing lifestyle, and then enters into a treaty with the United States that reserves this aboriginal water use, the water right thereby established retains a priority date of first or immemorial use.[22]

This does not mean, however, as the individual appellants argue, that the former Klamath Reservation will be subject to a "wilderness servitude" in favor of the Tribe. Apparently, appellants read the water rights decreed to the Tribe to require restoration of an 1864 level of water flow on former reservation lands now used by the Tribe to maintain traditional hunting and fishing lifestyles. We do not interpret the district court's decision so expansively.

In its opinion discussing the Tribe's hunting and fishing water rights, the district court stated "[t]he Indians are still entitled to as much water on the Reservation lands as they need to protect their hunting and fishing rights." 478 F. Supp. at 345. We interpret this statement to confirm to the Tribe the amount of water necessary to support its hunting and fishing rights as currently exercised to maintain the livelihood of Tribe members, not as these rights once were exercised by the Tribe in 1864. We find authority for such a construction of the Indians' rights in the Supreme Court's decision in *Washington v. Fishing Vessel Ass'n,* 443 U.S. (1979). There, citing *Arizona v. California,* 373 U.S. 546 (1963), a reserved water rights case, the court stated "that Indian treaty rights to a natural resource that once was thoroughly and exclusively exploited by the Indians secures so much as, but not more than, is necessary to provide the Indians with a livelihood—that is to say, a moderate living." 443 U.S. at 686. Implicit in this "moderate living" standard is the conclusion that Indian tribes are not generally entitled to the same level of exclusive use and exploitation of a natural resource that they enjoyed at the time they entered into the treaty reserving their interest in the resource, unless, of course, no lesser level will supply them with a moderate living. As limited by the "moderate living" standard enunciated in *Fishing Vessel,* we affirm the district court's decision that the Klamath Tribe is entitled to a reservation of water, with a priority date of immemorial use, sufficient to support exercise of treaty hunting and fishing rights. ***

IN RE THE GENERAL ADJUDICATION OF ALL RIGHTS TO USE WATER IN THE BIG HORN RIVER SYSTEM

753 P.2d 76 (Wyo. 1988)

***

The history of the Big Horn Basin for purposes of this case begins in the early 1800's when explorers, trappers and traders began traveling into northwestern Wyoming, part of the vast hunting grounds of the peripatetic Shoshone Indians. Neither group encroached on the other and relations were friendly. Nonetheless, in 1865, the United States, hoping to preserve the peace

---

22. In the present case, the Klamath Tribe, as we have noted, has depended upon the waters in question to support its hunting and fishing activities for over 1,000 years. It would be inconsistent with the principles we follow in today's decision to hold that the priority of the Tribe's water rights is any less ancient than the "immemorial" use that has been made of them. *See United States v. Shoshone Tribe,* 304 U.S. 111, 117 (1938).

and stability, reached an agreement delineating the area within which the Eastern Shoshone roamed, a 44,672,000 acre region comprising parts of Wyoming, Colorado and Utah. Following the Civil War, as the westward movement gained momentum, the United States government realized the size of the region set aside for Indians only was unrealistic, and on July 3, 1868, executed the Second Treaty of Fort Bridger with the Shoshone and Bannock Indians, establishing the Wind River Indian Reservation. ***

B. *Procedural History of the Instant Litigation*

On January 22, 1977, Wyoming enacted § 1–1054.1, W.S.1957 (now § 1–37–106, W.S.1977), authorizing the State to commence system-wide adjudications of water rights. The State of Wyoming filed the complaint commencing this litigation and naming the United States as a defendant on January 24, 1977, in the District Court of the Fifth Judicial District of Wyoming. ***

The case was divided into three phases: Phase I, Indian reserved water rights (appeal decided here); Phase II, non-Indian federal reserved water rights (completed); and Phase III, state water rights evidenced by a permit or certificate (pending). ***

The special master signed his 451–page Report Concerning Reserved Water Right Claims by and on Behalf of the Tribes in the Wind River Reservation on December 15, 1982, covering four years of conferences and hearings, involving more than 100 attorneys, transcripts of more than 15,000 pages and over 2,300 exhibits.

The report recognized a reserved water right for the Wind River Indian Reservation and determined that the purpose for which the reservation had been established was a permanent homeland for the Indians. A reserved water right for irrigation, stock watering, fisheries, wildlife and aesthetics, mineral and industrial, and domestic, commercial, and municipal uses was quantified and awarded. ***

The State of Wyoming, the United States, the Shoshone and Arapahoe Tribes, and numerous private parties presented objections to the master's report, and on May 10, 1983, Judge Joffe entered his Findings of Fact, Conclusions of Law and Judgment approving that portion of the master's report awarding reserved water rights for practicably irrigable acreage within the Wind River Indian Reservation and refusing to accept that portion of the master's report recommending an award of reserved water rights for other than agricultural purposes. ***

III. IS THERE A RESERVED WATER RIGHT FOR THE WIND RIVER INDIAN RESERVATION?

***

B. *Was There an Intent to Reserve Water?*

Both the special master and the district court undertook the rigorous analysis called for by *United States v. New Mexico, supra* 438 U.S. at 700: "Each time this Court has applied the 'implied-reservation-of-water doctrine,' it has carefully examined both the asserted water right and the specific purposes for which the land was reserved, and concluded that without the water the purposes of the reservation would be entirely defeated." ***

The treaty establishing the Wind River Indian Reservation, signed on July 3, 1868, ratified on February 16, 1869, and proclaimed on February 24, 1869, Treaty of Ft. Bridger, 15 Stat. 673 (1869), is silent on the subject of water for the reservation. Yet both the district court and the special master found an intent to reserve water. We affirm. ***

***

IV. PURPOSES OF THE WIND RIVER INDIAN RESERVATION

*** We have already decided that Congress intended to reserve water for the Wind River Indian Reservation when it was created in 1868, and we accept the proposition that the amount of water impliedly reserved is determined by the purposes for which the reservation was created. ***

A. *The Treaty*

*** Considering the well-established principles of treaty interpretation, the treaty itself, the ample evidence and testimony addressed, and the findings of the district court, we have no difficulty affirming the finding that it was the intent at the time to create a reservation with a sole agricultural purpose. Indian treaties should be interpreted generously, and liberally in favor of the Indians, and should not be given a crabbed or restrictive meaning. Nor should treaties be improperly construed in favor of Indians ***. Article 7 of the treaty refers to "said agricultural reservations." Article 6 authorizes allotments for farming purposes; Article 8 provides seeds and implements for farmers; in Article 9 "the United States agreed to pay each Indian farming a $20 annual stipend, but only $10 to 'roaming' Indians"; and Article 12 establishes a $50 prize to the ten best Indian farmers. The treaty does not encourage any other occupation or pursuit. The district court correctly found that the reference in Article 4 to "permanent homeland" does nothing more than permanently set aside lands for the Indians; it does not define the purpose of the reservation. Rather, the purpose of the permanent-home reservation is found in Articles 6, 8, 9, and 12 of the treaty. ***

Although the treaty did not force the Indians to become farmers and although it clearly contemplates that other activities would be permitted (hunting is mentioned in Article 4, lumbering and milling in Article 3, roaming in Article 9), the treaty encouraged only agriculture, and that was its primary purpose.

B. *Fisheries*

Reserved water rights for fisheries have been recognized where a treaty provision explicitly recognized an exclusive right to take fish on the reservation or the right to take fish at traditional off-reservation fishing grounds, in common with others. Instream fishery flows have also been recognized where the Indians were heavily, if not totally, dependent on fish for their livelihood. *United States v. Adair, supra* 723 F.2d at 1409; *Colville Confederated Tribes v. Walton, supra* 647 F.2d at 48. In the case at bar, the Tribes introduced evidence showing that fish had always been part of the Indians' diet. The master, erroneously concluding that a reserved right for fisheries should be implied when the tribe is "at least partially dependent upon fishing," awarded an instream flow right for fisheries. The district court, however, finding neither a dependency upon fishing for a livelihood nor a traditional lifestyle involving fishing, deleted the award. The district court did not err. The evidence is not sufficient to imply a fishery flow right absent a treaty provision.

C. *Mineral and Industrial*

The Tribes were denied a reserved water right for mineral and industrial development. All parties to the treaty were well aware before it was signed of the valuable mineral estate underlying the Wind River Indian Reservation. The question of whether, because the Indians own the minerals, the intent was that they should have the water necessary to develop them must be determined, of course, by the intent in 1868. Neither the Tribes nor the United States has cited this court to any provision of the treaty or other evidence indicating that the parties contemplated in 1868 that a purpose of the reservation would be for the Indians to develop the minerals. The fact that the Tribes have since used water for mineral and industrial purposes does not establish that water was impliedly reserved in 1868 for such uses. The district court did not err in denying a reserved water right for mineral and industrial uses.

D. *Municipal, Domestic and Commercial*

A reserved water right for municipal, domestic and commercial uses was included within the agricultural reserved water award. Domestic and related use has traditionally been subsumed in agricultural reserved rights. *** The court properly allowed a reserved water right for municipal, domestic, and commercial use.

E. *Livestock*

For the reasons stated above, the district court did not err in finding a sole agricultural purpose for the reservation or in subsuming livestock use within that purpose.

F. *Wildlife and Aesthetics*

The special master awarded 60% of historic flows for wildlife and aesthetic uses, consistent with his determination that the purpose of the reservation was to be a permanent homeland. The district court deleted this award, reciting not only that the purpose was solely agricultural, but that insufficient evidence had been presented to justify an award for these uses. The district court did not err in holding that the Tribes and the United States did not introduce sufficient evidence of a tradition of wildlife and aesthetic preservation which would justify finding this to be a purpose for which the reservation was created and for which water was impliedly reserved.

The district court did not err in finding a sole agricultural purpose in the creation of the Wind River Indian Reservation. The Treaty itself evidences no other purpose, and none of the extraneous evidence cited is sufficient to attribute a broader purpose.

V. SCOPE OF THE RESERVED WATER RIGHT

A. *Groundwater*

The logic which supports a reservation of surface water to fulfill the purpose of the reservation also supports reservation of groundwater. *** Acknowledging the above, we note that, nonetheless, not a single case applying the reserved water doctrine to groundwater is cited to us. *** The district court did not err in deciding there was no reserved groundwater right.

***

VI. QUANTIFICATION

A. *The Measure*

The measure of the Tribes' reserved water right is the water necessary to irrigate the practicably irrigable acreage on the reservation. In *Arizona v. California, supra* 373 U.S. at 600–601, a needs test was rejected as too uncertain, the Court opting instead for practicably irrigable acreage as the measure of a tribal agricultural reserved water right. Two subsequent non-Indian reserved water right cases, *Cappaert v. United States, supra* 426 U.S. 128 and *United States v. New Mexico, supra* 438 U.S. at 702, indicate that necessity is the measure of a reserved water right. *** The district court was correct in quantifying the Tribes' reserved water right by the amount of water necessary to irrigate all of the reservation's practicably irrigable acreage.

B. *Future Lands*

The Tribes and the United States claimed a reserved water right for lands on the reservation not yet developed for irrigation, but which were in their view, practicably irrigable acreage. Counsel for the State, the Tribes and the United States agreed upon a definition of practicably irrigable acreage: "those acres susceptible to sustained irrigation at reasonable costs." The determination of practicably irrigable acreage involves a two-part analysis, *i.e.*, the PIA must be susceptible of sustained irrigation (not only proof of the arability but also of the engineering feasibility of irrigating the land) and irrigable "at reasonable cost."

The United States presented evidence on all these factors to support its ultimate claim for 53,760 practicably irrigable acres (210,000 acre-feet/year)[.]

*** The Amended Judgment and Decree corrected the Riverton East figure by reducing it to 3,019 acres, which resulted in the total final award being 48,097 acres.

1. Arability

Over Wyoming's objection that the land classes did not consider economic factors and were not sufficiently specific, the master adopted this system:

Class 1: Class 1 lands are of high quality for irrigation, and will yield high returns with minimum production and management costs.

Class 2: Class 2 lands are good quality with only minor deficiencies.

Class 3: Class 3 consists of fair quality lands having more serious deficiencies than Class 2 lands.

Class 4: Class 4 lands are of marginal quality for irrigation and are used mainly for shallow-rooted crops or pasture.

Class 5: Class 5 lands are those lands which have been placed into a deferred status pending further investigation. There were no lands included in a deferred status.

Class 6: Class 6 lands do not meet the minimum requirements for arability under the land classification standards used.

The land classification system was first utilized to determine all arable acres. The arable acreage was then analyzed from an engineering standpoint. The resulting irrigable acres were then subjected to stringent economic analysis, including cropping pattern and crop yield analysis. The economic analysis requirement was satisfied. Wyoming proposed no alternative land classification system. We approve the system adopted by the master, finding it reasonable and fair to the parties. ***

2. Engineering Feasibility

The State next attacks the design work of Dr. Woldzion Mesghinna, the United States' irrigation engineer, because he had never before designed a system for Wyoming lands and because none of the systems he had designed were yet operational. *** The master praised Mesghinna's thorough work and found him not only credible, but "detached from any preconceived estimates of what should be the result." *** The special master, after weighing the testimony, accepted Dr. Mesghinna's climate work and found that it satisfied "any burden of the United States to prove the climate base for the engineering feasibility analysis. The State does not shift the burden back merely by asserting that greater efforts could have been made in the data collection." Credibility of the witness was for the trier of fact, and the master found the witness credible and his data reliable; we accept that finding. ***

3. Economic Feasibility

[The court determined that the United States had demonstrated the economic feasibility of irrigating 48,097 acres.]

C. *Historic Lands*

The district court awarded a reserved water right for 54,216 practicably irrigable acres currently and/or historically irrigated on the reservation, defining five types of historic lands:

(a) Adjudicated trust lands are lands with an uncancelled state permit or certificate of appropriation;

(b) Unadjudicated but currently irrigated trust lands are those being irrigated at the time of trial, but not carrying a state permit or certificate;

(c) Type VII trust lands are those previously irrigated but currently idle or retired;

(d) Type VIII trust lands are undeveloped arable lands, not currently irrigated but irrigable from existing canals (*i.e.*, within or near project areas); and

(e) Indian fee lands are those owned in fee by individual Indians.

*** [T]he master took evidence on arability, engineering feasibility and economic feasibility and found the United States' evidence to be "competent, generally convincing, and in most cases adequate in supporting Federal claims." As to the Tribes' claims for Indian fee land, the master found the evidence showed the land awarded a reserved water right to be PIA. The evidence the master accepted was different from evidence used to prove PIA for the future projects but it was sufficient to meet the stipulated definition of PIA. ***

[The priority date was properly set as 1868.]

THOMAS, JUSTICE, dissenting with whom **HANSCUM, DISTRICT JUDGE**, joins.

The purpose of establishing an Indian reservation, such as the Wind River Indian Reservation, is to provide a homeland for Indian peoples. If one is to assume that, pursuant to the reserved rights doctrine relating to water, there is an implied reservation of those waters essential to accomplish the purpose of the reservation of land, then I cannot agree that the implied reservation of water with respect to the Wind River Indian Reservation should be limited, as the majority has held in approving the judgment of the district court. The fault that I find with such a limitation is that it assumes that the Indian peoples will not enjoy the same style of evolution as other people, nor are they to have the benefits of modern civilization. I would understand that the homeland concept assumes that the homeland will not be a static place frozen in an instant of time but that the homeland will evolve and will be used in different ways as the Indian society develops. For that reason, I would hold that the implied reservation of water rights attaching to an Indian reservation assumes any use that is appropriate to the Indian homeland as it progresses and develops. The one thing that I would not assume is that using the reserved water as a salable commodity was contemplated in connection with the implied reservation of the water. I would limit its use to the territorial boundaries of the reservation.

Deeming it unnecessary to detail further the formula for allocation of water which involves the concept of practicably irrigable acreage (*Arizona v. California,* 460 U.S. 605 (1983)), I am convinced that there has to be some degree of pragmatism in determining practicably irrigable acreage. It is clear from the majority opinion that there was included in quantifying the water reserved to the Indian peoples lands not now irrigable but deemed to be practicably irrigable acreage upon the assumption of the development of future irrigation projects. I would be appalled, as most other concerned citizens should be, if the Congress of the United States, or any other governmental body, began expending money to develop water projects for irrigating these Wyoming lands when far more fertile lands in the midwestern states now are being removed from production due to poor market conditions. I am convinced that, because of this pragmatic concern, those lands which were included as practicably irrigable acreage, based upon the assumption of the construction of a future irrigation project, should not be included for the purpose of quantification of the Indian peoples' water rights. They may be irrigable academically, but not as a matter of practicality, and I would require their exclusion from any quantification. ***

HANSCUM, DISTRICT JUDGE, dissenting.

I join in the dissent. Specifically, I would agree with the dissent's proposed holding that the implied reservation of water rights attaching to an Indian reservation should assume any use that is appropriate to the Indian homeland as it progresses and develops.

I depart, however, when Justice Thomas proposes to limit water use to the territorial boundaries of the reservation, thus precluding marketability of the water. Justice Thomas would hold that, as a matter of law, marketing water off the reservation never could be appropriate to the progress and development of the Indian homeland.

I disagree. I would go that additional step. I would hold that sale of water off the reservation should be permitted, provided that, as a factual matter, it could be demonstrated that such marketing contributed to the progress and development of the Indian homeland. I can envision a variety of scenarios where such showing could be made successfully. To preclude the opportunity of proving such a nexus unduly would restrict and hamper the prospective development of the Indian homeland in the future.

IN RE THE GENERAL ADJUDICATION OF ALL RIGHTS TO USE WATER IN THE GILA RIVER SYSTEM AND SOURCE

35 P.3d 68 (Ariz. 2001)

ZLAKET, CHIEF JUSTICE.

***

PROCEDURAL HISTORY

In its September 1988 decision, the trial court stated that each Indian reservation [in the Gila River system] was entitled to

> such water as is necessary to effectuate the purpose of that reservation. While as to other types of federal lands courts have allowed controversy about what the purpose of the land is and how much water will satisfy that purpose, as to Indian reservations the courts have drawn a clear and distinct line. It is that the amount is measured by the amount of water necessary to irrigate all of the *practicably irrigable acreage* (PIA) on that reservation. ***

Generally, the "purpose of a federal reservation of land defines the scope and nature of impliedly reserved water rights." *United States v. Adair,* 723 F.2d 1394, 1419 (9th Cir.1983). However, when applying the *Winters* doctrine, it is necessary to distinguish between Indian and non-Indian reservations.

The government may exercise total dominion over water rights on federal non-Indian lands. *State of Montana ex rel. Greely v. Confederated Salish & Kootenai Tribes,* 712 P.2d 754, 767 (1985) ("[T]he United States can lease, sell, quitclaim, release, encumber or convey its own federal reserved water rights."). But unlike those attached to Indian lands, which have reserved water rights for "future needs and changes in use," *id.,* non-Indian reserved rights are narrowly quantified to meet the original, primary purpose of the reservation; water for secondary purposes must be acquired under state law. Thus, the primary purpose for which the federal government reserves non-Indian land is strictly construed after careful examination. The test for determining such a right is clear.

> For each federal claim of a reserved water right, the trier of fact must examine the documents reserving the land from the public domain and the underlying legislation authorizing the reservation; determine the precise federal purposes to be served by such legislation; determine whether water is essential for the primary purposes of the reservation; and finally determine the precise quantity of water—the minimal need *** required for such purposes.

Greely, 712 P.2d at 767 (quoting *United States v. City & County of Denver,* 656 P.2d 1, 20 (Colo. 1983)).

Indian reservations, however, are different. In its role as trustee of such lands, the government must act for the Indians' benefit. *See United States v. Mitchell,* 463 U.S. 206, 225–26, (1983). This fiduciary relationship is referred to as "one of the primary cornerstones of Indian law." Felix S. Cohen, Handbook of Federal Indian Law 221 (1982). Thus, treaties, statutes, and executive orders are construed liberally in the Indians' favor. *County of Yakima v. Confederated Tribes & Bands of the Yakima Indian Nation,* 502 U.S. 251, 269 (1992) (citations omitted). Such an approach is equally applicable to the federal government's actions with regard to water for Indian reservations. "The purposes of Indian reserved rights *** are given broader interpretation in order to further the federal goal of Indian self sufficiency."

The parties dispute the purposes of the several Indian reservations involved in this case. The United States and the tribal litigants argue that federal case law has preemptively determined that every Indian reservation was established as a permanent tribal homeland. The state litigants disagree, contending instead that the trial court must analyze each tribe's treaty or enabling documentation to determine that reservation's individual purpose. We need not decide whether federal case law has preemptively determined the issue. We agree with the Supreme Court that the essential purpose of Indian reservations is to provide Native American people with a "permanent home and abiding place," *Winters,* 207 U.S. at 565 that is, a "livable" environment.

While courts may choose to examine historical documents in determining the purpose and reason for creating a federal reservation on non-Indian lands, the utility of such an exercise with respect to Indian reservations is highly questionable.[2] This is so for a variety of reasons.

First, as pointed out by the state litigants, many Indian reservations were pieced together over time. For example, the boundaries of the Gila River Indian Community changed ten times from its creation in 1859 until 1915, resulting in overall growth from 64,000 to 371,422 acres. But some of the changes along the way actually decreased the size of the reservation or limited the scope of previous additions. If these alterations had different purposes, as the state litigants suggest, it might be argued that water reserved to a specific parcel could not be utilized elsewhere on the same reservation, or that water once available could no longer be accessed. Such an arbitrary patchwork of water rights would be unworkable and inconsistent with the concept of a permanent, unified homeland.

*** It is well known that in the nineteenth century, the federal government made conflicting promises. On one hand, it offered white settlers free land, an abundance of resources, and safety if they would travel to and inhabit the West. The government also assured Indians that they would be able to live on their lands in peace. The promises to the tribes were not kept. *** As recognized by former Arizona Congressman Morris K. Udall, the federal government "can be kindly described as having been less than diligent in its efforts to secure sufficient water supplies for the [Indian] community to develop its arable lands and achieve meaningful economic self-sufficiency and self-determination." 134 Cong. Rec. E562–02 (Mar. 8, 1988) (statement of Rep. Udall).

---

2. One commentator, in fact, suggests that "the effort to inform the quantification of federal [Indian] reserved rights with historical considerations is futile and should be abandoned." Martha C. Franks, *The Uses of the Practicably Irrigable Acreage Standard in the Quantification of Reserved Water Rights,* 31 Nat. Resources J. 549, 563 (1991). While we generally agree with this observation, we believe that tribal history may play an important role in quantifying the amount of water necessary to fulfill an Indian reservation's purpose as a permanent homeland.

*** Limiting an Indian reservation's purpose to agriculture, as the PIA standard implicitly does,

> assumes that the Indian peoples will not enjoy the same style of evolution as other people, nor are they to have the benefits of modern civilization. I would understand that the homeland concept assumes that the homeland will not be a static place frozen in an instant of time but that the homeland will evolve and will be used in different ways as the Indian society develops.

In re General Adjudication of All Rights to Use Water in the Big Horn River System, 753 P.2d 76, 119 (Wyo.1988) (Thomas, J., dissenting); *see also Walton* 647 F.2d at 47 (stating that courts consider Indians' "need to maintain themselves under changed circumstances" when determining a reservation's purpose).[4]

Other right holders are not constrained in this, the twenty-first century, to use water in the same manner as their ancestors in the 1800s. Although over 40% of the nation's population lived and worked on farms in 1880, less than 5% do today. U.S. Census Bureau, *Historical Statistics of the United States, Colonial Times to 1970,* 240, 457 (1975). Likewise, agriculture has steadily decreased as a percentage of our gross domestic product. *See* U.S. Census Bureau, *Statistical Abstract of the United States,* 881, 886 (1999) (demonstrating that agricultural output as a percentage of GDP has declined from 10.7% in 1930 to 2.84% in 1997). Just as the nation's economy has evolved, nothing should prevent tribes from diversifying their economies if they so choose and are reasonably able to do so. The permanent homeland concept allows for this flexibility and practicality. We therefore hold that the purpose of a federal Indian reservation is to serve as a "permanent home and abiding place" to the Native American people living there.

C. Primary–Secondary Purpose Test

Next arises the question of whether the primary-secondary purpose test applies to Indian reservations. [The court held that the test did not apply because of the broad purposes in establishing Indian reservations.]

D. Quantifying Winters Rights

The *Winters* doctrine retains the concept of "minimal need" by reserving "only that amount of water necessary to fulfill the purpose of the reservation, no more." *Cappaert,* 426 U.S. at 141. The method utilized in arriving at such an amount, however, must satisfy both present and future needs of the reservation as a livable homeland. *See Arizona I,* 373 U.S. at 599–600.

E. The PIA Standard

The trial court in this matter held that each Indian reservation was entitled to "the amount of water necessary to irrigate all of the *practicably irrigable acreage* (P.I.A.) on that reservation." Order, *supra,* at 17 (emphasis in original). The PIA standard was developed by Special Master Rifkind in *Arizona I,* 373 U.S. 546 (1963). That case dealt with the water rights of similarly-situated

4. Even where reservations were created so that tribes could engage in agricultural pursuits, Congress only envisioned this as "a first step in the 'civilizing' process." *Walton,* 647 F.2d at 47 n. 9 (*citing* 11 Cong. Rec. 905 (1881)).

tribes in Arizona, California, and Nevada. Without much amplification, the Supreme Court declared:

> We also agree with the Master's conclusion as to the quantity of water intended to be reserved. He found that the water was intended to satisfy the future as well as the present needs of the Indian Reservations and ruled that enough water was reserved to irrigate all the practicably irrigable acreage on the reservations.

Id. at 600. Other courts have since adopted the PIA standard in quantifying reserved water rights for Indian tribes. *See Walton,* 647 F.2d at 47–48 (applying PIA "to provide a homeland for the Indians to maintain their agrarian society"); *Greely,* 712 P.2d at 764 (utilizing PIA to fulfill a reservation's agricultural purpose).

PIA constitutes "those acres susceptible to sustained irrigation at reasonable costs." *Big Horn I,* 753 P.2d at 101. This implies a two-step process. First, it must be shown that crops can be grown on the land, considering arability and the engineering practicality of irrigation. Second, the economic feasibility of irrigation must be demonstrated. *See generally Arizona v. California,* 460 U.S. 605 (1983) [*Arizona II*] (adopting the Special Master's PIA analysis requiring this methodology); Andrew C. Mergen & Sylvia F. Liu, *A Misplaced Sensitivity: The Draft Opinions in* Wyoming v. United States, 68 U. Colo. L. Rev. 683, 696 (1997) (acknowledging that, since *Arizona II,* the economic feasibility requirement in PIA analysis has "become the norm"). This is accomplished by subjecting proposed irrigation projects to a cost-benefit analysis, "comparing the likely costs of the project to the likely financial returns. If the latter outweighs the former, the project can be found economically feasible, and the underlying land 'practicably irrigable' ***." Franks, *supra,* at 553.

The United States and tribal litigants argue that federal case law has preemptively established PIA as the standard by which to quantify reserved water rights on Indian reservations. We disagree. As observed by Special Master Tuttle in his *Arizona II* report, "the Court did not necessarily adopt this standard as the universal measure of Indian reserved water rights. *** " *Id.* at 556 n. 40 (quoting Special Master's Report at 90 (Feb. 22, 1981)). Indeed, nothing in *Arizona I* or *II* suggests otherwise.

On its face, PIA appears to be an objective method of determining water rights. But while there may be some "value of the certainty inherent in the practicably irrigable acreage standard," *Big Horn I,* 753 P.2d at 101, its flaws become apparent on closer examination.

The first objection to an across-the-board application of PIA lies in its potential for inequitable treatment of tribes based solely on geographical location. Arizona's topography is such that some tribes inhabit flat alluvial plains while others dwell in steep, mountainous areas. This diversity creates a dilemma that PIA cannot solve. As stated by two commentators:

> There can be little doubt that the PIA standard works to the advantage of tribes inhabiting alluvial plains or other relatively flat lands adjacent to stream courses. In contrast, tribes inhabiting mountainous or other agriculturally marginal terrains are at a severe disadvantage when it comes to demonstrating that their lands are practicably irrigable.

Mergen & Liu, *supra,* at 695. Tribes who fail to show either the engineering or economic feasibility of proposed irrigation projects run the risk of not receiving any reserved water under PIA. *See, e.g., State ex rel. Martinez v. Lewis,* 861 P.2d 235, 246–51 (N.M Ct. App.1993) (denying water rights to the Mescalero Apache Tribe, situated in a mountainous region of southern New Mexico, for failure to prove irrigation projects were economically feasible). This inequity is unacceptable and inconsistent with the idea of a permanent homeland.

Another concern with PIA is that it forces tribes to pretend to be farmers in an era when "large agricultural projects *** are risky, marginal enterprises. This is demonstrated by the fact that no federal project planned in accordance with the Principles and Guidelines [adopted by the Water Resources Council of the Federal Government] has been able to show a positive benefit/cost ratio in the last decade [1981 to 1991]." Franks, *supra* note 2, at 578. A permanent homeland requires water for multiple uses, which may or may not include agriculture. The PIA standard, however, forces "tribes to prove economic feasibility for a kind of enterprise that, judging from the evidence of both federal and private willingness to invest money, is simply no longer economically feasible in the West." *Id.*

*** The PIA standard also potentially frustrates the requirement that federally reserved water rights be tailored to minimal need. Rather than focusing on what is necessary to fulfill a reservation's overall design, PIA awards what may be an overabundance of water by including every irrigable acre of land in the equation.

For the foregoing reasons, we decline to approve the use of PIA as the exclusive quantification measure for determining water rights on Indian lands.

F. Proper Factors for Consideration

Recognizing that the most likely reason for PIA's endurance is that "no satisfactory substitute has emerged," Dan A. Tarlock, *One River, Three Sovereigns: Indian and Interstate Water Rights,* 22 Land & Water L. Rev. 631, 659 (1987), we now enter essentially uncharted territory. In *Gila III,* this court stated that determining the amount of water necessary to accomplish a reservation's purpose is a "fact-intensive inquir[y] that must be made on a reservation-by-reservation basis." 195 *Arizona* at 420, 989 P.2d at 748. We still adhere to the belief that this is the only way federally reserved rights can be tailored to meet each reservation's minimal need.

When *Big Horn I* went before the Supreme Court, one of the present state litigants, in an amicus brief, argued that there should be a "balancing of a myriad of factors" in quantifying reserved water rights. *** During oral argument in the present case, counsel for the Apache tribes made a similar argument. Considering the objective that tribal reservations be allocated water necessary to achieve their purpose as permanent homelands, such a multi-faceted approach appears best-suited to produce a proper outcome.

Tribes have already used this methodology in settling water rights claims with the federal government. One feature of such settlements has been the development of master land use plans specifying the quantity of water necessary for different purposes on the reservation. *See, e.g.,* S. Rep. 101–479 (1990) (Fort McDowell Indian Community utilized a land use plan in conjunction with its water rights settlement based on agricultural production, commercial development, industrial use, residential use, recreational use, and wilderness).

While we commend the creation of master land use plans as an effective means of demonstrating water requirements, tribes may choose to present evidence to the trial court in a different manner. The important thing is that the lower court should have before it actual and proposed uses, accompanied by the parties' recommendations regarding feasibility and the amount of water necessary to accomplish the homeland purpose. In viewing this evidence, the lower court should consider the following factors, which are not intended to be exclusive.

A tribe's history will likely be significant. Deference should be given to practices requiring water use that are embedded in Native American traditions. Some rituals may date back hundreds of years, and tribes should be granted water rights necessary to continue such practices into the future. An Indian reservation could not be a true homeland otherwise.

In addition to history, the court should consider tribal culture when quantifying federally reserved rights. Preservation of culture benefits both Indians and non-Indians; for this reason, Congress has recognized the "unique values of Indian culture" in our society. 25 U.S.C. § 1902 (1994) (recognizing the importance of culture when placing Indian children in foster care); *see also* 20 U.S.C. § 7801 (1994) (finding that education should "build on Indian culture"). Water uses that have particular cultural significance should be respected, where possible. The length of time a practice has been engaged in, its nature (*e.g.*, religious or otherwise), and its importance in a tribe's daily affairs may all be relevant.

The court should also consider the tribal land's geography, topography, and natural resources, including groundwater availability. As mentioned earlier, one of the biggest problems with PIA is that it does not allow for flexibility in this regard. It has also been observed that "irrigation is one of the most inefficient and ecologically damaging ways to use water. *** [I]ncreasing the use of water for irrigation runs counter to a historic trend in western water use—the transition from agricultural to less consumptive and higher-valued municipal and industrial uses." This does not mean that tribes are prohibited from including agriculture/irrigation as part of their development plans. However, future irrigation projects are subject to a PIA-type analysis: irrigation must be both practically and economically feasible. Tribes should be free to develop their reservations based on the surroundings they inhabit. We anticipate that any development plan will carefully consider natural resources (including potential water uses), so that the water actually granted will be put to its best use on the reservation.

In conjunction with natural resources, the court should look to a tribe's economic base in determining its water rights. Tribal development plans or other evidence should address, and the court should consider, "the optimal manner of creating jobs and income for the tribes [and] the most efficient use of the water. *** " Economic development and its attendant water use must be tied, in some manner, to a tribe's current economic station. Physical infrastructure, human resources, including the present and potential employment base, technology, raw materials, financial resources, and capital are all relevant in viewing a reservation's economic infrastructure.

Past water use on a reservation should also be considered when quantifying a tribe's rights. The historic use of water may indicate how a tribe has valued it. Logically, tribal prioritization of past water use will affect its future development. For example, a tribe that has never used water to irrigate is less likely to successfully and economically develop irrigation projects in the future. This does not mean that Indians may not use their water allocations for new purposes on a reservation. However, any proposed projects should be scrutinized to insure that they are practical and economical. Such projects should also be examined to determine that they are, in fact, appropriate to a particular homeland.

While it should never be the only factor, a tribe's present and projected future population may be considered in determining water rights. We recognize that the Supreme Court has rejected any quantification standard based solely on the "number of Indians." *Arizona II,* 460 U.S. at 617. However, if a federally reserved water right is to be tailored to a reservation's "minimal need," as we believe it must, then population necessarily must be part of the equation. To act without regard to population would ignore the fact that water will always be used, most importantly, for human needs. Therefore, the number of humans is a necessary element in quantifying water rights. Such consideration is not at odds with the need to satisfy tribes' "future as well as *** present needs." *Arizona I,* 373 U.S. at 600. Population forecasts are common in today's society and are recognized and relied upon by the legal system. It is therefore proper to use population evidence in conjunction with other factors in quantifying a tribe's *Winters* rights.

The state litigants argue that courts should act with sensitivity toward existing state water users when quantifying tribal water rights. *** They claim that this is necessary because when a water source is fully appropriated, there will be a gallon-for-gallon decrease in state users' water rights due to the tribes' federally reserved rights. *See Arizona II,* 460 U.S. at 621. When an Indian reservation is created, the government impliedly reserves water to carry out its purpose as a permanent homeland. *See Winters,* 207 U.S. at 566–67, 577. The court's function is to determine the amount of water necessary to effectuate this purpose, tailored to the reservation's minimal need. We believe that such a minimalist approach demonstrates appropriate sensitivity and consideration of existing users' water rights, and at the same time provides a realistic basis for measuring tribal entitlements.

Again, the foregoing list of factors is not exclusive. The lower court must be given the latitude to consider other information it deems relevant to determining tribal water rights. We require only that proposed uses be reasonably feasible. As with PIA, this entails a two-part analysis. First, development projects need to be achievable from a practical standpoint—they must not be pie-in-the-sky ideas that will likely never reach fruition. Second, projects must be economically sound. When water, a scarce resource, is put to efficient uses on the reservation, tribal economies and members are the beneficiaries.

CONCLUSION

We wish it were possible to dispose of this matter by establishing a bright line standard, easily applied, in order to relieve the lower court and the parties of having to engage in the difficult, time-consuming process that certainly lies ahead. Unfortunately, we cannot. ***

IN RE CSRBA (CASE NO. 49576), UNITED STATES OF AMERICA AND COEUR D'ALENE TRIBE

448 P.3d 322 (Idaho 2019)

STEGNER, JUSTICE.

These four appeals arise from a consolidated subcase that is a part of the broader Coeur d'Alene-Spokane River Basin Adjudication (CSRBA). The United States Department of the Interior (the United States), as trustee for the Coeur d'Alene Tribe (the Tribe), filed 353 claims in Idaho state court seeking judicial recognition of federal reserved water rights to fulfill the purposes of the Coeur d'Alene Tribe's Reservation (the Reservation). The Tribe joined the litigation. The State of Idaho (the State) and others objected to the claims asserted by the United States and the Tribe. The district court bifurcated the proceedings to decide only the entitlement to water at this stage, with the quantification stage to follow. After cross-motions for summary judgment, the district court allowed certain claims to proceed and disallowed others.

The district court specifically allowed reserved water rights for agriculture, fishing and hunting, and domestic purposes. The district court allowed reserved water rights for instream flows within the Reservation, but disallowed those for instream flows outside the Reservation. The district court disallowed other claims, including a claim on behalf of the Tribe to maintain the level of Lake Coeur d'Alene. The district court then determined priority dates for the various claims it found should proceed to quantification. Generally speaking, the district court held that the Tribe was entitled to a date-of-reservation priority date for the claims for consumptive uses, and a time immemorial priority date for nonconsumptive uses.

I. FACTUAL AND PROCEDURAL BACKGROUND

A. History of the Tribe and the Reservation.

In its summary judgment order, the district court adopted the history of the Tribe and the creation of the Reservation as set out by the United States Supreme Court in *Idaho v. United States* (hereafter *Idaho II*), 533 U.S. 262, 121 S. Ct. 2135, 150 L.Ed.2d 326 (2001). That history, as articulated by the U.S. Supreme Court, is as follows:

> The Coeur d'Alene Tribe once inhabited more than 3.5 million acres in what is now northern Idaho and northeastern Washington, including the area of Lake Coeur d'Alene and the St. Joe River. Tribal members traditionally used the lake and its related waterways for food, fiber, transportation, recreation, and cultural activities. The Tribe depended on submerged lands for everything from water potatoes harvested from the lake to fish weirs and traps anchored in riverbeds and banks.
>
> ... In 1867, in the face of immigration into the Tribe's aboriginal territory, President Johnson issued an Executive Order setting aside a reservation of comparatively modest size, although the Tribe was apparently unaware of this action until at least 1871, when it petitioned [Tribe's 1872 Petition] the Government to set aside a reservation. The Tribe found the 1867 boundaries unsatisfactory, due in part to their failure to make

adequate provision for fishing and other uses of important waterways. When the Tribe petitioned the Commissioner of Indian Affairs a second time, it insisted on a reservation that included key river valleys because "we are not as yet quite up to living on farming" and "for a while yet we need [to] have some hunting and fishing."

Following further negotiations, the Tribe in 1873 agreed to relinquish (for compensation) all claims to its aboriginal lands outside the bounds of a more substantial reservation that negotiators for the United States agreed to "set apart and secure" "for the exclusive use of the Coeur d'Alene Indians, and to protect ... from settlement or occupancy by other persons." The reservation boundaries described in the agreement covered part of the St. Joe River (then called the St. Joseph), and all of Lake Coeur d'Alene except a sliver cut off by the northern boundary.

Although by its own terms the agreement was not binding without congressional approval, later in 1873 President Grant issued an Executive Order directing that the reservation specified in the agreement be "withdrawn from sale and set apart as a reservation for the Coeur d'Alene Indians." The 1873 Executive Order set the northern boundary of the reservation directly across Lake Coeur d'Alene ....

As of 1885, Congress had neither ratified the 1873 agreement nor compensated the Tribe. This inaction prompted the Tribe to petition the Government again [Tribe's 1885 Petition], to "make with us a proper treaty of peace and friendship ... by which your petitioners may be properly and fully compensated for such portion of their lands not now reserved to them; [and] that their present reserve may be confirmed to them." In response, Congress authorized new negotiations to obtain the Tribe's agreement to cede land outside the borders of the 1873 reservation. In 1887, the Tribe agreed to cede

> "all right, title, and claim which they now have, or ever had, to all lands in said Territories [Washington, Idaho, and Montana] and elsewhere, except the portion of land within the boundaries of their present reservation in the Territory of Idaho, known as the Coeur d'Alene Reservation."

The Government, in return, promised to compensate the Tribe, and agreed that

> "[i]n consideration of the foregoing cession and agreements ... the Coeur d'Alene Reservation shall be held forever as Indian land and as homes for the Coeur d'Alene Indians ... and no part of said reservation shall ever be sold, occupied, open[ed] to white settlement, or otherwise disposed of without the consent of the Indians residing on said reservation."

As before, the agreement was not binding on either party until ratified by Congress.

In January 1888, not having as yet ratified any agreement with the Tribe, the Senate expressed uncertainty about the extent of the Tribe's reservation and adopted a resolution directing the Secretary of the Interior to "inform the Senate as to the extent of the present area and boundaries of the Coeur d'Alene Indian Reservation in the Territory of Idaho,"

> and specifically, "whether such area includes any portion, and if so, about how much of the navigable waters of Lake Coeur d'Alene, and of Coeur d'Alene and St. Joseph Rivers." The Secretary responded in February 1888 with a report of the Commissioner of Indian Affairs, stating that "the reservation appears to embrace all the navigable waters of Lake Coeur d'Alene, except a very small fragment cut off by the north boundary of the reservation," and that "[t]he St. Joseph River also flows through the reservation." ...
>
> ....
>
> Congress was not prepared to ratify the 1887 agreement, however, owing to a growing desire to obtain for the public not only any interest of the Tribe in land outside the 1873 reservation, but certain portions of the reservation itself. ...
>
> But Congress did not simply alter the 1873 boundaries unilaterally. Instead, the Tribe was understood to be entitled beneficially to the reservation as then defined, and the 1889 Indian Appropriations Act included a provision directing the Secretary of the Interior "to negotiate with the Coeur d'Alene tribe of Indians," and, specifically, to negotiate "for the purchase and release by said tribe of such portions of its reservation not agricultural and valuable chiefly for minerals and timber as such tribe shall consent to sell." Later that year, the Tribe and Government negotiators reached a new agreement under which the Tribe would cede the northern portion of the reservation, including approximately two-thirds of Lake Coeur d'Alene, in exchange for $500,000. The new boundary line, like the old one, ran across the lake, and General Simpson, a negotiator for the United States, reassured the Tribe that "you still have the St. Joseph River and the lower part of the lake." And, again, the agreement was not to be binding on either party until both it and the 1887 agreement were ratified by Congress.
>
> ....
>
> ... On March 3, 1891, Congress "accepted, ratified, and confirmed" both the 1887 and 1889 agreements with the Tribe.

Idaho II, 533 U.S. at 265-71, 121 S. Ct. 2135 (citations and footnotes omitted).

***

Federal reservations and accompanying reserved water rights may be created by executive order. ***

The United States Supreme Court and Ninth Circuit have held that the Coeur d'Alene Reservation was established by the 1873 Executive Order. *E.g., Idaho II,* 533 U.S. at 277, 279, 121 S. Ct. 2135; *Idaho v. Andrus,* 720 F.2d 1461, 1463 (9th Cir. 1983). The district court also found the Reservation was created by President Grant's Executive Order of November 8, 1873. We conclude the district court's finding in this regard was correct.

***

D. The purposes of the Tribe's Reservation.

1. The district court erred by applying the primary-secondary purpose distinction set out in *New Mexico.*

***

[In *United States v. New Mexico*, 438 U.S. 696 (1979) the Supreme Court ruled that National Forests are only entitled to reserved water in order to satisfy the "primary purposes" of the reservation. eds.] Because *New Mexico* did not involve an Indian reservation, at least two state supreme courts have found *New Mexico's* primary-secondary analysis inapplicable to Indian water rights cases. ***

First, the two rights have different origins. *Id.* Non-Indian "[f]ederal reserved water rights are created by the document that reserves the land from the public domain. By contrast, aboriginal-Indian reserved water rights exist from time immemorial and are merely recognized by the document that reserves the Indian land." *Id.*

Second, Montana found ownership to be an important distinction. *Id.* "The United States is not the owner of Indian reserved rights; it is a trustee for the benefit of the" tribes. *Id.* In contrast, the United States owns federal reserved rights in all other reservations and has the power to "lease, sell, quitclaim, release, encumber or convey its own federal reserved water rights." *Id.* Bearing these distinctions in mind, the Montana court held that Indian rights "are given broader interpretation in order to further the federal goal of Indian self-sufficiency." *Id.* at 768.

Similarly, the Supreme Court of Arizona held that Indian reservations should be distinguished from non-Indian reservations. *Gila V,* 35 P.3d at 77. *Gila V,* specifically disavowed Wyoming's application of the primary-secondary analysis in *Big Horn III. Id.* That court reasoned "[W]hile the purpose for which the federal government reserves other types of lands may be strictly construed, the purposes of Indian reservations are necessarily entitled to broader interpretation if the goal of Indian self-sufficiency is to be attained." *Id.* (quoting William C. Canby, Jr., *American Indian Law* 245-46 (1981)). While recognizing the same differences identified by the Supreme Court of Montana, Arizona identified others as well. *Gila V,* 35 P.3d at 74. One such difference is that, in the context of Indian reservations, the government, as trustee of such lands, must act for the Indians' benefit. *Id.* "Thus, treaties, statutes, and executive orders are construed liberally in the Indians' favor." *Gila V,* 35 P.3d at 74 (citing *Yakima Indian Nation,* 502 U.S. at 269, 112 S. Ct. 683).

The reasons given by the Montana and Arizona courts are persuasive as to why the purposes of Indian reservations should not be construed similarly to non-Indian federal reservations. Even more to the point, the primary-secondary distinction runs counter to the concept that the purpose of many Indian reservations was to establish a "home and abiding place" for the tribes. *Winters.,* 207 U.S. at 565, 28 S. Ct. 207. This leads to the consideration of a broader purpose that has been termed the homeland purpose theory, which is more consistent with both Supreme Court precedent and the well-established canons of construction regarding Indian reservations. Notably, the Ninth Circuit appears to have endorsed a homeland purpose theory but still used the *New Mexico* primary-secondary distinction when analyzing reservation purposes. *See Agua Caliente,* 849 F.3d at 1269. Notwithstanding the somewhat contradictory Ninth Circuit precedent, we find the homeland purpose theory is better suited to an Indian reservation. We are unpersuaded *New Mexico* and its primary-secondary analysis should apply to Indian Reservations.

b. *The homeland purpose theory should be recognized when established by the formative documents.*

The district court reasoned that utilization of the homeland purpose theory could be so expansive, that it would be "difficult to conceive a beneficial use of water that would not serve the expansive concept of 'the homeland.' " We share the district court's concerns; however, when viewed in the proper context, the homeland purpose theory is not without limits. The tenets of construction instead confine the homeland purpose theory to the parameters contemplated at the time surrounding the Reservation's creation and which are supported by the formative documents and circumstances. *See Arizona I,* 373 U.S. at 600, 83 S. Ct. 1468 ("[T]he United States did reserve the water rights for the Indians effective as of the time the Indian Reservations were created."); *Agua Caliente,* 849 F.3d at 1270 (Purposes are derived from "the documents] and circumstances surrounding [a reservation's] creation ...."). Moreover, the Supreme Court has announced that Indian reserved water rights are limited by the "necessity" requirement. *See New Mexico,* 438 U.S. at 700, 98 S. Ct. 3012 (citing *Arizona I,* 373 U.S. at 600-01, 83 S. Ct. 1468; *Winters,* 207 U.S. at 567, 28 S. Ct. 207).

***

[T]he general purpose of the Reservation was to provide a homeland for the Tribe and that purpose "is a broad one and must be liberally construed." *Agua Caliente,* 849 F.3d at 1270 (quoting *Walton I,* 647 F.2d at 47). The homeland purpose may require water for multiple uses or included purposes. *Gila V,* 35 P.3d at 78. Given the analysis thus far and the language of the Reservation's formative documents, the following uses or included purposes will be recognized as involving water rights: consumptive uses for both domestic (including groundwater) and agriculture; and nonconsumptive uses for hunting (wildlife habitat), fishing (fish habitat), plant gathering (including seeps and springs), and cultural activities—so long as they can be established as aboriginal uses (i.e., uses of water predating the creation of the Reservation).

***

F. The district court correctly concluded the Tribe's water rights include instream flows on the Reservation.

The United States claimed nonconsumptive water rights for the Tribe both within and outside of the Reservation boundaries to maintain the Tribe's fishery. Those claimed rights inside the Reservation include claims on both tribal and non-tribal-owned lands. For clarity, it is best to understand this dispute as involving three concentric circles. The innermost circle involves claimed water rights on Reservation property owned by the Tribe or members of the Tribe. Claims within this first circle are not at issue in these appeals. The middle circle includes claimed water rights to the instream flows within the Reservation, but on lands that neither the Tribe nor members of the Tribe own. These were allowed by the district court and that decision has been appealed by the State. The outermost circle involves claims for instream flows on non-tribal-owned land off of the Reservation. The United States and the Tribe claim an entitlement to these off-Reservation instream flows to enhance stream habitat and fish stocks to satisfy their on-Reservation fishing purpose. These outermost claims were rejected by the district court and that decision has been appealed by the United States and the Tribe.

[The Court next determined that when the Tribe agreed to convey all "right, title and claim which they now have or ever had" to the United States in an 1891 Act of Congress, it surrendered any right to off-reservation instream flow rights. eds.]

***

Here, the Tribe's expert, Dr. Dudley Reiser, has opined that upstream habitat is necessary for the health of Lake Coeur d'Alene's adfluvial fisheries. The instream flows claimed, both on and off the Reservation, are tied to the Tribe's fishing on tribal-owned lands on the Reservation. The fish species that the Tribe has historically fished, the Westslope Cutthroat Trout and Bull Trout, are adfluvial species. These species spend a significant part of their lives in Lake Coeur d'Alene, but spawn by migrating upstream and downstream in rivers and streams located both on and off the Reservation. These spawning areas are quite expansive within the Coeur d'Alene Basin. Fish can travel more than a hundred miles in search of spawning grounds.

The federal reserved water rights doctrine, as recognized in *Winters*, allows the United States to reserve waters "appurtenant" to federally reserved lands in order to fulfill the purposes of the reservation. *Cappaert*, 426 U.S. at 138, 96 S. Ct. 2062 (the government "reserves *appurtenant water* then unappropriated to the extent needed to accomplish the purpose of the reservation." (italics added)). However, the United States Supreme Court has never defined "appurtenant" in regards to a reserved water right.

Generally, "appurtenant" does not mean physical adjacency. *See John v. United States*, 720 F.3d 1214, 1229 (9th Cir. 2013). Rather, "[a]ppurtenancy has to do with the relationship between reserved federal land and the use of the water, not the location of the water." *Id.* at 1230 (alteration in original). This Court recognized that appurtenance is not dependent upon a "physical relationship" with the land. *See Joyce Livestock Co. v. United States*, 144 Idaho 1, 12, 156 P.3d 502, 514 (2007).

***

In sum, the district court correctly determined the entitlement to instream water rights. The Tribe is entitled to water rights on the Reservation. In the nomenclature previously used, this involves the two innermost concentric circles. The Tribe is entitled to control instream flows on the Reservation whether the land physically adjacent to the water is owned by the Tribe or not. However, the Tribe is not entitled to instream flows that are off of the Reservation. Those rights were extinguished when the Tribe conveyed all "right, title and claim which they now have or ever had" to the United States in the 1891 Act of Congress. 26 Stat. at 1027. As a result, the district court did not err in deciding the Tribe had an entitlement to instream water flows on the Reservation and in deciding the Tribe did not have an entitlement to off-Reservation instream flows.

NOTES AND QUESTIONS

1. *Consistency with Supreme Court precedent?* Which decision—*Adair*, *Wind River*, *Coeur d'Alene*, or *Gila River*—is more consistent with *Winters* and *Arizona v. California*? Which is better as a matter of policy? Which is more

likely to result in a workable legal standard? The Supreme Court agreed to examine the Wyoming Supreme Court's ruling on the PIA standard, but ended up affirming on a 4–4 vote. *Wyoming v. United States,* 492 U.S. 406 (1989). Justice O'Connor had drafted a majority opinion for the Court that would have reversed what she viewed as an overly-generous application of the PIA standard. Before the opinion was issued, however, it was discovered that Justice O'Connor had a conflict of interest that required her recusal from the matter. The Wyoming Supreme Court's decision was thus affirmed without opinion. *See* Andrew C. Mergen & Sylvia F. Liu, *A Misplaced Sensitivity: The Draft Opinions in* Wyoming v. United States, 68 U. Colo. L. Rev. 683 (1997) (draft majority and dissenting opinions reprinted as appendix).

2. *Moderate living standard?* How would you (or your expert) determine how much water is necessary in a given case to provide a tribe, first, with a moderate standard of living from fisheries, hunting and gathering as set out in the *Adair* case; and second, with only enough water to sustain such a moderate living?

3. *Theory of a new case.* If you were a lawyer representing a tribe in a water rights adjudication today, how would you structure your claims? What sort of a team would you want to assist you in determining what claims to file? Would you answer be different if you were in Arizona state court? What if you were in a federal court in Arizona?

4. *Change in use.* Changes in the place of use or nature of use under state law typically require a water right holder to seek the approval of the state administrative agency with regulatory authority over water use. *See* Robert E. Beck, Waters and Water Rights, § 14 (3rd Ed. 2009). The Supreme Court approved a stipulation permitting water reserved for agricultural purposes to be used for other purposes. *Arizona v. California,* 439 U.S. 419, 422 (1979); *see also United States v. Anderson,* 736 F.2d 1358, 1365 (9th Cir. 1984) (irrigation water may be used to augment instream flows). The Wyoming Supreme Court rejected the Wind River Reservation Tribes' proposed change in use from irrigation to instream flows without compliance with state law. *In re General Adjudication of the Big Horn River Sys.,* 835 P.2d 273 (Wyoming 1992). Why should state law govern the use of water rights established under federal law?

Note on Instream Flows for Fisheries

The United States Supreme Court has never weighed in on the issue of reserved rights for instream flows to protect Indian hunting, fishing and gathering rights. In *Cappaert v. United States,* 426 U.S. 128 (1976) the Court held that the United States impliedly reserved water for Devil's Hole, an underground pool containing desert pupfish, when President Truman added it to Death Valley National Monument in 1952. 66 Stat. 17. The federal government demonstrated that the groundwater pumping was lowering the level of the pool so as to endanger the fish. The Supreme Court approved an injunction limiting groundwater pumping that diminished the underground pool.

The Idaho Supreme Court in *Coeur d'Alene*, and the 9th circuit in *Adair* have provided the most complete analysis of tribal instream flow and lake level rights. The Idaho Supreme Court rejected federal and tribal claims to water for instream flows at off-reservation fisheries habitat but recognized such rights on-reservation without regard to land ownership (there is a considerable amount of non-Indian land on the reservation due to allotment). If off-reservation water withdrawals are limiting the amount of water needed for on-reservation instream flow rights, should the Tribe be able to limit the junior off-reservation uses? The *Cappaert* precedent makes the answer appear to be yes. Should the most junior right holder be limited first, or should diverters closest to the reservation be curtailed first? Would that be a question of state or federal law?

The Supreme Court of Washington has acknowledged the existence of Indian reserved rights to instream flows. *Dep't. of Ecology v. Yakima Reservation Irrigation Dist.*, 850 P.2d 1306, 1317 (Wash. 1993) ("Water to fulfill the fishing rights under the treaty may be found to have been reserved, if fishing was a primary purpose of the reservation."). On remand, the trial court explicitly held that the Yakama Nation's instream flow right extended off the reservation to support usual and accustomed fisheries. *In the Matter of the Determination of the Rights to the Use of Surface Waters of the Yakima River Drainage Basin*, No. 77–2–01484–5, Final Order Re: Treaty Reserved Water Rights at Usual and Accustomed Fishing Places at 3–4 (Yakima Sup. Ct. March 1, 1995); *In the Matter of the Determination of the Rights to the Use of Surface Waters of the Yakima River Drainage Basin*, No. 77–2–01484–5, Memorandum Opinion: Treaty Reserved Water Rights at Usual and Accustomed Fishing Places, Yakima Sup. Ct., Sept. 1, 1994. *See also Joint Board of Control of Flathead Irrigation Dist. v. United States*, 832 F.2d 1127, 1132 (9th Cir. 1987):

> The action of the BIA in establishing stream flow and pool levels necessary to protect tribal fisheries is not unreviewable. In making its determination, however, the BIA is acting as trustee for the Tribes. Because any aboriginal fishing rights secured by treaty are prior to all irrigation rights, neither the BIA nor the Tribes are subject to a duty of fair and equal distribution of reserved fishery waters. Only after fishery waters are protected does the BIA, acting as Officer-in-Charge of the irrigation project, have a duty to distribute fairly and equitably the *remaining* waters among irrigators of equal priority.

See also, United States v. Anderson, 591 F. Supp. 1, 5 (E.D. Wash. 1982), *aff'd in part & rev'd in part*, 736 F.2d 1358 (9th Cir. 1984) (water reserved to maintain favorable temperature conditions to support fishery); *Kittitas Reclamation Dist. v. Sunnyside Valley Irr. Dist.*, 763 F.2d 1032 (9th Cir. 1985) (court acted appropriately in ordering release of water to protect habitat for treaty fishery.

In *Baley v. United States*, 134 Fed.Cl. 619 (2017) the United States successfully defended a Fifth Amendment takings claim by irrigators who did not receive contract water from a Bureau of Reclamation project. The water was needed to support senior Indian reserved rights for fisheries habitat in the Klamath River, so that the junior state irrigation rights were not entitled to deliveries. The case is on appeal to the Federal Circuit.

Yurok tribal attorneys and fisheries staff on Blue Creek near its confluence with the Klamath River. Photograph by Robert Anderson.

III. STATE JURISDICTION AND MODERN ADJUDICATIONS

As demonstrated in the chapters about state-tribal jurisdiction, the general rule is that states lack regulatory and adjudicatory jurisdiction over tribes and tribal property within Indian country. Of course, Congress has power to grant jurisdiction to the states and their courts. In 1953 a statute known as the McCarran Amendment became law:

> Consent is hereby given to join the United States as a defendant in any suit (1) for the adjudication of rights to the use of water of a river system or other source, or (2) for the administration of such rights, where it appears that the United States is the owner of or is in the process of acquiring water rights by appropriation under State law, by purchase, by exchange, or otherwise, and the United States is a necessary party to such suit. The United States, when a party to any such suit, shall (1) be deemed to have waived any right to plead that the State laws are inapplicable or that the United States is not amenable thereto by reason of its sovereignty, and (2) shall be subject to the judgments, orders, and decrees of the court having jurisdiction, and may obtain review thereof, in the same

manner and to the same extent as a private individual under like circumstances: *Provided*, That no judgment for costs shall be entered against the United States in any such suit.

43 U.S.C. § 666.

While the statute does not mention federal reserved rights in general or Indian reserved water rights, it has been broadly construed by the Supreme Court to permit joinder of the United States and the inclusion of Indian water rights. *See Colo. River Conservation Dist. v. United States*, 424 U.S. 800 (1976) (state courts have authority to adjudicate federal reserved rights). However, the proceeding must be a comprehensive adjudication of all water right holders in a river system—state and federal. *Dugan v. Rank*, 372 U.S. 609, 618–19 (1963). As you read the following cases, consider whether the Supreme Court is faithful to the Indian law canons of construction. For a comprehensive review of the McCarran Amendment and general stream adjudications see John E. Thorson *et al.*, *Dividing Western Waters: A Century of Adjudicating Rivers and Streams*, 8 U. Denv. Water L. Rev. 355, 449–58 (2005) and John E. Thorson *et al.*, *Dividing Western Waters: A Century of Adjudicating Rivers and Streams, Part II*, 9 U. Denv. Water L. Rev. 299 (2006).

ARIZONA V. SAN CARLOS APACHE TRIBE

463 U.S. 545, 103 S. Ct. 3201, 77 L.Ed.2d 837 (1983)

JUSTICE BRENNAN delivered the opinion of the Court.

These consolidated cases form a sequel to our decision in *Colorado River Conservation District v. United States,* 424 U.S. 800 (1976). That case held that (1) the McCarran Amendment, 43 U.S.C. § 666, which waived the sovereign immunity of the United States as to comprehensive state water rights adjudications, provides state courts with jurisdiction to adjudicate Indian water rights held in trust by the United States, and (2) in light of the clear federal policies underlying the McCarran Amendment, a water rights suit brought by the United States in federal court was properly dismissed in favor of a concurrent comprehensive adjudication reaching the same issues in Colorado state court. The questions in this case are parallel: (1) What is the effect of the McCarran Amendment in those States which, unlike Colorado, were admitted to the Union subject to federal legislation that reserved "absolute jurisdiction and control" over Indian lands in the Congress of the United States? (2) If the courts of such States do have jurisdiction to adjudicate Indian water rights, should concurrent federal suits brought by Indian tribes, rather than by the United States, and raising only Indian claims, also be subject to dismissal under the doctrine of *Colorado River?* ***

II.

The two petitions considered here arise out of three separate consolidated appeals that were decided within three days of each other by the same panel of the Court of Appeals for the Ninth Circuit. In each of the underlying cases, either the United States as trustee or certain Indian tribes on their own behalf, or both, asserted the right to have certain Indian water rights in Arizona or Montana adjudicated in federal court.

The Montana Cases (No. 81–2188)

In January 1975, the Northern Cheyenne Tribe brought an action in the United States District Court for the District of Montana seeking an adjudication of its rights in certain streams in that State. Shortly thereafter, the United States brought two suits in the same Court, seeking a determination of water rights both on its own behalf and on behalf of a number of Indian Tribes, including the Northern Cheyenne, in the same streams. Each of the federal actions was a general adjudication which sought to determine the rights *inter sese* of *all* users of the stream, and not merely the rights of the plaintiffs. On motion of the Northern Cheyenne, its action was consolidated with one of the Government actions. The other concerned Tribes intervened as appropriate.

At about the time that all this activity was taking place in federal court, the State of Montana was preparing to begin a process of comprehensive water adjudication under a recently passed state statute. In July 1975, the Montana Department of Natural Resources and Conservation filed petitions in state court commencing comprehensive proceedings to adjudicate water rights in the same streams at issue in the federal cases.

Both sets of contestants having positioned themselves, nothing much happened for a number of years. The federal proceedings were stayed for a time pending our decision in *Colorado River*. When that decision came down, the State of Montana, one of the defendants in the federal suits, brought a motion to dismiss, which was argued in 1976, but not decided until 1979. Meanwhile, process was completed in the various suits, answers were submitted, and discovery commenced. Over in the state courts, events moved even more slowly, and no appreciable progress seems to have been made by 1979.

In April 1979, the United States brought four more suits in federal court, seeking to adjudicate its rights and the rights of various Indian tribes in other Montana streams. One month later, the Montana legislature amended its water adjudication procedures "to expedite and facilitate the adjudication of existing water rights." Act to Adjudicate Claims of Existing Water Rights in Montana, § 1(1), 1979 Mont. Laws 1901. The legislation provided for the initiation of comprehensive proceedings by order of the Montana Supreme Court, the appointment of water judges throughout the State, and the consolidation of all existing actions within each water division. It also provided, among other things, that the Montana Supreme Court should issue an order requiring all claimants not already involved in the state proceedings, including the United States on its own behalf or as trustee for the Indians, to file a statement of claim with the Department of Natural Resources and Conservation by a date set by the court or be deemed to have abandoned any water rights claim. *Id.*, § 16, 1979 Mont. Laws, at 1906–1907, codified at Mont. Code Ann. § 85–2–212 (1981). The Montana court issued the required order, and the United States was served with formal notice thereof. ***

The Arizona Cases (No. 81–2147)

In the mid–1970s, various water rights claimants in Arizona filed petitions in state court to initiate general adjudications to determine conflicting rights in a number of river systems. In early 1979, process was served in one of the proceedings on approximately 12,000 known potential water claimants, including the United States. In July 1981, process was served in another proceeding on approximately 58,000 known water claimants, again including the United States. In each case, the United States was joined both in its independent capacity and as trustee for various Indian tribes.

In March and April of 1979, a number of Indian tribes whose rights were implicated by the state water proceedings filed a series of suits in the United States District Court for the District of Arizona, asking variously for removal of the state adjudications to federal court, declaratory and injunctive relief preventing any further adjudication of their rights in state court, and independent federal determinations of their water rights. A number of defendants in the federal proceedings filed motions seeking remand or dismissal. The District Court, relying on *Colorado River,* remanded the removed actions, and dismissed most of the independent federal actions without prejudice. 484 F. Supp. 778 (D. Ariz. 1980). *** The Court of Appeals reversed, holding that the Enabling Act under which Arizona was admitted to statehood, 36 Stat. 557 (1910), and the Arizona Constitution, Art. 20, ¶ 4, both of which contain wording substantially identical to the Montana Enabling Act and Constitution, disabled Arizona from adjudicating Indian water claims. ***

We granted certiorari, in order to resolve a conflict among the circuits regarding the role of federal and state courts in adjudicating Indian water rights. We now reverse.

III. A.

At the outset of our analysis, a number of propositions are clear. First, the federal courts had jurisdiction here to hear the suits brought both by the United States and the Indian tribes. Second, it is also clear in this case, as it was in *Colorado River,* that a dismissal or stay of the federal suits would have been improper if there was no jurisdiction in the concurrent state actions to adjudicate the claims at issue in the federal suits. ***

Finally, it should be obvious that, to the extent that a claimed bar to state jurisdiction in these cases is premised on the respective state Constitutions, that is a question of state law over which the state courts have binding authority. Because, in each of these cases, the state courts have taken jurisdiction over the Indian water rights at issue here, we must assume, until informed otherwise, that—at least insofar as state law is concerned—such jurisdiction exists. We must therefore look, for our purposes, to the federal enabling acts and other federal legislation, in order to determine whether there is a federal bar to the assertion of state jurisdiction in these cases. *** [W]e are convinced that, whatever limitation the Enabling Acts or federal policy may have originally placed on state court jurisdiction over Indian water rights, those limitations were removed by the McCarran Amendment. ***

IV.

The second crucial issue in these cases is whether our analysis in *Colorado River* applies with full force to federal suits brought by Indian tribes, rather than by the United States, and seeking adjudication only of Indian water rights. *** The United States and the various Indian respondents raise a series of arguments why dismissal or stay of the federal suit is not appropriate when it is brought by an Indian tribe and only seeks to adjudicate Indian rights. (1) Indian rights have traditionally been left free of interference from the States. (2) State courts may be inhospitable to Indian rights. (3) The McCarran

Amendment, although it waived United States sovereign immunity in state comprehensive water adjudications, did not waive *Indian* sovereign immunity. It is therefore unfair to force Indian claimants to choose between waiving their sovereign immunity by intervening in the state proceedings and relying on the United States to represent their interests in state court, particularly in light of the frequent conflict of interest between Indian claims and other federal interests and the right of the Indians under 28 U.S.C. § 1362 to bring suit on their own behalf in federal court.[17] (4) Indian water rights claims are generally based on federal rather than state law. (5) Because Indian water claims are based on the doctrine of "reserved rights," and take priority over most water rights created by state law, they need not as a practical matter be adjudicated *inter sese* with other water rights, and could simply be incorporated into the comprehensive state decree at the conclusion of the state proceedings.

Each of these arguments has a good deal of force. We note, though, that very similar arguments were raised and rejected in *Eagle County* and *Colorado River*. More important, all of these arguments founder on one crucial fact: If the state proceedings have jurisdiction over the Indian water rights at issue here, as appears to be the case, then concurrent federal proceedings are likely to be duplicative and wasteful, generating "additional litigation through permitting inconsistent dispositions of property." *Colorado River,* 424 U.S., at 819. Moreover, since a judgment by either court would ordinarily be *res judicata* in the other, the existence of such concurrent proceedings creates the serious potential for spawning an unseemly and destructive race to see which forum can resolve the same issues first—a race contrary to the entire spirit of the McCarran Amendment and prejudicial, to say the least, to the possibility of reasoned decision making by either forum. The United States and many of the Indian tribes recognize these concerns, but in responding to them they cast aside the sort of sound argument generally apparent in the rest of their submissions and rely instead on vague statements of faith and hope. The United States, for example, states that adjudicating Indian water right rights in federal court, despite the existence of a comprehensive state proceeding, would not

> entail any duplication or potential for inconsistent judgments. The federal court will quantify the Indian rights only if it is asked to do so before the State court has embarked on the task. And, of course, once the United States district court has indicated its determination to perform that limited role, *we assume* the State tribunal will turn its attention to the typically more complex business of adjudicating all other claims on the stream. *In the usual case,* the federal court will have completed its function earlier and its quantification will simply be incorporated in the comprehensive State court decree.

Brief for the United States 30 (emphasis added).

---

17. This argument, of course, suffers from the flaw that, although the McCarran Amendment did not waive the sovereign immunity of Indians as *parties* to state comprehensive water adjudications, it did (as we made quite clear in *Colorado River*) waive sovereign immunity with regard to the Indian *rights* at issue in those proceedings. Moreover, contrary to the submissions by certain of the parties, any judgment against the United States, as trustee for the Indians, would ordinarily be binding on the Indians. In addition, there is no indication in these cases that the state courts would deny the Indian parties leave to intervene to protect their interests. Thus, although the Indians have the right to refuse to intervene even if they believe that the United States is not adequately representing their interests, the practical value of that right in this context is dubious at best.

Similarly, the Navajo Nation states:

> There is no reasonably foreseeable danger that [the federal action brought by the Navajo] will duplicate or delay state proceedings or waste judicial resources. While the Navajo claim proceeds in federal court, the state court *can* move forward to assess, quantify, and rank the 58,000 state claims. The Navajo federal action will be concluded long before the state court has finished its task.

Brief for the Navajo Nation 22 (emphasis added; footnote omitted).

The problem with these scenarios, however, is that they assume a cooperative attitude on the part of state courts, state legislatures, and state parties which is neither legally required nor realistically always to be expected. The state courts need not "turn their attention" to other matters if they are prompted by state parties to adjudicate the Indian claims first. Moreover, considering the specialized resources and experience of the state courts, it is not at all obvious that the federal actions "will be concluded long before" the state courts have issued at least preliminary judgments on the question of Indian water rights.

The McCarran Amendment, as interpreted in *Colorado River,* allows and encourages state courts to undertake the task of quantifying Indian water rights in the course of comprehensive water adjudications. Although adjudication of those rights in federal court instead might in the abstract be practical, and even wise, it will be neither practical nor wise as long as it creates the possibility of duplicative litigation, tension and controversy between the federal and state forums, hurried and pressured decisionmaking, and confusion over the disposition of property rights. ***

V.

Nothing we say today should be understood to represent even the slightest retreat from the general proposition we expressed so recently in *New Mexico v. Mescalero Apache Tribe*: "Because of their sovereign status, [Indian] tribes and their reservation lands are insulated in some respects by an 'historic immunity from state and local control,' *Mescalero Apache Tribe v. Jones,* 411 U.S. 145, 152 (1973), and tribes retain any aspect of their historical sovereignty not 'inconsistent with the overriding interests of the National Government.' *Washington v. Confederated Tribes,* [447 U.S. 134, 153 (1980)]." Nor should we be understood to retreat from the general proposition, expressed in *Colorado River,* that federal courts have a "virtually unflagging obligation *** to exercise the jurisdiction given them." 424 U.S., at 817. But water rights adjudication is a virtually unique type of proceeding, and the McCarran Amendment is a virtually unique federal statute, and we cannot in this context be guided by general propositions.

We also emphasize, as we did in *Colorado River,* that our decision in no way changes the substantive law by which Indian rights in state water adjudications must be judged. State courts, as much as federal courts, have a solemn obligation to follow federal law. Moreover, any state court decision alleged to abridge Indian water rights protected by federal law can expect to receive, if brought for review before this Court, a particularized and exacting scrutiny commensurate with the powerful federal interest in safeguarding those rights from state encroachment.

The judgment of the Court of Appeals in each of these cases is reversed and the cases are remanded for further proceedings consistent with this opinion.

JUSTICES STEVENS, BLACKMUN and **MARSHALL** dissented.

NOTES AND QUESTIONS

1. *Federal courts still available?* What options does an Indian tribe have now if it wishes to quantify its water rights? Can it go to federal court on its own? State court? Must the United States be a party to any such case? What are the advantages and disadvantages of these approaches? Remember that states have sovereign immunity from suit, which is protected by the Eleventh Amendment. How would you deal with that obstacle?

For a contested Indian reserved rights case heard in federal court over state objections, see *United States v. Adair*, 723 F.2d 1394, 1398–1407 (9th Cir. 1983):

> In September of 1975, the United States filed suit in federal district court seeking a declaration of water rights within the Williamson River drainage above the "reef" near Kirk, Oregon. In January of 1976, the State of Oregon initiated formal proceedings under state law to determine water rights in the Klamath Basin including that portion of the Williamson River drainage covered by the Government's suit. Later in 1976, the State of Oregon moved to intervene as a defendant in the United States suit. The Klamath Tribe also moved to intervene in the federal suit as a plaintiff. Both motions were granted. Subsequently, the State, joined by the individual defendants, moved for dismissal of the federal court water rights adjudication in favor of the state proceeding under the rule announced by the Supreme Court in *Colorado River Water Conservation District v. United States.* *** [By the time the federal court reached the merits of the case, there had been virtually no activity in the state court proceeding.]
>
> The district court limited its exercise of jurisdiction to a determination of the priority among federal water rights on lands roughly within the boundaries of the former Klamath Indian Reservation. It did not undertake a general stream adjudication. Proceeding in this fashion, it avoided the duplication of any state water rights adjudication and, we think, the pitfalls of piecemeal determination of water rights. In fact, the district court considered those factors identified as "secondary" in *Colorado River, see* 424 U.S. at 820, and found, correctly we think, that they did not counsel dismissal. Under these circumstances we cannot say that the district court abused its discretion. Because the district court had statutory jurisdiction to act as it did, and because we believe it would be an exercise in unwise and wasteful judicial administration inconsistent with the Supreme Court's decision in *San Carlos Apache Tribe* to vacate and cast aside the district court's carefully considered judgment in these matters, we proceed to a review of the merits of the district court's decision.

The remainder of the *Adair* decision is reprinted in Section 2 above. Do you think the result would have been the same in state court? Can you see differences between *Adair* and the *Wind River* and *Gila River* cases above, in which state courts dealt with similar questions of the purposes for which water was reserved?

2. *Form and scope of McCarran Amendment adjudications.* Under current interpretations of the McCarran Amendment, states usually control the procedures governing water rights adjudications. Tribes and the United States challenged Oregon's General Stream Adjudication procedure as falling below McCarran Amendment standards. The procedures were as follows:

> Upon petition by a claimant, or on its own initiative, the Oregon Water Resources Department [OWRD] may commence the adjudication of the rights of all claimants to a river or stream. Notice must be given to all interested parties. Those claimants who have already been issued water certificates through the permit system are not required to participate in the adjudication in order to preserve their rights as already determined. However, those with undetermined claims to the water of the system are required to appear and submit proof of their claims before the OWRD. The OWRD accepts claims and objections to claims, surveys the river system, takes evidence and holds hearings regarding contested claims. After these hearings, the OWRD makes findings of fact and an order determining the parties' water rights. This order is effective upon issuance unless a party wishes to contest the order and files a bond. After the order is filed, a judicial hearing is scheduled and notice of that hearing is given to the participants. Parties objecting to the department's order must file written exceptions with the court in order to preserve their objections. If no objections are filed, the court must enter a judgment affirming the order. Otherwise, a hearing is held at which contesting parties may offer evidence as in a normal civil case. The court may remand the case to the OWRD or other referee for further findings, followed by another judicial hearing. At the final judicial hearing, the court reviews the exceptions and then enters a judgment affirming or modifying the order as it considers proper. This judgment is appealable to the Oregon Court of Appeals in the same manner as any other civil judgment.

United States v. State of Oregon, 44 F.3d 758, 764 (9th Cir. 1994).

Oregon's adjudication excluded groundwater rights and post–1909 water right holders. The United States and the Klamath Tribes argued that the proceeding was neither "comprehensive" nor an "adjudication" within the meaning of the McCarran Amendment. Both arguments were rejected by the court of appeals.

When the Tribes sought Supreme Court review, the United States told the Supreme Court: "1. Petitioner [Tribes] correctly criticizes the court of appeals' reasoning that Oregon may require the United States to participate in its administrative proceedings. *** 2. Petitioner also correctly criticizes the court of appeals' ruling that Oregon's adjudication is sufficiently comprehensive to satisfy the McCarran Amendment. *** The United States agrees with petitioner that the judgment of the court of appeals conflicts with the rules properly governing joinder of the United States and the Indian Tribes in state water right adjudications under the McCarran Amendment. Further review of the issues raised here, however, does not appear warranted at this time." The Supreme Court followed the federal recommendation and refused to hear the case. What could the reasons be for the United States to oppose review of a decision it thought was wrongly decided?

3. *Utility and fairness of general stream adjudications.* The Supreme Court found that the McCarran amendment included tribal water rights in part because the Court believed this would serve judicial economy and finality in water litigation. Some reports suggest that this has not been the result of state adjudication:

> [T]here are frequent indications that tribes, the United States, and the states are weary of the fray and are beginning to question the incredible outlay of resources required for such massive adjudications. For example, in Arizona, the parties have struggled for the last ten to fifteen years just to establish a procedure to deal with the complexities of the federal rights of the United States and Indian tribes.

Scott B. McElroy & Jeff J. Davis, *Revisiting* Colorado River Water Conservation District v. United States—*There Must Be a Better Way*, 27 Ariz. St. L.J. 597, 600 (1995). For a sense of some of the inefficiencies, think about the typical state court docket, composed of family law, criminal, tort and commercial cases. How and when will an overloaded state court judge acquire the necessary expertise to do justice to a multi-year, multi-party water rights adjudication? Some states are better equipped than others to address these problems. Colorado, for example, has specialized water courts. Yet Colorado only has two Indian tribes within its borders, whereas Arizona has twenty-one.

4. General stream adjudications are very expensive and time-consuming, and few have been commenced in the past 20 years. Idaho's attempt to collect over $10,000,000 in filing fees from the United States was rejected by the Supreme Court. The Court ruled that while "the McCarran Amendment submits the United States generally to state adjective law, as well as to state substantive law of water rights, we do not believe it subjects the United States to the payment of the sort of fees that Idaho sought to exact here." *United States v. Idaho ex rel. Dir., Idaho Dep't of Water Res.*, 508 U.S. 1, 8 (1993).

5. Indian tribes have long been wary of bias against them in state courts. For an insightful discussion of the issue by a Justice of the Colorado Supreme Court see Gregory J. Hobbs, Jr., *State Water Politics Versus an Independent Judiciary: The Colorado and Idaho Experiences*, 5 U. Denv. Water L. Rev. 122, 122 (2001):

> A great privilege of being a state supreme court justice is the opportunity to author an important water opinion. It could also be one's last important opinion. Especially if the case involves a close, split decision of your court and you are up for reelection in a contested race.
>
> In May of 2000, Justice Cathy Silak lost reelection to the Idaho Supreme Court. In November of 1954, Chief Justice Mortimer Stone lost reelection to the Colorado Supreme Court. The unifying element of both defeats: each justice authored a decision with a one-vote-margin in favor of the United States in a highly contested water case.

IV. CONFLICTS OF INTEREST AND THE FEDERAL TRUST RESPONSIBILITY

As noted earlier in this chapter, the landmark *Winters* case coincided with the rise of the Bureau of Reclamation as the dominant force in water infrastructure in the west— resulting in over 60 years of dam and irrigation system construction for non-Indian irrigation and public works projects. as the next case illustrates, the federal government often deliberately or negligently ignored its trust responsibility to tribes. The result was that tribes had little opportunity to put water to use for agricultural or other homeland purposes, and their reserved rights to instream flows for fisheries habitat suffered greatly. As you will see, the Supreme Court rejected the justice department's attempt to rectify one instance of federal neglect. Is there another way to remediate the harm done?

NEVADA V. UNITED STATES

463 U.S. 110, 103 S. Ct. 2906, 77 L. Ed.2d 509 (1983)

REHNQUIST, JUSTICE.

In 1913 the United States sued to adjudicate water rights to the Truckee River for the benefit of the Pyramid Lake Indian Reservation and the planned Newlands Reclamation Project. Thirty-one years later, in 1944, the United States District Court for the District of Nevada entered a final decree in the case pursuant to a settlement agreement. In 1973 the United States filed the present action in the same court on behalf of the Pyramid Lake Indian Reservation seeking additional water rights to the Truckee River. The issue thus presented is whether the Government may partially undo the 1944 decree, or whether principles of *res judicata* prevent it, and the intervenor Pyramid Lake Paiute Tribe, from litigating this claim on the merits.

I

Nevada has, on the average, less precipitation than any other State in the Union. Except for drainage in the southeastern part of the State into the Colorado River, and drainage in the northern part of the State into the Columbia River, the rivers that flow in Nevada generally disappear into "sinks." Department of Agriculture Yearbook, *Climate and Man* (1941). The present litigation relates to water rights in the Truckee River, one of the three principal rivers flowing through west central Nevada. It rises in the High Sierra in Placer County, California, flows into and out of Lake Tahoe, and thence down the eastern slope of the Sierra Nevada mountains. It flows through Reno, Nevada, and after a course of some 120 miles debouches into Pyramid Lake, which has no outlet.

It has been said that Pyramid Lake is "widely considered the most beautiful desert lake in North America [and that its] fishery [has] brought it worldwide fame. A species of cutthroat trout *** grew to world record size in the desert lake and attracted anglers from throughout the world." S. Wheeler, The Desert Lake 90–92 (1967). The first recorded sighting of Pyramid Lake by non-Indians occurred in January of 1844 when Captain John C. Fremont and his party camped nearby. In his journal Captain Fremont reported that the Lake "broke upon our eyes like the ocean" and was "set like a gem in the mountains." 1 The Expeditions of John Charles Fremont 604–605 (1970). Commenting upon the fishery, as well as the Pyramid Lake Indians that his party was camping with, Captain Fremont wrote:

> An Indian brought in a large fish to trade, which we had the inexpressible satisfaction to find was a salmon trout; we gathered round him eagerly. The Indians were amused with our delight, and immediately brought in numbers; so that the camp was soon stocked. Their flavor was excellent—superior, in fact, to that of any fish I have ever known. They were of extraordinary size—about as large as the Columbia river salmon—generally from two to four feet in length.

Id., at 609.

When first viewed by Captain Fremont in early 1844, Pyramid Lake was some 50 miles long and 12 miles wide. Since that time the surface area of the Lake has been reduced by about 20,000 acres.

The origins of the cases before us are found in two historical events involving the Federal Government in this part of the country. First, in 1859 the Department of the Interior set aside nearly half a million acres in what is now western Nevada as a reservation for the area's Paiute Indians. In 1874 President Ulysses S. Grant by executive order confirmed the withdrawal as the Pyramid Lake Indian Reservation. The Reservation includes Pyramid Lake, the land surrounding it, the lower reaches of the Truckee River, and the bottom land alongside the lower Truckee.

Then, with the passage of the Reclamation Act of 1902, ch. 1093, 32 Stat. 388, the Federal Government was designated to play a more prominent role in the development of the West. That Act directed the Secretary of the Interior to withdraw from public entry arid lands in specified western States, reclaim the lands through irrigation projects, and then to restore the lands to entry pursuant to the homestead laws and certain conditions imposed by the Act itself. Accordingly, the Secretary withdrew from the public domain approximately 200,000 acres in western Nevada, which ultimately became the Newlands Reclamation Project. The Project was designed to irrigate a substantial area in the vicinity of Fallon, Nevada, with waters from both the Truckee and the Carson Rivers.

The Carson River, like the Truckee, rises on the eastern slope of the High Sierra in Alpine County, California, and flows north and northeast over a course of about 170 miles, finally disappearing into Carson sink. The Newlands Project accomplished the diversion of water from the Truckee River to the Carson River by constructing the Derby Diversion Dam on the Truckee River, and constructing the Truckee Canal through which the diverted waters would be transported to the Carson River. Experience in the early days of the Project indicated the necessity of a storage reservoir on the Carson River, and accordingly Lahontan Dam was constructed and Lahontan Reservoir behind that Dam was created. The combined waters of the Truckee and Carson Rivers impounded in Lahontan Reservoir are distributed for irrigation and related uses on downstream lands by means of lateral canals within the Newlands Reclamation Project.

Before the works contemplated by the Project went into operation, a number of private landowners had established rights to water in the Truckee River under Nevada law. The Government also asserted on behalf of the Indians of the Pyramid Lake Indian Reservation a reserved right under the so-called "implied-reservation-of-water" doctrine set forth in *Winters v. United States.* The United States therefore filed a complaint in the United States District Court for the District of Nevada in March, 1913, commencing what became known as the *Orr Ditch* litigation. The Government, for the benefit of both the Project and the Pyramid Lake Reservation, asserted a claim to 10,000 cubic feet of water per second for the Project and a claim to 500 cubic feet per second for the Reservation. The complaint named as defendants all water users on the Truckee River in Nevada. The Government expressly sought a final decree quieting title to the rights of all parties.

Following several years of hearings, a Special Master issued a report and proposed decree in July of 1924. The report awarded the Reservation an 1859 priority date in the Truckee River for 58.7 second feet and 12,412 acre feet annually of water to irrigate 3,130 acres of Reservation lands. The Project was awarded a 1902 priority date for 1,500 cubic feet per second to irrigate, to the extent the amount would allow, 232,800 acres of land within the Newlands Reclamation Project. In February of 1926 the District Court entered a temporary restraining order declaring the water rights as proposed by the Special Master. "One of the primary purposes" for entering a temporary order was to allow for an experimental period during which modifications of the declared rights could be made if necessary. App. to Nevada Petn. for Cert. at186.

Not until almost ten years later, in the midst of a prolonged drought, was interest stimulated in concluding the Orr Ditch litigation. Settlement negotiations were commenced in 1934 by the principal organizational defendants in the case, Washoe County Water Conservation District and the Sierra Pacific Power Co., and the representatives of the Project and the Reservation. The United States still acted on behalf of the Reservation's interests, but the Project was now under the management of the Truckee–Carson Irrigation District (TCID).[4] The defendants and TCID proposed an agreement along the lines of the temporary restraining order. The United States objected, demanding an increase in the Reservation's water rights to allow for the irrigation of an additional 2,745 acres of Reservation land. After some resistance, the Government's demand was accepted and a settlement agreement was signed on July 1, 1935. The District Court entered a final decree adopting the agreement on September 8, 1944. No appeal was taken. Thus, 31 years after its inception the *Orr Ditch* litigation came to a close.

On December 21, 1973 the Government instituted the action below seeking additional rights to the Truckee River for the Pyramid Lake Indian Reservation; the Pyramid Lake Paiute Tribe was permitted to intervene in support of the United States. The Government named as defendants all persons presently claiming water rights to the Truckee River and its tributaries in Nevada. The defendants include the defendants in the *Orr Ditch* litigation and their successors, approximately 3800 individual farmers that own land in the Newlands Reclamation Project, and the Truckee–Carson Irrigation District. The

4. The newly formed Truckee–Carson Irrigation District had assumed operational control of the Newlands Project pursuant to a contract entered into with the Government on December 18, 1926.

District Court certified the Project farmers as a class and directed TCID to represent their interests.

In its complaint the Government purported not to dispute the rights decreed in the *Orr Ditch* case. Instead, it alleged that *Orr Ditch* determined only the Reservation's right to "water for irrigation," not the claim now being asserted for "sufficient waters from the Truckee River [for] the maintenance and preservation of Pyramid Lake, [and for] the maintenance of the lower reaches of the Truckee River as a natural spawning ground for fish," App. to Nevada Petn. for Cert. at 155–156. The complaint further averred that in establishing the Reservation the United States had intended that the Pyramid Lake fishery be maintained. Since the additional water now being claimed is allegedly necessary for that purpose, the Government alleged that the executive order creating the Reservation must have impliedly reserved a right to this water.[7]

The defendants below asserted *res judicata* as an affirmative defense, saying that the United States and the Tribe were precluded by the *Orr Ditch* decree from litigating this claim. Following a separate trial on this issue, the District Court sustained the defense and dismissed the complaint in its entirety. ***

II

The Government opens the "Summary of Argument" portion of its brief by stating: "The court of appeals has simply permitted a reallocation of the water decreed in *Orr Ditch* to a single party—the United States—from reclamation uses to a Reservation use with an earlier priority. The doctrine of *res judicata* does not bar a single party from reallocating its water in this fashion. ***." We are bound to say that the Government's position, if accepted, would do away with half a century of decided case law relating to the Reclamation Act of 1902 and water rights in the public domain of the West.

It is undisputed that the primary purpose of the Government in bringing the *Orr Ditch* suit in 1913 was to secure water rights for the irrigation of land that would be contained in the Newlands Project, and that the Government was acting under the aegis of the Reclamation Act of 1902 in bringing that action. ***

In two leading cases, *Ickes v. Fox*, 300 U.S. 82 (1937), and *Nebraska v. Wyoming*, 325 U.S. 589, (1945), this Court has discussed the beneficial ownership of water rights in irrigation projects built pursuant to the Reclamation Act. In *Ickes v. Fox*, the Court said:

> Although the government diverted, stored and distributed the water, the contention of petitioner that thereby ownership of the water or water-rights became vested in the United States is not well founded.

7. Between 1920 and 1940 the surface area of Pyramid Lake was reduced by about 20,000 acres. The decline resulted in a delta forming at the mouth of the Truckee that prevented the fish indigenous to the Lake, the Lahontan cutthroat trout and the cui-ui, from reaching their spawning grounds in the Truckee River, resulting in the near extinction of both species. Efforts to restore the fishery have occurred since that time. Pyramid Lake has been stabilized for several years and, augmented by passage of the Washoe Project Act of 1956, ch. 809, § 4, 70 Stat. 777, the Lake is being restocked with cutthroat trout and cui-ui. Fish hatcheries operated by both the State of Nevada and the United States have been one source for replenishing the Lake. In 1976 the Marble Bluff Dam and Fishway was completed, enabling the fish to bypass the delta to their spawning grounds in the Truckee. Both the District Court and Court of Appeals observed that "these restoration efforts 'appear to justify optimism for eventual success.' "

> Appropriation was made not for the use of the government, but, under the Reclamation Act, for the use of the land owners; and by the terms of the law and of the contract already referred to, the water rights became the property of the land owners, wholly distinct from the property right of the government in the irrigation works. The government was and remains simply a carrier and distributor of the water (*ibid.*), with the right to receive the sum stipulated in the contracts as reimbursement for the cost of construction and annual charges for operation and maintenance of the works. As security therefor, it was provided that the government should have a lien upon the lands *and the water rights* appurtenent thereto—a provision which in itself imports that the water-rights belong to another than the lienor, that is to say, to the land owner.
>
> ***

In the light of these cases, we conclude that the Government is completely mistaken if it believes that the water rights confirmed to it by the *Orr Ditch* decree in 1944 for use in irrigating lands within the Newlands Reclamation Project were like so many bushels of wheat, to be bartered, sold, or shifted about as the Government might see fit. Once these lands were acquired by settlers in the Project, the Government's "ownership" of the water rights was at most nominal; the beneficial interest in the rights confirmed to the Government resided in the owners of the land within the Project to which these water rights became appurtenant upon the application of Project water to the land. ***

Both the briefs of the parties and the opinion of the Court of Appeals focus their analysis of *res judicata* on provisions relating to the relationship between private trustees and fiduciaries, especially those governing a breach of duty by the fiduciary to the beneficiary. While these undoubtedly provide useful analogies in a case such as this, they cannot be regarded as finally dispositive of the issues. This Court has long recognized "the distinctive obligation of trust incumbent by the Government" in its dealings with Indian tribes, *see, e.g., Seminole Nation v. United States*, 316 U.S. 286, 296 (1942). These concerns have been traditionally focused on the Bureau of Indian Affairs within the Department of the Interior.

But Congress in its wisdom, when it enacted the Reclamation Act of 1902, required the Secretary of the Interior to assume substantial obligations with respect to the reclamation of arid lands in the western part of the United States. Additionally, *** Congress provided for the inclusion of irrigable lands of the Pyramid Lake Indian Reservation within the Newlands Project, and further authorized the Secretary, after allotting five acres of such land to each Indian belonging to the Reservation, to reclaim and dispose of the remainder of the irrigable Reservation land to settlers under the Reclamation Act.

Today, *** it may well appear that Congress was requiring the Secretary of the Interior to carry water on at least two shoulders when it delegated to him both the responsibility for the supervision of the Indian tribes and the commencement of reclamation projects in areas adjacent to reservation lands. But Congress chose to do this, and it is simply unrealistic to suggest that the Government may not perform its obligation to represent Indian tribes in litigation when Congress has obliged it to represent other interests as well. In this regard, the Government cannot follow the fastidious standards of a private fiduciary, who would breach his duties to his single beneficiary solely by representing potentially conflicting interests without the beneficiary's consent. The Government does not "compromise" its obligation to one interest that Congress obliges it to represent by the mere fact that it simultaneously performs another task for another interest that Congress has obligated it by statute to do.

With these observations in mind, we turn to the principles of *res judicata* that we think are involved in this case.

III

*** Simply put, the doctrine of *res judicata* provides that when a final judgment has been entered on the merits of a case, "[i]t is a finality as to the claim or demand in controversy, concluding parties and those in privity with them, not only as to every matter which was offered and received to sustain or defeat the claim or demand, but as to any other admissible matter which might have been offered for that purpose." The final "judgment puts an end to the cause of action, which cannot again be brought into litigation between the parties upon any ground whatever."

To determine the applicability of *res judicata* to the facts before us, we must decide first if the "cause of action" which the Government now seeks to assert is the "same cause of action" that was asserted in *Orr Ditch;* we must then decide whether the parties in the instant proceeding are identical to or in privity with the parties in *Orr Ditch.* We address these questions in turn.

A

Definitions of what constitutes the "same cause of action" have not remained static over time. *** We find it unnecessary in this case to parse any minute differences which these differing tests might produce, because whatever standard may be applied the only conclusion allowed by the record in the *Orr Ditch* case is that the Government was given an opportunity to litigate the Reservation's entire water right to the Truckee, and that the Government intended to take advantage of that opportunity. ***

While the Government focuses more specifically on the Tribe's reliance on fishing in this later complaint, it seems quite clear to us that they are asserting the same reserved right for purposes of "fishing" and maintenance of "lands and waters" that was asserted in *Orr Ditch.*

B

Having decided that the cause of action asserted below is the same cause of action asserted in the *Orr Ditch* litigation, we must next determine which of the parties before us are bound by the earlier decree. As stated earlier, the general rule is that a prior judgment will bar the "parties" to the earlier lawsuit, "and those in privity with them," from relitigating the cause of action.

There is no doubt but that the United States was a party to the *Orr Ditch* proceeding, acting as a representative for the Reservation's interests and the interests of the Newlands Project, and cannot relitigate the Reservation's "implied-reservation-of-water" rights with those who can use the *Orr Ditch* decree as a defense. We also hold that the Tribe, whose interests were represented in *Orr Ditch* by the United States, can be bound by the *Orr Ditch* decree.[14] This

14. We, of course, do not pass judgment on the quality of representation that the Tribe received. In 1951 the Tribe sued the Government before the Indian Claims Commission for damages,

Court left little room for an argument to the contrary in *Heckman v. United States*, 224 U.S. 413 (1912), where it plainly said that "it could not, consistently with any principle, be tolerated that, after the United States on behalf of its wards had invoked the jurisdiction of its courts *** these wards should themselves be permitted to relitigate the question." We reaffirm that principle now.

It is so ordered.

JUSTICE BRENNAN, concurring.

The mere existence of a formal "conflict of interest" does not deprive the United States of authority to represent Indians in litigation, and therefore to bind them as well. If, however, the United States actually causes harm through a breach of its trust obligations the Indians should have a remedy against it. I join the Court's opinion on the understanding that it reaffirms that the Pyramid Lake Paiute Tribe has a remedy against the United States for the breach of duty that the United States has admitted.

In the final analysis, our decision today is that thousands of small farmers in northwestern Nevada can rely on specific promises made to their forebears two and three generations ago, and solemnized in a judicial decree, despite strong claims on the part of the Pyramid Lake Paiutes. The availability of water determines the character of life and culture in this region. Here, as elsewhere in the West, it is insufficient to satisfy all claims. In the face of such fundamental natural limitations, the rule of law cannot avert large measures of loss, destruction, and profound disappointment, no matter how scrupulously even-handed are the law's doctrines and administration. Yet the law can and should fix responsibility for loss and destruction that should have been avoided, and it can and should require that those whose rights are appropriated for the benefit of others receive appropriate compensation.

NOTES AND QUESTIONS

1. *Potential breach of trust action?* What relief could the tribe get from the United States after this decision? The Indian Claims Commission Act required all damages claims for pre–1946 damages against the United States to be filed by the close of 1951. Would that Act preclude recovery? In fact, Congress passed settlement legislation in 1990. Truckee–Carson–Pyramid Lake Water Rights Settlement Act of 1990, Pub. L. 101–618, title II, 104 Stat. 3289 (1990).

2. *Tribes as client or trust beneficiary?* The Justice Department represents the federal government in litigation. Who is the client when Indian water rights are being litigated? Is it the affected tribe, or the Secretary of the Interior, who has been assigned most Executive Branch responsibility as trustee to the tribes? The federal view is that the Secretary is the client, although tribes now typically have their own counsel and participate in the litigation as intervenors.

---

basing its claim of liability on the Tribe's receipt of less water for the fishery than it was entitled to. *Northern Paiute Tribe v. United States,* 30 Ind.Cl.Comm. 210 (1973). In a settlement the Tribe was given $8,000,000 in return for its waiver of further liability on the part of the United States.

3. *Settlement decisions.* Should the United States and other parties be able to settle a water rights case over the objection of the affected tribe?

4. *Hopelessly conflicted?* For a former insider's view of the many conflicts of interest within the Departments of the Interior and Justice, *see* Ann C. Juliano, *Conflicted Justice: The Department of Justice's Conflict of Interest in Representing Native American Tribes*, 37 Ga. L. Rev. 1307 (2003).

5. *Endless litigation?* In earlier litigation involving Pyramid Lake, a federal district court held that the Secretary of the Interior's fiduciary responsibility to the Pyramid Lake Paiutes precluded him from simply making a "judgment call" in favor of the Newlands Reclamation Project. *Pyramid Lake Paiute Tribe v. Morton*, 354 F. Supp. 252, 256 (D. D.C. 1973) ("In order to fulfill his fiduciary duty, the Secretary must insure, to the extent of his power, that all water not obligated by court decree or contract with the [Reclamation Project] goes to Pyramid Lake." For the latest in the long-running Pyramid Lake litigation, see, *United States v. Alpine Land & Reservoir Co.*, 510 F.3d 1035 (9th Cir. 2007) (holding that, despite years of non-use, the water rights on some non-Indian parcels had not been abandoned, and so could be transferred rather than returned to the Truckee River to benefit the ecology of Pyramid Lake, but also holding that water rights on other parcels had been forfeited under state law so that the water returned to the Truckee River); and *Pyramid Lake Paiute Tribe of Indians v. Nevada, Dep't of Wildlife*, 724 F.3d 1181, 1188 (9th Cir. 2013) ("Tribe's allegation that the State Engineer's decision [to allow change in use of irrigation water] will increase demand for Truckee River water in the Carson Division and thereby reduce flows to Pyramid Lake establishes a cognizable injury").

6. *What if the federal government will not assert tribal rights?* It is often the case that tribes request that the United States affirmatively assert rights on their behalf in litigation. It could be that the tribe wants instream flows for fisheries protection, or water for consumptive use on the reservation. In *Shoshone-Bannock Tribes v. Reno*, 56 F.3d 1476, (D.C. Cir. 1995) the court rejected the tribes' claim that the federal trust responsibility required the Justice Department to assert the Tribes' off-reservation instream flow claims in Idaho's Snake River Basin Adjudication. The court ruled that "the Attorney General's refusal to represent the Tribes in the Idaho proceeding is committed to her discretion. Judicial review of the Tribes' claim is consequently unavailable." *Id.* at 1477–78. In a case now on appeal, a federal district court refused to allow a complaint to be amended to assert that the Department of the Interior must claim reserved water rights on behalf of the Navajo Nation in litigation. The court reasoned that "unless there is a specific duty that has been placed on the government with respect to Indians, the government's general trust obligation is discharged by the government's compliance with general regulations and statutes not specifically aimed at protecting Indian tribes." Navajo Nation v. United States Department of the Interior, 2019 WL 3997370, at *7 (D. Ariz. 2019). For criticism of the court's approach, see Robert T. Anderson, *Indigenous Rights to Water and Environmental Protection*, 53 Harv. C.R. C.L. L. Rev. 337, 362-367 (2018) (critiquing judicial reluctance to rely on the trust responsibility to force prospective agency action).

V. ALLOTMENT WATER RIGHTS

UNITED STATES V. POWERS

305 U.S. 527, 59 S. Ct. 344, 83 L. Ed. 330 (1939)

JUSTICE MCREYNOLDS delivered the opinion of the Court.

By this proceeding (begun in 1934) the United States seek to prevent further taking of water from certain non-navigable streams within the Crow Indian Reservation. This water is essential to the cultivation of respondents' lands allotted more than twenty years ago to members of the tribe and presently held [by non-Indians] under properly acquired fee simple titles. The prayer of the bill is for a permanent injunction against "maintaining or using said dams and ditches, as aforesaid, and from diverting by means of said dams and ditches or in any other manner any of the waters from Lodge Grass Creek or Little Big Horn River and their tributaries; ***."

By Treaty of May 7, 1868, 15 Stat. 649, 650, 651, the United States set aside a large tract of arid land now within the State of Montana as a Reservation for the "absolute and undisturbed used and occupation" of Crow Indians, and they undertook to make their permanent homes thereon. It provides that whenever an individual Indian desires "to commence farming" he may select land, under stated conditions, which thereupon shall "cease to be held in common, but the same may be occupied and held in the exclusive possession of the person selecting it, and of his family, so long as he or they may continue to cultivate it." Also—

> The President may at any time order a survey of the reservation, and, when so surveyed, Congress shall provide for protecting the rights of settlers in their improvements, and may fix the character of the title held by each. *** When the head of a family or lodge shall have selected lands and received his certificate as above directed, and the agent shall be satisfied that he intends in good faith to commence cultivating the soil for a living, he shall be entitled to receive seeds and agricultural implements for the first year in value one hundred dollars, and for each succeeding year he shall continue to farm, for a period of three years more, he shall be entitled to receive seeds and implements as aforesaid in value twenty-five dollars per annum.

Article 6.

The treaty contains no definite provision concerning appropriation or use of waters. Although the lands are arid a considerable area is susceptible of cultivation under irrigation. ***

The [General Allotment Act] provides for allotments in severalty to Indians upon any reservation created for their use whenever in the President's opinion any part is advantageous for agricultural and grazing purposes. And it directs that after allotments are approved the Secretary of the Interior shall issue patents declaring the United States will hold the land for twenty-five years in trust and thereafter "will convey the same by patent to said Indian, or his heirs as aforesaid, in fee, discharged of said trust and free of all charge or incumbrance whatsoever ***." "In cases where the use of water for irrigation is necessary to render the lands within any Indian reservation available for agricultural purposes, the Secretary of the Interior is authorized to prescribe such rules and regulations as he may deem necessary to secure a just and equal distribution thereof among the Indians residing upon any such reservations; and no other appropriation or grant of water by any riparian proprietor shall be authorized or permitted to the damage of any other riparian proprietor." 25 U.S.C.A. § 381. ***

Commencing in 1901 allotments in severalty of tracts abutting or adjacent to the Little Big Horn River or Lodge Grass Creek were made to respondents' Indian predecessors. These culminated in the issuance of fee simple patents as provided by Act of May 8, 1906. Each patent undertook to convey the land "together with all the rights, privileges, immunities and appurtenances, of whatsoever nature, thereunto belonging," but contained no express provision concerning water rights. Respondents have succeeded to the interest of the original allottees either by *mesne* conveyances or by purchase at government sales of deceased allottees' lands.

The Little Big Horn River and its affluent, Lodge Grass Creek, under normal conditions may afford sufficient water to irrigate twenty thousand acres within the Reservation. Through private ditches respondents and their predecessors have long conveyed water from these streams in order to irrigate their lands and thus render them susceptible of cultivation. It is not suggested that water therefor can be obtained from any other source. ***

Respondents maintain that under the Treaty of 1868 waters within the Reservation were reserved for the equal benefit of tribal members (*Winters v. United States*, 207 U.S. 564 (1908)), and that when allotments of land were duly made for exclusive use and thereafter conveyed in fee, the right to use some portion of tribal waters essential for cultivation passed to the owners.

The respondents' claim to the extent stated is well founded.

Manifestly the Treaty of 1868 contemplated ultimate settlement by individual Indians upon designated tracts where they could make homes with exclusive right of cultivation for their support and with expectation of ultimate complete ownership. Without water productive cultivation has always been impossible. [The United States was not allowed to enjoin the non-Indian successors' use of water.]

No Name Creek Entering Omak Lake.†

COLVILLE CONFEDERATED TRIBES V. WALTON

752 F.2d 397 (9th Cir. 1985)

EUGENE A. WRIGHT, CIRCUIT JUDGE:

This dispute involves respective rights of the Colville Confederated Tribes (Tribe), Indian allottees and Walton to share in water from the No Name Creek Hydrological System, which was originally reserved for the Tribe under the *Winters* doctrine, when the Colville Reservation was created.

Walton and the Indian allottees seek water for irrigation. ***

All the former reservation land involved in this case passed into private ownership pursuant to the General Allotment Act of 1887. 24 Stat. 388. A row of seven allotments in the No Name Creek watershed was created in 1917. *Walton II,* 647 F.2d at 45. The United States holds allotments 892 to the north of Walton's property, and 901 and 903 to the south, in trust for the heirs of the original Indian allottees. The Tribe farms and irrigates these allotments under long-term leases. Allotment 526, which is also held in trust by the United States, is beneficially owned by the Tribe, but was properly excluded from the district court's allocation pursuant to the remand.

Walton owns allotments 525, 2371 and 894, which he purchased in 1948. These allotments originally passed out of the ownership of Indian allottees between 1921 and 1925.

---

†. This and the following photograph courtesy of Harry (Skip) Johnsen.

No Name Creek is a spring-fed creek which originates on allotment 892 and flows through Walton's allotments and the Indians' southern allotments into Omak Lake, a saline lake with no outlet. The creek and an underground aquifer underlying the Indians' northern allotments and the northern tip of Walton's allotment, number 525, constitute the No Name Creek Hydrological System.

In *Walton II,* we held that the United States reserved sufficient water, when the Colville Reservation was created, to allow the irrigation of all practicably irrigable acreage on the reservation. 647 F.2d at 48. We held also that a ratable share of this water reserved for irrigation passed to Indian allottees. This ratable share could in turn be conveyed to a non-Indian purchaser. However, the non-Indian purchaser's share is subject to loss if not put to use. *Id.*

In addition to water for irrigation, we held that sufficient water was reserved to allow the establishment of the Omak Lake Fishery and permit natural spawning of the Lahonton Cutthroat Trout. *Id.* at 48. This quantity of water, unrelated to irrigation, was not affected by the allotment of reservation lands and passage of title out of the Indians' hands.

We remanded the case to the district court to calculate the respective rights of the Tribe, Walton, and the individual allottees. The district court, in an unreported opinion, awarded 384 acre feet per year to Walton, 428.8 acre feet per year to the Indian allottees for irrigation, and 187.2 acre feet per year to the Tribe for the trout spawning program. The Tribe appealed. ***

II.

Law Applied. Reserved rights are "federal water rights" and "are not dependent upon state law or state procedures." *** This dispute involves relative shares of Colville's reserved waters, and is governed by federal law. We look to state law only for guidance.

III.

Walton's Allocation

***

A. Irrigable Acreage

An Indian allottee's share of water reserved for purposes of irrigation is limited by the relationship between the number of irrigable acres owned and the number of irrigable acres contained within the reservation. For example, an allottee who owns ten percent of the total number of irrigable acres within a reservation, is entitled to ten percent of the water reserved for irrigation purposes when the reservation was created. This in turn creates an upper limit on the share that may be conveyed to a non-Indian purchaser. *Walton II,* 647 F.2d at 51.

The district court found that Walton owned 170 irrigable acres. This is a finding of fact which we uphold unless clearly erroneous. ***

The Tribe argues that almost all of Walton's land is waterlogged and not irrigable. We need not determine whether Walton owns 170 acres of irrigable land. As we discuss more fully below, we conclude that Walton's predecessors exercised reasonable diligence in irrigating only 30 acres. If Walton owns at least 30 irrigable acres, irrigable acreage is no longer a limiting factor.

Walton's property beyond question contains at least 30 irrigable acres. Wilson W. Walton (Walton, Sr.) and W.B. Walton (Walton, Jr.) both testified they successfully farmed and irrigated 104–155 acres. Reporter's Transcript, Aug. 9, 1982 (testimony of Walton, Sr.) and May 5, 1982 (testimony of Walton, Jr.). The Waltons' testimony was supported by that of Al Blomdahl, former Chief Soil Conservation Officer for the Okanogan Office of the United States Department of Agriculture Soil Conservation Service, who testified that Wilson Walton was named Regional Conservation Farmer of the Year in the early 1960's. Reporter's Transcript, May 5, 1982, p. 217.

B. Reasonable Diligence

In *Walton II,* 647 F.2d at 51, we said:

> On remand [the district court] will need to determine the number of irrigable acres Walton owns and the amount of water he appropriated with reasonable diligence in order to determine the extent of his right to share in reserved water.

The district court interpreted this to mean that Walton's diligence in applying water beneficially was the determinative factor in calculating his share of the reserved waters. The district court found that "Walton exercised reasonable diligence in irrigating a minimum of 104 acres," and calculated his allocation accordingly. The court then made alternative findings as to the diligence of the preceding owners of the property dating back to the immediate grantees of the original Indian allottees.

1. Scope of the Mandate

In *Walton II,* we established the criteria governing the transfer of reserved water rights from an Indian allottee to a non-Indian purchaser. *** In *Walton II* we said:

> The non-Indian successor acquires a right to water being appropriated by the Indian allottee at the time title passes. The non-Indian also acquires a right, with a date-of-reservation priority date, to water that he or she appropriates with reasonable diligence after the passage of title. If the full measure of the Indian's reserved water right is not acquired by this means and maintained by continued use, it is lost to the non-Indian successor.

A careful reading leaves no doubt that the immediate grantee of the original allottee must exercise due diligence to perfect his or her inchoate right to the allottee's ratable share of reserved waters. This interpretation is supported by our reference to *Walton II* in subsequent cases. *See, e.g., United States v. Anderson,* 736 F.2d 1358, 1362 (9th Cir.1984) ("use it or lose it"); *United States v. Adair,* 723 F.2d 1394, 1417 (9th Cir.1983). Once perfected, the water right must be "maintained by continued use [or] it is lost." *Walton II,* 647 F.2d at 51.

The district court on remand was to "calculate the respective rights of the parties." *Id.* at 53. Calculating Walton's share required an investigation into the diligence with which the immediate grantee from the Indian allottees appropriated water, and the extent to which successor grantees, up to and including Walton, continued to use the water thus appropriated. Otherwise, any remote purchaser could appropriate enough water to irrigate all irrigable acreage with a priority date as of the creation of the Reservation. The reasonable diligence requirement of *Walton II* would be meaningless.

2. Appropriation

Walton's share of the Colvilles' reserved water is limited to that amount appropriated "with reasonable diligence after the passage of title" from the original Indian allottees (or their heirs), and "maintained by continued use" by each subsequent successor, including Walton. *Id.* at 51.

Under the doctrine of "prior appropriation", (followed by most western states, including Washington, *see* Morris, *Washington Water Rights—A Sketch,* 31 Wash. L. Rev. 243, 252–260 (1956)), "one acquires a right to water by diverting it from its natural source and applying it to some beneficial use." To perfect an "appropriation," one must intend to appropriate a quantity of water, and diligently put it to a beneficial use. ***

If diligently applied, the priority date of the water right relates back to the initial diversion. *See, e.g., Longmire v. Smith,* 67 P. 246, 249 (1901). The tests developed to determine whether or not an appropriator has been sufficiently diligent in applying water to a beneficial use to justify relating the priority date back to the initial diversion are appropriate to determine how much water Walton's predecessors appropriated with reasonable diligence, after the passage of title.

3. Intent/Due Diligence

An initial diversion of at least some water is an important indication of intent. When water is diverted for irrigation purposes, and the amount continuously and gradually increased, an intent to appropriate the quantity eventually used may logically be inferred. This could include enough water to irrigate all irrigable acres. Thus, intent and due diligence are necessarily interrelated.

The district court found that the owners between the Indian allottees and Walton exercised "diligence in beneficially applying water for agricultural purposes to the maximum extent reasonably possible given prevailing economic and technological conditions."

The court apparently inferred that these owners intended to appropriate enough water to irrigate at least 104 acres, as soon as technologically feasible. We find this conclusion unsupported by the record.

The amount of land irrigated remained fairly constant, throughout the 23–27 year period following purchase by the Whams, the first non-Indian purchasers. ***

We are unable to infer an intent to appropriate an increasing amount of water from over two decades of relatively static irrigation practices. Walton's share of the reserved water is thus limited to the amount utilized for irrigation throughout this period.

The district court found that the original non-Indian purchasers, the Whams, "irrigated about 30 acres employing gravity flow rill method as well as a small gasoline powered pump," and that they continued to irrigate the same amount of land until Walton bought the land in 1948. ***

We affirm the trial court's finding that sufficient water to irrigate 30 acres was appropriated with reasonable diligence by the original non-Indian purchasers and continually used by each subsequent owner, including Walton. Walton's right to this amount of water has a priority date as of the establishment of the Reservation. ***

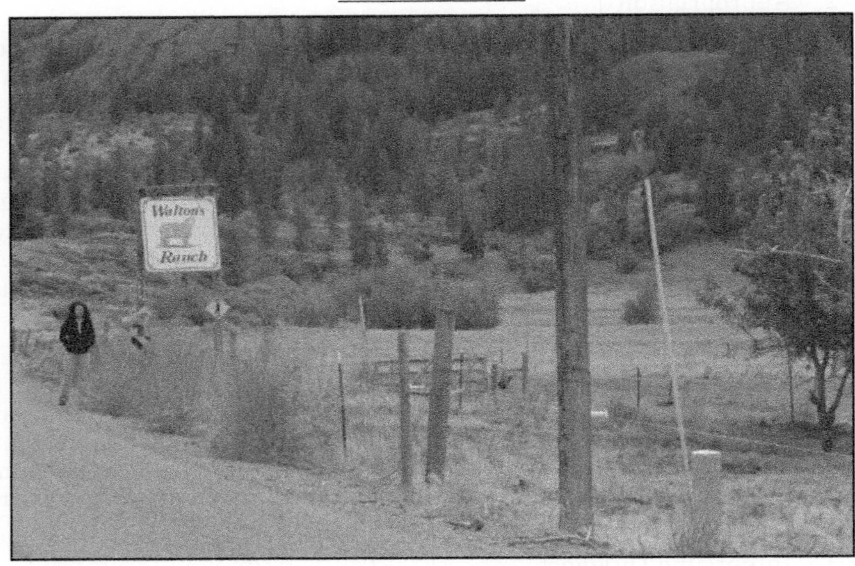

Walton's Ranch.

NOTES AND QUESTIONS

1. *Non–Indian successors.* Why should non-Indian successors obtain the right to any water with a date of reservation priority date? One commentator called the court's rationale "the classic circular argument of property law. The allottee was able to transfer a property interest because the allottee had a property interest. One could as easily decide that an allottee's right to the undeveloped part of the reservation water right is a mere opportunity to perfect the right while the land remains in trust, an opportunity that serves the trust purpose and expires when the land becomes subject to state law." Richard B. Collins, *Indian Allotment Water Rights*, 20 Land & Water L. Rev. 421, 446 (1985). Professor Collins, however, ends up supporting the result in *Walton* based on reasonable expectations supported by dicta in past decisions like *United States v. Powers. See also* David H. Getches, *Water Rights on Indian Allotments*, 26 S. D. L. Rev. 405 (1981) (non-Indian purchasers of allotments should acquire only the amount of water actually used by the Indian allottee during the trust period). Which rule is preferable?

2. *Due diligence of non-Indian successors.* As the *Walton* case demonstrates, determining the water rights of non-Indian purchasers of allotments can be complicated. What constitutes a "reasonable time" for putting water to use? Should it matter if the non-Indian purchaser is within an irrigation district and is awaiting federal funding for construction of the irrigation works? *See In re General Adjudication of All Rights to Use Water in Big Horn River System*, 48 P.3d 1040, 1055 (Wyo. 2002) ("We hold, under the circumstances of this case and presuming irrigation was not possible absent the project, in order to establish beneficial use of the reserved water within a reasonable time to retain the federal reserved right, the unsuccessful claimants must

demonstrate their efforts to put the lands under irrigation within a reasonable time and with due diligence, as defined by state law, after the federal project facilities became available to the properties.")

3. *Reacquired tribal lands.* Are there water rights associated with land that has fallen out of trust status and is subsequently acquired by a tribe? *See United States v. Anderson*, 736 F.2d 1358, 1362 (9th Cir. 1984) (water rights appurtenant to lands reacquired by tribe after allotment and sale to non-Indians carry a priority date, as to those water rights not lost to nonuse, as of the date of the creation of the reservation; land removed from tribal ownership and then returned to tribal ownership without appurtenant water rights acquires a reserved water right with a priority as of the date they were returned to tribal trust status).

4. *Regulatory authority over allotment water rights.* Tribes of course, have authority to regulate use of water decreed to the tribe and its members. Indian allotment owners are held to be entitled to use of a share of tribal water under 25 U.S.C. § 381 ("In cases where the use of water for irrigation is necessary to render the lands within any Indian reservation available for agricultural purposes, the Secretary of the Interior is authorized to prescribe such rules and regulations as he may deem necessary to secure a just and equal distribution thereof among the Indians residing upon any such reservations ***."). *Colville Confederated Tribes v. Walton*, 752 F.2d 397, 401 (9th Cir. 1985). The Solicitor of the Department of the Interior opined that "[t]he basic attributes of tribal and allottee interests in such water rights are as follows: 1. An Indian allottee has a right to a 'just and equal distribution' of water for irrigation purposes. 2. Indian tribes possess broad regulatory power over reservation water resources, including those to which allottees have rights. 3. The quantity of water to which an allottee may be entitled is not subject to precise formulae." Sol. Op. No. M–36982, *Entitlements to Water Under the Southern Arizona Water Rights Settlement Act (SAWRSA)* (March 30, 1995). Is this advice helpful?

5. *Jurisdiction over non-Indian water use.* What about tribal jurisdiction over non-Indian water use of surplus waters on non-Indian lands? There are few cases dealing with the matter. Regulation of water use should be subject to the same rules normally applied to the relative bounds of tribal and state jurisdiction. *Compare United States v. Anderson*, 736 F.2d 1358 (9th Cir. 1984) (state may regulate non-Indian use of surplus water on non-Indian land within Spokane Indian Reservation) *with Colville Confederated Tribes v. Walton*, 647 F.2d 42, 52 (9th Cir. 1981) (no state jurisdiction to regulate non-Indian use on portion of Colville Reservation). Tribes may also receive treatment as a state to regulate water quality under the Clean Water Act. *See* ch. 9 § 1. B, *supra*.

VI. INDIAN WATER RIGHT SETTLEMENTS

Indian water rights litigation is extremely time consuming and expensive—especially in the context of state general stream adjudications. Washington State's Yakima Basin Adjudication has been going on since 1975 and a final decree at the trial court level was finally entered in 2019. Some say the State may have to go back and adjudicate rights to groundwater in the basin—which were left out of the current adjudication. It took fifty years to decree final Indian rights in *Arizona v. California*. The Klamath Basin Adjudication commenced in 1975 and the merits of the quantification of the Indian reserved rights were concluded at the administrative stage in 2013 with trial court level review pending as of late 2019. Idaho's Snake River Basin Adjudication resulted in a settlement with the Nez Perce Tribe after a relatively brief seventeen years.

Another shortcoming of litigation is that the end result may simply be a "paper water right." This refers to the fact that after a water rights adjudication, the end result is a decree setting forth the amount of water each party to the case is entitled to use and a priority date for the right. In the case of Indian reserved rights, however, the decree often provides for water rights far beyond the amount actually put to use in the past. In such a case, there is a paper (or legal) right to water that requires infrastructure in order to be utilized. There is no guarantee that the infrastructure will ever be built. Settlements confirmed by federal legislation offer opportunities to obtain funding to remedy past inequities in water resource development. The following excerpt describes federal inaction after the decision in *Winters* and the premise for arguments in favor of federal appropriations for reservation water development.

ROBERT T. ANDERSON, *INDIAN WATER RIGHTS AND THE FEDERAL TRUST RESPONSIBILITY*

46 Nat. Resources J. 399, 430–31 (2006)

*** The federal government's zeal to develop non-Indian irrigation interests left tribal needs for irrigation, protection of fisheries and wildlife habitat, and domestic consumption to languish. The Bureau of Reclamation and its non-Indian constituents have always commanded the lion's share of resources within the Department of the Interior—both in terms of dollars for projects and of attorney staff to advise and defend reclamation programs. Shortly after the resounding victory for Indian water rights in *Winters*, the Indian Service sought additional legal assistance to assert and protect Indian reserved water. The water rights of tribes, however, were largely ignored. By 1913, the BIA complained of the favored status held by the Reclamation Service, which "had been generously staffed to assert and protect water rights for Reclamation projects." Since establishment of the Bureau of Reclamation in 1902, the federal government has enshrined the diversion of Indian water for non-Indian use as federal policy, and simply left the Indian tribes out of the development mix.[202]

---

202. One court of appeals noted this in 1956 when it evaluated an agreement entered into by the Secretary of the Interior purporting to greatly reduce the amount of water available to the Yakama Indian Nation.

> With an opportunity to study the history of the Winters rule, as it has stood now for nearly 50 years, we can readily perceive that the Secretary of the Interior, in acting as he did, improvidently bargained away extremely valuable rights belonging to the Indians. Perhaps the feature of the whole matter most worthy of criticism is the apparent failure of the Secretary, before approving such an arrangement, to obtain legal advice either from the Solicitor or from the Department of Justice, as to the validity or the advisability of the proposed agreement. Viewing this contract as an improvident disposal of three-fourths of that which justly belonged to the Indians, it cannot be said to be out of character with the

In addition to its failure to develop water for Indian agricultural uses, the federal government did virtually nothing to ensure that water remained instream to satisfy the needs of fish and wildlife preserved in treaties and agreements. This all was despite the fact that, in its dealings with Indians, the United States "has charged itself with moral obligations of the highest responsibility and trust." The extent to which the federal government meets this trust responsibility depends in part on funding from Congress and on any given Administration's priorities ***.

Congress has enacted twenty-seven Indian water right settlements into law since 1978. *See* Cohen's Handbook of Federal Indian Law 1247 (2012).

Recent scholarship covers a variety of Indian water rights topics and generally extols the virtues of Indian water settlements. *See* Robert T. Anderson, *Indian Water Rights, Practical Reasoning and Negotiated Settlements,* 98 Cal. L. Rev. 1133 (2010); Negotiating Tribal Water Rights: Fulfilling Promises in the Arid West (Bonnie G. Colby *et al.*, eds., 2005); Tribal Water Rights: Essays in Contemporary Law, Policy, and Economics (John E. Thorson *et al.*, eds., U. Ariz. Press 2006); *see also* Reid Peyton Chambers & John E. Echohawk, *Implementing the Winters Doctrine of Indian Reserved Water Rights: Protecting Indian Water and Economic Development Without Injuring Non–Indian Water Users?*, 27 Gonz. L. Rev. 447 (1992).

DANIEL C. MCCOOL, *NATIVE WATERS: CONTEMPORARY INDIAN WATER SETTLEMENTS AND THE SECOND TREATY ERA*

100–101 (2002)

Of all the reasons to negotiate, perhaps the most convincing is the opportunity to turn back a century of water loss and return ancestral waters to Indian people. Or, in the more arcane language of negotiations, a settlement can provide "wet water" rather than mere "paper water" won in court. David Getches writes, "negotiation is a more promising vehicle for reaching a meaningful, practical resolution that provides the Indians with deliverable water and non-Indians with genuine certainty." An OMB official made a similar point: "The big advantage of settlements is that you free up the resource; the Indians get some wet water and the Anglos get the [legal] cloud [on their rights] removed." An Indian attorney argued that "The goal that everyone should have is getting wet water." ***

> sort of thing which Congress and the Department of the Interior has been doing throughout the sad history of the Government's dealings with the Indians and the Indian tribes. That history largely supports the statement: "From the very beginnings of this nation, the chief issue around which federal Indian policy has revolved has been, not how to assimilate the Indian nations whose lands we usurped, but how best to transfer Indian lands and resources to non-Indians."

United States v. Ahtanum Irrigation Dist., 236 F.2d 321, 337 (9th Cir. 1956) (*citing* Dorothy Van de Mark, The Raid on the Reservations, Harper's Mag., Mar. 1956).

While each settlement is unique, a common component is the reduction of tribal claims to reserved water to a level acceptable to state-law water users, accompanied by a state and federal monetary contribution sufficient to allow the tribal water right to be utilized. This converts a potential "paper right" to wet water. The federal government has a general policy favoring the negotiation and settlement of Indian water rights, which is implemented through the following policy guidance.

CRITERIA AND PROCEDURES FOR THE PARTICIPATION OF THE FEDERAL GOVERNMENT IN THE NEGOTIATIONS FOR THE SETTLEMENT OF INDIAN WATER RIGHTS

55 Fed. Reg. 9223 (March 12, 1990).

***

Indian water rights are vested property rights for which the United States has a trust responsibility, with the United States holding legal title to such water in trust for the benefit of the Indians.

It is the policy of this Administration, as set forth by President Bush on June 21, 1989, in his statement signing into law H.R. 932, the 1989 Puyallup Tribe of Indians Settlement Act, that disputes regarding Indian water rights should be resolved through negotiated settlements rather than litigation.

Accordingly, the Department of the Interior adopts the following criteria and procedures to establish the basis for negotiation and settlements of claims concerning Indian water resources. *** The criteria provide a framework for negotiating settlements so that (1) The United States will be able to participate in water settlements consistent with the Federal Government's responsibilities as trustee to Indians; (2) Indians receive equivalent benefits for rights which they, and the United States as trustee, may release as part of a settlement; (3) Indians obtain the ability as part of each settlement to realize value from confirmed water rights resulting from settlement; and (4) The settlement contains appropriate cost-sharing by all parties benefiting from the settlement.

Criteria

1. These criteria are applicable to all negotiations involving Indian water rights claims settlements in which the Federal Government participates. Claims to be settled through negotiation may include, but are not limited to, claims:

(a) By tribes and U.S. Government to quantify reserved Indian water rights.

(b) By tribes against the U.S. Government.

(c) By tribes and the U.S. Government against third parties.

2. The Department of the Interior will support legislation authorizing those agreements to which is a signatory party.

3. Settlements should be completed in such a way that all outstanding water claims are resolved and finality is achieved.

4. The total cost of a settlement to all parties should not exceed the value of the existing claims as calculated by the Federal Government.

5. Federal contributions to a settlement should not exceed the sum of the following two elements:

a. First, calculable legal exposure—litigation cost and judgment obligations if the case is lost; Federal and non-Federal exposure should be calculated on a present value basis taking into account the size of the claim, value of the water, timing of the award, likelihood of loss.

b. Second, additional costs related to Federal trust or programmatic responsibilities (assuming the U.S. obligation as trustee can be compared to existing precedence.)—Federal contributions relating to programmatic responsibilities should be justified as to why such contributions cannot be funded through the normal budget process.

6. Settlements should include non-Federal cost-sharing proportionate to the benefits received by the non-Federal parties.

7. Settlements should be structured to promote economic efficiency on reservations and tribal self-sufficiency.

8. Operating capabilities and various resources of the Federal and non-Federal parties to the claims negotiations should be considered in structuring a settlement (*e.g.* operating criteria and water conservation in Federal and non-Federal projects).

9. If Federal cash contributions are part of a settlement and once such contributions are certified as deposited in the appropriate tribal treasury, the U.S. shall not bear any obligation or liability regarding the investment, management, or use of such funds.

10. Federal participation in Indian water rights negotiations should be conducive to long-term harmony and cooperation among all interested parties through respect for the sovereignty of the States and tribes in their respective jurisdictions.

11. Settlements should generally not include: ***

f. U.S. participation in an economically unjustified irrigation investment; however investments for delivery of water for households, gardens, or domestic livestock may be exempted from this criterion. ***

NOTES AND QUESTIONS

1. *Does the United States follow the Criteria and Procedures?* The government's position in water settlements, while ostensibly guided by the Criteria and Procedures, has been inconsistent and subject to frequent congressional overrides. McCool, *supra* at 119 ("The favored strategy was just to ignore [the criteria and procedures] and take negotiated agreements straight to Congress, with a conspicuous lack of OMB review.") Of course, the ability to overcome a threat of a Presidential veto depends on the strength of a given state's

congressional delegation, or on the ability to attach a settlement to a veto-proof appropriations bill.

2. *Do balanced budget goals mean no settlements?* President Clinton's first term was marked by successful efforts toward a balanced federal budget. The federal government's failure to conclude any Indian water rights settlements during that period based on budgetary constraints was severely criticized within Indian country and by state representatives. *See* Barbara A. Cosens, *The 1997 Water Rights Settlement Between the State of Montana and the Chippewa Cree Tribe of the Rocky Boy's Reservation: The Role of Community and of the Trustee*, 16 UCLA J. Envtl. L. & Pol'y 255, 257 (1998) ("The failure of the federal government to effectively participate in and support settlement discussions calls into question its ability to fulfill its role as trustee to the many Indian tribes still struggling to settle their water rights."). Any Indian water rights case can be settled if the federal budget is viewed as a bottomless pit to be used to buy out willing non-Indian users, provide compensation to tribes for past damages and limitations on future rights, build new projects to store water, and pay for conservation measures such as lining canals in order to make available water that otherwise is lost. How should the federal government determine the appropriate amount of funding for a given settlement? Should the fact that non-Indian neighbors of the tribes often received large subsidies under the Reclamation laws be taken into account? One of the most encouraging developments in recent years is the establishment of the Reclamation Water Settlement Fund to fund Indian water rights settlements without either decimating the budget of the Bureau of Indian Affairs or completely reordering the Bureau of Reclamation's operations. Omnibus Public Land Management Act of 2009, Pub. L. No. 111–11, § 10501, 123 Stat. 991, 1375 (2009). While funding is not scheduled to be available until 2020, its creation is a significant step in the right direction, and the current Administration is reliably rumored to favor advancing the timing of its availability. Access to this fund is a response to years of efforts by Indian and non-Indian advocates to encourage increased federal support for Indian water settlements. These efforts have been led by the Native American Rights Fund and the Western States Water Council. *See* Western States Water Council—Celebrating our 40th Anniversary at 21–22 (2005).

3. *The Snake River Basin Adjudication—a model for the future?* Congress passed the Snake River Water Rights Act of 2004 "to achieve a fair, equitable, and final settlement of the all claims of the Nez Perce Tribe, its members, and allottees and the United States on behalf of the Tribe, its members, and allottees to the water of the Snake River Basin within Idaho[.]" Snake River Water Rights Act of 2004, § 2 (2), Pub. L. 108–447, 108 Stat. 3431 (2004). The Act was passed as a rider to the fiscal year 2005 Consolidated Appropriations Act, a 657-page statute. The parties to the adjudication were heavily invested in negotiations to resolve not just tribal water rights disputes, but also to deal with Endangered Species Act (ESA) matters of grave concern to non-Indian water users in Idaho. Serious negotiations had begun in 1998 with the appointment of a mediator by the court. Ann R. Klee & Duane Mecham, *The Nez Perce Indian Water Right Settlement—Federal Perspective*, 42 Idaho L. Rev. 595, 602 (2006).

> The Settlement involved three major components with the first two serving as the incentive for the State of Idaho and private water users to support a favorable settlement of tribal claims. First was the desire for

> security for upper Snake River water users pursuant to a 30–year negotiated flow augmentation plan. Second was agreement on the fairly specific plan for an agreement under § 6 of the ESA for habitat protection and restoration in the Salmon and Clearwater Basins. Having satisfied those desires, private water users and the State supported a tribal settlement with the following primary components. The Settlement Act and "mediator's term sheet" provide: 1. water for a variety of tribal uses on the reservation; 2. recognition of allotment water rights and a due process requirement for tribal regulation of such rights; 3. for the transfer of on-reservation land valued at $7 million (estimated to be approximately 11,000 acres) from the federal Bureau of Land Management to the tribe; 4. a right to access and use of approximately 600 springs and fountains on federal lands in off-reservation areas; 5. tribal control of 200,000 acre feet of water from Dworshak reservoir; 6. authorization of nearly $90 million for tribal water and habitat related improvements; and 7. instream flows minimums at over 200 "locations selected by the Tribe as a matter of biological and cultural priority[.]" There is an additional $38 million allocated for a Salmon and Clearwater River Basins Habitat Fund. ***

Robert T. Anderson, *Indian Water Rights: Litigation and Settlements*, 42 Tulsa L. Rev. 23, 30–31 (2006).

Idaho's chief negotiator described the manner in which the settlement was slipped at the last minute into a 657 page appropriation bill:

> [I]n the final hours of a "Lame Duck" session, it was assured that the Congress would "approve, ratify and confirm" the Nez Perce Settlement Agreement as a part of an essential spending package for the federal government. In legislative parlance (borrowing from a sports analogy) this was the equivalent of throwing a Hail Mary pass with no time on the clock for a game-winning legislative touchdown.

Laurence Michael Bogert, *The Future is No Place to Place Your Better Days: Sovereignty, Certainty, Opportunity, and Governor Kempthorne's Shaping of the Nez Perce Agreement*, 42 Idaho L. Rev. 673, 691 (2006).

4. *Blackfeet, Choctaw-Chickasaw, and Pechanga.* Congress approved three settlements in the Water Infrastructure Improvements for the Nation Act, Pub. L. No. 114-322 (2016), 130 Stat. 1628: the Pechanga Band of Luiseno Mission Indians Water Rights Settlement Act, *id.*, §§ 3401-3413; the Choctaw Nation and Chickasaw Nation Water Settlement Act, *id.*, § 3608; and the Blackfeet Water Rights Settlement Act, *id.*, §§ 3701-3724. The Pechanga Settlement

> protects the Pechanga Band's access to groundwater in the region and provides the tribe with more than $30 million in federal funding to pay for water storage projects. The Agreement quantifies the water rights claims for the Pechanga Band in Southern California's Temecula Valley, which had been pending in an adjudication dating back to the 1950s; resolves potential liability for both the United States and other parties; and establishes a cooperative and efficient water management regime involving Pechanga and local agencies.

Department of the Interior Press Release (Nov. 29, 2017), https://www.doi.gov/pressreleases/interior-executes-water-rights-settlement-agreement-pechanga-band-luiseno-mission [https://perma.cc/P9L9-QADC]. The Oklahoma

Settlements provided the tribes with a secure right to stored water, and also protects fish and wildlife with minimum flows and lake levels, and establishes a management framework under state law that includes tribal participation. No federal appropriations are required for the settlement. *See* https://www.waterunityok.com for background information and the actual settlement. The Blackfeet Water Settlement provides the Tribe with approximately 800,000 acre feet of water for various uses on the reservation, and payments of nearly $500 million from the state and federal governments for infrastructure construction and rehabilitation. The tribe has a webpage with myriad information about the settlement. *See* https://blackfeetnation.com/watercompact/.

5. *Is litigation necessary for settlement?* Should tribes attempt to negotiate water rights settlements outside of a litigation context? How would the parties be brought to the table? Which parties should be there? How would such a settlement bind the parties to the agreement? What if the United States were unwilling to participate? Can a tribe settle its claims without the participation of the United States? Probably not, if the United States is correct in its assertion that it holds legal title to Indian water rights. Could a tribe get around this by signing a binding contract to defer for a term of years the exercise of its water rights? Don't forget about tribal sovereign immunity.

CHAPTER 11

AMERICAN INDIAN RELIGION AND CULTURE

■ ■ ■

Most American Indian religions comprise practices and beliefs centered on achieving harmonious relationships with all persons, other species, and the land. These spiritual beliefs pervade and infuse virtually every aspect of Indian life. American Indian culture is therefore not readily separable from religion, and both are integral to the identity of American Indian tribes. *See* Vine Deloria, Jr., God is Red: a Native View of Religion (2d ed. 1994). Both are also intimately connected to the specific places that organize and give meaning to morality and culture. As Frank Pommersheim writes, for many Native peoples, land "is the source of spiritual origins and sustaining myth which in turn provides a landscape of cultural and emotional meaning. The land often determines the values of the human landscape." Frank Pommersheim, *The Reservation as Place: A South Dakota Essay*, 34 S.D. L. Rev. 246, 250 (1989)*; see also* Rebecca Tsosie*, Land, Culture and Community: Reflections on Native Sovereignty and Property in America*, 34 Ind. L. Rev. 1291, 1302–1303 (2001). There are many important differences among American Indian religions, especially in terms of their site-specific beliefs and rituals, but Vine Deloria, Jr., has identified the following common themes:

> The Indian is confronted with a bountiful earth in which all things and experiences have a role to play. The task of the tribal religion, if such a religion can be said to have a task, is to determine the proper relationship that the people of the tribe must have with other living things and to develop the self-discipline within the tribal community so that man acts harmoniously with other creatures. The world that he experiences is dominated by the presence of power, the manifestation of life energies, the whole life-flow of a creation. Recognition that the human beings hold an important place in such a creation is tempered by the thought that they are dependent on everything in creation for their existence.

Deloria, *supra*, at 88.

As if paying perverse tribute to the all-encompassing nature of Indian religion, United States government agents and reformers were just as thoroughgoing in their efforts to stamp out Indian spiritual practices and beliefs. Assimilationist policies adopted during the late nineteenth and early twentieth centuries were astonishingly detailed, aimed at rooting out all aspects of American Indian difference. Religious or cultural ceremonies were banned by law, and Indian agents were charged to police hair length, funeral procedures, hunting and fishing practices, and beef slaughtering. *See* Cohen's Handbook of Federal Indian Law 77 (2012). As late as 1921, the Commissioner of Indian Affairs promulgated regulations prohibiting the "sun-dance and all other similar dances and so-called religious ceremonies." *See* Office of Indian Affairs, Circular No. 1665, April 26, 1921, *cited in* Felix Cohen, Handbook of Federal Indian Law 175 (1941). In addition to suppressing Indian culture and religion, the federal government supported and encouraged the practice of converting Indians to Christianity. *See* Allison Dussias, *Ghost Dance and Holy Ghost: The Echoes of 19th Century Christianization Policy in 20th Century Native American Free Exercise Cases*, 49 Stan. L. Rev. 773, 783–87 (1997).

Because of the deep connections between land and native culture and religion, deprivation of native land may have had an even more profound effect than direct suppression of religious practices. As Professor Jonathan Lear describes, when the Crow Indian Tribe was confined to a fraction of its former territory, and therefore unable to engage in the rituals and practices that gave meaning to being Crow, they suffered a form of cultural death more profound than what could have been achieved through criminalization of their spiritual practices. *See* Jonathan Lear, Radical Hope: Ethics in the Face of Cultural Devastation (2006):

> To make the point, allow me to speak in the first person as an imaginary Crow subject: Not only can I no longer plant a coup-stick, but nothing could count as my intending to do so. As it turns out, only in the context of vibrant tribal life can I have any of the mental states that are salient and important to me. The situation is even worse: these are the mental states that help to constitute me as a Crow subject. Insofar as I am a Crow subject there is nothing left for me to do; and there is nothing left for me to deliberate about, intend, or plan for. Insofar as I am a Crow subject, *I* have ceased to be.

Id. at 49–50.

As a result of this history, some commentators have argued that tribal sovereignty is crucial to the perpetuation of tribal religion and culture:

> Sovereignty is the necessary buffer that allows distinct, unique, and endemic cultures to survive. They survive not by remaining static—if that were the goal, then museums could substitute for Indian tribes—but by evolving in the way that all cultures do, and sometimes even into peoples that seem not to fit any of our romantic notions of what is "Indian." Crucial to survival of the culture is the survival of the governing structures that also evolve; the enactment of tribal sovereignty is itself an expression of tribal culture. The fate of tribal political structures and cultures is intertwined. To put it bluntly, without sovereign American Indian tribes, there would be no American Indians.

Sarah Krakoff, *The Virtues and Vices of Sovereignty*, 38 Conn. L. Rev. 797, 804–805 (2006). Professor Carole Goldberg makes a similar point: "Very simply, if Indians do not have a protected land base and some substantial measure of self-determination, Indian culture will fade and ultimately disappear." Carole Goldberg–Ambrose, *Not "Strictly" Racial: A Response to "Indians as Peoples,"* 39 UCLA. L. Rev. 169, 184 (1991). Professor Rebecca Tsosie's complementary argument is that tribes can and should exercise their "cultural sovereignty" to further the goals of retaining their distinct languages and cultures. *See* Rebecca Tsosie; *Reclaiming Native Stories: An Essay on Cultural Appropriation and Cultural Rights*, 34 Ariz. St. L.J. 299, 306–09 (2002); *see also*

Angela R. Riley, *"Straight Stealing": Towards an Indigenous System of Cultural Property Protection*, 80 Wash. L. Rev. 69 (2005).

According to this view, the earlier chapters on tribal sovereignty are just as, if not more, important to the protection of American Indian religion and culture as the materials in this chapter. Do you agree with this view? Is political independence linked to the perpetuation of culture? If so, how much political independence is required? Which aspects of sovereignty are most important to protect and perpetuate culture? If not, what other conditions are necessary to perpetuate a living culture? Can you have this discussion in the abstract, without knowing the particulars of what constitutes culture to a people? For discussion purposes, consider comparing, for example, stateless peoples such as Jews before the founding of Israel or Palestinians today. Consider also what culture means to American citizens of foreign descent, including Italian–Americans, African–Americans and others. Can you draw a meaningful distinction between these groups and American Indians for the purposes of determining what is required to perpetuate a living culture? Why would the construct of legal sovereignty be more important to American Indians than to these other groups?

I. CONSTITUTIONAL AND FEDERAL STATUTORY FRAMEWORK

The First Amendment of the United States Constitution provides that "Congress shall make no law respecting an establishment of religion, or prohibiting the free exercise thereof[.]" U.S. Const., amend. I. Policymakers who sought to suppress native religious practices seem not to have considered potential conflicts with the first clause of this provision, and there are no reported decisions evaluating such legal challenges. Cohen's Handbook of Federal Indian Law 965 n.154 (2012). With regard to the second clause, contemporary claims by Native people that the government has violated their rights to free exercise of religion have met with little success. The land-based and holistic features of Indian spiritual practices have often been viewed with skepticism and misunderstanding. And as the following cases reveal, Indian free exercise claims also present hard questions regarding the extent to which courts should protect minority religions, particularly ones that seem to place unique demands on government agencies. Despite these challenges, in recent times some progress has been made with regard to increasing legal protections for American Indian religious and cultural practices. The materials in this section describe the general constitutional and legislative framework, and Sections I, II, and III address in turn sacred site protection, cultural and religious practices, and cultural and religious resources and property.

LYNG V. NORTHWEST INDIAN CEMETERY PROTECTIVE ASSOCIATION

485 U.S. 439, 108 S. Ct. 1319, 99 L.Ed.2d 534 (1988)

JUSTICE O'CONNOR delivered the opinion of the Court.

This case requires us to consider whether the First Amendment's Free Exercise Clause prohibits the Government from permitting timber harvesting in, or constructing a road through, a portion of a National Forest that has traditionally been used for religious purposes by members of three American Indian tribes in northwestern California. We conclude that it does not.

As part of a project to create a paved 75–mile road linking two California towns, Gasquet and Orleans, the United States Forest Service has upgraded 49 miles of previously unpaved roads on federal land. In order to complete this project (the G–O road), the Forest Service must build a 6–mile paved segment through the Chimney Rock section of the Six Rivers National Forest. That section of the forest is situated between two other portions of the road that are already complete.

In 1977, the Forest Service issued a draft environmental impact statement that discussed proposals for upgrading an existing unpaved road that runs through the Chimney Rock area. In response to comments on the draft statement, the Forest Service commissioned a study of American Indian cultural and religious sites in the area. The Hoopa Valley Indian Reservation adjoins the Six Rivers National Forest, and the Chimney Rock area has historically been used for religious purposes by Yurok, Karok, and Tolowa Indians. The commissioned study, which was completed in 1979, found that the entire area "is significant as an integral and indispen[sable] part of Indian religious conceptualization and practice." Specific sites are used for certain rituals, and "successful use of the [area] is dependent upon and facilitated by certain qualities of the physical environment, the most important of which are privacy, silence, and an undisturbed natural setting." The study concluded that constructing a road along any of the available routes "would cause serious and irreparable damage to the sacred areas which are an integral and necessary part of the belief systems and lifeway of Northwest California Indian peoples." Accordingly, the report recommended that the G–O road not be completed.

In 1982, the Forest Service decided not to adopt this recommendation, and it prepared a final environmental impact statement for construction of the road. The Regional Forester selected a route that avoided archeological sites and was removed as far as possible from the sites used by contemporary Indians for specific spiritual activities. Alternative routes that would have avoided the Chimney Rock area altogether were rejected because they would have required the acquisition of private land, had serious soil stability problems, and would in any event have traversed areas having ritualistic value to American Indians. At about the same time, the Forest Service adopted a management plan allowing for the harvesting of significant amounts of timber in this area of the forest. The management plan provided for one-half mile protective zones around all the religious sites identified in the report that had been commissioned in connection with the G–O road.

After exhausting their administrative remedies, respondents—an Indian organization, individual Indians, nature organizations and individual members of those organizations, and the State of California—challenged the road-building and timber-harvesting decisions in the United States District Court for the Northern District of California. Respondents claimed that the Forest Service's decisions violated the Free Exercise Clause, the Federal Water Pollution Control Act (FWPCA), 86 Stat. 896, as amended, 33 U.S.C. § 1251 *et seq.*, the National Environmental Policy Act of 1969 (NEPA), 83 Stat. 852, 42 U.S.C. § 4321 *et seq.*, several other federal statutes, and governmental trust responsibilities to Indians living on the Hoopa Valley Reservation.

After a trial, the District Court issued a permanent injunction prohibiting the Government from constructing the Chimney Rock section of the G–O road or putting the timber-harvesting management plan into effect. See *Northwest Indian Cemetery Protective Assn. v. Peterson,* 565 F. Supp. 586 (N.D. Cal. 1983). The court found that both actions would violate the Free Exercise Clause because they "would seriously damage the salient visual, aural, and environmental qualities of the high country." *Id.,* at 594–595. *** [A divided panel of the Ninth Circuit affirmed the constitutional portion of the ruling.] *Northwest Indian Cemetery Protective Assn. v. Peterson,* 795 F.2d 688 (9th Cir. 1986). ***

III.

A.

The Free Exercise Clause of the First Amendment provides that "Congress shall make no law *** prohibiting the free exercise [of religion]." It is undisputed that the Indian respondents' beliefs are sincere and that the Government's proposed actions will have severe adverse effects on the practice of their religion. Those respondents contend that the burden on their religious practices is heavy enough to violate the Free Exercise Clause unless the Government can demonstrate a compelling need to complete the G–O road or to engage in timber harvesting in the Chimney Rock area. We disagree.

In *Bowen v. Roy,* 476 U.S. 693, (1986), we considered a challenge to a federal statute that required the States to use Social Security numbers in administering certain welfare programs. Two applicants for benefits under these programs contended that their religious beliefs prevented them from acceding to the use of a Social Security number for their 2–year–old daughter because the use of a numerical identifier would " 'rob the spirit' of [their] daughter and prevent her from attaining greater spiritual power." *Id.* at 696. Similarly, in this case, it is said that disruption of the natural environment caused by the G–O road will diminish the sacredness of the area in question and create distractions that will interfere with "training and ongoing religious experience of individuals using [sites within] the area for personal medicine and growth *** and as integrated parts of a system of religious belief and practice which correlates ascending degrees of personal power with a geographic hierarchy of power." ("Scarred hills and mountains, and disturbed rocks destroy the purity of the sacred areas, and [Indian] consultants repeatedly stressed the need of a training doctor to be undistracted by such disturbance"). The Court rejected this kind of challenge in *Roy:*

> The Free Exercise Clause simply cannot be understood to require the Government to conduct its own internal affairs in ways that comport with the religious beliefs of particular citizens. *** The Free Exercise Clause affords an individual protection from certain forms of governmental compulsion; it does not afford an individual a right to dictate the conduct of the Government's internal procedures.

476 U.S., at 699–700.

The building of a road or the harvesting of timber on publicly owned land cannot meaningfully be distinguished from the use of a Social Security number in *Roy.* In both cases, the challenged Government action would interfere significantly with private persons' ability to pursue spiritual fulfillment according to their own religious beliefs. In neither case, however, would the affected individuals be coerced by the Government's action into violating their religious beliefs; nor would either governmental action penalize religious activity by denying any person an equal share of the rights, benefits, and privileges enjoyed by other citizens.

***

Respondents insist, nonetheless, that the courts below properly relied on a factual inquiry into the degree to which the Indians' spiritual practices would become ineffectual if the G–O road were built. ***

*** It is true that this Court has repeatedly held that indirect coercion or penalties on the free exercise of religion, not just outright prohibitions, are subject to scrutiny under the First Amendment. Thus, for example, ineligibility for unemployment benefits, based solely on a refusal to violate the Sabbath, has been analogized to a fine imposed on Sabbath worship. *Sherbert, supra,* 374 U.S., at 404. This does not and cannot imply that incidental effects of government programs, which may make it more difficult to practice certain religions but which have no tendency to coerce individuals into acting contrary to their religious beliefs, require government to bring forward a compelling justification for its otherwise lawful actions. The crucial word in the constitutional text is "prohibit": "For the Free Exercise Clause is written in terms of what the government cannot do to the individual, not in terms of what the individual can exact from the government." *Sherbert, supra,* at 412 (Douglas, J., concurring).

Whatever may be the exact line between unconstitutional prohibitions on the free exercise of religion and the legitimate conduct by government of its own affairs, the location of the line cannot depend on measuring the effects of a governmental action on a religious objector's spiritual development. The Government does not dispute, and we have no reason to doubt, that the logging and road-building projects at issue in this case could have devastating effects on traditional Indian religious practices. Those practices are intimately and inextricably bound up with the unique features of the Chimney Rock area, which is known to the Indians as the "high country." Individual practitioners use this area for personal spiritual development; some of their activities are believed to be critically important in advancing the welfare of the Tribe, and indeed, of mankind itself. The Indians use this area, as they have used it for a very long time, to conduct a wide variety of specific rituals that aim to accomplish their religious goals. According to their beliefs, the rituals would not be efficacious if conducted at other sites than the ones traditionally used, and too much disturbance of the area's natural state would clearly render any meaningful continuation of traditional practices impossible. To be sure, the Indians themselves were far from unanimous in opposing the G–O road, and it seems less than certain that construction of the road will be so disruptive that it will doom their religion. Nevertheless, we can assume that the threat to the efficacy of at least some religious practices is extremely grave.

Even if we assume that we should accept the Ninth Circuit's prediction, according to which the G–O road will "virtually destroy the *** Indians' ability to practice their religion," 795 F.2d, at 693 (opinion below), the Constitution simply does not provide a principle that could justify upholding respondents' legal claims. However much we might wish that it were otherwise, government simply could not operate if it were required to satisfy every citizen's religious needs and desires. A broad range of government activities-from social welfare programs to foreign aid to conservation projects-will always be considered essential to the spiritual well-being of some citizens, often on the basis of sincerely held religious beliefs. Others will find the very same activities deeply offensive, and perhaps incompatible with their own search for spiritual fulfillment and with the tenets of their religion. The First Amendment must apply to all citizens alike, and it can give to none of them a veto over public programs that do not prohibit the free exercise of religion. The Constitution does not, and courts cannot, offer to reconcile the various competing demands on government, many of them rooted in sincere religious belief, that inevitably arise in so diverse a society as ours. That task, to the extent that it is feasible, is for the legislatures and other institutions. *Cf.* The Federalist No. 10 (suggesting that the effects of religious factionalism are best restrained through competition among a multiplicity of religious sects).

One need not look far beyond the present case to see why the analysis in *Roy,* but not respondents' proposed extension of *Sherbert* and its progeny, offers a sound reading of the Constitution. Respondents attempt to stress the limits of the religious servitude that they are now seeking to impose on the Chimney Rock area of the Six Rivers National Forest. While defending an injunction against logging operations and the construction of a road, they apparently do not *at present* object to the area's being used by recreational visitors, other Indians, or forest rangers. Nothing in the principle for which they contend, however, would distinguish this case from another lawsuit in which they (or similarly situated religious objectors) might seek to exclude all human activity but their own from sacred areas of the public lands. The Indian respondents insist that "*[p]rivacy* during the power quests is required for the practitioners to maintain the purity needed for a successful journey." Similarly: "The practices conducted in the high country entail intense meditation and require the practitioner to achieve a profound awareness of the natural environment. Prayer seats are oriented so there is an unobstructed view, and the practitioner must be surrounded by *undisturbed* naturalness." No disrespect for these practices is implied when one notes that such beliefs could easily require *de facto* beneficial ownership of some rather spacious tracts of public property. Even without anticipating future cases, the diminution of the Government's property rights, and the concomitant subsidy of the Indian religion, would in this case be far from trivial: the District Court's order permanently forbade commercial timber harvesting, or the construction of a two-lane road, anywhere within an area covering a full 27 sections (*i.e.* more than 17,000 acres) of public land.

The Constitution does not permit government to discriminate against religions that treat particular physical sites as sacred, and a law prohibiting the Indian respondents from visiting the Chimney Rock area would raise a different set of constitutional questions. Whatever rights the Indians may have to the use of the area, however, those rights do not divest the Government of its right to use what is, after all, *its* land. ***

B

Nothing in our opinion should be read to encourage governmental insensitivity to the religious needs of any citizen. The Government's rights to the use of its own land, for example, need not and should not discourage it from accommodating religious practices like those engaged in by the Indian respondents. It is worth emphasizing, therefore, that the Government has taken numerous steps in this very case to minimize the impact that construction of the G–O road will have on the Indians' religious activities. First, the Forest Service commissioned a comprehensive study of the effects that the project would have on the cultural and religious value of the Chimney Rock area. The resulting 423–page report was so sympathetic to the Indians' interests that it has constituted the principal piece of evidence relied on by respondents throughout this litigation.

Although the Forest Service did not in the end adopt the report's recommendation that the project be abandoned, many other ameliorative measures were planned. No sites where specific rituals take place were to be disturbed. In fact, a major factor in choosing among alternative routes for the road was the relation of the various routes to religious sites. ***

Except for abandoning its project entirely, and thereby leaving the two existing segments of road to dead-end in the middle of a National Forest, it is difficult to see how the Government could have been more solicitous. Such solicitude accords with "the policy of the United States to protect and preserve for American Indians their inherent right of freedom to believe, express, and exercise the traditional religions of the American Indian *** including but not limited to access to sites, use and possession of sacred objects, and the freedom to worship through ceremonials and traditional rites." American Indian Religious Freedom Act (AIRFA), Pub.L. 95–341, 92 Stat. 469, 42 U.S.C. § 1996.

Respondents, however, suggest that AIRFA goes further and in effect enacts their interpretation of the First Amendment into statutory law. Although this contention was rejected by the District Court, they seek to defend the judgment below by arguing that AIRFA authorizes the injunction against completion of the G–O road. This argument is without merit. After reciting several legislative findings, AIRFA "resolves" upon the policy quoted above. A second section of the statute, 92 Stat. 470, required an evaluation of federal policies and procedures, in consultation with native religious leaders, of changes necessary to protect and preserve the rights and practices in question. The required report dealing with this evaluation was completed and released in 1979. Nowhere in the law is there so much as a hint of any intent to create a cause of action or any judicially enforceable individual rights.

What is obvious from the face of the statute is confirmed by numerous indications in the legislative history. The sponsor of the bill that became AIRFA, Representative Udall, called it "a sense of Congress joint resolution," aimed at ensuring that "the basic right of the Indian people to exercise their traditional religious practices is not infringed without a clear decision on the part of the Congress or the administrators that such religious practices must yield to some higher consideration." 124 Cong. Rec. 21444 (1978). Representative Udall emphasized that the bill would not "confer special religious rights on Indians," would "not change any existing State or Federal law," and in fact "has no teeth in it." *Id.* at 21444–21445.

***

JUSTICE KENNEDY took no part in the consideration or decision of this case.

JUSTICE BRENNAN, with whom **JUSTICE MARSHALL** and **JUSTICE BLACKMUN** join, dissenting.

"[T]he Free Exercise Clause," the Court explains today, "is written in terms of what the government cannot do to the individual, not in terms of what the individual can exact from the government." *Ante,* at 1326. Pledging fidelity to this unremarkable constitutional principle, the Court nevertheless concludes that even where the Government uses federal land in a manner that threatens the very existence of a Native American religion, the Government is simply not "*doing*" anything to the practitioners of that faith. Instead, the Court believes that Native Americans who request that the Government refrain from destroying their religion effectively seek to exact from the Government *de facto* beneficial ownership of federal property. These two astonishing conclusions follow naturally from the Court's determination that federal land-use decisions that render the practice of a given religion impossible do not burden that religion in a manner cognizable under the Free Exercise Clause, because such decisions neither coerce conduct inconsistent with religious belief nor penalize religious activity. The constitutional guarantee we interpret today, however, draws no such fine distinctions between types of restraints on religious exercise, but rather is directed against any form of governmental action that frustrates or inhibits religious practice. Because the Court today refuses even to acknowledge the constitutional injury respondents will suffer, and because this refusal essentially leaves Native Americans with absolutely no constitutional protection against perhaps the gravest threat to their religious practices, I dissent.

I

For at least 200 years and probably much longer, the Yurok, Karok, and Tolowa Indians have held sacred an approximately 25–square–mile area of land situated in what is today the Blue Creek Unit of Six Rivers National Forest in northwestern California. As the Government readily concedes, regular visits to this area, known to respondent Indians as the "high country," have played and continue to play a "critical" role in the religious practices and rituals of these Tribes. Those beliefs, only briefly described in the Court's opinion, are crucial to a proper understanding of respondents' claims.

As the Forest Service's commissioned study, the Theodoratus Report, explains, for Native Americans religion is not a discrete sphere of activity separate from all others, and any attempt to isolate the religious aspects of Indian life "is in reality an exercise which forces Indian concepts into non-Indian categories." Thus, for most Native Americans, "[t]he area of worship cannot be delineated from social, political, cultur[al], and other areas o[f] Indian lifestyle." American Indian Religious Freedom, Hearings on S.J. Res. 102 Before the Senate Select Committee on Indian Affairs, 95th Cong., 2d Sess., 86 (1978) (statement of Barney Old Coyote, Crow Tribe). A pervasive feature of this lifestyle is the individual's relationship with the natural world; this relationship, which can accurately though somewhat incompletely be characterized as one of stewardship, forms the core of what might be called, for want of a better nomenclature, the Indian religious experience. While traditional Western religions view creation as the work of a deity "who institutes natural laws which then govern the operation of physical nature," tribal religions regard creation as an on-going process in which they are morally and religiously obligated to participate. Native Americans fulfill this duty through ceremonies and rituals designed to preserve and stabilize the earth and to protect humankind from disease and other catastrophes. Failure to conduct these ceremonies in the manner and place specified, adherents believe, will result in great harm to the earth and to the people whose welfare depends upon it.

In marked contrast to traditional Western religions, the belief systems of Native Americans do not rely on doctrines, creeds, or dogmas. Established or universal truths—the mainstay of Western religions—play no part in Indian faith. Ceremonies are communal efforts undertaken for specific purposes in accordance with instructions handed down from generation to generation. Commentaries on or interpretations of the rituals themselves are deemed absolute violations of the ceremonies, whose value lies not in their ability to explain the natural world or to enlighten individual believers but in their efficacy as protectors and enhancers of tribal existence. Where dogma lies at the heart of Western religions, Native American faith is inextricably bound to the use of land. The site-specific nature of Indian religious practice derives from the Native American perception that land is itself a sacred, living being. *See* Suagee, *American Indian Religious Freedom and Cultural Resources Management: Protecting Mother Earth's Caretakers,* 10 Am. Ind. L. Rev. 1, 10 (1982). Rituals are performed in prescribed locations not merely as a matter of traditional orthodoxy, but because land, like all other living things, is unique, and specific sites possess different spiritual properties and significance. Within this belief system, therefore, land is not fungible; indeed, at the time of the Spanish colonization of the American Southwest, "all *** Indians held in some form a belief in a sacred and indissoluble bond between themselves and the land in which their settlements were located." E. Spicer, Cycles of Conquest: The Impact of Spain, Mexico, and the United States on the Indians of the Southwest, 1533–1960, p. 576 (1962).

For respondent Indians, the most sacred of lands is the high country where, they believe, prehuman spirits moved with the coming of humans to the Earth. Because these spirits are seen as the source of religious power, or "medicine," many of the tribes' rituals and practices require frequent journeys to the area. ***

[The district court in this case] found that "use of the high country is essential to [respondents'] 'World Renewal' ceremonies *** which constitute the heart of the Northwest Indian religious belief system," and that " '[i]ntrusions on the sanctity of the Blue Creek high country are *** potentially destructive of the very core of Northwest [Indian] religious beliefs and practices.' " *Northwest Indian Cemetery Protective Assn. v. Peterson,* 565 F. Supp. 586, 594–595 (ND Cal.1983). Concluding that these burdens on respondents' religious practices were sufficient to trigger the protections of the Free Exercise Clause, the court found that the interests served by the G–O road and the management plan were insufficient to justify those burdens. In particular, the court found that the road would not improve access to timber resources in the Blue Creek Unit and indeed was unnecessary to the harvesting of that timber; that it would not significantly improve the administration of the Six Rivers National Forest; and that it would increase recreational access only marginally, and at the expense of the very pristine environment that makes the area suitable for primitive recreational use in the first place. The court further found that the unconnected segments of the road had independent utility, and that although completion of the Chimney Rock segment would reduce timber-hauling costs, it would not generate new jobs but would instead merely shift work from one area of the region to another. Finally, in enjoining the proposed harvesting activities, the court found that the Blue Creek Unit's timber resources were but a small fraction of those located in the entire National Forest and that the local timber industry would not suffer seriously if access to this fraction were foreclosed.

While the case was pending on appeal before the Court of Appeals for the Ninth Circuit, Congress passed the California Wilderness Act of 1984, Pub. L. 98–425, 98 Stat. 1619, which designates most of the Blue Creek Unit a wilderness area, and thus precludes logging and all other commercial activities in most of the area covered by the Forest Service's management plan. Thereafter, the Court of Appeals affirmed the District Court's determination that the proposed harvesting and construction activities violated respondents' constitutional rights. *** Like the lower court, the Court of Appeals found the Government's interests in building the road and permitting limited timber harvesting—interests which of course were considerably undermined by passage of the California Wilderness Act—did not justify the destruction of respondents' religion.

II

The Court does not for a moment suggest that the interests served by the G–O road are in any way compelling, or that they outweigh the destructive effect construction of the road will have on respondents' religious practices. Instead, the Court embraces the Government's contention that its prerogative as landowner should always take precedence over a claim that a particular use of federal property infringes religious practices.***

I *** cannot accept the Court's premise that the form of the government's restraint on religious practice, rather than its effect, controls our constitutional analysis. Respondents here have demonstrated that construction of the G–O road will completely frustrate the practice of their religion, for as the lower courts found, the proposed logging and construction activities will virtually destroy respondents' religion, and will therefore necessarily force them into abandoning those practices altogether. Indeed, the Government's proposed activities will restrain religious practice to a far greater degree here than in any of the cases cited by the Court today. None of the religious adherents in *Hobbie, Thomas,* and *Sherbert,* for example, claimed or could have claimed that the denial of unemployment benefits rendered the practice of their religions impossible; at most, the challenged laws made those practices more expensive. *** Here the threat posed by the desecration of sacred lands that are indisputably essential to respondents' religious practices is both more direct and more substantial than that raised by a compulsory school law that simply exposed Amish children to an alien value system. And of course respondents here do not even have the option, however unattractive it might be, of migrating to more hospitable locales; the site-specific nature of their belief system renders it nontransportable.

***

III

Today, the Court holds that a federal land-use decision that promises to destroy an entire religion does not burden the practice of that faith in a manner recognized by the Free Exercise Clause. Having thus stripped respondents and all other Native Americans of any constitutional protection against perhaps the most serious threat to their age-old religious practices, and indeed to their entire way of life, the Court assures us that nothing in its decision "should be read to encourage governmental insensitivity to the religious needs of any citizen." I find it difficult, however, to imagine conduct more insensitive to religious needs than the Government's determination to build a marginally useful road in the face of uncontradicted evidence that the road will render the practice of respondents' religion impossible. Nor do I believe that respondents will derive any solace from the knowledge that although the practice of their religion will become "more difficult" as a result of the Government's actions, they remain free to maintain their religious beliefs. Given today's ruling, that freedom amounts to nothing more than the right to believe that their religion will be destroyed. The safeguarding of such a hollow freedom not only makes a mockery of the " 'policy of the United States to protect and preserve for American Indians their inherent right of freedom to believe, express, and exercise the[ir] traditional religions,' " (quoting AIRFA), it fails utterly to accord with the dictates of the First Amendment.

I dissent.

NOTES AND QUESTIONS

1. The *Lyng* Court assumed for the purpose of its decision that the G–O road could "virtually destroy the *** Indians' ability to practice their religion." The Court nonetheless concluded that the government's actions did not trigger a Free Exercise violation. What test does the Lyng majority announce for the purpose of passing the first hurdle of a Free Exercise claim? What kind of government action would flunk this test in the context of Indian sacred sites on federal land? One commentator has suggested that few government actions short of barring American Indian religious practitioners from entry could flunk this test, and that Indian religions are therefore susceptible to destruction without constitutional redress, while relatively minor inconveniences to practitioners of western religions receive accommodation. *See* Scott Hardt, Comment, *The Sacred Public Lands: Improper Line Drawing in the Supreme Court's Free Exercise Analysis*, 60 U. Colo. L. Rev. 601, 657 (1989).

2. If the majority had concluded that the construction of the G–O road triggered a free exercise claim, and therefore reached the "compelling governmental interest" prong of the test, would the government have been able to meet its burden? If you accept Justice Brennan's characterization of the significance and effects of the G–O road (which were based on the findings of the courts below) the answer seems to be no. Why doesn't the majority want to reach the compelling governmental interest question? *See Lyng* at 452–53. ("Nothing in the principle for which [the Indian respondents] contend *** would distinguish this case from another lawsuit in which they *** might seek to exclude all human activity but their own from sacred areas of the public lands.") Can you think of a response to Justice O'Connor's concern? Could the Court draw a line short of allowing Indian religious claims to dictate all federal land use decisions?

3. Justice Brennan goes into far greater detail about the nature of the Yurok, Karok and Tolowas' religious practices. He also suggests that the *Lyng* majority has made light of the finding below that the G–O road would destroy the Indians' ability to practice their religion: "Remarkably, the Court treats this factual determination as nothing more than an assumption or 'prediction,' and suggests that it is 'less than certain that construction of the road will be

so disruptive that it will doom [respondents'] religion.'" *Lyng* at 464, n. 3 (Brennan, J. dissenting). Do you agree with Justice Brennan that the majority makes light of the findings below about the G–O road's effects? If so, what forces might be at work in Indian free exercise cases that create hurdles for legal practitioners pursuing such claims? What strategies can lawyers use to overcome such hurdles?

4. Some scholars have suggested that a property rights approach to protect access to sacred sites might be more successful than a Free Exercise approach. *See* Kristen A. Carpenter, *A Property Rights Approach to Sacred Sites Cases: Asserting a Place for Indians as Nonowners*, 52 UCLA L. Rev. 1061 (2005); Kevin J. Worthen, *Protecting the Sacred Sites of Indigenous People in U.S. Courts: Reconciling Native American Religion and the Right to Exclude*, 13 St. Thomas L. Rev. 239 (2000). In *Zuni Tribe v. Platt*, 730 F. Supp. 318 (D. Ariz. 1990), the court recognized a prescriptive easement over private property in circumstances where the Zuni tribe had historically and continuously accessed a path for its pilgrimages to its sacred place of origin. Prescriptive or adverse possession claims are recognized in only limited circumstances against the federal government, however. *See* Cohen's Handbook of Federal Indian Law 970, n. 187 (2012).

5. The *Lyng* Court held that the American Indian Religious Freedom Act, 42 U.S.C. § 1996 (AIRFA,) provides no "judicially enforceable individual rights." The AIRFA was passed in 1978 as part of a shift in federal policy from the prior stance of assimilation and elimination of Indian religion and culture. The AIRFA states that:

> [I]t shall be the policy of the United States to protect and preserve for American Indians their inherent right of freedom to believe, express, and exercise the traditional religions of the American Indian, Eskimo, Aleut, and Native Hawaiians, including but not limited to access to sites, use and possession of sacred objects, and the freedom to worship through ceremonies and traditional rights.

42 U.S.C. § 1996. According to *Lyng*, AIRFA's function is to provide guidance to federal agencies and express a policy preference, but, quoting Congressman Morris Udall, the Act " 'has no teeth to it.' " *Lyng*, *supra* at 455. The comment became a self-fulfilling prophecy. The AIRFA, on its own, did little to encourage federal agencies to prioritize the protection of American Indian religion. After *Lyng*, however, pressure increased on federal agencies to take the AIRFA's policy expression seriously, and on Congress to pass laws providing greater protection.

6. The tribes achieved through legislation what they had lost in the Supreme Court. In 1990, in large part due to active lobbying in the wake of *Lyng*, Congress designated the sacred high country as permanent wilderness under the Smith River National Recreation Area Act. The Act specifically included the G–O road within the new wilderness boundaries, putting an end to construction plans. *See* 16 U.S.C. § 460 bbb–3(b)(2)(H) (2000). Is Congress better suited to make this kind of decision about public land management? If so, are Indian religions, which are inevitably minority religions in our society, afforded the same protections under the free exercise clause as other practitioners? With regard to other sacred sites, further discussion of legislation and agency action appears in Section II below.

EMPLOYMENT DIVISION, DEPARTMENT OF HUMAN RESOURCES OF OREGON V. SMITH

494 U.S. 872, 110 S. Ct. 1595, 108 L.Ed.2d 876 (1990)

JUSTICE SCALIA delivered the opinion of the Court.

***

Oregon law prohibits the knowing or intentional possession of a "controlled substance" unless the substance has been prescribed by a medical practitioner. *** [T]he drug peyote, a hallucinogen derived from the plant *Lophophora williamsii Lemaire* [is a controlled substance].

Respondents Alfred Smith and Galen Black (hereinafter respondents) were fired from their jobs with a private drug rehabilitation organization because they ingested peyote for sacramental purposes at a ceremony of the Native American Church, of which both are members. When respondents applied to petitioner Employment Division (hereinafter petitioner) for unemployment compensation, they were determined to be ineligible for benefits because they had been discharged for work-related "misconduct." *** [When the Oregon Supreme Court's decision that the restriction was prohibited by the Free Exercise Clause first came before the U.S. Supreme Court, it remanded for a determination of whether sacramental peyote use violated the Oregon statute. *Employment Div., Dept. of Human Resources of Oregon v. Smith*, 485 U.S. 660 (1988) (*Smith I*). On remand the Oregon Supreme Court held that respondents' religiously inspired use of peyote fell within the prohibition of the Oregon statute, but affirmed its decision that the prohibition of such use violated the Free Exercise Clause.]

II

Respondents' claim for relief rests on our decisions in *Sherbert v. Verner, supra, Thomas v. Review Bd. of Indiana Employment Security Div., supra,* and *Hobbie v. Unemployment Appeals Comm'n of Florida,* 480 U.S. 136 (1987), in which [the Court held that a State could not deny unemployment insurance to individuals terminated for refusing to work on their Sabbath.] As we observed in *Smith I,* however, the conduct at issue in those cases was not prohibited by law. We held that distinction to be critical, for "if Oregon does prohibit the religious use of peyote, and if that prohibition is consistent with the Federal Constitution, there is no federal right to engage in that conduct in Oregon," and "the State is free to withhold unemployment compensation from respondents for engaging in work-related misconduct, despite its religious motivation." 485 U.S. at 672. Now that the Oregon Supreme Court has confirmed that Oregon does prohibit the religious use of peyote, we proceed to consider whether that prohibition is permissible under the Free Exercise Clause.

A.

The Free Exercise Clause of the First Amendment, which has been made applicable to the States by incorporation into the Fourteenth Amendment, *see*

Cantwell v. Connecticut, 310 U.S. 296 (1940), provides that "Congress shall make no law respecting an establishment of religion, or *prohibiting the free exercise thereof* ***." U.S. Const., Amdt. 1 (emphasis added). The free exercise of religion means, first and foremost, the right to believe and profess whatever religious doctrine one desires. Thus, the First Amendment obviously excludes all "governmental regulation of religious *beliefs* as such." *Sherbert v. Verner, supra,* 374 U.S., at 402. The government may not compel affirmation of religious belief, punish the expression of religious doctrines it believes to be false, impose special disabilities on the basis of religious views or religious status, or lend its power to one or the other side in controversies over religious authority or dogma.

But the "exercise of religion" often involves not only belief and profession but the performance of (or abstention from) physical acts: assembling with others for a worship service, participating in sacramental use of bread and wine, proselytizing, abstaining from certain foods or certain modes of transportation. It would be true, we think (though no case of ours has involved the point), that a State would be "prohibiting the free exercise [of religion]" if it sought to ban such acts or abstentions only when they are engaged in for religious reasons, or only because of the religious belief that they display. It would doubtless be unconstitutional, for example, to ban the casting of "statues that are to be used for worship purposes," or to prohibit bowing down before a golden calf.

Respondents in the present case, however, seek to carry the meaning of "prohibiting the free exercise [of religion]" one large step further. They contend that their religious motivation for using peyote places them beyond the reach of a criminal law that is not specifically directed at their religious practice, and that is concededly constitutional as applied to those who use the drug for other reasons. They assert, in other words, that "prohibiting the free exercise [of religion]" includes requiring any individual to observe a generally applicable law that requires (or forbids) the performance of an act that his religious belief forbids (or requires). ***

We have never held that an individual's religious beliefs excuse him from compliance with an otherwise valid law prohibiting conduct that the State is free to regulate. *** We first had occasion to assert that principle in *Reynolds v. United States,* 98 U.S. 145 (1878), where we rejected the claim that criminal laws against polygamy could not be constitutionally applied to those whose religion commanded the practice. ***

Respondents argue that even though exemption from generally applicable criminal laws need not automatically be extended to religiously motivated actors, at least the claim for a religious exemption must be evaluated under the balancing test set forth in *Sherbert v. Verner,* 374 U.S. 398 (1963). Under the *Sherbert* test, governmental actions that substantially burden a religious practice must be justified by a compelling governmental interest. Applying that test we have, on three occasions, invalidated state unemployment compensation rules that conditioned the availability of benefits upon an applicant's willingness to work under conditions forbidden by his religion. We have never invalidated any governmental action on the basis of the *Sherbert* test except the denial of unemployment compensation. Although we have sometimes purported to apply the *Sherbert* test in contexts other than that, we have always found the test satisfied. *** In *Lyng v. Northwest Indian Cemetery Protective Assn.,* 485 U.S. 439, (1988), we declined to apply *Sherbert* analysis to the

Government's logging and road construction activities on lands used for religious purposes by several Native American Tribes, even though it was undisputed that the activities "could have devastating effects on traditional religious practices." ***

Whether or not the decisions are that limited, they at least have nothing to do with an across-the-board criminal prohibition on a particular form of conduct. *** We conclude today that the sounder approach, and the approach in accord with the vast majority of our precedents, is to hold the [*Sherbert*] test inapplicable to such challenges. The government's ability to enforce generally applicable prohibitions of socially harmful conduct, like its ability to carry out other aspects of public policy, "cannot depend on measuring the effects of a governmental action on a religious objector's spiritual development." *Lyng, supra,* 485 U.S., at 451. To make an individual's obligation to obey such a law contingent upon the law's coincidence with his religious beliefs, except where the State's interest is "compelling"—permitting him, by virtue of his beliefs, "to become a law unto himself," *Reynolds v. United States,* 98 U.S. at 167—contradicts both constitutional tradition and common sense.

***

Nor is it possible to limit the impact of respondents' proposal by requiring a "compelling state interest" only when the conduct prohibited is "central" to the individual's religion. *Cf. Lyng v. Northwest Indian Cemetery Protective Assn.,* 485 U.S., at 474–76 (Brennan, J., dissenting). It is no more appropriate for judges to determine the "centrality" of religious beliefs before applying a "compelling interest" test in the free exercise field, than it would be for them to determine the "importance" of ideas before applying the "compelling interest" test in the free speech field. What principle of law or logic can be brought to bear to contradict a believer's assertion that a particular act is "central" to his personal faith? Judging the centrality of different religious practices is akin to the unacceptable "business of evaluating the relative merits of differing religious claims." ***

If the "compelling interest" test is to be applied at all, then, it must be applied across the board, to all actions thought to be religiously commanded. Moreover, if "compelling interest" really means what it says (and watering it down here would subvert its rigor in the other fields where it is applied), many laws will not meet the test. Any society adopting such a system would be courting anarchy, but that danger increases in direct proportion to the society's diversity of religious beliefs, and its determination to coerce or suppress none of them. Precisely because "we are a cosmopolitan nation made up of people of almost every conceivable religious preference," *Braunfeld v. Brown,* 366 U.S., at 606, and precisely because we value and protect that religious divergence, we cannot afford the luxury of deeming *presumptively invalid,* as applied to the religious objector, every regulation of conduct that does not protect an interest of the highest order. The rule respondents favor would open the prospect of constitutionally required religious exemptions from civic obligations of almost every conceivable kind—ranging from compulsory military service, to the payment of taxes, to health and safety regulation such as manslaughter and child neglect laws, compulsory vaccination laws, drug laws, and traffic laws, to social welfare legislation such as minimum wage laws, child labor laws, animal cruelty laws, environmental protection laws, and laws providing for equality of opportunity for the races. The First Amendment's protection of religious liberty does not require this.

Values that are protected against government interference through enshrinement in the Bill of Rights are not thereby banished from the political process. Just as a society that believes in the negative protection accorded to the press by the First Amendment is likely to enact laws that affirmatively foster the dissemination of the printed word, so also a society that believes in the negative protection accorded to religious belief can be expected to be solicitous of that value in its legislation as well. It is therefore not surprising that a number of States have made an exception to their drug laws for sacramental peyote use. *See, e.g.,* Ariz. Rev. Stat. Ann. §§ 13–3402(B)(1)–(3) (1989); Colo. Rev. Stat. § 12–22–317(3) (1985); N.M. Stat. Ann. § 30–31–6(D) (Supp. 1989). But to say that a nondiscriminatory religious-practice exemption is permitted, or even that it is desirable, is not to say that it is constitutionally required, and that the appropriate occasions for its creation can be discerned by the courts. It may fairly be said that leaving accommodation to the political process will place at a relative disadvantage those religious practices that are not widely engaged in; but that unavoidable consequence of democratic government must be preferred to a system in which each conscience is a law unto itself or in which judges weigh the social importance of all laws against the centrality of all religious beliefs.

***

Because respondents' ingestion of peyote was prohibited under Oregon law, and because that prohibition is constitutional, Oregon may, consistent with the Free Exercise Clause, deny respondents unemployment compensation when their dismissal results from use of the drug. The decision of the Oregon Supreme Court is accordingly reversed.

It is so ordered.

JUSTICE O'CONNOR, with whom **JUSTICE BRENNAN**, **JUSTICE MARSHALL**, and **JUSTICE BLACKMUN** join as to Parts I and II, concurring in the judgment.†

Although I agree with the result the Court reaches in this case, I cannot join its opinion. In my view, today's holding dramatically departs from well-settled First Amendment jurisprudence, appears unnecessary to resolve the question presented, and is incompatible with our Nation's fundamental commitment to individual religious liberty.

***

II

The Free Exercise Clause of the First Amendment commands that "Congress shall make no law *** prohibiting the free exercise [of religion]." *** Because the First Amendment does not distinguish between religious belief and religious conduct, conduct motivated by sincere religious belief, like the belief itself, must be at least presumptively protected by the Free Exercise Clause.

The Court today, however, interprets the Clause to permit the government to prohibit, without justification, conduct mandated by an individual's religious beliefs, so long as that prohibition is generally applicable. But a law that

†. Although Justice Brennan, Justice Marshall, and Justice Blackmun join Part I and II of this opinion, they do not concur in the judgment.

prohibits certain conduct—conduct that happens to be an act of worship for someone-manifestly does prohibit that person's free exercise of his religion. A person who is barred from engaging in religiously motivated conduct is barred from freely exercising his religion. Moreover, that person is barred from freely exercising his religion regardless of whether the law prohibits the conduct only when engaged in for religious reasons, only by members of that religion, or by all persons. It is difficult to deny that a law that prohibits religiously motivated conduct, even if the law is generally applicable, does not at least implicate First Amendment concerns.

***

To say that a person's right to free exercise has been burdened, of course, does not mean that he has an absolute right to engage in the conduct. Under our established First Amendment jurisprudence, we have recognized that the freedom to act, unlike the freedom to believe, cannot be absolute. Instead, we have respected both the First Amendment's express textual mandate and the governmental interest in regulation of conduct by requiring the government to justify any substantial burden on religiously motivated conduct by a compelling state interest and by means narrowly tailored to achieve that interest. The compelling interest test effectuates the First Amendment's command that religious liberty is an independent liberty, that it occupies a preferred position, and that the Court will not permit encroachments upon this liberty, whether direct or indirect, unless required by clear and compelling governmental interests "of the highest order," *Yoder, supra,* 406 U.S. at 215. "Only an especially important governmental interest pursued by narrowly tailored means can justify exacting a sacrifice of First Amendment freedoms as the price for an equal share of the rights, benefits, and privileges enjoyed by other citizens." *Roy, supra,* 476 U.S. at 728 (opinion concurring in part and dissenting in part).

***

Finally, the Court today suggests that the disfavoring of minority religions is an "unavoidable consequence" under our system of government and that accommodation of such religions must be left to the political process. In my view, however, the First Amendment was enacted precisely to protect the rights of those whose religious practices are not shared by the majority and may be viewed with hostility. The history of our free exercise doctrine amply demonstrates the harsh impact majoritarian rule has had on unpopular or emerging religious groups such as the Jehovah's Witnesses and the Amish. Indeed, the words of Justice Jackson in *West Virginia State Bd. of Ed. v. Barnette* 310 U.S. 586 (1940) are apt:

> The very purpose of a Bill of Rights was to withdraw certain subjects from the vicissitudes of political controversy, to place them beyond the reach of majorities and officials and to establish them as legal principles to be applied by the courts. One's right to life, liberty, and property, to free speech, a free press, freedom of worship and assembly, and other fundamental rights may not be submitted to vote; they depend on the outcome of no elections. 319 U.S. at 638.

*** The compelling interest test reflects the First Amendment's mandate of preserving religious liberty to the fullest extent possible in a pluralistic society. For the Court to deem this command a "luxury," is to denigrate "[t]he very purpose of a Bill of Rights."

[Justice O'Connor nevertheless concurred in the judgment because despite the fundamental interference with the Respondents' religious practices, granting an exemption for sacramental peyote use would unduly interfere with governmental interests in preventing the health risks of peyote and assuring uniform application and enforcement of criminal laws.]

[Justice Blackmun, with whom Justice Brennan and Justice Marshall join, dissented, agreeing with the test announced in Justice O'Connor's concurrence, but finding that Oregon's lack of prosecution of any sacramental peyote users, the careful way in which sacramental peyote was administered, and the number of federal and state governments that granted exemptions for religious peyote use, suggested there was no compelling interest in forbidding an exemption.]

NOTES AND QUESTIONS

1. *Commentary on* Smith. Scholarly response to the *Smith* decision has been largely critical. *See* Jesse H. Choper, *The Rise and Decline of the Constitutional Protection of Religious Liberty*, 70 Neb. L. Rev. 651, 685–88 (1991); John Delaney, *Police Power Absolutism and Nullifying the Free Exercise Clause: A Critique of* Oregon v. Smith, 25 Ind. L. Rev. 71, 75 (1991); Craig J. Dorsay & Lea Ann Easton, *Just Say "No" to the Free Exercise Clause*, 59 UMKC L. Rev. 555 (1991); *see also* Garrett Epps, *To an Unknown God: The Hidden History of* Employment Division v. Smith, 30 Ariz. St. L. J. 953, 956 (1996) ("*Smith* was one of the most unpopular decisions in the Court's recent history."). One theme in this criticism is an attack on *Smith*'s definition of "neutrality":

> In *Smith*, the generally applicable law was the prohibition on the use of hallucinogenic drugs. The Native American Church uses peyote as its sacrament. Application of the anti-drug laws to the sacramental use of peyote effectively destroys the practice of the Native American Church. Is this neutral?
>
> No, it is not. Christians and Jews use wine as part of their sacrament, and wine is not illegal. Even when wine was illegal during Prohibition, Congress exempted the sacramental use of wine from the proscription. The effect of laws prohibiting hallucinogenic drugs but not alcohol, or of allowing exemptions from one law but not the other, is to impose a burden on the practice of the Native American Church that is not imposed on Christians or Jews. It is no more neutral than operating courts on Saturday and not on Sunday.
>
> But perhaps this overstates the case. *** The difference in treatment can be said to be based on objective differences between the effects of the two substances. ***
>
> The only way to tell whether the difference in treatment between peyote and wine is the result of prejudice or the result of objective differences in the substances is to examine closely the purported governmental purpose. *** This, of course, is a rough description of the compelling interest test.

Michael W. McConnell, *Free Exercise Revisionism and the Smith Decision*, 57 U. Chi. L. Rev. 1109, 1134–1136 (1990). William Marshall responded that exemptions for free exercise would overly entangle courts in determining the centrality of religious practice and undermine the values of the Establishment Clause by favoring religious adherents over non-religious individuals. William P. Marshall, *In Defense of* Smith *and Free Exercise Revisionism*, 58 U. Chi. L. Rev. 308 (1991). Who is right?

2. *State Response to Peyote Use. Smith II* undermined the decisions of several state courts that the Free Exercise Clause prevented the criminalization of sacramental peyote use. The California Supreme Court held that the free exercise clause required the state to make an exception to its drug laws to accommodate sacramental use of peyote by a member of the Native American Church in 1964. *People v. Woody*, 394 P.2d 813 (Cal. 1964). In language resonating with the spirit of the 1960's, Justice Tobriner wrote for the Court:

> In a mass society, which presses at every point toward conformity, the protection of a self-expression, however unique, of the individual and the group becomes ever more important. The varying currents of the subcultures that flow into the mainstream of our national life give it depth and beauty. We preserve a greater value than an ancient tradition when we protect the rights of Indians who honestly practiced an old religion in using peyote one night in a desert Hogan near Needles, California.

Id. at 821–22. *Woody* was followed by two other state courts, *State v. Whittingham*, 504 P.2d 950 (Ariz. Ct. App. 1973); *Whitehorn v. State*, 561 P.2d 539 (Okla. Ct. App. 1977), and led other states to liberalize their peyote laws. By the time of *Smith II*, the federal government and twenty-three states had created legislative or regulatory exceptions to their narcotics laws in order to accommodate Indian religious use of peyote. McConnell, 57 U. Chi. L. Rev. at 1135; *cf.* Cohen's Handbook of Federal Indian Law 967 n.168 (2012) (discussing contemporary exemptions).

3. *Congressional action.* Justice O'Connor would have retained the substantial burden/compelling state interest test, but then would have held that Oregon had a compelling state interest in prohibiting the use of peyote, even for religious purposes. *See Smith* at 903–907 (O'Connor, J., concurring). As discussed below, Congress responded to *Smith* by enacting the Religious Freedom Restoration Act of 1993, 42 U.S.C. § 2000bb to 2000bb–4, restoring the compelling state interest test. In addition, Congress passed the American Indian Religious Freedom Act Amendments of 1994, 42 U.S.C. § 1996a, prohibiting states from penalizing an Indian who uses peyote in a traditional manner for religious purposes, save for some exceptions related to law enforcement, transportation, the military and prisons. Do you think these laws would have been passed if the O'Connor approach had prevailed? Are Indian religious practitioners better off with these legislative changes than they would have been with the O'Connor version of *Smith*?

4. *Exemption for Non–Indians?* With the AIRFA amendment permitting Indian religious peyote use, the remaining issues in dispute concern whether non-tribal members may claim similar exemptions for peyote use under either the Free Exercise or Equal Protection clauses. Courts have gone different ways, some extending the exemption and others refusing to. *Compare State v. Mooney*, 98 P.3d 420 (Utah 2004) (holding that plain language of AIRFA and preference for construing statutes to avoid constitutional issues required

interpretation of statute to cover use of peyote by non-Indian practitioners) *and United States v. Boyll*, 774 F. Supp. 1333 (D.N.M. 1991) (extending peyote exemption to non-Indian practitioner) *with Peyote Way Church of God v. Thornburgh*, 922 F.2d 1210 (5th Cir. 1991) (assuming without deciding that AIRFA only protected Indian practitioners and upholding provision against constitutional challenge). For further discussion and analysis of these issues, see Cohen's Handbook of Federal Indian Law 974-75 (2012).

Congressional Response: The Religious Freedom Restoration Act (RFRA)

Congress responded to the *Smith* decision by enacting the Religious Freedom Restoration Act, 42 U.S.C. §§ 2000bb–1–2000bb–4 (RFRA). The RFRA restored the substantial burden/compelling state interest test that the Court had articulated in *Sherbert v. Verner*, 374 U.S. 398 (1963) by providing that even a rule of general applicability may not substantially burden a person's exercise of religion unless the government shows that "application of the burden to the person (1) is in furtherance of a compelling governmental interest; and (2) is the least restrictive means of furthering that compelling governmental interest." 42 U.S.C. § 2000bb–1. In *City of Boerne v. Flores*, 521 U.S. 507 (1997), the Supreme Court held that RFRA was unconstitutional as applied to states because Congress had exceeded its powers under section five of the fourteenth amendment. With respect to federal agencies, however, RFRA is valid because it draws on the constitutional authority to create those agencies. *See Burwell v. Hobby Lobby Stores, Inc.*, 134 S. Ct. 2751, 2761 (2014); *see also Gonzales v. O Centro Espirita Beneficente Uniao do Vegetal*, 546 U.S. 418 (2006) (holding that United States failed to sufficiently justify criminalization of a hallucinogenic tea used in religious ceremonies under RFRA).

Three years after the *Boerne* decision, Congress enacted the Religious Land Use and Institutionalized Persons Act of 2000, 42 U.S.C. § 2000cc, *et seq.* (RLUIPA). Mindful of *Boerne*'s analysis, Congress grounded RLUIPA in its spending and commerce clause powers. *See* 42 U.S.C. §§ 2000cc–1(b)(1)–(2). RLUIPA prohibits state and local governments from imposing substantial burdens on the exercise of religion through prisoner or land-use regulations unless those burdens are the least restrictive means of achieving a compelling interest. 42 U.S.C. §§ 2000cc, 2000cc–1. In addition, RLUIPA replaced RFRA's original, constitution-based definition of "exercise of religion" with the following: "any exercise of religion, whether or not compelled by, or central to, a system of religious belief." 42 U.S.C. §§ 2000bb–2(4), 2000cc–5(7)(A). In the course of setting aside regulations mandating insurance coverage for birth control under the Affordable Care Act, the Court described RLUIPA as "an obvious effort to effect a complete separation from First Amendment case law," and held that RLUIPA's enhanced definition of exercise of religion applied to RFRA as well. *Burwell v. Hobby Lobby Stores, Inc.*, 134 S. Ct. 2751, 2761-62 (2014). In *Cutter v. Wilkinson*, 544 U.S. 709 (2005), the Supreme Court held that RLUIPA's provisions (applied to prisoners) did not violate the establishment clause, but did not consider whether Congress had exceeded its powers under the spending or commerce clauses.

After RFRA, RLUIPA and *Boerne*, the constitutional and legislative framework for free exercise claims is as follows. RFRA, with its substantial burden/compelling state interest test, applies to all federal government actions, as well as state prisoner or land use regulations. The *Smith* Court's approach, which limited *Sherbert* to its facts, still applies to other neutral state laws of general application, with exceptions made for religious use of Peyote as required by the AIRFA amendments, 42 U.S.C. § 1996a.

II. SACRED SITES AND LANDS

The *Lyng* decision articulated the test for free exercise limitations on federal land use decisions. But RFRA's reinstatement of the substantial burden/compelling state interest test gave new life to claims by American Indians that federal land use decisions should be modified or invalidated when they desecrate sacred sites or otherwise interfere with Indian spiritual practices. Now that Congress had weighed in, the courts did not have to fear that they were engaging in constitutional free-lancing when striking down governmental actions that burdened religion. Or so it seemed. Evaluate whether RFRA made any difference to the court's analysis in the following case.

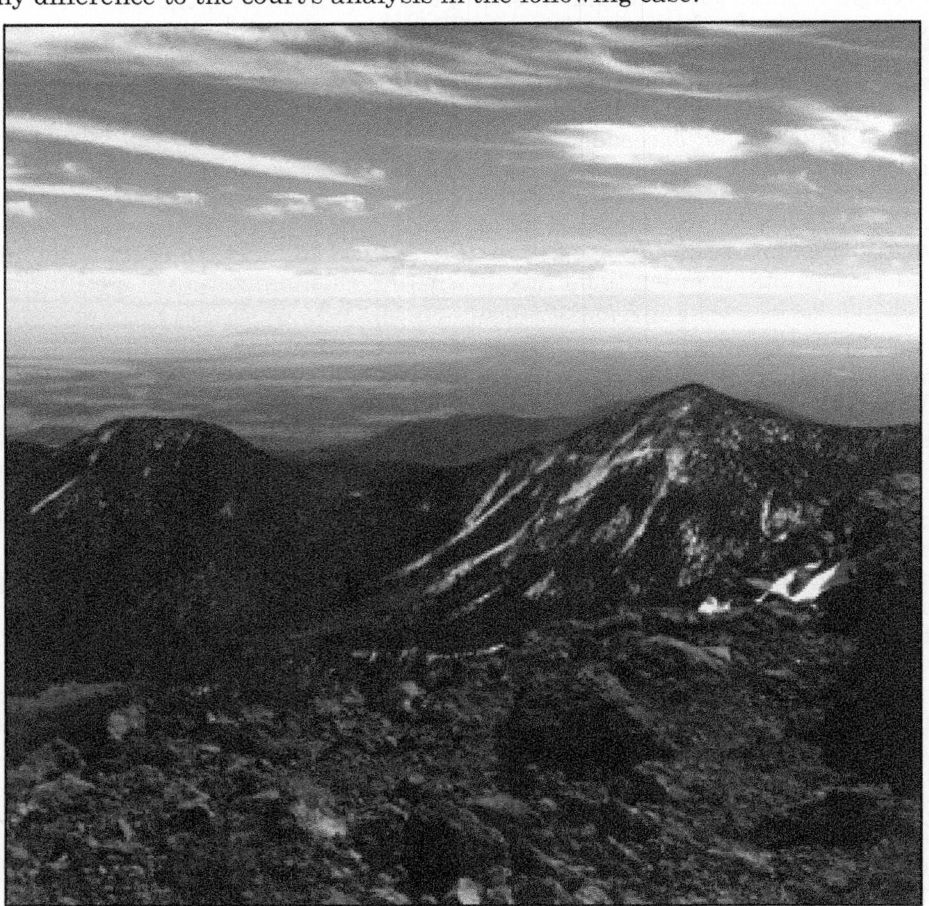

San Francisco Peaks. Photo by Sarah Krakoff, Fall 2012.

NAVAJO NATION V. UNITED STATES FOREST SERVICE

535 F.3d 1058 (9th Cir. 2008) (*en banc*)

BEA, CIRCUIT JUDGE:

In this case, American Indians ask us to prohibit the federal government from allowing the use of artificial snow for skiing on a portion of a public mountain sacred in their religion. At the heart of their claim is the planned use of recycled wastewater, which contains 0.0001% human waste, to make artificial snow. The Plaintiffs claim the use of such snow on a sacred mountain desecrates the entire mountain, deprecates their religious ceremonies, and injures their religious sensibilities. We are called upon to decide whether this government-approved use of artificial snow on government-owned park land violates the Religious Freedom Restoration Act of 1993 ("RFRA")[.] ***

Plaintiff Indian tribes and their members consider the San Francisco Peaks in Northern Arizona to be sacred in their religion. They contend that the use of recycled wastewater to make artificial snow for skiing on the Snowbowl, a ski area that covers approximately one percent of the San Francisco Peaks, will spiritually contaminate the entire mountain and devalue their religious exercises. The district court found the Plaintiffs' beliefs to be sincere; there is no basis to challenge that finding. The district court also found, however, that there are no plants, springs, natural resources, shrines with religious significance, or religious ceremonies that would be physically affected by the use of such artificial snow. No plants would be destroyed or stunted; no springs polluted; no places of worship made inaccessible, or liturgy modified. The Plaintiffs continue to have virtually unlimited access to the mountain, including the ski area, for religious and cultural purposes. On the mountain, they continue to pray, conduct their religious ceremonies, and collect plants for religious use.

Thus, the sole effect of the artificial snow is on the Plaintiffs' subjective spiritual experience. That is, the presence of the artificial snow on the Peaks is offensive to the Plaintiffs' feelings about their religion and will decrease the spiritual fulfillment Plaintiffs get from practicing their religion on the mountain. Nevertheless, a government action that decreases the spirituality, the fervor, or the satisfaction with which a believer practices his religion is not what Congress has labeled a "substantial burden"—a term of art chosen by Congress to be defined by reference to Supreme Court precedent—on the free exercise of religion. Where, as here, there is no showing the government has coerced the Plaintiffs to act contrary to their religious beliefs under the threat of sanctions, or conditioned a governmental benefit upon conduct that would violate the Plaintiffs' religious beliefs, there is no "substantial burden" on the exercise of their religion.

Were it otherwise, any action the federal government were to take, including action on its own land, would be subject to the personalized oversight of millions of citizens. Each citizen would hold an individual veto to prohibit the government action solely because it offends his religious beliefs, sensibilities, or tastes, or fails to satisfy his religious desires. Further, giving one religious sect a veto over the use of public park land would deprive others of the right to use what is, by definition, land that belongs to everyone.

"[W]e are a cosmopolitan nation made up of people of almost every conceivable religious preference." *Braunfeld v. Brown,* 366 U.S. 599, 606 (1961). Our nation recognizes and protects the expression of a great range of religious beliefs. Nevertheless, respecting religious credos is one thing; requiring the government to change its conduct to avoid any perceived slight to them is quite another. No matter how much we might wish the government to conform its conduct to our religious preferences, act in ways that do not offend our religious sensibilities, and take no action that decreases our spiritual fulfillment, no government—let alone a government that presides over a nation with as many religions as the United States of America—could function were it required to do so. *Lyng v. Nw. Indian Cemetery Protective Ass'n.,* 485 U.S. 439, 452 (1988).

I. Factual and Procedural Background

The Snowbowl ski area ("the Snowbowl") is located on federally owned public land and operates under a special use permit issued by the United States Forest Service ("the Forest Service"). Specifically, the Snowbowl is situated on Humphrey's Peak, the highest of the San Francisco Peaks ("the Peaks"), located within the Coconino National Forest in Northern Arizona. The Peaks cover about 74,000 acres. The Snowbowl sits on 777 acres, or approximately one percent of the Peaks.

*** The Snowbowl has been in operation since the 1930s and is the only downhill ski area within the Coconino National Forest.

The Peaks have long-standing religious and cultural significance to Indian tribes. The tribes believe the Peaks are a living entity. They conduct religious ceremonies, such as the Navajo Blessingway Ceremony, on the Peaks. The tribes also collect plants, water, and other materials from the Peaks for medicinal bundles and tribal healing ceremonies. According to the tribes, the presence of the Snowbowl desecrates for them the spirituality of the Peaks. Certain Indian religious practitioners believe the desecration of the Peaks has caused many disasters, including the September 11, 2001 terrorist attacks, the Columbia Space Shuttle accident, and increases in natural disasters.

***

With this brief background, we turn to the Plaintiffs' challenge in this case. In 2002, the Snowbowl submitted a proposal to the Forest Service to upgrade its operations. The proposal included a request for artificial snowmaking from recycled wastewater for use on the Snowbowl. *Id.* The Snowbowl had suffered highly variable snowfall for several years; this resulted in operating losses that threatened its ski operation. Indeed, the district court found that artificial snowmaking is "needed to maintain the viability of the Snowbowl as a public recreational resource."

The recycled wastewater to be used for snowmaking is classified as "A+" by the Arizona Department of Environmental Quality ("ADEQ").[6] A+ recycled

6. The recycled wastewater that will be used at the Snowbowl "will undergo specific advanced treatment requirements, including tertiary treatment with disinfection. In addition, the reclaimed water will comply with specific monitoring requirements, including frequent microbiological testing to assure pathogens are removed, and reporting requirements." *Navajo Nation,* 408 F.Supp.2d at 887. Further, the recycled wastewater will "comply with extensive treatment and monitoring requirements under three separate permit programs: the Arizona Pollutant Discharge Elimination System ('AZPDES') Permit, the Arizona Aquifer Protection Permit Program, and the Water Reuse Program." *Id.*

wastewater is the highest quality of recycled wastewater recognized by Arizona law and may be safely and beneficially used for many purposes, including irrigating school ground landscapes and food crops. Further, the ADEQ has specifically approved the use of recycled wastewater for snowmaking. ***

The Forest Service conducted an extensive review of the Snowbowl's proposal. As part of its review, the Forest Service made more than 500 contacts with Indian tribes, including between 40 and 50 meetings, to determine the potential impact of the proposal on the tribes. In a December 2004 Memorandum of Agreement, the Forest Service committed to, among other things: (1) continue to allow the tribes access to the Peaks, including the Snowbowl, for cultural and religious purposes; and (2) work with the tribes periodically to inspect the conditions of the religious and cultural sites on the Peaks and ensure the tribes' religious activities on the Peaks are uninterrupted.

The Forest Service's task is complicated by the number of sacred sites under its jurisdiction. In the Coconino National Forest alone, there are approximately a dozen mountains recognized as sacred by American Indian tribes. The district court found the tribes hold other landscapes to be sacred as well, such as canyons and canyon systems, rivers and river drainages, lakes, discrete mesas and buttes, rock formations, shrines, gathering areas, pilgrimage routes, and prehistoric sites. Within the Southwestern Region forest lands alone, there are between 40,000 and 50,000 prehistoric sites. The district court also found the Navajo and the Hualapai Plaintiffs consider the entire Colorado River to be sacred. New sacred areas are continuously being recognized by the Plaintiffs.

***

After an 11–day bench trial on the RFRA claim, the district court held that the proposed upgrades, including the use of recycled wastewater to make artificial snow on the Peaks, do not violate RFRA. The district court found that the upgrades did not bar the Plaintiffs' "access, use, or ritual practice on any part of the Peaks." As a result, the court held that the Plaintiffs had failed to demonstrate the Snowbowl upgrade "coerces them into violating their religious beliefs or penalizes their religious activity," as required to establish a substantial burden on the exercise of their religion under RFRA.

A three-judge panel of this court reversed the district court in part, holding that the use of recycled wastewater on the Snowbowl violates RFRA, and in one respect, that the Forest Service failed to comply with NEPA. *** We took the case *en banc* to revisit the panel's decision and to clarify our circuit's interpretation of "substantial burden" under RFRA.

***

III. Religious Freedom Restoration Act of 1993

Plaintiffs contend the use of artificial snow, made from recycled wastewater, on the Snowbowl imposes a substantial burden on the free exercise of their religion, in violation of the Religious Freedom Restoration Act of 1993 ("RFRA"), 42 U.S.C. §§ 2000bb *et seq.* We hold that the Plaintiffs have failed to establish a RFRA violation. The presence of recycled wastewater on the Peaks does not coerce the Plaintiffs to act contrary to their religious beliefs under the threat of sanctions, nor does it condition a governmental benefit upon conduct that would violate their religious beliefs, as required to establish a "substantial burden" on religious exercise under RFRA.[9]

RFRA was enacted in response to the Supreme Court's decision in *Employment Division v. Smith,* 494 U.S. 872 (1990).[10] *** Congress found that in *Smith,* the "Supreme Court virtually eliminated the requirement that the government justify burdens on religious exercise imposed by laws neutral toward religion." 42 U.S.C. § 2000bb(a)(4). Congress further found that "laws 'neutral' toward religion may burden religious exercise as surely as laws intended to interfere with religious exercise." *Id.* § 2000bb(a)(2). With the enactment of RFRA, Congress created a cause of action for persons whose exercise of religion is substantially burdened by a government action, regardless of whether the burden results from a neutral law of general applicability. RFRA states, in relevant part:

> (a) In general
>
> Government shall not substantially burden a person's exercise of religion even if the burden results from a rule of general applicability, except as provided in subsection (b) of this section.
>
> (b) Exception
>
> Government may substantially burden a person's exercise of religion only if it demonstrates that application of the burden to the person—
>
> (1) is in furtherance of a compelling governmental interest; and
>
> (2) is the least restrictive means of furthering that compelling governmental interest.

To establish a prima facie RFRA claim, a plaintiff must present evidence sufficient to allow a trier of fact rationally to find the existence of two elements. First, the activities the plaintiff claims are burdened by the government action must be an "exercise of religion." Second, the government action must "substantially burden" the plaintiff's exercise of religion. If the plaintiff cannot prove either element, his RFRA claim fails. Conversely, should the plaintiff establish a substantial burden on his exercise of religion, the burden of persuasion shifts to the government to prove that the challenged government action is in furtherance of a "compelling governmental interest" and is implemented by "the least restrictive means." If the government cannot so prove, the court must find a RFRA violation.

We now turn to the application of these principles to the facts of this case. The first question is whether the activities Plaintiffs claim are burdened by the use of recycled wastewater on the Snowbowl constitute an "exercise of religion." RFRA defines "exercise of religion" as "any exercise of religion, whether or not

---

9. The Defendants do not contend RFRA is inapplicable to the government's use and management of its own land, which is at issue in this case. Because this issue was not raised or briefed by the parties, we have no occasion to consider it. Therefore, we assume, without deciding, that RFRA applies to the government's use and management of its land, and conclude there is no RFRA violation in this case.

10. In *City of Boerne v. Flores,* 521 U.S. 507 (1997), the Supreme Court invalidated RFRA as applied to the States and their subdivisions, holding RFRA exceeded Congress's powers under the Enforcement Clause of the Fourteenth Amendment. *Id.* at 532, 536, 117 S. Ct. 2157. We have held that RFRA remains operative as to the federal government. *See Guam v. Guerrero,* 290 F.3d 1210, 1220–22 (9th Cir. 2002).

compelled by, or central to, a system of religious belief." 42 U.S.C. § 2000bb–2(4); 42 U.S.C. § 2000cc–5(7)(A). The Defendants do not contest the district court's holding that the Plaintiffs' religious beliefs are sincere and the Plaintiffs' religious activities on the Peaks constitute an "exercise of religion" within the meaning of RFRA.

The crux of this case, then, is whether the use of recycled wastewater on the Snowbowl imposes a "substantial burden" on the exercise of the Plaintiffs' religion. RFRA does not specifically define "substantial burden." Fortunately, we are not required to interpret the term by our own lights. Rather, we are guided by the express language of RFRA and decades of Supreme Court precedent.

A.

Our interpretation begins, as it must, with the statutory language. RFRA's stated purpose is to "restore the compelling interest test as set forth in *Sherbert v. Verner,* 374 U.S. 398 (1963) and *Wisconsin v. Yoder,* 406 U.S. 205 (1972) and to guarantee its application in all cases where free exercise of religion is substantially burdened." 42 U.S.C. § 2000bb(b)(1). RFRA further states "the compelling interest test as set forth in *** Federal court rulings [prior to *Smith*] is a workable test for striking sensible balances between religious liberty and competing prior governmental interests." *Id.* § 2000bb(a)(5).

Of course, the "compelling interest test" cited in the above-quoted RFRA provisions applies only if there is a substantial burden on the free exercise of religion. That is, the government is not required to prove a compelling interest for its action or that its action involves the least restrictive means to achieve its purpose, unless the plaintiff first proves the government action substantially burdens his exercise of religion. ***

B.

In *Sherbert,* a Seventh-day Adventist was fired by her South Carolina employer because she refused to work on Saturdays, her faith's day of rest. *Sherbert,* 374 U.S. at 399. Sherbert filed a claim for unemployment compensation benefits with the South Carolina Employment Security Commission, which denied her claim, finding she had failed to accept work without good cause. The Supreme Court held South Carolina could not, under the Free Exercise Clause, condition unemployment compensation so as to deny benefits to Sherbert because of the exercise of her faith. Such a condition unconstitutionally forced Sherbert "to choose between following the precepts of her religion and forfeiting benefits, on the one hand, and abandoning one of the precepts of her religion in order to accept work, on the other hand."

In *Yoder,* defendants, who were members of the Amish religion, were convicted of violating a Wisconsin law that required their children to attend school until the children reached the age of sixteen, under the threat of criminal sanctions for the parents. The defendants sincerely believed their children's attendance in high school was "contrary to the Amish religion and way of life." The Supreme Court reversed the defendants' convictions ***. According to the Court, the Wisconsin law "affirmatively compel[led the defendants], under threat of criminal sanction, to perform acts undeniably at odds with fundamental tenets of their religious beliefs."

The Supreme Court's decisions in *Sherbert* and *Yoder,* relied upon and incorporated by Congress into RFRA, lead to the following conclusion: Under RFRA, a "substantial burden" is imposed only when individuals are forced to choose between following the tenets of their religion and receiving a governmental benefit (*Sherbert*) or coerced to act contrary to their religious beliefs by the threat of civil or criminal sanctions (*Yoder*). Any burden imposed on the exercise of religion short of that described by *Sherbert* and *Yoder* is not a "substantial burden" within the meaning of RFRA, and does not require the application of the compelling interest test set forth in those two cases.

Applying *Sherbert* and *Yoder,* there is no "substantial burden" on the Plaintiffs' exercise of religion in this case. The use of recycled wastewater on a ski area that covers one percent of the Peaks does not force the Plaintiffs to choose between following the tenets of their religion and receiving a governmental benefit, as in *Sherbert.* The use of recycled wastewater to make artificial snow also does not coerce the Plaintiffs to act contrary to their religion under the threat of civil or criminal sanctions, as in *Yoder.* The Plaintiffs are not fined or penalized in any way for practicing their religion on the Peaks or on the Snowbowl. Quite the contrary: the Forest Service "has guaranteed that religious practitioners would still have access to the Snowbowl" and the rest of the Peaks for religious purposes. *Navajo Nation,* 408 F.Supp.2d at 905.

The only effect of the proposed upgrades is on the Plaintiffs' subjective, emotional religious experience. That is, the presence of recycled wastewater on the Peaks is offensive to the Plaintiffs' religious sensibilities. To plaintiffs, it will spiritually desecrate a sacred mountain and will decrease the spiritual fulfillment they get from practicing their religion on the mountain. Nevertheless, under Supreme Court precedent, the diminishment of spiritual fulfillment—serious though it may be—is not a "substantial burden" on the free exercise of religion.

The Supreme Court's decision in *Lyng v. Northwest Indian Cemetery Protective Ass'n,* 485 U.S. 439 (1988), is on point. ***

Like the Indians in *Lyng,* the Plaintiffs here challenge a government-sanctioned project, conducted on the government's own land, on the basis that the project will diminish their spiritual fulfillment. Even were we to assume, as did the Supreme Court in *Lyng,* that the government action in this case will "virtually destroy the *** Indians' ability to practice their religion," there is nothing to distinguish the road-building project in *Lyng* from the use of recycled wastewater on the Peaks. We simply cannot uphold the Plaintiffs' claims of interference with their faith and, at the same time, remain faithful to *Lyng*'s dictates.

***

Affirmed.

WILLIAM A. FLETCHER, CIRCUIT JUDGE, dissenting, joined by **JUDGE PREGERSON** and **JUDGE FISHER**:

***

I. Religious Freedom Restoration Act

[D]ivers great learned men have been heretical, whilst they have sought to fly up to the secrets of the Deity by the waxen wings of the senses.

— Sir Francis Bacon, *Of the Proficience and Advancement of Learning, Divine and Human* (Book I, 1605).

The majority holds that spraying 1.5 million gallons per day of treated sewage effluent on the most sacred mountain of southwestern Indian tribes does not "substantially burden" their "exercise of religion" in violation of RFRA. According to the majority, "no plants, springs, natural resources, shrines with religious significance, or religious ceremonies *** would be physically affected" by the use of the treated sewage effluent. Maj. op. at 1063. According to the majority, the "sole effect" of the dumping of the treated sewage effluent is on the Indians' "subjective spiritual experience." ***

B. Religious Freedom Restoration Act

Under the Religious Freedom Restoration Act of 1993 ("RFRA"), the federal government may not "substantially burden a person's exercise of religion even if the burden results from a rule of general applicability, except as provided in subsection (b)." "Exercise of religion" is defined to include "any exercise of religion, whether or not compelled by, or central to, a system of religious belief." Subsection (b) of § 2000bb–1 provides, "Government may substantially burden a person's exercise of religion only if it demonstrates that application of the burden to the person-(1) is in furtherance of a compelling governmental interest; and (2) is the least restrictive means of furthering that compelling governmental interest."

***

In several ways, RFRA provides greater protection for religious practices than did the Supreme Court's pre-*Smith* cases, which were based solely on the First Amendment. First, RFRA "goes beyond the constitutional language that forbids the 'prohibiting' of the free exercise of religion and uses the broader verb 'burden.' " *United States v. Bauer,* 84 F.3d 1549, 1558 (9th Cir.1996) (as amended).

Second, as the Supreme Court noted in *City of Boerne,* RFRA provides greater protection than did the First Amendment under the pre-*Smith* cases because "the Act imposes in every case a least restrictive means requirement—a requirement that was not used in the pre-*Smith* jurisprudence RFRA purported to codify." 521 U.S. at 535.

Third, in passing RLUIPA in 2000, Congress amended RFRA's definition of "exercise of religion." Under the amended definition—"any exercise of religion, whether or not compelled by, or central to, a system of religious belief"—RFRA now protects a broader range of conduct than was protected under the Supreme Court's interpretation of "exercise of religion" under the First Amendment. *See Guru Nanak Sikh Soc'y v. County of Sutter,* 456 F.3d 978, 995 n. 21 (9th Cir. 2006) (noting same). After 2000, RFRA plaintiffs must still prove that the burden on their religious exercise is "substantial," but the difficulty of showing a substantial burden is decreased because a broader range of religious exercise is now protected under RFRA. That is, some governmental actions were not previously considered burdens because they burdened non-protected religious exercise. Given the new broader definition of statutorily protected "exercise of religion," those actions have now become burdens within the meaning of RFRA.

Finally, and perhaps most important, RFRA provides broader protection because it applies *Sherbert* and *Yoder*'s compelling interest test "in all cases" where the exercise of religion is substantially burdened. 42 U.S.C. § 2000bb(b). Prior to *Smith,* the Court had refused to apply the compelling interest analysis in various contexts, exempting entire classes of free exercise cases from such heightened scrutiny. ***

C. The Majority's Misstatements of the Law under RFRA

The majority misstates the law under RFRA in three ways. First, it concludes that a "substantial burden" on the "exercise of religion" under RFRA occurs only when the government "has coerced the Plaintiffs to act contrary to their religious beliefs under threat of sanctions, or conditioned a governmental benefit upon conduct that would violate the Plaintiffs' religious beliefs." Maj. op. at 1063. Second, it ignores the impact of RLUIPA, and cases interpreting RLUIPA, on the definition of a "substantial burden" on the "exercise of religion" in RFRA. Third, it treats as an open question whether RFRA applies to the federal government's use of its own land. I discuss these misstatements in turn.

1. Definition of "Substantial Burden"

***

For six reasons, the majority is wrong in looking to *Sherbert* and *Yoder* for an exhaustive definition of what constitutes a "substantial burden." First, the majority's approach is inconsistent with the plain meaning of the phrase "substantial burden." Second, RFRA does not incorporate any pre-RFRA definition of "substantial burden." Third, even if RFRA did incorporate a pre-RFRA definition of "substantial burden," *Sherbert, Yoder,* and other pre-RFRA Supreme Court cases did not use the term in the restrictive manner employed by the majority. That is, the cases on which the majority relies did not state that interferences with the exercise of religion constituted a "substantial burden" only when imposed through the two mechanisms used in *Sherbert* and *Yoder.* Fourth, the purpose of RFRA was to expand rather than to contract protection for the exercise of religion. If a disruption of religious practices can qualify as a "substantial burden" under RFRA only when it is imposed by the same mechanisms as in *Sherbert* and *Yoder,* RFRA would permit interferences with religion that it was surely intended to prevent. Fifth, the majority's approach overrules fourteen years of contrary circuit precedent. Sixth, the majority's approach is inconsistent with our cases applying RLUIPA. The Supreme Court has instructed us that RLUIPA employs the same analytic frame-work and standard as RFRA.

***

NOTES AND QUESTIONS

1. *The conceptual difficulty of religious burdens.* The *Navajo Nation* court reinstated an interpretation of the "substantial burden" test that the plaintiffs and the dissent argued had been rejected by RFRA. Whether one agrees or not with the majority, a recurring challenge for plaintiffs in these cases is that land use burdens do not register as concretely as burdens to specific practices. If religious practitioners can still access the site, what is

affected, other than a subjective sense of "fulfillment," as the majority described it? To highlight this difficulty, consider that *Navajo Nation* was not the first case to challenge ski area expansion at the same site. In *Wilson v. Block*, Navajo and Hopi religious practitioners brought a free exercise challenge to the first significant expansion of the Snowbowl. 708 F.2d 735 (D.C. Cir. 1983). The *Wilson* court held that the expansion of the ski area did not substantially burden the plaintiffs' exercise of their religion. Do you think that the *Navajo Nation* plaintiffs faced a bigger hurdle to establish substantial burden because, despite the loss in *Wilson*, they are still practicing their religion and holding the San Francisco Peaks sacred? If so, is that fair?

Not all courts have embraced the restrictive definition of "substantial burden" adopted by the Ninth Circuit. The Tenth Circuit, for example, has defined it to include denying an individual "reasonable opportunities to engage in those activities" that are important to an individual's religion, and found that RLUIPA relaxed the definition of religious exercise under *Lyng* and RFRA. *See Grace Methodist Church v. City of Cheyenne*, 451 F.3d 643, 662 (10th Cir. 2006), A 2008 district court opinion relied on this standard to find that a military base could not be built next to a site sacred to the Comanche without satisfying RFRA's compelling interest test. *See Comanche Nation v. United States*, 2008 WL 4426621 (W.D. Okla. 2008).

2. *Need for empirical data?* Like *Wilson v. Block*, most other pre-RFRA free exercise cases challenging land use decisions about sacred sites were decided in favor of the government. *See Crow v. Gullett*, 541 F. Supp. 785 (D. S.D. 1982) (no substantial burden on Indian religious practitioners stemming from management of Bear Butte State Park); *Sequoyah Valley v. TVA*, 480 F. Supp. 608 (E.D. Tenn. 1979) (no Cherokee property interest, and therefore no free exercise claim, in case of flooding of sacred lands for reservoir); *Badoni v. Higginson*, 455 F. Supp. 641 (D. Utah 1977) (no substantial burden on religion stemming from flooding of Rainbow Bridge, a site sacred to the Navajo). *Lyng*, Section I, *supra*, affirmed the rejection of these claims, but then became a rallying point for the legislative and administrative changes that culminated in RFRA.

There has been no follow-up analysis of how the American Indian plaintiffs' religions have been affected by the many development projects that have been allowed to go forward. (Some projects, such as the G–O road in *Lyng*, were stopped by legislative or other means.) Would it be helpful in future free exercise and RFRA cases for the parties and courts to have some information about how, for example, Cherokee religion has been affected by the flooding of their sacred lands? What kind of study could be designed to elicit this information? How could the questions be framed to yield legally salient information? Would it have helped the *Navajo Nation* plaintiffs to point to studies or testimony indicating that the Snowbowl expansion approved in *Wilson* caused deterioration to their religious practice? What, under the *Navajo Nation*'s test for substantial burden, would have been enough? *See Burwell v. Hobby Lobby Stores, Inc.*, 134 S. Ct. 2751, 2779 (2014)(requirement to provide contraceptive insurance coverage "clearly imposes a substantial burden on those [religious] beliefs" precluding use of contraceptives).

Federal/Tribal Sacred Sites Agreements, Management and Litigation

Many American Indian sacred sites are located on federal public lands. In the wake of the *Lyng* decision, the American Indian Religious Freedom Coalition organized to put pressure on the federal government, concerned that otherwise a vast number of places of unique spiritual significance would be afforded virtually no protection in the administrative process. In response, Congress passed amendments to several statutes, including the National Historic Preservation Act (NHPA), 16 U.S.C. § 470, *et seq.* The amendments, adopted in 1992, add "properties of traditional and cultural importance to an Indian tribe or Native Hawaiian organization *** " to those that are eligible for inclusion in the National Register of Historic Places. *See* 16 U.S.C. § 470a (d)(6)(a). In addition, tribes and Native Hawaiian organizations must be included in the consultation process mandated by the NHPA when federal agency actions threaten to affect historic properties. *Id.* at § 470a (d)(6)(b). For a helpful and detailed explanation of the NHPA process, see Cohen's Handbook of Federal Indian Law 1288-95 (2012).

Providing further impetus to federal agencies, in 1996 President Clinton signed the "Indian Sacred Sites" Executive Order 13,007, 61 Fed. Reg. 26,771 (May 24, 1996). The Executive Order directs agencies to "accommodate access to and ceremonial use of Indian sacred sites by Indian religious practitioners." *Id.* Federal land management agencies have attempted to fashion management plans and agreements that accommodate American Indian spiritual beliefs and practices. A few of these have been subject to litigation on the grounds that the accommodations run afoul of the Constitution's establishment clause, but the courts have so far mostly rejected these challenges, as discussed further below.

Devil's Tower Management Plan and Litigation

Devil's Tower (known as Bear's Lodge to some American Indian tribes) is located in Wyoming. More than twenty Indian tribes have cultural and spiritual connections to Devil's Tower, and the Arapaho, Crow, Lakota, Cheyenne, Kiowa, and Shoshone have specific geographic and historical ties to the area. *See* Devil's Tower General Management Plan, Final, http://www.nps.gov/deto/parkmgmt/upload/~3949671.pdf [https://perma.cc/9JM8-CW4F].

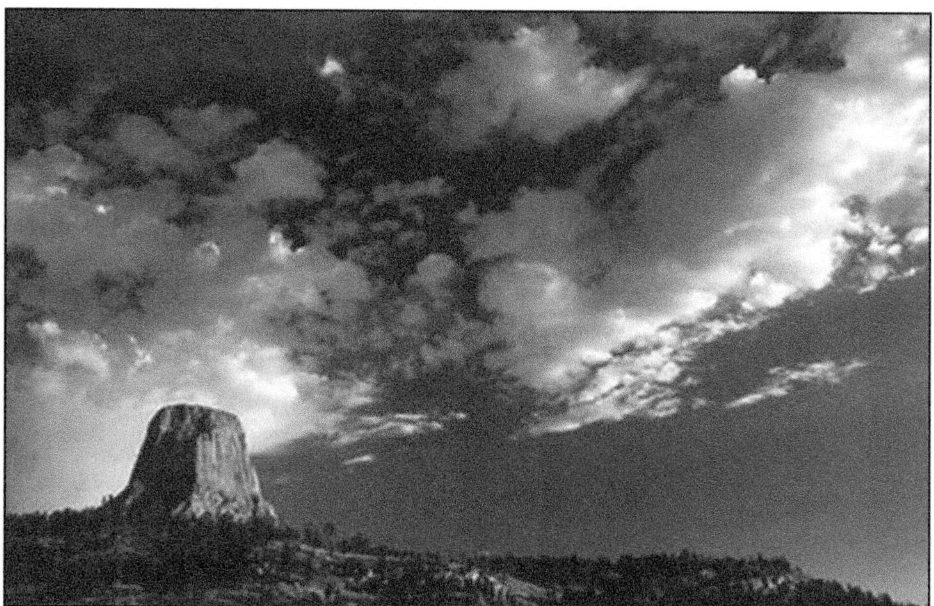

Devil's Tower. Photograph courtesy of Bradley Davis.

President Theodore Roosevelt designated Devils Tower as the first national monument in 1906. Its striking geological features have since made it a popular tourist destination, climbing mecca, and cultural icon. (Devil's Tower is the image Richard Dreyfus carves out of mashed potatoes in the hit 1977 movie *Close Encounters of the Third Kind*). The Tower's popularity created difficulties for American Indian religious practitioners, who found the increasing congestion, traffic, noise, and desecration to interfere with their spiritual beliefs and activities. After consulting with the affected tribes, in 1995 the National Park Service announced a plan to suspend commercial rock climbing licenses during the month of June, when tribal ceremonial activities are at their most active. Shortly thereafter a group of climbers filed a lawsuit in federal district court alleging that the mandatory commercial climbing ban violated the establishment clause. The court issued a preliminary injunction against the NPS in June 1996, finding that the ban favored one religious group over another. *See* No. 96–CV–063–D (D. Wyo. June 8, 1996). The NPS then revised the plan, downscaling the mandatory ban on commercial climbing to a voluntary ban. A smaller group of climbers filed a lawsuit against the revised plan, arguing that even a voluntary ban violated the establishment clause. The federal district court rejected this claim, finding that the mild accommodation sought not to establish religion, but merely to remove barriers to American Indian religious worship. *Bear Lodge Multiple Use Ass'n v. Babbitt* 2 F.Supp.2d 1448 (D.Wyo. 1998); *aff'd*, 175 F.3d 814 (10th Cir. 1999) (holding that the plaintiffs lacked standing); *cert. denied* 529 U.S. 1037 (2000). For more details on the consultation process and the interests at stake in the litigation, see Lloyd Burton & David Ruppert, *Bear's Lodge or Devil's Tower: Intercultural Relations, Legal Pluralism, and the Management of Sacred Sites on Public Lands*, 8 Cornell J.L. & Pub. Pol'y 201 (1999).

Rainbow Bridge Management Plan and Litigation

Rainbow Bridge

Rainbow Bridge is the largest natural bridge in the world with a span of 275 feet. Located in a remote and rugged corner of southern Utah, Rainbow Bridge received few non-American Indian visitors until after the construction of Glen Canyon Dam in 1963, which flooded Glen Canyon and created Lake Powell. The National Park Service manages both the Glen Canyon National Recreation Area and the Rainbow Bridge National Monument, though pursuant to different statutory mandates. With regard to Rainbow Bridge National Monument, the National Park Service must "conserve the scenery and the natural and historic objects and the wild life *** and *** provide for the enjoyment of the same in such manner and by such means as will leave them unimpaired for the enjoyment of future generations." 16 U.S.C. § 1 (2000). In contrast, concerning Glen Canyon National Recreation Area, the National Park Service is directed to "provide for public outdoor recreation use and enjoyment of Lake Powell and lands adjacent thereto in the States of Arizona and Utah *** " 16 U.S.C. § 460dd (2000).

Rainbow Bridge is considered sacred by many Navajo people, and also has religious and cultural significance to members of the Hopi, San Juan Paiute, and Pueblo tribes. Soon after the waters of Lake Powell began to allow easy tourist access to Rainbow Bridge, a group of Navajo plaintiffs filed a free exercise claim, which was rejected by the federal court on grounds that the Navajo had no property interest in the Monument (notwithstanding that Rainbow Bridge is within the exterior boundaries of the Navajo Nation), and that in any event the government interest in maintaining full water storage capacity at Lake Powell outweighed any burden on the plaintiffs. *See Badoni v. Higginson*, 455 F. Supp. 641 (D. Utah 1977).

In the ensuing years, visitors to Rainbow Bridge increased dramatically. "By 1986, approximately 65,000 visited the bridge just in the month of July—an average of 270 people at any one time over an eight-hour day. In 1995, visitation peaked at approximately 346,000 visitors. It was anticipated that if the increase in visitation continued, by 2000, visitation would approach 450,000." *Natural Arch and Bridge Society v. Alston*, 209 F.Supp.2d 1207, 1212 (D. Utah 2002), *aff'd*, 98 Fed.Appx. 711 (10th Cir. 2004) (unreported decision). The increased visitation was accompanied by various behaviors that damaged the monument, including defacing of petroglyphs, graffiti, litter, multiple trails resulting in harm to the delicate desert vegetation, and increased air and noise pollution.

The National Park Service engaged in a planning process attempting to balance the recreational mandate of Glen Canyon with the preservationist mandate of the Monument, and also to acknowledge concerns of the Navajo and other tribes regarding interference with their spiritual and cultural practices and beliefs. The result was a General Management Plan (GMP) that included guidelines on visitor numbers, voluntary restrictions on visitor access near to and under Rainbow Bridge, closure of areas for revegetation, other measures to reduce resource degradation, and interpretive signs and brochures attempting to educate the public about the cultural and religious significance of the Bridge to American Indians.

Members of the Natural Arch and Bridge Society challenged the GMP on establishment clause grounds, but the court upheld the GMP, noting the voluntary nature of the restrictions and the neutral and secular governmental purpose of accommodating religious beliefs and educating the public about different cultures:

> Had the Park Service demanded that visitors view Rainbow Bridge from the viewing area rather than walking up to or under the bridge, or prohibited visitor access to the bridge, then it could possibly be said that the Park Service had abandoned neutrality and intentionally promoted Native American religious beliefs over those of other cultures. Here, however, the 1993 GMP and Interpretive Prospectus contemplate the public's voluntary compliance with the policy. Its purpose is not to establish, promote, or advance religion; its purpose is to educate and inform the public about different cultures and increase sensitivity to the beliefs of others. In the words of the policy, its purpose is to "help visitors understand that different cultures perceive resources differently, *i.e.*, some neighboring American Indians regard Rainbow Bridge as sacred," and "generate visitor interest in the cultures and lifestyles, from prehistoric to present times, of the people of the Rainbow Bridge region."

209 F.Supp.2d 1207, 1223–24.

Other Federal/Tribal Sacred Sites Management Plans and Litigation

Like Devil's Tower and Rainbow Bridge, other sacred site protection plans draw competing interests and controversies. Land management agencies have a delicate balancing act to do, striving to meet their multiple statutory and Executive Order objectives while steering clear both of free exercise and establishment clause violations. What follows are just two more examples of the many struggles over these issues.

- The National Forest Service's Historic Preservation Plan for the Medicine Wheel National Historic Landmark and Medicine Mountain (HPP) provides protection for a prehistoric site consisting of a circular array of rocks eighty feet in diameter with a large rock pile in the center and "spokes" radiating there from. The Medicine Wheel HPP requires consultation with tribes before allowing activities that would harm the Wheel's spiritual values, and closes a road within view of the Wheel. The HPP has been upheld against a logging association's establishment clause challenge. *See Wyoming Saw Mills, Inc. v. United States Forest Service*, 179 F. Supp. 2d 1279 (2001), aff'd, 383 F.3d 1241 (10th Cir. 2004).
- The National Forest Service issued a management plan for Cave Rock, a natural rock formation on the shoreline of Lake Tahoe, that banned all rock climbing but allowed other forms of recreation to continue. Cave Rock is of central religious and cultural significance to the Washoe Indian Tribe, and when the management plan was being formulated members of the tribe participated and expressed their concern over the increasing use of Cave Rock as a recreation area, and in particular about desecration and interference with their religious practices due to rock climbing. Climbing had become popular in the area in the late 1980's, and climbers had fixed 325 bolts into the rock to serve as fixed anchors and made a number of unauthorized changes to the cave's entrance, including installation of a concrete floor in the cave and rock seating made up of boulders removed from their original locations. The Forest Service cited the Washoe Tribe's religious and cultural interests as well as Cave Rock's general archaeological and historic significance as justifications for the climbing ban. The Ninth Circuit upheld the plan and rejected an establishment clause challenge brought by The Access Fund, a rock climbing advocacy group. The court noted that the Forest Service grounded its decision in secular purposes consistent with its varied management obligations at the site, and that the accommodation to religious interests was therefore appropriate. *See The Access Fund v. United States Dep't of Agriculture*, 499 F.3d 1036 (9th Cir. 2007).

NOTES AND QUESTIONS

1. *Guidance for federal managers.* Consider each of the previous examples of agency action affecting American Indian sacred sites. Can you formulate general advice for federal land managers on how best to address likely conflicts? Is it possible to come up with a litigation-proof management plan? If not, what steps can the agencies take to ensure that they stand the best chance possible of having their plans upheld? Compare, for example, the Forest Service's planning process and decision in *Navajo Nation v. United States Forest Service* with the National Park Service's approach at Rainbow Bridge. For a helpful discussion of these issues, *see* Michelle Kay Albert, *Obligations and Opportunities to Protect Native American Sacred Sites on Public Lands*, 40 Colum. Hum. Rts. L. Rev. 479 (2009).

Litigation-proof plans may be elusive, but the Department of the Interior successfully defended a withdrawal of public lands from operation of the

General Mining Law in a large area surrounding the Grand Canyon National Park. The Southern Paiute, Hualapai, Havasupai, and Hopi Tribes have traditional, sacred, cultural, and religious sites throughout the withdrawn area, and the court stated that the agency did not exceed its statutory authority by relying on the tribes' interests to justify its decision. *See National Mining Association v. Zinke*, 877 F.3d 845, 869 (9th Cir. 2017).

2. *"Voluntary" restrictions.* To avoid establishment clause problems, the federal agencies at Devil's Tower and Rainbow Bridge have adopted voluntary, as opposed to mandatory, restrictions on non-Indian access to sacred sites. Does this leave American Indian religions uniquely vulnerable due to the specific geographically based nature of their spiritual beliefs? What kinds of evidence would you want to have in order to evaluate this concern?

3. Ad hoc *regulatory approaches?* After assessing federal agency responses to the Indian Sacred Sites Executive Order, Executive Order 13,007, *supra*, and the other statutory amendments (NHPA, RFRA) that followed *Lyng* and *Smith*, one commentator concluded that the flexible agency management approach is preferable to the outcome that might have pertained had *Lyng* been decided differently:

> Agency decisions can create the most efficient outcomes because, in considering the desires of each side, agencies are more likely to leave both parties to the dispute better off than if one side had the unilateral ability to determine the future of sacred site land. Although tribes *** might find agency accommodation less desirable than protection that would give them complete control over their sacred sites, agency protection, which can accommodate competing interests while still protecting sacred sites, is preferable from the perspective of society as a whole.
>
> Furthermore, the benefit of leaving land-use determinations in agency hands is especially high because sacred sites regulation is rarely a zero-sum game. *** [L]ands can often be used in a variety of different ways without foreclosing all other uses. Furthermore, even in instances of irreconcilable incompatibility, such as the flooding that destroyed the Cherokee burial sites in the Tennessee Valley, it still may be best to leave such decisions in the hands of individual agencies, so that these types of decisions can be made on a case-by-case basis and not as the result of sweeping rules that leave no room for compromise even when compromise is an option.

Marcia Yablon, Note, *Property Rights and Sacred Sites: Federal Regulatory Responses to American Indian Religious Claims on Public Land*, 113 Yale L.J. 1623, 1660 (2004). How well does the vocabulary of efficiency apply to deeply held spiritual beliefs? Even if there is something jarring about considering religious practice in such terms, does this view reflect a larger political reality in terms of what American Indian religions can expect to preserve in situations where they do not have total legal control over the land? Even if it does, would the situation today be all that different if *Lyng* had held that the compelling state interest test applied to federal land use decisions? In other words, would a constitutional victory for the tribes in *Lyng* actually have resulted in "sweeping rules that leave no room for compromise"? This concern still weighs on courts, as evident in *Navajo Nation, infra.*, but can you devise an adequate response to this "floodgates" argument? *Cf.* Kristen Carpenter, *Limiting Principles and Empowering Practices in American Indian Religious Freedoms*, 387

Conn. L. Rev. 387, 478 (2012) (arguing that courts can develop meaningful limiting principles in Indian religion cases, but "Congress and the Executive Branch, when motivated to address Indian issues, are better situated than the courts to negotiate with tribal governments over the contours of religious accommodation").

4. *Whose religion?* It might seem surprising that non-Indian visitors to public lands find voluntary restrictions troubling enough to sue about. What principles and beliefs might be behind these challenges? Consider the following visitor to Rainbow Bridge:

> "We've been coming here and walking under the bridge since 1974, so maybe you could say this is our religion," says Fred Woods, an Anglo visitor from Mesa, Ariz. Woods ignored the Park Service signs *** to lead his friends and family beneath the giant sandstone curve. As a small herd of tourists followed, scornful onlookers back at the viewing area audibly questioned their morals. Woods was undaunted: "You come all the way to see it, then they tell you not to get close to it because of someone else's religion. I don't see how they can do that."

Chris Smith & Elizabeth Manning, *The Sacred and Profane Collide in the West*, High Country News, May 26, 1997. Should agencies distinguish between Mr. Woods' claim that visiting Rainbow Bridge up close is his religion, and the religious and spiritual claims of American Indian tribes? If so, how?

5. *Presidential authority under the Antiquities Act.* On December 28, 2016, President Obama designated the Bears Ears National Monument pursuant to his authority under the Antiquities Act of 1906, Pub. L. No. 209, 54 U.S.C. § 320301 (codified as amended). The Monument was the first ever to be proposed by American Indian tribes. The Hopi, Navajo, Ute Mountain Ute, Uintah and Ouray Ute, and Zuni Tribes joined with conservation groups to protect a vast landscape in southeast Utah that contains sacred sites, historic artifacts, and traditional use areas for all five tribes. President Obama's Proclamation also noted the surfeit of geological, paleontological, and ecological features throughout the Bears Ears landscape, consistent with the other protective purposes of the Antiquities Act. The Bears Ears National Monument was celebrated by indigenous and non-indigenous communities alike for uniting conservation interests with concerns about justice for indigenous communities. The Monument was nonetheless reversed in 2017 by the Trump Administration in a Proclamation purporting to revoke the Monument's boundaries and shrink its acreage by eighty-five percent. Mining interests as well as non-indigenous Utah politicians were behind the reversal. Whether President Trump's revocation of the monument was authorized under the Antiquities Act is currently being litigated in federal court. For more background and history of Bears Ears and the Antiquities Act's role with regard to Native lands and sacred sites, see Sarah Krakoff, *Public Lands, Conservation, and the Possibility of Justice*, 53 Harv. Civ. Rts-Civ. Liberties L. Rev. 213 (2018).

III. CULTURAL AND RELIGIOUS PRACTICES AND BELIEFS

In addition to the sacramental use of Peyote, discussed in Section A above, American Indian religious practices that tend to become the subject of legal battles include the taking and possession of eagle parts and feathers, and the rights of American Indian prisoners.

Religious Use of Eagle Feathers and Parts

The eagle plays a central role in many American Indian religions. Possession of eagle feathers and parts is therefore not unusual among medicine men, religious dancers, and other religious practitioners. Taking and possession of eagles is prohibited by the Bald and Golden Eagle Protection Act (BGEPA), 16 U.S.C. § 668, but the Act, as amended in 1978, authorizes the Secretary of the Interior to create a permit system for the taking and possession of eagle parts "for the religious purposes of the Indian tribes," so long as the system is compatible with the goal of species preservation. 16 U.S.C. § 668a. The regulations implementing the permit system clarify that only members of federally recognized tribes may obtain permits. *See* 50 C.F.R. § 22.22.

In cases that preceded the Religious Freedom Restoration Act, 42 U.S.C. §§ 2000bb–1–2000bb–4, tribal members raised free exercise challenges to BGEPA's prohibitions. One federal district court rejected such a claim, finding that the government's compelling interests outweighed the burden on the religious practitioner. *See United States v. Thirty Eight (38) Golden Eagles*, 649 F. Supp. 269 (D. Nev. 1986). Other courts, however, upheld the claims in the context of criminal convictions. *See United States v. Abeyta*, 632 F. Supp. 1301 (D. N.M. 1986); *United States v. Gonzales*, 957 F. Supp. 1225 (D. N.M. 1997).

After RFRA, courts have split on the issue, both with regard to Indian and non-Indian practitioners. In a case involving a Canadian Indian who exchanged eagle feathers acquired in Canada for money and goods as part of a potlatch ceremony, the Ninth Circuit held that the permit system was the least restrictive means of serving the government's compelling interest in eagle protection. *See United States v. Antoine*, 318 F.3d 919 (9th Cir. 2003); *see also United States v. Vasquez-Ramos*, 531 F.3d 987 (9th Cir. 2008) (following *Antoine* and rejecting RFRA challenge brought by nonmember Indians). In *Gibson v. Babbitt*, 223 F.3d 1256, 1258 (11th Cir. 2000), the Eleventh Circuit rejected a challenge brought by an American Indian who was not a tribal member because "without the exemption the limited supply of bald and golden eagle parts will be distributed to a wider population and the delays will increase in providing eagle parts to members of federally recognized Indian Tribes, thereby vitiating the government's efforts to fulfill its treaty obligations to federally recognized Indian tribes." The Tenth Circuit, however, found that the government failed to meet its burden in the following case.

UNITED STATES V. HARDMAN

297 F.3d 1116 (10th Cir. 2002)

TACHA, CHIEF JUDGE.[†]

Appellants Raymond S. Hardman and Samuel Ray Wilgus, Jr., were convicted for unrelated counts of illegally possessing eagle feathers in violation of sections 703 and 668(a) of Title 16 of the United States Code, respectively. Appellee Joseluis Saenz had eagle feathers in his possession seized by the Bureau of Indian Affairs, but was not criminally prosecuted. He made a motion pursuant to Fed. R. Crim. P. 41(e) for the return of the feathers, and the district court granted the motion. The cases initially came to three separate panels of this court. Because of the conflicting panel outcomes and the factual and legal similarities among the cases, we simultaneously issued and vacated the panel opinions, and then *sua sponte* ordered that the cases be reheard *en banc*. We *** hold that the Religious Freedom Restoration Act controls all three cases, REMAND to the district court with respect to Mr. Hardman and Mr. Wilgus, and AFFIRM with respect to Mr. Saenz.

I. Background

A. Hardman

Mr. Hardman has been a practitioner of a Native American religion for many years. Although Mr. Hardman is not of Native American descent, his ex-wife and two children are enrolled members of the S'Kallum Tribe, a federally recognized tribe located in Washington State. Mr. Hardman resides within the boundaries of the Uintah and Ouray Reservation in Neola, Utah.

In 1993, when Mr. Hardman was still married to and living with his ex-wife, his son's godfather died. Mr. Hardman transported the body to Arizona so that appropriate religious services could be performed. As a part of the religious cleansing ritual, a Hopi tribal religious leader gave Mr. Hardman a bundle of prayer feathers—which included golden eagle feathers—to be kept in the truck that he had used to transport the body. Mr. Hardman claims that the feathers "hold a special prayer for me, my family, and the automobile they were in." After returning to his home, Mr. Hardman contacted the Utah Division of Wildlife Resources in order to obtain a permit to possess the feathers. He was informed, however, that he would not be allowed to apply because he was not a member of a federally recognized tribe.

Several years later, after Mr. Hardman and his wife separated, Mr. Hardman's estranged wife informed Ute tribal officers that he possessed golden eagle feathers without a permit. On September 24, 1996, Ute tribal fish and game officer Cleveland Murray went to Mr. Hardman's home and demanded the surrender of the eagle feathers. Under protest, Mr. Hardman surrendered the eagle feathers, which were hanging from the rear view mirror of his truck.

On March 10, 1997, Mr. Hardman was issued a federal violation notice for possessing golden eagle feathers without a permit in violation of the Migratory Bird Treaty Act ("MBTA"), 16 U.S.C. § 703. Mr. Hardman was not charged

---

†. The opinion is unanimous with respect to all but parts II.E.1.b and II.F. Judges Murphy and Briscoe do not join those portions of the opinion.

with a violation of the Bald and Golden Eagle Protection Act ("BGEPA"). On February 25, 1999, a bench trial was held before a magistrate judge. The court found Mr. Hardman guilty of violating the MBTA, sentenced him to pay a small fine, and placed him on two years' bench probation. Mr. Hardman appealed to the district court, which affirmed his conviction.

***

[Like Mr. Hardman, Mr. Wilgus is a non-Indian practitioner of American Indian religion who received eagle feathers from American Indians for religious purposes].

C. Saenz

Joseluis Saenz is a lineal descendant of the Chiricahua Apache. Chiricahua have been included as members of other, federally recognized Apache tribes, and there was once a Chiricahua Reservation. Since at least 1886, however, the Chiricahua have not been a federally recognized tribe.

Mr. Saenz follows the beliefs and traditions of the Chiricahua Apache religion. Eagle feathers are an integral part of his religious practices. In 1996, while New Mexico state officials were executing a search warrant at Mr. Saenz's home as part of an investigation unrelated to this case, the officers noticed items with eagle feathers hanging on the walls. Mr. Saenz had obtained these feathers as gifts in connection with various ceremonies. After contacting the U.S. Fish and Wildlife Service and determining that Mr. Saenz did not have a permit for the feathers, the officers seized the items and sent them to the Fish and Wildlife Service office in Albuquerque. In March 1997, the government brought criminal charges against Mr. Saenz under the BGEPA, 16 U.S.C. § 668(a), but the charges were dismissed on the government's motion in July 1997. After attempting to retrieve his feathers through administrative proceedings, Mr. Saenz filed a motion in federal district court under Fed. R. Crim. P. 41(e) for the return of property seized by a search warrant. *** The district court granted Mr. Saenz's motion and ordered the return of the feathers. The court did not consider the constitutional grounds, and based its decision entirely upon the BGEPA and RFRA. The United States appealed, arguing that the district court's analysis under RFRA was erroneous. *** A panel of this court found for Mr. Saenz under RFRA, and affirmed.

We now consider the parties' arguments en banc.

***

E. The Religious Freedom Restoration Act of 1993

*** [The Religious Freedom Restoration Act] states: "Government shall not substantially burden a person's exercise of religion even if the burden results from a rule of general applicability, except as provided in subsection (b) of this section." 42 U.S.C. § 2000bb–1(a). Subsection (b) provides that "[g]overnment may substantially burden a person's exercise of religion only if it demonstrates that application of the burden to the person—(1) is in furtherance of a compelling governmental interest; and (2) is the least restrictive means of furthering that compelling governmental interest." *Id.* § 2000bb–1(b). ***

Here, the government does not dispute that claimants' beliefs are sincerely held or that the regulations represent a substantial burden upon claimants' religious beliefs. The eagle feather is sacred in many Native American religions, including claimants'. Any scheme that limits their access to eagle feathers therefore must be seen as having a substantial effect on the exercise of religious belief. Given this, we next consider whether the regulations governing the BGEPA and MBTA: (1) advance a compelling government interest; and (2) are the least restrictive means of furthering that interest.

1. Compelling Interests

[W]e consider the interests that the United States argues are compelling: (a) protecting eagles and (b) preserving Native American culture and religion and pursuing the federal government's trust obligations to Native American tribes.

a. Protecting Eagles

There is dicta from the Supreme Court indicating that the protection of migratory birds might qualify as a compelling interest. *Missouri v. Holland,* 252 U.S. 416 (1920) (referring to the protection of migratory birds as "a national interest of very nearly the first magnitude."). We cannot ignore that the migratory bird in question here is the symbol of our nation, heightening the government's interest in keeping the species viable. Moreover, most other courts that have addressed this issue have agreed that the preservation of eagle species represents a compelling interest.

Claimants assert that the increased number of bald and golden eagles undercuts the compelling nature of the government's interest. This view finds some limited support in the case law. *United States v. Abeyta,* 632 F. Supp. 1301, 1307 (D. N.M.1986) (finding that the record did not support a compelling interest in golden eagle preservation). We disagree. The bald eagle would remain our national symbol whether there were 100 eagles or 100,000 eagles. The government's interest in preserving the species remains compelling in either situation. What might change depending on the number of birds existing is the scope of a program that we would accept as being narrowly tailored as the least restrictive means of achieving its interest. Thus, we agree that the government's interest in preserving eagle populations is compelling.

b. Protecting Native American Culture/Treaty Obligations

The government also asserts a compelling interest in preserving Native American culture and religion. The government is correct that it has a longstanding obligation to preserve Native American cultures. Along with Congress's power to "regulate Commerce *** with the Indian Tribes" comes an obligation of trust to protect the rights and interests of federally recognized tribes and to promote their self-determination. *Morton v. Mancari,* 417 U.S. 535, 552 (1974) (quoting U.S. Const. art. I, § 8, cl. 3); *see also Worcester v. Georgia,* 31 U.S. (6 Pet.) 515, 557 (1832); *Cherokee Nation v. Georgia,* 30 U.S. (5 Pet.) 1, 16, (1831). Thus, we have little trouble finding a compelling interest in protecting Indian cultures from extinction, growing from government's "historical obligation to respect Native American sovereignty and to protect Native American culture." *Rupert v. Director, U.S. Fish & Wildlife Serv.,* 957 F.2d 32, 35 (1st Cir. 1992).

*** In sum, the government's general interests in preserving Native American culture and religion in-and-of-themselves and in fulfilling trust obligations to Native Americans remain compelling interests.

2. Least Restrictive Means

The two dispositive questions under RFRA are whether application of the permitting process to claimants furthers the government's compelling interests, and whether it is the "least restrictive means" of furthering those interests. 42 U.S.C. § 2000bb–1(b). This statutory language must guide our analysis.

The statute directs that, in interpreting "least restrictive means," courts should view the Act as "restor[ing] the compelling interest test ***. Given these contours, we evaluate the regulatory scheme for the BGEPA and MBTA to determine whether they are sufficiently narrowly tailored and represent the least restrictive means of achieving a compelling interest. ***

F. Application to Hardman, Wilgus, and Saenz

1. Hardman and Wilgus

The government bears the burden of building a record that proves that the statutory and regulatory scheme in question is the least restrictive means of advancing the government's compelling interests. In these two cases, the RFRA claims were dismissed in light of *City of Boerne* as a matter of law before trial. The government thus has not had an opportunity to build a record with respect to either case. We therefore REMAND these cases to afford both parties an opportunity to develop a record, and for a determination as to whether these regulations represent the least restrictive means of advancing the government's interests.

2. Saenz

We are in a different situation with regard to Mr. Saenz. The government did build a record in the district court with respect to Mr. Saenz. Therefore, we examine the record to determine if the government has carried its burden of proving the least restrictive means of carrying out its interests. ***

a. Protecting Eagles

We first consider how excluding sincere practitioners of Native American religions who are not members of federally recognized tribes from applying for permits advances the government's interest in preserving the eagle population. Presumably, expanding the permit process to include non-Native American adherents would have no effect on bird populations—as long as the total number of permits available stayed constant, such an expansion would at worst create a longer wait list for parts. We do not, however, make rulings on presumptions. Instead, it is incumbent upon the government to build a record that either contradicts or confirms these presumptions.

Here, the government has not carried its burden. The government offers two arguments. First, the government presented an estimate of the number of members of federally-recognized tribes versus the number of Americans who identify themselves as having Indian ancestry. The apparent purpose of these estimates is to support an extrapolation that expanding the permitting process would expand the number of permit applicants, thereby further endangering eagle populations. The record contains no evidence indicating that increased permit applications would place increased pressure on eagle populations. Such a result seems highly unlikely, especially since the impact upon eagle populations is an explicit consideration in determining whether or not to grant a permit. Moreover, the data provided are largely irrelevant. The relevant comparison is between members of federally recognized tribes *who hold the eagle feather as sacred* and other persons *who hold a sincere religious belief that the eagle feather is sacred.* The government's estimation process is akin to attempting to extrapolate the number of practicing Catholics in the country by identifying the number of Irish–Americans. We will not engage in such extrapolation here.

Second, the government argues that increasing the wait for parts will increase poaching. As evidence, it cites cases in which practitioners from federally recognized tribes poached eagles rather than waiting for parts. From this, the government asks us to extrapolate that more applicants will lead to longer waits, which will lead to more poaching and further endanger the eagle. Assuming arguendo that there will be an increased wait for parts, the government's poaching argument misses the mark. The fact that some members of federally recognized tribes have poached eagles rather than waiting for parts does not, absent additional evidence, lead to the conclusion that increased waits will result in sufficient poaching to frustrate the government's interest in protecting eagle populations. In the absence of additional evidence, the opposite conclusion seems equally plausible. While the wait might increase for members of federally recognized tribes, it would decrease for sincere practitioners who are *not* members of federally recognized tribes, who currently have *no* legal access to eagle parts for religious purposes. This approach could result in an offsetting decrease in poaching by people who are not members of federally recognized tribes. People with no opportunity to receive eagle feathers might be more likely to poach than those who must simply wait. At any rate, these questions remain unanswered in the record in this case, and it was incumbent upon the government to answer them.

b. Protecting Native American Culture

We next consider to what degree excluding non-tribal members from the permitting scheme advances the government's interest in preserving Native American cultures and fulfilling trust obligations. We find that the United States has failed to build an adequate record on this question. The only evidence offered by the government that Native American culture would be endangered by expanding the permitting process to include all bona fide practitioners of Native American faiths is the speculative testimony of a Fish and Wildlife Service official, similar testimony from a member of the Mescalero Apache tribe, and evidence that there is currently a wait for parts. The government cannot carry its burden through mere speculation. The government has failed to present any hard evidence that there are substantial numbers of individuals who are not members of federally recognized tribes, but who are sincere practitioners of Native American faiths that hold eagle feathers to be sacred and could be expected to apply for permits. Thus, it has failed to show that broader eligibility would result in an increased wait substantial enough to endanger Native American cultures. The government gives no consideration to any offsetting increase in available parts from any recovery of bald and golden eagle population. Moreover, the government offers no evidence on the threshold question of whether allowing sincere practitioners who are not members of federally recognized tribes to possess eagle feathers, in addition to those who are members, truly threatens Native American culture. Allowing a wider variety of people to participate in Native American religion could just as easily *foster* Native American culture and religion by exposing it to a wider array of persons.[23]

Finally, the government has offered insufficient evidence regarding its trust obligations to federally recognized Native American tribes. It has not shown, for instance, that statutory protections for eagles (apart from the exception for religious purposes) were motivated by trust obligations. Nor has it shown precisely how restricting personal, individual permits for religious purposes to members of federally recognized tribes is connected to the government's sovereign-to-sovereign relationships with tribes. Thus, the government has not shown that broader permit eligibility would damage the government's ability to fulfill its trust obligations.

The government has failed to demonstrate how the permitting process advances its compelling interests. It leaves far too many questions unanswered. We therefore find that it has failed to carry its burden.

c. Setting the Interests in Equipoise

*** The First Circuit and Judge Murphy rightly point out that there is a great deal of interplay between the two compelling interests and that the ultimate test is whether the balance between the two interests struck by the government is achieved by the least restrictive means available. ***

This can be conceptualized as something of a sliding scale: At one extreme is a situation where nobody can hold eagle feathers, which would maximize eagle protection and set protection of Native American cultures at zero. At the other extreme is a situation where members of federally recognized tribes who are sincere practitioners of Native American religion are given full access to all the eagle feathers they desire, which minimizes protection of eagles. The government has essentially chosen a point somewhere along this continuum which attempts to strike some type of balance between the two extremes. The ultimate question for the court, then, is whether the point that the government has chosen constitutes means that minimize the impact on religious adherents who are not members of federally recognized tribes.

---

23. *** The concurrence questions whether we view the compelling interest as "limited to the maintenance of the viability of Native American cultural practices as a historical legacy within the contours of our modern culture," or as "guaranteeing that members of sovereign and semi-autonomous Indian nations have the ability to carry on their traditional way of life." *Infra,* at 1136–37 (Murphy, J., concurring).

We agree that simply guaranteeing that Native American cultural practices are somehow a part of our modern culture is too cramped a view of the compelling interest, and we wish to dispose of any notion that such a view is advanced by this opinion, or by Supreme Court jurisprudence. *** We do not express an opinion on whether distributing eagle feathers to sincere adherents of Native American faiths irrespective of whether they were members of federally recognized tribes or not, or of Native American lineage or not, would foster or inhibit this compelling interest. We simply emphasize that it is the government's burden to build a record clarifying how the regulations serve its interests. It may well be that it can do so on remand in *Hardman* and *Wilgus.* It has not, however, done so in *Saenz.*

Before that ultimate question can be addressed, however, we must first determine where along that continuum the government's present solution lies, and where other, less restrictive means would lie. This analysis is a necessary predicate to determining whether the government has properly set the interests in equipoise, and it requires that we compartmentalize our analysis somewhat. On appeal, it was the government's burden to show us how it was balancing the interests and that no other, less restrictive means existed to achieve a similar balance. From the record, we do not know how much, if at all, the government's regulatory scheme advances the interest in protecting eagles. *** The government's interest in preserving eagles might have something to do with the total number of people who are allowed to acquire eagle feathers, but it quite possibly has little to do with the question here, which is how those permits are distributed. We do not, however, have a sufficient factual record to state even that conclusion with certainty, and this requires us to remand in *Wilgus* and *Hardman* and is fatal to the government's case in *Saenz*. The government also has not shown how many eagles exist, in what direction the eagle population is trending, how many people can be expected to apply for permits if the regulations change, how much additional delay in delivering eagle feathers to applicants could be expected under various alternative schemes, and how much such delays might impact Native American culture.

Thus, it is impossible for us to address whether the government has offered the least restrictive means of *balancing* the questions, because it has not established where on the above-described continuum of interests the current regulatory scheme lies, nor has it described where other, less restrictive alternatives lie on that continuum. *** On remand, if the district court is presented with sufficient factual evidence to enable it to determine *** how the government has balanced the interests and should examine whether potentially broader, less burdensome regulations would allow it to strike a similar balance. But for the purposes of this appeal, we are simply not presented with adequate factual findings to make the necessary predicate determinations before proceeding to that step in the analysis.

III. Conclusion

*** We therefore REMAND with respect to Mr. Hardman and Mr. Wilgus, and AFFIRM with respect to Mr. Saenz.

NOTES AND QUESTIONS

1. *Balancing two compelling interests.* The *Hardman* court held that the government's interests were divided. On one hand, the government has a compelling interest in protecting eagles. On the other, the government has an obligation to protect Native culture and religion. At the same time, under RFRA, the government has to employ the least restrictive means when it imposes substantial burdens on any religious practitioners, whether Native or not. *Hardman* held that the government failed to meet its burden with respect to Saenz, who was Chiricahua Apache but not a member of a federally recognized tribe, and remanded the two cases involving non-Indians to the district court. On remand, the district court engaged in a searching and nuanced analysis of the competing interests, and found that the government failed to meet its obligations under RFRA. *See United States v. Hardman*, 622 F.Supp.2d 1129 (D.

Utah 2009); United *States v. Wilgus*, 622 F.Supp.2d 1308 (D. Utah 2009). The Tenth Circuit reversed, however, concluding that the government had made an adequate showing that restricting access to eagle feathers and parts was the least restrictive means to achieve its compelling interests in protecting eagles and furthering American Indian religion. *United States v. Wilgus*, 638 F.3d 1274 (10th Cir. 2011). The court, in its second bite at formulating the government's interest in protecting American Indian religion and culture, decided that the tie to federally recognized tribes was crucial, and that the government did not have a compelling interest in protecting Native religion and culture more generally:

> [T]his formulation of the governmental interest is consistent with the Supreme Court's longstanding interpretation of the federal government's relationship with Native American tribes. In *Morton v. Mancari*, 417 U.S. 535, 537–39 (1974), the Supreme Court considered an equal protection attack on a provision of the 1934 Indian Reorganization Act that gave Native Americans preference for employment in the Bureau of Indian Affairs. The Court began by noting that Congress has "plenary power" to legislate concerning the tribes, springing from both the Indian Commerce Clause of Article I of the Constitution, U.S. Const. art. I, § 8, cl. 3, and the treaty power of Article II, *id.* art. II, § 2, cl. 2. *Morton*, 417 U.S. at 551–52. The Court noted that, as a consequence of the forcible seizure of Indian lands by the United States, "the United States assumed the duty of furnishing ... protection [to the Native Americans], and with it the authority to do all that was required to perform that obligation." *Id.* at 552.
>
> Pursuant to this obligation to the tribes, Congress was empowered to "single out for special treatment *a constituency of tribal Indians*." *Id.* (emphasis added). The employment preference before the Court did not draw a distinction based on race, but rather one based on political constituency: "The preference, as applied, is granted to Indians not as a discrete racial group, but, rather, as members of quasi-sovereign tribal entities." *Id.* at 554. The preference was "political rather than racial, in nature." *Id.* at 553 n. 24. Thus the preference did not offend the equal protection component of the Due Process Clause of the Fifth Amendment. ***
>
> Similarly, here, even though we are not considering an equal protection or due process attack on the Eagle Act, we note that the language of the exception to the possession ban in the Eagle Act refers specifically to "the religious purposes of Indian tribes." 16 U.S.C. § 668a. The Act thus draws a distinction between Native Americans and non-Native Americans based on the "quasi-sovereign" status of the tribes. *Morton* itself characterized Congress' power over Indian affairs in terms of the tribes: "Resolution of the instant issue turns on ... the plenary power of Congress, based on a history of treaties and the assumption of a 'guardian-ward' status, to legislate on behalf of *federally recognized* Indian tribes." *Id.* at 551 (emphasis added). Thus, by adopting the federally-recognized tribes version of the compelling governmental interest in this case, we situate ourselves in the very heartland of federal power, as recognized by the Supreme Court in its *Morton* line of cases.

United States v. Wilgus, 638 F.3d at 1286-87. Do you agree with the court's narrower articulation of its interest in protecting American Indian religion and culture? One of the court's concerns was that if the interest was to promote

American Indian religion and culture generally, the government could be vulnerable to accusations of favoring or sponsoring a particular religion, potentially running afoul of the establishment clause. The tie to the federal government's constitutional relationship with federally recognized tribes keeps it on the sovereign-to-sovereign side of that line. *See id.* at 1287-88. How, then, does the court's conclusion concerning Saenz, the Chiricahua Apache practitioner whose RFRA rights were violated, fit into this formulation of the interest? Did the *Wilgus* court simply forget about Saenz, or can you make an argument that nonmember Indians should be treated differently than non-Indians with respect to furthering the government's interest in protecting the religion and culture of federally recognized tribes?

2. *Least Restrictive Means.* The Supreme Court gave all RFRA claims a shot of adrenaline when it decided *Burwell v. Hobby Lobby*, 134 S. Ct. 1751 (2014). *Hobby Lobby* held that the government cannot require a closely held corporation to comply with provisions of the Affordable Care Act (colloquially known as Obamacare) that require employer contributions for birth control devices if those devices violate the corporation's religious beliefs. *Hobby Lobby*'s articulation of the "least restrictive means" test is particularly relevant to the eagle feather cases. The Supreme Court described the test as "exceptionally demanding." *Id.* At 2780. The Fifth Circuit, relying on this language, held that the government had not met its burden at the summary judgment stage in a case involving RFRA challenges to the BGEPA and MBTA. *See McAllen Grace Brethren Church v. Salazar*, 764 F.3d 465 (5th Cir. 2014). Similar to the *Saenz*, *Hardman*, and *Wilgus* cases, one of the challengers, Robert Soto, was a member of the Lipan Apache, a non-federally recognized Indian tribe. The court remanded the case for evidentiary hearings, and cautioned that "[t]he burden on the Department is a high one: they must demonstrate that 'no alternative forms of regulation' would maintain [the relationship between federally recognized tribes and the federal government] without infringing upon the rights of others." *Id.* at 479-480.

Soto and the other challengers had proposed that such means could include allowing sincere religious practitioners to collect molted feathers or feathers from zoos. "While the Department urges that doing so would make it impossible to determine if the feathers possessed were truly molted or taken in some other way, the Department's difficulties with enforcement do not justify the diminishing of individual rights, especially if a less restrictive alternative could achieve the same goals without harming the rights of someone like Soto, a sincere adherent who is a member of a tribe that is not federally recognized." *Id.* at 476. What kind of evidence does the government need to produce on remand to uphold the current permit system?

3. *De-listing of the Bald Eagle.* Prompted by the Bald Eagle's impressive recovery, the Department of the Interior removed the Bald Eagle from the Endangered Species list. *See* 72 Fed. Reg. 37345 (July 9, 2007). American Indian tribes that hold the eagle sacred generally opposed the delisting. *See* Resolution of the National Congress of American Indians Opposing Delisting of the Bald Eagle (Resolution #ECWS–07–004, March 19, 2007), http://web.archive.org/web/20071028035612/;https://www.ncai.org/ncai/resolutions/doc/07-004_Bald_Eagle.pdf. In order to foster eagle recovery and at the same time avoid the burdens on their religion imposed by the permit system, some tribes, including the Iowa Tribe of Oklahoma and the Zuni Pueblo, have their own eagle

aviaries. Others, like the Hopi tribe, have established their own permit systems for taking eagles. *See Tawahongva*, 456 F.Supp.2d at 1123.

Despite the Bald Eagle's de-listing, courts have been reluctant to uphold RFRA claims in the context of taking live eagles. In *United States v. Friday*, 525 F.3d 938 (10th Cir. 2008), Winslow Friday, a Northern Arapahoe tribal member, raised a RFRA challenge to his conviction for killing a Bald Eagle. Mr. Friday had taken the eagle as part of his family's religious obligation with respect to the sacred Sun Dance, and had succeeded in having his indictment dismissed in the district court. The district court's dismissal was based in large part on its finding that the government had kept what is known as the "live-take permit" for religious practitioners a well kept secret. The Tenth Circuit reversed, holding that the government's permit system did not impose a substantial burden on Mr. Friday's religious practice. The Tenth Circuit revisited this factual finding, making new law with respect to appellate review of facts.

Other courts have also upheld the BGEPA's application to tribal members. *See United States v. Oliver*, 255 F.3d 588 (8th Cir. 2001) (*per curiam*); *United States v. Tawahongva*, 456 F. Supp.2d 1120 (D. Ariz. 2006). In *Tawahongva*, the government's evidence included its regular provision of live-take permits to Hopi tribal members, as well as information about the Hopi Tribe's own accessible and cost-free permit system established and administered pursuant to tribal law. *Id.* at 1123. In *United States v. Friday*, by contrast, there was testimony by a U.S. Fish and Wildlife officer that even he was not aware of the live-take permits. Given the courts' reluctance to allow eagle takings for religious purposes outside of the permit system, how might you advise tribal religious practitioners to pursue their concerns in this context? The Northern Araphaoe Tribe decided to request permits from the Fish and Wildlife Service. When the FWS refused to issue permits within the Tribe's reservation, the Tribe sued and won on the grounds that the FWS had not adopted the least restrictive means to furthering its twin interests in eagle protection and honoring the conflicting concerns of the Eastern Shoshone Tribe, which shares the reservation. *Northern Arapahoe Tribe v. Ashe*, 92 F.Supp.3d 1160, 1187-88 (D. Wyo. 2015). For an interesting empirical study of free exercise cases over the past twenty-five years, see Caleb C. Wolanek & Heidi Liu, *Applying Strict Scrutiny: And Empirical Analysis of Free Exercise Cases*, 78 Mont. L. Rev. 275 (2017).

4. *Religious Rights of American Indian Inmates*. American Indians are incarcerated at disproportionate rates and typically serve longer sentences farther from home than other offenders. Indian Law & Order Commission, *A Roadmap for Making Native America Safer*, Ch.5 (2013), http://www.aisc.ucla.edu/iloc/report/ [https://perma.cc/AN62-SQYT]. Many crimes by Indian prisoners are drug and alcohol related, and experts and spiritual leaders have emphasized the importance of traditional cultural and religious practices as an essential aspect of reform and rehabilitation. Yet prison officials are often particularly resistant to accommodating Indian religious beliefs and practices. Suzanne J. Crawford & Dennis F. Kelley, American Indian Religious Traditions: An Encyclopedia 774 (2005). Until 1987, the federal courts had mixed reactions to these claims. Some courts protected Indian religious practices, especially against restrictions on hair length. *See, e.g., Teterud v. Burns*, 522 F.2d 357 (8th Cir. 1975) (upholding right of Indian inmate to wear long braids); *Weaver v. Jago*, 675 F.2d 116 (6th Cir. 1982). Other courts rejected inmates' free exercise claims. *See, e.g., Cole v. Flick*, 758 F.2d 124 (3d Cir. 1985); *Capoeman v. Reed*, 754 F.2d 1512 (9th Cir. 1985). But starting in 1987, the free exercise

claims of prisoners were evaluated under the very deferential "legitimate penological interest" test articulated by the Supreme Court. *See Turner v. Safley*, 482 U.S. 78 (1987); *O'Lone v. Estate of Shabazz*, 482 U.S. 342 (1987). Most restrictions on American Indian religious practices were upheld under this standard. *See Iron Eyes v. Henry*, 907 F.2d 810 (8th Cir. 1990) (hair-length restriction reasonably related to legitimate penological interest); *Pollock v. Marshall*, 845 F.2d 656 (6th Cir. 1988) (same); *Standing Deer v. Carlson*, 831 F.2d 1525 (9th Cir. 1987) (upholding ban on head-bands). *But see Sample v. Borg*, 675 F. Supp. 574 (E.D. Cal. 1987) (finding restrictions on pipe ceremonies and other religious practices to violate free exercise rights of Indian inmates), *vacated as moot* 870 F.2d 563 (9th Cir. 1989).

As in the sacred sites and eagle contexts, the Religious Freedom Restoration Act and Religious Land Use and Institutionalized Persons Act revived the religious claims of American Indian inmates, providing that substantial burdens on religious practices must be narrowly tailored to achieve a compelling governmental interest. 42 U.S.C. § 2000cc–1. Court decisions conflict regarding whether religious restrictions on Indian inmates meet this exacting standard. *Warsoldier v. Woodford*, 418 F.3d 989 (9th Cir. 2005) (holding the hair length restriction was not justified under RLUIPA) and *Native American Council of Tribes v. Weber*, 750 F.3d 742 (8th Cir. 2013) (invalidating prohibition of religious use of tobacco under prison tobacco ban under RLUIPA) *with Knight v. Thompson*, 723 F.3d 1275 (11th Cir. 2013) (upholding prison short-hair policy against RLUIPA challenge) *and Fowler v. Crawford*, 534 F.3d 931 (8th Cir. 2008) (upholding denial of permission to a prisoner to use a sweat lodge against RLUIPA challenge); *cf. Yellowbear v. Lampbert*, 741 F.3d 48 (10th Cir. 2014) (reversing and remanding grant of summary judgment to prison officials in RLUIPA challenge to denial of access to sweat lodge).

The difficulty that American Indian inmates face in having their religious interests in hair length, pipe ceremonies, sweat lodges, and other practices and rituals accommodated, and the costliness and uncertainty of federal litigation even after RFRA, have led some advocates to try alternative strategies. State statutes, for example, can become a vehicle through which to educate prison officials and enact meaningful reforms even when litigation is a dead end. Leonard Foster, Director of the Corrections Project of the Navajo Nation Department of Behavioral Health Services and a long-time advocate for the religious rights of Native prisoners, drafted model legislation to protect the religious rights of American Indian prisoners, which has been passed in several states. *See, e.g.*, Colo. Rev. Stat. § 17–42–102 (requiring that state correctional facilities allow Native prisoners access to traditional spiritual leaders, ceremonial items and materials, and religious facilities). *See* "*The Fight for Native American Prisoners' Rights: The Red Road to Rehabilitation*," in A Seat at the Table: Huston Smith in Conversation with Native Americans on Religious Freedom 114–128 (Phil Cousineau, ed. 2006).

IV. PROTECTION OF AMERICAN INDIAN CULTURAL AND INTELLECTUAL PROPERTY

A. PROTECTION AND REPATRIATION OF CULTURAL SITES, OBJECTS, REMAINS AND OTHER TANGIBLE PROPERTY

The appropriation of Indian lands and intentional efforts to destroy Indian religion and culture were accompanied by an assumption that American Indians as such would disappear. Efforts were therefore made to collect various specimens and examples in order to preserve them for posterity. While a great deal of Indian cultural patrimony was also taken by private parties and sold, destroyed, or otherwise made permanently unavailable, the anthropological and historical instinct to preserve resulted in enormous volumes of American Indian physical cultural property being held by museums and government agencies. *See* Jack F. Trope & Walter R. Echohawk, *The Native American Graves Protection and Repatriation Act: Background and Legislative History*, 24 Ariz. St. L.J. 35 (1992). American Indian activism and pressure to reverse the trends of the past and provide protections against ongoing depredation resulted in the passage of several important statutes concerning American Indian cultural property, sacred remains, and archeological resources. *See id.* at 54.

Smithsonian Collection, Museum of the American Indian (1921), by Nathaniel L. Stebbins, Public domain.

1. The Native American Grave Protection and Repatriation Act (NAGPRA)

The Native American Graves Protection and Repatriation Act (NAGPRA), 25 U.S.C. §§ 3001–3013, enacted in 1990, provides American Indian tribes, Native Hawaiian organizations, and their lineal descendants with rights to repatriate human remains, funerary objects, sacred objects, and objects of cultural patrimony from federal agencies and museums funded or owned by the federal government. Criminal provisions of NAGPRA prohibit trafficking in American Indian human remains and cultural items. 18 U.S.C. § 1170. NAGPRA also creates a protective legal regime for access to cultural objects or remains, prohibiting their removal or disturbance from federal or tribal lands without tribal consent, and imposing criminal penalties for unauthorized excavation, removal or damage to such sites. 25 U.S.C. § 3002; *see* Cohen's Handbook on Federal Indian Law 1279-84 (2012) (describing these provisions in detail). To date, criminal prosecutions under NAGPRA have withstood challenges on vagueness and other grounds. *See United States v. Tidwell*, 191 F.3d 976 (9th Cir. 1999); *United States v. Kramer*, 168 F.3d 1196 (10th Cir. 1999); *United States v. Corrow*, 119 F.3d 796 (10th Cir. 1997).

NAGPRA's repatriation provisions require federal agencies and museums to summarize and compile inventories of the protected objects, and to engage in consultation with the relevant tribes, Native Hawaiian organizations, lineal descendants, and traditional religious leaders. 25 U.S.C. §§ 3003–3004. There are four limitations on the duty to repatriate: scientific study, right of possession, competing claim, and taking of property. *See* 25 U.S.C. § 3005(b); Cohen's Handbook on Federal Indian Law 1277-79 (2012). The National Park Service maintains a national on-line database that includes the number of remains that have been found and considered culturally identifiable, and also posts pending Notices of Intent to Repatriate. *See* National Park Service, NAGPRA, http://www.cr.nps.gov/nagpra/fed_notices/nagpradir/index2.htm.

NAGPRA's requirements have at times created tension with other groups interested in ancient remains. The most widely publicized of these controversies was the dispute over the so-called "Kennewick Man." Discovered on the banks of the Columbia River in 1996, this 9,300 year old skeleton became the subject of intense and emotional litigation. Indian tribes from the Columbia River basin made a claim for ownership under NAGPRA, and federal officials determined that the remains should be granted to the tribes. Scientists objected and sued for the right to study the skeleton, arguing that their findings would provide important information about the history of human habitation of North America. A federal district court ruled that the remains should be turned over to the scientists, and the Ninth Circuit upheld the decision on the grounds that there was insufficient establishment of a cultural affiliation between the present day tribes and the ancient skeleton. *See Bonnichsen v. United States*, 217 F. Supp. 2d 1116 (D. Or. 2002), *aff'd and remanded*, 367 F.3d 864 (9th Cir. 2004).

Early statements by scientist James Chatters that the skeleton's features were not distinctively Native American sparked a storm of discussion concerning whether Kennewick Man supported views that Europeans arrived earlier to North America than previously believed, and therefore pre-dated American Indian presence. Those views have since been discredited, and Chatters disavowed any comments misperceived as an assertion that Kennewick man was

Caucasian. *See Bonnichsen*, 217 F.Supp.2d at 1127 n.24. Yet the intensity of the debate over Kennewick man replayed familiar battles over rights to land and heritage, and also recycled Indian stereotypes in the context of a case construing a federal law intended to restore Indian control over culture:

> In a ***60 Minutes*** segment, television journalist Leslie Stahl suggested that Kennewick Man "could turn out to be the missing link between what we thought to be the truth and what is actually the truth—a truth, if it is the truth—that the Indians are not happy with and would just as soon leave well enough alone." In the same program, James Chatters proposed that tribal opposition to further testing was "based largely on fear, fear that if someone was here before they were, their status as sovereign nations, and all that goes with it—treaty rights, and lucrative casinos *** could be at risk." Although noting that Indians dismissed such charges as "nonsense," this widely watched program left the distinct impression that if Kennewick Man turned out to be non-Indian, tribal sovereignty would be directly threatened.

David Hurst Thomas, Skull Wars: Kennewick Man, Archaeology, and the Battle for Native American Identity 234 (2000). There is no evidence that Kennewick man is a descendant of any European group. But even if there were, would tribal sovereignty be threatened? Why or why not?

A stranger recent dispute involved the remains of Sac and Fox athlete Jim Thorpe, who some still regard as the greatest Olympian of all time. After Thorpe died in 1953, his third wife Patty intervened in his ritual burial ceremony in Oklahoma and, with the assistance of state officers, seized his casket and stored it while she considered various towns interested in having him buried there. Finally, she delivered his body to two small Pennsylvania towns which agreed to rename themselves Jim Thorpe, build a memorial in Thorpe's honor, and pay Patty an unspecified amount of money. The town buried Thorpe in the town cemetery for several years, but in 1957 moved him to the mausoleum that it had constructed in his honor. Thorpe's son John and other family members had always objected to the removal, but waited until 2010 to invoke the act in seeking to remove Thorpe's body to Oklahoma. Although NAGPRA had been enacted twenty years before, John did not want to bring the suit until his sister, who opposed removing her father's body yet again, had died. The language of NAGPRA is technically broad enough to cover the situation, as it requires repatriation by "any institution or State or local government agency (including any institution of higher learning) that receives Federal funds and has possession of, or control over, Native American cultural items." 25 U.S.C. § 3001(8). Reading this provision literally, however, would permit NAGPRA claims not only in situations like the Thorpe burial, but also in any family dispute over remains in a cemetery controlled by a state or local government. Finding that this was the rare situation where a court should resist a literal interpretation that reached a "clearly absurd result," the court held that NAGPRA could not be interpreted to reach remains of those buried consistent with the wishes of their next-of-kin. *Thorpe v. Borough of Jim Thorpe*, 770 F.3d 255, 264-66 (3d Cir. 2014).

2. The Archaeological Resources Protection Act

The Archaeological Resources Protection Act of 1979 prohibits the excavation, removal, alteration or destruction of archaeological resources from federal lands and "Indian lands" unless a permit for removal has been issued. 16 U.S.C. § 470aa, *et seq*. A permit for excavation on Indian lands requires tribal consent as well as the consent of the particular Indian owner of the land. ARPA references NAGPRA with regard to the requirements for disposition of American Indian remains or cultural objects discovered on public lands, and requires notification of affected tribes when issuance of a permit might harm religious or cultural sites. *See* 16 U.S.C. §§ 470 CC (b)(3) and CC(c). For further details about ARPA's substantive requirements and procedures, see Cohen's Handbook of Federal Indian Law 1285-88 (2012).

3. The National Historic Preservation Act

As discussed in Section II, *supra*, Congress amended the National Historic Preservation Act (NHPA), 16 U.S.C. § 470, *et seq*., in response to pressure from Indian tribes and others in the wake of the Supreme Court's decision in *Lyng*. The NHPA includes environmental review and consultation requirements analogous to the National Environmental Policy Act. The NHPA has been important both in prompting federal agencies to recognize and prioritize American Indian cultural and sacred sites, and in providing Indian tribes a vehicle through which to participate in and monitor federal lands management. *See, e.g., Pueblo of Sandia v. United States*, 50 F.3d 856 (10th Cir. 1995) (finding that the National Forest Service violated the NHPA by failing to evaluate Pueblo's cultural and religious use of canyon); *see also* Cohen's Handbook of Federal Indian Law 1288-1300 (2012) (describing NHPA's provisions and mechanics in detail).

4. The Indian Arts and Crafts Act

The Indian Arts and Crafts Act, 18 U.S.C. §§ 1158–1159, 25 U.S.C. § 305, *et seq*., prevents the sale of goods which are falsely represented to have been made by Indians or which are sold in a manner that conveys the impression that they are made by Indians. The Act authorizes the Indian Arts and Crafts Board to create distinctive trademarks for Indian tribes and artists, and imposes criminal and civil liability for those violating its "truth in marketing" provisions. The Act defines an Indian as either a member of any Indian tribe or someone who is certified as an Indian artisan by an Indian tribe. *See* 25 U.S.C. § 305e(d)(1); *see also* 25 C.F.R. § 309.2(a). For more on the IACA, see Cohen's Handbook of Federal Indian Law 1303-07 (2012).

5. Tribal Law

Not content to rely solely on the good will of Congress or the enforcement enthusiasm of the federal agencies, some American Indian tribes also provide for the protection of tangible cultural property under tribal law. One study found that at least twenty-nine tribes in the lower forty-eight states had code provisions addressing cultural property, and sixty-seven tribes had developed some form of cultural resources program. *See* Angela R. Riley, *"Straight Stealing": Towards an Indigenous System of Cultural Property Protection*, 80 Wash. L. Rev. 69, 101–109 (2005). Tribal laws may provide the best protection against the misappropriation of tribal cultural property, and can afford tribes with remedies for return that may be unavailable under federal or state laws.

As tribes exert their sovereign powers to protect their cultural property, they inevitably run into the tangle of questions created by the federal body of law defining tribal jurisdiction, discussed in earlier chapters. In *Chilkat Indian Village v. Johnson*, 870 F.2d 1469 (9th Cir. 1989), a Tlingit village in Alaska sued Michael Johnson, a non-Indian art dealer, and several tribal member defendants in federal court for, among other things, violating a tribal ordinance prohibiting the sale of tribal artifacts without permission of the Chilkat Indian Village Council. Over a period of many years, Johnson had doggedly attempted to convince individual tribal members to sell him the artifacts. He eventually succeeded despite knowledge of the tribal ordinance and repeated rebuffs by the Village Council, some of which included physically prohibiting Johnson from access to the location where the artifacts were kept. *See* Marilee Enge, *The Whale House Series*, The Anchorage Daily News, *available at*: http://www.ankn.uaf.edu/curriculum/Tlingit/WhaleHouse/part1.html. The Ninth Circuit held that the issue of whether the tribe had jurisdiction over Johnson was a matter of federal law, pursuant to *National Farmers Union, supra*. The court otherwise determined that the federal court lacked jurisdiction over the substantive claim for return of the artifacts, and the case ultimately went forward in tribal court. *See Chilkat Indian Village, IRA v. Johnson*, 20 Indian L. Rep. 6127 (Civ. No. 90–01) (Chilkat Tribal Ct. Nov. 3, 1993). After a trial at which Michael Johnson refused to appear, the tribal court found that Johnson and the tribal member defendants had violated the tribal ordinance, and ordered the return of the objects, which included four carved posts and a wooden rain screen described collectively as the "Whale House artifacts." Below is an excerpt from the tribal court opinion summarizing the testimony of one of the Village's witnesses:

> Plaintiff called as its first witness Joe Hotch, President of the Chilkat Indian Village Council. *** He began his testimony by explaining the significance of the traditional regalia (headpiece and shirt) which he wore while testifying. He then provided some demographic information about Klukwan.
>
> The village has a population which varies from 110–120 people in the winter, to 150–175 people in the summer. With the exception of about ten people, Mr. Hotch stated that all residents are Tlingit Indians. The tribe, which is organized and has a constitution and bylaws pursuant to section 16 of the Indian Reorganization Act, 25 U.S.C. § 476, collectively owns all of the land in the village, including all of the real property on which all residences are situated. Joe Hotch stated that the tribal council, of which he is president, is regarded by village members as the sole governing body. He stated that at various times some of the Tlingit defendants served as members of the council, including Evans Willard, David Light, Wes Willard, and Bill Thomas.
>
> Mr. Hotch, whose parents were Victor and Annie Hotch, is a member of the Eagle (or Wolf) moiety, Eagle Clan, and Bear and Killer Whale houses. ***
>
> Regarding the four house posts (sometimes called poles or totems) and rain screen here at issue, Joe Hotch testified that they were "clan trust property," with great spiritual significance to the Ganexteidi Clan, which has primary custodial rights over them. Mr. Hotch and other witnesses explained that the tribe on the whole also has an interest in the artifacts because they have tremendous significance not just for Ravens, but for all Eagles in Klukwan as well.

Joe Hotch described in eloquent terms the healing quality which the artifacts assume. For example, when a member of an opposite clan (of the Eagle moiety) died, and a potlatch was held as a part of the progression of Tlingit funeral arrangements, members of the grieving clan would be brought before the rain screen and told that it constituted medicine which would relieve the loss of their clan member.

Mr. Hotch also provided detailed testimony regarding how certain property is confirmed as being clan trust property, which includes presenting it in a ceremony in which members of the opposite "tribe" (*i.e.*, in this case members of clans of the Eagle moiety) are invited, which completes the confirmation of the clan trust status of property such as the Whale House artifacts, which, according to Mr. Hotch, were subject to this process. Joe Hotch recalled attending many ceremonies at the Whale House in which the artifacts played a central role.

He also recalled the two unsuccessful attempts in the mid–1970s to remove the artifacts from the Whale House in Klukwan. He recalled that in 1976 Estelle DeHaven Johnson, a Tlingit who was the granddaughter of "Chief Shotridge" of the Whale House, attempted to remove the artifacts with the backing of art dealer Michael Johnson. The attempt was thwarted when villagers (Victor Hotch in particular by some accounts) placed one or more skiffs (small vessels) in front of the door to the Whale House. Joe Hotch (and others) recalled that following the first unsuccessful removal attempt, Michael Johnson financed a federal court action to determine ownership of the artifacts, although the pendency of that action did not deter a second attempt to remove the artifacts later in 1976. That second attempt was unsuccessful when the village siren was sounded, trees were felled blocking exits of the village, and members of the tribe acted together to prevent the removal. ***

Id. at 6131. The *Chilkat* case was decided before *Alaska v. Native Village of Venetie*, discussed in ch. 5, *supra*. After *Venetie*, would a federal court require Johnson to exhaust his tribal court remedies? If so, how could the tribal court best support a ruling in favor of the tribe's jurisdiction over Johnson? What purposes, aside from the immediate objective of obtaining the Whale House artifacts, are served by providing a tribal law and a tribal forum for the resolution of this dispute?

B. PROTECTION OF INTANGIBLE PROPERTY

Stories, rituals, music, dances, names, medicines—these and other intangibles are the stuff of all cultures. For American Indians, protection and perpetuation of these intangible aspects of culture can be complicated for several reasons. The intellectual property law frameworks—copyright, patent, trademark, and laws governing publicity rights—are not always a perfect fit, and may at times work against tribal interests in maintaining collective, as opposed to individual, ownership. In some tribes, it is paramount that aspects of cultural or religious knowledge remain secret from outsiders, thus confounding conventional requirements for disclosure in order to obtain legal protection. *See* Rebecca Tsosie, *Reclaiming Native Stories: An Essay on Cultural Appropriation and Cultural Rights*, 34 Ariz. St. L. J. 299 (2002) (describing unique challenges to protecting tribal cultural property). Historical policies aimed at dismantling American Indian culture have resulted in the heightened vigilance with which many tribes guard their cultural practices and knowledge. This history, as well as widespread lack of information about the current status and existence of American Indian tribes, also informs disputes over sports mascots and product names. *See* Gavin Clarkson, *Racial Imagery and Native Americans: A First Look at the Empirical Evidence Behind the Indian Mascot Controversy*, 11 Cardozo J. Int'l & Comp. L. 393 (2003).

Legal efforts to protect and preserve intangible cultural property can be usefully, if not entirely cleanly, divided into two categories: efforts to prevent outsiders from misuse or appropriation, and efforts to promote growth and flourishing of tribal cultural life.

1. Preventing Misuse and Appropriation

American Indian names, images, and artwork pervade American society, often without permission or credit to tribes or Indian artists. People climb into their four-wheel drive Cherokees, trek cross-country in their Winnebagos, and spread Land O'Lakes butter on their waffles, hardly registering what many American Indian people experience as the appropriation of indigenous cultural property. The hiphop/funk duo Outkast, which has vigorously protested unauthorized downloading of its songs, spiced up its 2004 Grammy performance with buckskin bikini clad women in braids and feathers and an unauthorized broadcast of the sacred Navajo Beauty Way song. Angela R. Riley, *"Straight Stealing": Towards an Indigenous System of Cultural Property Protection*, 80 Wash. L. Rev. 69, 70–72 (2005). Pharrell Williams, pop superstar, posed in a faux Dakota headdress for the cover of UK Vogue in June, 2014, drawing immediate criticism from American Indian communities and their supporters. Williams apologized shortly thereafter, stating in an interview in *Rolling Stone Magazine*: "I respect and honor ever kind of race, background, culture. I am genuinely sorry."

The American Indian mascot represents a crucible for the struggle over indigenous control over representation. Until recently, approximately 2700 schools and professional sports teams used Native American mascots or team names. William N. Wright, *Not in Whose Name?: Evidentiary Issues in Legal Challenges to Native American Sports Teams and Mascots*, 40 Conn. L. Rev. 279, 283 (2007).

One of the better known mascots is Chief Wahoo of the Cleveland Indians, whose toothy grin adorns the team's memorabilia. Can you imagine a similarly stereotypical image of an Asian, an African, or a Latino being used to promote the Cleveland Africans, Asians, or Mexicans? Defenders of Indian mascots and associated imagery claim that they are honoring, not denigrating, Native people. *See* Wright, 40 Conn. L. Rev. at 289–291. Teams name themselves after Indians, defenders argue, to associate themselves with positive qualities, like native nobility, strength, or bravery. Opponents respond both that the other popular mascots so honored are all animals, and that this kind of adulation of the idealized Indian has a long and pernicious role in American culture and policy:

> *** Oren Lyons, the Haudenosaunee faithkeeper noted: "Army had a mule, Navy had a goat, Georgia had a bulldog and Syracuse had an Indian." *** "[S]uch honoring relegates Indians to the long-ago and thus makes them magically disappear from public consciousness and

> conscience," according to Michael Dorris, the Modoc writer. *** The Rev. Gary Cavendar, a member of the Sioux Nation, told a reporter that permitting the use of Indian names "[k]eeps us in a box. We're an ornament."
>
> Reinforcing the dehumanizing influence of these images is the fact that they are presented as ahistorical and contextless. *** In this vision of history, unfortunately embraced by members of the Supreme Court, those who did not "announc[e] their dependence on the Federal Government" were brave, but ultimately doomed, "sinking before our superior policy, our arts and our arms." By rendering native people as inhuman, timeless, and essentialized, these images help promote the myth of the vanishing Indian and in so doing, deprive Indians not just of their history but of their present reality. *** Suzan Shown Harjo, a Cheyenne/Muscogee activist, and plaintiff in a case challenging the right of the Washington football team to use the name "Redskins" states: "[W]e are not in the present tense or the future tense in the minds of the general population. If we were, policy would be better crafted for people who are not simply anomalies in the modern era."

Nell Jessup Newton, *Memory and Misrepresentation: Representing Crazy Horse*, 27 Conn. L. Rev. 1003, 1009–1011 (1995).

The end of American Indian team names and mascots? Of all of the cases against derogatory or offensive uses of American Indian names and images, the one against the National Football League's Washington, D.C. team, still known as the "Redskins" at the time of this writing, has the most notoriety. Efforts to eliminate use of the name through trademark litigation ran aground when the U.S. Supreme Court struck down the provision that allowed for cancellation of discriminatory marks. *Matal v. Tam*, 137 S. Ct. 1744, 1751 (2017) (holding that provision allowing for challenge of trademarks based on "disparagement," 15 U.S.C. §§ 1052(a), violated first amendment rights).

Despite the trademark decision, there are indicia of long-term success on the mascot and team name front. In 2001, the United States Commission on Civil Rights "call[ed] for an end to the use of Native American imagery and mascots by non-Native schools." Statement on the Use of Native American Images and Nicknames as Sports Symbols (Apr. 13, 2001), *available at* http://www.usccr.gov/press/archives/2001/041601st.htm. Even more important, in 2005 the National College Athletic Association prohibited schools with "hostile or abusive" mascots from hosting or displaying their mascots at post-season championships after February 2006. Gary T. Brown, *Policy applies core principles to mascot issue; February deadline set for affected schools to comply*, The NCAA News (Aug. 15, 2005), *available at* www.ncaa.org. Of the nineteen schools identified as having an offensive mascot, eleven agreed to change their mascots, and three refused to comply with the policy. *See* NCAA News Archive 2005 at www.ncaa.org. Five other teams, including the Florida State Seminoles and the Central Michigan University Chippewas, have been deemed exempt from the policy, *id.*, because the Florida State Seminole and Saginaw Chippewa tribes approved the imagery used. John Supinie, *Chief Concerns; Illinois Doesn't Have Support of the Tribe*, State Journal Register (Springfield, Ill.), May 19, 2006. If the images are offensive to Native people generally, should tribal approval make a difference? Or is lack of control over the image the basic problem? Florida State discontinued use of its buffoonish "Sammy Seminole" mascot, for example, after the Seminole Tribe of Florida complained.

What if the different tribes with the same name disagree on the use of the mascot? While the Seminole Tribe of Florida, for example, has approved the Florida State Seminole mascot and worked with the university on education and representation issues, the Seminole Nation of Oklahoma objects to the mascot use. Other Chippewa tribes, similarly, object to the CMU mascot.

Advertising and appropriation. The dispute over the use of the name of Crazy Horse, the revered Oglala Lakota leader, provides another window into the complexity of protecting intangible tribal property. When Hornell Brewing Co. first proposed selling its Original Crazy Horse Malt Liquor, members of the Rosebud Sioux Tribe attempted to convince them to refrain. When these attempts failed, tribal members and others convinced Congress to pass a statute banning the use of the name Crazy Horse in connection with the sale of liquor. 102 Pub. L. § 393, 633; 106 Stat. 1729 (1992). Hornell Brewing Co challenged the law on first amendment grounds and prevailed. *See Hornell Brewing Co. v. Brady*, 819 F. Supp. 1227 (E.D. N.Y. 1993).

A descendant of Crazy Horse then filed suit in the Rosebud Sioux Tribal Court alleging violations of tort and intellectual property law, and arguing that Tasunke Witko (Crazy Horse) was a spiritual leader for the Lakota people who abstained from alcohol, and that the use of his name to peddle malt liquor was deeply offensive to his family and tribe. The Rosebud Sioux Tribal Court found that the descendants had the right under tribal law to prevent unauthorized use of Crazy Horse's name, but also found that it lacked jurisdiction over the defendant brewing company. *In re Tasunke Witko* (Civ. No. 93–204) (Rbd. Sx. Tribal Ct. Oct. 25, 1994). The jurisdictional finding was reversed by the Rosebud Sioux Supreme Court, *see Estate of Tasunke Witko v. G. Heileman Brewing Co.* (*In re Tasunke Witko*), 23 Indian L. Rep. 6104 (Rbd. Sx. Sup. Ct. 1996). But when the defendants appealed the jurisdictional question to federal court, the Eighth Circuit held that the tribal court lacked jurisdiction over nonmember defendants who sold their product outside of the reservation. *Hornell Brewing Co. v. Rosebud Sioux Tribal Court*, 133 F.3d 1087, 1093 (8th Cir. 1998).

The story did not end there, however. Crazy Horse's descendants and the Rosebud Sioux Tribe continued to pursue the issue in federal court with Hornell and Heileman Brewing Company, which was eventually bought by Stroh's Brewing Co. In 2001, Heileman and Stroh's were dropped from the suit after agreeing to issue a public apology for misusing the name Crazy Horse, assign all intellectual property rights in the name of Crazy Horse to his descendants, destroy all packages and packaging materials related to Crazy Horse Malt Liquor, and agree never to use the name Crazy Horse in any commercial venture. In addition, Stroh's presented the Estate and Rosebud Sioux Tribe with 32 Pendleton blankets, 32 braids of sweet grass, 32 twists of tobacco (one for each of the 32 states in which the malt liquor had been distributed), and seven thoroughbred race horses (one for each of the seven malt liquor bottling facilities). *See* Estate of Tasunke Witko, *One Brewing Company Settles with the Family of Crazy Horse and Rosebud Sioux Tribe, available at* http://web.archive.org/web/20090422042836/; http:// ableza.org/CHorse.html. Hornell continued to package the malt liquor until finally agreeing to settle with the estate in 2004. *Crazy Horse Suit Finally Dismissed, Use of Brandname–Breweries*, Modern Brewery Age at 3 (Jan. 19, 2004). What role did law play in the resolution of this dispute? What role did tribal sovereignty play?

Some American Indian tribes have passed their own laws to protect intangible cultural property. *See* Angela R. Riley, *"Straight Stealing": Towards an Indigenous System of Cultural Property Protection*, 80 Wash. L. Rev. 69, 116–17 (2005). Advantages for tribes of fashioning their own legal protections include the ability to define cultural property accurately according to their tribal belief systems, and the potential for positive feedback effects on outside jurisdictions. *See id.* at 123–29 (describing ways in which tribal laws and customs have been acknowledged by other courts). As suggested by the Crazy Horse litigation, however, judicial restrictions on tribal jurisdiction over non-members may limit enforcement of such laws.

2. Promoting the Flourishing of Tribal Culture

The flip side of preventing misuse and appropriation of tribal culture is promoting its growth and flourishing from within tribal communities. As documented by Professor Riley, many tribes have offices or programs dedicated to cultural growth and preservation. *See* Riley, *supra*, at 101–114. These efforts are often made possible or enhanced by the presence of tribal and federal laws supporting Native culture and language. *Id.* (describing tribal laws promoting and protecting culture); *see also* Native American Languages Act, 25 U.S.C. §§ 2901–06 (expressing policy of protecting Native American languages and establishing a grant program).

American Indian tribal colleges have proven to be creative laboratories for the blending of old and new tribal teachings. Consider the approach taken by Dine' College in Tsaile, Navajo Nation:

> A herd of sheep grazed peacefully outside the library of Dine' College on a recent afternoon as a student casually strolled by with a laptop case in his right hand. "This is awesome," said an enthused Ferlin Clark, president of Dine' College ***. For Clark, the immediate image is symbolic to the school's entire purpose: to provide a balance between traditional Navajo knowledge and Western education. ***
>
> Since the groundbreaking of the school on April 13, 1971, implementing a Navajo viewpoint into curriculum has been a top goal ***. The school's core classes also include Navajo language, culture, history, philosophy and government. ***
>
> The institution is grounded in the philosophy and principles of *s'ah naagh bik'eh hzhn*, the Dine' traditional living system, which places human life in harmony with the natural world and the universe. *** Many years ago, educators and leaders came to a realization that instead of incorporating Navajo knowledge into Western education, it should be the other way around. "We said, 'Wait a minute. We're doing it backward,' " said Jack Jackson, director of Cultural and Legislative Affairs. *** "[Now] we're using Navajo knowledge to verify Western knowledge." ***
>
> Students are also encouraged to talk with the staff and faculty, especially the Navajo faculty who have knowledge of stories and traditional ways. ***
>
> In 2004, the 20th Navajo Nation Council and President Joe Shirley Jr. approved 20 years of funding that will provide the college with $4.2 million per year. "We basically secured the future viability of Dine' College ***," Clark said. ***

Natasha Kaye Johnson, *Mixing Old & New: Dine College Blends Two Cultures in Learning,* The Gallup Independent (Mar. 21, 2007), *available at* http://web.archive.org/web/20100317072640/; http://www.gallupindependent. com/2007/march/032107nkj_dneclgoldnew.html.

What role has American Indian law and the construct of legal sovereignty played in the context of Dine' College? Could you argue that Dine' College and its uniquely Navajo program would exist without legal sovereignty for Indian nations?

CHAPTER 12

ALASKA AND HAWAI'I

■ ■ ■

Every tribe's legal status under federal law is unique due to particular treaty provisions, statutes, Executive Orders, regulations, and litigation history, although each tribe's legal rights under federal law have common roots. Alaska and Hawai'i have among the highest percentages of indigenous people of any U.S. state. Native people in Alaska and Hawai'i are also subject to the same general principles of federal Indian law as the Indian tribes and Nations treated elsewhere in this book. Federal law, however, has at times treated these Native populations substantially differently from Indian tribes and nations in the other states. Those differences warrant separate treatment and explication.

I. ALASKA NATIVES†

Alaska was essentially unknown and unexplored by non-Native people in 1867 when the United States acquired Alaska from Russia pursuant to the Treaty of Cession. Treaty Concerning the Cession of Russian Possessions in North America, U.S.–Rus., 15 Stat. 539, T.S. No. 301 (1867). Article 3 of the Treaty provided that "[t]he uncivilized tribes will be subject to such laws and regulations as the United States may, from time to time, adopt in regard to aboriginal tribes of that country." In a case involving ownership of submerged lands near Anchorage, the Supreme Court stated that "By the Treaty of Cession in 1867 Russia ceded to the United States *** 'all the territory and dominion now possessed (by Russia) on the continent of America and in the adjacent islands.' 15 Stat. 539. The cession was effectively a quitclaim. It is undisputed that the United States thereby acquired whatever dominion Russia had possessed immediately prior to cession." *Alaska v. United States*, 422 U.S. 184, 192, n. 13 (1975). There was no real colonization of Alaska by the Russians. There were permanent settlements at Kodiak and Sitka (in the Aleutian chain and Southeast Alaska respectively), but "never more than 823 Russians" in Alaska. Robert D. Arnold, Alaska Native Land Claims 20 (1976). When the size of Alaska is considered—the state is as wide as the entire lower forty-eight states, and larger than Texas, California, and Montana combined—it is hard to conceive of Alaska as being "owned" by Russia in 1867.

Despite a few cases approving transfers of Native land in the early 20th century as if aboriginal title did not exist, "the general lesson gleaned from history and disposition of aboriginal claims in Alaska is that, like other indigenous Americans, Alaska Natives held claims to vast tracts of land by aboriginal title." David S. Case and David A. Voluck, Alaska Natives and American

---

†. The phrase "Alaska Native" is generally used as a collective reference to Alaska's various indigenous groups, and includes Indian, Aleut, Yupik and Inuit peoples.

Laws 62 (3d Ed. 2012); *see generally*, Cohen's Handbook of Federal Indian Law § 4.07[3] (2012). While the existence of Alaska Native claims to aboriginal title had been recognized by many from the early years of the 20th century, the enormous size of the state and relatively small non-Native population meant there was little urgency to address the issue. Because the United States acquired Alaska only three years before the end of treaty making, no treaties were signed with Alaska Natives. Nevertheless a number of Indian reservations were established by Executive Order and later pursuant to the Indian Reorganization Act. By 1950, more than 90 requests for reservations had been made by tribes in Alaska Native villages. Alaska Natives and the Land: Report of the Federal Field Committee at 443–448 (Table V–3) (1968); *see also* Case & Voluck, *supra*, at 69–95 (summarizing reservation policy in Alaska). The pro-reservation policy of the New Deal era was intensely opposed by most non-Native Alaskans and was abandoned by 1950, although existing reservations remained in place.

Alaska Native claims to aboriginal title in southeast Alaska were confirmed by the United States Court of Claims in 1959.

> The land and water owned and claimed by each local clan division in a village was usually well-defined as to area and use. Clan property included fishing streams, coastal waters and shores, hunting grounds, berrying areas, sealing rocks, house sites in the villages, and the rights to passes into the interior. *** The modes of living and of dealing with property among these Indians were regulated by rigidly enforced tradition and custom, and, except under special circumstances, there was no authority in a clan or clan division to sell, transfer or otherwise dispose of, in whole or in part, any claimed area of land or water. *** In addition to the areas which were claimed and used exclusively by individual houses, there were certain common areas which could be used by all the clans comprising a particular group of clans residing in a single geographical area. Certain designated offshore fishing and sea mammal hunting areas in larger bodies of water, channels and bays and stretches of open sea could also be used in common by all members of the various clans residing in a particular geographical area, but Indians residing in other geographical areas had no right to such use.

Tlingit and Haida Indians v. United States, 177 F. Supp. 452, 456 (Ct. Cl. 1959). The court's decision roughly coincided with the admission of Alaska as the 49th state. Like many other western states, Alaska's admission to the union was conditioned on its disclaimer of jurisdiction over Native property rights:

> As a compact with the United States said State and its people do agree and declare that they forever disclaim all right and title *** to any lands or other property (including fishing rights), the right or title to which may be held by any Indians, Eskimos, or Aleuts (hereinafter called natives) or held by the United States in trust for said natives; that all such lands or other property (including fishing rights), the right or title to which may be held by said natives or is held by the United States in trust for said natives, shall be and remain under the absolute jurisdiction and control of the United States until disposed of under its authority except to such extent as the Congress has prescribed or may hereafter prescribe ***.

Act of July 7, 1958, Pub L. No. 85–508, § 4, 72 Stat. 339. However, the Statehood Act also provided the new state with the right to select approximately 103 million acres of land that was "vacant, unappropriated and unreserved at the time of their selection." *Id.* § 6(b). As the state commenced its selections, Alaska Native Villages began to file protests with the Bureau of Land Management (BLM) within the Department of the Interior. The protests asserted that selected land was not "vacant" because it was subject to Native aboriginal title. In 1966, Secretary of the Interior Stewart Udall stopped processing state land selections and conveyances to the state and a formal "land freeze" was put in place in 1969. *See Alaska v. Udall*, 420 F.2d 938 (9th Cir. 1969). The discovery of oil at Prudhoe Bay led to intense pressure to extinguish aboriginal title in Alaska in order that a trans-Alaska pipeline might be built to transport the anticipated oil from Alaska's North Slope to the port at Valdez. Together, pressure from oil interests and Alaska Native groups resulted in the Alaska Native Claims Settlement Act (ANCSA).

A. THE ALASKA NATIVE CLAIMS SETTLEMENT ACT

ANCSA's extinguishment of aboriginal title was unambiguous:

> (a) *** All prior conveyances of public land and water areas in Alaska, or any interest therein, pursuant to Federal law, and all tentative approvals pursuant to section 6(g) of the Alaska Statehood Act, shall be regarded as an extinguishment of the aboriginal title thereto, if any.
>
> (b) *** All aboriginal titles, if any, and claims of aboriginal title in Alaska based on use and occupancy, including submerged land underneath all water areas, both inland and offshore, and including any aboriginal hunting or fishing rights that may exist, are hereby extinguished.
>
> (c) ***All claims against the United States, the State, and all other persons that are based on claims of aboriginal right, title, use, or occupancy of land or water areas in Alaska, or that are based on any statute or treaty of the United States relating to Native use and occupancy, or that are based on the laws of any other nation, including any such claims that are pending before any Federal or state court or the Indian Claims Commission, are hereby extinguished.

43 U.S.C. § 1603.

In exchange for the extinguishment, Alaska Natives alive on December 18, 1971, were permitted to enroll and be issued 100 shares of stock in one of thirteen regional corporations, according to their place of residence or origin. The State was divided into twelve regions largely based on existing Native associations, "with each region composed as far as practicable of Natives having a common heritage and sharing common interests." 43 U.S.C. § 1606. A thirteenth region was established for Alaska Natives who were not residing in Alaska at the time of the Settlement. The corporations were entitled to approximately 40 million acres of land and nearly a billion dollars from an "Alaska Native Fund" to be funded in nearly equal shares from congressional appropriations and royalties from mineral leasing activity in Alaska. 43 U.S.C. §§ 1605 & 1608. Another section, 43 U.S.C. § 1610(b)(1), identified over 200 Native

Villages with populations of twenty-five or more residents. The Villages so identified were entitled to make selections from the public lands:

> [T]he Secretary shall issue to the Village Corporation a patent to the surface estate in the number of acres shown in the following table [with the first column representing village population on the census date of 1970]:
>
> | | |
> |---|---|
> | 25 and 99 | 69,120 acres. |
> | 100 and 199 | 92,160 acres. |
> | 200 and 399 | 115,200 acres. |
> | 400 and 599 | 138,240 acres. |
> | 600 or more | 161,280 acres. |
>
> The lands patented shall be those selected by the Village Corporation pursuant to section 1611(a) of this title. In addition, the Secretary shall issue to the Village Corporation a patent to the surface estate in the lands selected pursuant to section 1611(b) of this title. [The Village Corporations were conveyed approximately 22 million acres. *See* 43 U.S.C. 1611(b).]
>
> (b) *** Immediately after selection by any Village Corporation for a Native village listed in section 1615 of this title which the Secretary finds is qualified for land benefits under this chapter, the Secretary shall issue to the Village Corporation a patent to the surface estate to 23,040 acres. The lands patented shall be the lands within the township or townships that enclose the Native village, and any additional lands selected by the Village Corporation from the surrounding townships withdrawn for the Native village by section 1615(a) of this title.
>
> (c) *** Each patent issued pursuant to subsections (a) and (b) of this section shall be subject to the requirements of this subsection. Upon receipt of a patent or patents:
>
> > (1) the Village Corporation shall first convey to any Native or non-Native occupant, without consideration, title to the surface estate in the tract occupied as of December 18, 1971 (except that occupancy of tracts located in the Pribilof Islands shall be determined as of the date of initial conveyance of such tracts to the appropriate Village Corporation) as a primary place of residence, or as a primary place of business, or as a subsistence campsite, or as headquarters for reindeer husbandry; ***

43 U.S.C. § 1613.

The Village corporations did not receive the subsurface estate. Instead, ANCSA provided that:

> When the Secretary issues a patent to a Village Corporation for the surface estate in lands pursuant to subsections (a) and (b) of this section, he shall issue to the Regional Corporation for the region in which the lands are located a patent to the subsurface estate in such lands *** Provided, That the right to explore, develop, or remove minerals from the subsurface

> estate in the lands within the boundaries of any Native village shall be subject to the consent of the Village Corporation.

43 U.S.C. § 1613(f). Regional Corporations received surface and subsurface title to an additional 16 million acres according to a formula designed to provide regions with larger land claims with more land. 43 U.S.C. § 1611(c); Case & Voluck, *supra*, at 162. Since the tribes on large former reservations exercised their option to take their entire reservation in fee simple, Alaska Natives ended up with approximately 45,000,000 acres of land. *Id.*; *see* 43 U.S.C. § 1618. In addition, individual Alaska Natives received approximately one million acres pursuant to the Alaska Native Allotment Act, Act of May 17, 1906, 34 Stat. 197. *See* Case & Voluck, *supra*, at 109.

NOTES AND QUESTIONS

1. *Scope of the extinguishment.* What about claims for trespass on aboriginal lands that occurred in the years before ANCSA became law? *See Inupiat Community of Arctic Slope v. United States*, 680 F.2d 122 (Ct. Cl. 1982) (ANCSA extinguished all prior claims based on aboriginal title, including those against United States for takings and breach of trust); *United States v. Atlantic Richfield Co.*, 612 F.2d 1132 (9th Cir. 1980) (ANCSA extinguished trespass claims against private parties).

2. ANCSA's corporate structure is exceedingly complex and the Act has been amended almost annually. The 45 million acres conveyed to the corporations are not subject to any restrictions on voluntary alienation of the land. Stock in the corporations, however, was restricted from most forms of alienation for only twenty years. After that the stock is freely alienable. For discussion of ANCSA and its evolution, *see* Case & Voluck, *supra*, at 179–198; Cohen's Handbook of Federal Indian Law 329-37 (2012). Congress's approach has been described by some as "termination in disguise" and by others as an "exercise in self-determination." Can you see why?

3. By the early 1980's, a consensus developed that Congress's goal of establishing economically viable corporations that could return profits and protect Native land and other assets after stock became alienable in 1991 would not be achieved. *See* Thomas Berger, Village Journey: The Report of the Alaska Native Review Commission (1985); S. Rep. No. 100–201 at 19–22, 100th Cong. 1st Sess. (1987), *reprinted in* 1987 U.S. Code Cong. & Ad. News 3269–72 (indicating that many Alaska Natives believed they would lose control over their corporations and, most importantly, over legal title to corporation lands, once shares became alienable). Many Regional corporations were in perilous financial condition, which Congress sought to remedy partially through innovative tax treatment made available only to Native corporations. *See Bay View, Inc. v. Ahtna, Inc.*, 105 F.3d 1281 (9th Cir. 1997) (dealing with legislation permitting the sale of Native corporation "net operating losses"). In 1988, Congress made a fundamental change in ANCSA's structure when it adopted what are popularly known as the "1991 amendments," and indefinitely extended the restrictions on alienation of Native corporation stock. Act of Feb. 3, 1988, Pub. L. 100–241, 101 Stat. 1788, *codified at* 43 U.S.C. § 1606(h)(1). Case & Voluck at 185-86. Corporations may lift the restrictions pursuant to a complicated set of procedures, 43 U.S.C. §§ 1629b, 1629c & 1629d, but no corporation has elected

to make its stock alienable. *See* Case & Voluck at 189, n. 129 (noting that one regional corporation's shareholders voted against removing the restrictions on alienation). The legislation also provided undeveloped and unleased Native Corporation lands with tax exemptions and protection from involuntary loss, such as adverse possession or liquidation in bankruptcy proceedings. 43 U.S.C. § 1636(d). The amendments authorized corporations to issue new stock to Natives born after 1971. 43 U.S.C. § 1606(g)(B). *See* Maude Blair, *Issuing New Stock in ANCSA Corporations*, 33 Alaska L. Rev. 273, 281 (2016). The Calista Corporation's website describes one new-stock issuance program. CALISTA CORPORATION, https://www.calistacorp.com/shareholders/shareholder-portal/descendant-enrollment-information/ [https://perma.cc/DL6E-XTA2] (last visited Sept. 16, 2019). *See also,* Cong. Research Serv., *The Alaska Land Transfer Acceleration Act: Background and Summary* (2005); *see also* Native American Technical Amendments Act of 2006, Pub. L. No. 109–221, § 102, codified at 43 U.S.C. § 1613a (dealing with reconveyances and land exchanges).

4. *Why corporations?* ANCSA required the creation of corporations to receive the land and money provided in the Settlement. Why not provide the assets to the institutions whose aboriginal claims made congressional action necessary? Part of the explanation might be that federal policy had not yet moved completely out of the termination era mindset that took hold in the 1950s. Washington State Senator Henry Jackson was a key figure in passage of ANCSA and he is reported to have had an "antipathy toward Indian reservations in general and Alaska reservations in particular." Charles F. Wilkinson, Blood Struggle: The Rise of Modern Native Nations 258 (2005). In addition, many of the Native leaders involved mistrusted the BIA and wanted to avoid the paternalism that historically marked the reservation model of Indian affairs. For a recent review of ANCSA's history and shortcomings, see Robert T. Anderson, *Sovereignty and Subsistence: Native Self-Government and Rights to Hunt, Fish, and Gather After ANCSA*, 33 Alaska L. Rev. 187 (2016).

5. *Indian country in Alaska after ANCSA?* Review the holding in *Alaska v. Native Village of Venetie, supra*, ch. 5. What is the status of the several thousand allotments held by Natives in restricted fee status? The allotments were obtained through the Alaska Native Allotment Act, Act of May 17, 1906, 34 Stat. 197, which authorized land selections by individual Natives from the public domain. How about "Native townsite" lots, which are also held in restricted fee status? *See Carlo v. Gustafson*, 512 F. Supp. 833 (D. Alaska 1981) (describing fiduciary responsibility of federal government under the Native Townsite Act).

6. *Land into trust in Alaska?* Could Indian country be created by the Secretary of the Interior taking land into trust under the IRA, 25 U.S.C. § 465? A Federal regulation implementing the statute used to declare that they do not apply to acquisitions in Alaska, except for those for the Metlakatla Indian Community. *See* 25 C.F.R. § 151.1. The regulation was declared unlawful in *Akiachak Native Community v. Salazar,* 935 F. Supp.2d 195 (D. D.C. 2013). In response, the Department of the Interior proposed an amendment to the current rules that would provide for trust acquisitions in Alaska. Proposed Rule, Land Acquisitions in the State of Alaska, 79 Fed. Reg. 24648 (May 1, 2014). Land may not me taken into trust under any final rule, however, until the State of Alaska's appeal is exhausted. *Akiachak Native Community v. Jewell,* 995 F. Supp.2d 7 (D.D.C. 2014). Assistant Secretary Kevin Washburn signed the Final Rule on December 18, 2014. 79 Fed. Reg. 76888 (Dec. 23, 2014). The

preamble to the Final Rule contains analysis of a number of Alaska-specific issues raised in comments to the proposed rule.

If a Village Corporation transferred its surface estate to a tribe to be taken into trust by the Secretary of the Interior, what would the effect be on the subsurface owned by a Regional Corporation? Would the subsurface be considered Indian country? Could the tribe deny access to the subsurface? These and many other questions were raised in comments to the proposed rule, and are addressed in the preamble to the Final Rule. *Id.*

B. TRIBAL GOVERNMENTS IN ALASKA

What about the tribal governments? ANCSA did not even mention the governmental powers exercised by Native tribes in Alaska, so many assumed that those powers continued to exist, as would normally be the case under federal law. Others felt that since they were not mentioned, they must have been terminated (or that tribes never existed because Alaska was "different"). The latter drew support for their argument from the section of ANCSA that revoked all reservations, except for the Annette Islands Reservation (Metlakatla), 43 U.S.C. § 1618. Also, one of the congressional findings stated that, "the settlement should be accomplished rapidly, with certainty, in conformity with the real economic and social needs of Natives, without litigation, with maximum participation by Natives in decisions affecting their rights and property, without establishing any permanent racially defined institutions, rights, privileges, or obligations, without creating a reservation system or lengthy wardship or trusteeship, and without adding to the categories of property and institutions enjoying special tax privileges or to the legislation establishing special relationships between the United States Government and the State of Alaska[.]" 43 U.S.C. § 1601(b). Native governments in Alaska argued that they were not "racially defined" and that as inherent sovereigns preexisting the establishment of the State of Alaska, one could hardly claim that their continued survival was in any way affected by ANCSA. The sovereign status of Alaska Native tribes has been recognized by all three branches of the federal government and confirmed in several Alaska Supreme Court rulings. *See* Cohen's Handbook of Federal Indian Law at 353-54 (2012 ed.)

In 1979, when the Department of the Interior published the first list of "Indian entities recognized and eligible to receive services from the United States," the list defined tribes to include "Eskimos and Aleuts," but stated that "[t]he list of eligible Alaskan entities will be published at a later date." 44 Fed Reg. at 7235. The 1982 list published a "preliminary list show[ing] those entities to which the Bureau of Indian Affairs gives priority for purposes of funding and services," including the traditional Alaska Native councils formerly recognized by the BIA under the Indian Reorganization Act. 47 Fed. Reg. 53133–53134 (Nov. 24, 1982). Similarly, both the 1975 Indian Self–Determination and Education Assistance Act and the 1978 Indian Child Welfare Act explicitly included Alaska Native entities recognized or established under ANCSA within the definition of tribes. 25 U.S.C. § 450b(e); 25 U.S.C. § 1903(8). In 1991, the Ninth Circuit held that Alaska Native Villages were entitled to be treated as tribes under federal law. *Native Village of Venetie I.R.A. Council,* 944 F.2d 548 (9th Cir. 1991); *cf. Chilkat Indian Village v. Johnson*, 870 F.2d 1469 (9th Cir.

1989) (evaluating Alaska Native village jurisdiction over non-Indian under standards applied to American Indian tribes). The Alaska Supreme Court, in contrast, ruled in 1988 that an Alaska Native Village was not entitled to sovereign immunity "because it, like most native groups in Alaska, is not self-governing or in any meaningful sense sovereign." *Native Village of Stevens v. Alaska Management & Planning*, 757 P.2d 32 (Alaska 1988).

In 1993, to respond to the confusion and frustration such decisions caused, the Solicitor of the Department of the Interior issued a comprehensive opinion declaring that Alaska Native Villages had the same legal status as federally recognized Indian tribes. Sol. Op. M–36,975 (Jan. 11, 1993). After reviewing the history of legal treatment of Alaska Native Villages, the Solicitor concluded that,

> By the time of enactment of the IRA (Indian Reorganization Act of 1934, as amended in 1936), the preponderant opinion was that Alaska Natives were subject to the same legal principles as Indians in the contiguous 48 states, and had the same powers and attributes as other Indian tribes, except to the extent limited or preempted by Congress.
>
> What constitutes a tribe in the contiguous 48 states is sometimes a difficult question. So also is it in Alaska. The history of Alaska is unique, but so is that of California, New Mexico and Oklahoma. While the Department's position with regard to the existence of tribes in Alaska may have vacillated between 1867 and the opening decades of this century, it is clear that for the last half century, Congress and the Department have dealt with Alaska Natives as though there were tribes in Alaska. The fact that the Congress and the Department may not have dealt with all Alaska Natives as tribes at all times prior to the 1930's did not preclude it from dealing with them as tribes subsequently.

Sol. Op. M–36,975, at 46, 47–48 (Jan. 11, 1993). In response to the opinion, and to comply with federal requirements, the Department of the Interior published a list of Alaska tribal entities, including roughly 225 Alaska Native villages and regional tribes that, it found, "have functioned as political entities exercising governmental authority and are, therefore, acknowledged to have 'the immunities and privileges available to other federally acknowledged Indian tribes by virtue of their status as Indian tribes as well as the responsibilities and obligations of such tribes.' " *Indian Entities Recognized and Eligible To Receive Services From the United States Bureau of Indian Affairs*, 58 Fed. Reg. 54364 (Oct. 21, 1993). The preamble to the list declared:

> The purpose of the current publication is to *** to eliminate any doubt as to the Department's intention by expressly and unequivocally acknowledging that the Department has determined that the villages and regional tribes listed below are distinctly Native communities and have the same status as tribes in the contiguous 48 states. *** This list is published to clarify that the villages and regional tribes listed below are not simply eligible for services, or recognized as tribes for certain narrow purposes. Rather, they have the same governmental status as other federally acknowledged Indian tribes by virtue of their status as Indian tribes with a government-to-government relationship with the United States; are entitled to the same protection, immunities, privileges as other acknowledged tribes; have the right, subject to general principles of Federal Indian law, to exercise the same inherent and delegated authorities available to

other tribes; and are subject to the same limitations imposed by law on other tribes.

58 Fed. Reg. 54364 (Oct. 21, 1993).

Because tribal legal status is determined by the federal government, not the states, *see U.S. v. Sandoval*, 231 U.S. 28 (1913), *supra* Ch. 5, this guidance should have established that cases like *Stevens* were wrongly decided. Before the Alaska Supreme Court could revisit the issue, however, the United States Supreme Court decided *Alaska v. Native Village of Venetie*, 522 U.S. 220 (1998), *supra* Ch. 5, holding that ANCSA corporation land was not "Indian country." The Alaska Supreme Court subsequently faced two questions: first, were Alaska Native Villages possessed of sovereign powers to govern; and second, if they were, what did such sovereign powers mean in the absence of legal territory for jurisdictional purposes? The court began to answer these questions in the next case.

JOHN V. BAKER

982 P.2d 738 (Alaska 1999)

FABE, JUSTICE.

I. INTRODUCTION

Seeking sole custody of his two children, John Baker, a member of Northway Village, filed a custody petition in the Northway Tribal Court. Anita John, the children's mother and a member of Mentasta Village, consented to Northway's jurisdiction. After the tribal court issued an order granting shared custody, Mr. Baker filed an identical suit in state superior court. Although Ms. John moved to dismiss based on the tribal court proceeding, the superior court denied the motion and awarded primary physical custody to Mr. Baker. Ms. John appeals, arguing that as a federally recognized tribe, Northway Village has the inherent sovereignty to adjudicate custody disputes between its members and that the superior court therefore should have dismissed the state case.

This appeal raises a question of first impression. We must decide whether the sovereign adjudicatory authority of Native tribes exists outside the confines of Indian country. After reviewing evidence of the intent of the Executive Branch, as well as relevant federal statutes and case law, we conclude that Native tribes do possess the inherent sovereign power to adjudicate child custody disputes between tribal members in their own courts. We therefore reverse and remand to the superior court to determine whether the tribal court's custody determination should be recognized by the superior court under the doctrine of comity.

II. FACTS AND PROCEEDINGS

Anita John and John Baker are Alaska Natives; Ms. John is a member of Mentasta Village and Mr. Baker is a member of Northway Village. Although they never married, Ms. John and Mr. Baker had two children together: John Jr., born in July 1991, and Emmanuel, born in June 1992. The family lived together in Ms. John's village until the parents ended their relationship in 1993. For the next two years, Ms. John and Mr. Baker cooperated in sharing custody of John Jr. and Emmanuel. This cooperation ended in July 1995 when Mr. Baker refused to return the children to Ms. John.

In July 1995 Mr. Baker filed a petition with the Northway Tribal Court requesting sole custody of John Jr. and Emmanuel. The tribal court sent a notice to the parties on August 10 informing them of their right to be present at the custody hearing, and both parents participated in the hearing held on August 29. At the conclusion of the hearing, Tribal Court Judge Lorraine Titus ordered the parents to share custody of the children on an alternating monthly schedule. Judge Titus stated, however, that this arrangement would be temporary and that she would reconsider the custody question in one year, before the oldest child entered school.

The parents followed the tribal court's order from September to December, deviating from the alternating schedule only so that Ms. John could care for the children while Mr. Baker was serving a sentence for DWI. During these months Mr. Baker appealed to the tribal court to change its custody order, but the court denied his request. Dissatisfied with the tribal court's custody determination, Mr. Baker filed a separate action in state court in December. In the affidavit accompanying the state complaint, required at that time under the Uniform Child Custody Jurisdiction Act (UCCJA), Mr. Baker misled the superior court by stating that he was "unaware of any custody proceeding regarding the children, except as provided herein, in Alaska, or any other jurisdiction." ***

III. DISCUSSION

Resolving this appeal requires us to examine the nature and scope of Native American self-government in Alaska. We must decide whether Northway Village had the jurisdiction to adjudicate a custody dispute involving children who are tribal members. If Northway possessed such jurisdiction, we must then decide whether the superior court should have dismissed Mr. Baker's identical state suit. ***

C. Tribes without Indian Country Can Adjudicate Internal Child Custody Disputes.

Today we must decide for the first time a question of significant complexity and import: Do Alaska Native villages have inherent, non-territorial sovereignty allowing them to resolve domestic disputes between their own members? After examining relevant federal pronouncements regarding sovereign power, we hold that Alaska Native tribes, by virtue of their inherent powers as sovereign nations, do possess that authority.

1. We defer to Congress's finding that Alaska Native tribes are sovereign powers under federal law.

We have previously held that tribal status is a non-justiciable political question. We therefore will defer to the determinations of Congress and the Executive Branch on the question of tribal status. If Congress or the Executive Branch recognizes a group of Native Americans as a sovereign tribe, we "must do the same."

Prior to 1993, no such recognition of Alaska villages had occurred. In *Native Village of Stevens v. Alaska Management & Planning*, we conducted an historical analysis and concluded that the federal government had never recognized Alaska villages as sovereign tribes. ***

In 1993, however, the Department of the Interior issued a list of federally recognized tribes that included Northway Village and most of the other Native villages in Alaska. In the list's preamble, the Department of Interior explained that it was issuing the list in order to clarify confusion over the tribal status of various Alaska Native entities. The Department believed that previous lists had been interpreted to mean that Native villages in Alaska, although qualifying for federal funding, were not recognized as sovereign tribes. It sought to rectify this misunderstanding and to reaffirm the sovereign status of the recognized tribes. In particular, the Department emphasized that the list included those Alaskan entities that the federal government historically had treated as tribes. ***

And for those who may have doubted the power of the Department of the Interior to recognize sovereign political bodies, a 1994 act of Congress appears to lay such doubts to rest. In the Federally Recognized Tribe List Act of 1994, [Act of Nov. 2, 1994, 108 Stat. 4791, *codified at* 25 U.S.C. § 479a, et seq.] Congress specifically directed the Department to publish annually "a list of all Indian tribes which the Secretary recognizes to be eligible for the special programs and services provided by the United States to Indians because of their status as Indians." The Department published tribal lists for 1995 through 1998, all of which include Alaska Native villages such as Northway, based on this specifically delegated authority. ***

Through the 1993 tribal list and the 1994 Tribe List Act, the federal government has recognized the historical tribal status of Alaska Native villages like Northway. In deference to that determination, we also recognize such villages as sovereign entities.

The fact that Northway Village is a federally recognized tribe answers only part of the question posed by this case. Alaska Native villages such as Northway are in a unique position: Unlike most other tribes, Alaska Native villages occupy no reservations and for the most part possess no Indian country. Mr. Baker and the dissent argue that the existence of tribal land—Indian country—is the cornerstone of tribal court jurisdiction and that Congress necessarily withdrew such jurisdiction from Alaska Native villages when it enacted ANCSA.

To evaluate this argument, we must decide how much authority tribes retain in the absence of reservation land. We must, in other words, determine the meaning of "sovereignty" in the context of Alaska's post-ANCSA landscape by asking whether ANCSA, to the extent that it eliminated Alaska's Indian country, also divested Alaska Native villages of their sovereign powers.

2. Tribes retain their sovereign powers to regulate internal domestic affairs unless Congress specifically withdraws their authority to act.

*** We begin our analysis of congressional intent with the established principle under federal law that "Indian tribes retain those fundamental attributes of sovereignty *** which have not been divested by Congress or by necessary implication of the tribe's dependent status." The United States Supreme Court explained in *United States v. Wheeler* that this starting point stems from the fact that tribal governance predates the founding of our nation: "The powers of Indian tribes are, in general, inherent powers of a limited sovereignty which has never been extinguished. Before the coming of the Europeans, the tribes were self-governing sovereign political communities ***. The sovereignty that the Indian tribes retain is of a unique and limited character." ***

The dissent, however, asks us to begin from the opposite premise. Rather than following the teachings of federal and state law that respect tribal sovereignty by presuming that sovereign power exists unless divested, the dissent quotes language from *Mescalero Apache Tribe v. Jones*, in which the United States Supreme Court noted that "Indians going beyond reservation boundaries have generally been held subject to non-discriminatory state law otherwise applicable to all citizens." From this statement the dissent deduces what it terms an "allocative principle." Based upon Mescalero's language, the dissent formulates a presumption that would reverse the basic rule and require courts, at least outside of Indian country, to refuse to recognize tribal jurisdiction unless an act of Congress specifically authorizes the exercise of tribal adjudicatory power. We refuse to accept this invitation to deny the existence of tribal sovereignty and to turn federal law on its head. ***

3. ANCSA itself and post-ANCSA federal statutes regarding tribal sovereignty all support Northway's jurisdiction over child custody matters.

Ample evidence exists that Congress did not intend for ANCSA to divest tribes of their powers to adjudicate domestic disputes between members. Congress intended ANCSA to free Alaska Natives from the dictates of "lengthy wardship or trusteeship," not to handicap tribes by divesting them of their sovereign powers. As a principal author of the law has explained, ANCSA "rejected the paternalism of the past and gave Alaska Natives an innovative way to retain their land and culture without forcing them into a failed reservation system."[85] But nowhere does the law express any intent to force Alaska Natives to abandon their sovereignty.

We noted above that the Tribe List Act shows Congress's determination that Alaska Native villages are sovereign entities. The inclusion of Alaska Native villages on the tribal lists makes clear that Alaska Natives "have the right, subject to general principles of Federal Indian law, to exercise the same inherent and delegated authorities available to other tribes." And since this court defers to determinations of tribal status by the Executive Branch or by Congress, we similarly accept their conclusion that, even after ANCSA, federally recognized Alaska Native tribes like Northway Village retain sovereignty to adjudicate domestic disputes between members.

***

Because the traditional reservation-based structure of tribal life in most states forms the backdrop for the federal cases, courts have not had occasion to tease apart the ideas of land-based sovereignty and membership sovereignty. Consequently, the federal decisions do not conclusively answer the question of what happens when a law like ANCSA separates membership and land completely by allowing a federally recognized tribe to redefine its relationship to state and federal governments by eliminating the idea of Indian country. But federal case law does provide significant support for our conclusion that federal tribes derive the power to adjudicate internal domestic

85. Senator Ted Stevens, Address Before the Alaska Legislature (Apr. 2, 1997), in Senate and House Joint Journal Supp. No. 9 at 5, 1997 House Journal 915, quoted in Donald C. Mitchell, Alaska v. Native Village of Venetie: *Statutory Construction or Judicial Usurpation? Why History Counts*, 14 Alaska L. Rev. 353, 440 (1997).

matters, including child custody disputes over tribal children, from a source of sovereignty independent of the land they occupy.

The federal decisions discussing the relationship between Indian country and tribal sovereignty indicate that the nature of tribal sovereignty stems from two intertwined sources: tribal membership and tribal land. The United States Supreme Court has recognized the dual nature of Indian sovereignty for more than a century and a half; the Court has explained that, under federal law, "Indian tribes are unique aggregations possessing attributes of sovereignty over both their members and their territory." *United States v. Mazurie*, 419 U.S. 544, 557 (1975) (*citing Worcester v. Georgia*, 6 Pet. 515, 557 (1832)). ***

We hold that the type of dispute before us today—an action for determination of custody of the children of a member of Northway Village—falls squarely within Northway's sovereign power to regulate the internal affairs of its members.

***

Although we recognize Northway's jurisdiction to adjudicate child custody disputes between village members, its jurisdiction is not exclusive. The State of Alaska can also exercise jurisdiction over such disputes. This is so because villages like Northway presumably do not occupy Indian country, and federal law suggests that the only bar to state jurisdiction over Indians and Indian affairs is the presence of Indian country. ***

By acknowledging tribal jurisdiction, we enhance the opportunity for Native villages and the state to cooperate in the child custody arena by sharing resources. Recognizing the ability and power of tribes to resolve internal disputes in their own forums, while preserving the right of access to state courts, can only help in the administration of justice for all.

***

We must also determine whether the superior court should have dismissed Mr. Baker's identical state suit. After examining whether states should afford tribal court judgments full faith and credit, we conclude that the comity doctrine provides the proper framework for deciding when state courts should recognize tribal court decisions.

*** Comity is the principle that "the courts of one state or jurisdiction will give effect to the laws and judicial decisions of another state or jurisdiction, not as a matter of obligation, but out of deference and mutual respect." ***

In certain limited circumstances, however, state recognition of tribal judgments may be inappropriate. *** [S]tate courts should afford no comity to proceedings in which any litigant is denied due process. *** But this due process analysis in no way requires tribes to use procedures identical to ours in their courts. The comity analysis is not an invitation for our courts to deny recognition to tribal judgments based on paternalistic notions of proper procedure. Instead, in deciding whether a party was denied due process, superior courts should strive to respect the cultural differences that influence tribal jurisprudence, as well as to recognize the practical limits experienced by smaller court systems.

*** Additionally, superior courts should not deny recognition to tribal judgments simply because they disagree with the outcome reached by the tribal judge or because they conclude that they could better resolve the dispute at issue. Thus, suggesting—as the superior court did in this case—that state jurisdiction was proper because "significant expertise will be required to resolve this difficult dispute," has no place in a comity analysis.

IV. CONCLUSION

Tribal courts in Alaska have jurisdiction to adjudicate custody disputes involving tribal members. This jurisdiction is concurrent with that of the state courts. We therefore REVERSE and REMAND to the superior court to determine whether the tribal court's resolution of the custody dispute between Ms. John and Mr. Baker should be recognized under the doctrine of comity.

MATTHEWS, CHIEF JUSTICE, joined by **COMPTON, JUSTICE**, dissenting.

***

Does inherent tribal jurisdiction over custody cases extend beyond Indian country? The majority answers "yes," concluding that tribal sovereignty prevails unless Congress provides otherwise. My answer is "no." Under established principles of federal Indian law, state law governs outside of Indian country unless Congress provides otherwise, and it has not so provided. Moreover, the United States Supreme Court has twice held that inherent tribal jurisdiction over custody applies only to cases arising within Indian country.

Today's opinion changes Alaska society. Alaska law no longer applies to every Alaskan. The doors of Alaska's courts will no longer be open to all Alaskans. More than one-sixth of Alaskan children,[1] regardless of where they reside, will be subject to the laws of one of 226 village tribal organizations. More than one-sixth of Alaskan adults, regardless of where they reside, will be subject to the domestic relations laws of one of 226 village tribal organizations. These laws, written or unwritten, may be different from the laws of the state, indeed they may conflict with the laws of the state. But their reach will be statewide, and even beyond, governing cases that arise in cities, towns, and villages which may be hundreds of miles from the village whose tribal laws are applied. And the family law cases of more than one out of six Alaskan children and adults now will be subject to adjudication not in the Alaska Court System, but in the tribal courts of one of 226 villages. Some tribal court cases will be decided fairly. Others will not be. But the only remedy Alaskans aggrieved by the application of conflicting laws or unfair decisions will have is to pursue "comity" litigation in the state courts. Relief through this vague doctrine will be uncertain, hard to obtain, and expensive.

Because today's opinion takes a long step away from the Alaska constitutional goal of equal rights under the law and is contrary to federal law, I dissent. Given the importance of this case to the future of Alaska's system of justice, I set forth my views in greater length than is normally required or appropriate in a dissenting opinion. ***

1. Of Alaska's estimated 1998 population of 621,400, 104,085 are Native Alaskans. *See* Alaska Population Overview: 1998 Estimates, Population Estimate by Race and Ethnicity, 1 (Alaska Dep't of Labor). In addition, Department of Labor estimates indicate that more than 30,000 Native Alaskan Indians, Eskimos, and Aleuts resided outside of Alaska in 1990. *See* Alaska Population Overview: 1997 Estimates, Population by Race and Tribal Group, Alaska and U.S.1980, 1990, Table 1.5, at 23 (Alaska Dep't of Labor).

NOTES AND QUESTIONS

1. The case returned twice to the Supreme Court. *See John v. Baker II*, 30 P.3d 68 (Alaska 2001) (reversing state lower court decision that tribal court opinion was not entitled to comity, but remanding to Northway Tribal Court to conduct new custody proceedings to account for passage of time since original 1995 order); *John v. Baker III*, 125 P.3d 323 (Alaska 2005) (holding that while tribal court had jurisdiction over custody, state superior court retained jurisdiction over related child support matter).

2. The *John v. Baker* dispute did not come within Indian Child Welfare Act (ICWA) jurisdiction, which does not include disputes between parents. Even in cases involving ICWA, Alaska formerly took the position that as a Pub. L 280 state, it had *exclusive* jurisdiction over child custody matters involving Native children until the Native government petitioned the federal government to resume ICWA jurisdiction. *See Native Village of Nenana v. Alaska Department of Health and Human Services*, 722 P.2d 219 (Alaska 1986) (construing 25 U.S.C. § 1918). The Alaska Supreme Court has since overruled this line of cases, holding that Alaska Native governments retain the right, under 25 U.S.C. § 1911(b), to have cases involving Native children transferred to Native courts absent good cause to the contrary. *See In re CRH*, 29 P.3d 849 (Alaska 2001). Even before *John v. Baker I* and *CRH*, Alaska law authorized the Bureau of Vital Statistics to recognize adoptions decreed by Alaska Native governments under tribal custom. *See Hernandez v. Lambert*, 951 P.2d 436, 441 (Alaska 1998); *see also Simmonds v. Parks*, 329 P.3d 995, 101 (Alaska 2014) ("tribal court judgments in ICWA-defined child custody proceedings are entitled to full faith and credit to the same extent as a judgment of a sister state"); *Native Village of Kaltag v. Jackson*, 344 Fed. Appx. 324 (9th Cir. 2009) (ICWA required state to grant full faith and credit to tribal adoption decree). Note that despite the concerns raised by the dissent in *John v. Baker I*, not all Native custody decrees have been accorded recognition. Following the court's guidance that "courts should consider whether the parties received notice of the proceedings and whether they were granted a full and fair opportunity to be heard," state courts have refused to recognize adoption decrees made by village resolution without notice to the opposing party. *See Starr v. George*, 175 P.3d 50 (Alaska 2008); *Evans v. Native Village of Selawik I.R.A, Council*, 65 P.3d 58 (Alaska 2003).

3. *How far does tribal jurisdiction go?* Can a tribe assert criminal jurisdiction over its own members to protect public safety in the village? How would it enforce such a judgment?

4. The Violence Against Women Act Amendments of 2013 that restored tribal criminal jurisdiction over domestic violence offenses, *see* ch. 8, *supra*, excluded Alaska tribes (aside from Metlakatla). In 2014, however, Congress amended the statute to make it fully applicable to all Alaska tribes. Pub. L. 113-275. *See* S. Rep. 113-260 (2014). How significant is this given the relatively small amount of Indian country in Alaska?

5. The prospects for increased exercise of tribal sovereignty in Alaska brightened with promulgation of a rule allowing land to be taken in trust for Alaska Tribes. The BIA summary of the rule states:

> Section 5 of the Indian Reorganization Act (IRA), as amended, authorizes the Secretary of the Interior (Secretary) to acquire land in trust for individual Indians and Indian tribes in the continental United States and Alaska. 25 U.S.C. § 465; 25 U.S.C. § 473a. For several decades, the Department's regulations at 25 C.F.R. part 151, which establish the process for taking land into trust, have included a provision stating that the regulations in part 151 do not cover the acquisition of land in trust status in the State of Alaska, except acquisitions for the Metlakatla Indian Community of the Annette Island Reserve or its members (the "Alaska Exception"). 25 C.F.R. § 151.1. This rule deletes the Alaska Exception, thereby allowing applications for land to be taken into trust in Alaska to proceed under the part 151 regulations. The Department retains its usual discretion to grant or deny land-into-trust applications and makes its decisions on a case-by-case basis in accordance with the requirements of part 151 and the IRA.

Land Acquisitions in the State of Alaska, 79 Fed. Reg. 76888 (2014). *See also, Akiachak Native Comty. v. U.S. Department of the Interior*, 827 F.3d 100 (D.C. Cir. 2016) (dismissing Alaska's appeal as moot). The state declined to seek Supreme Court review, so the rule is now in effect. The Craig Tribal Association is the first tribe in Alaska to have land taken in trust by the Secretary of the Interior under the new regulation. Land Acquisitions: Craig Tribal Association, 82 Fed. Reg. 4915 (2017) (1.08 acres). The Trump Administration announced a six month review process of the regulation and its legality. *Withdrawal of Sol. Op. M-37043. "Authority to Acquire Land into Trust in Alaska," Pending Review,* Sol. Op. M-37053 (June 29, 2018).

C. HUNTING, FISHING AND GATHERING RIGHTS

As noted above, ANCSA extinguished not only possessory rights, but also "any aboriginal hunting or fishing rights that may exist." 43 U.S.C. § 1603(b). This step was particularly unprecedented because, even more than for most indigenous peoples in the lower 48, the culture and livelihood of Alaska Native peoples centers around hunting and fishing. Congress did not intend that these needs would be ignored. The Conference Committee report declared that,

> The conference committee, after careful consideration, believes that all Native interests in subsistence resource lands can and will be protected by the Secretary through the exercise of his existing withdrawal authority. The Secretary could, for example, withdraw appropriate lands and classify them in a manner which would protect Native subsistence needs and requirements by closing appropriate lands to entry by non-residents when the subsistence resources of these lands are in short supply or otherwise threatened. The Conference Committee expects both the Secretary and the State to take any action necessary to protect the subsistence needs of the Natives.

H.R. Rep. No. 92–746 at 37 (1971). After the passage of ANCSA, Congress took several actions recognizing the unique importance of hunting and fishing to Alaska's Native peoples. The 1973 Trans–Alaska Oil Pipeline Act, for example, created strict liability for pipeline right-of-way holders whose actions interfered with "fish, wildlife, biotic or natural resources relied upon by Alaska

Natives." 16 U.S.C. § 1653. The 1972 Marine Mammal Protection Act and the 1973 Endangered Species Act both created specific exemptions for Alaska Native uses. 16 U.S.C. § 1371(b) (Marine Mammal Protection Act exemption); 16 U.S.C. § 1539(e) (Endangered Species Act exemption). But contrary to Congress' expectations, the Secretary did little to protect Native hunting, fishing, and gathering rights. By the late 1970s, it was clear that Congress needed to act. In 1980, when it passed the Alaska National Interest Lands Conservation Act (ANILCA) setting aside substantial lands for conservation purposes, Congress included a subsistence title.

TITLE VIII OF ANILCA

16 U.S.C. §§ 3111–3126

---

16 U.S.C. § 3111

The Congress finds and declares that—

(1) the continuation of the opportunity for subsistence uses by rural residents of Alaska, including both Natives and non-Natives, on the public lands and by Alaska Natives on Native lands is essential to Native physical, economic, traditional, and cultural existence and to non-Native physical, economic, traditional, and social existence;

(2) the situation in Alaska is unique in that, in most cases, no practical alternative means are available to replace the food supplies and other items gathered from fish and wildlife which supply rural residents dependent on subsistence uses;

(3) continuation of the opportunity for subsistence uses of resources on public and other lands in Alaska is threatened by the increasing population of Alaska, with resultant pressure on subsistence resources, by sudden decline in the populations of some wildlife species which are crucial subsistence resources, by increased accessibility of remote areas containing subsistence resources, and by taking of fish and wildlife in a manner inconsistent with recognized principles of fish and wildlife management;

(4) in order to fulfill the policies and purposes of the Alaska Native Claims Settlement Act [43 U.S.C.A. § 1601 *et seq.*] and as a matter of equity, it is necessary for the Congress to invoke its constitutional authority over Native affairs and its constitutional authority under the property clause and the commerce clause to protect and provide the opportunity for continued subsistence uses on the public lands by Native and non-Native rural residents; and

(5) the national interest in the proper regulation, protection, and conservation of fish and wildlife on the public lands in Alaska and the continuation of the opportunity for a subsistence way of life by residents of rural Alaska require that an administrative structure be established for the purpose of enabling rural residents who have personal knowledge of local conditions and requirements to have a meaningful role in the management of fish and wildlife and of subsistence uses on the public lands in Alaska.

16 U.S.C. § 3112.

It is hereby declared to be the policy of Congress that—

(1) consistent with sound management principles, and the conservation of healthy populations of fish and wildlife, the utilization of the public lands in Alaska is to cause the least adverse impact possible on rural residents who depend upon subsistence uses of the resources of such lands; consistent with management of fish and wildlife in accordance with recognized scientific principles and the purposes for each unit established, designated, or expanded by or pursuant to titles II through VII of this Act, the purpose of this subchapter is to provide the opportunity for rural residents engaged in a subsistence way of life to do so;

(2) nonwasteful subsistence uses of fish and wildlife and other renewable resources shall be the priority consumptive uses of all such resources on the public lands of Alaska when it is necessary to restrict taking in order to assure the continued viability of a fish or wildlife population or the continuation of subsistence uses of such population, the taking of such population for nonwasteful subsistence uses shall be given preference on the public lands over other consumptive uses; ***

16 U.S.C. § 3113.

As used in this Act, the term "subsistence uses" means the customary and traditional uses by rural Alaska residents of wild, renewable resources for direct personal or family consumption as food, shelter, fuel, clothing, tools, or transportation; for the making and selling of handicraft articles out of nonedible byproducts of fish and wildlife resources taken for personal or family consumption; for barter, or sharing for personal or family consumption; and for customary trade. For the purposes of this section, the term—

(1) "family" means all persons related by blood, marriage, or adoption, or any person living within the household on a permanent basis;

(2) "barter" means the exchange of fish or wildlife or their parts, taken for subsistence uses—

(A) for other fish or game or their parts; or

(B) for other food or for nonedible items other than money if the exchange is of a limited and noncommercial nature.

16 U.S.C. § 3114.

Except as otherwise provided in this Act and other Federal laws, the taking on public lands of fish and wildlife for nonwasteful subsistence uses shall be accorded priority over the taking on such lands of fish and wildlife for other purposes. Whenever it is necessary to restrict the taking of populations of fish and wildlife on such lands for subsistence uses in order to protect the continued viability of such populations, or to continue such uses, such priority shall be implemented through appropriate limitations based on the application of the following criteria:

(1) customary and direct dependence upon the populations as the mainstay of livelihood;

(2) local residency; and

(3) the availability of alternative resources.

NOTES AND QUESTIONS

1. Review the statute carefully. Where does the priority apply? What does it mean to "be the priority consumptive uses of all such resources on the public lands"? Federal laws setting aside lands for conservation purposes often prohibit hunting and fishing on those lands. Because of the importance of wild resources to Alaska Natives, most of the conservation system units established or expanded in ANILCA allow subsistence activities to take place.

2. Note that the law protects subsistence uses by not only Natives but all "rural Alaska residents." 16 U.S.C. § 3113. Why not simply adopt a preference for Alaska Natives? Many other federal statutes enacted before and after ANILCA provide for Native subsistence uses. The Marine Mammal Protection Act of 1972 generally prohibits the taking of marine mammals, unless such taking is by an Alaska Native who dwells on the Pacific coast and "(1) is for subsistence purposes; or (2) is done for purposes of creating and selling authentic native articles of handicrafts and clothing: Provided, That only authentic native articles of handicrafts and clothing may be sold in interstate commerce: And provided further, That any edible portion of marine mammals may be sold in native villages and towns in Alaska or for native consumption." 16 U.S.C. § 1371(b). Polar bear management agreements and treaties also contain special provisions dealing with Native harvests, 16 U.S.C. § 1423c, and regulations implementing the Pacific Halibut Convention provide for Native subsistence uses of halibut. 50 CFR § 300.65(g)(2)("A person is eligible to harvest subsistence halibut if he or she is a member of an Alaska Native tribe [listed in the following table] with customary and traditional uses of halibut."). In 1973, the Trans-Alaska Oil Pipeline Act imposed strict liability for any harm to the subsistence resources of Natives or others, 43 U.S.C. § 1653(a)(1), and the Endangered Species Act (ESA) presumptively exempted subsistence uses by Natives and "any non-Native permanent resident of an Alaskan Native village" from its coverage. 16 U.S.C. § 1539(e)(1); the Secretaries of the Interior and Commerce issued an order requiring early and substantial consultation between federal agencies implementing the ESA and affected Alaska Native tribes. Secretarial Order No. 3225 (Jan. 19, 2001). The 1978 Fish and Wildlife Improvement Act authorized the Secretary "to assure that the taking of migratory birds and the collection of their eggs, by the indigenous inhabitants of the State of Alaska, shall be permitted for their own nutritional and other essential needs." 16 U.S.C. § 712(1). Most recently, Congress passed the "Huna Tlingit Traditional Gull Egg Use Act'," which provides that the Secretary of the Interior "may allow the collection by members of the Hoonah Indian Association of the eggs of glaucous-winged gulls (Laurus glaucescens) within Glacier Bay National Park." Pub. L. No. 113-142 (July 25, 2014).

3. *State regulation under Title VIII of ANILCA.* When a Native preference provision was included in the proposed federal subsistence legislation in 1978, however, the State objected on the ground that the Alaska Constitution would bar enforcement of a "racially based" preference, so the neutral "rural" priority came into being. Was the State correct that a preference for Native subsistence uses would be racially based? Are there other substantial policy reasons for including protection for non-Native subsistence uses? Ironically, as will be seen below, the preference for rural residents created significant

problems under state law, and ultimately was held to be unlawful under the Alaska Constitution. Although ANILCA applied only to federal lands, Title VIII provided that the State could obtain management authority over subsistence on federal public lands, "if the State enacts and implements laws of general applicability which are consistent with, and which provide for the definition, preference, and participation specified in [ANILCA]." 16 U.S.C. § 3115(d). Any laws regulating subsistence uses had to be formulated with the advice and participation of regional councils and local advisory committees, which had the authority to evaluate and make recommendations on laws regulating such uses. 16 U.S.C. § 3115(a) & (d).

4. Anticipating the enactment of ANILCA, the State adopted a subsistence priority statute in 1978. Although the preference was not initially restricted to rural Alaskans, regulations adopted in 1982 brought state law into compliance with ANILCA's rural priority. In 1982, the Secretary of the Interior certified the State to regulate ANILCA rights. As a result, Alaska's 1978 subsistence priority statute became operative as to all state lands and to virtually all federally owned lands in Alaska.

BOBBY V. ALASKA

718 F. Supp.764 (D. Alaska 1989)

HOLLAND, CHIEF JUDGE.

This case raises important questions of first impression for the court with respect to the validity of regulations promulgated by the Alaska Board of Game for the implementation of subsistence hunting rights which are protected by federal law.

***

Th[e] complaint focused upon the closed season, individual bag limit, village harvest quota, and management area restrictions imposed on Lime Village residents by the Board of Game, as well as two collateral issues which are suggested by these regulations or the potential enforcement of them. Plaintiffs contend that the regulations are arbitrary, unreasonable, and unnecessary, and that they "fail to accord to plaintiff and his class the priority for non-wasteful subsistence uses required by Section 804 of ANILCA."

Plaintiffs seek a declaration that the closed season, bag limit, village harvest quota, and management area restrictions are unlawful. Plaintiffs seek an injunction from the court requiring the State to submit to the court, for approval and incorporation into a final judgment, regulations pertaining to the subsistence uses of moose and caribou by the plaintiffs.

***

Pursuant to [State law enacted to implement ANILCA], the Board of Game has undertaken from time to time the enactment of various regulations pertaining to the taking of moose and caribou by plaintiffs, residents of Lime Village, Alaska.

It is entirely clear that Congress understood that there would be state regulation of subsistence uses and made provision for the same in ANILCA. In this regard, ANILCA § 805(d), 16 U.S.C. § 3115(d), in authorizing state management of subsistence uses, provides in part:

> Laws establishing a system of local advisory committees and regional advisory councils consistent with this section [16 U.S.C. § 3115] shall provide that the *State rule-making authority shall consider* the advice and recommendations of the regional councils concerning the taking of fish and wildlife populations on public lands within their respective regions for subsistence uses ***. If a recommendation is not adopted by the State rulemaking authority, such authority shall set forth the factual basis and the reasons for its decision.

(Emphasis supplied.) Plaintiffs do not challenge the Board of Game's power to promulgate regulations.

Plaintiffs do challenge the Board of Game's various regulations which establish seasons and bag limits for the taking of moose and caribou. They contend these regulations are "arbitrary, unreasonable, and unnecessary, and they fail to accord to plaintiff and his class the priority for non-wasteful subsistence uses required by Section 804 [16 U.S.C. § 3114] of ANILCA." ***

[T]he issues presented here have to do with whether or not the Board of Game regulations imposing seasons and bag limits upon subsistence hunters are or are not "within the grant of power" accorded the Board of Game by Alaska's second subsistence law. *Id.* [Alaska's first subsistence law did not provide priority to rural residents, and was replaced to accord with the subsistence priority in ANILCA. The regulations at issue here were initially promulgated under the first subsistence law, but continued under the second.] The court's point of reference for purposes of evaluating the Board of Game regulations is Alaska's second subsistence law because, as discussed in the above background material, the State's regulatory scheme has "supplant[ed] the federal regulatory scheme." Regulations which are not within such grant are unlawful and must be enjoined as required by ANILCA § 807(a), 16 U.S.C. § 3117(a).

B. History of Adoption of Bag Limits & Seasons for Lime Village

***

[In 1985, the plaintiffs, all subsistence hunters residing in Lime Village,] submitted a proposal to the Board of Game for consideration during its March 1985 meeting. The proposal read:

> In order to provide for subsistence uses, it is proposed that with respect to moose and caribou there be no closed season and no individual bag limits for those domiciled in Lime Village in Unit 19." ***

[At the 1985 meeting, b]ased upon public testimony and the Kari Report [prepared by the Alaska Department of Fish and Game], the Board of Game found:

> (1) that the residents of Lime Village are "extremely dependent on moose and caribou in [game management unit] 19(A)."
>
> (2) that "the 40 residents of Lime Village are probably the most geographically isolated and subsistence dependent people in the state."

(3) that moose and caribou were particularly important to Lime Village residents and that these animals "supply the highest proportion of the food eaten by residents of the area."

(4) that Lime Village residents have "customarily harvested moose and caribou on an opportunistic basis throughout the year."

(5) that the moose populations were stable and that the caribou population in the area was at a high level and growing. *Id.*

The Board of Game concluded that establishing a management area for Lime Village would provide a reasonable opportunity for the residents of Lime Village and other Alaskans to harvest moose in the area, and that an increase in the caribou bag limit in the area as well as an increase in the length in the moose season would be a more reasonable mechanism for providing for subsistence uses than the then current, more limited, opportunities. *Id.*

Based on these findings, caribou hunting regulations for the Lime Village management area were reviewed by the Board of Game, increasing the caribou bag limit to five for Lime Village residents. The caribou season remained the same, August 10 through March 31. With respect to moose hunting, the Board of Game extended the season within the Lime Village management area to be open August 10 through September 25, November 20 through December 31, and February 1 through March 31, for a total of 148 days. Although based upon subsistence related information, these regulations were included in the generally applicable "big game" regulations. *Id.*

The Board of Game [subsequently] modified the applicable regulations by closing the Lime Village management area to hunting by persons other than those domiciled within the area. Within the Lime Village management area, moose hunting was allowed (open season) from August 10 through September 25, and November 20 through March 31, a total of 179 days. Additionally, the Board of Game raised the bag limit from one to two moose, and established a quota for the Lime Village management area of twenty moose, ten of which could be cows. *Id.*

***

The Alaska Boards of Game and Fisheries, or their equivalents, have regulated the taking of fish and game by commercial operators and by the general public in Alaska for almost thirty years. There has been significant competition between commercial interests and sport hunters and fishermen. Alaska's endorsement of the subsistence lifestyle pursuant to ANILCA has required that the state game managers deal with a new, third, competing claim upon available fish and game. This task has not been easy, as the history of the development of Alaska law regarding subsistence hunting and fishing indicates. Fish and game authorities have not only had to deal with another competing application of fish and game, but one entitled to "preference over other consumptive uses[.]" § 6, ch. 52 SLA 1986, AS 16.05.258(c). The job of dealing with subsistence was rendered even more difficult for the Board of Game because it has been caught between the demands of the courts of the State of Alaska and the Alaska Legislature.

The court commends the Board of Game for its efforts to fit subsistence in its proper place in light of the difficult (if not impossible) situation which arose from [these conflicts.] ***

As discussed hereinabove, plaintiffs claim that the Board of Game regulations establishing seasons and bag limits on the taking of moose and caribou are unlawful and therefore not valid. The court concludes that the Lime Village hunting regulations are indeed unlawful.

***

[T]he court feels constrained, as a result of its review of the transcripts of the Board of Game hearings which are part of the record, to observe that the Board of Game must in the future proceed with scrupulous care and caution in imposing seasons and bag limits on subsistence hunting. Bag limits and seasons are game management tools which have seen extensive use in Alaska and nationally. These restrictions have typically, if not universally, been used to regulate sport hunting. In this case, bag limits and seasons are being applied to a very different type of game use. In its purest form, the subsistence lifestyle is quite literally the gaining of one's sustenance off the land. Typically, the sport hunter does not go hungry if the season ends without his taking any game or if he has taken and eaten his bag limit. The subsistence hunter who is without meat during a closed season or who has with his family consumed a fixed bag limit will go hungry unless some other game or fish are available and in season. Hunger knows nothing of seasons, nor is it satisfied for long after one's bag limit has been consumed. ***

If bag limits and seasons are imposed on subsistence hunting, there must be substantial evidence in the record that such restrictions are not inconsistent with customary and traditional uses of the game in question. It must be clear in the record that subsistence uses will be accommodated, as regards both the quantity or volume of use and the duration of the use. Need is not the standard. Again, it matters not that other food sources may be available at any given time or place. The standard is customary and traditional use of game.

***

The record now before the court [also] does not provide an adequate basis for understanding or resolving the obvious conflict between a finding that Lime Village residents customarily and traditionally take moose and caribou "throughout the year" and a regulation that precludes them from taking moose during almost six months of the year and from taking caribou during just over four months of the year. The court concludes that the currently operative season regulations are necessarily arbitrary for they substantially fail to accommodate what the board has determined to be the customary and traditional use of moose and caribou for subsistence purposes without first eliminating other consumptive uses.

*** Because the Board of Game did not follow or articulate its use of the statutory analytical process for adopting bag limits as to subsistence hunting, those regulations are also arbitrary.

A specific aspect of the bag limit regulations on subsistence hunting by Lime Village residents requires further comment. There is substantial evidence in the March 1985 record that moose and caribou are taken by a few hunters who then share their take with the whole community. It appears well established by the record that customary and traditional uses of moose and caribou have a communal aspect at Lime Village. Simply put, the very young, the old, and the infirm of the community are provided with meat by the healthy adult members of the community who are skilled at hunting. It is not clear from the Board of Game findings or the discussions of the board members how this aspect of the Lime Village subsistence tradition of hunting and game-sharing interrelates with bag limits. The court is concerned that the established bag limits do not accommodate this traditional aspect of Lime Village hunting of moose and caribou.

***

On the basis of the extensive briefing by both plaintiffs and defendant on the State's motion for summary judgment, and in consideration of the nature of these proceedings (review of administrative rulemaking), the court is in a position as discussed above to rule on plaintiffs' claims. The court concludes that plaintiffs are entitled to the declaratory relief they seek with respect to 5 AAC §§ 88.025 and -.045. The current version of these regulations, as well as their precursers (including the 1985 version, AAC § 81.320), were not adopted in conformity with § 6, ch. 52, SLA 1986, AS 16.05.258. They impose seasons not consistent with the board's findings as to established customs of the people of Lime Village, and thereby unacceptably restrict the preference for subsistence uses dictated by § 6, ch. 52, SLA 1986, AS 16.05.258. The regulations impose bag limits which were not demonstrably of a size sufficient to accommodate the customary taking of moose or caribou at Lime Village. The Board of Game shall review its subsistence hunting regulations for Lime Village, Alaska, and shall submit to the court for review reenacted subsistence hunting regulations in accordance with Alaska's second subsistence law and this decision.

***

NOTES AND QUESTIONS

1. *Application of the priority?* The cooperative federalism regime operated for eight years, although the State suffered a string of defeats as it struggled to actually provide the rural priority. *See, e.g., Madison v. Alaska Department of Fish and Game*, 696 P.2d 168 (1985) (overturning state regulations that limited subsistence uses to rural residents as inconsistent with the Alaska subsistence statute); *Kenaitze Indian Tribe v. Alaska*, 860 F.2d 312, 313-14 (9th Cir. 1988) (striking down narrow state definition of rural); *United States* v. *Alexander*, 938 F.2d 942 (9th Cir. 1991) (finding invalid state regulation that barred any sales of herring roe even if part of customary trade); *Native Village of Quinhagak v. United States*, 35 F.3d 388 (9th Cir. 1994) (replacing restrictive state fishing regulations with federal protection); *Bobby v. Alaska*, 718 F. Supp. 764, 789 (D. Alaska 1989) (setting aside regulations that restricted moose and caribou hunting by residents of Lime Village); *Kwethluk IRA Council v. Alaska*, 740 F. Supp. 765 (D. Alaska 1990) (setting aside state regulations precluding emergency caribou hunt); *Katie John v. Alaska*, No. A85-698-CV, (D. Alaska 1990) (setting aside state regulations that restricted subsistence fishing at the site of historic Native Village of Batzulnetas in what is now Wrangell St. Elias National Park).

2. *The end of state management.* In *McDowell v. Alaska*, 785 P.2d 1 (Alaska 1989) the Alaska Supreme Court dealt an even more serious blow to the State's effort to manage subsistence activities pursuant to a rural priority. The court held that any state preference of rural over urban subsistence users

violated state constitutional provisions that ensured equal access to state natural resources. *Id.* at 9. The court recognized that the laws were enacted to comply with ANILCA, but held that this was not a compelling purpose because the federal government could regulate subsistence use if the state did not. *Id.* at 11. The court declared,

> When it becomes necessary for the propagation and preservation of wild game and fish for the use of the public, the people acting in their sovereign capacity, through their lawmaking power, may pass laws to regulate the right of each individual which he enjoys in common with every other member of the community to use of same. But when the sovereign undertakes to regulate or restrain the individual in its right as a member of the community to enjoy the right to take and use this common property of all, it must do so upon the same terms to all members of the community alike. The common right, which one individual of the whole community is entitled to enjoy as much as another, cannot be made by law the exclusive privilege of the people of a certain class or section upon terms and conditions that do not apply to the whole people alike. *** No special privileges or immunities [based on residence] can be conferred.

Id. at 11–12. Several efforts to amend the Alaska Constitution to allow for a rural preference failed and the federal government was obliged to administer the priority on federal public lands. In an unpublished 2006 opinion, the Ninth Circuit rejected a federal equal protection challenge to ANILCA's rural preference. *Alaska Constitutional Legal Defense Conservation Fund v. Kempthorne*, 198 Fed. Appx. 601, 602–603 (9th Cir. 2006); *see Katie John v. United States*, 720 F.3d 1214, 1221 (9th Cir. 2013), *cert. denied*, 134 S. Ct. 1759 (2014) (summarizing history of litigation over subsistence regulatory authority).

Questions also arise as to what is included in the definition of "public lands" under federal jurisdiction for subsistence management purposes. When the federal government first assumed management of subsistence uses in 1990, it refused to provide the priority to virtually any waters, and the following litigation ensued.

ALASKA V. BABBITT

72 F.3d 698 (9th Cir. 1995)
reaffirmed and adopted as majority opinion

JOHN V. UNITED STATES

247 F.3d 1032 (9th Cir. 2001) (*en banc*)

EUGENE A. WRIGHT, CIRCUIT JUDGE:

These appeals arise from the efforts of Katie John, Doris Charles and the other upper Ahtna Athabaskan Indians of Mentasta Village to continue subsistence fishing at Batzulnetas as they and their ancestors have done since time immemorial.[1] The fishery at Batzulnetas lies near the confluence of Tanada Creek and the Copper River and within Wrangell–St. Elias National Park. They also involve the claim by the state of Alaska that the Secretaries of the Interior and Agriculture, on behalf of the federal government, are attempting to exercise too much control over fish and wildlife management within the state.

The Alaska National Interest Lands Conservation Act (ANILCA), requires that subsistence fishing and hunting be given a priority over other uses of fish and wildlife on "public lands." The sole issue remaining in this appeal concerns the meaning of the definition of public lands in § 102 of ANILCA. Specifically, the parties dispute whether navigable waters fall within the statutory definition of public lands and are thus subject to federal management to implement ANILCA's subsistence priority.

The district court adopted a highly expansive definition of public lands, holding that the subsistence priority applies to all Alaskan waters subject to the federal navigational servitude. We disagree. Instead, we hold that the subsistence priority applies to navigable waters in which the United States has reserved water rights. We hold also that the federal agencies that administer the subsistence priority are responsible for identifying those waters. We therefore reverse and remand to the district court for further proceedings consistent with this opinion.

I. BACKGROUND

In 1958, Congress preserved aboriginal fishing rights in the Statehood Act. Act of July 7, 1958, Pub. L. 85–508, § 4, 72 Stat. 339. But in 1960, after assuming responsibility for fish and wildlife management, the state closed the fishery at Batzulnetas and other traditional subsistence fisheries. In 1971, Congress extinguished aboriginal fishing rights.

Congress expected that the state and the federal agencies would protect subsistence hunting and fishing. In 1980, frustrated with their failure to do so, Congress enacted ANILCA. Title VIII of ANILCA required that rural Alaska residents be accorded a priority for subsistence hunting and fishing on public lands. Pursuant to § 805(d) of ANILCA, Congress gave the state authority to implement the rural subsistence preference by enacting laws of general applicability consistent with ANILCA's operative provisions. In anticipation of ANILCA's passage, the state enacted laws consistent with Title VIII which gave rural residents a subsistence priority. In 1982, after Congress enacted ANILCA, the Secretary of the Interior certified the state to manage subsistence hunting and fishing on public lands.

Congress could not have anticipated the next chain of events. In 1989, the Alaska Supreme Court struck down the state act granting the rural subsistence preference as contrary to the Alaska state constitution. *McDowell v. Alaska,* 785 P.2d 1 (Alaska 1989). It stayed its decision to give the legislature

1. The following *amici curiae* also seek to continue subsistence fishing in particular navigable waters: the Peratrovich Plaintiffs whose ancestors fished in marine waters in the Alexander Archipelago and within the Tongass National Forest; the Tlingit, Haida and Tsimshian Indians of the Sitka Tribe whose ancestors also fished in marine waters; the Yup'ik Eskimos of the Villages of Quinhagak and Goodnews Bay whose ancestors fished at the mouths of the Kanektok and Goodnews Rivers; and the Native Alaskans of the Village of Elim and the Nome Eskimo Community whose ancestors fished along the coast of the Seward Peninsula in northern Norton Sound.

an opportunity to amend the constitution or otherwise bring its program into compliance with ANILCA. The legislature, however, failed to act during either its regular or special session.

In 1990, the federal government withdrew Alaska's certification and took over implementation of Title VIII. The Secretary of the Interior, on behalf of all concerned federal agencies, published temporary subsistence management regulations that adopted a very narrow definition of public lands, explaining that "navigable waters generally are not included within the definition of public lands." 55 Fed. Reg. 27,114, at 27,115 (June 29, 1990). The final regulations did not differ significantly. *See* 57 Fed. Reg. 22,940, at 22,942 (May 29, 1992).

Katie John and the state brought separate actions against the federal agencies; Katie John challenged the regulations that provided that public lands excluded navigable waters and the state challenged the federal government's authority to regulate in this area at all. The district court ordered these actions consolidated and that other actions raising similar issues be jointly managed.

Katie John argued that public lands include virtually all navigable waters, by virtue of the federal navigational servitude. The state contended that public lands exclude navigable waters. Prior to oral argument before the district court, the federal agencies agreed with the state. But at oral argument, those agencies modified their position, arguing that public lands include those navigable waters in which the federal government has an interest under the reserved water rights doctrine.

On cross-motions for summary judgment, the district court concluded that public lands include all navigable waters encompassed by the navigational servitude. Subsequently, the district court stayed its decision and certified the issue of whether public lands include navigable waters for interlocutory appeal.

II. ANALYSIS

*** Under ANILCA, "the term 'public lands' means land[s] situated in Alaska which *** are Federal lands." "The term 'Federal land' means lands the title to which is in the United States." 16 U.S.C. § 3102(2). And "[t]he term 'land' means lands, waters, and interests therein." 16 U.S.C. § 3102(1). In other words, public lands are lands, waters, and interests therein, the title to which is in the United States. *Amoco Production Co. v. Village of Gambell,* 480 U.S. 531, 548 n. 15 (1987).

As noted above, the parties dispute whether navigable waters are public lands. At one extreme, the state maintains that ANILCA's definition of public lands excludes all navigable waters because the federal government does not hold title to them by virtue of the navigational servitude or the reserved water rights doctrine. At the other extreme are Katie John and *amici curiae* Peratrovich Plaintiffs who argue that all navigable waters are public lands. Katie John says this is so because the navigational servitude defines the scope of public lands. *** In the middle are federal agencies contending that public lands include certain navigable waters, defined by the reserved water rights doctrine. ***

ANILCA's language and legislative history indicate clearly that Congress spoke to the precise question of whether *some* navigable waters may be public lands. They clearly indicate that subsistence uses include subsistence fishing. *See, e.g.,* 16 U.S.C. § 3113. And subsistence fishing has traditionally taken place in navigable waters. Thus, we have no doubt that Congress intended that public lands include at least some navigable waters. ***

Unfortunately, ANILCA's language and legislative history do not give us the clear direction necessary to find that Congress spoke to the precise question of *which* navigable waters are public lands. ANILCA itself refers only to "lands, waters, and interests therein, the title to which is in the United States." It makes no reference to navigable waters. The legislative history is also unhelpful, containing only a single reference to navigable waters. ***

A. Navigational Servitude

The navigational servitude describes the paramount interest of the United States in navigation and the navigable waters of the nation. *United States v. Certain Parcels of Land,* 666 F.2d 1236, 1238 (9th Cir. 1982). It derives from the Commerce Clause. *** It is "a concept of power, not of property." ***

We have held that the navigational servitude is not "public land" within the meaning of ANILCA because the United States does not hold title to it. ***

For this reason, we reject the argument that the navigational servitude is an "interest *** the title to which is in the United States," such that all navigable waters are public lands within the meaning of ANILCA. ***

C. Reserved Water Rights

Under the reserved water rights doctrine, when the United States withdraws its lands from the public domain and reserves them for a federal purpose, the United States implicitly reserves appurtenant waters then unappropriated to the extent needed to accomplish the purpose of the reservation. The United States may reserve "only that amount of water necessary to fulfill the purpose of the reservation." The United States' authority to reserve unappropriated waters derives from the Commerce Clause and the Property Clause.

In determining whether the reserved water rights doctrine applies, we must determine whether the United States intended to reserve unappropriated waters. Intent is inferred if those waters are necessary to accomplish the purposes for which the land was reserved. It follows that courts must conclude that "without the water the purposes of the reservation would be entirely defeated."

The United States has reserved vast parcels of land in Alaska for federal purposes through a myriad of statutes.[10] In doing so, it has also implicitly reserved appurtenant waters, including appurtenant navigable waters, to the extent needed to accomplish the purposes of the reservations. By virtue of its reserved water rights, the United States has interests in some navigable waters. Consequently, public lands subject to subsistence management under ANILCA include certain navigable waters.

For these reasons, we hold to be reasonable the federal agencies' conclusion that the definition of public lands includes those navigable waters in which the United States has an interest by virtue of the reserved water rights

10. These statutes include, but are not limited to, acts reserving land for national parks, forests and wildlife preserves, the Statehood Act, the Alaska Native Claims Settlement Act and ANILCA itself.

doctrine. We also hold that the federal agencies that administer the subsistence priority are responsible for identifying those waters.

III. CONCLUSION

We recognize that our holding may be inherently unsatisfactory. By holding that public lands include some specific navigable waters as a result of reserved water rights, we impose an extraordinary administrative burden on federal agencies. We accept a complicated regulatory scheme requiring federal and state management of navigable waters. Let us hope that the federal agencies will determine promptly which navigable waters are public lands subject to federal subsistence management. As long as federal *and* state regulation is necessary, we expect the federal agencies and the state to cooperate fully to protect and provide the opportunity for subsistence fishing in navigable waters.

If we were to adopt the state's position, that public lands exclude navigable waters, we would give meaning to the term "title" in the definition of the phrase "public lands." But we would undermine congressional intent to protect and provide the opportunity for subsistence fishing.

If we were to adopt Katie John's position, that public lands include all navigable waters, we would give federal agencies control over all such waters in Alaska. ANILCA does not support such a complete assertion of federal control and the federal agencies do not ask to have that control.

The issue raised by the parties cries out for a legislative, not a judicial, solution. If the Alaska Legislature were to amend the state constitution or otherwise comply with ANILCA's rural subsistence priority, the state could resume management of subsistence uses on public lands including navigable waters. Neither the heavy administrative burden nor the complicated regulatory scheme that may result from our decision would be necessary. If Congress were to amend ANILCA, it could clarify both the definition of public lands and its intent. Only legislative action by Alaska or Congress will truly resolve the problem.

Reversed and remanded.

[**CYNTHIA HOLCOMB HALL, CIRCUIT JUDGE**, dissented, arguing that ANILCA did not clearly include any navigable waters, and such questions were better left to Congress.]

Katie John as a young woman. Used with permission of Kathryn Martin.

Katie John persuades Alaska Governor Tony Knowles to drop the appeal to the U.S. Supreme Court in 2001. Used with permission of Kathryn Martin.

NOTES AND QUESTIONS

1. *Federal Reserved Waters and* Sturgeon v. Frost. The Secretaries of the Interior and Agriculture promulgated regulations in 1999 identifying the federal reserved waters where the federal priority would apply. 64 Fed. Reg. 1276 (Jan. 8, 1999). In 2005, the State of Alaska and a number of Native tribes and individuals sued the United States arguing, respectively, that either too many, or too few, waters were included in the delineation of federal reserved waters. The court of appeals upheld the regulations in *Katie John v. United States*, 720 F.3d 1214 (9th Cir. 2013), *cert. denied*, 134 S. Ct. 1759 (2014). Despite Native plaintiffs' failure to achieve a more expansive definition of public lands, the Alaska Native community regarded the *John* decision and denial of Supreme Court review as a significant victory because the lower court upheld federal jurisdiction over 60% of the Alaska's navigable inland waters. It then appeared that the litigation was over. That was incorrect.

Sturgeon *v.* Frost, 897 F.3d 927 (9th Cir. 2017), *rev'd*, Sturgeon *v.* Frost, 139 S. C. 1066 (2019).

The National Park Service (NPS) issued a citation to a moose hunter for using a hovercraft in a National Preserve. The Ninth Circuit upheld NPS jurisdiction by relying on the *Katie John* holding that the waters constitute "public lands" subject to Park Service regulatory power. *Sturgeon v. Frost*, 897 F.3d 927 (9th Cir. 2017). The Supreme Court reversed, *Sturgeon v. Frost*, 139 S. Ct. 1066 (2019), on the ground that the river was not "public land" for purposes of Park Service regulations. The Court reasoned that the federal reserved rights theory did not make the water public lands—at least for purposes of NPS jurisdiction.

Despite rejecting the "public lands" rationale for NPS authority, the Court dropped a footnote critical to the *Katie John* litigants and all rural subsistence users in Alaska:

> As noted earlier, the Ninth Circuit has held in three cases—the so-called *Katie John* trilogy—that the term "public lands," when used in ANILCA's subsistence-fishing provisions, encompasses navigable waters like the Nation River. [citations omitted] Those provisions are not at issue in this case, and we therefore do not disturb the Ninth Circuit's holdings that the Park Service may regulate subsistence fishing on navigable waters. See generally Brief for State of Alaska as *Amicus Curiae* 29–35 (arguing that this case does not implicate those decisions); Brief for Ahtna, Inc., as *Amicus Curiae* 30–36 (same).

Because the Supreme Court left in place the federal government's authority to enforce the subsistence priority, the *Katie John* decisions constitute binding precedent as to the duty and power to continue to enforce Title VIII on federal reserved waters. In September, 2019 the State of Alaska filed a petition for rulemaking asking the Department of the Interior to change the subsistence regulations by dropping the federally reserved navigable waters from its scope. Letter from Alaska Attorney General , Kevin Clarkson, to Secretary David Bernhardt, Department of the Interior (Sept. 17, 2019). If the request is granted, the federal subsistence priority for fishing would no longer apply in a meaningful way. The only areas covered would be non-navigable waters within federal lands, and waters above submerged land that was reserved by the United States prior to statehood—a very small set of waters. In its brief to the Supreme Court, the State Attorney General had argued that the "public lands" definition had a different meaning in Title VIII of ANILCA. Brief of Amicus Curiae State of Alaska in Support of Petitioner at 30, *Sturgeon II*, 139 S. Ct. 1066 (2019) (No. 17-949), 2018 WL 4063284, at *30. For a discussion of the case and possible solutions to the issues presented, see Robert T. Anderson, *The* Katie John *Litigation: The Long Search for Alaska Native Fishing Rights After ANCSA*, 51 Ariz. St. L. J. 845 (Forthcoming 2019).

2. *Fishing and Hunting Rights in the Waters of the Outer Continental Shelf.* Under federal law, submerged lands beneath navigable waters within three miles of a state's shoreline are part of the territory of the state. 43 U.S.C. § 1312. Alaska Native fishing rights in such waters, therefore, are part of the aboriginal rights "in Alaska" extinguished under ANCSA. *See* 43 U.S.C. § 1603(b). The Outer Continental Shelf (OCS), however, consisting of American waters outside this three-mile limit are not part of state territory, but rather are within the paramount control and dominion of the United States. *See United States v. Maine*, 420 U.S. 515, 522 (1975). Any aboriginal rights in these waters are therefore not extinguished by ANCSA. *See People of Village of Gambell v. Hodel*, 869 F.2d 1273, 1280 (9th Cir. 1989). The Supreme Court, however, has held that the OCS is not included in ANILCA's definition of public lands either, so that subsistence uses there are not subject to ANILCA's special protection. *Amoco Production Co. v. Village of Gambell*, 480 U.S. 531, 546–547 (1987). In *Native Village of Eyak v. Blank*, 688 F.3d 619 (9th Cir. 2012) (*en banc*), the court held that Alaska Natives did not retain aboriginal fishing rights in the OCS because they could not prove that they had "exclusive use" of the area. Judge William Fletcher wrote a sharp dissent, but was on the short end of a 6-5 vote.

Increased oil and gas development and other activity in areas of the OCS used by Alaska Natives may lead to further litigation, but it is complex and lengthy. The *Eyak* case was in litigation for over 14 years.

3. *Environmental protection?* Section 810 of ANILCA, 16 U.S.C. § 3120 provides that

> No withdrawal, reservation, lease, permit, or other use, occupancy or disposition of [public lands] which would significantly restrict subsistence uses shall be effected until the head of such Federal agency—
>
> ***
>
> (3) determines that (A) such a significant restriction of subsistence uses is necessary, consistent with sound management principles for the utilization of the public lands, (B) the proposed activity will involve the minimal amount of public lands necessary to accomplish the purposes of such use, occupancy, or other disposition, and (C) reasonable steps will be taken to minimize adverse impacts upon subsistence uses and resources resulting from such actions.

The Supreme Court has stated that

> The purpose of ANILCA § 810 is to protect Alaskan subsistence resources from unnecessary destruction. Section 810 does not prohibit all federal land use actions which would adversely affect subsistence resources but sets forth a procedure through which such effects must be considered and provides that actions which would significantly restrict subsistence uses can only be undertaken if they are necessary and if the adverse effects are minimized.

Amoco Production Co. v. Village of Gambell, 480 U.S. 531, 544 (1987). *See Native Village of Hoonah v. Morrison*, 170 F.3d 1223 (9th Cir. 1999) (effect on subsistence uses is only one of a number of considerations in evaluating a timber sale in National Forest).

4. *Restoration of aboriginal rights, or something else?* Given all the litigation and the fact that subsistence is now being managed on a piecemeal basis, should Congress revisit the issue of Native hunting and fishing rights? Could Congress create a Native preference applicable on federal, state and private lands in Alaska? What would you advise a member of Congress concerned about federal constitutional issues? At a 2013 hearing before the United States Senate Energy and Natural Resources Committee, several Alaska Native leaders suggested amendments to Title VIII to provide a Native preference for subsistence uses and Native co-management for resources on federal, Native and state lands. Hearing Before the Senate Energy and Natural Resources Committee, 113th Cong. 1st Sess. at 33-70 (Sept. 19, 2013) (S. Hrg. 113-118).

5. *Climate change: the new threat to Native subsistence activities.* The Arctic region has experienced dramatic warming in recent years. The warming, a result of global climate change caused by human emissions of carbon dioxide and other greenhouse gases, is already affecting the health and migratory patterns of the animals and plants that rural Alaskans depend on as well as Native subsistence activities including hunting, fishing, gathering of plants, and even basic travel. Some Native villages are also at risk of subsiding into the ocean due to coastal erosion caused by melting permafrost, decreased sea ice, and changing ocean patterns. The Native Village of Kivalina sued ExxonMobil Corp. and other defendants on a nuisance theory, alleging that the threat to their village, which is undergoing relocation planning due to severe erosion, was caused by defendants' greenhouse gas emissions. The Ninth Circuit dismissed the case, finding that the Supreme Court had already held that the Clean Air Act preempted federal common law regulation of domestic greenhouse gas emissions. *Native Vill. of Kivalina v. ExxonMobil Corp.*, 696 F.3d 849, 856 (9th Cir. 2012) (relying on *American Electric Power Co., Inc. v. Connecticut*, 131 S. Ct. 2527 (2011)). A case by youth climate change activists, is pending before the Alaska Supreme Court, *Esau Sinnok, et al. v. State of Alaska*, No. S-17297 (Alaska S.Ct) (oral argument held, Oct.9, 2019). In the case, 17 youths challenge the constitutionality of a state statute that promotes the development of fossil fuels. The statute, AS 44.99.115 Declaration of State Energy Policy, and the policies it calls on the legislature to implement, are alleged to exacerbate climate change and its impacts in violation of the due process clause and several other provisions of the Alaska Constitution. A decision is expected by the summer of 2020.

II. HAWAI`I

Central components of indigenous survival include control of some aboriginal lands and resources, along with recognition by the United States government. Treaties and agreements ratified by Congress charted the course for most tribes in the contiguous 48 states, and Alaska Native land claims were dealt with through the Alaska Native Claims Settlement Act. The 2010 census puts the Native Hawaiian population at over 290,000, making them the largest indigenous group in the United States; at over 21% of the population of Hawaii, Native Hawaiians also comprise the largest indigenous population of any state. The United States, however, has not officially recognized Native Hawaiian sovereignty since annexing Hawaii over a century ago.

Native Hawaiians have been pressing claims to land and sovereignty for many years and are in the midst of dramatic developments. In 2008, the Hawai'i Supreme Court precluded the transfer of certain state trust lands from the state to third parties due to Native Hawaiian land and sovereignty claims, only to be reversed by the United States Supreme Court the next year. The Hawaii legislature then acted to preserve state trust land lands from most transfers absent a super majority vote. Meanwhile, the House of Representatives passed the "Native Hawaiian Government Reorganization Act," H.R. 505, 110th Cong. (2007), which would provide federal recognition of a sovereign Native Hawaiian government within the framework of federal Indian law. The bill failed to pass in the Senate, and although introduced in the next two sessions of Congress, it was not proposed in the 113th Congress and appears to be dead. In lieu of federal legislation, the Department of Interior is exploring administrative options to provide federal recognition to Native Hawaiians.

As a brief historical review demonstrates, Native Hawaiian claims to sovereignty and land are rooted in a history of treaty relationships with the Kingdom of Hawai`i as constituted after western contact. Prior to contact, Native Hawaiians lived within a political system closely tied to land use and ownership patterns. Most authorities date inhabitation of the Hawaiian Islands by Polynesian peoples at about 1,700 years ago. Cohen's Handbook of Federal Indian Law 357 (2012), *citing* Patrick V. Kirch, On the Road of the Winds 230–245 (2000). Prior to western contact and for a time thereafter, the eight major islands were governed by a system of local chiefs who controlled land use, but retained ownership of all land in trust for the people through a hierarchical system. *Id.*

> The land tenure system provided that each High Chief controlled the land within his boundaries, which could consist of a region on an island, one island, or several islands. The High Chief would keep some land for his own use and distribute the rest to Konohiki (lesser ranking chiefs) loyal to him. The Konohiki were allocated *ahupua'a*, a pie shaped parcel of land, generally contiguous with a valley, starting at two mountain ridges and widening as it reached the ocean. The *ahupua'a* provided them with access to all necessary resources, from fresh water and timber, to cultivatable lands, fish ponds and the ocean. The Konohiki would allocate strips of land, called ili, to Maka' ãinana (the common people) that included access to all these resources. [The Maka' ãinana organized to perform public works projects and had what might be considered a symbiotic relationship with the Konohiki and the High Chiefs.]

From Mauka to Makai: The River of Justice Must Flow Freely, Report on the Reconciliation Process between the Federal Government and Native Hawaiians 22 (Department of the Interior and Department of Justice, Oct. 23, 2000).

Shortly after Captain Cook landed on the islands in 1778 and 1779, the islands were consolidated as one kingdom under Kamehameha I. The consolidation was completed in 1810. *Id.* "Beginning about 1820, missionaries arrived, of whom Congregationalists from New England *** sought to teach Hawaiians to abandon religious beliefs and customs that were contrary to Christian teachings and practices." *Rice v. Cayetano*, 528 U.S. 495, 500–501 (2000). Foreigners gradually expanded their influence in the Islands as merchants and missionaries emigrated and emphasized international trade. Non–Native advisors to Kamehameha encouraged a shift in property ownership from the traditional system to a western-style fee simple. A division of land known as the Mahele ended the interlocking system of land among the King, chiefs and common people and substituted a fee simple system. Cohen's Handbook of Federal Indian Law 359 (2012). The end result was that by the 1850s, the king held nearly a million acres of land; the government owned 1.5 million acres; chiefs and *konohiki* 1.5 million acres; while the commoners received approximately 30,000 acres. Also, foreigners were authorized to own land. *Id.* at 357-58. By the end of the 19th Century, non-Native Hawaiians held over 60% of the fee simple lands and dominated Hawai`i's economy. *Id.* at 360.

Through a series of illegal acts, non-Native interests overthrew the Hawaiian monarchy in 1893. In 1898, the United States annexed Hawai`i through a joint resolution, J. Res. 55, July 7, 1898, 30 Stat. 750, which made Hawai`i part of the United States and transferred "all public, Government, or Crown lands" to the United States. One hundred years after the overthrow, Congress described and apologized for these acts in the Joint Resolution below. What is its legal effect?

JOINT RESOLUTION TO ACKNOWLEDGE THE 100TH ANNIVERSARY OF THE JANUARY 17, 1893 OVERTHROW OF THE KINGDOM OF HAWAI`I

Pub. L. No. 103–150, 107 Stat. 1510 (1993)†

Whereas, prior to the arrival of the first Europeans in 1778, the Native Hawaiian people lived in a highly organized self-sufficient, subsistent social system based on communal land tenure with a sophisticated language, culture, and religion;

Whereas[,] a unified monarchical government of the Hawaiian Islands was established in 1810 under Kamehameha I, the first King of Hawai`i;

Whereas, from 1826 until 1893, the United States recognized the independence of the Kingdom of Hawai`i, extended full and complete diplomatic recognition to the Hawaiian Government, and entered into treaties and conventions with the Hawaiian monarchs to govern commerce and navigation in 1826, 1842, 1849, 1875, and 1887;

†. Internal quotation marks omitted.

Whereas[,] the Congregational Church (now known as the United Church of Christ), through its American Board of Commissioners for Foreign Missions, sponsored and sent more than 100 missionaries to the Kingdom of Hawai`i between 1820 and 1850;

Whereas, on January 14, 1893, John L. Stevens (hereafter referred to in this Resolution as the "United States Minister"), the United States Minister assigned to the sovereign and independent Kingdom of Hawai`i conspired with a small group of non-Hawaiian residents of the Kingdom of Hawai`i, including citizens of the United States, to overthrow the indigenous and lawful Government of Hawai`i;

Whereas, in pursuance of the conspiracy to overthrow the Government of Hawai`i, the United States Minister and the naval representatives of the United States caused armed naval forces of the United States to invade the sovereign Hawaiian nation on January 16, 1893, and to position themselves near the Hawaiian Government buildings and the Iolani Palace to intimidate Queen Liliuokalani and her Government;

Whereas, on the afternoon of January 17, 1893, a Committee of Safety that represented the American and European sugar planters, descendents of missionaries, and financiers deposed the Hawaiian monarchy and proclaimed the establishment of a Provisional Government;

Whereas[,] the United States Minister thereupon extended diplomatic recognition to the Provisional Government that was formed by the conspirators without the consent of the Native Hawaiian people or the lawful Government of Hawai`i and in violation of treaties between the two nations and of international law;

Whereas, soon thereafter, when informed of the risk of bloodshed with resistance, Queen Liliuokalani issued the following statement yielding her authority to the United States Government rather than to the Provisional Government:

> I[,] Liliuokalani, by the Grace of God and under the Constitution of the Hawaiian Kingdom, Queen, do hereby solemnly protest against any and all acts done against myself and the Constitutional Government of the Hawaiian Kingdom by certain persons claiming to have established a Provisional Government of and for this Kingdom.
>
> That I yield to the superior force of the United States of America whose Minister Plenipotentiary, His Excellency John L. Stevens, has caused United States troops to be landed at Honolulu and declared that he would support the Provisional Government.
>
> Now to avoid any collision of armed forces, and perhaps the loss of life, I do this under protest and impelled by said force yield my authority until such time as the Government of the United States shall, upon facts being presented to it, undo the action of its representatives and reinstate me in the authority which I claim as the Constitutional Sovereign of the Hawaiian Islands.
>
> Done at Honolulu this 17th day of January, A.D. 1893.;

Whereas, without the active support and intervention by the United States diplomatic and military representatives, the insurrection against the

Government of Queen Liliuokalani would have failed for lack of popular support and insufficient arms;

Whereas[,] on February 1, 1893, the United States Minister raised the American flag and proclaimed Hawai'i to be a protectorate of the United States;

Whereas, the report of a Presidentially established investigation conducted by former Congressman James Blount into the events surrounding the insurrection and overthrow of January 17, 1893, concluded that the United States diplomatic and military representatives had abused their authority and were responsible for the change in government;

Whereas, as a result of this investigation, the United States Minister to Hawai`i was recalled from his diplomatic post and the military commander of the United States armed forces stationed in Hawai`i was disciplined and forced to resign his commission;

Whereas, in a message to Congress on December 18, 1893, President Grover Cleveland reported fully and accurately on the illegal acts of the conspirators, described such acts as an "act of war, committed with the participation of a diplomatic representative of the United States and without authority of Congress", and acknowledged that by such acts the government of a peaceful and friendly people was overthrown;

Whereas[,] President Cleveland further concluded that a "substantial wrong has thus been done which a due regard for our national character as well as the rights of the injured people requires we should endeavor to repair" and called for the restoration of the Hawaiian monarchy;

Whereas[,] the Provisional Government protested President Cleveland's call for the restoration of the monarchy and continued to hold state power and pursue annexation to the United States;

Whereas[,] the Provisional Government successfully lobbied the Committee on Foreign Relations of the Senate (hereafter referred to in this Resolution as the "Committee") to conduct a new investigation into the events surrounding the overthrow of the monarchy;

Whereas[,] the Committee and its chairman, Senator John Morgan, conducted hearings in Washington, D.C., from December 27, 1893, through February 26, 1894, in which members of the Provisional Government justified and condoned the actions of the United States Minister and recommended annexation of Hawai`i;

Whereas, although the Provisional Government was able to obscure the role of the United States in the illegal overthrow of the Hawaiian monarchy, it was unable to rally the support from two-thirds of the Senate needed to ratify a treaty of annexation;

Whereas, on July 4, 1894, the Provisional Government declared itself to be the Republic of Hawai`i;

Whereas, on January 24, 1895, while imprisoned in Iolani Palace, Queen Liliuokalani was forced by representatives of the Republic of Hawai`i to officially abdicate her throne;

Whereas, in the 1896 United States Presidential election, William McKinley replaced Grover Cleveland;

Whereas, on July 7, 1898, as a consequence of the Spanish–American War, President McKinley signed the Newlands Joint Resolution that provided for the annexation of Hawai`i;

Whereas, through the Newlands Resolution, the self-declared Republic of Hawai`i ceded sovereignty over the Hawaiian Islands to the United States;

Whereas, the Republic of Hawai`i also ceded 1,800,000 acres of crown, government and public lands of the Kingdom of Hawai`i, without the consent of or compensation to the Native Hawaiian people of Hawai`i or their sovereign government;

Whereas[,] the Congress, through the Newlands Resolution, ratified the cession, annexed Hawai`i as part of the United States, and vested title to the lands in Hawai`i in the United States;

Whereas[,] the Newlands Resolution also specified that treaties existing between Hawai`i and foreign nations were to immediately cease and be replaced by United States treaties with such nations;

Whereas[,] the Newlands Resolution effected the transaction between the Republic of Hawai`i and the United States Government;

Whereas[,] the indigenous Hawaiian people never directly relinquished their claims to their inherent sovereignty as a people or over their national lands to the United States, either through their monarchy or through a plebiscite or referendum;

Whereas, on April 30, 1900, President McKinley signed the Organic Act that provided a government for the territory of Hawai`i and defined the political structure and powers of the newly established Territorial Government and its relationship with the United States;

Whereas, on August 21, 1959, Hawai`i became the 50th State of the United States;

Whereas[,] the health and well-being of the Native Hawaiian people is intrinsically tied to their deep feelings and attachment to the land;

Whereas[,] the long-range economic and social changes in Hawai`i over the nineteenth and early twentieth centuries have been devastating to the population and to the health and well-being of the Hawaiian people; ***

Whereas[,] the Native Hawaiian people are determined to preserve, develop and transmit to future generations their ancestral territory, and their cultural identity in accordance with their own spiritual and traditional beliefs, customs, practices, language, and social institutions;

Whereas, in order to promote racial harmony and cultural understanding, the Legislature of the State of Hawai`i has determined that the year 1993 should serve Hawai`i as a year of special reflection on the rights and dignities of the Native Hawaiians in the Hawaiian and the American societies;

Whereas[,] the Eighteenth General Synod of the United Church of Christ in recognition of the denomination's historical complicity in the illegal overthrow of the Kingdom of Hawai`i in 1893 directed the Office of the President of the United Church of Christ to offer a public apology to the Native Hawaiian people and to initiate the process of reconciliation between the United Church of Christ and the Native Hawaiians; and

Whereas[,] it is proper and timely for the Congress on the occasion of the impending one hundredth anniversary of the event, to acknowledge the historic significance of the illegal overthrow of the Kingdom of Hawai`i, to express deep regret to the Native Hawaiian people, and to support the reconciliation efforts of the State of Hawai'i and the United Church of Christ with Native Hawaiians: Now, therefore, be it

Resolved by the Senate and House of Representatives of the United State of American in Congress assembled,

***

The Congress—

(1) on the occasion of the 100th anniversary of the illegal overthrow of the Kingdom of Hawai`i on January 17, 1893, acknowledges the historical significance of this event which resulted in the suppression of the inherent sovereignty of the Native Hawaiian people;

(2) recognizes and commends the efforts of reconciliation initiated by the State of Hawai`i and the United Church of Christ with Native Hawaiians;

(3) apologizes to Native Hawaiians on behalf of the people of the United States for the overthrow of the Kingdom of Hawai`i on January 17, 1893 with the participation of agents and citizens of the United States, and the deprivation of the rights of Native Hawaiians to self-determination;

(4) expresses its commitment to acknowledge the ramifications of the overthrow of the Kingdom of Hawai`i, in order to provide a proper foundation for reconciliation between the United States and the Native Hawaiian people; and

(5) urges the President of the United States to also acknowledge the ramifications of the overthrow of the Kingdom of Hawai`i and to support reconciliation efforts between the United States and the Native Hawaiian people.

***

As used in this Joint Resolution, the term "Native Hawaiian" means any individual who is a descendent of the aboriginal people who, prior to 1778, occupied and exercised sovereignty in the area that now constitutes the State of Hawai`i.

*** Disclaimer

Nothing in this Joint Resolution is intended to serve as a settlement of any claims against the United States.

Approved November 23, 1993.

A. CLAIMS TO LAND

When Hawai`i became a state in 1959, the United States transferred 1.4 million acres of the lands it had acquired from the Kingdom of Hawai`i in trust to the State of Hawai`i. After Congress issued the Apology Resolution above, the Office of Hawaiian Affairs challenged state title over the ceded lands, arguing that it was the result of illegal annexation. In *Office of Hawaiian Affairs v. Housing and Community Development Corporation of Hawai`i*, 177 P.3d 884

(Hawai`i 2008) the Hawai`i Supreme Court relied on the Apology Resolution and similar state laws when it affirmed a ruling precluding the State defendants from selling or otherwise transferring to third parties any lands from the public lands trust created in the Statehood Act until the claims of the Native Hawaiians to those lands were resolved. The Hawai`i Supreme Court reasoned as follows.

> In sum, all of the aforementioned pronouncements indicate that the issue of native Hawaiian title to the ceded lands will be addressed through the political process. In this case, Congress, the Hawai`i state legislature, the parties, and the trial court all recognize (1) the cultural importance of the land to native Hawaiians, (2) that the ceded lands were illegally taken from the native Hawaiian monarchy, (3) that future reconciliation between the state and the native Hawaiian people is contemplated, and, (4) once any ceded lands are alienated from the public lands trust, they will be gone forever. For present purposes, this court need not speculate as to what a future settlement might entail—*i.e.*, whether such settlement would involve monetary payment, transfer of lands, ceded or otherwise, a combination of money and land, or the creation of a sovereign Hawaiian nation; it is enough that Congress, the legislature, and the governor have all expressed their desire to reach such a settlement. In other words, the aforementioned pronouncements as they relate and impact the plaintiffs' claim for injunctive relief clearly support the plaintiffs' position that the State has a fiduciary duty as trustee to protect the ceded lands pending a resolution of native Hawaiian claims. As such, we believe that the plaintiffs have met the first prong of the three-part test for issuance of a permanent injunction, *i.e.*, prevailing on the merits of their claim.

Id. at 923. The Supreme Court granted review.

HAWAI`I V. OFFICE OF HAWAIIAN AFFAIRS

556 U.S. 163 (2009)

ALITO, J., delivered the opinion for a unanimous Court.

This case presents the question whether Congress stripped the State of Hawaii of its authority to alienate its sovereign territory by passing a joint resolution to apologize for the role that the United States played in overthrowing the Hawaiian monarchy in the late 19th century. Relying on Congress' joint resolution, the Supreme Court of Hawaii permanently enjoined the State from alienating certain of its lands, pending resolution of native Hawaiians' land claims that the court described as "unrelinquished." We reverse.

I

In 1893, "[a] so-called Committee of Safety, a group of professionals and businessmen, with the active assistance of John Stevens, the United States Minister to Hawaii, acting with the United States Armed Forces, replaced the [Hawaiian] monarchy with a provisional government." *Rice v. Cayetano,* 528 U.S. 495, 504–505 (2000). ***

In 1959, Congress admitted Hawaii to the Union. *See* Pub.L. 86–3, 73 Stat. 4 (hereinafter Admission Act). Under the Admission Act, with exceptions not relevant here, "the United States grant[ed] to the State of Hawaii, effective upon its admission into the Union, the United States' title to all the public lands and other public property within the boundaries of the State of Hawaii, title to which is held by the United States immediately prior to its admission into the Union." § 5(b), *id.*, at 5. These lands, "together with the proceeds from the sale or other disposition of [these] lands and the income therefrom, shall be held by [the] State as a public trust" to promote various public purposes, including supporting public education, bettering conditions of Native Hawaiians, developing home ownership, making public improvements, and providing lands for public use. § 5(f), *id.*, at 6. Hawaii state law also authorizes the State to use or sell the ceded lands, provided that the proceeds are held in trust for the benefit of the citizens of Hawaii.

In 1993, Congress enacted a joint resolution "to acknowledge the historic significance of the illegal overthrow of the Kingdom of Hawaii, to express its deep regret to the Native Hawaiian people, and to support the reconciliation efforts of the State of Hawaii and the United Church of Christ with Native Hawaiians." Joint Resolution to Acknowledge the 100th Anniversary of the January 17, 1893 Overthrow of the Kingdom of Hawaii, Pub.L. 103–150, 107 Stat. 1510, 1513 (hereinafter Apology Resolution). ***

Finally, § 3 of the Apology Resolution states that "Nothing in this Joint Resolution is intended to serve as a settlement of any claims against the United States." *Id.*, at 1514.

B

This suit involves a tract of former crown land on Maui, now known as the "Leiali'i parcel," that was ceded in "absolute fee" to the United States at annexation and has been held by the State since 1959 as part of the trust established by § 5(f) of the Admission Act. The Housing Finance and Development Corporation (HFDC)—Hawaii's affordable housing agency—received approval to remove the Leiali'i parcel from the § 5(f) trust and redevelop it. In order to transfer the Leiali'i parcel out of the public trust, HFDC was required to compensate respondent Office of Hawaiian Affairs (OHA), which was established to receive and manage funds from the use or sale of the ceded lands for the benefit of native Hawaiians. Haw. Const., Art. XII, §§ 4–6.

In this case, however, OHA demanded more than monetary compensation. Relying on the Apology Resolution, respondent OHA demanded that HFDC include a disclaimer preserving any native Hawaiian claims to ownership of lands transferred from the public trust for redevelopment. HFDC declined to include the requested disclaimer because "to do so would place a cloud on title, rendering title insurance unavailable."

Again relying on the Apology Resolution, respondents then sued the State, its Governor, HFDC (since renamed), and its officials. Respondents sought "to enjoin the defendants from selling or otherwise transferring the Leiali'i parcel to third parties and selling or otherwise transferring to third parties any of the ceded lands in general until a determination of the native Hawaiians' claims to the ceded lands is made." *Office of Hawaiian Affairs v. Housing and Community Development Corp. of Hawaii,* 177 P.3d 884, 899 (2008). Respondents "alleged that an injunction was proper because, in light of the Apology

Resolution, any transfer of ceded lands by the State to third-parties would amount to a breach of trust. *** " 177 P.3d, at 898.

The state trial court entered judgment against respondents, but the Supreme Court of Hawaii vacated the lower court's ruling. Relying on a "plain reading of the Apology Resolution," which "dictate[d]" its conclusion, 177 P.3d, at 922, the State Supreme Court ordered "an injunction against the defendants from selling or otherwise transferring to third parties (1) the Leiali'i parcel and (2) any other ceded lands from the public lands trust until the claims of the native Hawaiians to the ceded lands have been resolved," 177 P.3d, at 928. In doing so, the court rejected petitioners' argument that "the State has the undoubted and explicit power to sell ceded lands pursuant to the terms of the Admission Act and pursuant to state law." 177 P.3d, at 920 (internal quotation marks and alterations omitted).

II

[Although the respondents argued that the Supreme Court had no jurisdiction because the case below was decided on state rather than federal law grounds, the Court found that the Supreme Court of Hawaii made clear that the federal Apology Resolution formed the center of the plaintiffs' legal claims, creating jurisdiction to review the decision.]

III

Turning to the merits, we must decide whether the Apology Resolution "strips Hawaii of its sovereign authority to sell, exchange, or transfer" the lands that the United States held in "absolute fee" (30 Stat. 750) and "grant[ed] to the State of Hawaii, effective upon its admission into the Union" (73 Stat. 5). We conclude that the Apology Resolution has no such effect.

A

***

The resolution's first substantive provision uses six verbs, all of which are conciliatory or precatory. Specifically, Congress "acknowledge[d] the historical significance" of the Hawaiian monarchy's overthrow, "recognize[d] and commend[ed] efforts of reconciliation" with native Hawaiians, "apologize[d] to [n]ative Hawaiians" for the monarchy's overthrow, "expresse[d] [Congress's] commitment to acknowledge the ramifications of the overthrow," and "urge[d] the President of the United States to also acknowledge the ramifications of the overthrow. *** " § 1. ***

The Apology Resolution's second and final substantive provision is a disclaimer, which provides: "Nothing in this Joint Resolution is intended to serve as a settlement of any claims against the United States." § 3. By its terms, § 3 speaks only to those who may or may not have "claims *against the United States*." The court below, however, held that the only way to save § 3 from superfluity is to construe it as a congressional recognition- and preservation-of claims *against Hawaii* and as "the *foundation* (or starting point) for reconciliation" between the State and native Hawaiians. 177 P.3d, at 902.

***

B

Rather than focusing on the operative words of the law, the court below directed its attention to the 37 "whereas" clauses that preface the Apology Resolution. *See* 107 Stat. 1510–1513. "Based on a plain reading of" the "whereas" clauses, the Supreme Court of Hawaii held that "Congress has clearly recognized that the native Hawaiian people have unrelinquished claims over the ceded lands." 177 P.3d, at 901. That conclusion is wrong for at least three reasons.

First, "whereas" clauses like those in the Apology Resolution cannot bear the weight that the lower court placed on them. ***

Second, even if the "whereas" clauses had some legal effect, they did not "chang[e] the legal landscape and restructur[e] the rights and obligations of the State." 177 P.3d, at 900. As we have emphasized, "repeals by implication are not favored and will not be presumed unless the intention of the legislature to repeal [is] clear and manifest." *National Assn. of Home Builders v. Defenders of Wildlife,* 551 U.S. 644, 662 (2007). The Apology Resolution reveals no indication—much less a "clear and manifest" one—that Congress intended to amend or repeal the State's rights and obligations under Admission Act (or any other federal law); nor does the Apology Resolution reveal any evidence that Congress intended *sub silentio* to "cloud" the title that the United States held in "absolute fee" and transferred to the State in 1959. On that score, we find it telling that even respondent OHA has now abandoned its argument, made below, that "Congress *** enacted the Apology Resolution and thus *** change[d]" the Admission Act. App. 114a. ***

Third, the Apology Resolution would raise grave constitutional concerns if it purported to "cloud" Hawaii's title to its sovereign lands more than three decades after the State's admission to the Union. We have emphasized that "Congress cannot, after statehood, reserve or convey submerged lands that have already been bestowed upon a State." *Idaho v. United States,* 533 U.S. 262, 280, n. 9, 121 S. Ct. 2135, 150 L.Ed.2d 326 (2001) (internal quotation marks and alteration omitted). *** And that proposition applies *a fortiori* where virtually all of the State's public lands—not just its submerged ones are at stake. In light of those concerns, we must not read the Apology Resolution's nonsubstantive "whereas" clauses to create a retroactive "cloud" on the title that Congress granted to the State of Hawaii in 1959. *See, e.g., Clark v. Martinez,* 543 U.S. 371, 381–382, 125 S. Ct. 716, 160 L.Ed.2d 734 (2005) (the canon of constitutional avoidance "is a tool for choosing between competing plausible interpretations of a statutory text, resting on the reasonable presumption that Congress did not intend the alternative which raises serious constitutional doubts").

When a state supreme court incorrectly bases a decision on federal law, the court's decision improperly prevents the citizens of the State from addressing the issue in question through the processes provided by the State's constitution. Here, the State Supreme Court incorrectly held that Congress, by adopting the Apology Resolution, took away from the citizens of Hawaii the authority to resolve an issue that is of great importance to the people of the State. Respondents defend that decision by arguing that they have both state-law property rights in the land in question and "broader moral and political claims for compensation for the wrongs of the past." Brief for Respondents 18. But we have no authority to decide questions of Hawaiian law or to provide redress for past wrongs except as provided for by federal law. The judgment of the Supreme Court of Hawaii is reversed, and the case is remanded for further proceedings not inconsistent with this opinion.

It is so ordered.

NOTES AND QUESTIONS

1. After the Supreme Court's ruling, the Hawai`i legislature passed an Act to "establish a more comprehensive process for the sale of state-owned land, and to reserve a larger oversight role of the legislature to assure that key information about certain sales or exchanges of land is shared with the legislature." 2009 Haw. Sess. Laws, Act 176, § 1, *codified at* Haw. Rev. Stat. 171-64.7. To accomplish that purpose, the Act requires the adoption of a concurrent resolution by at least two-thirds majority vote of each house of the legislature when the State administration sells, transfers, or exchanges ceded lands, although it has been limited in some degree by subsequent amendments. *Id.* In *Office of Hawaiian Affairs v. Housing and Community Development Corporation of Hawai`i*, 219 P.3d 1111 (Hawai`i 2009) the court dismissed a continuing challenge to the state ceded land management regime as not ripe in light of the legislation requiring a two-thirds vote to sell, transfer, or exchange ceded lands.

2. If the legislature approves the transfer of ceded lands by the required majority, could an affected party successfully challenge the transfer as a matter of state law? On what basis?

3. The Court makes an analogy to the automatic conveyance of submerged lands to a state upon its admission to the Union, which under the Equal Footing Doctrine may only be reserved by the United States through congressional action prior to statehood. *See* ch. 9, I. C., *supra*. Does that fit with the statutory conveyance by the United States of surface lands which may be burdened by aboriginal title?

B. NATIVE HAWAIIAN CLAIMS TO SOVEREIGNTY

Prior to western contact, Native Hawaiians were clearly self-governing and evolved into a kingdom that engaged in international relations with the United States and other nations during the 19th Century. The federal government, however, has never dealt with Hawaiian Natives in the same government-to-government fashion as it has with tribes in the contiguous 48 states and Alaska. At the same time, the Hawaiian Homes Commission Act of 1920, Pub. L. 67–34, 42 Stat. 108, and a number of subsequent federal laws, have recognized unique obligations to Native Hawaiians. Recall that in *Rice v. Cayetano*, Ch. 4, *supra*, the Supreme Court set aside, on Fifteenth Amendment grounds, the criterion that limited voting eligibility for the Trustees of the Office of Hawaiian Affairs to Native Hawaiians. The State (through its lawyer, now-Supreme Court Chief Justice John Roberts) argued that the voting limitation was not racially-based, but rather premised upon the status of Native

Hawaiians as a politically-based classification. The Court avoided addressing the argument:

> The most far reaching of the State's arguments is that exclusion of non-Hawaiians from voting is permitted under our cases allowing the differential treatment of certain members of Indian tribes. The decisions of this Court, interpreting the effect of treaties and congressional enactments on the subject, have held that various tribes retained some elements of quasi-sovereign authority, even after cession of their lands to the United States. See *Brendale v. Confederated Tribes and Bands of Yakima Nation*, 492 U.S. 408, 425 (1989) (plurality opinion); *Oliphant v. Suquamish Tribe*, 435 U.S. 191, 208 (1978). The retained tribal authority relates to self-governance. *Brendale*, *supra*, at 425 (plurality opinion). In reliance on that theory the Court has sustained a federal provision giving employment preferences to persons of tribal ancestry. *Mancari*, 417 U.S., at 553–555. The *Mancari* case, and the theory upon which it rests, are invoked by the State to defend its decision to restrict voting for the OHA trustees, who are charged so directly with protecting the interests of native Hawaiians.
>
> If Hawaii's restriction were to be sustained under *Mancari* we would be required to accept some beginning premises not yet established in our case law. Among other postulates, it would be necessary to conclude that Congress, in reciting the purposes for the transfer of lands to the State—and in other enactments such as the Hawaiian Homes Commission Act and the Joint Resolution of 1993—has determined that native Hawaiians have a status like that of Indians in organized tribes, and that it may, and has, delegated to the State a broad authority to preserve that status. These propositions would raise questions of considerable moment and difficulty. It is a matter of some dispute, for instance, whether Congress may treat the native Hawaiians as it does the Indian tribes. *Compare* Van Dyke, *The Political Status of the Native Hawaiian People*, 17 Yale L. & Pol'y Rev. 95 (1998), *with* Benjamin, *Equal Protection and the Special Relationship: The Case of Native Hawaiians*, 106 Yale L.J. 537 (1996). We can stay far off that difficult terrain, however.
>
> The State's argument fails for a more basic reason. Even were we to take the substantial step of finding authority in Congress, delegated to the State, to treat Hawaiians or native Hawaiians as tribes, Congress may not authorize a State to create a voting scheme of this sort.

Rice v. Cayetano, 528 U.S. 495, 518–519 (2000).

In the years since the Supreme Court's decision, Congress repeatedly considered legislation to recognize a sovereign Native Hawaiian government and allow Native Hawaiians to organize such a government according to their wishes. In 2010 the House passed a bill to provide a process for the reorganization of the Native Hawaiian government as well as to recognize a government-to-government relationship between the United States and the Native Hawaiian government. The bill set forth provisions such as:

- Qualified Native Hawaiian Constituent: the bill establishes criteria for determining who is a qualified Native Hawaiian constituent for the purposes of establishing a membership and voting roll. The provision includes various criteria such as certifying that the individual is (1) a direct lineal descendant of the aboriginal, indigenous native people who resided in Hawai`i prior to statehood and that the individual has (2) maintained a significant cultural, social, or civic connection to the Native Hawaiian community, such as by residing in the State of Hawai`i or has been a member of at least one Native Hawaiian membership organization.

- Negotiations: the bill provided that upon reaffirmation of the relationship between the United States and the Native Hawaiian government, the United States and the State of Hawai`i can enter into negotiations with the Native Hawaiian government addressing matters such as (1) the transfer of State of Hawai`i lands, surplus Federal lands, and natural resources (2) the exercise of civil and criminal jurisdiction (3) the exercise of authority to tax and (4) grievances regarding assertions of historical wrongs committed against Native Hawaiians by the United States or by the State of Hawai`i.
- Governmental Authority: the bill clarifies that the Native Hawaiian government shall be vested with the inherent powers and privileges of self-government of a native government under existing law, with the exception of certain federal laws such as the Indian Gaming Regulatory Act (IGRA). The bill's provisions state that the Native Hawaiian government and Native Hawaiians may not conduct gaming activities as a matter of claimed inherent authority or under the authority of IGRA. The bill also states that the Indian Trade and Intercourse Act, 25 U.S.C. § 177, is inapplicable to any purchase, grant, lease, title, or other conveyance of lands from Native Hawaiians that occurred prior to the date of the United States' recognition of the Native Hawaiian government.

Native Hawaiian Government Reorganization Act, H.R. 2314, 111th Cong. (2010); S. 675, 112th Cong. (2011). The bill failed to pass in the Senate and has yet to be proposed again.

NOTES AND QUESTIONS

1. *Constitutionality.* Does Congress have the power to recognize Native Hawaiians as an "Indian tribe" under federal law? The Court in *Rice v. Cayetano* called it "difficult ground." What would *United States v. Sandoval, supra* ch. 4, indicate? If *Sandoval* does not control, what authority governs Congress's power to recognize indigenous peoples as tribes with a government-to-government relationship with the United States?

2. *Political strategy.* When an earlier version of the 2010 Bill, H.R. 505, passed the House in 2007 the Office of Management and Budget, which speaks for the White House on most legislative matters, issued a "Statement of Administration Policy" on October 22, 2007 on behalf of the Bush Administration:

> The Administration strongly opposes passage of H.R. 505. As the U.S. Civil Rights Commission recently noted, this legislation "would discriminate on the basis of race or national origin and further subdivide the American people into discrete subgroups according to varying degrees of

privilege." *** *If H.R. 505 were presented to the President, his senior advisors would recommend that he veto the bill.* ***

Given the substantial historical and cultural differences between Native Hawaiians as a group and members of federally recognized Indian tribes, the Administration believes that tribal recognition is inappropriate and unwise for Native Hawaiians and would raise serious constitutional concerns.

If you were an advocate for Native Hawaiians in favor of the Bill, how would you counter these arguments?

3. Native Hawaiians cannot seek federal recognition as a tribe through the administrative process set forth in 25 C.F.R. Part 83, under which most unrecognized groups pursue federal acknowledgement. The regulations provide that they apply "only to those American Indian groups indigenous to the continental United States which are not currently acknowledged as Indian tribes by the Department," 25 C.F.R. § 83.3(a), and define the "continental United States" as the "contiguous 48 states and Alaska." 25 C.F.R. § 83.1. As noted in a Ninth Circuit opinion, by these regulations "the Department of Interior was hanging out a sign that said: 'No Hawaiians need apply.'" *Kawaiiola v. Norton*, 386 F.3d 1271, 1274 (9th Cir. 2004). The court nevertheless held that the regulations were constitutional, finding that the relationship between the United States and Indian tribes was historically political, rather than race-based, and that the decision whether to enter into a government-to-government relationship with an indigenous group was at the core of this kind of political decision-making. *Id.* at 1278. The regulations were thus subject to the rational basis review articulated in *Morton v. Mancari* rather than strict scrutiny. *Id.* Given the distinctive history and relationship of the United States with Native Hawaiians, the court found that the decision to exclude them from the acknowledgement regulations passed this rational basis test. *Id.* at 1281–1283.

The Department of the Interior may be having a change of heart. The Department adopted a final rule, effective November 14, 2016, which establishes a process for the Native Hawaiian government to seek a formal relationship with the federal government:

> The final rule sets forth an administrative procedure and criteria that the Secretary would use if the Native Hawaiian community forms a unified government that then seeks a formal government-to-government relationship with the United States. The rule does not provide a process for reorganizing a Native Hawaiian government. The decision to reorganize a Native Hawaiian government and to establish a formal government-to-government relationship is for the Native Hawaiian community to make as an exercise of self-determination.
>
> Congress already federally acknowledged or recognized the Native Hawaiian community by establishing a special political and trust relationship through over 150 enactments. This unique special political and trust relationship exists even though Native Hawaiians have not had an organized government since the overthrow of the Kingdom of Hawaii in 1893. Accordingly, this rule provides a process and criteria for reestablishing a formal government-to-government relationship that would enable a reorganized Native Hawaiian government to represent the Native Hawaiian

community and conduct government-to-government relations with the United States under the Constitution and applicable Federal law. The term "formal government-togovernment relationship" in this rule refers to the working relationship with the United States that will occur if the Native Hawaiian community reorganizes and submits a request consistent with the rule's criteria.

Importantly, the process set out in this rule is optional and Federal action will occur only upon an express, formal request from the reorganized Native Hawaiian government. The rule also provides a process for public comment on the request and a process for the Secretary to receive, evaluate, and act on the request.

Procedures for Reestablishing a Government-to-Government Relationship With the Native Hawaiian Community, 81 Fed. Reg. 71278 (2016) (codified at 43 C.F.R. pt. 50).

Prior to the issuance of the Final Rule, the Advanced Notice of Proposed Rulemaking stated that the Secretary was seeking comments solely on five threshold questions:

- Should the Secretary propose an administrative rule that would facilitate the reestablishment of a government-to-government relationship with the Native Hawaiian community?
- Should the Secretary assist the Native Hawaiian community in reorganizing its government, with which the United States could reestablish a government-to-government relationship?
- If so, what process should be established for drafting and ratifying a reorganized Native Hawaiian government's constitution or other governing document?
- Should the Secretary instead rely on the reorganization of a Native Hawaiian government through a process established by the Native Hawaiian community and facilitated by the State of Hawaii, to the extent such a process is consistent with Federal law?
- If so, what conditions should the Secretary establish as prerequisites to Federal acknowledgment of a government-to-government relationship with the reorganized Native Hawaiian government?

Procedures for Reestablishing a Government-to-Government Relationship With the Native Hawaiian Community, 79 Fed. Reg. 35297 (2014). How would you answer these questions?

In summarizing the public comments received on the ANPRM, the Department stated that numerous commenters expressed support for the rule in its effort to help the Native Hawaiian community achieve parity in Federal policy compared to other indigenous communities in the United States. Additionally, commenters highlighted potential benefits to a government-to-government relationship, for example by enabling more direct management of assets and resources by Native Hawaiians in accordance with customary and traditional practices. Many commenters also expressed opposition to the rule, with comments ranging from the rule being impermissibly race-based to discontent that the reestablishment of the formal government-to-government relationship does not affect the title or status of Federal lands in Hawai`i.

Procedures for Reestablishing a Government-to-Government Relationship With the Native Hawaiian Community, 81 Fed. Reg. 71293 (2016). Crucially, federal action will only occur once a request is made by a reorganized Native Hawaiian government. What are the benefits and downsides to a formal government-to-government relationship?

4. The preamble to the Final Rule proclaims that "Congress already federally acknowledged or recognized the Native Hawaiian community by establishing a special political and trust relationship through over 150 enactments. This unique special political and trust relationship exists even though Native Hawaiians have not had an organized government since the overthrow of the Kingdom of Hawaii in 1893." Note 1, *supra*. Do you think a court will view that statement as binding when considering current legislation making Hawaiians eligible for various federal programs available to members of federally recognized tribes? Remember that the Supreme Court has stated: "In reference to [federal recognition], it is the rule of this court to follow the action of the executive and other political departments of the government, whose more special duty it is to determine such affairs. If by them those Indians are recognized as a tribe, this court must do the same. If they are a tribe of Indians, then, by the Constitution of the United States, they are placed, for certain purposes, within the control of the laws of Congress." *United States v. Holliday*, 70 U.S. 407, 419 (1865).

5. *Education for Native Hawaiians* The unique status of Native Hawaiians has raised difficult questions in the context of schools too. Recall that in *Morton v. Mancari*, the Court held that classifications based on American Indians tribes' political status are not subject to strict scrutiny under the equal protection clause. *See* ch. 4. In *Rice*, the Court avoided the equal protection question, holding instead that the 15th Amendment dictated the outcome in that case. The Kamehameha schools, founded in 1887, have an admissions policy that favors those with Native Hawaiian ancestry. The policy has been repeatedly challenged as discriminatory, on various legal grounds. In the latest case, the Ninth Circuit rejected a federal civil rights law claim in a narrow 8–7 *en banc* opinion. *See Doe v. Kamehameha Schools/Bernice Pauahi Bishop Estate*, 470 F.3d 827 (9th Cir. 2006). For further discussion on the Kamehameha Schools, *see* Melody Kapilialoha MacKenzie, et al., Native Hawaiian Law: A Treatise, Ch. 5: Native Hawaiians and U.S. Law (2015).

CHAPTER 13

INDIGENOUS PEOPLES' RIGHTS IN INTERNATIONAL AND COMPARATIVE CONTEXTS

■ ■ ■

Federal Indian law was, at its origins, a creature of the law of nations. As the materials in Chapters 2–3 make clear, nascent concepts of international law were used to justify the taking of Indian lands and the assertion of power over Indian peoples, even while these concepts also recognized some measure of Indian autonomy. This was true in the early stages of European arrival and treaty-making, but also in Chief Justice Marshall's self-consciously uncomfortable acceptance of the discovery doctrine in his trilogy. *See* S. James Anaya, Indigenous Peoples in International Law 23–26 (1996). The use of international law to justify unilateral assumptions of federal authority simultaneously embedded and excused norms of dominance and racial superiority. *See* Robert A. Williams, Jr., *Columbus's Legacy: Law as an Instrument of Racial Discrimination*, 8 Ariz. J. Int'l & Comp. L. 51, 67–74 (1991). Yet in contemporary times, indigenous peoples, through activism, legal advocacy, and persistent and patient politics, are shaping international law into something more redeeming. Indigenous peoples have taken the core notion of nations being bound by laws generated beyond their jurisdictional boundaries and transformed that idea into concrete expressions of international commitment, as well as positive law binding on individual countries. *See* Kristen A. Carpenter & Angela R. Riley, *Indigenous Peoples and the Jurisgenerative Moment in International Human Rights*, 102 Cal. L. Rev. 173 (2014).

This chapter first describes the international human rights framework for indigenous peoples, and then turns to the development of indigenous rights law in other countries.

I. INDIGENOUS RIGHTS IN INTERNATIONAL LAW

The most exciting development for indigenous peoples in the international law arena has been the growing recognition of group or community rights. In particular, the adoption by the United Nations General Assembly of the United Nations Declaration on the Rights of Indigenous Peoples was the culmination of more than two decades of work and activism by indigenous communities throughout the world:

> The UN General Assembly's adoption of the UN Declaration on the Rights of Indigenous Peoples on September 13, 2007 marked the end of a long journey, a milestone in the long and arduous march of what have come to be known as "indigenous peoples" through the major institution of organized intergovernmental society: the United Nations. It was a day

of celebration for indigenous leaders and their rank and file scattered around the globe, united in a common fate of conquest, dispossession, marginalization and neglect, but also in the joy of rising again.

When the United Nations Working Group on Indigenous Populations was established in 1982, one of its key missions was the establishment of a declaration of rights of indigenous peoples. Indigenous peoples from around the world trekked to the Palais des Nations in Geneva each summer afterwards to articulate their claims to the members of the Working Group and state delegations. In 1993, under the inspirational leadership of long-time Chairperson Mrs. Erica–Irene Daes, agreement was reached by the Working Group on a "Draft Declaration on the Rights of Indigenous Peoples." This draft became the basis for discussion within the UN Commission on Human Rights, which was replaced in 2006 by the Human Rights Council. In its first substantive decision, the Council on June 29, 2006, by a vote of 30 in favor, 2 against and 12 abstentions, adopted a revised text of the Declaration, and passed it on to the General Assembly for its final approval.

S. James Anaya & Siegfried Wiessner, *The UN Declaration on the Rights of Indigenous Peoples: Towards Re-empowerment*, Jurist Legal News & Research, Univ. of Pittsburgh School of Law (Oct. 3, 2007), http://jurist.law.pitt.edu/forumy/2007/10/un-declaration-on-rights-of-indigenous.php.

Review the Declaration carefully. Do rights that American Indian tribes possess map onto some of the Declaration's provisions? Are there any provisions that seem inconsistent with statements of U.S. law?

Note that although the Declaration was developed by the group originally called the "Working Group on Indigenous Populations" the Declaration concerns "Indigenous Peoples." This change was important to the indigenous participants in the working group meetings. What is the significance of the different words? Also note that Article 3 declares the right of indigenous peoples to "self-determination." The decision to include Article 3 in the 1993 Draft Declaration met with a standing ovation from indigenous participants. Dr. Erica–Irene A. Daes, *The Concepts of Self–Determination and Autonomy of Indigenous Peoples in the Draft United Nations Declaration on the Rights of Indigenous Peoples*, 14 St. Thomas L. Rev. 259, 261 (2001). But governmental concern about this principle was a significant factor leading to the long delay before the Declaration was finally approved. *Id.* at 262. How does the Declaration define self-determination? Why was this term so important to the indigenous participants?

UNITED NATIONS DECLARATION ON THE RIGHTS OF INDIGENOUS PEOPLES

June 29, 2006

The Human Rights Council,

Affirming that indigenous peoples are equal to all other peoples, while recognizing the right of all peoples to be different, to consider themselves different, and to be respected as such,

***

Solemnly proclaims the following United Nations Declaration on the Rights of Indigenous Peoples as a standard of achievement to be pursued in a spirit of partnership and mutual respect:

Article 1

Indigenous peoples have the right to the full enjoyment, as a collective or as individuals, of all human rights and fundamental freedoms as recognized in the Charter of the United Nations, the Universal Declaration of Human Rights and international human rights law.

Article 2

Indigenous peoples and individuals are free and equal to all other peoples and individuals and have the right to be free from any kind of discrimination, in the exercise of their rights, in particular that based on their indigenous origin or identity.

Article 3

Indigenous peoples have the right to self-determination. By virtue of that right they freely determine their political status and freely pursue their economic, social and cultural development.

Article 4

Indigenous peoples, in exercising their right to self-determination, have the right to autonomy or self-government in matters relating to their internal and local affairs, as well as ways and means for financing their autonomous functions.

Article 5

Indigenous peoples have the right to maintain and strengthen their distinct political, legal, economic, social and cultural institutions, while retaining their right to participate fully, if they so choose, in the political, economic, social and cultural life of the State.

Article 6

Every indigenous individual has the right to a nationality.

Article 7

1. Indigenous individuals have the rights to life, physical and mental integrity, liberty and security of person.

2. Indigenous peoples have the collective right to live in freedom, peace and security as distinct peoples and shall not be subjected to any act of genocide or any other act of violence, including forcibly removing children of the group to another group.

Article 8

1. Indigenous peoples and individuals have the right not to be subjected to forced assimilation or destruction of their culture.

2. States shall provide effective mechanisms for prevention of, and redress for [any actions depriving them of rights outlined herein].

***

Article 9

Indigenous peoples and individuals have the right to belong to an indigenous community or nation, in accordance with the traditions and customs of the community or nation concerned. No discrimination of any kind may arise from the exercise of such a right.

Article 10

Indigenous peoples shall not be forcibly removed from their lands or territories. No relocation shall take place without the free, prior and informed consent of the indigenous peoples concerned and after agreement on just and fair compensation and, where possible, with the option of return.

Article 11

1. Indigenous peoples have the right to practise and revitalize their cultural traditions and customs. This includes the right to maintain, protect and develop the past, present and future manifestations of their cultures, such as archaeological and historical sites, artefacts, designs, ceremonies, technologies and visual and performing arts and literature.

2. States shall provide redress through effective mechanisms, which may include restitution, developed in conjunction with indigenous peoples, with respect to their cultural, intellectual, religious and spiritual property taken without their free, prior and informed consent or in violation of their laws, traditions and customs.

Article 12

1. Indigenous peoples have the right to manifest, practise, develop and teach their spiritual and religious traditions, customs and ceremonies; the right to maintain, protect and have access in privacy to their religious and cultural sites; the right to the use and control of their ceremonial objects; and the right to the repatriation of their human remains.

2. States shall seek to enable the access and/or repatriation of ceremonial objects and human remains in their possession through fair, transparent and effective mechanisms developed in conjunction with indigenous peoples concerned.

Article 13

1. Indigenous peoples have the right to revitalize, use, develop and transmit to future generations their histories, languages, oral traditions,

philosophies, writing systems and literatures, and to designate and retain their own names for communities, places and persons.

2. States shall take effective measures to ensure that this right is protected and also to ensure that indigenous peoples can understand and be understood in political, legal and administrative proceedings, where necessary through the provision of interpretation or by other appropriate means.

Article 14

1. Indigenous peoples have the right to establish and control their educational systems and institutions providing education in their own languages, in a manner appropriate to their cultural methods of teaching and learning.

2. Indigenous individuals, particularly children, have the right to all levels and forms of education of the State without discrimination.

3. States shall, in conjunction with indigenous peoples, take effective measures, in order for indigenous individuals, particularly children, including those living outside their communities, to have access, when possible, to an education in their own culture and provided in their own language.

Article 15

1. Indigenous peoples have the right to the dignity and diversity of their cultures, traditions, histories and aspirations which shall be appropriately reflected in education and public information.

2. States shall take effective measures, in consultation and cooperation with the indigenous peoples concerned, to combat prejudice and eliminate discrimination and to promote tolerance, understanding and good relations among indigenous peoples and all other segments of society.

Article 16

1. Indigenous peoples have the right to establish their own media in their own languages and to have access to all forms of non-indigenous media without discrimination.

2. States shall take effective measures to ensure that State-owned media duly reflect indigenous cultural diversity. States, without prejudice to ensuring full freedom of expression, should encourage privately owned media to adequately reflect indigenous cultural diversity.

Article 17

1. Indigenous individuals and peoples have the right to enjoy fully all rights established under applicable international and domestic labour law.

2. States shall, in consultation and cooperation with indigenous peoples, take specific measures to protect indigenous children from economic exploitation and from performing any work that is likely to be hazardous or to interfere with the child's education, or to be harmful to the child's health or physical, mental, spiritual, moral or social development, taking into account their special vulnerability and the importance of education for their empowerment.

3. Indigenous individuals have the right not to be subjected to any discriminatory conditions of labour and, *inter alia*, employment or salary.

Article 18

Indigenous peoples have the right to participate in decision-making in matters which would affect their rights, through representatives chosen by themselves in accordance with their own procedures, as well as to maintain and develop their own indigenous decision-making institutions.

Article 19

States shall consult and cooperate in good faith with the indigenous peoples concerned through their own representative institutions in order to obtain their free, prior and informed consent before adopting and implementing legislative or administrative measures that may affect them.

Article 20

1. Indigenous peoples have the right to maintain and develop their political, economic and social systems or institutions, to be secure in the enjoyment of their own means of subsistence and development, and to engage freely in all their traditional and other economic activities.

2. Indigenous peoples deprived of their means of subsistence and development are entitled to just and fair redress.

Article 21

1. Indigenous peoples have the right, without discrimination, to the improvement of their economic and social conditions, including, *inter alia*, in the areas of education, employment, vocational training and retraining, housing, sanitation, health and social security.

2. States shall take effective measures and, where appropriate, special measures to ensure continuing improvement of their economic and social conditions. Particular attention shall be paid to the rights and special needs of indigenous elders, women, youth, children and persons with disabilities.

Article 22

1. Particular attention shall be paid to the rights and special needs of indigenous elders, women, youth, children and persons with disabilities in the implementation of this Declaration.

2. States shall take measures, in conjunction with indigenous peoples, to ensure that indigenous women and children enjoy the full protection and guarantees against all forms of violence and discrimination.

Article 23

Indigenous peoples have the right to determine and develop priorities and strategies for exercising their right to development. In particular, indigenous peoples have the right to be actively involved in developing and determining health, housing and other economic and social programmes affecting them and, as far as possible, to administer such programmes through their own institutions.

Article 24

1. Indigenous peoples have the right to their traditional medicines and to maintain their health practices, including the conservation of their vital medicinal plants, animals and minerals. Indigenous individuals also have the right to access, without any discrimination, to all social and health services.

2. Indigenous individuals have an equal right to the enjoyment of the highest attainable standard of physical and mental health. States shall take the necessary steps with a view to achieving progressively the full realization of this right.

Article 25

Indigenous peoples have the right to maintain and strengthen their distinctive spiritual relationship with their traditionally owned or otherwise occupied and used lands, territories, waters and coastal seas and other resources and to uphold their responsibilities to future generations in this regard.

Article 26

1. Indigenous peoples have the right to the lands, territories and resources which they have traditionally owned, occupied or otherwise used or acquired.

2. Indigenous peoples have the right to own, use, develop and control the lands, territories and resources that they possess by reason of traditional ownership or other traditional occupation or use, as well as those which they have otherwise acquired.

3. States shall give legal recognition and protection to these lands, territories and resources. Such recognition shall be conducted with due respect to the customs, traditions and land tenure systems of the indigenous peoples concerned.

Article 27

States shall establish and implement, in conjunction with indigenous peoples concerned, a fair, independent, impartial, open and transparent process, giving due recognition to indigenous peoples' laws, traditions, customs and land tenure systems, to recognize and adjudicate the rights of indigenous peoples pertaining to their lands, territories and resources, including those which were traditionally owned or otherwise occupied or used. Indigenous peoples shall have the right to participate in this process.

Article 28

1. Indigenous peoples have the right to redress, by means that can include restitution or, when this is not possible, just, fair and equitable compensation, for the lands, territories and resources which they have traditionally owned or otherwise occupied or used, and which have been confiscated, taken, occupied, used or damaged without their free, prior and informed consent.

2. Unless otherwise freely agreed upon by the peoples concerned, compensation shall take the form of lands, territories and resources equal in quality, size and legal status or of monetary compensation or other appropriate redress.

Article 29

1. Indigenous peoples have the right to the conservation and protection of the environment and the productive capacity of their lands or territories and resources. States shall establish and implement assistance programmes for indigenous peoples for such conservation and protection, without discrimination.

2. States shall take effective measures to ensure that no storage or disposal of hazardous materials shall take place in the lands or territories of indigenous peoples without their free, prior and informed consent.

3. States shall also take effective measures to ensure, as needed, that programmes for monitoring, maintaining and restoring the health of indigenous peoples, as developed and implemented by the peoples affected by such materials, are duly implemented.

Article 30

1. Military activities shall not take place in the lands or territories of indigenous peoples, unless justified by a significant threat to relevant public interest or otherwise freely agreed with or requested by the indigenous peoples concerned.

***

Article 31

1. Indigenous peoples have the right to maintain, control, protect and develop their cultural heritage, traditional knowledge and traditional cultural expressions, as well as the manifestations of their sciences, technologies and cultures, including human and genetic resources, seeds, medicines, knowledge of the properties of fauna and flora, oral traditions, literatures, designs, sports and traditional games and visual and performing arts. They also have the right to maintain, control, protect and develop their intellectual property over such cultural heritage, traditional knowledge, and traditional cultural expressions.

2. In conjunction with indigenous peoples, States shall take effective measures to recognize and protect the exercise of these rights.

Article 32

1. Indigenous peoples have the right to determine and develop priorities and strategies for the development or use of their lands or territories and other resources.

2. States shall consult and cooperate in good faith with the indigenous peoples concerned through their own representative institutions in order to obtain their free and informed consent prior to the approval of any project affecting their lands or territories and other resources, particularly in connection with the development, utilization or exploitation of their mineral, water or other resources.

3. States shall provide effective mechanisms for just and fair redress for any such activities, and appropriate measures shall be taken to mitigate adverse environmental, economic, social, cultural or spiritual impact.

Article 33

1. Indigenous peoples have the right to determine their own identity or membership in accordance with their customs and traditions. This does not impair the right of indigenous individuals to obtain citizenship of the States in which they live.

2. Indigenous peoples have the right to determine the structures and to select the membership of their institutions in accordance with their own procedures.

Article 34

Indigenous peoples have the right to promote, develop and maintain their institutional structures and their distinctive customs, spirituality, traditions, procedures, practices and, in the cases where they exist, juridical systems or customs, in accordance with international human rights standards.

Article 35

Indigenous peoples have the right to determine the responsibilities of individuals to their communities.

Article 36

1. Indigenous peoples, in particular those divided by international borders, have the right to maintain and develop contacts, relations and cooperation, including activities for spiritual, cultural, political, economic and social purposes, with their own members as well as other peoples across borders.

2. States, in consultation and cooperation with indigenous peoples, shall take effective measures to facilitate the exercise and ensure the implementation of this right.

Article 37

1. Indigenous peoples have the right to the recognition, observance and enforcement of treaties, agreements and other constructive arrangements concluded with States or their successors and to have States honour and respect such treaties, agreements and other constructive arrangements.

2. Nothing in this Declaration may be interpreted as diminishing or eliminating the rights of indigenous peoples contained in treaties, agreements and other constructive arrangements.

Article 38

States, in consultation and cooperation with indigenous peoples, shall take the appropriate measures, including legislative measures, to achieve the ends of this Declaration.

Article 39

Indigenous peoples have the right to have access to financial and technical assistance from States and through international cooperation, for the enjoyment of the rights contained in this Declaration.

Article 40

Indigenous peoples have the right to access to and prompt decision through just and fair procedures for the resolution of conflicts and disputes with States or other parties, as well as to effective remedies for all infringements of their individual and collective rights. Such a decision shall give due consideration to the customs, traditions, rules and legal systems of the indigenous peoples concerned and international human rights.

Article 41

The organs and specialized agencies of the United Nations system and other intergovernmental organizations shall contribute to the full realization of the provisions of this Declaration through the mobilization, *inter alia*, of financial cooperation and technical assistance. Ways and means of ensuring participation of indigenous peoples on issues affecting them shall be established.

Article 42

The United Nations, its bodies, including the Permanent Forum on Indigenous Issues, and specialized agencies, including at the country level, and States shall promote respect for and full application of the provisions of this Declaration and follow up the effectiveness of this Declaration.

Article 43

The rights recognized herein constitute the minimum standards for the survival, dignity and well-being of the indigenous peoples of the world.

Article 44

All the rights and freedoms recognized herein are equally guaranteed to male and female indigenous individuals.

Article 45

Nothing in this Declaration may be construed as diminishing or extinguishing the rights indigenous peoples have now or may acquire in the future.

Article 46

1. Nothing in this Declaration may be interpreted as implying for any State, people, group or person any right to engage in any activity or to perform any act contrary to the Charter of the United Nations.

2. In the exercise of the rights enunciated in the present Declaration, human rights and fundamental freedoms of all shall be respected. The exercise of the rights set forth in this Declaration shall be subject only to such limitations as are determined by law, in accordance with international human rights obligations. Any such limitations shall be non-discriminatory and strictly necessary solely for the purpose of securing due recognition and respect for the rights and freedoms of others and for meeting the just and most compelling requirements of a democratic society.

3. The provisions set forth in this Declaration shall be interpreted in accordance with the principles of justice, democracy, respect for human rights, equality, non-discrimination, good governance and good faith.

NOTES AND QUESTIONS

1. *The U.N. Declaration's Enforceability.* There are two major types of international law—international instruments setting forth expressly agreed upon standards, and international customary law. With regard to the first type, the instruments come in two groupings: (1) treaties, conventions, covenants and other agreements that are legally binding in countries that have ratified them; (2) declarations, resolutions, and other non-binding statements that have moral, but not necessarily legal, force in countries to which they apply. International customary law is legally binding on nations, and consists of rules originating in international custom. Yet nations are only bound by those rules of international customary law that they believe themselves obligated to follow. Like common law more generally, United States courts consider, discern, and then accept or reject a particular norm as meeting the standards for enforceability. There is interplay between the two major types of international law, in that norms codified in binding or non-binding instruments may then become the basis of enforceable international customary law.

The U.N. Declaration on the Rights of Indigenous Peoples (UNDRIP) falls into the second category of instruments, and is therefore not binding on nations. Nonetheless, many of the rights recognized in the Declaration are arguably within the realm of internationally accepted customs that should be binding as principles of international customary law. *See* S. James Anaya, International Human Rights and Indigenous Peoples 98–104 (2009). Professor Anaya has argued that the Declaration's provisions recognizing rights to the preservation of culture, language, religion and identity have the requisite level of international consensus. *See id.* at 100. Likewise, the provisions supporting political and economic self-determination as well as land rights reflect customary norms and practices. *See id.* at 100–01. "Furthermore, no state opposed the provision of the Declaration that mandates the observance of treaties between states and indigenous peoples." *Id.* at 101. Do you agree that there is widespread international support for the foregoing norms? Do you think United States courts could be persuaded to agree? What aspects of federal Indian law could you draw on to support or oppose these arguments? For a brief history of the development of the Declaration by one of the key participants, see Robert T. Coulter, *The U.N. Declaration on the Rights of Indigenous Peoples: A Historic Change in International Law*, 45 Idaho L. Rev. 539 (2009).

2. *The votes against the U.N. Declaration.* The United States was one of only four countries voting against it, along with Australia, New Zealand and Canada. (Eleven other countries abstained.) Within a few years, however, Australia, New Zealand, Canada, and finally, in 2010, the United States, all endorsed the Declaration. Two of the states that had initially abstained, Colombia and Samoa, also have since endorsed the declaration. In its statement of support, the United States announced that the Declaration

> [W]hile not legally binding or a statement of current international law—has both moral and political force ... [T]he Declaration] expresses aspirations of the United States, aspirations that this country seeks to achieve within the structure of the United States Constitution, laws, and international obligations, while also seeking, where appropriate, to improve our laws and policies. U.S. Support for the Declaration goes hand in hand with the U.S. commitment to address the consequences of a history in which,

> as President Obama recognized, "few have been more marginalized and ignored by Washington as long as Native Americans—our First Americans."

Announcement of U.S. Statement of Support for the United Nations Declaration on the Rights of Indigenous Peoples, http://www.state.gov/r/pa/prs/ps/.

Do these shifts in position lend further support to Professor Anaya's arguments that many of the rights embodied in the Declaration have the status of customary international law? Or do the numerous qualifications in statements like that of the United States indicate the opposite? As UN Special Rapporteur on the Rights of Indigenous Peoples, Anaya firmly disagreed that the Declaration is non-binding or solely aspirational. S. James Anaya, Report of the Special Rapporteur on the Rights of Indigenous Peoples 4 (August 2013),http://unsr.jamesanaya.org/annual-reports/report-to-the-general-assembly-a-68-317-14-august-2013.

New Zealand Delegation to the Ninth United Nations Forum on Indigenous Issues celebrates New Zealand's endorsement of the Declaration (2010), by Broddi Sigurðarson, Creative Commons License.

3. *Implementation of UNDRIP.* Although not directly enforceable, the UNDRIP has already shaped domestic laws and practice. As early as 2007, the high court of Belize extensively discussed UNDRIP in finding that the government failed to sufficiently protect Maya lands and illegally granted concessions for oil exploration of those lands. *Cal v. Attorney General* (Belize, 2007). The court's decision was based largely on the Belize Constitution, yet the court noted that although UN Declarations were "not ordinarily binding on member states ... where these resolutions or Declarations contain principles of general international law, states are not expected to disregard them." Observing that the declaration was adopted by an "overwhelming number" of states, including Belize, the Court found that the "Declaration, embodying as it does, general

principles of international law relating to indigenous peoples and their lands and resources, is of such force that the defendants, representing the Government of Belize, will not disregard it." *Id.* at ¶¶ 131–133. In 2013, the Indonesian Constitutional Court similarly relied on UNDRIP to find that the government's action in asserting ownership of forests customarily used by indigenous peoples and evicting them from their traditional lands violated the Indonesian Constitution. Decision No. 35/PUU-X/2012.

UNDRIP may also affect decisions by regional human rights tribunals. In 2010, the African Commission on Human and Peoples' Rights issued a landmark decision recognizing for the first time indigenous peoples' rights over traditionally owned land. The decision found human rights violations in Kenya's 1973 eviction of the Endorois people from their ancestral lands for the creation of the Lake Bogoria National Reserve, ordering restitution of lands, free access to the Reserve, and adequate monetary compensation. Although the decision was based on the African Charter of Human Rights, the tribunal relied both on UNDRIP (which Kenya had declined to approve) and other UN and regional human rights instruments and decisions in interpreting the African Charter. *See Ctr. for Minority Rights Development v. Kenya*, No. 276/2003 (2010), http://www.achpr.org/communications/decision/276.03/.

Judicial decisions are not the only or even the primary influence of the UNDRIP on domestic law and practice. Some countries have implemented the UNDRIP by amending their constitutions. *See, e.g.*, Const. of Bolivia, Pt. I, Title II, ch. IV (Rights of the Nations and Rural Native Indigeouns Peoples); Const. of Ecuador, Art. 11, § 3 (incorporating rights and guarantees in international human rights instruments). Other nations have enacted legislation recognizing indigenous rights. Japan, for example, recognized the Ainu as an indigenous people for the first time several months after approving the Declaration. It was likely not a coincidence that the legislation came just a few weeks before Japan hosted a conference on indigenous peoples in Hokkaido, the traditional Ainu homeland. Norimutsu Orishi, *Recognition for a People Who Faded as Japan Grew*, New York Times, July 3, 2008. In all of these developments, however, implementation of declared legal rights is a continuing challenge.

4. *Role of the Special Rapporteur.* The UN Special Rapporteur on the Rights of Indigenous Peoples can also influence implementation of principles consistent with UNDRIP. The Rapporteur has authority to make official investigations and country visits, issue annual reports to the General Assembly, and request that countries remediate human rights violations. For example, by working with the Ecuadoran Assembly during its constitutional revision, the Rapporteur helped produce "one of the most progressive constitutions in the world" on indigenous peoples rights. Report of the Special Rapporteur,http://unsr.jamesanaya.org/annual-reports/report-to-the-general-assembly-a-68-317-14-august-2013. In another instance, the Rapporteur was able to arrange a consultation between indigenous peoples and legislative bodies in Asian countries that had not yet recognized the existence of indigenous peoples within their borders. *Id.*

In a 2017 report, the Special Rapporteur examined the relationship between climate change and the rights of indigenous peoples. The report addressed the role that indigenous peoples can play in mitigation and adaption, as well as the unique and disproportionate vulnerabilities of indigenous peoples to climate change impacts. The report described how the UNDRIP principles should be implemented to address these concerns, working within the framework of other international law instruments. *See* 2017 Report of the Special Rapporteur on the Rights of Indigenous Peoples, Sept. 15, 2017, https://www.refworld.org/pdfid/59c2720c4.pdf [https://perma.cc/9263-9DUB].

5. *Influence on U.S. Law.* Several other sources of binding and non-binding international law may influence federal policy towards American Indians. The Universal Declaration of Human Rights, adopted by the United Nations in 1948, for example, guarantees entitlement to fundamental rights regardless of "race, colour, sex, language, religion, political or other opinion, national or social origin, property, birth or other status," "the right to own property alone as well as in association with others" and freedom from arbitrary deprivation of property, as well as "economic, social and cultural rights indispensable for his dignity and the free development of his personality." The United States has also ratified the International Covenant on Civil and Political Rights (ICCPR), *opened for signature* Dec. 16, 1966, 999 U.N.T.S. 171, *reprinted in* Basic Documents in International Law 276 (Ian Brownlie ed., 4th ed. 1995), and the International Convention on the Elimination of All Forms of Racial Discrimination (ICERD), *adopted* Mar. 7, 1966, 660 U.N.T.S. 195, *reprinted in* Basic Documents in International Law 311 (Ian Brownlie ed. 4th ed. 1995). The Senate ratified both treaties, however, with stipulations that they were not self-executing. The Supreme Court has declared that neither the Universal Declaration nor the ICCPR are directly enforceable in United States courts. *See Sosa v. Alvarez-Machain*, 542 U.S. 692, 733 (2004); *Medellin v. Texas*, 522 U.S. 491, 508 (2008). Relying on this principle, lower courts have so far refused to consider claims based on UNDRIP. *See, e.g., El v. United States*, 122 Fed. Cl. 707, 707-710 (2015) (no Court of Claims jurisdiction to hear UNDRIP claims); *Joyner-El v. Giammarella*, 2010 WL 1685957 *3 n.4, *citing Sosa v. Alvarez-Machain*, 542 U.S. 692, 733 (2004).

The United States must still comply with the ICCPR's and ICERD's reporting requirements, and ratification of both treaties likely renders some of their provisions enforceable as a matter of international customary law. *Cf. Sosa v. Alvarez-Machain*, 542 U.S. at 732-735 (finding that specific, universally accepted principles of international customary law may be enforceable). These documents may also be used as a guide to the interpretation of domestic law, or to inform executive agency action. *See* Cohen's Handbook of Federal Indian Law 457, 460-61 (2012).

Human rights principles may also have less direct influence. In 2007, Amnesty International began denouncing the United States, alleging human rights violations in U.S. creation of a system that led to epidemic rates of violence against women. Amnesty International, *Maze of Injustice: The Failure to Protect Indigenous Women from Sexual Violence in the U.S.A* (2007). The following year, the UN Committee on the Elimination of Racial Discrimination recommended that the United States address the high rates of rape and sexual violence against Native women. UN Doc. CERD/C/USA/CO/6 (May 8, 2008). In 2010, the United States enacted the Tribal Law and Order Act of 2010, acknowledging the Amnesty International Report in doing so. Sen. Rep. No. 111-93 at 19 (Oct. 29, 2009). More recently, this movement led to the authorization of tribal jurisdiction over non-Indian perpetrators of domestic violence in the 2013 reauthorization of the Violence Against Women Act. *See* Ch.5 § IV, *supra.*

6. *UNDRIP and* Adoptive Couple v. Baby Girl. As discussed in Chapter 7 § V, after the Supreme Court's decision in *Adoptive Couple v. Baby Girl*, the South Carolina Supreme Court ordered "Baby Veronica" transferred from her Cherokee father to the adoptive parents. Concerned about protection of her human rights, Baby Girl's court-appointed attorney, the National Indian Child Welfare Association, and the National Congress of American Indians submitted a "statement of information about the case to the UN Special Rapporteur for Indigenous Peoples Rights. Rapporteur Anaya responded with this statement:

> Veronica's human rights as a child and as member of the Cherokee Nation, an indigenous people, should be fully and adequately considered in the ongoing judicial and administrative proceedings that will determine her future upbringing ... I urge the relevant authorities, as well as all parties involved in the custody dispute, to ensure the best interests of Veronica, fully taking into account her rights to maintain her cultural identity and to maintain relations with her indigenous family and people.

Nevertheless, the South Carolina and Oklahoma courts ordered Veronica transferred without a hearing as to whether this was in her best interests or providing visitation rights to her Cherokee father or grandparents. *See* Kristen A. Carpenter & Lorie Graham, *Human Rights to Culture, Family, & Self-Determination: The Case of* Adoptive Couple v. Baby Girl, in Indigenous People and Human Rights (Stefan Kirchner & Joan Policastri eds. forthcoming). What provisions of the UNDRIP are implicated by the case?

7. *ICCPR Article 27 in Action.* Article 27 of the ICCPR has been the basis for several decisions favorable to indigenous communities. The Article provides:

> In those States in which ethnic, religious or linguistic minorities exist, persons belonging to such minorities shall not be denied the right, in community with other members of their group to enjoy their own culture, to profess and practice their own religion, or to use their own language.

The ICCPR established a Human Rights Committee to hear complaints brought pursuant to the Covenant, and the Optional Protocol to the ICCPR established procedures for implementation. Individuals can file petitions against states that have ratified the Optional Protocol. *See* Cohen's Handbook of Federal Indian Law 457-58 (2012); *see also* Sian Lewis–Anthony, *Treaty-Based Procedures for Making Human Rights Complaints with the UN System* in Guide to International Human Rights Practice 41–49 (Hurst Hannum, ed., 1992 ed.).

The Human Rights Committee relied on Article 27 in a case involving a Canadian woman's challenge to Section 12(1)(b) of Canada's Indian Act, which denied Indian status and benefits to any female Indian who married a non-Indian. The Committee found that the Act's provisions violated the woman's legal right to reside on her Band's reserve. See *Lovelace v. Canada*, Communication No. 24/1977, *adopted* 30 July 1981, *reprinted in* Human Rights Committee, Selected Decisions Under the Optional Protocol, Second to Sixteenth Sessions at 83, U.N. Doc. CCPR/C/op/1, U.N. Sales No. E.84.XIV.2 (1985). The

Human Rights Committee has also found that Article 27's protection of the right to culture may be violated by governmental authorization of leasing or other intrusions into indigenous lands. *See* Bernard Ominayak, *Chief of the Lubicon Lake Band v. Canada*, Communication No. 167/1984, *Fourteenth Annual Report of the Human Rights Committee*, Annex IX(A), U.N. Doc. A/45/40 (1990), *reprinted in* 2 Official Records of the Human Rights Committee 1989/90 at 381, U.N. Doc. CCPR/9/Add.1, U.N. Sales No. E.94.XIV.12 (1995). *See* also S. James Anaya, *Indigenous Rights Norms in Contemporary International Law*, 8 Ariz. J. Int'l & Comp. L. 1, 18 (1991) (analyzing the *Lubicon* case and other cases construing Article 27 in the context of cultural rights to land).

8. *ILO Convention No. 169*. The International Labour Organisation on Indigenous and Tribal Peoples, Convention No. 169, was, until the ratification of the U.N. Declaration on the Rights of Indigenous Peoples, the strongest international law statement on the group rights of indigenous peoples. *See* Convention Concerning Indigenous and Tribal Peoples in Independent Countries (ILO 169) 72 ILO Official Bull. 59 (entered into force on Sept. 5, 1991). ILO Convention No. 169 was adopted by the International Labour Conference at the urging of indigenous groups who wanted to replace the 1957 ILO Convention No. 107, which was assimilationist and integrationist in tone. ILO Convention No. 169 uses the term "peoples", as opposed to communities, and while it also contains qualifying language that arguably softens any inference of rights to self-determination, the matter is one for interpretation by the International Labour Office. See S. James Anaya, Indigenous Peoples in International Law 49 (1996). Among the provisions included in the Convention are rights to equality, control over development, health care, safety, education, and land, and respect for indigenous customary laws. For more on the substantive provisions of the Convention, *see* Claire Charters, *Reparations for Indigenous Peoples: Global International Instruments and Institutions*, in Reparations for Indigenous Peoples: International & Comparative Perspectives 166–168 (Federico Lenzerini, ed. 2008).

ILO Convention No. 169 is a multilateral treaty binding on the nations that ratify it. It establishes a supervisory system, which includes reporting requirements for participating states as well as complaint procedures. Several states in the Americas have adopted the Convention, but many others have not. *See* Lee Sweptson, *A New Step in the International Law on Indigenous and Tribal Peoples: ILO Convention No. 169 of 1989*, 15 Okla. City L. Rev. 677, 692 (1990). Nonetheless, increasing recognition of the norms embodied in ILO Convention No. 169, whether through ratification, analogous domestic law, or other international law, heightens the argument that these rights are part of the body of customary international law. *See* S. James Anaya & Robert A. Williams, Jr., *The Protection of Indigenous Peoples' Rights Over Lands and Natural Resources Under the Inter–American Human Rights System*, 14 Harv. Hum. Rts. J. 33, 53–55 (2001).

9. *The Inter–American Commission on Human Rights*. Like the United Nations, the Organization of American States (OAS) adopted a Charter and Declaration of the Rights and Duties of Man in the wake of World War II. The United States is an OAS member. Whether the Declaration is binding on the United States under international law is uncertain, but the Inter–American Commission on Human Rights (IACHR) has jurisdiction to monitor member compliance with certain provisions of the Declaration.

Mary and Carrie Dann, members of the Western Shoshone Tribe, filed a petition against the United States before the Inter–American Commission claiming that denial of their aboriginal property rights violated rights protected under the Declaration. The IACHR issued a decision finding that the United States had denied the Dann sisters of their aboriginal lands through unfair procedures, which included the Indian Claims Commission process. See *Case of Mary and Carrie Dann v. United States*, Case No. 11.140 (Judgment on the Merits), Inter–Am C. H.R. No 75/02 (Dec. 27, 2002). The Dann sisters brought the IACHR petition after having exhausted their domestic remedies in federal court. See *United States v. Dann*, 470 U.S. 39 (1985); 865 F.2d 1528 (9th Cir. 1989) (holding, on remand, that 1934 Taylor Grazing Act withdrew unappropriated land from public domain and therefore ended possibility of affirming individual aboriginal rights). The United States refused to take any of the actions recommended by the IACHR, and seized the Dann sisters' cattle, which they had been grazing on the disputed lands. *See* S. James Anaya & Robert A. Williams, Jr., *The Protection of Indigenous Peoples' Rights Over Lands and Natural Resources Under the Inter–American Human Rights System*, 14 Harv. Hum. Rts. J. 33 (2001) (discussing this and other IACHR cases). The Dann sisters' petition, while unavailing in terms of the specific relief sought, is part of a larger movement to take indigenous issues outside of the confines of domestic legal systems. What are the benefits, even if only symbolic, of doing so? Are there any risks?

The Organization of American States also has a formal court, the Inter–American Court of Human Rights, the decisions of which are legally binding on OAS member states that have both ratified the American Convention on Human Rights and acceded to the Court's jurisdiction. Nicaragua has done both, and also has a troubled history with regard to treatment of its aboriginal people. The following case was a landmark decision for the Court and for the parties.

MAYAGNA (SUMO) AWAS TINGNI COMMUNITY V. NICARAGUA

Inter–Am. Ct. H.R., Case No. 11.577
Judgment of August 31, 2001

[The Awas Tingni community alleged that Nicaragua violated the American Convention on Human Rights by approving of destructive logging on indigenous lands without consulting with or obtaining agreement from the community, and also by failing to carry out Nicaragua's legal obligation to demarcate and secure indigenous lands.]

VIII

VIOLATION OF ARTICLE 25

Right to Judicial Protection

***

111. The Court has noted that Article 25 of the Convention has established, in broad terms,

> the obligation of the States to offer, to all persons under their jurisdiction, effective legal remedy against acts that violate their fundamental rights. It also establishes that the right protected therein applies not only to rights included in the Convention, but also to those recognized by the Constitution or the law.

112. The Court has also reiterated that the right of every person to simple and rapid remedy or to any other effective remedy before the competent judges or courts, to protect them against acts which violate their fundamental rights, "is one of the basic mainstays, not only of the American Convention, but also of the Rule of Law in a democratic society, in the sense set forth in the Convention".

***

114. This Court has further stated that for the State to comply with the provisions of the aforementioned article, it is not enough for the remedies to exist formally, since they must also be effective.

***

a) Existence of a procedure for indigenous land titling and demarcation:

116. Article 5 of the 1995 Constitution of Nicaragua states that:

> Freedom, justice, respect for the dignity of the human person, political, social, and ethnic pluralism, recognition of the various forms of property, free international cooperation and respect for free self-determination are principles of the Nicaraguan nation. *** The State recognizes the existence of the indigenous peoples, who have the rights, duties and guarantees set forth in the Constitution, and especially those of maintaining and developing their identity and culture, having their own forms of social organization and managing their local affairs, as well as maintaining communal forms of ownership of their lands, and also the use and enjoyment of those lands, in accordance with the law. An autonomous regime is established in the *** Constitution for the communities of the Atlantic Coast.
>
> The various forms of property: public, private, associative, cooperative, and communitarian, must be guaranteed and promoted with no discrimination, to produce wealth, and all of them while functioning freely must carry out a social function.

117. Article 89 of the Constitution further states that:

> The Communities of the Atlantic Coast are an inseparable part of the Nicaraguan people, and as such they have the same rights and the same obligations.
>
> The Communities of the Atlantic Coast have the right to maintain and develop their cultural identity within national unity; to have their own forms of social organization and to manage their local affairs according to their traditions.

> The State recognizes the communal forms of land ownership of the Community of the Atlantic Coast. It also recognizes the use and enjoyment of the waters and forests on their communal lands.

118. Article 180 of said Constitution states that:

> The Communities of the Atlantic Coast have the right to live and develop under the forms of social organization which correspond to their historical and cultural traditions.
>
> The State guarantees these communities the enjoyment of their natural resources, the effectiveness of their communal forms of property and free election of their authorities and representatives.

It also guarantees preservation of their cultures and languages, religions and customs.

***

120. Decree No. 16–96 of August 23, 1996, pertaining to the creation of the National Commission for the Demarcation of the Lands of the Indigenous Communities of the Atlantic Coast, established that "the State recognizes communal forms of property of the lands of the Communities of the Atlantic Coast," and pointed out that "it is necessary to establish an appropriate administrative body to begin the process of demarcation of the traditional lands of the indigenous communities". To this end, the decree entrusts that national commission, among other functions, with that of identifying the lands which the various indigenous communities have traditionally occupied, to conduct a geographical analysis process to determine the communal areas and those belonging to the State, to prepare a demarcation project and to seek funding for this project.

121. Law No. 14, published on January 13, 1986 in La Gaceta No. 8, Official Gazette of the Republic of Nicaragua, called "Amendment to the Agrarian Reform Law," establishes in Article 31 that:

> The State will provide the necessary lands for the Miskito, Sumo, Rama, and other ethnic communities of the Atlantic of Nicaragua, so as to improve their standard of living and contribute to the social and economic development of the [N]ation.

122. Based on the above, the Court believes that the existence of norms recognizing and protecting indigenous communal property in Nicaragua is evident.

123. Now then, it would seem that the procedure for titling of lands occupied by indigenous groups has not been clearly regulated in Nicaraguan legislation. According to the State, the legal framework to carry out the process of land titling for indigenous communities in the country is that set forth in Law No. 14, "Amendment to the Agrarian Reform Law," and that process should take place through the Nicaraguan Agrarian Reform Institute (INRA). *** However, this Court considers that Law No. 14 does not establish a specific procedure for demarcation and titling of lands held by indigenous communities, taking into account their specific characteristics.

124. The rest of the body of evidence in the instant case also shows that the State does not have a specific procedure for indigenous land titling. Several of the witnesses and expert witnesses ***, expressed that in Nicaragua there is

a general lack of knowledge, an uncertainty as to what must be done and to whom should a request for demarcation and titling be submitted.

125. In addition, a March, 1998 document, "General diagnostic study on land tenure in the indigenous communities of the Atlantic Coast," prepared by the Central American and Caribbean Research Council and supplied by the State in the present case (*supra* paras. 64, 65, 80 and 96), recognizes " *** lack of legislation assigning specific authority to INRA to grant title to indigenous communal lands" and points out that it is possible that the existence of "legal ambiguities has *** contributed to the pronounced delay in the response by INRA to indigenous demands for communal titling." That diagnostic study adds that

***

[Nicaragua] lacks a clear legal delimitation on the status of national lands in relation to indigenous communal lands. *** [B]eyond the relation between national and communal land, the very concept of indigenous communal land lacks a clear definition.

126. On the other hand, it has been proven that since 1990 no title deeds have been issued to indigenous communities.

127. In light of the above, this Court concludes that there is no effective procedure in Nicaragua for delimitation, demarcation, and titling of indigenous communal lands.

***

138. The Court believes it necessary to make the rights recognized by the Nicaraguan Constitution and legislation effective, in accordance with the American Convention. Therefore, pursuant to Article 2 of the American Convention, the State must adopt in its domestic law the necessary legislative, administrative, or other measures to create an effective mechanism for delimitation and titling of the property of the members of the Awas Tingni Mayagna Community, in accordance with the customary law, values, customs and mores of that Community.

139. From all the above, the Court concludes that the State violated Article 25 of the American Convention, to the detriment of the members of the Mayagna (Sumo) Awas Tingni Community, in connection with articles 1(1) and 2 of the Convention.

IX.

Violation of Article 21

Right to Private Property

***

Considerations of the Court

142. Article 21 of the Convention declares that:

1. Everyone has the right to the use and enjoyment of his property. The law may subordinate such use and enjoyment to the interest of society.

2. No one shall be deprived of his property except upon payment of just compensation, for reasons of public utility or social interest, and in the cases and according to the forms established bylaw.

3. Usury and any other form of exploitation of man by man shall by prohibited by law.

143. Article 21 of the American Convention recognizes the right to private property. In this regard, it establishes: a) that "[e]veryone has the right to the use and enjoyment of his property"; b) that such use and enjoyment can be subordinate, according to a legal mandate, to "social interest"; c) that a person may be deprived of his or her property for reasons of "public utility or social interest, and in the cases and according to the forms established by law"; and d) that when so deprived, a just compensation must be paid.

144. "Property" can be defined as those material things which can be possessed, as well as any right which may be part of a person's patrimony; that concept includes all movables and immovables, corporeal and incorporeal elements and any other intangible object capable of having value.

145. During the study and consideration of the preparatory work for the American Convention on Human Rights, the phrase "[e]veryone has the right to the use and enjoyment of private property, but the law may subordinate its use and enjoyment to public interest" was replaced by "[e]veryone has the right to the use and enjoyment of his property. The law may subordinate such use and enjoyment to the social interest." In other words, it was decided to refer to the "use and enjoyment of his property" instead of "private property."

***

148. Through an evolutionary interpretation of international instruments for the protection of human rights, taking into account applicable norms of interpretation and pursuant to Article 29(b) of the Convention—which precludes a restrictive interpretation of rights—, it is the opinion of this Court that Article 21 of the Convention protects the right to property in a sense which includes, among others, the rights of members of the indigenous communities within the framework of communal property, which is also recognized by the Constitution of Nicaragua.

149. Given the characteristics of the instant case, some specifications are required on the concept of property in indigenous communities. Among indigenous peoples there is a communitarian tradition regarding a communal form of collective property of the land, in the sense that ownership of the land is not centered on an individual but rather on the group and its community. Indigenous groups, by the fact of their very existence, have the right to live freely in their own territory; the close ties of indigenous people with the land must be recognized and understood as the fundamental basis of their cultures, their spiritual life, their integrity, and their economic survival. For indigenous communities, relations to the land are not merely a matter of possession and production but a material and spiritual element which they must fully enjoy, even to preserve their cultural legacy and transmit it to future generations.

***

151. Indigenous peoples' customary law must be especially taken into account for the purpose of this analysis. As a result of customary practices, possession

of the land should suffice for indigenous communities lacking real title to property of the land to obtain official recognition of that property, and for consequent registration.

152. As has been pointed out, Nicaragua recognizes communal property of indigenous peoples, but has not regulated the specific procedure to materialize that recognition, and therefore no such title deeds have been granted since 1990. Furthermore, in the instant case the State has not objected to the claim of the Awas Tingni Community to be declared owner, even though the extent of the area claimed is disputed.

153. It is the opinion of the Court that, pursuant to Article 5 of the Constitution of Nicaragua, the members of the Awas Tingni Community have a communal property right to the lands they currently inhabit, without detriment to the rights of other indigenous communities. Nevertheless, the Court notes that the limits of the territory on which that property right exists have not been effectively delimited and demarcated by the State. This situation has created a climate of constant uncertainty among the members of the Awas Tingni Community, insofar as they do not know for certain how far their communal property extends geographically and, therefore, they do not know until where they can freely use and enjoy their respective property. Based on this understanding, the Court considers that the members of the Awas Tingni Community have the right that the State

> a) carry out the delimitation, demarcation, and titling of the territory belonging to the Community; and
>
> b) abstain from carrying out, until that delimitation, demarcation, and titling have been done, actions that might lead the agents of the State itself, or third parties acting with its acquiescence or its tolerance, to affect the existence, value, use or enjoyment of the property located in the geographical area where the members of the Community live and carry out their activities.

Based on the above, and taking into account the criterion of the Court with respect to applying Article 29(b) of the Convention (*supra* para. 148), the Court believes that, in light of Article 21 of the Convention, the State has violated the right of the members of the Mayagna Awas Tingni Community to the use and enjoyment of their property, and that it has granted concessions to third parties to utilize the property and resources located in an area which could correspond, fully or in part, to the lands which must be delimited, demarcated, and titled.

154. Together with the above, we must recall what has already been established by this court, based on Article 1(1) of the American Convention, regarding the obligation of the State to respect the rights and freedoms recognized by the Convention and to organize public power so as to ensure the full enjoyment of human rights by the persons under its jurisdiction. According to the rules of law pertaining to the international responsibility of the State and applicable under International Human Rights Law, actions or omissions by any public authority, whatever its hierarchic position, are chargeable to the State which is responsible under the terms set forth in the American Convention.

155. For all the above, the Court concludes that the State violated Article 21 of the American Convention, to the detriment of the members of the Mayagna

(Sumo) Awas Tingni Community, in connection with articles 1(1) and 2 of the Convention.

NOTES AND QUESTIONS

1. The Inter–American Court found that Nicaragua violated the right of judicial protection embodied in Article 25 and the right to property in Article 21. The Court also imposed a reparative remedy on Nicaragua, requiring the country to invest $50,000 in public works and services for the Awas Tingni community. The case had real effects. The logging in the Awas Tingni area ceased, and the Nicaraguan government passed a law and administrative procedure for recognizing indigenous title to land. In 2008, seven years after the *Awas Tingni* decision, the community was granted title to its traditional lands.

The Inter–American Court expanded the protection for indigenous property rights in its later decisions. In two cases involving different communities of the Enxet–Langua of Paraguay, the Court held that where the state had failed to adequately protect indigenous communal property rights, Article 21 provided indigenous peoples with continuing rights in ancestral lands long ago sold to private owners. *See Sawhoyamaxa Indigenous Community vs. Paraguay*, Inter Am. Ct. H.R. (Ser. C) No 146 (Mar. 29, 2006); *Yakye Axa Indigenous Community v. Paraguay*, Inter. Am. Ct. H.R. (Ser. C) No. 125 (June 17, 2005). Finding that the expropriation had left the community homeless and impoverished, the Court also held that the Paraguay's actions had denied the Enxet–Langua of the right to life protected by Article 4 of the Convention. Although the Court ordered Paraguay to secure the return of the ancestral lands or provide the communities equivalent lands, Paraguay failed to comply for many years. In 2013, the Sawhoyamaxa, who had been living beside a highway since their expulsion, determined to occupy the lands themselves. In 2014, Paraguay finally enacted a bill to acquire land for their benefit.

2. Consider the definitions of property provided by the Inter–American Court. How do they compare to conceptions under United States law?

3. *International law's influence on domestic law.* The *Awas Tingni* case influenced the Belize decision in *Cal v. Attorney General, supra.* Following the approach in *Awas Tingni*, the Inter–American Commission found that Belize violated Art. 23 of the American Declaration. See *Maya Indigenous Communities of the Toledo Dist. v. Belize* (24 October 2003), case 12.053, report No. 96/03. The domestic case, referencing the newly ratified U.N. Declaration on the Rights of Indigenous Peoples, then followed. *See Cal v. Attorney General, supra.* International law thus has the potential to influence the development of each country's laws regarding the rights of indigenous peoples. Consider again the *Dann* case, discussed above. Should United States courts or law makers see federal Indian law in a new light due to the emerging norms in the international context? What arguments would support using international law norms as an interpretive guide for U.S. law? Are there reasons to pursue claims against the United States in international forums aside from getting concrete results in particular cases? Consider, for example, the petition filed by Sheila Watt–Cloutier before the Inter–American Commission on Human Rights, which alleged that the United States violated various human rights provisions

due to its contributions to global warming, which is already having serious effects on the subsistence culture and economy of the Inuit peoples of the polar region. *See Petition to the Inter American Commission on Human Rights Seeking Relief from Violation Resulting from Global Warming Caused by Acts and Omissions of the United States* (submitted Dec. 7, 2005).

II. RIGHTS OF INDIGENOUS PEOPLE IN OTHER NATIONS

On every continent, indigenous peoples who live in countries where they represent a minority of the population struggle with issues of self-rule and land rights. The countries most analogous to the United States are those that share origins in the United Kingdom. The similar histories and patterns of colonization, as well as inherited legal doctrines, make Australia, New Zealand, and Canada apt comparisons. Yet it is important to keep in mind that the Sami in Norway, Sweden and Finland, the Maya in Belize, the Ainu in Japan, and the many other indigenous peoples throughout Asia, Africa, and the rest of the world also grapple with their treatment under domestic law, even as they increasingly turn also to international law for redress. For an interesting survey of international and comparative law in many diverse regions, *see* Reparations for Indigenous Peoples: International & Comparative Perspectives (Federico Lenzerini, ed. 2008). Below are brief introductions to the legal status of indigenous peoples in Australia, New Zealand and Canada.

A. AUSTRALIA

As described eloquently by two scholars of aboriginal law, Australia has only recently begun to recognize that its indigenous peoples have formal legal rights to their land. The *Mabo* case that they mention, and that is set out below, was a dramatic turnaround in the development of Australian law:

> Australia stands geographically remote from Europe and its founding country, England—and has become more remote constitutionally in recent years, with prevalence of Bills of Rights, which Australia lacks at the federal level. *** In Australia as elsewhere, colonial policies and eugenics were globalizing forces across a range of areas dominated by notions of European superiority. *** In its isolation, Australia has only recently confronted a number of legacies of its treatment of its indigenous population including *** the denial of any recognition of traditional ownership of indigenous lands until the *Mabo* case in 1992.

Barbara Ann Hocking & Margaret Stephenson, *Why the Persistent Absence of a Foundational Principle? Indigenous Australians, Proprietary and Family Reparations* in Reparations for Indigenous Peoples: International & Comparative Perspectives 477–78 (Federico Lenzerini, ed. 2008).

MABO V. QUEENSLAND

107 A.L.R. 1 (1992) (High Court of Australia).

BRENNAN J.

The Murray Islands lie in the Torres Strait. *** The Islands are surrounded for the most part by fringing reefs. The people who were in occupation of these Islands before first European contact and who have continued to occupy those Islands to the present day are known as the Meriam people. Although outsiders, relatively few in number, have lived on the Murray Islands from time to time and worked as missionaries, government officials, or fishermen, there has not been a permanent immigrant population. Anthropological records and research show that the present inhabitants of the Islands are descended from the people described in early European reports. The component of foreign ancestry among the present population is small compared with most communities living in the Torres Strait. The Meriam people of today retain a strong sense of affiliation with their forbears and with the society and culture of earlier times. They have a strong sense of identity with their Islands. The plaintiffs are members of the Meriam people. In this case, the legal rights of the members of the Meriam people to the land of the Murray Islands are in question.

***

Annexation of the Murray Islands

***

In September 1879, Captain Pennefather on the instructions of H.M. Chester visited the Murray Islands where (as he reported) he "mustered the natives" and informed them "that they would be held amenable to British law now the island was annexed". ***

In about February 1882, the Queensland Government "reserved" Murray Island for native inhabitants.

***

The Theory of Universal and Absolute Crown Ownership

***

Oversimplified, the chief question in this case is whether these transactions had the effect on 1 August 1879 of vesting in the Crown absolute ownership of, legal possession of and exclusive power to confer title to, all land in the Murray Islands. The defendant submits that that was the legal consequence of the Letters Patent and of the events which brought them into effect. If that submission be right, the Queen took the land occupied by Meriam people on 1 August 1879 without their knowing of the expropriation; they were no longer entitled without the consent of the Crown to continue to occupy the land they had occupied for centuries past.

***

On analysis, the defendant's argument is that, when the territory of a settled colony became part of the Crown's dominions, the law of England so far as applicable to colonial conditions became the law of the colony and, by that law, the Crown acquired the absolute beneficial ownership of all land in the territory so that the colony became the Crown's demesne and no right or interest in any land in the territory could thereafter be possessed by any other person unless granted by the Crown.

***

The proposition that, when the Crown assumed sovereignty over an Australian colony, it became the universal and absolute beneficial owner of all the land therein, invites critical examination. *** According to the cases, the common law itself took from indigenous inhabitants any right to occupy their traditional land, exposed them to deprivation of the religious, cultural and economic sustenance which the land provides, vested the land effectively in the control of the Imperial authorities without any right to compensation and made the indigenous inhabitants intruders in their own homes and mendicants for a place to live. Judged by any civilized standard, such a law is unjust and its claim to be part of the common law to be applied in contemporary Australia must be questioned. This Court must now determine whether, by the common law of this country, the rights and interests of the Meriam people of today are to be determined on the footing that their ancestors lost their traditional rights and interests in the land of the Murray Islands on 1 August 1879.

***

Although our law is the prisoner of its history, it is not now bound by decisions of courts in the hierarchy of an Empire then concerned with the development of its colonies. It is not immaterial to the resolution of the present problem that, since the Australia Act 1986 came into operation, the law of this country is entirely free of Imperial control. The law which governs Australia is Australian law. *** The peace and order of Australian society is built on the legal system. It can be modified to bring it into conformity with contemporary notions of justice and human rights, but it cannot be destroyed. It is not possible, *a priori*, to distinguish between cases that express a skeletal principle and those which do not, but no case can command unquestioning adherence if the rule it expresses seriously offends the values of justice and human rights (especially equality before the law) which are aspirations of the contemporary Australian legal system. If a postulated rule of the common law expressed in earlier cases seriously offends those contemporary values, the question arises whether the rule should be maintained and applied. Whenever such a question arises, it is necessary to assess whether the particular rule is an essential doctrine of our legal system and whether, if the rule were to be overturned, the disturbance to be apprehended would be disproportionate to the benefit flowing from the overturning.

***

The Acquisition of Sovereignty

***

Although the question whether a territory has been acquired by the Crown is not justiciable before municipal courts, those courts have jurisdiction to determine the consequences of an acquisition under municipal law. Accordingly, the municipal courts must determine the body of law which is in force in the new territory. By the common law, the law in force in a newly-acquired territory depends on the manner of its acquisition by the Crown. Although the manner in which a sovereign state might acquire new territory is a matter for international law, the common law has had to march in step with international law in order to provide the body of law to apply in a territory newly acquired by the Crown.

International law recognized conquest, cession, and occupation of territory that was *terra nullius* as three of the effective ways of acquiring sovereignty. No other way is presently relevant ***. The great voyages of European discovery opened to European nations the prospect of occupying new and valuable territories that were already inhabited. As among themselves, the European nations parcelled out the territories newly discovered to the sovereigns of the respective discoverers, *Worcester v. Georgia*, 31 US 350, 369 (1832), provided the discovery was confirmed by occupation and provided the indigenous inhabitants were not organized in a society that was united permanently for political action. To these territories the European colonial nations applied the doctrines relating to acquisition of territory that was *terra nullius*. They recognized the sovereignty of the respective European nations over the territory of "backward peoples" and, by State practice, permitted the acquisition of sovereignty of such territory by occupation rather than by conquest. Various justifications for the acquisition of sovereignty over the territory of "backward peoples" were advanced. The benefits of Christianity and European civilization had been seen as a sufficient justification from mediaeval times, *see* Williams, The American Indian in Western Legal Thought, 78 (1990), and *Johnson v. McIntosh*, 21 US 240, 253 (1823). Another justification for the application of the theory of *terra nullius* to inhabited territory—a justification first advanced by Vattel at the end of the 18th century—was that new territories could be claimed by occupation if the land were uncultivated, for Europeans had a right to bring lands into production if they were left uncultivated by the indigenous inhabitants. It may be doubted whether, even if these justifications were accepted, the facts would have sufficed to permit acquisition of the Murray Islands as though the Islands were *terra nullius*. The Meriam people were *** devoted gardeners. In 1879, having accepted the influence of the London Missionary Society, they were living peacefully in a land-based society under some sort of governance by the Mamoose and the London Missionary Society. However that may be, it is not for this Court to canvass the validity of the Crown's acquisition of sovereignty over the Islands which, in any event, was consolidated by uninterrupted control of the Islands by Queensland authorities.

The enlarging of the concept of *terra nullius* by international law to justify the acquisition of inhabited territory by occupation on behalf of the acquiring sovereign raised some difficulties in the expounding of the common law doctrines as to the law to be applied when inhabited territories were acquired by occupation (or "settlement", to use the term of the common law). ***

***

The facts as we know them today do not fit the "absence of law" or "barbarian" theory underpinning the colonial reception of the common law of England. That being so, there is no warrant for applying in these times rules of the

English common law which were the product of that theory. It would be a curious doctrine to propound today that, when the benefit of the common law was first extended to Her Majesty's indigenous subjects in the Antipodes, its first fruits were to strip them of their right to occupy their ancestral lands. Yet the supposedly barbarian nature of indigenous people provided the common law of England with the justification for denying them their traditional rights and interests in land ***.

***

As the indigenous inhabitants of a settled colony were regarded as "low in the scale of social organization", they and their occupancy of colonial land were ignored in considering the title to land in a settled colony. Ignoring those rights and interests, the Crown's sovereignty over a territory which had been acquired under the enlarged notion of terra nullius was equated with Crown ownership of the lands therein ***. The theory that the indigenous inhabitants of a "settled" colony had no proprietary interest in the land thus depended on a discriminatory denigration of indigenous inhabitants, their social organization and customs. As the basis of the theory is false in fact and unacceptable in our society, there is a choice of legal principle to be made in the present case. This Court can either apply the existing authorities and proceed to inquire whether the Meriam people are higher "in the scale of social organization" than the Australian Aborigines whose claims were "utterly disregarded" by the existing authorities or the Court can overrule the existing authorities, discarding the distinction between inhabited colonies that were terra nullius and those which were not.

The theory of *terra nullius* has been critically examined in recent times by the International Court of Justice in its *Advisory Opinion on Western Sahara* (62) (1975) ICJR, at p 39. *** The court was unanimously of the opinion that Western Sahara at the time of colonization by Spain in 1884 was not a territory belonging to no-one (*terra nullius*).

If the international law notion that inhabited land may be classified as *terra nullius* no longer commands general support, the doctrines of the common law which depend on the notion that native peoples may be "so low in the scale of social organization" that it is "idle to impute to such people some shadow of the rights known to our law" can hardly be retained. If it were permissible in past centuries to keep the common law in step with international law, it is imperative in today's world that the common law should neither be nor be seen to be frozen in an age of racial discrimination. The fiction by which the rights and interests of indigenous inhabitants in land were treated as non-existent was justified by a policy which has no place in the contemporary law of this country.

***

It was only by fastening on the notion that a settled colony was *terra nullius* that it was possible to predicate of the Crown the acquisition of ownership of land in a colony already occupied by indigenous inhabitants. It was only on the hypothesis that there was nobody in occupation that it could be said that the Crown was the owner because there was no other. If that hypothesis be rejected, the notion that sovereignty carried ownership in its wake must be rejected too. Though the rejection of the notion of *terra nullius* clears away the fictional impediment to the recognition of indigenous rights and interests in colonial land, it would be impossible for the common law to recognize such rights and interests if the basic doctrines of the common law are inconsistent with their recognition.

***

Once it is accepted that indigenous inhabitants in occupation of a territory when sovereignty is acquired by the Crown are capable of enjoying—whether in community, as a group or as individuals—proprietary interests in land, the rights and interests in the land which they had theretofore enjoyed under the customs of their community are seen to be a burden on the radical title which the Crown acquires.

***

As none of the grounds advanced for attributing to the Crown an universal and absolute ownership of colonial land is acceptable, we must now turn to consider a further obstacle advanced against the survival of the rights and interests of indigenous inhabitants on the Crown's acquisition of sovereignty.

***

The proposition that pre-existing rights and interests in land must be established, if at all, under the new legal system introduced on an acquisition of sovereignty is axiomatic, and the proposition that treaties do not create rights enforceable in municipal courts is well established. However, the relevant question is whether the rights and interests in land derived from the old regime survive the acquisition of sovereignty or do they achieve recognition only upon an express act of recognition by the new sovereign? ***

***

The preferable rule, supported by the authorities cited, is that a mere change in sovereignty does not extinguish native title to land. (The term "native title" conveniently describes the interests and rights of indigenous inhabitants in land, whether communal, group or individual, possessed under the traditional laws acknowledged by and the traditional customs observed by the indigenous inhabitants.) The preferable rule equates the indigenous inhabitants of a settled colony with the inhabitants of a conquered colony in respect of their rights and interests in land and recognizes in the indigenous inhabitants of a settled colony the rights and interests *** as surviving to the benefit of the residents of a conquered colony.

***

It must be acknowledged that, to state the common law in this way involves the overruling of cases which have held the contrary. To maintain the authority of those cases would destroy the equality of all Australian citizens before the law. The common law of this country would perpetuate injustice if it were to continue to embrace the enlarged notion of *terra nullius* and to persist in characterizing the indigenous inhabitants of the Australian colonies as people too low in the scale of social organization to be acknowledged as possessing rights and interests in land. Moreover, to reject the theory that the Crown acquired absolute beneficial ownership of land is to bring the law into conformity with Australian history. The dispossession of the indigenous inhabitants of Australia was not worked by a transfer of beneficial ownership when sovereignty was acquired by the Crown, but by the recurrent exercise of a paramount power to exclude the indigenous inhabitants from their traditional lands as colonial settlement expanded and land was granted to the colonists. Dispossession is attributable not to a failure of native title to survive the acquisition of sovereignty, but to its subsequent extinction by a paramount power. Before examining the power to extinguish native title, it is necessary to say something about the nature and incidents of the native title which, surviving the Crown's acquisition of sovereignty, burdens the Crown's radical title.

The nature and incidents of native title

Native title has its origin in and is given its content by the traditional laws acknowledged by and the traditional customs observed by the indigenous inhabitants of a territory. The nature and incidents of native title must be ascertained as a matter of fact by reference to those laws and customs. *** Though these are matters of fact, some general propositions about native title can be stated without reference to evidence.

First, unless there are pre-existing laws of a territory over which the Crown acquires sovereignty which provide for the alienation of interests in land to strangers, the rights and interests which constitute a native title can be possessed only by the indigenous inhabitants and their descendants. Native title, though recognized by the common law, is not an institution of the common law and is not alienable by the common law. ***

Of course, since European settlement of Australia, many clans or groups of indigenous people have been physically separated from their traditional land and have lost their connexion with it. But that is not the universal position. It is clearly not the position of the Meriam people. Where a clan or group has continued to acknowledge the laws and (so far as practicable) to observe the customs based on the traditions of that clan or group, whereby their traditional connexion with the land has been substantially maintained, the traditional community title of that clan or group can be said to remain in existence. The common law can, by reference to the traditional laws and customs of an indigenous people, identify and protect the native rights and interests to which they give rise. However, when the tide of history has washed away any real acknowledgment of traditional law and any real observance of traditional customs, the foundation of native title has disappeared. A native title which has ceased with the abandoning of laws and customs based on tradition cannot be revived for contemporary recognition. Australian law can protect the interests of members of an indigenous clan or group, whether communally or individually, only in conformity with the traditional laws and customs of the people to whom the clan or group belongs and only where members of the clan or group acknowledge those laws and observe those customs (so far as it is practicable to do so). Once traditional native title expires, the Crown's radical title expands to a full beneficial title, for then there is no other proprietor than the Crown.

It follows that a right or interest possessed as a native title cannot be acquired from an indigenous people by one who, not being a member of the indigenous people, does not acknowledge their laws and observe their customs; nor can such a right or interest be acquired by a clan, group or member of the indigenous people unless the acquisition is consistent with the laws and customs of that people. *** Here, the fact is that strangers were not allowed to settle on the Murray Islands and, even after annexation in 1879, strangers who were living on the Islands were deported. The Meriam people asserted an exclusive right to occupy the Murray Islands and, as a community, held a proprietary interest in the Islands. They have maintained their identity as a people and they observe customs which are traditionally based. ***

Secondly, native title, being recognized by the common law (though not as a common law tenure), may be protected by such legal or equitable remedies as are appropriate to the particular rights and interests established by the evidence, whether proprietary or personal and usufructuary in nature and whether possessed by a community, a group or an individual. *** Here, the Meriam people have maintained their own identity and their own customs. The Murray Islands clearly remain their home country. Their land disputes have been dealt with over the years by the Island Court in accordance with the customs of the Meriam people.

***

The extinguishing of native title

Sovereignty carries the power to create and to extinguish private rights and interests in land within the Sovereign's territory. It follows that, on a change of sovereignty, rights and interests in land that may have been indefeasible under the old regime become liable to extinction by exercise of the new sovereign power. The sovereign power may or may not be exercised with solicitude for the welfare of indigenous inhabitants but, in the case of common law countries, the courts cannot review the merits, as distinct from the legality, of the exercise of sovereign power. *United States v. Santa Fe Pacific Railroad Company* 314 US 339, 347 (1941); *Tee–Hit–Ton Indians v. United States* 348 US 272, 281–285 (1954). However, under the constitutional law of this country, the legality (and hence the validity) of an exercise of a sovereign power depends on the authority vested in the organ of government purporting to exercise it: municipal constitutional law determines the scope of authority to exercise a sovereign power over matters governed by municipal law, including rights and interests in land.

[A]n interest validly granted by the Crown, or a right or interest dependent on an interest validly granted by the Crown cannot be extinguished by the Crown without statutory authority. As the Crown is not competent to derogate from a grant once made, a statute which confers a power on the Crown will be presumed (so far as consistent with the purpose for which the power is conferred) to stop short of authorizing any impairment of an interest in land granted by the Crown or dependent on a Crown grant. But, as native title is not granted by the Crown, there is no comparable presumption affecting the conferring of any executive power on the Crown the exercise of which is apt to extinguish native title.

However, the exercise of a power to extinguish native title must reveal a clear and plain intention to do so, whether the action be taken by the Legislature or by the Executive. This requirement, which flows from the seriousness of the consequences to indigenous inhabitants of extinguishing their traditional rights and interests in land, has been repeatedly emphasized by courts dealing with the extinguishing of the native title of Indian bands in North America. It is unnecessary for our purposes to consider the several juristic foundations—proclamation, policy, treaty or occupation—on which native title has been rested in Canada and the United States but reference to the leading cases in each jurisdiction reveals that, whatever the juristic foundation assigned by those courts might be, native title is not extinguished unless there be a clear and plain intention to do so. That approach has been followed in New Zealand. It is patently the right rule.

***

The Crown did not purport to extinguish native title to the Murray Islands when they were annexed in 1879. ***

***

Native title was not extinguished by the creation of reserves nor by the mere appointment of "trustees" to control a reserve where no grant of title was made. To reserve land from sale is to protect native title from being extinguished by alienation under a power of sale. To appoint trustees to control a reserve does not confer on the trustees a power to interfere with the rights and interests in land possessed by indigenous inhabitants under a native title. Nor is native title impaired by a declaration that land is reserved not merely for use by the indigenous inhabitants of the land but "for use of Aboriginal Inhabitants of the State" generally.

***

A Crown grant which vests in the grantee an interest in land which is inconsistent with the continued right to enjoy a native title in respect of the same land necessarily extinguishes the native title. *** But where the Crown has not granted interests in land or reserved and dedicated land inconsistently with the right to continued enjoyment of native title by the indigenous inhabitants, native title survives and is legally enforceable.

***

After this lengthy examination of the problem, it is desirable to state in summary form what I hold to be the common law of Australia with reference to land titles:

1. The Crown's acquisition of sovereignty over the several parts of Australia cannot be challenged in an Australian municipal court.

2. On acquisition of sovereignty over a particular part of Australia, the Crown acquired a radical title to the land in that part.

3. Native title to land survived the Crown's acquisition of sovereignty and radical title. The rights and privileges conferred by native title were unaffected by the Crown's acquisition of radical title but the acquisition of sovereignty exposed native title to extinguishment by a valid exercise of sovereign power inconsistent with the continued right to enjoy native title.

4. Where the Crown has validly alienated land by granting an interest that is wholly or partially inconsistent with a continuing right to enjoy native title, native title is extinguished to the extent of the inconsistency. Thus native title has been extinguished by grants of estates of freehold or of leases but not necessarily by the grant of lesser interests (*e.g.*, authorities to prospect for minerals).

5. Where the Crown has validly and effectively appropriated land to itself and the appropriation is wholly or partially inconsistent with a continuing right to enjoy native title, native title is extinguished to the extent of the inconsistency. Thus native title has been extinguished to parcels of the waste lands of the Crown that have been validly appropriated for use (whether by dedication, setting aside, reservation or other valid means) and used for roads, railways, post offices and other permanent public works which preclude the continuing concurrent enjoyment of native title. Native title continues where the waste lands of the Crown have not been so appropriated or used or where the appropriation and use is consistent with the continuing concurrent enjoyment of native title over the land (*e.g.*, land set aside as a national park).

6. Native title to particular land (whether classified by the common law as proprietary, usufructuary or otherwise), its incidents and the persons entitled thereto are ascertained according to the laws and customs of the indigenous people who, by those laws and customs, have a connection with the land. It is immaterial that the laws and customs have undergone some change since the Crown acquired sovereignty provided the general nature of the connection between the indigenous people and the land remains. Membership of the indigenous people depends on biological descent from the indigenous people and on mutual recognition of a particular person's membership by that person and by the elders or other persons enjoying traditional authority among those people.

7. Native title to an area of land which a clan or group is entitled to enjoy under the laws and customs of an indigenous people is extinguished if the clan or group, by ceasing to acknowledge those laws, and (so far as practicable) observe those customs, loses its connection with the land or on the death of the last of the members of the group or clan.

8. Native title over any parcel of land can be surrendered to the Crown voluntarily by all those clans or groups who, by the traditional laws and customs of the indigenous people, have a relevant connection with the land but the rights and privileges conferred by native title are otherwise inalienable to persons who are not members of the indigenous people to whom alienation is permitted by the traditional laws and customs.

9. If native title to any parcel of the waste lands of the Crown is extinguished, the Crown becomes the absolute beneficial owner.

***

[The Court declared that the Murray Islands are not Crown lands; that the Meriam people are entitled to possession, use and enjoyment of most of the island of Mer; and that the Queensland Parliament and Council has the power to extinguish the Meriam peoples' title subject to any inconsistencies with the laws of Australia.]

NOTES AND QUESTIONS

1. Six Justices agreed with Justice Brennan that the doctrine of *terra nullius* should be overruled, and that native title survived colonization. But

only three Justices out of seven thought that its extinguishment by an inconsistent Crown grant might be subject to compensation. How does *Mabo*'s articulation and recognition of native title differ from that in *Tee–Hit–Ton*?

2. How does Justice Brennan's reasoning differ from Chief Justice Marshall's in *Johnson v. M'Intosh*? Note that Justice Brennan cites to international law decisions, as well as to United States case law. Justice Brennan also explicitly repudiates the racist underpinnings of the *terra nullius* doctrine. Is the functional outcome of *Mabo* distinguishable from that of the Marshall trilogy? Even if not, is there something gained by explicitly rejecting the colonialist assumptions?

3. *Land Rights Legislation*. The doctrine of *terra nullius* prevailed in Australia until 1992 when *Mabo* overruled it, but a powerful aboriginal land rights movement preceded the decision. Starting in the 1960's, Aborigine communities began organizing against leasing and other uses of their lands. In 1971, the Supreme Court of the Northern Territory rejected claims to aboriginal title in *Milirrpum v. Nabalco Pty. Ltd*, 17 F.L.R. 141 (N.T. Sup. Ct 1971). The case involved the government's issuance of mining leases in the Gove Peninsula without consulting the Yirrkala people, the aboriginal inhabitants of the area. The case ignited the aboriginal protest movement, which culminated in occupation of the grounds of Parliament. Subsequently, a government sympathetic to aboriginal concerns came to power and declared a moratorium on mineral leases in aboriginal reserves in the Northern Territory. The government also commissioned a report and recommendations concerning land transfers to aboriginal groups in the Northern Territory. The report, drafted by Justice Woodward who had represented the Yirrkala people, made several recommendations favorable to aboriginal land rights, and reforms followed. Among them, in 1976 the Aboriginal Land Rights Act was passed. The Act recognized aboriginal land claims in the Northern Territory based on spiritual ties, and established mechanisms for aboriginal people to acquire title through land trusts. The Crown retained the mineral estate under any aboriginal lands. The Minister of Aboriginal Affairs appoints the members of the land trusts, choosing from lists submitted by Aboriginal Land Councils, which are similar to tribal governments.

The Aboriginal Land Rights Act of 1976 also established an Aboriginal Land Commissioner to decide land claims cases. The Commissioner holds hearings and makes recommendations to the Minister of Aboriginal Affairs, who issues final decisions. In 1981, the Land Acquisition Act was passed, which provided the authority for the Commonwealth to compel the sale of land to meet obligations pursuant to aboriginal claims. The 1981 Act was necessary to provide some redress to the vast majority of aboriginal peoples whose traditional lands were in private ownership. *See* Heather McRae, et al., Aboriginal Legal Issues (3d ed. 2003).

Following *Mabo*, the federal government passed new land rights legislation. The Native Title Act of 1993 recognized native title; established standards and procedures for future native title issues; and validated past acts that native title invalidated. For a comprehensive analysis of the Act, *see* Beth Ganz, *Indigenous Peoples and Land Tenure: An Issue of Human Rights and Environmental Protection*, 9 Geo. Int'l Envtl. L. Rev. 173 (1996). Under the Native Title Act, there is pending legislation that would authorize indigenous rights in national parks and pastoral leasehold lands as well as the transfer of Crown lands. *See* Jon Altman, et al., *Native Title and Indigenous Australian Utilization of Wildlife: Policy Perspectives*, Aus. Nat'l U. (Jan. 2019).

As of 2017, native title has been recognized to exist in over 1 million square kilometers of Australian land and water, and 629 registered Indigenous Land Use Agreements have been put into effect. Additional helpful sources on *Mabo* and land rights generally include: *Mabo* and Native Title: Origins and Institutional Implications (William G. Sanders, ed. 1994); Garth Nettheim, et al., Indigenous Peoples and Governance Structures: A Comparative Analysis of Land and Resource Management Rights (2002); and Maureen Tehan, *A Hope Disillusioned, an Opportunity Lost? Reflections on Common Law Native Title and Ten Years of the Native Title Act*, 27 Melbourne U. L. Rev. 523 (2003).

4. *Sovereignty for Aborigines of Australia?* To date, Australian courts have not recognized any aboriginal sovereign rights over territory or members. Thus while aboriginal communities govern themselves according to their own traditions and customs, and also exercise authority through the Aboriginal Land Councils, they are not recognized as having inherent authority by the Australian government. *See, e.g., Coe v. Commonwealth*, 53 A.L.J.R. 403 (Austl. 1979). Does Australia's belated vote in support of the UN Declaration on the Rights of Indigenous Peoples strengthen aboriginal arguments for inherent sovereignty? Review Articles 3 and 4 of the Declaration, *supra*.

5. *Apologies and Reparations.* For reasons similar to those advanced by the architects of the United States' Allotment policies, Australia maintained an official policy of separating aboriginal children from their families. The policies and programs, resulting in what have become known as the "Stolen Generations," began in the nineteenth century and persisted through the 1960's. Recently, the Australian government issued an official apology for the policies, stating that "We apologise for the laws and policies of successive parliaments and governments that have inflicted profound grief, suffering and loss on these our fellow Australians." *Apology to Australia's Indigenous Peoples*, Government Business, Motion No. 1, Feb. 13, 2008 (Australian Parliament). The apology was not accompanied by monetary or other concrete forms of reparations, but several regional governments have afforded reparations. The Governments of South Australia and New South Wales, for example, offered $117 million and $73 million respectively to establish funds and programs for survivors of the Stolen Generation. The continuing harm to aboriginal peoples from the decades of intentional destruction of their families includes many of the same social and economic challenges faced by American Indians in the United States. For more on the Stolen Generations and the issue of reparations, *see* Barbara Ann Hocking & Margaret Stephenson, *Why the Persistent Absence of a Foundational Principle? Indigenous Australians, Proprietary and Family Reparations* in Reparations for Indigenous Peoples: International & Comparative Perspectives 481–496 (Federico Lenzerini, ed. 2008).

B. NEW ZEALAND

Despite their geographic proximity and similar histories of European arrival, the structure of indigenous rights varies greatly between Australia and

New Zealand. Formal legal rights for the Maori people of Aotearoa, as they call their homeland, date back to the Treaty of Waitangi, entered into in 1840:

> Before colonization, Maori controlled Aotearoa New Zealand. Colonization removed that control, along with control of much of its land and natural resources. The primary facilitator of this was a treaty between Maori and the British Queen—the Treaty of Waitangi—that was later breached by the incoming settlers and the resulting colonial government. *** Since the 1970's a comprehensive attempt at reparations has been embarked upon *** [which] has entailed the creation of an independent body to inquire into Maori grievances, *** enabled courts to adjudicate on some breaches of indigenous rights, and has negotiated reparations settlements for a wide range of grievances.

Catherine J. Iorns Magallanes, *Reparations for Maori Grievances in Aotearoa New Zealand*, in Reparations for Indigenous Peoples: International & Comparative Perspectives 523 (Federico Lenzerini, ed. 2008); *see also* Claudia Orange, The Treaty of Waitangi (1987).

THE TREATY OF WAITANGI

(1840)

HER MAJESTY VICTORIA Queen of the United Kingdom of Great Britain and Ireland regarding with Her Royal Favour the Native Chiefs and Tribes of New Zealand and anxious to protect their just Rights and Property and to secure to them the enjoyment of Peace and Good Order has deemed it necessary in consequence of the great number of Her Majesty's Subjects who have already settled in New Zealand and the rapid extension of Emigration both from Europe and Australia which is still in progress to constitute and appoint a functionary properly authorised to treat with the Aborigines of New Zealand for the recognition of Her Majesty's Sovereign authority over the whole or any part of those islands—Her Majesty therefore being desirous to establish a settled form of Civil Government with a view to avert the evil consequences which must result from the absence of the necessary Laws and Institutions alike to the native population and to Her subjects has been graciously pleased to empower and to authorise me William Hobson a Captain in Her Majesty's Royal Navy Consul and Lieutenant–Governor of such parts of New Zealand as may be or hereafter shall be ceded to her Majesty to invite the confederated and independent Chiefs of New Zealand to concur in the following Articles and Conditions.

Article the first [Article 1]

The Chiefs of the Confederation of the United Tribes of New Zealand and the separate and independent Chiefs who have not become members of the Confederation cede to Her Majesty the Queen of England absolutely and without reservation all the rights and powers of Sovereignty which the said Confederation or Individual Chiefs respectively exercise or possess, or may be supposed to exercise or to possess over their respective Territories as the sole sovereigns thereof.

Article the second [Article 2]

Her Majesty the Queen of England confirms and guarantees to the Chiefs and Tribes of New Zealand and to the respective families and individuals thereof the full exclusive and undisturbed possession of their Lands and Estates Forests Fisheries and other properties which they may collectively or individually possess so long as it is their wish and desire to retain the same in their possession; but the Chiefs of the United Tribes and the individual Chiefs yield to Her Majesty the exclusive right of Preemption over such lands as the proprietors thereof may be disposed to alienate at such prices as may be agreed upon between the respective Proprietors and persons appointed by Her Majesty to treat with them in that behalf.

Article the third [Article 3]

In consideration thereof Her Majesty the Queen of England extends to the Natives of New Zealand Her royal protection and imparts to them all the Rights and Privileges of British Subjects.

(signed) William Hobson, Lieutenant–Governor.

Now therefore We the Chiefs of the Confederation of the United Tribes of New Zealand being assembled in Congress at Victoria in Waitangi and We the Separate and Independent Chiefs of New Zealand claiming authority over the Tribes and Territories which are specified after our respective names, having been made fully to understand the Provisions of the foregoing Treaty, accept and enter into the same in the full spirit and meaning thereof in witness of which we have attached our signatures or marks at the places and the dates respectively specified. Done at Waitangi this Sixth day of February in the year of Our Lord one thousand eight hundred and forty.

NOTES AND QUESTIONS

1. *The Treaty in practice in the nineteenth and early twentieth centuries.* The Treaty had some initial success, in that in the 1840's and 1850's, a tentative peace was reached between the settlers and the Maori, and many Maori prospered with the new contact and opportunity for trade. In the 1860's, however, conflicts arose over land and resources, eventually resulting in wars on the North Island, known as the New Zealand wars. Maori leaders wanted to retain control over their land and resisted the increasing imposition of outside governance. The settlers wanted more access to land and resources, and the New Zealand government was eager to oblige. More than four million acres of Maori land were confiscated pursuant to the New Zealand Settlements Act of 1863. Thousands more acres were lost in the following decades under the auspices of the Native Land Court, which was established in 1865. The court, which was operated according to the settlers' legal system, converted customary Maori title to individual title, thus making it easier for settlers to obtain land. Many of the practices were deceptive or fraudulent. In the 1870's the New Zealand government began an aggressive program of purchasing Maori lands. Losses through the Native Land Court and to the government resulted, by the 1910's, in only one quarter of the North Island remaining to the Maori and a mere 1% of the South Island, most of which had been obtained earlier by the Crown. *See* Catherine J Iorns Magallanes, *Reparations for Maori Grievances*

in Aotearoa New Zealand, in Reparations for Indigenous Peoples: International & Comparative Perspectives 532–36 (Federico Lenzerini, ed. 2008). For an excellent public resource, *see also The Treaty in Practice*, http://www.nzhistory.net.nz/politics/treaty/the-treaty-in-practice/early-crown-policy.

2. *The problem of translation*. Continuing sources of conflict surrounding the Treaty of Waitangi stem from disparities between the English version and the Maori language version. In Article 1, the English version refers to sovereignty, whereas the Maori word is *kawanatanga*, which does not refer to sovereignty, but to governance. The Maori version thus recognizes British governance over matters within their territory, but does not cede Maori authority over relations between and among themselves. *See* Iorns Magallanes, *supra* at 530. Does the Maori interpretation lead to a version of retained sovereignty similar to that recognized by Chief Justice Marshall in *Worcester*?

In Article 2, the English version describes the Maori as retaining "full exclusive and undisturbed possession" of their lands and resources, whereas the Maori version refers to retention of *te tino rangatiratang* over their lands, villages and treasures. "This phrase refers to the highest or absolute chieftanship, and would be the best Maori term to use to refer to sovereignty." Iorns Magallanes, *supra*, at 530. Finally, also in Article 2, the English version refers to the right of preemption, whereas the Maori version refers only to purchases of land that Maori were willing to sell. For the full Maori text, *see Maori Text—Read The Treaty*, http://www.nzhistory.net.nz/politics/read-the-treaty/maori-text.

3. *The Treaty in the modern era*. The Maori protest movement, sparked by paternalistic legislation passed in 1967, culminated in a land march in 1975 by thousands of Maori of all ages. The march covered the length of the North Island ending at the New Zealand Parliament, and highlighted the extensive land loss by Maori people, from 66 million acres in 1840, to approximately three million. Maori activism resulted in a revitalization of the Treaty of Waitangi and a range of legal and social measures to restore the Maori population. The Treaty of Waitangi Act of 1975 authorized a Waitangi tribunal to investigate complaints of government conduct inconsistent with the principles of the Treaty. Initially the Tribunal was limited to present or future actions, but in 1985 the Act was amended to allow inquiry into historical grievances going back to 1840. The Tribunal lacks sanctioning or enforcement powers, but makes recommendations for government action. The Tribunal has had to consider the language difference between the two versions of the Treaty, and while to date it has rejected the interpretation that Maori retained sovereignty in Article 1, it has found that Maori retention of land and other resources in Article 2 includes the authority to control them. *See* Iorns Magallanes, *supra*, at 538.

Court decisions have also revived Maori rights. In *New Zealand Maori Council v. Attorney General*, 1 N.Z.L.R. 641 (1987), the court of appeals described the Crown's obligations to safeguard Maori rights as "analogous to fiduciary duties." The Crown should provide "active protection" to Maori people and their resources. In *Huakina Development Trust v. Waikato Valley Authority* 2 N.Z.L.R. 188 (1987), the court described the Treaty as part of the "fabric of New Zealand society" and relied on Maori cultural and spiritual values to interpret its provisions.

4. *The Treaty of Waitangi (Fisheries Claims) Settlement Act of 1992.* Following successful litigation brought by Maori people concerning violations of their customary fishing rights, *see Te Weehi v. Regional Fisheries Offices*, 1 N.Z.L.R. 680 (1986), Parliament passed legislation implementing a settlement. The Treaty of Waitangi (Fisheries Claims) Settlement Act of 1992 waived all Maori commercial fishing claims in exchange for government funding for a joint venture purchase of Sealords, New Zealand's largest fishing company. The Maori also received twenty percent of future commercial fishing quotas for all new species brought under New Zealand's management system. Traditional Maori fishing rights for personal and customary use were also retained. The New Zealand High Court ruled, however, that urban and individual Maori not members of a sub-tribe, or hapu, could be excluded from the settlement. *See Te Waka Hi Ika o Te Arawa v. Treaty of Waitangi Fisheries Commission*, 1 N.Z.L.R. 285 (2000). For more on the Settlement Act, *see* Michael A. Burnett, *The Dilemma of Commercial Fishing Rights of Indigenous Peoples: A Comparative Study of the Common Law Nations*, 19 Suffolk Transnat'l L. Rev. 389 (1996); *see also* Iorns Magallanes, *supra*, at 557–60. In 2011, the Marine and Coastal Area (Takutai Moana) Act was passed, which replaced Crown ownership with a "no ownership" principle, and restored Maori ability to seek customary rights and title through negotiation or the courts. *See* NZ Pub. Act 2011, No. 3, March 31, 2011.

5. *Current conditions.* Today, the Maori comprise approximately 15% of the population of New Zealand and have considerable political and legal clout. Just as important, Maori culture and traditions have survived and evolved, and the country as a whole is moving towards reconciliation, albeit not always easily or smoothly. As Professor Iorns Magallanes observes, "New Zealand has embarked upon a significant modern effort to effect reparations for Maori grievances arising out of colonization. *** [T]he New Zealand experience has shown that it is possible for indigenous peoples to obtain concrete and meaningful reparations for past injustices." Iorns Magallanes, *supra* at 562.

C. CANADA

Like the United States, Canada is home to many diverse indigenous peoples. There are more than 600 First Nations in Canada, with 11 languages and more than fifty dialects. *See* Bradford W. Morse, *Indigenous Peoples of Canada and Their Efforts to Achieve True Reparations*, in Reparations for Indigenous Peoples: International & Comparative Perspectives 271 n.1 (Federico Lenzerini, ed. 2008). Also like the United States, as well as New Zealand, treaties play a foundational role in the legal relationship between the Canadian government and the First Nations of Canada. The Royal Proclamation of 1763 was the region's first constitutional document, and it contained provisions recognizing and affirming the treaty process which have never been repealed. When Canada became a national government in 1867, it assumed control over Indian affairs under the British North America Act of 1867, and entered into treaties with First Nations beginning in 1871. Many tribes and bands lack treaties, however, and litigation about the rights of these groups forms the basis of a good deal of modern Canadian Indian law.

Other similarities between the United States and Canada include periods of ignoring or marginalizing the solemn promises made in treaties. The low point for judicial disparagement of treaty rights came in 1927. In *R v. Syliboy*, the court held that hunting and fishing rights held by Nova Scotia Indians were unenforceable because:

> [T]he Indians were never recognized as an independent power. *** The savages rights of sovereignty even of ownership were never recognized. Nova Scotia had passed to Great Britain not by gift or purchase from or even by conquest of the Indians but by Treaty with France, which had acquired it by priority of discovery and ancient possession; and the Indians passed with it.

R. v. Syliboy, [1929] 1 D.L.R. 307 (Co.Ct. 1928). *Syliboy* was rooted in the assimilationist policies of the time. In 1871, Canada passed the Indian Act of 1876, Act of April 12, 1876, ch. 18, 1876 Can.Stat. 43, which, in addition to other measures, effectively allowed provincial abrogation of treaty rights. In subsequent amendments to the Act, provincial authority to abrogate treaties was repealed, but Indians on reserves were still subject to provincial authority if federal law did not apply. *See* 3 Can. Rev. Stat. Ch. 149 (1952) (amending the Indian Act of 1876).

Despite the similarities, there are key differences between Canada and the United States with regard to the legal relationship with indigenous peoples. First, Canada still engages in treaty making, and the treaty process is an important feature of contemporary policy. *See* Morse, *supra*, at 293–306 (discussing land claims and treaty negotiations from 1975 to the present). Second, Canada constitutionalized its recognition of aboriginal rights in the Constitution Act of 1982, relevant portions of which are excerpted below.

CONSTITUTION ACT

1982

Part I, Canadian Charter of Rights and Freedoms

***

25. The guarantee in this Charter of certain rights and freedoms shall not be construed so as to abrogate or derogate from any aboriginal, treaty or other rights or freedoms that pertain to the aboriginal peoples of Canada including

(a) any rights or freedoms that have been recognized by the Royal Proclamation of October 7, 1763; and

(b) any rights or freedoms that may be acquired by the aboriginal peoples of Canada by way of land claims settlement.

***

Part II, Rights of the Aboriginal Peoples of Canada

35. (1) The existing aboriginal and treaty rights of the aboriginal peoples of Canada are hereby recognized and affirmed.

(2) In this Act, "aboriginal peoples of Canada" includes the Indian, Inuit, and Metis peoples of Canada.

(3) For greater certainty, in subsection (1) "treaty rights" includes rights that now exist by way of land claims agreements or may be so acquired.

(4) Notwithstanding any other provision of this Act, the aboriginal and treaty rights referred to in subsection (1) are guaranteed equally to male and female persons.

35.1 The government of Canada and the provincial governments are committed to the principal that, before any amendment is made to Class 24 of section 91 of the "Constitution Act, 1867", to section 25 of this Act or to this Part,

(a) a constitutional conference that includes in its agenda an item relating to the proposed amendment, composed of the Prime Minister of Canada and the first ministers of the provinces, will be convened by the Prime Minister of Canada; and

(b) the Prime Minister of Canada will invite representatives of the aboriginal peoples of Canada to participate in the discussions on that item.

The Constitution Act's provisions have had a profound effect on the law and politics of aboriginal rights in Canada. The stance of the *Syliboy* court has been firmly rejected, *see Simon v. The Queen* [1985] 2 S.C.R. 387, and the Supreme Court of Canada has issued decisions recognizing and affirming the Canadian government's unique obligations to First Nations, and to aboriginal rights to land, hunting and fishing.

GUERIN V. THE QUEEN

Supreme Court of Canada
[1984] 2 S.C.R. 335

[The Musqueam Indian Band sued the Crown for damages flowing from the lease of a portion of the Band's Reserve to a golf club. The Reserve included over 400 acres within the Charter area of the City of Vancouver. In 1956 the Shaughnessy Heights Golf Club wanted to obtain land from the Reserve, and the Musqueam Band agreed to surrender 162 acres to the Crown for lease to the club. The final lease terms were far less favorable than the one that the Band had agreed to when it met with government officials.]

IV. Fiduciary Relationship

The issue of the Crown's liability was dealt with in the courts below on the basis of the existence or non-existence of a trust. ***

In my view, the nature of Indian title and the framework of the statutory scheme established for disposing of Indian land places upon the Crown an equitable obligation, enforceable by the courts, to deal with the land for the benefit of the Indians. This obligation does not amount to a trust in the private law sense. It is rather a fiduciary duty. If, however, the Crown breaches this fiduciary duty it will be liable to the Indians in the same way and to the same extent as if such a trust were in effect.

The fiduciary relationship between the Crown and the Indians has its roots in the concept of aboriginal, native or Indian title. The fact that Indian bands have a certain interest in lands does not, however, in itself give rise to a fiduciary relationship between the Indians and the Crown. The conclusion that the Crown is a fiduciary depends upon the further proposition that the Indian interest in the land is inalienable except upon surrender to the Crown.

An Indian band is prohibited from directly transferring its interest to a third party. Any sale or lease of land can only be carried out after a surrender has taken place, with the Crown then acting on the band's behalf. The Crown took this responsibility upon itself in the Royal Proclamation of 1763. It is still recognized in the surrender provisions of the Indian Act. The surrender requirement, and the responsibility it entails, are the source of a distinct fiduciary obligation owed by the Crown to the Indians. In order to explore the character of this obligation, however, it is first necessary to consider the basis of aboriginal title and the nature of the interest in land which it represents.

(a) The existence of Indian title

In *Calder et al. v. A.G. B.C.*, [1973] S.C.R. 313, [1973], this court recognized aboriginal title as a legal right derived from the Indians' historic occupation and possession of their tribal lands. With Judson and Hall JJ. writing the principal judgments, the court split three-three on the major issue of whether the Nishga Indians' aboriginal title to their ancient tribal territory had been extinguished by general land enactments in British Columbia. The court also split on the issue of whether the Royal Proclamation of 1763 was applicable to Indian lands in that province. Judson and Hall JJ. were in agreement, however, that aboriginal title existed in Canada (at least where it has not been extinguished by appropriate legislative action) independently of the Royal Proclamation of 1763. Judson J. stated expressly that the Proclamation was not the "exclusive" source of Indian title. Hall J. said that "aboriginal Indian title does not depend on treaty, executive order or legislative enactment."

The Royal Proclamation of 1763 reserved " ***under our Sovereignty, Protection, and Dominion, for the use of the said Indians, all the Lands and Territories not included within the Limits of Our said Three new Governments, or within the limits of the Territory granted to the Hudson's Bay Company, as also all the Lands and Territories lying to the Westward of the Sources of the Rivers which fall into the Sea from the West and North West as aforesaid." In recognizing that the Proclamation is not the sole source of Indian title the decision went beyond the judgment of the Privy Council in *St. Catherine's Milling & Lumber Co. v. The Queen* (1888), 14 App. Cas. 46. In that case Lord Watson acknowledged the existence of aboriginal title but said it had its origin in the Royal Proclamation. In this respect Calder is consistent with the position of Chief Justice Marshall in the leading American cases of *Johnson and Graham's Lessee v. M'Intosh*, 21 U.S. 240 (1823), and *Worcester v. State of Georgia*, 31 U.S. 530 (1832), cited by Judson and Hall JJ.in their respective judgments.

In *Johnson v. M'Intosh* Marshall C.J., although he acknowledged the Royal Proclamation of 1763 as one basis for recognition of Indian title, was none the less of opinion that the rights of Indians in the lands they traditionally occupied prior to European colonization both predated and survived the claims to sovereignty made by various European nations in the territories of the North American continent. The principle of discovery which justified these claims gave the ultimate title in the land in a particular area to the nation which had discovered and claimed it. In that respect at least the Indians' rights in the land were obviously diminished; but their rights of occupancy and possession remained unaffected. ***

***

It does not matter, in my opinion, that the present case is concerned with the interest of an Indian band in a reserve rather than with unrecognized aboriginal title in traditional tribal lands. The Indian interest in the land is the same in both cases. It is worth noting, however, that the reserve in question here was created out of the ancient tribal territory of the Musqueam band by the unilateral action of the Colony of British Columbia, prior to Confederation.

(b) The Nature of Indian Title

In the *St. Catherine's Milling* case, *supra*, the Privy Council held that the Indians had a "personal and usufructuary right" in the lands which they had traditionally occupied. *** Chief Justice Marshall took a similar view in *Johnson v. M'Intosh*, supra, saying, "All our institutions recognize the absolute title of the Crown, subject only to the Indian right of occupancy."

***

Indians have a legal right to occupy and possess certain lands, the ultimate title to which is in the Crown. While their interest does not, strictly speaking, amount to beneficial ownership, neither is its nature completely exhausted by the concept of a personal right. It is true that the *sui generis* interest which the Indians have in the land is personal in the sense that it cannot be transferred to a grantee, but it is also true, as will presently appear, that the interest gives rise upon surrender to a distinctive fiduciary obligation on the part of the Crown to deal with the land for the benefit of the surrendering Indians. These two aspects of Indian title go together, since the Crown's original purpose in declaring the Indians' interest to be inalienable otherwise than to the Crown was to facilitate the Crown's ability to represent the Indians in dealings with third parties. The nature of the Indians' interest is therefore best characterized by its general inalienability, coupled with the fact that the Crown is under an obligation to deal with the land on the Indians' behalf when the interest is surrendered. Any description of Indian title which goes beyond these two features is both unnecessary and potentially misleading.

(c) The Crown's Fiduciary Obligation

The concept of fiduciary obligation originated long ago in the notion of breach of confidence, one of the original heads of jurisdiction in chancery. In the present appeal its relevance is based on the requirement of a "surrender" before Indian land can be alienated.

The Royal Proclamation of 1763 provided that no private person could purchase from the Indians any lands that the Proclamation had reserved to them, and provided further that all purchases had to be by and in the name of the Crown, in a public assembly of the Indians held by the governor or commander-in-chief of the colony in which the lands in question lay. As Lord

Watson pointed out in *St. Catherine's Milling*, this policy with respect to the sale or transfer of the Indians' interest in land has been continuously maintained by the British Crown, by the governments of the colonies when they became responsible for the administration of Indian affairs and, after 1867, by the federal government of Canada. Successive federal statutes, predecessors to the present Indian Act, have all provided for the general inalienability of Indian reserve land except upon surrender to the Crown, the relevant provisions in the present Act being ss. 37–41.

The purpose of this surrender requirement is clearly to interpose the Crown between the Indians and prospective purchasers or lessees of their land, so as to prevent the Indians from being exploited. ***

This discretion on the part of the Crown, far from ousting, as the Crown contends, the jurisdiction of the courts to regulate the relationship between the Crown and the Indians, has the effect of transforming the Crown's obligation into a fiduciary one. ***

***

Section 18(1) of the Indian Act confers upon the Crown a broad discretion in dealing with surrendered land. In the present case, the document of surrender *** by which the Musqueam band surrendered the land at issue, confirms this discretion in the clause conveying the land to the Crown "in trust to lease *** upon such terms as the Government of Canada may deem most conducive to our Welfare and that of our people". When, as here, an Indian band surrenders its interest to the Crown, a fiduciary obligation takes hold to regulate the manner in which the Crown exercises its discretion in dealing with the land on the Indians' behalf.

***

(d) Breach of the Fiduciary Obligation

The trial judge found that the Crown's agents promised the band to lease the land in question on certain specified terms and then, after surrender, obtained a lease on different terms. The lease obtained was much less valuable. As already mentioned, the surrender document did not make reference to the "oral" terms. I would not wish to say that those terms had none the less somehow been incorporated as conditions into the surrender. They were not formally assented to by a majority of the electors of the band, nor were they accepted by the Governor in Council. ***

None the less, the Crown, in my view, was not empowered by the surrender document to ignore the oral terms which the band understood would be embodied in the lease. The oral representations form the backdrop against which the Crown's conduct in discharging its fiduciary obligation must be measured. They inform and confine the field of discretion within which the Crown was free to act. After the Crown's agents had induced the band to surrender its land on the understanding that the land would be leased on certain terms, it would be unconscionable to permit the Crown simply to ignore those terms. When the promised lease proved impossible to obtain, the Crown, instead of proceeding to lease the land on different, unfavourable terms, should have returned to the band to explain what had occurred and seek the band's counsel on how to proceed. The existence of such unconscionability is the key to a conclusion that the Crown breached its fiduciary duty. Equity will not countenance unconscionable behaviour in a fiduciary, whose duty is that of utmost loyalty to his principal.

While the existence of the fiduciary obligation which the Crown owes to the Indians is dependent on the nature of the surrender process, the standard of conduct which the obligation imports is both more general and more exacting than the terms of any particular surrender. In the present case the relevant aspect of the required standard of conduct is defined by a principle analogous to that which underlies the doctrine of promissory or equitable estoppel. The Crown cannot promise the band that it will obtain a lease of the latter's land on certain stated terms, thereby inducing the band to alter its legal position by surrendering the land, and then simply ignore that promise to the band's detriment.

In obtaining without consultation a much less valuable lease than that promised, the Crown breached the fiduciary obligation it owed the band. It must make good the loss suffered in consequence.

NOTES AND QUESTIONS

1. How does the *Guerin* Court define the nature and scope of the fiduciary obligation? Consider how the *Guerin* definitions compare to the United States Supreme Court's articulation of the trust obligation in *Mitchell I*, *Mitchell II*, *Navajo Nation*, and *White Mountain Apache*, discussed in preceding chapters.

2. The rights of the Musqueam Indian Band were also at issue in another leading case in the post-Constitution Act era. In *Sparrow v. R.*, [1990] 1 S.C.R. 1075, a member of the Musqueam Band was charged with violating Canada's Fisheries Act for fishing with a drift net that exceeded the length prescribed by the Band's government issued permit. The Band member argued that Section 35(1) of the Constitution invalidated the permit's restriction because he was exercising his aboriginal right to fish. The Court found that the Band's aboriginal fishing rights were not abrogated by the Fisheries Act, and then articulated a test for determining whether the government could nonetheless regulate the Band's rights:

> Section 35(1) suggests that while regulation affecting aboriginal rights is not precluded, such regulation must be enacted according to a valid objective. *** By giving aboriginal rights constitutional status and priority, Parliament and the provinces have sanctioned challenges to social and economic policy objectives embodied in legislation to the extent that aboriginal rights are affected. Implicit in this constitutional scheme is the obligation of the legislature to satisfy the test of justification. The way in which a legislative objective is to be attained must uphold the honour of the Crown and must be in keeping with the unique contemporary relationship, grounded in history and policy, between the Crown and Canada's aboriginal peoples. The extent of legislative or regulatory impact on an existing aboriginal right may be scrutinized so as to ensure recognition and affirmation.

Id. at 1110. The Court then explained that a *prima facie* infringement of Section 35(1) could be made out by showing that the government limitation is unreasonable, imposes an undue hardship, and denies to the rights holders their preferred means of exercising that right. If the challenger to the government restriction makes out a *prima facie* case, then the government must show that the restriction is justified by a valid legislative objective, and that the regulatory means of achieving that objective are also justified. *See id.* at 1111–1113. This "justification test" is similar to forms of heightened scrutiny that the United States Supreme Court applies in the Equal Protection context. Compare *Sparrow* to *Dion*, the case in which the Supreme Court held that federal legislation abrogated Indian treaty rights to hunt eagles. Can you recall why the Court's conclusion that the statute abrogated the treaty right did not include an analysis of whether the abrogation was justified?

3. The *Guerin* Court also touches on the issue of aboriginal title, but leaves the matter relatively undefined. The Supreme Court of Canada refined the contours of aboriginal title in the following case.

DELGAMUUKW V. BRITISH COLUMBIA

Supreme Court of Canada,
[1997] 3 S.C.R. 1010.

The judgment of **LAMER C.J.** and **CORY** and **MAJOR J.J.** was delivered by **THE CHIEF JUSTICE**

I. Introduction

This appeal is the latest in a series of cases in which it has fallen to this Court to interpret and apply the guarantee of existing aboriginal rights found in s. 35(1) of the Constitution Act, 1982. Although that line of decisions, commencing with *R. v. Sparrow*, [1990] 1 S.C.R. 1075, proceeding through the *Van der Peet* trilogy (*R. v. Van der Peet*, [1996] 2 S.C.R. 507, *R. v. N.T.C. Smokehouse Ltd.*, [1996] 2 S.C.R. 672, and *R. v. Gladstone*, [1996] 2 S.C.R. 723), and ending in *R. v. Pamajewon*, [1996] 2 S.C.R. 821, *R. v. Adams*, [1996] 3 S.C.R. 101, and *R. v. Côté*, [1996] 3 S.C.R. 139, have laid down the jurisprudential framework for s. 35(1), this appeal raises a set of interrelated and novel questions which revolve around a single issue—the nature and scope of the constitutional protection afforded by s. 35(1) to common law aboriginal title.

***

V. Analysis

***

This appeal requires us to apply not only the first principle in *Van der Peet*, but the second principle as well, and adapt the laws of evidence so that the aboriginal perspective on their practices, customs and traditions and on their relationship with the land, are given due weight by the courts. In practical terms, this requires the courts to come to terms with the oral histories of aboriginal societies, which, for many aboriginal nations, are the only record of their past. Given that the aboriginal rights recognized and affirmed by s. 35(1) are defined by reference to pre-contact practices or, as I will develop below, in the case of title, pre-sovereignty occupation, those histories play a crucial role in the litigation of aboriginal rights.

A useful and informative description of aboriginal oral history is provided by the Report of the Royal Commission on Aboriginal Peoples (1996), vol. 1 (*Looking Forward, Looking Back*), at p. 33:

> The Aboriginal tradition in the recording of history is neither linear nor steeped in the same notions of social progress and evolution [as in the non-Aboriginal tradition]. Nor is it usually human-centred in the same way as the western scientific tradition, for it does not assume that human beings are anything more than one—and not necessarily the most important—element of the natural order of the universe. Moreover, the Aboriginal historical tradition is an oral one, involving legends, stories and accounts handed down through the generations in oral form. It is less focused on establishing objective truth and assumes that the teller of the story is so much a part of the event being described that it would be arrogant to presume to classify or categorize the event exactly or for all time.
>
> In the Aboriginal tradition the purpose of repeating oral accounts from the past is broader than the role of written history in western societies. It may be to educate the listener, to communicate aspects of culture, to socialize people into a cultural tradition, or to validate the claims of a particular family to authority and prestige. ***
>
> Oral accounts of the past include a good deal of subjective experience. They are not simply a detached recounting of factual events but, rather, are "facts enmeshed in the stories of a lifetime". They are also likely to be rooted in particular locations, making reference to particular families and communities. This contributes to a sense that there are many histories, each characterized in part by how a people see themselves, how they define their identity in relation to their environment, and how they express their uniqueness as a people.

Many features of oral histories would count against both their admissibility and their weight as evidence of prior events in a court that took a traditional approach to the rules of evidence. The most fundamental of these is their broad social role not only "as a repository of historical knowledge for a culture" but also as an expression of "the values and mores of [that] culture." *** The difficulty with these features of oral histories is that they are tangential to the ultimate purpose of the fact-finding process at trial—the determination of the historical truth. Another feature of oral histories which creates difficulty is that they largely consist of out-of-court statements, passed on through an unbroken chain across the generations of a particular aboriginal nation to the present-day. These out-of-court statements are admitted for their truth and therefore conflict with the general rule against the admissibility of hearsay.

Notwithstanding the challenges created by the use of oral histories as proof of historical facts, the laws of evidence must be adapted in order that this type of evidence can be accommodated and placed on an equal footing with the types of historical evidence that courts are familiar with, which largely consists of historical documents. This is a long-standing practice in the interpretation of treaties between the Crown and aboriginal peoples. To quote Dickson C.J., given that most aboriginal societies "did not keep written records", the failure to do so would "impose an impossible burden of proof" on aboriginal peoples, and "render nugatory" any rights that they have (*Simon v. The Queen*, [1985] 2 S.C.R. 387, at p. 408). This process must be undertaken on a case-by-case basis. ***

***

In my opinion, the trial judge expected too much of the oral history of the appellants, as expressed in the recollections of aboriginal life of members of the appellant nations. He expected that evidence to provide definitive and precise evidence of pre-contact aboriginal activities on the territory in question. However, as I held in *Van der Peet*, this will be almost an impossible burden to meet. Rather, if oral history cannot conclusively establish pre-sovereignty (after this decision) occupation of land, it may still be relevant to demonstrate that current occupation has its origins prior to sovereignty. This is exactly what the appellants sought to do.

***

(e) Conclusion

The trial judge's treatment of the various kinds of oral histories did not satisfy the principles I laid down in *Van der Peet*. These errors are particularly worrisome because oral histories were of critical importance to the appellants' case. They used those histories in an attempt to establish their occupation and use of the disputed territory, an essential requirement for aboriginal title. The trial judge, after refusing to admit, or giving no independent weight to these oral histories, reached the conclusion that the appellants had not demonstrated the requisite degree of occupation for "ownership". Had the trial judge assessed the oral histories correctly, his conclusions on these issues of fact might have been very different.

***

C. What is the content of aboriginal title, how is it protected by s. 35 of the Constitution Act, 1982, and what is required for its proof?

***

Although cases involving aboriginal title have come before this Court and Privy Council before, there has never been a definitive statement from either court on the *content* of aboriginal title. In *St. Catherine's Milling*, the Privy Council, as I have mentioned, described the aboriginal title as a "personal and usufructuary right", but declined to explain what that meant because it was not "necessary to express any opinion upon the point" (at p. 55). Similarly, in *Calder*, *Guerin*, and *Paul*, the issues were the extinguishment of, the fiduciary duty arising from the surrender of, and statutory easements over land held pursuant to, aboriginal title, respectively; the content of title was not at issue and was not directly addressed.

Although the courts have been less than forthcoming, I have arrived at the conclusion that the content of aboriginal title can be summarized by two propositions: first, that aboriginal title encompasses the right to exclusive use and occupation of the land held pursuant to that title for a variety of purposes, which need not be aspects of those aboriginal practices, customs and traditions which are integral to distinctive aboriginal cultures; and second, that those protected uses must not be irreconcilable with the nature of the group's attachment to that land. ***

(d) Aboriginal Title Under s. 35(1) of the Constitution Act, 1982

Aboriginal title at common law is protected in its full form by s. 35(1). This conclusion flows from the express language of s. 35(1) itself, which states in full: "[t]he *existing* aboriginal and treaty rights of the aboriginal peoples of Canada are hereby recognized and affirmed" (emphasis added). On a plain reading of the provision, s. 35(1) did not create aboriginal rights; rather, it accorded constitutional status to those rights which were "existing" in 1982. The provision, at the very least, constitutionalized those rights which aboriginal peoples possessed at common law, since those rights existed at the time s. 35(1) came into force. Since aboriginal title was a common law right whose existence was recognized well before 1982 (e.g., *Calder, supra*), s. 35(1) has constitutionalized it in its full form.

***

The acknowledgement that s. 35(1) has accorded constitutional status to common law aboriginal title raises a further question—the relationship of aboriginal title to the "aboriginal rights" protected by s. 35(1). ***

***

The picture which emerges from *Adams* is that the aboriginal rights which are recognized and affirmed by s. 35(1) fall along a spectrum with respect to their degree of connection with the land. At the one end, there are those aboriginal rights which are practices, customs and traditions that are integral to the distinctive aboriginal culture of the group claiming the right. However, the "*occupation and use of the land*" where the activity is taking place is not "*sufficient to support a claim of title to the land*" (emphasis in original). Nevertheless, those activities receive constitutional protection. In the middle, there are activities which, out of necessity, take place on land and indeed, might be intimately related to a particular piece of land. Although an aboriginal group may not be able to demonstrate title to the land, it may nevertheless have a site-specific right to engage in a particular activity. ***

***

Because aboriginal rights can vary with respect to their degree of connection with the land, some aboriginal groups may be unable to make out a claim to title, but will nevertheless possess aboriginal rights that are recognized and affirmed by s. 35(1), including site-specific rights to engage in particular activities. ***

***

VI. Conclusion and Disposition

***

[T]his litigation has been both long and expensive, not only in economic but in human terms as well. By ordering a new trial, I do not necessarily encourage the parties to proceed to litigation and to settle their dispute through the courts. As was said in *Sparrow*, s. 35(1) "provides a solid constitutional base upon which subsequent negotiations can take place". Those negotiations should also include other aboriginal nations which have a stake in the territory claimed. Moreover, the Crown is under a moral, if not a legal, duty to enter into and conduct those negotiations in good faith. Ultimately, it is through negotiated settlements, with good faith and give and take on all sides, reinforced by the judgments of this Court, that we will achieve what I stated in *Van der Peet*, *supra*, to be a basic purpose of s. 35(1)—"the reconciliation of the pre-existence of aboriginal societies with the sovereignty of the Crown". Let us face it, we are all here to stay.

NOTES AND QUESTIONS

1. *Delgamuukw* addressed evidentiary issues as well as substantive standards for a claim of aboriginal title. Note also the exhortatory nature of the opinion's final sentence. The Court's words acknowledged the difficult nature of these conflicts, and the intense feelings of all involved. And yet matters became even more fraught in the aftermath of a subsequent treaty rights case. In *R. v. Marshall* [1999] 3 S.C.R. 456, the Court held that the treaty right to fish could be a defense to the charge of fishing without a license. The decision was controversial because it appeared to acknowledge a treaty right not only to fish for subsistence purposes, but also for commercial trade. *Id.* at par. 4. An uproar followed, involving non-Native fears of being unable to regulate or conserve their fisheries, and Native claims of near-blanket exemptions. The Supreme Court attempted to tamp down the concerns in *Marshall II*, a re-hearing of the case that resulted in an opinion acknowledging that the government can limit treaty rights to earn a moderate livelihood from fishing if the limitations are justified on conservation or other grounds of public importance. *See R. v. Marshall*, [1999] 3 S.C.R. 533

2. While the *Delgamuukw* decision is widely (and correctly) hailed as a tremendous victory for aboriginal Nations in Canada, Chief Justice Lamer's opinion has language that may indicate considerable leeway in infringing upon aboriginal title.

> In my opinion, the development of agriculture, forestry, mining, and hydroelectric power, the general economic development of the interior of British Columbia, protection of the environment or endangered species, the building of infrastructure and the settlement of foreign populations to support those aims, are the kinds of objectives that *** can justify the infringement of aboriginal title. Whether a particular measure or government act can be explained by reference to one of those objectives, however, is ultimately a question of fact that will have to be examined on a case-by-case basis.

Delgamuukw, *supra*, ¶ 165. The claims at issue in *Delgamuukw* were remanded in 1997, but no further judicial proceedings have occurred. Instead, prolonged negotiations have ensued. For a comprehensive report on the treaty process in British Columbia see BC Treaty Commission, http://www.bctreaty.net/files/publications.php (last visited Sept. 13, 2013).

3. The *Delgamuukw* court draws a distinction between aboriginal "rights" and aboriginal "title." Where does that distinction come from? Is it based on aboriginal law, or a colonizing view of what is permissible under Canadian law? More recent cases dealing with the content of aboriginal rights, title and Crown duties of consultation when infringing upon aboriginal rights or title, include, *R. v. Marshall*, [2005] 2 S.C.R. 220; *Haida Nation v. British*

Columbia, [2004] 3 S.C.R. 511; *Taku River Tlingit First Nation v. British Columbia*, [2004] 3 S.C.R. 550.

4. As these cases reveal, First Nations law in Canada is vital and evolving. Sources addressing ongoing treaty negotiations include Patrick Macklem, Indigenous Differences and the Constitution of Canada (2001) and John Borrows, *Ground Rules: Indigenous Treaties in Canada and New Zealand*, 22 N.Z.U. L. Rev. 188 (2006). For more about the Canadian Supreme Court's jurisprudence, see Gordon Christie, *Developing Case Law: The Future of Consultation and Accommodation*, 39 U. Brit. Colo. L. Rev. 139 (2006); Kent McNeil, *Aboriginal Title and the Supreme Court: What's Happening?*, 69 Sask. L. Rev. 281 (2006); *The Power of Promises: Rethinking Indian Treaties in the Pacific Northwest* (Alexandra Harmon ed., 2005); John Borrows, *Frozen Rights in Canada: Constitutional Interpretation and the Trickster*, 22 Am. Ind. L. Rev. 37 (1997). Finally, for an in-depth treatment of the history, politics, and law of aboriginal peoples in Canada, consult the multi-volume report issued by the Royal Commission on Aboriginal Peoples, *Report of the Royal Commission on Aboriginal Peoples (Looking Forward, Looking Back)* (1996), http://www.aadnc-aandc.gc.ca/eng/1100100014597/1100100014637#chp3. *See also* John J. Borrows & Leonard I. Rotman, Aboriginal Legal Issues: Cases, Materials and Commentary (3rd ed. 2007); Robert T. Anderson, *Aboriginal Title in the Canadian Legal System: The story of* Delgamuukw v. British Columbia, *in* Indian Law Stories 621 (C. Goldberg, K. Washburn & P. Frickey, eds. 2011).

5. The Canadian Supreme Court returned to fundamental questions of aboriginal title in *Tsilhqot'in Nation v. British Columbia*, [2014] SCC 44 (Can.). The Xeni Gwet'in First Nations (as part of the larger Tsilhqot'in Nation) asserted aboriginal title to a portion of their territory in central British Columbia that was about to be logged pursuant to a provincial license. The trial extended for 339 days over a five-year period, after which the trial court concluded that the Xeni Gwet'in had established aboriginal title to portions of the claimed area. The court of appeal reversed, holding that title had not been established, but that rights to "hunt, trap and harvest" should be recognized. The Xeni Gwet'in appealed, seeking reinstatement of the trial court's determination of aboriginal title and revocation of the forest harvest permits as an unjustified infringement on aboriginal title.

On appeal, the Canadian Supreme Court posed several questions, and summarized the governing legal principles.

> What is the test for Aboriginal title to land? If title is established, what rights does it confer? Does the British Columbia *Forest Act*, R.S.B.C. 1996, c. 157, apply to land covered by Aboriginal title? What are the constitutional constraints on provincial regulation of land under Aboriginal title? Finally, how are broader public interests to be reconciled with the rights conferred by Aboriginal title? *** [As for governing legal principles], [t]he jurisprudence ... establishes a number of propositions that touch on the issues that arise in this case, including:
>
> - Radical or underlying Crown title is subject to Aboriginal land interests where they are established.
> - Aboriginal title gives the Aboriginal group the right to use and control the land and enjoy its benefits.

- Governments can infringe Aboriginal rights conferred by Aboriginal title but only where they can justify the infringements on the basis of a compelling and substantial purpose and establish that they are consistent with the Crown's fiduciary duty to the group.
- Resource development on claimed land to which title has not been established requires the government to consult with the claimant Aboriginal group.
- Governments are under a legal duty to negotiate in good faith to resolve claims to ancestral lands.

The Court engaged in an extended discussion of the three elements needed to prove aboriginal title: 1) sufficiency of occupation; 2) continuity of occupation; and 3) exclusivity of occupation. The Court ruled that western common law notions of property rights must be melded with the "Aboriginal perspective" in evaluating these factors. "[O]ne looks to the Aboriginal culture and practices, and compares them in a culturally sensitive way with what was required at common law to establish title on the basis of occupation." Occupation need not be confined to specific sites of settlement but extends to areas regularly used for hunting, fishing or otherwise exploiting resources and "over which the group exercised effective control at the time of assertion of European sovereignty."

Applying the test, the Court found that the trial court had ample support in the record to affirm its decision. The Court then held that any infringement on aboriginal title must "be undertaken in accordance with the Crown's procedural duty to consult and must also be justified on the basis of a compelling and substantial public interest, and must be consistent with the Crown's fiduciary duty to the Aboriginal group." This means that the Xeni Gwet'in have "the right to determine, subject to the inherent limits of group title held for future generations, the uses to which the land is put and to enjoy its economic fruits."

The Court also held that the constitutional obligation to respect aboriginal title extends to the Provinces, and that licenses to harvest timber unlawfully infringe on aboriginal rights unless there has been prior consultation and consent, or prior consultation coupled with a "compelling and substantial legislative objective in the public interest." In other words any federal or provincial legislation must conform with "s. 35 of the *Constitution Act, 1982*, which directly addresses the requirement that these [aboriginal property] interests must be respected by the government, unless the government can justify incursion on them for a compelling purpose and in conformity with its fiduciary duty to affected Aboriginal groups."

6. The *Xeni Gwet'in First Nations* decision represents a significant advance for aboriginal land claims in British Columbia (the Province is the size of California, Washington and Oregon combined). It is the first decision to confirm aboriginal title to specific lands, and it effectively set aside a provincial timber license based on the failure to abide by the law governing aboriginal title.

The trial court had also recognized Xeni Gwet'in aboriginal title to private lands, but those rights were disavowed on appeal. The Supreme Court noted that a number of non-aboriginal residents of the aboriginal area supported the

First Nation's claim. What do you think were the tactics leading up to that decision, and does that give you any indication of how governance matters might be worked out? Recall the hope expressed in *Delgamuukw v. British Columbia* that the litigation set the stage for "the reconciliation of the pre-existence of aboriginal societies with the sovereignty of the Crown." Do you think the *Xeni Gwet'in* decision will advance that cause?

7. The Canada Supreme Court decided two more cases dealing with aboriginal rights and the Crown's duty to consult. *Clyde River (Hamlet) v. Petroleum Geo-Services Inc (Clyde River)*, 2017 SCC 40, 2017 Carswell Nat 3470 (Crown failed to discharge its duty to consult and accommodate when authorizing offshore oil and gas exploration in area important to Inuit peoples for marine mammal harvest); and *Chippewas of the Thames First Nation v. Enbridge Pipelines Inc.*, 2017 SCC 41, 2017 SCC 41, 2017 Carswell Nat 3468 (National Energy Board provided First Nation with adequate opportunity to participate in decision-making process regarding pipeline approval when Nation was allowed to participate in hearing and was provided adequate funding for its participation). For an in-depth discussion of the cases, see Nigel Bankes, *Clarifying the Parameters of the Crown's Duty to Consult and Accommodate in the Context of Decision-Making by Energy Tribunals*, 36 J. Energy & Nat. Resources L. 163 (2018).

EPILOGUE

PERSPECTIVES ON AMERICAN INDIAN LAW

■ ■ ■

Students who have made their way through all or part of this casebook now have the basic outline of the many areas that fall under the heading "American Indian law." The next step for most future practitioners of Indian law is to dive even deeper into the weeds of one of the Indian law sub-topics. Some of you will have to master complex jurisdictional rules to prepare for work in a tribal legal department; others will plunge into Indian country definitions to work for the Federal Defenders or United States Attorney's office, and so forth. For law students who do not plan to pursue a career in American Indian law, the likely path is to leave the field behind, perhaps remembering a handful of key concepts, notable decisions, or striking phrases. (Even if you think you have left the field, however, do not be surprised if you are confronted with an Indian law issue in your practice in a commercial, labor, property or family law context.) Each of these paths leaves little time to contemplate the larger questions that beg to be asked about the field. We therefore close with a short discussion designed to encourage students to consider those questions.

First, we offer a vigorous caveat. Any distillation of lengthy and dense scholarly arguments inevitably oversimplifies them. Further, to the extent that particular authors are quoted or associated with certain approaches, readers should keep in mind that most scholars write in a range of modes throughout their careers, and that there is fluidity both within the approaches and even within each individual writer. With the disclaimers out of the way, what follows are brief descriptions of scholarly understandings of the field of Indian law.

Foundationalist

Foundationalist scholarship seeks to reconnect Indian law to its precedential, jurisprudential, and constitutional roots. According to the foundationalist view, Indian law is best understood as consisting of the principles articulated in the Marshall trilogy, in particular in *Worcester v. Georgia*. Felix Cohen's subsequent articulation of those principles in his treatise might be described as the quintessential foundationalist summary of Indian law doctrine:

> (1) An Indian tribe possesses, in the first instance, all the powers of any sovereign state. (2) Conquest renders the tribe subject to the legislative power of the United States and, in substance, terminates the external powers of sovereignty of the tribe, *e.g.*, its power to enter into treaties with foreign nations, but does not by itself affect the internal sovereignty of the tribe, *e.g.*, *i.e.*, its powers of local self-government. (3) These powers are subject to qualification by Congress, but, save as thus expressly qualified,

> full powers of internal sovereignty are vested in the Indian tribes and in their duly constituted organs of government.

Felix S. Cohen, Handbook of Federal Indian Law 123 (1941). To foundationalists, these core doctrinal principles are the best tools to mitigate the harsh but inevitable reality that American Indian nations have been subsumed within the American legal system, largely against their will. According to the foundationalist view, the main problem with recent Supreme Court cases, particularly in the areas of tribal jurisdiction over nonmembers and state regulation of tribal affairs, is that the Court has strayed from this foundational core. For a forceful articulation of the foundationalist perspective, see David Getches, *Conquering the Cultural Frontier: The New Subjectivism of the Supreme Court in Indian Law*, 84 Cal. L. Rev. 1573 (1996) (showing ways that recent cases depart from the animating roots of Indian law). The classic, and still relevant, foundationalist text by a contemporary scholar is Charles F. Wilkinson, American Indians, Time and the Law: Native Societies in a Modern Constitutional Democracy (1987).[†]

Critical

It is difficult to read the Marshall trilogy, *Kagama, Lone Wolf, Tee-Hit Ton*, and many other early and even contemporary (e.g., *Oliphant, Strate v. A-1 Contractors, Nevada v. Hicks*) Indian law cases and not conclude that racism at worst, misunderstanding of Indians at best, has played some part in how the Justices construe the law. The critical Indian law perspective posits that the racist narrative not only influences, but constructs and perpetuates the colonized legal status of American Indians. Professor Robert Williams is the leading scholar in the critical camp, and his thorough historical research leaves little doubt about Indian law's racist origins. *See* Robert A. Williams, Jr., The American Indian in Western Legal Thought: The Discourses of Conquest (1990). He takes a very different view of the principles distilled in the Marshall trilogy than the foundationalists do. Williams contends that the Marshall model of Indian rights comprises four elements: (1) recognition of the exclusive right of the United States to exercise supremacy over Indian tribes on the basis of tribes' presumed inferiority; (2) the doctrine of discovery as the principle that expresses the scope of white privilege; (3) the perpetuation of racist language to characterize Indians as savages and justify their subjugation; and (4) absolution for the Justices of any responsibility in this racist and colonialist state of affairs on the basis of purported deference to realpolitik. *See* Robert A. Williams, Jr., Like a Loaded Weapon: The Rehnquist Court, Indian Rights, and the Legal History of Racism in America 58 (2005).

Professor Williams concludes that only a thorough repudiation of the early cases and their debased view of Indian people will achieve a reformation in the way judges decide contemporary Indian law disputes. Just as the Supreme Court in *Brown v. Board of Education* rejected the racist narrative of *Plessy v. Ferguson* and *Dred Scott*, so too should the Court cleanse Indian law by

---

†. Additional sources that take a foundational approach include but are not limited to: David H. Getches, *Beyond Indian Law: The Rehnquist Court's Pursuit of State's Rights, Color-Blind Justice and Mainstream Values*, 86 Minn. L. Rev. 267 (2001); John LaVelle, *Sanctioning a Tyranny: The Diminishment of* Ex Parte Young, *Expansion of* Hans *Immunity, and Denial of Indian Rights in* Coeur d'Alene Tribe, 31 Ariz. St. L.J. 787 (1999); Judith V. Royster, *The Legacy of Allotment*, 27 Ariz. St. L.J. 1 (1995); Richard Collins, *Indian Consent to American Government*, 31 Ariz. L. Rev. 365 (1989).

explicitly confronting its tainted roots. *See* Williams, Like a Loaded Weapon at xxi. Professor Williams recommends a return to what he sees as the only redeeming aspect of the Marshall trilogy, which was its incorporation of international law principles. The contemporary context of indigenous rights in international law offers, according to Williams, a better context for considering the rights of American Indians.

Other critical perspectives adopt a similar view of Indian law, but offer different prescriptions. Professor Robert Odawi Porter, for example, offers various domestic solutions for adopting a less constrained vision of sovereignty for Indian nations. *See* Robert Odawi Porter, *A Proposal to the Hanodaganyas to Decolonize Federal Indian Control Law*, 31 U. Mich. J. L. Ref. 899 (1998); *see also* Robert N. Clinton, *Redressing the Legacy of Conquest: A Vision Quest for a Decolonized Federal Indian Law*, 46 Ark. L. Rev. (1993).[††]

Another critical approach, which relies on settler-colonial theory, examines how federal Indian law historically defined tribes and tribal members in order to separate indigenous peoples from their land. Indian law therefore paved the way for manifest destiny and the non-Indian settlement of the west. These critical approaches nonetheless also describe how tribes have been able to use the apparatus of Indian law to reclaim rights to land and self-determination. *See* Bethany R. Berger, Red: Racism and the American Indian, 56 UCLA L. Rev. 591 (2009); Sarah Krakoff, *Inextricably Political: Race Membership and Tribal Sovereignty*, 87 Wash. L. Rev. 1041 (2012); Addie Rolnick, *The Promise of* Mancari: *Indian Political Rights as Racial Remedy*, 86 NYU L. Rev. 958 (2011). In a similar vein, Professor Maggie Blackhawk argues that federal Indian law is central, not peripheral, to a full understanding of the limitations and promises of American public law. She takes a critically descriptive approach to the field, documenting key moments when Indian law defined the republic, sometimes for better and sometimes for worse. *See* Maggie Blackhawk, *Federal Indian Law as Paradigm within Public Law*, 132 Harv. L. Rev. 1787 (2019).

Critical scholarship may also emerge from foundationalist approaches. Thus, Professor Robert Clinton's thoroughgoing rejection of basic elements of contemporary Indian Law, Robert N. Clinton, *There is No Federal Supremacy Clause for Indian Tribes*, 34 Ariz. St. L.J. 113 (2002), is closely related to his earlier foundationalist examination of the meaning and early interpretation of the Indian Commerce Clause. Robert N. Clinton, *The Dormant Indian Commerce Clause*, 27 Conn. L. Rev. 1055 (1995).

Pragmatist

Pragmatist scholarship stakes somewhat of a middle ground. In essence, the pragmatist position is that American Indian law is imperfect in many ways, including its racist origins, yet also includes principles, including the interpretive approach adopted by Chief Justice Marshall in *Worcester*, that may be the best tools for protecting tribal rights in light of power structures. *See* Philip P. Frickey, *Congressional Intent, Practical Reasoning, and the*

---

††. Additional sources taking a critical approach include but are not limited to: Jo Carillo, *Identity as Idiom:* Mashpee *Reconsidered*, 28 Indiana L. Rev. 511 (1995); Robert Odawi Porter, *The Demise Of The Ongwehoweh And The Rise Of The Native Americans: Redressing The Genocidal Act Of Forcing American Citizenship Upon Indigenous Peoples*, 15 Harv. BlackLetter L.J. 107 (1999).

Dynamic Nature of Federal Indian Law, 78 Cal. L. Rev. 1137 (1990); *see also* Robert Laurence, *Learning to Live with Congressional Plenary Power Over Indians: An Essay in Response to Professor Williams' Algebra*, 30 Ariz. L. Rev. 413, 422 (1988). In practical terms, the pragmatist approach may differ little from the foundationalist one. Under both views, American Indian law should hew to the overriding norm of preserving the retained sovereignty of tribes and adopt interpretive approaches consistent with that norm. Indeed, some scholarship might fairly be called either pragmatist or foundationalist. Felix Cohen's magisterial *Handbook on Federal Indian Law*, for example, might be described as a great foundationalist document, in that it shows the thread of measured protection for tribal sovereignty that runs throughout judicial decisions, treaties, and historical practice, but is also informed by Cohen's deeply realist perspective. Contemporary articles that might fall within this description include Dean Nell Newton's *Plenary Power Over Indians: Its Scope, Sources and Limitations*, 132 U. Pa. L. Rev 195 (1984) and Professor Frickey's *Marshalling Past and Present: Colonialism, Constitutionalism, and Interpretation in Federal Indian Law*, 107 Harv. L. Rev. 381 (1993). The pragmatist approach retains deep awareness of the limitations of understanding the law solely from a doctrinal perspective, and is attuned to the ways that conflicting policy concerns and structures of power influence the implementation of law. For more elaboration on this point, as well as additional details about the foundationalist and pragmatist approaches, see Sarah Krakoff, *Undoing Indian Law One Case at a Time: Judicial Minimalism and Tribal Sovereignty*, 50 American U. L. Rev. 1177, 1198-99 (2001).

Pragmatist scholarship also recognizes the limitations of looking solely to the judiciary as a law-making branch. Professor Michalyn Steele has argued that Congress is a better audience than the courts for arguments in support of tribal sovereignty. *See* Michalyn Steele, *Plenary Power, Political Questions, and Sovereignty in Indian Affairs*, 63 UCLA L. Rev. 666 (2016). And in a series of articles, Professor Kirsten Matoy Carlson has undertaken empirical examinations of the Congress's role in Indian law. *See* Kirsten Matoy Carlson, *Lobying as Strategy for Tribal Resilience*, 2018 B.Y.U. L. Rev. 1159 (2018); *Congress, Tribal Recognition, and Legislative-Administrative Multiplicity*, 91 Ind. L.J. 955 (2016); *Congress and Indians*, 86 Colo. L. Rev. 77 (2015). Finally pragmatist scholarship recognizes that even for powerful nations, "sovereignty" is never absolute, but is always constrained by legal rules, political forces, and the need to work with other sovereign entities. *See* Sam Deloria, *Commentary on Nation Building: The Future of Indian Nations*, 34 Ariz. St. L. J. 55, 55-56 (2002). Pragmatist work therefore often focuses on the importance of negotiated or cooperative resolution of conflicts in Indian law. Thus work on achieving indigenous water rights, see Robert T. Anderson, *Indigenous Rights to Water & Environmental Protection*, 53 Harv. C.R.-C.L. L. Rev. (2018); Robert T. Anderson, *Indian Water Rights, Practical Reasoning and Negotiated Settlements,* 98 Cal. L. Rev. 1133 (2010); Robert T. Anderson, *Indian Water Rights and the Federal Trust Responsibility*, 46 Nat. Resources J. 399 (2006); Daniel McCool, Native Waters: Contemporary Indian Water Settlements and the Second Treaty Era (2002); Negotiating Tribal Water Rights: Fulfilling Promises in the Arid West (Bonnie G. Colby *et al.* eds. 2005), full faith and credit agreements, P.S. Deloria & Robert Laurence, *Negotiating Tribal-State Full Faith and Credit Agreements: The Topology of the Negotiation and the Merits of the Question*, 28 Ga. L. Rev. 365, 373-74 (1994), tribal-state tax agreements,

Matthew L.M. Fletcher, *The Power to Tax, The Power to Destroy, and the Michigan's Tribal-State Tax Agreements*, 82 U. Det. Mercy L. Rev. 1 (2004), and agreements for protection of sacred sites, Kristen A. Carpenter, *Limiting Principles and Empowering Practices in American Indian Religious Freedoms*, 387 Conn. L. Rev. 387 (2012), all fall within this pragmatist mode. *See also* Robert T. Anderson, *The* Katie John *Litigation: The Long Search for Alaska Native Subsistence Protections After ANCSA*, 51 Ariz. St. L.J. 845 (Forthcoming 2019)(describing the shortcomings of the Alaska Native Claims Settlement Act and offering suggestions for congressional reform), Frank Pommersheim, Braid of Feathers: American Indian Law and Contemporary Tribal Life 153-154, 158-161 (1995) (advocating various negotiated resolutions of tribal-state conflicts). Consistent with the pragmatic recognition of the power differentials in tribal, state, and federal power relations, however, these scholars typically recognize the dangers of negotiation, and the need for legal and normative ground rules to inform cooperative exercises of sovereignty.

Tribal Realism

Many contemporary scholars conduct research aimed at addressing how law actually works in Indian country. This work takes seriously Professor Frank Pommersheim's call to move beyond a discourse of federal law and domination and instead obtain a "reservation perspective" on American Indian Law. *See* Frank Pommersheim, Braid of Feathers: American Indian Law and Contemporary Tribal Life 3 (1995). Using a variety of methodological approaches, these scholars investigate tribal courts and institutions, the effects of federal law on either or both, the impacts of law on Indian people and vice versa, and a range of other topics that go beyond doctrinal analysis or critique. A recurrent theme in this literature is that Indian nations and people are agents in the making of Indian law. Another is that federal courts are poorly served by the dearth of information about tribal life that appears to make its way into judicial chambers. Dean Rennard Strickland was an early leader in this area. His historical research on the Cherokee Nation's traditional legal system remains a standard bearer in the field. *See Fire and the Spirits: Cherokee Law from Clan to Court* (1975). Professor Carole Goldberg's work about the efficacy of law enforcement in Public Law 280 states, and the meanings and uses of tribal membership requirements provide other examples of this approach. *See, e.g.*, Carole Goldberg, *Public Law 280 and the Problem of Lawlessness in California Indian Country*, 44 UCLA L. Rev. 1405 (1997); Carole Goldberg, *Members Only? Designing Citizenship Requirements for Indian Nations*, 50 U. Kan. L. Rev. 437 (2002); Carole Goldberg, *Descent into Race*, 49 UCLA L. Rev. 1373 (2002).

There is also a growing body of work on the ways that tribal governments use their sovereignty and respond to federal limitations on that sovereignty. *See, e.g.*, Elizabeth Kronk Warner, *Justice Brandeis and Indian Country: Lessons from the Tribal Environmental Laboratory*, 47 Ariz. St. L.J. 857 (2015) and *Examining Tribal Environmental Law*, 39 Colum. J. Envt'l L. 41 (2014); Bethany R. Berger, *Justice and the Outsider: Jurisdiction over Nonmembers in Tribal Legal Systems*, 37 Ariz. St. L.J. 1047 (2005); Sarah Krakoff, *A Narrative of Sovereignty: Illuminating the Paradox of the Domestic Dependent Nation*, 83 Oregon L. Rev. 1109 (2004). In a similar vein, some scholars are examining how tribes in the U.S. are incorporating international indigenous rights norms into their own laws, and reciprocally how tribal law is influencing the development of international law. *See* Kristen A. Carpenter & Angela R. Riley, *Indigenous Peoples and the Jurisgenerative Moment in Indigenous Human Rights*, 102 Cal. L. Rev. 173 (2014). For an important body of economic and sociological work along these lines, see the many publications produced under the auspices of the Harvard Project on Indian Economic Development. There are too many other articles emerging in this vein to list, but some additional authors are Matthew Fletcher, Elizabeth Kronk, Stacey Leeds, Justin Richland, Ezra Rosser, Wenona Singel, Paul Spruhan, Melissa Tatum, Gloria Valencia-Weber, Dean Kevin Washburn, and Christine Zuni-Cruz, among others. And to drive home the point that these categories are fluid and that authors move among them, a recent major work that recounts the role that tribes played in the emergence of modern tribal sovereignty is Charles Wilkinson's Blood Struggle: The Rise of Modern Indian Nations (2005).

Skeptic

The skeptical position is not adopted by many academics. Rather, it is the view expressed through some judicial opinions and by some practitioners that there really is no distinctive body of law that is "American Indian law," and that general legal principles and doctrines instead should control disputes between tribes or tribal members and non-Indians. Three examples of Supreme Court cases that drift toward the skeptical view, even if they stop short of adopting it explicitly, are *Plains Commerce Bank v. Long Family Land and Cattle Co.*, 128 S. Ct. 2709 (2008) (no tribal court jurisdiction over lawsuit brought by tribal members against non-Indian bank), *Wagnon v. Prairie Band of Potawatomi Nation*, 546 U.S. 95 (2005) (Indian law taxation principles not applied to state taxation of fuel sold at tribal gas station on grounds that tax is imposed on off-reservation distributor), and *Arizona Department of Revenue v. Blaze Construction*, 526 U.S. 32 (1999) (Indian law taxation principles not applied to state taxation of Indian-owned company doing business on Indian reservation pursuant to a federal contract). *Plains Commerce*, *Wagnon* and *Blaze* represent the skeptics' tendency to narrow the category of cases to which Indian law principles apply by focusing on factual distinctions that become controlling. In *Plains Commerce*, the Court focused exclusively on the fact that the remedy sought by the tribal member plaintiffs would have affected a sale of non-Indian fee land between non-Indians. In *Wagnon*, the Court found controlling the fact that the legal incidence of the tax fell on a non-Indian, off-reservation distributor. In *Blaze*, the Court adopted a new bright line test that states may tax federal contractors, regardless of whether they are working in Indian country. In each of these cases, the Court's focus on factual distinctions allowed it to avoid the application of Indian law principles which, in ordinary fashion, would have likely dictated an outcome for the other party.

The skeptical view would likely do away, judicially, with the doctrine of tribal sovereign immunity, and would endorse imposing state laws and regulations in Indian country unless Congress prohibited doing so. The skeptics would take the final step towards flipping the presumptions created by *Worcester* and coalesced by Cohen and others since. Protecting tribes would be largely in Congress's hands, and courts would be free to impose ordinary legal principles unless otherwise directed to do so by Congress.

NOTES AND QUESTIONS

1. *What role should federal courts play in redefining American Indian law?* How would each of the foregoing perspectives address that question? Think, for example, about whether the terms "activist" and "conservative" have the same meaning that they seem to in the constitutional law context. To carry out the skeptics' view that there is no tribal sovereign immunity, would the Court be engaging in judicial activism in the sense that they would have to overturn prior precedent? What about the possibility that carrying out the critical prescription would require overturning almost all early Indian law precedents? If so, is doing so in either context justified by other overriding norms and goals that the judiciary is charged with enforcing?

2 *What role should tribal institutions play in redefining Indian Law?* What does each perspective have to say about this? If a tribe has a sales tax that it is imposing on all consumer transactions within its boundaries and a non-Indian challenges that tax, can the tribe look to any of the above perspectives on Indian law to support its position that it retains the inherent power to tax even transient activity in Indian country? Relatedly, what role should tribal norms play in informing the interpretive approaches of Indian law? For a thoughtful view on this, see N. Bruce Duthu, American Indians and the Law 191-201 (2008).

3. *How do sovereign Indian nations fit within a democracy?* Indian nations remain geographically distinct and continue to be ruled by their own laws, even after all the inroads and modifications made to that simple understanding from *Worcester*. Yet the inroads include depriving tribes of territorial jurisdiction in ways that call into question whether they can really have their own "laws," as opposed to norms or customs. In general, it is the nature of a law that it applies throughout a geographic jurisdiction, not just to selected persons with certain relationships to one another. Certainly, there is still a geographic aspect to tribal jurisdiction. But to the extent that it has been eroded, it has largely been in the name of ensuring that the larger sovereign, the United States, can ensure all of its citizens equal and constitutional treatment. *Duro*, for example, expresses this constitutional nervousness, as does Justice Kennedy's concurrence in *Lara*. How do any of the above views of Indian law address this tension?

4. Finally, what should American Indian law do, and whose interest does it or should it serve? We will leave you with those questions to ponder. In our view, they inescapably inform the answers to more focused questions about the field. We hope the introduction provided here helps to guide you regarding how to think about this, and spurs you on to learn even more.

APPENDIX

THE CONSTITUTION OF THE UNITED STATES

■ ■ ■

We the People of the United States, in Order to form a more perfect Union, establish Justice, insure domestic Tranquility, provide for the common defence, promote the general Welfare, and secure the Blessings of Liberty to ourselves and our Posterity, do ordain and establish this Constitution for the United States of America.

ARTICLE I

Section 1. All legislative Powers herein granted shall be vested in a Congress of the United States, which shall consist of a Senate and House of Representatives.

Section 2. [1] The House of Representatives shall be composed of Members chosen every second Year by the People of the several States, and the Electors in each State shall have the Qualifications requisite for Electors of the most numerous Branch of the State Legislature.

[2] No Person shall be a Representative who shall not have attained to the Age of twenty five Years, and been seven Years a Citizen of the United States, and who shall not, when elected, be an Inhabitant of that State in which he shall be chosen.

[3] Representatives and direct Taxes shall be apportioned among the several States which may be included within this Union, according to their respective Numbers, which shall be determined by adding to the whole Number of free Persons, including those bound to Service for a Term of Years, and excluding Indians not taxed, three fifths of all other Persons. The actual Enumeration shall be made within three Years after the first Meeting of the Congress of the United States, and within every subsequent Term of ten Years, in such Manner as they shall by Law direct. The Number of Representatives shall not exceed one for every thirty Thousand, but each State shall have at Least one Representative; and until such enumeration shall be made, the State of New Hampshire shall be entitled to chuse three, Massachusetts eight, Rhode Island and Providence Plantations one, Connecticut five, New York six, New Jersey four, Pennsylvania eight, Delaware one, Maryland six, Virginia ten, North Carolina five, South Carolina five, and Georgia three.

[4] When vacancies happen in the Representation from any State, the Executive Authority thereof shall issue Writs of Election to fill such Vacancies.

[5] The House of Representatives shall chuse their Speaker and other Officers; and shall have the sole Power of Impeachment.

Section 3. [1] The Senate of the United States shall be composed of two Senators from each State, chosen by the Legislature thereof, for six Years; and each Senator shall have one Vote.

[2] Immediately after they shall be assembled in Consequence of the first Election, they shall be divided as equally as may be into three Classes. The Seats of the Senators of the first Class shall be vacated at the Expiration of the second Year, of the second Class at the Expiration of the fourth Year, and of the third Class at the Expiration of the sixth Year, so that one third may be chosen every second Year; and if Vacancies happen by Resignation, or otherwise, during the Recess of the Legislature of any State, the Executive thereof may make temporary Appointments until the next Meeting of the Legislature, which shall then fill such Vacancies.

[3] No Person shall be a Senator who shall not have attained to the Age of thirty Years, and been nine Years a Citizen of the United States, and who shall not, when elected, be an Inhabitant of that State for which he shall be chosen.

[4] The Vice President of the United States shall be President of the Senate, but shall have no Vote, unless they be equally divided.

[5] The Senate shall chuse their other Officers, and also a President pro tempore, in the Absence of the Vice President, or when he shall exercise the Office of President of the United States.

[6] The Senate shall have the sole Power to try all Impeachments. When sitting for that Purpose, they shall be on Oath or Affirmation. When the President of the United States is tried, the Chief Justice shall preside: And no Person shall be convicted without the Concurrence of two thirds of the Members present.

[7] Judgment in Cases of Impeachment shall not extend further than to removal from Office, and disqualification to hold and enjoy any Office of honor, Trust, or Profit under the United States: but the Party convicted shall nevertheless be liable and subject to Indictment, Trial, Judgment, and Punishment, according to Law.

Section 4. [1] The Times, Places and Manner of holding Elections for Senators and Representatives, shall be prescribed in each State by the Legislature thereof; but the Congress may at any time by Law make or alter such Regulations, except as to the Places of chusing Senators.

[2] The Congress shall assemble at least once in every Year, and such Meeting shall be on the first Monday in December, unless they shall by Law appoint a different Day.

Section 5. [1] Each House shall be the Judge of the Elections, Returns, and Qualifications of its own Members, and a Majority of each shall constitute a Quorum to do Business; but a smaller Number may adjourn from day to day, and may be authorized to compel the Attendance of absent Members, in such Manner, and under such Penalties as each House may provide.

[2] Each House may determine the Rules of its Proceedings, punish its Members for disorderly Behaviour, and, with the Concurrence of two thirds, expel a Member.

[3] Each House shall keep a Journal of its Proceedings, and from time to time publish the same, excepting such Parts as may in their Judgment require Secrecy; and the Yeas and Nays of the Members of either House on any question shall, at the Desire of one fifth of those Present, be entered on the Journal.

[4] Neither House, during the Session of Congress, shall without the Consent of the other, adjourn for more than three days, nor to any other Place than that in which the two Houses shall be sitting.

Section 6. [1] The Senators and Representatives shall receive a Compensation for their Services, to be ascertained by Law, and paid out of the Treasury of the United States. They shall in all Cases, except Treason, Felony, and Breach of the Peace, be privileged from Arrest during their Attendance at the Session of their respective Houses, and in going to and returning from the same; and for any Speech or Debate in either House, they shall not be questioned in any other Place.

[2] No Senator or Representative shall, during the Time for which he was elected, be appointed to any civil Office under the Authority of the United States, which shall have been created, or the Emoluments whereof shall have been encreased during such time; and no Person holding any Office under the United States, shall be a Member of either House during his Continuance in Office.

Section 7. [1] All Bills for raising Revenue shall originate in the House of Representatives; but the Senate may propose or concur with Amendments as on other Bills.

[2] Every Bill which shall have passed the House of Representatives and the Senate, shall, before it become a Law, be presented to the President of the United States; If he approve he shall sign it, but if not he shall return it, with his Objections to that House in which it shall have originated, who shall enter the Objections at large on their Journal, and proceed to reconsider it. If after such Reconsideration two thirds of that House shall agree to pass the Bill, it shall be sent, together with the Objections, to the other House, by which it shall likewise be reconsidered, and if approved by two thirds of that House, it shall become a Law. But in all such Cases the Votes of both Houses shall be determined by Yeas and Nays, and the Names of the Persons voting for and against the Bill shall be entered on the Journal of each House respectively. If any Bill shall not be returned by the President within ten Days (Sundays excepted) after it shall have been presented to him, the Same shall be a Law, in like Manner as if he had signed it, unless the Congress by their Adjournment prevent its Return, in which Case it shall not be a Law.

[3] Every Order, Resolution, or Vote to which the Concurrence of the Senate and House of Representatives may be necessary (except on a question of Adjournment) shall be presented to the President of the United States; and before the Same shall take Effect, shall be approved by him, or being disapproved by him, shall be repassed by two thirds of the Senate and House of Representatives, according to the Rules and Limitations prescribed in the Case of a Bill.

Section 8. [1] The Congress shall have Power To lay and collect Taxes, Duties, Imposts and Excises, to pay the Debts and provide for the common Defence and general Welfare of the United States; but all Duties, Imposts and Excises shall be uniform throughout the United States;

[2] To borrow Money on the credit of the United States;

[3] To regulate Commerce with foreign Nations, and among the several States, and with the Indian Tribes;

[4] To establish an uniform Rule of Naturalization, and uniform Laws on the subject of Bankruptcies throughout the United States;

[5] To coin Money, regulate the Value thereof, and of foreign Coin, and fix the Standard of Weights and Measures;

[6] To provide for the Punishment of counterfeiting the Securities and current Coin of the United States;

[7] To establish Post Offices and Post Roads;

[8] To promote the Progress of Science and useful Arts, by securing for limited Times to Authors and Inventors the exclusive Right to their respective Writings and Discoveries;

[9] To constitute Tribunals inferior to the supreme Court;

[10] To define and punish Piracies and Felonies committed on the high Seas, and Offences against the Law of Nations;

[11] To declare War, grant Letters of Marque and Reprisal, and make Rules concerning Captures on Land and Water;

[12] To raise and support Armies, but no Appropriation of Money to that Use shall be for a longer Term than two Years;

[13] To provide and maintain a Navy;

[14] To make Rules for the Government and Regulation of the land and naval Forces;

[15] To provide for calling forth the Militia to execute the Laws of the Union, suppress Insurrections and repel Invasions;

[16] To provide for organizing, arming, and disciplining, the Militia, and for governing such Part of them as may be employed in the Service of the United States, reserving to the States respectively, the Appointment of the Officers, and the Authority of training the Militia according to the discipline prescribed by Congress;

[17] To exercise exclusive Legislation in all Cases whatsoever, over such District (not exceeding ten Miles square) as may, by Cession of particular States and the Acceptance of Congress, become the Seat of the Government of the United States, and to exercise like Authority over all Places purchased by the Consent of the Legislature of the State in which the Same shall be, for the Erection of Forts, Magazines, Arsenals, dock-Yards, and other needful Buildings;—And

[18] To make all Laws which shall be necessary and proper for carrying into Execution the foregoing Powers, and all other Powers

vested by this Constitution in the Government of the United States, or in any Department or Officer thereof.

Section 9. [1] The Migration or Importation of such Persons as any of the States now existing shall think proper to admit, shall not be prohibited by the Congress prior to the Year one thousand eight hundred and eight, but a Tax or duty may be imposed on such Importation, not exceeding ten dollars for each Person.

[2] The Privilege of the Writ of Habeas Corpus shall not be suspended, unless when in Cases of Rebellion or Invasion the public Safety may require it.

[3] No Bill of Attainder or ex post facto Law shall be passed.

[4] No Capitation, or other direct, Tax shall be laid, unless in Proportion to the Census or Enumeration herein before directed to be taken.

[5] No Tax or Duty shall be laid on Articles exported from any State.

[6] No Preference shall be given by any Regulation of Commerce or Revenue to the Ports of one State over those of another: nor shall Vessels bound to, or from, one State, be obliged to enter, clear, or pay Duties in another.

[7] No Money shall be drawn from the Treasury, but in Consequence of Appropriations made by Law; and a regular Statement and Account of the Receipts and Expenditures of all public Money shall be published from time to time.

[8] No Title of Nobility shall be granted by the United States: And no Person holding any Office of Profit or Trust under them, shall, without the Consent of the Congress, accept of any present, Emolument, Office, or Title, of any kind whatever, from any King, Prince, or foreign State.

Section 10. [1] No State shall enter into any Treaty, Alliance, or Confederation; grant Letters of Marque and Reprisal; coin Money; emit Bills of Credit; make any Thing but gold and silver Coin a Tender in Payment of Debts; pass any Bill of Attainder, ex post facto Law, or Law impairing the Obligation of Contracts, or grant any Title of Nobility.

[2] No State shall, without the Consent of the Congress, lay any Imposts or Duties on Imports or Exports, except what may be absolutely necessary for executing its inspection Laws: and the net Produce of all Duties and Imposts, laid by any State on Imports or Exports, shall be for the Use of the Treasury of the United States; and all such Laws shall be subject to the Revision and Controul of the Congress.

[3] No State shall, without the Consent of Congress, lay any Duty of Tonnage, keep Troops, or Ships of War in time of Peace, enter into any Agreement or Compact with another State, or with a foreign Power, or engage in War, unless actually invaded, or in such imminent Danger as will not admit of delay.

ARTICLE II

Section 1. [1] The executive Power shall be vested in a President of the United States of America. He shall hold his Office during the Term of four Years, and, together with the Vice President, chosen for the same Term, be elected, as follows:

[2] Each State shall appoint, in such Manner as the Legislature thereof may direct, a Number of Electors, equal to the whole Number of Senators and Representatives to which the State may be entitled in the Congress: but no Senator or Representative, or Person holding an Office of Trust or Profit under the United States, shall be appointed an Elector.

[3] The electors shall meet in their respective States, and vote by ballot for two Persons, of whom one at least shall not be an Inhabitant of the same State with themselves. And they shall make a List of all the Persons voted for, and of the Number of Votes for each; which List they shall sign and certify, and transmit sealed to the Seat of the Government of the United States, directed to the President of the Senate. The President of the Senate shall, in the Presence of the Senate and House of Representatives, open all the Certificates, and the Votes shall then be counted. The Person having the greatest Number of Votes shall be the President, if such Number be a Majority of the whole Number of Electors appointed; and if there be more than one who have such Majority, and have an equal Number of Votes, then the House of Representatives shall immediately chuse by Ballot one of them for President; and if no Person have a Majority, then from the five highest on the List the said House shall in like Manner chuse the President. But in chusing the President, the Votes shall be taken by States, the Representation from each State having one Vote; A quorum for this Purpose shall consist of a Member or Members from two thirds of the States, and a Majority of all the States shall be necessary to a Choice. In every Case, after the Choice of the President, the Person having the greatest Number of Votes of the Electors shall be the Vice President. But if there should remain two or more who have equal Votes, the Senate shall chuse from them by Ballot the Vice-President.

[4] The Congress may determine the Time of chusing the Electors, and the Day on which they shall give their Votes; which Day shall be the same throughout the United States.

[5] No Person except a natural born Citizen, or a Citizen of the United States, at the time of the Adoption of this Constitution, shall be eligible to the Office of President; neither shall any Person be eligible to that Office who shall not have attained to the Age of thirty five Years, and been fourteen Years a Resident within the United States.

[6] In Case of the Removal of the President from Office, or of his Death, Resignation, or Inability to discharge the Powers and Duties of the said Office, the Same shall devolve on the Vice President, and the Congress may by Law provide for the Case of Removal, Death, Resignation or Inability, both of the President and Vice President, declaring what Officer shall then act as President, and such Officer shall act accordingly, until the Disability be removed, or a President shall be elected.

[7] The President shall, at stated Times, receive for his Services, a Compensation, which shall neither be encreased nor diminished during the Period for which he shall have been elected, and he shall not receive within that Period any other Emolument from the United States, or any of them.

[8] Before he enter on the Execution of his Office, he shall take the following Oath or Affirmation: "I do solemnly swear (or affirm) that I will faithfully execute the Office of President of the United States, and will to the best of my Ability, preserve, protect and defend the Constitution of the United States."

Section 2. [1] The President shall be Commander in Chief of the Army and Navy of the United States, and of the Militia of the several States, when called into the actual Service of the United States; he may require the Opinion, in writing, of the principal Officer in each of the executive Departments, upon any Subject relating to the Duties of their respective Offices, and he shall have Power to grant Reprieves and Pardons for Offenses against the United States, except in Cases of Impeachment.

[2] He shall have Power, by and with the Advice and Consent of the Senate, to make Treaties, provided two thirds of the Senators present concur; and he shall nominate, and by and with the Advice and Consent of the Senate, shall appoint Ambassadors, other public Ministers and Consuls, Judges of the supreme Court, and all other Officers of the United States, whose Appointments are not herein otherwise provided for, and which shall be established by Law: but the Congress may by Law vest the Appointment of such inferior Officers, as they think proper, in the President alone, in the Courts of Law, or in the Heads of Departments.

[3] The President shall have Power to fill up all Vacancies that may happen during the Recess of the Senate, by granting Commissions which shall expire at the End of their next Session.

Section 3. He shall from time to time give to the Congress Information of the State of the Union, and recommend to their Consideration such Measures as he shall judge necessary and expedient; he may, on extraordinary Occasions, convene both Houses, or either of them, and in Case of Disagreement between them, with Respect to the Time of Adjournment, he may adjourn them to such Time as he shall think proper; he shall receive Ambassadors and other public Ministers; he shall take Care that the Laws be faithfully executed, and shall Commission all the Officers of the United States.

Section 4. The President, Vice President and all civil Officers of the United States, shall be removed from Office on Impeachment for, and Conviction of, Treason, Bribery, or other high Crimes and Misdemeanors.

ARTICLE III

Section 1. The judicial Power of the United States, shall be vested in one supreme Court, and in such inferior Courts as the Congress may from time to time ordain and establish. The Judges, both of the supreme and inferior Courts, shall hold their Offices during good Behaviour, and shall, at stated Times, receive for their Services, a Compensation, which shall not be diminished during their Continuance in Office.

Section 2. [1] The judicial Power shall extend to all Cases, in Law and Equity, arising under this Constitution, the Laws of the United States, and Treaties made, or which shall be made, under their Authority;—to all Cases affecting Ambassadors, other public Ministers and Consuls;—to all Cases of admiralty and maritime Jurisdiction; — to Controversies to which the United States shall be a Party;—to Controversies between two or more States; — between a State and Citizens of another State;—between Citizens of different States;—between Citizens of the same State claiming Lands under Grants of different States, and between a State, or the Citizens thereof, and foreign States, Citizens or Subjects.

[2] In all Cases affecting Ambassadors, other public Ministers and Consuls, and those in which a State shall be Party, the supreme Court shall have original Jurisdiction. In all the other Cases before mentioned, the supreme Court shall have appellate Jurisdiction, both as to Law and Fact, with such Exceptions, and under such Regulations as the Congress shall make.

[3] The Trial of all Crimes, except in Cases of Impeachment, shall be by Jury; and such Trial shall be held in the State where the said Crimes shall have been committed; but when not committed within any State, the Trial shall be at such Place or Places as the Congress may by Law have directed.

Section 3. [1] Treason against the United States, shall consist only in levying War against them, or in adhering to their Enemies, giving them Aid and Comfort. No Person shall be convicted of Treason unless on the Testimony of two Witnesses to the same overt Act, or on Confession in open Court.

[2] The Congress shall have Power to declare the Punishment of Treason, but no Attainder of Treason shall work Corruption of Blood, or Forfeiture except during the Life of the Person attainted.

ARTICLE IV

Section 1. Full Faith and Credit shall be given in each State to the public Acts, Records, and judicial Proceedings of every other State. And the Congress may by general Laws prescribe the Manner in which such Acts, Records and Proceedings shall be proved, and the Effect thereof.

Section 2. [1] The Citizens of each State shall be entitled to all Privileges and Immunities of Citizens in the several States.

[2] A person charged in any State with Treason, Felony, or other Crime, who shall flee from Justice, and be found in another State, shall on Demand of the executive Authority of the State from which he fled, be delivered up, to be removed to the State having Jurisdiction of the Crime.

[3] No Person held to Service or Labour in one State, under the Laws thereof, escaping into another, shall, in Consequence of any Law or Regulation therein, be discharged from such Service or Labour, but shall be delivered up on Claim of the Party to whom such Service or Labour may be due.

Section 3. [1] New States may be admitted by the Congress into this Union; but no new State shall be formed or erected within the Jurisdiction of any other State; nor any State be formed by the Junction of two or more

States, or Parts of States, without the Consent of the Legislatures of the States concerned as well as of the Congress.

[2] The Congress shall have Power to dispose of and make all needful Rules and Regulations respecting the Territory or other Property belonging to the United States; and nothing in this Constitution shall be so construed as to Prejudice any Claims of the United States, or of any particular State.

Section 4. The United States shall guarantee to every State in this Union a Republican Form of Government, and shall protect each of them against Invasion; and on Application of the Legislature, or of the Executive (when the Legislature cannot be convened) against domestic Violence.

ARTICLE V

The Congress, whenever two thirds of both Houses shall deem it necessary, shall propose Amendments to this Constitution, or on the Application of the Legislatures of two thirds of the several States, shall call a Convention for proposing Amendments, which, in either Case, shall be valid to all Intents and Purposes, as Part of this Constitution, when ratified by the Legislatures of three fourths of the several States, or by Conventions in three fourths thereof, as the one or the other Mode of Ratification may be proposed by the Congress; Provided that no Amendment which may be made prior to the Year One thousand eight hundred and eight shall in any Manner affect the first and fourth Clauses in the Ninth Section of the first Article; and that no State, without its Consent, shall be deprived of its equal Suffrage in the Senate.

ARTICLE VI

[1] All Debts contracted and Engagements entered into, before the Adoption of this Constitution, shall be as valid against the United States under this Constitution, as under the Confederation.

[2] This Constitution, and the Laws of the United States which shall be made in Pursuance thereof; and all Treaties made, or which shall be made, under the Authority of the United States, shall be the supreme Law of the Land; and the Judges in every State shall be bound thereby, any Thing in the Constitution or Laws of any State to the Contrary notwithstanding.

[3] The Senators and Representatives before mentioned, and the Members of the several State Legislatures, and all executive and judicial Officers, both of the United States and of the several States, shall be bound by Oath or Affirmation, to support this Constitution; but no religious Test shall ever be required as a Qualification to any Office or public Trust under the United States.

ARTICLE VII

The Ratification of the Conventions of nine States, shall be sufficient for the Establishment of this Constitution between the States so ratifying the Same.

ARTICLES IN ADDITION TO, AND AMENDMENT OF, THE CONSTITUTION OF THE UNITED STATES OF AMERICA, PROPOSED BY CONGRESS, AND RATIFIED BY THE LEGISLATURES OF THE SEVER-

AL STATES, PURSUANT TO THE FIFTH ARTICLE OF THE ORIGINAL CONSTITUTION.

AMENDMENT I [1791]

Congress shall make no law respecting an establishment of religion, or prohibiting the free exercise thereof; or abridging the freedom of speech, or of the press; or the right of the people peaceably to assemble, and to petition the Government for a redress of grievances.

AMENDMENT II [1791]

A well regulated Militia, being necessary to the security of a free State, the right of the people to keep and bear Arms, shall not be infringed.

AMENDMENT III [1791]

No Soldier shall, in time of peace be quartered in any house, without the consent of the Owner, nor in time of war, but in a manner to be prescribed by law.

AMENDMENT IV [1791]

The right of the people to be secure in their persons, houses, papers, and effects, against unreasonable searches and seizures, shall not be violated, and no Warrants shall issue, but upon probable cause, supported by Oath or affirmation, and particularly describing the place to be searched, and the persons or things to be seized.

AMENDMENT V [1791]

No person shall be held to answer for a capital, or otherwise infamous crime, unless on a presentment or indictment of a Grand Jury, except in cases arising in the land or naval forces, or in the Militia, when in actual service in time of War or public danger; nor shall any person be subject for the same offence to be twice put in jeopardy of life or limb; nor shall be compelled in any criminal case to be a witness against himself, nor be deprived of life, liberty, or property, without due process of law; nor shall private property be taken for public use, without just compensation.

AMENDMENT VI [1791]

In all criminal prosecutions, the accused shall enjoy the right to a speedy and public trial, by an impartial jury of the State and district wherein the crime shall have been committed, which district shall have been previously ascertained by law, and to be informed of the nature and cause of the accusation; to be confronted with the witnesses against him; to have compulsory process for obtaining witnesses in his favor, and to have the Assistance of Counsel for his defence.

AMENDMENT VII [1791]

In Suits at common law, where the value in controversy shall exceed twenty dollars, the right of trial by jury shall be preserved, and no fact tried by a jury, shall be otherwise re-examined in any Court of the United States, than according to the rules of the common law.

AMENDMENT VIII [1791]

Excessive bail shall not be required, nor excessive fines imposed, nor cruel and unusual punishments inflicted.

AMENDMENT IX [1791]

The enumeration in the Constitution, of certain rights, shall not be construed to deny or disparage others retained by the people.

AMENDMENT X [1791]

The powers not delegated to the United States by the Constitution, nor prohibited by it to the States, are reserved to the States respectively, or to the people.

AMENDMENT XI [1798]

The Judicial power of the United States shall not be construed to extend to any suit in law or equity, commenced or prosecuted against one of the United States by Citizens of another State, or by Citizens or Subjects of any Foreign State.

AMENDMENT XII [1804]

The Electors shall meet in their respective states and vote by ballot for President and Vice-President, one of whom, at least, shall not be an inhabitant of the same state with themselves; they shall name in their ballots the person voted for as President, and in distinct ballots the person voted for as Vice-President, and they shall make distinct lists of all persons voted for as President, and of all persons voted for as Vice-President, and of the number of votes for each, which lists they shall sign and certify, and transmit sealed to the seat of the government of the United States, directed to the President of the Senate;—The President of the Senate shall, in the presence of the Senate and House of Representatives, open all the certificates and the votes shall then be counted;—The person having the greatest number of votes for President, shall be the President, if such number be a majority of the whole number of Electors appointed; and if no person have such majority, then from the persons having the highest numbers not exceeding three on the list of those voted for as President, the House of Representatives shall choose immediately, by ballot, the President. But in choosing the President, the votes shall be taken by states, the representation from each state having one vote; a quorum for this purpose shall consist of a member or members from two-thirds of the states, and a majority of all the states shall be necessary to a choice. And if the House of Representatives shall not choose a President whenever the right of choice shall devolve upon them, before the fourth day of March next following, then the Vice-President shall act as President, as in the case of the death or other constitutional disability of the President. The person having the greatest number of votes as Vice-President, shall be the Vice-President, if such number be a majority of the whole number of Electors appointed, and if no person have a majority, then from the two highest numbers on the list, the Senate shall choose the Vice-President; a quorum for the purpose shall consist of two-thirds of the whole number of Senators, and a majority of the whole number shall be necessary to a choice. But no person constitutionally ineligible to the office of President shall be eligible to that of Vice-President of the United States.

AMENDMENT XIII [1865]

Section 1. Neither slavery nor involuntary servitude, except as a punishment for crime whereof the party shall have been duly convicted, shall exist within the United States, or any place subject to their jurisdiction.

Section 2. Congress shall have power to enforce this article by appropriate legislation.

AMENDMENT XIV [1868]

Section 1. All persons born or naturalized in the United States, and subject to the jurisdiction thereof, are citizens of the United States and of the State wherein they reside. No State shall make or enforce any law which shall abridge the privileges or immunities of citizens of the United States; nor shall any State deprive any person of life, liberty, or property, without due process of law; nor deny to any person within its jurisdiction the equal protection of the laws.

Section 2. Representatives shall be apportioned among the several States according to their respective numbers, counting the whole number of persons in each State, excluding Indians not taxed. But when the right to vote at any election for the choice of electors for President and Vice President of the United States, Representatives in Congress, the Executive and Judicial officers of a State, or the members of the Legislature thereof, is denied to any of the male inhabitants of such State, being twenty-one years of age, and citizens of the United States, or in any way abridged, except for participation in rebellion, or other crime, the basis of representation therein shall be reduced in the proportion which the number of such male citizens shall bear to the whole number of male citizens twenty-one years of age in such State.

Section 3. No person shall be a Senator or Representative in Congress, or elector of President and Vice President, or hold any office, civil or military, under the United States, or under any State, who, having previously taken an oath, as a member of Congress, or as an officer of the United States, or as a member of any State legislature, or as an executive or judicial officer of any State, to support the Constitution of the United States, shall have engaged in insurrection or rebellion against the same, or given aid or comfort to the enemies thereof. But Congress may by a vote of two-thirds of each House, remove such disability.

Section 4. The validity of the public debt of the United States, authorized by law, including debts incurred for payment of pensions and bounties for services in suppressing insurrection or rebellion, shall not be questioned. But neither the United States nor any State shall assume or pay any debt or obligation incurred in aid of insurrection or rebellion against the United States, or any claim for the loss or emancipation of any slave; but all such debts, obligations and claims shall be held illegal and void.

Section 5. The Congress shall have power to enforce, by appropriate legislation, the provisions of this article.

AMENDMENT XV [1870]

Section 1. The right of citizens of the United States to vote shall not be denied or abridged by the United States or by any State on account of race, color, or previous condition of servitude.

Section 2. The Congress shall have power to enforce this article by appropriate legislation.

AMENDMENT XVI [1913]

The Congress shall have power to lay and collect taxes on incomes, from whatever source derived, without apportionment among the several States, and without regard to any census or enumeration.

AMENDMENT XVII [1913]

[1] The Senate of the United States shall be composed of two Senators from each State, elected by the people thereof, for six years; and each Senator shall have one vote. The electors in each State shall have the qualifications requisite for electors of the most numerous branch of the State legislatures.

[2] When vacancies happen in the representation of any State in the Senate, the executive authority of such State shall issue writs of election to fill such vacancies: Provided, That the legislature of any State may empower the executive thereof to make temporary appointments until the people fill the vacancies by election as the legislature may direct.

[3] This amendment shall not be so construed as to affect the election or term of any Senator chosen before it becomes valid as part of the Constitution.

AMENDMENT XVIII [1919]

Section 1. After one year from the ratification of this article the manufacture, sale, or transportation of intoxicating liquors within, the importation thereof into, or the exportation thereof from the United States and all territory subject to the jurisdiction thereof for beverage purposes is hereby prohibited.

Section 2. The Congress and the several States shall have concurrent power to enforce this article by appropriate legislation.

Section 3. This article shall be inoperative unless it shall have been ratified as an amendment to the Constitution by the legislatures of the several States, as provided in the Constitution, within seven years from the date of the submission hereof to the States by the Congress.

AMENDMENT XIX [1920]

[1] The right of citizens of the United States to vote shall not be denied or abridged by the United States or by any State on account of sex.

[2] Congress shall have power to enforce this article by appropriate legislation.

AMENDMENT XX [1933]

Section 1. The terms of the President and Vice President shall end at noon on the 20th day of January, and the terms of Senators and Representatives at noon on the 3d day of January, of the years in which such terms would have ended if this article had not been ratified; and the terms of their successors shall then begin.

Section 2. The Congress shall assemble at least once in every year, and such meeting shall begin at noon on the 3d day of January, unless they shall by law appoint a different day.

Section 3. If, at the time fixed for the beginning of the term of the President, the President elect shall have died, the Vice President elect shall become President. If a President shall not have been chosen before the time fixed for the beginning of his term, or if the President elect shall have failed to qualify, then the Vice President elect shall act as President until a President shall have qualified; and the Congress may by law provide for the case wherein neither a President elect nor a Vice President elect shall have qualified, declaring who shall then act as President, or the manner in which one who is to act shall be selected, and such person shall act accordingly until a President or Vice President shall have qualified.

Section 4. The Congress may by law provide for the case of the death of any of the persons from whom the House of Representatives may choose a President whenever the right of choice shall have devolved upon them, and for the case of the death of any of the persons from whom the Senate may choose a Vice President whenever the right of choice shall have devolved upon them.

Section 5. Sections 1 and 2 shall take effect on the 15th day of October following the ratification of this article.

Section 6. This article shall be inoperative unless it shall have been ratified as an amendment to the Constitution by the legislatures of three-fourths of the several States within seven years from the date of its submission.

AMENDMENT XXI [1933]

Section 1. The eighteenth article of amendment to the Constitution of the United States is hereby repealed.

Section 2. The transportation or importation into any State, Territory, or possession of the United States for delivery or use therein of intoxicating liquors, in violation of the laws thereof, is hereby prohibited.

Section 3. This article shall be inoperative unless it shall have been ratified as an amendment to the Constitution by conventions in the several States, as provided in the Constitution, within seven years from the date of the submission hereof to the States by the Congress.

AMENDMENT XXII [1951]

Section 1. No person shall be elected to the office of the President more than twice, and no person who has held the office of President, or acted as President, for more than two years of a term to which some other person was elected President shall be elected to the office of the President more than once. But this Article shall not apply to any person holding the office of President when this Article was proposed by the Congress, and shall not prevent any person who may be holding the office of President, or acting as President, during the term within which this Article becomes operative from holding the office of President or acting as President during the remainder of such term.

Section 2. This article shall be inoperative unless it shall have been ratified as an amendment to the Constitution by the legislatures of three-fourths of the several States within seven years from the date of its submission to the States by the Congress.

AMENDMENT XXIII [1961]

Section 1. The District constituting the seat of Government of the United States shall appoint in such manner as the Congress may direct:

A number of electors of President and Vice President equal to the whole number of Senators and Representatives in Congress to which the District would be entitled if it were a State, but in no event more than the least populous State; they shall be in addition to those appointed by the States, but they shall be considered, for the purposes of the election of President and Vice President, to be electors appointed by a State; and they shall meet in the District and perform such duties as provided by the twelfth article of amendment.

Section 2. The Congress shall have power to enforce this article by appropriate legislation.

AMENDMENT XXIV [1964]

Section 1. The right of citizens of the United States to vote in any primary or other election for President or Vice President, for electors for President or Vice President, or for Senator or Representative in Congress, shall not be denied or abridged by the United States or any State by reason of failure to pay any poll tax or other tax.

Section 2. The Congress shall have power to enforce this article by appropriate legislation.

AMENDMENT XXV [1967]

Section 1. In case of the removal of the President from office or of his death or resignation, the Vice President shall become President.

Section 2. Whenever there is a vacancy in the office of the Vice President, the President shall nominate a Vice President who shall take office upon confirmation by a majority vote of both Houses of Congress.

Section 3. Whenever the President transmits to the President pro tempore of the Senate and the Speaker of the House of Representatives his written declaration that he is unable to discharge the powers and duties of his office, and until he transmits to them a written declaration to the contrary, such powers and duties shall be discharged by the Vice President as Acting President.

Section 4. Whenever the Vice President and a majority of either the principal officers of the executive departments or of such other body as Congress may by law provide, transmit to the President pro tempore of the Senate and the Speaker of the House of Representatives their written declaration that the President is unable to discharge the powers and duties of his office, the Vice President shall immediately assume the powers and duties of the office as Acting President.

Thereafter, when the President transmits to the President pro tempore of the Senate and the Speaker of the House of Representatives his written declaration that no inability exists, he shall resume the powers and duties of his office unless the Vice President and a majority of either the principal officers of the executive department or of such other body as Congress may by law provide, transmit within four days to the President pro tempore of the Senate and the Speaker of the House of Representatives their written declaration that the President is unable to discharge the powers and duties of his office. Thereupon Congress shall decide the issue, assembling within forty-eight hours for that purpose if not in session. If the Congress, within twenty-one days after receipt of the latter written declaration, or, if Congress is not in session, within twenty-one days after Congress is required to assemble, determines by two-thirds vote of both Houses that the President is unable to discharge the powers and duties of his office, the Vice President shall continue to discharge the same as Acting President; otherwise, the President shall resume the powers and duties of his office.

AMENDMENT XXVI [1971]

Section 1. The right of citizens of the United States, who are eighteen years of age or older, to vote shall not be denied or abridged by the United States or by any State on account of age.

Section 2. The Congress shall have power to enforce this article by appropriate legislation.

AMENDMENT XXVII [1992]

No law, varying the compensation for the services of the Senators and Representatives, shall take effect, until an election of Representatives shall have intervened.

INDEX

REFERENCES ARE TO PAGES

■ ■ ■